THE FOUNDATIONS OF ENGLISH LITERATURE

THE FOUNDATIONS OF ENGLISH LITERATURE

An Anthology of Pre-Restoration British Literature

Edited with Introductions by
A. M. RAIN

WHITLOCK PUBLISHING
Alfred, NY

First Whitlock Publishing edition 2025

Whitlock Publishing
Alfred, New York

Editorial matter © Alyra Rain

ISBN 13: 978-1-943115-57-0

Cover art from Wikimedia Commons

This book was set in Garamond on #50 acid-free paper that meets ANSI standards for archival quality.

CONTENTS

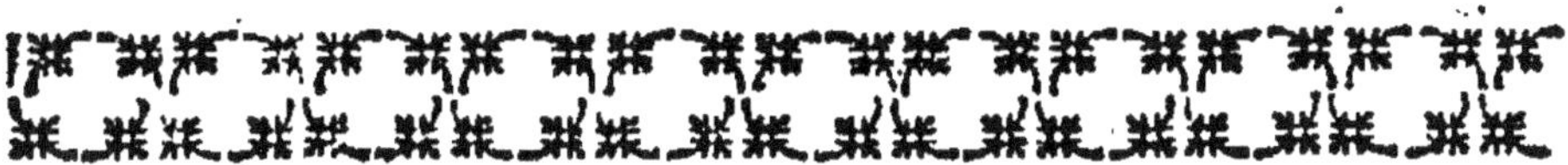

MEDIEVAL PERIOD

LATE FIFTH CENTURY—1485

EARLY MODERN PERIOD

1485-1603

SEVENTEENTH CENTURY

1603-1660

Acknowledgements

I would like to thank the entire Alfred University English division for their contributions, both to this anthology and to my time at Alfred in general. Dr. Susan Mayberry and Dr. Allen Grove worked tirelessly to help me edit, assisting me in the creation of a project that I can truly be proud of. I would never have been equipped to write the introductions for this book without Professor Susan Morehouse and Dr. Juliana Gray teaching me to write well. Dr. Melissa Ryan, Dr. Robert Reginio, and Dr. Chloe Hansen provided me with essential moral support during this project.

I am also grateful to my dear friends for their support in various capacities and the fact that they never complained about how often I mentioned this book in conversation. Similarly, I am thankful for my family's encouragement, help, and love. Finally, I would like to honor my grandmother, Gale Scholes Siess, who adored literature but never got to see this anthology's completion. Oma, I know you would be proud of me.

Introduction

"If this were played upon a stage now, I could condemn it as an improbable fiction."
— William Shakespeare, *Twelfth Night*

The anthology also provides a window into the development of the English language. Written in Old English, the original version of "Cædmon's Hymn" is incomprehensible to most modern English-speaking readers. *Beowulf* and *Sir Gawain and the Green Knight* are provided in translation while *The Canterbury Tales* requires substantial footnotes. Moving closer to the present, texts like Shakespeare's plays and John Donne's poetry contain archaic spellings and pairs of words that no longer rhyme due to linguistic evolution. In the most recent text included, *Paradise Lost*, Milton employs words, sentence structures, and abbreviations that are no longer standard. By examining works from different time periods, readers can follow its progression of language into something similar to modern-day English.

It is impossible thematically to summarize such a sweeping anthology. The main themes are universal, like freedom, grief, honor, love, and fear. Additionally, religious norms and levels of tolerance were rapidly evolving, which is reflected throughout the collection: *Beowulf* chronicles an earlier pagan society; "Cædmon's Hymn" and its composition illustrate the development of Christianity and monastic life; *The Canterbury Tales* are told on a religious pilgrimage; *Doctor Faustus* examines morality through a deal with the Devil; and *Paradise Lost* reimagines the Fall in part through Satan's perspective. As our primary and primal cultural stories were written, England evolved from a newly Catholic society with deeply pagan roots to a Protestant society focused on the role of church in government. The accessibility of reading and writing itself changed drastically between the ninth century and the seventeenth, as more of the general population became literate and writing was no longer dominated by the clergy. When Johannes Gutenberg invented his moveable type printing press in mid-fifteenth-century Germany, literature became more available to the masses; in Elizabethan England, the publishing industry blossomed in London with the Stationer's Register, the first effective method of copyright and literary licensing.

Alyra Rain, an avid reader and writer for her entire life, is passionate about everything in this anthology but especially Shakespeare's plays. She is from Delmar, New York.

Timeline

700s	The first known fragment of *The Dream of the Rood* is carved on a stone cross in Northumbria (now Scotland).
c. 731	Bede completes his *Ecclesiastical History of the English People*, written in Latin. It contains the story of Cædmon and "Cædmon's Hymn."
899	Alfred the Great, King of the Saxons, dies.
late 900s	The *Exeter Book*, the largest surviving collection of Old English poetry, is compiled. It contains *The Seafarer* and *The Wife's Lament*.
late 900s–early 1000s	The earliest extant *Beowulf* manuscript is produced; the story might have originated much earlier.
1066	William the Conquerer takes England in the Norman Conquest.
late 1300s	The first extant manuscript of *Sir Gawain and the Green Knight* originates in the north of England.
late 1300s–early 1400s	Julian of Norwich writes her *Revelations of Divine Love*, the first surviving English book known to be written by a woman.
1399	Geoffrey Chaucer writes "The Complaint of Chaucer to His Purse."
c. 1400	*The Canterbury Tales* are published following Chaucer's death.
c. 1440	Johannes Gutenberg invents his printing press in Germany.
1455–85	The houses of Lancaster and York battle for control of the throne in the Wars of the Roses; peace is made when they combine into the house of Tudor.
late 1400s	*Everyman* is written by an unknown author. It is published in 1530.
1509	King Henry VII dies and is succeeded by his son Henry VIII.
1513	Henry VIII launches his first invasion of France. Scotland responds by invading England.
1533	Henry VIII divorces his first wife, Catherine of Aragon. England splits from the Catholic Church and establishes the Church of England.

1547	Henry VIII dies and is succeeded by his nine-year-old son Edward VI.
1553	King Edward VI dies and is succeeded by his sister Mary I.
1554–55	Princess Elizabeth writes "Written with a Diamond on Her Window at Woodstock" while on house arrest.
1555	The "Oxford Martyrs," three major Protestant leaders, are burnt at the stake.
1558	Queen Mary I dies and is succeeded by her sister Elizabeth I.
1587	Mary, Queen of Scots is beheaded after the discovery of a Catholic plot to put her on the English throne.
1588	The English navy defeats the Spanish Armada in Queen Elizabeth I's most important military victory.
1592-93	Christopher Marlowe writes *Doctor Faustus*; William Shakespeare writes *Richard III*.
1593	Marlowe dies.
1590s	John Donne writes "The Flea" as a young law student.
1598	*Hero and Leander* is published, after being completed by George Chapman after Marlowe's death.
1599	*The Passionate Shepherd to his Love* is published, six years after Marlowe's death.
1600	Sir Walter Raleigh publishes *The Nymph's Reply to the Shepherd*.
1602	The first recorded performance of Shakespeare's *Twelfth Night*.
c. 1603	Queen Elizabeth I dies and is succeeded by James VI of Scotland as James I of England. He becomes the patron of Shakespeare's company.
1605	King James VI and I survives the Gunpowder Plot, a plan by Catholic dissident Guy Fawkes to blow up Parliament.
1605-06	Ben Johnson writes *Volpone*.
1609	Shakespeare's cycle of 154 sonnets is published in quarto form.
1611	The King James Version of the Bible is published in English.
1616	Shakespeare dies suddenly of unknown causes.
1618	The Thirty Years' War begins in continental Europe.

1621	Donne becomes Dean of Saint Paul's.
1625	King James VI and I dies and is succeeded by his son Charles I.
1631	Donne dies after delivering his final sermon, "Death's Duel."
c. 1631	John Milton writes "L'Allegro" and "Il Penseroso," two pastoral poems.
1633	Donne's *Songs and Sonnets* and *Holy Sonnets* are first published. George Herbert publishes *The Temple*.
1642	Civil war begins between King Charles's Royalist forces and supporters of Parliamentary power.
1645	Charles flees to Scotland after a defeat by Parliamentary forces.
1648	Robert Herrick publishes *The Hesperides*, a book of hundreds of poems, including "To the Virgins, to Make Much of Time" and "Upon Julia's Breasts."
1649	King Charles I is tried for treason and executed in an unprecedented move by Parliament. The English Commonwealth is established; Parliament and the Army Council of Officers govern England.
1649-50	Oliver Cromwell leads a brutally violent re-conquest of Ireland.
1650	Richard Lovelace publishes his poetry collection *Lucasta*, which includes "To Lucasta, Going to the Warres." Henry Vaughan publishes *Silex scintillans*.
1650s	Andrew Marvell writes "To His Coy Mistress."
1652	Richard Crashaw's "The Flaming Heart" and "On our crucified Lord naked and bloody" are published.
1653	Oliver Cromwell takes over government of England as Lord Protector.
1658	Oliver Cromwell dies. His son Richard becomes Lord Protector, but he lacks his father's power and soon resigns, opening the door for the restoration of the monarchy.
1660	The Restoration: King Charles II, son of Charles I, ascends to the English throne, restoring the monarchy to power.
1667	Milton publishes *Paradise Lost*. His goal for decades has been to write a great English epic.
1670	*Revelations of Divine Love* is published after centuries of obscurity.

THE MEDIEVAL PERIOD
End of fifth century-1485

ABSTRACT

The Medieval Period, or the Middle Ages, prevailed in England from the collapse of Roman rule in the late fifth century until the royal House of Tudor began its reign in 1485. By far the longest historical period covered in this anthology, it saw multiple waves of colonization and invasion from the Continent: first an influx of Germanic migration, then Viking invasions, and finally the Norman Conquest.

EARLY MIDDLE AGES
c. 600-1066

The Roman Empire colonized most of England from the early first century to late in the fifth century. When the empire collapsed, England was left in economic distress and without a stable government. The Roman retreat also led to increased immigration from Germanic peoples originating in northern Europe. Their language combined with existing dialects to form Old Englishm which replaced British Latin as the area's dominant language. Germanic settlers established new cultures, most notably Anglian culture established by the Angles (from whom the name England originated) and Saxon culture established by the Saxons. By the 700s, these had merged to form the dominant Anglo-Saxon society. *Beowulf*, an epic poem dating to the late 900s or earlier, is set in sixth century Scandinavia, suggesting that its subject matter might have originated during this Germanic migration.

In the 500s and 600s, small fiefdoms began to form, ruled by kings who collected tribute money from the regions they controlled. This period also saw the Christianization of the formerly pagan Anglo-Saxons—missionaries came from Ireland as well as directly from the Pope in Rome. Britannia, the Roman province that encompassed England and southern Scotland, had been Christian before the fall of the Roman Empire, but the Germanic immigrants brought Germanic paganism with them. This caused England to return to paganism before being Christianized a second time. The first Archbishop of Canterbury, Augustine of Canterbury, was consecrated in 597. Conversion of the population was gradual with a relative absence of violence. Christianity spread from Kent in the southeast of England, where the first missionaries arrived, to the north and west.

During the 600s, the powerful kingdom of Mercia came to dominate the Midlands region, taking over most of modern-day England. In the 700s, England was controlled by central Mercia and its neighbors Wessex to the south, East

Anglia to the east, and Northumbria, which reached into modern-day Scotland, to the north. During this period, the monk Bede, also known as the Venerable Bede, wrote his *Ecclesiastical History of the English People*. Composed in Latin, it provides an invaluable record for historians and literary scholars. Bede travelled across Britain collecting information for the *History*, which he completed in about 731. Among many important contributions, the *History* contains the only surviving account of the poet Cædmon. Known in some scholarly circles as the Father of English History, Bede was canonized in 1899. The earliest known fragment of the poem "The Dream of the Rood" also originated in the 700s, when it was carved on the Ruthwell Cross, an ornate stone monument in Northumbria.

Large-scale Viking raids began to threaten the English kingdoms in the late 700s. By the late 800s, Mercia, East Anglia, and Northumbria fell to the Danish force known as the Viking Great Army. The main resistance to Scandinavian invasions was mounted by King Alfred of Wessex, later Alfred the Great or Alfred, King of the Saxons. In 878, Alfred won an important battle that helped push back the Danes to the eastern portion of England. He managed to gather large forces from the various Anglo-Saxon kingdoms to counter the invasion. Many citizens viewed the Viking raids as punishment from God, which probably inspired Alfred's efforts to found monasteries and increase religious education.

The 800s was an important period in literary history in that it established the legend of King Arthur, who became a mythical British folk hero. The first mentions of Arthur, in two Welsh history books dating from the 800s or 900s, portray him as a real historical figure from the period of Germanic immigration. He ostensibly led native Britons against the Anglo-Saxons. However, these books were written hundreds of years after Arthur supposedly lived, and most historians agree that he is a purely legendary figure. The late 900s also saw the compilation of the *Exeter Book*, one of the most important records of poetry in Old English. The earliest extant *Beowulf* manuscript was most likely produced not long after the *Exeter Book*.

King Alfred's line, the House of Wessex, continued to rule most of England until a succession crisis at the end of the 900s led to a Danish family invading and claiming the throne. Edward the Confessor, the last king from the House of Wessex, returned from exile in Normandy in 1042 to take power. Edward's reign offered unity, but he died childless, causing another crisis of succession. This instability inspired William, Duke of Normandy, to invade England in the Norman Conquest of 1066, which historians now define as the beginning of the High Middle Ages.

HIGH MIDDLE AGES
1066-1272

Normandy, in northern France, lies across the English Channel just 20 miles from the British Isles; the region provided a strategic launching point for William the Conqueror's forces during the 1066 Norman conquest. Facing little effective opposition, French invaders quickly spread throughout

England. They then invaded Wales, a series of campaigns that took about one hundred years to complete. By the time William of Normandy died in 1087, England was controlled by powerful Norman nobles. Norman rule also caused French to become the language of the nobility in England, a linguistic impact that has lasted into modern times. French remained the second language of English elites for centuries after that. In the late 1000s, England's wealth grew, enabling Norman rulers to fund invasions further into France. William's death, however, caused a succession crisis between his three sons. Full-scale civil war, caused by further crises of succession, started around 1135, ending with a peace treaty in 1154 led by William's great-grandson, who took power and became King Henry II.

In 1136, cleric Geoffrey of Monmouth popularized the legend of King Arthur with his book *Historia Regum Britanniae*. Written in Latin, *The History of the Kings of Britain* is historically inaccurate but retains literary importance. It provides the source for many details of the modern legend of King Arthur, including the characters of Merlin and Guinevere. In the later 1100s, French writers invented other knights of the round table such as Lancelot, Gawain, and Percival, establishing Arthurian romance as an important medieval genre. This set the stage for the emergence of *Sir Gawain and the Green Knight* in the 1300s. The *History* also originated the story of King Lear, later dramatized by William Shakespeare.

While focusing most of his attention on war in France, Henry II managed to invade and colonize Ireland. In religious matters, he clashed with Thomas Becket, the Archbishop of Canterbury, over the privileges of the Church. Becket was murdered by the King's knights in 1170, either on the King's orders or after the knights misinterpreted them. Becket was canonized shortly afterwards, and his shrine in Canterbury became an important site of religious pilgrimages; the shrine gives its name to *The Canterbury Tales*.

King Henry II married the powerful Duchess Eleanor of Aquitaine, whose marriage to King Louis VII of France had recently been annulled. Eleanor controlled Aquitaine, then a large region in central France, meaning that Henry II gained joint control of the region upon their marriage. They had seven surviving children, all of whom became either monarchs, dukes, or duchesses. Eleanor would later rule jointly over Aquitaine with two of her sons, King Richard I and later King John.

Sixteen years before Henry's death, his children began looking to acquire power. He had four surviving sons: Henry the Young King[1], who predeceased his father; Richard the Lionheart; Geoffrey II, Duke of Brittany; and John. The eldest three staged a rebellion against their father in 1173, but despite Eleanor's support, the attempt failed. William the Lion, King of Scotland, also participated in this conflict, a serious mistake during his otherwise largely successful forty-nine year reign. The failure of the revolt and the ensuing Treaty of Falaise allowed England to gain more power over Scotland.

1: Henry was called this because he ruled as titular King of England during his father's reign, at the time a French tradition, while he was a young adult. However, because he lacked real power, Henry the Young King rebelled against his father along with his brothers.

Upon Henry II's death in 1189, Richard I, also known as Richard the Lionheart, took control as the eldest surviving son. He spent most of his reign defending his lands in France as well as participating in the Third Crusade, which failed to capture Jerusalem. Richard died in 1199; his brother John succeeded him. King John was unpopular due to failed military campaigns in France which caused rebellions across England. When he died in 1216, his nine-year-old son Henry III became King. Henry and his council of regents managed to end the uprisings by strengthening England's ties to the papacy, gaining support for Henry from the Pope. Converting the rebellions into a religious cause also helped turn the popular tide in the King's favor; following the end of the war, his regents began restoring royal authority. In 1225, however, the second iteration of the Magna Carta limited the power of the Crown and guaranteed certain rights to the people.

Henry III took full control of his kingdom at the age of twenty, going on to rule for fifty-six years, the longest-reigning English monarch until King George III[2]. Most historians agree that Henry's death in 1272 marks the end of the High Middle Ages and the beginning of the Late Middle Ages.

LATE MIDDLE AGES
1272-1485

Edward I[3] succeeded his father Henry III in 1272. His reign was characterized by the dominance of the Crown, as he rebuilt castles and tightened the monarchy's governance of England. Edward also invaded and further colonized Wales. He invaded Scotland in 1296 but failed to achieve victory; this war continued into the reign of his son, Edward II, before ending in defeat in 1328 with continued Scottish independence.

Edward II became King upon his father's death in 1307, but his reign was unpopular because of several military failures. Together with her lover, the exiled Lord Mortimer, Edward's wife Isabella defeated her husband in a 1327 coup. Edward and Isabella's son Edward III went on to depose them in 1330.

Edward III's reign became successful militarily when he invaded France, beginning the Hundred Years' War during which England conquered territory on the Continent. His son Edward the Black Prince became an important commander in these wars. While the Black Prince likely died from chronic dysentery, the Black Death, the first and deadliest outbreak of the bubonic plague, began to spread throughout England in the 1340s, crippling society and hindering Edward's successes.

After Edward III's son the Black Prince died in battle, Edward was succeeded by ten-year-old Richard in 1377. While his uncle John of Gaunt acted as

2: George III reigned for almost sixty years despite severe mental illness. Queen Elizabeth II, however, remains Britain's longest reigning monarch.

3: While several kings named Edward ruled before the Norman Conquest, the numbering of English monarchs begins with the Conquest in 1066. Previous rulers are instead distinguished by epithets, such as Edward the Confessor.

unofficial regent for the young king, Richard II exerted more control over his kingdom than did most child rulers, especially regarding his opposition to war. However, Richard's reign suffered from economic problems caused by the Black Death, culminating with the Peasants' Revolt in 1381. His years as king also saw continuous power struggles between the English nobles. Richard's cousin Henry of Bolingbroke, John of Gaunt's son, succeeded in deposing Richard in 1399. Ruling as Henry IV, he became the House of Lancaster's first monarch. This development helped provide for Geoffrey Chaucer's literary success at the end of his life, since John of Gaunt was his patron and close friend. It also served as fodder for Shakespeare's English history plays.

The medieval period inspired most of Shakespeare's history plays. Most historians agree that Shakespeare's *Richard II* allocates the titular king a less positive reputation than he deserved. Shakespeare attributes the source of the Wars of the Roses to Richard's failed reign, for example, which is probably untrue. However, the popular plays of the 1400s were not historical dramas, but plays focusing on religious topics. Morality plays like *Everyman* depict human protagonists surrounded by supporting characters who are allegorical representations of concepts such as kindness, sin, and beauty. This genre reached its height in the mid-to-late 1400s, with *Everyman* representing the last surviving morality play. Another important literary development in the 1400s was the moveable-type printing press, invented by Johannes Gutenberg around 1440 in Germany. The printing press made written documents such as the Gutenberg Bible much more widely available throughout Europe.

Henry IV became the first English ruler since the Norman Conquest to speak English as his first language rather than French. After a reign characterized by rebellions and assassination attempts, Henry IV died in 1413. His son Henry V assumed the throne. Henry V's reign was more successful than that of his father. He managed to sustain important military victories during the Hundred Years' War with France, but he fell ill and died in 1422. Shakespeare's second dramatic tetralogy (*Richard II*; *Henry IV, Parts 1 and 2*; *Henry V*) portrays these historical events. Henry V's infant son Henry VI subsequently became King of England.

During Henry VI's minority, France recouped significant territory in the ongoing Hundred Years' War. Female military savior Joan of Arc was instrumental in these victories. The death of Henry V, his young son's inability to command an army, and the infighting among English nobles allowed France to gain the upper hand. England would forfeit the Hundred Years' War in 1453, which ended any hope of English monarchs acquiring the French throne. Nonetheless, their official royal titles retained claims of French sovereignty until 1801, after France became a republic in 1792.

The Wars of the Roses, a series of civil wars fought between the House of York and the House of Lancaster for control of the English Crown, lasted for approximately thirty years. The Houses of Lancaster and York descended from the French Plantagenet dynasty via Edward III, meaning that members of both houses believed they had inherited legitimate rights to the English throne. After Lancasterian Henry VI came of age, he began to display signs of mental instability, causing his cousin Richard, Duke of York, to claim the throne. While scholars remain uncertain about whether Henry was insane, suffered from a disability, or merely possessed a personality incompatible with leadership, the Wars of the Roses began in 1455 with York kidnapping Henry. York was killed in battle in 1460. His son Edward then took up the claim and succeeded in defeating the Lancasters in 1461, after which he was officially crowned King Edward IV.

Edward IV ruled from 1461 to 1469, when his closest advisor the Earl of Warwick rebelled against him in an attempt to crown Edward's brother George, Duke of Clarence. After this coup failed, Edward reassumed the throne. Continuing rebellions forced him to flee to the Continent in 1470, at which time Henry VI was restored as King in what is known as the "Readeption." With French support, Edward IV re-invaded England, defeated Warwick, and then eliminated Henry's sole heir, Edward of Westminster, at the decisive Battle of Tewkesbury in 1471. Henry later died imprisoned in the Tower of London. Shakespeare depicts these events in his trilogy on Henry VI: *Henry VI, Parts 1,2, and 3*.

The next twelve years were relatively peaceful, and Edward IV died in 1483. He was succeeded by his twelve-year-old son Edward V, who was quickly deposed by his uncle Richard, Duke of Gloucester, afterwards Richard III. Edward and his nine-year-old brother were taken to the Tower of London and subsequently disappeared. A popular theory, supported by William Shakespeare in the concluding play of his first tetralogy, *Richard III*, suggests that the princes were murdered on Richard's command in order to solidify his claim to the throne. This assertion, however, has never been proven.

Richard's ascension to the throne caused a rebellion during which many of his Yorkish supporters defected. Henry Tudor, a Lancasterian descendent who returned from French exile, defeated Richard two years later at the Battle of Bosworth Field and took the throne as Henry VII. This victory began the Tudor dynasty, which ended with Queen Elizabeth I's death in 1603. When Lancasterian Henry VII married Elizabeth of York, the older sister of Edward V, the couple officially united the houses of Lancaster and York. Henry's ascension in 1485 marks the beginning of the Early Modern period. Overall, more than 100,000 people died during the Wars of the Roses.

The rose emblems of the houses of Lancaster (left, a red rose), York (center, a white rose), and Tudor (right, a combination of the two). The Wars of the Roses get their name from these floral emblems.

TIMELINE

476	The western Roman Empire collapses, leaving England with no governmental structure.
700s	The first known excerpt of *The Dream of the Rood* appears in Northumbria (now Scotland).
c. 731	The Venerable Bede completes his *Ecclesiastical History of the English People.*
899	Alfred the Great, King of the Saxons, dies.
Late 900s	The *Exeter Book* is compiled.
c. Late 900s	The earliest extant *Beowulf* manuscript is produced.
1066	William of Normandy begins to take England in the Norman Conquest.
c. 1136	Geoffrey of Monmouth completes *Historia Regum Britanniae.*
1154	Civil war within the Norman nobility ends.
1173	Henry II's eldest three sons and his wife rebel against him.
1225	The definitive version of the Magna Carta charter grants certain rights to English citizens.
1337	The Hundred Years' War begins.
1340s	The Black Death arrives in England.
Late 1300s	The first extant manuscript of *Sir Gawain and the Green Knight* is written.
c. 1400	Julian of Norwich writes her *Revelations of Divine Love.*
1399	Geoffrey Chaucer writes "The Complaint of Chaucer to His Purse."
c. 1400	*The Canterbury Tales* are published just after Chaucer's death.
c. 1440	Johannes Gutenberg invents his moveable-type printing press in Germany.
1455-85	The Wars of the Roses take place.
1471-83	Edward IV (House of York) rules in relative peace.
1483	Richard III deposes his nephew Henry V and takes power; Henry and his younger brother disappear.
Late 1400s	The morality play *Everyman* is written.
1485	The Early Modern Period starts with the reign of Henry VII and the beginning of the Royal House of Tudor.

THE DREAM OF THE ROOD

Lo! choicest of dreams I will relate,
What dream I dreamt in middle of night
When mortal men reposed in rest.
Methought I saw a wondrous wood
5   Tower aloft with light bewound,
Brightest of trees; that beacon was all
Begirt with gold; jewels were standing
Four at surface of earth, likewise were there five
Above on the shoulder-brace. All angels of God beheld it,
10   Fair through future ages; 'twas no criminal's cross indeed,
But holy spirits beheld it there,
Men upon earth, all this glorious creation.
Strange was that victor-tree, and stained with sins was I,
With foulness defiled. I saw the glorious tree
15   With vesture adorned winsomely shine,
Begirt with gold; bright gems had there
Worthily decked the tree of the Lord.
Yet through that gold I might perceive
Old strife of the wretched, that first it gave
20   Blood on the stronger [right][1] side. With sorrows was I oppressed,
Afraid for that fair sight; I saw the ready beacon
Change in vesture and hue; at times with moisture covered,
Soiled with course of blood; at times with treasure adorned.
Yet lying there a longer while,
25   Beheld I sad the Saviour's tree
Until I heard that words it uttered;
The best of woods gan speak these words:
"'Twas long ago (I remember it still)
That I was hewn at end of a grove,
30   Stripped from off my stem; strong foes laid hold of me there,
Wrought for themselves a show, bade felons raise me up;
Men bore me on their shoulders, till on a mount they set me;
Fiends many fixed me there. Then saw I mankind's Lord
Hasten with mickle might, for He would sty upon me.
35   There durst I not 'gainst word of the Lord
Bow down or break, when saw I tremble
The surface of earth; I might then all
My foes have felled, yet fast I stood.

1: Brackets are used for clarifications.

The Hero young begirt Himself, Almighty God was He,
40   Strong and stern of mind; He stied on the gallows high,
Bold in sight of many, for man He would redeem.
I shook when the Hero clasped me, yet durst not bow to earth,
Fall to surface of earth, but firm I must there stand.
A rood was I upreared; I raised the mighty King,
45   The Lord of Heaven; I durst not bend me.
They drove their dark nails through me; the wounds are seen upon me,
The open gashes of guile; I durst harm none of them.
They mocked us both together; all moistened with blood was I,
Shed from side of the man, when forth He sent His spirit.
50   Many have I on that mount endured
Of cruel fates; I saw the Lord of Hosts
Strongly outstretched; darkness had then
Covered with clouds the corse of the Lord,
The brilliant brightness; the shadow continued,
55   Wan 'neath the welkin. There wept all creation,
Bewailed the King's death; Christ was on the cross.
Yet hastening thither they came from afar
To the Son of the King: that all I beheld.
Sorely with sorrows was I oppressed; yet I bowed 'neath the hands of men,
60   Lowly with mickle might. Took they there Almighty God,
Him raised from the heavy torture; the battle-warriors left me
To stand bedrenched with blood; all wounded with darts was I.
There laid they the weary of limb, at head of His corse they stood,
Beheld the Lord of Heaven, and He rested Him there awhile,
65   Worn from the mickle war. Began they an earth-house to work,
Men in the murderers' sight, carved it of brightest stone,
Placed therein victories' Lord. Began sad songs to sing
The wretched at eventide; then would they back return
Mourning from the mighty prince; all lonely rested He there.
70   Yet weeping we then a longer while
Stood at our station: the [voice] arose
Of battle-warriors; the corse grew cold,
Fair house of life. Then one gan fell
Us all to earth; 'twas a fearful fate!
75   One buried us in deep pit, yet of me the thanes of the Lord,
His friends, heard tell; [from earth they raised me],
And me begirt with gold and silver.
Now thou mayst hear, my dearest man,
That bale of woes have I endured,
80   Of sorrows sore. Now the time is come,
That me shall honor both far and wide
Men upon earth, and all this mighty creation
Will pray to this beacon. On me God's Son

Suffered awhile; so glorious now
85 I tower to Heaven, and I may heal
Each one of those who reverence me;
Of old I became the hardest of pains,
Most loathsome to ledes [nations], the way of life,
Right way, I prepared for mortal men.
90 Lo! the Lord of Glory honored me then
Above the grove, the guardian of Heaven,
As He His mother, even Mary herself,
Almighty God before all men
Worthily honored above all women.
95 Now thee I bid, my dearest man,
That thou this sight shalt say to men,
Reveal in words, 'tis the tree of glory,
On which once suffered Almighty God
For the many sins of all mankind,
100 And also for Adam's misdeeds of old.
Death tasted He there; yet the Lord arose
With His mickle might for help to men.
Then stied He to Heaven; again shall come
Upon this mid-earth to seek mankind
105 At the day of doom the Lord Himself,
Almighty God, and His angels with Him;
Then He will judge, who hath right of doom,
Each one of men as here before
In this vain life he hath deserved.
110 No one may there be free from fear
In view of the word that the Judge will speak.
He will ask 'fore the crowd, where is the man
Who for name of the Lord would bitter death
Be willing to taste, as He did on the tree.
115 But then they will fear, and few will bethink them
What they to Christ may venture to say.
Then need there no one be filled with fear
Who bears in his breast the best of beacons;
But through the rood a kingdom shall seek
120 From earthly way each single soul
That with the Lord thinketh to dwell."
Then I prayed to the tree with joyous heart,
With mickle might, when I was alone
With small attendance; the thought of my mind
125 For the journey was ready; I've lived through many
Hours of longing. Now 'tis hope of my life
That the victory-tree I am able to seek,
Oftener than all men I alone may

Honor it well; my will to that
130 Is mickle in mind, and my plea for protection
To the rood is directed. I've not many mighty
Of friends on earth; but hence went they forth
From joys of the world, sought glory's King;
Now live they in Heaven with the Father on high,
135 In glory dwell, and I hope for myself
On every day when the rood of the Lord,
Which here on earth before I viewed,
In this vain life may fetch me away
And bring me then, where bliss is mickle,
140 Joy in the Heavens, where the folk of the Lord
Is set at the feast, where bliss is eternal;
And may He then set me where I may hereafter
In glory dwell, and well with the saints
Of joy partake. May the Lord be my friend,
145 Who here on earth suffered before
On the gallows-tree for the sins of man!
He us redeemed, and gave to us life,
A heavenly home. Hope was renewed,
With blessing and bliss, for the sufferers of burning.
150 The Son was victorious on that fateful journey,
Mighty and happy, when He came with a many,
With a band of spirits to the kingdom of God,
The Ruler Almighty, for joy to the angels
And to all the saints, who in Heaven before
155 In glory dwelt, when their Ruler came,
Almighty God, where was His home.

CÆDMON

Cædmon is the first English poet whose name scholars know. There is no information about his family, upbringing, or career, but by 658 he worked as a cowherd at a monastery now called Whitby Abbey. The abbess at the time was the Abbey's founder, St. Hilda, venerated both by the Roman Catholic Church and the Church of England. About fifty years after Cædmon's death, Bede recorded Cædmon's story in Bede's Ecclesiastical History of the English People (ca. 731). While some scholars believe that Cædmon was a bard or scop before finding work at the abbey, Bede wrote that Cædmon sheepishly left the mead hall when guests began to sing songs and tell stories. This entire account of Cædmon is according to Bede.

c. 658, Cædmon had a dream in which someone asked him to sing about the Creation. Miraculously, he did so, using verses that he had never heard before. When he woke up, he informed his supervisor, who escorted him to the Abbess, St. Hilda. She proclaimed that his inspiration was divine, testing him by requesting that he turn a piece of sacred history into poetry. He produced that poetry by the next morning, so Hilda invited him to take monastic vows to become a monk. For the rest of his life, Cædmon composed poetry based on religious texts, writing many splendid poems. Only his original hymn, however, from his original dream, survives. Bede's legend tells us that Cædmon received a premonition of his death, which usually only happened to the most saintly and pious followers of God. He died c. 680, around the time that St. Hilda died.

Scholars are divided on whether the version of "Cædmon's Hymn" that survives in Old English is the original. Bede wrote his History in Latin, and therefore the first source for "Cædmon's Hymn" is in Latin. Later Anglo-Saxon sources may have translated the hymn back into Old English, instead of having access to the original. Cædmon was illiterate and spoke his poems aloud in Old English; they were transcribed by monks. This means that an Old English original version of "Cædmon's Hymn" predates Bede's Latin translation, but might now be lost.

TIMELINE

c. 658   Cædmon is working as a cowherd for Whitby Abbey, when he receives a blessing from God in a dream that allows him to convert scripture into poetry.

c. 658   "Cædmon's Hymn," his only surviving poem.

c. 680   Cædmon dies.

731   Bede records Cædmon's story in his *Ecclesiastical History of the English People*.

Cædmon's Hymn

Modern English

Now must we hymn the Master of heaven,
The might of the Maker, the deeds of the Father,
The thought of His heart. He, Lord everlasting,
Established of old the source of all wonders:
Creator all-holy, He hung the bright heaven,
A roof high upreared, o'er the children of men;
The King of mankind then created for mortals
The world in its beauty, the earth spread beneath them,
He, Lord everlasting, omnipotent God.

Old English

This is a constructed common ancestor of all the extant versions of the hymn.[2]

Nu scylun hergan   hefaenricaes uard,
metudæs maecti,   end his modgidanc,
uerc uuldurfadur—   sue he uundra gihuaes,
eci dryctin,   or astelidæ!
He aerist scop   eordu barnum
heben til hrofe,   haleg sceppend;
tha middungeard,   moncynnæs uard,
eci dryctin,   æfter tiadæ
firum foldu,   frea allmectig.

2: O'Donnell, Daniel Paul, ed. Cædmon's Hymn: A Multimedia Study, Edition and Archive. 2005. 1.1 Internet Reprint, vol. A.8, SEENET, 2018, caedmon. seenet.org/index.html.

The Four Major Codices

Old English poetry exists primarily in fragments or in one of four major surviving manuscripts. Many manuscripts were lost during the sixteenth century when King Henry VIII's separation from the Catholic Church led him to dissolve Catholic monasteries across England and destroy their libraries. The first of the four major collections, the *Junius Manuscript* (tenth century), contains four poems on biblical subjects, compiled by at least two different scribes and illustrated by two artists. It was formerly called the "Cædmon manuscript" because early scholars theorized that its poems were the work of Cædmon (see page 12); this theory has been discredited.

The second major manuscript is the *Exeter Book* or *Codex Exoniensis*, which also originated in the tenth century and is the largest known manuscript of Old English literature. It contains over thirty poems and more than ninety riddles. *The Exeter Book* is notable for the diverse genres and themes represented in its poems, in contrast to the *Junius Manuscript*, which consists solely of religious poems. The *Exeter Book* is the source for "Riddle V," "The Seafarer," and "The Wife's Lament." It is also the source for two of the four known surviving poems by Cynewulf, one of a very few Old English poets whose name and works are both known to us. Cynewulf likely flourished in the ninth century; he wrote in the Anglian dialect, indicating that he was from the north of England.

The third major manuscript or codex, the *Vercelli Book*, also originated in the late tenth century. It was rediscovered in a medieval library in Vercelli, Italy in 1822, where it is still housed today. The *Vercelli Book* comprises twenty-four prose texts and six poems, all of which deal with religious subjects. It contains Cynewulf's other two known poems, signed with his runic acrostic signature, including the most complete surviving version of "The Dream of the Rood" (pages 8-11). "The Dream," however, exists in fragments as early as an 8th-century stone carving, making it older than the other poems.

The fourth major codex is the *Nowell Codex*, sometimes referred to as the *Beowulf Manuscript*. It likely originated just after the turn of the first millennium, in the early eleventh century. In addition to *Beowulf*, the manuscript boasts three fictional prose texts and one poetic translation of a story from the Book of Judith, a book contained in Catholic and Orthodox Bibles today. About three-fourths of *Judith* is missing from the manuscript. The *Nowell Codex* was damaged in a fire in the 18th century, explaining the many missing fragments of *Beowulf*; *Judith* was already fragmented before that fire.

Because these four codices contain the majority of surviving Old English poetry, they are invaluable resources for modern scholars and readers.

RIDDLE V: A SHIELD

A lonely warrior, I am wounded with iron,
Scarred with sword-points, sated with battle-play,
Weary of weapons. I have witnessed much fighting,
Much stubborn strife. From the strokes of war
5   I have no hope for help or release
Ere I pass from the world with the proud warrior band.
With brands and billies they beat upon me;
The hard edges hack me; the handwork of smiths
In crowds I encounter; with courage I endure
10 Ever bitterer battles. No balm may I find,
And no doctor to heal me in the whole field of battle,
To bind me with ointments and bring me to health,
But my grievous gashes grow ever sorer
Through death-dealing strokes by day and night.

THE SEAFARER

I will sing of myself a song that is true,
Tell of my travels and troublesome days,
How often I endured days of hardship;
Bitter breast-care I have borne as my portion,
5   Have seen from my ship sorrowful shores,
Awful welling of waves; oft on watch I have been
On the narrow night-wakes at the neck of the ship,
When it crashed into cliffs; with cold often pinched
Were my freezing feet, by frost bound tight
10 In its blighting clutch; cares then burned me,
Hot around my heart. Hunger tore within
My sea-weary soul. To conceive this is hard
For the landsman who lives on the lonely shore—
How, sorrowful and sad on a sea ice-cold,
15 I eked out my exile through the awful winter
. . . . [3]deprived of my kinsmen,
Hung about by icicles; hail flew in showers.
There I heard naught but the howl of the sea,
The ice-cold surge with a swan-song at times;
20 The note of the gannet for gayety served me,

3: This is the notation for a missing fragment of an early text. The section
has not been omitted by choice; it has not survived to the modern day.

The sea-bird's song for sayings of people,
For the mead-drink of men the mew's sad note.
Storms beat on the cliffs, 'mid the cry of gulls,
Icy of feather; and the eagle screamed,
25   The dewy-winged bird. No dear friend comes
With merciful kindness my misery to conquer.
Of this little can he judge who has joy in his life,
And, settled in the city, is sated with wine,
And proud and prosperous— how painful it is
30   When I wearily wander on the waves full oft!
Night shadows descended; it snowed from the north;
The world was fettered with frost; hail fell to the earth,
The coldest of corns. Yet course now desires
Which surge in my heart for the high seas,
35   That I test the terrors of the tossing waves;
My soul constantly kindles in keenest impatience
To fare itself forth and far off hence
To seek the strands of stranger tribes.
There is no one in this world so o'erweening in power,
40   So good in his giving, so gallant in his youth,
So daring in his deeds, so dear to his lord,
But that he leaves the land and longs for the sea.
By the grace of God he will gain or lose;
Nor hearkens he to harp nor has heart for gift-treasures,
45   Nor in the wiles of a wife nor in the world rejoices.
Save in the welling of waves no whit takes he pleasure;
But he ever has longing who is lured by the sea.
The forests are in flower and fair are the hamlets;
The woods are in bloom, the world is astir:
50   Everything urges one eager to travel,
Sends the seeker of seas afar
To try his fortune on the terrible foam.
The cuckoo warns in its woeful call;
The summer-ward sings, sorrow foretelling,
55   Heavy to the heart. Hard is it to know
For the man of pleasure, what many with patience
Endure who dare the dangers of exile!
In my bursting breast now burns my heart,
My spirit sallies over the sea-floods wide,
60   Sails o'er the waves, wanders afar
To the bounds of the world and back at once,
Eagerly, longingly; the lone flyer beckons
My soul unceasingly to sail o'er the whale-path,
Over the waves of the sea.

THE WIFE'S LAMENT

Sorrowfully I sing my song of woe,
My tale of trials. In truth I may say
That the buffets I have borne since my birth in the world
Were never more than now, either new or old.
5   Ever the evils of exile I endure!
Long since went my lord from the land of his birth,
Over the welling waves. Woeful at dawn I asked
Where lingers my lord, in what land does he dwell?
Then I fared into far lands and faithfully sought him,
10   A weary wanderer in want of comfort.
His treacherous tribesmen contrived a plot,
Dark and dastardly, to drive us apart
The width of a world, where with weary hearts
We live in loneliness, and longing consumes me.
15   My master commanded me to make my home here.
Alas, in this land my loved ones are few,
My faithful friends! Hence I feel great sorrow
That the man well-matched with me I have found
To be sad in soul and sorrowful in mind,
20   Concealing his thoughts and thinking of murder,
Though blithe in his bearing. Oft we bound us by oath
That the day of our death should draw us apart,
Nothing less end our love. Alas, all is changed!
Now is as naught, as if never it were,
25   Our faith and our friendship. Far and near I shall
Endure the hate of one dear to my heart!
He condemned me to dwell in a darksome wood,
Under an oak-tree in an earth-cave drear.
Old is the earth-hall. I am anxious with longing.
30   Dim are the dales, dark the hills tower,
Bleak the tribe-dwellings, with briars entangled,
Unblessed abodes. Here bitterly I have suffered
The faring of my lord afar. Friends there are on earth
Living in love, in lasting bliss,
35   While, wakeful at dawn, I wander alone
Under the oak-tree the earth-cave near.
Sadly I sit there the summer-long day,
Wearily weeping my woeful exile,
My many miseries. Hence I may not ever

40 Cease my sorrowing, my sad bewailing,
  Nor all the longings of my life of woe.
  Always may the young man be mournful of spirit,
  Unhappy of heart, and have as his portion
  Many sorrows of soul, unceasing breast-cares,
45 Though now blithe of behavior. Unbearable likewise
  Be his joys in the world. Wide be his exile
  To far-away folk-lands where my friend sits alone,
  A stranger under stone-cliffs, by storm made hoary,
  A weary-souled wanderer, by waters encompassed,
50 In his lonely lodging. My lover endures
  Unmeasured mind-care: he remembers too oft
  A happier home. To him is fate cruel
  Who lingers and longs for the loved one's return!

Epic Poetry

Epic poetry, long narrative poems about the feats of heroes, is one of the oldest, most influential genres in the world. Composed before the invention of writing as we know it today, folk epics were passed down orally by scops or bards, as seen in *Beowulf*. The first surviving epic poem, *The Epic of Gilgamesh*, originated around 4,000 years ago in the Sumerian civilization. Scholars believe that ancient epics were composed in verse so that storytellers could memorize and retell them more easily. *The Epic of Gilgamesh* probably consisted of about 3,000 lines when it was complete (it survives only in segments). The most famous Western epics, Homer's *The Iliad* and *The Odyssey*, are much longer at about 15,000 lines each. *The Mahabharata* originated in India between the third century BCE and the third century CE; it contains over 200,000 lines, though different parts were composed at different times. All these poems were dispersed in their narrative entirety by storytellers reciting from memory.

While scholars may disagree on the precise definition of an epic, most works share common elements:

1) The central hero possesses superhuman abilities, accomplishing things no one else can.
   - In *Beowulf*, the titular hero swims to the bottom of a lake to kill Grendel's mother, spending several hours underwater without breathing.
2) The epic begins with an invocation to a muse and a statement of theme.
   - Homer begins *The Odyssey* by requesting help from the Greek muse of poetry; he then summarizes the lessons in Odysseus's story.
3) The epic relies on epithets (descriptive terms that follow character names) and sustained epic similes.
   - *Beowulf* frequently refers to its hero as "Beowulf, son of Ecgtheow."
   - An epic simile in *The Iliad* reads "as when the shudder of the west wind suddenly rising scatters across the water, and the water darkens beneath it, so darkening were settled the ranks of Achaians and Trojans in the plain." This simile compares the combatants in the Trojan War to a windswept ocean.
4) Divine intervention, or intervention from supernatural forces, takes place.
   - In Dante's *The Inferno*, the first book of *The Divine Comedy*, an angel, who saw the danger from heaven, saves the protagonist from some monsters in Hell.
5) The setting of the epic is vast, like a kingdom, the entire world, or Heaven and Hell.
   - In *The Odyssey*, Odysseus travels thousands of miles in the Mediterranean Sea, encountering many different kingdoms, and islands with different types of magic.

6) The style of the epic is elevated throughout, with sophisticated language, including elaborate descriptions.

     o   John Milton uses elevated language in *Paradise Lost*:

> We may with more successful hope resolve
> To wage by force or guile eternal Warr
> Irreconcileable, to our grand Foe,
> Who now triumphs, and in th' excess of joy
> Sole reigning holds the Tyranny of Heav'n.

This passage, spoken by Satan, includes sophisticated words, like "guile," "irreconcilable," and "tyranny." Milton also uses unusual sentence structures to enhance his writing, like the last line of this excerpt, which is flipped from the conventional structure. He creates an elevated style by combining these elements with tools such as simile, allusion, and personification.

7) Epics contain catalogues of things, characters, or ideas, such as *The Iliad's* ships and *Beowulf's* previous kings.

8) Characters often undergo a descent into Hell or the underworld, which is the central plot of *The Inferno*.

These characteristics are not always present, but they provide a solid framework through which to view epics. The epics of different cultures also have unique characteristics, passed down through oral tradition.

TIMELINE

~2500-1300 BCE	*The Epic of Gilgamesh*, Sumer.
~800-700 BCE	*The Iliad* and *The Odyssey*, Greece, recorded by Homer.
~300 BCE-300 CE	*The Mahabharata*, India.
29-19 BCE	*The Aeneid*, Rome, by Virgil.
~700-1000 CE	*Beowulf*, England.
1321	*The Divine Comedy*, Italy, by Dante Alighieri.
~1380-1390	*Troilus and Criseyde* by Geoffrey Chaucer.
1596	*The Faerie Queene* by Edmund Spenser.
1674	*Paradise Lost* by John Milton.

Introduction to *Beowulf* and its Translation

Most study of early English literature is dependent upon translation. Unless students have studied and are fluent in Old English, texts such as *Beowulf* are unreadable without a translation, because the English language has changed so much since they were written. This is obvious in "Cædmon's Hymn" (find the original and the translation side-by-side on page 13). Middle English texts like *The Canterbury Tales* require extensive line notes with translations of certain words and explanations of archaic spellings. Even texts in Early Modern English such as Shakespeare's plays need clarification for elements like puns and double entendres that are no longer in use today. Thus, a translator has significant power to shape the reader's interpretation and understanding of the text. This introduction will provide context for the translated texts in this anthology, compare different translations, and explain why certain translations were chosen.

In 2018, Dr. Emily Wilson, a professor of classical studies, published her translation of Homer's *The Odyssey*. Her translation was *The Odyssey's* first major English translation by a woman, and she used iambic pentameter rather than the free verse used by other translators. Her research sparked a discussion about how the identity and approach of the translator affects the text. *Beowulf*, the longest translated text in this anthology, is available in many different translations, each with pros and cons. Today's most widely read translation is Seamus Heaney's 1999 *Beowulf: A New Verse Translation*. Heaney, an Irish poet and 1995 Nobel Prize in Literature winner, uses poetic verse instead of prose in order to preserve the rhythm of the original *Beowulf*. His translation is widely admired for staying true to *Beowulf's* poetic roots while making the folk epic comprehensible to modern readers.

Just as Wilson's identity as a woman impacts her translation of *The Odyssey*, Heaney's Irish identity contributes notable elements to his translation of *Beowulf*. Heaney is more sympathetic towards Grendel, a main antagonist who is an outsider shunned by the Danes. Other translators, most of whom are English, identify with the in-group of warlike men, while Heaney as a citizen of a Catholic country long controlled by Protestant England is able to empathize with the outcast Grendel, said to be descended from the biblical Cain. Below are two versions of the same passage describing Grendel, the first from Heaney in verse and the second from Ernest Kirtlan's 1913 prose translation:

> So times were pleasant for the people there
> until finally one, a fiend out of hell,
> began to work his evil in the world.
> Grendel was the name of this grim demon
> haunting the marshes, marauding round the heath
> and the desolate fens; he had dwelt for a time
> in misery among the banished monsters,

> Cain's clan, whom the Creator had outlawed
> and condemned as outcasts (Heaney 99-107).

> So noble men lived in joy, and were all blessed till one began to do evil,
> a devil from hell; and this grim spirit was called Grendel. And he was a
> march-stepper, who ruled on the moorlands, the fens, and the stronghold.
> For a while he kept guard, this unhappy creature, over the land of the
> race of monsters, since the Creator had proscribed him. On the race of
> Cain the Eternal Lord brought death as vengeance, when he slew Abel
> (Kirtlan 25-26).

Neither translator portrays Grendel as good, and both indicate he originated in
hell. However, Heaney emphasizes Grendel's time "in misery among the banished
monsters" while Kirtlan portrays him as ruling over "the land of the race of
monsters." Here's another contrasting portrayal from the early descriptions of
Grendel:

> So Grendel waged his lonely war,
> inflicting constant cruelties on the people,
> atrocious hurt. He took over Heorot,
> haunting the glittering hall after dark,
> but the throne itself, the treasure-seat,
> he was kept from approaching; he was the Lord's outcast
> (Heaney 164-169).

> Thus the foe of mankind, the terrible and lonesome traveller, often
> he did them even greater despite. And he took up his dwelling in the
> treasure-decked Hall of Hart in the dark night, nor could he come near
> the throne the treasure of God, nor did he know His love (Kirtlan 29).

Here, Heaney emphasizes Grendel's loneliness with "lonely war," and calls him "the
Lord's outcast." Kirtlan, instead, emphasizes that he is "terrible and lonesome,"
while saying that he does not "know [God's] love."

Because this anthology is restricted to texts that are out of copyright,
Heaney's translation of *Beowulf* could not be included. Instead, we use J. Lesslie
Hall's 1892 translation, which is still one of the most popular and faithful to the
original poem. Hall was a professor of English and history at the College of
William and Mary, with a doctorate from Johns Hopkins University.

While the identities of *Beowulf* translators can be examined, the poet's identity
is unknown. General scholarly consensus places the poem's creation in the eighth
century. The poet most likely recorded a folk epic handed down to them by oral
tradition. Scholars disagree about how much creative liberty the poet allowed
themself in their rendition of the poem. The most important and well-known
aspect of the *Beowulf* poet's identity is their religion. *Beowulf* probably started out as
a pagan epic, as evidenced by the nonreligious heroes and supernatural monsters

such as dragons, but there is considerable Christian influence in the version of the poem that survives, which leads scholars to believe that the *Beowulf* poet was Christian. When the poem was recorded around 800 CE, most people other than clergy members such as monks and nuns were illiterate. Debate about the *Beowulf* poet's identity continues, but most scholars agree that they recorded, rather than composed, a poem passed down orally from the earlier Anglo-Saxons, that they lived in England, and that they were a Christian whose religious devotion became superimposed upon the originally pagan poem.

Beowulf

Summary

Hrothgar, king of the Danes, or Scyldings, builds a great mead-hall, or palace, in which he hopes to feast his liegemen and to give them presents. The joy of king and retainers is, however, of short duration. Grendel, the monster, is seized with hateful jealousy. He cannot brook the sounds of joyance that reach him down in his fen-dwelling near the hall. Oft and anon he goes to the joyous building, bent on direful mischief. Thane after thane is ruthlessly carried off and devoured, while no one is found strong enough and bold enough to cope with the monster. For twelve years he persecutes Hrothgar and his vassals.

Over sea, a day's voyage off, Beowulf, of the Geats, nephew of Higelac, king of the Geats, hears of Grendel's doings and of Hrothgar's misery. He resolves to crush the fell monster and relieve the aged king. With fourteen chosen companions, he sets sail for Dane-land. Reaching that country, he soon persuades Hrothgar of his ability to help him. The hours that elapse before night are spent in beer-drinking and conversation. When Hrothgar's bedtime comes he leaves the hall in charge of Beowulf, telling him that never before has he given to another the absolute wardship of his palace. All retire to rest, Beowulf, as it were, sleeping upon his arms.

Grendel comes, the great march-stepper, bearing God's anger. He seizes and kills one of the sleeping warriors. Then he advances towards Beowulf. A fierce and desperate hand-to-hand struggle ensues. No arms are used, both combatants trusting to strength and hand-grip. Beowulf tears Grendel's shoulder from its socket, and the monster retreats to his den, howling and yelling with agony and fury. The wound is fatal.

The next morning, at early dawn, warriors in numbers flock to the hall Heorot, to hear the news. Joy is boundless. Glee runs high. Hrothgar and his retainers are lavish of gratitude and of gifts.

Grendel's mother, however, comes the next night to avenge his death. She is furious and raging. While Beowulf is sleeping in a room somewhat apart from the quarters of the other warriors, she seizes one of Hrothgar's favorite counsellors, and carries him off and devours him. Beowulf is called. Determined to leave Heorot entirely purified, he arms himself, and goes down to look for the female monster. After traveling through the waters many hours, he meets her near the sea-bottom. She drags him to her den. There he sees Grendel lying dead. After a desperate and almost fatal struggle with the woman, he slays her, and swims upward in triumph, taking with him Grendel's head.

Joy is renewed at Heorot. Congratulations crowd upon the victor. Hrothgar literally pours treasures into the lap of Beowulf; and it is agreed among the vassals of the king that Beowulf will be their next liegelord.

Beowulf leaves Dane-land. Hrothgar weeps and laments at his departure.

When the hero arrives in his own land, Higelac treats him as a distinguished guest. He is the hero of the hour.

Beowulf subsequently becomes king of his own people, the Geats. After he has been ruling for fifty years, his own neighborhood is wofully harried by a fire-spewing dragon. Beowulf determines to kill him. In the ensuing struggle both Beowulf and the dragon are slain. The grief of the Geats is inexpressible. They determine, however, to leave nothing undone to honor the memory of their lord. A great funeral-pyre is built, and his body is burnt. Then a memorial-barrow is made, visible from a great distance, that sailors afar may be constantly reminded of the prowess of the national hero of Geatland.

The poem closes with a glowing tribute to his bravery, his gentleness, his goodness of heart, and his generosity.

GLOSSARY OF NAMES

Ælfhere.—A kinsman of Wiglaf.

Æschere.—Confidential friend of King Hrothgar. Elder brother of Yrmenlaf. Killed by Grendel.

Beanstan.—Father of Breca.

Beowulf.—Son of Scyld, the founder of the dynasty of Scyldings. Father of Healfdene, and grandfather of Hrothgar.

Beowulf.—The hero of the poem. Sprung from the stock of Geats, son of Ecgtheow. Brought up by his maternal grandfather Hrethel, and figuring in manhood as a devoted liegeman of his uncle Higelac. A hero from his youth. Has the strength of thirty men. Engages in a swimming-match with Breca. Goes to the help of Hrothgar against the monster Grendel. Vanquishes Grendel and his mother. Afterwards becomes king of the Geats. Late in life attempts to kill a fire-spewing dragon, and is slain. Is buried with great honors.

Breca.—Beowulf's opponent in the famous swimming-match.

Brondings.—A people ruled by Breca.

Brosinga mene.—A famous collar once owned by the Brosings.

Cain.—Progenitor of Grendel and other monsters.

Dæghrefn.—A warrior of the Hugs, killed by Beowulf.

Danes.—Subjects of Scyld and his descendants, and hence often called Scyldings. Other names for them are Victory-Scyldings, Honor-Scyldings, Armor-Danes, Bright-Danes, East-Danes, West-Danes, North-Danes, South-Danes, Ingwins, Hrethmen.

Ecglaf.—Father of Unferth, who taunts Beowulf.

Ecgtheow.—Father of Beowulf, the hero of the poem. A widely-known Wægmunding warrior. Marries Hrethel's daughter. After slaying Heatholaf, a Wylfing, he flees his country.

Ecgwela.—A king of the Danes before Scyld.

Elan.—Sister of Hrothgar, and probably wife of Ongentheow, king of the Swedes.

Eagle Cape.—A promontory in Geat-land, under which took place Beowulf's last encounter.

Eadgils.—Son of Ohthere and brother of Eanmund.

Eanmund.—Son of Ohthere and brother of Eadgils. The reference to these brothers is vague, and variously understood. Heyne supposes as follows: Raising a revolt against their father, they are obliged to leave Sweden. They go to the land of the Geats; with what intention, is not known, but probably to conquer and plunder. The Geatish king, Heardred, is slain by one of the brothers, probably Eanmund.

Eofor.—A Geatish hero who slays Ongentheow in war, and is rewarded by Hygelac with the hand of his only daughter.

Eormenric.—A Gothic king, from whom Hama took away the famous Brosinga mene.

Eomær.—Son of Offa and Thrytho, king and queen of the Angles.

Finn.—King of the North-Frisians and the Jutes. Marries Hildeburg. At his court takes place the horrible slaughter in which the Danish general, Hnæf, fell. Later on, Finn himself is slain by Danish warriors.

Fin-land.—The country to which Beowulf was driven by the currents in his swimming-match.

Fitela.—Son and nephew of King Sigemund, whose praises are sung in XIV.

Folcwalda.—Father of Finn.

Franks.—Introduced occasionally in referring to the death of Higelac.

Frisians.—A part of them are ruled by Finn. Some of them were engaged in the struggle in which Higelac was slain.

Freaware.—Daughter of King Hrothgar. Married to Ingeld, a Heathobard prince.

Froda.—King of the Heathobards, and father of Ingeld.

Garmund.—Father of Offa.

Geats, Geatmen.—The race to which the hero of the poem belongs. Also called Weder-Geats, or Weders, War-Geats, Sea-Geats. They are ruled by Hrethel, Hæthcyn, Higelac, and Beowulf.

Gepids.—Named in connection with the Danes and Swedes.

Grendel.—A monster of the race of Cain. Dwells in the fens and moors. Is furiously envious when he hears sounds of joy in Hrothgar's palace. Causes the king untold agony for years. Is finally conquered by Beowulf, and dies of his wound. His hand and arm are hung up in Hrothgar's hall Heorot. His head is cut off by Beowulf when he goes down to fight with Grendel's mother.

Guthlaf.—A Dane of Hnæf's party.

Half-Danes.—Branch of the Danes to which Hnæf belonged.

Halga.—Surnamed the Good. Younger brother of Hrothgar.

Hama.—Takes the Brosinga mene from Eormenric.

Hæreth.—Father of Higelac's queen, Hygd.

Hæthcyn.—Son of Hrethel and brother of Higelac. Kills his brother Herebeald accidentally. Is slain at Ravenswood, fighting against Ongentheow.

Helmings.—The race to which Queen Wealhtheow belonged.

Heming.—A kinsman of Garmund, perhaps nephew.

Hengest.—A Danish leader. Takes command on the fall of Hnæf.

Herebeald.—Eldest son of Hrethel, the Geatish king, and brother of Higelac. Killed by his younger brother Hæthcyn.

Heremod.—A Danish king of a dynasty before the Scylding line. Was a source of great sorrow to his people.

Hereric.—Referred to as uncle of Heardred, but otherwise unknown.

Hetwars.—Another name for the Franks.

Healfdene.—Grandson of Scyld and father of Hrothgar. Ruled the Danes long and well.

Heardred.—Son of Higelac and Hygd, king and queen of the Geats. Succeeds his father, with Beowulf as regent. Is slain by the sons of Ohthere.

Heathobards.—Race of Lombards, of which Froda is king. After Froda falls in battle with the Danes, Ingeld, his son, marries Hrothgar's daughter, Freaware, in order to heal the feud.

Heatholaf.—A Wylfing warrior slain by Beowulf's father.

Heathoremes.—The people on whose shores Breca is cast by the waves during his contest with Beowulf.

Heorogar.—Elder brother of Hrothgar, and surnamed 'Weoroda Ræswa,' Prince of the Troopers.

Hereward.—Son of the above.

Heort, Heorot.—The great mead-hall which King Hrothgar builds. It is invaded by Grendel for twelve years. Finally cleansed by Beowulf, the Geat. It is called Heort on account of the hart-antlers which decorate it.

Hildeburg.—Wife of Finn, daughter of Hoce, and related to Hnæf,—probably his sister.

Hnæf.—Leader of a branch of the Danes called Half-Danes. Killed in the struggle at Finn's castle.

Hondscio.—One of Beowulf's companions. Killed by Grendel just before Beowulf grappled with that monster.

Hoce.—Father of Hildeburg and probably of Hnæf.

Hrethel.—King of the Geats, father of Higelac, and grandfather of Beowulf.

Hrethmen.—Another name for the Danes.

Hrethric.—Son of Hrothgar.

Hreosna-beorh.—A promontory in Geat-land, near which Ohthere's sons made plundering raids.

Hrothgar.—The Danish king who built the hall Heort, but was long unable to enjoy it on account of Grendel's persecutions. Marries Wealhtheow, a Helming lady. Has two sons and a daughter. Is a typical Teutonic king, lavish of gifts. A devoted liegelord, as his lamentations over slain liegemen prove. Also very appreciative of kindness, as is shown by his loving gratitude to Beowulf.

Hrothmund.—Son of Hrothgar.

Hrothulf.—Probably a son of Halga, younger brother of Hrothgar. Certainly on terms of close intimacy in Hrothgar's palace.

Hrunting.—Unferth's sword, lent to Beowulf.

Hugs.—A race in alliance with the Franks and Frisians at the time of Higelac's fall.

Hun.—A Frisian warrior, probably general of the Hetwars. Gives Hengest a beautiful sword.

Hunferth.—Sometimes used for Unferth.

Hygelac, Higelac.—King of the Geats, uncle and liegelord of Beowulf, the hero of the poem.—His second wife is the lovely Hygd, daughter of Hæreth. The son of their union is Heardred. Is slain in a war with the Hugs, Franks, and Frisians combined. Beowulf is regent, and afterwards king of the Geats.

Hygd.—Wife of Higelac, and daughter of Hæreth. There are some indications that she married Beowulf after she became a widow.

Ingeld.—Son of the Heathobard king, Froda. Marries Hrothgar's daughter, Freaware, in order to reconcile the two peoples.

Ingwins.—Another name for the Danes.

Jutes.—Name sometimes applied to Finn's people.

Lafing.—Name of a famous sword presented to Hengest by Hun.

Merewing.—A Frankish king, probably engaged in the war in which Higelac was slain.

Nægling.—Beowulf's sword.

Offa.—King of the Angles, and son of Garmund. Marries the terrible Thrytho who is so strongly contrasted with Hygd.

Ohthere.—Son of Ongentheow, king of the Swedes. He is father of Eanmund and Eadgils.

Onela.—Brother of Ohthere.

Ongentheow.—King of Sweden, of the Scylfing dynasty. Married, perhaps, Elan, daughter of Healfdene.

Oslaf.—A Dane of Hnæf's party.

Ravenswood.—The forest near which Hæthcyn was slain.

Scefing.—Applied to Scyld, and meaning 'son of Scef.'

Scyld.—Founder of the dynasty to which Hrothgar, his father, and grandfather belonged. He dies, and his body is put on a vessel, and set adrift. He goes from Daneland just as he had come to it—in a bark.

Scyldings.—The descendants of Scyld. They are also called Honor-Scyldings, Victory-Scyldings, War-Scyldings, etc. (See 'Danes,' above.)

Scylfings.—A Swedish royal line to which Wiglaf belonged.

Sigemund.—Son of Wæls, and uncle and father of Fitela. His struggle with a dragon is related in connection with Beowulf's deeds of prowess.

Swerting.—Grandfather of Higelac, and father of Hrethel.

Swedes.—People of Sweden, ruled by the Scylfings.

Thrytho.—Wife of Offa, king of the Angles. Known for her fierce and unwomanly disposition. She is introduced as a contrast to the gentle Hygd, queen of Higelac.

Unferth.—Son of Ecglaf, and seemingly a confidential courtier of Hrothgar. Taunts Beowulf for having taken part in the swimming-match. Lends Beowulf his sword when he goes to look for Grendel's mother. In the MS. sometimes written Hunferth.

Wæls.—Father of Sigemund.

Wægmunding.—A name occasionally applied to Wiglaf and Beowulf, and perhaps derived from a common ancestor, Wægmund.

Weders.—Another name for Geats or Wedergeats.

Wayland.—A fabulous smith mentioned in this poem and in other old Teutonic literature.

Wendels.—The people of Wulfgar, Hrothgar's messenger. (Perhaps = Vandals.)

Wealhtheow.—Wife of Hrothgar. Her queenly courtesy is well shown in the poem.

Weohstan, or Wihstan.—A Wægmunding, and father of Wiglaf.

Whale's Ness.—A prominent promontory, on which Beowulf's mound was built.

Wiglaf.—Son of Wihstan, and related to Beowulf. He remains faithful to Beowulf in the fatal struggle with the fire-drake. Would rather die than leave his lord in his dire emergency.

Wonred.—Father of Wulf and Eofor.

Wulf.—Son of Wonred. Engaged in the battle between Higelac's and Ongentheow's forces, and had a hand-to-hand fight with Ongentheow himself. Ongentheow disables him, and is thereupon slain by Eofor.

Wulfgar.—Lord of the Wendels, and retainer of Hrothgar.

Wylfings.—A people to whom belonged Heatholaf, who was slain by Ecgtheow.

Yrmenlaf.—Younger brother of Æschere, the hero whose death grieved Hrothgar so deeply.

LIST OF WORDS AND PHRASES

ATHELING.—Prince, nobleman.

BAIRN.—Son, child.

BARROW.—Mound, rounded hill, funeral-mound.

BATTLE-SARK.—Armor.

BEAKER.—Cup, drinking-vessel.

BEGEAR.—Prepare.

BIGHT.—Bay, sea.

BILL.—Sword.

BOSS.—Ornamental projection.

BRACTEATE.—A round ornament on a necklace.

BRAND.—Sword.

BURN.—Stream.

BURNIE.—Armor.

CARLE.—Man, hero.

EARL.—Nobleman, any brave man.

EKE.—Also.

EMPRISE.—Enterprise, undertaking.

ERST.—Formerly.

ERST-WORTHY.—Worthy for a long time past.

FAIN.—Glad.

FERRY.—Bear, carry.

FEY.—Fated, doomed.
FLOAT.—Vessel, ship.
FOIN.—To lunge (Shaks.).
GLORY OF KINGS.—God.
GREWSOME.—Cruel, fierce.
HEFT.—Handle, hilt; used by synecdoche for 'sword.'
HELM.—Helmet, protector.
HENCHMAN.—Retainer, vassal.
HIGHT.—Am (was) named.
HOLM.—Ocean, curved surface of the sea.
HIMSEEMED.—(It) seemed to him.
LIEF.—Dear, valued.
MERE.—Sea; in compounds, 'mere-ways,' 'mere-currents,' etc.
MICKLE.—Much.
NATHLESS.—Nevertheless.
NAZE.—Edge (nose).
NESS.—Edge.
NICKER.—Sea-beast.
QUIT, QUITE.—Requite.
RATHE.—Quickly.
REAVE.—Bereave, deprive.
SAIL-ROAD.—Sea.
SETTLE.—Seat, bench.
SKINKER.—One who pours.
SOOTHLY.—Truly.
SWINGE.—Stroke, blow.
TARGE, TARGET.—Shield.
THROUGHLY.—Thoroughly.
TOLD.—Counted.
UNCANNY.—Ill-featured, grizzly.
UNNETHE.—Difficult.
WAR-SPEED.—Success in war.
WEB.—Tapestry (that which is 'woven').
WEEDED.—Clad (cf. widow's weeds).
WEEN.—Suppose, imagine.
WEIRD.—Fate, Providence.
WHILOM.—At times, formerly, often.
WIELDER.—Ruler. Often used of God; also in compounds, as 'Wielder of Glory,' 'Wielder of Worship.'
WIGHT.—Creature.
WOLD.—Plane, extended surface.
WOT.—Knows.
YOUNKER.—Youth.

BEOWULF

Lo! the Spear-Danes' glory through splendid achievements
The folk-kings' former fame we have heard of,
How princes displayed then their prowess-in-battle.
Oft Scyld the Scefing from scathers in numbers
5   From many a people their mead-benches tore.
Since first he found him friendless and wretched,
The earl had had terror: comfort he got for it,
Waxed 'neath the welkin, world-honor gained,
Till all his neighbors o'er sea were compelled to
10   Bow to his bidding and bring him their tribute:
An excellent atheling! After was borne him
A son and heir, young in his dwelling,
Whom God-Father sent to solace the people.
He had marked the misery malice had caused them,
15   That reaved of their rulers they wretched had erstwhile
Long been afflicted. The Lord, in requital,
Wielder of Glory, with world-honor blessed him.
Famed was Beowulf, far spread the glory
Of Scyld's great son in the lands of the Danemen.
20   So the carle that is young, by kindnesses rendered
The friends of his father, with fees in abundance
Must be able to earn that when age approacheth
Eager companions aid him requitingly,
When war assaults him serve him as liegemen:
25   By praise-worthy actions must honor be got
'Mong all of the races. At the hour that was fated
Scyld then departed to the All-Father's keeping
Warlike to wend him; away then they bare him
To the flood of the current, his fond-loving comrades,
30   As himself he had bidden, while the friend of the Scyldings
Word-sway wielded, and the well-lovèd land-prince
Long did rule them. The ring-stemmèd vessel,
Bark of the atheling, lay there at anchor,
Icy in glimmer and eager for sailing;
35   The belovèd leader laid they down there,
Giver of rings, on the breast of the vessel,
The famed by the mainmast. A many of jewels,
Of fretted embossings, from far-lands brought over,
Was placed near at hand then; and heard I not ever
40   That a folk ever furnished a float more superbly

With weapons of warfare, weeds for the battle,
Bills and burnies; on his bosom sparkled
Many a jewel that with him must travel
On the flush of the flood afar on the current.
45   And favors no fewer they furnished him soothly,
Excellent folk-gems, than others had given him
Who when first he was born outward did send him
Lone on the main, the merest of infants:
And a gold-fashioned standard they stretched under heaven
50   High o'er his head, let the holm-currents bear him,
Seaward consigned him: sad was their spirit,
Their mood very mournful. Men are not able
Soothly to tell us, they in halls who reside,
Heroes under heaven, to what haven he hied.

55   In the boroughs then Beowulf, bairn of the Scyldings,
Belovèd land-prince, for long-lasting season
Was famed mid the folk (his father departed,
The prince from his dwelling), till afterward sprang
Great-minded Healfdene; the Danes in his lifetime
60   He graciously governed, grim-mooded, agèd.
Four bairns of his body born in succession
Woke in the world, war-troopers' leader
Heorogar, Hrothgar, and Halga the good;
Heard I that Elan was Ongentheow's consort,
65   The well-beloved bedmate of the War-Scylfing leader.
Then glory in battle to Hrothgar was given,
Waxing of war-fame, that willingly kinsmen
Obeyed his bidding, till the boys grew to manhood,
A numerous band. It burned in his spirit
70   To urge his folk to found a great building,
A mead-hall grander than men of the era
Ever had heard of, and in it to share
With young and old all of the blessings
The Lord had allowed him, save life and retainers.
75   Then the work I find afar was assigned
To many races in middle-earth's regions,
To adorn the great folk-hall. In due time it happened
Early 'mong men, that 'twas finished entirely,
The greatest of hall-buildings; Heorot he named it
80   Who wide-reaching word-sway wielded 'mong earlmen.
His promise he brake not, rings he lavished,
Treasure at banquet. Towered the hall up
High and horn-crested, huge between antlers:
It battle-waves bided, the blasting fire-demon;

85 Ere long then from hottest hatred must sword-wrath
Arise for a woman's husband and father.
Then the mighty war-spirit endured for a season,
Bore it bitterly, he who bided in darkness,
That light-hearted laughter loud in the building
90 Greeted him daily; there was dulcet harp-music,
Clear song of the singer. He said that was able
To tell from of old earthmen's beginnings,
That Father Almighty earth had created,
The winsome wold that the water encircleth,
95 Set exultingly the sun's and the moon's beams
To lavish their lustre on land-folk and races,
And earth He embellished in all her regions
With limbs and leaves; life He bestowed too
On all the kindreds that live under heaven.
100 So blessed with abundance, brimming with joyance,
The warriors abided, till a certain one gan to
Dog them with deeds of direfullest malice,
A foe in the hall-building: this horrible stranger
Was Grendel entitled, the march-stepper famous
105 Who dwelt in the moor-fens, the marsh and the fastness;
The wan-mooded being abode for a season
In the land of the giants, when the Lord and Creator
Had banned him and branded. For that bitter murder,
The killing of Abel, all-ruling Father
110 The kindred of Cain crushed with His vengeance;
In the feud He rejoiced not, but far away drove him
From kindred and kind, that crime to atone for,
Meter of Justice. Thence ill-favored creatures,
Elves and giants, monsters of ocean,
115 Came into being, and the giants that longtime
Grappled with God; He gave them requital.

When the sun was sunken, he set out to visit
The lofty hall-building, how the Ring-Danes had used it
For beds and benches when the banquet was over.
120 Then he found there reposing many a noble
Asleep after supper; sorrow the heroes,
Misery knew not. The monster of evil
Greedy and cruel tarried but little,
Fell and frantic, and forced from their slumbers
125 Thirty of thanemen; thence he departed
Leaping and laughing, his lair to return to,
With surfeit of slaughter sallying homeward.
In the dusk of the dawning, as the day was just breaking,

Was Grendel's prowess revealed to the warriors:
130 Then, his meal-taking finished, a moan was uplifted,
Morning-cry mighty. The man-ruler famous,
The long-worthy atheling, sat very woful,
Suffered great sorrow, sighed for his liegemen,
When they had seen the track of the hateful pursuer,
135 The spirit accursèd: too crushing that sorrow,
Too loathsome and lasting. Not longer he tarried,
But one night after continued his slaughter
Shameless and shocking, shrinking but little
From malice and murder; they mastered him fully.
140 He was easy to find then who otherwhere looked for
A pleasanter place of repose in the lodges,
A bed in the bowers. Then was brought to his notice
Told him truly by token apparent
The hall-thane's hatred: he held himself after
145 Further and faster who the foeman did baffle.
So ruled he and strongly strove against justice
Lone against all men, till empty uptowered
The choicest of houses. Long was the season:
Twelve-winters' time torture suffered
150 The friend of the Scyldings, every affliction,
Endless agony; hence it after became
Certainly known to the children of men
Sadly in measures, that long against Hrothgar
Grendel struggled:—his grudges he cherished,
155 Murderous malice, many a winter,
Strife unremitting, and peacefully wished he
Life-woe to lift from no liegeman at all of
The men of the Dane-folk, for money to settle,
No counsellor needed count for a moment
160 On handsome amends at the hands of the murderer;
The monster of evil fiercely did harass,
The ill-planning death-shade, both elder and younger,
Trapping and tricking them. He trod every night then
The mist-covered moor-fens; men do not know where
165 Witches and wizards wander and ramble.
So the foe of mankind many of evils
Grievous injuries, often accomplished,
Horrible hermit; Heort he frequented,
Gem-bedecked palace, when night-shades had fallen
170 (Since God did oppose him, not the throne could he touch,
The light-flashing jewel, love of Him knew not).
'Twas a fearful affliction to the friend of the Scyldings
Soul-crushing sorrow. Not seldom in private

Sat the king in his council; conference held they
175 What the braves should determine 'gainst terrors unlooked for.
At the shrines of their idols often they promised
Gifts and offerings, earnestly prayed they
The devil from hell would help them to lighten
Their people's oppression. Such practice they used then,
180 Hope of the heathen; hell they remembered
In innermost spirit, God they knew not,
Judge of their actions, All-wielding Ruler,
No praise could they give the Guardian of Heaven,
The Wielder of Glory. Woe will be his who
185 Through furious hatred his spirit shall drive to
The clutch of the fire, no comfort shall look for,
Wax no wiser; well for the man who,
Living his life-days, his Lord may face
And find defence in his Father's embrace!

190 So Healfdene's kinsman constantly mused on
His long-lasting sorrow; the battle-thane clever
Was not anywise able evils to 'scape from:
Too crushing the sorrow that came to the people,
Loathsome and lasting the life-grinding torture,
195 Greatest of night-woes. So Higelac's liegeman,
Good amid Geatmen, of Grendel's achievements
Heard in his home: of heroes then living
He was stoutest and strongest, sturdy and noble.
He bade them prepare him a bark that was trusty;
200 He said he the war-king would seek o'er the ocean,
The folk-leader noble, since he needed retainers.
For the perilous project prudent companions
Chided him little, though loving him dearly;
They egged the brave atheling, augured him glory.
205 The excellent knight from the folk of the Geatmen
Had liegemen selected, likest to prove them
Trustworthy warriors; with fourteen companions
The vessel he looked for; a liegeman then showed them,
A sea-crafty man, the bounds of the country.
210 Fast the days fleeted; the float was a-water,
The craft by the cliff. Clomb to the prow then
Well-equipped warriors: the wave-currents twisted
The sea on the sand; soldiers then carried
On the breast of the vessel bright-shining jewels,
215 Handsome war-armor; heroes outshoved then,
Warmen the wood-ship, on its wished-for adventure.
The foamy-necked floater fanned by the breeze,

Likest a bird, glided the waters,
Till twenty and four hours thereafter
220 The twist-stemmed vessel had traveled such distance
That the sailing-men saw the sloping embankments,
The sea cliffs gleaming, precipitous mountains,
Nesses enormous: they were nearing the limits
At the end of the ocean. Up thence quickly
225 The men of the Weders clomb to the mainland,
Fastened their vessel (battle weeds rattled,
War burnies clattered), the Wielder they thanked
That the ways o'er the waters had waxen so gentle.
Then well from the cliff edge the guard of the Scyldings
230 Who the sea-cliffs should see to, saw o'er the gangway
Brave ones bearing beauteous targets,
Armor all ready, anxiously thought he,
Musing and wondering what men were approaching.
High on his horse then Hrothgar's retainer
235 Turned him to coastward, mightily brandished
His lance in his hands, questioned with boldness.
"Who are ye men here, mail-covered warriors
Clad in your corslets, come thus a-driving
A high riding ship o'er the shoals of the waters,
240 And hither 'neath helmets have hied o'er the ocean?
I have been strand-guard, standing as warden,
Lest enemies ever anywise ravage
Danish dominions with army of war-ships.
More boldly never have warriors ventured
245 Hither to come; of kinsmen's approval,
Word-leave of warriors, I ween that ye surely
Nothing have known. Never a greater one
Of earls o'er the earth have I had a sight of
Than is one of your number, a hero in armor;
250 No low-ranking fellow adorned with his weapons,
But launching them little, unless looks are deceiving,
And striking appearance. Ere ye pass on your journey
As treacherous spies to the land of the Scyldings
And farther fare, I fully must know now
255 What race ye belong to. Ye far-away dwellers,
Sea-faring sailors, my simple opinion
Hear ye and hearken: haste is most fitting
Plainly to tell me what place ye are come from."

The chief of the strangers rendered him answer,
260 War-troopers' leader, and word-treasure opened:
"We are sprung from the lineage of the people of Geatland,

And Higelac's hearth-friends. To heroes unnumbered
My father was known, a noble head-warrior
Ecgtheow titled; many a winter
265 He lived with the people, ere he passed on his journey,
Old from his dwelling; each of the counsellors
Widely mid world-folk well remembers him.
We, kindly of spirit, the lord of thy people,
The son of King Healfdene, have come here to visit,
270 Folk-troop's defender: be free in thy counsels!
To the noble one bear we a weighty commission,
The helm of the Danemen; we shall hide, I ween,
Naught of our message. Thou know'st if it happen,
As we soothly heard say, that some savage despoiler,
275 Some hidden pursuer, on nights that are murky
By deeds very direful 'mid the Danemen exhibits
Hatred unheard of, horrid destruction
And the falling of dead. From feelings least selfish
I am able to render counsel to Hrothgar,
280 How he, wise and worthy, may worst the destroyer,
If the anguish of sorrow should ever be lessened,
Comfort come to him, and care-waves grow cooler,
Or ever hereafter he agony suffer
And troublous distress, while towereth upward
285 The handsomest of houses high on the summit."
Bestriding his stallion, the strand-watchman answered,
The doughty retainer: "The difference surely
'Twixt words and works, the warlike shield-bearer
Who judgeth wisely well shall determine.
290 This band, I hear, beareth no malice
To the prince of the Scyldings. Pass ye then onward
With weapons and armor. I shall lead you in person;
To my war-trusty vassals command I shall issue
To keep from all injury your excellent vessel,
295 Your fresh-tarred craft, 'gainst every opposer
Close by the sea-shore, till the curved-neckèd bark shall
Waft back again the well-beloved hero
O'er the way of the water to Weder dominions.
To warrior so great 'twill be granted sure
300 In the storm of strife to stand secure."
Onward they fared then (the vessel lay quiet,
The broad-bosomed bark was bound by its cable,
Firmly at anchor); the boar-signs glistened
Bright on the visors vivid with gilding,
305 Blaze-hardened, brilliant; the boar acted warden.
The heroes hastened, hurried the liegemen,

Descended together, till they saw the great palace,
The well-fashioned wassail-hall wondrous and gleaming:
'Mid world-folk and kindreds that was widest reputed
310 Of halls under heaven which the hero abode in;
Its lustre enlightened lands without number.
Then the battle-brave hero showed them the glittering
Court of the bold ones, that they easily thither
Might fare on their journey; the aforementioned warrior
315 Turning his courser, quoth as he left them:
"'Tis time I were faring; Father Almighty
Grant you His grace, and give you to journey
Safe on your mission! To the sea I will get me
'Gainst hostile warriors as warden to stand."

320 The highway glistened with many-hued pebble,
A by-path led the liegemen together.
Firm and hand-locked the war-burnie glistened,
The ring-sword radiant rang 'mid the armor
As the party was approaching the palace together
325 In warlike equipments. 'Gainst the wall of the building
Their wide-fashioned war-shields they weary did set then,
Battle-shields sturdy; benchward they turned then;
Their battle-sarks rattled, the gear of the heroes;
The lances stood up then, all in a cluster,
330 The arms of the seamen, ashen-shafts mounted
With edges of iron: the armor-clad troopers
Were decked with weapons. Then a proud-mooded hero
Asked of the champions questions of lineage:
"From what borders bear ye your battle-shields plated,
335 Gilded and gleaming, your gray-colored burnies,
Helmets with visors and heap of war-lances?—
To Hrothgar the king I am servant and liegeman.
'Mong folk from far-lands found I have never
Men so many of mien more courageous.
340 I ween that from valor, nowise as outlaws,
But from greatness of soul ye sought for King Hrothgar."
Then the strength-famous earlman answer rendered,
The proud-mooded Wederchief replied to his question,
Hardy 'neath helmet: "Higelac's mates are we;
345 Beowulf hight I. To the bairn of Healfdene,
The famous folk-leader, I freely will tell
To thy prince my commission, if pleasantly hearing
He'll grant we may greet him so gracious to all men."
Wulfgar replied then (he was prince of the Wendels,
350 His boldness of spirit was known unto many,

His prowess and prudence): "The prince of the Scyldings,
The friend-lord of Danemen, I will ask of thy journey,
The giver of rings, as thou urgest me do it,
The folk-chief famous, and inform thee early
355   What answer the good one mindeth to render me."
He turned then hurriedly where Hrothgar was sitting,
Old and hoary, his earlmen attending him;
The strength-famous went till he stood at the shoulder
Of the lord of the Danemen, of courteous thanemen
360   The custom he minded. Wulfgar addressed then
His friendly liegelord: "Folk of the Geatmen
O'er the way of the waters are wafted hither,
Faring from far-lands: the foremost in rank
The battle-champions Beowulf title.
365   They make this petition: with thee, O my chieftain,
To be granted a conference; O gracious King Hrothgar,
Friendly answer refuse not to give them!
In war-trappings weeded worthy they seem
Of earls to be honored; sure the atheling is doughty
370   Who headed the heroes hitherward coming."

Hrothgar answered, helm of the Scyldings:
"I remember this man as the merest of striplings.
His father long dead now was Ecgtheow titled,
Him Hrethel the Geatman granted at home his
375   One only daughter; his battle-brave son
Is come but now, sought a trustworthy friend.
Seafaring sailors asserted it then,
Who valuable gift-gems of the Geatmen carried
As peace-offering thither, that he thirty men's grapple
380   Has in his hand, the hero-in-battle.
The holy Creator usward sent him,
To West-Dane warriors, I ween, for to render
'Gainst Grendel's grimness gracious assistance:
I shall give to the good one gift-gems for courage.
385   Hasten to bid them hither to speed them,
To see assembled this circle of kinsmen;
Tell them expressly they're welcome in sooth to
The men of the Danes." To the door of the building
Wulfgar went then, this word-message shouted:
390   "My victorious liegelord bade me to tell you,
The East-Danes' atheling, that your origin knows he,
And o'er wave-billows wafted ye welcome are hither,
Valiant of spirit. Ye straightway may enter
Clad in corslets, cased in your helmets,

395 To see King Hrothgar. Here let your battle-boards,
Wood-spears and war-shafts, await your conferring.”
The mighty one rose then, with many a liegeman,
An excellent thane-group; some there did await them,
And as bid of the brave one the battle-gear guarded.
400 Together they hied them, while the hero did guide them,
’Neath Heorot’s roof; the high-minded went then
Sturdy ’neath helmet till he stood in the building.
Beowulf spake (his burnie did glisten,
His armor seamed over by the art of the craftsman):
405 “Hail thou, Hrothgar! I am Higelac’s kinsman
And vassal forsooth; many a wonder
I dared as a stripling. The doings of Grendel,
In far-off fatherland I fully did know of:
Sea-farers tell us, this hall-building standeth,
Excellent edifice, empty and useless
410 To all the earlmen after evenlight’s glimmer
’Neath heaven’s bright hues hath hidden its glory.
This my earls then urged me, the most excellent of them,
Carles very clever, to come and assist thee,
Folk-leader Hrothgar; fully they knew of
415 The strength of my body. Themselves they beheld me
When I came from the contest, when covered with gore
Foes I escaped from, where five I had bound,
The giant-race wasted, in the waters destroying
The nickers by night, bore numberless sorrows,
420 The Weders avenged (woes had they suffered)
Enemies ravaged; alone now with Grendel
I shall manage the matter, with the monster of evil,
The giant, decide it. Thee I would therefore
Beg of thy bounty, Bright-Danish chieftain,
425 Lord of the Scyldings, this single petition:
Not to refuse me, defender of warriors,
Friend-lord of folks, so far have I sought thee,
That I may unaided, my earlmen assisting me,
This brave-mooded war-band, purify Heorot.
430 I have heard on inquiry, the horrible creature
From veriest rashness recks not for weapons;
I this do scorn then, so be Higelac gracious,
My liegelord belovèd, lenient of spirit,
To bear a blade or a broad-fashioned target,
435 A shield to the onset; only with hand-grip
The foe I must grapple, fight for my life then,
Foeman with foeman; he fain must rely on
The doom of the Lord whom death layeth hold of.

I ween he will wish, if he win in the struggle,
440 To eat in the war-hall earls of the Geat-folk,
Boldly to swallow them, as of yore he did often
The best of the Hrethmen! Thou needest not trouble
A head-watch to give me; he will have me dripping
And dreary with gore, if death overtake me,
445 Will bear me off bleeding, biting and mouthing me,
The hermit will eat me, heedless of pity,
Marking the moor-fens; no more wilt thou need then
Find me my food. If I fall in the battle,
Send to Higelac the armor that serveth
450 To shield my bosom, the best of equipments,
Richest of ring-mails; 'tis the relic of Hrethla,
The work of Wayland. Goes Weird as she must go!"

Hrothgar discoursed, helm of the Scyldings:
"To defend our folk and to furnish assistance,
455 Thou soughtest us hither, good friend Beowulf.
The fiercest of feuds thy father engaged in,
Heatholaf killed he in hand-to-hand conflict
'Mid Wilfingish warriors; then the Wederish people
For fear of a feud were forced to disown him.
460 Thence flying he fled to the folk of the South-Danes,
The race of the Scyldings, o'er the roll of the waters;
I had lately begun then to govern the Danemen,
The hoard-seat of heroes held in my youth,
Rich in its jewels: dead was Heregar,
465 My kinsman and elder had earth-joys forsaken,
Healfdene his bairn. He was better than I am!
That feud thereafter for a fee I compounded;
O'er the weltering waters to the Wilfings I sent
Ornaments old; oaths did he swear me.
470 It pains me in spirit to any to tell it,
What grief in Heorot Grendel hath caused me,
What horror unlooked-for, by hatred unceasing.
Waned is my war-band, wasted my hall-troop;
Weird hath offcast them to the clutches of Grendel.
475 God can easily hinder the scather
From deeds so direful. Oft drunken with beer
O'er the ale-vessel promised warriors in armor
They would willingly wait on the wassailing-benches
A grapple with Grendel, with grimmest of edges.
480 Then this mead-hall at morning with murder was reeking,
The building was bloody at breaking of daylight,
The bench-deals all flooded, dripping and bloodied,

The folk-hall was gory: I had fewer retainers,
Dear-beloved warriors, whom death had laid hold of.
485 Sit at the feast now, thy intents unto heroes,
Thy victor-fame show, as thy spirit doth urge thee!"
For the men of the Geats then together assembled,
In the beer-hall blithesome a bench was made ready;
There warlike in spirit they went to be seated,
490 Proud and exultant. A liegeman did service,
Who a beaker embellished bore with decorum,
And gleaming-drink poured. The gleeman sang whilom
Hearty in Heorot; there was heroes' rejoicing,
A numerous war-band of Weders and Danemen.

495 Unferth spoke up, Ecglaf his son,
Who sat at the feet of the lord of the Scyldings,
Opened the jousting (the journey of Beowulf,
Sea-farer doughty, gave sorrow to Unferth
And greatest chagrin, too, for granted he never
500 That any man else on earth should attain to,
Gain under heaven, more glory than he):
"Art thou that Beowulf with Breca did struggle,
On the wide sea-currents at swimming contended,
Where to humor your pride the ocean ye tried,
505 From vainest vaunting adventured your bodies
In care of the waters? And no one was able
Nor lief nor loth one, in the least to dissuade you
Your difficult voyage; then ye ventured a-swimming,
Where your arms outstretching the streams ye did cover,
510 The mere-ways measured, mixing and stirring them,
Glided the ocean; angry the waves were,
With the weltering of winter. In the water's possession,
Ye toiled for a seven-night; he at swimming outdid thee,
In strength excelled thee. Then early at morning
515 On the Heathoremes' shore the holm-currents tossed him,
Sought he thenceward the home of his fathers,
Beloved of his liegemen, the land of the Brondings,
The peace-castle pleasant, where a people he wielded,
Had borough and jewels. The pledge that he made thee
520 The son of Beanstan hath soothly accomplished.
Then I ween thou wilt find thee less fortunate issue,
Though ever triumphant in onset of battle,
A grim grappling, if Grendel thou darest
For the space of a night near-by to wait for!"
525 Beowulf answered, offspring of Ecgtheow:
"My good friend Unferth, sure freely and wildly,

Thou fuddled with beer of Breca hast spoken,
Hast told of his journey! A fact I allege it,
That greater strength in the waters I had then,
530 Ills in the ocean, than any man else had.
We made agreement as the merest of striplings
Promised each other (both of us then were
Younkers in years) that we yet would adventure
Out on the ocean; it all we accomplished.
535 While swimming the sea-floods, sword-blade unscabbarded
Boldly we brandished, our bodies expected
To shield from the sharks. He sure was unable
To swim on the waters further than I could,
More swift on the waves, nor would I from him go.
540 Then we two companions stayed in the ocean
Five nights together, till the currents did part us,
The weltering waters, weathers the bleakest,
And nethermost night, and the north-wind whistled
Fierce in our faces; fell were the billows.
545 The mere fishes' mood was mightily ruffled:
And there against foemen my firm-knotted corslet,
Hand-jointed, hardy, help did afford me;
My battle-sark braided, brilliantly gilded,
Lay on my bosom. To the bottom then dragged me,
550 A hateful fiend-scather, seized me and held me,
Grim in his grapple: 'twas granted me, nathless,
To pierce the monster with the point of my weapon,
My obedient blade; battle offcarried
The mighty mere-creature by means of my hand-blow.

555 "So ill-meaning enemies often did cause me
Sorrow the sorest. I served them, in quittance,
With my dear-lovèd sword, as in sooth it was fitting;
They missed the pleasure of feasting abundantly,
Ill-doers evil, of eating my body,
560 Of surrounding the banquet deep in the ocean;
But wounded with edges early at morning
They were stretched a-high on the strand of the ocean,
Put to sleep with the sword, that sea-going travelers
No longer thereafter were hindered from sailing
565 The foam-dashing currents. Came a light from the east,
God's beautiful beacon; the billows subsided,
That well I could see the nesses projecting,
The blustering crags. Weird often saveth
The undoomed hero if doughty his valor!
570 But me did it fortune to fell with my weapon

Nine of the nickers. Of night-struggle harder
'Neath dome of the heaven heard I but rarely,
Nor of wight more woful in the waves of the ocean;
Yet I 'scaped with my life the grip of the monsters,
575 Weary from travel. Then the waters bare me
To the land of the Finns, the flood with the current,
The weltering waves. Not a word hath been told me
Of deeds so daring done by thee, Unferth,
And of sword-terror none; never hath Breca
580 At the play of the battle, nor either of you two,
Feat so fearless performèd with weapons
Glinting and gleaming . . . .
. . . . I utter no boasting;
Though with cold-blooded cruelty thou killedst thy brothers,
585 Thy nearest of kin; thou needs must in hell get
Direful damnation, though doughty thy wisdom.
I tell thee in earnest, offspring of Ecglaf,
Never had Grendel such numberless horrors,
The direful demon, done to thy liegelord,
590 Harrying in Heorot, if thy heart were as sturdy,
Thy mood as ferocious as thou dost describe them.
He hath found out fully that the fierce-burning hatred,
The edge-battle eager, of all of your kindred,
Of the Victory-Scyldings, need little dismay him:
595 Oaths he exacteth, not any he spares
Of the folk of the Danemen, but fighteth with pleasure,
Killeth and feasteth, no contest expecteth
From Spear-Danish people. But the prowess and valor
Of the earls of the Geatmen early shall venture
600 To give him a grapple. He shall go who is able
Bravely to banquet, when the bright-light of morning
Which the second day bringeth, the sun in its ether-robes,
O'er children of men shines from the southward!"
Then the gray-haired, war-famed giver of treasure
605 Was blithesome and joyous, the Bright-Danish ruler
Expected assistance; the people's protector
Heard from Beowulf his bold resolution.
There was laughter of heroes; loud was the clatter,
The words were winsome. Wealhtheow advanced then,
610 Consort of Hrothgar, of courtesy mindful,
Gold-decked saluted the men in the building,
And the freeborn woman the beaker presented
To the lord of the kingdom, first of the East-Danes,
Bade him be blithesome when beer was a-flowing,
615 Lief to his liegemen; he lustily tasted

Of banquet and beaker, battle-famed ruler.
The Helmingish lady then graciously circled
'Mid all the liegemen lesser and greater:
Treasure-cups tendered, till time was afforded
620 That the decorous-mooded, diademed folk-queen
Might bear to Beowulf the bumper o'errunning;
She greeted the Geat-prince, God she did thank,
Most wise in her words, that her wish was accomplished,
That in any of earlmen she ever should look for
625 Solace in sorrow. He accepted the beaker,
Battle-bold warrior, at Wealhtheow's giving,
Then equipped for combat quoth he in measures,
Beowulf spake, offspring of Ecgtheow:
"I purposed in spirit when I mounted the ocean,
630 When I boarded my boat with a band of my liegemen,
I would work to the fullest the will of your people
Or in foe's-clutches fastened fall in the battle.
Deeds I shall do of daring and prowess,
Or the last of my life-days live in this mead-hall."
635 These words to the lady were welcome and pleasing,
The boast of the Geatman; with gold trappings broidered
Went the freeborn folk-queen her fond-lord to sit by.
Then again as of yore was heard in the building
Courtly discussion, conquerors' shouting,
640 Heroes were happy, till Healfdene's son would
Go to his slumber to seek for refreshing;
For the horrid hell-monster in the hall-building knew he
A fight was determined, since the light of the sun they
No longer could see, and lowering darkness
645 O'er all had descended, and dark under heaven
Shadowy shapes came shying around them.
The liegemen all rose then. One saluted the other,
Hrothgar Beowulf, in rhythmical measures,
Wishing him well, and, the wassail-hall giving
650 To his care and keeping, quoth he departing:
"Not to any one else have I ever entrusted,
But thee and thee only, the hall of the Danemen,
Since high I could heave my hand and my buckler.
Take thou in charge now the noblest of houses;
655 Be mindful of honor, exhibiting prowess,
Watch 'gainst the foeman! Thou shalt want no enjoyments,
Survive thou safely adventure so glorious!"

Then Hrothgar departed, his earl-throng attending him,
Folk-lord of Scyldings, forth from the building;

660 The war-chieftain wished then Wealhtheow to look for,
The queen for a bedmate. To keep away Grendel
The Glory of Kings had given a hall-watch,
As men heard recounted: for the king of the Danemen
He did special service, gave the giant a watcher:
665 And the prince of the Geatmen implicitly trusted
His warlike strength and the Wielder's protection.
His armor of iron off him he did then,
His helmet from his head, to his henchman committed
His chased-handled chain-sword, choicest of weapons,
670 And bade him bide with his battle-equipments.
The good one then uttered words of defiance,
Beowulf Geatman, ere his bed he upmounted:
"I hold me no meaner in matters of prowess,
In warlike achievements, than Grendel does himself;
675 Hence I seek not with sword-edge to sooth him to slumber,
Of life to bereave him, though well I am able.
No battle-skill has he, that blows he should strike me,
To shatter my shield, though sure he is mighty
In strife and destruction; but struggling by night we
680 Shall do without edges, dare he to look for
Weaponless warfare, and wise-mooded Father
The glory apportion, God ever-holy,
On which hand soever to him seemeth proper."
Then the brave-mooded hero bent to his slumber,
685 The pillow received the cheek of the noble;
And many a martial mere-thane attending
Sank to his slumber. Seemed it unlikely
That ever thereafter any should hope to
Be happy at home, hero-friends visit
690 Or the lordly troop-castle where he lived from his childhood;
They had heard how slaughter had snatched from the wine-hall,
Had recently ravished, of the race of the Scyldings
Too many by far. But the Lord to them granted
The weaving of war-speed, to Wederish heroes
695 Aid and comfort, that every opponent
By one man's war-might they worsted and vanquished,
By the might of himself; the truth is established
That God Almighty hath governed for ages
Kindreds and nations. A night very lurid
700 The trav'ler-at-twilight came tramping and striding.
The warriors were sleeping who should watch the horned-building,
One only excepted. 'Mid earthmen 'twas 'stablished,
Th' implacable foeman was powerless to hurl them
To the land of shadows, if the Lord were unwilling;

705 But serving as warder, in terror to foemen,
He angrily bided the issue of battle.

'Neath the cloudy cliffs came from the moor then
Grendel going, God's anger bare he.
The monster intended some one of earthmen
710 In the hall-building grand to entrap and make way with:
He went under welkin where well he knew of
The wine-joyous building, brilliant with plating,
Gold-hall of earthmen. Not the earliest occasion
He the home and manor of Hrothgar had sought:
715 Ne'er found he in life-days later nor earlier
Hardier hero, hall-thanes more sturdy!
Then came to the building the warrior marching,
Bereft of his joyance. The door quickly opened
On fire-hinges fastened, when his fingers had touched it;
720 The fell one had flung then—his fury so bitter—
Open the entrance. Early thereafter
The foeman trod the shining hall-pavement,
Strode he angrily; from the eyes of him glimmered
A lustre unlovely likest to fire.
725 He beheld in the hall the heroes in numbers,
A circle of kinsmen sleeping together,
A throng of thanemen: then his thoughts were exultant,
He minded to sunder from each of the thanemen
The life from his body, horrible demon,
730 Ere morning came, since fate had allowed him
The prospect of plenty. Providence willed not
To permit him any more of men under heaven
To eat in the night-time. Higelac's kinsman
Great sorrow endured how the dire-mooded creature
735 In unlooked-for assaults were likely to bear him.
No thought had the monster of deferring the matter,
But on earliest occasion he quickly laid hold of
A soldier asleep, suddenly tore him,
Bit his bone-prison, the blood drank in currents,
740 Swallowed in mouthfuls: he soon had the dead man's
Feet and hands, too, eaten entirely.
Nearer he strode then, the stout-hearted warrior
Snatched as he slumbered, seizing with hand-grip,
Forward the foeman foined with his hand;
745 Caught he quickly the cunning deviser,
On his elbow he rested. This early discovered
The master of malice, that in middle-earth's regions,
'Neath the whole of the heavens, no hand-grapple greater

In any man else had he ever encountered:
750   Fearful in spirit, faint-mooded waxed he,
      Not off could betake him; death he was pondering,
      Would fly to his covert, seek the devils' assembly:
      His calling no more was the same he had followed
      Long in his lifetime. The liege-kinsman worthy
755   Of Higelac minded his speech of the evening,
      Stood he up straight and stoutly did seize him.
      His fingers crackled; the giant was outward,
      The earl stepped farther. The famous one minded
      To flee away farther, if he found an occasion,
760   And off and away, avoiding delay,
      To fly to the fen-moors; he fully was ware of
      The strength of his grapple in the grip of the foeman.
      'Twas an ill-taken journey that the injury-bringing,
      Harrying harmer to Heorot wandered:
765   The palace re-echoed; to all of the Danemen,
      Dwellers in castles, to each of the bold ones,
      Earlmen, was terror. Angry they both were,
      Archwarders raging. Rattled the building;
      'Twas a marvellous wonder that the wine-hall withstood then
770   The bold-in-battle, bent not to earthward,
      Excellent earth-hall; but within and without it
      Was fastened so firmly in fetters of iron,
      By the art of the armorer. Off from the sill there
      Bent mead-benches many, as men have informed me,
775   Adorned with gold-work, where the grim ones did struggle.
      The Scylding wise men weened ne'er before
      That by might and main-strength a man under heaven
      Might break it in pieces, bone-decked, resplendent,
      Crush it by cunning, unless clutch of the fire
780   In smoke should consume it. The sound mounted upward
      Novel enough; on the North Danes fastened
      A terror of anguish, on all of the men there
      Who heard from the wall the weeping and plaining,
      The song of defeat from the foeman of heaven,
785   Heard him hymns of horror howl, and his sorrow
      Hell-bound bewailing. He held him too firmly
      Who was strongest of main-strength of men of that era.

      For no cause whatever would the earlmen's defender
      Leave in life-joys the loathsome newcomer,
790   He deemed his existence utterly useless
      To men under heaven. Many a noble
      Of Beowulf brandished his battle-sword old,

Would guard the life of his lord and protector,
The far-famous chieftain, if able to do so;
795　While waging the warfare, this wist they but little,
Brave battle-thanes, while his body intending
To slit into slivers, and seeking his spirit:
That the relentless foeman nor finest of weapons
Of all on the earth, nor any of war-bills
800　Was willing to injure; but weapons of victory
Swords and suchlike he had sworn to dispense with.
His death at that time must prove to be wretched,
And the far-away spirit widely should journey
Into enemies' power. This plainly he saw then
805　Who with mirth of mood malice no little
Had wrought in the past on the race of the earthmen
(To God he was hostile), that his body would fail him,
But Higelac's hardy henchman and kinsman
Held him by the hand; hateful to other
810　Was each one if living. A body-wound suffered
The direful demon, damage incurable
Was seen on his shoulder, his sinews were shivered,
His body did burst. To Beowulf was given
Glory in battle; Grendel from thenceward
815　Must flee and hide him in the fen-cliffs and marshes,
Sick unto death, his dwelling must look for
Unwinsome and woful; he wist the more fully
The end of his earthly existence was nearing,
His life-days' limits. At last for the Danemen,
820　When the slaughter was over, their wish was accomplished.
The comer-from-far-land had cleansed then of evil,
Wise and valiant, the war-hall of Hrothgar,
Saved it from violence. He joyed in the night-work,
In repute for prowess; the prince of the Geatmen
825　For the East-Danish people his boast had accomplished,
Bettered their burdensome bale-sorrows fully,
The craft-begot evil they erstwhile had suffered
And were forced to endure from crushing oppression,
Their manifold misery. 'Twas a manifest token,
830　When the hero-in-battle the hand suspended,
The arm and the shoulder (there was all of the claw
Of Grendel together) 'neath great-stretching hall-roof.

In the mist of the morning many a warrior
Stood round the gift-hall, as the story is told me:
835　Folk-princes fared then from far and from near
Through long-stretching journeys to look at the wonder,

The footprints of the foeman. Few of the warriors
Who gazed on the foot-tracks of the inglorious creature
His parting from life pained very deeply,
840 How, weary in spirit, off from those regions
In combats conquered he carried his traces,
Fated and flying, to the flood of the nickers.
There in bloody billows bubbled the currents,
The angry eddy was everywhere mingled
845 And seething with gore, welling with sword-blood;
He death-doomed had hid him, when reaved of his joyance
He laid down his life in the lair he had fled to,
His heathenish spirit, where hell did receive him.
Thence the friends from of old backward turned them,
850 And many a younker from merry adventure,
Striding their stallions, stout from the seaward,
Heroes on horses. There were heard very often
Beowulf's praises; many often asserted
That neither south nor north, in the circuit of waters,
855 O'er outstretching earth-plain, none other was better
'Mid bearers of war-shields, more worthy to govern,
'Neath the arch of the ether. Not any, however,
'Gainst the friend-lord muttered, mocking-words uttered
Of Hrothgar the gracious (a good king he).
860 Oft the famed ones permitted their fallow-skinned horses
To run in rivalry, racing and chasing,
Where the fieldways appeared to them fair and inviting,
Known for their excellence; oft a thane of the folk-lord,
A man of celebrity, mindful of rhythms,
865 Who ancient traditions treasured in memory,
New word-groups found properly bound:
The bard after 'gan then Beowulf's venture
Wisely to tell of, and words that were clever
To utter skilfully, earnestly speaking,
870 Everything told he that he heard as to Sigmund's
Mighty achievements, many things hidden,
The strife of the Wælsing, the wide-going ventures
The children of men knew of but little,
The feud and the fury, but Fitela with him,
875 When suchlike matters he minded to speak of,
Uncle to nephew, as in every contention
Each to other was ever devoted:
A numerous host of the race of the scathers
They had slain with the sword-edge. To Sigmund accrued then
880 No little of glory, when his life-days were over,
Since he sturdy in struggle had destroyed the great dragon,

The hoard-treasure's keeper; 'neath the hoar-grayish stone he,
The son of the atheling, unaided adventured
The perilous project; not present was Fitela,
885 Yet the fortune befell him of forcing his weapon
Through the marvellous dragon, that it stood in the wall,
Well-honored weapon; the worm was slaughtered.
The great one had gained then by his glorious achievement
To reap from the ring-hoard richest enjoyment,
890 As best it did please him: his vessel he loaded,
Shining ornaments on the ship's bosom carried,
Kinsman of Wæls: the drake in heat melted.
He was farthest famed of fugitive pilgrims,
· Mid wide-scattered world-folk, for works of great prowess,
895 War-troopers' shelter: hence waxed he in honor.
Afterward Heremod's hero-strength failed him,
His vigor and valor. 'Mid venomous haters
To the hands of foemen he was foully delivered,
Offdriven early. Agony-billows
900 Oppressed him too long, to his people he became then,
To all the athelings, an ever-great burden;
And the daring one's journey in days of yore
Many wise men were wont to deplore,
Such as hoped he would bring them help in their sorrow,
905 That the son of their ruler should rise into power,
Holding the headship held by his fathers,
Should govern the people, the gold-hoard and borough,
The kingdom of heroes, the realm of the Scyldings.
He to all men became then far more beloved,
910 Higelac's kinsman, to kindreds and races,
To his friends much dearer; him malice assaulted.—
Oft running and racing on roadsters they measured
The dun-colored highways. Then the light of the morning
Was hurried and hastened. Went henchmen in numbers
915 To the beautiful building, bold ones in spirit,
To look at the wonder; the liegelord himself then
From his wife-bower wending, warden of treasures,
Glorious trod with troopers unnumbered,
Famed for his virtues, and with him the queen-wife
920 Measured the mead-ways, with maidens attending.

Hrothgar discoursed (to the hall-building went he,
He stood by the pillar, saw the steep-rising hall-roof
Gleaming with gold-gems, and Grendel his hand there)
"For the sight we behold now, thanks to the Wielder
925 Early be offered! Much evil I bided,

Snaring from Grendel: God can e'er 'complish
Wonder on wonder, Wielder of Glory!
But lately I reckoned ne'er under heaven
Comfort to gain me for any of sorrows,
930 While the handsomest of houses horrid with bloodstain
Gory uptowered; grief had offfrightened
Each of the wise ones who weened not that ever
The folk-troop's defences 'gainst foes they should strengthen,
'Gainst sprites and monsters. Through the might of the Wielder
935 A doughty retainer hath a deed now accomplished
Which erstwhile we all with our excellent wisdom
Failed to perform. May affirm very truly
What woman soever in all of the nations
Gave birth to the child, if yet she surviveth,
940 That the long-ruling Lord was lavish to herward
In the birth of the bairn. Now, Beowulf dear,
Most excellent hero, I'll love thee in spirit
As bairn of my body; bear well henceforward
The relationship new. No lack shall befall thee
945 Of earth-joys any I ever can give thee.
Full often for lesser service I've given
Hero less hardy hoard-treasure precious,
To a weaker in war-strife. By works of distinction
Thou hast gained for thyself now that thy glory shall flourish
950 Forever and ever. The All-Ruler quite thee
With good from His hand as He hitherto did thee!"
Beowulf answered, Ecgtheow's offspring:
"That labor of glory most gladly achieved we,
The combat accomplished, unquailing we ventured
955 The enemy's grapple; I would grant it much rather
Thou wert able to look at the creature in person,
Faint unto falling, the foe in his trappings!
On murder-bed quickly I minded to bind him,
With firm-holding fetters, that forced by my grapple
960 Low he should lie in life-and-death struggle
'Less his body escape; I was wholly unable,
Since God did not will it, to keep him from going,
Not held him that firmly, hated opposer;
Too swift was the foeman. Yet safety regarding
965 He suffered his hand behind him to linger,
His arm and shoulder, to act as watcher;
No shadow of solace the woe-begone creature
Found him there nathless: the hated destroyer
Liveth no longer, lashed for his evils,
970 But sorrow hath seized him, in snare-meshes hath him

Close in its clutches, keepeth him writhing
In baleful bonds: there banished for evil
The man shall wait for the mighty tribunal,
How the God of glory shall give him his earnings."
975   Then the soldier kept silent, son of old Ecglaf,
From boasting and bragging of battle-achievements,
Since the princes beheld there the hand that depended
'Neath the lofty hall-timbers by the might of the nobleman,
Each one before him, the enemy's fingers;
980   Each finger-nail strong steel most resembled,
The heathen one's hand-spur, the hero-in-battle's
Claw most uncanny; quoth they agreeing,
That not any excellent edges of brave ones
Was willing to touch him, the terrible creature's
985   Battle-hand bloody to bear away from him.

Then straight was ordered that Heorot inside
With hands be embellished: a host of them gathered,
Of men and women, who the wassailing-building
The guest-hall begeared. Gold-flashing sparkled
990   Webs on the walls then, of wonders a many
To each of the heroes that look on such objects.
The beautiful building was broken to pieces
Which all within with irons was fastened,
Its hinges torn off: only the roof was
995   Whole and uninjured when the horrible creature
Outlawed for evil off had betaken him,
Hopeless of living. 'Tis hard to avoid it
(Whoever will do it!); but he doubtless must come to
The place awaiting, as Wyrd hath appointed,
1000   Soul-bearers, earth-dwellers, earls under heaven,
Where bound on its bed his body shall slumber
When feasting is finished. Full was the time then
That the son of Healfdene went to the building;
The excellent atheling would eat of the banquet.
1005   Ne'er heard I that people with hero-band larger
Bare them better tow'rds their bracelet-bestower.
The laden-with-glory stooped to the bench then
(Their kinsmen-companions in plenty were joyful,
Many a cupful quaffing complaisantly),
1010   Doughty of spirit in the high-tow'ring palace,
Hrothgar and Hrothulf. Heorot then inside
Was filled with friendly ones; falsehood and treachery
The Folk-Scyldings now nowise did practise.
Then the offspring of Healfdene offered to Beowulf

1015 A golden standard, as reward for the victory,
A banner embossed, burnie and helmet;
Many men saw then a song-famous weapon
Borne 'fore the hero. Beowulf drank of
The cup in the building; that treasure-bestowing
1020 He needed not blush for in battle-men's presence.
Ne'er heard I that many men on the ale-bench
In friendlier fashion to their fellows presented
Four bright jewels with gold-work embellished.
'Round the roof of the helmet a head-guarder outside
1025 Braided with wires, with bosses was furnished,
That swords-for-the-battle fight-hardened might fail
Boldly to harm him, when the hero proceeded
Forth against foemen. The defender of earls then
Commanded that eight steeds with bridles
1030 Gold-plated, gleaming, be guided to hallward,
Inside the building; on one of them stood then
An art-broidered saddle embellished with jewels;
'Twas the sovereign's seat, when the son of King Healfdene
Was pleased to take part in the play of the edges;
1035 The famous one's valor ne'er failed at the front when
Slain ones were bowing. And to Beowulf granted
The prince of the Ingwins, power over both,
O'er war-steeds and weapons; bade him well to enjoy them.
In so manly a manner the mighty-famed chieftain,
1040 Hoard-ward of heroes, with horses and jewels
War-storms requited, that none e'er condemneth
Who willeth to tell truth with full justice.

And the atheling of earlmen to each of the heroes
Who the ways of the waters went with Beowulf,
1045 A costly gift-token gave on the mead-bench,
Offered an heirloom, and ordered that that man
With gold should be paid for, whom Grendel had erstwhile
Wickedly slaughtered, as he more of them had done
Had far-seeing God and the mood of the hero
1050 The fate not averted: the Father then governed
All of the earth-dwellers, as He ever is doing;
Hence insight for all men is everywhere fittest,
Forethought of spirit! much he shall suffer
Of lief and of loathsome who long in this present
1055 Useth the world in this woful existence.
There was music and merriment mingling together
Touching Healfdene's leader; the joy-wood was fingered,
Measures recited, when the singer of Hrothgar

On mead-bench should mention the merry hall-joyance
1060 Of the kinsmen of Finn, when onset surprised them:
"The Half-Danish hero, Hnæf of the Scyldings,
On the field of the Frisians was fated to perish.
Sure Hildeburg needed not mention approving
The faith of the Jutemen: though blameless entirely,
1065 When shields were shivered she was shorn of her darlings,
Of bairns and brothers: they bent to their fate
With war-spear wounded; woe was that woman.
Not causeless lamented the daughter of Hoce
The decree of the Wielder when morning-light came and
1070 She was able 'neath heaven to behold the destruction
Of brothers and bairns, where the brightest of earth-joys
She had hitherto had: all the henchmen of Finn
War had offtaken, save a handful remaining,
That he nowise was able to offer resistance
1075 To the onset of Hengest in the parley of battle,
Nor the wretched remnant to rescue in war from
The earl of the atheling; but they offered conditions,
Another great building to fully make ready,
A hall and a high-seat, that half they might rule with
1080 The sons of the Jutemen, and that Folcwalda's son would
Day after day the Danemen honor
When gifts were giving, and grant of his ring-store
To Hengest's earl-troop ever so freely,
Of his gold-plated jewels, as he encouraged the Frisians
1085 On the bench of the beer-hall. On both sides they swore then
A fast-binding compact; Finn unto Hengest
With no thought of revoking vowed then most solemnly
The woe-begone remnant well to take charge of,
His Witan advising; the agreement should no one
1090 By words or works weaken and shatter,
By artifice ever injure its value,
Though reaved of their ruler their ring-giver's slayer
They followed as vassals, Fate so requiring:
Then if one of the Frisians the quarrel should speak of
1095 In tones that were taunting, terrible edges
Should cut in requital. Accomplished the oath was,
And treasure of gold from the hoard was uplifted.
The best of the Scylding braves was then fully
Prepared for the pile; at the pyre was seen clearly
1100 The blood-gory burnie, the boar with his gilding,
The iron-hard swine, athelings many
Fatally wounded; no few had been slaughtered.
Hildeburg bade then, at the burning of Hnæf,

The bairn of her bosom to bear to the fire,
1105 That his body be burned and borne to the pyre.
The woe-stricken woman wept on his shoulder,
In measures lamented; upmounted the hero.
The greatest of dead-fires curled to the welkin,
On the hill's-front crackled; heads were a-melting,
1110 Wound-doors bursting, while the blood was a-coursing
From body-bite fierce. The fire devoured them,
Greediest of spirits, whom war had offcarried
From both of the peoples; their bravest were fallen.

"Then the warriors departed to go to their dwellings,
1115 Reaved of their friends, Friesland to visit,
Their homes and high-city. Hengest continued
Biding with Finn the blood-tainted winter,
Wholly unsundered; of fatherland thought he
Though unable to drive the ring-stemmèd vessel
1120 O'er the ways of the waters; the wave-deeps were tossing,
Fought with the wind; winter in ice-bonds
Closed up the currents, till there came to the dwelling
A year in its course, as yet it revolveth,
If season propitious one alway regardeth,
1125 World-cheering weathers. Then winter was gone,
Earth's bosom was lovely; the exile would get him,
The guest from the palace; on grewsomest vengeance
He brooded more eager than on oversea journeys,
Whe'r onset-of-anger he were able to 'complish,
1130 The bairns of the Jutemen therein to remember.
Nowise refused he the duties of liegeman
When Hun of the Frisians the battle-sword Láfing,
Fairest of falchions, friendly did give him:
Its edges were famous in folk-talk of Jutland.
1135 And savage sword-fury seized in its clutches
Bold-mooded Finn where he bode in his palace,
When the grewsome grapple Guthlaf and Oslaf
Had mournfully mentioned, the mere-journey over,
For sorrows half-blamed him; the flickering spirit
1140 Could not bide in his bosom. Then the building was covered
With corpses of foemen, and Finn too was slaughtered,
The king with his comrades, and the queen made a prisoner.
The troops of the Scyldings bore to their vessels
All that the land-king had in his palace,
1145 Such trinkets and treasures they took as, on searching,
At Finn's they could find. They ferried to Daneland
The excellent woman on oversea journey,

Led her to their land-folk." The lay was concluded,
The gleeman's recital. Shouts again rose then,
1150   Bench-glee resounded, bearers then offered
Wine from wonder-vats. Wealhtheo advanced then
Going 'neath gold-crown, where the good ones were seated
Uncle and nephew; their peace was yet mutual,
True each to the other. And Unferth the spokesman
1155   Sat at the feet of the lord of the Scyldings:
Each trusted his spirit that his mood was courageous,
Though at fight he had failed in faith to his kinsmen.
Said the queen of the Scyldings: "My lord and protector,
Treasure-bestower, take thou this beaker;
1160   Joyance attend thee, gold-friend of heroes,
And greet thou the Geatmen with gracious responses!
So ought one to do. Be kind to the Geatmen,
In gifts not miserly; anear and afar now
Peace thou enjoyest. Report hath informed me
1165   Thou'lt have for a bairn the battle-brave hero.
Now is Heorot cleansèd, ring-palace gleaming;
Give while thou mayest many rewards,
And bequeath to thy kinsmen kingdom and people,
On wending thy way to the Wielder's splendor.
1170   I know good Hrothulf, that the noble young troopers
He'll care for and honor, lord of the Scyldings,
If earth-joys thou endest earlier than he doth;
I reckon that recompense he'll render with kindness
Our offspring and issue, if that all he remember,
1175   What favors of yore, when he yet was an infant,
We awarded to him for his worship and pleasure."
Then she turned by the bench where her sons were carousing,
Hrethric and Hrothmund, and the heroes' offspring,
The war-youth together; there the good one was sitting
1180   'Twixt the brothers twain, Beowulf Geatman.

A beaker was borne him, and bidding to quaff it
Graciously given, and gold that was twisted
Pleasantly proffered, a pair of arm-jewels,
Rings and corslet, of collars the greatest
1185   I've heard of 'neath heaven. Of heroes not any
More splendid from jewels have I heard 'neath the welkin,
Since Hama off bore the Brosingmen's necklace,
The bracteates and jewels, from the bright-shining city,
Eormenric's cunning craftiness fled from,
1190   Chose gain everlasting. Geatish Higelac,
Grandson of Swerting, last had this jewel

When tramping 'neath banner the treasure he guarded,
The field-spoil defended; Fate offcarried him
When for deeds of daring he endured tribulation,
1195 Hate from the Frisians; the ornaments bare he
O'er the cup of the currents, costly gem-treasures,
Mighty folk-leader, he fell 'neath his target;
The corpse of the king then came into charge of
The race of the Frankmen, the mail-shirt and collar:
1200 Warmen less noble plundered the fallen,
When the fight was finished; the folk of the Geatmen
The field of the dead held in possession.
The choicest of mead-halls with cheering resounded.
Wealhtheo discoursed, the war-troop addressed she:
1205 "This collar enjoy thou, Beowulf worthy,
Young man, in safety, and use thou this armor,
Gems of the people, and prosper thou fully,
Show thyself sturdy and be to these liegemen
Mild with instruction! I'll mind thy requital.
1210 Thou hast brought it to pass that far and near
Forever and ever earthmen shall honor thee,
Even so widely as ocean surroundeth
The blustering bluffs. Be, while thou livest,
A wealth-blessèd atheling. I wish thee most truly
1215 Jewels and treasure. Be kind to my son, thou
Living in joyance! Here each of the nobles
Is true unto other, gentle in spirit,
Loyal to leader. The liegemen are peaceful,
The war-troops ready: well-drunken heroes,
1220 Do as I bid ye." Then she went to the settle.
There was choicest of banquets, wine drank the heroes:
Weird they knew not, destiny cruel,
As to many an earlman early it happened,
When evening had come and Hrothgar had parted
1225 Off to his manor, the mighty to slumber.
Warriors unnumbered warded the building
As erst they did often: the ale-settle bared they,
'Twas covered all over with beds and pillows.
Doomed unto death, down to his slumber
1230 Bowed then a beer-thane. Their battle-shields placed they,
Bright-shining targets, up by their heads then;
O'er the atheling on ale-bench 'twas easy to see there
Battle-high helmet, burnie of ring-mail,
And mighty war-spear. 'Twas the wont of that people
1235 To constantly keep them equipped for the battle,
At home or marching—in either condition—

At seasons just such as necessity ordered
As best for their ruler; that people was worthy.

They sank then to slumber. With sorrow one paid for
1240 His evening repose, as often betid them
While Grendel was holding[1] the gold-bedecked palace,
Ill-deeds performing, till his end overtook him,
Death for his sins. 'Twas seen very clearly,
Known unto earth-folk, that still an avenger
1245 Outlived the loathed one, long since the sorrow
Caused by the struggle; the mother of Grendel,
Devil-shaped woman, her woe ever minded,
Who was held to inhabit the horrible waters,
The cold-flowing currents, after Cain had become a
1250 Slayer-with-edges to his one only brother,
The son of his sire; he set out then banished,
Marked as a murderer, man-joys avoiding,
Lived in the desert. Thence demons unnumbered
Fate-sent awoke; one of them Grendel,
1255 Sword-cursèd, hateful, who at Heorot met with
A man that was watching, waiting the struggle,
Where a horrid one held him with hand-grapple sturdy;
Nathless he minded the might of his body,
The glorious gift God had allowed him,
1260 And folk-ruling Father's favor relied on,
His help and His comfort: so he conquered the foeman,
The hell-spirit humbled: he unhappy departed then,
Reaved of his joyance, journeying to death-haunts,
Foeman of man. His mother moreover
1265 Eager and gloomy was anxious to go on
Her mournful mission, mindful of vengeance
For the death of her son. She came then to Heorot
Where the Armor-Dane earlmen all through the building
Were lying in slumber. Soon there became then
1270 Return to the nobles, when the mother of Grendel
Entered the folk-hall; the fear was less grievous
By even so much as the vigor of maidens,
War-strength of women, by warrior is reckoned,
When well-carved weapon, worked with the hammer,
1275 Blade very bloody, brave with its edges,
Strikes down the boar-sign that stands on the helmet.
Then the hard-edgèd weapon was heaved in the building,
The brand o'er the benches, broad-lindens many
Hand-fast were lifted; for helmet he recked not,
1280 For armor-net broad, whom terror laid hold of.

She went then hastily, outward would get her
Her life for to save, when some one did spy her;
Soon she had grappled one of the athelings
Fast and firmly, when fenward she hied her;
1285 That one to Hrothgar was liefest of heroes
In rank of retainer where waters encircle,
A mighty shield-warrior, whom she murdered at slumber,
A broadly-famed battle-knight. Beowulf was absent,
But another apartment was erstwhile devoted
1290 To the glory-decked Geatman when gold was distributed.
There was hubbub in Heorot. The hand that was famous
She grasped in its gore; grief was renewed then
In homes and houses: 'twas no happy arrangement
In both of the quarters to barter and purchase
1295 With lives of their friends. Then the well-agèd ruler,
The gray-headed war-thane, was woful in spirit,
When his long-trusted liegeman lifeless he knew of,
His dearest one gone. Quick from a room was
Beowulf brought, brave and triumphant.
1300 As day was dawning in the dusk of the morning,
Went then that earlman, champion noble,
Came with comrades, where the clever one bided
Whether God all gracious would grant him a respite
After the woe he had suffered. The war-worthy hero
1305 With a troop of retainers trod then the pavement
(The hall-building groaned), till he greeted the wise one,
The earl of the Ingwins; asked if the night had
Fully refreshed him, as fain he would have it.

Hrothgar rejoined, helm of the Scyldings:
1310 "Ask not of joyance! Grief is renewed to
The folk of the Danemen. Dead is Æschere,
Yrmenlaf's brother, older than he,
My true-hearted counsellor, trusty adviser,
Shoulder-companion, when fighting in battle
1315 Our heads we protected, when troopers were clashing,
And heroes were dashing; such an earl should be ever,
An erst-worthy atheling, as Æschere proved him.
The flickering death-spirit became in Heorot
His hand-to-hand murderer; I can not tell whither
1320 The cruel one turned in the carcass exulting,
By cramming discovered. The quarrel she wreaked then,
That last night igone Grendel thou killedst
In grewsomest manner, with grim-holding clutches,
Since too long he had lessened my liege-troop and wasted

1325 My folk-men so foully. He fell in the battle
With forfeit of life, and another has followed,
A mighty crime-worker, her kinsman avenging,
And henceforth hath 'stablished her hatred unyielding,
As it well may appear to many a liegeman,
1330 Who mourneth in spirit the treasure-bestower,
Her heavy heart-sorrow; the hand is now lifeless
Which availed you in every wish that you cherished.
Land-people heard I, liegemen, this saying,
Dwellers in halls, they had seen very often
1335 A pair of such mighty march-striding creatures,
Far-dwelling spirits, holding the moorlands:
One of them wore, as well they might notice,
The image of woman, the other one wretched
In guise of a man wandered in exile,
1340 Except he was huger than any of earthmen;
Earth-dwelling people entitled him Grendel
In days of yore: they know not their father,
Whe'r ill-going spirits any were borne him
Ever before. They guard the wolf-coverts,
1345 Lands inaccessible, wind-beaten nesses,
Fearfullest fen-deeps, where a flood from the mountains
'Neath mists of the nesses netherward rattles,
The stream under earth: not far is it henceward
Measured by mile-lengths that the mere-water standeth,
1350 Which forests hang over, with frost-whiting covered,
A firm-rooted forest, the floods overshadow.
There ever at night one an ill-meaning portent
A fire-flood may see; 'mong children of men
None liveth so wise that wot of the bottom;
1355 Though harassed by hounds the heath-stepper seek for,
Fly to the forest, firm-antlered he-deer,
Spurred from afar, his spirit he yieldeth,
His life on the shore, ere in he will venture
To cover his head. Uncanny the place is:
1360 Thence upward ascendeth the surging of waters,
Wan to the welkin, when the wind is stirring
The weathers unpleasing, till the air groweth gloomy,
And the heavens lower. Now is help to be gotten
From thee and thee only! The abode thou know'st not,
1365 The dangerous place where thou'rt able to meet with
The sin-laden hero: seek if thou darest!
For the feud I will fully fee thee with money,
With old-time treasure, as erstwhile I did thee,
With well-twisted jewels, if away thou shalt get thee."

1370 Beowulf answered, Ecgtheow's son:
"Grieve not, O wise one! for each it is better,
His friend to avenge than with vehemence wail him;
Each of us must the end-day abide of
His earthly existence; who is able accomplish
1375 Glory ere death! To battle-thane noble
Lifeless lying, 'tis at last most fitting.
Arise, O king, quick let us hasten
To look at the footprint of the kinsman of Grendel!
I promise thee this now: to his place he'll escape not,
1380 To embrace of the earth, nor to mountainous forest,
Nor to depths of the ocean, wherever he wanders.
Practice thou now patient endurance
Of each of thy sorrows, as I hope for thee soothly!"
Then up sprang the old one, the All-Wielder thanked he,
1385 Ruler Almighty, that the man had outspoken.
Then for Hrothgar a war-horse was decked with a bridle,
Curly-maned courser. The clever folk-leader
Stately proceeded: stepped then an earl-troop
Of linden-wood bearers. Her footprints were seen then
1390 Widely in wood-paths, her way o'er the bottoms,
Where she faraway fared o'er fen-country murky,
Bore away breathless the best of retainers
Who pondered with Hrothgar the welfare of country.
The son of the athelings then went o'er the stony,
1395 Declivitous cliffs, the close-covered passes,
Narrow passages, paths unfrequented,
Nesses abrupt, nicker-haunts many;
One of a few of wise-mooded heroes,
He onward advanced to view the surroundings,
1400 Till he found unawares woods of the mountain
O'er hoar-stones hanging, holt-wood unjoyful;
The water stood under, welling and gory.
'Twas irksome in spirit to all of the Danemen,
Friends of the Scyldings, to many a liegeman
1405 Sad to be suffered, a sorrow unlittle
To each of the earlmen, when to Æschere's head they
Came on the cliff. The current was seething
With blood and with gore (the troopers gazed on it).
The horn anon sang the battle-song ready.
1410 The troop were all seated; they saw 'long the water then
Many a serpent, mere-dragons wondrous
Trying the waters, nickers a-lying
On the cliffs of the nesses, which at noonday full often
Go on the sea-deeps their sorrowful journey,

1415 Wild-beasts and wormkind; away then they hastened
   Hot-mooded, hateful, they heard the great clamor,
   The war-trumpet winding. One did the Geat-prince
   Sunder from earth-joys, with arrow from bowstring,
   From his sea-struggle tore him, that the trusty war-missile
1420 Pierced to his vitals; he proved in the currents
   Less doughty at swimming whom death had offcarried.
   Soon in the waters the wonderful swimmer
   Was straitened most sorely with sword-pointed boar-spears,
   Pressed in the battle and pulled to the cliff-edge;
1425 The liegemen then looked on the loath-fashioned stranger.
   Beowulf donned then his battle-equipments,
   Cared little for life; inlaid and most ample,
   The hand-woven corslet which could cover his body,
   Must the wave-deeps explore, that war might be powerless
1430 To harm the great hero, and the hating one's grasp might
   Not peril his safety; his head was protected
   By the light-flashing helmet that should mix with the bottoms,
   Trying the eddies, treasure-emblazoned,
   Encircled with jewels, as in seasons long past
1435 The weapon-smith worked it, wondrously made it,
   With swine-bodies fashioned it, that thenceforward no longer
   Brand might bite it, and battle-sword hurt it.
   And that was not least of helpers in prowess
   That Hrothgar's spokesman had lent him when straitened;
1440 And the hilted hand-sword was Hrunting entitled,
   Old and most excellent 'mong all of the treasures;
   Its blade was of iron, blotted with poison,
   Hardened with gore; it failed not in battle
   Any hero under heaven in hand who it brandished,
1445 Who ventured to take the terrible journeys,
   The battle-field sought; not the earliest occasion
   That deeds of daring 'twas destined to 'complish.
   Ecglaf's kinsman minded not soothly,
   Exulting in strength, what erst he had spoken
1450 Drunken with wine, when the weapon he lent to
   A sword-hero bolder; himself did not venture
   'Neath the strife of the currents his life to endanger,
   To fame-deeds perform; there he forfeited glory,
   Repute for his strength. Not so with the other
1455 When he clad in his corslet had equipped him for battle.

   Beowulf spake, Ecgtheow's son:
   "Recall now, oh, famous kinsman of Healfdene,
   Prince very prudent, now to part I am ready,

Gold-friend of earlmen, what erst we agreed on,
1460 Should I lay down my life in lending thee assistance,
When my earth-joys were over, thou wouldst evermore serve me
In stead of a father; my faithful thanemen,
My trusty retainers, protect thou and care for,
Fall I in battle: and, Hrothgar belovèd,
1465 Send unto Higelac the high-valued jewels
Thou to me hast allotted. The lord of the Geatmen
May perceive from the gold, the Hrethling may see it
When he looks on the jewels, that a gem-giver found I
Good over-measure, enjoyed him while able.
1470 And the ancient heirloom Unferth permit thou,
The famed one to have, the heavy-sword splendid
The hard-edgèd weapon; with Hrunting to aid me,
I shall gain me glory, or grim-death shall take me."
The atheling of Geatmen uttered these words and
1475 Heroic did hasten, not any rejoinder
Was willing to wait for; the wave-current swallowed
The doughty-in-battle. Then a day's-length elapsed ere
He was able to see the sea at its bottom.
Early she found then who fifty of winters
1480 The course of the currents kept in her fury,
Grisly and greedy, that the grim one's dominion
Some one of men from above was exploring.
Forth did she grab them, grappled the warrior
With horrible clutches; yet no sooner she injured
1485 His body unscathèd: the burnie out-guarded,
That she proved but powerless to pierce through the armor,
The limb-mail locked, with loath-grabbing fingers.
The sea-wolf bare then, when bottomward came she,
The ring-prince homeward, that he after was powerless
1490 (He had daring to do it) to deal with his weapons,
But many a mere-beast tormented him swimming,
Flood-beasts no few with fierce-biting tusks did
Break through his burnie, the brave one pursued they.
The earl then discovered he was down in some cavern
1495 Where no water whatever anywise harmed him,
And the clutch of the current could come not anear him,
Since the roofed-hall prevented; brightness a-gleaming
Fire-light he saw, flashing resplendent.
The good one saw then the sea-bottom's monster,
1500 The mighty mere-woman; he made a great onset
With weapon-of-battle, his hand not desisted
From striking, that war-blade struck on her head then
A battle-song greedy. The stranger perceived then

The sword would not bite, her life would not injure,
1505 But the falchion failed the folk-prince when straitened:
Erst had it often onsets encountered,
Oft cloven the helmet, the fated one's armor:
'Twas the first time that ever the excellent jewel
Had failed of its fame. Firm-mooded after,
1510 Not heedless of valor, but mindful of glory,
Was Higelac's kinsman; the hero-chief angry
Cast then his carved-sword covered with jewels
That it lay on the earth, hard and steel-pointed;
He hoped in his strength, his hand-grapple sturdy.
1515 So any must act whenever he thinketh
To gain him in battle glory unending,
And is reckless of living. The lord of the War-Geats
(He shrank not from battle) seized by the shoulder
The mother of Grendel; then mighty in struggle
1520 Swung he his enemy, since his anger was kindled,
That she fell to the floor. With furious grapple
She gave him requital early thereafter,
And stretched out to grab him; the strongest of warriors
Faint-mooded stumbled, till he fell in his traces,
1525 Foot-going champion. Then she sat on the hall-guest
And wielded her war-knife wide-bladed, flashing,
For her son would take vengeance, her one only bairn.
His breast-armor woven bode on his shoulder;
It guarded his life, the entrance defended
1530 'Gainst sword-point and edges. Ecgtheow's son there
Had fatally journeyed, champion of Geatmen,
In the arms of the ocean, had the armor not given,
Close-woven corslet, comfort and succor,
And had God most holy not awarded the victory,
1535 All-knowing Lord; easily did heaven's
Ruler most righteous arrange it with justice;
Uprose he erect ready for battle.

Then he saw mid the war-gems a weapon of victory,
An ancient giant-sword, of edges a-doughty,
1540 Glory of warriors: of weapons 'twas choicest,
Only 'twas larger than any man else was
Able to bear to the battle-encounter,
The good and splendid work of the giants.
He grasped then the sword-hilt, knight of the Scyldings,
1545 Bold and battle-grim, brandished his ring-sword,
Hopeless of living, hotly he smote her,
That the fiend-woman's neck firmly it grappled,

Broke through her bone-joints, the bill fully pierced her
Fate-cursèd body, she fell to the ground then:
1550   The hand-sword was bloody, the hero exulted.
The brand was brilliant, brightly it glimmered,
Just as from heaven gemlike shineth
The torch of the firmament. He glanced 'long the building,
And turned by the wall then, Higelac's vassal
1555   Raging and wrathful raised his battle-sword
Strong by the handle. The edge was not useless
To the hero-in-battle, but he speedily wished to
Give Grendel requital for the many assaults he
Had worked on the West-Danes not once, but often,
1560   When he slew in slumber the subjects of Hrothgar,
Swallowed down fifteen sleeping retainers
Of the folk of the Danemen, and fully as many
Carried away, a horrible prey.
He gave him requital, grim-raging champion,
1565   When he saw on his rest-place weary of conflict
Grendel lying, of life-joys bereavèd,
As the battle at Heorot erstwhile had scathed him;
His body far bounded, a blow when he suffered,
Death having seized him, sword-smiting heavy,
1570   And he cut off his head then. Early this noticed
The clever carles who as comrades of Hrothgar
Gazed on the sea-deeps, that the surging wave-currents
Were mightily mingled, the mere-flood was gory:
Of the good one the gray-haired together held converse,
1575   The hoary of head, that they hoped not to see again
The atheling ever, that exulting in victory
He'd return there to visit the distinguished folk-ruler:
Then many concluded the mere-wolf had killed him.
The ninth hour came then. From the ness-edge departed
1580   The bold-mooded Scyldings; the gold-friend of heroes
Homeward betook him. The strangers sat down then
Soul-sick, sorrowful, the sea-waves regarding:
They wished and yet weened not their well-loved friend-lord
To see any more. The sword-blade began then,
1585   The blood having touched it, contracting and shriveling
With battle-icicles; 'twas a wonderful marvel
That it melted entirely, likest to ice when
The Father unbindeth the bond of the frost and
Unwindeth the wave-bands, He who wieldeth dominion
1590   Of times and of tides: a truth-firm Creator.
Nor took he of jewels more in the dwelling,
Lord of the Weders, though they lay all around him,

Than the head and the handle handsome with jewels;
The brand early melted, burnt was the weapon:
1595 So hot was the blood, the strange-spirit poisonous
That in it did perish. He early swam off then
Who had bided in combat the carnage of haters,
Went up through the ocean; the eddies were cleansèd,
The spacious expanses, when the spirit from farland
1600 His life put aside and this short-lived existence.
The seamen's defender came swimming to land then
Doughty of spirit, rejoiced in his sea-gift,
The bulky burden which he bore in his keeping.
The excellent vassals advanced then to meet him,
1605 To God they were grateful, were glad in their chieftain,
That to see him safe and sound was granted them.
From the high-minded hero, then, helmet and burnie
Were speedily loosened: the ocean was putrid,
The water 'neath welkin weltered with gore.
1610 Forth did they fare, then, their footsteps retracing,
Merry and mirthful, measured the earth-way,
The highway familiar: men very daring
Bare then the head from the sea-cliff, burdening
Each of the earlmen, excellent-valiant.
1615 Four of them had to carry with labor
The head of Grendel to the high towering gold-hall
Upstuck on the spear, till fourteen most-valiant
And battle-brave Geatmen came there going
Straight to the palace: the prince of the people
1620 Measured the mead-ways, their mood-brave companion.
The atheling of earlmen entered the building,
Deed-valiant man, adorned with distinction,
Doughty shield-warrior, to address King Hrothgar:
Then hung by the hair, the head of Grendel
1625 Was borne to the building, where beer-thanes were drinking,
Loth before earlmen and eke 'fore the lady:
The warriors beheld then a wonderful sight.

Beowulf spake, offspring of Ecgtheow:
"Lo! we blithely have brought thee, bairn of Healfdene,
1630 Prince of the Scyldings, these presents from ocean
Which thine eye looketh on, for an emblem of glory.
I came off alive from this, narrowly 'scaping:
In war 'neath the water the work with great pains I
Performed, and the fight had been finished quite nearly,
1635 Had God not defended me. I failed in the battle
Aught to accomplish, aided by Hrunting,

Though that weapon was worthy, but the Wielder of earth-folk
Gave me willingly to see on the wall a
Heavy old hand-sword hanging in splendor
1640 (He guided most often the lorn and the friendless),
That I swung as a weapon. The wards of the house then
I killed in the conflict (when occasion was given me).
Then the battle-sword burned, the brand that was lifted,
As the blood-current sprang, hottest of war-sweats;
1645 Seizing the hilt, from my foes I offbore it;
I avenged as I ought to their acts of malignity,
The murder of Danemen. I then make thee this promise,
Thou'lt be able in Heorot careless to slumber
With thy throng of heroes and the thanes of thy people
1650 Every and each, of greater and lesser,
And thou needest not fear for them from the selfsame direction
As thou formerly fearedst, oh, folk-lord of Scyldings,
End-day for earlmen." To the age-hoary man then,
The gray-haired chieftain, the gold-fashioned sword-hilt,
1655 Old-work of giants, was thereupon given;
Since the fall of the fiends, it fell to the keeping
Of the wielder of Danemen, the wonder-smith's labor,
And the bad-mooded being abandoned this world then,
Opponent of God, victim of murder,
1660 And also his mother; it went to the keeping
Of the best of the world-kings, where waters encircle,
Who the scot divided in Scylding dominion.
Hrothgar discoursed, the hilt he regarded,
The ancient heirloom where an old-time contention's
1665 Beginning was graven: the gurgling currents,
The flood slew thereafter the race of the giants,
They had proved themselves daring: that people was loth to
The Lord everlasting, through lash of the billows
The Father gave them final requital.
1670 So in letters of rune on the clasp of the handle
Gleaming and golden, 'twas graven exactly,
Set forth and said, whom that sword had been made for,
Finest of irons, who first it was wrought for,
Wreathed at its handle and gleaming with serpents.
1675 The wise one then said (silent they all were)
Son of old Healfdene: "He may say unrefuted
Who performs 'mid the folk-men fairness and truth
(The hoary old ruler remembers the past),
That better by birth is this bairn of the nobles!
1680 Thy fame is extended through far-away countries,
Good friend Beowulf, o'er all of the races,

Thou holdest all firmly, hero-like strength with
Prudence of spirit. I'll prove myself grateful
As before we agreed on; thou granted for long shalt
1685 Become a great comfort to kinsmen and comrades,
A help unto heroes. Heremod became not
Such to the Scyldings, successors of Ecgwela;
He grew not to please them, but grievous destruction,
And diresome death-woes to Danemen attracted;
1690 He slew in anger his table-companions,
Trustworthy counsellors, till he turned off lonely
From world-joys away, wide-famous ruler:
Though high-ruling heaven in hero-strength raised him,
In might exalted him, o'er men of all nations
1695 Made him supreme, yet a murderous spirit
Grew in his bosom: he gave then no ring-gems
To the Danes after custom; endured he unjoyful
Standing the straits from strife that was raging,
Longsome folk-sorrow. Learn then from this,
1700 Lay hold of virtue! Though laden with winters,
I have sung thee these measures. 'Tis a marvel to tell it,
How all-ruling God from greatness of spirit
Giveth wisdom to children of men,
Manor and earlship: all things He ruleth.
1705 He often permitteth the mood-thought of man of
The illustrious lineage to lean to possessions,
Allows him earthly delights at his manor,
A high-burg of heroes to hold in his keeping,
Maketh portions of earth-folk hear him,
1710 And a wide-reaching kingdom so that, wisdom failing him,
He himself is unable to reckon its boundaries;
He liveth in luxury, little debars him,
Nor sickness nor age, no treachery-sorrow
Becloudeth his spirit, conflict nowhere,
1715 No sword-hate, appeareth, but all of the world doth
Wend as he wisheth; the worse he knoweth not,
Till arrant arrogance inward pervading,
Waxeth and springeth, when the warder is sleeping,
The guard of the soul: with sorrows encompassed,
1720 Too sound is his slumber, the slayer is near him,
Who with bow and arrow aimeth in malice.

"Then bruised in his bosom he with bitter-toothed missile
Is hurt 'neath his helmet: from harmful pollution
He is powerless to shield him by the wonderful mandates
1725 Of the loath-cursèd spirit; what too long he hath holden

Him seemeth too small, savage he hoardeth,
Nor boastfully giveth gold-plated rings,
The fate of the future flouts and forgetteth
Since God had erst given him greatness no little,
1730 Wielder of Glory. His end-day anear,
It afterward happens that the bodily-dwelling
Fleetingly fadeth, falls into ruins;
Another lays hold who doleth the ornaments,
The nobleman's jewels, nothing lamenting,
1735 Heedeth no terror. Oh, Beowulf dear,
Best of the heroes, from bale-strife defend thee,
And choose thee the better, counsels eternal;
Beware of arrogance, world-famous champion!
But a little-while lasts thy life-vigor's fulness;
1740 'Twill after hap early, that illness or sword-edge
Shall part thee from strength, or the grasp of the fire,
Or the wave of the current, or clutch of the edges,
Or flight of the war-spear, or age with its horrors,
Or thine eyes' bright flashing shall fade into darkness:
1745 'Twill happen full early, excellent hero,
That death shall subdue thee. So the Danes a half-century
I held under heaven, helped them in struggles
'Gainst many a race in middle-earth's regions,
With ash-wood and edges, that enemies none
1750 On earth molested me. Lo! offsetting change, now,
Came to my manor, grief after joyance,
When Grendel became my constant visitor,
Inveterate hater: I from that malice
Continually travailed with trouble no little.
1755 Thanks be to God that I gained in my lifetime,
To the Lord everlasting, to look on the gory
Head with mine eyes, after long-lasting sorrow!
Go to the bench now, battle-adornèd
Joy in the feasting: of jewels in common
1760 We'll meet with many when morning appeareth."
The Geatman was gladsome, ganged he immediately
To go to the bench, as the clever one bade him.
Then again as before were the famous-for-prowess,
Hall-inhabiters, handsomely banqueted,
1765 Feasted anew. The night-veil fell then
Dark o'er the warriors. The courtiers rose then;
The gray-haired was anxious to go to his slumbers,
The hoary old Scylding. Hankered the Geatman,
The champion doughty, greatly, to rest him:
1770 An earlman early outward did lead him,

Flagged from his faring, from far-country springing,
Who for etiquette's sake all of a liegeman's
Needs regarded, such as seamen at that time
Were bounden to feel. The big-hearted rested;
1775 The building uptowered, spacious and gilded,
The guest within slumbered, till the sable-clad raven
Blithely foreboded the beacon of heaven.
Then the bright-shining sun o'er the bottoms came going;
The warriors hastened, the heads of the peoples
1780 Were ready to go again to their peoples,
The high-mooded farer would faraway thenceward
Look for his vessel. The valiant one bade then,
Offspring of Ecglaf, off to bear Hrunting,
To take his weapon, his well-beloved iron;
1785 He him thanked for the gift, saying good he accounted
The war-friend and mighty, nor chid he with words then
The blade of the brand: 'twas a brave-mooded hero.
When the warriors were ready, arrayed in their trappings,
The atheling dear to the Danemen advanced then
1790 On to the dais, where the other was sitting,
Grim-mooded hero, greeted King Hrothgar.

Beowulf spake, Ecgtheow's offspring:
"We men of the water wish to declare now
Fared from far-lands, we're firmly determined
1795 To seek King Higelac. Here have we fitly
Been welcomed and feasted, as heart would desire it;
Good was the greeting. If greater affection
I am anywise able ever on earth to
Gain at thy hands, ruler of heroes,
1800 Than yet I have done, I shall quickly be ready
For combat and conflict. O'er the course of the waters
Learn I that neighbors alarm thee with terror,
As haters did whilom, I hither will bring thee
For help unto heroes henchmen by thousands.
1805 I know as to Higelac, the lord of the Geatmen,
Though young in years, he yet will permit me,
By words and by works, ward of the people,
Fully to furnish thee forces and bear thee
My lance to relieve thee, if liegemen shall fail thee,
1810 And help of my hand-strength; if Hrethric be treating,
Bairn of the king, at the court of the Geatmen,
He thereat may find him friends in abundance:
Faraway countries he were better to seek for
Who trusts in himself." Hrothgar discoursed then,

1815   Making rejoinder: "These words thou hast uttered
         All-knowing God hath given thy spirit!
         Ne'er heard I an earlman thus early in life
         More clever in speaking: thou'rt cautious of spirit,
         Mighty of muscle, in mouth-answers prudent.
1820   I count on the hope that, happen it ever
         That missile shall rob thee of Hrethel's descendant,
         Edge-horrid battle, and illness or weapon
         Deprive thee of prince, of people's protector,
         And life thou yet holdest, the Sea-Geats will never
1825   Find a more fitting folk-lord to choose them,
         Gem-ward of heroes, than thou mightest prove thee,
         If the kingdom of kinsmen thou carest to govern.
         Thy mood-spirit likes me the longer the better,
         Beowulf dear: thou hast brought it to pass that
1830   To both these peoples peace shall be common,
         To Geat-folk and Danemen, the strife be suspended,
         The secret assailings they suffered in yore-days;
         And also that jewels be shared while I govern
         The wide-stretching kingdom, and that many shall visit
1835   Others o'er the ocean with excellent gift-gems:
         The ring-adorned bark shall bring o'er the currents
         Presents and love-gifts. This people I know
         Tow'rd foeman and friend firmly established,
         After ancient etiquette everywise blameless."
1840   Then the warden of earlmen gave him still farther,
         Kinsman of Healfdene, a dozen of jewels,
         Bade him safely seek with the presents
         His well-beloved people, early returning.
         Then the noble-born king kissed the distinguished,
1845   Dear-lovèd liegeman, the Dane-prince saluted him,
         And claspèd his neck; tears from him fell,
         From the gray-headed man: he two things expected,
         Agèd and reverend, but rather the second,
         That bold in council they'd meet thereafter.
1850   The man was so dear that he failed to suppress the
         Emotions that moved him, but in mood-fetters fastened
         The long-famous hero longeth in secret
         Deep in his spirit for the dear-beloved man
         Though not a blood-kinsman. Beowulf thenceward,
1855   Gold-splendid warrior, walked o'er the meadows
         Exulting in treasure: the sea-going vessel
         Riding at anchor awaited its owner.
         As they pressed on their way then, the present of Hrothgar
         Was frequently referred to: a folk-king indeed that

1860　Everyway blameless, till age did debar him
　　　The joys of his might, which hath many oft injured.

　　　Then the band of very valiant retainers
　　　Came to the current; they were clad all in armor,
　　　In link-woven burnies. The land-warder noticed
1865　The return of the earlmen, as he erstwhile had seen them;
　　　Nowise with insult he greeted the strangers
　　　From the naze of the cliff, but rode on to meet them;
　　　Said the bright-armored visitors vesselward traveled
　　　Welcome to Weders. The wide-bosomed craft then
1870　Lay on the sand, laden with armor,
　　　With horses and jewels, the ring-stemmèd sailer:
　　　The mast uptowered o'er the treasure of Hrothgar.
　　　To the boat-ward a gold-bound brand he presented,
　　　That he was afterwards honored on the ale-bench more highly
1875　As the heirloom's owner. Set he out on his vessel,
　　　To drive on the deep, Dane-country left he.
　　　Along by the mast then a sea-garment fluttered,
　　　A rope-fastened sail. The sea-boat resounded,
　　　The wind o'er the waters the wave-floater nowise
1880　Kept from its journey; the sea-goer traveled,
　　　The foamy-necked floated forth o'er the currents,
　　　The well-fashioned vessel o'er the ways of the ocean,
　　　Till they came within sight of the cliffs of the Geatmen,
　　　The well-known headlands. The wave-goer hastened
1885　Driven by breezes, stood on the shore.
　　　Prompt at the ocean, the port-ward was ready,
　　　Who long in the past outlooked in the distance,
　　　At water's-edge waiting well-lovèd heroes;
　　　He bound to the bank then the broad-bosomed vessel
1890　Fast in its fetters, lest the force of the waters
　　　Should be able to injure the ocean-wood winsome.
　　　Bade he up then take the treasure of princes,
　　　Plate-gold and fretwork; not far was it thence
　　　To go off in search of the giver of jewels:
1895　Hrethel's son Higelac at home there remaineth,
　　　Himself with his comrades close to the sea-coast.
　　　The building was splendid, the king heroic,
　　　Great in his hall, Hygd very young was,
　　　Fine-mooded, clever, though few were the winters
1900　That the daughter of Hæreth had dwelt in the borough;
　　　But she nowise was cringing nor stingy of presents,
　　　Of ornaments rare, to the race of the Geatmen.
　　　Thrytho nursed anger, excellent folk-queen,

Hot-burning hatred: no hero whatever
1905 'Mong household companions, her husband excepted
Dared to adventure to look at the woman
With eyes in the daytime; but he knew that death-chains
Hand-wreathed were wrought him: early thereafter,
When the hand-strife was over, edges were ready,
1910 That fierce-raging sword-point had to force a decision,
Murder-bale show. Such no womanly custom
For a lady to practise, though lovely her person,
That a weaver-of-peace, on pretence of anger
A belovèd liegeman of life should deprive.
1915 Soothly this hindered Heming's kinsman;
Other ale-drinking earlmen asserted
That fearful folk-sorrows fewer she wrought them,
Treacherous doings, since first she was given
Adorned with gold to the war-hero youthful,
1920 For her origin honored, when Offa's great palace
O'er the fallow flood by her father's instructions
She sought on her journey, where she afterwards fully,
Famed for her virtue, her fate on the king's-seat
Enjoyed in her lifetime, love did she hold with
1925 The ruler of heroes, the best, it is told me,
Of all of the earthmen that oceans encompass,
Of earl-kindreds endless; hence Offa was famous
Far and widely, by gifts and by battles,
Spear-valiant hero; the home of his fathers
1930 He governed with wisdom, whence Eomær did issue
For help unto heroes, Heming's kinsman,
Grandson of Garmund, great in encounters.

Then the brave one departed, his band along with him,
Seeking the sea-shore, the sea-marches treading,
1935 The wide-stretching shores. The world-candle glimmered,
The sun from the southward; they proceeded then onward,
Early arriving where they heard that the troop-lord,
Ongentheow's slayer, excellent, youthful
Folk-prince and warrior was distributing jewels,
1940 Close in his castle. The coming of Beowulf
Was announced in a message quickly to Higelac,
That the folk-troop's defender forth to the palace
The linden-companion alive was advancing,
Secure from the combat courtward a-going.
1945 The building was early inward made ready
For the foot-going guests as the good one had ordered.
He sat by the man then who had lived through the struggle,

Kinsman by kinsman, when the king of the people
Had in lordly language saluted the dear one,
1950 In words that were formal. The daughter of Hæreth
Coursed through the building, carrying mead-cups:
She loved the retainers, tendered the beakers
To the high-minded Geatmen. Higelac 'gan then
Pleasantly plying his companion with questions
1955 In the high-towering palace. A curious interest
Tormented his spirit, what meaning to see in
The Sea-Geats' adventures: "Beowulf worthy,
How throve your journeying, when thou thoughtest suddenly
Far o'er the salt-streams to seek an encounter,
1960 A battle at Heorot? Hast bettered for Hrothgar,
The famous folk-leader, his far-published sorrows
Any at all? In agony-billows
I mused upon torture, distrusted the journey
Of the belovèd liegeman; I long time did pray thee
1965 By no means to seek out the murderous spirit,
To suffer the South-Danes themselves to decide on
Grappling with Grendel. To God I am thankful
To be suffered to see thee safe from thy journey."
Beowulf answered, bairn of old Ecgtheow:
1970 "'Tis hidden by no means, Higelac chieftain,
From many of men, the meeting so famous,
What mournful moments of me and of Grendel
Were passed in the place where he pressing affliction
On the Victory-Scyldings scathefully brought,
1975 Anguish forever; that all I avengèd,
So that any under heaven of the kinsmen of Grendel
Needeth not boast of that cry-in-the-morning,
Who longest liveth of the loth-going kindred,
Encompassed by moorland. I came in my journey
1980 To the royal ring-hall, Hrothgar to greet there:
Soon did the famous scion of Healfdene,
When he understood fully the spirit that led me,
Assign me a seat with the son of his bosom.
The troop was in joyance; mead-glee greater
1985 'Neath arch of the ether not ever beheld I
'Mid hall-building holders. The highly-famed queen,
Peace-tie of peoples, oft passed through the building,
Cheered the young troopers; she oft tendered a hero
A beautiful ring-band, ere she went to her sitting.
1990 Oft the daughter of Hrothgar in view of the courtiers
To the earls at the end the ale-vessel carried,
Whom Freaware I heard then hall-sitters title,

When nail-adorned jewels she gave to the heroes:
Gold-bedecked, youthful, to the glad son of Froda
1995 Her faith has been plighted; the friend of the Scyldings,
The guard of the kingdom, hath given his sanction,
And counts it a vantage, for a part of the quarrels,
A portion of hatred, to pay with the woman.
Somewhere not rarely, when the ruler has fallen,
2000 The life-taking lance relaxeth its fury
For a brief breathing-spell, though the bride be charming!

"It well may discomfit the prince of the Heathobards
And each of the thanemen of earls that attend him,
When he goes to the building escorting the woman,
2005 That a noble-born Daneman the knights should be feasting:
There gleam on his person the leavings of elders
Hard and ring-bright, Heathobards' treasure,
While they wielded their arms, till they misled to the battle
Their own dear lives and belovèd companions.
2010 He saith at the banquet who the collar beholdeth,
An ancient ash-warrior who earlmen's destruction
Clearly recalleth (cruel his spirit),
Sadly beginneth sounding the youthful
Thane-champion's spirit through the thoughts of his bosom,
2015 War-grief to waken, and this word-answer speaketh:
'Art thou able, my friend, to know when thou seest it
The brand which thy father bare to the conflict
In his latest adventure, 'neath visor of helmet,
The dearly-loved iron, where Danemen did slay him,
2020 And brave-mooded Scyldings, on the fall of the heroes,
(When vengeance was sleeping) the slaughter-place wielded?
E'en now some man of the murderer's progeny
Exulting in ornaments enters the building,
Boasts of his blood-shedding, offbeareth the jewel
2025 Which thou shouldst wholly hold in possession!'
So he urgeth and mindeth on every occasion
With woe-bringing words, till waxeth the season
When the woman's thane for the works of his father,
The bill having bitten, blood-gory sleepeth,
2030 Fated to perish; the other one thenceward
'Scapeth alive, the land knoweth thoroughly.
Then the oaths of the earlmen on each side are broken,
When rancors unresting are raging in Ingeld
And his wife-love waxeth less warm after sorrow.
2035 So the Heathobards' favor not faithful I reckon,
Their part in the treaty not true to the Danemen,

Their friendship not fast. I further shall tell thee
More about Grendel, that thou fully mayst hear,
Ornament-giver, what afterward came from
2040 The hand-rush of heroes. When heaven's bright jewel
O'er earthfields had glided, the stranger came raging,
The horrible night-fiend, us for to visit,
Where wholly unharmed the hall we were guarding.
To Hondscio happened a hopeless contention,
2045 Death to the doomed one, dead he fell foremost,
Girded war-champion; to him Grendel became then,
To the vassal distinguished, a tooth-weaponed murderer,
The well-beloved henchman's body all swallowed.
Not the earlier off empty of hand did
2050 The bloody-toothed murderer, mindful of evils,
Wish to escape from the gold-giver's palace,
But sturdy of strength he strove to outdo me,
Hand-ready grappled. A glove was suspended
Spacious and wondrous, in art-fetters fastened,
2055 Which was fashioned entirely by touch of the craftman
From the dragon's skin by the devil's devices:
He down in its depths would do me unsadly
One among many, deed-doer raging,
Though sinless he saw me; not so could it happen
2060 When I in my anger upright did stand.
'Tis too long to recount how requital I furnished
For every evil to the earlmen's destroyer;
'Twas there, my prince, that I proudly distinguished
Thy land with my labors. He left and retreated,
2065 He lived his life a little while longer:
Yet his right-hand guarded his footstep in Heorot,
And sad-mooded thence to the sea-bottom fell he,
Mournful in mind. For the might-rush of battle
The friend of the Scyldings, with gold that was plated,
2070 With ornaments many, much requited me,
When daylight had dawned, and down to the banquet
We had sat us together. There was chanting and joyance:
The age-stricken Scylding asked many questions
And of old-times related; oft light-ringing harp-strings,
2075 Joy-telling wood, were touched by the brave one;
Now he uttered measures, mourning and truthful,
Then the large-hearted land-king a legend of wonder
Truthfully told us. Now troubled with years
The age-hoary warrior afterward began to
2080 Mourn for the might that marked him in youth-days;
His breast within boiled, when burdened with winters

Much he remembered. From morning till night then
We joyed us therein as etiquette suffered,
Till the second night season came unto earth-folk.
2085 Then early thereafter, the mother of Grendel
Was ready for vengeance, wretched she journeyed;
Her son had death ravished, the wrath of the Geatmen.
The horrible woman avengèd her offspring,
And with mighty mainstrength murdered a hero.
2090 There the spirit of Æschere, agèd adviser,
Was ready to vanish; nor when morn had lightened
Were they anywise suffered to consume him with fire,
Folk of the Danemen, the death-weakened hero,
Nor the belovèd liegeman to lay on the pyre;
2095 She the corpse had offcarried in the clutch of the foeman
’Neath mountain-brook’s flood. To Hrothgar ’twas saddest
Of pains that ever had preyed on the chieftain;
By the life of thee the land-prince then me
Besought very sadly, in sea-currents’ eddies
2100 To display my prowess, to peril my safety,
Might-deeds accomplish; much did he promise.
I found then the famous flood-current’s cruel,
Horrible depth-warder. A while unto us two
Hand was in common; the currents were seething
2105 With gore that was clotted, and Grendel’s fierce mother’s
Head I offhacked in the hall at the bottom
With huge-reaching sword-edge, hardly I wrested
My life from her clutches; not doomed was I then,
But the warden of earlmen afterward gave me
2110 Jewels in quantity, kinsman of Healfdene.

“So the belovèd land-prince lived in decorum;
I had missed no rewards, no meeds of my prowess,
But he gave me jewels, regarding my wishes,
Healfdene his bairn; I’ll bring them to thee, then,
2115 Atheling of earlmen, offer them gladly.
And still unto thee is all my affection:
But few of my folk-kin find I surviving
But thee, dear Higelac!” Bade he in then to carry
The boar-image, banner, battle-high helmet,
2120 Iron-gray armor, the excellent weapon,
In song-measures said: “This suit-for-the-battle
Hrothgar presented me, bade me expressly,
Wise-mooded atheling, thereafter to tell thee
The whole of its history, said King Heregar owned it,
2125 Dane-prince for long: yet he wished not to give then

The mail to his son, though dearly he loved him,
Hereward the hardy. Hold all in joyance!"
I heard that there followed hard on the jewels
Two braces of stallions of striking resemblance,
2130 Dappled and yellow; he granted him usance
Of horses and treasures. So a kinsman should bear him,
No web of treachery weave for another,
Nor by cunning craftiness cause the destruction
Of trusty companion. Most precious to Higelac,
2135 The bold one in battle, was the bairn of his sister,
And each unto other mindful of favors.
I am told that to Hygd he proffered the necklace,
Wonder-gem rare that Wealhtheow gave him,
The troop-leader's daughter, a trio of horses
2140 Slender and saddle-bright; soon did the jewel
Embellish her bosom, when the beer-feast was over.
So Ecgtheow's bairn brave did prove him,
War-famous man, by deeds that were valiant,
He lived in honor, belovèd companions
2145 Slew not carousing; his mood was not cruel,
But by hand-strength hugest of heroes then living
The brave one retained the bountiful gift that
The Lord had allowed him. Long was he wretched,
So that sons of the Geatmen accounted him worthless,
2150 And the lord of the liegemen loth was to do him
Mickle of honor, when mead-cups were passing;
They fully believed him idle and sluggish,
An indolent atheling: to the honor-blest man there
Came requital for the cuts he had suffered.
2155 The folk-troop's defender bade fetch to the building
The heirloom of Hrethel, embellished with gold,
So the brave one enjoined it; there was jewel no richer
In the form of a weapon 'mong Geats of that era;
In Beowulf's keeping he placed it and gave him
2160 Seven of thousands, manor and lordship.
Common to both was land 'mong the people,
Estate and inherited rights and possessions,
To the second one specially spacious dominions,
To the one who was better. It afterward happened
2165 In days that followed, befell the battle-thanes,
After Higelac's death, and when Heardred was murdered
With weapons of warfare 'neath well-covered targets,
When valiant battlemen in victor-band sought him,
War-Scylfing heroes harassed the nephew
2170 Of Hereric in battle. To Beowulf's keeping

Turned there in time extensive dominions:
He fittingly ruled them a fifty of winters
(He a man-ruler wise was, manor-ward old) till
A certain one 'gan, on gloom-darkening nights, a
2175 Dragon, to govern, who guarded a treasure,
A high-rising stone-cliff, on heath that was grayish:
A path 'neath it lay, unknown unto mortals.
Some one of earthmen entered the mountain,
The heathenish hoard laid hold of with ardor;
2180 *   *   *   *   *   *   *
*   *   *   *   *   *   *
*   *   *   *   *   *   *
*   *   *   *   *   *   *
*   *   *   *   *   *   *
2185
*   *   *   *   *   *   *

He sought of himself who sorely did harm him,
But, for need very pressing, the servant of one of
The sons of the heroes hate-blows evaded,
2190 Seeking for shelter and the sin-driven warrior
Took refuge within there. He early looked in it,
*   *   *   *   *   *   *
*   *   *   *   *   *   *
*   *   *   *   * when the onset surprised him,
2195 He a gem-vessel saw there: many of suchlike
Ancient ornaments in the earth-cave were lying,
As in days of yore some one of men of
Illustrious lineage, as a legacy monstrous,
There had secreted them, careful and thoughtful,
2200 Dear-valued jewels. Death had offsnatched them,
In the days of the past, and the one man moreover
Of the flower of the folk who fared there the longest,
Was fain to defer it, friend-mourning warder,
A little longer to be left in enjoyment
2205 Of long-lasting treasure. A barrow all-ready
Stood on the plain the stream-currents nigh to,
New by the ness-edge, unnethe of approaching:
The keeper of rings carried within a
Ponderous deal of the treasure of nobles,
2210 Of gold that was beaten, briefly he spake then:
"Hold thou, O Earth, now heroes no more may,
The earnings of earlmen. Lo! erst in thy bosom
Worthy men won them; war-death hath ravished,
Perilous life-bale, all my warriors,
2215 Liegemen belovèd, who this life have forsaken,

Who hall-pleasures saw. No sword-bearer have I,
And no one to burnish the gold-plated vessel,
The high-valued beaker: my heroes are vanished.
The hardy helmet behung with gilding
2220 Shall be reaved of its riches: the ring-cleansers slumber
Who were charged to have ready visors-for-battle,
And the burnie that bided in battle-encounter
O'er breaking of war-shields the bite of the edges
Moulds with the hero. The ring-twisted armor,
2225 Its lord being lifeless, no longer may journey
Hanging by heroes; harp-joy is vanished,
The rapture of glee-wood, no excellent falcon
Swoops through the building, no swift-footed charger
Grindeth the gravel. A grievous destruction
2230 No few of the world-folk widely hath scattered!"
So, woful of spirit one after all
Lamented mournfully, moaning in sadness
By day and by night, till death with its billows
Dashed on his spirit. Then the ancient dusk-scather
2235 Found the great treasure standing all open,
He who flaming and fiery flies to the barrows,
Naked war-dragon, nightly escapeth
Encompassed with fire; men under heaven
Widely beheld him. 'Tis said that he looks for
2240 The hoard in the earth, where old he is guarding
The heathenish treasure; he'll be nowise the better.
So three-hundred winters the waster of peoples
Held upon earth that excellent hoard-hall,
Till the forementioned earlman angered him bitterly:
2245 The beat-plated beaker he bare to his chieftain
And fullest remission for all his remissness
Begged of his liegelord. Then the hoard was discovered,
The treasure was taken, his petition was granted
The lorn-mooded liegeman. His lord regarded
2250 The old-work of earth-folk—'twas the earliest occasion.
When the dragon awoke, the strife was renewed there;
He snuffed 'long the stone then, stout-hearted found he
The footprint of foeman; too far had he gone
With cunning craftiness close to the head of
2255 The fire-spewing dragon. So undoomed he may 'scape from
Anguish and exile with ease who possesseth
The favor of Heaven. The hoard-warden eagerly
Searched o'er the ground then, would meet with the person
That caused him sorrow while in slumber reclining:
2260 Gleaming and wild he oft went round the cavern,

All of it outward; not any of earthmen
Was seen in that desert. Yet he joyed in the battle,
Rejoiced in the conflict: oft he turned to the barrow,
Sought for the gem-cup; this he soon perceived then
2265 That some man or other had discovered the gold,
The famous folk-treasure. Not fain did the hoard-ward
Wait until evening; then the ward of the barrow
Was angry in spirit, the loathèd one wished to
Pay for the dear-valued drink-cup with fire.
2270 Then the day was done as the dragon would have it,
He no longer would wait on the wall, but departed
Fire-impelled, flaming. Fearful the start was
To earls in the land, as it early thereafter
To their giver-of-gold was grievously ended.

2275 The stranger began then to vomit forth fire,
To burn the great manor; the blaze then glimmered
For anguish to earlmen, not anything living
Was the hateful air-goer willing to leave there.
The war of the worm widely was noticed,
2280 The feud of the foeman afar and anear,
How the enemy injured the earls of the Geatmen,
Harried with hatred: back he hied to the treasure,
To the well-hidden cavern ere the coming of daylight.
He had circled with fire the folk of those regions,
2285 With brand and burning; in the barrow he trusted,
In the wall and his war-might: the weening deceived him.
Then straight was the horror to Beowulf published,
Early forsooth, that his own native homestead,
The best of buildings, was burning and melting,
2290 Gift-seat of Geatmen. 'Twas a grief to the spirit
Of the good-mooded hero, the greatest of sorrows:
The wise one weened then that wielding his kingdom
'Gainst the ancient commandments, he had bitterly angered
The Lord everlasting: with lorn meditations
2295 His bosom welled inward, as was nowise his custom.
The fire-spewing dragon fully had wasted
The fastness of warriors, the water-land outward,
The manor with fire. The folk-ruling hero,
Prince of the Weders, was planning to wreak him.
2300 The warmen's defender bade them to make him,
Earlmen's atheling, an excellent war-shield
Wholly of iron: fully he knew then
That wood from the forest was helpless to aid him,
Shield against fire. The long-worthy ruler

2305 Must live the last of his limited earth-days,
Of life in the world and the worm along with him,
Though he long had been holding hoard-wealth in plenty.
Then the ring-prince disdained to seek with a war-band,
With army extensive, the air-going ranger;
2310 He felt no fear of the foeman's assaults and
He counted for little the might of the dragon,
His power and prowess: for previously dared he
A heap of hostility, hazarded dangers,
War-thane, when Hrothgar's palace he cleansèd,
2315 Conquering combatant, clutched in the battle
The kinsmen of Grendel, of kindred detested.
'Twas of hand-fights not least where Higelac was slaughtered,
When the king of the Geatmen with clashings of battle,
Friend-lord of folks in Frisian dominions,
2320 Offspring of Hrethrel perished through sword-drink,
With battle-swords beaten; thence Beowulf came then
On self-help relying, swam through the waters;
He bare on his arm, lone-going, thirty
Outfits of armor, when the ocean he mounted.
2325 The Hetwars by no means had need to be boastful
Of their fighting afoot, who forward to meet him
Carried their war-shields: not many returned from
The brave-mooded battle-knight back to their homesteads.
Ecgtheow's bairn o'er the bight-courses swam then,
2330 Lone-goer lorn to his land-folk returning,
Where Hygd to him tendered treasure and kingdom,
Rings and dominion: her son she not trusted,
To be able to keep the kingdom devised him
'Gainst alien races, on the death of King Higelac.
2335 Yet the sad ones succeeded not in persuading the atheling
In any way ever, to act as a suzerain
To Heardred, or promise to govern the kingdom;
Yet with friendly counsel in the folk he sustained him,
Gracious, with honor, till he grew to be older,
2340 Wielded the Weders. Wide-fleeing outlaws,
Ohthere's sons, sought him o'er the waters:
They had stirred a revolt 'gainst the helm of the Scylfings,
The best of the sea-kings, who in Swedish dominions
Distributed treasure, distinguished folk-leader.
2345 'Twas the end of his earth-days; injury fatal
By swing of the sword he received as a greeting,
Offspring of Higelac; Ongentheow's bairn
Later departed to visit his homestead,

When Heardred was dead; let Beowulf rule them,
2350   Govern the Geatmen: good was that folk-king.

He planned requital for the folk-leader's ruin
In days thereafter, to Eadgils the wretched
Becoming an enemy. Ohthere's son then
Went with a war-troop o'er the wide-stretching currents
2355   With warriors and weapons: with woe-journeys cold he
After avenged him, the king's life he took.
So he came off uninjured from all of his battles,
Perilous fights, offspring of Ecgtheow,
From his deeds of daring, till that day most momentous
2360   When he fate-driven fared to fight with the dragon.
With eleven companions the prince of the Geatmen
Went lowering with fury to look at the fire-drake:
Inquiring he'd found how the feud had arisen,
Hate to his heroes; the highly-famed gem-vessel
2365   Was brought to his keeping through the hand of th' informer.
That in the throng was thirteenth of heroes,
That caused the beginning of conflict so bitter,
Captive and wretched, must sad-mooded thenceward
Point out the place: he passed then unwillingly
2370   To the spot where he knew of the notable cavern,
The cave under earth, not far from the ocean,
The anger of eddies, which inward was full of
Jewels and wires: a warden uncanny,
Warrior weaponed, wardered the treasure,
2375   Old under earth; no easy possession
For any of earth-folk access to get to.
Then the battle-brave atheling sat on the naze-edge,
While the gold-friend of Geatmen gracious saluted
His fireside-companions: woe was his spirit,
2380   Death-boding, wav'ring; Weird very near him,
Who must seize the old hero, his soul-treasure look for,
Dragging aloof his life from his body:
Not flesh-hidden long was the folk-leader's spirit.
Beowulf spake, Ecgtheow's son:
2385   "I survived in my youth-days many a conflict,
Hours of onset: that all I remember.
I was seven-winters old when the jewel-prince took me,
High-lord of heroes, at the hands of my father,
Hrethel the hero-king had me in keeping,
2390   Gave me treasure and feasting, our kinship remembered;
Not ever was I any less dear to him
Knight in the boroughs, than the bairns of his household,

Herebald and Hæthcyn and Higelac mine.
To the eldest unjustly by acts of a kinsman
2395   Was murder-bed strewn, since him Hæthcyn from horn-bow
His sheltering chieftain shot with an arrow,
Erred in his aim and injured his kinsman,
One brother the other, with blood-sprinkled spear:
'Twas a feeless fight, finished in malice,
2400   Sad to his spirit; the folk-prince however
Had to part from existence with vengeance untaken.
So to hoar-headed hero 'tis heavily crushing
To live to see his son as he rideth
Young on the gallows: then measures he chanteth,
2405   A song of sorrow, when his son is hanging
For the raven's delight, and aged and hoary
He is unable to offer any assistance.
Every morning his offspring's departure
Is constant recalled: he cares not to wait for
2410   The birth of an heir in his borough-enclosures,
Since that one through death-pain the deeds hath experienced.
He heart-grieved beholds in the house of his son the
Wine-building wasted, the wind-lodging places
Reaved of their roaring; the riders are sleeping,
2415   The knights in the grave; there's no sound of the harp-wood,
Joy in the yards, as of yore were familiar.

"He seeks then his chamber, singeth a woe-song
One for the other; all too extensive
Seemed homesteads and plains. So the helm of the Weders
2420   Mindful of Herebald heart-sorrow carried,
Stirred with emotion, nowise was able
To wreak his ruin on the ruthless destroyer:
He was unable to follow the warrior with hatred,
With deeds that were direful, though dear he not held him.
2425   Then pressed by the pang this pain occasioned him,
He gave up glee, God-light elected;
He left to his sons, as the man that is rich does,
His land and fortress, when from life he departed.
Then was crime and hostility 'twixt Swedes and Geatmen,
2430   O'er wide-stretching water warring was mutual,
Burdensome hatred, when Hrethel had perished,
And Ongentheow's offspring were active and valiant,
Wished not to hold to peace oversea, but
Round Hreosna-beorh often accomplished
2435   Cruelest massacre. This my kinsman avengèd,
The feud and fury, as 'tis found on inquiry,

Though one of them paid it with forfeit of life-joys,
With price that was hard: the struggle became then
Fatal to Hæthcyn, lord of the Geatmen.
2440 Then I heard that at morning one brother the other
With edges of irons egged on to murder,
Where Ongentheow maketh onset on Eofor:
The helmet crashed, the hoary-haired Scylfing
Sword-smitten fell, his hand then remembered
2445 Feud-hate sufficient, refused not the death-blow.
The gems that he gave me, with jewel-bright sword I
'Quited in contest, as occasion was offered:
Land he allowed me, life-joy at homestead,
Manor to live on. Little he needed
2450 From Gepids or Danes or in Sweden to look for
Trooper less true, with treasure to buy him;
'Mong foot-soldiers ever in front I would hie me,
Alone in the vanguard, and evermore gladly
Warfare shall wage, while this weapon endureth
2455 That late and early often did serve me
When I proved before heroes the slayer of Dæghrefn,
Knight of the Hugmen: he by no means was suffered
To the king of the Frisians to carry the jewels,
The breast-decoration; but the banner-possessor
2460 Bowed in the battle, brave-mooded atheling.
No weapon was slayer, but war-grapple broke then
The surge of his spirit, his body destroying.
Now shall weapon's edge make war for the treasure,
And hand and firm-sword." Beowulf spake then,
2465 Boast-words uttered—the latest occasion:
"I braved in my youth-days battles unnumbered;
Still am I willing the struggle to look for,
Fame-deeds perform, folk-warden prudent,
If the hateful despoiler forth from his cavern
2470 Seeketh me out!" Each of the heroes,
Helm-bearers sturdy, he thereupon greeted
Belovèd co-liegemen—his last salutation:
"No brand would I bear, no blade for the dragon,
Wist I a way my word-boast to 'complish
2475 Else with the monster, as with Grendel I did it;
But fire in the battle hot I expect there,
Furious flame-burning: so I fixed on my body
Target and war-mail. The ward of the barrow
I'll not flee from a foot-length, the foeman uncanny.
2480 At the wall 'twill befall us as Fate decreeth,
Each one's Creator. I am eager in spirit,

With the wingèd war-hero to away with all boasting.
Bide on the barrow with burnies protected,
Earls in armor, which of us two may better
2485 Bear his disaster, when the battle is over.
'Tis no matter of yours, and man cannot do it,
But me and me only, to measure his strength with
The monster of malice, might-deeds to 'complish.
I with prowess shall gain the gold, or the battle,
2490 Direful death-woe will drag off your ruler!"
The mighty champion rose by his shield then,
Brave under helmet, in battle-mail went he
'Neath steep-rising stone-cliffs, the strength he relied on
Of one man alone: no work for a coward.
2495 Then he saw by the wall who a great many battles
Had lived through, most worthy, when foot-troops collided,
Stone-arches standing, stout-hearted champion,
Saw a brook from the barrow bubbling out thenceward:
The flood of the fountain was fuming with war-flame:
2500 Not nigh to the hoard, for season the briefest
Could he brave, without burning, the abyss that was yawning,
The drake was so fiery. The prince of the Weders
Caused then that words came from his bosom,
So fierce was his fury; the firm-hearted shouted:
2505 His battle-clear voice came in resounding
'Neath the gray-colored stone. Stirred was his hatred,
The hoard-ward distinguished the speech of a man;
Time was no longer to look out for friendship.
The breath of the monster issued forth first,
2510 Vapory war-sweat, out of the stone-cave:
The earth re-echoed. The earl 'neath the barrow
Lifted his shield, lord of the Geatmen,
Tow'rd the terrible stranger: the ring-twisted creature's
Heart was then ready to seek for a struggle.
2515 The excellent battle-king first brandished his weapon,
The ancient heirloom, of edges unblunted,
To the death-planners twain was terror from other.
The lord of the troopers intrepidly stood then
'Gainst his high-rising shield, when the dragon coiled him
2520 Quickly together: in corslet he bided.
He went then in blazes, bended and striding,
Hasting him forward. His life and body
The targe well protected, for time-period shorter
Than wish demanded for the well-renowned leader,
2525 Where he then for the first day was forced to be victor,
Famous in battle, as Fate had not willed it.

The lord of the Geatmen uplifted his hand then,
Smiting the fire-drake with sword that was precious,
That bright on the bone the blade-edge did weaken,
2530 Bit more feebly than his folk-leader needed,
Burdened with bale-griefs. Then the barrow-protector,
When the sword-blow had fallen, was fierce in his spirit,
Flinging his fires, flamings of battle
Gleamed then afar: the gold-friend of Weders
2535 Boasted no conquests, his battle-sword failed him
Naked in conflict, as by no means it ought to,
Long-trusty weapon. 'Twas no slight undertaking
That Ecgtheow's famous offspring would leave
The drake-cavern's bottom; he must live in some region
2540 Other than this, by the will of the dragon,
As each one of earthmen existence must forfeit.
'Twas early thereafter the excellent warriors
Met with each other. Anew and afresh
The hoard-ward took heart (gasps heaved then his bosom):
2545 Sorrow he suffered encircled with fire
Who the people erst governed. His companions by no means
Were banded about him, bairns of the princes,
With valorous spirit, but they sped to the forest,
Seeking for safety. The soul-deeps of one were
2550 Ruffled by care: kin-love can never
Aught in him waver who well doth consider.

The son of Weohstan was Wiglaf entitled,
Shield-warrior precious, prince of the Scylfings,
Ælfhere's kinsman: he saw his dear liegelord
2555 Enduring the heat 'neath helmet and visor.
Then he minded the holding that erst he had given him,
The Wægmunding warriors' wealth-blessèd homestead,
Each of the folk-rights his father had wielded;
He was hot for the battle, his hand seized the target,
2560 The yellow-bark shield, he unsheathed his old weapon,
Which was known among earthmen as the relic of Eanmund,
Ohthere's offspring, whom, exiled and friendless,
Weohstan did slay with sword-edge in battle,
And carried his kinsman the clear-shining helmet,
2565 The ring-made burnie, the old giant-weapon
That Onela gave him, his boon-fellow's armor,
Ready war-trappings: he the feud did not mention,
Though he'd fatally smitten the son of his brother.
Many a half-year held he the treasures,
2570 The bill and the burnie, till his bairn became able,

Like his father before him, fame-deeds to 'complish;
Then he gave him 'mong Geatmen a goodly array of
Weeds for his warfare; he went from life then
Old on his journey. 'Twas the earliest time then
2575 That the youthful champion might charge in the battle
Aiding his liegelord; his spirit was dauntless.
Nor did kinsman's bequest quail at the battle:
This the dragon discovered on their coming together.
Wiglaf uttered many a right-saying,
2580 Said to his fellows, sad was his spirit:
"I remember the time when, tasting the mead-cup,
We promised in the hall the lord of us all
Who gave us these ring-treasures, that this battle-equipment,
Swords and helmets, we'd certainly quite him,
2585 Should need of such aid ever befall him:
In the war-band he chose us for this journey spontaneously,
Stirred us to glory and gave me these jewels,
Since he held and esteemed us trust-worthy spearmen,
Hardy helm-bearers, though this hero-achievement
2590 Our lord intended alone to accomplish,
Ward of his people, for most of achievements,
Doings audacious, he did among earth-folk.
The day is now come when the ruler of earthmen
Needeth the vigor of valiant heroes:
2595 Let us wend us towards him, the war-prince to succor,
While the heat yet rageth, horrible fire-fight.
God wot in me, 'tis mickle the liefer
The blaze should embrace my body and eat it
With my treasure-bestower. Meseemeth not proper
2600 To bear our battle-shields back to our country,
'Less first we are able to fell and destroy the
Long-hating foeman, to defend the life of
The prince of the Weders. Well do I know 'tisn't
Earned by his exploits, he only of Geatmen
2605 Sorrow should suffer, sink in the battle:
Brand and helmet to us both shall be common,
Shield-cover, burnie." Through the bale-smoke he stalked then,
Went under helmet to the help of his chieftain,
Briefly discoursing: "Beowulf dear,
2610 Perform thou all fully, as thou formerly saidst,
In thy youthful years, that while yet thou livedst
Thou wouldst let thine honor not ever be lessened.
Thy life thou shalt save, mighty in actions,
Atheling undaunted, with all of thy vigor;
2615 I'll give thee assistance." The dragon came raging,

Wild-mooded stranger, when these words had been uttered
('Twas the second occasion), seeking his enemies,
Men that were hated, with hot-gleaming fire-waves;
With blaze-billows burned the board to its edges:
2620 The fight-armor failed then to furnish assistance
To the youthful spear-hero: but the young-agèd stripling
Quickly advanced 'neath his kinsman's war-target,
Since his own had been ground in the grip of the fire.
Then the warrior-king was careful of glory,
2625 He soundly smote with sword-for-the-battle,
That it stood in the head by hatred driven;
Nægling was shivered, the old and iron-made
Brand of Beowulf in battle deceived him.
'Twas denied him that edges of irons were able
2630 To help in the battle; the hand was too mighty
Which every weapon, as I heard on inquiry,
Outstruck in its stroke, when to struggle he carried
The wonderful war-sword: it waxed him no better.
Then the people-despoiler—third of his onsets—
2635 Fierce-raging fire-drake, of feud-hate was mindful,
Charged on the strong one, when chance was afforded,
Heated and war-grim, seized on his neck
With teeth that were bitter; he bloody did wax with
Soul-gore seething; sword-blood in waves boiled.

2640 Then I heard that at need of the king of the people
The upstanding earlman exhibited prowess,
Vigor and courage, as suited his nature;
He his head did not guard, but the high-minded liegeman's
Hand was consumed, when he succored his kinsman,
2645 So he struck the strife-bringing strange-comer lower,
Earl-thane in armor, that in went the weapon
Gleaming and plated, that 'gan then the fire
Later to lessen. The liegelord himself then
Retained his consciousness, brandished his war-knife,
2650 Battle-sharp, bitter, that he bare on his armor:
The Weder-lord cut the worm in the middle.
They had felled the enemy (life drove out then
Puissant prowess), the pair had destroyed him,
Land-chiefs related: so a liegeman should prove him,
2655 A thaneman when needed. To the prince 'twas the last of
His era of conquest by his own great achievements,
The latest of world-deeds. The wound then began
Which the earth-dwelling dragon erstwhile had wrought him
To burn and to swell. He soon then discovered

2660   That bitterest bale-woe in his bosom was raging,
       Poison within. The atheling advanced then,
       That along by the wall, he prudent of spirit
       Might sit on a settle; he saw the giant-work,
       How arches of stone strengthened with pillars
2665   The earth-hall eternal inward supported.
       Then the long-worthy liegeman laved with his hand the
       Far-famous chieftain, gory from sword-edge,
       Refreshing the face of his friend-lord and ruler,
       Sated with battle, unbinding his helmet.
2670   Beowulf answered, of his injury spake he,
       His wound that was fatal (he was fully aware
       He had lived his allotted life-days enjoying
       The pleasures of earth; then past was entirely
       His measure of days, death very near):
2675   "My son I would give now my battle-equipments,
       Had any of heirs been after me granted,
       Along of my body. This people I governed
       Fifty of winters: no king 'mong my neighbors
       Dared to encounter me with comrades-in-battle,
2680   Try me with terror. The time to me ordered
       I bided at home, mine own kept fitly,
       Sought me no snares, swore me not many
       Oaths in injustice. Joy over all this
       I'm able to have, though ill with my death-wounds;
2685   Hence the Ruler of Earthmen need not charge me
       With the killing of kinsmen, when cometh my life out
       Forth from my body. Fare thou with haste now
       To behold the hoard 'neath the hoar-grayish stone,
       Well-lovèd Wiglaf, now the worm is a-lying,
2690   Sore-wounded sleepeth, disseized of his treasure.
       Go thou in haste that treasures of old I,
       Gold-wealth may gaze on, together see lying
       The ether-bright jewels, be easier able,
       Having the heap of hoard-gems, to yield my
2695   Life and the land-folk whom long I have governed."

       Then heard I that Wihstan's son very quickly,
       These words being uttered, heeded his liegelord
       Wounded and war-sick, went in his armor,
       His well-woven ring-mail, 'neath the roof of the barrow.
2700   Then the trusty retainer treasure-gems many
       Victorious saw, when the seat he came near to,
       Gold-treasure sparkling spread on the bottom,
       Wonder on the wall, and the worm-creature's cavern,

The ancient dawn-flier's, vessels a-standing,
2705   Cups of the ancients of cleansers bereavèd,
Robbed of their ornaments: there were helmets in numbers,
Old and rust-eaten, arm-bracelets many,
Artfully woven. Wealth can easily,
Gold on the sea-bottom, turn into vanity
2710   Each one of earthmen, arm him who pleaseth!
And he saw there lying an all-golden banner
High o'er the hoard, of hand-wonders greatest,
Linkèd with lacets: a light from it sparkled,
That the floor of the cavern he was able to look on,
2715   To examine the jewels. Sight of the dragon
Not any was offered, but edge offcarried him.
Then I heard that the hero the hoard-treasure plundered,
The giant-work ancient reaved in the cavern,
Bare on his bosom the beakers and platters,
2720   As himself would fain have it, and took off the standard,
The brightest of beacons; the bill had erst injured
(Its edge was of iron), the old-ruler's weapon,
Him who long had watched as ward of the jewels,
Who fire-terror carried hot for the treasure,
2725   Rolling in battle, in middlemost darkness,
Till murdered he perished. The messenger hastened,
Not loth to return, hurried by jewels:
Curiosity urged him if, excellent-mooded,
Alive he should find the lord of the Weders
2730   Mortally wounded, at the place where he left him.
'Mid the jewels he found then the famous old chieftain,
His liegelord belovèd, at his life's-end gory:
He thereupon 'gan to lave him with water,
Till the point of his word piercèd his breast-hoard.
2735   Beowulf spake (the gold-gems he noticed),
The old one in sorrow: "For the jewels I look on
Thanks do I utter for all to the Ruler,
Wielder of Worship, with words of devotion,
The Lord everlasting, that He let me such treasures
2740   Gain for my people ere death overtook me.
Since I've bartered the agèd life to me granted
For treasure of jewels, attend ye henceforward
The wants of the war-thanes; I can wait here no longer.
The battle-famed bid ye to build them a grave-hill,
2745   Bright when I'm burned, at the brim-current's limit;
As a memory-mark to the men I have governed,
Aloft it shall tower on Whale's-Ness uprising,
That earls of the ocean hereafter may call it

Beowulf's barrow, those who barks ever-dashing
2750 From a distance shall drive o'er the darkness of waters."
The bold-mooded troop-lord took from his neck then
The ring that was golden, gave to his liegeman,
The youthful war-hero, his gold-flashing helmet,
His collar and war-mail, bade him well to enjoy them:
2755 "Thou art latest left of the line of our kindred,
Of Wægmunding people: Weird hath offcarried
All of my kinsmen to the Creator's glory,
Earls in their vigor: I shall after them fare."
'Twas the aged liegelord's last-spoken word in
2760 His musings of spirit, ere he mounted the fire,
The battle-waves burning: from his bosom departed
His soul to seek the sainted ones' glory.

It had wofully chanced then the youthful retainer
To behold on earth the most ardent-belovèd
2765 At his life-days' limit, lying there helpless.
The slayer too lay there, of life all bereavèd,
Horrible earth-drake, harassed with sorrow:
The round-twisted monster was permitted no longer
To govern the ring-hoards, but edges of war-swords
2770 Mightily seized him, battle-sharp, sturdy
Leavings of hammers, that still from his wounds
The flier-from-farland fell to the earth
Hard by his hoard-house, hopped he at midnight
Not e'er through the air, nor exulting in jewels
2775 Suffered them to see him: but he sank then to earthward
Through the hero-chief's handwork. I heard sure it throve then
But few in the land of liegemen of valor,
Though of every achievement bold he had proved him,
To run 'gainst the breath of the venomous scather,
2780 Or the hall of the treasure to trouble with hand-blows,
If he watching had found the ward of the hoard-hall
On the barrow abiding. Beowulf's part of
The treasure of jewels was paid for with death;
Each of the twain had attained to the end of
2785 Life so unlasting. Not long was the time till
The tardy-at-battle returned from the thicket,
The timid truce-breakers ten all together,
Who durst not before play with the lances
In the prince of the people's pressing emergency;
2790 But blushing with shame, with shields they betook them,
With arms and armor where the old one was lying:
They gazed upon Wiglaf. He was sitting exhausted,

Foot-going fighter, not far from the shoulders
Of the lord of the people, would rouse him with water;
2795 No whit did it help him; though he hoped for it keenly,
He was able on earth not at all in the leader
Life to retain, and nowise to alter
The will of the Wielder; the World-Ruler's power
Would govern the actions of each one of heroes,
2800 As yet He is doing. From the young one forthwith then
Could grim-worded greeting be got for him quickly
Whose courage had failed him. Wiglaf discoursed then,
Weohstan his son, sad-mooded hero,
Looked on the hated: "He who soothness will utter
2805 Can say that the liegelord who gave you the jewels,
The ornament-armor wherein ye are standing,
When on ale-bench often he offered to hall-men
Helmet and burnie, the prince to his liegemen,
As best upon earth he was able to find him,—
2810 That he wildly wasted his war-gear undoubtedly
When battle o'ertook him. The troop-king no need had
To glory in comrades; yet God permitted him,
Victory-Wielder, with weapon unaided
Himself to avenge, when vigor was needed.
2815 I life-protection but little was able
To give him in battle, and I 'gan, notwithstanding,
Helping my kinsman (my strength overtaxing):
He waxed the weaker when with weapon I smote on
My mortal opponent, the fire less strongly
2820 Flamed from his bosom. Too few of protectors
Came round the king at the critical moment.
Now must ornament-taking and weapon-bestowing,
Home-joyance all, cease for your kindred,
Food for the people; each of your warriors
2825 Must needs be bereavèd of rights that he holdeth
In landed possessions, when faraway nobles
Shall learn of your leaving your lord so basely,
The dastardly deed. Death is more pleasant
To every earlman than infamous life is!"

2830 Then he charged that the battle be announced at the hedge
Up o'er the cliff-edge, where the earl-troopers bided
The whole of the morning, mood-wretched sat them,
Bearers of battle-shields, both things expecting,
The end of his lifetime and the coming again of
2835 The liegelord belovèd. Little reserved he
Of news that was known, who the ness-cliff did travel,

But he truly discoursed to all that could hear him:
"Now the free-giving friend-lord of the folk of the Weders,
The folk-prince of Geatmen, is fast in his death-bed,
2840 By the deeds of the dragon in death-bed abideth;
Along with him lieth his life-taking foeman
Slain with knife-wounds: he was wholly unable
To injure at all the ill-planning monster
With bite of his sword-edge. Wiglaf is sitting,
2845 Offspring of Wihstan, up over Beowulf,
Earl o'er another whose end-day hath reached him,
Head-watch holdeth o'er heroes unliving,
For friend and for foeman. The folk now expecteth
A season of strife when the death of the folk-king
2850 To Frankmen and Frisians in far-lands is published.
The war-hatred waxed warm 'gainst the Hugmen,
When Higelac came with an army of vessels
Faring to Friesland, where the Frankmen in battle
Humbled him and bravely with overmight 'complished
2855 That the mail-clad warrior must sink in the battle,
Fell 'mid his folk-troop: no fret-gems presented
The atheling to earlmen; aye was denied us
Merewing's mercy. The men of the Swedelands
For truce or for truth trust I but little;
2860 But widely 'twas known that near Ravenswood Ongentheow
Sundered Hæthcyn the Hrethling from life-joys,
When for pride overweening the War-Scylfings first did
Seek the Geatmen with savage intentions.
Early did Ohthere's age-laden father,
2865 Old and terrible, give blow in requital,
Killing the sea-king, the queen-mother rescued,
The old one his consort deprived of her gold,
Onela's mother and Ohthere's also,
And then followed the feud-nursing foemen till hardly,
2870 Reaved of their ruler, they Ravenswood entered.
Then with vast-numbered forces he assaulted the remnant,
Weary with wounds, woe often promised
The livelong night to the sad-hearted war-troop:
Said he at morning would kill them with edges of weapons,
2875 Some on the gallows for glee to the fowls.
Aid came after to the anxious-in-spirit
At dawn of the day, after Higelac's bugle
And trumpet-sound heard they, when the good one proceeded
And faring followed the flower of the troopers.

2880 "The blood-stainèd trace of Swedes and Geatmen,
The death-rush of warmen, widely was noticed,
How the folks with each other feud did awaken.
The worthy one went then with well-beloved comrades,
Old and dejected to go to the fastness,
2885 Ongentheo earl upward then turned him;
Of Higelac's battle he'd heard on inquiry,
The exultant one's prowess, despaired of resistance,
With earls of the ocean to be able to struggle,
'Gainst sea-going sailors to save the hoard-treasure,
2890 His wife and his children; he fled after thenceward
Old 'neath the earth-wall. Then was offered pursuance
To the braves of the Swedemen, the banner to Higelac.
They fared then forth o'er the field-of-protection,
When the Hrethling heroes hedgeward had thronged them.
2895 Then with edges of irons was Ongentheow driven,
The gray-haired to tarry, that the troop-ruler had to
Suffer the power solely of Eofor:
Wulf then wildly with weapon assaulted him,
Wonred his son, that for swinge of the edges
2900 The blood from his body burst out in currents,
Forth 'neath his hair. He feared not however,
Gray-headed Scylfing, but speedily quited
The wasting wound-stroke with worse exchange,
When the king of the thane-troop thither did turn him:
2905 The wise-mooded son of Wonred was powerless
To give a return-blow to the age-hoary man,
But his head-shielding helmet first hewed he to pieces,
That flecked with gore perforce he did totter,
Fell to the earth; not fey was he yet then,
2910 But up did he spring though an edge-wound had reached him.
Then Higelac's vassal, valiant and dauntless,
When his brother lay dead, made his broad-bladed weapon,
Giant-sword ancient, defence of the giants,
Bound o'er the shield-wall; the folk-prince succumbed then,
2915 Shepherd of people, was pierced to the vitals.
There were many attendants who bound up his kinsman,
Carried him quickly when occasion was granted
That the place of the slain they were suffered to manage.
This pending, one hero plundered the other,
2920 His armor of iron from Ongentheow ravished,
His hard-sword hilted and helmet together;
The old one's equipments he carried to Higelac.
He the jewels received, and rewards 'mid the troopers
Graciously promised, and so did accomplish:

2925 The king of the Weders requited the war-rush,
Hrethel's descendant, when home he repaired him,
To Eofor and Wulf with wide-lavished treasures,
To each of them granted a hundred of thousands
In land and rings wrought out of wire:
2930 None upon mid-earth needed to twit him
With the gifts he gave them, when glory they conquered;
And to Eofor then gave he his one only daughter,
The honor of home, as an earnest of favor.
That's the feud and hatred—as ween I 'twill happen—
2935 The anger of earthmen, that earls of the Swedemen
Will visit on us, when they hear that our leader
Lifeless is lying, he who longtime protected
His hoard and kingdom 'gainst hating assailers,
Who on the fall of the heroes defended of yore
2940 The deed-mighty Scyldings, did for the troopers
What best did avail them, and further moreover
Hero-deeds 'complished. Now is haste most fitting,
That the lord of liegemen we look upon yonder,
And that one carry on journey to death-pyre
2945 Who ring-presents gave us. Not aught of it all
Shall melt with the brave one—there's a mass of bright jewels,
Gold beyond measure, grewsomely purchased
And ending it all ornament-rings too
Bought with his life; these fire shall devour,
2950 Flame shall cover, no earlman shall wear
A jewel-memento, nor beautiful virgin
Have on her neck rings to adorn her,
But wretched in spirit bereavèd of gold-gems
She shall oft with others be exiled and banished,
2955 Since the leader of liegemen hath laughter forsaken,
Mirth and merriment. Hence many a war-spear
Cold from the morning shall be clutched in the fingers,
Heaved in the hand, no harp-music's sound shall
Waken the warriors, but the wan-coated raven
2960 Fain over fey ones freely shall gabble,
Shall say to the eagle how he sped in the eating,
When, the wolf his companion, he plundered the slain."
So the high-minded hero was rehearsing these stories
Loathsome to hear; he lied as to few of
2965 Weirds and of words. All the war-troop arose then,
'Neath the Eagle's Cape sadly betook them,
Weeping and woful, the wonder to look at.
They saw on the sand then soulless a-lying,
His slaughter-bed holding, him who rings had given them

2970 In days that were done; then the death-bringing moment
Was come to the good one, that the king very warlike,
Wielder of Weders, with wonder-death perished.
First they beheld there a creature more wondrous,
The worm on the field, in front of them lying,
2975 The foeman before them: the fire-spewing dragon,
Ghostly and grisly guest in his terrors,
Was scorched in the fire; as he lay there he measured
Fifty of feet; came forth in the night-time
To rejoice in the air, thereafter departing
2980 To visit his den; he in death was then fastened,
He would joy in no other earth-hollowed caverns.
There stood round about him beakers and vessels,
Dishes were lying and dear-valued weapons,
With iron-rust eaten, as in earth's mighty bosom
2985 A thousand of winters there they had rested:
That mighty bequest then with magic was guarded,
Gold of the ancients, that earlman not any
The ring-hall could touch, save Ruling-God only,
Sooth-king of Vict'ries gave whom He wished to
2990 (He is earth-folk's protector) to open the treasure,
E'en to such among mortals as seemed to Him proper.

Then 'twas seen that the journey prospered him little
Who wrongly within had the ornaments hidden
Down 'neath the wall. The warden erst slaughtered
2995 Some few of the folk-troop: the feud then thereafter
Was hotly avengèd. 'Tis a wonder where,
When the strength-famous trooper has attained to the end of
Life-days allotted, then no longer the man may
Remain with his kinsmen where mead-cups are flowing.
3000 So to Beowulf happened when the ward of the barrow,
Assaults, he sought for: himself had no knowledge
How his leaving this life was likely to happen.
So to doomsday, famous folk-leaders down did
Call it with curses—who 'complished it there—
3005 That that man should be ever of ill-deeds convicted,
Confined in foul-places, fastened in hell-bonds,
Punished with plagues, who this place should e'er ravage.
He cared not for gold: rather the Wielder's
Favor preferred he first to get sight of.
3010 Wiglaf discoursed then, Wihstan his son:
"Oft many an earlman on one man's account must
Sorrow endure, as to us it hath happened.
The liegelord belovèd we could little prevail on,

Kingdom's keeper, counsel to follow,
3015 Not to go to the guardian of the gold-hoard, but let him
Lie where he long was, live in his dwelling
Till the end of the world. Met we a destiny
Hard to endure: the hoard has been looked at,
Been gained very grimly; too grievous the fate that
3020 The prince of the people pricked to come thither.
I was therein and all of it looked at,
The building's equipments, since access was given me,
Not kindly at all entrance permitted
Within under earth-wall. Hastily seized I
3025 And held in my hands a huge-weighing burden
Of hoard-treasures costly, hither out bare them
To my liegelord belovèd: life was yet in him,
And consciousness also; the old one discoursed then
Much and mournfully, commanded to greet you,
3030 Bade that remembering the deeds of your friend-lord
Ye build on the fire-hill of corpses a lofty
Burial-barrow, broad and far-famous,
As 'mid world-dwelling warriors he was widely most honored
While he reveled in riches. Let us rouse us and hasten
3035 Again to see and seek for the treasure,
The wonder 'neath wall. The way I will show you,
That close ye may look at ring-gems sufficient
And gold in abundance. Let the bier with promptness
Fully be fashioned, when forth we shall come,
3040 And lift we our lord, then, where long he shall tarry,
Well-beloved warrior, 'neath the Wielder's protection."
Then the son of Wihstan bade orders be given,
Mood-valiant man, to many of heroes,
Holders of homesteads, that they hither from far,
3045 Leaders of liegemen, should look for the good one
With wood for his pyre: "The flame shall now swallow
(The wan fire shall wax) the warriors' leader
Who the rain of the iron often abided,
When, sturdily hurled, the storm of the arrows
3050 Leapt o'er linden-wall, the lance rendered service,
Furnished with feathers followed the arrow."
Now the wise-mooded son of Wihstan did summon
The best of the braves from the band of the ruler
Seven together; 'neath the enemy's roof he
3055 Went with the seven; one of the heroes
Who fared at the front, a fire-blazing torch-light
Bare in his hand. No lot then decided
Who that hoard should havoc, when hero-earls saw it

Lying in the cavern uncared-for entirely,
3060 Rusting to ruin: they rued then but little
That they hastily hence hauled out the treasure,
The dear-valued jewels; the dragon eke pushed they,
The worm o'er the wall, let the wave-currents take him,
The waters enwind the ward of the treasures.
3065 There wounden gold on a wain was uploaded,
A mass unmeasured, the men-leader off then,
The hero hoary, to Whale's-Ness was carried.

The folk of the Geatmen got him then ready
A pile on the earth strong for the burning,
3070 Behung with helmets, hero-knights' targets,
And bright-shining burnies, as he begged they should have them;
Then wailing war-heroes their world-famous chieftain,
Their liegelord beloved, laid in the middle.
Soldiers began then to make on the barrow
3075 The largest of dead-fires: dark o'er the vapor
The smoke-cloud ascended, the sad-roaring fire,
Mingled with weeping (the wind-roar subsided)
Till the building of bone it had broken to pieces,
Hot in the heart. Heavy in spirit
3080 They mood-sad lamented the men-leader's ruin;
And mournful measures the much-grieving widow
   *   *   *   *   *   *   *
   *   *   *   *   *   *   *
   *   *   *   *   *   *   *
3085 *   *   *   *   *   *   *
   *   *   *   *   *   *   *
   *   *   *   *   *   *   *

The men of the Weders made accordingly
A hill on the height, high and extensive,
3090 Of sea-going sailors to be seen from a distance,
And the brave one's beacon built where the fire was,
In ten-days' space, with a wall surrounded it,
As wisest of world-folk could most worthily plan it.
They placed in the barrow rings and jewels,
3095 All such ornaments as erst in the treasure
War-mooded men had won in possession:
The earnings of earlmen to earth they entrusted,
The gold to the dust, where yet it remaineth
As useless to mortals as in foregoing eras.
3100 'Round the dead-mound rode then the doughty-in-battle,
Bairns of all twelve of the chiefs of the people,
More would they mourn, lament for their ruler,

Speak in measure, mention him with pleasure,
Weighed his worth, and his warlike achievements
3105 Mightily commended, as 'tis meet one praise his
Liegelord in words and love him in spirit,
When forth from his body he fares to destruction.
So lamented mourning the men of the Geats,
Fond-loving vassals, the fall of their lord,
3110 Said he was kindest of kings under heaven,
Gentlest of men, most winning of manner,
Friendliest to folk-troops and fondest of honor.

Sir Gawain and the Green Knight

[1]Siþen þe sege & þe assaut watȝ sesed at Troye,
Þe borȝ brittened & brent to brondeȝ & askeȝ,
Þe tulk þat þe trammes of tresoun þer wroȝt,
Watȝ tried for his tricherie, þe trewest on erthe;
Hit watȝ Ennias þe athel, & his highe kynde,
Þat siþen depreced prouinces, & patrounes bicome
Welneȝe of al þe wele in þe west iles,
Fro riche Romulus to Rome ricchis hym swyþe,
With gret bobbaunce þat burȝe he biges vpon fyrst,
& neuenes hit his aune nome, as hit now hat;
Ticius to Tuskan [turnes,] & teldes bigynnes;
Langaberde in Lumbardie lyftes vp homes;
& fer ouer þe French flod Felix Brutus
On mony bonkkes ful brode Bretayn he setteȝ,
wyth wynne;
Where werre, & wrake, & wonder,
Bi syþeȝ hatȝ wont þer-inne,
& oft boþe blysse & blunder
Ful skete hatȝ skyfted synne.

I

Of the making of Britain

After the siege and the assault of Troy, when that burg was destroyed and burnt to ashes, and the traitor slain for his treason, the noble Æneas and his kin sailed forth to become princes and patrons of well-nigh all the Western Isles. Thus Romulus built Rome (and gave to the city his own name, which it bears even to this day); and Ticius turned him to Tuscany; and Langobard raised him up dwellings in Lombardy; and Felix Brutus sailed far over the French flood, and founded the kingdom of Britain, wherein have been war and waste and wonder, and bliss and bale, oft-times since.

And in that kingdom of Britain have been wrought more gallant deeds than in any other; but of all British kings Arthur was the most valiant, as I have heard tell, therefore will I set forth a wondrous adventure that fell out in his time. And if ye will listen to me, but for a little while, I will tell it even as it stands in story stiff and strong, fixed in the letter, as it hath long been known in the land.

---

1   This is the first paragraph in the original Middle English.

How Arthur held high feast at Camelot

KING ARTHUR LAY AT CAMELOT UPON A CHRISTMAS-TIDE, with many a gallant lord and lovely lady, and all the noble brotherhood of the Round Table. There they held rich revels with gay talk and jest; one while they would ride forth to joust and tourney, and again back to the court to make carols; for there was the feast holden fifteen days with all the mirth that men could devise, song and glee, glorious to hear, in the daytime, and dancing at night. Halls and chambers were crowded with noble guests, the bravest of knights and the loveliest of ladies, and Arthur himself was the comeliest king that ever held a court. For all this fair folk were in their youth, the fairest and most fortunate under heaven, and the king himself of such fame that it were hard now to name so valiant a hero.

New Year's Day

NOW THE NEW YEAR HAD BUT NEWLY COME IN, and on that day a double portion was served on the high table to all the noble guests, and thither came the king with all his knights, when the service in the chapel had been sung to an end. And they greeted each other for the New Year, and gave rich gifts, the one to the other (and they that received them were not wroth, that may ye well believe!), and the maidens laughed and made mirth till it was time to get them to meat. Then they washed and sat them down to the feast in fitting rank and order, and Guinevere the queen, gaily clad, sat on the high daïs. Silken was her seat, with a fair canopy over her head, of rich tapestries of Tars, embroidered, and studded with costly gems; fair she was to look upon, with her shining grey eyes, a fairer woman might no man boast himself of having seen.

But Arthur would not eat till all were served, so full of joy and gladness was he, even as a child; he liked not either to lie long, or to sit long at meat, so worked upon him his young blood and his wild brain. And another custom he had also, that came of his nobility, that he would never eat upon an high day till he had been advised of some knightly deed, or some strange and marvellous tale, of his ancestors, or of arms, or of other ventures. Or till some knight should seek of him leave to joust with another, that they might set their lives in jeopardy, one against another, as fortune might favour them. Such was the king's custom when he sat in hall at each high feast with his noble knights, therefore on that New Year tide, he abode, fair of face, on the throne, and made much mirth withal.

Of the noble knights there present

THUS THE KING SAT BEFORE THE HIGH TABLE, and spake of many things; and there good Sir Gawain was seated by Guinevere the queen, and on her other side sat Agravain, *à la dure main*; both were the king's sister's sons and full gallant knights. And at the end of the table was Bishop Bawdewyn, and Ywain, King Urien's son, sat at the other side alone. These were worthily served on the daïs, and at the lower tables sat many valiant knights. Then they bare the first course with the blast of trumpets and waving f banners, with the sound of drums and pipes, of song and lute, that many a heart was uplifted at the melody. Many were the dainties, and rare the meats, so great was the plenty they might scarce find room on the board to set on the dishes. Each helped himself as he liked best, and to each two were twelve dishes, with great plenty of beer and wine.

The coming of the Green Knight

Now I will say no more of the service, but that ye may know there was no lack, for there drew near a venture that the folk might well have left their labour to gaze upon. As the sound of the music ceased, and the first course had been fitly served, there came in at the hall door one terrible to behold, of stature greater than any on earth; from neck to loin so strong and thickly made, and with limbs so long and so great that he seemed even as a giant. And yet he was but a man, only the mightiest that might mount a steed; broad of chest and shoulders and slender of waist, and all his features of like fashion; but men marvelled much at his colour, for he rode even as a knight, yet was green all over.

The fashion of the knight

For he was clad all in green, with a straight coat, and a mantle above; all decked and lined with fur was the cloth and the hood that was thrown back from his locks and lay on his shoulders. Hose had he of the same green, and spurs of bright gold with silken fastenings richly worked; and all his vesture was verily green. Around his waist and his saddle were bands with fair stones set upon silken work, 'twere too long to tell of all the trifles that were embroidered thereon— birds and insects in gay gauds of green and gold.

Of the knight's steed

All the trappings of his steed were of metal of like enamel, even the stirrups that he stood in stained of the same, and stirrups and saddle-bow alike gleamed and shone with green stones. Even the steed on which he rode was of the same hue, a green horse, great and strong, and hard to hold, with broidered bridle, meet for the rider.

The knight was thus gaily dressed in green, his hair falling around his shoulders, on his breast hung a beard, as thick and green as a bush, and the beard and the hair of his head were clipped all round above his elbows. The lower part of his sleeves were fastened with clasps in the same wise as a king's mantle. The horse's mane was crisped and plaited with many a knot folded in with gold thread about the fair green, here a twist of the hair, here another of gold. The tail was twined in like manner, and both were bound about with a band of bright green set with many a precious stone; then they were tied aloft in a cunning knot, whereon rang many bells of burnished gold. Such a steed might no other ride, nor had such ever been looked upon in that hall ere that time; and all who saw that knight spake and said that a man might scarce abide his stroke.

The arming of the knight

The knight bore no helm nor hauberk, neither gorget nor breast-plate, neither shaft nor buckler to smite nor to shield, but in one hand he had a holly-bough, that is greenest when the groves are bare, and in his other an axe, huge and uncomely, a cruel weapon in fashion, if one would picture it. The head was an ell-yard long, the metal all of green steel and gold, the blade burnished bright, with a broad edge, as well shapen to shear as a sharp razor. The steel was set into a strong staff, all bound round with iron, even to the end, and engraved with green in cunning work. A lace was twined about it, that looped at the head, and all adown the handle it was clasped with tassels on buttons of bright green richly broidered.

The knight halted in the entrance of the hall, looking to the high daïs, and greeted no man, but looked ever upwards; and the first words he spake were, "Where is the ruler of this folk? I would gladly look upon that hero, and have speech with him." He cast his eyes on the knights, and mustered them up and down, striving ever to see who of them was of most renown.

Then was there great gazing to behold that chief, for each man marvelled what it might mean that a knight and his steed should have even such a hue as the green grass; and that seemed even greener than green enamel on bright gold. All looked on him as he stood, and drew near unto him wondering greatly what he might be; for many marvels had they seen, but none such as this, and phantasm and faërie did the folk deem it. Therefore were the gallant knights slow to answer, and gazed astounded, and sat stone still in a deep silence through that goodly hall, as if a slumber were fallen upon them. I deem it was not all for doubt, but some for courtesy that they might give ear unto his errand.

Then Arthur beheld this adventure before his high daïs, and knightly he greeted him, for discourteous was he never. "Sir," he said, "thou art welcome to this place—lord of this hall am I, and men call me Arthur. Light thee down, and tarry awhile, and what thy will is, that shall we learn after."

Of the knight's challenge

"Nay," quoth the stranger, "so help me He that sitteth on high, 'twas not mine errand to tarry any while in this dwelling; but the praise of this thy folk and thy city is lifted up on high, and thy warriors are holden for the best and the most valiant of those who ride mail-clad to the fight. The wisest and the worthiest of this world are they, and well proven in all knightly sports. And here, as I have heard tell, is fairest courtesy, therefore have I come hither as at this time. Ye may be sure by the branch that I bear here that I come in peace, seeking no strife. For had I willed to journey in warlike guise I have at home both hauberk and helm, shield and shining spear, and other weapons to mine hand, but since I seek no war my raiment is that of peace. But if thou be as bold as all men tell thou wilt freely grant me the boon I ask."

And Arthur answered, "Sir Knight, if thou cravest battle here thou shalt not fail for lack of a foe."

And the knight answered, "Nay, I ask no fight, in faith here on the benches are but beardless children, were I clad in armour on my steed there is no man here might match me. Therefore I ask in this court but a Christmas jest, for that it is Yule-tide, and New Year, and there are many here. If any one in this hall holds himself so hardy, so bold both of blood and brain, as to dare strike me one stroke for another, I will give him as a gift this axe, which is heavy enough, in sooth, to handle as he may list, and I will abide the first blow, unarmed as I sit. If any knight be so bold as to prove my words let him come swiftly to me here, and take this weapon, I quit claim to it, he may keep it as his own, and I will abide his stroke, firm on the floor. Then shalt thou give me the right to deal him another, the respite of a year from to-day shall he have. Now pledge me thy word, and let see whether any here dare say aught.

THE SILENCE OF THE KNIGHTS

Now if the knights had been astounded at the first, yet stiller were they all, high and low, when they had heard his words. The knight on his steed straightened himself in the saddle, and rolled his eyes fiercely round the hall, red they gleamed under his green and bushy brows. He frowned and twisted his beard, waiting to see who should rise, and when none answered he cried aloud in mockery, "What, is this Arthur's hall, and these the knights whose renown hath run through many realms? Where are now your pride and your conquests, your wrath, and anger, and mighty words? Now are the praise and the renown of the Round Table overthrown by one man's speech, since all keep silence for dread ere ever they have seen a blow!"

With that he laughed so loudly that the blood rushed to the king's fair face for very shame; he waxed wroth, as did all his knights, and sprang to his feet, and drew near to the stranger and said, "Now by heaven foolish is thine asking, and thy folly shall find its fitting answer. I know no man aghast at thy great words. Give me here thine axe and I shall grant thee the boon thou hast asked." Lightly he sprang to him and caught at his hand, and the knight, fierce of aspect, lighted down from his charger.

Then Arthur took the axe and gripped the haft, and swung it round, ready to strike. And the knight stood before him, taller by the head than any in the hall; he stood, and stroked his beard, and drew down his coat, no more dismayed for the king's threats than if one had brought him a drink of wine.

HOW SIR GAWAIN DARED THE VENTURE

Then Gawain, who sat by the queen, leaned forward to the king and spake, "I beseech ye, my lord, let this venture be mine. Would ye but bid me rise from this seat, and stand by your side, so that my liege lady thought it not ill, then would I come to your counsel before this goodly court. For I think it not seemly that such challenge should be made in your hall that ye yourself should undertake it, while there are many bold knights who sit beside ye, none are there, methinks, of readier will under heaven, or more valiant in open field. I am the weakest, I wot, and the feeblest of wit, and it will be the less loss of my life if ye seek sooth. For save that ye are mine uncle naught is there in me to praise, no virtue is there in my body save your blood, and since this challenge is such folly that it beseems ye not to take it, and I have asked it from ye first, let it fall to me, and if I bear myself ungallantly then let all this court blame me."

Then they all spake with one voice that the king should leave this venture and grant it to Gawain.

Then Arthur commanded the knight to rise, and he rose up quickly and knelt down before the king, and caught hold of the weapon; and the king loosed his hold of it, and lifted up his hand, and gave him his blessing, and bade him be strong both of heart and hand. "Keep thee well, nephew," quoth Arthur, "that thou give him but the one blow, and if thou redest him rightly I trow thou shalt well abide the stroke he may give thee after."

The making of the covenant

Gawain stepped to the stranger, axe in hand, and he, never fearing, awaited his coming. Then the Green Knight spake to Sir Gawain, "Make we our covenant ere we go further. First, I ask thee, knight, what is thy name? Tell me truly, that I may know thee."

"In faith," quoth the good knight, "Gawain am I, who give thee this buffet, let what may come of it; and at this time twelvemonth will I take another at thine hand with whatsoever weapon thou wilt, and none other."

Then the other answered again, "Sir Gawain, so may I thrive as I am fain to take this buffet at thine hand," and he quoth further, "Sir Gawain, it liketh me well that I shall take at thy fist that which I have asked here, and thou hast readily and truly rehearsed all the covenant that I asked of the king, save that thou shalt swear me, by thy troth, to seek me thyself wherever thou hopest that I may be found, and win thee such reward as thou dealest me to-day, before this folk."

"Where shall I seek thee?" quoth Gawain. "Where is thy place? By Him that made me, I wot never where thou dwellest, nor know I thee, knight, thy court, nor thy name. But teach me truly all that pertaineth thereto, and tell me thy name, and I shall use all my wit to win my way thither, and that I swear thee for sooth, and by my sure troth."

"That is enough in the New Year, it needs no more," quoth the Green Knight to the gallant Gawain, "if I tell thee truly when I have taken the blow, and thou hast smitten me; then will I teach thee of my house and home, and mine own name, then mayest thou ask thy road and keep covenant. And if I waste no words then farest thou the better, for thou canst dwell in thy land, and seek no further. But take now thy toll, and let see how thy strikest."

"Gladly will I," quoth Gawain, handling his axe.

THE GIVING OF THE BLOW

THEN THE GREEN KNIGHT swiftly made him ready, he bowed down his head, and laid his long locks on the crown that his bare neck might be seen. Gawain gripped his axe and raised it on high, the left foot he set forward on the floor, and let the blow fall lightly on the bare neck. The sharp edge of the blade sundered the bones, smote through the neck, and clave it in two, so that the edge of the steel bit on the ground, and the head rolled even to the horse's feet.

THE MARVEL OF THE GREEN KNIGHT

THE BLOOD SPURTED FORTH, and glistened on the green raiment, but the knight neither faltered nor fell; he started forward with out-stretched hand, and caught the head, and lifted it up; then he turned to his steed, and took hold of the bridle, set his foot in the stirrup, and mounted. His head he held by the hair, in his hand. Then he seated himself in his saddle as if naught ailed him, and he were not headless. He turned his steed about, the grim corpse bleeding freely the while, and they who looked upon him doubted them much for the covenant.

For he held up the head in his hand, and turned the face towards them that sat on the high daïs, and it lifted up the eye-lids and looked upon them, and spake as ye shall hear. "Look, Gawain, that thou art ready to go as thou hast promised, and seek leally till thou find me, even as thou hast sworn in this hall in the hearing of these knights. Come thou, I charge thee, to the Green Chapel, such a stroke as thou hast dealt thou hast deserved, and it shall be promptly paid thee on New Year's morn. Many men know me as the knight of the Green Chapel, and if thou askest thou shalt not fail to find me. Therefore it behoves thee to come, or to yield thee as recreant."

With that he turned his bridle, and galloped out at the hall door, his head in his hands, so that the sparks flew from beneath his horse's hoofs. Whither he went none knew, no more than they wist whence he had come; and the king and Gawain they gazed and laughed, for in sooth this had proved a greater marvel than any they had known aforetime.

Though Arthur the king was astonished at his heart, yet he let no sign of it be seen, but spake in courteous wise to the fair queen: "Dear lady, be not dismayed, such craft is well suited to Christmas-tide when we seek jesting, laughter and song, and fair carols of knights and ladies. But now I may well get me to meat, for I have seen a marvel I may not forget." Then he looked on Sir Gawain, and said gaily, "Now, fair nephew, hang up thine axe, since it has hewn enough," and they hung it on the dossal above the daïs, where all men might look on it for a marvel, and by its true token tell of the wonder. Then the twain sat them down together, the king and the good knight, and men served them with a double portion, as was the share of the noblest, with all manner of meat and of minstrelsy. And they spent that day in gladness, but Sir Gawain must well bethink him of the heavy venture to which he had set his hand.

II

THIS BEGINNING OF ADVENTURES had Arthur at the New Year, for he yearned to hear gallant tales, though his words were few when he sat at the feast. But now had they stern work on hand. Gawain was glad to begin the jest in the hall, but ye need have no marvel if the end be heavy. For though a man be merry in mind when he has well drunk, yet a year runs full swiftly, and the beginning but rarely matches the end.

THE WANING OF THE YEAR

FOR YULE WAS NOW OVER-PAST, and the year after, each season in its turn following the other. For after Christmas comes crabbed Lent, that will have fish for flesh and simpler cheer. But then the weather of the world chides with winter; the cold withdraws itself, the clouds uplift, and the rain falls in warm showers on the fair plains. Then the flowers come forth, meadows and groves are clad in green, the birds make ready to build, and sing sweetly for solace of the soft summer that follows thereafter. The blossoms bud and blow in the hedgerows rich and rank, and noble notes enough are heard in the fair woods.

After the season of summer, with the soft winds, when zephyr breathes lightly on seeds and herbs, joyous indeed is the growth that waxes thereout when the dew drips from the leaves beneath the blissful glance of the bright sun. But then comes harvest and hardens the grain, warning it to wax ripe ere the winter. The drought drives the dust on high, flying over the face of the land; the angry wind of the welkin wrestles with the sun; the leaves fall from the trees and light upon the ground, and all brown are the groves that but now were green, and ripe is the fruit that once was flower. So the year passes into many yesterdays, and winter comes again, as it needs no sage to tell us.

SIR GAWAIN BETHINKS HIM OF HIS COVENANT

WHEN THE MICHAELMAS MOON WAS COME IN WITH WARNINGS OF WINTER, Sir Gawain bethought him full oft of his perilous journey. Yet till All Hallows Day he lingered with Arthur, and on that day they made a great feast for the hero's sake, with much revel and richness of the Round Table. Courteous knights and comely ladies, all were in sorrow for the love of that knight, and though they spake no word of it many were joyless for his sake.

And after meat, sadly Sir Gawain turned to his uncle, and spake of his journey, and said, "Liege lord of my life, leave from you I crave. Ye know well how the matter stands without more words, to-morrow am I bound to set forth in search of the Green Knight."

Then came together all the noblest knights, Ywain and Erec, and many another. Sir Dodinel le Sauvage, Launcelot and Lionel, and Lucan the Good, Sir Bors and Sir Bedivere, valiant knights both, and many another hero, with Sir Mador de la Porte, and they all drew near, heavy at heart, to take counsel with Sir Gawain. Much sorrow and weeping was there in the hall to think that so worthy a knight as Gawain should wend his way to seek a deadly blow, and should no more wield his sword in fight. But the knight made ever good cheer, and said, "Nay, wherefore should I shrink? What may a man do but prove his fate?"

THE ARMING OF SIR GAWAIN

HE DWELT THERE ALL THAT DAY, and on the morn he arose and asked betimes for his armour; and they brought it unto him on this wise: first, a rich carpet was stretched on the floor (and brightly did the gold gear glitter upon it), then the knight stepped on to it, and handled the steel; clad he was in a doublet of silk, with a close hood, lined fairly throughout. Then they set the steel shoes upon his feet, and wrapped his legs with greaves, with polished knee-caps fastened with knots of gold. Then they cased his thighs in cuisses closed with thongs, and brought him the byrny of bright steel rings sewn upon a fair stuff. Well burnished braces they set on each arm with good elbow-pieces, and gloves of mail, and all the goodly gear that should shield him in his need. And they cast over all a rich surcoat, and set the golden spurs on his heels, and girt him with a trusty sword fastened with a silken bawdrick. When he was thus clad his harness was costly, for the least loop or latchet gleamed with gold. So armed as he was he hearkened Mass and made his offering at the high altar. Then he came to the king, and the knights of his court, and courteously took leave of lords and ladies, and they kissed him, and commended him to Christ.

With that was Gringalet ready, girt with a saddle that gleamed gaily with many golden fringes, enriched and decked anew for the venture. The bridle was all barred about with bright gold buttons, and all the covertures and trappings of the steed, the crupper and the rich skirts, accorded with the saddle; spread fair with the rich red gold that glittered and gleamed in the rays of the sun.

Then the knight called for his helmet, which was well lined throughout, and set it high on his head, and hasped it behind. He wore a light kerchief over the vintail, that was broidered and studded with fair gems on a broad silken ribbon, with birds of gay colour, and many a turtle and true-lover's knot interlaced thickly, even as many a maiden had wrought them. But the circlet which crowned his helmet was yet more precious, being adorned with a device in diamonds. Then they brought him his shield, which was of bright red, with the pentangle painted thereon in gleaming gold.

WHEREFORE SIR GAWAIN BARE THE PENTANGLE

AND WHY THAT NOBLE PRINCE bare the pentangle I am minded to tell you, though my tale tarry thereby. It is a sign that Solomon set ere-while, as betokening truth; for it is a figure with five points and each line overlaps the other, and no-where hath it beginning or end, so that in English it is called "the endless knot." And therefore was it well suiting to this knight and to his arms, since Gawain was faithful in five and five-fold, for pure was he as gold, void of all villainy and endowed with all virtues. Therefore he bare the pentangle on shield and surcoat as truest of heroes and gentlest of knights.

For first he was faultless in his five senses; and his five fingers never failed him; and all his trust upon earth was in the five wounds that Christ bare on the cross, as the Creed tells. And wherever this knight found himself in stress of battle he deemed well that he drew his strength from the five joys which the Queen of Heaven had of her Child. And for this cause did he bear an image of Our Lady on the one half of his shield, that whenever he looked upon it he might not lack for aid. And the fifth five that the hero used were frankness and fellowship above all, purity and courtesy that never failed him, and compassion that surpasses all; and in these five virtues was that hero wrapped and clothed. And all these, fivefold, were linked one in the other, so that they had no end, and were fixed on five points that never failed, neither at any side were they joined or sundered, nor could ye find beginning or end. And therefore on his shield was the knot shapen, red-gold upon red, which is the pure pentangle. Now was Sir Gawain ready, and he took his lance in hand, and bade them all *Farewell*, he deemed it had been for ever.

How Sir Gawain went forth

THEN HE SMOTE THE STEED with his spurs, and sprang on his way, so that sparks flew from the stones after him. All that saw him were grieved at heart, and said one to the other, "By Christ, 'tis great pity that one of such noble life should be lost! I' faith, 'twere not easy to find his equal upon earth. The king had done better to have wrought more warily. Yonder knight should have been made a duke; a gallant leader of men is he, and such a fate had beseemed him better than to be hewn in pieces at the will of an elfish man, for mere pride. Who ever knew a king to take such counsel as to risk his knights on a Christmas jest?" Many were the tears that flowed from their eyes when that goodly knight rode from the hall. He made no delaying, but went his way swiftly, and rode many a wild road, as I heard say in the book.

Of Sir Gawain's journey

SO RODE SIR GAWAIN through the realm of Logres, on an errand that he held for no jest. Often he lay companionless at night, and must lack the fare that he liked. No comrade had he save his steed, and none save God with whom to take counsel. At length he drew nigh to North Wales, and left the isles of Anglesey on his left hand, crossing over the fords by the foreland over at Holyhead, till he came into the wilderness of Wirral, that is loved neither of God nor of man, and there he abode but a little time. And ever he asked, as he fared, of all whom he met, if they had heard any tidings of a Green Knight in the country thereabout, or of a Green Chapel? And all answered him, Nay, never in their lives had they seen any man of such a hue. And the knight wended his way by many a strange road and many a rugged path, and the fashion of his countenance changed full often ere he saw the Green Chapel.

Many a cliff did he climb in that unknown land, where afar from his friends he rode as a stranger. Never did he come to a stream or a ford but he found a foe before him, and that one so marvellous, so foul and fell, that it behoved him to fight. So many wonders did that knight behold that it were too long to tell the tenth part of them. Sometimes he fought with dragons and wolves; sometimes with wild men that dwelt in the rocks; another while with bulls, and bears, and wild boars, or with giants of the high moorland that drew near to him. Had he not been a doughty knight, enduring, and of well-proved valour, doubtless he had been slain, for he was oft in danger of death. Yet he cared not so much for the strife, what he deemed worse was when the cold clear water was shed from the clouds, and froze ere it fell on the fallow ground. More nights than enough he slept in his harness on the bare rocks, near slain with the sleet, while the stream leapt bubbling from the crest of the hills, and hung in hard icicles over his head.

Thus in peril and pain, and many a hardship, the knight rode alone till Christmas Eve, and in that tide he made his prayer to the Blessed Virgin that she would guide his steps and lead him to some dwelling. On that morning he rode by a hill, and came into a thick forest, wild and drear; on each side were high hills, and thick woods below them of great hoar oaks, a hundred together, of hazel and hawthorn with their trailing boughs intertwined, and rough ragged moss spreading everywhere. On the bare twigs the birds chirped piteously, for pain of the cold. The knight upon Gringalet rode lonely beneath them, through marsh and mire, much troubled at heart lest he should fail to see the service of the Lord, who on that self-same night was born of a Maiden for the cure of our grief; and therefore he said, sighing, "I beseech Thee, Lord, and Mary Thy gentle Mother, for some shelter where I may hear Mass, and Thy mattins at morn. This I ask meekly, and thereto I pray my Paternoster, Ave, and Credo." Thus he rode praying, and lamenting his misdeeds, and he crossed himself, and said, "May the Cross of Christ speed me."

How Sir Gawain came to a fair castle on Christmas Eve

Now that knight had crossed himself but thrice ere he was aware in the wood of a dwelling within a moat, above a lawn, on a mound surrounded by many mighty trees that stood round the moat. 'Twas the fairest castle that ever a knight owned; built in a meadow with a park all about it, and a spiked palisade, closely driven, that enclosed the trees for more than two miles. The knight was ware of the hold from the side, as it shone through the oaks. Then he lifted off his helmet, and thanked Christ and S. Julian that they had courteously granted his prayer, and hearkened to his cry. "Now," quoth the knight, "I beseech ye, grant me fair hostel." Then he pricked Gringalet with his golden spurs, and rode gaily towards the great gate, and came swiftly to the bridge end.

The bridge was drawn up and the gates close shut; the walls were strong and thick, so that they might fear no tempest. The knight on his charger abode on the bank of the deep double ditch that surrounded the castle. The walls were set deep in the water, and rose aloft to a wondrous height; they were of hard hewn stone up to the corbels, which were adorned beneath the battlements with fair carvings, and turrets set in between with many a loophole; a better barbican Sir Gawain had never looked upon. And within he beheld the high hall, with its tower and many windows with carven cornices, and chalk-white chimneys on the turreted roofs that shone fair in the sun. And everywhere, thickly scattered on the castle battlements, were pinnacles, so many that it seemed as if it were all wrought out of paper, so white was it.

The knight on his steed deemed it fair enough, if he might come to be sheltered within it to lodge there while that the Holy-day lasted. He called aloud, and soon there came a porter of kindly countenance, who stood on the wall and greeted this knight and asked his errand.

"Good sir," quoth Gawain, "wilt thou go mine errand to the high lord of the castle, and crave for me lodging?"

"Yea, by S. Peter," quoth the porter. "In sooth I trow that ye be welcome to dwell here so long as it may like ye."

How Sir Gawain was welcomed

Then he went, and came again swiftly, and many folk with him to receive the knight. They let down the great drawbridge, and came forth and knelt on their knees on the cold earth to give him worthy welcome. They held wide open the great gates, and he greeted them courteously, and rode over the bridge. Then men came to him and held his stirrup while he dismounted, and took and stabled his steed. There came down knights and squires to bring the guest with joy to the hall. When he raised his helmet there were many to take it from his hand, fain to serve him, and they took from him sword and shield.

Sir Gawain gave good greeting to the nobles and the mighty men who came to do him honour. Clad in his shining armour they led him to the hall, where a great fire burnt brightly on the floor; and the lord of the household came forth from his chamber to meet the hero fitly. He spake to the knight, and said: "Ye are welcome to do here as it likes ye. All that is here is your own to have at your will and disposal."

"Gramercy!" quote Gawain, "may Christ requite ye."

As friends that were fain each embraced the other; and Gawain looked on the knight who greeted him so kindly, and thought 'twas a bold warrior that owned that burg.

Of mighty stature he was, and of high age; broad and flowing was his beard, and of a bright hue. He was stalwart of limb, and strong in his stride, his face fiery red, and his speech free: in sooth he seemed one well fitted to be a leader of valiant men.

Then the lord led Sir Gawain to a chamber, and commanded folk to wait upon him, and at his bidding there came men enough who brought the guest to a fair bower. The bedding was noble, with curtains of pure silk wrought with gold, and wondrous coverings of fair cloth all embroidered. The curtains ran on ropes with rings of red gold, and the walls were hung with carpets of Orient, and the same spread on the floor. There with mirthful speeches they took from the guest his byrny and all his shining armour, and brought him rich robes of the choicest in its stead. They were long and flowing, and became him well, and when he was clad in them all who looked on the hero thought that surely God had never made a fairer knight: he seemed as if he might be a prince without peer in the field where men strive in battle.

Then before the hearth-place, whereon the fire burned, they made ready a chair for Gawain, hung about with cloth and fair cushions; and there they cast around him a mantle of brown samite, richly embroidered and furred within with costly skins of ermine, with a hood of the same, and he seated himself in that rich seat, and warmed himself at the fire and was cheered at heart. And while he sat thus the serving men set up a table on trestles, and covered it with a fair white cloth, and set thereon salt-cellar, and napkin, and silver spoons; and the knight washed at his will, and set him down to meat.

The folk served him courteously with many dishes seasoned of the best, a double portion. All kinds of fish were there, some baked in bread, some broiled on the embers, some sodden, some stewed and savoured with spices, with all sorts of cunning devices to his taste. And often he called it a feast, when they spake gaily to him all together, and said, "Now take ye this penance, and it shall be for your amendment." Much mirth thereof did Sir Gawain make.

Sir Gawain tells his name

THEN THEY QUESTIONED THAT PRINCE COURTEOUSLY of whence he came; and he told them that he was of the court of Arthur, who is the rich royal King of the Round Table, and that it was Gawain himself who was within their walls, and would keep Christmas with them, as the chance had fallen out. And when the lord of the castle heard those tidings he laughed aloud for gladness, and all men in that keep were joyful that they should be in the company of him to whom belonged all fame, and valour, and courtesy, and whose honour was praised above that of all men on earth. Each said softly to his fellow, "Now shall we see courteous bearing, and the manner of speech befitting courts. What charm lieth in gentle speech shall we learn without asking, since here we have welcomed the fine father of courtesy. God has surely shewn us His grace since He sends us such a guest as Gawain! When men shall sit and sing, blithe for Christ's birth, this knight shall bring us to the knowledge of fair manners, and it may be that hearing him we may learn the cunning speech of love."

By the time the knight had risen from dinner it was near nightfall. Then chaplains took their way to the chapel, and rang loudly, even as they should, for the solemn evensong of the high feast. Thither went the lord, and the lady also, and entered with her maidens into a comely closet, and thither also went Gawain. Then the lord took him by the sleeve and led him to a seat, and called him by his name, and told him he was of all men in the world the most welcome. And Sir Gawain thanked him truly, and each kissed the other, and they sat gravely together throughout the service.

THE LADY OF THE CASTLE

THEN WAS THE LADY FAIN TO LOOK UPON THAT KNIGHT; and she came forth from her closet with many fair maidens. The fairest of ladies was she in face, and figure, and colouring, fairer even than Guinevere, so the knight thought. She came through the chancel to greet the hero, another lady held her by the left hand, older than she, and seemingly of high estate, with many nobles about her. But unlike to look upon were those ladies, for if the younger were fair, the elder was yellow. Rich red were the cheeks of the one, rough and wrinkled those of the other; the kerchiefs of the one were broidered with many glistening pearls, her throat and neck bare, and whiter than the snow that lies on the hills; the neck of the other was swathed in a gorget, with a white wimple over her black chin. Her forehead was wrapped in silk with many folds, worked with knots, so that naught of her was seen save her black brows, her eyes, her nose, and her lips, and those were bleared, and ill to look upon. A worshipful lady in sooth one might call her! In figure was she short and broad, and thickly made—far fairer to behold was she whom she led by the hand.

When Gawain beheld that fair lady, who looked at him graciously, with leave of the lord he went towards them, and, bowing low, he greeted the elder, but the younger and fairer he took lightly in his arms, and kissed her courteously, and greeted her in knightly wise. Then she hailed him as friend, and he quickly prayed to be counted as her servant, if she so willed. Then they took him between them, and talking, led him to the chamber, to the hearth, and bade them bring spices, and they brought them in plenty with the good wine that was wont to be drunk at such seasons. Then the lord sprang to his feet and bade them make merry, and took off his hood, and hung it on a spear, and bade him win the worship thereof who should make most mirth that Christmas-tide. "And I shall try, by my faith, to fool it with the best, by the help of my friends, ere I lose my raiment." Thus with gay words the lord made trial to gladden Gawain with jests that night, till it was time to bid them light the tapers, and Sir Gawain took leave of them and gat him to rest.

OF THE CHRISTMAS FEAST

IN THE MORN WHEN ALL MEN CALL TO MIND how Christ our Lord was born on earth to die for us, there is joy, for His sake, in all dwellings of the world; and so was there here on that day. For high feast was held, with many dainties and cunningly cooked messes. On the daïs sat gallant men, clad in their best. The ancient dame sat on the high seat, with the lord of the castle beside her. Gawain and the fair lady sat together, even in the midst of the board, when the feast was served; and so throughout all the hall each sat in his degree, and was served in order. There was meat, there was mirth, there was much joy, so that to tell thereof would take me too long, though peradventure I might strive to declare it. But Gawain and that fair lady had much joy of each other's company through her sweet words and courteous converse. And there was music made before each prince, trumpets and drums, and merry piping; each man hearkened his minstrel, and they too hearkened theirs.

How the feast came to an end but Gawain abode at the castle

So they held high feast that day and the next, and the third day thereafter, and the joy on S. John's Day was fair to hearken, for 'twas the last of the feast, and the guests would depart in the grey of the morning. Therefore they awoke early, and drank wine, and danced fair carols, and at last, when it was late, each man took his leave to wend early on his way. Gawain would bid his host farewell, but the lord took him by the hand, and led him to his own chamber beside the hearth, and there he thanked him for the favour he had shown him in honouring his dwelling at that high season, and gladdening his castle with his fair countenance. "I wis, sir, that while I live I shall be held the worthier that Gawain has been my guest at God's own feast."

"Gramercy, sir," quoth Gawain, "in good faith, all the honour is yours, may the High King give it ye, and I am but at your will to work your behest, inasmuch as I am beholden to ye in great and small by rights."

Then the lord did his best to persuade the knight to tarry with him, but Gawain answered that he might in no wise do so. Then the host asked him courteously what stern behest had driven him at the holy season from the king's court, to fare all alone, ere yet the feast was ended?

"Forsooth," quoth the knight, "ye say but the truth: 'tis a high quest and a pressing that hath brought me afield, for I am summoned myself to a certain place, and I know not whither in the world I may wend to find it; so help me Christ, I would give all the kingdom of Logres an I might find it by New Year's morn. Therefore, sir, I make request of ye that ye tell me truly if ye ever heard word of the Green Chapel, where it may be found, and the Green Knight that keeps it. For I am pledged by solemn compact sworn between us to meet that knight at the New Year if so I were on life; and of that same New Year it wants but little—I' faith, I would look on that hero more joyfully than on any other fair sight! Therefore, by your will, it behoves me to leave ye, for I have but barely three days, and I would as fain fall dead as fail of mine errand."

Then the lord quoth, laughing, "Now must ye needs stay, for I will show ye your goal, the Green Chapel, ere your term be at an end, have ye no fear! But ye can take your ease, friend, in your bed, till the fourth day, and go forth on the first of the year, and come to that place at mid-morn to do as ye will. Dwell here till New Year's Day, and then rise and set forth, and ye shall be set in the way; 'tis not two miles hence."

Then was Gawain glad, and he laughed gaily. "Now I thank ye for this above all else. Now my quest is achieved I will dwell here at your will, and otherwise do as ye shall ask."

Then the lord took him, and set him beside him, and bade the ladies be fetched for their greater pleasure, tho' between themselves they had solace. The lord, for gladness, made merry jest, even as one who wist not what to do for joy;

and he cried aloud to the knight, "Ye have promised to do the thing I bid ye: will ye hold to this behest, here, at once?"

"Yea, forsooth," said that true knight, "while I abide in your burg I am bound by your behest."

"Ye have travelled from far," said the host, "and since then ye have waked with me, ye are not well refreshed by rest and sleep, as I know. Ye shall therefore abide in your chamber, and lie at your ease to-morrow at Mass-tide, and go to meat when ye will with my wife, who shall sit with ye, and comfort ye with her company till I return; and I shall rise early and go forth to the chase." And Gawain agreed to all this courteously.

Sir Gawain makes a covenant with his host

"Sir knight," quoth the host, "we will make a covenant. Whatsoever I win in the wood shall be yours, and whatever may fall to your share, that shall ye exchange for it. Let us swear, friend, to make this exchange, however our hap may be, for worse or for better."

"I grant ye your will," quoth Gawain the good; "if ye list so to do, it liketh me well."

"Bring hither the wine-cup, the bargain is made," so said the lord of that castle. They laughed each one, and drank of the wine, and made merry, these lords and ladies, as it pleased them. Then with gay talk and merry jest they arose, and stood, and spoke softly, and kissed courteously, and took leave of each other. With burning torches, and many a serving man, was each led to his couch; yet ere they gat them to bed the old lord oft repeated their covenant, for he knew well how to make sport.

III

The first day's hunting

Full early, ere daylight, the folk rose up; the guests who would depart called their grooms, and they made them ready, and saddled the steeds, tightened up the girths, and trussed up their mails. The knights, all arrayed for riding, leapt up lightly, and took their bridles, and each rode his way as pleased him best.

The lord of the land was not the last. Ready for the chase, with many of his men, he ate a sop hastily when he had heard Mass, and then with blast of the bugle fared forth to the field. He and his nobles were to horse ere daylight glimmered upon the earth.

Then the huntsmen coupled their hounds, unclosed the kennel door, and called them out. They blew three blasts gaily on the bugles, the hounds bayed fiercely, and they that would go a-hunting checked and chastised them. A hundred hunters there were of the best, so I have heard tell. Then the trackers gat them to the trysting-place and uncoupled the hounds, and the forest rang again with their gay blasts.

At the first sound of the hunt the game quaked for fear, and fled, trembling, along the vale. They betook them to the heights, but the liers in wait turned them back with loud cries; the harts they let pass them, and the stags with their spreading antlers, for the lord had forbidden that they should be slain, but the hinds and the does they turned back, and drave down into the valleys. Then might ye see much shooting of arrows. As the deer fled under the boughs a broad whistling shaft smote and wounded each sorely, so that, wounded and bleeding, they fell dying on the banks. The hounds followed swiftly on their tracks, and hunters, blowing the horn, sped after them with ringing shouts that well-nigh burst the cliffs asunder. What game escaped those that shot was run down at the outer ring. Thus were they driven on the hills, and harassed at the waters, so well did the men know their work, and the greyhounds were so great and swift that they ran them down as fast as the hunters could slay them. Thus the lord passed the day in mirth and joyfulness, even to nightfall.

How the lady of the castle came to Sir Gawain

So the lord roamed the woods, and Gawain, that good knight, lay ever a-bed, curtained about, under the costly coverlet, while the daylight gleamed on the walls. And as he lay half slumbering, he heard a little sound at the door, and he raised his head, and caught back a corner of the curtain, and waited to see what it might be. It was the lovely lady, the lord's wife; she shut the door softly behind her, and turned towards the bed; and Gawain laid him down softly and made as if he slept. And she came lightly to the bedside, within the curtain, and sat herself down beside him, to wait till he wakened. The knight lay there awhile, and marvelled within himself what her coming might betoken; and he said to himself, "'Twere more seemly if I asked her what hath brought her hither." Then he made feint to waken, and turned towards her, and opened his eyes as one astonished, and crossed himself; and she looked on him laughing, with her cheeks red and white, lovely to behold.

"Good morrow, Sir Gawain," said that fair lady; "ye are but a careless sleeper, since one can enter thus. Now are ye taken unawares, and lest ye escape me I shall bind you in your bed; of that be ye assured!" Laughing, she spake these words.

"Good morrow, fair lady," quoth Gawain blithely. "I will do your will, as it likes me well. For I yield me readily, and pray your grace, and that is best, by my faith, since I needs must do so." Thus he jested again, laughing. "But an ye would, fair lady, grant me this grace that ye pray your prisoner to rise. I would get me from bed, and array me better, then could I talk with ye in more comfort."

"Nay, forsooth, fair sir," quoth the lady, "ye shall not rise, I will rede ye better. I shall keep ye here, since ye can do no other, and talk with my knight whom I have captured. For I know well that ye are Sir Gawain, whom all the world worships, wheresoever ye may ride. Your honour and your courtesy are praised by lords and ladies, by all who live. Now ye are here and we are alone, my lord and his men are afield; the serving men in their beds, and my maidens also, and the door shut upon us. And since in this hour I have him that all men love, I shall use my time well with speech, while it lasts. Ye are welcome to my company, for it behoves me in sooth to be your servant."

"In good faith," quoth Gawain, "I think me that I am not he of whom ye speak, for unworthy am I of such service as ye here proffer. In sooth, I were glad if I might set myself by word or service to your pleasure; a pure joy would it be to me!"

"In good faith, Sir Gawain," quoth the gay lady, "the praise and the prowess that pleases all ladies I lack them not, nor hold them light; yet are there ladies enough who would liever now have the knight in their hold, as I have ye here, to dally with your courteous words, to bring them comfort and to ease their cares, than much of the treasure and the gold that are theirs. And now, through the grace of Him who upholds the heavens, I have wholly in my power that which they all desire!"

Thus the lady, fair to look upon, made him great cheer, and Sir Gawain, with modest words, answered her again: "Madam," he quoth, "may Mary requite ye, for in good faith I have found in ye a noble frankness. Much courtesy have other folk shown me, but the honour they have done me is naught to the worship of yourself, who knoweth but good."

"By Mary," quoth the lady, "I think otherwise; for were I worth all the women alive, and had I the wealth of the world in my hand, and might choose me a lord to my liking, then, for all that I have seen in ye, Sir Knight, of beauty and courtesy and blithe semblance, and for all that I have hearkened and hold for true, there should be no knight on earth to be chosen before ye!"

"Well I wot," quoth Sir Gawain, "that ye have chosen a better; but I am proud that ye should so prize me, and as your servant do I hold ye my sovereign, and your knight am I, and may Christ reward ye."

So they talked of many matters till mid-morn was past, and ever the lady shewed her love to him, and the knight turned her speech aside. For though she were the brightest of maidens, yet had he forborne to shew her love for the danger that awaited him, and the blow that must be given without delay.

Then the lady prayed her leave from him, and he granted it readily. And she gave him good-day, with laughing glance, but he must needs marvel at her words:

"Now He that speeds fair speech reward ye this disport; but that ye be Gawain my mind misdoubts me greatly."

"Wherefore?" quoth the knight quickly, fearing lest he had lacked in some courtesy.

And the lady spake: "So true a knight as Gawain is holden, and one so perfect in courtesy, would never have tarried so long with a lady but he would of his courtesy have craved a kiss at parting."

How the lady kissed Sir Gawain

Then quoth Gawain, "I wot I will do even as it may please ye, and kiss at your commandment, as a true knight should who forbears to ask for fear of displeasure."

At that she came near and bent down and kissed the knight, and each commended the other to Christ, and she went forth from the chamber softly.

Then Sir Gawain arose and called his chamberlain and chose his garments, and when he was ready he gat him forth to Mass, and then went to meat, and made merry all day till the rising of the moon, and never had a knight fairer lodging than had he with those two noble ladies, the elder and the younger.

And ever the lord of the land chased the hinds through holt and heath till eventide, and then with much blowing of bugles and baying of hounds they bore the game homeward; and by the time daylight was done all the folk had returned to that fair castle. And when the lord and Sir Gawain met together, then were they both well pleased. The lord commanded them all to assemble in the great hall, and the ladies to descend with their maidens, and there, before them all, he bade the men fetch in the spoil of the day's hunting, and he called unto Gawain, and counted the tale of the beasts, and showed them unto him, and said, "What think ye of this game, Sir Knight? Have I deserved of ye thanks for my woodcraft?"

"Yea, I wis," quoth the other, "here is the fairest spoil I have seen this seven year in the winter season."

How the covenant was kept

"And all this do I give ye, Gawain," quoth the host, "for by accord of covenant ye may claim it as your own."

"That is sooth," quoth the other, "I grant you that same; and I have fairly won this within walls, and with as good will do I yield it to ye." With that he clasped his hands round the lord's neck and kissed him as courteously as he might. "Take ye here my spoils, no more have I won; ye should have it freely, though it were greater than this."

"'Tis good," said the host, "gramercy thereof. Yet were I fain to know where ye won this same favour, and if it were by your own wit?"

"Nay," answered Gawain, "that was not in the bond. Ask me no more: ye have taken what was yours by right, be content with that."

They laughed and jested together, and sat them down to supper, where they were served with many dainties; and after supper they sat by the hearth, and wine was served out to them; and oft in their jesting they promised to observe on the morrow the same covenant that they had made before, and whatever chance might betide to exchange their spoil, be it much or little, when they met at night. Thus they renewed their bargain before the whole court, and then the night-drink was served, and each courteously took leave of the other and gat him to bed.

Of the second day's hunting

By the time the cock had crowed thrice the lord of the castle had left his bed; Mass was sung and meat fitly served. The folk were forth to the wood ere the day broke, with hound and horn they rode over the plain, and uncoupled their dogs among the thorns. Soon they struck on the scent, and the hunt cheered on the hounds who were first to seize it, urging them with shouts. The others hastened to the cry, forty at once, and there rose such a clamour from the pack that the rocks rang again. The huntsmen followed hard after with shouting and blasts of the horn; and the hounds drew together to a thicket betwixt the water and a high crag in the cliff beneath the hillside. As the rough rocks were ill for riding the huntsmen sprang to earth and hastened on foot, and cast about round the hill and the thicket. The knights wist well what beast was within, and would drive him forth with the bloodhounds. And as they beat the bushes, suddenly over the beaters there rushed forth a wondrous great and fierce boar, long since had he left the herd to roam by himself. Grunting, he cast many to the ground, and fled forth at his best speed, without more mischief. The men hallooed loudly and cried, "*Hay! Hay!*" and blew the horns to urge on the hounds, and rode swiftly after the boar. Many a time did he turn to bay and tare the hounds, and they yelped, and howled shrilly. Then the men made ready their arrows and shot at him, but the points were turned on his thick hide, and the barbs would not bite upon him, for the shafts shivered in pieces, and the head but leapt again wherever it hit.

But when the boar felt the stroke of the arrows he waxed mad with rage, and turned on the hunters and tare many, so that, affrighted, they fled before him. But the lord on a swift steed pursued him, blowing his bugle; as a gallant knight he rode through the woodland chasing the boar till the sun grew low.

So did the hunters this day, while Sir Gawain lay in his bed lapped in rich gear; and the lady forgat not to salute him, for early was she at his side, to cheer his mood.

Of the lady and Sir Gawain

She came to the bedside and looked on the knight, and Gawain gave her fit greeting, and she greeted him again with ready words, and sat her by his side and laughed, and with a sweet look she spoke to him:

"Sir, if ye be Gawain, I think it a wonder that ye be so stern and cold, and care not for the courtesies of friendship, but if one teach ye to know them ye cast the lesson out of your mind. Ye have soon forgotten what I taught ye yesterday, by all the truest tokens that I knew!"

"What is that?" quoth the knight. "I trow I know not. If it be sooth that ye say, then is the blame mine own."

"But I taught ye of kissing," quoth the fair lady. "Wherever a fair countenance is shown him, it behoves a courteous knight quickly to claim a kiss."

"Nay, my dear," said Sir Gawain, "cease that speech; that durst I not do lest I were denied, for if I were forbidden I wot I were wrong did I further entreat."

"I' faith," quoth the lady merrily, "ye may not be forbid, ye are strong enough to constrain by strength an ye will, were any so discourteous as to give ye denial."

"Yea, by Heaven," said Gawain, "ye speak well; but threats profit little in the land where I dwell, and so with a gift that is given not of good will! I am at your commandment to kiss when ye like, to take or to leave as ye list."

Then the lady bent her down and kissed him courteously.

How the lady strove to beguile Sir Gawain with words of love

And as they spake together she said, "I would learn somewhat from ye, an ye would not be wroth, for young ye are and fair, and so courteous and knightly as ye are known to be, the head of all chivalry, and versed in all wisdom of love and war—'tis ever told of true knights how they adventured their lives for their true love, and endured hardships for her favours, and avenged her with valour, and eased her sorrows, and brought joy to her bower; and ye are the fairest knight of your time, and your fame and your honour are everywhere, yet I have sat by ye here twice, and never a word have heard of love! Ye who are so courteous and skilled in such lore ought surely to teach one so young and unskilled some little craft of true love! Why are ye so unlearned who art otherwise so famous? Or is it that ye deem me unworthy to hearken to your teaching? For shame, Sir Knight! I come hither alone and sit at your side to learn of ye some skill; teach me of your wit, while my lord is from home."

"In good faith," quoth Gawain, "great is my joy and my profit that so fair a lady as ye are should deign to come hither, and trouble ye with so poor a man, and make sport with your knight with kindly countenance, it pleaseth me much. But that I, in my turn, should take it upon me to tell of love and such like matters to ye who know more by half, or a hundred fold, of such craft than I do, or ever shall in all my lifetime, by my troth 'twere folly indeed! I will work your will to the best of my might as I am bounden, and evermore will I be your servant, so help me Christ!"

Then often with guile she questioned that knight that she might win him to woo her, but he defended himself so fairly that none might in any wise blame him, and naught but bliss and harmless jesting was there between them. They laughed and talked together till at last she kissed him, and craved her leave of him, and went her way.

How the boar was slain

Then the knight arose and went forth to Mass, and afterward dinner was served, and he sat and spake with the ladies all day. But the lord of the castle rode ever over the land chasing the wild boar, that fled through the thickets, slaying the best of his hounds and breaking their backs in sunder; till at last he was so weary he might run no longer, but made for a hole in a mound by a rock. He got the mound at his back and faced the hounds, whetting his white tusks and foaming at the mouth. The huntsmen stood aloof, fearing to draw nigh him; so many of them had been already wounded that they were loth to be torn with his tusks, so fierce he was and mad with rage. At length the lord himself came up, and saw the beast at bay, and the men standing aloof. Then quickly he sprang to the ground and drew out a bright blade, and waded through the stream to the boar.

When the beast was ware of the knight with weapon in hand, he set up his bristles and snorted loudly, and many feared for their lord lest he should be slain. Then the boar leapt upon the knight so that beast and man were one atop of the other in the water; but the boar had the worst of it, for the man had marked, even as he sprang, and set the point of his brand to the beast's chest, and drove it up to the hilt, so that the heart was split in twain, and the boar fell snarling, and was swept down by the water to where a hundred hounds seized on him, and the men drew him to shore for the dogs to slay.

Then was there loud blowing of horns and baying of hounds, the huntsmen smote off the boar's head, and hung the carcase by the four feet to a stout pole, and so went on their way homewards. The head they bore before the lord himself, who had slain the beast at the ford by force of his strong hand.

It seemed him o'er long ere he saw Sir Gawain in the hall, and he blew a blast on his horn to let all men know that he was come again to take his part in the covenant. And when he saw Gawain the lord laughed aloud, and bade them call the ladies and the household together, and he showed them the game, and told them the tale, how they had hunted the wild boar through the woods, and of his length and breadth and height; and Sir Gawain commended his deeds and praised him for his valour, well proven, for so mighty a beast had he never seen before.

THE KEEPING OF THE COVENANT

THEN THEY HANDLED THE HUGE HEAD, and the lord said aloud, "Now, Gawain, this game is your own by sure covenant, as ye right well know."

"'Tis sooth," quoth the knight, "and as truly will I give ye all I have gained." He took the host round the neck, and kissed him courteously twice. "Now are we quits," he said, "this eventide, of all the covenants that we made since I came hither."

And the lord answered, "By S. Giles, ye are the best I know; ye will be rich in a short space if ye drive such bargains!"

Then they set up the tables on trestles, and covered them with fair cloths, and lit waxen tapers on the walls. The knights sat and were served in the hall, and much game and glee was there round the hearth, with many songs, both at supper and after; songs of Christmas, and new carols, with all the mirth one may think of. And ever that lovely lady sat by the knight, and with still stolen looks made such feint of pleasing him, that Gawain marvelled much, and was wroth with himself, but he could not for his courtesy return her fair glances, but dealt with her cunningly, however she might strive to wrest the thing.

When they had tarried in the hall so long as it seemed them good, they turned to the inner chamber and the wide hearth-place, and there they drank wine, and the host proffered to renew the covenant for New Year's Eve; but the knight craved leave to depart on the morrow, for it was nigh to the term when he must fulfil his pledge. But the lord would withhold him from so doing, and prayed him to tarry, and said,

"As I am a true knight I swear my troth that ye shall come to the Green Chapel to achieve your task on New Year's morn, long before prime. Therefore abide ye in your bed, and I will hunt in this wood, and hold ye to the covenant to exchange with me against all the spoil I may bring hither. For twice have I tried ye, and found ye true, and the morrow shall be the third time and the best. Make we merry now while we may, and think on joy, for misfortune may take a man whensoever it wills."

Then Gawain granted his request, and they brought them drink, and they gat them with lights to bed.

OF THE THIRD DAY'S HUNTING

SIR GAWAIN LAY AND SLEPT SOFTLY, but the lord, who was keen on woodcraft, was afoot early. After Mass he and his men ate a morsel, and he asked for his steed; all the knights who should ride with him were already mounted before the hall gates.

'Twas a fair frosty morning, for the sun rose red in ruddy vapour, and the welkin was clear of clouds. The hunters scattered them by a forest side, and the rocks rang again with the blast of their horns. Some came on the scent of a fox, and a hound gave tongue; the huntsmen shouted, and the pack followed in a crowd on the trail. The fox ran before them, and when they saw him they pursued him with noise and much shouting, and he wound and turned through many a thick grove, often cowering and hearkening in a hedge. At last by a little ditch he leapt out of a spinney, stole away slily by a copse path, and so out of the wood and away from the bounds. But he went, ere he wist, to a chosen tryst, and three started forth on him at once, so he must needs double back, and betake him to the wood again.

Then was it joyful to hearken to the hounds; when all the pack had met together and had sight of their game they made as loud a din as if all the lofty cliffs had fallen clattering together. The huntsmen shouted and threatened, and followed close upon him so that he might scarce escape, but Reynard was wily, and he turned and doubled upon them, and led the lord and his men over the hills, now on the slopes, now in the vales, while the knight at home slept through the cold morning beneath his costly curtains.

HOW THE LADY CAME FOR THE THIRD TIME TO SIR GAWAIN

BUT THE FAIR LADY OF THE CASTLE ROSE BETIMES, and clad herself in a rich mantle that reached even to the ground, and was bordered and lined with costly furs. On her head she wore no golden circlet, but a network of precious stones, that gleamed and shone through her tresses in clusters of twenty together. Thus she came into the chamber and set open a window, and called to him gaily, "Sir Knight, how may ye sleep? The morning is so fair."

Sir Gawain was deep in slumber, and in his dream he vexed him much for the destiny that should befall him on the morrow, when he should meet the knight at the Green Chapel, and abide his blow; but when the lady spake he heard her, and came to himself, and roused from his dream and answered swiftly. The lady came laughing, and kissed him courteously, and he welcomed her fittingly with a cheerful countenance. He saw her so glorious and gaily dressed, so faultless of features and complexion, that it warmed his heart to look upon her.

They spake to each other smiling, and all was bliss and good cheer between them. They exchanged fair words, and much happiness was therein, yet was there a gulf between them, and she might win no more of her knight, for that gallant prince watched well his words—he would neither take her love, nor frankly refuse it. He cared for his courtesy, lest he be deemed churlish, and yet more for his honour lest he be traitor to his host. "God forbid," quoth he to himself, "that it should so befall." Thus with courteous words did he set aside all the special speeches that came from her lips.

Then spake the lady to the knight, "Ye deserve blame if ye hold not that lady who sits beside ye above all else in the world, if ye have not already a love whom ye hold dearer, and like better, and have sworn such firm faith to that lady that ye care not to loose it—as I scarce may believe. And now I pray ye straitly that ye tell me that in truth, and hide it not."

And the knight answered, "By S. John" (and he smiled as he spake) "no such love have I, nor do I think to have yet awhile."

"That is the worst word I may hear," quoth the lady, "but in sooth I have mine answer; kiss me now courteously, and I will go hence; I can but mourn as a maiden that loves much."

Sighing, she stooped down and kissed him, and then she rose up and spake as she stood, "Now, dear, at our parting do me this grace: give me some gift, if it were but thy glove, that I may bethink me of my knight, and lessen my mourning."

The lady would fain have a parting gift from Gawain

"Now, I wis," quoth the knight, "I would that I had here but the least thing that I possess on earth that I might leave ye as love-token, great or small, for ye have deserved forsooth more reward than I might give ye. But it is not to your honour to have at this time a glove for reward as gift from Gawain, and I am here on a strange errand, and have no man with me, nor mails with goodly things— that mislikes me much, lady, at this time; but each man must fare as he is taken, if for sorrow and ill."

She would give him her ring

"Nay, knight highly honoured," quoth that lovesome lady, "though I have naught of yours, yet shall ye have somewhat of mine." With that she reached him a ring of red gold with a sparkling stone therein, that shone even as the sun (wit ye well, it was worth many marks); but the knight refused it, and spake readily,

"I will take no gift, lady, at this time. I have none to give, and none will I take."

She prayed him to take it, but he refused her prayer, and sware in sooth that he would not have it.

Or her girdle

The lady was sorely vexed, and said, "If ye refuse my ring as too costly, that ye will not be so highly beholden to me, I will give ye my girdle as a lesser gift." With that she loosened a lace that was fastened at her side, knit upon her kirtle under her mantle. It was wrought of green silk, and gold, only braided by the fingers, and that she offered to the knight, and besought him though it were of little worth that he would take it, and he said nay, he would touch neither gold nor gear ere God give him grace to achieve the adventure for which he had come hither. "And therefore, I pray ye, displease ye not, and ask me no longer, for I may not grant it. I am dearly beholden to ye for the favour ye have shown me, and ever, in heat and cold, will I be your true servant."

The virtue of the girdle

"Now," said the lady, "ye refuse this silk, for it is simple in itself, and so it seems, indeed; lo, it is small to look upon and less in cost, but whoso knew the virtue that is knit therein he would, peradventure, value it more highly. For whatever knight is girded with this green lace, while he bears it knotted about him there is no man under heaven can overcome him, for he may not be slain for any magic on earth."

How Sir Gawain took the girdle

Then Gawain bethought him, and it came into his heart that this were a jewel for the jeopardy that awaited him when he came to the Green Chapel to seek the return blow—could he so order it that he should escape unslain, 'twere a craft worth trying. Then he bare with her chiding, and let her say her say, and she pressed the girdle on him and prayed him to take it, and he granted her prayer, and she gave it him with good will, and besought him for her sake never to reveal it but to hide it loyally from her lord; and the knight agreed that never should any man know it, save they two alone. He thanked her often and heartily, and she kissed him for the third time.

Then she took her leave of him, and when she was gone Sir Gawain arose, and clad him in rich attire, and took the girdle, and knotted it round him, and hid it beneath his robes. Then he took his way to the chapel, and sought out a priest privily, and prayed him to teach him better how his soul might be saved when he should go hence; and there he shrived him, and showed his misdeeds, both great and small, and besought mercy and craved absolution; and the priest assoiled him, and set him as clean as if Doomsday had been on the morrow. And afterwards Sir Gawain made him merry with the ladies, with carols, and all kinds of joy, as never he did but that one day, even to nightfall; and all the men marvelled at him, and said that never since he came thither had he been so merry.

The death of the fox

Meanwhile the lord of the castle was abroad chasing the fox; awhile he lost him, and as he rode through a spinney he heard the hounds near at hand, and Reynard came creeping through a thick grove, with all the pack at his heels. Then the lord drew out his shining brand, and cast it at the beast, and the fox swerved aside for the sharp edge, and would have doubled back, but a hound was on him ere he might turn, and right before the horse's feet they all fell on him, and worried him fiercely, snarling the while.

Then the lord leapt from his saddle, and caught the fox from their jaws, and held it aloft over his head, and hallooed loudly, and the hunters hied them thither, blowing their horns; all that bare bugles blew them at once, and all the others shouted. 'Twas the merriest meeting that ever men heard, the clamour that was raised at the death of the fox. They rewarded the hounds, stroking them and rubbing their heads, and took Reynard and stripped him of his coat; then blowing their horns, they turned them homewards, for it was nigh nightfall.

How Sir Gawain kept not all the covenant

The lord was gladsome at his return, and found a bright fire on the hearth, and the knight beside it, the good Sir Gawain, who was in joyous mood for the pleasure he had had with the ladies. He wore a robe of blue, that reached even to the ground, and a surcoat richly furred, that became him well. A hood like to the surcoat fell on his shoulders, and all alike were done about with fur. He met the host in the midst of the floor, and jesting, he greeted him, and said, "Now shall I be first to fulfil our covenant which we made together when there was no lack of wine." Then he embraced the knight, and kissed him thrice, as solemnly as he might.

"Of a sooth," quoth the other, "ye have good luck in the matter of this covenant, if ye made a good exchange!"

"Yea, it matters naught of the exchange," quoth Gawain, "since what I owe is swiftly paid."

"Marry," said the other, "mine is behind, for I have hunted all this day, and naught have I got but this foul fox-skin, and that is but poor payment for three such kisses as ye have here given me."

"Enough," quoth Sir Gawain, "I thank ye, by the Rood."

Then the lord told them of his hunting, and how the fox had been slain.

With mirth and minstrelsy, and dainties at their will, they made them as merry as a folk well might till 'twas time for them to sever, for at last they must needs betake them to their beds. Then the knight took his leave of the lord, and thanked him fairly.

"For the fair sojourn that I have had here at this high feast may the High King give ye honour. I give ye myself, as one of your servants, if ye so like; for I must needs, as ye know, go hence with the morn, and ye will give me, as ye promised, a guide to show me the way to the Green Chapel, an God will suffer me on New Year's Day to deal the doom of my weird."

"By my faith," quoth the host, "all that ever I promised, that shall I keep with good will." Then he gave him a servant to set him in the way, and lead him by the downs, that he should have no need to ford the stream, and should fare by the shortest road through the groves; and Gawain thanked the lord for the honour done him. Then he would take leave of the ladies, and courteously he kissed them, and spake, praying them to receive his thanks, and they made like reply; then with many sighs they commended him to Christ, and he departed courteously from that folk. Each man that he met he thanked him for his service and his solace, and the pains he had been at to do his will; and each found it as hard to part from the knight as if he had ever dwelt with him.

How Sir Gawain took leave of his host

Then they led him with torches to his chamber, and brought him to his bed to rest. That he slept soundly I may not say, for the morrow gave him much to think on. Let him rest a while, for he was near that which he sought, and if ye will but listen to me I will tell ye how it fared with him thereafter.

IV

Now the New Year drew nigh, and the night passed, and the day chased the darkness, as is God's will; but wild weather wakened therewith. The clouds cast the cold to the earth, with enough of the north to slay them that lacked clothing. The snow drave smartly, and the whistling wind blew from the heights, and made great drifts in the valleys. The knight, lying in his bed, listened, for though his eyes were shut he might sleep but little, and hearkened every cock that crew.

He arose ere the day broke, by the light of a lamp that burned in his chamber, and called to his chamberlain, bidding him bring his armour and saddle his steed. The other gat him up, and fetched his garments, and robed Sir Gawain.

The robing of Sir Gawain

First he clad him in his clothes to keep off the cold, and then in his harness, which was well and fairly kept. Both hauberk and plates were well burnished, the rings of the rich byrny freed from rust, and all as fresh as at first, so that the knight was fain to thank them. Then he did on each piece, and bade them bring his steed, while he put the fairest raiment on himself; his coat with its fair cognizance, adorned with precious stones upon velvet, with broidered seams, and all furred within with costly skins. And he left not the lace, the lady's gift, that Gawain forgot not, for his own good. When he had girded on his sword he wrapped the gift twice about him, swathed around his waist. The girdle of green silk set gaily and well upon the royal red cloth, rich to behold, but the knight ware it not for pride of the pendants, polished though they were, with fair gold that gleamed brightly on the ends, but to save himself from sword and knife, when it behoved him to abide his hurt without question. With that the hero went forth, and thanked that kindly folk full often.

How Sir Gawain went forth from the castle

Then was Gringalet ready, that was great and strong, and had been well cared for and tended in every wise; in fair condition was that proud steed, and fit for a journey. Then Gawain went to him, and looked on his coat, and said by his sooth, "There is a folk in this place that thinketh on honour; much joy may they have, and the lord who maintains them, and may all good betide that lovely lady all her life long. Since they for charity cherish a guest, and hold honour in their hands, may He who holds the heaven on high requite them, and also ye all. And if I might live anywhile on earth, I would give ye full reward, readily, if so I might." Then he set foot in the stirrup and bestrode his steed, and his squire gave him his shield, which he laid on his shoulder. Then he smote Gringalet with his golden spurs, and the steed pranced on the stones and would stand no longer.

By that his man was mounted, who bare his spear and lance, and Gawain quoth, "I commend this castle to Christ, may He give it ever good fortune." Then the drawbridge was let down, and the broad gates unbarred and opened on both sides; the knight crossed himself, and passed through the gateway, and praised the porter, who knelt before the prince, and gave him good-day, and commended him to God. Thus the knight went on his way with the one man who should guide him to that dread place where he should receive rueful payment.

The two went by hedges where the boughs were bare, and climbed the cliffs where the cold clings. Naught fell from the heavens, but 'twas ill beneath them; mist brooded over the moor and hung on the mountains; each hill had a cap, a great cloak, of mist. The streams foamed and bubbled between their banks, dashing sparkling on the shores where they shelved downwards. Rugged and dangerous was the way through the woods, till it was time for the sun-rising. Then were they on a high hill; the snow lay white beside them, and the man who rode with Gawain drew rein by his master.

THE SQUIRE'S WARNING

"SIR," HE SAID, "I have brought ye hither, and now ye are not far from the place that ye have sought so specially. But I will tell ye for sooth, since I know ye well, and ye are such a knight as I well love, would ye follow my counsel ye would fare the better.

OF THE KNIGHT OF THE GREEN CHAPEL

"THE PLACE WHITHER YE GO is accounted full perilous, for he who liveth in that waste is the worst on earth, for he is strong and fierce, and loveth to deal mighty blows; taller is he than any man on earth, and greater of frame than any four in Arthur's court, or in any other. And this is his custom at the Green Chapel: there may no man pass by that place, however proud his arms, but he does him to death by force of his hand, for he is a discourteous knight, and shews no mercy. Be he churl or chaplain who rides by that chapel, monk or mass-priest, or any man else, he thinks it as pleasant to slay them as to pass alive himself. Therefore, I tell ye, as sooth as ye sit in saddle, if ye come there and that knight know it, ye shall be slain, though ye had twenty lives; trow me that truly! He has dwelt here full long and seen many a combat; ye may not defend ye against his blows. Therefore, good Sir Gawain, let the man be, and get ye away some other road; for God's sake seek ye another land, and there may Christ speed ye! And I will hie me home again, and I promise ye further that I will swear by God and the saints, or any other oath ye please, that I will keep counsel faithfully, and never let any wit the tale that ye fled for fear of any man."

Sir Gawain is none dismayed

"GRAMERCY," QUOTH GAWAIN, BUT ILL PLEASED. "Good fortune be his who wishes me good, and that thou wouldst keep faith with me I well believe; but didst thou keep it never so truly, an I passed here and fled for fear as thou sayest, then were I a coward knight, and might not be held guiltless. So I will to the chapel let chance what may, and talk with that man, even as I may list, whether for weal or for woe as fate may have it. Fierce though he may be in fight, yet God knoweth well how to save His servants."

"Well," quoth the other, "now that ye have said so much that ye will take your own harm on yourself, and ye be pleased to lose your life, I will neither let nor keep ye. Have here your helm and the spear in your hand, and ride down this same road beside the rock till ye come to the bottom of the valley, and there look a little to the left hand, and ye shall see in that vale the chapel, and the grim man who keeps it. Now fare ye well, noble Gawain; for all the gold on earth I would not go with ye nor bear ye fellowship one step further." With that the man turned his bridle into the wood, smote the horse with his spurs as hard as he could, and galloped off, leaving the knight alone.

Quoth Gawain, "I will neither greet nor groan, but commend myself to God, and yield me to His will."

Then the knight spurred Gringalet, and rode adown the path close in by a bank beside a grove. So he rode through the rough thicket, right into the dale, and there he halted, for it seemed him wild enough. No sign of a chapel could he see, but high and burnt banks on either side and rough rugged crags with great stones above. An ill-looking place he thought it.

Then he drew in his horse and looked around to seek the chapel, but he saw none and thought it strange. Then he saw as it were a mound on a level space of land by a bank beside the stream where it ran swiftly, the water bubbled within as if boiling. The knight turned his steed to the mound, and lighted down and tied the rein to the branch of a linden; and he turned to the mound and walked round it, questioning with himself what it might be. It had a hole at the end and at either side, and was overgrown with clumps of grass, and it was hollow within as an old cave or the crevice of a crag; he knew not what it might be.

The finding of the chapel

"AH," QUOTH GAWAIN, "can this be the Green Chapel? Here might the devil say his mattins at midnight! Now I wis there is wizardry here. 'Tis an ugly oratory, all overgrown with grass, and 'twould well beseem that fellow in green to say his devotions on devil's wise. By my five wits, 'tis the foul fiend himself who hath set me this tryst, to destroy me here! This is a chapel of mischance: ill-luck betide it, 'tis the cursedest kirk that ever I came in!"

Helmet on head and lance in hand, he came up to the rough dwelling, when he heard over the high hill beyond the brook, as it were in a bank, a wondrous fierce noise, that rang in the cliff as if it would cleave asunder. 'Twas as if one ground a scythe on a grindstone, it whirred and whetted like water on a mill-wheel and rushed and rang, terrible to hear.

"By God," quoth Gawain, "I trow that gear is preparing for the knight who will meet me here. Alas! naught may help me, yet should my life be forfeit, I fear not a jot!" With that he called aloud. "Who waiteth in this place to give me tryst? Now is Gawain come hither: if any man will aught of him let him hasten hither now or never."

THE COMING OF THE GREEN KNIGHT

"STAY," QUOTH ONE ON THE BANK above his head, "and ye shall speedily have that which I promised ye." Yet for a while the noise of whetting went on ere he appeared, and then he came forth from a cave in the crag with a fell weapon, a Danish axe newly dight, wherewith to deal the blow. An evil head it had, four feet large, no less, sharply ground, and bound to the handle by the lace that gleamed brightly. And the knight himself was all green as before, face and foot, locks and beard, but now he was afoot. When he came to the water he would not wade it, but sprang over with the pole of his axe, and strode boldly over the brent that was white with snow.

Sir Gawain went to meet him, but he made no low bow. The other said, "Now, fair sir, one may trust thee to keep tryst. Thou art welcome, Gawain, to my place. Thou hast timed thy coming as befits a true man. Thou knowest the covenant set between us: at this time twelve months agone thou didst take that which fell to thee, and I at this New Year will readily requite thee. We are in this valley, verily alone, here are no knights to sever us, do what we will. Have off thy helm from thine head, and have here thy pay; make me no more talking than I did then when thou didst strike off my head with one blow."

"Nay," quoth Gawain, "by God that gave me life, I shall make no moan whatever befall me, but make thou ready for the blow and I shall stand still and say never a word to thee, do as thou wilt."

With that he bent his head and shewed his neck all bare, and made as if he had no fear, for he would not be thought a-dread.

HOW SIR GAWAIN FAILED TO STAND THE BLOW

THEN THE GREEN KNIGHT MADE HIM READY, and grasped his grim weapon to smite Gawain. With all his force he bore it aloft with a mighty feint of slaying him: had it fallen as straight as he aimed he who was ever doughty of deed had been slain by the blow. But Gawain swerved aside as the axe came gliding down to slay him as he stood, and shrank a little with the shoulders, for the sharp iron. The other heaved up the blade and rebuked the prince with many proud words:

OF THE GREEN KNIGHT'S REPROACHES

"THOU ART NOT GAWAIN," HE SAID, "who is held so valiant, that never feared he man by hill or vale, but *thou* shrinkest for fear ere thou feelest hurt. Such cowardice did I never hear of Gawain! Neither did *I* flinch from thy blow, or make strife in King Arthur's hall. My head fell to my feet, and yet I fled not, but thou didst wax faint of heart ere any harm befell. Wherefore must I be deemed the braver knight."

Quoth Gawain, "I shrank once, but so will I no more, though an *my* head fall on the stones I cannot replace it. But haste, Sir Knight, by thy faith, and bring me to the point, deal me my destiny, and do it out of hand, for I will stand thee a stroke and move no more till thine axe have hit me—my troth on it."

"Have at thee, then," quoth the other, and heaved aloft the axe with fierce mien, as if he were mad. He struck at him fiercely but wounded him not, withholding his hand ere it might strike him.

Gawain abode the stroke, and flinched in no limb, but stood still as a stone or the stump of a tree that is fast rooted in the rocky ground with a hundred roots.

Then spake gaily the man in green, "So now thou hast thine heart whole it behoves me to smite. Hold aside thy hood that Arthur gave thee, and keep thy neck thus bent lest it cover it again."

Then Gawain said angrily, "Why talk on thus? Thou dost threaten too long. I hope thy heart misgives thee."

HOW THE GREEN KNIGHT DEALT THE BLOW

"FOR SOOTH," QUOTH THE OTHER, "so fiercely thou speakest I will no longer let thine errand wait its reward." Then he braced himself to strike, frowning with lips and brow, 'twas no marvel that he who hoped for no rescue misliked him. He lifted the axe lightly and let it fall with the edge of the blade on the bare neck. Though he struck swiftly it hurt him no more than on the one side where it severed the skin. The sharp blade cut into the flesh so that the blood ran over his shoulder to the ground. And when the knight saw the blood staining the snow, he sprang forth, swift-foot, more than a spear's length, seized his helmet and set it on his head, cast his shield over his shoulder, drew out his bright sword, and spake boldly (never since he was born was he half so blithe), "Stop, Sir Knight, bid me no more blows. I have stood a stroke here without flinching, and if thou give me another, I shall requite thee, and give thee as good again. By the covenant made betwixt us in Arthur's hall but one blow falls to me here. Halt, therefore."

OF THE THREE COVENANTS

THEN THE GREEN KNIGHT DREW OFF from him, and leaned on his axe, setting the shaft on the ground, and looked on Gawain as he stood all armed and faced him fearlessly—at heart it pleased him well. Then he spake merrily in a loud voice, and said to the knight, "Bold sir, be not so fierce, no man here hath done thee wrong, nor will do, save by covenant, as we made at Arthur's court. I promised thee a blow and thou hast it—hold thyself well paid! I release thee of all other claims. If I had been so minded I might perchance have given thee a rougher buffet. First I menaced thee with a feigned one, and hurt thee not for the covenant that we made in the first night, and which thou didst hold truly. All the gain didst thou give me as a true man should. The other feint I proffered thee for the morrow: my fair wife kissed thee, and thou didst give me her kisses—for both those days I gave thee two blows without scathe—true man, true return. But the third time thou didst fail, and therefore hadst thou that blow. For 'tis my weed thou wearest, that same woven girdle, my own wife wrought it, that do I wot for sooth. Now know I well thy kisses, and thy conversation, and the wooing of my wife, for 'twas mine own doing. I sent her to try thee, and in sooth I think thou art the most faultless knight that ever trode earth. As a pearl among white peas is of more worth than they, so is Gawain, i' faith, by other knights. But thou didst lack a little, Sir Knight, and wast wanting in loyalty, yet that was for no evil work, nor for wooing neither, but because thou lovedst thy life—therefore I blame thee the less."

The shame of Sir Gawain

Then the other stood a great while still, sorely angered and vexed within himself; all the blood flew to his face, and he shrank for shame as the Green Knight spake; and the first words he said were, "Cursed be ye, cowardice and covetousness, for in ye is the destruction of virtue." Then he loosed the girdle, and gave it to the knight. "Lo, take there the falsity, may foul befall it! For fear of thy blow cowardice bade me make friends with covetousness and forsake the customs of largess and loyalty, which befit all knights. Now am I faulty and false and have been afeard: from treachery and untruth come sorrow and care. I avow to thee, Sir Knight, that I have ill done; do then thy will. I shall be more wary hereafter."

Then the other laughed and said gaily, "I wot I am whole of the hurt I had, and thou hast made such free confession of thy misdeeds, and hast so borne the penance of mine axe-edge, that I hold thee absolved from that sin, and purged as clean as if thou hadst never sinned since thou wast born. And this girdle that is wrought with gold and green, like my raiment, do I give thee, Sir Gawain, that thou mayest think upon this chance when thou goest forth among princes of renown, and keep this for a token of the adventure of the Green Chapel, as it chanced between chivalrous knights. And thou shalt come again with me to my dwelling and pass the rest of this feast in gladness." Then the lord laid hold of him, and said, "I wot we shall soon make peace with my wife, who was thy bitter enemy."

How Sir Gawain would keep the girdle

"Nay, forsooth," said Sir Gawain and seized his helmet and took it off swiftly, and thanked the knight: "I have fared ill, may bliss betide thee, and may He who rules all things reward thee swiftly. Commend me to that courteous lady, thy fair wife, and to the other my honoured ladies, who have beguiled their knight with skilful craft. But 'tis no marvel if one be made a fool and brought to sorrow by women's wiles, for so was Adam beguiled, and many a mighty man of old, Samson, and David, and Solomon—if one might love a woman and believe her not, 'twere great gain! And since all they were beguiled by women, methinks 'tis the less blame to me that I was misled! But as for thy girdle, that will I take with good will, not for gain of the gold, nor for samite, nor silk, nor the costly pendants, neither for weal nor for worship, but in sign of my frailty. I shall look upon it when I ride in renown and remind myself of the fault and faintness of the flesh; and so when pride uplifts me for prowess of arms, the sight of this lace shall humble my heart. But one thing would I pray, if it displease thee not: since thou art lord of yonder land wherein I have dwelt, tell me what thy rightful name may be, and I will ask no more."

HOW THE MARVEL WAS WROUGHT

"THAT WILL I TRULY," quoth the other. "Bernlak de Hautdesert am I called in this land. Morgain le Fay dwelleth in mine house, and through knowledge of clerkly craft hath she taken many. For long time was she the mistress of Merlin, who knew well all you knights of the court. Morgain the goddess is she called therefore, and there is none so haughty but she can bring him low. She sent me in this guise to yon fair hall to test the truth of the renown that is spread abroad of the valour of the Round Table. She taught me this marvel to betray your wits, to vex Guinevere and fright her to death by the man who spake with his head in his hand at the high table. That is she who is at home, that ancient lady, she is even thine aunt, Arthur's half-sister, the daughter of the Duchess of Tintagel, who afterward married King Uther. Therefore I bid thee, knight, come to thine aunt, and make merry in thine house; my folk love thee, and I wish thee as well as any man on earth, by my faith, for thy true dealing."

But Sir Gawain said nay, he would in no wise do so; so they embraced and kissed, and commended each other to the Prince of Paradise, and parted right there, on the cold ground. Gawain on his steed rode swiftly to the king's hall, and the Green Knight got him whithersoever he would.

HOW SIR GAWAIN CAME AGAIN TO CAMELOT

SIR GAWAIN, WHO HAD THUS WON grace of his life, rode through wild ways on Gringalet; oft he lodged in a house, and oft without, and many adventures did he have and came off victor full often, as at this time I cannot relate in tale. The hurt that he had in his neck was healed, he bare the shining girdle as a baldric bound by his side, and made fast with a knot 'neath his left arm, in token that he was taken in a fault—and thus he came in safety again to the court.

Then joy awakened in that dwelling when the king knew that the good Sir Gawain was come, for he deemed it gain. King Arthur kissed the knight, and the queen also, and many valiant knights sought to embrace him. They asked him how he had fared, and he told them all that had chanced to him—the adventure of the chapel, the fashion of the knight, the love of the lady—at last of the lace. He showed them the wound in the neck which he won for his disloyalty at the hand of the knight, the blood flew to his face for shame as he told the tale.

SIR GAWAIN MAKES CONFESSION OF HIS FAULT

"LO, LADY," HE QUOTH, and handled the lace, "this is the bond of the blame that I bear in my neck, this is the harm and the loss I have suffered, the cowardice and covetousness in which I was caught, the token of my covenant in which I was taken. And I must needs wear it so long as I live, for none may hide his harm, but undone it may not be, for if it hath clung to thee once, it may never be severed."

THE KNIGHTS WEAR THE LACE IN HONOUR OF GAWAIN

THEN THE KING COMFORTED THE KNIGHT, and the court laughed loudly at the tale, and all made accord that the lords and the ladies who belonged to the Round Table, each hero among them, should wear bound about him a baldric of bright green for the sake of Sir Gawain. And to this was agreed all the honour of the Round Table, and he who ware it was honoured the more thereafter, as it is testified in the best book of romance.

THE END OF THE TALE

THAT IN ARTHUR'S DAYS this adventure befell, the book of Brutus bears witness.
Many a venture herebefore
Hath fallen such as this:
May He that bare the crown of thorn
Bring us unto His bliss.

Amen

Julian of Norwich

Little is known about the life of English anchoress and mystic Julian of Norwich. Julian may not have been her real name since the church she served was called St. Julian's Church, perhaps the source of that name. According to her writings, Julian was born around 1343, most likely spending her entire life in the then-major city of Norwich near England's eastern coast. By the 1390s, she had become an anchoress; these religious figures secluded themselves in a small cell attached to a church. Anchorites were relatively common in England from the eleventh century until Henry VIII's dissolution of the monasteries in the 1530s.

Julian's life prior to becoming an anchoress, including the details of her family, is obscure. Some scholars who analyze her observations on the maternal qualities of God believe that she had children before isolating herself. Because the Black Death, the first wave of bubonic plague, reached Norwich during Julian's childhood, she could have lost her family (her birth family, her own husband and children, or both) in one of many plague outbreaks.

When she was thirty, Julian writes, she experienced an illness that almost killed her. She could have already been an anchoress at the time, though the fact that visitors were allowed to see her would have been unusual, or she could have been living outside the church still. Whatever the case, this illness caused her to have sixteen visions of Jesus Christ. When she recovered after about a week, Julian wrote down the details of her visions. This first manuscript, known by scholars as the *Short Text*, survived in the form of a copy written by a scribe. We know that Julian became an anchoress by the 1390s from a 1394 will in which twelve shillings were left to her. Decades after her visions, certainly while she was already an anchoress, Julian revisited her experiences in the *Long Text*, contemplating their meanings. This anthology includes an abridged version of the *Short Text*.

As an anchoress, Julian became a spiritual adviser within her church. She was treated as a sort of living link to God—the ceremony to bring anchorites into their cells involved singing funeral psalms as though they were dead before sealing their cell door. Julian's cell would have had a window looking into the church so that she could observe services. She would have offered prayers on behalf of those who visited her, likely including the important Catholic mystic Margery Kempe who visited Julian for advice around 1414. The last mention of Julian by name dates to 1416, indicating that she died sometime after.

Julian's work was overlooked until 1670, when an English monk living in France published it. Serenus de Cressy was a Catholic convert and a scholar of Catholic church history who published several forgotten texts, including Julian's; he titled her contributions *Revelations of Divine Love*.

TIMELINE

c. 1343	Julian is born in Norwich, England.
c. 1373	Julian falls ill and has sixteen visions of Jesus Christ; she writes the *Short Text*.
By 1394	Julian becomes an anchoress, isolating herself in a cell attached to St. Julian's Church in Norwich.
c. 1390s	Julian revisits her visions in the *Long Text*.
c. 1414	Margery Kempe visits Julian.
After 1416	Julian dies.
1670	Julian's writings are published with the title *Revelations of Divine Love* by an English Benedictine monk and scholar.

REVELATIONS OF DIVINE LOVE

By Julian of Norwich

THIS IS A REVELATION OF LOVE that Jesus Christ, our endless bliss, made in Sixteen Shewings, or Revelations particular.

Of the which the First is of His precious crowning with thorns; and therewith was comprehended and specified the Trinity, with the Incarnation, and unity betwixt God and man's soul; with many fair shewings of endless wisdom and teachings of love: in which all the Shewings that follow be grounded and oned.

The Second is the changing of colour of His fair face in token of His dearworthy Passion.

The Third is that our Lord God, Allmighty Wisdom, All-Love, right as verily as He hath made everything that is, all-so verily He doeth and worketh all-thing that is done.

The Fourth is the scourging of His tender body, with plenteous shedding of His blood.

The Fifth is that the Fiend is overcome by the precious Passion of Christ.

The Sixth is the worshipful thanking by our Lord God in which He rewardeth His blessed servants in Heaven.

The Seventh is our often feeling of weal and woe; (the feeling of weal is gracious touching and lightening, with true assuredness of endless joy; the feeling of woe is temptation by heaviness and irksomeness of our fleshly living;) with ghostly understanding that we are kept all as securely in Love in woe as in weal, by the Goodness of God.

The Eighth is of the last pains of Christ, and His cruel dying.

The Ninth is of the pleasing which is in the Blissful Trinity by the hard Passion of Christ and His rueful dying: in which joy and pleasing He willeth that we be solaced and mirthed with Him, till when we come to the fulness in Heaven.

The Tenth is, our Lord Jesus sheweth in love His blissful heart even cloven in two, rejoicing.

The Eleventh is an high ghostly Shewing of His dearworthy Mother.

The Twelfth is that our Lord is most worthy Being.

The Thirteenth is that our Lord God willeth we have great regard to all the deeds that He hath done: in the great nobleness of the making of all things; and the excellency of man's making, which is above all his works; and the precious Amends that He hath made for man's sin, turning all our blame into endless worship. In which Shewing also our Lord saith: *Behold and see! For by the same Might, Wisdom, and Goodness that I have done all this, by the same Might, Wisdom, and Goodness I shall make well all that is not well; and thou shalt see it.* And in this He willeth that we keep us in the Faith and truth of Holy Church, not desiring to see into His secret things now, save as it belongeth to us in this life.

The Fourteenth is that our Lord is the Ground of our Prayer. Herein were seen two properties: the one is rightful prayer, the other is steadfast trust; which He willeth should both be alike large; and thus our prayer pleaseth Him and He of His Goodness fulfilleth it.

The Fifteenth is that we shall suddenly be taken from all our pain and from all our woe, and of His Goodness we shall come up above, where we shall have our Lord Jesus for our meed and be fulfilled with joy and bliss in Heaven.

The Sixteenth is that the Blissful Trinity, our Maker, in Christ Jesus our Saviour endlessly dwelleth in our soul, worshipfully ruling and protecting all things, us mightily and wisely saving and keeping, for love; and we shall not be overcome of our Enemy.

These Revelations were shewed to a simple creature unlettered, the year of our Lord , the Thirteenth day of May. Which creature had afore desired three gifts of God. The First was mind of His Passion; the Second was bodily sickness in youth, at thirty years of age; the Third was to have of God's gift three wounds.

As to the First, methought I had some feeling in the Passion of Christ, but yet I desired more by the grace of God. Methought I would have been that time with Mary Magdalene, and with other that were Christ's lovers, and therefore I desired a bodily sight wherein I might have more knowledge of the bodily pains of our Saviour and of the compassion of our Lady and of all His true lovers that saw, that time, His pains. For I would be one of them and suffer with Him. Other sight nor shewing of God desired I never none, till the soul were disparted from the body. The cause of this petition was that after the shewing I should have the more true mind in the Passion of Christ.

The Second came to my mind with contrition; I freely desiring that sickness to be so hard as to death, that I might in that sickness receive all my rites of Holy Church, myself thinking that I should die, and that all creatures might suppose the same that saw me: for I would have no manner of comfort of earthly life. In this sickness I desired to have all manner of pains bodily and ghostly that I should have if I should die, (with all the dreads and tempests of the fiends) except the outpassing of the soul. And this I meant for that I would be purged, by the mercy of God, and afterward live more to the worship of God because of that sickness. And that for the more furthering in my death: for I desired to be soon with my God.

These two desires of the Passion and the sickness I desired with a condition, saying thus: *Lord, Thou knowest what I would,—if it be Thy will that I have it—; and if it be not Thy will, good Lord, be not displeased: for I will nought but as Thou wilt.*

For the Third petition, by the grace of God and teaching of Holy Church I conceived a mighty desire to receive three wounds in my life: that is to say, the wound of very contrition, the wound of kind compassion, and the wound of steadfast longing toward God. And all this last petition I asked without any condition.

These two desires aforesaid passed from my mind, but the third dwelled with me continually.

And when I was thirty years old and a half, God sent me a bodily sickness, in which I lay three days and three nights; and on the fourth night I took all my rites of Holy Church, and weened not to have lived till day. And after this I languored forth two days and two nights, and on the third night I weened oftentimes to have passed; and so weened they that were with me.

And being in youth as yet, I thought it great sorrow to die;—but for nothing that was in earth that meliked to live for, nor for no pain that I had fear of: for I trusted in God of His mercy. But it was to have lived that I might have loved God better, and longer time, that I might have the more knowing and loving of God in bliss of Heaven. For methought all the time that I had lived here so little and so short in regard of that endless bliss,—I thought it was as nothing. Wherefore I thought: *Good Lord, may my living no longer be to Thy worship!* And I understood by my reason and by my feeling of my pains that I should die; and I assented fully with all the will of my heart to be at God's will.

Thus I dured till day, and by then my body was dead from the middle downwards, as to my feeling. Then was I minded to be set upright, backward leaning, with help,—for to have more freedom of my heart to be at God's will, and thinking on God while my life would last.

My Curate was sent for to be at my ending, and by that time when he came I had set my eyes, and might not speak. He set the Cross before my face and said: *I have brought thee the Image of thy Maker and Saviour: look thereupon and comfort thee therewith.*

Methought I was well as it was, for my eyes were set uprightward unto Heaven, where I trusted to come by the mercy of God; but nevertheless I assented to set my eyes on the face of the Crucifix, if I might; and so I did. For methought I might longer dure to look even-forth than right up.

After this my sight began to fail, and it was all dark about me in the chamber, as if it had been night, save in the Image of the Cross whereon I beheld a common light; and I wist not how. All that was away from the Cross was of horror to me, as if it had been greatly occupied by the fiends.

After this the upper part of my body began to die, so far forth that scarcely I had any feeling;—with shortness of breath. And then I weened in sooth to have passed.

And in this moment suddenly all my pain was taken from me, and I was as whole (and specially in the upper part of my body) as ever I was afore.

I marvelled at this sudden change; for methought it was a privy working of God, and not of nature. And yet by the feeling of this ease I trusted never the more to live; nor was the feeling of this ease any full ease unto me: for methought I had liefer have been delivered from this world.

Then came suddenly to my mind that I should desire the second wound of our Lord's gracious gift: that my body might be fulfilled with mind and feeling of His blessed Passion. For I would that His pains were my pains, with compassion and afterward longing to God. But in this I desired never bodily sight nor shewing of God, but compassion such as a kind soul might have with our Lord Jesus, that for love would be a mortal man: and therefore I desired to suffer with Him.

The First Revelation

In this moment suddenly I saw the red blood trickle down from under the Garland hot and freshly and right plenteously, as it were in the time of His Passion when the Garland of thorns was pressed on His blessed head who was both God and Man, the same that suffered thus for me. I conceived truly and mightily that it was Himself shewed it me, without any mean.

And in the same Shewing suddenly the Trinity fulfilled my heart most of joy. And so I understood it shall be in heaven without end to all that shall come there. For the Trinity is God: God is the Trinity; the Trinity is our Maker and Keeper, the Trinity is our everlasting love and everlasting joy and bliss, by our Lord Jesus Christ. And this was shewed in the First Shewing and in all: for where Jesus appeareth, the blessed Trinity is understood, as to my sight.

And I said: *Benedicite Domine!* This I said for reverence in my meaning, with mighty voice; and full greatly was astonied for wonder and marvel that I had, that He that is so reverend and dreadful will be so homely with a sinful creature living in wretched flesh.

This Shewing I took for the time of my temptation,—for methought by the sufferance of God I should be tempted of fiends ere I died. Through this sight of the blessed Passion, with the Godhead that I saw in mine understanding, I knew well that *It* was strength enough for me, yea, and for all creatures living, against all the fiends of hell and ghostly temptation.

In this Shewing He brought our blessed Lady to my understanding. I saw her ghostly, in bodily likeness: a simple maid and a meek, young of age and little waxen above a child, in the stature that she was when she conceived. Also God shewed in part the wisdom and the truth of her soul: wherein I understood the reverent beholding in which she beheld her God and Maker, marvelling with great reverence that He would be born of her that was a simple creature of His making. And this wisdom and truth: knowing the greatness of her Maker and the littleness of herself that was made,—caused her to say full meekly to Gabriel: *Lo me, God's handmaid!* In this sight I understood soothly that she is more than all that God made beneath her in worthiness and grace; for above her is nothing that is made but the blessed Manhood of Christ, as to my sight.

In this same time our Lord shewed me a spiritual sight of His homely loving.

I saw that He is to us everything that is good and comfortable for us: He is our clothing that for love wrappeth us, claspeth us, and all encloseth us for tender love, that He may never leave us; being to us all-thing that is good, as to mine understanding.

Also in this He shewed me a little thing, the quantity of an hazel-nut, in the palm of my hand; and it was as round as a ball. I looked thereupon with eye of my understanding, and thought: *What may this be?* And it was answered generally thus: *it is all that is made.* I marvelled how it might last, for methought it might suddenly have fallen to naught for littleness. And I was answered in my understanding: *It lasteth, and ever shall last for that God loveth it.* And so All-thing hath the Being by the love of God.

In this Little Thing I saw three properties. The first is that God made it, the second is that God loveth it, the third, that God keepeth it. But what is to me verily the Maker, the Keeper, and the Lover,—I cannot tell; for till I am Substantially oned to Him, I may never have full rest nor very bliss: that is to say, till I be so fastened to Him, that there is right nought that is made betwixt my God and me.

It needeth us to have knowing of the littleness of creatures and to hold as nought all-thing that is made, for to love and have God that is unmade. For this is the cause why we be not all in ease of heart and soul: that we seek here rest in those things that are so little, wherein is no rest, and know not our God that is All-mighty, All-wise, All-good. For He is the Very Rest. God willeth to be known, and it pleaseth Him that we rest in Him; for all that is beneath Him sufficeth not us. And this is the cause why that no soul is rested till it is made nought as to all things that are made. When it is willingly made nought, for love, to have Him that is all, then is it able to receive spiritual rest.

Also our Lord God shewed that it is full great pleasance to Him that a helpless soul come to Him simply and plainly and homely. For this is the natural yearnings of the soul, by the touching of the Holy Ghost (as by the understanding that I have in this Shewing): *God, of Thy Goodness, give me Thyself: for Thou art enough to me, and I may nothing ask that is less that may be full worship to Thee; and if I ask anything that is less, ever me wanteth,—but only in Thee I have all.*

And these words are full lovely to the soul, and full near touch they the will of God and His Goodness. For His Goodness comprehendeth all His creatures and all His blessed works, and overpasseth without end. For He is the endlessness, and He hath made us only to Himself, and restored us by His blessed Passion, and keepeth us in His blessed love; and all this of His Goodness.

This Shewing was made to learn our soul wisely to cleave to the Goodness of God.

And in that time the custom of our praying was brought to mind: how we use for lack of understanding and knowing of Love, to take many means whereby to beseech Him.

Then saw I truly that it is more worship to God, and more very delight, that we faithfully pray to Himself of His Goodness and cleave thereunto by His Grace, with true understanding, and steadfast by love, than if we took all the means that heart can think. For if we took all these means, it is too little, and not full worship to God: but in His Goodness is all the whole, and *there* faileth right nought.

For this, as I shall tell, came to my mind in the same time: We pray to God for the sake of His holy flesh and His precious blood, His holy Passion, His dearworthy death and wounds: and all the blessed kindness, the endless life that we have of all this, is His Goodness. And we pray Him for the sake of His sweet Mother's love that Him bare; and all the help we have of her is of His Goodness. And we pray by His holy Cross that he died on, and all the virtue and the help that we have of the Cross, it is of His Goodness. And on the same wise, all the help that we have of special saints and all the blessed Company of Heaven, the dearworthy love and endless friendship that we have of them, it is of His Goodness. For God of His Goodness hath ordained means to help us, full fair and many: of which the chief and principal mean is the blessed nature that He took of the Maid, with all the means that go afore and come after which belong to our redemption and to endless salvation. Wherefore it pleaseth Him that we seek Him and worship through means, understanding that He is the Goodness of all.

For the Goodness of God is the highest prayer, and it cometh down to the lowest part of our need. It quickeneth our soul and bringeth it on life, and maketh it for to waxen in grace and virtue. It is nearest in nature; and readiest in grace: for *it* is the same grace that the soul seeketh, and ever shall seek till we know verily that He hath us all in Himself enclosed.

For He hath no despite of that He hath made, nor hath He any disdain to serve us at the simplest office that to our body belongeth in nature, for love of the soul that He hath made to His own likeness.

For as the body is clad in the cloth, and the flesh in the skin, and the bones in the flesh, and the heart in the whole, so are we, soul and body, clad in the Goodness of God, and enclosed. Yea, and more homely: for all these may waste and wear away, but the Goodness of God is ever whole; and more near to us, without any likeness; for truly our Lover desireth that our soul cleave to Him with all its might, and that we be ever-more cleaving to His Goodness. For of all things that heart may think, this pleaseth most God, and soonest speedeth the soul.

For our soul is so specially loved of Him that is highest, that it overpasseth the knowing of all creatures: that is to say, there is no creature that is made that may fully know how much and how sweetly and how tenderly our Maker loveth us. And therefore we may with grace and His help stand in spiritual beholding, with everlasting marvel of this high, overpassing, inestimable Love that Almighty God hath to us of His Goodness. And therefore we may ask of our Lover with reverence all that we will.

For our natural Will is to have God, and the Good Will of God is to have us; and we may never cease from willing nor from longing till we have Him in fullness of joy: and then may we no more desire.

For He willeth that we be occupied in knowing and loving till the time that we shall be fulfilled in Heaven; and therefore was this lesson of Love shewed, with all that followeth, as ye shall see. For the strength and the Ground of all was shewed in the First Sight. For of all things the beholding and the loving of the Maker maketh the soul to seem less in his own sight, and most filleth him with reverent dread and true meekness; with plenty of charity to his even-Christians.

Because of the Shewing I am not good but if I love God the better: and in as much as ye love God the better, it is more to you than to me. I say not this to them that be wise, for they wot it well; but I say it to you that be simple, for ease and comfort: for we are all one in comfort. For truly it was not shewed me that God loved me better than the least soul that is in grace; for I am certain that there be many that never had Shewing nor sight but of the common teaching of Holy Church, that love God better than I. For if I look singularly to myself, I am right nought; but in the general Body I am, I hope, in oneness of charity with all mine even-Christians.

For in this oneness standeth the life of all mankind that shall be saved. For God is all that is good, as to my sight, and God hath made all that is made, and God loveth all that He hath made: and he that loveth generally all his even-Christians for God, he loveth all that is. For in mankind that shall be saved is comprehended all: that is to say, all that is made and the Maker of all. For in man is God, and God is in all. And I hope by the grace of God he that beholdeth it thus shall be truly taught and mightily comforted, if he needeth comfort.

I speak of them that shall be saved, for in this time God shewed me none other. But in all things I believe as Holy Church believeth, preacheth, and teacheth. For the Faith of Holy Church, the which I had aforehand understood and, as I hope, by the grace of God earnestly kept in use and custom, stood continually in my sight: I willing and meaning never to receive anything that might be contrary thereunto. And with this intent I beheld the Shewing with all my diligence: for in all this blessed Shewing I beheld it as one in God's meaning.

All this was shewed by three ways: that is to say, by bodily sight, and by word formed in mine understanding, and by spiritual sight. But the spiritual sight I cannot nor may not shew it as openly nor as fully as I would. But I trust in our Lord God Almighty that He shall of His goodness, and for your love, make you to take it more spiritually and more sweetly than I can or may tell it.

The Second Revelation

And after this I saw with bodily sight in the face of the crucifix that hung before me, on the which I gazed continually, a part of His Passion: despite, spitting and sullying, and buffetting, and many languoring pains, more than I can tell, and often changing of colour. And one time I saw half the face, beginning at the ear, over-gone with dry blood till it covered to the mid-face. And after that the other half was covered on the same wise, the whiles in this first part it vanished even as it came.

This saw I bodily, troublously and darkly; and I desired more bodily sight, to have seen more clearly. And I was answered in my reason: *If God will shew thee more, He shall be thy light: thee needeth none but Him.* For I saw Him sought.

For we are now so blind and unwise that we never seek God till He of His goodness shew Himself to us. And when we aught see of Him graciously, then are we stirred by the same grace to seek with great desire to see Him more blissfully.

And thus I saw Him, and sought Him; and I had Him, I wanted Him. And this is, and should be, our common working in this life, as to my sight.

One time mine understanding was led down into the sea-ground, and there I saw hills and dales green, seeming as it were moss-be-grown, with wrack and gravel. Then I understood thus: that if a man or woman were under the broad water, if he might have sight of God so as God is with a man continually, he should be safe in body and soul, and take no harm: and overpassing, he should have more solace and comfort than all this world can tell. For He willeth we should believe that we see Him continually though that to us it seemeth but little of sight; and in this belief He maketh us evermore to gain grace. For He will be seen and He will be sought: He will be abided and he will be trusted.

This Second Shewing was so low and so little and so simple, that my spirits were in great travail in the beholding,—mourning, full of dread, and longing: for I was some time in doubt whether it was a Shewing. And then diverse times our good Lord gave me more sight, whereby I understood truly that it was a Shewing. It was a figure and likeness of our foul deeds' shame that our fair, bright, blessed Lord bare for our sins: it made me to think of the Holy Vernacle at Rome, which He hath portrayed with His own blessed face when He was in His hard Passion, with steadfast will going to His death, and often changing of colour. Of the brownness and blackness, the ruefulness and wastedness of this Image many marvel how it might be, since that He portrayed it with His blessed Face who is the fairness of heaven, flower of earth, and the fruit of the Maiden's womb. Then how might this Image be so darkening in colour and so far from fair?—I desire to tell like as I have understood by the grace of God:—

We know in our Faith, and believe by the teaching and preaching of Holy Church, that the blessed Trinity made Mankind to His image and to His likeness. In the same manner-wise we know that when man fell so deep and so wretchedly by sin, there was none other help to restore man but through Him that made man. And He that made man for love, by the same love He would restore man to the same bliss, and overpassing; and like as we were like-made to the Trinity in our first making, our Maker would that we should be like Jesus Christ, Our Saviour, in heaven without end, by the virtue of our again-making.

Then atwix these two, He would for love and worship of man make Himself as like to man in this deadly life, in our foulness and our wretchedness, as man might be without guilt. This is that which is meant where it is said afore: it was the image and likeness of our foul black deeds' shame wherein our fair, bright, blessed Lord God was hid. But full certainly I dare say, and we ought to trow it, that so fair a man was never none but He, till what time His fair colour was changed with travail and sorrow and Passion and dying. Of this it is spoken in the Eighth Revelation, where it treateth more of the same likeness. And where it speaketh of the Vernacle of Rome, it meaneth by reason of diverse changing of colour and countenance, sometime more comfortably and life-like, sometime more ruefully and death-like, as it may be seen in the Eighth Revelation.

And this dim vision was a learning, to mine understanding, that the continual seeking of the soul pleaseth God full greatly: for it may do no more than seek, suffer and trust. And this is wrought in the soul that hath it, by the Holy Ghost; and the clearness of finding, *it* is of His special grace, when it is His will. The seeking, with faith, hope, and charity, pleaseth our Lord, and the finding pleaseth the soul and fulfilleth it with joy. And thus was I learned, to mine understanding, that seeking is as good as beholding, for the time that He will suffer the soul to be in travail. It is God's will that *we seek Him*, to the beholding of Him, for by *that* He shall shew us Himself of His special grace when He will. And how a soul shall have Him in its beholding, He shall teach Himself: and that is most worship to Him and profit to thyself, and the soul thus most receiveth of meekness and virtues with the grace and leading of the Holy Ghost. For a soul that only fasteneth itself on to God with very trust, either by seeking or in beholding, it is the most worship that it may do to Him, as to my sight.

These are two workings that may be seen in this Vision: the one is seeking, the other is beholding. The seeking is common,—that every soul may have with His grace,—and ought to have that discretion and teaching of the Holy Church. It is God's will that we have three things in our seeking:—The first is that we seek earnestly and diligently, without sloth, and, as it may be through His grace, without unreasonable heaviness and vain sorrow. The second is, that we abide Him steadfastly for His love, without murmuring and striving against Him, to our life's end: for it shall last but awhile. The third is that we trust in Him mightily of full assured faith. For it is His will that we know that He shall appear suddenly and blissfully to all that love Him.

For His working is privy, and He willeth to be perceived; and His appearing shall be swiftly sudden; and He willeth to be trusted. For He is full gracious and homely: Blessed may He be!

THE THIRD REVELATION

AND AFTER THIS I SAW God in a Point, that is to say, in mine understanding,— by which sight I saw that He is in all things.

I beheld and considered, seeing and knowing in sight, with a soft dread, and thought: *What is sin?*

For I saw truly that God doeth all-thing, be it never so little. And I saw truly that nothing is done by hap nor by adventure, but all things by the foreseeing wisdom of God: if it be hap or adventure in the sight of man, our blindness and our unforesight is the cause. For the things that are in the foreseeing wisdom of God from without beginning, (which rightfully and worshipfully and continually He leadeth to the best end,) as they come about fall to us suddenly, ourselves unwitting; and thus by our blindness and our unforesight we say: these be haps and adventures. But to our Lord God they be not so.

Wherefore me behoveth needs to grant that all-thing that is done, it is well-done: for our Lord God doeth all. For in this time the working of creatures was not shewed, but the working of our Lord God in the creature: for He is in the Mid-point of all thing, and all He doeth. And I was certain He doeth no sin.

And here I saw verily that sin is no deed: for in all this was not sin shewed. And I would no longer marvel in this, but beheld our Lord, what He would shew.

And thus, as much as it might be for the time, the rightfulness of God's working was shewed to the soul.

Rightfulness hath two fair properties: it is right and it is full. And so are all the works of our Lord God: thereto needeth neither the working of mercy nor grace: for they be all rightful: wherein faileth nought.

But in another time He gave a Shewing for the beholding of sin nakedly, as I shall tell: where He useth working of mercy and grace.

And this vision was shewed, to mine understanding, for that our Lord would have the soul turned truly unto the beholding of Him, and generally of all His works. For they are full good; and all His doings are easy and sweet, and to great ease bringing the soul that is turned from the beholding of the blind Deeming of man unto the fair sweet Deeming of our Lord God. For a man beholdeth some deeds well done and some deeds evil, but our Lord beholdeth them not so: for as all that hath being in nature is of Godly making, so is all that is done, in property of God's doing. For it is easy to understand that the best deed is well done: and so well as the best deed is done—the highest—so well is the least deed done; and all thing in its property and in the order that our Lord hath ordained it to from without beginning. For there is no doer but He.

I saw full surely that he changeth never His purpose in no manner of thing, nor never shall, without end. For there was no thing unknown to Him in His rightful ordinance from without beginning. And therefore all-thing was set in order ere anything was made, as it should stand without end; and no manner of thing shall fail of that point. For He made all things in fulness of goodness, and therefore the blessed Trinity is ever full pleased in all His works.

And all this shewed He full blissfully, signifying thus: *See! I am God: see! I am in all thing: see! I do all thing: see! I lift never mine hands off my works, nor ever shall, without end: see! I lead all thing to the end I ordained it to from without beginning, by the same Might, Wisdom and Love whereby I made it. How should any thing be amiss?*

Thus mightily, wisely, and lovingly was the soul examined in this Vision. Then saw I soothly that me behoved, of need, to assent, with great reverence enjoying in God.

The Fourth Revelation

And after this I saw, beholding, the body plenteously bleeding in seeming of the Scourging, as thus:—The fair skin was broken full deep into the tender flesh with sharp smiting all about the sweet body. So plenteously the hot blood ran out that there was neither seen skin nor wound, but as it were all blood. And when it came where it should have fallen down, then it vanished. Notwithstanding, the bleeding continued awhile: till it might be seen and considered. And this was so plenteous, to my sight, that methought if it had been so in kind and in substance at that time, it should have made the bed all one blood, and have passed over about.

And then came to my mind that God hath made waters plenteous in earth to our service and to our bodily ease for tender love that He hath to us, but yet liketh Him better that we take full homely His blessed blood to wash us of sin: for there is no water that is made that He liketh so well to give us. For it is most plenteous as it is most precious: and that by the virtue of His blessed Godhead; and it is of our Kind, and all-blissfully belongeth to us by the virtue of His precious love.

The dearworthy blood of our Lord Jesus Christ as verily as it is most precious, so verily it is most plenteous. Behold and see! The precious plenty of His dearworthy blood descended down into Hell and burst her bands and delivered all that were there which belonged to the Court of Heaven. The precious plenty of His dearworthy blood overfloweth all Earth, and is ready to wash all creatures of sin, which be of goodwill, have been, and shall be. The precious plenty of His dearworthy blood ascended up into Heaven to the blessed body of our Lord Jesus Christ, and there is in Him, bleeding and praying for us to the Father,—and is, and shall be as long as it needeth;—and ever shall be as long as it needeth. And evermore it floweth in all Heavens enjoying the salvation of all mankind, that are there, and shall be—fulfilling the number that faileth.

THE FIFTH REVELATION

AND AFTER THIS, ere God shewed any words, He suffered me for a convenient time to give heed unto Him and all that I had seen, and all intellect that was therein, as the simplicity of the soul might take it. Then He, without voice and opening of lips, formed in my soul these words: *Herewith is the Fiend overcome.* These words said our Lord, meaning His blessed Passion as He shewed it afore.

On this shewed our Lord that the Passion of Him is the overcoming of the Fiend. God shewed that the Fiend hath now the same malice that he had afore the Incarnation. And as sore he travaileth, and as continually he seeth that all souls of salvation escape him, worshipfully, by the virtue of Christ's precious Passion. And that is his sorrow, and full evil is he ashamed: for all that God suffereth him to do turneth for us to joy and for him to shame and woe. And he hath as much sorrow when God giveth him leave to work, as when he worketh not: and that is for that he may never do as ill as he would: for his might is all taken into God's hand.

But in God there may be no wrath, as to my sight: for our good Lord endlessly hath regard to His own worship and to the profit of all that shall be saved. With might and right He withstandeth the Reproved, the which of malice and wickedness busy them to contrive and to do against God's will. Also I saw our Lord scorn his malice and set at nought his unmight; and He willeth that we do so. For this sight I laughed mightily, and that made them to laugh that were about me, and their laughing was a pleasure to me. I thought that I would that all mine even-Christians had seen as I saw, and then would they all laugh with me. But I saw not Christ laugh. For I understood that we may laugh in comforting of ourselves and joying in God for that the devil is overcome. And when I saw Him scorn his malice, it was by leading of mine understanding into our Lord: that is to say, it was an inward shewing of verity, without changing of look. For, as to my sight, it is a worshipful property of God's that He is ever the same.

And after this I fell into a graveness, and said: *I see three things: I see game, scorn, and earnest. I see a game, in that the Fiend is overcome; I see scorn, in that God scorneth him, and he shall be scorned; and I see earnest, in that he is overcome by the blissful Passion and Death of our Lord Jesus Christ that was done in full earnest and with sober travail.*

When I said, *he is scorned,*—I meant that God scorneth him, that is to say, because He seeth him now as he shall do without end. For in this word God shewed that the Fiend is condemned. And this meant I when I said: *he shall be scorned:* he shall be scorned at Doomsday, generally of all that shall be saved, to whose consolation he hath great ill-will. For then he shall see that all the woe and tribulation that he hath done to them shall be turned to increase of their joy, without end; and all the pain and tribulation that he would have brought them to shall endlessly go with him to hell.

THE SIXTH REVELATION

AFTER THIS OUR GOOD LORD SAID: *I thank thee for thy travail, and especially for thy youth.*
And in this Shewing mine understanding was lifted up into Heaven where I saw our Lord as a lord in his own house, which hath called all his dear worthy servants and friends to a stately feast. Then I saw the Lord take no place in His own house, but I saw Him royally reign in His house, fulfilling it with joy and mirth, Himself endlessly to gladden and to solace His dearworthy friends, full homely and full courteously, with marvellous melody of endless love, in His own fair blessed Countenance. Which glorious Countenance of the Godhead fulfilleth the Heavens with joy and bliss.

God shewed three degrees of bliss that every soul shall have in Heaven that willingly hath served God in any degree in earth. The first is the worshipful thanks of our Lord God that he shall receive when he is delivered of pain. This thanking is so high and so worshipful that the soul thinketh it filleth him though there were no more. For methought that all the pain and travail that might be suffered by all living men might not deserve the worshipful thanks that one man shall have that willingly hath served God. The second is that all the blessed creatures that are in Heaven shall see that worshipful thanking, and He maketh his service known to all that are in Heaven. And here this example was shewed:—A king, if he thank his servants, it is a great worship to them, and if he maketh it known to all the realm, then is the worship greatly increased.—The third is, that as new and as gladdening as it is received in that time, right so shall it last without end.

And I saw that homely and sweetly was this shewed, and that the age of every man shall be made known in Heaven, and he shall be rewarded for his willing service and for his time. And specially the age of them that willingly and freely offer their youth unto God, passingly is rewarded and wonderfully is thanked.

For I saw that whene'er what time a man or woman is truly turned to God,—for one day's service and for his endless will he shall have all these three decrees of bliss. And the more the loving soul seeth this courtesy of God, the liefer he is to serve him all the days of his life.

THE SEVENTH REVELATION

AND AFTER THIS HE SHEWED a sovereign ghostly pleasante in my soul. I was fulfilled with the everlasting sureness, mightily sustained without any painful dread. This feeling was so glad and so ghostly that I was in all peace and in rest, that there was nothing in earth that should have grieved me.

This lasted but a while, and I was turned and left to myself in heaviness, and weariness of my life, and irksomeness of myself, that scarcely I could have patience to live. There was no comfort nor none ease to me but faith, hope, and charity; and these I had in truth, but little in feeling.

And anon after this our blessed Lord gave me again the comfort and the rest in soul, in satisfying and sureness so blissful and so mighty that no dread, no sorrow, no pain bodily that might be suffered should have distressed me. And then the pain shewed again to my feeling, and then the joy and the pleasing, and now that one, and now that other, divers times—I suppose about twenty times. And in the time of joy I might have said with Saint Paul: *Nothing shall dispart me from the charity of Christ*; and in the pain I might have said with Peter: *Lord, save me: I perish!*

This Vision was shewed me, according to mine understanding, for that it is speedful to some souls to feel on this wise: sometime to be in comfort, and sometime to fail and to be left to themselves. God willeth that we know that He keepeth us even alike secure in woe and in weal. And for profit of man's soul, a man is sometime left to himself; although sin is not always the cause: for in this time I sinned not wherefore I should be left to myself—for it was so sudden. Also I deserved not to have this blessed feeling. But freely our Lord giveth when He will; and suffereth us to be in woe sometime. And both is one love.

For it is God's will that we hold us in comfort with all our might: for bliss is lasting without end, and pain is passing and shall be brought to nought for them that shall be saved. And therefore it is not God's will that we follow the feelings of pain in sorrow and mourning for them, but that we suddenly pass over, and hold us in endless enjoyment.

THE EIGHT REVELATION

AFTER THIS CHRIST SHEWED a part of His Passion near His dying.

I saw His sweet face as it were dry and bloodless with pale dying. And later, more pale, dead, languoring; and then turned more dead unto blue; and then more brown-blue, as the flesh turned more deeply dead. For His Passion shewed to me most specially in His blessed face (and chiefly in His lips): there I saw these four colours, though it were afore fresh, ruddy, and pleasing, to my sight. This was a pitiful change to see, this deep dying. And also the inward moisture clotted and dried, to my sight, and the sweet body was brown and black, all turned out of fair, life-like colour of itself, unto dry dying.

For that same time that our Lord and blessed Saviour died upon the Rood, it was a dry, hard wind, and wondrous cold, as to my sight, and what time all the precious blood was bled out of the sweet body that might pass therefrom, yet there dwelled a moisture in the sweet flesh of Christ, as it was shewed.

Bloodlessness and pain dried within; and blowing of wind and cold coming from without met together in the sweet body of Christ. And these four,—twain without, and twain within—dried the flesh of Christ by process of time. And though this pain was bitter and sharp, it was full long lasting, as to my sight, and painfully dried up all the lively spirits of Christ's flesh. Thus I saw the sweet flesh dry in seeming by part after part, with marvellous pains. And as long as any spirit had life in Christ's flesh, so long suffered He pain.

This long pining seemed to me as if He had been seven nights dead, dying, at the point of outpassing away, suffering the last pain. And when I said it seemed to me as if He had been seven night dead, it meaneth that the sweet body was so discoloured, so dry, so shrunken, so deathly, and so piteous, as if He had been seven night dead, continually dying. And methought the drying of Christ's flesh was the most pain, and the last, of His Passion.

And in this dying was brought to my mind the words of Christ: *I thirst*.

For I saw in Christ a double thirst: one bodily; another spiritual.

For this word was shewed for the bodily thirst: the which I understood was caused by failing of moisture. For the blessed flesh and bones was left all alone without blood and moisture. The blessed body dried alone long time with wringing of the nails and weight of the body. For I understood that for tenderness of the sweet hands and of the sweet feet, by the greatness, hardness, and grievousness of the nails the wounds waxed wide and the body sagged, for weight by long time hanging. And therewith was piercing and pressing of the head, and binding of the Crown all baked with dry blood, with the sweet hair clinging, and the dry flesh, to the thorns, and the thorns to the flesh drying; and in the beginning while the flesh was fresh and bleeding, the continual sitting of the thorns made the wounds wide. And furthermore I saw that the sweet skin and the tender flesh, with the hair and the blood, was all raised and loosed about from the bone, with the thorns where-through it were rent in many pieces, as a cloth that were sagging, as if it would hastily have fallen off, for heaviness and looseness, while it had natural moisture. And that was great sorrow and dread to me: for methought I would not for my life have seen it fall. How it was done I saw not; but understood it was with the sharp thorns and the violent and grievous setting on of the Garland of Thorns, unsparingly and without pity. This continued awhile, and soon it began to change, and I beheld and marvelled how it might be. And then I saw it was because it began to dry, and stint a part of the weight, and set about the Garland. And thus it encircled all about, as it were garland upon garland. The Garland of the Thorns was dyed with the blood, and that other garland of Blood and the head, all was one colour, as clotted blood when it is dry. The skin of the flesh that shewed (of the face and of the body), was small-rimpled with a tanned colour, like a dry board when it is aged; and the face more brown than the body.

I saw four manner of dryings: the first was bloodlessness; the second was pain following after; the third, hanging up in the air, as men hang a cloth to dry; the fourth, that the bodily Kind asked liquid and there was no manner of comfort ministered to Him in all His woe and distress. Ah! hard and grievous was his pain, but much more hard and grievous it was when the moisture failed and began to dry thus, shrivelling.

These were the pains that shewed in the blessed head: the first wrought to the dying, while it had moisture; and that other, slow, with shrinking drying, and with blowing of the wind from without, that dried and pained Him with cold more than mine heart can think.

And other pains—for which pains I saw that all is too little that I can say: for it may not be told.

The which Shewing of Christ's pains filled me full of pain. For I wist well He suffered but once, but this was as if He would shew it me and fill me with mind as I had afore desired. And in all this time of Christ's pains I felt no pain but for Christ's pains. Then thought-me: *I knew but little what pain it was that I asked*; and, as a wretch, repented me, thinking: *If I had wist what it had been, loth me had been to have prayed it.* For methought it passed bodily death, my pains.

I thought: *Is any pain like this?* And I was answered in my reason: *Hell is another pain: for there is despair. But of all pains that lead to salvation this is the most pain, to see thy Love suffer. How might any pain be more to me than to see Him that is all my life, all my bliss, and all my joy, suffer?* Here felt I soothfastly that I loved Christ so much above myself that there was no pain that might be suffered like to that sorrow that I had to see Him in pain.

Here I saw a part of the compassion of our Lady, Saint Mary: for Christ and she were so oned in love that the greatness of her loving was cause of the greatness of her pain. For in this Shewing I saw a Substance of Nature's Love, continued by Grace, that creatures have to Him: which Kind Love was most fully shewed in His sweet Mother, and overpassing; for so much as she loved Him more than all other, her pains passed all other. For ever the higher, the mightier, the sweeter that the love be, the more sorrow it is to the lover to see that body in pain that is loved.

And all His disciples and all His true lovers suffered pains more than their own bodily dying. For I am sure by mine own feeling that the least of them loved Him so far above himself that it passeth all that I can say.

Here saw I a great oneing betwixt Christ and us, to mine understanding: for when He was in pain, we were in pain.

And all creatures that ought suffer pain, suffered with Him: that is to say, all creatures that God hath made to our service. The firmament, the earth, failed for sorrow in their Nature in the time of Christ's dying. For it belongeth naturally to their property to know Him for their God, in whom all their virtue standeth: when He failed, then behoved it needs to them, because of kindness between them, to fail with Him, as much as they might, for sorrow of His pains.

And thus they that were His friends suffered pain for love. And, generally, *all*: that is to say, they that knew Him not suffered for failing of all manner of comfort save the mighty, privy keeping of God. I speak of two manner of folk, as they may be understood by two persons: the one was Pilate, the other was Saint Dionyse of France, which was at that time a Paynim. For when he saw wondrous and marvellous sorrows and dreads that befell in that time, he said: *Either the world is now at an end, or He that is Maker of Kind suffereth.* Wherefore he did write on an altar: This is the Altar of Unknown God. God that of His goodness maketh the planets and the elements to work of Kind to the blessed man and the cursed, in that time made withdrawing of it from both; wherefore it was that they that knew Him not were in sorrow that time.

In this time I would have looked up from the Cross, but I durst not. For I wist well that while I beheld in the Cross I was surely-safe; therefore I would not assent to put my soul in peril: for away from the Cross was no sureness, for frighting of fiends.

Then had I a proffer in my reason, as if it had been friendly said to me: *Look up to Heaven to His Father.* And then saw I well, with the faith that I felt, that there was nothing betwixt the Cross and Heaven that might have harmed me. Either me behoved to look up or else to answer. I answered inwardly with all the might of my soul, and said: *Nay; I may not: for Thou art my Heaven.* This I said for that I would not. For I would liever have been in that pain till Doomsday than to come to Heaven otherwise than by Him. For I wist well that He that bound me so sore, He should unbind me when that He would. Thus was I learned to choose Jesus to my Heaven, whom I saw only in pain at that time: meliked no other Heaven than Jesus, which shall be my bliss when I come there.

And this hath ever been a comfort to me, that I chose Jesus to my Heaven, by His grace, in all this time of Passion and sorrow; and that hath been a learning to me that I should evermore do so: choose only Jesus to my Heaven in weal and woe.

And though I as a wretched creature had repented me (I said afore if I had wist what pain it would be, I had been loth to have prayed), here saw I truly that it was reluctance and frailty of the flesh without assent of the soul: to which God assigneth no blame. Repenting and willing choice be two contraries which I felt both in one at that time. And these be of our two parts: the one outward, the other inward. The outward part is our deadly flesh-hood, which is now in pain and woe, and shall be, in this life: whereof I felt much in this time; and that part it was that repented. The inward part is an high, blissful life, which is all in peace and in love: and this was more inwardly felt; and this part is that in which mightily, wisely and with steadfast will I chose Jesus to my Heaven.

And in this I saw verily that the inward part is master and sovereign to the outward, and doth not charge itself with, nor take heed to, the will of that: but all the intent and will is set to be oned unto our Lord Jesus. That the outward part should draw the inward to assent was not shewed to me; but that the inward draweth the outward by grace, and both shall be oned in bliss without end, by the virtue of Christ,—*this* was shewed.

THE NINTH REVELATION

THEN SAID OUR GOOD LORD JESUS CHRIST: *Art thou well pleased that I suffered for thee?* I said: *Yea, good Lord, I thank Thee; Yea, good Lord, blessed mayst Thou be.* Then said Jesus, our kind Lord: *If thou art pleased, I am pleased: it is a joy, a bliss, an endless satisfying to me that ever suffered I Passion for thee; and if I might suffer more, I would suffer more.*

In this feeling my understanding was lifted up into Heaven, and there I saw three heavens: of which sight I marvelled greatly. And though I see three heavens—and all in the blessed manhood of Christ—none is more, none is less, none is higher, none is lower, but they are even-like in bliss.

For the First Heaven, Christ shewed me His Father; in no bodily likeness, but in His property and in His working. That is to say, I saw in Christ that the Father is. The working of the Father is this, that He giveth meed to His Son Jesus Christ. This gift and this meed is so blissful to Jesus that His Father might have given Him no meed that might have pleased Him better. The first heaven, that is the pleasing of the Father, shewed to me as one heaven; and it was full blissful: for He is full pleased with all the deeds that Jesus hath done about our salvation.

Wherefore we be not only His by His buying, but also by the courteous gift of His Father we be His bliss, we be His meed, we be His worship, we be His crown. (And this was a singular marvel and a full delectable beholding, that we be His crown!) This that I say is so great bliss to Jesus that He setteth at nought all His travail, and His hard Passion, and His cruel and shameful death.

And in these words: *If that I might suffer more, I would suffer more,*—I saw in truth that as often as He *might* die, so often He *would,* and love should never let Him have rest till He had done it. And I beheld with great diligence for to learn how often He would die if He might. And verily the number passed mine understanding and my wits so far that my reason might not, nor could, comprehend it. And when He had thus oft died, or should, yet He would set it at nought, for love: for all seemeth Him but little in regard of His love.

For though the sweet manhood of Christ might suffer but once, the goodness in Him may never cease of proffer: every day He is ready to the same, if it might be. For if He said He would for my love make new Heavens and new Earth, it were but little in comparison; for this might be done every day if He would, without any travail. But to die for my love so often that the number passeth creature's reason, it is the highest proffer that our Lord God might make to man's soul, as to my sight. Then meaneth He thus: *How should it not be that I should not do for thy love all that I might of deeds which grieve me not, sith I would, for thy love, die so often, having no regard to my hard pains?*

And here saw I, for the Second Beholding in this blessed Passion *the love that made Him to suffer passeth as far all His pains as Heaven is above Earth.* For the pains was a noble, worshipful deed done in a time by the working of love: but Love was without beginning, is, and shall be without ending. For which love He said full sweetly these words: *If I might suffer more, I would suffer more.* He said not, *If it were needful to suffer more:* for though it were not needful, if He *might* suffer more, He would.

This deed, and this work about our salvation, was ordained as well as God might ordain it. And here I saw a Full Bliss in Christ: for His bliss should not have been full, if it might any better have been done.

THE TENTH REVELATION

THEN WITH A GLAD CHEER our Lord looked unto His Side and beheld, rejoicing. With His sweet looking He led forth the understanding of His creature by the same wound into His Side within. And then he shewed a fair, delectable place, and large enough for all mankind that shall be saved to rest in peace and in love. And therewith He brought to mind His dearworthy blood and precious water which he let pour all out for love. And with the sweet beholding He shewed His blessed heart even cloven in two.

And with this sweet enjoying, He shewed unto mine understanding, in part, *the blessed Godhead,* stirring then the poor soul to understand, as it may be said, that is, to think on, the *endless* Love that was without beginning, and is, and shall be ever. And with this our good Lord said full blissfully: *Lo, how that I loved thee,* as if

He had said: *My darling, behold and see thy Lord, thy God that is thy Maker and thine end-less joy, see what satisfying and bliss I have in thy salvation; and for my love rejoice thou with me.*

And also, for more understanding, this blessed word was said: *Lo, how I loved thee! Behold and see that I loved thee so much ere I died for thee that I would die for thee; and now I have died for thee and suffered willingly that which I may. And now is all my bitter pain and all my hard travail turned to endless joy and bliss to me and to thee. How should it now be that thou shouldst anything pray that pleaseth me but that I should full gladly grant it thee? For my pleasing is thy holiness and thine endless joy and bliss with me.*

This is the understanding, simply as I can say it, of this blessed word: *Lo, how I loved thee.* This shewed our good Lord for to make us glad and merry.

THE ELEVENTH REVELATION

AND WITH THIS SAME CHEER of mirth and joy our good Lord looked down on the right side and brought to my mind where our Lady stood in the time of His Passion; and said: *Wilt thou see her?* And in this sweet word it was as if He had said: *I wot well that thou wouldst see my blessed Mother: for, after myself, she is the highest joy that I might shew thee, and most pleasance and worship to me; and most she is desired to be seen of my blessed creatures.* And for the high, marvellous, singular love that He hath to this sweet Maiden, His blessed Mother, our Lady Saint Mary, He shewed her highly rejoicing, as by the meaning of these sweet words; as if He said: *Wilt thou see how I love her, that thou mightest joy with me in the love that I have in her and she in me?*

And also (unto more understanding this sweet word) our Lord speaketh to all mankind that shall be saved, as it were all to one person, as if He said: *Wilt thou see in her how thou art loved? For thy love I made her so high, so noble and so worthy; and this pleaseth me, and so will I that it doeth thee.*

For after Himself she is the most blissful sight.

But hereof am I not learned to long to see her bodily presence while I am here, but the virtues of her blessed soul: her truth, her wisdom, her charity; whereby I may learn to know myself and reverently dread my God. And when our good Lord had shewed this and said this word: *Wilt thou see her?* I answered and said: *Yea, good Lord, I thank Thee; yea, good Lord, if it be Thy will.* Oftentimes I prayed this, and I weened to have seen her in bodily presence, but I saw her not so. And Jesus in that word shewed me ghostly sight of her: right as I had seen her afore little and simple, so He shewed her then high and noble and glorious, and pleasing to Him above all creatures.

And He willeth that it be known; that so all those that please them in Him should please them in her, and in the pleasance that He hath in her and she in Him. And, to more understanding, He shewed this example: *As if a man love a creature singularly, above all creatures,* he willeth to make all creatures to love and to have pleasance in that creature that he loveth so greatly. And in this word that Jesus said: *Wilt thou see her?* methought it was the most pleasing word that He might have given me of her, with that ghostly Shewing that He gave me of her. For our Lord shewed me nothing in special but our Lady Saint Mary; and her He shewed three times. The first was as she was with Child; the second was as she was in her sorrows under the Cross; the third is as she is now in pleasing, worship, and joy.

"And he wil that it be knowen that al those that lyke in him should lyken in hir and in the lykyng that he hath in hir and she in him."

THE TWELFTH REVELATION

AND AFTER THIS OUR LORD shewed Himself more glorified, as to my sight, than I saw Him before in the Shewing wherein I was learned that our soul shall never have rest till it cometh to Him, knowing that He is fulness of joy, homely and courteous, blissful and very life.

Our Lord Jesus oftentimes said: *I it am, I it am: I it am that is highest, I it am that thou lovest, I it am that thou enjoyest, I it am that thou servest, I it am that thou longest for, I it am that thou desirest, I it am that thou meanest, I it am that is all. I it am that Holy Church preacheth and teacheth thee, I it am that shewed me here to thee.* The number of the words passeth my wit and all my understanding and all my powers. And they are the highest, as to my sight: for therein is comprehended—I cannot tell,—but the joy that I saw in the Shewing of them passeth all that heart may wish for and soul may desire. Therefore the words be not declared here; but every man after the grace that God giveth him in understanding and loving, receive them in our Lord's meaning.

THE THIRTEENTH REVELATION

AFTER THIS THE LORD brought to my mind the longing that I had to Him afore. And I saw that nothing letted me but sin. And so I looked, generally, upon us all, and methought: *If sin had not been, we should all have been clean and like to our Lord, as He made us.*

And thus, in my folly, afore this time often I wondered why by the great foreseeing wisdom of God the beginning of sin was not letted: for then, methought, all should have been well. This stirring of mind was much to be forsaken, but nevertheless mourning and sorrow I made therefor, without reason and discretion.

But Jesus, who in this Vision informed me of all that is needful to me, answered by this word and said: *It behoved that there should be sin; but all shall be well, and all shall be well, and all manner of thing shall be well.*

In this naked word *sin*, our Lord brought to my mind, generally, *all that is not good*, and the shameful despite and the utter noughting that He bare for us in this life, and His dying; and all the pains and passions of all His creatures, ghostly and bodily; (for we be all partly noughted, and we shall be noughted following our Master, Jesus, till we be full purged, that is to say, till we be fully noughted of our deadly flesh and of all our inward affections which are not very good;) and the beholding of this, with all pains that ever were or ever shall be,—and with all these I understand the Passion of Christ for most pain, and overpassing. All this was shewed in a touch and quickly passed over into comfort: for our good Lord would not that the soul were affeared of this terrible sight.

But I saw not *sin*: for I believe it hath no manner of substance nor no part of being, nor could it be known but by the pain it is cause of.

And thus pain, *it* is something, as to my sight, for a time; for it purgeth, and maketh us to know ourselves and to ask mercy. For the Passion of our Lord is comfort to us against all this, and so is His blessed will. And for the tender love that our good Lord hath to all that shall be saved, He comforteth readily and sweetly, signifying thus: *It is sooth that sin is cause of all this pain; but all shall be well, and all shall be well, and all manner of thing shall be well.*

These words were said full tenderly, showing no manner of blame to me nor to any that shall be saved. Then were it a great unkindness to blame or wonder on God for my sin, since He blameth not me for sin.

And in these words I saw a marvellous high mystery hid in God, which mystery He shall openly make known to us in Heaven: in which knowing we shall verily see the cause why He suffered sin to come. In which sight we shall endlessly joy in our Lord God.

Thus I saw how Christ hath compassion on us for the cause of sin. And right as I was afore in the Shewing of the Passion of Christ fulfilled with pain and compassion, like so in this sight I was fulfilled, in part, with compassion of all mine even-Christians—for that well, well beloved people that shall be saved. For God's servants, Holy Church, shall be shaken in sorrow and anguish, tribulation in this world, as men shake a cloth in the wind.

And as to this our Lord answered in this manner: *A great thing shall I make hereof in Heaven of endless worship and everlasting joys.*

Yea, so far forth I saw, that our Lord joyeth of the tribulations of His servants, with ruth and compassion. On each person that He loveth, to His bliss for to bring them, He layeth something that is no blame in His sight, whereby they are blamed and despised in this world, scorned, mocked, and outcasted. And this He doeth for to hinder the harm that they should take from the pomp and the vain-glory of this wretched life, and make their way ready to come to Heaven, and up-raise them in His bliss everlasting. For He saith: *I shall wholly break you of your vain affections and your vicious pride; and after that I shall together gather you, and make you mild and meek, clean and holy, by oneing to me.*

And then I saw that each kind compassion that man hath on his even-Christians with charity, it is Christ in him.

That same noughting that was shewed in His Passion, it was shewed again here in this Compassion. Wherein were two manner of understandings in our Lord's meaning. The one was the bliss that we are brought to, wherein He willeth that we rejoice. The other is for comfort in our pain: for He willeth that we perceive that it shall all be turned to worship and profit by virtue of His passion, that we perceive that we suffer not alone but with Him, and see Him to be our Ground, and that we see His pains and His noughting passeth so far all that we may suffer, that it may not be fully thought.

The beholding of this will save us from murmuring and despair in the feeling of our pains. And if we see soothly that our sin deserveth it, yet His love excuseth us, and of His great courtesy He doeth away all our blame, and beholdeth us with ruth and pity as children innocent and unloathful.

And yet in this I desired, as far as I durst, that I might have full sight of Hell and Purgatory. But it was not my meaning to make proof of anything that belongeth to the Faith: for I believed soothfastly that Hell and Purgatory is for the same end that Holy Church teacheth, but my meaning was that I might have seen, for learning in all things that belong to my Faith: whereby I might live the more to God's worship and to my profit.

But for all my desire, I could see of this right nought, save as it is aforesaid in the First Shewing, where I saw that the devil is reproved of God and endlessly condemned. In which sight I understood as to all creatures that are of the devil's condition in this life, and therein end, that there is no more mention made of them afore God and all His Holy than of the devil,—notwithstanding that they be of mankind—whether they be christened or not.

For though the Revelation was made of goodness in which was made little mention of evil, yet I was not drawn thereby from any point of the Faith that Holy Church teacheth me to believe. For I had sight of the Passion of Christ in diverse Shewings,—the First, the Second, the Fifth, and the Eighth,—wherein I had in part a feeling of the sorrow of our Lady, and of His true friends that saw Him in pain; but I saw not so properly specified the Jews that did Him to death. Notwithstanding I knew in my Faith that they were accursed and condemned without end, saving those that converted, by grace. And I was strengthened and taught generally to keep me in the Faith in every point, and in all as I had before understood: hoping that I was therein with the mercy and the grace of God; desiring and praying in my purpose that I might continue therein unto my life's end.

And it is God's will that we have great regard to all His deeds that He hath done, but evermore it needeth us to leave the beholding what the Deed shall be. And let us desire to be like our brethren which be saints in Heaven, that will right nought but God's will and are well pleased both with hiding and with shewing. For I saw soothly in our Lord's teaching, the more we busy us to know His secret counsels in this or any other thing, the farther shall we be from the knowing thereof.

Our Lord God shewed two manner of secret things. One is this great Secret Counsel with all the privy points that belong thereto: and these secret things He willeth we should know as *being*, but as *hid* until the time that He will clearly shew them to us. The other are the secret things that He willeth to make open and known to us; for He would have us understand that it is His will that we should know them. They are secrets to us not only for that He willeth that they be secrets to us, but they are secrets to us for our blindness and our ignorance; and thereof He hath great ruth, and therefore He will Himself make them more open to us, whereby we may know Him and love Him and cleave to Him. For all that is speedful for us to learn and to know, full courteously will our Lord shew us: and of that is this Shewing, with all the preaching and teaching of Holy Church.

God shewed full great pleasance that He hath in all men and women that mightily and meekly and with all their will take the preaching and teaching of Holy Church. For it is His Holy Church: He is the Ground, He is the Substance, He is the Teaching, He is the Teacher, He is the End, He is the Meed for which every kind soul travaileth.

And *this* of the Shewing is made known, and shall be known to every soul to which the Holy Ghost declareth it. And I hope truly that all those that seek this, He shall speed: for they seek God.

All this that I have now told, and more that I shall tell after, is comforting against sin. For in the Third Shewing when I saw that God doeth all that is done, I saw no sin: and then I saw that all *is* well. But when God shewed me for sin, then said He: *All* shall *be well.*

THE FOURTEENTH REVELATION

After this our Lord shewed concerning Prayer. In which Shewing I see two conditions in our Lord's signifying: one is rightfulness, another is sure trust.

But yet oftentimes our trust is not full: for we are not sure that God heareth us, as we think because of our unworthiness, and because we feel right nought, (for we are as barren and dry oftentimes after our prayers as we were afore); and this, in our feeling our folly, is cause of our weakness. For thus have I felt in myself.

And all this brought our Lord suddenly to my mind, and shewed these words, and said: *I am Ground of thy beseeching: first it is my will that thou have it; and after, I make thee to will it; and after, I make thee to beseech it and thou beseechest it. How should it then be that thou shouldst not have thy beseeching?*

And thus in the first reason, with the three that follow, our good Lord sheweth a mighty comfort, as it may be seen in the same words. And in the first reason,— where He saith: *And thou beseechest it*, there He sheweth His full great pleasance, and endless meed that He will give us for our beseeching. And in the second reason, where He saith: *How should it then be?* etc., this was said for an impossible thing. For it is most impossible that we should beseech mercy and grace, and not have it. For everything that our good Lord maketh us to beseech, Himself hath ordained it to us from without beginning. Here may we see that our beseeching is not cause of God's goodness; and that shewed He soothfastly in all these sweet words when He saith: *I am the Ground.*—And our good Lord willeth that this be known of His lovers in earth; and the more that we know it the more should we beseech, if it be wisely taken; and so is our Lord's meaning.

Beseeching is a true, gracious, lasting will of the soul, oned and fastened into the will of our Lord by the sweet inward work of the Holy Ghost. Our Lord Himself, He is the first receiver of our prayer, as to my sight, and taketh it full thankfully and highly enjoying; and He sendeth it up above and setteth it in the Treasure, where it shall never perish. It is there afore God with all His Holy continually received, ever speeding the help of our needs; and when we shall receive our bliss it shall be given us for a degree of joy, with endless worshipful thanking from Him.

Full glad and merry is our Lord of our prayer; and He looketh thereafter and He willeth to have it because with His grace He maketh us like to Himself in condition as we are in kind: and so is His blissful will. Therefore He saith thus: *Pray inwardly, though thee thinketh it savour thee not: for it is profitable, though thou feel not, though thou see nought; yea, though thou think thou canst not. For in dryness and in barrenness, in sickness and in feebleness, then is thy prayer well-pleasant to me, though thee thinketh it savour thee nought but little. And so is all thy believing prayer in my sight.* For the meed and the endless thanks that He will give us, *therefor* He is covetous to have us pray continually in His sight. God accepteth the goodwill and the travail of His servant, howsoever we feel: wherefore it pleaseth Him that we work both in our prayers and in good living, by His help and His grace, reasonably with discretion keeping our powers turned to Him, till when that we have Him that we seek, in fulness of joy: that is, Jesus. And that shewed He in the Fifteenth Revelation, farther on, in this word: *Thou shalt have me to thy meed.*

And also to prayer belongeth thanking. Thanking is a true inward knowing, with great reverence and lovely dread turning ourselves with all our mights unto the working that our good Lord stirreth us to, enjoying and thanking inwardly. And sometimes, for plenteousness it breaketh out with voice, and saith: *Good Lord, I thank Thee! Blessed mayst Thou be!* And sometime when the heart is dry and feeleth not, or else by temptation of our enemy,—then it is driven by reason and by grace to cry upon our Lord with voice, rehearing His blessed Passion and His great Goodness; and the virtue of our Lord's word turneth into the soul and quickeneth the heart and entereth it by His grace into true working, and maketh it pray right blissfully. And truly to enjoy our Lord, it is a full blissful thanking in His sight.

The Fifteenth Revelation

Afore this time I had great longing and desire of God's gift to be delivered of this world and of this life. For oftentimes I beheld the woe that is here, and the weal and the bliss that is being there: (and if there had been no pain in this life but the absence of our Lord, methought it was some-time more than I might bear;) and this made me to mourn, and eagerly to long. And also from mine own wretchedness, sloth, and weakness, me liked not to live and to travail, as me fell to do.

And to all this our courteous Lord answered for comfort and patience, and said these words: *Suddenly thou shalt be taken from all thy pain, from all thy sickness, from all thy distress and from all thy woe. And thou shalt come up above and thou shalt have me to thy meed, and thou shalt be fulfilled of love and of bliss. And thou shalt never have no manner of pain, no manner of misliking, no wanting of will; but ever joy and bliss without end. What should it then aggrieve thee to suffer awhile, seeing that it is my will and my worship?*

And in this word: *Suddenly thou shalt be taken,*—I saw that God rewardeth man for the patience that he hath in abiding God's will, and for his time, and for that man lengtheneth his patience over the time of his living. For not-knowing of his time of passing, that is a great profit: for if a man knew his time, he should not have patience over that time; but, as God willeth, while the soul is in the body it seemeth to itself that it is ever at the point to be taken. For all this life and this languor that we have here is but a point, and when we are taken suddenly out of pain into bliss then pain shall be nought.

And in this time I saw a body lying on the earth, which body shewed heavy and horrible, without shape and form, as it were a swollen quag of stinking mire. And suddenly out of this body sprang a full fair creature, a little Child, fully shapen and formed, nimble and lively, whiter than lily; which swiftly glided up into heaven. And the swollenness of the body betokeneth great wretchedness of our deadly flesh, and the littleness of the Child betokeneth the cleanness of purity in the soul. And methought: *With this body abideth no fairness of this Child, and on this Child dwelleth no foulness of this body.*

It is more blissful that man be taken from pain, than that pain be taken from man; for if pain be taken from us it may come again: therefore it is a sovereign comfort and blissful beholding in a loving soul that we shall be taken from pain. For in this behest I saw a marvellous compassion that our Lord hath in us for our woe, and a courteous promising of clear deliverance. For He willeth that we be comforted in the overpassing; and *that* He shewed in these words: *And thou shalt come up above, and thou shalt have me to thy meed, and thou shalt be fulfilled of joy and bliss.*

It is God's will that we set the point of our thought in this blissful beholding as often as we may,—and as long time keep us therein with His grace; for this is a blessed contemplation to the soul that is led of God, and full greatly to His worship, for the time that it lasteth. And when we fall again to our heaviness, and spiritual blindness, and feeling of pains spiritual and bodily, by our frailty, it is God's will that we know that He hath not forgotten us. And so signifieth He in these words: *And thou shalt never more have pain; no manner of sickness, no manner of misliking, no wanting of will; but ever joy and bliss without end. What should it then aggrieve thee to suffer awhile, seeing it is my will and my worship?*

It is God's will that we take His behests and His comfortings as largely and as mightily as we may take them, and also He willeth that we take our abiding and our troubles as lightly as we may take them, and set them at nought. For the more lightly we take them, and the less price we set on them, for love, the less pain we shall have in the feeling of them, and the more thanks and meed we shall have for them.

THE SIXTEENTH REVELATION

AND THEN OUR LORD OPENED MY SPIRITUAL EYE and shewed me my soul in midst of my heart. I saw the Soul so large as it were an endless world, and as it were a blissful kingdom. And by the conditions that I saw therein I understood that it is a worshipful City. In the midst of that City sitteth our Lord Jesus, God and Man, a fair Person of large stature, highest Bishop, most majestic King, most worshipful Lord; and I saw Him clad majestically. And worshipfully He sitteth in the Soul, even-right in peace and rest. And the Godhead ruleth and sustaineth heaven and earth and all that is,—sovereign Might, sovereign Wisdom, and sovereign Goodness,—but the place that Jesus taketh in *our Soul* He shall never remove it, without end, as to my sight: for in us is His *homliest* home and His *endless* dwelling.

And in this He shewed the satisfying that He hath of the making of Man's Soul. For as well as the Father might make a creature, and as well as the Son could make a creature, so well would the Holy Ghost that Man's Soul were made: and so it was done. And therefore the blessed Trinity enjoyeth without end in the making of Man's Soul: for He saw from without beginning what should please

Him without end. All thing that He hath made sheweth His Lordship,—as understanding was given at the same time by example of a creature that is to see great treasures and kingdoms belonging to a lord; and when it had seen all the nobleness beneath, then, marvelling, it was moved to seek above to the high place where the lord dwelleth, knowing, by reason, that his dwelling is in the worthiest place. And thus I understood in verity that our Soul may never have rest in things that are beneath itself. And when it cometh above all creatures into the Self, yet may it not abide in the beholding of its Self, but all the beholding is blissfully set in God that is the Maker dwelling therein. For in Man's Soul is His very dwelling; and the highest light and the brightest shining of the City is the glorious love of our Lord, as to my sight.

And what may make us more to enjoy in God than to see in Him that He enjoyeth in the highest of all His works? For I saw in the same Shewing that if the blessed Trinity might have made Man's Soul any better, any fairer, any nobler than it was made, He should not have been full pleased with the making of Man's Soul. And He willeth that our hearts be mightily raised above the deepness of the earth and all vain sorrows, and rejoice in Him.

Geoffrey Chaucer

Geoffrey Chaucer was born in the early 1340s, probably in London. Although disputed, the commonly accepted year cited for his birth is 1343. While not much is known about his childhood or personal life, Chaucer's career as a  civil servant allows his public life to be uncommonly well-documented for a writer of the period. His father, John Chaucer, was a wealthy vintner (winemaker) and merchant. His mother was Agnes de Compton, whose family owned extensive properties in London. Nothing is known of Chaucer's early education, but it would have been customary for him to be fluent in French. He held his first documented position in 1357, as a servant in the household of Elizabeth, Countess of Ulster, who was married to the third son of King Edward III. Privileged children were typically placed into royal households. Such placement would have enabled Chaucer to meet John of Gaunt, fourth son of Edward III and Chaucer's most important literary patron and friend.

By 1359, Chaucer was serving in France with Edward's army. After he was captured as a prisoner of war, Edward paid his £16 ransom, the equivalent of over $15,000 today. In 1360, he served as a messenger between France and England during their peace negotiations. While we know little of Chaucer's career between 1360 and 1365, he likely either served the King, possibly travelling in continental Europe, or studied law in preparation for his career. The next record occurs in 1366, when he went on a diplomatic mission to Spain. He also married Philippa Roet around this time, a lady-in-waiting to Edward's queen consort. Her family was wealthy and her father was an important French knight. John of Gaunt later married her sister, Katherine.

Chaucer and Philippa had three or four children, two sons and one or two daughters. Their son Thomas Chaucer served in Parliament fifteen times, became Speaker of the House of Commons, and served as an advisor and diplomat to four English kings. Geoffrey Chaucer wrote his astronomical "Treatise on the Astrolabe" for his other son, Lewis. A woman who became a nun known as "Elizabeth Chaucy" may have been a daughter, and the other, Agnes, was an attendant at the coronation of King Henry IV.

During the next few years (1367-69), Chaucer served Edward III in various positions such as a yeoman, esquire, diplomat, and military officer. In 1369, Chaucer and Philippa were official mourners for Edward's queen consort. He wrote his first important poem, *Book of the Duchess*, between 1369 and 1370. An elegy for John of Gaunt's first wife who died of the plague in 1369, the *Book* takes considerable inspiration from French literature, but it is also original in its use of a mourner figure in an elegy. Chaucer gives that mourner, representative of John of Gaunt, a complex relationship with the poet/narrator. Chaucer's distinct use of a first-person narrator, who reflects both similarities to and distinct differences from the poet, is reiterated throughout his works. Despite being a serious elegy, the *Book* contains the first hints of Chaucer's later masterful comic writing, displayed in full force in *The Canterbury Tales*.

Another important aspect of the *Book* is that Chaucer wrote it in English. In the early Middle Ages, Middle English was considered a vulgar language; the nobility almost exclusively spoke French. Chaucer read extensively in French, which heavily inspired his early works. Latin was the other literary language at the time, used for scientific or religious treatises, or works intended for a wide Continental audience. Chaucer, however, wrote all of his important works in English. Because he pioneered the use of English in sophisticated, widely read poetry, he became known as the father of English literature.

In the 1370s, Chaucer's career flourished as he received generous payment from both Edward III and John of Gaunt. In 1374, he was made a comptroller for the Port of London, an important and lucrative position which allowed him to benefit from the fines he levied. When Edward died in 1377, Chaucer's position was confirmed by his successor, ten-year-old King Richard II. Chaucer participated in various diplomatic missions to France, Italy, and Belgium throughout the 1370s. His travels in Italy exposed him to Petrarch and Boccaccio, both of whom considerably influenced his later writing. His only poetry of the decade is *The House of Fame*, a comic poem written as a dream vision in which Chaucer visits the home of the goddess Fame and learns about the importance of preserving stories. The poem is inspired by Roman mythology and features a temple to Venus, as well as a summary of the *Aeneid*. The *House of Fame* cannot be reliably dated, but scholars consider it most likely to be Chaucer's second major work, placing it in the late 1370s.

Chaucer's probable third work, *The Parliament of Fowls*, dates to the early 1380s. Here he uses birds to create an allegory about each social class at court—nobles are eagles and hawks, merchants are waterfowl, and the landed farmers are turtle doves. Chaucer also examines themes of courtly love and nature in the *Parliament*. His next work, *Troilus and Criseyde*, a retelling of the tragic love story of Troilus and Cressida, is set during the Trojan War. Another text referencing Roman stories, this poem is impressive for its complex titular characters and takes inspiration from Italian writers like Dante and Petrarch. The 1380s likewise produced *The Legend of Good Women*, a long poem that is a collection of stories about women such as Cleopatra and Lucrece who were betrayed by men. A notable feature is its framing device, a humorous prologue in which the god of love forces Chaucer to write about good women. However, critics find this framework weak and the stories in the *Legend* monotonous. Criticism of *The Legend of Good Women* may have inspired the much stronger framing device of a religious pilgrimage in *The Canterbury Tales*, which Chaucer likely began working on during this decade.

Chaucer was appointed to an additional comptrollership in 1382, but in 1385 he moved from London to Kent, becoming a justice of the peace; his positions at the London port were passed on to others in 1386. He became a Knight of the Shire in Kent in 1386, which made him a member of Parliament. Scholars are unsure why Chaucer left London, but one theory is that his wife was in poor health, dying in 1387. There was also political strife during this time: Richard II and John of Gaunt had their power usurped by a group of barons. Chaucer could have been removed from his positions because of his close associations with the King and his family. In 1388, Chaucer's debts accrued lawsuits, forcing him to sell his royal pension. Established courtiers, some of whom were Chaucer's friends, were executed in 1388. Nonetheless, Richard II regained control of the throne in 1389 and appointed Chaucer as Clerk of the King's Works, where he oversaw the upkeep of buildings like the Palace of Westminster and the Tower of London.

As the clerk of the King's works, Chaucer earned a generous salary. However, after being robbed, he changed jobs in 1391 to become a forester on the King's land. He was in royal favor for the next decade, receiving numerous gifts from Richard. He also maintained his close relationship with John of Gaunt and Gaunt's son Henry. In 1399, Gaunt died, and Henry rebelled against Richard II to become King Henry IV. The new King continued to be generous to Chaucer, leasing him a home in the garden of Westminster Abbey in 1399. Chaucer died of unknown causes in October of 1400. He was buried in Westminster Abbey. In 1556, his body was moved and he became the first poet buried in what is now known as Westminster's "Poet's Corner." Other writers who are buried or honored in Poet's Corner include Edmund Spenser, William Shakespeare, Charles Dickens, Lord Byron, and T.S. Eliot.

Chaucer never finished his most famous work, *The Canterbury Tales*. The *Tales* is inspired by Italian author Boccaccio's *The Decameron*, which uses a framing device in which ten nobles are quarantined to avoid the plague, each telling a tale every day. Chaucer makes innovative changes to this storytelling framework, including the fact that his characters are not noble but range from an upper-class knight to lower middle-class workers. This type of story is known as an "estates satire," because it satirizes the three estates, or social classes. The clergy were known as the first estate, the royalty and nobility were the second, and the commoners were the third. Chaucer also interconnects the tales with dialogue, giving his characters strong personalities and flaws. He adds the character of the Host, as well as the personae of the naive narrator, who is quite different from the astute satirist, and hence becomes Chaucer's parody of himself. The *Tales* features a group of thirty pilgrims traveling from Southwark, near London, to Canterbury. Chaucer originally planned to have each of them tell four tales, two on the way to Canterbury and two on the way back, for a total of 120 tales. However, only twenty-four tales were completed. Scholars speculate that Chaucer stopped working on the *Tales* years before his death, overwhelmed by the task he had set himself.

What Chaucer managed to accomplish with his incomplete manuscript is nevertheless significant. He creates complex, fascinating, and funny characters in his Prologue, figures who parody the flaws as well as represent the strengths of medieval England's three estates. The tales themselves demonstrate conflicts between the pilgrims caused by social class differences and personal whim. Chaucer also compiled stories from a wide variety of genres—from courtly romances and religious allegories to raunchy fabliaux, a French genre of bawdy stories. Additionally, the purported religious pilgrimage that the characters come together for contrasts with the very irreligious tales and the less-than-holy motivations of religious characters like the Prioress and the Pardoner. The *Tales'* importance as a famous work of complex poetry written in Middle English, at a time when sophisticated writers generally wrote in French or Latin, cannot be overstated.

TIMELINE

1340-45	Chaucer is born, probably in London
1357	Chaucer serves in his first court position
1359	Chaucer first serves King Edward III in the military.
1366	Chaucer marries Philippa Roet
~1370	*Book of the Duchess*
1374	Chaucer becomes comptroller for the Port of London
late 1370s	*House of Fame*
early 1380s	*The Parliament of Fowls*
mid 1380s	*Troilus and Criseyde; The Legend of Good Women; The Canterbury Tales* are probably started
1385-86	Chaucer leaves London and his jobs as comptroller
1387	Chaucer's wife, Philippa, dies
1389	Chaucer becomes Clerk of the King's Works
1391	Chaucer becomes a forester for the King
1399	John of Gaunt dies; his son Henry takes the throne
1400	Chaucer dies

THE CANTERBURY TALES

BY GEOFFREY CHAUCER

THE PROLOGUE

When that Aprilis, with his showers swoot*,   *sweet
The drought of March hath pierced to the root,
And bathed every vein in such licour,
Of which virtue engender'd is the flower;
5 When Zephyrus eke with his swoote breath
Inspired hath in every holt* and heath   *grove, forest
The tender croppes* and the younge sun   *twigs, boughs
Hath in the Ram* his halfe course y-run,   *Aries
And smalle fowles make melody,
10 That sleepen all the night with open eye,
(So pricketh them nature in their corages*);   *hearts, inclinations
Then longe folk to go on pilgrimages,
And palmers for to seeke strange strands,
To *ferne hallows couth* in sundry lands;   *distant saints known*
15 And specially, from every shire's end
Of Engleland, to Canterbury they wend,
The holy blissful Martyr for to seek,
That them hath holpen*, when that they were sick.   *helped
Befell that, in that season on a day,
20 In Southwark at the Tabard as I lay,
Ready to wenden on my pilgrimage
To Canterbury with devout corage,
At night was come into that hostelry
Well nine and twenty in a company
25 Of sundry folk, *by aventure y-fall   *who had by chance
In fellowship*, and pilgrims were they all,   fallen into company.*
That toward Canterbury woulde ride.
The chamber, and the stables were wide,
And *well we weren eased at the best.*   *we were well provided
30 And shortly, when the sunne was to rest,   with the best*
So had I spoken with them every one,
That I was of their fellowship anon,
And made forword* early for to rise,   *promise
To take our way there as I you devise*.   *describe, relate
35 But natheless, while I have time and space,
Ere that I farther in this tale pace,

Me thinketh it accordant to reason,
To tell you alle the condition
Of each of them, so as it seemed me,
40   And which they weren, and of what degree;
And eke in what array that they were in:
And at a Knight then will I first begin.

A Knight there was, and that a worthy man,
That from the time that he first began
45   To riden out, he loved chivalry,
Truth and honour, freedom and courtesy.
Full worthy was he in his Lorde's war,
And thereto had he ridden, no man farre*,   *farther
As well in Christendom as in Heatheness,
50   And ever honour'd for his worthiness
At Alisandre* he was when it was won.   *Alexandria
Full often time he had the board begun
Above alle nations in Prusse.
In Lettowe* had he reysed,** and in Russe,   *Lithuania; **journeyed
55   No Christian man so oft of his degree.
In Grenade at the siege eke had he be
Of Algesir, and ridden in Belmarie.
At Leyes was he, and at Satalie,[1]
When they were won; and in the Greate Sea
60   At many a noble army had he be.
At mortal battles had he been fifteen,
And foughten for our faith at Tramissene.[2]
In listes thries, and aye slain his foe.
This ilke* worthy knight had been also   *same
65   Some time with the lord of Palatie,
Against another heathen in Turkie:
And evermore *he had a sovereign price*.   *He was held in very
And though that he was worthy he was wise,   high esteem.*
And of his port as meek as is a maid.
70   He never yet no villainy ne said
In all his life, unto no manner wight.
He was a very perfect gentle knight.
But for to telle you of his array,
His horse was good, but yet he was not gay.
75   Of fustian he weared a gipon*,   *short doublet
Alle *besmotter'd with his habergeon,*   *soiled by his coat of mail.*
For he was late y-come from his voyage,

____

1: These places are supposedly in Africa.
2: The Knight fought against pagans.

And wente for to do his pilgrimage.
With him there was his son, a younge Squire,
A lover, and a lusty bacheler,
80   With lockes crulle* as they were laid in press.   *curled
Of twenty year of age he was I guess.
Of his stature he was of even length,
And *wonderly deliver*, and great of strength.   *wonderfully nimble*
And he had been some time in chevachie*,   *cavalry raids
85   In Flanders, in Artois, and Picardie,
And borne him well, *as of so little space*,   *in such a short time*
In hope to standen in his lady's grace.
Embroider'd was he, as it were a mead
All full of freshe flowers, white and red.
90   Singing he was, or fluting all the day;
He was as fresh as is the month of May.
Short was his gown, with sleeves long and wide.
Well could he sit on horse, and faire ride.
He coulde songes make, and well indite,
95   Joust, and eke dance, and well pourtray and write.
So hot he loved, that by nightertale*   *night-time
He slept no more than doth the nightingale.
Courteous he was, lowly, and serviceable,
And carv'd before his father at the table.[3]
100   A Yeoman had he, and servants no mo'
At that time, for *him list ride so*   *it pleased him so to ride*
And he was clad in coat and hood of green.
A sheaf of peacock arrows bright and keen
Under his belt he bare full thriftily.
105   Well could he dress his tackle yeomanly:
His arrows drooped not with feathers low;
And in his hand he bare a mighty bow.
A nut-head* had he, with a brown visiage: *nut-brown hair
Of wood-craft coud* he well all the usage: *knew
110   Upon his arm he bare a gay bracer*,   *small shield
And by his side a sword and a buckler,
And on that other side a gay daggere,
Harnessed well, and sharp as point of spear:
A Christopher on his breast of silver sheen.
115   An horn he bare, the baldric was of green:
A forester was he soothly* as I guess.   *certainly

There was also a Nun, a Prioress,
That of her smiling was full simple and coy;

3: This was customary for squires of the highest degree.

Her greatest oathe was but by Saint Loy;
120 And she was cleped* Madame Eglentine.   *called
Full well she sang the service divine,
Entuned in her nose full seemly;
And French she spake full fair and fetisly*   *properly
After the school of Stratford atte Bow,
125 For French of Paris was to her unknow.
At meate was she well y-taught withal;
She let no morsel from her lippes fall,
Nor wet her fingers in her sauce deep.
Well could she carry a morsel, and well keep,
130 That no droppe ne fell upon her breast.
In courtesy was set full much her lest*.   *pleasure
Her over-lippe wiped she so clean,
That in her cup there was no farthing* seen   *speck
Of grease, when she drunken had her draught;
135 Full seemely after her meat she raught*:   *reached out her hand
And *sickerly she was of great disport*,   *surely she was of a
And full pleasant, and amiable of port,   lively disposition*
And *pained her to counterfeite cheer   *took pains to assume a
Of court,* and be estately of mannere,   courtly disposition*
140 And to be holden digne* of reverence.   *worthy
But for to speaken of her conscience,
She was so charitable and so pitous,*   *full of pity
She woulde weep if that she saw a mouse
Caught in a trap, if it were dead or bled.
145 Of smalle houndes had she, that she fed
With roasted flesh, and milk, and *wastel bread.*   *finest white bread*
But sore she wept if one of them were dead,
Or if men smote it with a yarde* smart: *staff
And all was conscience and tender heart.
150 Full seemly her wimple y-pinched was;
Her nose tretis;* her eyen gray as glass[4];   *well-formed
Her mouth full small, and thereto soft and red;
But sickerly she had a fair forehead.
It was almost a spanne broad I trow;
155 For *hardily she was not undergrow*.   *certainly she was not small*
Full fetis* was her cloak, as I was ware.   *neat
Of small coral about her arm she bare
A pair of beades, gauded all with green;
And thereon hung a brooch of gold full sheen,
160 On which was first y-written a crown'd A,
And after, *Amor vincit omnia.*   *love conquers all*

———————————

4: Then a mark of beauty.

Another Nun also with her had she,
[That was her chapelleine, and Priestes three.]

A Monk there was, a fair *for the mast'ry*, *above all others*
165 An out-rider, that loved venery*; *hunting
A manly man, to be an abbot able.
Full many a dainty horse had he in stable:
And when he rode, men might his bridle hear
Jingeling in a whistling wind as clear,
170 And eke as loud, as doth the chapel bell,
There as this lord was keeper of the cell.
The rule of Saint Maur and of Saint Benet*, *Benedict
Because that it was old and somedeal strait
This ilke* monk let olde thinges pace, *same
175 And held after the newe world the trace.
He *gave not of the text a pulled hen,* *he cared nothing for the text*
That saith, that hunters be not holy men:
Ne that a monk, when he is cloisterless;
Is like to a fish that is waterless;
180 This is to say, a monk out of his cloister.
This ilke text held he not worth an oyster;
And I say his opinion was good.
Why should he study, and make himselfe wood* *mad
Upon a book in cloister always pore,
185 Or swinken* with his handes, and labour, *toil
As Austin bid? how shall the world be served?
Let Austin have his swink to him reserved.
Therefore he was a prickasour* aright: *hard rider
Greyhounds he had as swift as fowl of flight;
190 Of pricking* and of hunting for the hare *riding
Was all his lust,* for no cost would he spare. *pleasure
I saw his sleeves *purfil'd at the hand *worked at the end with a
With gris,* and that the finest of the land.   fur called "gris"*
And for to fasten his hood under his chin,
195 He had of gold y-wrought a curious pin;
A love-knot in the greater end there was.
His head was bald, and shone as any glass,
And eke his face, as it had been anoint;
He was a lord full fat and in good point;
200 His eyen steep,* and rolling in his head, *deep-set
That steamed as a furnace of a lead.
His bootes supple, his horse in great estate,
Now certainly he was a fair prelate;
He was not pale as a forpined* ghost; *wasted
205 A fat swan lov'd he best of any roast.

His palfrey was as brown as is a berry.
A Friar there was, a wanton and a merry,
A limitour[5], a full solemne man.
In all the orders four is none that can*   *knows
210 So much of dalliance and fair language.
He had y-made full many a marriage
Of younge women, at his owen cost.
Unto his order he was a noble post;
Full well belov'd, and familiar was he
215 With franklins *over all* in his country,   *everywhere*
And eke with worthy women of the town:
For he had power of confession,
As said himselfe, more than a curate,
For of his order he was licentiate.
220 Full sweetely heard he confession,
And pleasant was his absolution.
He was an easy man to give penance,
There as he wist to have a good pittance: *where he would get
For unto a poor order for to give   good payment*
225 Is signe that a man is well y-shrive.
For if he gave, he *durste make avant*,   *dared to boast*
He wiste* that the man was repentant.   *knew
For many a man so hard is of his heart,
He may not weep although him sore smart.
230 Therefore instead of weeping and prayeres,
Men must give silver to the poore freres.
His tippet was aye farsed* full of knives   *stuffed
And pinnes, for to give to faire wives;
And certainly he had a merry note:
235 Well could he sing and playen *on a rote*;   *from memory*
Of yeddings* he bare utterly the prize.   *songs
His neck was white as is the fleur-de-lis.
Thereto he strong was as a champion,
And knew well the taverns in every town.
240 And every hosteler and gay tapstere,
Better than a lazar* or a beggere,   *leper
For unto such a worthy man as he
Accordeth not, as by his faculty,
To have with such lazars acquaintance.
245 It is not honest, it may not advance,
As for to deale with no such pouraille*,   *offal, refuse
But all with rich, and sellers of vitaille*.   *victuals

5: Limitour: A friar with licence or privilege to beg, or exercise other functions, within a certain district: as, "the limitour of Holderness".

	And *ov'r all there as* profit should arise,	*in every place where*
	Courteous he was, and lowly of service;	
250	There n'as no man nowhere so virtuous.	
	He was the beste beggar in all his house:	
	And gave a certain farme for the grant,[6]	
	None of his bretheren came in his haunt.	
	For though a widow hadde but one shoe,	
255	So pleasant was his In Principio,[7]	
	Yet would he have a farthing ere he went;	
	His purchase was well better than his rent.	
	And rage he could and play as any whelp,	
	In lovedays*; there could he muchel** help.	*days to settle quarrels; **greatly
260	For there was he not like a cloisterer,	
	With threadbare cope as is a poor scholer;	
	But he was like a master or a pope.	
	Of double worsted was his semicope*,	*short cloak
	That rounded was as a bell out of press.	
265	Somewhat he lisped for his wantonness,	
	To make his English sweet upon his tongue;	
	And in his harping, when that he had sung,	
	His eyen* twinkled in his head aright,	*eyes
	As do the starres in a frosty night.	
270	This worthy limitour was call'd Huberd.	
	A Merchant was there with a forked beard,	
	In motley, and high on his horse he sat,	
	Upon his head a Flandrish beaver hat.	
	His bootes clasped fair and fetisly*.	*neatly
275	His reasons aye spake he full solemnly,	
	Sounding alway th' increase of his winning.	
	He would the sea were kept* for any thing	*safeguarded from attack
	Betwixte Middleburg[8] and Orewell[9]	
	Well could he in exchange shieldes* sell	*crown coins
280	This worthy man full well his wit beset*;	*employed
	There wiste* no wight** that he was in debt,	*knew **man
	So *estately was he of governance*	*so well he managed*
	With his bargains, and with his chevisance*.	*business contract
	For sooth he was a worthy man withal,	
285	But sooth to say, I n'ot* how men him call.	*know not
	A Clerk there was of Oxenford* also,	*Oxford
	That unto logic hadde long y-go*.	*devoted himself

6: The farm is used as a payment of rent; he paid for his license to beg.

7: A part of a Mass service.

8: In the Netherlands.

9: In Essex.

As leane was his horse as is a rake,
And he was not right fat, I undertake;
290 But looked hollow*, and thereto soberly**.   *thin; **poorly
Full threadbare was his *overest courtepy*,   *uppermost short cloak*
For he had gotten him yet no benefice,
Ne was not worldly, to have an office.
For him was lever* have at his bed's head   *rather
295 Twenty bookes, clothed in black or red,
Of Aristotle, and his philosophy,
Than robes rich, or fiddle, or psalt'ry.
But all be that he was a philosopher,
Yet hadde he but little gold in coffer,
300 But all that he might of his friendes hent*,   *obtain
On bookes and on learning he it spent,
And busily gan for the soules pray
Of them that gave him wherewith to scholay*   *study
Of study took he moste care and heed.
305 Not one word spake he more than was need;
And that was said in form and reverence,
And short and quick, and full of high sentence.
Sounding in moral virtue was his speech,
And gladly would he learn, and gladly teach.
310 A Sergeant of the Law, wary and wise,
That often had y-been at the Parvis,[10]
There was also, full rich of excellence.
Discreet he was, and of great reverence:
He seemed such, his wordes were so wise,
315 Justice he was full often in assize,
By patent, and by plein* commission;   *full
For his science, and for his high renown,
Of fees and robes had he many one.
So great a purchaser was nowhere none.
320 All was fee simple to him, in effect
His purchasing might not be in suspect*   *suspicion
Nowhere so busy a man as he there was
And yet he seemed busier than he was
In termes had he case' and doomes* all   *judgements
325 That from the time of King Will. were fall.
Thereto he could indite, and make a thing
There coulde no wight *pinch at* his writing.   *find fault with*
And every statute coud* he plain by rote   *knew
He rode but homely in a medley* coat,   *multicoloured
330 Girt with a seint* of silk, with barres small;   *sash

10: St. Paul's, where lawyers met their clients.

Of his array tell I no longer tale.

A Frankelin* was in this company;   *Rich landowner
White was his beard, as is the daisy.
Of his complexion he was sanguine.
335 Well lov'd he in the morn a sop in wine.
To liven in delight was ever his won*,   *wont
For he was Epicurus' owen son,
That held opinion, that plein* delight   *full
Was verily felicity perfite.
340 An householder, and that a great, was he;
Saint Julian[11] he was in his country.
His bread, his ale, was alway *after one*;   *pressed on one*
A better envined* man was nowhere none;   *stored with wine
Withoute bake-meat never was his house,
345 Of fish and flesh, and that so plenteous,
It snowed in his house of meat and drink,
Of alle dainties that men coulde think.
After the sundry seasons of the year,
So changed he his meat and his soupere.
350 Full many a fat partridge had he in mew*,   *cage
And many a bream, and many a luce* in stew**   *pike **fish-pond
Woe was his cook, *but if* his sauce were   *unless*
Poignant and sharp, and ready all his gear.
His table dormant* in his hall alway   *fixed
355 Stood ready cover'd all the longe day.
At sessions there was he lord and sire.
Full often time he was *knight of the shire*   *Member of Parliament*
An anlace*, and a gipciere** all of silk,   *dagger **purse
Hung at his girdle, white as morning milk.
360 A sheriff had he been, and a countour*   *accountant
Was nowhere such a worthy vavasour*.   *important landowner
An Haberdasher, and a Carpenter,
A Webbe*, a Dyer, and a Tapiser**,   *weaver **tapestry-maker
Were with us eke, cloth'd in one livery,
365 Of a solemn and great fraternity.[12]
Full fresh and new their gear y-picked* was.   *spruce
Their knives were y-chaped* not with brass,   *mounted
But all with silver wrought full clean and well,
Their girdles and their pouches *every deal*.   *in every part*
370 Well seemed each of them a fair burgess,
To sitten in a guild-hall, on the dais.

––––––––––––––––––

11: The patron saint of hospitality.
12: They are members of a guild for clothmakers.

Evereach, for the wisdom that he can*,   *knew
Was shapely* for to be an alderman.   *fitted
For chattels hadde they enough and rent,
375   And eke their wives would it well assent:
And elles certain they had been to blame.
It is full fair to be y-clep'd madame,
And for to go to vigils all before,
And have a mantle royally y-bore.

380   A Cook they hadde with them for the nones*,   *occasion
To boil the chickens and the marrow bones,
And powder merchant tart and galingale.
Well could he know a draught of London ale.
He could roast, and stew, and broil, and fry,
385   Make mortrewes, and well bake a pie.
But great harm was it, as it thoughte me,
That, on his shin a mormal* hadde he.   *ulcer
For blanc manger,[13] that made he with the best.

A Shipman was there, *wonned far by West*:   *who dwelt far to the
390   For ought I wot, be was of Dartemouth.   West*
He rode upon a rouncy*, as he couth,   *hack
All in a gown of falding* to the knee.   *coarse cloth
A dagger hanging by a lace had he
About his neck under his arm adown;
395   The hot summer had made his hue all brown;
And certainly he was a good fellaw.
Full many a draught of wine he had y-draw
From Bourdeaux-ward, while that the chapmen sleep;
Of nice conscience took he no keep.
400   If that he fought, and had the higher hand,
By water he sent them home to every land.   *he drowned his
But of his craft to reckon well his tides,   prisoners*
His streames and his strandes him besides,
His herberow*, his moon, and lodemanage**,   *harbourage; **pilotage
405   There was none such, from Hull unto Carthage
Hardy he was, and wise, I undertake:
With many a tempest had his beard been shake.
He knew well all the havens, as they were,
From Scotland to the Cape of Finisterre,
410   And every creek in Bretagne and in Spain:
His barge y-cleped was the Magdelain.

––––––––––––

13: A type of white pudding.

With us there was a Doctor of Physic;
In all this worlde was there none him like
To speak of physic, and of surgery:
415 For he was grounded in astronomy.
He kept his patient a full great deal
In houres by his magic natural.
Well could he fortune* the ascendent   *make fortunate
Of his images for his patient,.
420 He knew the cause of every malady,
Were it of cold, or hot, or moist, or dry,
And where engender'd, and of what humour.
He was a very perfect practisour
The cause y-know,* and of his harm the root,   *known
425 Anon he gave to the sick man his boot*   *remedy
Full ready had he his apothecaries,
To send his drugges and his lectuaries
For each of them made other for to win
Their friendship was not newe to begin
430 Well knew he the old Esculapius,
And Dioscorides, and eke Rufus;
Old Hippocras, Hali, and Gallien;
Serapion, Rasis, and Avicen;
Averrois, Damascene, and Constantin;
435 Bernard, and Gatisden, and Gilbertin.[14]
Of his diet measurable was he,
For it was of no superfluity,
But of great nourishing, and digestible.
His study was but little on the Bible.
440 In sanguine* and in perse** he clad was all   *red **blue
Lined with taffeta, and with sendall*.   *fine silk
And yet *he was but easy of dispense*:   *he spent very little*
He kept *that he won in the pestilence*.   *the money he made
during the plague*
445 For gold in physic is a cordial;
Therefore he loved gold in special.

A good Wife was there of beside Bath,
But she was somedeal deaf, and that was scath*.   *damage; pity
Of cloth-making she hadde such an haunt*,   *skill
450 She passed them of Ypres, and of Gaunt.
In all the parish wife was there none,
That to the off'ring* before her should gon,   *the offering at mass
And if there did, certain so wroth was she,

14: These are the authors of important medical textbooks of the time.

That she was out of alle charity
455 Her coverchiefs* were full fine of ground   *head-dresses
I durste swear, they weighede ten pound
That on the Sunday were upon her head.
Her hosen weren of fine scarlet red,
Full strait y-tied, and shoes full moist* and new   *fresh, not old
460 Bold was her face, and fair and red of hue.
She was a worthy woman all her live,
Husbands at the church door had she had five,
Withouten other company in youth;
But thereof needeth not to speak as nouth*.   *now
465 And thrice had she been at Jerusalem;
She hadde passed many a strange stream
At Rome she had been, and at Bologne,
In Galice at Saint James*, and at Cologne;   *a shrine in Spain
She coude* much of wand'rng by the Way.   *knew
470 Gat-toothed* was she, soothly for to say.   *gap-toothed[15]
Upon an ambler easily she sat,
Y-wimpled well, and on her head an hat
As broad as is a buckler or a targe.
A foot-mantle about her hippes large,
475 And on her feet a pair of spurres sharp.
In fellowship well could she laugh and carp*   *jest, talk
Of remedies of love she knew perchance
For of that art she coud* the olde dance.   *knew

A good man there was of religion,
480 That was a poore Parson of a town:
But rich he was of holy thought and werk*.   *work
He was also a learned man, a clerk,
That Christe's gospel truly woulde preach.
His parishens* devoutly would he teach.   *parishioners
485 Benign he was, and wonder diligent,
And in adversity full patient:
And such he was y-proved *often sithes*.   *oftentimes*
Full loth were him to curse for his tithes,
But rather would he given out of doubt,
490 Unto his poore parishens about,
Of his off'ring, and eke of his substance.
He could in little thing have suffisance.   *he was satisfied
Wide was his parish, and houses far asunder,   with very little*
But he ne left not, for no rain nor thunder,
495 In sickness and in mischief to visit

15: A sign of wantonness and promiscuity.

The farthest in his parish, *much and lit*,   *great and small*
Upon his feet, and in his hand a staff.
This noble ensample to his sheep he gaf*,   *gave
That first he wrought, and afterward he taught.
500 Out of the gospel he the wordes caught,
And this figure he added yet thereto,
That if gold ruste, what should iron do?
For if a priest be foul, on whom we trust,
No wonder is a lewed* man to rust: *unlearned
505 And shame it is, if that a priest take keep,
To see a shitten shepherd and clean sheep:
Well ought a priest ensample for to give,
By his own cleanness, how his sheep should live.
He sette not his benefice to hire,
510 And left his sheep eucumber'd in the mire,
And ran unto London, unto Saint Paul's,
To seeke him a chantery* for souls,   *donation
Or with a brotherhood to be withold:*   *detained
But dwelt at home, and kepte well his fold,
515 So that the wolf ne made it not miscarry.
He was a shepherd, and no mercenary.
And though he holy were, and virtuous,
He was to sinful men not dispitous*   *severe
Nor of his speeche dangerous nor dign*   *disdainful
520 But in his teaching discreet and benign.
To drawen folk to heaven, with fairness,
By good ensample, was his business:
But it were any person obstinate,   *but if it were*
What so he were of high or low estate,
525 Him would he snibbe* sharply for the nones**.   *reprove **occasion
A better priest I trow that nowhere none is.
He waited after no pomp nor reverence,
Nor maked him a *spiced conscience*,   *artificial conscience*
But Christe's lore, and his apostles' twelve,
530 He taught, and first he follow'd it himselve.

With him there was a Ploughman, was his brother,
That had y-laid of dung full many a fother*.   *ton
A true swinker* and a good was he,   *hard worker
Living in peace and perfect charity.
535 God loved he beste with all his heart
At alle times, were it gain or smart*,   *pain, loss
And then his neighebour right as himselve.
He woulde thresh, and thereto dike*, and delve,   *dig ditches
For Christe's sake, for every poore wight,

540   Withouten hire, if it lay in his might.
       His tithes payed he full fair and well,
       Both of his *proper swink*, and his chattel**   *his own labour* **goods
       In a tabard* he rode upon a mare.   *sleeveless jerkin

       There was also a Reeve, and a Millere,
545   A Sompnour, and a Pardoner also,
       A Manciple, and myself, there were no mo'.

       The Miller was a stout carle for the nones,
       Full big he was of brawn, and eke of bones;
       That proved well, for *ov'r all where* he came,   *wheresoever*
550   At wrestling he would bear away the ram.[16]
       He was short-shouldered, broad, a thicke gnarr*,   *stump of wood
       There was no door, that he n'old* heave off bar,   *could not
       Or break it at a running with his head.
       His beard as any sow or fox was red,
555   And thereto broad, as though it were a spade.
       Upon the cop* right of his nose he had   *head
       A wart, and thereon stood a tuft of hairs
       Red as the bristles of a sowe's ears.
       His nose-thirles* blacke were and wide.   *nostrils
560   A sword and buckler bare he by his side.
       His mouth as wide was as a furnace.
       He was a jangler, and a goliardais*,   *buffoon
       And that was most of sin and harlotries.
       Well could he steale corn, and tolle thrice
565   And yet he had a thumb of gold, pardie.
       A white coat and a blue hood weared he
       A baggepipe well could he blow and soun',
       And therewithal he brought us out of town.

       A gentle Manciple was there of a temple,
570   Of which achatours* mighte take ensample   *buyers
       For to be wise in buying of vitaille*.   *victuals
       For whether that he paid, or took *by taile*,   *on credit
       Algate* he waited so in his achate**,   *always **purchase
       That he was aye before in good estate.
575   Now is not that of God a full fair grace
       That such a lewed* mannes wit shall pace**   *unlearned **surpass
       The wisdom of an heap of learned men?
       Of masters had he more than thries ten,
       That were of law expert and curious:

16: The usual prize at a wrestling match.

580   Of which there was a dozen in that house,
     Worthy to be stewards of rent and land
     Of any lord that is in Engleland,
     To make him live by his proper good,
     In honour debtless, *but if he were wood*,   *unless he were mad*
585   Or live as scarcely as him list desire;
     And able for to helpen all a shire
     In any case that mighte fall or hap;
     And yet this Manciple *set their aller cap*   *outwitted them all*

     The Reeve* was a slender choleric man   *land-steward
590   His beard was shav'd as nigh as ever he can.
     His hair was by his eares round y-shorn;
     His top was docked like a priest beforn
     Full longe were his legges, and full lean
     Y-like a staff, there was no calf y-seen
595   Well could he keep a garner* and a bin*   *storeplaces for grain
     There was no auditor could on him win
     Well wist he by the drought, and by the rain,
     The yielding of his seed and of his grain
     His lorde's sheep, his neat*, and his dairy   *cattle
600   His swine, his horse, his store, and his poultry,
     Were wholly in this Reeve's governing,
     And by his cov'nant gave he reckoning,
     Since that his lord was twenty year of age;
     There could no man bring him in arrearage
605   There was no bailiff, herd, nor other hine*   *servant
     That he ne knew his *sleight and his covine*   *tricks and cheating*
     They were adrad* of him, as of the death   *in dread
     His wonning* was full fair upon an heath   *abode
     With greene trees y-shadow'd was his place.
610   He coulde better than his lord purchase
     Full rich he was y-stored privily
     His lord well could he please subtilly,
     To give and lend him of his owen good,
     And have a thank, and yet* a coat and hood.   *also
615   In youth he learned had a good mistere*   *trade
     He was a well good wright, a carpentere
     This Reeve sate upon a right good stot*,   *steed
     That was all pomely* gray, and highte** Scot.   *dappled **called
     A long surcoat of perse* upon he had,   *sky-blue
620   And by his side he bare a rusty blade.
     Of Norfolk was this Reeve, of which I tell,
     Beside a town men clepen* Baldeswell,   *call
     Tucked he was, as is a friar, about,

hindmost of the group

And ever rode the *hinderest of the rout*.

625 A Sompnour* was there with us in that place,   *summoner[17]
That had a fire-red cherubinnes face,
For sausefleme* he was, with eyen narrow.   *red or pimply
As hot he was and lecherous as a sparrow,
With scalled browes black, and pilled* beard: *scanty
630 Of his visage children were sore afeard.
There n'as quicksilver, litharge, nor brimstone,
Boras, ceruse, nor oil of tartar none,
Nor ointement that woulde cleanse or bite,
That him might helpen of his whelkes* white,   *pustules
635 Nor of the knobbes* sitting on his cheeks.   *buttons
Well lov'd he garlic, onions, and leeks,
And for to drink strong wine as red as blood.
Then would he speak, and cry as he were wood;
And when that he well drunken had the wine,
640 Then would he speake no word but Latin.
A fewe termes knew he, two or three,
That he had learned out of some decree;
No wonder is, he heard it all the day.
And eke ye knowen well, how that a jay
645 Can clepen* "Wat," as well as can the Pope.   *call
But whoso would in other thing him grope*,   *search
Then had he spent all his philosophy,
Aye, *Questio quid juris*, would he cry.   *I ask which law (applies)*

He was a gentle harlot* and a kind;   *a low fellow
650 A better fellow should a man not find.
He woulde suffer, for a quart of wine,
A good fellow to have his concubine
A twelvemonth, and excuse him at the full.
Full privily a *finch eke could he pull*.   *"fleece" a man*
655 And if he found owhere* a good fellaw,   *anywhere
He woulde teach him to have none awe
In such a case of the archdeacon's curse;
But if a manne's soul were in his purse;   *unless*
For in his purse he should y-punished be.
660 "Purse is the archedeacon's hell," said he.
But well I wot, he lied right indeed:
Of cursing ought each guilty man to dread,
For curse will slay right as assoiling* saveth;   *absolving
And also 'ware him of a significavit*.   *a writ of excommunication

---

17: One who summoned people to appear at ecclesiastical courts.

665   In danger had he at his owen guise
       The younge girles[18] of the diocese,
       And knew their counsel, and was of their rede*.   *counsel
       A garland had he set upon his head,
       As great as it were for an alestake*:   *The post of an alehouse sign
670   A buckler had he made him of a cake.

       With him there rode a gentle Pardonere[19]
       Of Ronceval, his friend and his compere,
       That straight was comen from the court of Rome.
       Full loud he sang, "Come hither, love, to me"
675   This Sompnour *bare to him a stiff burdoun*,   *sang the bass*
       Was never trump of half so great a soun'.
       This Pardoner had hair as yellow as wax,
       But smooth it hung, as doth a strike* of flax: *strip
       By ounces hung his lockes that he had,
680   And therewith he his shoulders oversprad.
       Full thin it lay, by culpons* one and one,   *locks, shreds
       But hood for jollity, he weared none,
       For it was trussed up in his wallet.
       Him thought he rode all of the *newe get*,   *latest fashion*
685   Dishevel, save his cap, he rode all bare.
       Such glaring eyen had he, as an hare.
       A vernicle* had he sew'd upon his cap.   *image of Christ
       His wallet lay before him in his lap,
       Bretful* of pardon come from Rome all hot.   *brimful
690   A voice he had as small as hath a goat.
       No beard had he, nor ever one should have.
       As smooth it was as it were new y-shave;
       I trow he were a gelding or a mare.
       But of his craft, from Berwick unto Ware,
695   Ne was there such another pardonere.
       For in his mail* he had a pillowbere**,   *bag; **pillowcase
       Which, as he saide, was our Lady's veil:
       He said, he had a gobbet* of the sail   *piece
       That Sainte Peter had, when that he went
700   Upon the sea, till Jesus Christ him hent*.   *took hold of
       He had a cross of latoun* full of stones,   *copper
       And in a glass he hadde pigge's bones.
       But with these relics, whenne that he fond
       A poore parson dwelling upon lond,
705   Upon a day he got him more money

____

18: Young people of both sexes.
19: A seller of pardons and indulgences.

Than that the parson got in moneths tway;
And thus with feigned flattering and japes*,   *jests
He made the parson and the people his apes.
But truely to tellen at the last,
710   He was in church a noble ecclesiast.
Well could he read a lesson or a story,
But alderbest* he sang an offertory: *best of all
For well he wiste, when that song was sung,
He muste preach, and well afile* his tongue,   *polish
715   To winne silver, as he right well could:
Therefore he sang full merrily and loud.

Now have I told you shortly in a clause
Th' estate, th' array, the number, and eke the cause
Why that assembled was this company
720   In Southwark at this gentle hostelry,
That highte the Tabard, fast by the Bell.
But now is time to you for to tell
How that we baren us that ilke night,   *what we did that same night*
When we were in that hostelry alight.
725   And after will I tell of our voyage,
And all the remnant of our pilgrimage.
But first I pray you of your courtesy,
That ye *arette it not my villainy*,   *count it not rudeness in me*
Though that I plainly speak in this mattere.
730   To tellen you their wordes and their cheer;
Not though I speak their wordes properly.
For this ye knowen all so well as I,
Whoso shall tell a tale after a man,
He must rehearse, as nigh as ever he can,
735   Every word, if it be in his charge,
All speak he ne'er so rudely and so large;   *let him speak*
Or elles he must tell his tale untrue,
Or feigne things, or finde wordes new.
He may not spare, although he were his brother;
740   He must as well say one word as another.
Christ spake Himself full broad in Holy Writ,
And well ye wot no villainy is it.
Eke Plato saith, whoso that can him read,
The wordes must be cousin to the deed.
745   Also I pray you to forgive it me,
All have I not set folk in their degree,   *although I have*
Here in this tale, as that they shoulden stand:
My wit is short, ye may well understand.
Great cheere made our Host us every one,

750 And to the supper set he us anon:
    And served us with victual of the best.
    Strong was the wine, and well to drink us lest*.   *pleased
    A seemly man Our Hoste was withal
    For to have been a marshal in an hall.
755 A large man he was with eyen steep*,   *deep-set
    A fairer burgess is there none in Cheap[20]:
    Bold of his speech, and wise and well y-taught,
    And of manhoode lacked him right naught.
    Eke thereto was he right a merry man,
760 And after supper playen he began,
    And spake of mirth amonges other things,
    When that we hadde made our reckonings;
    And saide thus; "Now, lordinges, truly
    Ye be to me welcome right heartily:
765 For by my troth, if that I shall not lie,
    I saw not this year such a company
    At once in this herberow*, am is now.   *inn
    Fain would I do you mirth, an* I wist* how.   *if I knew*
    And of a mirth I am right now bethought.
770 To do you ease*, and it shall coste nought.   *pleasure
    Ye go to Canterbury; God you speed,
    The blissful Martyr *quite you your meed*;   *grant you what you
    And well I wot, as ye go by the way,   deserve*
    Ye *shapen you* to talken and to play: *intend to*
775 For truely comfort nor mirth is none
    To ride by the way as dumb as stone:
    And therefore would I make you disport,
    As I said erst, and do you some comfort.
    And if you liketh all by one assent
780 Now for to standen at my judgement,
    And for to worken as I shall you say
    To-morrow, when ye riden on the way,
    Now by my father's soule that is dead,
    But ye be merry, smiteth off mine head.   *unless you are merry,
785 Hold up your hands withoute more speech.   smite off*

    Our counsel was not longe for to seech*:   *seek
    Us thought it was not worth to *make it wise*,   *discuss it at length*
    And granted him withoute more avise*,   *consideration
    And bade him say his verdict, as him lest.
790 Lordings (quoth he), now hearken for the best;
    But take it not, I pray you, in disdain;

20: Cheapside, the wealthiest area of London at the time.

This is the point, to speak it plat* and plain.   *flat
That each of you, to shorten with your way
In this voyage, shall tellen tales tway,
795   To Canterbury-ward, I mean it so,
And homeward he shall tellen other two,
Of aventures that whilom have befall.
And which of you that bear'th him best of all,
That is to say, that telleth in this case
800   Tales of best sentence and most solace,
Shall have a supper *at your aller cost*   *at the cost of you all*
Here in this place, sitting by this post,
When that ye come again from Canterbury.
And for to make you the more merry,
805   I will myselfe gladly with you ride,
Right at mine owen cost, and be your guide.
And whoso will my judgement withsay,
Shall pay for all we spenden by the way.
And if ye vouchesafe that it be so,
810   Tell me anon withoute wordes mo'*, *more
And I will early shape me therefore."

This thing was granted, and our oath we swore
With full glad heart, and prayed him also,
That he would vouchesafe for to do so,
815   And that he woulde be our governour,
And of our tales judge and reportour,
And set a supper at a certain price;
And we will ruled be at his device,
In high and low: and thus by one assent,
820   We be accorded to his judgement.
And thereupon the wine was fet* anon.   *fetched.
We drunken, and to reste went each one,
Withouten any longer tarrying
A-morrow, when the day began to spring,
825   Up rose our host, and was *our aller cock*,   *the cock to wake us all*
And gather'd us together in a flock,
And forth we ridden all a little space,
Unto the watering of Saint Thomas:
And there our host began his horse arrest,
830   And saide; "Lordes, hearken if you lest.
Ye *weet your forword,* and I it record.   *know your promise*
If even-song and morning-song accord,
Let see now who shall telle the first tale.
As ever may I drinke wine or ale,
835   Whoso is rebel to my judgement,

Shall pay for all that by the way is spent.
Now draw ye cuts*, ere that ye farther twin**.   *lots **go
He which that hath the shortest shall begin."
"Sir Knight (quoth he), my master and my lord,
840 Now draw the cut, for that is mine accord.
Come near (quoth he), my Lady Prioress,
And ye, Sir Clerk, let be your shamefastness,
Nor study not: lay hand to, every man."
Anon to drawen every wight began,
845 And shortly for to tellen as it was,
Were it by a venture, or sort*, or cas**,   *lot **chance
The sooth is this, the cut fell to the Knight,
Of which full blithe and glad was every wight;
And tell he must his tale as was reason,
850 By forword, and by composition,
As ye have heard; what needeth wordes mo'?
And when this good man saw that it was so,
As he that wise was and obedient
To keep his forword by his free assent,
855 He said; "Sithen* I shall begin this game,   *since
Why, welcome be the cut in Godde's name.
Now let us ride, and hearken what I say."
And with that word we ridden forth our way;
And he began with right a merry cheer
860 His tale anon, and said as ye shall hear.

The Miller's Tale

The Prologue

When that the Knight had thus his tale told
In all the rout was neither young nor old,
That he not said it was a noble story,
And worthy to be *drawn to memory*;   *recorded*
5   And *namely the gentles* every one.   *especially the gentlefolk*
Our Host then laugh'd and swore, "So may I gon,*   *prosper
This goes aright; *unbuckled is the mail;*   *the budget is opened*
Let see now who shall tell another tale:
For truely this game is well begun.
10 Now telleth ye, Sir Monk, if that ye conne*,   *know
Somewhat, to quiten* with the Knighte's tale."   *match
The Miller that fordrunken was all pale,
So that unnethes* upon his horse he sat,   *with difficulty
He would avalen* neither hood nor hat,   *uncover
15 Nor abide* no man for his courtesy,   *give way to
But in Pilate's voice[21] he gan to cry,
And swore by armes, and by blood, and bones,
"I can a noble tale for the nones*   *occasion,
With which I will now quite* the Knighte's tale."   *match
20 Our Host saw well how drunk he was of ale,
And said; "Robin, abide, my leve* brother,   *dear
Some better man shall tell us first another:
Abide, and let us worke thriftily."
By Godde's soul," quoth he, "that will not I,
25 For I will speak, or elles go my way!"
Our Host answer'd; "*Tell on a devil way*;   *devil take you!*
Thou art a fool; thy wit is overcome."
"Now hearken," quoth the Miller, "all and some:
But first I make a protestatioun.
30 That I am drunk, I know it by my soun':
And therefore if that I misspeak or say,
Wite it the ale of Southwark, I you pray: *blame it on*
For I will tell a legend and a life
Both of a carpenter and of his wife,
35 How that a clerk hath *set the wrighte's cap*."   *fooled the carpenter*
The Reeve answer'd and saide, "*Stint thy clap*,   *hold your tongue*

21: A harsh, gruff voice, like that of Pontius Pilate.

Let be thy lewed drunken harlotry.
It is a sin, and eke a great folly
To apeiren* any man, or him defame,   *injure
40   And eke to bringe wives in evil name.
Thou may'st enough of other thinges sayn."
This drunken Miller spake full soon again,
And saide, "Leve brother Osewold,
Who hath no wife, he is no cuckold.
45   But I say not therefore that thou art one;
There be full goode wives many one.
Why art thou angry with my tale now?
I have a wife, pardie, as well as thou,
Yet *n'old I*, for the oxen in my plough,   *I would not*
50   Taken upon me more than enough,
To deemen* of myself that I am one;   *judge
I will believe well that I am none.
An husband should not be inquisitive
Of Godde's privity, nor of his wife.
55   So he may finde Godde's foison* there,   *treasure
Of the remnant needeth not to enquere."
What should I more say, but that this Millere
He would his wordes for no man forbear,
But told his churlish* tale in his mannere;   *boorish, rude
60   Me thinketh, that I shall rehearse it here.
And therefore every gentle wight I pray,
For Godde's love to deem not that I say
Of evil intent, but that I must rehearse
Their tales all, be they better or worse,
65   Or elles falsen* some of my mattere.   *falsify
And therefore whoso list it not to hear,
Turn o'er the leaf, and choose another tale;
For he shall find enough, both great and smale,
Of storial* thing that toucheth gentiless,   *historical, true
70   And eke morality and holiness.
Blame not me, if that ye choose amiss.
The Miller is a churl, ye know well this,
So was the Reeve, with many other mo',
And harlotry* they tolde bothe two.   *ribald tales
75   *Avise you* now, and put me out of blame;   *be warned*
And eke men should not make earnest of game*.   *jest, fun

THE TALE

Whilom there was dwelling in Oxenford
   A riche gnof*, that *guestes held to board*,   *miser; *took in boarders*

And of his craft he was a carpenter.
With him there was dwelling a poor scholer,
5   Had learned art, but all his fantasy
Was turned for to learn astrology.
He coude* a certain of conclusions   *knew
To deeme* by interrogations,   *determine
If that men asked him in certain hours,
10 When that men should have drought or elles show'rs:
Or if men asked him what shoulde fall
Of everything, I may not reckon all.

This clerk was called Hendy* Nicholas;   *gentle, handsome
Of derne* love he knew and of solace;   *secret, earnest
15 And therewith he was sly and full privy,
And like a maiden meek for to see.
A chamber had he in that hostelry
Alone, withouten any company,
Full *fetisly y-dight* with herbes swoot*,   *neatly decorated*
20 And he himself was sweet as is the root   *sweet
Of liquorice, or any setewall*.   *valerian
His Almagest[22], and bookes great and small,
His astrolabe, belonging to his art,
His augrim* stones, layed fair apart   *counting
25 On shelves couched* at his bedde's head,   *laid, set
His press y-cover'd with a falding* red.   *coarse cloth
And all above there lay a gay psalt'ry
On which he made at nightes melody,
So sweetely, that all the chamber rang:
30 And *Angelus ad virginem* he sang.   *Ave Maria*
And after that he sung the kinge's note;
Full often blessed was his merry throat.
And thus this sweete clerk his time spent
After *his friendes finding and his rent.*   *Attending to his friends,
35 This carpenter had wedded new a wife,   and providing for the
Which that he loved more than his life: cost of his lodging*
Of eighteen year, I guess, she was of age.
Jealous he was, and held her narr'w in cage,
For she was wild and young, and he was old,
40 And deemed himself belike* a cuckold.   *perhaps
He knew not Cato, for his wit was rude,
That bade a man wed his similitude.
Men shoulde wedden after their estate,
For youth and eld* are often at debate.   *age

22: Ptolemy's astrological book.

45   But since that he was fallen in the snare,
       He must endure (as other folk) his care.
       Fair was this younge wife, and therewithal
       As any weasel her body gent* and small.   *slim, neat
       A seint* she weared, barred all of silk,   *girdle
50   A barm-cloth* eke as white as morning milk   *apron
       Upon her lendes*, full of many a gore**.   *loins; **plait
       White was her smock*, and broider'd all before,   *robe or gown
       And eke behind, on her collar about
       Of coal-black silk, within and eke without.
55   The tapes of her white volupere*   *head-kerchief
       Were of the same suit of her collere;
       Her fillet broad of silk, and set full high:
       And sickerly* she had a likerous** eye.   *certainly; **lascivious
       Full small y-pulled were her browes two,
60   And they were bent*, and black as any sloe.   *arched
       She was well more *blissful on to see*   *pleasant to look upon*
       Than is the newe perjenete* tree;   *young pear-tree
       And softer than the wool is of a wether.
       And by her girdle hung a purse of leather,
65   Tassel'd with silk, and *pearled with latoun*.   *set with brass pearls*
       In all this world to seeken up and down
       There is no man so wise, that coude thenche*   *imagine
       So gay a popelot*, or such a wench.   *young woman
       Full brighter was the shining of her hue,
70   Than in the Tower the noble* forged new.   *a shiny gold coin
       But of her song, it was as loud and yern*,   *lively
       As any swallow chittering on a bern*.   *barn
       Thereto* she coulde skip, and *make a game*   *also; *romp*
       As any kid or calf following his dame.
75   Her mouth was sweet as braket[23], or as methe*   *mead
       Or hoard of apples, laid in hay or heath.
       Wincing* she was as is a jolly colt,   *skittish
       Long as a mast, and upright as a bolt.
       A brooch she bare upon her low collere,
80   As broad as is the boss of a bucklere.
       Her shoon were laced on her legges high;
       She was a primerole,* a piggesnie**,   *primrose; **darling
       For any lord t' have ligging* in his bed,   *lying
       Or yet for any good yeoman to wed.

85   Now, sir, and eft* sir, so befell the case,   *again
       That on a day this Hendy Nicholas

23: A sweet drink made from honey and spices.

Fell with this younge wife to rage* and play, *toy, play the rogue
While that her husband was at Oseney,[24]
As clerkes be full subtle and full quaint.
90   And privily he caught her by the queint,* *cunt
And said; "Y-wis,* but if I have my will, *assuredly
For *derne love of thee, leman, I spill."* *for earnest love of thee
And helde her fast by the haunche bones, my mistress, I perish*
And saide "Leman, love me well at once,
95   Or I will dien, all so God me save."
And she sprang as a colt doth in the trave[25]:
And with her head she writhed fast away,
And said; "I will not kiss thee, by my fay*. *faith
Why let be," quoth she, "let be, Nicholas,
100   Or I will cry out harow* and alas! *help
Do away your handes, for your courtesy."
This Nicholas gan mercy for to cry,
And spake so fair, and proffer'd him so fast,
That she her love him granted at the last,
105   And swore her oath by Saint Thomas of Kent,
That she would be at his commandement,
When that she may her leisure well espy.
"My husband is so full of jealousy,
That but* ye waite well, and be privy, *unless
110   I wot right well I am but dead," quoth she.
"Ye muste be full derne* as in this case." *secret
"Nay, thereof care thee nought," quoth Nicholas:
"A clerk had *litherly beset his while*, *ill spent his time*
But if he could a carpenter beguile." *unless
115   And thus they were accorded and y-sworn
To wait a time, as I have said beforn.
When Nicholas had done thus every deal*, *whit
And thwacked her about the lendes* well, *loins
He kiss'd her sweet, and taketh his psalt'ry
120   And playeth fast, and maketh melody.
Then fell it thus, that to the parish church,
Of Christe's owen workes for to wirch*, *work
This good wife went upon a holy day;
Her forehead shone as bright as any day,
125   So was it washen, when she left her werk.
Now was there of that church a parish clerk,
The which that was y-cleped Absolon.
Curl'd was his hair, and as the gold it shone,

24: An abbey near Oxford.
25: A pen for unruly horses.

	And strutted* as a fanne large and broad;	*stretched
130	Full straight and even lay his jolly shode*.	*head of hair
	His rode* was red, his eyen grey as goose,	*complexion
	With Paule's windows carven on his shoes[26]	
	In hosen red he went full fetisly*.	*daintily, neatly
	Y-clad he was full small and properly,	
135	All in a kirtle* of a light waget*;	*girdle; **sky blue
	Full fair and thicke be the pointes set,	
	And thereupon he had a gay surplice,	
	As white as is the blossom on the rise*.	*twig
	A merry child he was, so God me save;	
140	Well could he letten blood, and clip, and shave,	
	And make a charter of land, and a quittance.	
	In twenty manners could he trip and dance,	
	After the school of Oxenforde tho*,	*then
	And with his legges caste to and fro;	
145	And playen songes on a small ribible*;	*fiddle
	Thereto he sung sometimes a loud quinible*	*treble
	And as well could he play on a gitern.*	*guitar
	In all the town was brewhouse nor tavern,	
	That he not visited with his solas*,	*mirth, sport
150	There as that any *garnard tapstere* was.	*licentious barmaid*
	But sooth to say he was somedeal squaimous*	*squeamish
	Of farting, and of speeche dangerous.	
	This Absolon, that jolly was and gay,	
	Went with a censer on the holy day,	
155	Censing* the wives of the parish fast;	*burning incense for
	And many a lovely look he on them cast,	
	And namely* on this carpenter's wife:	*especially
	To look on her him thought a merry life.	
	She was so proper, and sweet, and likerous.	
160	I dare well say, if she had been a mouse,	
	And he a cat, he would *her hent anon*.	*have soon caught her*
	This parish clerk, this jolly Absolon,	
	Hath in his hearte such a love-longing!	
	That of no wife took he none offering;	
165	For courtesy he said he woulde none.	
	The moon at night full clear and brighte shone,	
	And Absolon his gitern hath y-taken,	
	For paramours he thoughte for to waken,	
	And forth he went, jolif* and amorous,	*joyous
170	Till he came to the carpentere's house,	
	A little after the cock had y-crow,	

26: His shoes were ornamented like the windows of St. Paul's.

And *dressed him* under a shot window,   *stationed himself.*
That was upon the carpentere's wall.
He singeth in his voice gentle and small;
175 "Now, dear lady, if thy will be,
I pray that ye will rue* on me;"   *take pity
Full well accordant to his giterning.
This carpenter awoke, and heard him sing,
And spake unto his wife, and said anon,
180 What Alison, hear'st thou not Absolon,
That chanteth thus under our bower* wall?"   *chamber
And she answer'd her husband therewithal;
"Yes, God wot, John, I hear him every deal."
This passeth forth; what will ye bet* than well?   *better

185 From day to day this jolly Absolon
So wooeth her, that him is woebegone.
He waketh all the night, and all the day,
To comb his lockes broad, and make him gay.
He wooeth her *by means and by brocage*,   *by presents and by agents*
190 And swore he woulde be her owen page.
He singeth brokking* as a nightingale.   *quavering
He sent her piment[27], mead, and spiced ale,
And wafers* piping hot out of the glede**:   *cakes; **coals
And, *for she was of town, he proffer'd meed.*   *As she was from town,
195 For some folk will be wonnen for richess,   he offered wealth.*
And some for strokes, and some with gentiless.
Sometimes, to show his lightness and mast'ry,
He playeth Herod[28] on a scaffold high.
But what availeth him as in this case?
200 So loveth she the Hendy Nicholas,
That Absolon may *blow the bucke's horn*:   *"go whistle"*
He had for all his labour but a scorn.
And thus she maketh Absolon her ape,
And all his earnest turneth to a jape*.   *jest
205 Full sooth is this proverb, it is no lie;
Men say right thus alway; the nighe sly
Maketh oft time the far lief to be loth.[29]
For though that Absolon be wood* or wroth   *mad
Because that he far was from her sight,
210 This nigh Nicholas stood still in his light.
Now bear thee well, thou Hendy Nicholas,

27: A drink made with wine, honey, and spices.
28: He acted a leading role in a church mystery-play.
29: A proverb: the cunning one near at hand often makes the loving one far off
odious.

For Absolon may wail and sing "Alas!"
And so befell, that on a Saturday
This carpenter was gone to Oseney,
215 And Hendy Nicholas and Alison
Accorded were to this conclusion,
That Nicholas shall *shape him a wile*   *devise a stratagem*
The silly jealous husband to beguile;
And if so were the game went aright,
220 She shoulde sleepen in his arms all night;
For this was her desire and his also.
And right anon, withoute wordes mo',
This Nicholas no longer would he tarry,
But doth full soft unto his chamber carry
225 Both meat and drinke for a day or tway.
And to her husband bade her for to say,
If that he asked after Nicholas,
She shoulde say, "She wist* not where he was;   *knew
Of all the day she saw him not with eye;
230 She trowed* he was in some malady,   *believed
For no cry that her maiden could him call
He would answer, for nought that might befall."
Thus passed forth all thilke* Saturday,   *that
That Nicholas still in his chamber lay,
235 And ate, and slept, and didde what him list
Till Sunday, that* the sunne went to rest.   *when
This silly carpenter *had great marvaill*   *wondered greatly*
Of Nicholas, or what thing might him ail,
And said; "I am adrad*, by Saint Thomas!   *afraid, in dread
240 It standeth not aright with Nicholas:
God shielde that he died suddenly.   *heaven forbid!*
This world is now full fickle sickerly*.   *certainly
I saw to-day a corpse y-borne to chirch,
That now on Monday last I saw him wirch*.   *work
245 "Go up," quod he unto his knave*, "anon;   *servant.
Clepe* at his door, or knocke with a stone: *call
Look how it is, and tell me boldely."
This knave went him up full sturdily,
And, at the chamber door while that he stood,
250 He cried and knocked as that he were wood:*   *mad
"What how? what do ye, Master Nicholay?
How may ye sleepen all the longe day?"
But all for nought, he hearde not a word.
An hole he found full low upon the board,
255 Where as the cat was wont in for to creep,
And at that hole he looked in full deep,

And at the last he had of him a sight.
This Nicholas sat ever gaping upright,
As he had kyked* on the newe moon.   *looked
260 Adown he went, and told his master soon,
In what array he saw this ilke* man.   *same

This carpenter to *blissen him* began,   *bless, cross himself*
And said: "Now help us, Sainte Frideswide[30].
A man wot* little what shall him betide.   *knows
265 This man is fall'n with his astronomy
Into some woodness* or some agony.   *madness
I thought aye well how that it shoulde be.
Men should know nought of Godde's privity*.   *secrets
Yea, blessed be alway a lewed* man,   *unlearned
270 That *nought but only his believe can*.   *knows no more than
So far'd another clerk with astronomy: his "credo."*
He walked in the fieldes for to *pry
Upon* the starres, what there should befall,   *keep watch on*
Till he was in a marle pit y-fall.
275 He saw not that. But yet, by Saint Thomas!
Me rueth sore of Hendy Nicholas: *I am very sorry for*
He shall be *rated of* his studying,   *chidden for*
If that I may, by Jesus, heaven's king!
Get me a staff, that I may underspore*   *lever up
280 While that thou, Robin, heavest off the door:
He shall out of his studying, as I guess."
And to the chamber door he gan him dress*   *apply himself.
His knave was a strong carl for the nonce,
And by the hasp he heav'd it off at once;
285 Into the floor the door fell down anon.
This Nicholas sat aye as still as stone,
And ever he gap'd upward into the air.
The carpenter ween'd* he were in despair,   *thought
And hent* him by the shoulders mightily,   *caught
290 And shook him hard, and cried spitously;*   *angrily
"What, Nicholas? what how, man? look adown:
Awake, and think on Christe's passioun.
I crouche thee from elves, and from wights*.   *witches
Therewith the night-spell said he anon rights*,   *properly
295 On the four halves* of the house about,   *corners
And on the threshold of the door without.
"Lord Jesus Christ, and Sainte Benedight,
Blesse this house from every wicked wight,

30: The patroness of a large Oxford priory.

From the night mare, the white Pater-noster;
300   Where wonnest* thou now, Sainte Peter's sister?"   *dwellest
And at the last this Hendy Nicholas
Gan for to sigh full sore, and said; "Alas!
Shall all time world be lost eftsoones* now?"   *forthwith
This carpenter answer'd; "What sayest thou?
305   What? think on God, as we do, men that swink.*"   *labor
This Nicholas answer'd; "Fetch me a drink;
And after will I speak in privity
Of certain thing that toucheth thee and me:
I will tell it no other man certain."
310   This carpenter went down, and came again,
And brought of mighty ale a large quart;
And when that each of them had drunk his part,
This Nicholas his chamber door fast shet*,   *shut
And down the carpenter by him he set,
315   And saide; "John, mine host full lief* and dear,   *loved
Thou shalt upon thy truthe swear me here,
That to no wight thou shalt my counsel wray*:   *betray
For it is Christes counsel that I say,
And if thou tell it man, thou art forlore:*   *lost
320   For this vengeance thou shalt have therefor,
That if thou wraye* me, thou shalt be wood**."   *betray; **mad
"Nay, Christ forbid it for his holy blood!"
Quoth then this silly man; "I am no blab,*   *talker
Nor, though I say it, am I *lief to gab*.   *fond of speech*
325   Say what thou wilt, I shall it never tell
To child or wife, by *him that harried Hell*."   *Christ*
"Now, John," quoth Nicholas, "I will not lie,
I have y-found in my astrology,
As I have looked in the moone bright,
330   That now on Monday next, at quarter night,
Shall fall a rain, and that so wild and wood*,   *mad
That never half so great was Noe's flood.
This world," he said, "in less than half an hour
Shall all be dreint*, so hideous is the shower: *drowned
335   Thus shall mankinde drench*, and lose their life."   *drown
This carpenter answer'd; "Alas, my wife!
And shall she drench? alas, mine Alisoun!"
For sorrow of this he fell almost adown,
And said; "Is there no remedy in this case?"
340   "Why, yes, for God," quoth Hendy Nicholas;
"If thou wilt worken after *lore and rede*;   *learning and advice*
Thou may'st not worken after thine own head.
For thus saith Solomon, that was full true:

Work all by counsel, and thou shalt not rue*.   *repent
345 And if thou worke wilt by good counseil,
I undertake, withoute mast or sail,
Yet shall I save her, and thee, and me.
Hast thou not heard how saved was Noe,
When that our Lord had warned him beforn,
350 That all the world with water *should be lorn*?"   *should perish*
"Yes," quoth this carpenter," *full yore ago*."   *long since*
"Hast thou not heard," quoth Nicholas, "also
The sorrow of Noe, with his fellowship,
That he had ere he got his wife to ship?[31]
355 *Him had been lever, I dare well undertake,   *At that time he would have
At thilke time, than all his wethers black,   given all his black wethers,
That she had had a ship herself alone.*   if she had had an ark to
And therefore know'st thou what is best to be done?   herself.*
This asketh haste, and of an hasty thing
360 Men may not preach or make tarrying.
Anon go get us fast into this inn*   *house
A kneading trough, or else a kemelin*,   *brewing-tub
For each of us; but look that they be large,
In whiche we may swim* as in a barge: *float
365 And have therein vitaille suffisant
But for one day; fie on the remenant;
The water shall aslake* and go away   *slacken, abate
Aboute prime* upon the nexte day.   *early morning
But Robin may not know of this, thy knave*,   *servant
370 Nor eke thy maiden Gill I may not save:
Ask me not why: for though thou aske me
I will not telle Godde's privity.
Sufficeth thee, *but if thy wit be mad*,   *unless thou be out of thy wits*
To have as great a grace as Noe had;
375 Thy wife shall I well saven out of doubt.
Go now thy way, and speed thee hereabout.
But when thou hast for her, and thee, and me,
Y-gotten us these kneading tubbes three,
Then shalt thou hang them in the roof full high,
380 So that no man our purveyance* espy: *foresight, providence
And when thou hast done thus as I have said,
And hast our vitaille fair in them y-laid,
And eke an axe to smite the cord in two
When that the water comes, that we may go,
385 And break an hole on high upon the gable

31: According to the old mysteries, Noah's wife refused to come into the ark, and bade her husband row forth and get him a new wife, because he was leaving her friends in the town to drown. Shem and his brothers got her onto the ship by force.

Into the garden-ward, over the stable,
That we may freely passe forth our way,
When that the greate shower is gone away.
Then shalt thou swim as merry, I undertake,
390   As doth the white duck after her drake:
Then will I clepe,* 'How, Alison? How, John?   *call
Be merry: for the flood will pass anon.'
And thou wilt say, 'Hail, Master Nicholay,
Good-morrow, I see thee well, for it is day.'
395   And then shall we be lordes all our life
Of all the world, as Noe and his wife.
But of one thing I warne thee full right,
Be well advised, on that ilke* night,   *same
When we be enter'd into shippe's board,
400   That none of us not speak a single word,
Nor clepe nor cry, but be in his prayere,
For that is Godde's owen heste* dear.   *command
Thy wife and thou must hangen far atween*,   *asunder
For that betwixte you shall be no sin,
405   No more in looking than there shall in deed.
This ordinance is said: go, God thee speed
To-morrow night, when men be all asleep,
Into our kneading tubbes will we creep,
And sitte there, abiding Godde's grace.
410   Go now thy way, I have no longer space
To make of this no longer sermoning:
Men say thus: Send the wise, and say nothing:
Thou art so wise, it needeth thee nought teach.
Go, save our lives, and that I thee beseech."
415   This silly carpenter went forth his way,
Full oft he said, "Alas! and Well-a-day!,'
And to his wife he told his privity,
And she was ware, and better knew than he
What all this *quainte cast was for to say*.   *strange contrivance meant*
420   But natheless she fear'd as she would dey,
And said: "Alas! go forth thy way anon.
Help us to scape, or we be dead each one.
I am thy true and very wedded wife;
Go, deare spouse, and help to save our life."
425   Lo, what a great thing is affection!
Men may die of imagination,
So deeply may impression be take.
This silly carpenter begins to quake:
He thinketh verily that he may see
430   This newe flood come weltering as the sea

To drenchen* Alison, his honey dear.   *drown
He weepeth, waileth, maketh *sorry cheer*;   *dismal countenance*
He sigheth, with full many a sorry sough.*   *groan
He go'th, and getteth him a kneading trough,
435 And after that a tub, and a kemelin,
And privily he sent them to his inn:
And hung them in the roof full privily.
With his own hand then made he ladders three,
To climbe by *the ranges and the stalks*   *the rungs and the uprights*
440 Unto the tubbes hanging in the balks*;   *beams
And victualed them, kemelin, trough, and tub,
With bread and cheese, and good ale in a jub*,   *jug
Sufficing right enough as for a day.
But ere that he had made all this array,
445 He sent his knave*, and eke his wench** also,   *servant; **maid
Upon his need* to London for to go.   *business
And on the Monday, when it drew to night,
He shut his door withoute candle light,
And dressed* every thing as it should be.   *prepared
450 And shortly up they climbed all the three.
They satte stille well *a furlong way*.   *the time it would take to
"Now, Pater noster, clum," said Nicholay,   walk a furlong*
And "clum," quoth John; and "clum," said Alison:
This carpenter said his devotion,
455 And still he sat and bidded his prayere,
Awaking on the rain, if he it hear.
The deade sleep, for weary business,
Fell on this carpenter, right as I guess,
About the curfew-time[32], or little more,
460 For *travail of his ghost* he groaned sore,   *anguish of spirit*
And eft he routed, for his head mislay.   *and then he snored,
Adown the ladder stalked Nicholay;   for his head lay awry*
And Alison full soft adown she sped.
Withoute wordes more they went to bed,
465 *There as* the carpenter was wont to lie: *where*
There was the revel, and the melody.
And thus lay Alison and Nicholas,
In business of mirth and in solace,
Until the bell of laudes* gan to ring,   *morning service, at 3.a.m.
470 And friars in the chancel went to sing.
This parish clerk, this amorous Absolon,
That is for love alway so woebegone,
Upon the Monday was at Oseney

32: 8PM.

With company, him to disport and play;
475 And asked upon cas* a cloisterer**   *occasion; **monk
Full privily after John the carpenter;
And he drew him apart out of the church,
And said, "I n'ot;* I saw him not here wirch**   *know not; **work
Since Saturday; I trow that he be went
480 For timber, where our abbot hath him sent.
And dwellen at the Grange a day or two:
For he is wont for timber for to go,
Or else he is at his own house certain.
Where that he be, I cannot *soothly sayn.*"   *say certainly*
485 This Absolon full jolly was and light,
And thought, "Now is the time to wake all night,
For sickerly* I saw him not stirring   *certainly
About his door, since day began to spring.
So may I thrive, but I shall at cock crow
490 Full privily go knock at his window,
That stands full low upon his bower* wall: *chamber
To Alison then will I tellen all
My love-longing; for I shall not miss
That at the leaste way I shall her kiss.
495 Some manner comfort shall I have, parfay*,   *by my faith
My mouth hath itched all this livelong day:
That is a sign of kissing at the least.
All night I mette* eke I was at a feast.   *dreamt
Therefore I will go sleep an hour or tway,
500 And all the night then will I wake and play."
When that the first cock crowed had, anon
Up rose this jolly lover Absolon,
And him arrayed gay, *at point devise.*   *with exact care*
But first he chewed grains* and liquorice,   *spices
505 To smelle sweet, ere he had combed his hair.
Under his tongue a true love[33] he bare,
For thereby thought he to be gracious.
Then came he to the carpentere's house,
And still he stood under the shot window;
510 Unto his breast it raught*, it was so low;   *reached
And soft he coughed with a semisoun'.*   *low tone
"What do ye, honeycomb, sweet Alisoun?
My faire bird, my sweet cinamome*,   *cinnamon, sweet spice
Awaken, leman* mine, and speak to me.   *mistress
515 Full little thinke ye upon my woe,
That for your love I sweat *there as* I go.   *wherever

____

33: Some type of sweet herb.

No wonder is that I do swelt* and sweat.   *faint
I mourn as doth a lamb after the teat
Y-wis*, leman, I have such love-longing,   *certainly
520   That like a turtle* true is my mourning.   *turtle-dove
I may not eat, no more than a maid."
"Go from the window, thou jack fool," she said:
"As help me God, it will not be, 'come ba* me.'   *kiss
I love another, else I were to blame",
525   Well better than thee, by Jesus, Absolon.
Go forth thy way, or I will cast a stone;
And let me sleep; *a twenty devil way*.   *twenty devils take ye!*
"Alas!" quoth Absolon, "and well away!
That true love ever was so ill beset:
530   Then kiss me, since that it may be no bet*,   *better
For Jesus' love, and for the love of me."
"Wilt thou then go thy way therewith?" , quoth she.
"Yea, certes, leman," quoth this Absolon.
"Then make thee ready," quoth she, "I come anon."
535   And unto Nicholas she said *full still*:   *in a low voice*
"Now peace, and thou shalt laugh anon thy fill."
This Absolon down set him on his knees,
And said; "I am a lord at all degrees:
For after this I hope there cometh more;
540   Leman, thy grace, and, sweete bird, thine ore.*"   *favour
The window she undid, and that in haste.
"Have done," quoth she, "come off, and speed thee fast,
Lest that our neighebours should thee espy."
Then Absolon gan wipe his mouth full dry.
545   Dark was the night as pitch or as the coal,
And at the window she put out her hole,
And Absolon him fell ne bet ne werse,
But with his mouth he kiss'd her naked erse*   *arse
Full savourly. When he was ware of this,
550   Aback he start, and thought it was amiss;
For well he wist a woman hath no beard.
He felt a thing all rough, and long y-hair'd,
And saide; "Fy, alas! what have I do?"
"Tee hee!" quoth she, and clapt the window to;
555   And Absolon went forth at sorry pace.
"A beard, a beard," said Hendy Nicholas;
"By God's corpus, this game went fair and well."
This silly Absolon heard every deal*,   *word
And on his lip he gan for anger bite;
560   And to himself he said, "I shall thee quite*.   *requite, be even with
Who rubbeth now, who frotteth* now his lips   *rubs

With dust, with sand, with straw, with cloth, with chips,
But Absolon? that saith full oft, "Alas!
My soul betake I unto Sathanas,
565 But me were lever* than all this town," quoth he   *rather
I this despite awroken* for to be.   *revenged
Alas! alas! that I have been y-blent*."   *deceived
His hote love is cold, and all y-quent.*   *quenched
For from that time that he had kiss'd her erse,
570 Of paramours he *sette not a kers,*   *cared not a rush*
For he was healed of his malady;
Full often paramours he gan defy,
And weep as doth a child that hath been beat.
A softe pace he went over the street
575 Unto a smith, men callen Dan* Gerveis,   *master
That in his forge smithed plough-harness;
He sharped share and culter busily.
This Absolon knocked all easily,
And said; "Undo, Gerveis, and that anon."
580 "What, who art thou?" "It is I, Absolon."
"What? Absolon, what? Christe's sweete tree*,   *cross
Why rise so rath*? hey! Benedicite,   *early
What aileth you? some gay girl, God it wote,
Hath brought you thus upon the viretote:
585 By Saint Neot, ye wot well what I mean."
This Absolon he raughte* not a bean   *cared
Of all his play; no word again he gaf*,   *spoke
For he had *more tow on his distaff*   *more serious business*
Than Gerveis knew, and saide; "Friend so dear,
590 That hote culter in the chimney here
Lend it to me, I have therewith to don*:   *do
I will it bring again to thee full soon."
Gerveis answered; "Certes, were it gold,
Or in a poke* nobles all untold,   *purse
595 Thou shouldst it have, as I am a true smith.
Hey! Christe's foot, what will ye do therewith?"
"Thereof," quoth Absolon, "be as be may;
I shall well tell it thee another day:"
And caught the culter by the colde stele*.   *handle
600 Full soft out at the door he gan to steal,
And went unto the carpentere's wall
He coughed first, and knocked therewithal
Upon the window, light as he did ere*.   *before
This Alison answered; "Who is there
605 That knocketh so? I warrant him a thief."
"Nay, nay," quoth he, "God wot, my sweete lefe*,   *love

I am thine Absolon, my own darling.
Of gold," quoth he, "I have thee brought a ring,
My mother gave it me, so God me save!
610 Full fine it is, and thereto well y-grave*:   *engraved
This will I give to thee, if thou me kiss."
Now Nicholas was risen up to piss,
And thought he would *amenden all the jape*;   *improve the joke*
He shoulde kiss his erse ere that he scape:
615 And up the window did he hastily,
And out his erse he put full privily
Over the buttock, to the haunche bone.
And therewith spake this clerk, this Absolon,
"Speak, sweete bird, I know not where thou art."
620 This Nicholas anon let fly a fart,
As great as it had been a thunder dent*;   *peal, clap
That with the stroke he was well nigh y-blent*;   *blinded
But he was ready with his iron hot,
And Nicholas amid the erse* he smote.   *arse
625 Off went the skin an handbreadth all about.
The hote culter burned so his tout,
That for the smart he weened* he would die;   *thought
As he were wood*, for woe he gan to cry,   *mad
"Help! water, water, help for Godde's heart!"
630 This carpenter out of his slumber start,
And heard one cry "Water," as he were wood*,   *mad
And thought, "Alas! now cometh Noe's flood."
He sat him up withoute wordes mo'
And with his axe he smote the cord in two;
635 And down went all; he found neither to sell
Nor bread nor ale, till he came to the sell*,   *threshold
Upon the floor, and there in swoon he lay.
Up started Alison and Nicholay,
And cried out an "harow*!" in the street.   *help
640 The neighbours alle, bothe small and great
In ranne, for to gauren* on this man,   *stare
That yet in swoone lay, both pale and wan:
For with the fall he broken had his arm.
But stand he must unto his owen harm,
645 For when he spake, he was anon borne down
With Hendy Nicholas and Alisoun.
They told to every man that he was wood*;   *mad
He was aghaste* so of Noe's flood,   *afraid
Through phantasy, that of his vanity
650 He had y-bought him kneading-tubbes three,
And had them hanged in the roof above;

And that he prayed them for Godde's love
To sitten in the roof for company.
The folk gan laughen at his phantasy.
655   Into the roof they kyken* and they gape,   *peep, look.
And turned all his harm into a jape*.   *jest
For whatsoe'er this carpenter answer'd,
It was for nought, no man his reason heard.
With oathes great he was so sworn adown,
660   That he was holden wood in all the town.
For every clerk anon right held with other;
They said, "The man was wood, my leve* brother;"   *dear
And every wight gan laughen at his strife.
Thus swived* was the carpentere's wife,   *enjoyed
665   For all his keeping* and his jealousy;   *care
And Absolon hath kiss'd her nether eye;
And Nicholas is scalded in the tout.
This tale is done, and God save all the rout*.   *company

The Wife of Bath's Tale

The Prologue

Experience, though none authority*   *authoritative texts
Were in this world, is right enough for me
To speak of woe that is in marriage:
For, lordings, since I twelve year was of age,
5 (Thanked be God that *is etern on live),*   *lives eternally*
Husbands at the church door have I had five,
For I so often have y-wedded be,
And all were worthy men in their degree.
But me was told, not longe time gone is
10 That sithen* Christe went never but ones   *since
To wedding, in the Cane* of Galilee,   *Cana
That by that ilk* example taught he me,   *same
That I not wedded shoulde be but once.
Lo, hearken eke a sharp word for the nonce,* *occasion
15 Beside a welle Jesus, God and man,
Spake in reproof of the Samaritan:
"Thou hast y-had five husbandes," said he;
"And thilke* man, that now hath wedded thee, *that
Is not thine husband:" thus said he certain;
20 What that he meant thereby, I cannot sayn.
But that I aske, why the fifthe man
Was not husband to the Samaritan?
How many might she have in marriage?
Yet heard I never tellen *in mine age*   *in my life*
25 Upon this number definitioun.
Men may divine, and glosen* up and down; *comment
But well I wot, express without a lie,
God bade us for to wax and multiply;
That gentle text can I well understand.
30 Eke well I wot, he said, that mine husband
Should leave father and mother, and take to me;
But of no number mention made he,
Of bigamy or of octogamy;
Why then should men speak of it villainy?* *as if it were a disgrace

35 Lo here, the wise king Dan* Solomon,   *Lord
I trow that he had wives more than one;

As would to God it lawful were to me
To be refreshed half so oft as he!
What gift* of God had he for all his wives?   *special favor, license
40 No man hath such, that in this world alive is.
God wot, this noble king, *as to my wit,*   *as I understand*
The first night had many a merry fit
With each of them, so *well was him on live.*   *so well he lived*
Blessed be God that I have wedded five!
45 Welcome the sixth whenever that he shall.
For since I will not keep me chaste in all,
When mine husband is from the world y-gone,
Some Christian man shall wedde me anon.
For then th' apostle saith that I am free
50 To wed, *a' God's half,* where it liketh me.   *on God's part*
He saith, that to be wedded is no sin;
Better is to be wedded than to brin.*   *burn
What recketh* me though folk say villainy**   *care; **evil
Of shrewed* Lamech, and his bigamy?   *impious, wicked
55 I wot well Abraham was a holy man,
And Jacob eke, as far as ev'r I can.*   *know
And each of them had wives more than two;
And many another holy man also.
Where can ye see, *in any manner age,*   *in any period*
60 That highe God defended* marriage   *forbade
By word express? I pray you tell it me;
Or where commanded he virginity?
I wot as well as you, it is no dread,*   *doubt
Th' apostle, when he spake of maidenhead,
65 He said, that precept thereof had he none:
Men may counsel a woman to be one,*   *a virgin
But counseling is no commandement;
He put it in our owen judgement.
For, hadde God commanded maidenhead,
70 Then had he damned* wedding out of dread;**   *condemned; **doubt
And certes, if there were no seed y-sow,*   *sown
Virginity then whereof should it grow?
Paul durste not commanden, at the least,
A thing of which his Master gave no hest.*   *command
75 The dart* is set up for virginity;   *goal
Catch whoso may, who runneth best let see.
But this word is not ta'en of every wight,
But there as God will give it of his might.   *except where*
I wot well that th' apostle was a maid,
80 But natheless, although he wrote and said,
He would that every wight were such as he,

All is but counsel to virginity.
And, since to be a wife he gave me leave
Of indulgence, so is it no repreve*   *scandal, reproach
85   To wedde me, if that my make* should die,   *mate, husband
Without exception* of bigamy;   *charge, reproach
All were it good no woman for to touch   *though it might be*
(He meant as in his bed or in his couch),
For peril is both fire and tow t'assemble
90   Ye know what this example may resemble.
This is all and some, he held virginity
More profit than wedding in frailty:
(*Frailty clepe I, but if* that he and she   *frailty I call it, unless*
Would lead their lives all in chastity),
95   I grant it well, I have of none envy
Who maidenhead prefer to bigamy;
It liketh them t' be clean in body and ghost;*   *soul
Of mine estate* I will not make a boast.   *condition

For, well ye know, a lord in his household
100 Hath not every vessel all of gold;
Some are of tree, and do their lord service.
God calleth folk to him in sundry wise,
And each one hath of God a proper gift,
Some this, some that, as liketh him to shift.*   *appoint, distribute
105 Virginity is great perfection,
And continence eke with devotion:
But Christ, that of perfection is the well,*   *fountain
Bade not every wight he should go sell
All that he had, and give it to the poor,
110 And in such wise follow him and his lore:*   *doctrine
He spake to them that would live perfectly, —
And, lordings, by your leave, that am not I;
I will bestow the flower of mine age
In th' acts and in the fruits of marriage.
115 Tell me also, to what conclusion*   *end, purpose
Were members made of generation,
And of so perfect wise a wight* y-wrought?   *being
Trust me right well, they were not made for nought.
Glose whoso will, and say both up and down,
120 That they were made for the purgatioun
Of urine, and of other thinges smale,
And eke to know a female from a male:
And for none other cause? say ye no?
Experience wot well it is not so.
125 So that the clerkes* be not with me wroth,   *scholars

I say this, that they were made for both,
That is to say, *for office, and for ease*   *for duty and for pleasure*
Of engendrure, there we God not displease.
Why should men elles in their bookes set,
130   That man shall yield unto his wife her debt?
Now wherewith should he make his payement,
If he us'd not his silly instrument?
Then were they made upon a creature
To purge urine, and eke for engendrure.
135   But I say not that every wight is hold,*   *obliged
That hath such harness* as I to you told,   *equipment
To go and use them in engendrure;
Then should men take of chastity no cure.*   *care
Christ was a maid, and shapen* as a man,   *fashioned
140   And many a saint, since that this world began,
Yet ever liv'd in perfect chastity.
I will not vie* with no virginity.   *contend
Let them with bread of pured* wheat be fed,   *purified
And let us wives eat our barley bread.
145   And yet with barley bread, Mark tell us can,
Our Lord Jesus refreshed many a man.
In such estate as God hath *cleped us,*   *called us to*
I'll persevere, I am not precious,*   *over-dainty
In wifehood I will use mine instrument
150   As freely as my Maker hath it sent.
If I be dangerous* God give me sorrow;   *sparing of my favours
Mine husband shall it have, both eve and morrow,
When that him list come forth and pay his debt.
A husband will I have, I *will no let,*   *will bear no hindrance*
155   Which shall be both my debtor and my thrall,*   *slave
And have his tribulation withal
Upon his flesh, while that I am his wife.
I have the power during all my life
Upon his proper body, and not he;
160   Right thus th' apostle told it unto me,
And bade our husbands for to love us well;
All this sentence me liketh every deal.*   *whit

Up start the Pardoner, and that anon;
"Now, Dame," quoth he, "by God and by Saint John,
165   Ye are a noble preacher in this case.
I was about to wed a wife, alas!
What? should I bie* it on my flesh so dear?   *suffer for
Yet had I lever* wed no wife this year."   *rather
"Abide,"* quoth she; "my tale is not begun   *be patient

170   Nay, thou shalt drinken of another tun
       Ere that I go, shall savour worse than ale.
       And when that I have told thee forth my tale
       Of tribulation in marriage,
       Of which I am expert in all mine age,
175   (This is to say, myself hath been the whip),
       Then mayest thou choose whether thou wilt sip
       Of *thilke tunne,* that I now shall broach.   *that tun*
       Beware of it, ere thou too nigh approach,
       For I shall tell examples more than ten:
180   Whoso will not beware by other men,
       By him shall other men corrected be:
       These same wordes writeth Ptolemy;
       Read in his Almagest, and take it there."
       "Dame, I would pray you, if your will it were,"
185   Saide this Pardoner, "as ye began,
       Tell forth your tale, and spare for no man,
       And teach us younge men of your practique."
       "Gladly," quoth she, "since that it may you like.
       But that I pray to all this company,
190   If that I speak after my fantasy,
       To take nought agrief* what I may say;   *to heart
       For mine intent is only for to play.

       Now, Sirs, then will I tell you forth my tale.
       As ever may I drinke wine or ale
195   I shall say sooth; the husbands that I had
       Three of them were good, and two were bad
       The three were goode men, and rich, and old
       Unnethes mighte they the statute hold   *they could with difficulty
       In which that they were bounden unto me.   obey the law*
200   Yet wot well what I mean of this, pardie.*   *by God
       As God me help, I laugh when that I think
       How piteously at night I made them swink,*   *labour
       But, *by my fay, I told of it no store:*   *by my faith, I held it
       They had me giv'n their land and their treasor,   of no account*
205   Me needed not do longer diligence
       To win their love, or do them reverence.
       They loved me so well, by God above,
       That I *tolde no dainty* of their love.   *cared nothing for*
       A wise woman will busy her ever-in-one*   *constantly
210   To get their love, where that she hath none.
       But, since I had them wholly in my hand,
       And that they had me given all their land,
       Why should I take keep* them for to please,   *care

But* it were for my profit, or mine ease?   *unless
215   I set them so a-worke, by my fay,
      That many a night they sange, well-away!
      The bacon was not fetched for them, I trow,
      That some men have in Essex at Dunmow.[34]
      I govern'd them so well after my law,
220   That each of them full blissful was and fawe*   *fain
      To bringe me gay thinges from the fair.
      They were full glad when that I spake them fair,
      For, God it wot, I *chid them spiteously.*   *rebuked them angrily*
      Now hearken how I bare me properly.

225   Ye wise wives, that can understand,
      Thus should ye speak, and *bear them wrong on hand,*   *make them
      For half so boldely can there no man   believe falsely*
      Swearen and lien as a woman can.
      (I say not this by wives that be wise,
230   *But if* it be when they them misadvise.)*   *unless*; *act unadvisedly
      A wise wife, if that she can* her good,   *knows
      Shall *beare them on hand* the cow is wood,   *make them believe*
      And take witness of her owen maid
      Of their assent: but hearken how I said.
235   "Sir olde kaynard*, is this thine array?   *dog
      Why is my neigheboure's wife so gay?
      She is honour'd *over all where* she go'th,   *wheresoever*
      I sit at home, I have no *thrifty cloth.*   *good clothes*
      What dost thou at my neigheboure's house?
240   Is she so fair? art thou so amorous?
      What rown'st* thou with our maid? benedicite,   *whisperest
      Sir olde lechour, let thy japes* be.   *tricks
      And if I have a gossip, or a friend
      (Withoute guilt), thou chidest as a fiend,
245   If that I walk or play unto his house.
      Thou comest home as drunken as a mouse,
      And preachest on thy bench, with evil prefe:*   *proof
      Thou say'st to me, it is a great mischief
      To wed a poore woman, for costage:*   *expense
250   And if that she be rich, of high parage;*   * birth
      Then say'st thou, that it is a tormentry
      To suffer her pride and melancholy.
      And if that she be fair, thou very knave,
      Thou say'st that every holour* will her have;   *whoremonger
255   She may no while in chastity abide,

34: At Dunmow prevailed the custom of giving bacon to the married pair who had
lived together for a year without quarrel.

       That is assailed upon every side.
       Thou say'st some folk desire us for richess,
       Some for our shape, and some for our fairness,
       And some, for she can either sing or dance,
260   And some for gentiless and dalliance,
       Some for her handes and her armes smale:
       Thus goes all to the devil, by thy tale;
       Thou say'st, men may not keep a castle wall
       That may be so assailed *over all.*   *everywhere*
265   And if that she be foul, thou say'st that she
       Coveteth every man that she may see;
       For as a spaniel she will on him leap,
       Till she may finde some man her to cheap;*   *buy
       And none so grey goose goes there in the lake,
270   (So say'st thou) that will be without a make.*   *mate
       And say'st, it is a hard thing for to weld*   *wield, govern
       A thing that no man will, *his thankes, held.*   *hold with his goodwill*
       Thus say'st thou, lorel,* when thou go'st to bed,   *good-for-nothing
       And that no wise man needeth for to wed,
275   Nor no man that intendeth unto heaven.
       With wilde thunder dint* and fiery leven**   *stroke; **lightning
       Mote* thy wicked necke be to-broke. *may
       Thou say'st, that dropping houses, and eke smoke,
       And chiding wives, make men to flee
280   Out of their owne house; ah! ben'dicite,
       What aileth such an old man for to chide?
       Thou say'st, we wives will our vices hide,
       Till we be fast,* and then we will them shew.   *wedded
       Well may that be a proverb of a shrew.*   *ill-tempered wretch
285   Thou say'st, that oxen, asses, horses, hounds,
       They be *assayed at diverse stounds,*   *tested at various seasons*
       Basons and lavers, ere that men them buy,
       Spoones, stooles, and all such husbandry,
       And so be pots, and clothes, and array,*   *raiment
290   But folk of wives make none assay,
       Till they be wedded, — olde dotard shrew! —
       And then, say'st thou, we will our vices shew.
       Thou say'st also, that it displeaseth me,
       But if * that thou wilt praise my beauty,   *unless
295   And but* thou pore alway upon my face,   *unless
       And call me faire dame in every place;
       And but* thou make a feast on thilke** day   *unless; **that
       That I was born, and make me fresh and gay;
       And but thou do to my norice* honour,   *nurse
300   And to my chamberere* within my bow'r,   *chamber-maid

And to my father's folk, and mine allies;*   *relations
Thus sayest thou, old barrel full of lies.
And yet also of our prentice Jenkin,
For his crisp hair, shining as gold so fine,
305 And for he squireth me both up and down,
Yet hast thou caught a false suspicioun:
I will him not, though thou wert dead to-morrow.
But tell me this, why hidest thou, *with sorrow,*   *sorrow on thee!*
The keyes of thy chest away from me?
310 It is my good* as well as thine, pardie.   *property
What, think'st to make an idiot of our dame?
Now, by that lord that called is Saint Jame,
Thou shalt not both, although that thou wert wood,*   *furious
Be master of my body, and my good,*   *property
315 The one thou shalt forego, maugre* thine eyen.   *in spite of
What helpeth it of me t'inquire and spyen?
I trow thou wouldest lock me in thy chest.
Thou shouldest say, 'Fair wife, go where thee lest;
Take your disport; I will believe no tales;
320 I know you for a true wife, Dame Ales.'*   *Alice
We love no man, that taketh keep* or charge   *care
Where that we go; we will be at our large.
Of alle men most blessed may he be,
The wise astrologer Dan* Ptolemy,   *Lord
325 That saith this proverb in his Almagest:
'Of alle men his wisdom is highest,
That recketh not who hath the world in hand.
By this proverb thou shalt well understand,
Have thou enough, what thar* thee reck or care   *needs, behoves
330 How merrily that other folkes fare?
For certes, olde dotard, by your leave,
Ye shall have queint* right enough at eve.   *cunt
He is too great a niggard* that will werne**   *miser; **forbid
A man to light a candle at his lantern;
335 He shall have never the less light, pardie.
Have thou enough, thee thar* not plaine** thee   *need; **complain
Thou say'st also, if that we make us gay
With clothing and with precious array,
That it is peril of our chastity.
340 And yet, — with sorrow! — thou enforcest thee,
And say'st these words in the apostle's name:
'In habit made with chastity and shame*   *modesty
Ye women shall apparel you,' quoth he,
'And not in tressed hair and gay perrie,*   *jewels
345 As pearles, nor with gold, nor clothes rich.'

After thy text nor after thy rubrich
I will not work as muchel as a gnat.
Thou say'st also, I walk out like a cat;
For whoso woulde singe the catte's skin
350   Then will the catte well dwell in her inn;*   *house
And if the catte's skin be sleek and gay,
She will not dwell in house half a day,
But forth she will, ere any day be daw'd,
To shew her skin, and go a caterwaw'd.*   *caterwauling
355   This is to say, if I be gay, sir shrew,
I will run out, my borel* for to shew.   *apparel, fine clothes
Sir olde fool, what helpeth thee to spyen?
Though thou pray Argus with his hundred eyen
To be my wardecorps,* as he can best   *body-guard
360   In faith he shall not keep me, *but me lest:*   *unless I please*
Yet could I *make his beard,* so may I the.   *make a jest of him*
"Thou sayest eke, that there be thinges three,   *thrive
Which thinges greatly trouble all this earth,
And that no wighte may endure the ferth:*   *fourth
365   O lefe* sir shrew, may Jesus short** thy life.   *pleasant; **shorten
Yet preachest thou, and say'st, a hateful wife
Y-reckon'd is for one of these mischances.
Be there *none other manner resemblances*   *no other kind of
That ye may liken your parables unto,   comparison*
370   But if a silly wife be one of tho?*   *those
Thou likenest a woman's love to hell;
To barren land where water may not dwell.
Thou likenest it also to wild fire;
The more it burns, the more it hath desire
375   To consume every thing that burnt will be.
Thou sayest, right as wormes shend* a tree,   *destroy
Right so a wife destroyeth her husbond;
This know they well that be to wives bond."

Lordings, right thus, as ye have understand,
380   *Bare I stiffly mine old husbands on hand,*   *made them believe*
That thus they saiden in their drunkenness;
And all was false, but that I took witness
On Jenkin, and upon my niece also.
O Lord! the pain I did them, and the woe,
385   'Full guilteless, by Godde's sweete pine;*   *pain
For as a horse I coulde bite and whine;
I coulde plain,* an'** I was in the guilt,   *complain; **even though
Or elles oftentime I had been spilt*   *ruined
Whoso first cometh to the nilll, first grint;*   *is ground

390	I plained first, so was our war y-stint.* *stopped
	They were full glad to excuse them full blive* *quickly
	Of things that they never *aguilt their live.* *were guilty in their lives*
	Of wenches would I *beare them on hand,* *falsely accuse them*
	When that for sickness scarcely might they stand,
395	Yet tickled I his hearte for that he
	Ween'd* that I had of him so great cherte:** *though; **affection
	I swore that all my walking out by night
	Was for to espy wenches that he dight:* *adorned
	Under that colour had I many a mirth.
400	For all such wit is given us at birth;
	Deceit, weeping, and spinning, God doth give
	To women kindly*, while that they may live. *naturally
	And thus of one thing I may vaunte me,
	At th' end I had the better in each degree,
405	By sleight, or force, or by some manner thing,
	As by continual murmur or grudging,* *complaining
	Namely* a-bed, there hadde they mischance, *especially
	There would I chide, and do them no pleasance:
	I would no longer in the bed abide,
410	If that I felt his arm over my side,
	Till he had made his ransom unto me,
	Then would I suffer him do his nicety.* *folly
	And therefore every man this tale I tell,
	Win whoso may, for all is for to sell;
415	With empty hand men may no hawkes lure;
	For winning would I all his will endure,
	And make me a feigned appetite,
	And yet in bacon* had I never delight: *i.e. of Dunmow
	That made me that I ever would them chide.
420	For, though the Pope had sitten them beside,
	I would not spare them at their owen board,
	For, by my troth, I quit* them word for word *repaid
	As help me very God omnipotent,
	Though I right now should make my testament
425	I owe them not a word, that is not quit* *repaid
	I brought it so aboute by my wit,
	That they must give it up, as for the best
	Or elles had we never been in rest.
	For, though he looked as a wood* lion, *furious
430	Yet should he fail of his conclusion.
	Then would I say, "Now, goode lefe* tak keep** *dear; **heed
	How meekly looketh Wilken oure sheep!
	Come near, my spouse, and let me ba* thy cheek *kiss
	Ye shoulde be all patient and meek,

435   And have a *sweet y-spiced* conscience,   *tender, nice*
       Since ye so preach of Jobe's patience.
       Suffer alway, since ye so well can preach,
       And but* ye do, certain we shall you teach   *unless
       That it is fair to have a wife in peace.
440   One of us two must bowe* doubteless: *give way
       And since a man is more reasonable
       Than woman is, ye must be suff'rable.
       What aileth you to grudge* thus and groan?   *complain
       Is it for ye would have my queint* alone?   *cunt
445   Why, take it all: lo, have it every deal,*   *bit
       Peter! shrew* you but ye love it well   *curse
       For if I woulde sell my *belle chose*,   *beautiful thing*
       I coulde walk as fresh as is a rose,
       But I will keep it for your owen tooth.
450   Ye be to blame, by God, I say you sooth."
       Such manner wordes hadde we on hand.

       Now will I speaken of my fourth husband.
       My fourthe husband was a revellour;
       This is to say, he had a paramour,
455   And I was young and full of ragerie,*   *wantonness
       Stubborn and strong, and jolly as a pie.*   *magpie
       Then could I dance to a harpe smale,
       And sing, y-wis,* as any nightingale,   *certainly
       When I had drunk a draught of sweete wine.
460   Metellius, the foule churl, the swine,
       That with a staff bereft his wife of life
       For she drank wine, though I had been his wife,
       Never should he have daunted me from drink:
       And, after wine, of Venus most I think.
465   For all so sure as cold engenders hail,
       A liquorish mouth must have a liquorish tail.
       In woman vinolent* is no defence,**   *full of wine; *resistance
       This knowe lechours by experience.
       But, lord Christ, when that it rememb'reth me
470   Upon my youth, and on my jollity,
       It tickleth me about mine hearte-root;
       Unto this day it doth mine hearte boot,*   *good
       That I have had my world as in my time.
       But age, alas! that all will envenime,*   *poison, embitter
475   Hath me bereft my beauty and my pith:*   *vigour
       Let go; farewell; the devil go therewith.
       The flour is gon, there is no more to tell,
       The bran, as I best may, now must I sell.

But yet to be right merry will I fand.*   *try
480   Now forth to tell you of my fourth husband,
      I say, I in my heart had great despite,
      That he of any other had delight;
      But he was quit,* by God and by Saint Joce: *requited, paid back
      I made for him of the same wood a cross;
485   Not of my body in no foul mannere,
      But certainly I made folk such cheer,
      That in his owen grease I made him fry
      For anger, and for very jealousy.
      By God, in earth I was his purgatory,
490   For which I hope his soul may be in glory.
      For, God it wot, he sat full oft and sung,
      When that his shoe full bitterly him wrung.*   *pinched
      There was no wight, save God and he, that wist
      In many wise how sore I did him twist.
495   He died when I came from Jerusalem,
      And lies in grave under the *roode beam:*   *cross*
      Although his tomb is not so curious
      As was the sepulchre of Darius,
      Which that Apelles wrought so subtlely.
500   It is but waste to bury them preciously.
      Let him fare well, God give his soule rest,
      He is now in his grave and in his chest.

      Now of my fifthe husband will I tell:
      God let his soul never come into hell.
505   And yet was he to me the moste shrew;*   *cruel, ill-tempered
      That feel I on my ribbes all *by rew,*   *in a row*
      And ever shall, until mine ending day.
      But in our bed he was so fresh and gay,
      And therewithal so well he could me glose,*   *flatter
510   When that he woulde have my belle chose,
      Though he had beaten me on every bone,
      Yet could he win again my love anon.
      I trow, I lov'd him better, for that he
      Was of his love so dangerous* to me.   *sparing, difficult
515   We women have, if that I shall not lie,
      In this matter a quainte fantasy.
      Whatever thing we may not lightly have,
      Thereafter will we cry all day and crave.
      Forbid us thing, and that desire we;
520   Press on us fast, and thenne will we flee.
      With danger* utter we all our chaffare;**   *difficulty; **merchandise
      Great press at market maketh deare ware,

And too great cheap is held at little price;
This knoweth every woman that is wise.
525   My fifthe husband, God his soule bless,
Which that I took for love and no richess,
He some time was *a clerk of Oxenford,*   *a scholar of Oxford*
And had left school, and went at home to board
With my gossip,* dwelling in oure town: *godmother
530   God have her soul, her name was Alisoun.
She knew my heart, and all my privity,
Bet than our parish priest, so may I the.*   *thrive
To her betrayed I my counsel all;
For had my husband pissed on a wall,
535   Or done a thing that should have cost his life,
To her, and to another worthy wife,
And to my niece, which that I loved well,
I would have told his counsel every deal.*   *bit
And so I did full often, God it wot,
540   That made his face full often red and hot
For very shame, and blam'd himself, for he
Had told to me so great a privity.*   *secret
And so befell that ones in a Lent
(So oftentimes I to my gossip went,
545   For ever yet I loved to be gay,
And for to walk in March, April, and May
From house to house, to heare sundry tales),
That Jenkin clerk, and my gossip, Dame Ales,
And I myself, into the fieldes went.
550   Mine husband was at London all that Lent;
I had the better leisure for to play,
And for to see, and eke for to be sey*   *seen
Of lusty folk; what wist I where my grace*   *favour
Was shapen* for to be, or in what place?   *appointed
555   Therefore made I my visitations
To vigilies,* and to processions,   *festival-eves
To preachings eke, and to these pilgrimages,
To plays of miracles, and marriages,
And weared upon me gay scarlet gites.*   *gowns
560   These wormes, nor these mothes, nor these mites
On my apparel frett* them never a deal**   *fed; **whit
And know'st thou why? for they were used* well.   *worn
Now will I telle forth what happen'd me:
I say, that in the fieldes walked we,
565   Till truely we had such dalliance,
This clerk and I, that of my purveyance*   *foresight
I spake to him, and told him how that he,

If I were widow, shoulde wedde me.
For certainly, I say for no bobance,*   *boasting
570 Yet was I never without purveyance*   *foresight
Of marriage, nor of other thinges eke:
I hold a mouse's wit not worth a leek,
That hath but one hole for to starte* to,   *escape
And if that faile, then is all y-do.* *done
575 *I bare him on hand* he had enchanted me   *falsely assured him*
(My dame taughte me that subtilty);
And eke I said, I mette* of him all night,   *dreamed
He would have slain me, as I lay upright,
And all my bed was full of very blood;
580 But yet I hop'd that he should do me good;
For blood betoken'd gold, as me was taught.
And all was false, I dream'd of him right naught,
But as I follow'd aye my dame's lore,
As well of that as of other things more.
585 But now, sir, let me see, what shall I sayn?
Aha! by God, I have my tale again.
When that my fourthe husband was on bier,
I wept algate* and made a sorry cheer,**   *always; **countenance
As wives must, for it is the usage;
590 And with my kerchief covered my visage;
But, for I was provided with a make,*   *mate
I wept but little, that I undertake*   *promise
To churche was mine husband borne a-morrow
With neighebours that for him made sorrow,
595 And Jenkin, oure clerk, was one of tho:*   *those
As help me God, when that I saw him go
After the bier, methought he had a pair
Of legges and of feet so clean and fair,
That all my heart I gave unto his hold.*   *keeping
600 He was, I trow, a twenty winter old,
And I was forty, if I shall say sooth,
But yet I had always a colte's tooth.
Gat-toothed* I was, and that became me well,   *gap-toothed
I had the print of Sainte Venus' seal.
605 As help me God, I was a lusty one,
And fair, and rich, and young, and *well begone:*   *in a good way*
For certes I am all venerian*   *under the influence of Venus
In feeling, and my heart is martian;*   *under the influence of Mars
Venus me gave my lust and liquorishness,
610 And Mars gave me my sturdy hardiness.
Mine ascendant was Taure,* and Mars therein: *Taurus
Alas, alas, that ever love was sin!

I follow'd aye mine inclination
By virtue of my constellation:
615 That made me that I coulde not withdraw
My chamber of Venus from a good fellaw.
Yet have I Marte's mark upon my face,
And also in another privy place.
For God so wisly* be my salvation,   *certainly
620 I loved never by discretion,
But ever follow'd mine own appetite,
All* were he short, or long, or black, or white,   *whether
I took no keep,* so that he liked me,   *heed
How poor he was, neither of what degree.
625 What should I say? but that at the month's end
This jolly clerk Jenkin, that was so hend,*   *courteous
Had wedded me with great solemnity,
And to him gave I all the land and fee
That ever was me given therebefore:
630 But afterward repented me full sore.
He woulde suffer nothing of my list.*   *pleasure
By God, he smote me ones with his fist,
For that I rent out of his book a leaf,
That of the stroke mine eare wax'd all deaf.
635 Stubborn I was, as is a lioness,
And of my tongue a very jangleress,*   *prater
And walk I would, as I had done beforn,
From house to house, although he had it sworn:*   *had sworn to
For which he oftentimes woulde preach prevent it
640 And me of olde Roman gestes* teach   *stories
How that Sulpitius Gallus left his wife
And her forsook for term of all his
For nought but open-headed* he her say**   *bare-headed; **saw
Looking out at his door upon a day.
645 Another Roman told he me by name,
That, for his wife was at a summer game
Without his knowing, he forsook her eke.
And then would he upon his Bible seek
That ilke* proverb of Ecclesiast,   *same
650 Where he commandeth, and forbiddeth fast,
Man shall not suffer his wife go roll about.
Then would he say right thus withoute doubt:
"Whoso that buildeth his house all of sallows,*   *willows
And pricketh his blind horse over the fallows,
655 And suff'reth his wife to *go seeke hallows,*   *make pilgrimages*
Is worthy to be hanged on the gallows."
But all for nought; I *sette not a haw*   *cared nothing for*

Of his proverbs, nor of his olde saw;
Nor would I not of him corrected be.
660 I hate them that my vices telle me,
And so do more of us (God wot) than I.
This made him wood* with me all utterly;   *furious
I woulde not forbear* him in no case.   *endure
Now will I say you sooth, by Saint Thomas,
665 Why that I rent out of his book a leaf,
For which he smote me, so that I was deaf.
He had a book, that gladly night and day
For his disport he would it read alway;
He call'd it Valerie, and Theophrast,
670 And with that book he laugh'd alway full fast.
And eke there was a clerk sometime at Rome,
A cardinal, that highte Saint Jerome,
That made a book against Jovinian,
Which book was there; and eke Tertullian,
675 Chrysippus, Trotula, and Heloise,
That was an abbess not far from Paris;
And eke the Parables* of Solomon,   *Proverbs
Ovide's Art, and bourdes* many one;   *jests
And alle these were bound in one volume.
680 And every night and day was his custume
(When he had leisure and vacation
From other worldly occupation)
To readen in this book of wicked wives.
He knew of them more legends and more lives
685 Than be of goodde wives in the Bible.
For, trust me well, it is an impossible
That any clerk will speake good of wives,
(*But if* it be of holy saintes' lives)   *unless*
Nor of none other woman never the mo'.
690 Who painted the lion, tell it me, who?
By God, if women haddde written stories,
As clerkes have within their oratories,
They would have writ of men more wickedness
Than *all the mark of Adam* may redress   *all men*
695 The children of Mercury and of Venus,
Be in their working full contrarious.
Mercury loveth wisdom and science,
And Venus loveth riot and dispence.*   *extravagance
And for their diverse disposition,
700 Each falls in other's exaltation.
As thus, God wot, Mercury is desolate
In Pisces, where Venus is exaltate,

And Venus falls where Mercury is raised.
Therefore no woman by no clerk is praised.
705   The clerk, when he is old, and may not do
Of Venus' works not worth his olde shoe,
Then sits he down, and writes in his dotage,
That women cannot keep their marriage.
But now to purpose, why I tolde thee
710   That I was beaten for a book, pardie.

Upon a night Jenkin, that was our sire,*   *goodman
Read on his book, as he sat by the fire,
Of Eva first, that for her wickedness
Was all mankind brought into wretchedness,
715   For which that Jesus Christ himself was slain,
That bought us with his hearte-blood again.
Lo here express of women may ye find
That woman was the loss of all mankind.
Then read he me how Samson lost his hairs
720   Sleeping, his leman cut them with her shears,
Through whiche treason lost he both his eyen.
Then read he me, if that I shall not lien,
Of Hercules, and of his Dejanire,
That caused him to set himself on fire.
725   Nothing forgot he of the care and woe
That Socrates had with his wives two;
How Xantippe cast piss upon his head.
This silly man sat still, as he were dead,
He wip'd his head, and no more durst he sayn,
730   But, "Ere the thunder stint* there cometh rain."   *ceases
Of Phasiphae, that was queen of Crete,
For shrewedness* he thought the tale sweet.   *wickedness
Fy, speak no more, it is a grisly thing,
Of her horrible lust and her liking.
735   Of Clytemnestra, for her lechery
That falsely made her husband for to die,
He read it with full good devotion.
He told me eke, for what occasion
Amphiorax at Thebes lost his life:
740   My husband had a legend of his wife
Eryphile, that for an ouche* of gold   *clasp, collar
Had privily unto the Greekes told,
Where that her husband hid him in a place,
For which he had at Thebes sorry grace.
745   Of Luna told he me, and of Lucie;
They bothe made their husbands for to die,

That one for love, that other was for hate.
Luna her husband on an ev'ning late
Empoison'd had, for that she was his foe:
750 Lucia liquorish lov'd her husband so,
That, for he should always upon her think,
She gave him such a manner* love-drink,   *sort of
That he was dead before it were the morrow:
And thus algates* husbands hadde sorrow.   *always
755 Then told he me how one Latumeus
Complained to his fellow Arius
That in his garden growed such a tree,
On which he said how that his wives three
Hanged themselves for heart dispiteous.
760 "O leve* brother," quoth this Arius,   *dear
"Give me a plant of thilke* blessed tree,   *that
And in my garden planted shall it be."
Of later date of wives hath he read,
That some have slain their husbands in their bed,
765 And let their *lechour dight them* all the night,   *lover ride them*
While that the corpse lay on the floor upright:
And some have driven nails into their brain,
While that they slept, and thus they have them slain:
Some have them given poison in their drink:
770 He spake more harm than hearte may bethink.
And therewithal he knew of more proverbs,
Than in this world there groweth grass or herbs.
"Better (quoth he) thine habitation
Be with a lion, or a foul dragon,
775 Than with a woman using for to chide.
Better (quoth he) high in the roof abide,
Than with an angry woman in the house,
They be so wicked and contrarious:
They hate that their husbands loven aye."
780 He said, "A woman cast her shame away
When she cast off her smock;" and farthermo',
"A fair woman, but* she be chaste also,   *except
Is like a gold ring in a sowe's nose.
Who coulde ween,* or who coulde suppose   *think
785 The woe that in mine heart was, and the pine?*   *pain
And when I saw that he would never fine*   *finish
To readen on this cursed book all night,
All suddenly three leaves have I plight*   *plucked
Out of his book, right as he read, and eke
790 I with my fist so took him on the cheek,
That in our fire he backward fell adown.

And he up start, as doth a wood* lion,   *furious
And with his fist he smote me on the head,
That on the floor I lay as I were dead.
795   And when he saw how still that there I lay,
He was aghast, and would have fled away,
Till at the last out of my swoon I braid,*   *woke
"Oh, hast thou slain me, thou false thief?" I said
"And for my land thus hast thou murder'd me?
800   Ere I be dead, yet will I kisse thee."
And near he came, and kneeled fair adown,
And saide", "Deare sister Alisoun,
As help me God, I shall thee never smite:
That I have done it is thyself to wite,*   *blame
805   Forgive it me, and that I thee beseek."*   *beseech
And yet eftsoons* I hit him on the cheek,   *immediately; again
And saidde, "Thief, thus much am I awreak.*   *avenged
Now will I die, I may no longer speak."

But at the last, with muche care and woe
810   We fell accorded* by ourselves two: *agreed
He gave me all the bridle in mine hand
To have the governance of house and land,
And of his tongue, and of his hand also.
I made him burn his book anon right tho.*   *then
815   And when that I had gotten unto me
By mast'ry all the sovereignety,
And that he said, "Mine owen true wife,
Do *as thee list,* the term of all thy life,   *as pleases thee*
Keep thine honour, and eke keep mine estate;
820   After that day we never had debate.
God help me so, I was to him as kind
As any wife from Denmark unto Ind,
And also true, and so was he to me:
I pray to God that sits in majesty
825   So bless his soule, for his mercy dear.
Now will I say my tale, if ye will hear. —

The Friar laugh'd when he had heard all this:
"Now, Dame," quoth he, "so have I joy and bliss,
This is a long preamble of a tale."
830   And when the Sompnour heard the Friar gale,*   *speak
"Lo," quoth this Sompnour, "Godde's armes two,
A friar will intermete* him evermo':   *interpose
Lo, goode men, a fly and eke a frere
Will fall in ev'ry dish and eke mattere.

835   What speak'st thou of perambulation?*   *preamble
  What? amble or trot; or peace, or go sit down:
  Thou lettest* our disport in this mattere."   *hinder
  "Yea, wilt thou so, Sir Sompnour?" quoth the Frere;
  "Now by my faith I shall, ere that I go,
840   Tell of a Sompnour such a tale or two,
  That all the folk shall laughen in this place."
  "Now do, else, Friar, I beshrew* thy face,"   *curse
  Quoth this Sompnour; "and I beshrewe me,
  But if* I telle tales two or three   *unless
845   Of friars, ere I come to Sittingbourne,
  That I shall make thine hearte for to mourn:
  For well I wot thy patience is gone."
  Our Hoste cried, "Peace, and that anon;"
  And saide, "Let the woman tell her tale.
850   Ye fare* as folk that drunken be of ale.   *behave
  Do, Dame, tell forth your tale, and that is best."
  "All ready, sir," quoth she, "right as you lest,*   *please
  If I have licence of this worthy Frere."
  "Yes, Dame," quoth he, "tell forth, and I will hear."

THE TALE

  In olde dayes of the king Arthour,
  Of which that Britons speake great honour,
  All was this land full fill'd of faerie;*   *fairies
  The Elf-queen, with her jolly company,
5   Danced full oft in many a green mead
  This was the old opinion, as I read;
  I speak of many hundred years ago;
  But now can no man see none elves mo',
  For now the great charity and prayeres
10   Of limitours,* and other holy freres,   *begging friars
  That search every land and ev'ry stream
  As thick as motes in the sunne-beam,
  Blessing halls, chambers, kitchenes, and bowers,
  Cities and burghes, castles high and towers,
15   Thorpes* and barnes, shepens** and dairies,   *villages; **stables
  This makes that there be now no faeries:
  For *there as* wont to walke was an elf,   *where*
  There walketh now the limitour himself,
  In undermeles* and in morrowings**,   *evenings; **mornings
20   And saith his matins and his holy things,
  As he goes in his limitatioun.*   *begging district
  Women may now go safely up and down,
  In every bush, and under every tree;

There is none other incubus but he;
25   And he will do to them no dishonour.

And so befell it, that this king Arthour
Had in his house a lusty bacheler,
That on a day came riding from river:
And happen'd, that, alone as she was born,
30   He saw a maiden walking him beforn,
Of which maiden anon, maugre* her head,   *in spite of
By very force he reft her maidenhead:
For which oppression was such clamour,
And such pursuit unto the king Arthour,
35   That damned* was this knight for to be dead   *condemned
By course of law, and should have lost his head;
(Paraventure such was the statute tho),*   *then
But that the queen and other ladies mo'
So long they prayed the king of his grace,
40   Till he his life him granted in the place,
And gave him to the queen, all at her will
To choose whether she would him save or spill*   *destroy
The queen thanked the king with all her might;
And, after this, thus spake she to the knight,
45   When that she saw her time upon a day.
"Thou standest yet," quoth she, "in such array,*   *a position
That of thy life yet hast thou no surety;
I grant thee life, if thou canst tell to me
What thing is it that women most desiren:
50   Beware, and keep thy neck-bone from the iron*   *executioner's axe
And if thou canst not tell it me anon,
Yet will I give thee leave for to gon
A twelvemonth and a day, to seek and lear*   *learn
An answer suffisant* in this mattere.   *satisfactory
55   And surety will I have, ere that thou pace,*   *go
Thy body for to yielden in this place."
Woe was the knight, and sorrowfully siked;*   *sighed
But what? he might not do all as him liked.
And at the last he chose him for to wend,*   *depart
60   And come again, right at the yeare's end,
With such answer as God would him purvey:*   *provide
And took his leave, and wended forth his way.

He sought in ev'ry house and ev'ry place,
Where as he hoped for to finde grace,
65   To learne what thing women love the most:
But he could not arrive in any coast,

Where as he mighte find in this mattere
Two creatures *according in fere.*   *agreeing together*
Some said that women loved best richess,
70   Some said honour, and some said jolliness,
Some rich array, and some said lust* a-bed,   *pleasure
And oft time to be widow and be wed.
Some said, that we are in our heart most eased
When that we are y-flatter'd and y-praised.
75   He *went full nigh the sooth,* I will not lie;   *came very near the truth*
A man shall win us best with flattery;
And with attendance, and with business
Be we y-limed,* bothe more and less.   *caught with bird-lime
And some men said that we do love the best
80   For to be free, and do *right as us lest,*   *whatever we please*
And that no man reprove us of our vice,
But say that we are wise, and nothing nice,*   *foolish
For truly there is none among us all,
If any wight will *claw us on the gall,*   *scratch us on the sore place*
85   That will not kick, for that he saith us sooth:
Assay,* and he shall find it, that so do'th.   *try
For be we never so vicious within,
We will be held both wise and clean of sin.
And some men said, that great delight have we
90   For to be held stable and eke secre,*   *discreet
And in one purpose steadfastly to dwell,
And not bewray* a thing that men us tell.   *give away
But that tale is not worth a rake-stele.*   *rake-handle
Pardie, we women canne nothing hele,*   *hide
95   Witness on Midas; will ye hear the tale?
Ovid, amonges other thinges smale*   *small
Saith, Midas had, under his longe hairs,
Growing upon his head two ass's ears;
The whiche vice he hid, as best he might,
100 Full subtlely from every man's sight,
That, save his wife, there knew of it no mo';
He lov'd her most, and trusted her also;
He prayed her, that to no creature
She woulde tellen of his disfigure.
105 She swore him, nay, for all the world to win,
She would not do that villainy or sin,
To make her husband have so foul a name:
She would not tell it for her owen shame.
But natheless her thoughte that she died,
110 That she so longe should a counsel hide;
Her thought it swell'd so sore about her heart

That needes must some word from her astart
And, since she durst not tell it unto man
Down to a marish fast thereby she ran,
115 Till she came there, her heart was all afire:
And, as a bittern bumbles* in the mire,   *makes a humming noise
She laid her mouth unto the water down
"Bewray me not, thou water, with thy soun'"
Quoth she, "to thee I tell it, and no mo',
120 Mine husband hath long ass's eares two!
Now is mine heart all whole; now is it out;
I might no longer keep it, out of doubt."
Here may ye see, though we a time abide,
Yet out it must, we can no counsel hide.
125 The remnant of the tale, if ye will hear,
Read in Ovid, and there ye may it lear.*   *learn

This knight, of whom my tale is specially,
When that he saw he might not come thereby,
That is to say, what women love the most,
130 Within his breast full sorrowful was his ghost.*   *spirit
But home he went, for he might not sojourn,
The day was come, that homeward he must turn.
And in his way it happen'd him to ride,
In all his care,* under a forest side,   *trouble, anxiety
135 Where as he saw upon a dance go
Of ladies four-and-twenty, and yet mo',
Toward this ilke* dance he drew full yern,**   *same; **eagerly
The hope that he some wisdom there should learn;
But certainly, ere he came fully there,
140 Y-vanish'd was this dance, he knew not where;
No creature saw he that bare life,
Save on the green he sitting saw a wife,
A fouler wight there may no man devise.*   *imagine, tell
Against* this knight this old wife gan to rise,   *to meet
145 And said, "Sir Knight, hereforth* lieth no way.   *from here
Tell me what ye are seeking, by your fay.
Paraventure it may the better be:
These olde folk know muche thing." quoth she.
My leve* mother," quoth this knight, "certain,   *dear
150 I am but dead, but if* that I can sayn   *unless
What thing it is that women most desire:
Could ye me wiss,* I would well *quite your hire."*   *instruct;
"Plight me thy troth here in mine hand," quoth she,   *reward you*
"The nexte thing that I require of thee
155 Thou shalt it do, if it be in thy might,

And I will tell it thee ere it be night."
"Have here my trothe," quoth the knight; "I grant."
"Thenne," quoth she, "I dare me well avaunt,*   *boast, affirm
Thy life is safe, for I will stand thereby,
160   Upon my life the queen will say as I:
Let see, which is the proudest of them all,
That wears either a kerchief or a caul,
That dare say nay to that I shall you teach.
Let us go forth withoute longer speech
165   Then *rowned she a pistel* in his ear,   *she whispered a secret*
And bade him to be glad, and have no fear.

When they were come unto the court, this knight
Said, he had held his day, as he had hight,*   *promised
And ready was his answer, as he said.
170   Full many a noble wife, and many a maid,
And many a widow, for that they be wise, —
The queen herself sitting as a justice, —
Assembled be, his answer for to hear,
And afterward this knight was bid appear.
175   To every wight commanded was silence,
And that the knight should tell in audience,
What thing that worldly women love the best.
This knight he stood not still, as doth a beast,
But to this question anon answer'd
180   With manly voice, that all the court it heard,
"My liege lady, generally," quoth he,
"Women desire to have the sovereignty
As well over their husband as their love
And for to be in mast'ry him above.
185   This is your most desire, though ye me kill,
Do as you list, I am here at your will."
In all the court there was no wife nor maid
Nor widow, that contraried what he said,
But said, he worthy was to have his life.
190   And with that word up start that olde wife
Which that the knight saw sitting on the green.
"Mercy," quoth she, "my sovereign lady queen,
Ere that your court departe, do me right.
I taughte this answer unto this knight,
195   For which he plighted me his trothe there,
The firste thing I would of him requere,
He would it do, if it lay in his might.
Before this court then pray I thee, Sir Knight,"
Quoth she, "that thou me take unto thy wife,

200   For well thou know'st that I have kept* thy life.   *preserved
        If I say false, say nay, upon thy fay."*   *faith
        This knight answer'd, "Alas, and well-away!
        I know right well that such was my behest.*   *promise
        For Godde's love choose a new request
205   Take all my good, and let my body go."
        "Nay, then," quoth she, "I shrew* us bothe two,   *curse
        For though that I be old, and foul, and poor,
        I n'ould* for all the metal nor the ore,   *would not
        That under earth is grave,* or lies above   *buried
210   But if thy wife I were and eke thy love."
        "My love?" quoth he, "nay, my damnation,
        Alas! that any of my nation
        Should ever so foul disparaged be.
        But all for nought; the end is this, that he
215   Constrained was, that needs he muste wed,
        And take this olde wife, and go to bed.

        Now woulde some men say paraventure
        That for my negligence I do no cure*   *take no pains
        To tell you all the joy and all th' array
220   That at the feast was made that ilke* day.   *same
        To which thing shortly answeren I shall:
        I say there was no joy nor feast at all,
        There was but heaviness and muche sorrow:
        For privily he wed her on the morrow;
225   And all day after hid him as an owl,
        So woe was him, his wife look'd so foul
        Great was the woe the knight had in his thought
        When he was with his wife to bed y-brought;
        He wallow'd, and he turned to and fro.
230   This olde wife lay smiling evermo',
        And said, "Dear husband, benedicite,
        Fares every knight thus with his wife as ye?
        Is this the law of king Arthoures house?
        Is every knight of his thus dangerous?*   *fastidious, miserly
235   I am your owen love, and eke your wife
        I am she, which that saved hath your life
        And certes yet did I you ne'er unright.
        Why fare ye thus with me this firste night?
        Ye fare like a man had lost his wit.
240   What is my guilt? for God's love tell me it,
        And it shall be amended, if I may."
        "Amended!" quoth this knight; "alas, nay, nay,
        It will not be amended, never mo';

Thou art so loathly, and so old also,
245 And thereto* comest of so low a kind,   *in addition
That little wonder though I wallow and wind;*   *writhe, turn about
So woulde God, mine hearte woulde brest!"*   *burst
"Is this," quoth she, "the cause of your unrest?"
"Yea, certainly," quoth he; "no wonder is."
250 "Now, Sir," quoth she, "I could amend all this,
If that me list, ere it were dayes three,
So well ye mighte bear you unto me.   *if you could conduct yourself
But, for ye speaken of such gentleness   well towards me*
As is descended out of old richess,
255 That therefore shalle ye be gentlemen;
Such arrogancy is *not worth a hen.*   *worth nothing*
Look who that is most virtuous alway,
Prive and apert, and most intendeth aye   *in private and public*
To do the gentle deedes that he can;
260 And take him for the greatest gentleman.
Christ will,* we claim of him our gentleness,   *wills, requires
Not of our elders* for their old richess.   *ancestors
For though they gave us all their heritage,
For which we claim to be of high parage,*   *birth, descent
265 Yet may they not bequeathe, for no thing,
To none of us, their virtuous living
That made them gentlemen called to be,
And bade us follow them in such degree.
Well can the wise poet of Florence,
270 That highte Dante, speak of this sentence:*   *sentiment
Lo, in such manner* rhyme is Dante's tale.   *kind of
'Full seld'* upriseth by his branches smale   *seldom
Prowess of man, for God of his goodness
Wills that we claim of him our gentleness;'
275 For of our elders may we nothing claim
But temp'ral things that man may hurt and maim.
Eke every wight knows this as well as I,
If gentleness were planted naturally
Unto a certain lineage down the line,
280 Prive and apert, then would they never fine*   *cease
To do of gentleness the fair office
Then might they do no villainy nor vice.
Take fire, and bear it to the darkest house
Betwixt this and the mount of Caucasus,
285 And let men shut the doores, and go thenne,*   *thence
Yet will the fire as fair and lighte brenne*   *burn
As twenty thousand men might it behold;
Its office natural aye will it hold,   *it will perform its natural duty*

        On peril of my life, till that it die.
290   Here may ye see well how that gentery*   *gentility, nobility
        Is not annexed to possession,
        Since folk do not their operation
        Alway, as doth the fire, lo, *in its kind*   *from its very nature*
        For, God it wot, men may full often find
295   A lorde's son do shame and villainy.
        And he that will have price* of his gent'ry,   *esteem, honour
        For* he was boren of a gentle house,   *because
        And had his elders noble and virtuous,
        And will himselfe do no gentle deedes,
300   Nor follow his gentle ancestry, that dead is,
        He is not gentle, be he duke or earl;
        For villain sinful deedes make a churl.
        For gentleness is but the renomee*   *renown
        Of thine ancestors, for their high bounte,*   *goodness, worth
305   Which is a strange thing to thy person:
        Thy gentleness cometh from God alone.
        Then comes our very* gentleness of grace;   *true
        It was no thing bequeath'd us with our place.
        Think how noble, as saith Valerius,
310   Was thilke* Tullius Hostilius,   *that
        That out of povert' rose to high
        Read in Senec, and read eke in Boece,
        There shall ye see express, that it no drede* is,   *doubt
        That he is gentle that doth gentle deedes.
315   And therefore, leve* husband, I conclude,   *dear
        Albeit that mine ancestors were rude,
        Yet may the highe God, — and so hope I, —
        Grant me His grace to live virtuously:
        Then am I gentle when that I begin
320   To live virtuously, and waive* sin.   *forsake
        "And whereas ye of povert' me repreve,*   *reproach
        The highe God, on whom that we believe,
        In wilful povert' chose to lead his life:
        And certes, every man, maiden, or wife
325   May understand that Jesus, heaven's king,
        Ne would not choose a virtuous living.
        Glad povert' is an honest thing, certain;   *poverty cheerfully endured*
        This will Senec and other clerkes sayn
        Whoso that *holds him paid of* his povert',   *is satisfied with*
330   I hold him rich though he hath not a shirt.
        He that coveteth is a poore wight
        For he would have what is not in his might
        But he that nought hath, nor coveteth to have,

Is rich, although ye hold him but a knave.*   *slave, abject wretch
335   *Very povert' is sinne,* properly.   *the only true poverty is sin*
Juvenal saith of povert' merrily:
The poore man, when he goes by the way
Before the thieves he may sing and play
Povert' is hateful good, and, as I guess,
340   A full great *bringer out of business;*   *deliver from trouble*
A great amender eke of sapience
To him that taketh it in patience.
Povert' is this, although it seem elenge*   *strange
Possession that no wight will challenge
345   Povert' full often, when a man is low,
Makes him his God and eke himself to know
Povert' a spectacle* is, as thinketh me   *a pair of spectacles
Through which he may his very* friendes see.   *true
And, therefore, Sir, since that I you not grieve,
350   Of my povert' no more me repreve.*   *reproach
"Now, Sir, of elde* ye repreve me: *age
And certes, Sir, though none authority*   *text, dictum
Were in no book, ye gentles of honour
Say, that men should an olde wight honour,
355   And call him father, for your gentleness;
And authors shall I finden, as I guess.
Now there ye say that I am foul and old,
Then dread ye not to be a cokewold.*   *cuckold
For filth, and elde, all so may I the,*   *thrive
360   Be greate wardens upon chastity.
But natheless, since I know your delight,
I shall fulfil your wordly appetite.
Choose now," quoth she, "one of these thinges tway,
To have me foul and old till that I dey,*   *die
365   And be to you a true humble wife,
And never you displease in all my life:
Or elles will ye have me young and fair,
And take your aventure of the repair*   *resort
That shall be to your house because of me, —
370   Or in some other place, it may well be?
Now choose yourselfe whether that you liketh.
This knight adviseth* him and sore he siketh,**   *considered; **sighed
But at the last he said in this mannere;
"My lady and my love, and wife so dear,
375   I put me in your wise governance,
Choose for yourself which may be most pleasance
And most honour to you and me also;
I *do no force* the whether of the two: *care not*

For as you liketh, it sufficeth me."
380 "Then have I got the mastery," quoth she,
"Since I may choose and govern as me lest."* *pleases
"Yea, certes wife," quoth he, "I hold it best."
"Kiss me," quoth she, "we are no longer wroth,* *quarreling
For by my troth I will be to you both;
385 This is to say, yea, bothe fair and good.
I pray to God that I may *sterve wood,* *die mad*
But* I to you be all so good and true, *unless
As ever was wife since the world was new;
And but* I be to-morrow as fair to seen, *unless
390 As any lady, emperess or queen,
That is betwixt the East and eke the West
Do with my life and death right as you lest.* *please
Cast up the curtain, and look how it is."
And when the knight saw verily all this,
395 That she so fair was, and so young thereto,
For joy he hent* her in his armes two: *took
His hearte bathed in a bath of bliss,
A thousand times *on row* he gan her kiss: *in succession*
And she obeyed him in every thing
400 That mighte do him pleasance or liking.
And thus they live unto their lives' end
In perfect joy; and Jesus Christ us send
Husbandes meek and young, and fresh in bed,
And grace to overlive them that we wed.
405 And eke I pray Jesus to short their lives,
That will not be governed by their wives.
And old and angry niggards* of dispence,** *misers; **expense
God send them soon a very pestilence!

THE PARDONER'S TALE

THE PROLOGUE

    Our Hoste gan to swear as he were wood;
    "Harow!" quoth he, "by nailes and by blood,
    This was a cursed thief, a false justice.
    As shameful death as hearte can devise
5   Come to these judges and their advoca's.*   *advocates, counsellors
    Algate* this sely** maid is slain, alas!   *nevertheless; **innocent
    Alas! too deare bought she her beauty.
    Wherefore I say, that all day man may see
    That giftes of fortune and of nature
10 Be cause of death to many a creature.
    Her beauty was her death, I dare well sayn;
    Alas! so piteously as she was slain.
    Of bothe giftes, that I speak of now
    Men have full often more harm than prow,*   *profit
15 But truely, mine owen master dear,
    This was a piteous tale for to hear;
    But natheless, pass over; 'tis *no force.*   *no matter*
    I pray to God to save thy gentle corse,*   *body
    And eke thine urinals, and thy jordans,
20 Thine Hippocras, and eke thy Galliens,
    And every boist* full of thy lectuary,   *box
    God bless them, and our lady Sainte Mary.
    So may I the',* thou art a proper man,   *thrive
    And like a prelate, by Saint Ronian;
25 Said I not well? Can I not speak *in term?*   *in set form*
    But well I wot thou dost* mine heart to erme,**   *makest; **grieve
    That I have almost caught a cardiacle:*   *heartache
    By corpus Domini, but* I have triacle,**   *unless; **a remedy
    Or else a draught of moist and corny ale,
30 Or but* I hear anon a merry tale,   *unless
    Mine heart is brost* for pity of this maid.   *burst, broken
    Thou *bel ami,* thou Pardoner," he said,   *good friend*
    "Tell us some mirth of japes* right anon."   *jokes
    "It shall be done," quoth he, "by Saint Ronion.
35 But first," quoth he, "here at this ale-stake*   *ale-house sign
    I will both drink, and biten on a cake."
    But right anon the gentles gan to cry,

"Nay, let him tell us of no ribaldry.
Tell us some moral thing, that we may lear*   *learn
40   Some wit,* and thenne will we gladly hear."   *wisdom, sense
"I grant y-wis,"* quoth he; "but I must think   *surely
Upon some honest thing while that I drink."

THE TALE

Lordings (quoth he), in churche when I preach,
I *paine me* to have an hautein** speech,   *take pains*; **loud
And ring it out, as round as doth a bell,
For I know all by rote that I tell.
5   My theme is always one, and ever was;
Radix malorum est cupiditas.[35]
First I pronounce whence that I come,
And then my bulles shew I all and some;
Our liege lorde's seal on my patent,
10   That shew I first, *my body to warrent,*   *for the protection of my
That no man be so hardy, priest nor clerk,   person*
Me to disturb of Christe's holy werk.
And after that then tell I forth my tales.
Bulles of popes, and of cardinales,
15   Of patriarchs, and of bishops I shew,
And in Latin I speak a wordes few,
To savour with my predication,
And for to stir men to devotion
Then show I forth my longe crystal stones,
20   Y-crammed fall of cloutes* and of bones;   *rags, fragments
Relics they be, as *weene they* each one.   *as my listeners think*
Then have I in latoun* a shoulder-bone   *brass
Which that was of a holy Jewe's sheep.
"Good men," say I, "take of my wordes keep;*   *heed
25   If that this bone be wash'd in any well,
If cow, or calf, or sheep, or oxe swell,
That any worm hath eat, or worm y-stung,
Take water of that well, and wash his tongue,
And it is whole anon; and farthermore
30   Of pockes, and of scab, and every sore
Shall every sheep be whole, that of this well
Drinketh a draught; take keep* of that I tell.   *heed
"If that the goodman, that the beastes oweth,*   *own
Will every week, ere that the cock him croweth,
35   Fasting, y-drinken of this well a draught,

35: The love of money is the root of all evil.

As thilke holy Jew our elders taught,
His beastes and his store shall multiply.
And, Sirs, also it healeth jealousy;
For though a man be fall'n in jealous rage,
40 Let make with this water his pottage,
And never shall he more his wife mistrist,*   *mistrust
Though he the sooth of her defaulte wist;   *though he truly knew
All had she taken priestes two or three.[36]   her sin*
Here is a mittain* eke, that ye may see;   *glove, mitten
45 He that his hand will put in this mittain,
He shall have multiplying of his grain,
When he hath sowen, be it wheat or oats,
So that he offer pence, or elles groats.
And, men and women, one thing warn I you;
50 If any wight be in this churche now
That hath done sin horrible, so that he
Dare not for shame of it y-shriven* be;   *confessed
Or any woman, be she young or old,
That hath y-made her husband cokewold,*   *cuckold
55 Such folk shall have no power nor no grace
To offer to my relics in this place.
And whoso findeth him out of such blame,
He will come up and offer in God's name;
And I assoil* him by the authority   *absolve
60 Which that by bull y-granted was to me."

By this gaud* have I wonne year by year   *jest, trick
A hundred marks, since I was pardonere.
I stande like a clerk in my pulpit,
And when the lewed* people down is set,   *ignorant
65 I preache so as ye have heard before,
And telle them a hundred japes* more.   *jests, deceits
Then pain I me to stretche forth my neck,
And east and west upon the people I beck,
As doth a dove, sitting on a bern;*   *barn
70 My handes and my tongue go so yern,*   *briskly
That it is joy to see my business.
Of avarice and of such cursedness*   *wickedness
Is all my preaching, for to make them free
To give their pence, and namely* unto me.   *especially
75 For mine intent is not but for to win,
And nothing for correction of sin.
I recke never, when that they be buried,

36: Even if she had committed adultery with two or three priests.

Though that their soules go a blackburied*.   *damned
For certes *many a predication   *preaching is often inspired
80   Cometh oft-time of evil intention;*   by evil motives*
Some for pleasance of folk, and flattery,
To be advanced by hypocrisy;
And some for vainglory, and some for hate.
For, when I dare not otherwise debate,
85   Then will I sting him with my tongue smart*   *sharply
In preaching, so that he shall not astart*   *escape
To be defamed falsely, if that he
Hath trespass'd* to my brethren or to me.   *offended
For, though I telle not his proper name,
90   Men shall well knowe that it is the same
By signes, and by other circumstances.
Thus *quite I* folk that do us displeasances: *I am revenged on*
Thus spit I out my venom, under hue
Of holiness, to seem holy and true.
95   But, shortly mine intent I will devise,
I preach of nothing but of covetise.
Therefore my theme is yet, and ever was, —
Radix malorum est cupiditas.
Thus can I preach against the same vice
100 Which that I use, and that is avarice.
But though myself be guilty in that sin,
Yet can I maken other folk to twin*   *depart
From avarice, and sore them repent.
But that is not my principal intent;
105 I preache nothing but for covetise.
Of this mattere it ought enough suffice.
Then tell I them examples many a one,
Of olde stories longe time gone;
For lewed* people love tales old;   *unlearned
110 Such thinges can they well report and hold.
What? trowe ye, that whiles I may preach
And winne gold and silver for* I teach,   *because
That I will live in povert' wilfully?
Nay, nay, I thought it never truely.
115 For I will preach and beg in sundry lands;
I will not do no labour with mine hands,
Nor make baskets for to live thereby,
Because I will not beggen idlely.
I will none of the apostles counterfeit;*   *imitate (in poverty)
120 I will have money, wool, and cheese, and wheat,
All* were it given of the poorest page,   *even if
Or of the pooreste widow in a village:

All should her children sterve* for famine.   *die
Nay, I will drink the liquor of the vine,
125 And have a jolly wench in every town.
But hearken, lordings, in conclusioun;
Your liking is, that I shall tell a tale
Now I have drunk a draught of corny ale,
By God, I hope I shall you tell a thing
130 That shall by reason be to your liking;
For though myself be a full vicious man,
A moral tale yet I you telle can,
Which I am wont to preache, for to win.
Now hold your peace, my tale I will begin.

135 In Flanders whilom was a company
Of younge folkes, that haunted folly,
As riot, hazard, stewes,* and taverns;   *brothels
Where as with lutes, harpes, and giterns,*   *guitars
They dance and play at dice both day and night,
140 And eat also, and drink over their might;
Through which they do the devil sacrifice
Within the devil's temple, in cursed wise,
By superfluity abominable.
Their oathes be so great and so damnable,
145 That it is grisly* for to hear them swear.   *dreadful
Our blissful Lorde's body they to-tear;*   *tore to pieces
Them thought the Jewes rent him not enough,
And each of them at other's sinne lough.*   *laughed
And right anon in come tombesteres*   *dancers
150 Fetis* and small, and younge fruitesteres.**   *dainty; **fruit-girls
Singers with harpes, baudes,* waferers,**   *revellers; **cake-sellers
Which be the very devil's officers,
To kindle and blow the fire of lechery,
That is annexed unto gluttony.
155 The Holy Writ take I to my witness,
That luxury is in wine and drunkenness.
Lo, how that drunken Lot unkindely*   *unnaturally
Lay by his daughters two unwittingly,
So drunk he was he knew not what he wrought.
160 Herodes, who so well the stories sought,
When he of wine replete was at his feast,
Right at his owen table gave his hest*   *command
To slay the Baptist John full guilteless.
Seneca saith a good word, doubteless:
165 He saith he can no difference find
Betwixt a man that is out of his mind,

And a man whiche that is drunkelew:*   *a drunkard
But that woodness,* y-fallen in a shrew,*   *madness;
Persevereth longer than drunkenness.   **one evil-tempered

170 O gluttony, full of all cursedness;
   O cause first of our confusion,
   Original of our damnation,
   Till Christ had bought us with his blood again!
   Looke, how deare, shortly for to sayn,
175 Abought* was first this cursed villainy: *atoned for
   Corrupt was all this world for gluttony.
   Adam our father, and his wife also,
   From Paradise, to labour and to woe,
   Were driven for that vice, it is no dread.*   *doubt
180 For while that Adam fasted, as I read,
   He was in Paradise; and when that he
   Ate of the fruit defended* of the tree,   *forbidden
   Anon he was cast out to woe and pain.
   O gluttony! well ought us on thee plain.
185 Oh! wist a man how many maladies
   Follow of excess and of gluttonies,
   He woulde be the more measurable*   *moderate
   Of his diete, sitting at his table.
   Alas! the shorte throat, the tender mouth,
190 Maketh that east and west, and north and south,
   In earth, in air, in water, men do swink*   *labour
   To get a glutton dainty meat and drink.
   Of this mattere, O Paul! well canst thou treat
   Meat unto womb,* and womb eke unto meat,   *belly
195 Shall God destroye both, as Paulus saith.
   Alas! a foul thing is it, by my faith,
   To say this word, and fouler is the deed,
   When man so drinketh of the *white and red,*   *i.e. wine*
   That of his throat he maketh his privy
200 Through thilke cursed superfluity
   The apostle saith, weeping full piteously,
   There walk many, of which you told have I, —
   I say it now weeping with piteous voice, —
   That they be enemies of Christe's crois;*   *cross
205 Of which the end is death; womb* is their God.   *belly
   O womb, O belly, stinking is thy cod,*   *bag
   Full fill'd of dung and of corruptioun;
   At either end of thee foul is the soun.
   How great labour and cost is thee to find!*   *supply
210 These cookes how they stamp, and strain, and grind,

And turne substance into accident,
To fulfill all thy likerous talent!
Out of the harde bones knocke they
The marrow, for they caste naught away
215 That may go through the gullet soft and swoot*   *sweet
Of spicery and leaves, of bark and root,
Shall be his sauce y-maked by delight,
To make him have a newer appetite.
But, certes, he that haunteth such delices
220 Is dead while that he liveth in those vices.

A lecherous thing is wine, and drunkenness
Is full of striving and of wretchedness.
O drunken man! disfgur'd is thy face,
Sour is thy breath, foul art thou to embrace:
225 And through thy drunken nose sowneth the soun',
As though thous saidest aye, Samsoun! Samsoun!
And yet, God wot, Samson drank never wine.
Thou fallest as it were a sticked swine;
Thy tongue is lost, and all thine honest cure;*   *care
230 For drunkenness is very sepulture*   *tomb
Of manne's wit and his discretion.
In whom that drink hath domination,
He can no counsel keep, it is no dread.*   *doubt
Now keep you from the white and from the red,
235 And namely* from the white wine of Lepe,   *especially
That is to sell in Fish Street and in Cheap.
This wine of Spaine creepeth subtilly —
In other wines growing faste by,
Of which there riseth such fumosity,
240 That when a man hath drunken draughtes three,
And weeneth that he be at home in Cheap,
He is in Spain, right at the town of Lepe,
Not at the Rochelle, nor at Bourdeaux town;
And thenne will he say, Samsoun! Samsoun!
245 But hearken, lordings, one word, I you pray,
That all the sovreign actes, dare I say,
Of victories in the Old Testament,
Through very God that is omnipotent,
Were done in abstinence and in prayere:
250 Look in the Bible, and there ye may it lear.*   *learn
Look, Attila, the greate conqueror,
Died in his sleep, with shame and dishonour,
Bleeding aye at his nose in drunkenness:
A captain should aye live in soberness

255 And o'er all this, advise* you right well   *consider, bethink
     What was commanded unto Lemuel;
     Not Samuel, but Lemuel, say I.
     Reade the Bible, and find it expressly
     Of wine giving to them that have justice.
260 No more of this, for it may well suffice.

     And, now that I have spoke of gluttony,
     Now will I you *defende hazardry.*   *forbid gambling*
     Hazard is very mother of leasings,*   *lies
     And of deceit, and cursed forswearings:
265 Blasphem' of Christ, manslaughter, and waste also
     Of chattel* and of time; and furthermo'   *property
     It is repreve,* and contrar' of honour,   *reproach
     For to be held a common hazardour.
     And ever the higher he is of estate,
270 The more he is holden desolate.*   *undone, worthless
     If that a prince use hazardry,
     In alle governance and policy
     He is, as by common opinion,
     Y-hold the less in reputation.
275 Chilon, that was a wise ambassador,
     Was sent to Corinth with full great honor
     From Lacedemon, to make alliance;
     And when he came, it happen'd him, by chance,
     That all the greatest that were of that land,
280 Y-playing atte hazard he them fand.*   *found
     For which, as soon as that it mighte be,
     He stole him home again to his country
     And saide there, "I will not lose my name,
     Nor will I take on me so great diffame,*   *reproach
285 You to ally unto no hazardors.*   *gamblers
     Sende some other wise ambassadors,
     For, by my troth, me were lever* die,   *rather
     Than I should you to hazardors ally.
     For ye, that be so glorious in honours,
290 Shall not ally you to no hazardours,
     As by my will, nor as by my treaty."
     This wise philosopher thus said he.
     Look eke how to the King Demetrius
     The King of Parthes, as the book saith us,
295 Sent him a pair of dice of gold in scorn,
     For he had used hazard therebeforn:
     For which he held his glory and renown
     At no value or reputatioun.

Lordes may finden other manner play
300   Honest enough to drive the day away.

Now will I speak of oathes false and great
A word or two, as olde bookes treat.
Great swearing is a thing abominable,
And false swearing is more reprovable.
305   The highe God forbade swearing at all;
Witness on Matthew: but in special
Of swearing saith the holy Jeremie,
Thou thalt swear sooth thine oathes, and not lie:
And swear in doom* and eke in righteousness;   *judgement
310   But idle swearing is a cursedness.*   *wickedness
Behold and see, there in the firste table
Of highe Godde's hestes* honourable,   *commandments
How that the second best of him is this,
Take not my name in idle* or amiss.   *in vain
315   Lo, rather* he forbiddeth such swearing,   *sooner
Than homicide, or many a cursed thing;
I say that as by order thus it standeth;
This knoweth he that his hests* understandeth,   *commandments
How that the second hest of God is that.
320   And farthermore, I will thee tell all plat,*   *flatly, plainly
That vengeance shall not parte from his house,
That of his oathes is outrageous.
"By Godde's precious heart, and by his nails,
And by the blood of Christ, that is in Hailes,[37]
325   Seven is my chance, and thine is cinque and trey:
By Godde's armes, if thou falsely play,
This dagger shall throughout thine hearte go."
This fruit comes of the *bicched bones two,*   *two cursed bones (dice)*
Forswearing, ire, falseness, and homicide.
330   Now, for the love of Christ that for us died,
Leave your oathes, bothe great and smale.
But, Sirs, now will I ell you forth my tale.

These riotoures three, of which I tell,
Long *erst than* prime rang of any bell,   *before
335   Were set them in a tavern for to drink;
And as they sat, they heard a belle clink
Before a corpse, was carried to the grave.
That one of them gan calle to his knave,*   *servant
"Go bet," quoth he, "and aske readily

37: An abbey in Gloucestershire.

340 What corpse is this, that passeth here forth by;	
And look that thou report his name well."	
"Sir," quoth the boy, "it needeth never a deal;*	*whit
It was me told ere ye came here two hours;	
He was, pardie, an old fellow of yours,	
345 And suddenly he was y-slain to-night;	
Fordrunk* as he sat on his bench upright,	*completely drunk
There came a privy thief, men clepe Death,	
That in this country all the people slay'th,	
And with his spear he smote his heart in two,	
350 And went his way withoute wordes mo'.	
He hath a thousand slain this pestilence;	
And, master, ere you come in his presence,	
Me thinketh that it were full necessary	
For to beware of such an adversary;	
355 Be ready for to meet him evermore.	
Thus taughte me my dame; I say no more."	
"By Sainte Mary," said the tavernere,	
"The child saith sooth, for he hath slain this year,	
Hence ov'r a mile, within a great village,	
360 Both man and woman, child, and hind, and page;	
I trow his habitation be there;	
To be advised* great wisdom it were,	*watchful, on one's guard
Ere* that he did a man a dishonour."	*lest
"Yea, Godde's armes," quoth this riotour,	
365 "Is it such peril with him for to meet?	
I shall him seek, by stile and eke by street.	
I make a vow, by Godde's digne* bones."	*worthy
Hearken, fellows, we three be alle ones:*	*at one
Let each of us hold up his hand to other,	
370 And each of us become the other's brother,	
And we will slay this false traitor Death;	
He shall be slain, he that so many slay'th,	
By Godde's dignity, ere it be night."	
Together have these three their trothe plight	
375 To live and die each one of them for other	
As though he were his owen sworen brother.	
And up they start, all drunken, in this rage,	
And forth they go towardes that village	
Of which the taverner had spoke beforn,	
380 And many a grisly* oathe have they sworn,	*dreadful
And Christe's blessed body they to-rent;*	*tore to pieces
"Death shall be dead, if that we may him hent."*	*catch
When they had gone not fully half a mile,	
Right as they would have trodden o'er a stile,	

385 An old man and a poore with them met.
     This olde man full meekely them gret,*   *greeted
     And saide thus; "Now, lordes, God you see!"*   *look on graciously
     The proudest of these riotoures three
     Answer'd again; "What? churl, with sorry grace,
390 Why art thou all forwrapped* save thy face?   *closely wrapt up
     Why livest thou so long in so great age?"
     This olde man gan look on his visage,
     And saide thus; "For that I cannot find
     A man, though that I walked unto Ind,
395 Neither in city, nor in no village go,
     That woulde change his youthe for mine age;
     And therefore must I have mine age still
     As longe time as it is Godde's will.
     And Death, alas! he will not have my life.
400 Thus walk I like a resteless caitife,*   *miserable wretch
     And on the ground, which is my mother's gate,
     I knocke with my staff, early and late,
     And say to her, 'Leve* mother, let me in.   *dear
     Lo, how I wane, flesh, and blood, and skin;
405 Alas! when shall my bones be at rest?
     Mother, with you I woulde change my chest,
     That in my chamber longe time hath be,
     Yea, for an hairy clout to *wrap in me.'*   *wrap myself in*
     But yet to me she will not do that grace,
410 For which fall pale and welked* is my face.   *withered
     But, Sirs, to you it is no courtesy
     To speak unto an old man villainy,
     But* he trespass in word or else in deed.   *except
     In Holy Writ ye may yourselves read;
415 'Against* an old man, hoar upon his head,   *to meet
     Ye should arise:' therefore I you rede,*   *advise
     Ne do unto an old man no harm now,
     No more than ye would a man did you
     In age, if that ye may so long abide.
420 And God be with you, whether ye go or ride
     I must go thither as I have to go."
     "Nay, olde churl, by God thou shalt not so,"
     Saide this other hazardor anon;
     "Thou partest not so lightly, by Saint John.
425 Thou spakest right now of that traitor Death,
     That in this country all our friendes slay'th;
     Have here my troth, as thou art his espy;*   *spy
     Tell where he is, or thou shalt it abie,*   *suffer for
     By God and by the holy sacrament;

430 For soothly thou art one of his assent
    To slay us younge folk, thou false thief."
    "Now, Sirs," quoth he, "if it be you so lief*   *desire
    To finde Death, turn up this crooked way,
    For in that grove I left him, by my fay,
435 Under a tree, and there he will abide;
    Nor for your boast he will him nothing hide.
    See ye that oak? right there ye shall him find.
    God save you, that bought again mankind,
    And you amend!" Thus said this olde man;
440 And evereach of these riotoures ran,
    Till they came to the tree, and there they found
    Of florins fine, of gold y-coined round,
    Well nigh a seven bushels, as them thought.
    No longer as then after Death they sought;
445 But each of them so glad was of the sight,
    For that the florins were so fair and bright,
    That down they sat them by the precious hoard.
    The youngest of them spake the firste word:
    "Brethren," quoth he, "*take keep* what I shall say;   *heed*
450 My wit is great, though that I bourde* and play   *joke, frolic
    This treasure hath Fortune unto us given
    In mirth and jollity our life to liven;
    And lightly as it comes, so will we spend.
    Hey! Godde's precious dignity! who wend*   *weened, thought
455 Today that we should have so fair a grace?
    But might this gold he carried from this place
    Home to my house, or elles unto yours
    (For well I wot that all this gold is ours),
    Then were we in high felicity.
460 But truely by day it may not be;
    Men woulde say that we were thieves strong,
    And for our owen treasure do us hong.*   *have us hanged
    This treasure muste carried be by night,
    As wisely and as slily as it might.
465 Wherefore I rede,* that cut** among us all   *advise; **lots
    We draw, and let see where the cut will fall:
    And he that hath the cut, with hearte blithe
    Shall run unto the town, and that full swithe,*   *quickly
    And bring us bread and wine full privily:
470 And two of us shall keepe subtilly
    This treasure well: and if he will not tarry,
    When it is night, we will this treasure carry,
    By one assent, where as us thinketh best."
    Then one of them the cut brought in his fist,

475   And bade them draw, and look where it would fall;
       And it fell on the youngest of them all;
       And forth toward the town he went anon.
       And all so soon as that he was y-gone,
       The one of them spake thus unto the other;
480   "Thou knowest well that thou art my sworn brother,
       Thy profit will I tell thee right anon.   *what is for thine advantage*
       Thou knowest well that our fellow is gone,
       And here is gold, and that full great plenty,
       That shall departed* he among us three.   *divided
485   But natheless, if I could shape* it so   *contrive
       That it departed were among us two,
       Had I not done a friende's turn to thee?"
       Th' other answer'd, "I n'ot* how that may be;   *know not
       He knows well that the gold is with us tway.
490   What shall we do? what shall we to him say?"
       "Shall it be counsel?"* said the firste shrew;**   *secret; **wretch
       "And I shall tell to thee in wordes few
       What we shall do, and bring it well about."
       "I grante," quoth the other, "out of doubt,
495   That by my truth I will thee not bewray."*   *betray
       "Now," quoth the first, "thou know'st well we be tway,
       And two of us shall stronger be than one.
       Look; when that he is set,* thou right anon   *sat down
       Arise, as though thou wouldest with him play;
500   And I shall rive* him through the sides tway,   *stab
       While that thou strugglest with him as in game;
       And with thy dagger look thou do the same.
       And then shall all this gold departed* be,   *divided
       My deare friend, betwixte thee and me:
505   Then may we both our lustes* all fulfil,   *pleasures
       And play at dice right at our owen will."
       And thus accorded* be these shrewes** tway   *agreed; **wretches
       To slay the third, as ye have heard me say.
       The youngest, which that wente to the town,
510   Full oft in heart he rolled up and down
       The beauty of these florins new and bright.
       "O Lord!" quoth he, "if so were that I might
       Have all this treasure to myself alone,
       There is no man that lives under the throne
515   Of God, that shoulde have so merry as I."
       And at the last the fiend our enemy
       Put in his thought, that he should poison buy,
       With which he mighte slay his fellows twy.*   *two
       For why, the fiend found him *in such living,*   *leading such a (bad) life*

520   That he had leave to sorrow him to bring.
       For this was utterly his full intent
       To slay them both, and never to repent.
       And forth he went, no longer would he tarry,
       Into the town to an apothecary,
525   And prayed him that he him woulde sell
       Some poison, that he might *his rattes quell,*   *kill his rats*
       And eke there was a polecat in his haw,*   *farm-yard, hedge
       That, as he said, his eapons had y-slaw:*   *slain
       And fain he would him wreak,* if that he might,   *revenge
530   Of vermin that destroyed him by night.
       Th'apothecary answer'd, "Thou shalt have
       A thing, as wisly* God my soule save,   *surely
       In all this world there is no creature
       That eat or drank hath of this confecture,
535   Not but the mountance* of a corn of wheat,   *amount
       That he shall not his life *anon forlete;*   *immediately lay down*
       Yea, sterve* he shall, and that in lesse while   *die
       Than thou wilt go apace* nought but a mile: *quickly
       This poison is so strong and violent."
540   This cursed man hath in his hand y-hent*   *taken
       This poison in a box, and swift he ran
       Into the nexte street, unto a man,
       And borrow'd of him large bottles three;
       And in the two the poison poured he;
545   The third he kepte clean for his own drink,
       For all the night he shope him* for to swink**   *purposed; **labour
       In carrying off the gold out of that place.
       And when this riotour, with sorry grace,
       Had fill'd with wine his greate bottles three,
550   To his fellows again repaired he.
       What needeth it thereof to sermon* more?   *talk, discourse
       For, right as they had cast* his death before,   *plotted
       Right so they have him slain, and that anon.
       And when that this was done, thus spake the one;
555   "Now let us sit and drink, and make us merry,
       And afterward we will his body bury."
       And with that word it happen'd him *par cas*   *by chance*
       To take the bottle where the poison was,
       And drank, and gave his fellow drink also,
560   For which anon they sterved* both the two.   *died
       But certes I suppose that Avicen[38]
       Wrote never in no canon, nor no fen*,   *chapter

––––––––––––

38: A famed medical writer.

More wondrous signes of empoisoning,
Than had these wretches two ere their ending.
565 Thus ended be these homicides two,
And eke the false empoisoner also.
O cursed sin, full of all cursedness!
O trait'rous homicide! O wickedness!
O glutt'ny, luxury, and hazardry!
570 Thou blasphemer of Christ with villany,*   *outrage, impiety
And oathes great, of usage and of pride!
Alas! mankinde, how may it betide,
That to thy Creator, which that thee wrought,
And with his precious hearte-blood thee bought,
575 Thou art so false and so unkind,* alas!   *unnatural
Now, good men, God forgive you your trespass,
And ware* you from the sin of avarice.   *keep
Mine holy pardon may you all warice,*   *heal
So that ye offer *nobles or sterlings,*   *gold or silver coins*
580 Or elles silver brooches, spoons, or rings.
Bowe your head under this holy bull.
Come up, ye wives, and offer of your will;
Your names I enter in my roll anon;
Into the bliss of heaven shall ye gon;
585 I you assoil* by mine high powere,   *absolve
You that will offer, as clean and eke as clear
As ye were born. Lo, Sires, thus I preach;
And Jesus Christ, that is our soules' leech,*   *healer
So grante you his pardon to receive;
590 For that is best, I will not deceive.
But, Sirs, one word forgot I in my tale;
I have relics and pardon in my mail,
As fair as any man in Engleland,
Which were me given by the Pope's hand.
595 If any of you will of devotion
Offer, and have mine absolution,
Come forth anon, and kneele here adown
And meekely receive my pardoun.
Or elles take pardon, as ye wend,*   *go
600 All new and fresh at every towne's end,
So that ye offer, always new and new,
Nobles or pence which that be good and true.
'Tis an honour to evereach* that is here,   *each one
That ye have a suffisant* pardonere   *suitable
605 T'assoile* you in country as ye ride,   *absolve
For aventures which that may betide.
Paraventure there may fall one or two

Down of his horse, and break his neck in two.
Look, what a surety is it to you all,
610   That I am in your fellowship y-fall,
That may assoil* you bothe *more and lass,*   *absolve; *great and small*
When that the soul shall from the body pass.
I rede* that our Hoste shall begin,   *advise
For he is most enveloped in sin.
615   Come forth, Sir Host, and offer first anon,
And thou shalt kiss; the relics every one,
Yea, for a groat; unbuckle anon thy purse.
"Nay, nay," quoth he, "then have I Christe's curse!
Let be," quoth he, "it shall not be, *so the'ch.*   *so may I thrive*
620   Thou wouldest make me kiss thine olde breech,
And swear it were a relic of a saint,
Though it were with thy *fundament depaint'.*   *stained by your bottom*
But, by the cross which that Saint Helen fand,*   *found[39]
I would I had thy coilons* in mine hand,   *testicles
625   Instead of relics, or of sanctuary.
Let cut them off, I will thee help them carry;
They shall be shrined in a hogge's turd."
The Pardoner answered not one word;
So wroth he was, no worde would he say.
630   "Now," quoth our Host, "I will no longer play
With thee, nor with none other angry man."
But right anon the worthy Knight began
(When that he saw that all the people lough*),   *laughed
"No more of this, for it is right enough.
635   Sir Pardoner, be merry and glad of cheer;
And ye, Sir Host, that be to me so dear,
I pray you that ye kiss the Pardoner;
And, Pardoner, I pray thee draw thee ner,*   *nearer
And as we didde, let us laugh and play."
640   Anon they kiss'd, and rode forth their way.

39: Saint Helen supposedly found Christ's true cross.

Chaucer's Retraction of The Canterbury Tales

Now pray I to you all that hear this little treatise or read it, that if there be anything in it that likes them, that thereof they thank our Lord Jesus Christ, of whom proceedeth all wit and all goodness; and if there be anything that displeaseth them, I pray them also that they arette [ascribe] it to the default of mine unconning [unskillfulness], and not to my will, that would fain have said better if I had had conning; for the book saith, all that is written for our doctrine is written. Wherefore I beseech you meekly for the mercy of God that ye pray for me, that God have mercy on me and forgive me my guilts, and namely my translations and of inditing in worldly vanities, which I revoke in my Retractions, as is the Book of Troilus, the Book also of Fame, the Book of Twenty-five Ladies, the Book of the Duchess, the Book of Saint Valentine's Day and of the Parliament of Birds, the Tales of Canter bury, all those that sounen unto sin, [tend towards sin] the Book of the Lion, and many other books, if they were in my mind or remembrance, and many a song and many a lecherous lay, of the which Christ for his great mercy forgive me the sins. But of the translation of Boece de Consolatione, and other books of consolation and of legend of lives of saints, and homilies, and moralities, and devotion, that thank I our Lord Jesus Christ, and his mother, and all the saints in heaven, beseeching them that they from henceforth unto my life's end send me grace to bewail my guilts, and to study to the salvation of my soul, and grant me grace and space of very repentance, penitence, confession, and satisfaction, to do in this present life, through the benign grace of Him that is King of kings and Priest of all priests, that bought us with his precious blood of his heart, so that I may be one of them at the day of doom that shall be saved: Qui cum Patre et Spiritu Sancto vivis et regnas Deus per omnia secula[40]. Amen.

40: He who lives and reigns with the Father and Holy Spirit, God, world without end.

THE COMPLAINT OF CHAUCER TO HIS PURSE

To yow, my purse, and to noon other wight*   *person
Complayne I, for ye be my lady dere!
I am so sory, now that ye been lyght;
For certes, but* ye make me hevy chere,   *unless
Me were as leef be layd upon my bere*;   *I were as happy*; *bier[41]
For which unto your mercy thus I crye:
Beth hevy ageyn, or elles mot* I dye!   *might

Now voucheth sauf this day, *or yt be nyght,*   *ere it is night*
That I of yow* the blisful soun* may here,   *you; **sound
Or see your colour lyk the sonne* bryght,   *sun
That of yelownesse hadde never pere*.   *peer
Ye be my lyf, ye be *myn hertes stere,*   *my heart's steerer*
Quene of comfort and of good companye:
Beth hevy ageyn*, or elles moote** I dye!   *again; **might

Now purse, that ben to me my *lyves lyght*   *life's light*
And saveour, as doun in this world here,
Out of this toune helpe me thurgh your myght,
Syn* that ye wole** nat ben my tresorere;   *since; **will
For I am shave as nye* as any frere**.   *close; **friar
But yet I pray unto your curtesye:
Beth hevy agen, or elles moote I dye!

Lenvoy de Chaucer   *Envoy to Henry IV*
O conquerour of *Brutes Albyon*,   *Brutus's England*
Which that by lyne and free eleccion
Been verray kyng, this song to yow I sende;   *are very king*
And ye*, that mowen** alle oure harmes amende, *you; **may
Have mynde* upon my supplicacion!   *mind

41: On which a coffin is placed.

Everyman

CHARACTERS

EVERYMAN
GOD: ADONAI
DEATH
MESSENGER
FELLOWSHIP
COUSIN
KINDRED
GOODS
GOOD-DEEDS
STRENGTH
DISCRETION
FIVE-WITS
BEAUTY
KNOWLEDGE
CONFESSION
ANGEL
DOCTOR

Here beginneth a treatise how the high Father of Heaven sendeth Death to summon every creature to come and give account of their lives in this world and is in manner of a moral play.

Messenger. I pray you all give your audience,
And hear this matter with reverence,
By figure a moral play--
The *Summoning of Everyman* called it is,
5 That of our lives and ending shows
How transitory we be all day.
This matter is wondrous precious,
But the intent of it is more gracious,
And sweet to bear away.
10 The story saith,--Man, in the beginning,
Look well, and take good heed to the ending,
Be you never so gay!
Ye think sin in the beginning full sweet,
Which in the end causeth thy soul to weep,
15 When the body lieth in clay.
Here shall you see how *Fellowship* and *Jollity*,

Both *Strength*, *Pleasure*, and *Beauty*,
Will fade from thee as flower in May.
For ye shall hear, how our heaven king
20 Calleth *Everyman* to a general reckoning:
Give audience, and hear what he doth say.

God. I perceive here in my majesty,
How that all creatures be to me unkind,
Living without dread in worldly prosperity:
25 Of ghostly sight the people be so blind,
Drowned in sin, they know me not for their God;
In worldly riches is all their mind,
They fear not my rightwiseness, the sharp rod;
My law that I shewed, when I for them died,
30 They forget clean, and shedding of my blood red;
I hanged between two, it cannot be denied;
To get them life I suffered to be dead;
I healed their feet, with thorns hurt was my head:
I could do no more than I did truly,
35 And now I see the people do clean forsake me.
They use the seven deadly sins damnable;
As pride, covetise, wrath, and lechery,
Now in the world be made commendable;
And thus they leave of angels the heavenly company;
40 Everyman liveth so after his own pleasure,
And yet of their life they be nothing sure:
I see the more that I them forbear
The worse they be from year to year;
All that liveth appaireth[7] fast,
45 Therefore I will in all the haste
Have a reckoning of Everyman's person
For and I leave the people thus alone
In their life and wicked tempests,
Verily they will become much worse than beasts;
50 For now one would by envy another up eat;
Charity they all do clean forget.
I hoped well that Everyman
In my glory should make his mansion,
And thereto I had them all elect;
55 But now I see, like traitors deject,
They thank me not for the pleasure that I to them meant,
Nor yet for their being that I them have lent;
I proffered the people great multitude of mercy,
And few there be that asketh it heartily;
60 They be so cumbered with worldly riches,

That needs on them I must do justice,
On Everyman living without fear.
Where art thou, *Death*, thou mighty messenger?

Death. Almighty God, I am here at your will,
65   Your commandment to fulfil.

God. Go thou to *Everyman*,
And show him in my name
A pilgrimage he must on him take,
Which he in no wise may escape;
70   And that he bring with him a sure reckoning
Without delay or any tarrying.

Death. Lord, I will in the world go run over all,
And cruelly outsearch both great and small;
Every man will I beset that liveth beastly
75   Out of God's laws, and dreadeth not folly:
He that loveth riches I will strike with my dart,
His sight to blind, and from heaven to depart,
Except that alms be his good friend,
In hell for to dwell, world without end.
80   Lo, yonder I see *Everyman* walking;
Full little he thinketh on my coming;
His mind is on fleshly lusts and his treasure,
And great pain it shall cause him to endure
Before the Lord Heaven King.
85   *Everyman*, stand still; whither art thou going
Thus gaily? Hast thou thy Maker forget?

Everyman. Why askst thou?
Wouldest thou wete?

Death. Yea, sir, I will show you;
90   In great haste I am sent to thee
From God out of his majesty.

Everyman. What, sent to me?

Death. Yea, certainly.
Though thou have forget him here,
95   He thinketh on thee in the heavenly sphere,
As, or we depart, thou shalt know.

Everyman. What desireth God of me?

Death. That shall I show thee;
A reckoning he will needs have
100 Without any longer respite.

Everyman. To give a reckoning longer leisure I crave;
This blind matter troubleth my wit.

Death. On thee thou must take a long journey:
Therefore thy book of count with thee thou bring;
For turn again thou can not by no way,
105 And look thou be sure of thy reckoning:
For before God thou shalt answer, and show
Thy many bad deeds and good but a few;
How thou hast spent thy life, and in what wise,
Before the chief lord of paradise.
110 Have ado that we were in that way,
For, wete thou well, thou shalt make none attournay.

Everyman. Full unready I am such reckoning to give.
I know thee not: what messenger art thou?

Death. I am *Death*, that no man dreadeth.
115 For every man I rest and no man spareth;
For it is God's commandment
That all to me should be obedient.

Everyman. O *Death*, thou comest when I had thee least in mind;
In thy power it lieth me to save,
120 Yet of my good will I give thee, if ye will be kind,
Yea, a thousand pound shalt thou have,
And defer this matter till another day.

Death. Everyman, it may not be by no way;
I set not by gold, silver, nor riches,
125 Ne by pope, emperor, king, duke, ne princes.
For and I would receive gifts great,
All the world I might get;
But my custom is clean contrary.
I give thee no respite: come hence, and not tarry.

130 *Everyman.* Alas, shall I have no longer respite?
I may say *Death* giveth no warning:
To think on thee, it maketh my heart sick,
For all unready is my book of reckoning.
But twelve year and I might have abiding,
135 My counting book I would make so clear,
That my reckoning I should not need to fear.

Wherefore, *Death*, I pray thee, for God's mercy,
Spare me till I be provided of remedy.

Death. Thee availeth not to cry, weep, and pray:
140 But haste thee lightly that you were gone the journey,
And prove thy friends if thou can.
For, wete thou well, the tide abideth no man,
And in the world each living creature
For *Adam's* sin must die of nature.

145 *Everyman*. *Death*, if I should this pilgrimage take,
And my reckoning surely make,
Show me, for saint *charity*,
Should I not come again shortly?

Death. No, *Everyman*; and thou be once there,
150 Thou mayst never more come here,
Trust me verily.

Everyman. O gracious God, in the high seat celestial,
Have mercy on me in this most need;
Shall I have no company from this vale terrestrial
155 Of mine acquaintance that way me to lead?

Death. Yea, if any be so hardy,
That would go with thee and bear thee company.
Hie thee that you were gone to God's magnificence,
Thy reckoning to give before his presence.
160 What, weenest thou thy life is given thee,
And thy worldly goods also?

Everyman. I had wend so, verily.

Death. Nay, nay; it was but lent thee;
For as soon as thou art go,
165 Another awhile shall have it, and then go therefro
Even as thou hast done.
Everyman, thou art mad; thou hast thy wits five,
And here on earth will not amend thy life,
For suddenly I do come.

170 *Everyman*. O wretched caitiff, whither shall I flee,
That I might scape this endless sorrow!
Now, gentle *Death*, spare me till to-morrow,
That I may amend me
With good advisement.

175 *Death*. Nay, thereto I will not consent,
Nor no man will I respite,
But to the heart suddenly I shall smite
Without any advisement.
And now out of thy sight I will me hie;
180 See thou make thee ready shortly,
For thou mayst say this is the day
That no man living may scape away.

Everyman. Alas, I may well weep with sighs deep;
Now have I no manner of company
185 To help me in my journey, and me to keep;
And also my writing is full unready.
How shall I do now for to excuse me?
I would to God I had never be gete!
To my soul a full great profit it had be;
190 For now I fear pains huge and great.
The time passeth; Lord, help that all wrought;
For though I mourn it availeth nought.
The day passeth, and is almost a-go;
I wot not well what for to do.
195 To whom were I best my complaint to make?
What, and I to *Fellowship* thereof spake,
And showed him of this sudden chance?
For in him is all mine affiance;
We have in the world so many a day
200 Be on good friends in sport and play.
I see him yonder, certainly;
I trust that he will bear me company;
Therefore to him will I speak to ease my sorrow.
Well met, good *Fellowship*, and good morrow!

205 *Fellowship speaketh*. *Everyman*, good morrow by this day.
Sir, why lookest thou so piteously?
If any thing be amiss, I pray thee, me say,
That I may help to remedy.

Everyman. Yea, good *Fellowship*, yea,
210 I am in great jeopardy.

Fellowship. My true friend, show to me your mind;
I will not forsake thee, unto my life's end,
In the way of good company.

Everyman. That was well spoken, and lovingly.

215 *Fellowship.* Sir, I must needs know your heaviness;
I have pity to see you in any distress;
If any have you wronged ye shall revenged be,
Though I on the ground be slain for thee,--
Though that I know before that I should die.

220 *Everyman.* Verily, *Fellowship*, gramercy.

Fellowship. Tush! by thy thanks I set not a straw.
Show me your grief, and say no more.

Everyman. If I my heart should to you break,
And then you to turn your mind from me,
225 And would not me comfort, when you hear me speak,
Then should I ten times sorrier be.

Fellowship. Sir, I say as I will do in deed.

Everyman. Then be you a good friend at need:
I have found you true here before.

230 *Fellowship.* And so ye shall evermore;
For, in faith, and thou go to Hell,
I will not forsake thee by the way!

Everyman. Ye speak like a good friend; I believe you well;
I shall deserve it, and I may.

235 *Fellowship.* I speak of no deserving, by this day.
For he that will say and nothing do
Is not worthy with good company to go;
Therefore show me the grief of your mind,
As to your friend most loving and kind.

240 *Everyman.* I shall show you how it is;
Commanded I am to go a journey,
A long way, hard and dangerous,
And give a strait count without delay
Before the high judge Adonai.
245 Wherefore I pray you, bear me company,
As ye have promised, in this journey.

Fellowship. That is matter indeed! Promise is duty,
But, and I should take such a voyage on me,
I know it well, it should be to my pain:

250   Also it make me afeard, certain.
       But let us take counsel here as well as we can,
       For your words would fear a strong man.

       Everyman. Why, ye said, If I had need,
       Ye would me never forsake, quick nor dead,
255   Though it were to hell truly.

       Fellowship. So I said, certainly,
       But such pleasures be set aside, thee sooth to say:
       And also, if we took such a journey,
       When should we come again?

260   *Everyman.* Nay, never again till the day of doom.

       Fellowship. In faith, then will not I come there!
       Who hath you these tidings brought?

       Everyman. Indeed, *Death* was with me here.

       Fellowship. Now, by God that all hath bought,
265   If *Death* were the messenger,
       For no man that is living to-day
       I will not go that loath journey--
       Not for the father that begat me!

       Everyman. Ye promised other wise, pardie.

270   *Fellowship.* I wot well I say so truly;
       And yet if thou wilt eat, and drink, and make good cheer,
       Or haunt to women, the lusty company,
       I would not forsake you, while the day is clear,
       Trust me verily!

275   *Everyman.* Yea, thereto ye would be ready;
       To go to mirth, solace, and play,
       Your mind will sooner apply
       Than to bear me company in my long journey.

       Fellowship. Now, in good faith, I will not that way.
280   But and thou wilt murder, or any man kill,
       In that I will help thee with a good will!

       Everyman. O that is a simple advice indeed!
       Gentle *fellow*, help me in my necessity;

We have loved long, and now I need,
285   And now, gentle *Fellowship*, remember me.

Fellowship. Whether ye have loved me or no,
By Saint John, I will not with thee go.

Everyman. Yet I pray thee, take the labour, and do so much for me
To bring me forward, for saint charity,
290   And comfort me till I come without the town.

Fellowship. Nay, and thou would give me a new gown,
I will not a foot with thee go;
But and you had tarried I would not have left thee so.
And as now, God speed thee in thy journey,
295   For from thee I will depart as fast as I may.

Everyman. Whither away, *Fellowship*? will you forsake me?

Fellowship. Yea, by my fay, to God I betake thee.

Everyman. Farewell, good *Fellowship*; for this my heart is sore;
Adieu for ever, I shall see thee no more.

300   *Fellowship.* In faith, *Everyman*, farewell now at the end;
For you I will remember that parting is mourning.

Everyman. Alack! shall we thus depart indeed?
Our Lady, help, without any more comfort,
Lo, *Fellowship* forsaketh me in my most need:
305   For help in this world whither shall I resort?
Fellowship herebefore with me would merry make;
And now little sorrow for me doth he take.
It is said, in prosperity men friends may find,
Which in adversity be full unkind.
310   Now whither for succour shall I flee,
Sith that *Fellowship* hath forsaken me?
To my kinsmen I will truly,
Praying them to help me in my necessity;
I believe that they will do so,
315   For kind will creep where it may not go.
I will go say, for yonder I see them go.
Where be ye now, my friends and kinsmen?

Kindred. Here be we now at your commandment.
Cousin, I pray you show us your intent
320   In any wise, and not spare.

Cousin. Yea, *Everyman,* and to us declare
If ye be disposed to go any whither,
For wete you well, we will live and die together.

Kindred. In wealth and woe we will with you hold,
325   For over his kin a man may be bold.

Everyman. Gramercy, my friends and kinsmen kind.
Now shall I show you the grief of my mind:
I was commanded by a messenger,
That is an high king's chief officer;
330   He bade me go a pilgrimage to my pain,
And I know well I shall never come again;
Also I must give a reckoning straight,
For I have a great enemy, that hath me in wait,
Which intendeth me for to hinder.

335   *Kindred.* What account is that which ye must render?
That would I know.

Everyman. Of all my works I must show
How I have lived and my days spent;
Also of ill deeds, that I have used
340   In my time, sith life was me lent;
And of all virtues that I have refused.
Therefore I pray you go thither with me,
To help to make mine account, for saint *charity.*

Cousin. What, to go thither? Is that the matter?
345   Nay, *Everyman,* I had liefer fast bread and water
All this five year and more.

Everyman. Alas, that ever I was bore!
For now shall I never be merry
If that you forsake me.

350   *Kindred.* Ah, sir; what, ye be a merry man!
Take good heart to you, and make no moan.
But one thing I warn you, by Saint Anne,
As for me, ye shall go alone.

Everyman. My *Cousin,* will you not with me go?

355   *Cousin.* No, by our Lady; I have the cramp in my toe.
Trust not to me, for, so God me speed,
I will deceive you in your most need.

Kindred. It availeth not us to tice.
Ye shall have my maid with all my heart;
360 She loveth to go to feasts, there to be nice,
And to dance, and abroad to start:
I will give her leave to help you in that journey,
If that you and she may agree.

Everyman. Now show me the very effect of your mind.
365 Will you go with me, or abide behind?

Kindred. Abide behind? yea, that I will and I may!
Therefore farewell until another day.

Everyman. How should I be merry or glad?
For fair promises to me make,
370 But when I have most need, they me forsake.
I am deceived; that maketh me sad.

Cousin. Cousin *Everyman*, farewell now,
For verily I will not go with you;
Also of mine own an unready reckoning
375 I have to account; therefore I make tarrying.
Now, God keep thee, for now I go.

Everyman. Ah, *Jesus*, is all come hereto?
Lo, fair words maketh fools feign;
They promise and nothing will do certain.
380 My kinsmen promised me faithfully
For to abide with me steadfastly,
And now fast away do they flee:
Even so *Fellowship* promised me.
What friend were best me of to provide?
385 I lose my time here longer to abide.
Yet in my mind a thing there is;--
All my life I have loved riches;
If that my good now help me might,
He would make my heart full light.
390 I will speak to him in this distress.--
Where art thou, my *Goods* and riches?

Goods. Who calleth me? *Everyman?* what haste thou hast!
I lie here in corners, trussed and piled so high,
And in chests I am locked so fast,
395 Also sacked in bags, thou mayst see with thine eye,
I cannot stir; in packs low I lie.
What would ye have, lightly me say.

Everyman. Come hither, *Good,* in all the haste thou may,
For of counsel I must desire thee.

400   *Goods.* Sir, and ye in the world have trouble or adversity,
That can I help you to remedy shortly.

Everyman. It is another disease that grieveth me;
In this world it is not, I tell thee so.
I am sent for another way to go,
405   To give a straight account general
Before the highest *Jupiter* of all;
And all my life I have had joy and pleasure in thee.
Therefore I pray thee go with me,
For, peradventure, thou mayst before God Almighty
410   My reckoning help to clean and purify;
For it is said ever among,
That money maketh all right that is wrong.

Goods. Nay, *Everyman,* I sing another song,
I follow no man in such voyages;
415   For and I went with thee
Thou shouldst fare much the worse for me;
For because on me thou did set thy mind,
Thy reckoning I have made blotted and blind,
That thine account thou cannot make truly;
420   And that hast thou for the love of me.

Everyman. That would grieve me full sore,
When I should come to that fearful answer.
Up, let us go thither together.

Goods. Nay, not so, I am too brittle, I may not endure;
425   I will follow no man one foot, be ye sure.

Everyman. Alas, I have thee loved, and had great pleasure
All my life-days on good and treasure.

Goods. That is to thy damnation without lesing,
For my love is contrary to the love everlasting.
430   But if thou had me loved moderately during,
As, to the poor give part of me,
Then shouldst thou not in this dolour be,
Nor in this great sorrow and care.

Everyman. Lo, now was I deceived or I was ware,
435   And all I may wyte my spending of time.

Goods. What, weenest thou that I am thine?

Everyman. I had wend so.

Goods. Nay, *Everyman,* I say no;
As for a while I was lent thee,
440   A season thou hast had me in prosperity;
My condition is man's soul to kill;
If I save one, a thousand I do spill;
Weenest thou that I will follow thee?
Nay, from this world, not verily.

445   *Everyman.* I had wend otherwise.

Goods. Therefore to thy soul *Good* is a thief;
For when thou art dead, this is my guise
Another to deceive in the same wise
As I have done thee, and all to his soul's reprief.

450   *Everyman.* O false *Good,* cursed thou be!
Thou traitor to God, that hast deceived me,
And caught me in thy snare.

Goods. Marry, thou brought thyself in care,
Whereof I am glad,
455   I must needs laugh, I cannot be sad.

Everyman. Ah, *Good,* thou hast had long my heartly love;
I gave thee that which should be the Lord's above.
But wilt thou not go with me in deed?
I pray thee truth to say.

460   *Goods.* No, so God me speed,
Therefore farewell, and have good day.

Everyman. O, to whom shall I make my moan
For to go with me in that heavy journey?
First *Fellowship* said he would with me gone;
465   His words were very pleasant and gay,
But afterward he left me alone.
Then spake I to my kinsmen all in despair,
And also they gave me words fair,
They lacked no fair speaking,
470   But all forsake me in the ending.
Then went I to my *Goods* that I loved best,
In hope to have comfort, but there had I least;
For my *Goods* sharply did me tell

        That he bringeth many into hell.
475   Then of myself I was ashamed,
        And so I am worthy to be blamed;
        Thus may I well myself hate.
        Of whom shall I now counsel take?
        I think that I shall never speed
480   Till that I go to my *Good-Deed*,
        But alas, she is so weak,
        That she can neither go nor speak;
        Yet will I venture on her now.--
        My *Good-Deeds*, where be you?

485   *Good-Deeds.* Here I lie cold in the ground;
        Thy sins hath me sore bound,
        That I cannot stir.

        Everyman. O, *Good-Deeds*, I stand in fear;
        I must you pray of counsel,
490   For help now should come right well.

        Goods-Deeds. Everyman, I have understanding
        That ye be summoned account to make
        Before *Messias*, of Jerusalem King;
        And you do by me that journey what you will I take.

495   *Everyman.* Therefore I come to you, my moan to make;
        I pray you, that ye will go with me.

        Good-Deeds. I would full fain, but I cannot stand verily.

        Everyman. Why, is there anything on you fall?

        Good-Deeds. Yea, sir, I may thank you of all;
500   If ye had perfectly cheered me,
        Your book of account now full ready had be.
        Look, the books of your works and deeds eke;
        Oh, see how they lie under the feet,
        To your soul's heaviness.

505   *Everyman.* Our Lord *Jesus*, help me!
        For one letter here I can not see.

        Good-Deeds. There is a blind reckoning in time of
        distress!

        Everyman. Good-Deeds, I pray you, help me in this need,
510   Or else I am for ever damned indeed;

Therefore help me to make reckoning
Before the redeemer of all thing,
That king is, and was, and ever shall.

Good-Deeds. Everyman, I am sorry of your fall,
515   And fain would I help you, and I were able.

Everyman. Good-Deeds, your counsel I pray you give me.

Good-Deeds. That shall I do verily;
Though that on my feet I may not go,
I have a sister, that shall with you also,
520   Called *Knowledge*, which shall with you abide,
To help you to make that dreadful reckoning.

Knowledge. Everyman, I will go with thee, and be thy guide,
In thy most need to go by thy side.

Everyman. In good condition I am now in every thing,
525   And am wholly content with this good thing;
Thanked be God my Creator.

Good-Deeds. And when he hath brought thee there,
Where thou shalt heal thee of thy smart,
Then go you with your reckoning and your *Good-Deeds* together
530   For to make you joyful at heart
Before the blessed Trinity.

Everyman. My *Good-Deeds*, gramercy;
I am well content, certainly,
With your words sweet.

535   *Knowledge*. Now go we together lovingly,
To *Confession*, that cleansing river.

Everyman. For joy I weep; I would we were there;
But, I pray you, give me cognition
Where dwelleth that holy man, *Confession*.

540   *Knowledge*. In the house of salvation:
We shall find him in that place,
That shall us comfort by God's grace.
Lo, this is *Confession*; kneel down and ask mercy,
For he is in good conceit with God almighty.

545   *Everyman*. O glorious fountain that all uncleanness doth clarify,
Wash from me the spots of vices unclean,

That on me no sin may be seen;
I come with *Knowledge* for my redemption,
Repent with hearty and full contrition;
550　For I am commanded a pilgrimage to take,
And great accounts before God to make.
Now, I pray you, *Shrift*, mother of salvation,
Help my good deeds for my piteous exclamation.

Confession. I know your sorrow well, *Everyman*;
555　Because with *Knowledge* ye come to me,
I will you comfort as well as I can,
And a precious jewel I will give thee,
Called penance, wise voider of adversity;
Therewith shall your body chastised be,
560　With abstinence and perseverance in God's service:
Here shall you receive that scourge of me,
Which is penance strong, that ye must endure,
To remember thy Saviour was scourged for thee
With sharp scourges, and suffered it patiently;
565　So must thou, or thou scape that painful pilgrimage;
Knowledge, keep him in this voyage,
And by that time *Good-Deeds* will be with thee.
But in any wise, be sure of mercy,
For your time draweth fast, and ye will saved be;
570　Ask God mercy, and He will grant truly,
When with the scourge of penance man doth him bind,
The oil of forgiveness then shall he find.

Everyman. Thanked be God for his gracious work!
For now I will my penance begin;
575　This hath rejoiced and lighted my heart,
Though the knots be painful and hard within.

Knowledge. *Everyman*, look your penance that ye fulfil,
What pain that ever it to you be,
And *Knowledge* shall give you counsel at will,
580　How your accounts ye shall make clearly.

Everyman. O eternal God, O heavenly figure,
O way of rightwiseness, O goodly vision,
Which descended down in a virgin pure
Because he would *Everyman* redeem,
585　Which *Adam* forfeited by his disobedience:
O blessed Godhead, elect and high-divine,
Forgive my grievous offence;
Here I cry thee mercy in this presence.

O ghostly treasure, O ransomer and redeemer
590 Of all the world, hope and conductor,
Mirror of joy, and founder of mercy,
Which illumineth heaven and earth thereby,
Hear my clamorous complaint, though it late be;
Receive my prayers; unworthy in this heavy life,
595 Though I be, a sinner most abominable,
Yet let my name be written in *Moses'* table;
O *Mary*, pray to the Maker of all thing,
Me for to help at my ending,
And save me from the power of my enemy,
600 For *Death* assaileth me strongly;
And, Lady, that I may by means of thy prayer
Of your Son's glory to be partaker,
By the means of his passion I it crave,
I beseech you, help my soul to save.--
605 *Knowledge*, give me the scourge of penance;
My flesh therewith shall give a quittance:
I will now begin, if God give me grace.

Knowledge. Everyman, God give you time and space:
Thus I bequeath you in the hands of our Saviour,
610 Thus may you make your reckoning sure.

Everyman. In the name of the Holy Trinity,
My body sore punished shall be:
Take this body for the sin of the flesh;
Also thou delightest to go gay and fresh,
615 And in the way of damnation thou did me bring;
Therefore suffer now strokes and punishing.
Now of penance I will wade the water clear,
To save me from purgatory, that sharp fire.

Good-Deeds. I thank God, now I can walk and go;
620 And am delivered of my sickness and woe.
Therefore with *Everyman* I will go, and not spare;
His good works I will help him to declare.

Knowledge. Now, *Everyman*, be merry and glad;
Your *Good-Deeds* cometh now; ye may not be sad;
625 Now is your *Good-Deeds* whole and sound,
Going upright upon the ground.

Everyman. My heart is light, and shall be evermore;
Now will I smite faster than I did before.

Good-Deeds. Everyman, pilgrim, my special friend,
630   Blessed be thou without end;
For thee is prepared the eternal glory.
Ye have me made whole and sound,
Therefore I will bide by thee in every stound.

Everyman. Welcome, my *Good-Deeds*; now I hear thy voice,
635   I weep for very sweetness of love.

Knowledge. Be no more sad, but ever rejoice,
God seeth thy living in his throne above;
Put on this garment to thy behove,
Which is wet with your tears,
640   Or else before God you may it miss,
When you to your journey's end come shall.

Everyman. Gentle *Knowledge*, what do you it call?

Knowledge. It is a garment of sorrow:
From pain it will you borrow;
645   Contrition it is,
That getteth forgiveness;
It pleaseth God passing well.

Good-Deeds. Everyman, will you wear it for your heal?

Everyman. Now blessed be *Jesu, Mary's* Son!
650   For now have I on true contrition.
And let us go now without tarrying;
Good-Deeds, have we clear our reckoning?

Good-Deeds. Yea, indeed I have it here.

Everyman. Then I trust we need not fear;
655   Now, friends, let us not part in twain.

Knowledge. Nay, *Everyman*, that will we not, certain.

Good-Deeds. Yet must thou lead with thee
Three persons of great might.

Everyman. Who should they be?

660   *Good-Deeds. Discretion* and *Strength* they hight,
And thy *Beauty* may not abide behind.

Knowledge. Also ye must call to mind
Your *Five-wits* as for your counsellors.

Good-Deeds. You must have them ready at all hours.

665   *Everyman.* How shall I get them hither?

Knowledge. You must call them all together,
And they will hear you incontinent.

Everyman. My friends, come hither and be present
Discretion, Strength, my *Five-wits,* and *Beauty.*

670   *Beauty.* Here at your will we be all ready.
What will ye that we should do?

Good-Deeds. That ye would with *Everyman* go,
And help him in his pilgrimage,
Advise you, will ye with him or not in that voyage?

675   *Strength.* We will bring him all thither,
To his help and comfort, ye may believe me.

Discretion. So will we go with him all together.

Everyman. Almighty God, loved thou be,
I give thee laud that I have hither brought
680   *Strength, Discretion, Beauty,* and *Five-wits;* lack I nought;
And my *Good-Deeds,* with *Knowledge* clear,
All be in my company at my will here;
I desire no more to my business.

Strength. And I, *Strength,* will by you stand in distress,
685   Though thou would in battle fight on the ground.

Five-wits. And though it were through the world round,
We will not depart for sweet nor sour.

Beauty. No more will I unto death's hour,
Whatsoever thereof befall.

690   *Discretion. Everyman,* advise you first of all;
Go with a good advisement and deliberation;
We all give you virtuous monition
That all shall be well.

Everyman. My friends, hearken what I will tell:
695   I pray God reward you in his heavenly sphere.
Now hearken, all that be here,
For I will make my testament
Here before you all present.

In alms half my good I will give with my hands twain
700 In the way of charity, with good intent,
And the other half still shall remain
In quiet to be returned there it ought to be.
This I do in despite of the fiend of hell
To go quite out of his peril
705 Ever after and this day.

Knowledge. Everyman, hearken what I say;
Go to priesthood, I you advise,
And receive of him in any wise
The holy sacrament and ointment together;
710 Then shortly see ye turn again hither;
We will all abide you here.

Five-Wits. Yea, *Everyman,* hie you that ye ready were,
There is no emperor, king, duke, ne baron,
That of God hath commission,
715 As hath the least priest in the world being;
For of the blessed sacraments pure and benign,
He beareth the keys and thereof hath the cure
For man's redemption, it is ever sure;
Which God for our soul's medicine
720 Gave us out of his heart with great pine;
Here in this transitory life, for thee and me
The blessed sacraments seven there be,
Baptism, confirmation, with priesthood good,
And the sacrament of God's precious flesh and blood,
725 Marriage, the holy extreme unction, and penance;
These seven be good to have in remembrance,
Gracious sacraments of high divinity.

Everyman. Fain would I receive that holy body
And meekly to my ghostly father I will go.

730 *Five-wits. Everyman,* that is the best that ye can do:
God will you to salvation bring,
For priesthood exceedeth all other thing;
To us Holy Scripture they do teach,
And converteth man from sin heaven to reach;
735 God hath to them more power given,
Than to any angel that is in heaven;
With five words he may consecrate
God's body in flesh and blood to make,
And handleth his maker between his hands;
740 The priest bindeth and unbindeth all bands,

Both in earth and in heaven;
Thou ministers all the sacraments seven;
Though we kissed thy feet thou were worthy;
Thou art surgeon that cureth sin deadly:
745 No remedy we find under God
But all only priesthood.
Everyman, God gave priests that dignity,
And setteth them in his stead among us to be;
Thus be they above angels in degree.

750 *Knowledge.* If priests be good it is so surely;
But when Jesus hanged on the cross with great smart
There he gave, out of his blessed heart,
The same sacrament in great torment:
He sold them not to us, that Lord Omnipotent.
755 Therefore Saint Peter the apostle doth say
That Jesu's curse hath all they
Which God their Saviour do buy or sell,
Or they for any money do take or tell.
Sinful priests giveth the sinners example bad;
760 Their children sitteth by other men's fires, I have heard;
And some haunteth women's company,
With unclean life, as lusts of lechery
These be with sin made blind.

Five-wits. I trust to God no such may we find;
765 Therefore let us priesthood honour,
And follow their doctrine for our souls' succour;
We be their sheep, and they shepherds be
By whom we all be kept in surety.
Peace, for yonder I see *Everyman* come,
770 Which hath made true satisfaction.

Good-Deeds. Methinketh it is he indeed.

Everyman. Now Jesu be our alder speed.
I have received the sacrament for my redemption,
And then mine extreme unction:
775 Blessed be all they that counselled me to take it!
And now, friends, let us go without longer respite;
I thank God that ye have tarried so long.
Now set each of you on this rod your hand,
And shortly follow me:
780 I go before, there I would be; God be our guide.

Strength. Everyman, we will not from you go,
Till ye have gone this voyage long.

Discretion. I, *Discretion*, will bide by you also.

Knowledge. And though this pilgrimage be never so strong,
785   I will never part you fro:
Everyman, I will be as sure by thee
As ever I did by Judas Maccabee.

Everyman. Alas, I am so faint I may not stand,
My limbs under me do fold;
790   Friends, let us not turn again to this land,
Not for all the world's gold,
For into this cave must I creep
And turn to the earth and there to sleep.

Beauty. What, into this grave? alas!

795   *Everyman.* Yea, there shall you consume more and less.

Beauty. And what, should I smother here?

Everyman. Yea, by my faith, and never more appear.
In this world live no more we shall,
But in heaven before the highest Lord of all.

800   *Beauty.* I cross out all this; adieu by Saint *John*;
I take my cap in my lap and am gone.

Everyman. What, *Beauty*, whither will ye?

Beauty. Peace, I am deaf; I look not behind me,
Not and thou would give me all the gold in thy chest.

805   *Everyman.* Alas, whereto may I trust?
Beauty goeth fast away hie;
She promised with me to live and die.

Strength. *Everyman*, I will thee also forsake and deny;
Thy game liketh me not at all.

810   *Everyman.* Why, then ye will forsake me all.
Sweet *Strength*, tarry a little space.

Strength. Nay, sir, by the rood of grace
I will hie me from thee fast,
Though thou weep till thy heart brast.

815   *Everyman.* Ye would ever bide by me, ye said.

Strength. Yea, I have you far enough conveyed;
Ye be old enough, I understand,
Your pilgrimage to take on hand;
I repent me that I hither came.

820   *Everyman. Strength*, you to displease I am to blame;
Will you break promise that is debt?

Strength. In faith, I care not;
Thou art but a fool to complain,
You spend your speech and waste your brain;
825   Go thrust thee into the ground.

Everyman. I had wend surer I should you have found.
He that trusteth in his *Strength*
She him deceiveth at the length.
Both *Strength* and *Beauty* forsaketh me,
830   Yet they promised me fair and lovingly.

Discretion. Everyman, I will after *Strength* be gone,
As for me I will leave you alone.

Everyman. Why, *Discretion*, will ye forsake me?

Discretion. Yea, in faith, I will go from thee,
835   For when *Strength* goeth before
I follow after evermore.

Everyman. Yet, I pray thee, for the love of the Trinity,
Look in my grave once piteously.

Discretion. Nay, so nigh will I not come.
840   Farewell, every one!

Everyman. O all thing faileth, save God alone;
Beauty, Strength, and *Discretion*;
For when *Death* bloweth his blast,
They all run from me full fast.

845   *Five-wits. Everyman*, my leave now of thee I take;
I will follow the other, for here I thee forsake.

Everyman. Alas! then may I wail and weep,
For I took you for my best friend.

Five-wits. I will no longer thee keep;
850   Now farewell, and there an end.

Everyman. O Jesu, help, all hath forsaken me!

Good-Deeds. Nay, *Everyman*, I will bide with thee,
I will not forsake thee indeed;
Thou shalt find me a good friend at need.

855   *Everyman.* Gramercy, *Good-Deeds*; now may I true friends see;
They have forsaken me every one;
I loved them better than my *Good-Deeds* alone.
Knowledge, will ye forsake me also?

Knowledge. Yea, *Everyman*, when ye to death do go:
860   But not yet for no manner of danger.

Everyman. Gramercy, *Knowledge*, with all my heart.

Knowledge. Nay, yet I will not from hence depart,
Till I see where ye shall be come.

Everyman. Methinketh, alas, that I must be gone,
865   To make my reckoning and my debts pay,
For I see my time is nigh spent away.
Take example, all ye that this do hear or see,
How they that I loved best do forsake me,
Except my *Good-Deeds* that bideth truly.

870   *Good-Deeds.* All earthly things is but vanity:
Beauty, *Strength*, and *Discretion*, do man forsake,
Foolish friends and kinsmen, that fair spake,
All fleeth save *Good-Deeds*, and that am I.

Everyman. Have mercy on me, God most mighty;
875   And stand by me, thou Mother and Maid, holy *Mary*.

Good-Deeds. Fear not, I will speak for thee.

Everyman. Here I cry God mercy.

Good-Deeds. Short our end, and minish our pain;
Let us go and never come again.

880   *Everyman.* Into thy hands, Lord, my soul I commend;
Receive it, Lord, that it be not lost;
As thou me boughtest, so me defend,
And save me from the fiend's boast,
That I may appear with that blessed host
885   That shall be saved at the day of doom.
In manus tuas--of might's most
For ever--*commendo spiritum meum.*

Knowledge. Now hath he suffered that we all shall endure;
The *Good-Deeds* shall make all sure.
890 Now hath he made ending;
Methinketh that I hear angels sing
And make great joy and melody,
Where *Everyman's* soul received shall be.

Angel. Come, excellent elect spouse to Jesu:
895 Hereabove thou shalt go
Because of thy singular virtue:
Now the soul is taken the body fro;
Thy reckoning is crystal-clear.
Now shalt thou into the heavenly sphere,
900 Unto the which all ye shall come
That liveth well before the day of doom.

Doctor. This moral men may have in mind;
Ye hearers, take it of worth, old and young,
And forsake pride, for he deceiveth you in the end,
905 And remember *Beauty*, *Five-wits*, *Strength*, and *Discretion*,
They all at the last do *Everyman* forsake,
Save his *Good-Deeds*, there doth he take.
But beware, and they be small
Before God, he hath no help at all.
910 None excuse may be there for *Everyman*:
Alas, how shall he do then?
For after death amends may no man make,
For then mercy and pity do him forsake.
If his reckoning be not clear when he do come,
915 God will say--*ite maledicti in ignem æternum.*
And he that hath his account whole and sound,
High in heaven he shall be crowned;
Unto which place God bring us all thither
That we may live body and soul together.
920 Thereto help the Trinity,
Amen, say ye, for saint *Charity*.

THUS ENDETH THIS MORALL PLAY OF
EVERYMAN.

THE EARLY MODERN PERIOD
1485-1603

ABSTRACT

Beginning approximately with the conclusion of the Wars of the Roses in 1485, the Early Modern Period in English literary history was characterized by religious conflict and reformation. It saw a widespread increase in the availability of books and newspapers caused by the introduction of the printing press, which enabled more citizens to become literate, allowing them to read the Bible on their own for the first time. Additionally, literature was increasingly written in or translated into English. This linguistic transformation led to significant religious upheaval during the historical period called the Reformation along with blossoming cultural accomplishments in the Renaissance. The Early Modern period produced significant achievements in poetry and drama, and marked the beginning of a new age of literacy in Europe.

THE END OF THE WARS OF THE ROSES

The Wars of the Roses began in 1445 between the two major English royal houses, Lancaster and York. In 1485, Henry Tudor killed King Richard III, the last York monarch, at the Battle of Bosworth Field and took the throne as King Henry VII. Henry was the only remaining male descendent of the house of Lancaster; thus when he married Elizabeth of York in 1486, he united the two families into the House of Tudor. William Shakespeare depicted these wars in his history plays.

Henry VII's reign was largely peaceful, as he purposefully avoided involving England in foreign conflicts. He built up significant wealth for the Crown and oversaw the marriage of Catherine of Aragon to his elder son, Arthur. Catherine was the youngest daughter of Isabella I of Castile and Ferdinand II of Aragon, who were the politically powerful joint rulers of Spain. Prince Arthur died less than five months after their marriage. Henry VII died in 1509 and was succeeded by his surviving son, Henry VIII, who then married Catherine himself.

THE REIGN OF KING HENRY VIII, THE REFORMATION, AND SEPARATION FROM THE CATHOLIC CHURCH

King Henry VIII's more than thirty-seven-year rule caused radical changes in England after he separated the nation from the Catholic Church and declared himself the head of the Church of England. He was married six times, first to Catherine of Aragon, his brother's widow and a devout Spanish Catholic. Catherine produced only one living child, a daughter named Mary. Desperate for a male heir, Henry became determined to annul his marriage and remarry a younger woman who would give him the son required by primogeniture, the system in which an eldest son inherits the father's titles and property.

Early in his reign, the handsome, athletic Henry's public image was positive, and his court was a cultural center of the Renaissance. Highly educated, with access to an extensive library, he wrote and read in English, French, and Latin.

Henry VIII's reign was marked by multiple wars with France and Scotland. He invaded France in 1513, 1521, and 1544, eventually signing peace treaties each time. He held an important but unstable alliance with Charles V, who was both the king of Spain and the Holy Roman Emperor. Charles and other European monarchs encouraged Henry to invade France to capture land, but did not provide sufficient financial support to enable decisive victories. England and Scotland also continued their long feud under Henry, with major conflicts in 1513 and 1542 and minor tensions throughout his reign.

In 1517, the German priest and professor of theology Martin Luther published his *Ninety-five Theses*, in which he detailed corruption in the Catholic Church and argued that the only way to be forgiven for sin was inward repentance. He criticized the church for selling indulgences, which were certificates that sinners could purchase in order to be absolved of their transgressions. Luther sent his *Theses* to an archbishop on October 31st, 1517; that day is now credited with the beginning of the Protestant Reformation.

While Henry was staunchly Catholic at the beginning of his reign, he became increasingly antagonistic toward the Church with the Pope's refusal to annul his marriage. He believed that his then forty-year-old wife's barrenness was a sign that God disapproved of their union. In 1531, after twenty-two years of marriage to Catherine of Aragon, Henry banished her from court, and married Anne Boleyn in 1532. His marriage to Catherine was finally annulled in 1533, less than four months before Anne gave birth to a daughter—the future Queen Elizabeth I. In 1534, Parliament passed the Acts of Supremacy, which declared the King of England to be the head of the Church of England, officially separating England from the Catholic Church.

Serving as the King's chief minister, Thomas Cromwell oversaw England's separation from the Catholic Church. Cromwell was, however, disliked by many in court because of his controversial ideas—he believed that almost every relic of the Catholic Church was sinful, including pilgrimages and religious artwork. He campaigned extensively in 1538 to root out what the Church of England considered Catholic idolatry, eventually dismantling Thomas Becket's shrine in Canterbury. Becket was a twelfth century Archbishop of Canterbury who was martyred for his refusal to accept King Henry II's church policies, subsequently becoming a saint. Consequently, Pope Paul III excommunicated King Henry VIII. This did not stop the King from sanctioning the destruction of Catholic property, however, as he allowed the complete dismantling of saintly shrines in 1540, and the dissolution of all remaining monasteries in 1542. Monastic lands and funds henceforth became property of the Crown. This dissolution caused the loss or destruction of many early English manuscripts, in a tragic blow to the future study of history and literature.

Overseeing Anne Boleyn's execution in 1536, after she miscarried two sons, Henry became engaged to Jane Seymour, Anne's former lady-in-waiting, the following day. She gave birth to a son, Edward, in 1537 but died from complications after the birth. Henry would have no more children; some modern medical professionals believe that he had genetic fertility issues.

Parliament passed the Crown of Ireland Act in 1542, which granted Henry VIII and subsequent English monarchs the title of "King [or Queen] of Ireland." After this, the crown confiscated Irish-owned lands to house English settlers, banned Catholicism, destroyed monasteries, and restructured the government to abolish the traditional Irish system of clans. This caused multiple rebellions in Ireland throughout the Tudor dynasty.

Henry's final marriage in 1543 was to the widowed Catherine Parr. Catherine was a religious reformer who encouraged Henry to do away with the Catholic traditions that he still maintained in the Church of England. She also induced him to add his daughters back into the line of succession. Mary and Elizabeth were reinstated in the Third Succession Act below Henry's son Edward. At the end of his life, Henry suffered from obesity, painful boils, and gout. He died in 1547 at the age of fifty-five, and was succeeded by Edward.

King Edward VI and the Crisis of His Succession

King Edward VI was the first English monarch to be brought up as a Protestant. He became king upon his father's death in January 1547, and was crowned on 20 February, at the age of nine. As provided for in Henry's will, a regency council of sixteen people formed to help him rule. Edward's uncle Edward Seymour was declared Lord Protector of the Realm and Duke of Somerset. The Duke began to rule mostly by himself, without consulting the Privy Council, buying and bribing the loyalty of other members of the court. King Edward deferred to the Duke of Somerset and the Privy Council for most of his decisions.

King Edward's reign, like his father's, saw conflict between England and Scotland. The Duke of Somerset led a campaign in 1547 that was initially successful, but by 1548, Scotland allied itself with France, and Somerset faced financial difficulties supporting his large armies. Major armed revolts in England broke out in 1549. The two most threatening were caused by the forced conversion of England to Protestantism and by landlords enclosing public lands as private property. Somerset was blamed, particularly for the second rebellion, because he made proclamations that misled farmers into thinking the landlords were acting illegally.

After the disastrous rebellions, Somerset was arrested, and John Dudley, Earl of Warwick, became his successor as *de facto* leader of the council. In 1552, Somerset tried to overthrow Warwick, and was beheaded on charges of felony. Warwick encouraged King Edward's direct involvement in his government. Historians debate whether Edward, still in his teens, remained essentially a puppet or a ruler in his own right. His greatest influence over his kingdom occurred in religious matters. Warwick himself was a more calculating ruler than Somerset. He focused on preventing wars that England could not afford, and signed a peace treaty with France in 1550. Warwick also allowed the expert merchant Sir Thomas Gresham to handle financial reforms, which put England's finances on an upward trajectory, although the economy did not fully recover until the reign of Elizabeth I.

Throughout Edward's reign, his closest and most trusted counselor was Thomas Cranmer, the Archbishop of Canterbury. Edward was fervently Protestant, and with his consent, Cranmer purged the Anglican Church of lingering Catholic traditions, turning it into a clearly Protestant institution. The Crown also continued to seize church property and sell its lands, which aided England's economic recovery. The Reformation under Cranmer was often unpopular, both with Catholic traditionalists and with radical reformers who thought that reforms did not go far enough. Cranmer published the first *Book of Common Prayer* in 1549, which standardized religious services across England. Controversy over the *Book* incited one of the major rebellions that year. In 1550, priests were replaced with government-appointed ministers; in 1552, Cranmer published a revised *Book of Common Prayer*, addressing ambiguities in the first edition. The Church of England at last reached a unified official liturgy. Unfortunately, it was quickly destabilized by King Edward's decline in health.

In 1553, Edward became ill with lung issues. While he was dying, he authored a line of succession contrary to that of his father, writing that sixteen-year-old Lady Jane Grey, his first cousin, would inherit the throne. Edward did not want the Catholic Mary to become queen, knowing that she would reverse his reforms. Warwick, who had become Duke of Northumberland, convinced the rest of the councillors to sign the new line of succession into law. Historians debate whether Edward himself wanted to change the order of succession, or whether Northumberland, who was Lady Jane Grey's father-in-law, persuaded him to do so. However, most modern scholars believe that Edward either instigated the initiative or believed in it wholeheartedly.

King Edward VI died at the age of fifteen, on July 6th, 1553, of what most historians agree was pneumonia. Thomas Cranmer performed the funeral rites at the King's burial in Westminster Abbey. The issue of succession rose to the forefront as soon as knowledge of Edward's death became public. Mary immediately wrote to the Privy Council proclaiming herself queen. Lady Jane Grey was publicly declared queen on 10 July, while Northumberland secured her safety in the Tower of London as she waited to be crowned. Meantime, Mary gained a significant following of both Catholics and Protestants because the British people considered her to be the rightful queen under Henry VIII's acts of succession.

On July 19th, the Privy Council was swayed by the public's overwhelming support of Mary and officially declared her queen, ending Jane's nine-day reign. Although Northumberland declared Mary queen on the Council's orders, he was subsequently arrested and beheaded; Jane was later beheaded as well.

THE REIGN OF "BLOODY" MARY

After sustaining public support, Mary was officially crowned Queen Mary I in October 1553, at the age of thirty-seven. She was England's first undisputed queen regnant (a queen who reigns alone, at an equivalent rank to a king). Her first acts released high-ranking Catholics from prison. The same year, Mary imprisoned Protestant leaders in the Tower of London, including Archbishop of Canterbury Thomas Cranmer and King Edward's chaplain Hugh Latimer. She then repealed Edward's religious reformations and declared her parents' marriage legal. Mary also began to look for a husband in order to produce an heir and prevent her Protestant sister Elizabeth from coming to power. Her counselors and the House of Commons advised her to marry an Englishman, but Mary sought alliances with the Catholic continent and married Prince Phillip of Spain, the son of Charles V, in 1554. Her marriage was unpopular with her subjects, with Protestants fearing that Philip would bring the Spanish Inquisition to England.

In 1554 and 1555, Mary experienced a months-long false pregnancy. Modern medical professionals believe that it was caused by her strong desire to have a child. The false pregnancy brought disgrace to Mary's court, and she fell into depression. This event brought Mary even closer to her Catholic faith—she considered the false pregnancy a punishment from God for allowing Protestantism to remain in England.

In 1554, Parliament officially returned the Church of England to control by the papacy in Rome. Mary then brought back the Heresy Acts, making heresy once more punishable by death. The first Protestants were burned at the stake in February 1555. In October, Latimer and fellow bishop Nicholas Ridley were also burned. After being forced to watch these executions, Cranmer denounced Protestantism. However, Mary refused to pardon him for heresy, and he dramatically renounced Catholicism before his execution in March 1556. Immediately after Cranmer's execution, Mary appointed the last Catholic Archbishop of Canterbury, Reginald Pole. Together, Latimer, Ridley and Cranmer became known as the Oxford Martyrs. Mary also placed her half-sister Elizabeth under house arrest during this time, fearing that she would lead a Protestant revolt.

Mary ordered the executions of a total of 283 Protestant officials, earning her the pejorative nickname "Bloody Mary" by later historians. The burnings were so unpopular with the English people that even Philip and Mary's Catholic advisors warned they were going too far. Public deaths persisted, however, and executed Protestants were widely perceived as martyrs.

The ever-present conflict between France and England reached significant heights during Mary's reign. In response to France aiding an invasion that sought to replace Mary with Elizabeth, England and Spain declared war on France in 1557. The Pope's alliance with France caused issues between England and the papacy. England won a decisive early battle but lost Calais in 1558, which was a blow to Mary's reputation. Both the war with France and years of poor harvests contributed to economic strain throughout England. Mary's advisors looked for new financial opportunities, which included trade with Africa's Atlantic coast and tariffs on imported goods.

By spring of 1558, Mary's health was in serious decline. She experienced another false pregnancy, and suffered throughout the summer from, most likely, either ovarian cysts or uterine cancer. She died on November 17th, 1558, in London, at the age of forty-two. Despite Mary's hesitancy to pass the crown to her Protestant sister, she respected the will of her father, King Henry VIII, and officially declared Elizabeth her heir less than two weeks before her death.

THE RENAISSANCE

There are no official dates for the English Renaissance, but most scholars maintain that it began with the Tudor dynasty in 1485, reaching its height during Queen Elizabeth I's reign. It was a period of great achievement in English literature, culture, and political power. Nineteenth-century scholars referred to it as the Renaissance, French for "rebirth," because of the renewal of interest in ancient Greek and Roman culture. English playwrights were heavily influenced by early dramatists while Renaissance scholars consulted philosophers like Plato, Aristotle, and Socrates. There were significant advances in painting, more specifically portraiture, though the development of visual arts was stunted by the destruction of Catholic iconography. Music was less impacted by religious conflict, flourishing at the Tudor courts. Additionally, England launched voyages to Africa, Asia, and North America in order to learn more about the world around them (while simultaneously gaining wealth through colonization, exploitation, or trade). Poetry and plays, however, were the defining achievement of the English Renaissance, including the works of Sir Philip Sidney, Edmund Spenser, William Shakespeare, John Donne, and many others.

"THE VIRGIN QUEEN" ELIZABETH

Queen Elizabeth I ascended the throne at the age of twenty-five. Hoping she would put an end to Catholic persecution of Protestants and improve England's financial situation, the English public welcomed her. Elizabeth's most important advisor became William Cecil, Lord Burghley; she also relied heavily upon her spymaster, Sir Francis Walsingham. After Elizabeth was officially crowned in January 1559, the first major problem she addressed involved religion. She needed to appease her own subjects, both Protestant and Catholic, while preventing a potential crusade against England by continental Catholics.

Hence, Elizabeth led Parliament to propose a church that retained many Catholic influences but was largely based on her brother Edward VI's Protestant reforms. She appointed as many bishops as she could, including the new Archbishop of Canterbury, since Reginald Pole had died the same day as Mary. For the Archbishopric of Canterbury, Elizabeth chose Matthew Parker, her mother Anne Boleyn's favorite chaplain and one of the founders of Anglican belief. Later in 1559, Parliament passed another Act of Supremacy, requiring all public officials to swear an oath recognizing the monarch as Supreme Head of the Church of England. In 1562, refusal to swear the oath became a treasonous offense. Additionally, a new Act of Uniformity required all citizens to attend an Anglican church and follow the 1559 *Book of Common Prayer*. However, the heresy laws were repealed, and the penalties for practicing Catholicism were not severe.

The so-called "marriage question" was a dominating factor in Elizabeth's early reign. The Queen never married nor did she have children, at least legitimately. However, she entertained the idea of wedded union to many different suitors both to appease her subjects and to dangle the tempting possibility of marriage to create alliances with the Continent. Historians agree that Elizabeth was in love with her childhood friend Robert Dudley. However, Cecil and other royal advisors made it clear that a marriage between Dudley and the Queen was unacceptable, because of the former disgrace of his family and the gossip surrounding their relationship. In 1559, Elizabeth turned down a proposal by Queen Mary's husband King Philip II of Spain. She more seriously considered proposals by King Eric XIV of Sweden and King Frederick II of Denmark. She also entered negotiation to marry Philip's cousin, King Charles II, Archduke of Austria. Most historians believe that Elizabeth never intended to marry, but simply used the possibility to maintain her power and form alliances. From the very beginning of her reign, the Queen claimed she was married to her kingdom and its people, and a cult of goddess-like depictions formed around her virginity.

Another threat to Elizabeth's early reign was a potential French invasion of England—Continental Catholics wanted to replace Elizabeth with Mary, Queen of Scots. The 1560 Treaty of Edinburgh temporarily solved this problem, removing troops from Scotland and establishing a Protestant church there before Mary returned from France, where she grew up. In 1562, England began occupying Le Havre, a city in Normandy, France, after French Protestant reformers took the city and requested help from Elizabeth. The Queen sent troops, hoping to retake Calais, a territory lost under Mary four years earlier. However, French reformers settled a treaty with French Catholics; Elizabeth refused to withdraw her forces until France ceded Calais, but English forces were defeated in 1563. In 1564, England accepted French ownership of Calais in exchange for payment, establishing a shaky peace.

In 1565, Mary, Queen of Scots married Henry Stuart, Lord Darnley. They had one child, the future King James I of England, whose reign initiated the royal House of Stuart. A council led by James Hepburn, Earl of Bothwell most likely ordered Darnley assassinated in 1567, for unspecific political reasons. That same year, Mary married Bothwell, which created suspicion about her involvement with Darnley's death, sinking her popularity. She was forced to abdicate after which her one-year-old son James became King of Scotland and was reared as Protestant. Mary was subsequently imprisoned by the Scottish lords, escaping to England in 1568. Elizabeth considered restoring her cousin to the Scottish throne but instead imprisoned her in England. The following year, Catholic nobles in the north of England rebelled against Elizabeth with a plot to put Mary on the throne. The Queen subsequently had over 750 rebels executed, which caused the Pope to excommunicate her in 1570 for "oppress[ing] the followers of the Catholic faith." The plot was unknown to Mary, who experienced no repercussions but remained imprisoned.

Elizabeth continued marriage negotiations, though some historians believe that by this time advisors such as William Cecil knew she would never marry. She considered the future King Henry III of France in 1570, and her last serious courtship occurred with his brother Francis, Duke of Anjou between 1572 and 1581.

Elizabeth's policies included nautical exploration and the beginnings of colonization. In 1580, she knighted Sir Francis Drake after his circumnavigation of the globe. In 1583, Sir Humphrey Gilbert established an English colony in modern-day Newfoundland, Canada while in 1585 Sir Walter Raleigh founded the colony of Virginia, named for the "Virgin Queen" Elizabeth. The Queen granted both men charters, enabling them to claim land for the Crown. One of the last major events of her reign was the establishment of the charter of the East India Company in 1600. Possessing a private military larger than that of England, the company went on to colonize most of India.

Throughout her reign, Elizabeth confronted problems controlling her second kingdom, Ireland. Its population was (and still is) highly Catholic, making many people hostile to the Queen's Protestant reforms. In 1582, a group of southern Irish Catholics revolted against English rule; the English military response caused the starvation of more than 30,000 Irish citizens. Later, in 1593, the Nine Years' War began, with Irish rebels backed by Spain fighting against an English army. It took until 1603, just a few days after Elizabeth's death, for a peace treaty to be signed.

In 1586, Sir Francis Walsingham uncovered the Babington Plot, another ploy to assassinate Elizabeth and place Mary, Queen of Scots on the throne. After suffering nineteen years of imprisonment in England, Mary agreed to the plan in a letter that was confiscated afterwards by her enemies, causing her to be tried and executed in 1587.

Spain turned out to be another major source of difficulty during Queen Elizabeth's reign. Elizabeth's former brother-in-law Philip II ruled the Netherlands; in 1585, Elizabeth sent an English army to aid Protestant Dutch rebels. During the same year, she signed the Treaty of Nonsuch, promising ongoing military aid to the Dutch. Philip considered this an act of war, sparking an Anglo-Spanish conflict which lasted until 1604. In 1587, Sir Francis Drake led a raid on Cádiz, Spain, destroying ships that intended to invade England. Elizabeth's most important military victory became the 1588 defeat of the Spanish Armada when the English navy, assisted by severe storms in the English Channel, prevented the Armada's attempted invasion of England. Elizabeth gave her rousing "Speech to the Troops at Tilbury" (page XXX) before the English army knew that the Armada had been defeated. In 1589, however, the English navy suffered a catastrophic defeat when they attempted a counterattack on Spain. Spain would send three more armadas to England during the Queen's reign: storms destroyed a second in 1596 and a third in 1597, while a fourth in 1601 successfully invaded Ireland for three months before surrendering.

In addition to conflicts in Spain and Ireland, Elizabeth's late reign was marked with infighting among her advisors, conflicts over succession, and economic issues[1] caused by drawn-out wars as well as poor harvests. In 1590, Walsingham died; his death, among others, caused Elizabeth's government to fracture internally, crippling her decision-making power during her later reign. Persecution of Catholics also increased during this time, as Elizabeth allowed law enforcement to interrogate Catholics and spy on their homes. The arts, however, flourished during her late reign, which became the most productive period for poets and playwrights like William Shakespeare. In 1596, Edmund Spenser's epic poem *The Faerie Queene* was first published in its entirety, for which Elizabeth granted Spenser a pension, an unusually strong patronage gesture for her.

When William Cecil died in 1598, his advisory position was filled by his son, Robert Cecil, who began working on the matter of the Queen's succession by secretly writing to James VI of Scotland. After James accepted Robert's advice about how best to approach Elizabeth, she began to accept him as a potential successor. In 1602, Elizabeth's health began to decline after the deaths of several of her close friends. The Virgin Queen died on March 24th, 1603.[2] Her public funeral was lavish—despite the strife that occurred during her final years, the nation truly mourned her forty-five- year reign. Queen Elizabeth I was buried next to her sister Mary I in Westminster Abbey.

ELIZABETHAN DRAMA

While William Shakespeare (page 360) continues to reign as the best-known dramatist to emerge from the Elizabethan Era, most Early Modern scholars insist that even without Shakespeare, the Elizabethan Era would still be known as the golden age of English drama. Audiences then and now celebrate numerous other playwrights from the period beginning with Queen Elizabeth's ascension in 1558 and ending with Parliament's ban on play performance and the ensuing closure of the public theaters in 1642. These writers include Thomas Kyd, Christopher Marlowe (page 295), Ben Jonson (page 599), Thomas Nashe, George Peele, Robert Greene, George Chapman, Thomas Dekker, Michael Drayton, Thomas Heywood, and John Webster. In addition to works by Shakespeare and Marlowe, this collection contains Jonson's *Volpone*, a play that considerably influenced future writers.

1: The "Golden Speech" on page XXX addresses these issues.
2: Before the eighteenth century, March 25th was considered New Year's Day, meaning that Elizabeth died on the last day of 1602 in the British version of the Julian calendar in use at the time.

TIMELINE

1485	The Wars of the Roses end with King Henry VII taking the throne.
1509	King Henry VII dies and is succeeded by his son, King Henry VIII.
1530	The morality play *Everyman*, written in the late 1400s, is published.
1533	Henry VIII annulls his marriage to Catherine of Aragon; England separates from the Catholic Church.
1542	The Crown of Ireland Act grants the monarch of England rule over Ireland as well.
1547	Henry VIII dies and is succeeded by his son, King Edward VI.
1553	Edward VI dies and is succeeded by his sister, Queen Mary I.
1554	Mary marries Phillip of Spain.
1554-55	Then-princess Elizabeth writes "Written with a Diamond on Her Window at Woodstock" while on house arrest.
1555-56	Mary has the three Protestant leaders known as the "Oxford Martyrs" burnt at the stake.
1556	Mary's husband becomes King Philip II of Spain, briefly uniting the two realms.
1558	Mary dies and is succeeded by her sister, Queen Elizabeth I.
1559	The new Act of Supremacy requires all public officials to recognize Elizabeth as head of the church.
1567-68	Mary, Queen of Scots abdicates the throne of Scotland and flees to England, where she is imprisoned.
1570	Pope Pius V condemns Elizabeth in *Regnans in Excelsis*.
c. 1570	Elizabeth writes "The Doubt of Future Foes."
1582	A rebellion in Ireland leads to the starvation of around 30,000 Irish citizens.
1587-88	The trial and execution of Mary, Queen of Scots, due to her implication in a plot to assassinate Elizabeth.
1588	The English navy defeats the Spanish Armada after Elizabeth gives her Speech to the Troops at Tilbury. Christopher Marlowe writes "The Passionate Shepherd to His Love."
1591	Sir Philip Sidney's sonnet cycle *Astrophil and Stella* is first printed.
1592	William Shakespeare's first plays are recorded in London.
c. 1593	Marlowe writes *Doctor Faustus* and *Hero and Leander*; he then dies under mysterious circumstances.

1594	Shakespeare and his fellow actors form the Lord Chamberlain's Men.
1596	Edmund Spenser's *The Faerie Queene* is first published in its entirety.
1598	Ben Jonson is imprisoned for murder, converting to Catholicism in jail; his *Every Man in His Humour* is released with great success. Marlowe's *Hero and Leander* is published posthumously.
1600	Sir Walter Raleigh publishes "The Nymph's Reply to the Shepherd."
1601	Queen Elizabeth gives her "Golden Speech."
1602	The first recorded performance of *Twelfth Night* takes place.
1603	Elizabeth dies and is succeeded by King James VI of Scotland as James I of England, her first cousin twice removed; the Lord Chamberlain's Men become the King's Men. Shakespeare writes *Othello*.

Queen Elizabeth

Written With a Diamond on Her Window at Woodstock

Much suspected by[1] me
Nothing proved can be,
Quoth Elizabeth prisoner.

A Letter to Mary, Queen of Scots, 24 February 1567[2]

Madam,

My ears have been so astounded and my heart so frightened to hear of the horrible and abominable murder of your husband and my own cousin that I have scarcely spirit to write: yet I cannot conceal that I grieve more for you than him. I should not do the office of a faithful cousin and friend, if I did not urge you to preserve your honour, rather than look through your fingers at revenge on those who have done you that pleasure as most people say. I counsel you so to take this matter to heart, that you may show the world what a noble Princess and loyal woman you are. I write thus vehemently not that I doubt, but for affection.[3]

Regnans in Excelsis[4,5]

He that reigneth on high, to whom is given all power in heaven and earth, has committed one holy Catholic and apostolic Church, outside of which there is no salvation, to one alone upon earth, namely to Peter, the first of the apostles, and to Peter's successor, the pope of Rome, to be by him governed in fullness of power. Him alone He has made ruler over all peoples and kingdoms, to pull up, destroy, scatter, disperse, plant and build, so that he may preserve His faithful people (knit together with the girdle of charity) in the unity of the Spirit and present them safe and spotless to their Saviour.

1. In obedience to which duty, we (who by God's goodness are called to the aforesaid government of the Church) spare no pains and labour with all our might that unity and the Catholic religion (which their Author, for the trial of His children's faith and our correction, has suffered to be afflicted with such great

---

1: Of.

2: From the National Archives of the United Kingdom, translated from French. This is the first twelve lines.

3: Mary soon married one of the chief conspirators in her first husband's murder.

4: "Reigning on high;" this papal bull is named for the first three words of its Latin text.

5: Credit to Lara Eakins of tudorhistory.org for putting this public domain document into electronic format.

troubles) may be preserved entire. But the number of the ungodly has so much grown in power that there is no place left in the world which they have not tried to corrupt with their most wicked doctrines; and among others, Elizabeth, the pretended queen of England and the servant of crime, has assisted in this, with whom as in a sanctuary the most pernicious of all have found refuge. This very woman, having seized the crown and monstrously usurped the place of supreme head of the Church in all England to gether with the chief authority and jurisdiction belonging to it, has once again reduced this same kingdom- which had already been restored to the Catholic faith and to good fruits- to a miserable ruin.

2. Prohibiting with a strong hand the use of the true religion, which after its earlier overthrow by Henry VIII (a deserter therefrom) Mary, the lawful queen of famous memory, had with the help of this See restored, she has followed and embraced the errors of the heretics. She has removed the royal Council, composed of the nobility of England, and has filled it with obscure men, being heretics; oppressed the followers of the Catholic faith; instituted false preachers and ministers of impiety; abolished the sacrifice of the mass, prayers, fasts, choice of meats, celibacy, and Catholic ceremonies; and has ordered that books of manifestly heretical content be propounded to the whole realm and that impious rites and institutions after the rule of Calvin, entertained and observed by herself, be also observed by her subjects. She has dared to eject bishops, rectors of churches and other Catholic priests from their churches and benefices, to bestow these and other things ecclesiastical upon heretics, and to determine spiritual causes; has forbidden the prelates, clergy and people to acknowledge the Church of Rome or obey its precepts and canonical sanctions; has forced most of them to come to terms with her wicked laws, to abjure the authority and obedience of the pope of Rome, and to accept her, on oath, as their only lady in matters temporal and spiritual; has imposed penalties and punishments on those who would not agree to this and has exacted then of those who perserved in the unity of the faith and the aforesaid obedience; has thrown the Catholic prelates and parsons into prison where many, worn out by long languishing and sorrow, have miserably ended their lives. All these matter and manifest and notorius among all the nations; they are so well proven by the weighty witness of many men that there remains no place for excuse, defence or evasion.

3. We, seeing impieties and crimes multiplied one upon another the persecution of the faithful and afflictions of religion daily growing more severe under the guidance and by the activity of the said Elizabeth -and recognising that her mind is so fixed and set that she has not only despised the pious prayers and admonitions with which Catholic princes have tried to cure and convert her but has not even permitted the nuncios sent to her in this matter by this See to cross into England, are compelled by necessity to take up against her the weapons of juctice, though we cannot forbear to regret that we should be forced to turn, upon one whose ancestors have so well deserved of the Christian community. Therefore, resting upon the authority of Him whose pleasure it was to place us (though unequal to such a burden) upon this supreme justice-seat, we do out of the fullness of our apostolic power declare the foresaid Elizabeth to be a heretic

and favourer of heretics, and her adherents in the matters aforesaid to have in-
curred the sentence of excommunication and to be cut off from the unity of the
body of Christ.

4. And moreover (we declare) her to be deprived of her pretended title to the
aforesaid crown and of all lordship, dignity and privilege whatsoever.

5. And also (declare) the nobles, subjects and people of the said realm and
all others who have in any way sworn oaths to her, to be forever absolved from
such an oath and from any duty arising from lordshop. fealty and obedience; and
we do, by authority of these presents , so absolve them and so deprive the same
Elizabeth of her pretended title to the crown and all other the abovesaid matters.
We charge and command all and singular the nobles, subjects, peoples and others
afore said that they do not dare obey her orders, mandates and laws. Those who
shall act to the contrary we include in the like sentence of excommunication.

6. Because in truth it may prove too difficult to take these presents wheresoev-
er it shall be necessary, we will that copies made under the hand of a notary public
and sealed with the seal of a prelate of the Church or of his court shall have such
force and trust in and out of judicial proceedings, in all places among the nations,
as these presents would themselves have if they were exhibted or shown.

Given at St. Peter's at Rome, on 27 April 1570 of the Incarnation; in the fifth
year of our pontificate.

THE DOUBT OF FUTURE FOES

    The doubt[6] of future foes exiles my present joy,
    And wit me warns to shun such snares as threaten mine annoy.
    For falsehood now doth flow, and subjects' faith doth ebb;
    Which would not be if Reason ruled, or Wisdom weaved the web.
5   But clouds of toys untried do cloak aspiring minds,
    Which turn to rain of late repent by course of changed winds.
    The top of hope supposed the root of ruth will be;
    And fruitless all their graffed guiles, as shortly ye shall see.
    Those dazzled eyes with pride, which great ambition blinds,
10   Shall be unseal'd by worthy wights whose foresight falsehood finds.
    The Daughter of Debate that eke discord doth sow,
    Shall reap no gain where former rule hath taught still peace to grow.
    No foreign banish'd wight shall anchor in this port;
    Our realm it brooks no strangers' force, let them elsewhere resort.
15   Our rusty sword with rest shall first his edge employ,
    To poll their tops that seek such change, and gape for joy.

6: Fear.

Speech to the Troops at Tilbury[7]

My loving people, we have been persuaded by some that are careful of our safety to take heed how we commit ourself to armed multitudes for fear of treachery; but I assure you, I do not desire to live to distrust my faithful and loving people. Let tyrants fear. I have always so behaved myself that, under God, I have placed my chiefest strength and safe guard in the loyal hearts and good will of my subjects, and therefore I am come amongst you, as you see, at this time, not for my recreation and disport, but being resolved, in the midst and heat of the battle, to live or die amongst you all, to lay down my life for my God and for my kingdom and for my people, my honour, and my blood, even in the dust. I know I have the body of a weak and feeble woman, but I have the heart and stomach of a king, and a king of England too, and think foul scorn that Parma or Spain, or any prince of Europe should dare to invade the borders of my realm; the which, rather than any dishonour shall grow by me, I myself will take up arms, I myself will be your general, judge, and rewarder of every one of your virtues in the field. I know, already for your forwardness, you have deserved rewards and crowns; and we do assure you, in the word of a prince, they shall be duly paid you. In the meantime my lieutenant-general shall be in my stead, than whom never prince commanded a more noble or worthy subject, not doubting but by your obedience to my general, by your concord in the camp, and your valour in the field, we shall shortly have a famous victory over those enemies of my God, of my kingdom, and of my people.

Golden Speech[8]

Mr Speaker, we perceive by you, whom we did constitute the mouth of our Lower House, how with even consent they are fallen into the due consideration of the precious gift of thankfulness, most usually least esteemed, where it is best deserved. And therefore we charge you tell them how acceptable such sacrifice is worthily received of a loving King, who doubteth much whether the given thanks can be of more poise [i.e. weight] then the owed is to them: and suppose that they have done more for us, then they themselves believe. And this is our reason: Who keeps their Sovereign from the lapse of error, in which, by ignorance, and not by intent, they might have fallen; what thanks they deserve, we know, though you may guess. And as nothing is more dear unto us than the loving conservation of our subjects' hearts, what an undeserved doubt might we have incurred, if the abusers of our liberality, the thrallers of our people, the wringers of the poor, had not been told us! Which, ere our heart or hand should agree unto, we wish we had neither: and do thank you the more, supposing that such griefs touch not

---

7: Credit to Lara Eakins of tudorhistory.org for putting this public domain document into electronic format.

8: From the National Archives of the United Kingdom. This is the first transcription produced of the speech, moreso constituting a summary. The spelling has been modernized in this anthology by the editor.

some amongst you in particular. We trust there resides, in their conceits of us, no such simple cares of their good, whom we so dearly prize, that our hand should pass ought that might injure any, though they doubt not it is lawful for our kingly state to grant gifts of sundry sorts of whom we make election, either for service done, or merit to be deserved, as being for a King to make choice on whom to bestow benefits, more to one then another. You must not beguile yourselves, nor wrong us, to think that the glossing lustre of a glistering glory of a King's title may so extol us, that we think all is lawful what we list, not caring what we do: Lord, how far should you be off from our conceits! For our part we vow unto you, that we suppose Physicians aromatical favours, which in the top of their potion they deceive the Patient with, or gilded drugs that they cover their bitter sweet with, are not more beguilers of senses, then the vanting [vaunting] boast of a kingly name may deceive the ignorant of such an office. I grant, that such a Prince as cares but for the dignity, nor passes not how the rains be guided, so he rule, to such a one it may seem an easy business. But you are cumbered (I dare assure) with no such Prince, but such a one, as looks how to give account afore another Tribunal seat then this world affords, and that hopes, that if we discharge with conscience what he bids, will not lay to our charge the fault that our Substitutes (not being our crime) fall in. We think ourselves most fortunately born under such a star, as we have been enabled by God's power to have saved you under our reign, from foreign foes, from Tyrant's rule, and from your own ruin; and do confess, that we pass not so much to be a Queen, as to be a Queen of such Subjects, for whom (God is witness, without boast or vaunt) we would willingly lose our life, ere see such to perish. I bless God, he hath given me never this fault of fear; for he knows best, whether ever fear possessed me, for all my dangers: I know it is his gift; and not to hide his glory, I say it. For were it not for conscience, and for your sake, I would willingly yield another my place, so great is my pride in reigning, as she that wisheth no longer to be, then Best and Most would have me so. You know our presence can not assist each action, but must distribute in sundry sorts to diverse kinds our commands. If they (as the greatest number be commonly the worst) should (as I doubt not but some do) abuse their charge, annoy whom they should help, and dishonour their king, whom they should serve: yet we verily believe, that all you will (in your best judgement) discharge us from such guilts. Thus we commend us to your constant faith, and yourselves to your best fortunes.

Christopher Marlowe

Christopher Marlowe, also known as Kit Marlowe, was born in late February of 1564. He was born in Canterbury, to shoemaker John Marlowe and his wife Catherine. Marlowe began studying at the King's School in Canterbury in 1579, enrolling in Corpus Christi College, Cambridge, in 1581. Becoming fluent in Latin, he earned his BA in 1584, and stayed until 1587 for an MA, which could mean that he intended to take orders in the Church of England. He probably wrote his first major plays, *Dido, Queen of Carthage* and *Tamburlaine, Part I*, while at Cambridge. Both were most likely performed in 1587.

The controversial intrigue that permeated Marlowe's life began at Cambridge. The university hesitated to grant his master's degree based on his frequent absences, along with a rumor that he planned to move to Riems in northern France, where a large number of British Roman Catholics took refuge, to become a priest. Queen Elizabeth I's Privy Council sent Corpus Christi College a letter that attested his absences were "on matters touching the benefit of his country." This document became the source of scholarly speculation that Marlowe was a spy in Sir Francis Walsingham's secret service. However, we know nothing of how he benefited his country as all records of what he did have been lost.

After earning his degree, Marlowe moved to London to work as a playwright and poet. He wrote the well-known lyric poem "The Passionate Shepherd to his Love" around this time, as well as *Tamburlaine, Part II*, which followed the successful *Part I*. His use of blank verse (unrhymed iambic pentameter known as Marlowe's "mighty line") in *Tamburlaine* inspired many of his contemporaries, causing blank verse to become the predominant literary meter in Elizabethan England. *The Jew of Malta* followed these works; he probably wrote his most famous play, *Doctor Faustus*, between 1590 and 1593. Marlowe's last major works were the play *Edward II* and the poem *Hero and Leander*. Based on the Greek myth about lovers separated by a river, *Hero and Leander* was unfinished when Marlowe died; poet George Chapman completed and published it in 1598. Almost all of Marlowe's works were published posthumously, including *Dido, Queen of Carthage* in 1594, "The Passionate Shepherd" in 1599, and *Doctor Faustus* in 1601.

Marlowe developed an unsavory reputation during his literary career in London. His contemporaries thought of him as an atheist (and occasionally a Catholic), a violent spy, and a homosexual. Some scholars suggest that rumors of Marlowe's homosexuality were invented as further evidence against him near the end of his life while others cite queer themes in his writing, like his sympathetic portrayal of Edward II, whom he depicted in love with another man. His alleged atheism is contested; a few modern scholars believe that he invented it along with stories of his Catholicism to help his career as a spy.

Marlowe's friendships with London writers Thomas Watson and Thomas Kyd caused difficulties for him. Marlowe and Watson were imprisoned in 1589 for the death of William Bradley in a barroom brawl. Marlowe was released after two weeks, while Watson, whose sword had actually killed Bradley, was released after five months. Kyd was arrested for inciting violence against French Protestant refugees in 1593. When a heretical manuscript was found in his home, Kyd alleged that it was Marlowe's, since they had been roommates in the past, and a warrant was issued for Marlowe's arrest. Marlowe was staying with Thomas Walsingham, cousin of spymaster Francis Walsingham, in Kent at the time. He went before the Privy Council on May 20th, 1593; they commanded him to report to them daily.

On May 30th, 1593, Marlowe spent the day in a public house with three men, Ingram Frizer, Nicholas Skeres, and Robert Poley. Frizer worked for Thomas Walsingham; Skeres and Poley were secret government employees who helped uncover the plot to kill Queen Elizabeth that led to the execution of Mary, Queen of Scots in 1586. Marlowe and Frizer allegedly argued about who should pay the bill after dinner. Marlowe took Frizer's dagger, cutting him with it, after which Frizer stole it back and killed Marlowe by stabbing him above the eye. All of this was believed by the coroner; Marlowe was buried in an unmarked grave on June 1st, while Frizer was soon pardoned.

Speculation about Marlowe's death is common. The three witnesses were all professional secret agents or the like, and many scholars believe that they could have lied to the coroner about the events that led to Marlowe's death. Some believe that Marlowe's murder was a planned assassination on the orders of a high-ranking figure such as Sir Walter Raleigh or Sir William Cecil, perhaps even Queen Elizabeth herself. Others think that because Marlowe's relationship with Thomas Walsingham was romantic or sexual, someone close to Walsingham (perhaps his wife or Frizer himself) ordered Marlowe's death out of jealousy or fear for Walsingham's reputation. One still-popular but widely disproved theory asserts that Marlowe faked his death to save himself from going to trial for his alleged atheism, went into hiding, then assumed a new identity—perhaps even that of William Shakespeare.

Marlowe was widely respected as a writer by his contemporaries. Ben Jonson, Michael Drayton, Thomas Nashe, and William Shakespeare all honored Marlowe after his death. Shakespeare quotes Marlowe's *Hero and Leander* in *As You Like It*. Marlowe is remembered as a pioneer of Elizabethan drama and blank verse, inspiring generations of English poets and writers. In 1891, the Marlowe Memorial was unveiled in Canterbury, and in 2002, Marlowe received a memorial window in Westminster Abbey's Poets' Corner.

TIMELINE

1564	Marlowe is born in Canterbury.
1581	Marlowe begins studying at Corpus Christi College, Cambridge.
1587	Marlowe earns his master's degree from Corpus Christi, after the intervention of the Privy Council on his behalf.
c. 1587	*Dido, Queen of Carthage*; *Tamburlaine, Part I*.
c. 1588	"The Passionate Shepherd to His Love;" *Tamburlaine, Part II*.
1589	Marlowe and his friend Thomas Watson are imprisoned after a deadly argument with William Bradley.
c. 1589	*The Jew of Malta*.
c. 1592	*Doctor Faustus*; *Edward II*.
c. 1593	*Hero and Leander*.
1593	Marlowe dies under suspicious circumstances.

THE TRAGICAL HISTORY OF DOCTOR FAUSTUS

By Christopher Marlowe

From The Quarto of 1604

The Tragicall History of D. Faustus. As it Hath Bene Acted by the Right Honorable the Earle of Nottingham His Servants. Written by Ch. Marl.

DRAMATIS PERSONAE

THE POPE.
CARDINAL OF LORRAIN.
THE EMPEROR OF GERMANY.
DUKE OF VANHOLT.
FAUSTUS.
VALDES and CORNELIUS, friends to FAUSTUS.
WAGNER, servant to FAUSTUS.
Clown.
ROBIN.
RALPH.
Vintner.
Horse-courser.
A Knight.
An Old Man.
Scholars, Friars, and Attendants.
DUCHESS OF VANHOLT.
LUCIFER.
BELZEBUB.
MEPHISTOPHILIS.
Good Angel.
Evil Angel.
The Seven Deadly Sins.
Devils.
Spirits in the shapes of ALEXANDER THE GREAT, of his Paramour and of HELEN.
Chorus.

THE TRAGICAL HISTORY OF DOCTOR FAUSTUS

Enter CHORUS.

CHORUS. Not marching now in fields of Thrasymene,
Where Mars did mate the Carthaginians;
Nor sporting in the dalliance of love,
In courts of kings where state is overturn'd;
5   Nor in the pomp of proud audacious deeds,
Intends our Muse to vaunt her heavenly verse:
Only this, gentlemen,—we must perform
The form of Faustus' fortunes, good or bad:
To patient judgments we appeal our plaud,
10   And speak for Faustus in his infancy.
Now is he born, his parents base of stock,
In Germany, within a town call'd Rhodes:
Of riper years, to Wertenberg he went,
Whereas his kinsmen chiefly brought him up.
15   So soon he profits in divinity,
The fruitful plot of scholarism grac'd,
That shortly he was grac'd with doctor's name,
Excelling all whose sweet delight disputes
In heavenly matters of theology;
20   Till swoln with cunning, of a self-conceit,
His waxen wings did mount above his reach,
And, melting, heavens conspir'd his overthrow;
For, falling to a devilish exercise,
And glutted now with learning's golden gifts,
25   He surfeits upon cursed necromancy;
Nothing so sweet as magic is to him,
Which he prefers before his chiefest bliss:
And this the man that in his study sits.

                                        [Exit.]

FAUSTUS discovered in his study.

FAUSTUS. Settle thy studies, Faustus, and begin
30   To sound the depth of that thou wilt profess:
Having commenc'd, be a divine in shew,
Yet level at the end of every art,
And live and die in Aristotle's works.
Sweet Analytics, 'tis thou hast ravish'd me!
35   *Bene disserere est finis logices.*
Is, to dispute well, logic's chiefest end?
Affords this art no greater miracle?

Then read no more; thou hast attain'd that end:
A greater subject fitteth Faustus' wit:
40 Bid Economy farewell, and Galen come,
Seeing, *Ubi desinit philosophus, ibi incipit medicus:*
Be a physician, Faustus; heap up gold,
And be eterniz'd for some wondrous cure:
Summum bonum medicinae sanitas,
45 The end of physic is our body's health.
Why, Faustus, hast thou not attain'd that end?
Is not thy common talk found aphorisms?
Are not thy bills hung up as monuments,
Whereby whole cities have escap'd the plague,
50 And thousand desperate maladies been eas'd?
Yet art thou still but Faustus, and a man.
Couldst thou make men to live eternally,
Or, being dead, raise them to life again,
Then this profession were to be esteem'd.
55 Physic, farewell! Where is Justinian?

[Reads.]

Si una eademque res legatur duobus, alter rem, alter valorem rei, &c.
A pretty case of paltry legacies!

[Reads.]

Exhoereditare filium non potest pater, nisi, &c.
Such is the subject of the institute,
60 And universal body of the law:
This study fits a mercenary drudge,
Who aims at nothing but external trash;
Too servile and illiberal for me.
When all is done, divinity is best:
65 Jerome's Bible, Faustus; view it well.

[Reads.]

Stipendium peccati mors est.
Ha!
Stipendium, &c.
The reward of sin is death: that's hard.

[Reads.]

70 *Si peccasse negamus, fallimur, et nulla est in nobis veritas;*
If we say that we have no sin, we deceive ourselves, and there's no truth in
us. Why, then, belike we must sin, and so consequently die:
Ay, we must die an everlasting death.
What doctrine call you this, *Che sera, sera,*
75 What will be, shall be? Divinity, adieu!
These metaphysics of magicians,
And necromantic books are heavenly;
Lines, circles, scenes, letters, and characters;

Ay, these are those that Faustus most desires.
80   O, what a world of profit and delight,
     Of power, of honour, of omnipotence,
     Is promis'd to the studious artizan!
     All things that move between the quiet poles
     Shall be at my command: emperors and kings
85   Are but obeyed in their several provinces,
     Nor can they raise the wind, or rend the clouds;
     But his dominion that exceeds in this,
     Stretcheth as far as doth the mind of man;
     A sound magician is a mighty god:
90   Here, Faustus, tire thy brains to gain a deity.

                    Enter WAGNER.

     Wagner, commend me to my dearest friends,
     The German Valdes and Cornelius;
     Request them earnestly to visit me.

     WAGNER. I will, sir.
                                                        [Exit.]

     FAUSTUS. Their conference will be a greater help to me
95   Than all my labours, plod I ne'er so fast.

              Enter GOOD ANGEL and EVIL ANGEL.

     GOOD ANGEL. O, Faustus, lay that damned book aside,
     And gaze not on it, lest it tempt thy soul,
     And heap God's heavy wrath upon thy head!
     Read, read the Scriptures:—that is blasphemy.

100 EVIL ANGEL. Go forward, Faustus, in that famous art
     Wherein all Nature's treasure is contain'd:
     Be thou on earth as Jove is in the sky,
     Lord and commander of these elements.
                                               [Exeunt Angels.]

     FAUSTUS. How am I glutted with conceit of this!
105 Shall I make spirits fetch me what I please,
     Resolve me of all ambiguities,
     Perform what desperate enterprise I will?
     I'll have them fly to India for gold,
     Ransack the ocean for orient pearl,
110 And search all corners of the new-found world

For pleasant fruits and princely delicates;
I'll have them read me strange philosophy,
And tell the secrets of all foreign kings;
I'll have them wall all Germany with brass,
115   And make swift Rhine circle fair Wertenberg;
I'll have them fill the public schools with silk,
Wherewith the students shall be bravely clad;
I'll levy soldiers with the coin they bring,
And chase the Prince of Parma from our land,
120   And reign sole king of all the provinces;
Yea, stranger engines for the brunt of war,
Than was the fiery keel at Antwerp's bridge,
I'll make my servile spirits to invent.

Enter VALDES and CORNELIUS.

Come, German Valdes, and Cornelius,
125   And make me blest with your sage conference.
Valdes, sweet Valdes, and Cornelius,
Know that your words have won me at the last
To practice magic and concealed arts:
Yet not your words only, but mine own fantasy,
130   That will receive no object; for my head
But ruminates on necromantic skill.
Philosophy is odious and obscure;
Both law and physic are for petty wits;
Divinity is basest of the three,
135   Unpleasant, harsh, contemptible, and vile:
'Tis magic, magic, that hath ravish'd me.
Then, gentle friends, aid me in this attempt;
And I, that have with concise syllogisms
Gravell'd the pastors of the German church,
140   And made the flowering pride of Wertenberg
Swarm to my problems, as the infernal spirits
On sweet Musaeus when he came to hell,
Will be as cunning as Agrippa was,
Whose shadow made all Europe honour him.

145   VALDES. Faustus, these books, thy wit, and our experience,
Shall make all nations to canonize us.
As Indian Moors obey their Spanish lords,
So shall the spirits of every element
Be always serviceable to us three;
150   Like lions shall they guard us when we please;
Like Almain rutters with their horsemen's staves,

Or Lapland giants, trotting by our sides;
Sometimes like women, or unwedded maids,
Shadowing more beauty in their airy brows
155   Than have the white breasts of the queen of love:
From Venice shall they drag huge argosies,
And from America the golden fleece
That yearly stuffs old Philip's treasury;
If learned Faustus will be resolute.

160   FAUSTUS. Valdes, as resolute am I in this
As thou to live: therefore object it not.

CORNELIUS. The miracles that magic will perform
Will make thee vow to study nothing else.
He that is grounded in astrology,
165   Enrich'd with tongues, well seen in minerals,
Hath all the principles magic doth require:
Then doubt not, Faustus, but to be renowm'd,
And more frequented for this mystery
Than heretofore the Delphian oracle.
170   The spirits tell me they can dry the sea,
And fetch the treasure of all foreign wrecks,
Ay, all the wealth that our forefathers hid
Within the massy entrails of the earth:
Then tell me, Faustus, what shall we three want?

175   FAUSTUS. Nothing, Cornelius. O, this cheers my soul!
Come, shew me some demonstrations magical,
That I may conjure in some lusty grove,
And have these joys in full possession.

VALDES. Then haste thee to some solitary grove,
180   And bear wise Bacon's and Albertus' works,
The Hebrew Psalter, and New Testament;
And whatsoever else is requisite
We will inform thee ere our conference cease.

CORNELIUS. Valdes, first let him know the words of art;
185   And then, all other ceremonies learn'd,
Faustus may try his cunning by himself.

VALDES. First I'll instruct thee in the rudiments,
And then wilt thou be perfecter than I.

FAUSTUS. Then come and dine with me, and, after meat,
190   We'll canvass every quiddity thereof;

For, ere I sleep, I'll try what I can do:
This night I'll conjure, though I die therefore.

[Exeunt.]

Enter two SCHOLARS.

FIRST SCHOLAR. I wonder what's become of Faustus, that was wont to make our schools ring with sic probo.

195   SECOND SCHOLAR. That shall we know, for see, here comes his boy.

Enter WAGNER.

FIRST SCHOLAR. How now, sirrah! where's thy master?

WAGNER. God in heaven knows.

SECOND SCHOLAR. Why, dost not thou know?

WAGNER. Yes, I know; but that follows not.

200   FIRST SCHOLAR. Go to, sirrah! leave your jesting, and tell us where he is.

WAGNER. That follows not necessary by force of argument, that you, being licentiates, should stand upon: therefore acknowledge your error, and be attentive.

SECOND SCHOLAR. Why, didst thou not say thou knewest?

205   WAGNER. Have you any witness on't?

FIRST SCHOLAR. Yes, sirrah, I heard you.

WAGNER. Ask my fellow if I be a thief.

SECOND SCHOLAR. Well, you will not tell us?

WAGNER. Yes, sir, I will tell you: yet, if you were not dunces, you would never
210   ask me such a question; for is not he corpus naturale? and is not that mobile? then wherefore should you ask me such a question? But that I am by nature phlegmatic, slow to wrath, and prone to lechery (to love, I would say), it were not for you to come within forty foot of the place of execution, although I do not doubt to see you both hanged the next sessions. Thus having triumphed over
215   you, I will set my countenance like a precisian, and begin to speak thus: Truly, my dear brethren, my master is within at dinner, with Valdes and Cornelius, as this wine, if it could speak, would inform your worships: and so, the Lord bless you, preserve you, and keep you, my dear brethren, my dear brethren!

[Exit.]

FIRST SCHOLAR. Nay, then, I fear he is fallen into that damned art for
220   which they two are infamous through the world.

SECOND SCHOLAR. Were he a stranger, and not allied to me, yet should I grieve for him. But, come, let us go and inform the Rector, and see if he by his grave counsel can reclaim him.

FIRST SCHOLAR. O, but I fear me nothing can reclaim him!

225   SECOND SCHOLAR. Yet let us try what we can do.

                                                                    [Exeunt.]

                        Enter FAUSTUS to conjure.

FAUSTUS. Now that the gloomy shadow of the earth,
Longing to view Orion's drizzling look,
Leaps from th' antartic world unto the sky,
And dims the welkin with her pitchy breath,
230   Faustus, begin thine incantations,
And try if devils will obey thy hest,
Seeing thou hast pray'd and sacrific'd to them.
Within this circle is Jehovah's name,
Forward and backward anagrammatiz'd,
235   Th' abbreviated names of holy saints,
Figures of every adjunct to the heavens,
And characters of signs and erring stars,
By which the spirits are enforc'd to rise:
Then fear not, Faustus, but be resolute,
240   And try the uttermost magic can perform.—
Sint mihi dei Acherontis propitii! Valeat numen triplex Jehovoe!
Ignei, aerii, aquatani spiritus, salvete! Orientis princeps
Belzebub, inferni ardentis monarcha, et Demogorgon, propitiamus
vos, ut appareat et surgat Mephistophilis, quod tumeraris:
245   per Jehovam, Gehennam, et consecratam aquam quam nunc spargo,
signumque crucis quod nunc facio, et per vota nostra, ipse nunc
surgat nobis dicatus Mephistophilis!
                        Enter MEPHISTOPHILIS.
I charge thee to return, and change thy shape;
Thou art too ugly to attend on me:
250   Go, and return an old Franciscan friar;
That holy shape becomes a devil best.

                                                        [Exit MEPHISTOPHILIS.]

I see there's virtue in my heavenly words:
Who would not be proficient in this art?
How pliant is this Mephistophilis,
255   Full of obedience and humility!
Such is the force of magic and my spells:
No, Faustus, thou art conjuror laureat,
That canst command great Mephistophilis:
Quin regis Mephistophilis fratris imagine.

Re-enter MEPHISTOPHILIS like a Franciscan friar.

260   MEPHIST. Now, Faustus, what wouldst thou have me do?

FAUSTUS. I charge thee wait upon me whilst I live,
To do whatever Faustus shall command,
Be it to make the moon drop from her sphere,
Or the ocean to overwhelm the world.

265   MEPHIST. I am a servant to great Lucifer,
And may not follow thee without his leave:
No more than he commands must we perform.

FAUSTUS. Did not he charge thee to appear to me?

MEPHIST. No, I came hither of mine own accord.

270   FAUSTUS. Did not my conjuring speeches raise thee? speak.

MEPHIST. That was the cause, but yet per accidens;
For, when we hear one rack the name of God,
Abjure the Scriptures and his Saviour Christ,
We fly, in hope to get his glorious soul;
275   Nor will we come, unless he use such means
Whereby he is in danger to be damn'd.
Therefore the shortest cut for conjuring
Is stoutly to abjure the Trinity,
And pray devoutly to the prince of hell.

280   FAUSTUS. So Faustus hath
Already done; and holds this principle,
There is no chief but only Belzebub;
To whom Faustus doth dedicate himself.
This word "damnation" terrifies not him,
285   For he confounds hell in Elysium:
His ghost be with the old philosophers!
But, leaving these vain trifles of men's souls,
Tell me what is that Lucifer thy lord?
MEPHIST. Arch-regent and commander of all spirits.

290   FAUSTUS. Was not that Lucifer an angel once?

MEPHIST. Yes, Faustus, and most dearly lov'd of God.

FAUSTUS. How comes it, then, that he is prince of devils?

MEPHIST. O, by aspiring pride and insolence;
For which God threw him from the face of heaven.

295   FAUSTUS. And what are you that live with Lucifer?

       MEPHIST. Unhappy spirits that fell with Lucifer,
       Conspir'd against our God with Lucifer,
       And are for ever damn'd with Lucifer.

       FAUSTUS. Where are you damn'd?

300   MEPHIST. In hell.

       FAUSTUS. How comes it, then, that thou art out of hell?

       MEPHIST. Why, this is hell, nor am I out of it:
       Think'st thou that I, who saw the face of God,
       And tasted the eternal joys of heaven,
305   Am not tormented with ten thousand hells,
       In being depriv'd of everlasting bliss?
       O, Faustus, leave these frivolous demands,
       Which strike a terror to my fainting soul!

       FAUSTUS. What, is great Mephistophilis so passionate
310   For being deprived of the joys of heaven?
       Learn thou of Faustus manly fortitude,
       And scorn those joys thou never shalt possess.
       Go bear these tidings to great Lucifer:
       Seeing Faustus hath incurr'd eternal death
315   By desperate thoughts against Jove's deity,
       Say, he surrenders up to him his soul,
       So he will spare him four and twenty years,
       Letting him live in all voluptuousness;
       Having thee ever to attend on me,
320   To give me whatsoever I shall ask,
       To tell me whatsoever I demand,
       To slay mine enemies, and aid my friends,
       And always be obedient to my will.
       Go and return to mighty Lucifer,
325   And meet me in my study at midnight,
       And then resolve me of thy master's mind.

       MEPHIST. I will, Faustus.

                                                        [Exit.]

       FAUSTUS. Had I as many souls as there be stars,
       I'd give them all for Mephistophilis.
330   By him I'll be great emperor of the world,
       And make a bridge thorough the moving air,
       To pass the ocean with a band of men;

I'll join the hills that bind the Afric shore,
And make that country continent to Spain,
335 And both contributory to my crown:
The Emperor shall not live but by my leave,
Nor any potentate of Germany.
Now that I have obtain'd what I desir'd,
I'll live in speculation of this art,
340 Till Mephistophilis return again.

[Exit.]

Enter WAGNER and CLOWN.

WAGNER. Sirrah boy, come hither.

CLOWN. How, boy! swowns, boy! I hope you have seen many boys with such pickadevaunts as I have: boy, quotha!

WAGNER. Tell me, sirrah, hast thou any comings in?

345 CLOWN. Ay, and goings out too; you may see else.

WAGNER. Alas, poor slave! see how poverty jesteth in his nakedness! the villain is bare and out of service, and so hungry, that I know he would give his soul to the devil for a shoulder of mutton, though it were blood-raw.

CLOWN. How! my soul to the devil for a shoulder of mutton, though 350 'twere blood-raw! not so, good friend: by'r lady, I had need have it well roasted, and good sauce to it, if I pay so dear.

WAGNER. Well, wilt thou serve me, and I'll make thee go like Qui mihi discipulus?[1]

CLOWN. How, in verse?

355 WAGNER. No, sirrah; in beaten silk and staves-acre.

CLOWN. How, how, knaves-acre! ay, I thought that was all the land his father left him. Do you hear? I would be sorry to rob you of your living.

WAGNER. Sirrah, I say in staves-acre.

CLOWN. Oho, oho, staves-acre! why, then, belike, if I were your man, I 360 should be full of vermin.

WAGNER. So thou shalt, whether thou beest with me or no. But, sirrah, leave your jesting, and bind yourself presently unto me for seven years, or I'll turn all the lice about thee into familiars, and they shall tear thee in pieces.

1: He who is my student. Wagner is offering the clown clothes.

365   CLOWN. Do you hear, sir? you may save that labour; they are too familiar
      with me already: swowns, they are as bold with my flesh as if they had
      paid for their meat and drink.

      WAGNER. Well, do you hear, sirrah? hold, take these guilders.

                                                                    [Gives money.]

      CLOWN. Gridirons! what be they?

370   WAGNER. Why, French crowns.

      CLOWN. Mass, but for the name of French crowns, a man were as good
      have as many English counters. And what should I do with these?

      WAGNER. Why, now, sirrah, thou art at an hour's warning, whensoever or
      wheresoever the devil shall fetch thee.

375   CLOWN. No, no; here, take your gridirons again.

      WAGNER. Truly, I'll none of them.

      CLOWN. Truly, but you shall.

      WAGNER. Bear witness I gave them him.

      CLOWN. Bear witness I give them you again.

380   WAGNER. Well, I will cause two devils presently to fetch thee away.—
      Baliol and Belcher!

      CLOWN. Let your Baliol and your Belcher come here, and I'll knock
      them, they were never so knocked since they were devils: say I should kill
      one of them, what would folks say? "Do ye see yonder tall fellow in the
385   round slop? he has killed the devil." So I should be called Kill-devil all the
      parish over.

          Enter two DEVILS; and the CLOWN runs up and down crying.

      WAGNER. Baliol and Belcher,—spirits, away!

                                                                    [Exeunt DEVILS.]

      CLOWN. What, are they gone? a vengeance on them! they have vile long
      nails. There was a he-devil and a she-devil: I'll tell you how you shall know
390   them; all he-devils has horns, and all she-devils has clifts and cloven feet.

      WAGNER. Well, sirrah, follow me.

      CLOWN. But, do you hear? if I should serve you, would you teach me to
      raise up Banios and Belcheos?

WAGNER. I will teach thee to turn thyself to any thing, to a dog, or a cat,
400 or a mouse, or a rat, or any thing.

CLOWN. How! a Christian fellow to a dog, or a cat, a mouse, or a rat! no,
no, sir; if you turn me into any thing, let it be in the likeness of a little pretty
frisking flea, that I may be here and there and every where: O, I'll tickle the
pretty wenches' plackets! I'll be amongst them, i'faith.

405 WAGNER. Well, sirrah, come.

CLOWN. But, do you hear, Wagner?

WAGNER. How!—Baliol and Belcher!

CLOWN. O Lord! I pray, sir, let Banio and Belcher go sleep.

WAGNER. Villain, call me Master Wagner, and let thy left eye be diametarily
410 fixed upon my right heel, with quasi vestigiis nostris insistere.[2]

[Exit.]

CLOWN. God forgive me, he speaks Dutch fustian. Well, I'll follow him;
I'll serve him, that's flat.

[Exit.]

FAUSTUS discovered in his study.

FAUSTUS. Now, Faustus, must
Thou needs be damn'd, and canst thou not be sav'd:
415 What boots it, then, to think of God or heaven?
Away with such vain fancies, and despair;
Despair in God, and trust in Belzebub:
Now go not backward; no, Faustus, be resolute:
Why waver'st thou? O, something soundeth in mine ears,
420 "Abjure this magic, turn to God again!"
Ay, and Faustus will turn to God again.
To God? he loves thee not;
The god thou serv'st is thine own appetite,
Wherein is fix'd the love of Belzebub:
425 To him I'll build an altar and a church,
And offer lukewarm blood of new-born babes.

Enter GOOD ANGEL and EVIL ANGEL.

GOOD ANGEL. Sweet Faustus, leave that execrable art.
2: As if to follow in our footsteps.

FAUSTUS. Contrition, prayer, repentance—what of them?

GOOD ANGEL. O, they are means to bring thee unto heaven!

430   EVIL ANGEL. Rather illusions, fruits of lunacy,
That make men foolish that do trust them most.

GOOD ANGEL. Sweet Faustus, think of heaven and heavenly things.

EVIL ANGEL. No, Faustus; think of honour and of wealth.
                                       [Exeunt ANGELS.]

FAUSTUS. Of wealth!
435   Why, the signiory of Embden shall be mine.
When Mephistophilis shall stand by me,
What god can hurt thee, Faustus? thou art safe
Cast no more doubts.—Come, Mephistophilis,
And bring glad tidings from great Lucifer;—
440   Is't not midnight?—come, Mephistophilis,
Veni, veni, Mephistophile!

                    Enter MEPHISTOPHILIS.

Now tell me what says Lucifer, thy lord?

MEPHIST. That I shall wait on Faustus whilst he lives,
So he will buy my service with his soul.

445   FAUSTUS. Already Faustus hath hazarded that for thee.

MEPHIST. But, Faustus, thou must bequeath it solemnly,
And write a deed of gift with thine own blood;
For that security craves great Lucifer.
If thou deny it, I will back to hell.

450   FAUSTUS. Stay, Mephistophilis, and tell me, what good will my soul do
thy lord?

MEPHIST. Enlarge his kingdom.

FAUSTUS. Is that the reason why he tempts us thus?

MEPHIST. Solamen miseris socios habuisse doloris.

455   FAUSTUS. Why, have you any pain that torture others!

MEPHIST. As great as have the human souls of men.
But, tell me, Faustus, shall I have thy soul?
And I will be thy slave, and wait on thee,
And give thee more than thou hast wit to ask.

460   FAUSTUS. Ay, Mephistophilis, I give it thee.

      MEPHIST. Then, Faustus, stab thine arm courageously,
      And bind thy soul, that at some certain day
      Great Lucifer may claim it as his own;
      And then be thou as great as Lucifer.

465   FAUSTUS. [Stabbing his arm] Lo, Mephistophilis, for love of thee,
      I cut mine arm, and with my proper blood
      Assure my soul to be great Lucifer's,
      Chief lord and regent of perpetual night!
      View here the blood that trickles from mine arm,
470   And let it be propitious for my wish.

      MEPHIST. But, Faustus, thou must
      Write it in manner of a deed of gift.

      FAUSTUS. Ay, so I will [Writes]. But, Mephistophilis,
      My blood congeals, and I can write no more.

475   MEPHIST. I'll fetch thee fire to dissolve it straight.

                                                          [Exit.]

      FAUSTUS. What might the staying of my blood portend?
      Is it unwilling I should write this bill?
      Why streams it not, that I may write afresh?
      FAUSTUS GIVES TO THEE HIS SOUL: ah, there it stay'd!
480   Why shouldst thou not? is not thy soul shine own?
      Then write again, FAUSTUS GIVES TO THEE HIS SOUL.

            Re-enter MEPHISTOPHILIS with a chafer of coals.

      MEPHIST. Here's fire; come, Faustus, set it on.

      FAUSTUS. So, now the blood begins to clear again;
      Now will I make an end immediately.

                                                        [Writes.]

485   MEPHIST. O, what will not I do to obtain his soul?

                                                        [Aside.]

      FAUSTUS. Consummatum est; this bill is ended,
      And Faustus hath bequeath'd his soul to Lucifer.
      But what is this inscription on mine arm?
      Homo, fuge: whither should I fly?
490   If unto God, he'll throw me down to hell.

My senses are deceiv'd; here's nothing writ:—
I see it plain; here in this place is writ,
Homo, fuge: yet shall not Faustus fly.

MEPHIST. I'll fetch him somewhat to delight his mind.

              [Aside, and then exit.]

Re-enter MEPHISTOPHILIS with DEVILS, who give crowns and
   rich apparel to FAUSTUS, dance, and then depart.

495 FAUSTUS. Speak, Mephistophilis, what means this show?

MEPHIST. Nothing, Faustus, but to delight thy mind withal,
And to shew thee what magic can perform.

FAUSTUS. But may I raise up spirits when I please?

MEPHIST. Ay, Faustus, and do greater things than these.

500 FAUSTUS. Then there's enough for a thousand souls.
Here, Mephistophilis, receive this scroll,
A deed of gift of body and of soul:
But yet conditionally that thou perform
All articles prescrib'd between us both.

505 MEPHIST. Faustus, I swear by hell and Lucifer
To effect all promises between us made!

FAUSTUS. Then hear me read them. [Reads] ON THESE CONDITIONS
FOLLOWING. FIRST, THAT FAUSTUS MAY BE A SPIRIT IN FORM AND
SUBSTANCE. SECONDLY, THAT MEPHISTOPHILIS SHALL BE HIS
510 SERVANT, AND AT HIS COMMAND. THIRDLY, THAT MEPHISTOPHILIS
SHALL DO FOR HIM, AND BRING HIM WHATSOEVER HE DESIRES.
FOURTHLY, THAT HE SHALL BE IN HIS CHAMBER OR HOUSE
INVISIBLE. LASTLY, THAT HE SHALL APPEAR TO THE SAID JOHN
FAUSTUS, AT ALL TIMES, IN WHAT FORM OR SHAPE SOEVER
515 HE PLEASE. I, JOHN FAUSTUS, OF WERTENBERG, DOCTOR, BY
THESE PRESENTS, DO GIVE BOTH BODY AND SOUL TO LUCIFER
PRINCE OF THE EAST, AND HIS MINISTER MEPHISTOPHILIS; AND
FURTHERMORE GRANT UNTO THEM, THAT, TWENTY-FOUR YEARS
BEING EXPIRED, THE ARTICLES ABOVE-WRITTEN INVIOLATE,
520 FULL POWER TO FETCH OR CARRY THE SAID JOHN FAUSTUS, BODY
AND SOUL, FLESH, BLOOD, OR GOODS, INTO THEIR HABITATION
WHERESOEVER. BY ME, JOHN FAUSTUS.

MEPHIST. Speak, Faustus, do you deliver this as your deed?

FAUSTUS. Ay, take it, and the devil give thee good on't!

525   MEPHIST. Now, Faustus, ask what thou wilt.

FAUSTUS. First will I question with thee about hell.
Tell me, where is the place that men call hell?

MEPHIST. Under the heavens.

FAUSTUS. Ay, but whereabout?

530   MEPHIST. Within the bowels of these elements,
Where we are tortur'd and remain for ever:
Hell hath no limits, nor is circumscrib'd
In one self place; for where we are is hell,
And where hell is, there must we ever be:
535   And, to conclude, when all the world dissolves,
And every creature shall be purified,
All places shall be hell that are not heaven.

FAUSTUS. Come, I think hell's a fable.

MEPHIST. Ay, think so still, till experience change thy mind.

540   FAUSTUS. Why, think'st thou, then, that Faustus shall be damn'd?

MEPHIST. Ay, of necessity, for here's the scroll
Wherein thou hast given thy soul to Lucifer.

FAUSTUS. Ay, and body too: but what of that?
Think'st thou that Faustus is so fond to imagine
545   That, after this life, there is any pain?
Tush, these are trifles and mere old wives' tales.

MEPHIST. But, Faustus, I am an instance to prove the contrary,
For I am damn'd, and am now in hell.

FAUSTUS. How! now in hell!
550   Nay, an this be hell, I'll willingly be damn'd here:
What! walking, disputing, &c.
But, leaving off this, let me have a wife,
The fairest maid in Germany;
For I am wanton and lascivious,
555   And cannot live without a wife.

MEPHIST. How! a wife!
I prithee, Faustus, talk not of a wife.

FAUSTUS. Nay, sweet Mephistophilis, fetch me one, for I will have one.

MEPHIST. Well, thou wilt have one? Sit there till I come: I'll fetch thee a
560   wife in the devil's name.

                                                                          [Exit.]

Enter MEPHISTOPHILIS with a DEVIL drest like a WOMAN,
                          with fire-works.

MEPHIST. Tell me, Faustus, how dost thou like thy wife?

FAUSTUS. A plague on her for a hot whore!

MEPHIST. Tut, Faustus,
Marriage is but a ceremonial toy;
565   If thou lovest me, think no more of it.
I'll cull thee out the fairest courtezans,
And bring them every morning to thy bed:
She whom thine eye shall like, thy heart shall have,
Be she as chaste as was Penelope,
570   As wise as Saba, or as beautiful
As was bright Lucifer before his fall.
Hold, take this book, peruse it thoroughly:

                                                                    [Gives book.]

The iterating of these lines brings gold;
The framing of this circle on the ground
575   Brings whirlwinds, tempests, thunder, and lightning;
Pronounce this thrice devoutly to thyself,
And men in armour shall appear to thee,
Ready to execute what thou desir'st.

FAUSTUS. Thanks, Mephistophilis: yet fain would I have a book wherein
580   I might behold all spells and incantations, that I might raise up spirits when
I please.

MEPHIST. Here they are in this book.

                                                                  [Turns to them.]

FAUSTUS. Now would I have a book where I might see all characters and
planets of the heavens, that I might know their motions and dispositions.

585   MEPHIST. Here they are too.

                                                                  [Turns to them.]

FAUSTUS. Nay, let me have one book more,—and then I have done,—
wherein I might see all plants, herbs, and trees, that grow upon the earth.

MEPHIST. Here they be.

FAUSTUS. O, thou art deceived.

590 MEPHIST. Tut, I warrant thee.

[Turns to them.]

FAUSTUS. When I behold the heavens, then I repent,
And curse thee, wicked Mephistophilis,
Because thou hast depriv'd me of those joys.

MEPHIST. Why, Faustus,
595 Thinkest thou heaven is such a glorious thing?
I tell thee, 'tis not half so fair as thou,
Or any man that breathes on earth.

FAUSTUS. How prov'st thou that?

MEPHIST. 'Twas made for man, therefore is man more excellent.

600 FAUSTUS. If it were made for man, 'twas made for me:
I will renounce this magic and repent.

Enter GOOD ANGEL and EVIL ANGEL.

GOOD ANGEL. Faustus, repent; yet God will pity thee.

EVIL ANGEL. Thou art a spirit; God cannot pity thee.

FAUSTUS. Who buzzeth in mine ears I am a spirit?
605 Be I a devil, yet God may pity me;
Ay, God will pity me, if I repent.

EVIL ANGEL. Ay, but Faustus never shall repent.

[Exeunt ANGELS.]

FAUSTUS. My heart's so harden'd, I cannot repent:
Scarce can I name salvation, faith, or heaven,
610 But fearful echoes thunder in mine ears,
"Faustus, thou art damn'd!" then swords, and knives,
Poison, guns, halters, and envenom'd steel
Are laid before me to despatch myself;
And long ere this I should have slain myself,
615 Had not sweet pleasure conquer'd deep despair.
Have not I made blind Homer sing to me
Of Alexander's love and Oenon's death?

And hath not he, that built the walls of Thebes
With ravishing sound of his melodious harp,
620 Made music with my Mephistophilis?
Why should I die, then, or basely despair?
I am resolv'd; Faustus shall ne'er repent.—
Come, Mephistophilis, let us dispute again,
And argue of divine astrology.
625 Tell me, are there many heavens above the moon
Are all celestial bodies but one globe,
As is the substance of this centric earth?

MEPHIST. As are the elements, such are the spheres,
Mutually folded in each other's orb,
630 And, Faustus,
All jointly move upon one axletree,
Whose terminine is term'd the world's wide pole;
Nor are the names of Saturn, Mars, or Jupiter
Feign'd, but are erring stars.

635 FAUSTUS. But, tell me, have they all one motion, both situ et tempore?

MEPHIST. All jointly move from east to west in twenty-four hours upon the
poles of the world; but differ in their motion upon the poles of the zodiac.

FAUSTUS. Tush,
These slender trifles Wagner can decide:
640 Hath Mephistophilis no greater skill?
Who knows not the double motion of the planets?
The first is finish'd in a natural day;
The second thus; as Saturn in thirty years; Jupiter in twelve;
Mars in four; the Sun, Venus, and Mercury in a year; the Moon in
645 twenty-eight days. Tush, these are freshmen's suppositions.
But, tell me, hath every sphere a dominion or intelligentia?

MEPHIST. Ay.

FAUSTUS. How many heavens or spheres are there?

MEPHIST. Nine; the seven planets, the firmament, and the empyreal heaven.

650 FAUSTUS. Well, resolve me in this question; why have we not conjunctions,
oppositions, aspects, eclipses, all at one time, but in some years we have
more, in some less?

MEPHIST. Per inoequalem motum respectu totius.[3]

3: By an irregular movement in relation to the whole system.

FAUSTUS. Well, I am answered. Tell me who made the world?

655 MEPHIST. I will not.

FAUSTUS. Sweet Mephistophilis, tell me.

MEPHIST. Move me not, for I will not tell thee.

FAUSTUS. Villain, have I not bound thee to tell me any thing?

MEPHIST. Ay, that is not against our kingdom; but this is. Think thou on
660 hell, Faustus, for thou art damned.

FAUSTUS. Think, Faustus, upon God that made the world.

MEPHIST. Remember this.
                                                                  [Exit.]

FAUSTUS. Ay, go, accursed spirit, to ugly hell!
'Tis thou hast damn'd distressed Faustus' soul.
665 Is't not too late?

              Re-enter GOOD ANGEL and EVIL ANGEL.

EVIL ANGEL. Too late.

GOOD ANGEL. Never too late, if Faustus can repent.

EVIL ANGEL. If thou repent, devils shall tear thee in pieces.

GOOD ANGEL. Repent, and they shall never raze thy skin.
                                                        [Exeunt ANGELS.]

670 FAUSTUS. Ah, Christ, my Saviour,
Seek to save distressed Faustus' soul!

        Enter LUCIFER, BELZEBUB, and MEPHISTOPHILIS.

LUCIFER. Christ cannot save thy soul, for he is just:
There's none but I have interest in the same.

FAUSTUS. O, who art thou that look'st so terrible?

675 LUCIFER. I am Lucifer,
And this is my companion-prince in hell.

FAUSTUS. O, Faustus, they are come to fetch away thy soul!

LUCIFER. We come to tell thee thou dost injure us;
Thou talk'st of Christ, contrary to thy promise:
680 Thou shouldst not think of God: think of the devil,
And of his dam too.

FAUSTUS. Nor will I henceforth: pardon me in this,
And Faustus vows never to look to heaven,
Never to name God, or to pray to him,
685   To burn his Scriptures, slay his ministers,
And make my spirits pull his churches down.

LUCIFER. Do so, and we will highly gratify thee. Faustus, we are come
from hell to shew thee some pastime: sit down, and thou shalt see all the
Seven Deadly Sins appear in their proper shapes.

690   FAUSTUS. That sight will be as pleasing unto me,
As Paradise was to Adam, the first day
Of his creation.

LUCIFER. Talk not of Paradise nor creation; but mark this show: talk of
the devil, and nothing else.—Come away!

Enter the SEVEN DEADLY SINS.

695   Now, Faustus, examine them of their several names and dispositions.

FAUSTUS. What art thou, the first?

PRIDE. I am Pride. I disdain to have any parents. I am like to Ovid's flea;
I can creep into every corner of a wench; sometimes, like a perriwig, I sit
upon her brow; or, like a fan of feathers, I kiss her lips; indeed, I do—what
700   do I not? But, fie, what a scent is here! I'll not speak another word, except
the ground were perfumed, and covered with cloth of arras.

FAUSTUS. What art thou, the second?

COVETOUSNESS. I am Covetousness, begotten of an old churl, in an old
leathern bag: and, might I have my wish, I would desire that this house and
705   all the people in it were turned to gold, that I might lock you up in my good
chest: O, my sweet gold!

FAUSTUS. What art thou, the third?

WRATH. I am Wrath. I had neither father nor mother: I leapt out of a
lion's mouth when I was scarce half-an-hour old; and ever since I have run
710   up and down the world with this case of rapiers, wounding myself when I
had nobody to fight withal. I was born in hell; and look to it, for some of
you shall be my father.

FAUSTUS. What art thou, the fourth?

ENVY. I am Envy, begotten of a chimney-sweeper and an oyster-wife. I
715   cannot read, and therefore wish all books were burnt. I am lean with seeing

others eat. O, that there would come a famine through all the world, that all might die, and I live alone! then thou shouldst see how fat I would be. But must thou sit, and I stand? come down, with a vengeance!

FAUSTUS. Away, envious rascal!—What art thou, the fifth?

720 GLUTTONY. Who I, sir? I am Gluttony. My parents are all dead, and the devil a penny they have left me, but a bare pension, and that is thirty meals a-day and ten bevers, —a small trifle to suffice nature. O, I come of a royal parentage! my grandfather was a Gammon of Bacon, my grandmother a Hogshead of Claret-wine; my godfathers were these, Peter Pickle-herring and Martin Martle-
725 mas-beef; O, but my godmother, she was a jolly gentlewoman, and well-beloved in every good town and city; her name was Mistress Margery March-beer. Now, Faustus, thou hast heard all my progeny; wilt thou bid me to supper?

FAUSTUS. No, I'll see thee hanged: thou wilt eat up all my victuals.

GLUTTONY. Then the devil choke thee!

730 FAUSTUS. Choke thyself, glutton!—What art thou, the sixth?

SLOTH. I am Sloth. I was begotten on a sunny bank, where I have lain ever since; and you have done me great injury to bring me from thence: let me be carried thither again by Gluttony and Lechery. I'll not speak another word for a king's ransom.

735 FAUSTUS. What are you, Mistress Minx, the seventh and last?

LECHERY. Who I, sir? I am one that loves an inch of raw mutton better than an ell of fried stock-fish; and the first letter of my name begins with L.

FAUSTUS. Away, to hell, to hell!

[Exeunt the SINS.]

LUCIFER. Now, Faustus, how dost thou like this?

740 FAUSTUS. O, this feeds my soul!

LUCIFER. Tut, Faustus, in hell is all manner of delight.

FAUSTUS. O, might I see hell, and return again,
How happy were I then!

LUCIFER. Thou shalt; I will send for thee at midnight.
745 In meantime take this book; peruse it throughly,
And thou shalt turn thyself into what shape thou wilt.

FAUSTUS. Great thanks, mighty Lucifer!
This will I keep as chary as my life.

LUCIFER. Farewell, Faustus, and think on the devil.

750   FAUSTUS. Farewell, great Lucifer.

                   [Exeunt LUCIFER and BELZEBUB.]
     Come, Mephistophilis.

                         [Exeunt.]

           Enter CHORUS.

CHORUS. Learned Faustus,
     To know the secrets of astronomy
     Graven in the book of Jove's high firmament,
755   Did mount himself to scale Olympus' top,
     Being seated in a chariot burning bright,
     Drawn by the strength of yoky dragons' necks.
     He now is gone to prove cosmography,
     And, as I guess, will first arrive at Rome,
760   To see the Pope and manner of his court,
     And take some part of holy Peter's feast,
     That to this day is highly solemniz'd.

                         [Exit.]

       Enter FAUSTUS and MEPHISTOPHILIS.

FAUSTUS. Having now, my good Mephistophilis,
     Pass'd with delight the stately town of Trier,
765   Environ'd round with airy mountain-tops,
     With walls of flint, and deep-entrenched lakes,
     Not to be won by any conquering prince;
     From Paris next, coasting the realm of France,
     We saw the river Maine fall into Rhine,
770   Whose banks are set with groves of fruitful vines;
     Then up to Naples, rich Campania,
     Whose buildings fair and gorgeous to the eye,
     The streets straight forth, and pav'd with finest brick,
     Quarter the town in four equivalents:
775   There saw we learned Maro's golden tomb,
     The way he cut, an English mile in length,
     Thorough a rock of stone, in one night's space;
     From thence to Venice, Padua, and the rest,
     In one of which a sumptuous temple stands,
780   That threats the stars with her aspiring top.
     Thus hitherto hath Faustus spent his time:
     But tell me now what resting-place is this?
     Hast thou, as erst I did command,
     Conducted me within the walls of Rome?

785   MEPHIST. Faustus, I have; and, because we will not be unprovided, I have taken up his Holiness' privy-chamber for our use.

FAUSTUS. I hope his Holiness will bid us welcome.

MEPHIST.
Tut, 'tis no matter; man; we'll be bold with his good cheer.
790   And now, my Faustus, that thou mayst perceive
What Rome containeth to delight thee with,
Know that this city stands upon seven hills
That underprop the groundwork of the same:
Just through the midst runs flowing Tiber's stream
795   With winding banks that cut it in two parts;
Over the which four stately bridges lean,
That make safe passage to each part of Rome:
Upon the bridge call'd Ponte Angelo
Erected is a castle passing strong,
800   Within whose walls such store of ordnance are,
And double cannons fram'd of carved brass,
As match the days within one complete year;
Besides the gates, and high pyramides,
Which Julius Caesar brought from Africa.

805   FAUSTUS. Now, by the kingdoms of infernal rule,
Of Styx, of Acheron, and the fiery lake
Of ever-burning Phlegethon, I swear
That I do long to see the monuments
And situation of bright-splendent Rome:
810   Come, therefore, let's away.

MEPHIST. Nay, Faustus, stay: I know you'd fain see the Pope,
And take some part of holy Peter's feast,
Where thou shalt see a troop of bald-pate friars,
Whose summum bonum is in belly-cheer.

815   FAUSTUS. Well, I'm content to compass then some sport,
And by their folly make us merriment.
Then charm me, that I
May be invisible, to do what I please,
Unseen of any whilst I stay in Rome.
                               [Mephistophilis charms him.]

820   MEPHIST. So, Faustus; now
Do what thou wilt, thou shalt not be discern'd.

      Sound a Sonnet. Enter the POPE and the CARDINAL OF
         LORRAIN to the banquet, with FRIARS attending.

POPE. My Lord of Lorrain, will't please you draw near?

FAUSTUS. Fall to, and the devil choke you, an you spare!

POPE. How now! who's that which spake?—Friars, look about.

825   FIRST FRIAR. Here's nobody, if it like your Holiness.

POPE. My lord, here is a dainty dish was sent me from the Bishop of Milan.

FAUSTUS. I thank you, sir.

[Snatches the dish.]

POPE. How now! who's that which snatched the meat from me? will no man look?—My lord, this dish was sent me from the Cardinal of Florence.

830   FAUSTUS. You say true; I'll ha't.

[Snatches the dish.]

POPE. What, again!—My lord, I'll drink to your grace.

FAUSTUS. I'll pledge your grace.

[Snatches the cup.]

C. OF LOR. My lord, it may be some ghost, newly crept out of Purgatory, come to beg a pardon of your Holiness.

835   POPE. It may be so.—Friars, prepare a dirge to lay the fury of this ghost.—
Once again, my lord, fall to.

[The POPE crosses himself.]

FAUSTUS. What, are you crossing of yourself? Well, use that trick no more,
I would advise you.

[The POPE crosses himself again.]

Well, there's the second time. Aware the third; I give you fair warning.

[The POPE crosses himself again, and FAUSTUS hits him a box of the
ear; and they all run away.]

840   Come on, Mephistophilis; what shall we do?

MEPHIST. Nay, I know not: we shall be cursed with bell, book, and candle.

FAUSTUS. How! bell, book, and candle,—candle, book, and bell,—
Forward and backward, to curse Faustus to hell!
Anon you shall hear a hog grunt, a calf bleat, and an ass bray,
845   Because it is Saint Peter's holiday.

Re-enter all the FRIARS to sing the Dirge.

FIRST FRIAR.
Come, brethren, let's about our business with good devotion. [They sing.]
CURSED BE HE THAT STOLE AWAY HIS HOLINESS' MEAT FROM
THE TABLE! maledicat Dominus![4] CURSED BE HE THAT STRUCK HIS
HOLINESS A BLOW ON THE FACE! maledicat Dominus! CURSED BE
850   HE THAT TOOK FRIAR SANDELO A BLOW ON THE PATE! male-
dicat Dominus! CURSED BE HE THAT DISTURBETH OUR HOLY
DIRGE! maledicat Dominus! CURSED BE HE THAT TOOK AWAY HIS
HOLINESS' WINE! maledicat Dominus! Et omnes Sancti! Amen!

[MEPHISTOPHILIS and FAUSTUS beat the FRIARS, and fling fire-
works among them; and so exeunt.]

Enter CHORUS.

CHORUS. When Faustus had with pleasure ta'en the view
855   Of rarest things, and royal courts of kings,
He stay'd his course, and so returned home;
Where such as bear his absence but with grief,
I mean his friends and near'st companions,
Did gratulate his safety with kind words,
860   And in their conference of what befell,
Touching his journey through the world and air,
They put forth questions of astrology,
Which Faustus answer'd with such learned skill
As they admir'd and wonder'd at his wit.
865   Now is his fame spread forth in every land:
Amongst the rest the Emperor is one,
Carolus the Fifth, at whose palace now
Faustus is feasted 'mongst his noblemen.
What there he did, in trial of his art,
870   I leave untold; your eyes shall see't perform'd.

[Exit.]

Enter ROBIN the Ostler, with a book in his hand.

ROBIN. O, this is admirable! here I ha' stolen one of Doctor Faustus' con-
juring books, and, i'faith, I mean to search some circles for my own use. Now
will I make all the maidens in our parish dance at my pleasure, stark naked,
before me; and so by that means I shall see more than e'er I felt or saw yet.

Enter RALPH, calling ROBIN.

875   RALPH. Robin, prithee, come away; there's a gentleman tarries to have his
horse, and he would have his things rubbed and made clean: he keeps such
a chafing with my mistress about it; and she has sent me to look thee out;
prithee, come away.

4: May the Lord curse him.

880 ROBIN. Keep out, keep out, or else you are blown up, you are dismembered, Ralph: keep out, for I am about a roaring piece of work.

RALPH. Come, what doest thou with that same book? thou canst not read?

ROBIN. Yes, my master and mistress shall find that I can read, he for his forehead, she for her private study; she's born to bear with me, or else my art fails.

885 RALPH. Why, Robin, what book is that?

ROBIN. What book! why, the most intolerable book for conjuring that e'er was invented by any brimstone devil.

RALPH. Canst thou conjure with it?

ROBIN. I can do all these things easily with it; first, I can make thee
890 drunk with ippocras at any tabern in Europe for nothing; that's one of my conjuring works.

RALPH. Our Master Parson says that's nothing.

ROBIN. True, Ralph: and more, Ralph, if thou hast any mind to Nan Spit, our kitchen-maid, then turn her and wind her to thy own use, as often as
895 thou wilt, and at midnight.

RALPH. O, brave, Robin! shall I have Nan Spit, and to mine own use? On that condition I'll feed thy devil with horse-bread as long as he lives, of free cost.

ROBIN. No more, sweet Ralph: let's go and make clean our boots, which lie foul upon our hands, and then to our conjuring in the devil's name.

[Exeunt.]

Enter ROBIN and RALPH with a silver goblet.

900 ROBIN. Come, Ralph: did not I tell thee, we were for ever made by this Doctor Faustus' book? ecce, signum! here's a simple purchase for horse-keepers: our horses shall eat no hay as long as this lasts.

RALPH. But, Robin, here comes the Vintner.

ROBIN. Hush! I'll gull him supernaturally.

Enter VINTNER.

905 Drawer, I hope all is paid; God be with you!—Come, Ralph.

VINTNER. Soft, sir; a word with you. I must yet have a goblet paid from you, ere you go.

ROBIN. I a goblet, Ralph, I a goblet!—I scorn you; and you are but a, &c. I a goblet! search me.

910   VINTNER. I mean so, sir, with your favour.

[Searches ROBIN.]

ROBIN. How say you now?

VINTNER. I must say somewhat to your fellow.—You, sir!

RALPH. Me, sir! me, sir! search your fill. [VINTNER searches him.] Now, sir, you may be ashamed to burden honest men with a matter of truth.

915   VINTNER. Well, tone of you hath this goblet about you.

ROBIN. You lie, drawer, 'tis afore me [Aside].—Sirrah you, I'll teach you to impeach honest men;—stand by;—I'll scour you for a goblet;—stand aside you had best, I charge you in the name of Belzebub.—Look to the goblet, Ralph [Aside to RALPH].

920   VINTNER. What mean you, sirrah?

ROBIN. I'll tell you what I mean. [Reads from a book] Sanctobulorum Periphrasticon—nay, I'll tickle you, Vintner.—Look to the goblet, Ralph [Aside to RALPH].—[Reads] Polypragmos Belseborams framanto pacosti-phos tostu, Mephistophilis, &c.

Enter MEPHISTOPHILIS, sets squibs at their backs, and then exit.
They run about.

925   VINTNER. O, nomine Domini! what meanest thou, Robin? thou hast no goblet.

RALPH. Peccatum peccatorum!—Here's thy goblet, good Vintner.
[Gives the goblet to VINTNER, who exits.]

ROBIN. Misericordia pro nobis! what shall I do? Good devil, forgive me now, and I'll never rob thy library more.

Re-enter MEPHISTOPHILIS.

MEPHIST. Monarch of Hell, under whose black survey
930   Great potentates do kneel with awful fear,
Upon whose altars thousand souls do lie,
How am I vexed with these villains' charms?
From Constantinople am I hither come,
Only for pleasure of these damned slaves.

935   ROBIN. How, from Constantinople! you have had a great journey: will you take sixpence in your purse to pay for your supper, and be gone?

MEPHIST. Well, villains, for your presumption, I transform thee into an
ape, and thee into a dog; and so be gone!

[Exit.]

ROBIN. How, into an ape! that's brave: I'll have fine sport with the boys;
940 I'll get nuts and apples enow.

RALPH. And I must be a dog.

ROBIN. I'faith, thy head will never be out of the pottage-pot.

[Exeunt.]

Enter EMPEROR, FAUSTUS, and a KNIGHT, with ATTENDANTS.

EMPEROR. Master Doctor Faustus, I have heard strange report of thy
knowledge in the black art, how that none in my empire nor in the whole
945 world can compare with thee for the rare effects of magic: they say thou hast
a familiar spirit, by whom thou canst accomplish what thou list. This, there-
fore, is my request, that thou let me see some proof of thy skill, that mine
eyes may be witnesses to confirm what mine ears have heard reported: and
here I swear to thee, by the honour of mine imperial crown, that, whatever
950 thou doest, thou shalt be no ways prejudiced or endamaged.

KNIGHT. I'faith, he looks much like a conjurer.

[Aside.]

FAUSTUS. My gracious sovereign, though I must confess myself far inferi-
or to the report men have published, and nothing answerable to the honour
of your imperial majesty, yet, for that love and duty binds me thereunto, I
955 am content to do whatsoever your majesty shall command me.

EMPEROR. Then, Doctor Faustus, mark what I shall say.
As I was sometime solitary set
Within my closet, sundry thoughts arose
About the honour of mine ancestors,
960 How they had won by prowess such exploits,
Got such riches, subdu'd so many kingdoms,
As we that do succeed, or they that shall
Hereafter possess our throne, shall
(I fear me) ne'er attain to that degree
965 Of high renown and great authority:
Amongst which kings is Alexander the Great,
Chief spectacle of the world's pre-eminence,
The bright shining of whose glorious acts
Lightens the world with his reflecting beams,

970   As when I hear but motion made of him,
      It grieves my soul I never saw the man:
      If, therefore, thou, by cunning of thine art,
      Canst raise this man from hollow vaults below,
      Where lies entomb'd this famous conqueror,
975   And bring with him his beauteous paramour,
      Both in their right shapes, gesture, and attire
      They us'd to wear during their time of life,
      Thou shalt both satisfy my just desire,
      And give me cause to praise thee whilst I live.

980   FAUSTUS. My gracious lord, I am ready to accomplish your request, so far
      forth as by art and power of my spirit I am able to perform.

      KNIGHT. I'faith, that's just nothing at all.

                                                              [Aside.]

      FAUSTUS. But, if it like your grace, it is not in my ability to present before
      your eyes the true substantial bodies of those two deceased princes, which
985   long since are consumed to dust.

      KNIGHT. Ay, marry, Master Doctor, now there's a sign of grace in you,
      when you will confess the truth.

                                                              [Aside.]

      FAUSTUS. But such spirits as can lively resemble Alexander and his par-
      amour shall appear before your grace, in that manner that they both lived
990   in, in their most flourishing estate; which I doubt not shall sufficiently
      content your imperial majesty.

      EMPEROR. Go to, Master Doctor; let me see them presently.

      KNIGHT. Do you hear, Master Doctor? you bring Alexander and his
      paramour before the Emperor!

995   FAUSTUS. How then, sir?

      KNIGHT. I'faith, that's as true as Diana turned me to a stag.

      FAUSTUS. No, sir; but, when Actaeon died, he left the horns for you.—
      Mephistophilis, be gone.

                                            [Exit MEPHISTOPHILIS.]

      KNIGHT. Nay, an you go to conjuring, I'll be gone.

                                                              [Exit.]

1000 FAUSTUS. I'll meet with you anon for interrupting me so. —Here they are,
      my gracious lord.

Re-enter MEPHISTOPHILIS with SPIRITS in the shapes of
ALEXANDER and his PARAMOUR.

EMPEROR. Master Doctor, I heard this lady, while she lived, had a wart or
mole in her neck: how shall I know whether it be so or no?

FAUSTUS. Your highness may boldly go and see.

1005   EMPEROR. Sure, these are no spirits, but the true substantial bodies of
those two deceased princes.

[Exeunt Spirits.]

FAUSTUS. Wilt please your highness now to send for the knight that was so
pleasant with me here of late?

EMPEROR. One of you call him forth.

[Exit ATTENDANT.]

Re-enter the KNIGHT with a pair of horns on his head.

1010   How now, sir knight! why, I had thought thou hadst been a bachelor, but
now I see thou hast a wife, that not only gives thee horns, but makes thee
wear them. Feel on thy head.

KNIGHT. Thou damned wretch and execrable dog,
Bred in the concave of some monstrous rock,
1015   How dar'st thou thus abuse a gentleman?
Villain, I say, undo what thou hast done!

FAUSTUS. O, not so fast, sir! there's no haste: but, good, are you remem-
bered how you crossed me in my conference with the Emperor? I think I
have met with you for it.

1020   EMPEROR. Good Master Doctor, at my entreaty release him: he hath
done penance sufficient.

FAUSTUS. My gracious lord, not so much for the injury he offered me here
in your presence, as to delight you with some mirth, hath Faustus worthily
requited this injurious knight; which being all I desire, I am content to re-
1025   lease him of his horns:—and, sir knight, hereafter speak well of scholars.—
Mephistophilis, transform him straight. [MEPHISTOPHILIS removes the
horns.] —Now, my good lord, having done my duty, I humbly take my leave.

EMPEROR. Farewell, Master Doctor: yet, ere you go,
Expect from me a bounteous reward.

[Exeunt EMPEROR, KNIGHT, and ATTENDANTS.]

1030 FAUSTUS. Now, Mephistophilis, the restless course
      That time doth run with calm and silent foot,
      Shortening my days and thread of vital life,
      Calls for the payment of my latest years:
      Therefore, sweet Mephistophilis, let us
1035 Make haste to Wertenberg.

      MEPHIST. What, will you go on horse-back or on foot?

      FAUSTUS. Nay, till I'm past this fair and pleasant green, I'll walk on foot.

                    Enter a HORSE-COURSER.

      HORSE-COURSER. I have been all this day seeking one Master Fustian:
      mass, see where he is!—God save you, Master Doctor!

1040 FAUSTUS. What, horse-courser! you are well met.

      HORSE-COURSER. Do you hear, sir? I have brought you forty dollars
      for your horse.

      FAUSTUS. I cannot sell him so: if thou likest him for fifty, take him.

      HORSE-COURSER. Alas, sir, I have no more!—I pray you, speak for me.

1045 MEPHIST. I pray you, let him have him: he is an honest fellow, and he has
      a great charge, neither wife nor child.

      FAUSTUS. Well, come, give me your money [HORSE-COURSER gives
      FAUSTUS the money]: my boy will deliver him to you. But I must tell you
      one thing before you have him; ride him not into the water, at any hand.

1050 HORSE-COURSER. Why, sir, will he not drink of all waters?

      FAUSTUS. O, yes, he will drink of all waters; but ride him not into the water:
      ride him over hedge or ditch, or where thou wilt, but not into the water.

      HORSE-COURSER. Well, sir.—Now am I made man for ever: I'll not
      leave my horse for forty: if he had but the quality of hey-ding-ding, hey-
1055 ding-ding, I'd make a brave living on him: he has a buttock as slick as an eel
      [Aside].—Well, God b'wi'ye, sir: your boy will deliver him me: but, hark
      you, sir; if my horse be sick or ill at ease, if I bring his water to you, you'll
      tell me what it is?

      FAUSTUS. Away, you villain! what, dost think I am a horse-doctor?
                                          [Exit HORSE-COURSER.]
1060 What art thou, Faustus, but a man condemn'd to die?
      Thy fatal time doth draw to final end;

Despair doth drive distrust into my thoughts:
Confound these passions with a quiet sleep:
Tush, Christ did call the thief upon the Cross;
1065   Then rest thee, Faustus, quiet in conceit.

[Sleeps in his chair.]

Re-enter HORSE-COURSER, all wet, crying.

HORSE-COURSER. Alas, alas! Doctor Fustian, quoth a? mass, Doctor Lopus
was never such a doctor: has given me a purgation, has purged me of forty
dollars; I shall never see them more. But yet, like an ass as I was, I would not be
ruled by him, for he bade me I should ride him into no water: now I, thinking
1070   my horse had had some rare quality that he would not have had me know of, I,
like a venturous youth, rid him into the deep pond at the town's end. I was no
sooner in the middle of the pond, but my horse vanished away, and I sat upon
a bottle of hay, never so near drowning in my life. But I'll seek out my doctor,
and have my forty dollars again, or I'll make it the dearest horse!—O, yonder is
1075   his snipper-snapper.—Do you hear? you, hey-pass, where's your master?

MEPHIST. Why, sir, what would you? you cannot speak with him.

HORSE-COURSER. But I will speak with him.

MEPHIST. Why, he's fast asleep: come some other time.

HORSE-COURSER. I'll speak with him now, or I'll break his glass-windows
1080   about his ears.

MEPHIST. I tell thee, he has not slept this eight nights.

HORSE-COURSER. An he have not slept this eight weeks, I'll speak
with him.

MEPHIST. See, where he is, fast asleep.

1085   HORSE-COURSER. Ay, this is he.—God save you, Master Doctor, Master
Doctor, Master Doctor Fustian! forty dollars, forty dollars for a bottle of hay!

MEPHIST. Why, thou seest he hears thee not.

HORSE-COURSER. So-ho, ho! so-ho, ho! [Hollows in his ear.] No, will
you not wake? I'll make you wake ere I go. [Pulls FAUSTUS by the leg, and
1090   pulls it away.] Alas, I am undone! what shall I do?

FAUSTUS. O, my leg, my leg!—Help, Mephistophilis! call the officers.—My
leg, my leg!

MEPHIST. Come, villain, to the constable.

HORSE-COURSER. O Lord, sir, let me go, and I'll give you forty dollars more!

1095 MEPHIST. Where be they?

HORSE-COURSER. I have none about me: come to my ostry, and I'll give them you.

MEPHIST. Be gone quickly.

[HORSE-COURSER runs away.]

FAUSTUS. What, is he gone? farewell he! Faustus has his leg again, and the
1100 Horse-courser, I take it, a bottle of hay for his labour: well, this trick shall cost him forty dollars more.

Enter WAGNER.

How now, Wagner! what's the news with thee?

WAGNER. Sir, the Duke of Vanholt doth earnestly entreat your company.

FAUSTUS. The Duke of Vanholt! an honourable gentleman, to whom I must
1105 be no niggard[5] of my cunning. —Come, Mephistophilis, let's away to him.

[Exeunt.]

Enter the DUKE OF VANHOLT, the DUCHESS, and FAUSTUS.

DUKE. Believe me, Master Doctor, this merriment hath much pleased me.

FAUSTUS. My gracious lord, I am glad it contents you so well. —But it may be, madam, you take no delight in this. I have heard that great-bellied women do long for some dainties or other: what is it, madam? tell me, and
1110 you shall have it.

DUCHESS. Thanks, good Master Doctor: and, for I see your courteous intent to pleasure me, I will not hide from you the thing my heart desires; and, were it now summer, as it is January and the dead time of the winter, I would desire no better meat than a dish of ripe grapes.

1115 FAUSTUS. Alas, madam, that's nothing!—Mephistophilis, be gone. [Exit MEPHISTOPHILIS.] Were it a greater thing than this, so it would content you, you should have it.

Re-enter MEPHISTOPHILIS with grapes.

Here they be, madam: wilt please you taste on them?

DUKE. Believe me, Master Doctor, this makes me wonder above the rest,
1120 that being in the dead time of winter and in the month of January, how you should come by these grapes.

5: Miser.

FAUSTUS. If it like your grace, the year is divided into two circles over the whole world, that, when it is here winter with us, in the contrary circle it is summer with them, as in India, Saba, and farther countries in the east; and 1125   by means of a swift spirit that I have, I had them brought hither, as you see. —How do you like them, madam? be they good?

DUCHESS. Believe me, Master Doctor, they be the best grapes that e'er I tasted in my life before.

FAUSTUS. I am glad they content you so, madam.

1130   DUKE. Come, madam, let us in, where you must well reward this learned man for the great kindness he hath shewed to you.

DUCHESS. And so I will, my lord; and, whilst I live, rest beholding for this courtesy.

FAUSTUS. I humbly thank your grace.

1135   DUKE. Come, Master Doctor, follow us, and receive your reward.

[Exeunt.]

Enter WAGNER.

WAGNER. I think my master means to die shortly,
For he hath given to me all his goods:
And yet, methinks, if that death were near,
He would not banquet, and carouse, and swill
1140   Amongst the students, as even now he doth,
Who are at supper with such belly-cheer
As Wagner ne'er beheld in all his life.
See, where they come! belike the feast is ended.

[Exit.]

Enter FAUSTUS with two or three SCHOLARS, and MEPHISTOPHILIS.

FIRST SCHOLAR. Master Doctor Faustus, since our conference about fair 1145   ladies, which was the beautifulest in all the world, we have determined with ourselves that Helen of Greece was the admirablest lady that ever lived: therefore, Master Doctor, if you will do us that favour, as to let us see that peerless dame of Greece, whom all the world admires for majesty, we should think ourselves much beholding unto you.

1150   FAUSTUS. Gentlemen,
For that I know your friendship is unfeign'd,
And Faustus' custom is not to deny
The just requests of those that wish him well,
You shall behold that peerless dame of Greece,
1155   No otherways for pomp and majesty

Than when Sir Paris cross'd the seas with her,
And brought the spoils to rich Dardania.
Be silent, then, for danger is in words.
                    [Music sounds, and HELEN passeth over the stage.]

SECOND SCHOLAR. Too simple is my wit to tell her praise,
1160   Whom all the world admires for majesty.

THIRD SCHOLAR. No marvel though the angry Greeks pursu'd
With ten years' war the rape of such a queen,
Whose heavenly beauty passeth all compare.

FIRST SCHOLAR. Since we have seen the pride of Nature's works,
1165   And only paragon of excellence,
Let us depart; and for this glorious deed
Happy and blest be Faustus evermore!

FAUSTUS. Gentlemen, farewell: the same I wish to you.
                                        [Exeunt SCHOLARS.]

Enter an OLD MAN.

OLD MAN. Ah, Doctor Faustus, that I might prevail
1170   To guide thy steps unto the way of life,
By which sweet path thou mayst attain the goal
That shall conduct thee to celestial rest!
Break heart, drop blood, and mingle it with tears,
Tears falling from repentant heaviness
1175   Of thy most vile and loathsome filthiness,
The stench whereof corrupts the inward soul
With such flagitious crimes of heinous sin
As no commiseration may expel,
But mercy, Faustus, of thy Saviour sweet,
1180   Whose blood alone must wash away thy guilt.

FAUSTUS. Where art thou, Faustus? wretch, what hast thou done?
Damn'd art thou, Faustus, damn'd; despair and die!
Hell calls for right, and with a roaring voice
Says, "Faustus, come; thine hour is almost come;"
1185   And Faustus now will come to do thee right.
                            [MEPHISTOPHILIS gives him a dagger.]

OLD MAN. Ah, stay, good Faustus, stay thy desperate steps!
I see an angel hovers o'er thy head,
And, with a vial full of precious grace,
Offers to pour the same into thy soul:
1190   Then call for mercy, and avoid despair.

FAUSTUS. Ah, my sweet friend, I feel
Thy words to comfort my distressed soul!
Leave me a while to ponder on my sins.

OLD MAN. I go, sweet Faustus; but with heavy cheer,
1195 Fearing the ruin of thy hopeless soul.

[Exit.]

FAUSTUS. Accursed Faustus, where is mercy now?
I do repent; and yet I do despair:
Hell strives with grace for conquest in my breast:
What shall I do to shun the snares of death?

1200 MEPHIST. Thou traitor, Faustus, I arrest thy soul
For disobedience to my sovereign lord:
Revolt, or I'll in piece-meal tear thy flesh.

FAUSTUS. Sweet Mephistophilis, entreat thy lord
To pardon my unjust presumption,
1205 And with my blood again I will confirm
My former vow I made to Lucifer.

MEPHIST. Do it, then, quickly, with unfeigned heart,
Lest greater danger do attend thy drift.

FAUSTUS. Torment, sweet friend, that base and crooked age,
1210 That durst dissuade me from thy Lucifer,
With greatest torments that our hell affords.

MEPHIST. His faith is great; I cannot touch his soul;
But what I may afflict his body with
I will attempt, which is but little worth.

1215 FAUSTUS. One thing, good servant, let me crave of thee,
To glut the longing of my heart's desire,—
That I might have unto my paramour
That heavenly Helen which I saw of late,
Whose sweet embracings may extinguish clean
1220 Those thoughts that do dissuade me from my vow,
And keep mine oath I made to Lucifer.

MEPHIST. Faustus, this, or what else thou shalt desire,
Shall be perform'd in twinkling of an eye.

Re-enter HELEN.

FAUSTUS. Was this the face that launch'd a thousand ships,
1225 And burnt the topless towers of Ilium—
Sweet Helen, make me immortal with a kiss.—

[Kisses her.]

Her lips suck forth my soul: see, where it flies!—
Come, Helen, come, give me my soul again.
Here will I dwell, for heaven is in these lips,
1230 And all is dross that is not Helena.
I will be Paris, and for love of thee,
Instead of Troy, shall Wertenberg be sack'd;
And I will combat with weak Menelaus,
And wear thy colours on my plumed crest;
1235 Yea, I will wound Achilles in the heel,
And then return to Helen for a kiss.
O, thou art fairer than the evening air
Clad in the beauty of a thousand stars;
Brighter art thou than flaming Jupiter
1240 When he appear'd to hapless Semele;
More lovely than the monarch of the sky
In wanton Arethusa's azur'd arms;
And none but thou shalt be my paramour!

[Exeunt.]

Enter the OLD MAN.

OLD MAN. Accursed Faustus, miserable man,
1245 That from thy soul exclud'st the grace of heaven,
And fly'st the throne of his tribunal-seat!

Enter DEVILS.

Satan begins to sift me with his pride:
As in this furnace God shall try my faith,
My faith, vile hell, shall triumph over thee.
1250 Ambitious fiends, see how the heavens smile
At your repulse, and laugh your state to scorn!
Hence, hell! for hence I fly unto my God.
[Exeunt,—on one side, DEVILS, on the other, OLD MAN.]

Enter FAUSTUS, with SCHOLARS.

FAUSTUS. Ah, gentlemen!

FIRST SCHOLAR. What ails Faustus?

1255 FAUSTUS. Ah, my sweet chamber-fellow, had I lived with thee, then had I
lived still! but now I die eternally. Look, comes he not? comes he not?

SECOND SCHOLAR. What means Faustus?

THIRD SCHOLAR. Belike he is grown into sickness by being over-solitary.

FIRST SCHOLAR. If it be so, we'll have physicians to cure him. —'Tis but
1260 a surfeit; never fear, man.

FAUSTUS. A surfeit of deadly sin, that hath damned both body and soul.

SECOND SCHOLAR. Yet, Faustus, look up to heaven; remember God's
mercies are infinite.

FAUSTUS. But Faustus' offence can ne'er be pardoned: the serpent that
1265 tempted Eve may be saved, but not Faustus. Ah, gentlemen, hear me with
patience, and tremble not at my speeches! Though my heart pants and quivers
to remember that I have been a student here these thirty years, O, would I had
never seen Wertenberg, never read a book! and what wonders I have done, all
Germany can witness, yea, all the world; for which Faustus hath lost both Ger-
1270 many and the world, yea, heaven itself, heaven, the seat of God, the throne of
the blessed, the kingdom of joy; and must remain in hell for ever, hell, ah, hell,
for ever! Sweet friends, what shall become of Faustus, being in hell for ever?

THIRD SCHOLAR. Yet, Faustus, call on God.

FAUSTUS. On God, whom Faustus hath abjured! on God, whom Faustus
1275 hath blasphemed! Ah, my God, I would weep! but the devil draws in my
tears. Gush forth blood, instead of tears! yea, life and soul! O, he stays my
tongue! I would lift up my hands; but see, they hold them, they hold them!

ALL. Who, Faustus?

FAUSTUS. Lucifer and Mephistophilis. Ah, gentlemen, I gave them my
1280 soul for my cunning!

ALL. God forbid!

FAUSTUS. God forbade it, indeed; but Faustus hath done it: for vain plea-
sure of twenty-four years hath Faustus lost eternal joy and felicity. I writ
them a bill with mine own blood: the date is expired; the time will come,
1285 and he will fetch me.

FIRST SCHOLAR. Why did not Faustus tell us of this before, that divines
might have prayed for thee?

FAUSTUS. Oft have I thought to have done so; but the devil threatened to tear
me in pieces, if I named God, to fetch both body and soul, if I once gave ear
1290 to divinity: and now 'tis too late. Gentlemen, away, lest you perish with me.

SECOND SCHOLAR. O, what shall we do to save Faustus?

FAUSTUS. Talk not of me, but save yourselves, and depart.

THIRD SCHOLAR. God will strengthen me; I will stay with Faustus.

FIRST SCHOLAR. Tempt not God, sweet friend; but let us into the next
1295   room, and there pray for him.

FAUSTUS. Ay, pray for me, pray for me; and what noise soever ye hear,
come not unto me, for nothing can rescue me.

SECOND SCHOLAR. Pray thou, and we will pray that God may have
mercy upon thee.

1300   FAUSTUS. Gentlemen, farewell: if I live till morning, I'll visit you; if not,
Faustus is gone to hell.

ALL. Faustus, farewell.
                    [Exeunt SCHOLARS.—The clock strikes eleven.]

FAUSTUS. Ah, Faustus,
Now hast thou but one bare hour to live,
1305   And then thou must be damn'd perpetually!
Stand still, you ever-moving spheres of heaven,
That time may cease, and midnight never come;
Fair Nature's eye, rise, rise again, and make
Perpetual day; or let this hour be but
1310   A year, a month, a week, a natural day,
That Faustus may repent and save his soul!
O lente, lente currite, noctis equi!
The stars move still, time runs, the clock will strike,
The devil will come, and Faustus must be damn'd.
1315   O, I'll leap up to my God!—Who pulls me down?—
See, see, where Christ's blood streams in the firmament!
One drop would save my soul, half a drop: ah, my Christ!—
Ah, rend not my heart for naming of my Christ!
Yet will I call on him: O, spare me, Lucifer!—
1320   Where is it now? 'tis gone: and see, where God
Stretcheth out his arm, and bends his ireful brows!
Mountains and hills, come, come, and fall on me,
And hide me from the heavy wrath of God!
No, no!
1325   Then will I headlong run into the earth:
Earth, gape! O, no, it will not harbour me!
You stars that reign'd at my nativity,
Whose influence hath allotted death and hell,
Now draw up Faustus, like a foggy mist.
1330   Into the entrails of yon labouring clouds,
That, when you vomit forth into the air,
My limbs may issue from your smoky mouths,
So that my soul may but ascend to heaven!
[The clock strikes the half-hour.]

1335 Ah, half the hour is past! 'twill all be past anon
      O God,
      If thou wilt not have mercy on my soul,
      Yet for Christ's sake, whose blood hath ransom'd me,
      Impose some end to my incessant pain;
1340 Let Faustus live in hell a thousand years,
      A hundred thousand, and at last be sav'd!
      O, no end is limited to damned souls!
      Why wert thou not a creature wanting soul?
      Or why is this immortal that thou hast?
1345 Ah, Pythagoras' metempsychosis, were that true,
      This soul should fly from me, and I be chang'd
      Unto some brutish beast! all beasts are happy,
      For, when they die,
      Their souls are soon dissolv'd in elements;
1350 But mine must live still to be plagu'd in hell.
      Curs'd be the parents that engender'd me!
      No, Faustus, curse thyself, curse Lucifer
      That hath depriv'd thee of the joys of heaven.

                                              [The clock strikes twelve.]

      O, it strikes, it strikes! Now, body, turn to air,
1355 Or Lucifer will bear thee quick to hell!

                                              [Thunder and lightning.]

      O soul, be chang'd into little water-drops,
      And fall into the ocean, ne'er be found!

                        Enter DEVILS.

      My God, my god, look not so fierce on me!
      Adders and serpents, let me breathe a while!
1360 Ugly hell, gape not! come not, Lucifer!
      I'll burn my books!—Ah, Mephistophilis!

                                              [Exeunt DEVILS with FAUSTUS.]

                        Enter CHORUS.

      CHORUS. Cut is the branch that might have grown full straight,
      And burned is Apollo's laurel-bough,
      That sometime grew within this learned man.
1365 Faustus is gone: regard his hellish fall,
      Whose fiendful fortune may exhort the wise,
      Only to wonder at unlawful things,
      Whose deepness doth entice such forward wits
      To practice more than heavenly power permits.

                                              [Exit.]

      Terminat hora diem; terminat auctor opus.[6]
      6: The hour finishes the day; the author finishes his work.

Hero and Leander

First Sestiad

On Hellespont, guilty of true-love's blood,
In view and opposite two cities stood,
Sea-borderers, disjoined by Neptune's might;
The one Abydos, the other Sestos hight.
5 At Sestos Hero dwelt; Hero the fair,
Whom young Apollo courted for her hair,
And offered as a dower his burning throne,
Where she should sit for men to gaze upon.
The outside of her garments were of lawn,
10 The lining purple silk, with gilt stars drawn;
Her wide sleeves green, and bordered with a grove,
Where Venus in her naked glory strove
To please the careless and disdainful eyes
Of proud Adonis, that before her lies.
15 Her kirtle blue, whereon was many a stain,
Made with the blood of wretched lovers slain.
Upon her head she ware a myrtle wreath,
From whence her veil reached to the ground beneath.
Her veil was artificial flowers and leaves
20 Whose workmanship both man and beast deceives.
Many would praise the sweet smell as she passed,
When 'twas the odour which her breath forth cast;
And there for honey bees have sought in vain,
And, beat from thence, have lighted there again.
25 About her neck hung chains of pebblestone,
Which, lightened by her neck, like diamonds shone.
She ware no gloves; for neither sun nor wind
Would burn or parch her hands, but to her mind,
Or warm or cool them, for they took delight
30 To play upon those hands, they were so white.
Buskins of shells, all silvered used she,
And branched with blushing coral to the knee;
Where sparrows perched of hollow pearl and gold,
Such as the world would wonder to behold.
35 Those with sweet water oft her handmaid fills,
Which, as she went, would chirrup through the bills.
Some say for her the fairest Cupid pined

And looking in her face was strooken blind.
But this is true: so like was one the other,
40 As he imagined Hero was his mother.
And oftentimes into her bosom flew,
About her naked neck his bare arms threw,
And laid his childish head upon her breast,
And, with still panting rocked, there took his rest.
45 So lovely fair was Hero, Venus' nun,
As Nature wept, thinking she was undone,
Because she took more from her than she left,
And of such wondrous beauty her bereft.
Therefore, in sign her treasure suffered wrack,
50 Since Hero's time hath half the world been black.

Amorous Leander, beautiful and young,
(whose tragedy divine Musaeus sung,)
Dwelt at Abydos; since him dwelt there none
For whom succeeding times make greater moan.
55 His dangling tresses, that were never shorn,
Had they been cut, and unto Colchos borne,
Would have allured the vent'rous youth of Greece
To hazard more than for the golden fleece.
Fair Cynthia wished his arms might be her sphere;
60 Grief makes her pale, because she moves not there.
His body was as straight as Circe's wand;
Jove might have sipped out nectar from his hand.
Even as delicious meat is to the taste,
So was his neck in touching, and surpassed
65 The white of Pelop's shoulder. I could tell ye
How smooth his breast was and how white his belly;
And whose immortal fingers did imprint
That heavenly path with many a curious dint
That runs along his back, but my rude pen
70 Can hardly blazon forth the loves of men,
Much less of powerful gods. Let it suffice
That my slack Muse sings of Leander's eyes,
Those orient cheeks and lips, exceeding his
That leaped into the water for a kiss
75 Of his own shadow and, despising many,
Died ere he could enjoy the love of any.
Had wild Hippolytus Leander seen
Enamoured of his beauty had he been.
His presence made the rudest peasant melt
80 That in the vast uplandish country dwelt.
The barbarous Thracian soldier, moved with nought,

Was moved with him and for his favour sought.
Some swore he was a maid in man's attire,
For in his looks were all that men desire,
85 A pleasant smiling cheek, a speaking eye,
A brow for love to banquet royally;
And such as knew he was a man, would say,
"Leander, thou art made for amorous play.
Why art thou not in love, and loved of all?
90 Though thou be fair, yet be not thine own thrall."

The men of wealthy Sestos every year,
(For his sake whom their goddess held so dear,
Rose-cheeked Adonis) kept a solemn feast.
Thither resorted many a wandering guest
95 To meet their loves. Such as had none at all,
Came lovers home from this great festival.
For every street like to a firmament
Glistered with breathing stars who, where they went,
Frighted the melancholy earth which deemed
100 Eternal heaven to burn, for so it seemed,
As if another Phaeton had got
The guidance of the sun's rich chariot.
But far above the loveliest Hero shined
And stole away th' enchanted gazer's mind,
105 For like sea nymphs' enveigling Harmony,
So was her beauty to the standers by.
Nor that night-wandering, pale, and wat'ry star
(When yawning dragons draw her thirling car
From Latmus' mount up to the gloomy sky
110 Where, crowned with blazing light and majesty,
She proudly sits) more overrules the flood
Than she the hearts of those that near her stood.
Even as, when gaudy nymphs pursue the chase,
Wretched Ixion's shaggy footed race,
115 Incensed with savage heat, gallop amain
From steep pine-bearing mountains to the plain.
So ran the people forth to gaze upon her,
And all that viewed her were enamoured on her.
And as in fury of a dreadful fight,
120 Their fellows being slain or put to flight,
Poor soldiers stand with fear of death dead strooken,
So at her presence all surprised and tooken,
Await the sentence of her scornful eyes.
He whom she favours lives, the other dies.
125 There might you see one sigh, another rage;

And some, (their violent passions to assuage)
Compile sharp satires, but alas too late,
For faithful love will never turn to hate.
And many seeing great princes were denied
130   Pin'd as they went, and thinking on her died.
On this feast day, O cursed day and hour,
Went Hero thorough Sestos from her tower
To Venus' temple, where unhappily
As after chanced, they did each other spy.

135   So fair a church as this had Venus none.
The walls were of discoloured jasper stone
Wherein was Proteus carved, and o'erhead
A lively vine of green sea agate spread,
Where by one hand lightheaded Bacchus hung,
140   And, with the other, wine from grapes out wrung.
Of crystal shining fair the pavement was.
The town of Sestos called it Venus' glass.
There might you see the gods in sundry shapes
Committing heady riots, incest, rapes.
145   For know, that underneath this radiant floor
Was Danae's statue in a brazen tower,
Jove slyly stealing from his sister's bed,
To dally with Idalian Ganymede,
And for his love Europa bellowing loud,
150   And tumbling with the Rainbow in a cloud;
Blood quaffing Mars heaving the iron net
Which limping Vulcan and his Cyclops set;
Love kindling fire to burn such towns as Troy;
Sylvanus weeping for the lovely boy
155   That now is turned into a cypress tree,
Under whose shade the wood gods love to be.
And in the midst a silver altar stood.
There Hero, sacrificing turtle's blood,
Vailed to the ground, vailing her eyelids close,
160   And modestly they opened as she rose.
Thence flew Love's arrow with the golden head,
And thus Leander was enamoured.
Stone still he stood, and evermore he gazed
Till with the fire that from his countenance blazed
165   Relenting Hero's gentle heart was strook.
Such force and virtue hath an amorous look.

It lies not in our power to love or hate,
For will in us is overruled by fate.

When two are stripped, long ere the course begin
170 We wish that one should lose, the other win.
And one especially do we affect
Of two gold ingots like in each respect.
The reason no man knows; let it suffice
What we behold is censured by our eyes.
175 Where both deliberate, the love is slight:
Who ever loved, that loved not at first sight?

He kneeled, but unto her devoutly prayed.
Chaste Hero to herself thus softly said,
"Were I the saint he worships, I would hear him;"
180 And, as she spake those words, came somewhat near him.
He started up, she blushed as one ashamed,
Wherewith Leander much more was inflamed.
He touched her hand; in touching it she trembled.
Love deeply grounded, hardly is dissembled.
185 These lovers parleyed by the touch of hands;
True love is mute, and oft amazed stands.
Thus while dumb signs their yielding hearts entangled,
The air with sparks of living fire was spangled,
And night, deep drenched in misty Acheron,
190 Heaved up her head, and half the world upon
Breathed darkness forth (dark night is Cupid's day).
And now begins Leander to display
Love's holy fire, with words, with sighs, and tears,
Which like sweet music entered Hero's ears,
195 And yet at every word she turned aside,
And always cut him off as he replied.
At last, like to a bold sharp sophister,
With cheerful hope thus he accosted her.
"Fair creature, let me speak without offence.
200 I would my rude words had the influence
To lead thy thoughts as thy fair looks do mine,
Then shouldst thou be his prisoner, who is thine.
Be not unkind and fair; misshapen stuff
Are of behaviour boisterous and rough.
205 O shun me not, but hear me ere you go.
God knows I cannot force love as you do.
My words shall be as spotless as my youth,
Full of simplicity and naked truth.
This sacrifice, (whose sweet perfume descending
210 From Venus' altar, to your footsteps bending)
Doth testify that you exceed her far,
To whom you offer, and whose nun you are.

Why should you worship her? Her you surpass
As much as sparkling diamonds flaring glass.
215   A diamond set in lead his worth retains;
A heavenly nymph, beloved of human swains,
Receives no blemish, but ofttimes more grace;
Which makes me hope, although I am but base:
Base in respect of thee, divine and pure,
220   Dutiful service may thy love procure.
And I in duty will excel all other,
As thou in beauty dost exceed Love's mother.
Nor heaven, nor thou, were made to gaze upon,
As heaven preserves all things, so save thou one.
225   A stately builded ship, well rigged and tall,
The ocean maketh more majestical.
Why vowest thou then to live in Sestos here
Who on Love's seas more glorious wouldst appear?
Like untuned golden strings all women are,
230   Which long time lie untouched, will harshly jar.
Vessels of brass, oft handled, brightly shine.
What difference betwixt the richest mine
And basest mould, but use? For both, not used,
Are of like worth. Then treasure is abused
235   When misers keep it; being put to loan,
In time it will return us two for one.
Rich robes themselves and others do adorn;
Neither themselves nor others, if not worn.
Who builds a palace and rams up the gate
240   Shall see it ruinous and desolate.
Ah, simple Hero, learn thyself to cherish.
Lone women like to empty houses perish.
Less sins the poor rich man that starves himself
In heaping up a mass of drossy pelf,
245   Than such as you. His golden earth remains
Which, after his decease, some other gains.
But this fair gem, sweet in the loss alone,
When you fleet hence, can be bequeathed to none.
Or, if it could, down from th'enameled sky
250   All heaven would come to claim this legacy,
And with intestine broils the world destroy,
And quite confound nature's sweet harmony.
Well therefore by the gods decreed it is
We human creatures should enjoy that bliss.
255   One is no number; maids are nothing then
Without the sweet society of men.
Wilt thou live single still? One shalt thou be,

Though never singling Hymen couple thee.
Wild savages, that drink of running springs,
260 Think water far excels all earthly things,
But they that daily taste neat wine despise it.
Virginity, albeit some highly prize it,
Compared with marriage, had you tried them both,
Differs as much as wine and water doth.
265 Base bullion for the stamp's sake we allow;
Even so for men's impression do we you,
By which alone, our reverend fathers say,
Women receive perfection every way.
This idol which you term virginity
270 Is neither essence subject to the eye
No, nor to any one exterior sense,
Nor hath it any place of residence,
Nor is't of earth or mould celestial,
Or capable of any form at all.
275 Of that which hath no being do not boast;
Things that are not at all are never lost.
Men foolishly do call it virtuous;
What virtue is it that is born with us?
Much less can honour be ascribed thereto;
280 Honour is purchased by the deeds we do.
Believe me, Hero, honour is not won
Until some honourable deed be done.
Seek you for chastity, immortal fame,
And know that some have wronged Diana's name?
285 Whose name is it, if she be false or not
So she be fair, but some vile tongues will blot?
But you are fair, (ay me) so wondrous fair,
So young, so gentle, and so debonair,
As Greece will think if thus you live alone
290 Some one or other keeps you as his own.
Then, Hero, hate me not nor from me fly
To follow swiftly blasting infamy.
Perhaps thy sacred priesthood makes thee loath.
Tell me, to whom mad'st thou that heedless oath?"

295 "To Venus," answered she and, as she spake,
Forth from those two tralucent cisterns brake
A stream of liquid pearl, which down her face
Made milk-white paths, whereon the gods might trace
To Jove's high court. He thus replied: "The rites
300 In which love's beauteous empress most delights
Are banquets, Doric music, midnight revel,

Plays, masks, and all that stern age counteth evil.
Thee as a holy idiot doth she scorn
For thou in vowing chastity hast sworn
305 To rob her name and honour, and thereby
Committ'st a sin far worse than perjury,
Even sacrilege against her deity,
Through regular and formal purity.
To expiate which sin, kiss and shake hands.
310 Such sacrifice as this Venus demands."

Thereat she smiled and did deny him so,
As put thereby, yet might he hope for moe.
Which makes him quickly re-enforce his speech,
And her in humble manner thus beseech.
315 "Though neither gods nor men may thee deserve,
Yet for her sake, whom you have vowed to serve,
Abandon fruitless cold virginity,
The gentle queen of love's sole enemy.
Then shall you most resemble Venus' nun,
320 When Venus' sweet rites are performed and done.
Flint-breasted Pallas joys in single life,
But Pallas and your mistress are at strife.
Love, Hero, then, and be not tyrannous,
But heal the heart that thou hast wounded thus,
325 Nor stain thy youthful years with avarice.
Fair fools delight to be accounted nice.
The richest corn dies, if it be not reaped;
Beauty alone is lost, too warily kept."

These arguments he used, and many more,
330 Wherewith she yielded, that was won before.
Hero's looks yielded but her words made war.
Women are won when they begin to jar.
Thus, having swallowed Cupid's golden hook,
The more she strived, the deeper was she strook.
335 Yet, evilly feigning anger, strove she still
And would be thought to grant against her will.
So having paused a while at last she said,
"Who taught thee rhetoric to deceive a maid?
Ay me, such words as these should I abhor
340 And yet I like them for the orator."

With that Leander stooped to have embraced her
But from his spreading arms away she cast her,
And thus bespake him: "Gentle youth, forbear

To touch the sacred garments which I wear.
345 Upon a rock and underneath a hill
Far from the town (where all is whist and still,
Save that the sea, playing on yellow sand,
Sends forth a rattling murmur to the land,
Whose sound allures the golden Morpheus
350 In silence of the night to visit us)
My turret stands and there, God knows, I play,
With Venus' swans and sparrows all the day.
A dwarfish beldam bears me company,
That hops about the chamber where I lie,
355 And spends the night (that might be better spent)
In vain discourse and apish merriment.
Come thither." As she spake this, her tongue tripped,
For unawares "come thither" from her slipped.
And suddenly her former colour changed,
360 And here and there her eyes through anger ranged.
And like a planet, moving several ways,
At one self instant she, poor soul, assays,
Loving, not to love at all, and every part
Strove to resist the motions of her heart.
365 And hands so pure, so innocent, nay, such
As might have made heaven stoop to have a touch,
Did she uphold to Venus, and again
Vowed spotless chastity, but all in vain.
Cupid beats down her prayers with his wings,
370 Her vows above the empty air he flings,
All deep enraged, his sinewy bow he bent,
And shot a shaft that burning from him went,
Wherewith she strooken, looked so dolefully,
As made love sigh to see his tyranny.
375 And as she wept her tears to pearl he turned,
And wound them on his arm and for her mourned.
Then towards the palace of the destinies
Laden with languishment and grief he flies,
And to those stern nymphs humbly made request
380 Both might enjoy each other, and be blest.
But with a ghastly dreadful countenance,
Threatening a thousand deaths at every glance,
They answered Love, nor would vouchsafe so much
As one poor word, their hate to him was such.
385 Hearken a while and I will tell you why.
Heaven's winged herald, Jove-borne Mercury,
The selfsame day that he asleep had laid
Enchanted Argus, spied a country maid

Whose careless hair instead of pearl t'adorn it
390 Glistered with dew, as one that seemed to scorn it;
Her breath as fragrant as the morning rose,
Her mind pure, and her tongue untaught to gloze.
Yet proud she was (for lofty pride that dwells
In towered courts is oft in shepherds' cells.)
395 And too too well the fair vermilion knew,
And silver tincture of her cheeks, that drew
The love of every swain. On her this god
Enamoured was, and with his snaky rod
Did charm her nimble feet, and made her stay,
400 The while upon a hillock down he lay
And sweetly on his pipe began to play,
And with smooth speech her fancy to assay,
Till in his twining arms he locked her fast
And then he wooed with kisses; and at last,
405 As shepherds do, her on the ground he laid
And, tumbling in the grass, he often strayed
Beyond the bounds of shame, in being bold
To eye those parts which no eye should behold.
And, like an insolent commanding lover
410 Boasting his parentage, would needs discover
The way to new Elysium, but she,
Whose only dower was her chastity,
Having striv'n in vain was now about to cry
And crave the help of shepherds that were nigh.
415 Herewith he stayed his fury, and began
To give her leave to rise. Away she ran;
After went Mercury who used such cunning
As she, to hear his tale, left off her running.
Maids are not won by brutish force and might,
420 But speeches full of pleasure, and delight.
And, knowing Hermes courted her, was glad
That she such loveliness and beauty had
As could provoke his liking, yet was mute
And neither would deny nor grant his suit.
425 Still vowed he love. She, wanting no excuse
To feed him with delays, as women use,
Or thirsting after immortality, -
All women are ambitious naturally -
Imposed upon her lover such a task
430 As he ought not perform nor yet she ask.
A draught of flowing nectar she requested,
Wherewith the king of gods and men is feasted.
He, ready to accomplish what she willed,

Stole some from Hebe (Hebe Jove's cup filled)
435 And gave it to his simple rustic love.
Which being known (as what is hid from Jove?)
He inly stormed and waxed more furious
Than for the fire filched by Prometheus,
And thrusts him down from heaven. He, wandering here,
440 In mournful terms, with sad and heavy cheer,
Complained to Cupid. Cupid for his sake,
To be revenged on Jove did undertake.
And those on whom heaven, earth, and hell relies,
I mean the adamantine Destinies,
445 He wounds with love, and forced them equally
To dote upon deceitful Mercury.
They offered him the deadly fatal knife
That shears the slender threads of human life.
At his fair feathered feet the engines laid
450 Which th' earth from ugly Chaos' den upweighed.
These he regarded not but did entreat
That Jove, usurper of his father's seat,
Might presently be banished into hell,
And aged Saturn in Olympus dwell.
455 They granted what he craved, and once again
Saturn and Ops began their golden reign.
Murder, rape, war, lust, and treachery,
Were with Jove closed in Stygian empery.
But long this blessed time continued not.
460 As soon as he his wished purpose got
He reckless of his promise did despise
The love of th' everlasting Destinies.
They seeing it both love and him abhorred
And Jupiter unto his place restored.
465 And but that Learning in despite of Fate
Will mount aloft and enter heaven gate
And to the seat of Jove itself advance,
Hermes had slept in hell with Ignorance.
Yet as a punishment they added this,
470 That he and Poverty should always kiss.
And to this day is every scholar poor;
Gross gold from them runs headlong to the boor.
Likewise the angry Sisters thus deluded,
To venge themselves on Hermes, have concluded
475 That Midas' brood shall sit in honour's chair,
To which the Muses' sons are only heir;
And fruitful wits, that in aspiring are,
Shall discontent run into regions far;

And few great lords in virtuous deeds shall joy
480 But be surprised with every garish toy,
And still enrich the lofty servile clown,
Who with encroaching guile keeps learning down.
Then Muse not Cupid's suit no better sped,
Seeing in their loves the Fates were injured.

SECOND SESTIAD

By this, sad Hero, with love unacquainted,
Viewing Leander's face, fell down and fainted.
He kissed her and breathed life into her lips,
Wherewith as one displeased away she trips.
5   Yet, as she went, full often looked behind,
And many poor excuses did she find
To linger by the way, and once she stayed,
And would have turned again, but was afraid,
In offering parley, to be counted light.
10 So on she goes and in her idle flight
Her painted fan of curled plumes let fall,
Thinking to train Leander therewithal.
He, being a novice, knew not what she meant
But stayed, and after her a letter sent,
15 Which joyful Hero answered in such sort,
As he had hope to scale the beauteous fort
Wherein the liberal Graces locked their wealth,
And therefore to her tower he got by stealth.
Wide open stood the door, he need not climb,
20 And she herself before the pointed time
Had spread the board, with roses strowed the room,
And oft looked out, and mused he did not come.
At last he came. O who can tell the greeting
These greedy lovers had at their first meeting.
25 He asked, she gave, and nothing was denied.
Both to each other quickly were affied.
Look how their hands, so were their hearts united,
And what he did she willingly requited.
(Sweet are the kisses, the embracements sweet,
30 When like desires and affections meet,
For from the earth to heaven is Cupid raised,
Where fancy is in equal balance peised.)
Yet she this rashness suddenly repented
And turned aside, and to herself lamented
35 As if her name and honour had been wronged
By being possessed of him for whom she longed.

Ay, and she wished, albeit not from her heart
That he would leave her turret and depart.
The mirthful god of amorous pleasure smiled
40 To see how he this captive nymph beguiled.
For hitherto he did but fan the fire,
And kept it down that it might mount the higher.
Now waxed she jealous lest his love abated,
Fearing her own thoughts made her to be hated.
45 Therefore unto him hastily she goes
And, like light Salmacis, her body throws
Upon his bosom where with yielding eyes
She offers up herself a sacrifice
To slake his anger if he were displeased.
50 O, what god would not therewith be appeased?
Like Aesop's cock this jewel he enjoyed
And as a brother with his sister toyed
Supposing nothing else was to be done,
Now he her favour and good will had won.
55 But know you not that creatures wanting sense
By nature have a mutual appetence,
And, wanting organs to advance a step,
Moved by love's force unto each other lep?
Much more in subjects having intellect
60 Some hidden influence breeds like effect.
Albeit Leander rude in love and raw,
Long dallying with Hero, nothing saw
That might delight him more, yet he suspected
Some amorous rites or other were neglected.
65 Therefore unto his body hers he clung.
She, fearing on the rushes to be flung,
Strived with redoubled strength; the more she strived
The more a gentle pleasing heat revived,
Which taught him all that elder lovers know.
70 And now the same gan so to scorch and glow
As in plain terms (yet cunningly) he craved it.
Love always makes those eloquent that have it.
She, with a kind of granting, put him by it
And ever, as he thought himself most nigh it,
75 Like to the tree of Tantalus, she fled
And, seeming lavish, saved her maidenhead.
Ne'er king more sought to keep his diadem,
Than Hero this inestimable gem.
Above our life we love a steadfast friend,
80 Yet when a token of great worth we send,
We often kiss it, often look thereon,

And stay the messenger that would be gone.
No marvel then, though Hero would not yield
So soon to part from that she dearly held.
85   Jewels being lost are found again, this never;
'Tis lost but once, and once lost, lost forever.

Now had the morn espied her lover's steeds,
Whereat she starts, puts on her purple weeds,
And red for anger that he stayed so long
90   All headlong throws herself the clouds among.
And now Leander, fearing to be missed,
Embraced her suddenly, took leave, and kissed.
Long was he taking leave, and loath to go,
And kissed again as lovers use to do.
95   Sad Hero wrung him by the hand and wept
Saying, "Let your vows and promises be kept."
Then standing at the door she turned about
As loath to see Leander going out.
And now the sun that through th' horizon peeps,
100   As pitying these lovers, downward creeps,
So that in silence of the cloudy night,
Though it was morning, did he take his flight.
But what the secret trusty night concealed
Leander's amorous habit soon revealed.
105   With Cupid's myrtle was his bonnet crowned,
About his arms the purple riband wound
Wherewith she wreathed her largely spreading hair.
Nor could the youth abstain, but he must wear
The sacred ring wherewith she was endowed
110   When first religious chastity she vowed.
Which made his love through Sestos to be known,
And thence unto Abydos sooner blown
Than he could sail; for incorporeal fame
Whose weight consists in nothing but her name,
115   Is swifter than the wind, whose tardy plumes
Are reeking water and dull earthly fumes.
Home when he came, he seemed not to be there,
But, like exiled air thrust from his sphere,
Set in a foreign place; and straight from thence,
120   Alcides like, by mighty violence
He would have chased away the swelling main
That him from her unjustly did detain.
Like as the sun in a diameter
Fires and inflames objects removed far,
125   And heateth kindly, shining laterally,

So beauty sweetly quickens when 'tis nigh,
But being separated and removed,
Burns where it cherished, murders where it loved.
Therefore even as an index to a book,
130   So to his mind was young Leander's look.
O, none but gods have power their love to hide,
Affection by the countenance is descried.
The light of hidden fire itself discovers,
And love that is concealed betrays poor lovers,
135   His secret flame apparently was seen.
Leander's father knew where he had been
And for the same mildly rebuked his son,
Thinking to quench the sparkles new begun.
But love resisted once grows passionate,
140   And nothing more than counsel lovers hate.
For as a hot proud horse highly disdains
To have his head controlled, but breaks the reins,
Spits forth the ringled bit, and with his hooves
Checks the submissive ground; so he that loves,
145   The more he is restrained, the worse he fares.
What is it now, but mad Leander dares?
"O Hero, Hero!" thus he cried full oft;
And then he got him to a rock aloft,
Where having spied her tower, long stared he on't,
150   And prayed the narrow toiling Hellespont
To part in twain, that he might come and go;
But still the rising billows answered, "No."
With that he stripped him to the ivory skin
And, crying "Love, I come," leaped lively in.
155   Whereat the sapphire visaged god grew proud,
And made his capering Triton sound aloud,
Imagining that Ganymede, displeased,
Had left the heavens; therefore on him he seized.
Leander strived; the waves about him wound,
160   And pulled him to the bottom, where the ground
Was strewed with pearl, and in low coral groves
Sweet singing mermaids sported with their loves
On heaps of heavy gold, and took great pleasure
To spurn in careless sort the shipwrack treasure.
165   For here the stately azure palace stood
Where kingly Neptune and his train abode.
The lusty god embraced him, called him "Love,"
And swore he never should return to Jove.
But when he knew it was not Ganymede,
170   For under water he was almost dead,

He heaved him up and, looking on his face,
Beat down the bold waves with his triple mace,
Which mounted up, intending to have kissed him,
And fell in drops like tears because they missed him.
175   Leander, being up, began to swim
And, looking back, saw Neptune follow him,
Whereat aghast, the poor soul 'gan to cry
"O, let me visit Hero ere I die!"
The god put Helle's bracelet on his arm,
180   And swore the sea should never do him harm.
He clapped his plump cheeks, with his tresses played
And, smiling wantonly, his love bewrayed.
He watched his arms and, as they opened wide
At every stroke, betwixt them would he slide
185   And steal a kiss, and then run out and dance,
And, as he turned, cast many a lustful glance,
And threw him gaudy toys to please his eye,
And dive into the water, and there pry
Upon his breast, his thighs, and every limb,
190   And up again, and close beside him swim,
And talk of love. Leander made reply,
"You are deceived; I am no woman, I."
Thereat smiled Neptune, and then told a tale,
How that a shepherd, sitting in a vale,
195   Played with a boy so fair and kind,
As for his love both earth and heaven pined;
That of the cooling river durst not drink,
Lest water nymphs should pull him from the brink.
And when he sported in the fragrant lawns,
200   Goat footed satyrs and upstaring fauns
Would steal him thence. Ere half this tale was done,
"Ay me," Leander cried, "th' enamoured sun
That now should shine on Thetis' glassy bower,
Descends upon my radiant Hero's tower.
205   O, that these tardy arms of mine were wings!"
And, as he spake, upon the waves he springs.
Neptune was angry that he gave no ear,
And in his heart revenging malice bare.
He flung at him his mace but, as it went,
210   He called it in, for love made him repent.
The mace, returning back, his own hand hit
As meaning to be venged for darting it.
When this fresh bleeding wound Leander viewed,
His colour went and came, as if he rued
215   The grief which Neptune felt. In gentle breasts

Relenting thoughts, remorse, and pity rests.
And who have hard hearts and obdurate minds,
But vicious, harebrained, and illiterate hinds?
The god, seeing him with pity to be moved,
220   Thereon concluded that he was beloved.
(Love is too full of faith, too credulous,
With folly and false hope deluding us.)
Wherefore, Leander's fancy to surprise,
To the rich Ocean for gifts he flies.
225   'Tis wisdom to give much; a gift prevails
When deep persuading oratory fails.

By this Leander, being near the land,
Cast down his weary feet and felt the sand.
Breathless albeit he were he rested not
230   Till to the solitary tower he got,
And knocked and called. At which celestial noise
The longing heart of Hero much more joys
Than nymphs and shepherds when the timbrel rings,
Or crooked dolphin when the sailor sings.
235   She stayed not for her robes but straight arose
And, drunk with gladness, to the door she goes,
Where seeing a naked man, she screeched for fear
(Such sights as this to tender maids are rare)
And ran into the dark herself to hide.
240   (Rich jewels in the dark are soonest spied).
Unto her was he led, or rather drawn
By those white limbs which sparkled through the lawn.
The nearer that he came, the more she fled,
And, seeking refuge, slipped into her bed.
245   Whereon Leander sitting thus began,
Through numbing cold, all feeble, faint, and wan.
"If not for love, yet, love, for pity sake,
Me in thy bed and maiden bosom take.
At least vouchsafe these arms some little room,
250   Who, hoping to embrace thee, cheerly swum.
This head was beat with many a churlish billow,
And therefore let it rest upon thy pillow."
Herewith affrighted, Hero shrunk away,
And in her lukewarm place Leander lay,
255   Whose lively heat, like fire from heaven fet,
Would animate gross clay and higher set
The drooping thoughts of base declining souls
Than dreary Mars carousing nectar bowls.
His hands he cast upon her like a snare.

260 She, overcome with shame and sallow fear,
Like chaste Diana when Actaeon spied her,
Being suddenly betrayed, dived down to hide her.
And, as her silver body downward went,
With both her hands she made the bed a tent,
265 And in her own mind thought herself secure,
O'ercast with dim and darksome coverture.
And now she lets him whisper in her ear,
Flatter, entreat, promise, protest and swear;
Yet ever, as he greedily assayed
270 To touch those dainties, she the harpy played,
And every limb did, as a soldier stout,
Defend the fort, and keep the foeman out.
For though the rising ivory mount he scaled,
Which is with azure circling lines empaled,
275 Much like a globe (a globe may I term this,
By which love sails to regions full of bliss)
Yet there with Sisyphus he toiled in vain,
Till gentle parley did the truce obtain.
Wherein Leander on her quivering breast
280 Breathless spoke something, and sighed out the rest;
Which so prevailed, as he with small ado
Enclosed her in his arms and kissed her too.
And every kiss to her was as a charm,
And to Leander as a fresh alarm,
285 So that the truce was broke and she, alas,
(Poor silly maiden) at his mercy was.
Love is not full of pity (as men say)
But deaf and cruel where he means to prey.
Even as a bird, which in our hands we wring,
290 Forth plungeth and oft flutters with her wing,
She trembling strove. This strife of hers (like that
Which made the world) another world begat
Of unknown joy. Treason was in her thought,
And cunningly to yield herself she sought.
295 Seeming not won, yet won she was at length.
In such wars women use but half their strength.
Leander now, like Theban Hercules,
Entered the orchard of th' Hesperides;
Whose fruit none rightly can describe but he
300 That pulls or shakes it from the golden tree.
And now she wished this night were never done,
And sighed to think upon th' approaching sun;
For much it grieved her that the bright daylight
Should know the pleasure of this blessed night,

305 And them, like Mars and Erycine, display
Both in each other's arms chained as they lay.
Again, she knew not how to frame her look,
Or speak to him, who in a moment took
That which so long so charily she kept,
310 And fain by stealth away she would have crept,
And to some corner secretly have gone,
Leaving Leander in the bed alone.
But as her naked feet were whipping out,
He on the sudden clinged her so about,
315 That, mermaid-like, unto the floor she slid.
One half appeared, the other half was hid.
Thus near the bed she blushing stood upright,
And from her countenance behold ye might
A kind of twilight break, which through the hair,
320 As from an orient cloud, glimpsed here and there,
And round about the chamber this false morn
Brought forth the day before the day was born.
So Hero's ruddy cheek Hero betrayed,
And her all naked to his sight displayed,
325 Whence his admiring eyes more pleasure took
Than Dis, on heaps of gold fixing his look.
By this, Apollo's golden harp began
To sound forth music to the ocean,
Which watchful Hesperus no sooner heard
330 But he the bright day-bearing car prepared
And ran before, as harbinger of light,
And with his flaring beams mocked ugly night,
Till she, o'ercome with anguish, shame, and rage,
Danged down to hell her loathsome carriage.

THE PASSIONATE SHEPHERD TO HIS LOVE

BY CHRISTOPHER MARLOWE

Come live with me and be my love,
And we will all the pleasures prove
That hills and vallies, dales and fields,
Woods or steepy mountain yields.

5   And we will sit upon the rocks,
Seeing the shepherds feed their flocks
By shallow rivers to whose falls
Melodious birds sing madrigals.

And I will make thee beds of roses
10   And a thousand fragrant posies,
A cup of flowers and a kirtle
Embroidered all with leaves of myrtle.

A gown made of the finest wooll
Which from our pretty lambs we pull;
15   Fair-linèd slippers for the cold,
With buckles of the purest gold.

A belt of straw and ivy-buds,
With coral clasps and amber studs;
An if these pleasures may thee move,
20   Come live with me, and be my love.

The shepherd-swains shall dance and sing
For thy delight each May-morning:
If these delights thy mind may move,
Then live with me, and be my love.

THE NYMPH'S REPLY TO THE SHEPHERD

By Sir Walter Raleigh

If all the world and love were young,
And truth in every shepherd's tongue,
These pretty pleasures might me move
To live with thee and be thy love.

5 Time drives the flocks from field to fold
When rivers rage and rocks grow cold,
And Philomel becometh dumb;
The rest complains of cares to come.

The flowers do fade, and wanton fields
10 To wayward winter reckoning yields;
A honey tongue, a heart of gall,
Is fancy's spring but sorrow's fall.

Thy gowns, thy shoes, thy beds of roses,
Thy cap, thy kirtle, and thy posies
15 Soon break, soon wither, soon forgotten, -
In folly ripe, in reason rotten.

Thy belt of straw and ivy buds,
Thy coral clasps and amber studs,
All these in me no means can move
20 To come to thee and be thy love.

But could youth last and love still breed,
Had joys no date nor age no need,
Then these delights my mind might move
To live with thee and be thy love.

William Shakespeare

William Shakespeare was born in April of 1564 and baptized on April 26th. Though unknown, his birthday is often celebrated on April 23rd, which is the feast day of Saint George, the patron saint of England. The third of eight children, Shakespeare was baptized in Stratford-Upon-Avon in central England. His father, John Shakespeare, was a successful glovemaker, and his mother, Mary Arden, came from a wealthy farming family. Young Will would have attended a grammar school due to his middle-class social position, receiving an extensive education in classical Latin. Many of his later works take inspiration from ancient Greek and Roman dramas.

Nothing is recorded of Shakespeare's childhood until his hasty marriage at the age of eighteen, in 1582, to twenty-six-year-old Anne Hathaway. They were betrothed for months before this marriage, and six months later, Anne gave birth to their daughter Susanna. The couple had twins, Judith and Hamnet, in 1585. Their only son Hamnet died at the age of eleven; scholars speculate that this family tragedy influenced *Hamlet*. Some scholars believe that Anne and Shakespeare's relationship was strained, pointing out that she was not included in his will except with the bequest of his "second best bed." However, others argue that common law at the time automatically gave Anne one-third of her husband's estate upon his death and that the second-best bed could refer to their marriage bed.

In 1592, Shakespeare appeared on the theatrical scene in London, more than ninety miles from Stratford. We are not certain when he began writing, but by 1592 several of his plays had been performed in London. These early plays include *The Two Gentlemen of Verona*, *The Taming of the Shrew*, *Henry VI* (parts I, II, and III), *Titus Andronicus*, and *Richard III*. Shakespeare himself acted in most performances of his plays.

In 1594, Shakespeare joined the professional acting company the Lord Chamberlain's Men. It became the only group allowed to perform his plays; he wrote many works especially for the company, including *A Midsummer Night's Dream*, *Romeo and Juliet*, *Julius Caesar*, *Henry V*, *Hamlet*, *Twelfth Night*, *Othello*, *King Lear*, *Macbeth*, *The Tempest*, as well as others. The company occasionally performed plays by other dramatists such as Ben Jonson (*Every Man in His Humour*, *Sejanus His Fall*, *Volpone*) and perhaps Christopher Marlowe.

The Lord Chamberlain's Men owned and operated several playhouses, including one called "The Theatre," between 1594 and 1597. They then moved to the Curtain Theatre until the Globe Theatre was built in 1599. One of the most successful acting companies of the era, they became the King's Men in 1603 after King James I of England ascended the throne and became their new patron. Many famous actors of the time were company members, such as William Kempe, known for playing comic fool roles like Bottom in *A Midsummer Night's Dream*, and Richard Burbage, who played the lead tragedian in *Hamlet*, *Othello*, *King Lear*, and *Macbeth*, among others. Shakespeare himself played principal roles, although he appears to have stopped acting to focus on playwriting between 1600 and 1610.

The chronology of Shakespeare's plays can be estimated at best. Some of his works whose titles were recorded are now lost. These include *Love's Labour's Won*, a possible sequel to the early play *Love's Labour's Lost*; this may also have simply been an alternate title for a different comedy such as *All's Well That Ends Well*. *Cardenio* is another lost play, attributed to Shakespeare and another playwright named John Fletcher, who succeeded him as playwright for the King's Men. Scholars believe *Cardenio* to have been based on the character of the same name in *Don Quixote* by Miguel de Cervantes. This anthology includes the most accurate estimation of Shakespeare's life and works, based on the timeline used by the modern Royal Shakespeare Company. This timeline does not delineate all his works.

Shakespeare also wrote poetry. He published two narrative poems, *Venus and Adonis* and *The Rape of Lucrece*; two narrative poems published elsewhere are credited to him. His sonnets, however, have become his most famous poetic works. He published his collection of 154 sonnets in 1609. The overarching themes of this sonnet cycle include mortality, time, procreation, love, lust, and beauty. They appear to depict a sort of love triangle between the aging poet, the "fair youth," an attractive young man referred to in sonnets 1-126, and the "dark lady," a dark-complexioned woman referred to in sonnets 127-154. This thematic structure was uncommon for the time, as most sonnet cycles would focus on only two romantic lovers, one of which is the poet. Shakespeare's sonnets have become a primary source for speculation that Shakespeare was gay or bisexual, since many of the poems to the fair youth make it clear that a male poet writes romantically to and erotically about a young man. Some scholars hypothesize that the sonnets about the fair youth were written to Henry Wriothesley, 3rd Earl of Southampton and one of Shakespeare's patrons, to whom Shakespeare's narrative poems were dedicated. For more information about sonnets, see page 578.

We are not certain when Shakespeare completely retired from acting and playwriting, but he is not credited for any plays composed after 1613. He died on April 23rd, 1616, at the age of fifty-two. No explanation has been offered for his sudden death. He was buried in Stratford's Holy Trinity Church, the same location of his infant baptism. His grave bears a carving that threatens to curse "he that moves my bones."

Both of Shakespeare's daughters, Susanna and Judith, married before his death. He left the majority of his estate to Susanna in his will, requesting that the benefits be passed down to her son. She had no sons, however, only a daughter named Elizabeth.

Many of Shakespeare's plays were published posthumously. In 1623, the First Folio, titled *Mr. William Shakespear's Comedies, Histories, & Tragedies*, was published by John Heminges and Henry Condell. Many of Shakespeare's plays had been previously published in quarto form, smaller and less durable books than the Folio. Editions also exist of "bad quartos," meaning unlicensed publications of plays. Acting companies obtained these quartos by sending people into various play audiences to write down the script in an early form of piracy. Compiled by Heminges and Condell, two members of the Lord Chamberlain's Men, the First Folio has become the primary source for eighteen of Shakespeare's plays. Editors for the first time catalogued his plays into comedies, tragedies, and histories, which remains a popular system of categorization. However, modern scholars often delineate other categories, such as "problem plays," which refers to plays whose primary tone is neither comedic or tragic, such as *All's Well That Ends Well*, *Measure For Measure*, and *Troilus and Cressida*. In 1931, critic W.W. Lawrence defined a problem play as one in which "a perplexing and distressing complication in human life is presented in a spirit of high seriousness... to probe the complicated interrelations of character and action, in a situation admitting of different ethical interpretations." Another such category is "late romances," which includes *Pericles, Prince of Tyre*, *Cymbeline*, *The Winter's Tale*, and *The Tempest*. These plays include more spectacular and elaborate staging and are dominated by neither tragic nor comic themes.

Overall, William Shakespeare is an incredibly important figure in British literary history, and literature in general. He is commonly referenced in texts written after his time; his sonnets feature prominently at weddings, funerals, and other occasions; and his plays are still some of the most widely performed today—over 400 years after his death. Shakespeare's impact on modern literature and popular culture cannot be overstated.

TIMELINE

1564	William Shakespeare is born.
1582	Shakespeare marries Anne Hathaway.
1583-85	Anne gives birth to their three children.
1585-92	Shakespeare writes his first plays: *The Two Gentlemen of Verona; The Taming of the Shrew; Henry VI parts 1, 2, and 3; Titus Andronicus.*
1592	Shakespeare is recorded in the London theatrical scene.
1592-93	*Richard III; Edward III* (disputed authorship, thought to be written partially but not entirely by Shakespeare).
1594	Shakespeare and others form the Lord Chamberlain's Men.
1596	Shakespeare's son Hamnet dies aged eleven.
1594-99	*The Comedy of Errors; Love's Labours Lost; Love's Labours Won* (either a lost sequel or an early draft of a later comedy); *Richard II; Romeo and Juliet; A Midsummer Night's Dream; King John; The Merchant of Venice; Henry IV, parts 1 and 2; The Merry Wives of Windsor; Much Ado About Nothing; Henry V.*
1599	The Globe Theatre is completed and becomes the home of the Lord Chamberlain's Men.
1599-1603	*Julius Caesar; As You Like It; Hamlet; Twelfth Night; Troilus and Cressida.*
1603	Queen Elizabeth dies; James VI and I ascends the throne, the Lord Chamberlain's Men become the King's Men.
After 1603	*Measure for Measure; Othello; All's Well That Ends Well; King Lear; Timon of Athens* (disputed, collaborative authorship unknown); *Macbeth; Antony and Cleopatra; Pericles, Prince of Tyre; Coriolanus; The Winter's Tale; Cymbeline; The Tempest; Henry VIII* (originally titled *All Is True*); *The Two Noble Kinsmen.*
1613	Shakespeare retires; the Globe Theatre burns down.
1616	Shakespeare dies in Stratford from unknown causes.

Twelfth Night, or What You Will

By William Shakespeare

Dramatis Personæ

ORSINO, Duke of Illyria.
VALENTINE, Gentleman attending on the Duke
CURIO, Gentleman attending on the Duke
VIOLA, in love with the Duke.
SEBASTIAN, a young Gentleman, twin brother to Viola.
A SEA CAPTAIN, friend to Viola
ANTONIO, a Sea Captain, friend to Sebastian.
OLIVIA, a rich Countess.
MARIA, Olivia's Woman.
SIR TOBY BELCH, Uncle of Olivia.
SIR ANDREW AGUECHEEK.
MALVOLIO, Steward to Olivia.
FABIAN, Servant to Olivia.
CLOWN, Servant to Olivia.
PRIEST
Lords, Sailors, Officers, Musicians, and other Attendants.

ACT I.

SCENE I. An Apartment in the Duke's Palace.

Enter Orsino, Duke of Illyria, Curio, other Lords; Musicians attending.

DUKE.
If music be the food of love, play on,
Give me excess of it; that, surfeiting,
The appetite may sicken and so die.
That strain again, it had a dying fall;
5   O, it came o'er my ear like the sweet sound
That breathes upon a bank of violets,
Stealing and giving odour. Enough; no more;
'Tis not so sweet now as it was before.
O spirit of love, how quick and fresh art thou,
10   That notwithstanding thy capacity
Receiveth as the sea, nought enters there,
Of what validity and pitch soever,
But falls into abatement and low price
Even in a minute! So full of shapes is fancy,
15   That it alone is high fantastical.

CURIO.
 Will you go hunt, my lord?

DUKE.
 What, Curio?

CURIO.
 The hart.

DUKE.
 Why so I do, the noblest that I have.
20 O, when mine eyes did see Olivia first,
 Methought she purg'd the air of pestilence;
 That instant was I turn'd into a hart,
 And my desires, like fell and cruel hounds,
 E'er since pursue me. How now? what news from her?

Enter Valentine.

VALENTINE.
25 So please my lord, I might not be admitted,
 But from her handmaid do return this answer:
 The element itself, till seven years' heat,
 Shall not behold her face at ample view;
 But like a cloistress she will veiled walk,
30 And water once a day her chamber round
 With eye-offending brine: all this to season
 A brother's dead love, which she would keep fresh
 And lasting in her sad remembrance.

DUKE.
 O, she that hath a heart of that fine frame
35 To pay this debt of love but to a brother,
 How will she love, when the rich golden shaft
 Hath kill'd the flock of all affections else
 That live in her; when liver, brain, and heart,
 These sovereign thrones, are all supplied and fill'd
40 Her sweet perfections with one self king!
 Away before me to sweet beds of flowers,
 Love-thoughts lie rich when canopied with bowers.

[Exeunt.]

SCENE II. The sea-coast.

Enter Viola, a Captain and Sailors.

VIOLA.
 What country, friends, is this?

CAPTAIN.
This is Illyria, lady.

VIOLA.
And what should I do in Illyria?
My brother he is in Elysium.
5 Perchance he is not drown'd. What think you, sailors?

CAPTAIN.
It is perchance that you yourself were sav'd.

VIOLA.
O my poor brother! and so perchance may he be.

CAPTAIN.
True, madam; and to comfort you with chance,
Assure yourself, after our ship did split,
10 When you, and those poor number sav'd with you,
Hung on our driving boat, I saw your brother,
Most provident in peril, bind himself,
(Courage and hope both teaching him the practice)
To a strong mast that liv'd upon the sea;
15 Where, like Arion on the dolphin's back,
I saw him hold acquaintance with the waves
So long as I could see.

VIOLA.
For saying so, there's gold!
Mine own escape unfoldeth to my hope,
20 Whereto thy speech serves for authority,
The like of him. Know'st thou this country?

CAPTAIN.
Ay, madam, well, for I was bred and born
Not three hours' travel from this very place.

VIOLA.
Who governs here?

CAPTAIN.
25 A noble duke, in nature as in name.

VIOLA.
What is his name?

CAPTAIN.
Orsino.

VIOLA.
Orsino! I have heard my father name him.
He was a bachelor then.

CAPTAIN.
30   And so is now, or was so very late;
For but a month ago I went from hence,
And then 'twas fresh in murmur, (as, you know,
What great ones do, the less will prattle of)
That he did seek the love of fair Olivia.

VIOLA.
35   What's she?

CAPTAIN.
A virtuous maid, the daughter of a count
That died some twelvemonth since; then leaving her
In the protection of his son, her brother,
Who shortly also died; for whose dear love
40   They say, she hath abjur'd the company
And sight of men.

VIOLA.
O that I served that lady,
And might not be delivered to the world,
Till I had made mine own occasion mellow,
45   What my estate is.

CAPTAIN.
That were hard to compass,
Because she will admit no kind of suit,
No, not the Duke's.

VIOLA.
There is a fair behaviour in thee, Captain;
50   And though that nature with a beauteous wall
Doth oft close in pollution, yet of thee
I will believe thou hast a mind that suits
With this thy fair and outward character.
I pray thee, and I'll pay thee bounteously,
55   Conceal me what I am, and be my aid
For such disguise as haply shall become
The form of my intent. I'll serve this duke;
Thou shalt present me as an eunuch to him.
It may be worth thy pains; for I can sing,
60   And speak to him in many sorts of music,

That will allow me very worth his service.
What else may hap, to time I will commit;
Only shape thou thy silence to my wit.

CAPTAIN.
Be you his eunuch and your mute I'll be;
65 When my tongue blabs, then let mine eyes not see.

VIOLA.
I thank thee. Lead me on.

[*Exeunt.*]

SCENE III. A Room in Olivia's House.
Enter Sir Toby and Maria.

SIR TOBY.
What a plague means my niece to take the death of her brother thus? I am
sure care's an enemy to life.

MARIA.
By my troth, Sir Toby, you must come in earlier o' nights; your cousin, my
lady, takes great exceptions to your ill hours.

SIR TOBY.
5 Why, let her except, before excepted.

MARIA.
Ay, but you must confine yourself within the modest limits of order.

SIR TOBY.
Confine? I'll confine myself no finer than I am. These clothes are good
enough to drink in, and so be these boots too; and they be not, let them hang
themselves in their own straps.

MARIA.
10 That quaffing and drinking will undo you: I heard my lady talk of it yes-
terday; and of a foolish knight that you brought in one night here to be
her wooer.

SIR TOBY.
Who? Sir Andrew Aguecheek?

MARIA.
Ay, he.

SIR TOBY.
15 He's as tall a man as any's in Illyria.

MARIA.
 What's that to th' purpose?

SIR TOBY.
 Why, he has three thousand ducats a year.

MARIA.
 Ay, but he'll have but a year in all these ducats. He's a very fool, and a
prodigal.

SIR TOBY.
20 Fie, that you'll say so! he plays o' the viol-de-gamboys, and speaks three or four
languages word for word without book, and hath all the good gifts of nature.

MARIA.
 He hath indeed, almost natural: for, besides that he's a fool, he's a great
quarreller; and, but that he hath the gift of a coward to allay the gust he
hath in quarrelling, 'tis thought among the prudent he would quickly have
25 the gift of a grave.

SIR TOBY.
 By this hand, they are scoundrels and substractors that say so of him. Who
are they?

MARIA.
 They that add, moreover, he's drunk nightly in your company.

SIR TOBY.
 With drinking healths to my niece; I'll drink to her as long as there is a pas-
30 sage in my throat, and drink in Illyria. He's a coward and a coystril that will not
drink to my niece till his brains turn o' the toe like a parish top. What, wench!
Castiliano vulgo: for here comes Sir Andrew Agueface.

Enter Sir Andrew.

AGUECHEEK.
 Sir Toby Belch! How now, Sir Toby Belch?

SIR TOBY.
 Sweet Sir Andrew!

SIR ANDREW.
35 Bless you, fair shrew.

MARIA.
 And you too, sir.

SIR TOBY.
 Accost, Sir Andrew, accost.

SIR ANDREW.
What's that?

SIR TOBY.
My niece's chamber-maid.

SIR ANDREW.
40   Good Mistress Accost, I desire better acquaintance.

MARIA.
My name is Mary, sir.

SIR ANDREW.
Good Mistress Mary Accost,——

SIR TOBY.
You mistake, knight: accost is front her, board her, woo her, assail her.

SIR ANDREW.
By my troth, I would not undertake her in this company. Is that the meaning
45   of accost?

MARIA.
Fare you well, gentlemen.

SIR TOBY.
And thou let part so, Sir Andrew, would thou mightst never draw sword again.

SIR ANDREW.
And you part so, mistress, I would I might never draw sword again. Fair
lady, do you think you have fools in hand?

MARIA.
50   Sir, I have not you by the hand.

SIR ANDREW.
Marry, but you shall have, and here's my hand.

MARIA.
Now, sir, thought is free. I pray you, bring your hand to th' buttery bar and
let it drink.

SIR ANDREW.
Wherefore, sweetheart? What's your metaphor?

MARIA.
55   It's dry, sir.

SIR ANDREW.
 Why, I think so; I am not such an ass but I can keep my hand dry. But what's your jest?

MARIA.
 A dry jest, sir.

SIR ANDREW.
 Are you full of them?

MARIA.
60 Ay, sir, I have them at my fingers' ends: marry, now I let go your hand, I am barren.

                 [*Exit Maria.*]

SIR TOBY.
 O knight, thou lack'st a cup of canary: When did I see thee so put down?

SIR ANDREW.
 Never in your life, I think, unless you see canary put me down. Methinks sometimes I have no more wit than a Christian or an ordinary man has; but
65 I am a great eater of beef, and I believe that does harm to my wit.

SIR TOBY.
 No question.

SIR ANDREW.
 And I thought that, I'd forswear it. I'll ride home tomorrow, Sir Toby.

SIR TOBY.
 Pourquoy, my dear knight?

SIR ANDREW.
 What is *pourquoy?* Do, or not do? I would I had bestowed that time in the
70 tongues that I have in fencing, dancing, and bear-baiting. O, had I but followed the arts!

SIR TOBY.
 Then hadst thou had an excellent head of hair.

SIR ANDREW.
 Why, would that have mended my hair?

SIR TOBY.
 Past question; for thou seest it will not curl by nature.

SIR ANDREW.
75 But it becomes me well enough, does't not?

SIR TOBY.
 Excellent, it hangs like flax on a distaff; and I hope to see a huswife take thee between her legs, and spin it off.

SIR ANDREW.
 Faith, I'll home tomorrow, Sir Toby; your niece will not be seen, or if she be, it's four to one she'll none of me; the Count himself here hard by woos her.

SIR TOBY.
80 She'll none o' the Count; she'll not match above her degree, neither in estate, years, nor wit; I have heard her swear't. Tut, there's life in't, man.

SIR ANDREW.
 I'll stay a month longer. I am a fellow o' the strangest mind i' the world; I delight in masques and revels sometimes altogether.

SIR TOBY.
 Art thou good at these kick-shawses, knight?

SIR ANDREW.
85 As any man in Illyria, whatsoever he be, under the degree of my betters; and yet I will not compare with an old man.

SIR TOBY.
 What is thy excellence in a galliard, knight?

SIR ANDREW.
 Faith, I can cut a caper.

SIR TOBY.
 And I can cut the mutton to't.

SIR ANDREW.
90 And I think I have the back-trick simply as strong as any man in Illyria.

SIR TOBY.
 Wherefore are these things hid? Wherefore have these gifts a curtain before 'em? Are they like to take dust, like Mistress Mall's picture? Why dost thou not go to church in a galliard, and come home in a coranto? My very walk should be a jig; I would not so much as make water but in a sink-a-pace.
95 What dost thou mean? Is it a world to hide virtues in? I did think, by the excellent constitution of thy leg, it was formed under the star of a galliard.

SIR ANDREW.
 Ay, 'tis strong, and it does indifferent well in a dam'd-colour'd stock. Shall we set about some revels?

SIR TOBY.
 What shall we do else? Were we not born under Taurus?

SIR ANDREW.

100 Taurus? That's sides and heart.

SIR TOBY.

No, sir, it is legs and thighs. Let me see thee caper. Ha, higher: ha, ha, excellent!

[*Exeunt.*]

SCENE IV. A Room in the Duke's Palace.
Enter Valentine and Viola in man's attire.

VALENTINE.

If the duke continue these favours towards you, Cesario, you are like to be much advanced; he hath known you but three days, and already you are no stranger.

VIOLA.

You either fear his humour or my negligence, that you call in question the
5 continuance of his love. Is he inconstant, sir, in his favours?

VALENTINE.

No, believe me.

Enter Duke, Curio and Attendants.

VIOLA.

I thank you. Here comes the Count.

DUKE.

Who saw Cesario, ho?

VIOLA.

On your attendance, my lord, here.

DUKE.

10 Stand you awhile aloof.—Cesario,
Thou know'st no less but all; I have unclasp'd
To thee the book even of my secret soul.
Therefore, good youth, address thy gait unto her,
Be not denied access, stand at her doors,
15 And tell them, there thy fixed foot shall grow
Till thou have audience.

VIOLA.

Sure, my noble lord,
If she be so abandon'd to her sorrow
As it is spoke, she never will admit me.

DUKE.

20 Be clamorous and leap all civil bounds,
    Rather than make unprofited return.

VIOLA.

Say I do speak with her, my lord, what then?

DUKE.

O then unfold the passion of my love,
Surprise her with discourse of my dear faith;
25 It shall become thee well to act my woes;
She will attend it better in thy youth,
Than in a nuncio's of more grave aspect.

VIOLA.

I think not so, my lord.

DUKE.

Dear lad, believe it;
30 For they shall yet belie thy happy years,
That say thou art a man: Diana's lip
Is not more smooth and rubious; thy small pipe
Is as the maiden's organ, shrill and sound,
And all is semblative a woman's part.
35 I know thy constellation is right apt
For this affair. Some four or five attend him:
All, if you will; for I myself am best
When least in company. Prosper well in this,
And thou shalt live as freely as thy lord,
40 To call his fortunes thine.

VIOLA.

I'll do my best
To woo your lady. [*Aside.*] Yet, a barful strife!
Whoe'er I woo, myself would be his wife.

[*Exeunt.*]

SCENE V. A ROOM IN OLIVIA'S HOUSE.
Enter Maria and Clown.

MARIA.

Nay; either tell me where thou hast been, or I will not open my lips so wide as
a bristle may enter, in way of thy excuse: my lady will hang thee for thy absence.

CLOWN.

Let her hang me: he that is well hanged in this world needs to fear no colours.

MARIA.
 Make that good.

CLOWN.
5 He shall see none to fear.

MARIA.
 A good lenten answer. I can tell thee where that saying was born, of I fear
no colours.

CLOWN.
 Where, good Mistress Mary?

MARIA.
 In the wars, and that may you be bold to say in your foolery.

CLOWN.
10 Well, God give them wisdom that have it; and those that are fools, let them
use their talents.

MARIA.
 Yet you will be hanged for being so long absent; or to be turned away; is
not that as good as a hanging to you?

CLOWN.
 Many a good hanging prevents a bad marriage; and for turning away, let
15 summer bear it out.

MARIA.
 You are resolute then?

CLOWN.
 Not so, neither, but I am resolved on two points.

MARIA.
 That if one break, the other will hold; or if both break, your gaskins fall.

CLOWN.
 Apt, in good faith, very apt! Well, go thy way; if Sir Toby would leave drink-
20 ing, thou wert as witty a piece of Eve's flesh as any in Illyria.

MARIA.
 Peace, you rogue, no more o' that. Here comes my lady: make your excuse
wisely, you were best.

[Exit.]

Enter Olivia with Malvolio.

CLOWN.
Wit, and't be thy will, put me into good fooling! Those wits that think they
have thee, do very oft prove fools; and I that am sure I lack thee, may pass for
25   a wise man. For what says Quinapalus? Better a witty fool than a foolish wit.
God bless thee, lady!

OLIVIA.
Take the fool away.

CLOWN.
Do you not hear, fellows? Take away the lady.

OLIVIA.
Go to, y'are a dry fool; I'll no more of you. Besides, you grow dishonest.

CLOWN.
30   Two faults, madonna, that drink and good counsel will amend: for give the
dry fool drink, then is the fool not dry; bid the dishonest man mend himself,
if he mend, he is no longer dishonest; if he cannot, let the botcher mend
him. Anything that's mended is but patched; virtue that transgresses is but
patched with sin, and sin that amends is but patched with virtue. If that this
35   simple syllogism will serve, so; if it will not, what remedy? As there is no
true cuckold but calamity, so beauty's a flower. The lady bade take away the
fool, therefore, I say again, take her away.

OLIVIA.
Sir, I bade them take away you.

CLOWN.
Misprision in the highest degree! Lady, *cucullus non facit monachum:* that's as much
40   to say, I wear not motley in my brain. Good madonna, give me leave to prove
you a fool.

OLIVIA.
Can you do it?

CLOWN.
Dexteriously, good madonna.

OLIVIA.
Make your proof.

CLOWN.
45   I must catechize you for it, madonna. Good my mouse of virtue, answer me.

OLIVIA.
Well sir, for want of other idleness, I'll 'bide your proof.

CLOWN.
Good madonna, why mourn'st thou?

OLIVIA.
Good fool, for my brother's death.

CLOWN.
I think his soul is in hell, madonna.

OLIVIA.
50   I know his soul is in heaven, fool.

CLOWN.
The more fool you, madonna, to mourn for your brother's soul being in
heaven. Take away the fool, gentlemen.

OLIVIA.
What think you of this fool, Malvolio? doth he not mend?

MALVOLIO.
Yes; and shall do, till the pangs of death shake him. Infirmity, that decays
55   the wise, doth ever make the better fool.

CLOWN.
God send you, sir, a speedy infirmity, for the better increasing your folly!
Sir Toby will be sworn that I am no fox; but he will not pass his word for
twopence that you are no fool.

OLIVIA.
How say you to that, Malvolio?

MALVOLIO.
60   I marvel your ladyship takes delight in such a barren rascal; I saw him put
down the other day with an ordinary fool, that has no more brain than a
stone. Look you now, he's out of his guard already; unless you laugh and
minister occasion to him, he is gagged. I protest I take these wise men, that
crow so at these set kind of fools, no better than the fools' zanies.

OLIVIA.
65   O, you are sick of self-love, Malvolio, and taste with a distempered appetite.
To be generous, guiltless, and of free disposition, is to take those things for
bird-bolts that you deem cannon bullets. There is no slander in an allowed fool,
though he do nothing but rail; nor no railing in a known discreet man, though
he do nothing but reprove.

CLOWN.
70   Now Mercury endue thee with leasing, for thou speak'st well of fools!

Enter Maria.

MARIA.
Madam, there is at the gate a young gentleman much desires to speak with you.

OLIVIA.
From the Count Orsino, is it?

MARIA.
I know not, madam; 'tis a fair young man, and well attended.

OLIVIA.
Who of my people hold him in delay?

MARIA.
75   Sir Toby, madam, your kinsman.

OLIVIA.
Fetch him off, I pray you; he speaks nothing but madman. Fie on him!
[*Exit Maria.*]
Go you, Malvolio. If it be a suit from the Count, I am sick, or not at home.
What you will, to dismiss it.
[*Exit Malvolio.*]
Now you see, sir, how your fooling grows old, and people dislike it.

CLOWN.
80   Thou hast spoke for us, madonna, as if thy eldest son should be a fool:
whose skull Jove cram with brains, for here he comes, one of thy kin has a
most weak *pia mater.*

Enter Sir Toby.

OLIVIA.
By mine honour, half drunk. What is he at the gate, cousin?

SIR TOBY.
A gentleman.

OLIVIA.
85   A gentleman? What gentleman?

SIR TOBY.
'Tis a gentleman here. A plague o' these pickle-herrings! How now, sot?

CLOWN.
Good Sir Toby.

OLIVIA.
Cousin, cousin, how have you come so early by this lethargy?

SIR TOBY.
 Lechery! I defy lechery. There's one at the gate.

OLIVIA.
90 Ay, marry, what is he?

SIR TOBY.
Let him be the devil an he will, I care not: give me faith, say I. Well, it's all one.
[Exit.]

OLIVIA.
 What's a drunken man like, fool?

CLOWN.
 Like a drowned man, a fool, and a madman: one draught above heat makes him a fool, the second mads him, and a third drowns him.

OLIVIA.
95 Go thou and seek the coroner, and let him sit o' my coz; for he's in the third degree of drink; he's drowned. Go, look after him.

CLOWN.
 He is but mad yet, madonna; and the fool shall look to the madman.
[Exit Clown.]

Enter Malvolio.

MALVOLIO.
 Madam, yond young fellow swears he will speak with you. I told him you were sick; he takes on him to understand so much, and therefore comes to
100 speak with you. I told him you were asleep; he seems to have a foreknowledge of that too, and therefore comes to speak with you. What is to be said to him, lady? He's fortified against any denial.

OLIVIA.
 Tell him, he shall not speak with me.

MALVOLIO.
 Has been told so; and he says he'll stand at your door like a sheriff's post,
105 and be the supporter of a bench, but he'll speak with you.

OLIVIA.
 What kind o' man is he?

MALVOLIO.
 Why, of mankind.

OLIVIA.
 What manner of man?

MALVOLIO.
Of very ill manner; he'll speak with you, will you or no.

OLIVIA.
110   Of what personage and years is he?

MALVOLIO.
Not yet old enough for a man, nor young enough for a boy; as a squash is before 'tis a peascod, or a codling, when 'tis almost an apple. 'Tis with him in standing water, between boy and man. He is very well-favoured, and he speaks very shrewishly. One would think his mother's milk were scarce out
115   of him.

OLIVIA.
Let him approach. Call in my gentlewoman.

MALVOLIO.
Gentlewoman, my lady calls.

                                                      [Exit.]

Enter Maria.

OLIVIA.
Give me my veil; come, throw it o'er my face.
We'll once more hear Orsino's embassy.

Enter Viola.

VIOLA.
120   The honourable lady of the house, which is she?

OLIVIA.
Speak to me; I shall answer for her. Your will?

VIOLA.
Most radiant, exquisite, and unmatchable beauty,—I pray you, tell me if this be the lady of the house, for I never saw her. I would be loath to cast away my speech; for besides that it is excellently well penned, I have taken
125   great pains to con it. Good beauties, let me sustain no scorn; I am very comptible, even to the least sinister usage.

OLIVIA.
Whence came you, sir?

VIOLA.
I can say little more than I have studied, and that question's out of my part. Good gentle one, give me modest assurance, if you be the lady of the
130   house, that I may proceed in my speech.

OLIVIA.
Are you a comedian?

VIOLA.
No, my profound heart: and yet, by the very fangs of malice I swear, I am not that I play. Are you the lady of the house?

OLIVIA.
If I do not usurp myself, I am.

VIOLA.
135 Most certain, if you are she, you do usurp yourself; for what is yours to bestow is not yours to reserve. But this is from my commission. I will on with my speech in your praise, and then show you the heart of my message.

OLIVIA.
Come to what is important in't: I forgive you the praise.

VIOLA.
Alas, I took great pains to study it, and 'tis poetical.

OLIVIA.
140 It is the more like to be feigned; I pray you keep it in. I heard you were saucy at my gates; and allowed your approach, rather to wonder at you than to hear you. If you be mad, be gone; if you have reason, be brief: 'tis not that time of moon with me to make one in so skipping a dialogue.

MARIA.
Will you hoist sail, sir? Here lies your way.

VIOLA.
145 No, good swabber, I am to hull here a little longer. Some mollification for your giant, sweet lady. Tell me your mind. I am a messenger.

OLIVIA.
Sure, you have some hideous matter to deliver, when the courtesy of it is so fearful. Speak your office.

VIOLA.
It alone concerns your ear. I bring no overture of war, no taxation of hom-
150 age; I hold the olive in my hand: my words are as full of peace as matter.

OLIVIA.
Yet you began rudely. What are you? What would you?

VIOLA.
The rudeness that hath appeared in me have I learned from my entertain-
ment. What I am and what I would are as secret as maidenhead: to your ears, divinity; to any other's, profanation.

OLIVIA.
155   Give us the place alone: we will hear this divinity.

                                                              [*Exit Maria.*]

   Now, sir, what is your text?

VIOLA.
   Most sweet lady—

OLIVIA.
   A comfortable doctrine, and much may be said of it. Where lies your text?

VIOLA.
   In Orsino's bosom.

OLIVIA.
160   In his bosom? In what chapter of his bosom?

VIOLA.
   To answer by the method, in the first of his heart.

OLIVIA.
   O, I have read it; it is heresy. Have you no more to say?

VIOLA.
   Good madam, let me see your face.

OLIVIA.
   Have you any commission from your lord to negotiate with my face? You are
165   now out of your text: but we will draw the curtain and show you the picture.
   [*Unveiling.*] Look you, sir, such a one I was this present. Is't not well done?

VIOLA.
   Excellently done, if God did all.

OLIVIA.
   'Tis in grain, sir; 'twill endure wind and weather.

VIOLA.
   'Tis beauty truly blent, whose red and white
170   Nature's own sweet and cunning hand laid on.
   Lady, you are the cruel'st she alive
   If you will lead these graces to the grave,
   And leave the world no copy.

OLIVIA.
   O, sir, I will not be so hard-hearted; I will give out divers schedules of my
175   beauty. It shall be inventoried and every particle and utensil labelled to my
   will: as, item, two lips indifferent red; item, two grey eyes with lids to them;
   item, one neck, one chin, and so forth. Were you sent hither to praise me?

VIOLA.
I see you what you are, you are too proud;
But, if you were the devil, you are fair.
180   My lord and master loves you. O, such love
Could be but recompens'd though you were crown'd
The nonpareil of beauty!

OLIVIA.
How does he love me?

VIOLA.
185   With adorations, fertile tears,
With groans that thunder love, with sighs of fire.

OLIVIA.
Your lord does know my mind, I cannot love him:
Yet I suppose him virtuous, know him noble,
Of great estate, of fresh and stainless youth;
190   In voices well divulg'd, free, learn'd, and valiant,
And in dimension and the shape of nature,
A gracious person. But yet I cannot love him.
He might have took his answer long ago.

VIOLA.
If I did love you in my master's flame,
195   With such a suff'ring, such a deadly life,
In your denial I would find no sense,
I would not understand it.

OLIVIA.
Why, what would you?

VIOLA.
Make me a willow cabin at your gate,
200   And call upon my soul within the house;
Write loyal cantons of contemned love,
And sing them loud even in the dead of night;
Hallow your name to the reverberate hills,
And make the babbling gossip of the air
205   Cry out Olivia! O, you should not rest
Between the elements of air and earth,
But you should pity me.

OLIVIA.
You might do much.
What is your parentage?

VIOLA.
210   Above my fortunes, yet my state is well:
      I am a gentleman.

OLIVIA.
      Get you to your lord;
      I cannot love him: let him send no more,
      Unless, perchance, you come to me again,
215   To tell me how he takes it. Fare you well:
      I thank you for your pains: spend this for me.

VIOLA.
      I am no fee'd post, lady; keep your purse;
      My master, not myself, lacks recompense.
      Love make his heart of flint that you shall love,
220   And let your fervour like my master's be
      Plac'd in contempt. Farewell, fair cruelty.

                                                    [*Exit.*]

OLIVIA.
      What is your parentage?
      'Above my fortunes, yet my state is well:
      I am a gentleman.' I'll be sworn thou art;
225   Thy tongue, thy face, thy limbs, actions, and spirit,
      Do give thee five-fold blazon. Not too fast: soft, soft!
      Unless the master were the man. How now?
      Even so quickly may one catch the plague?
      Methinks I feel this youth's perfections
230   With an invisible and subtle stealth
      To creep in at mine eyes. Well, let it be.
      What ho, Malvolio!

                     Enter Malvolio.

MALVOLIO.
      Here, madam, at your service.

OLIVIA.
      Run after that same peevish messenger
235   The County's man: he left this ring behind him,
      Would I or not; tell him, I'll none of it.
      Desire him not to flatter with his lord,
      Nor hold him up with hopes; I am not for him.
      If that the youth will come this way tomorrow,
240   I'll give him reasons for't. Hie thee, Malvolio.

MALVOLIO.
Madam, I will.

[*Exit.*]

OLIVIA.
I do I know not what, and fear to find
Mine eye too great a flatterer for my mind.
Fate, show thy force, ourselves we do not owe.
245 What is decreed must be; and be this so!

[*Exit.*]

ACT II.

SCENE I. The sea-coast.
Enter Antonio and Sebastian.

ANTONIO.
Will you stay no longer? Nor will you not that I go with you?

SEBASTIAN.
By your patience, no; my stars shine darkly over me; the malignancy of
my fate might perhaps distemper yours; therefore I shall crave of you your
leave that I may bear my evils alone. It were a bad recompense for your love,
5 to lay any of them on you.

ANTONIO.
Let me know of you whither you are bound.

SEBASTIAN.
No, sooth, sir; my determinate voyage is mere extravagancy. But I perceive in
you so excellent a touch of modesty, that you will not extort from me what
I am willing to keep in. Therefore it charges me in manners the rather to
10 express myself. You must know of me then, Antonio, my name is Sebastian,
which I called Roderigo; my father was that Sebastian of Messaline whom I
know you have heard of. He left behind him myself and a sister, both born in
an hour. If the heavens had been pleased, would we had so ended! But you,
sir, altered that, for some hour before you took me from the breach of the
15 sea was my sister drowned.

ANTONIO.
Alas the day!

SEBASTIAN.
A lady, sir, though it was said she much resembled me, was yet of many
accounted beautiful. But though I could not with such estimable wonder
overfar believe that, yet thus far I will boldly publish her, she bore a mind

20 that envy could not but call fair. She is drowned already, sir, with salt water,
though I seem to drown her remembrance again with more.

ANTONIO.
Pardon me, sir, your bad entertainment.

SEBASTIAN.
O good Antonio, forgive me your trouble.

ANTONIO.
If you will not murder me for my love, let me be your servant.

SEBASTIAN.
25 If you will not undo what you have done, that is, kill him whom you have re-
covered, desire it not. Fare ye well at once; my bosom is full of kindness, and I
am yet so near the manners of my mother, that upon the least occasion more,
mine eyes will tell tales of me. I am bound to the Count Orsino's court: farewell.
[*Exit.*]

ANTONIO.
The gentleness of all the gods go with thee!
30 I have many enemies in Orsino's court,
Else would I very shortly see thee there:
But come what may, I do adore thee so,
That danger shall seem sport, and I will go.

[*Exit.*]

SCENE II. A STREET.
Enter Viola; Malvolio at several doors.

MALVOLIO.
Were you not even now with the Countess Olivia?

VIOLA.
Even now, sir; on a moderate pace I have since arrived but hither.

MALVOLIO.
She returns this ring to you, sir; you might have saved me my pains, to have
taken it away yourself. She adds, moreover, that you should put your lord
5 into a desperate assurance she will none of him. And one thing more, that
you be never so hardy to come again in his affairs, unless it be to report your
lord's taking of this. Receive it so.

VIOLA.
She took the ring of me: I'll none of it.

MALVOLIO.
Come sir, you peevishly threw it to her; and her will is it should be so returned.
10   If it be worth stooping for, there it lies in your eye; if not, be it his that finds it.
[Exit.]

VIOLA.
I left no ring with her; what means this lady?
Fortune forbid my outside have not charm'd her!
She made good view of me, indeed, so much,
That methought her eyes had lost her tongue,
15   For she did speak in starts distractedly.
She loves me, sure, the cunning of her passion
Invites me in this churlish messenger.
None of my lord's ring? Why, he sent her none.
I am the man; if it be so, as 'tis,
20   Poor lady, she were better love a dream.
Disguise, I see thou art a wickedness
Wherein the pregnant enemy does much.
How easy is it for the proper false
In women's waxen hearts to set their forms!
25   Alas, our frailty is the cause, not we,
For such as we are made of, such we be.
How will this fadge? My master loves her dearly,
And I, poor monster, fond as much on him,
And she, mistaken, seems to dote on me.
30   What will become of this? As I am man,
My state is desperate for my master's love;
As I am woman (now alas the day!)
What thriftless sighs shall poor Olivia breathe!
O time, thou must untangle this, not I,
35   It is too hard a knot for me t'untie!
[Exit.]

SCENE III. A ROOM IN OLIVIA'S HOUSE.
Enter Sir Toby and Sir Andrew.

SIR TOBY.
Approach, Sir Andrew; not to be abed after midnight, is to be up betimes;
and diluculo surgere, thou know'st.

SIR ANDREW.
Nay, by my troth, I know not; but I know to be up late is to be up late.

SIR TOBY.
A false conclusion; I hate it as an unfilled can. To be up after midnight, and
5   to go to bed then is early: so that to go to bed after midnight is to go to bed
betimes. Does not our lives consist of the four elements?

SIR ANDREW.
Faith, so they say, but I think it rather consists of eating and drinking.

SIR TOBY.
Th'art a scholar; let us therefore eat and drink.
Marian, I say! a stoup of wine.

Enter Clown.

SIR ANDREW.
10   Here comes the fool, i' faith.

CLOWN.
How now, my hearts? Did you never see the picture of "we three"?

SIR TOBY.
Welcome, ass. Now let's have a catch.

SIR ANDREW.
By my troth, the fool has an excellent breast. I had rather than forty
shillings I had such a leg, and so sweet a breath to sing, as the fool has. In
15   sooth, thou wast in very gracious fooling last night when thou spok'st of
Pigrogromitus, of the Vapians passing the equinoctial of Queubus; 'twas
very good, i' faith. I sent thee sixpence for thy leman. Hadst it?

CLOWN.
I did impeticos thy gratillity; for Malvolio's nose is no whipstock. My lady
has a white hand, and the Myrmidons are no bottle-ale houses.

SIR ANDREW.
20   Excellent! Why, this is the best fooling, when all is done. Now, a song.

SIR TOBY.
Come on, there is sixpence for you. Let's have a song.

SIR ANDREW.
There's a testril of me too: if one knight give a—

CLOWN.
Would you have a love-song, or a song of good life?

SIR TOBY.
A love-song, a love-song.

SIR ANDREW.
25   Ay, ay. I care not for good life.

CLOWN. [*sings.*]
O mistress mine, where are you roaming?
O stay and hear, your true love's coming,

That can sing both high and low.
Trip no further, pretty sweeting.
30 *Journeys end in lovers meeting,*
Every wise man's son doth know.

SIR ANDREW.
 Excellent good, i' faith.

SIR TOBY.
 Good, good.

CLOWN.
 What is love? 'Tis not hereafter,
35 *Present mirth hath present laughter.*
 What's to come is still unsure.
 In delay there lies no plenty,
 Then come kiss me, sweet and twenty.
 Youth's a stuff will not endure.

SIR ANDREW.
40 A mellifluous voice, as I am true knight.

SIR TOBY.
 A contagious breath.

SIR ANDREW.
 Very sweet and contagious, i' faith.

SIR TOBY.
 To hear by the nose, it is dulcet in contagion. But shall we make the welkin
dance indeed? Shall we rouse the night-owl in a catch that will draw three
45 souls out of one weaver? Shall we do that?

SIR ANDREW.
 And you love me, let's do't: I am dog at a catch.

CLOWN.
 By'r lady, sir, and some dogs will catch well.

SIR ANDREW.
 Most certain. Let our catch be, "Thou knave."

CLOWN.
 "Hold thy peace, thou knave" knight? I shall be constrain'd in't to call
50 thee knave, knight.

SIR ANDREW.
 'Tis not the first time I have constrained one to call me knave. Begin, fool;
it begins "Hold thy peace."

CLOWN.
I shall never begin if I hold my peace.

SIR ANDREW.
Good, i' faith! Come, begin.

[Catch sung.]

Enter Maria.

MARIA.
55 What a caterwauling do you keep here! If my lady have not called up her
steward Malvolio, and bid him turn you out of doors, never trust me.

SIR TOBY.
My lady's a Cataian, we are politicians, Malvolio's a Peg-a-Ramsey, and [*Sings.*]
Three merry men be we. Am not I consanguineous? Am I not of her blood? Til-
ly-vally! "Lady"! *There dwelt a man in Babylon, Lady, Lady.*

CLOWN.
60 Beshrew me, the knight's in admirable fooling.

SIR ANDREW.
Ay, he does well enough if he be disposed, and so do I too; he does it with
a better grace, but I do it more natural.

SIR TOBY.
[*Sings.*] *O' the twelfth day of December—*

MARIA.
For the love o' God, peace!

Enter Malvolio.

MALVOLIO.
65 My masters, are you mad? Or what are you? Have you no wit, manners, nor
honesty, but to gabble like tinkers at this time of night? Do ye make an ale-
house of my lady's house, that ye squeak out your coziers' catches without
any mitigation or remorse of voice? Is there no respect of place, persons,
nor time, in you?

SIR TOBY.
70 We did keep time, sir, in our catches. Sneck up!

MALVOLIO.
Sir Toby, I must be round with you. My lady bade me tell you that, though
she harbours you as her kinsman she's nothing allied to your disorders. If
you can separate yourself and your misdemeanours, you are welcome to the
house; if not, and it would please you to take leave of her, she is very willing
75 to bid you farewell.

SIR TOBY.
 [*Sings.*] *Farewell, dear heart, since I must needs be gone.*

MARIA.
 Nay, good Sir Toby.

CLOWN.
 [*Sings.*] *His eyes do show his days are almost done.*

MALVOLIO.
 Is't even so?

SIR TOBY.
80 [*Sings.*] *But I will never die.*

CLOWN.
 [*Sings.*] *Sir Toby, there you lie.*

MALVOLIO.
 This is much credit to you.

SIR TOBY.
 [*Sings.*] *Shall I bid him go?*

CLOWN.
 [*Sings.*] *What and if you do?*

SIR TOBY.
85 [*Sings.*] *Shall I bid him go, and spare not?*

CLOWN.
 [*Sings.*] *O, no, no, no, no, you dare not.*

SIR TOBY.
 Out o' tune? sir, ye lie. Art any more than a steward? Dost thou think, because thou art virtuous, there shall be no more cakes and ale?

CLOWN.
 Yes, by Saint Anne, and ginger shall be hot i' the mouth too.

SIR TOBY.
90 Th'art i' the right. Go, sir, rub your chain with crumbs. A stoup of wine, Maria!

MALVOLIO.
 Mistress Mary, if you prized my lady's favour at anything more than contempt, you would not give means for this uncivil rule; she shall know of it, by this hand.

[Exit.]

MARIA.
Go shake your ears.

SIR ANDREW.
95   'Twere as good a deed as to drink when a man's a-hungry, to challenge him the field, and then to break promise with him and make a fool of him.

SIR TOBY.
Do't, knight. I'll write thee a challenge; or I'll deliver thy indignation to him by word of mouth.

MARIA.
Sweet Sir Toby, be patient for tonight. Since the youth of the Count's was
100   today with my lady, she is much out of quiet. For Monsieur Malvolio, let me alone with him. If I do not gull him into a nayword, and make him a common recreation, do not think I have wit enough to lie straight in my bed. I know I can do it.

SIR TOBY.
Possess us, possess us, tell us something of him.

MARIA.
105   Marry, sir, sometimes he is a kind of Puritan.

SIR ANDREW.
O, if I thought that, I'd beat him like a dog.

SIR TOBY.
What, for being a Puritan? Thy exquisite reason, dear knight?

SIR ANDREW.
I have no exquisite reason for't, but I have reason good enough.

MARIA.
The devil a Puritan that he is, or anything constantly but a time-pleaser,
110   an affectioned ass that cons state without book and utters it by great swarths; the best persuaded of himself, so crammed (as he thinks) with excellencies, that it is his grounds of faith that all that look on him love him. And on that vice in him will my revenge find notable cause to work.

SIR TOBY.
What wilt thou do?

MARIA.
115   I will drop in his way some obscure epistles of love, wherein by the colour of his beard, the shape of his leg, the manner of his gait, the expressure of his eye, forehead, and complexion, he shall find himself most feelingly personated. I can write very like my lady your niece; on a forgotten matter we can hardly make distinction of our hands.

SIR TOBY.
120 Excellent! I smell a device.

SIR ANDREW.
 I have't in my nose too.

SIR TOBY.
 He shall think, by the letters that thou wilt drop, that they come from my niece, and that she is in love with him.

MARIA.
 My purpose is indeed a horse of that colour.

SIR ANDREW.
125 And your horse now would make him an ass.

MARIA.
 Ass, I doubt not.

SIR ANDREW.
 O 'twill be admirable!

MARIA.
 Sport royal, I warrant you. I know my physic will work with him. I will plant you two, and let the fool make a third, where he shall find the letter.
130 Observe his construction of it. For this night, to bed, and dream on the event. Farewell.

[Exit.]

SIR TOBY.
 Good night, Penthesilea.

SIR ANDREW.
 Before me, she's a good wench.

SIR TOBY.
 She's a beagle true bred, and one that adores me. What o' that?

SIR ANDREW.
135 I was adored once too.

SIR TOBY.
 Let's to bed, knight. Thou hadst need send for more money.

SIR ANDREW.
 If I cannot recover your niece, I am a foul way out.

SIR TOBY.
 Send for money, knight; if thou hast her not i' th' end, call me cut.

SIR ANDREW.
If I do not, never trust me, take it how you will.

SIR TOBY.
140 Come, come, I'll go burn some sack, 'tis too late to go to bed now. Come,
knight, come, knight.

[Exeunt.]

SCENE IV. A ROOM IN THE DUKE'S PALACE.
Enter Duke, Viola, Curio and others.

DUKE.
Give me some music. Now, good morrow, friends.
Now, good Cesario, but that piece of song,
That old and antique song we heard last night;
Methought it did relieve my passion much,
5   More than light airs and recollected terms
Of these most brisk and giddy-paced times.
Come, but one verse.

CURIO.
He is not here, so please your lordship, that should sing it.

DUKE.
Who was it?

CURIO.
10   Feste, the jester, my lord, a fool that the Lady Olivia's father took much
delight in. He is about the house.

DUKE.
Seek him out, and play the tune the while.

[Exit Curio. Music plays.]

Come hither, boy. If ever thou shalt love,
In the sweet pangs of it remember me:
15   For such as I am, all true lovers are,
Unstaid and skittish in all motions else,
Save in the constant image of the creature
That is belov'd. How dost thou like this tune?

VIOLA.
It gives a very echo to the seat
20   Where love is throned.

DUKE.
Thou dost speak masterly.
My life upon't, young though thou art, thine eye

Hath stayed upon some favour that it loves.
Hath it not, boy?

VIOLA.
25   A little, by your favour.

DUKE.
  What kind of woman is't?

VIOLA.
  Of your complexion.

DUKE.
  She is not worth thee, then. What years, i' faith?

VIOLA.
  About your years, my lord.

DUKE.
30   Too old, by heaven! Let still the woman take
      An elder than herself; so wears she to him,
      So sways she level in her husband's heart.
      For, boy, however we do praise ourselves,
      Our fancies are more giddy and unfirm,
35   More longing, wavering, sooner lost and worn,
      Than women's are.

VIOLA.
  I think it well, my lord.

DUKE.
  Then let thy love be younger than thyself,
  Or thy affection cannot hold the bent:
40   For women are as roses, whose fair flower
      Being once display'd, doth fall that very hour.

VIOLA.
  And so they are: alas, that they are so;
  To die, even when they to perfection grow!

                    Enter Curio and Clown.

DUKE.
  O, fellow, come, the song we had last night.
45   Mark it, Cesario, it is old and plain;
      The spinsters and the knitters in the sun,
      And the free maids, that weave their thread with bones

Do use to chant it: it is silly sooth,
And dallies with the innocence of love
50 Like the old age.

CLOWN.
Are you ready, sir?

DUKE.
Ay; prithee, sing.

            [Music.]

The Clown's song:

Come away, come away, death.
And in sad cypress let me be laid.
55 *Fly away, fly away, breath;*
I am slain by a fair cruel maid.
 My shroud of white, stuck all with yew,
  O, prepare it!
 My part of death no one so true
60 *Did share it.*

Not a flower, not a flower sweet,
On my black coffin let there be strown:
Not a friend, not a friend greet
My poor corpse where my bones shall be thrown:
65 *A thousand thousand sighs to save,*
  Lay me, O, where
 Sad true lover never find my grave,
  To weep there.

DUKE.
There's for thy pains.

CLOWN.
70 No pains, sir; I take pleasure in singing, sir.

DUKE.
I'll pay thy pleasure, then.

CLOWN.
Truly sir, and pleasure will be paid one time or another.

DUKE.
Give me now leave to leave thee.

CLOWN.
Now the melancholy god protect thee, and the tailor make thy doublet of
75 changeable taffeta, for thy mind is a very opal. I would have men of such con-
stancy put to sea, that their business might be everything, and their intent ev-
erywhere, for that's it that always makes a good voyage of nothing. Farewell.
[*Exit Clown.*]

DUKE.
Let all the rest give place.

[*Exeunt Curio and Attendants.*]

Once more, Cesario,
80 Get thee to yond same sovereign cruelty.
Tell her my love, more noble than the world,
Prizes not quantity of dirty lands;
The parts that fortune hath bestow'd upon her,
Tell her I hold as giddily as fortune;
85 But 'tis that miracle and queen of gems
That nature pranks her in attracts my soul.

VIOLA.
But if she cannot love you, sir?

DUKE.
I cannot be so answer'd.

VIOLA.
Sooth, but you must.
90 Say that some lady, as perhaps there is,
Hath for your love as great a pang of heart
As you have for Olivia: you cannot love her;
You tell her so. Must she not then be answer'd?

DUKE.
There is no woman's sides
95 Can bide the beating of so strong a passion
As love doth give my heart: no woman's heart
So big, to hold so much; they lack retention.
Alas, their love may be called appetite,
No motion of the liver, but the palate,
100 That suffer surfeit, cloyment, and revolt;
But mine is all as hungry as the sea,
And can digest as much. Make no compare
Between that love a woman can bear me
And that I owe Olivia.

VIOLA.
105 Ay, but I know—

DUKE.
What dost thou know?

VIOLA.
Too well what love women to men may owe.
In faith, they are as true of heart as we.
My father had a daughter loved a man,
110   As it might be perhaps, were I a woman,
I should your lordship.

DUKE.
And what's her history?

VIOLA.
A blank, my lord. She never told her love,
But let concealment, like a worm i' th' bud,
115   Feed on her damask cheek: she pined in thought,
And with a green and yellow melancholy
She sat like patience on a monument,
Smiling at grief. Was not this love, indeed?
We men may say more, swear more, but indeed,
120   Our shows are more than will; for still we prove
Much in our vows, but little in our love.

DUKE.
But died thy sister of her love, my boy?

VIOLA.
I am all the daughters of my father's house,
And all the brothers too: and yet I know not.
125   Sir, shall I to this lady?

DUKE.
Ay, that's the theme.
To her in haste. Give her this jewel; say
My love can give no place, bide no denay.

                                          [Exeunt.]

SCENE V. OLIVIA'S GARDEN.
Enter Sir Toby, Sir Andrew and Fabian.

SIR TOBY.
Come thy ways, Signior Fabian.

FABIAN.
Nay, I'll come. If I lose a scruple of this sport, let me be boiled to death
with melancholy.

SIR TOBY.
Wouldst thou not be glad to have the niggardly rascally sheep-biter come
5 by some notable shame?

FABIAN.
I would exult, man. You know he brought me out o' favour with my lady
about a bear-baiting here.

SIR TOBY.
To anger him we'll have the bear again, and we will fool him black and blue,
shall we not, Sir Andrew?

SIR ANDREW.
10 And we do not, it is pity of our lives.

Enter Maria.

SIR TOBY.
Here comes the little villain. How now, my metal of India?

MARIA.
Get ye all three into the box-tree. Malvolio's coming down this walk; he
has been yonder i' the sun practising behaviour to his own shadow this half
hour: observe him, for the love of mockery; for I know this letter will make
15 a contemplative idiot of him. Close, in the name of jesting! [*The men hide
themselves.*] Lie thou there; [*Throws down a letter*] for here comes the trout that
must be caught with tickling.

[*Exit Maria.*]

Enter Malvolio.

MALVOLIO.
'Tis but fortune, all is fortune. Maria once told me she did affect me, and
I have heard herself come thus near, that should she fancy, it should be
20 one of my complexion. Besides, she uses me with a more exalted respect
than anyone else that follows her. What should I think on't?

SIR TOBY.
Here's an overweening rogue!

FABIAN.
O, peace! Contemplation makes a rare turkey-cock of him; how he jets
under his advanced plumes!

SIR ANDREW.
25 'Slight, I could so beat the rogue!

SIR TOBY.
Peace, I say.

MALVOLIO.
To be Count Malvolio.

SIR TOBY.
Ah, rogue!

SIR ANDREW.
Pistol him, pistol him.

SIR TOBY.
30   Peace, peace.

MALVOLIO.
There is example for't. The lady of the Strachy married the yeoman of
the wardrobe.

SIR ANDREW.
Fie on him, Jezebel!

FABIAN.
O, peace! now he's deeply in; look how imagination blows him.

MALVOLIO.
35   Having been three months married to her, sitting in my state—

SIR TOBY.
O for a stone-bow to hit him in the eye!

MALVOLIO.
Calling my officers about me, in my branched velvet gown; having come
from a day-bed, where I have left Olivia sleeping.

SIR TOBY.
Fire and brimstone!

FABIAN.
40   O, peace, peace.

MALVOLIO.
And then to have the humour of state; and after a demure travel of regard,
telling them I know my place as I would they should do theirs, to ask for my
kinsman Toby.

SIR TOBY.
Bolts and shackles!

FABIAN.
45   O, peace, peace, peace! Now, now.

MALVOLIO.
 Seven of my people, with an obedient start, make out for him. I frown the
while, and perchance wind up my watch, or play with some rich jewel. Toby
approaches; curtsies there to me—

SIR TOBY.
 Shall this fellow live?

FABIAN.
50   Though our silence be drawn from us with cars, yet peace!

MALVOLIO.
 I extend my hand to him thus, quenching my familiar smile with an austere
regard of control—

SIR TOBY.
 And does not Toby take you a blow o' the lips then?

MALVOLIO.
 Saying 'Cousin Toby, my fortunes having cast me on your niece, give me
55   this prerogative of speech—'

SIR TOBY.
 What, what?

MALVOLIO.
 'You must amend your drunkenness.'

SIR TOBY.
 Out, scab!

FABIAN.
 Nay, patience, or we break the sinews of our plot.

MALVOLIO.
60   'Besides, you waste the treasure of your time with a foolish knight—'

SIR ANDREW.
 That's me, I warrant you.

MALVOLIO.
 'One Sir Andrew.'

SIR ANDREW.
 I knew 'twas I, for many do call me fool.

MALVOLIO.
 [*Taking up the letter*.] What employment have we here?

FABIAN.

65   Now is the woodcock near the gin.

SIR TOBY.

O, peace! And the spirit of humours intimate reading aloud to him!

MALVOLIO.

By my life, this is my lady's hand: these be her very C's, her U's, and her T's, and thus makes she her great P's. It is in contempt of question, her hand.

SIR ANDREW.

Her C's, her U's, and her T's. Why that?

MALVOLIO.

70   [*Reads.*] *To the unknown beloved, this, and my good wishes.* Her very phrases! By your leave, wax. Soft! and the impressure her Lucrece, with which she uses to seal: 'tis my lady. To whom should this be?

FABIAN.

This wins him, liver and all.

MALVOLIO.

[*Reads.*]
    Jove knows I love,
75   *But who?*
    Lips, do not move,
    No man must know.
'No man must know.' What follows? The numbers alter'd! 'No man must know.'—If this should be thee, Malvolio?

SIR TOBY.

80   Marry, hang thee, brock!

MALVOLIO.

    I may command where I adore,
    But silence, like a Lucrece knife,
    With bloodless stroke my heart doth gore;
    M.O.A.I. doth sway my life.

FABIAN.

85   A fustian riddle!

SIR TOBY.

Excellent wench, say I.

MALVOLIO.

'M.O.A.I. doth sway my life.'—Nay, but first let me see, let me see, let me see.

FABIAN.
What dish o' poison has she dressed him!

SIR TOBY.
And with what wing the staniel checks at it!

MALVOLIO.
90 'I may command where I adore.' Why, she may command me: I serve her,
she is my lady. Why, this is evident to any formal capacity. There is no ob-
struction in this. And the end—what should that alphabetical position por-
tend? If I could make that resemble something in me! Softly! 'M.O.A.I.'—

SIR TOBY.
O, ay, make up that:—he is now at a cold scent.

FABIAN.
95 Sowter will cry upon't for all this, though it be as rank as a fox.

MALVOLIO.
'M'—Malvolio; 'M!' Why, that begins my name!

FABIAN.
Did not I say he would work it out? The cur is excellent at faults.

MALVOLIO.
'M'—But then there is no consonancy in the sequel; that suffers under
probation: 'A' should follow, but 'O' does.

FABIAN.
100 And 'O' shall end, I hope.

SIR TOBY.
Ay, or I'll cudgel him, and make him cry 'O!'

MALVOLIO.
And then 'I' comes behind.

FABIAN.
Ay, and you had any eye behind you, you might see more detraction at your
heels than fortunes before you.

MALVOLIO.
105 'M.O.A.I.' This simulation is not as the former: and yet, to crush this a little,
it would bow to me, for every one of these letters are in my name. Soft, here
follows prose.

[Reads.] If this fall into thy hand, revolve. In my stars I am above thee, but be not afraid of greatness. Some are born great, some achieve greatness, and some have
110 *greatness thrust upon 'em. Thy fates open their hands, let thy blood and spirit embrace them. And, to inure thyself to what thou art like to be, cast thy humble slough and appear fresh. Be opposite with a kinsman, surly with servants. Let thy tongue tang arguments of state; put thyself into the trick of singularity. She thus advises thee that sighs for thee. Remember who commended thy yellow stockings, and wished*
115 *to see thee ever cross-gartered. I say, remember. Go to, thou art made, if thou desir'st to be so. If not, let me see thee a steward still, the fellow of servants, and not worthy to touch Fortune's fingers. Farewell. She that would alter services with thee,*
The Fortunate Unhappy.

Daylight and champian discovers not more! This is open. I will be proud,
120 I will read politic authors, I will baffle Sir Toby, I will wash off gross acquaintance, I will be point-device, the very man. I do not now fool myself, to let imagination jade me; for every reason excites to this, that my lady loves me. She did commend my yellow stockings of late, she did praise my leg being cross-gartered, and in this she manifests herself to my love,
125 and with a kind of injunction, drives me to these habits of her liking. I thank my stars, I am happy. I will be strange, stout, in yellow stockings, and cross-gartered, even with the swiftness of putting on. Jove and my stars be praised!—Here is yet a postscript. *[Reads.] Thou canst not choose but know who I am. If thou entertain'st my love, let it appear in thy smiling; thy smiles*
130 *become thee well. Therefore in my presence still smile, dear my sweet, I prithee.* Jove, I thank thee. I will smile, I will do everything that thou wilt have me.

[Exit.]

FABIAN.
 I will not give my part of this sport for a pension of thousands to be paid from the Sophy.

SIR TOBY.
 I could marry this wench for this device.

SIR ANDREW.
135 So could I too.

SIR TOBY.
 And ask no other dowry with her but such another jest.

Enter Maria.

SIR ANDREW.
 Nor I neither.

FABIAN.
 Here comes my noble gull-catcher.

SIR TOBY.
Wilt thou set thy foot o' my neck?

SIR ANDREW.
140 Or o' mine either?

SIR TOBY.
Shall I play my freedom at tray-trip, and become thy bond-slave?

SIR ANDREW.
I' faith, or I either?

SIR TOBY.
Why, thou hast put him in such a dream, that when the image of it leaves
him he must run mad.

MARIA.
145 Nay, but say true, does it work upon him?

SIR TOBY.
Like aqua-vitae with a midwife.

MARIA.
If you will then see the fruits of the sport, mark his first approach before
my lady: he will come to her in yellow stockings, and 'tis a colour she abhors,
and cross-gartered, a fashion she detests; and he will smile upon her, which
150 will now be so unsuitable to her disposition, being addicted to a melancholy
as she is, that it cannot but turn him into a notable contempt. If you will see
it, follow me.

SIR TOBY.
To the gates of Tartar, thou most excellent devil of wit!

SIR ANDREW.
I'll make one too.

[*Exeunt.*]

ACT III.

SCENE I. Olivia's garden.
Enter Viola and Clown with a tabor.

VIOLA.
Save thee, friend, and thy music. Dost thou live by thy tabor?

CLOWN.
No, sir, I live by the church.

VIOLA.
Art thou a churchman?

CLOWN.
No such matter, sir. I do live by the church, for I do live at my house, and
my house doth stand by the church.

VIOLA.
So thou mayst say the king lies by a beggar, if a beggar dwell near him; or
the church stands by thy tabor, if thy tabor stand by the church.

CLOWN.
You have said, sir. To see this age! A sentence is but a chev'ril glove to a
good wit. How quickly the wrong side may be turned outward!

VIOLA.
Nay, that's certain; they that dally nicely with words may quickly make
them wanton.

CLOWN.
I would, therefore, my sister had had no name, sir.

VIOLA.
Why, man?

CLOWN.
Why, sir, her name's a word; and to dally with that word might make my sis-
ter wanton. But indeed, words are very rascals, since bonds disgraced them.

VIOLA.
Thy reason, man?

CLOWN.
Troth, sir, I can yield you none without words, and words are grown so
false, I am loath to prove reason with them.

VIOLA.
I warrant thou art a merry fellow, and car'st for nothing.

CLOWN.
Not so, sir, I do care for something. But in my conscience, sir, I do not
care for you. If that be to care for nothing, sir, I would it would make you
invisible.

VIOLA.
Art not thou the Lady Olivia's fool?

CLOWN.
No, indeed, sir; the Lady Olivia has no folly. She will keep no fool, sir, till
she be married, and fools are as like husbands as pilchards are to herrings, the
husband's the bigger. I am indeed not her fool, but her corrupter of words.

VIOLA.
I saw thee late at the Count Orsino's.

CLOWN.
Foolery, sir, does walk about the orb like the sun; it shines everywhere. I
would be sorry, sir, but the fool should be as oft with your master as with
my mistress. I think I saw your wisdom there.

VIOLA.
30   Nay, and thou pass upon me, I'll no more with thee. Hold, there's expenses
for thee.

CLOWN.
Now Jove, in his next commodity of hair, send thee a beard!

VIOLA.
By my troth, I'll tell thee, I am almost sick for one, though I would not have
it grow on my chin. Is thy lady within?

CLOWN.
35   Would not a pair of these have bred, sir?

VIOLA.
Yes, being kept together, and put to use.

CLOWN.
I would play Lord Pandarus of Phrygia, sir, to bring a Cressida to this Troilus.

VIOLA.
I understand you, sir; 'tis well begged.

CLOWN.
The matter, I hope, is not great, sir, begging but a beggar: Cressida was a
40   beggar. My lady is within, sir. I will conster to them whence you come; who
you are and what you would are out of my welkin. I might say "element", but
the word is overworn.

[*Exit.*]

VIOLA.
This fellow is wise enough to play the fool,
And to do that well, craves a kind of wit:
45   He must observe their mood on whom he jests,
The quality of persons, and the time,
And like the haggard, check at every feather
That comes before his eye. This is a practice
As full of labour as a wise man's art:
50   For folly, that he wisely shows, is fit;
But wise men, folly-fall'n, quite taint their wit.

Enter Sir Toby and Sir Andrew.

SIR TOBY.
Save you, gentleman.

VIOLA.
And you, sir.

SIR ANDREW.
Dieu vous garde, monsieur.

VIOLA.
55   *Et vous aussi; votre serviteur.*

SIR ANDREW.
I hope, sir, you are, and I am yours.

SIR TOBY.
Will you encounter the house? My niece is desirous you should enter, if your trade be to her.

VIOLA.
I am bound to your niece, sir, I mean, she is the list of my voyage.

SIR TOBY.
60   Taste your legs, sir, put them to motion.

VIOLA.
My legs do better understand me, sir, than I understand what you mean by bidding me taste my legs.

SIR TOBY.
I mean, to go, sir, to enter.

VIOLA.
I will answer you with gait and entrance: but we are prevented.

Enter Olivia and Maria.

65   Most excellent accomplished lady, the heavens rain odours on you!

SIR ANDREW.
That youth's a rare courtier. 'Rain odours,' well.

VIOLA.
My matter hath no voice, lady, but to your own most pregnant and vouch-safed ear.

SIR ANDREW.
'Odours,' 'pregnant,' and 'vouchsafed.'—I'll get 'em all three ready.

OLIVIA.
70 Let the garden door be shut, and leave me to my hearing.
       [*Exeunt Sir Toby, Sir Andrew and Maria.*]
Give me your hand, sir.

VIOLA.
My duty, madam, and most humble service.

OLIVIA.
What is your name?

VIOLA.
Cesario is your servant's name, fair princess.

OLIVIA.
75 My servant, sir! 'Twas never merry world,
Since lowly feigning was call'd compliment:
Y'are servant to the Count Orsino, youth.

VIOLA.
And he is yours, and his must needs be yours.
Your servant's servant is your servant, madam.

OLIVIA.
80 For him, I think not on him: for his thoughts,
Would they were blanks rather than fill'd with me!

VIOLA.
Madam, I come to whet your gentle thoughts
On his behalf.

OLIVIA.
O, by your leave, I pray you.
85 I bade you never speak again of him.
But would you undertake another suit,
I had rather hear you to solicit that
Than music from the spheres.

VIOLA.
Dear lady—

OLIVIA.
90 Give me leave, beseech you. I did send,
After the last enchantment you did here,

A ring in chase of you. So did I abuse
Myself, my servant, and, I fear me, you.
Under your hard construction must I sit;
95 To force that on you in a shameful cunning,
Which you knew none of yours. What might you think?
Have you not set mine honour at the stake,
And baited it with all th' unmuzzled thoughts
That tyrannous heart can think? To one of your receiving
100 Enough is shown. A cypress, not a bosom,
Hides my heart: so let me hear you speak.

VIOLA.
I pity you.

OLIVIA.
That's a degree to love.

VIOLA.
No, not a grize; for 'tis a vulgar proof
105 That very oft we pity enemies.

OLIVIA.
Why then methinks 'tis time to smile again.
O world, how apt the poor are to be proud!
If one should be a prey, how much the better
To fall before the lion than the wolf! [*Clock strikes.*]
110 The clock upbraids me with the waste of time.
Be not afraid, good youth, I will not have you.
And yet, when wit and youth is come to harvest,
Your wife is like to reap a proper man.
There lies your way, due west.

VIOLA.
115 Then westward ho!
Grace and good disposition attend your ladyship!
You'll nothing, madam, to my lord by me?

OLIVIA.
Stay:
I prithee tell me what thou think'st of me.

VIOLA.
120 That you do think you are not what you are.

OLIVIA.
If I think so, I think the same of you.

VIOLA.
Then think you right; I am not what I am.

OLIVIA.
I would you were as I would have you be.

VIOLA.
Would it be better, madam, than I am?
125   I wish it might, for now I am your fool.

OLIVIA.
O what a deal of scorn looks beautiful
In the contempt and anger of his lip!
A murd'rous guilt shows not itself more soon
Than love that would seem hid. Love's night is noon.
130   Cesario, by the roses of the spring,
By maidhood, honour, truth, and everything,
I love thee so, that maugre all thy pride,
Nor wit nor reason can my passion hide.
Do not extort thy reasons from this clause,
135   For that I woo, thou therefore hast no cause;
But rather reason thus with reason fetter:
Love sought is good, but given unsought is better.

VIOLA.
By innocence I swear, and by my youth,
I have one heart, one bosom, and one truth,
140   And that no woman has; nor never none
Shall mistress be of it, save I alone.
And so adieu, good madam; never more
Will I my master's tears to you deplore.

OLIVIA.
Yet come again: for thou perhaps mayst move
145   That heart, which now abhors, to like his love.

[Exeunt.]

SCENE II. A ROOM IN OLIVIA'S HOUSE.
Enter Sir Toby, Sir Andrew and Fabian.

SIR ANDREW.
No, faith, I'll not stay a jot longer.

SIR TOBY.
Thy reason, dear venom, give thy reason.

FABIAN.
You must needs yield your reason, Sir Andrew.

SIR ANDREW.
Marry, I saw your niece do more favours to the Count's servingman than
5   ever she bestowed upon me; I saw't i' th' orchard.

SIR TOBY.
Did she see thee the while, old boy? Tell me that.

SIR ANDREW.
As plain as I see you now.

FABIAN.
This was a great argument of love in her toward you.

SIR ANDREW.
'Slight! will you make an ass o' me?

FABIAN.
10   I will prove it legitimate, sir, upon the oaths of judgment and reason.

SIR TOBY.
And they have been grand-jurymen since before Noah was a sailor.

FABIAN.
She did show favour to the youth in your sight only to exasperate you, to
awake your dormouse valour, to put fire in your heart and brimstone in your
liver. You should then have accosted her, and with some excellent jests, fire-
15   new from the mint, you should have banged the youth into dumbness. This
was looked for at your hand, and this was balked: the double gilt of this op-
portunity you let time wash off, and you are now sailed into the north of my
lady's opinion; where you will hang like an icicle on Dutchman's beard, un-
less you do redeem it by some laudable attempt, either of valour or policy.

SIR ANDREW.
20   And't be any way, it must be with valour, for policy I hate; I had as lief be
a Brownist as a politician.

SIR TOBY.
Why, then, build me thy fortunes upon the basis of valour. Challenge me
the Count's youth to fight with him. Hurt him in eleven places; my niece
shall take note of it, and assure thyself there is no love-broker in the world
25   can more prevail in man's commendation with woman than report of valour.

FABIAN.
There is no way but this, Sir Andrew.

SIR ANDREW.
 Will either of you bear me a challenge to him?

SIR TOBY.
 Go, write it in a martial hand, be curst and brief; it is no matter how witty,
so it be eloquent and full of invention. Taunt him with the licence of ink. If
30 thou 'thou'st' him some thrice, it shall not be amiss, and as many lies as will
lie in thy sheet of paper, although the sheet were big enough for the bed of
Ware in England, set 'em down. Go about it. Let there be gall enough in thy
ink, though thou write with a goose-pen, no matter. About it.

SIR ANDREW.
 Where shall I find you?

SIR TOBY.
35 We'll call thee at the cubiculo. Go.

[Exit Sir Andrew.]

FABIAN.
 This is a dear manikin to you, Sir Toby.

SIR TOBY.
 I have been dear to him, lad, some two thousand strong, or so.

FABIAN.
 We shall have a rare letter from him; but you'll not deliver it.

SIR TOBY.
 Never trust me then. And by all means stir on the youth to an answer. I
40 think oxen and wainropes cannot hale them together. For Andrew, if he
were opened and you find so much blood in his liver as will clog the foot of
a flea, I'll eat the rest of th' anatomy.

FABIAN.
 And his opposite, the youth, bears in his visage no great presage of cruelty.

Enter Maria.

SIR TOBY.
 Look where the youngest wren of nine comes.

MARIA.
45 If you desire the spleen, and will laugh yourselves into stitches, follow
me. Yond gull Malvolio is turned heathen, a very renegado; for there is no
Christian that means to be saved by believing rightly can ever believe such
impossible passages of grossness. He's in yellow stockings.

SIR TOBY.
And cross-gartered?

MARIA.
50   Most villainously; like a pedant that keeps a school i' th' church. I have dogged him like his murderer. He does obey every point of the letter that I dropped to betray him. He does smile his face into more lines than is in the new map with the augmentation of the Indies. You have not seen such a thing as 'tis. I can hardly forbear hurling things at him. I know my lady will
55   strike him. If she do, he'll smile and take't for a great favour.

SIR TOBY.
Come, bring us, bring us where he is.

                              [*Exeunt.*]

SCENE III. A street.
Enter Sebastian and Antonio.

SEBASTIAN.
I would not by my will have troubled you,
But since you make your pleasure of your pains,
I will no further chide you.

ANTONIO.
I could not stay behind you: my desire,
5   More sharp than filed steel, did spur me forth;
And not all love to see you, though so much,
As might have drawn one to a longer voyage,
But jealousy what might befall your travel,
Being skilless in these parts; which to a stranger,
10   Unguided and unfriended, often prove
Rough and unhospitable. My willing love,
The rather by these arguments of fear,
Set forth in your pursuit.

SEBASTIAN.
My kind Antonio,
15   I can no other answer make but thanks,
And thanks, and ever thanks; and oft good turns
Are shuffled off with such uncurrent pay.
But were my worth, as is my conscience, firm,
You should find better dealing. What's to do?
20   Shall we go see the relics of this town?

ANTONIO.
Tomorrow, sir; best first go see your lodging.

SEBASTIAN.
 I am not weary, and 'tis long to night;
 I pray you, let us satisfy our eyes
 With the memorials and the things of fame
25 That do renown this city.

ANTONIO.
 Would you'd pardon me.
 I do not without danger walk these streets.
 Once in a sea-fight, 'gainst the Count his galleys,
 I did some service, of such note indeed,
30 That were I ta'en here, it would scarce be answer'd.

SEBASTIAN.
 Belike you slew great number of his people.

ANTONIO.
 Th' offence is not of such a bloody nature,
 Albeit the quality of the time and quarrel
 Might well have given us bloody argument.
35 It might have since been answered in repaying
 What we took from them, which for traffic's sake,
 Most of our city did. Only myself stood out,
 For which, if I be lapsed in this place,
 I shall pay dear.

SEBASTIAN.
40 Do not then walk too open.

ANTONIO.
 It doth not fit me. Hold, sir, here's my purse.
 In the south suburbs, at the Elephant,
 Is best to lodge. I will bespeak our diet
 Whiles you beguile the time and feed your knowledge
45 With viewing of the town. There shall you have me.

SEBASTIAN.
 Why I your purse?

ANTONIO.
 Haply your eye shall light upon some toy
 You have desire to purchase; and your store,
 I think, is not for idle markets, sir.

SEBASTIAN.
50 I'll be your purse-bearer, and leave you for an hour.

ANTONIO.
To th' Elephant.

SEBASTIAN.
I do remember.

[*Exeunt.*]

SCENE IV. OLIVIA'S GARDEN.
Enter Olivia and Maria.

OLIVIA.
I have sent after him. He says he'll come;
How shall I feast him? What bestow of him?
For youth is bought more oft than begg'd or borrow'd.
I speak too loud.—
5   Where's Malvolio?—He is sad and civil,
And suits well for a servant with my fortunes;
Where is Malvolio?

MARIA.
He's coming, madam:
But in very strange manner. He is sure possessed, madam.

OLIVIA.
10   Why, what's the matter? Does he rave?

MARIA.
No, madam, he does nothing but smile: your ladyship were best to have
some guard about you if he come, for sure the man is tainted in 's wits.

OLIVIA.
Go call him hither. I'm as mad as he,
If sad and merry madness equal be.

Enter Malvolio.

15   How now, Malvolio?

MALVOLIO.
Sweet lady, ho, ho!

OLIVIA.
Smil'st thou? I sent for thee upon a sad occasion.

MALVOLIO.
Sad, lady? I could be sad: this does make some obstruction in the blood,
this cross-gartering. But what of that? If it please the eye of one, it is with
20   me as the very true sonnet is: 'Please one and please all.'

OLIVIA.
 Why, how dost thou, man? What is the matter with thee?

MALVOLIO.
 Not black in my mind, though yellow in my legs. It did come to his hands,
and commands shall be executed. I think we do know the sweet Roman hand.

OLIVIA.
 Wilt thou go to bed, Malvolio?

MALVOLIO.
25   To bed? Ay, sweetheart, and I'll come to thee.

OLIVIA.
 God comfort thee! Why dost thou smile so, and kiss thy hand so oft?

MARIA.
 How do you, Malvolio?

MALVOLIO.
 At your request? Yes, nightingales answer daws!

MARIA.
 Why appear you with this ridiculous boldness before my lady?

MALVOLIO.
30   'Be not afraid of greatness.' 'Twas well writ.

OLIVIA.
 What mean'st thou by that, Malvolio?

MALVOLIO.
 'Some are born great'—

OLIVIA.
 Ha?

MALVOLIO.
 'Some achieve greatness'—

OLIVIA.
35   What say'st thou?

MALVOLIO.
 'And some have greatness thrust upon them.'

OLIVIA.
 Heaven restore thee!

MALVOLIO.
'Remember who commended thy yellow stockings'—

OLIVIA.
Thy yellow stockings?

MALVOLIO.
40   'And wished to see thee cross-gartered.'

OLIVIA.
Cross-gartered?

MALVOLIO.
'Go to: thou art made, if thou desir'st to be so:'—

OLIVIA.
Am I made?

MALVOLIO.
'If not, let me see thee a servant still.'

OLIVIA.
45   Why, this is very midsummer madness.

Enter Servant.

SERVANT.
Madam, the young gentleman of the Count Orsino's is returned; I could
hardly entreat him back. He attends your ladyship's pleasure.

OLIVIA.
I'll come to him.

[Exit Servant.]

Good Maria, let this fellow be looked to. Where's my cousin Toby? Let
50   some of my people have a special care of him; I would not have him mis-
carry for the half of my dowry.

[Exeunt Olivia and Maria.]

MALVOLIO.
O ho, do you come near me now? No worse man than Sir Toby to look to
me. This concurs directly with the letter: she sends him on purpose, that I may
appear stubborn to him; for she incites me to that in the letter. 'Cast thy humble
55   slough,' says she; 'be opposite with a kinsman, surly with servants, let thy tongue
tang with arguments of state, put thyself into the trick of singularity,' and con-
sequently, sets down the manner how: as, a sad face, a reverend carriage, a slow
tongue, in the habit of some sir of note, and so forth. I have limed her, but it
is Jove's doing, and Jove make me thankful! And when she went away now, 'Let

60 this fellow be looked to;' 'Fellow!' not 'Malvolio', nor after my degree, but 'fellow'. Why, everything adheres together, that no dram of a scruple, no scruple of a scruple, no obstacle, no incredulous or unsafe circumstance. What can be said? Nothing that can be can come between me and the full prospect of my hopes. Well, Jove, not I, is the doer of this, and he is to be thanked.

Enter Sir Toby, Fabian and Maria.

SIR TOBY.

65 Which way is he, in the name of sanctity? If all the devils of hell be drawn in little, and Legion himself possessed him, yet I'll speak to him.

FABIAN.

Here he is, here he is. How is't with you, sir? How is't with you, man?

MALVOLIO.

Go off, I discard you. Let me enjoy my private. Go off.

MARIA.

Lo, how hollow the fiend speaks within him! Did not I tell you? Sir Toby,
70 my lady prays you to have a care of him.

MALVOLIO.

Ah, ha! does she so?

SIR TOBY.

Go to, go to; peace, peace, we must deal gently with him. Let me alone. How do you, Malvolio? How is't with you? What, man! defy the devil! Consider, he's an enemy to mankind.

MALVOLIO.

75 Do you know what you say?

MARIA.

La you, an you speak ill of the devil, how he takes it at heart! Pray God he be not bewitched.

FABIAN.

Carry his water to th' wise woman.

MARIA.

Marry, and it shall be done tomorrow morning, if I live. My lady would
80 not lose him for more than I'll say.

MALVOLIO.

How now, mistress!

MARIA.

O Lord!

SIR TOBY.
Prithee hold thy peace, this is not the way. Do you not see you move him?
Let me alone with him.

FABIAN.
85   No way but gentleness, gently, gently. The fiend is rough, and will not
be roughly used.

SIR TOBY.
Why, how now, my bawcock? How dost thou, chuck?

MALVOLIO.
Sir!

SIR TOBY.
Ay, biddy, come with me. What, man, 'tis not for gravity to play at cher-
90   ry-pit with Satan. Hang him, foul collier!

MARIA.
Get him to say his prayers, good Sir Toby, get him to pray.

MALVOLIO.
My prayers, minx?

MARIA.
No, I warrant you, he will not hear of godliness.

MALVOLIO.
Go, hang yourselves all! You are idle, shallow things. I am not of your ele-
95   ment. You shall know more hereafter.

[*Exit.*]

SIR TOBY.
Is't possible?

FABIAN.
If this were played upon a stage now, I could condemn it as an improbable
fiction.

SIR TOBY.
His very genius hath taken the infection of the device, man.

MARIA.
100   Nay, pursue him now, lest the device take air and taint.

FABIAN.
Why, we shall make him mad indeed.

MARIA.
The house will be the quieter.

SIR TOBY.
Come, we'll have him in a dark room and bound. My niece is already in the belief that he's mad. We may carry it thus for our pleasure, and his penance,
105   till our very pastime, tired out of breath, prompt us to have mercy on him, at which time we will bring the device to the bar, and crown thee for a finder of madmen. But see, but see!

Enter Sir Andrew.

FABIAN.
More matter for a May morning.

SIR ANDREW.
Here's the challenge, read it. I warrant there's vinegar and pepper in't.

FABIAN.
110   Is't so saucy?

SIR ANDREW.
Ay, is't, I warrant him. Do but read.

SIR TOBY.
Give me. [*Reads.*] *Youth, whatsoever thou art, thou art but a scurvy fellow.*

FABIAN.
Good, and valiant.

SIR TOBY.
Wonder not, nor admire not in thy mind, why I do call thee so, for I will show thee no
115   *reason for't.*

FABIAN.
A good note, that keeps you from the blow of the law.

SIR TOBY.
Thou comest to the Lady Olivia, and in my sight she uses thee kindly: but thou liest in thy throat; that is not the matter I challenge thee for.

FABIAN.
Very brief, and to exceeding good sense—less.

SIR TOBY.
120   *I will waylay thee going home; where if it be thy chance to kill me—*

FABIAN.
Good.

SIR TOBY.
Thou kill'st me like a rogue and a villain.

FABIAN.
Still you keep o' th' windy side of the law. Good.

SIR TOBY.
Fare thee well, and God have mercy upon one of our souls! He may have mercy upon mine, but
125   *my hope is better, and so look to thyself. Thy friend, as thou usest him, and thy sworn enemy,*
                                                                   Andrew Aguecheek.
If this letter move him not, his legs cannot. I'll give't him.

MARIA.
You may have very fit occasion for't. He is now in some commerce with my
lady, and will by and by depart.

SIR TOBY.
130   Go, Sir Andrew. Scout me for him at the corner of the orchard, like a
bum-baily. So soon as ever thou seest him, draw, and as thou draw'st, swear
horrible, for it comes to pass oft that a terrible oath, with a swaggering
accent sharply twanged off, gives manhood more approbation than ever
proof itself would have earned him. Away.

SIR ANDREW.
135   Nay, let me alone for swearing.
                                                                   [*Exit.*]

SIR TOBY.
Now will not I deliver his letter, for the behaviour of the young gentle-
man gives him out to be of good capacity and breeding; his employment
between his lord and my niece confirms no less. Therefore this letter,
being so excellently ignorant, will breed no terror in the youth. He will
140   find it comes from a clodpole. But, sir, I will deliver his challenge by word
of mouth, set upon Aguecheek notable report of valour, and drive the
gentleman (as I know his youth will aptly receive it) into a most hideous
opinion of his rage, skill, fury, and impetuosity. This will so fright them
both that they will kill one another by the look, like cockatrices.

Enter Olivia and Viola.

FABIAN.
145   Here he comes with your niece; give them way till he take leave, and pres-
ently after him.

SIR TOBY.
I will meditate the while upon some horrid message for a challenge.
       [*Exeunt Sir Toby, Fabian and Maria.*]

OLIVIA.
I have said too much unto a heart of stone,
And laid mine honour too unchary on't:
150 There's something in me that reproves my fault:
But such a headstrong potent fault it is,
That it but mocks reproof.

VIOLA.
With the same 'haviour that your passion bears
155 Goes on my master's griefs.

OLIVIA.
Here, wear this jewel for me, 'tis my picture.
Refuse it not, it hath no tongue to vex you.
And I beseech you come again tomorrow.
What shall you ask of me that I'll deny,
160 That honour sav'd, may upon asking give?

VIOLA.
Nothing but this, your true love for my master.

OLIVIA.
How with mine honour may I give him that
Which I have given to you?

VIOLA.
I will acquit you.

OLIVIA.
165 Well, come again tomorrow. Fare thee well;
A fiend like thee might bear my soul to hell.
             [*Exit.*]

Enter Sir Toby and Fabian.

SIR TOBY.
Gentleman, God save thee.

VIOLA.
And you, sir.

SIR TOBY.
That defence thou hast, betake thee to't. Of what nature the wrongs are
170 thou hast done him, I know not, but thy intercepter, full of despite, bloody

as the hunter, attends thee at the orchard end. Dismount thy tuck, be yare in thy preparation, for thy assailant is quick, skilful, and deadly.

VIOLA.
 You mistake, sir; I am sure no man hath any quarrel to me. My remembrance is very free and clear from any image of offence done to any man.

SIR TOBY.
175　You'll find it otherwise, I assure you. Therefore, if you hold your life at any price, betake you to your guard, for your opposite hath in him what youth, strength, skill, and wrath, can furnish man withal.

VIOLA.
 I pray you, sir, what is he?

SIR TOBY.
 He is knight, dubbed with unhatched rapier, and on carpet consideration,
180　but he is a devil in private brawl. Souls and bodies hath he divorced three, and his incensement at this moment is so implacable that satisfaction can be none but by pangs of death and sepulchre. Hob, nob is his word; give't or take't.

VIOLA.
 I will return again into the house and desire some conduct of the lady. I am no fighter. I have heard of some kind of men that put quarrels purposely
185　on others to taste their valour: belike this is a man of that quirk.

SIR TOBY.
 Sir, no. His indignation derives itself out of a very competent injury; therefore, get you on and give him his desire. Back you shall not to the house, unless you undertake that with me which with as much safety you might answer him. Therefore on, or strip your sword stark naked, for meddle you
190　must, that's certain, or forswear to wear iron about you.

VIOLA.
 This is as uncivil as strange. I beseech you, do me this courteous office, as to know of the knight what my offence to him is. It is something of my negligence, nothing of my purpose.

SIR TOBY.
 I will do so. Signior Fabian, stay you by this gentleman till my return.
[Exit Sir Toby.]

VIOLA.
195　Pray you, sir, do you know of this matter?

FABIAN.
 I know the knight is incensed against you, even to a mortal arbitrement, but nothing of the circumstance more.

VIOLA.
I beseech you, what manner of man is he?

FABIAN.
Nothing of that wonderful promise, to read him by his form, as you are
200 like to find him in the proof of his valour. He is indeed, sir, the most skilful,
bloody, and fatal opposite that you could possibly have found in any part of
Illyria. Will you walk towards him? I will make your peace with him if I can.

VIOLA.
I shall be much bound to you for't. I am one that had rather go with sir
priest than sir knight: I care not who knows so much of my mettle.

[*Exeunt.*]

Enter Sir Toby and Sir Andrew.

SIR TOBY.
205 Why, man, he's a very devil. I have not seen such a firago. I had a pass
with him, rapier, scabbard, and all, and he gives me the stuck-in with such a
mortal motion that it is inevitable; and on the answer, he pays you as surely
as your feet hits the ground they step on. They say he has been fencer to
the Sophy.

SIR ANDREW.
210 Pox on't, I'll not meddle with him.

SIR TOBY.
Ay, but he will not now be pacified: Fabian can scarce hold him yonder.

SIR ANDREW.
Plague on't, an I thought he had been valiant, and so cunning in fence, I'd
have seen him damned ere I'd have challenged him. Let him let the matter
slip, and I'll give him my horse, grey Capilet.

SIR TOBY.
215 I'll make the motion. Stand here, make a good show on't. This shall end
without the perdition of souls. [*Aside.*] Marry, I'll ride your horse as well as
I ride you.

Enter Fabian and Viola.

[*To Fabian.*] I have his horse to take up the quarrel. I have persuaded him
the youth's a devil.

FABIAN.
220 He is as horribly conceited of him, and pants and looks pale, as if a bear
were at his heels.

SIR TOBY.
There's no remedy, sir, he will fight with you for's oath sake. Marry, he
hath better bethought him of his quarrel, and he finds that now scarce to
be worth talking of. Therefore, draw for the supportance of his vow; he
225   protests he will not hurt you.

VIOLA.
[*Aside.*] Pray God defend me! A little thing would make me tell them how
much I lack of a man.

FABIAN.
Give ground if you see him furious.

SIR TOBY.
Come, Sir Andrew, there's no remedy, the gentleman will for his honour's sake
230   have one bout with you. He cannot by the duello avoid it; but he has promised
me, as he is a gentleman and a soldier, he will not hurt you. Come on: to't.

SIR ANDREW.
[*Draws.*] Pray God he keep his oath!

Enter Antonio.

VIOLA.
[*Draws.*] I do assure you 'tis against my will.

ANTONIO.
Put up your sword. If this young gentleman
235   Have done offence, I take the fault on me.
If you offend him, I for him defy you.

SIR TOBY.
You, sir? Why, what are you?

ANTONIO.
[*Draws.*] One, sir, that for his love dares yet do more
Than you have heard him brag to you he will.

SIR TOBY.
240   [*Draws.*] Nay, if you be an undertaker, I am for you.

Enter Officers.

FABIAN.
O good Sir Toby, hold! Here come the officers.

SIR TOBY.
[*To Antonio.*] I'll be with you anon.

VIOLA.
[*To Sir Andrew.*] Pray, sir, put your sword up, if you please.

SIR ANDREW.
Marry, will I, sir; and for that I promised you, I'll be as good as my word.
245 He will bear you easily, and reins well.

FIRST OFFICER.
This is the man; do thy office.

SECOND OFFICER.
Antonio, I arrest thee at the suit
Of Count Orsino.

ANTONIO.
You do mistake me, sir.

FIRST OFFICER.
250 No, sir, no jot. I know your favour well,
Though now you have no sea-cap on your head.—
Take him away, he knows I know him well.

ANTONIO.
I must obey. This comes with seeking you;
But there's no remedy, I shall answer it.
255 What will you do? Now my necessity
Makes me to ask you for my purse. It grieves me
Much more for what I cannot do for you,
Than what befalls myself. You stand amaz'd,
But be of comfort.

SECOND OFFICER.
260 Come, sir, away.

ANTONIO.
I must entreat of you some of that money.

VIOLA.
What money, sir?
For the fair kindness you have show'd me here,
And part being prompted by your present trouble,
265 Out of my lean and low ability
I'll lend you something. My having is not much;
I'll make division of my present with you.
Hold, there's half my coffer.

ANTONIO.
Will you deny me now?
270 Is't possible that my deserts to you
Can lack persuasion? Do not tempt my misery,
Lest that it make me so unsound a man
As to upbraid you with those kindnesses
That I have done for you.

VIOLA.
275 I know of none,
Nor know I you by voice or any feature.
I hate ingratitude more in a man
Than lying, vainness, babbling, drunkenness,
Or any taint of vice whose strong corruption
280 Inhabits our frail blood.

ANTONIO.
O heavens themselves!

SECOND OFFICER.
Come, sir, I pray you go.

ANTONIO.
Let me speak a little. This youth that you see here
I snatch'd one half out of the jaws of death,
285 Reliev'd him with such sanctity of love;
And to his image, which methought did promise
Most venerable worth, did I devotion.

FIRST OFFICER.
What's that to us? The time goes by. Away!

ANTONIO.
But O how vile an idol proves this god!
290 Thou hast, Sebastian, done good feature shame.
In nature there's no blemish but the mind;
None can be call'd deform'd but the unkind.
Virtue is beauty, but the beauteous evil
Are empty trunks, o'erflourished by the devil.

FIRST OFFICER.
295 The man grows mad, away with him. Come, come, sir.

ANTONIO.
Lead me on.

[Exeunt Officers with Antonio.]

VIOLA.
  Methinks his words do from such passion fly
  That he believes himself; so do not I.
  Prove true, imagination, O prove true,
300 That I, dear brother, be now ta'en for you!

SIR TOBY.
  Come hither, knight; come hither, Fabian. We'll whisper o'er a couplet or
  two of most sage saws.

VIOLA.
  He nam'd Sebastian. I my brother know
  Yet living in my glass; even such and so
305 In favour was my brother, and he went
  Still in this fashion, colour, ornament,
  For him I imitate. O if it prove,
  Tempests are kind, and salt waves fresh in love!

                                                                      [*Exit.*]

SIR TOBY.
  A very dishonest paltry boy, and more a coward than a hare. His dishonesty
310 appears in leaving his friend here in necessity, and denying him; and for his
  cowardship, ask Fabian.

FABIAN.
  A coward, a most devout coward, religious in it.

SIR ANDREW.
  'Slid, I'll after him again and beat him.

SIR TOBY.
  Do, cuff him soundly, but never draw thy sword.

SIR ANDREW.
315 And I do not—

                                                                      [*Exit.*]

FABIAN.
  Come, let's see the event.

SIR TOBY.
  I dare lay any money 'twill be nothing yet.

                                                                    [*Exeunt.*]

ACT IV.
SCENE I. The Street before Olivia's House.
Enter Sebastian and Clown.

CLOWN.
Will you make me believe that I am not sent for you?

SEBASTIAN.
Go to, go to, thou art a foolish fellow.
Let me be clear of thee.

CLOWN.
Well held out, i' faith! No, I do not know you, nor I am not sent to you
5   by my lady, to bid you come speak with her; nor your name is not Master
Cesario; nor this is not my nose neither. Nothing that is so, is so.

SEBASTIAN.
I prithee vent thy folly somewhere else,
Thou know'st not me.

CLOWN.
Vent my folly! He has heard that word of some great man, and now applies
10   it to a fool. Vent my folly! I am afraid this great lubber, the world, will prove
a cockney. I prithee now, ungird thy strangeness, and tell me what I shall
vent to my lady. Shall I vent to her that thou art coming?

SEBASTIAN.
I prithee, foolish Greek, depart from me.
There's money for thee; if you tarry longer
15   I shall give worse payment.

CLOWN.
By my troth, thou hast an open hand. These wise men that give fools mon-
ey get themselves a good report—after fourteen years' purchase.

Enter Sir Andrew, Sir Toby and Fabian.

SIR ANDREW.
Now sir, have I met you again? There's for you.

[Striking Sebastian.]

SEBASTIAN.
Why, there's for thee, and there, and there.
20   Are all the people mad?

[Beating Sir Andrew.]

SIR TOBY.
Hold, sir, or I'll throw your dagger o'er the house.

CLOWN.
 This will I tell my lady straight. I would not be in some of your coats for
twopence.

[*Exit Clown.*]

SIR TOBY.
 Come on, sir, hold!

SIR ANDREW.
25   Nay, let him alone, I'll go another way to work with him. I'll have an action
 of battery against him, if there be any law in Illyria. Though I struck him
 first, yet it's no matter for that.

SEBASTIAN.
 Let go thy hand!

SIR TOBY.
 Come, sir, I will not let you go. Come, my young soldier, put up your iron:
30   you are well fleshed. Come on.

SEBASTIAN.
 I will be free from thee. What wouldst thou now?
 If thou dar'st tempt me further, draw thy sword.

[*Draws.*]

SIR TOBY.
 What, what? Nay, then, I must have an ounce or two of this malapert blood
from you.

[*Draws.*]

Enter Olivia.

OLIVIA.
35   Hold, Toby! On thy life I charge thee hold!

SIR TOBY.
 Madam.

OLIVIA.
 Will it be ever thus? Ungracious wretch,
 Fit for the mountains and the barbarous caves,
 Where manners ne'er were preach'd! Out of my sight!
40   Be not offended, dear Cesario.
 Rudesby, be gone!

[*Exeunt Sir Toby, Sir Andrew and Fabian.*]

I prithee, gentle friend,
Let thy fair wisdom, not thy passion, sway
In this uncivil and unjust extent
45 Against thy peace. Go with me to my house,
And hear thou there how many fruitless pranks
This ruffian hath botch'd up, that thou thereby
Mayst smile at this. Thou shalt not choose but go.
Do not deny. Beshrew his soul for me,
50 He started one poor heart of mine, in thee.

SEBASTIAN.
What relish is in this? How runs the stream?
Or I am mad, or else this is a dream.
Let fancy still my sense in Lethe steep;
If it be thus to dream, still let me sleep!

OLIVIA.
55 Nay, come, I prithee. Would thou'dst be ruled by me!

SEBASTIAN.
Madam, I will.

OLIVIA.
O, say so, and so be!

                [*Exeunt.*]

SCENE II. A ROOM IN OLIVIA'S HOUSE.
Enter Maria and Clown.

MARIA.
Nay, I prithee, put on this gown and this beard; make him believe thou art
Sir Topas the curate. Do it quickly. I'll call Sir Toby the whilst.

                [*Exit Maria.*]

CLOWN.
Well, I'll put it on, and I will dissemble myself in't, and I would I were the
first that ever dissembled in such a gown. I am not tall enough to become
5 the function well, nor lean enough to be thought a good student, but to be
said, an honest man and a good housekeeper goes as fairly as to say, a care-
ful man and a great scholar. The competitors enter.

Enter Sir Toby and Maria.

SIR TOBY.
Jove bless thee, Master Parson.

CLOWN.
Bonos dies, Sir Toby: for as the old hermit of Prague, that never saw pen
10   and ink, very wittily said to a niece of King Gorboduc, 'That that is, is': so
I, being Master Parson, am Master Parson; for what is 'that' but 'that'? and
'is' but 'is'?

SIR TOBY.
To him, Sir Topas.

CLOWN.
What ho, I say! Peace in this prison!

SIR TOBY.
15   The knave counterfeits well. A good knave.

MALVOLIO.
[*Within.*] Who calls there?

CLOWN.
Sir Topas the curate, who comes to visit Malvolio the lunatic.

MALVOLIO.
Sir Topas, Sir Topas, good Sir Topas, go to my lady.

CLOWN.
Out, hyperbolical fiend! how vexest thou this man? Talkest thou nothing
20   but of ladies?

SIR TOBY.
Well said, Master Parson.

MALVOLIO.
Sir Topas, never was man thus wronged. Good Sir Topas, do not think I am
mad. They have laid me here in hideous darkness.

CLOWN.
Fie, thou dishonest Satan! I call thee by the most modest terms, for I am
25   one of those gentle ones that will use the devil himself with courtesy. Say'st
thou that house is dark?

MALVOLIO.
As hell, Sir Topas.

CLOWN.
Why, it hath bay windows transparent as barricadoes, and the clerestories
toward the south-north are as lustrous as ebony; and yet complainest thou
30   of obstruction?

MALVOLIO.
I am not mad, Sir Topas. I say to you this house is dark.

CLOWN.
Madman, thou errest. I say there is no darkness but ignorance, in which thou art more puzzled than the Egyptians in their fog.

MALVOLIO.
I say this house is as dark as ignorance, though ignorance were as dark as
35   hell; and I say there was never man thus abused. I am no more mad than you are. Make the trial of it in any constant question.

CLOWN.
What is the opinion of Pythagoras concerning wildfowl?

MALVOLIO.
That the soul of our grandam might haply inhabit a bird.

CLOWN.
What think'st thou of his opinion?

MALVOLIO.
40   I think nobly of the soul, and no way approve his opinion.

CLOWN.
Fare thee well. Remain thou still in darkness. Thou shalt hold the opinion of Pythagoras ere I will allow of thy wits, and fear to kill a woodcock, lest thou dispossess the soul of thy grandam. Fare thee well.

MALVOLIO.
Sir Topas, Sir Topas!

SIR TOBY.
45   My most exquisite Sir Topas!

CLOWN.
Nay, I am for all waters.

MARIA.
Thou mightst have done this without thy beard and gown. He sees thee not.

SIR TOBY.
To him in thine own voice, and bring me word how thou find'st him. I would we were well rid of this knavery. If he may be conveniently delivered, I would
50   he were, for I am now so far in offence with my niece that I cannot pursue with any safety this sport to the upshot. Come by and by to my chamber.

                                     [Exeunt Sir Toby and Maria.]

CLOWN.
[*Singing.*]
  Hey, Robin, jolly Robin,
  Tell me how thy lady does.

MALVOLIO.
Fool!

CLOWN.
55   *My lady is unkind, perdy.*

MALVOLIO.
Fool!

CLOWN.
  Alas, why is she so?

MALVOLIO.
Fool, I say!

CLOWN.
  She loves another—
60 Who calls, ha?

MALVOLIO.
Good fool, as ever thou wilt deserve well at my hand, help me to a candle, and pen, ink, and paper. As I am a gentleman, I will live to be thankful to thee for't.

CLOWN.
Master Malvolio?

MALVOLIO.
Ay, good fool.

CLOWN.
65 Alas, sir, how fell you besides your five wits?

MALVOLIO.
Fool, there was never man so notoriously abused. I am as well in my wits, fool, as thou art.

CLOWN.
But as well? Then you are mad indeed, if you be no better in your wits than a fool.

MALVOLIO.
70 They have here propertied me; keep me in darkness, send ministers to me, asses, and do all they can to face me out of my wits.

CLOWN.
Advise you what you say: the minister is here. [*As Sir Topas*] Malvolio, Mal-
volio, thy wits the heavens restore. Endeavour thyself to sleep, and leave thy
vain bibble-babble.

MALVOLIO.
75 Sir Topas!

CLOWN.
[*As Sir Topas*] Maintain no words with him, good fellow. [*As himself*] Who,
I, sir? not I, sir. God buy you, good Sir Topas. [*As Sir Topas*] Marry, amen.
[*As himself*] I will sir, I will.

MALVOLIO.
Fool, fool, fool, I say!

CLOWN.
80 Alas, sir, be patient. What say you, sir? I am shent for speaking to you.

MALVOLIO.
Good fool, help me to some light and some paper. I tell thee I am as well
in my wits as any man in Illyria.

CLOWN.
Well-a-day that you were, sir!

MALVOLIO.
By this hand, I am. Good fool, some ink, paper, and light, and convey
85 what I will set down to my lady. It shall advantage thee more than ever the
bearing of letter did.

CLOWN.
I will help you to't. But tell me true, are you not mad indeed? or do you
but counterfeit?

MALVOLIO.
Believe me, I am not. I tell thee true.

CLOWN.
Nay, I'll ne'er believe a madman till I see his brains. I will fetch you light,
90 and paper, and ink.

MALVOLIO.
Fool, I'll requite it in the highest degree: I prithee be gone.

CLOWN.
[*Singing.*]
  I am gone, sir, and anon, sir,

I'll be with you again,
In a trice, like to the old Vice,
95   *Your need to sustain;*
Who with dagger of lath, in his rage and his wrath,
Cries 'ah, ha!' to the devil:
Like a mad lad, 'Pare thy nails, dad.
Adieu, goodman devil.'

[*Exit.*]

SCENE III. OLIVIA'S GARDEN.
Enter Sebastian.

SEBASTIAN.
This is the air; that is the glorious sun,
This pearl she gave me, I do feel't and see't,
And though 'tis wonder that enwraps me thus,
Yet 'tis not madness. Where's Antonio, then?
5   I could not find him at the Elephant,
Yet there he was, and there I found this credit,
That he did range the town to seek me out.
His counsel now might do me golden service.
For though my soul disputes well with my sense
10   That this may be some error, but no madness,
Yet doth this accident and flood of fortune
So far exceed all instance, all discourse,
That I am ready to distrust mine eyes
And wrangle with my reason that persuades me
15   To any other trust but that I am mad,
Or else the lady's mad; yet if 'twere so,
She could not sway her house, command her followers,
Take and give back affairs and their dispatch,
With such a smooth, discreet, and stable bearing
20   As I perceive she does. There's something in't
That is deceivable. But here the lady comes.

Enter Olivia and a Priest.

OLIVIA.
Blame not this haste of mine. If you mean well,
Now go with me and with this holy man
Into the chantry by: there, before him
25   And underneath that consecrated roof,
Plight me the full assurance of your faith,
That my most jealous and too doubtful soul

May live at peace. He shall conceal it
Whiles you are willing it shall come to note,
30   What time we will our celebration keep
According to my birth. What do you say?

SEBASTIAN.
I'll follow this good man, and go with you,
And having sworn truth, ever will be true.

OLIVIA.
Then lead the way, good father, and heavens so shine,
35   That they may fairly note this act of mine!

[Exeunt.]

ACT V.

SCENE I. The Street before Olivia's House.
Enter Clown and Fabian.

FABIAN.
Now, as thou lov'st me, let me see his letter.

CLOWN.
Good Master Fabian, grant me another request.

FABIAN.
Anything.

CLOWN.
Do not desire to see this letter.

FABIAN.
5   This is to give a dog, and in recompense desire my dog again.

Enter Duke, Viola, Curio and Lords.

DUKE.
Belong you to the Lady Olivia, friends?

CLOWN.
Ay, sir, we are some of her trappings.

DUKE.
I know thee well. How dost thou, my good fellow?

CLOWN.
Truly, sir, the better for my foes, and the worse for my friends.

DUKE.
10   Just the contrary; the better for thy friends.

CLOWN.
No, sir, the worse.

DUKE.
How can that be?

CLOWN.
Marry, sir, they praise me, and make an ass of me. Now my foes tell me
plainly I am an ass: so that by my foes, sir, I profit in the knowledge of my-
self, and by my friends I am abused. So that, conclusions to be as kisses, if
your four negatives make your two affirmatives, why then, the worse for my
friends, and the better for my foes.

DUKE.
Why, this is excellent.

CLOWN.
By my troth, sir, no; though it please you to be one of my friends.

DUKE.
Thou shalt not be the worse for me; there's gold.

CLOWN.
But that it would be double-dealing, sir, I would you could make it another.

DUKE.
O, you give me ill counsel.

CLOWN.
Put your grace in your pocket, sir, for this once, and let your flesh and
blood obey it.

DUKE.
Well, I will be so much a sinner to be a double-dealer: there's another.

CLOWN.
Primo, secundo, tertio, is a good play, and the old saying is, the third pays for
all; the triplex, sir, is a good tripping measure; or the bells of Saint Bennet,
sir, may put you in mind—one, two, three.

DUKE.
You can fool no more money out of me at this throw. If you will let your
lady know I am here to speak with her, and bring her along with you, it may
awake my bounty further.

CLOWN.
Marry, sir, lullaby to your bounty till I come again. I go, sir, but I would not
have you to think that my desire of having is the sin of covetousness: but
as you say, sir, let your bounty take a nap, I will awake it anon.

[Exit Clown.]

Enter Antonio and Officers.

VIOLA.
35   Here comes the man, sir, that did rescue me.

DUKE.
That face of his I do remember well.
Yet when I saw it last it was besmear'd
As black as Vulcan, in the smoke of war.
A baubling vessel was he captain of,
40   For shallow draught and bulk unprizable,
With which such scathful grapple did he make
With the most noble bottom of our fleet,
That very envy and the tongue of loss
Cried fame and honour on him. What's the matter?

FIRST OFFICER.
45   Orsino, this is that Antonio
That took the *Phoenix* and her fraught from Candy,
And this is he that did the *Tiger* board
When your young nephew Titus lost his leg.
Here in the streets, desperate of shame and state,
50   In private brabble did we apprehend him.

VIOLA.
He did me kindness, sir; drew on my side,
But in conclusion, put strange speech upon me.
I know not what 'twas, but distraction.

DUKE.
Notable pirate, thou salt-water thief,
55   What foolish boldness brought thee to their mercies,
Whom thou, in terms so bloody and so dear,
Hast made thine enemies?

ANTONIO.
Orsino, noble sir,
Be pleased that I shake off these names you give me:
60   Antonio never yet was thief or pirate,
Though, I confess, on base and ground enough,
Orsino's enemy. A witchcraft drew me hither:
That most ingrateful boy there by your side
From the rude sea's enraged and foamy mouth
65   Did I redeem; a wreck past hope he was.
His life I gave him, and did thereto add

My love, without retention or restraint,
All his in dedication. For his sake
Did I expose myself, pure for his love,
70   Into the danger of this adverse town;
Drew to defend him when he was beset;
Where being apprehended, his false cunning
(Not meaning to partake with me in danger)
Taught him to face me out of his acquaintance,
75   And grew a twenty years' removed thing
While one would wink; denied me mine own purse,
Which I had recommended to his use
Not half an hour before.

VIOLA.
How can this be?

DUKE.
80   When came he to this town?

ANTONIO.
Today, my lord; and for three months before,
No int'rim, not a minute's vacancy,
Both day and night did we keep company.

Enter Olivia and Attendants.

DUKE.
Here comes the Countess, now heaven walks on earth.
85   But for thee, fellow, fellow, thy words are madness.
Three months this youth hath tended upon me;
But more of that anon. Take him aside.

OLIVIA.
What would my lord, but that he may not have,
Wherein Olivia may seem serviceable?
90   Cesario, you do not keep promise with me.

VIOLA.
Madam?

DUKE.
Gracious Olivia—

OLIVIA.
What do you say, Cesario? Good my lord—

VIOLA.
My lord would speak, my duty hushes me.

OLIVIA.
95   If it be aught to the old tune, my lord,
It is as fat and fulsome to mine ear
As howling after music.

DUKE.
Still so cruel?

OLIVIA.
Still so constant, lord.

DUKE.
100   What, to perverseness? You uncivil lady,
To whose ingrate and unauspicious altars
My soul the faithfull'st off'rings hath breathed out
That e'er devotion tender'd! What shall I do?

OLIVIA.
Even what it please my lord that shall become him.

DUKE.
105   Why should I not, had I the heart to do it,
Like to the Egyptian thief at point of death,
Kill what I love?—a savage jealousy
That sometime savours nobly. But hear me this:
Since you to non-regardance cast my faith,
110   And that I partly know the instrument
That screws me from my true place in your favour,
Live you the marble-breasted tyrant still.
But this your minion, whom I know you love,
And whom, by heaven I swear, I tender dearly,
115   Him will I tear out of that cruel eye
Where he sits crowned in his master's spite.—
Come, boy, with me; my thoughts are ripe in mischief:
I'll sacrifice the lamb that I do love,
To spite a raven's heart within a dove.

VIOLA.
120   And I, most jocund, apt, and willingly,
To do you rest, a thousand deaths would die.

OLIVIA.
Where goes Cesario?

VIOLA.
After him I love
More than I love these eyes, more than my life,
125   More, by all mores, than e'er I shall love wife.

If I do feign, you witnesses above
Punish my life for tainting of my love.

OLIVIA.
Ah me, detested! how am I beguil'd!

VIOLA.
Who does beguile you? Who does do you wrong?

OLIVIA.
130   Hast thou forgot thyself? Is it so long?
Call forth the holy father.

                                                         [*Exit an Attendant.*]

DUKE.
[*To Viola.*] Come, away!

OLIVIA.
Whither, my lord? Cesario, husband, stay.

DUKE.
Husband?

OLIVIA.
135   Ay, husband. Can he that deny?

DUKE.
Her husband, sirrah?

VIOLA.
No, my lord, not I.

OLIVIA.
Alas, it is the baseness of thy fear
That makes thee strangle thy propriety.
140   Fear not, Cesario, take thy fortunes up.
Be that thou know'st thou art, and then thou art
As great as that thou fear'st.

                          Enter Priest.

O, welcome, father!
Father, I charge thee, by thy reverence
145   Here to unfold—though lately we intended
To keep in darkness what occasion now
Reveals before 'tis ripe—what thou dost know
Hath newly passed between this youth and me.

PRIEST.
A contract of eternal bond of love,
150   Confirmed by mutual joinder of your hands,
Attested by the holy close of lips,
Strengthen'd by interchangement of your rings,
And all the ceremony of this compact
Sealed in my function, by my testimony;
155   Since when, my watch hath told me, toward my grave,
I have travelled but two hours.

DUKE.
O thou dissembling cub! What wilt thou be
When time hath sowed a grizzle on thy case?
Or will not else thy craft so quickly grow
160   That thine own trip shall be thine overthrow?
Farewell, and take her; but direct thy feet
Where thou and I henceforth may never meet.

VIOLA.
My lord, I do protest—

OLIVIA.
O, do not swear.
165   Hold little faith, though thou has too much fear.

Enter Sir Andrew.

SIR ANDREW.
For the love of God, a surgeon! Send one presently to Sir Toby.

OLIVIA.
What's the matter?

SIR ANDREW.
'Has broke my head across, and has given Sir Toby a bloody coxcomb too.
For the love of God, your help! I had rather than forty pound I were at home.

OLIVIA.
170   Who has done this, Sir Andrew?

SIR ANDREW.
The Count's gentleman, one Cesario. We took him for a coward, but he's
the very devil incardinate.

DUKE.
My gentleman, Cesario?

SIR ANDREW.
'Od's lifelings, here he is!—You broke my head for nothing; and that that
175   I did, I was set on to do't by Sir Toby.

VIOLA.
Why do you speak to me? I never hurt you:
You drew your sword upon me without cause,
But I bespake you fair and hurt you not.

Enter Sir Toby, drunk, led by the Clown.

SIR ANDREW.
If a bloody coxcomb be a hurt, you have hurt me. I think you set nothing by
180   a bloody coxcomb. Here comes Sir Toby halting, you shall hear more: but if
he had not been in drink, he would have tickled you othergates than he did.

DUKE.
How now, gentleman? How is't with you?

SIR TOBY.
That's all one; 'has hurt me, and there's th' end on't. Sot, didst see Dick
Surgeon, sot?

CLOWN.
185   O, he's drunk, Sir Toby, an hour agone; his eyes were set at eight i' th' morning.

SIR TOBY.
Then he's a rogue, and a passy measures pavin. I hate a drunken rogue.

OLIVIA.
Away with him. Who hath made this havoc with them?

SIR ANDREW.
I'll help you, Sir Toby, because we'll be dressed together.

SIR TOBY.
Will you help? An ass-head, and a coxcomb, and a knave, a thin-faced knave,
190   a gull?

OLIVIA.
Get him to bed, and let his hurt be looked to.

[Exeunt Clown, Fabian, Sir Toby and Sir Andrew.]

Enter Sebastian.

SEBASTIAN.
I am sorry, madam, I have hurt your kinsman;
But had it been the brother of my blood,
I must have done no less with wit and safety.

195 You throw a strange regard upon me, and by that
     I do perceive it hath offended you.
     Pardon me, sweet one, even for the vows
     We made each other but so late ago.

DUKE.
     One face, one voice, one habit, and two persons!
200 A natural perspective, that is, and is not!

SEBASTIAN.
     Antonio, O my dear Antonio!
     How have the hours rack'd and tortur'd me
     Since I have lost thee.

ANTONIO.
     Sebastian are you?

SEBASTIAN.
205 Fear'st thou that, Antonio?

ANTONIO.
     How have you made division of yourself?
     An apple cleft in two is not more twin
     Than these two creatures. Which is Sebastian?

OLIVIA.
     Most wonderful!

SEBASTIAN.
210 Do I stand there? I never had a brother:
     Nor can there be that deity in my nature
     Of here and everywhere. I had a sister,
     Whom the blind waves and surges have devoured.
     Of charity, what kin are you to me?
215 What countryman? What name? What parentage?

VIOLA.
     Of Messaline: Sebastian was my father;
     Such a Sebastian was my brother too:
     So went he suited to his watery tomb.
     If spirits can assume both form and suit,
220 You come to fright us.

SEBASTIAN.
     A spirit I am indeed,
     But am in that dimension grossly clad,
     Which from the womb I did participate.

Were you a woman, as the rest goes even,
225   I should my tears let fall upon your cheek,
And say, 'Thrice welcome, drowned Viola.'

VIOLA.
My father had a mole upon his brow.

SEBASTIAN.
And so had mine.

VIOLA.
And died that day when Viola from her birth
230   Had numbered thirteen years.

SEBASTIAN.
O, that record is lively in my soul!
He finished indeed his mortal act
That day that made my sister thirteen years.

VIOLA.
If nothing lets to make us happy both
235   But this my masculine usurp'd attire,
Do not embrace me till each circumstance
Of place, time, fortune, do cohere and jump
That I am Viola; which to confirm,
I'll bring you to a captain in this town,
240   Where lie my maiden weeds; by whose gentle help
I was preserv'd to serve this noble count.
All the occurrence of my fortune since
Hath been between this lady and this lord.

SEBASTIAN.
[*To Olivia.*] So comes it, lady, you have been mistook.
245   But nature to her bias drew in that.
You would have been contracted to a maid;
Nor are you therein, by my life, deceived:
You are betroth'd both to a maid and man.

DUKE.
Be not amazed; right noble is his blood.
250   If this be so, as yet the glass seems true,
I shall have share in this most happy wreck.
[*To Viola.*] Boy, thou hast said to me a thousand times
Thou never shouldst love woman like to me.

VIOLA.
And all those sayings will I over-swear,
255   And all those swearings keep as true in soul

As doth that orbed continent the fire
That severs day from night.

DUKE.
 Give me thy hand,
 And let me see thee in thy woman's weeds.

VIOLA.
260   The captain that did bring me first on shore
 Hath my maid's garments. He, upon some action,
 Is now in durance, at Malvolio's suit,
 A gentleman and follower of my lady's.

OLIVIA.
 He shall enlarge him. Fetch Malvolio hither.
265   And yet, alas, now I remember me,
 They say, poor gentleman, he's much distract.

Enter Clown, with a letter and Fabian.

A most extracting frenzy of mine own
 From my remembrance clearly banished his.
 How does he, sirrah?

CLOWN.
270   Truly, madam, he holds Belzebub at the stave's end as well as a man in his
 case may do. Has here writ a letter to you. I should have given it you today
 morning, but as a madman's epistles are no gospels, so it skills not much when
 they are delivered.

OLIVIA.
 Open 't, and read it.

CLOWN.
275   Look then to be well edified, when the fool delivers the madman. *By the
 Lord, madam,—*

OLIVIA.
 How now, art thou mad?

CLOWN.
 No, madam, I do but read madness: an your ladyship will have it as it ought
 to be, you must allow *vox.*

OLIVIA.
280   Prithee, read i' thy right wits.

CLOWN.
 So I do, madonna. But to read his right wits is to read thus; therefore
perpend, my princess, and give ear.

OLIVIA.
 [*To Fabian.*] Read it you, sirrah.

FABIAN.
 [*Reads.*] *By the Lord, madam, you wrong me, and the world shall know it. Though you have*
285   *put me into darkness and given your drunken cousin rule over me, yet have I the benefit of*
my senses as well as your ladyship. I have your own letter that induced me to the semblance
I put on; with the which I doubt not but to do myself much right or you much shame. Think
of me as you please. I leave my duty a little unthought of, and speak out of my injury.
                          The madly-used Malvolio.

OLIVIA.
290   Did he write this?

CLOWN.
 Ay, madam.

DUKE.
 This savours not much of distraction.

OLIVIA.
 See him delivered, Fabian, bring him hither.
                                                        [*Exit Fabian.*]
 My lord, so please you, these things further thought on,
295   To think me as well a sister, as a wife,
 One day shall crown th' alliance on't, so please you,
 Here at my house, and at my proper cost.

DUKE.
 Madam, I am most apt t' embrace your offer.
 [*To Viola.*] Your master quits you; and for your service done him,
300   So much against the mettle of your sex,
 So far beneath your soft and tender breeding,
 And since you call'd me master for so long,
 Here is my hand; you shall from this time be
 Your master's mistress.

OLIVIA.
305   A sister? You are she.

                  Enter Fabian and Malvolio.

DUKE.
 Is this the madman?

OLIVIA.
Ay, my lord, this same.
How now, Malvolio?

MALVOLIO.
Madam, you have done me wrong,
310   Notorious wrong.

OLIVIA.
Have I, Malvolio? No.

MALVOLIO.
Lady, you have. Pray you peruse that letter.
You must not now deny it is your hand,
Write from it, if you can, in hand, or phrase,
315   Or say 'tis not your seal, not your invention:
You can say none of this. Well, grant it then,
And tell me, in the modesty of honour,
Why you have given me such clear lights of favour,
Bade me come smiling and cross-garter'd to you,
320   To put on yellow stockings, and to frown
Upon Sir Toby, and the lighter people;
And acting this in an obedient hope,
Why have you suffer'd me to be imprison'd,
Kept in a dark house, visited by the priest,
325   And made the most notorious geck and gull
That e'er invention played on? Tell me why?

OLIVIA.
Alas, Malvolio, this is not my writing,
Though I confess, much like the character:
But out of question, 'tis Maria's hand.
330   And now I do bethink me, it was she
First told me thou wast mad; then cam'st in smiling,
And in such forms which here were presuppos'd
Upon thee in the letter. Prithee, be content.
This practice hath most shrewdly pass'd upon thee.
335   But when we know the grounds and authors of it,
Thou shalt be both the plaintiff and the judge
Of thine own cause.

FABIAN.
Good madam, hear me speak,
And let no quarrel, nor no brawl to come,
340   Taint the condition of this present hour,
Which I have wonder'd at. In hope it shall not,

Most freely I confess, myself and Toby
Set this device against Malvolio here,
Upon some stubborn and uncourteous parts
345   We had conceiv'd against him. Maria writ
The letter, at Sir Toby's great importance,
In recompense whereof he hath married her.
How with a sportful malice it was follow'd
May rather pluck on laughter than revenge,
350   If that the injuries be justly weigh'd
That have on both sides passed.

OLIVIA.
Alas, poor fool, how have they baffled thee!

CLOWN.
Why, 'some are born great, some achieve greatness, and some have great-
ness thrown upon them.' I was one, sir, in this interlude, one Sir Topas, sir,
355   but that's all one. 'By the Lord, fool, I am not mad.' But do you remember?
'Madam, why laugh you at such a barren rascal? And you smile not, he's
gagged'? And thus the whirligig of time brings in his revenges.

MALVOLIO.
I'll be revenged on the whole pack of you.

[Exit.]

OLIVIA.
He hath been most notoriously abus'd.

DUKE.
360   Pursue him, and entreat him to a peace:
He hath not told us of the captain yet.
When that is known, and golden time convents,
A solemn combination shall be made
Of our dear souls.—Meantime, sweet sister,
365   We will not part from hence.—Cesario, come:
For so you shall be while you are a man;
But when in other habits you are seen,
Orsino's mistress, and his fancy's queen.

[Exeunt.]

Clown sings:

When that I was and a little tiny boy,
370   *With hey, ho, the wind and the rain,*
  A foolish thing was but a toy,
   For the rain it raineth every day.

But when I came to man's estate,
    With hey, ho, the wind and the rain,
375   'Gainst knaves and thieves men shut their gate,
    For the rain it raineth every day.

But when I came, alas, to wive,
    With hey, ho, the wind and the rain,
By swaggering could I never thrive,
380   For the rain it raineth every day.

But when I came unto my beds,
    With hey, ho, the wind and the rain,
With toss-pots still had drunken heads,
    For the rain it raineth every day.

385   A great while ago the world begun,
    With hey, ho, the wind and the rain,
But that's all one, our play is done,
    And we'll strive to please you every day.

[Exit.]

OTHELLO

BY WILLIAM SHAKESPEARE

DRAMATIS PERSONÆ

DUKE OF VENICE
BRABANTIO, a Senator of Venice and Desdemona's father
Other Senators
GRATIANO, Brother to Brabantio
LODOVICO, Kinsman to Brabantio
OTHELLO, a noble Moor in the service of Venice
CASSIO, his Lieutenant
IAGO, his Ancient
MONTANO, Othello's predecessor in the government of Cyprus
RODERIGO, a Venetian Gentleman
CLOWN, Servant to Othello

DESDEMONA, Daughter to Brabantio and Wife to Othello
EMILIA, Wife to Iago
BIANCA, Mistress to Cassio

Officers, Gentlemen, Messenger, Musicians, Herald, Sailor, Attendants, &c.

SCENE: The First Act in Venice; during the rest of the Play at a Seaport in Cyprus.

ACT I

SCENE I. VENICE. A STREET.
Enter Roderigo and Iago.

RODERIGO.
Tush, never tell me, I take it much unkindly
That thou, Iago, who hast had my purse,
As if the strings were thine, shouldst know of this.

IAGO.
'Sblood, but you will not hear me.
5   If ever I did dream of such a matter,
Abhor me.

RODERIGO.
Thou told'st me, thou didst hold him in thy hate.

IAGO.
Despise me if I do not. Three great ones of the city,
In personal suit to make me his lieutenant,
10   Off-capp'd to him; and by the faith of man,
I know my price, I am worth no worse a place.
But he, as loving his own pride and purposes,
Evades them, with a bombast circumstance,
Horribly stuff'd with epithets of war:
15   And in conclusion,
Nonsuits my mediators: for "Certes," says he,
"I have already chose my officer."
And what was he?
Forsooth, a great arithmetician,
20   One Michael Cassio, a Florentine,
A fellow almost damn'd in a fair wife,
That never set a squadron in the field,
Nor the division of a battle knows
More than a spinster, unless the bookish theoric,
25   Wherein the toged consuls can propose
As masterly as he: mere prattle without practice
Is all his soldiership. But he, sir, had the election,
And I, of whom his eyes had seen the proof
At Rhodes, at Cyprus, and on other grounds,
30   Christian and heathen, must be belee'd and calm'd
By debitor and creditor, this counter-caster,
He, in good time, must his lieutenant be,
And I, God bless the mark, his Moorship's ancient.

RODERIGO.
By heaven, I rather would have been his hangman.

IAGO.
35   Why, there's no remedy. 'Tis the curse of service,
Preferment goes by letter and affection,
And not by old gradation, where each second
Stood heir to the first. Now sir, be judge yourself
Whether I in any just term am affin'd
40   To love the Moor.

RODERIGO.
I would not follow him, then.

IAGO.
O, sir, content you.
I follow him to serve my turn upon him:
We cannot all be masters, nor all masters

45 Cannot be truly follow'd. You shall mark
Many a duteous and knee-crooking knave
That, doting on his own obsequious bondage,
Wears out his time, much like his master's ass,
For nought but provender, and when he's old, cashier'd.
50 Whip me such honest knaves. Others there are
Who, trimm'd in forms, and visages of duty,
Keep yet their hearts attending on themselves,
And throwing but shows of service on their lords,
Do well thrive by them, and when they have lin'd their coats,
55 Do themselves homage. These fellows have some soul,
And such a one do I profess myself. For, sir,
It is as sure as you are Roderigo,
Were I the Moor, I would not be Iago:
In following him, I follow but myself.
60 Heaven is my judge, not I for love and duty,
But seeming so for my peculiar end.
For when my outward action doth demonstrate
The native act and figure of my heart
In complement extern, 'tis not long after
65 But I will wear my heart upon my sleeve
For daws to peck at: I am not what I am.

RODERIGO.
What a full fortune does the thick-lips owe,
If he can carry't thus!

IAGO.
Call up her father,
70 Rouse him, make after him, poison his delight,
Proclaim him in the streets; incense her kinsmen,
And though he in a fertile climate dwell,
Plague him with flies: though that his joy be joy,
Yet throw such changes of vexation on't,
75 As it may lose some color.

RODERIGO.
Here is her father's house, I'll call aloud.

IAGO.
Do, with like timorous accent and dire yell
As when, by night and negligence, the fire
Is spied in populous cities.

RODERIGO.
80 What ho, Brabantio! Signior Brabantio, ho!

IAGO.
Awake! what ho, Brabantio! Thieves, thieves!
Look to your house, your daughter, and your bags!
Thieves, thieves!

Brabantio appears above at a window.

BRABANTIO.
What is the reason of this terrible summons?
85   What is the matter there?

RODERIGO.
Signior, is all your family within?

IAGO.
Are your doors locked?

BRABANTIO.
Why, wherefore ask you this?

IAGO.
Zounds, sir, you're robb'd, for shame put on your gown,
90   Your heart is burst, you have lost half your soul;
Even now, now, very now, an old black ram
Is tupping your white ewe. Arise, arise,
Awake the snorting citizens with the bell,
Or else the devil will make a grandsire of you:
95   Arise, I say.

BRABANTIO.
What, have you lost your wits?

RODERIGO.
Most reverend signior, do you know my voice?

BRABANTIO.
Not I. What are you?

RODERIGO.
My name is Roderigo.

BRABANTIO.
100   The worser welcome.
I have charg'd thee not to haunt about my doors;
In honest plainness thou hast heard me say
My daughter is not for thee; and now in madness,
Being full of supper and distempering draughts,

105 Upon malicious bravery, dost thou come
To start my quiet.

RODERIGO.
Sir, sir, sir,—

BRABANTIO.
But thou must needs be sure
My spirit and my place have in them power
110 To make this bitter to thee.

RODERIGO.
Patience, good sir.

BRABANTIO.
What tell'st thou me of robbing?
This is Venice. My house is not a grange.

RODERIGO.
Most grave Brabantio,
115 In simple and pure soul I come to you.

IAGO.
Zounds, sir, you are one of those that will not serve God if the devil bid you. Because we come to do you service, and you think we are ruffians, you'll have your daughter cover'd with a Barbary horse; you'll have your nephews neigh to you; you'll have coursers for cousins and gennets for germans.

BRABANTIO.
120 What profane wretch art thou?

IAGO.
I am one, sir, that comes to tell you your daughter and the Moor are now making the beast with two backs.

BRABANTIO.
Thou art a villain.

IAGO.
You are a senator.

BRABANTIO.
125 This thou shalt answer. I know thee, Roderigo.

RODERIGO.
Sir, I will answer anything. But I beseech you,
If 't be your pleasure, and most wise consent,
(As partly I find it is) that your fair daughter,

At this odd-even and dull watch o' the night,
130   Transported with no worse nor better guard,
But with a knave of common hire, a gondolier,
To the gross clasps of a lascivious Moor:
If this be known to you, and your allowance,
We then have done you bold and saucy wrongs.
135   But if you know not this, my manners tell me,
We have your wrong rebuke. Do not believe
That from the sense of all civility,
I thus would play and trifle with your reverence.
Your daughter (if you have not given her leave)
140   I say again, hath made a gross revolt,
Tying her duty, beauty, wit, and fortunes
In an extravagant and wheeling stranger
Of here and everywhere. Straight satisfy yourself:
If she be in her chamber or your house,
145   Let loose on me the justice of the state
For thus deluding you.

BRABANTIO.
Strike on the tinder, ho!
Give me a taper! Call up all my people!
This accident is not unlike my dream,
150   Belief of it oppresses me already.
Light, I say, light!

                                        [Exit from above.]

IAGO.
Farewell; for I must leave you:
It seems not meet nor wholesome to my place
To be produc'd, as if I stay I shall,
155   Against the Moor. For I do know the state,
However this may gall him with some check,
Cannot with safety cast him, for he's embark'd
With such loud reason to the Cyprus wars,
Which even now stand in act, that, for their souls,
160   Another of his fathom they have none
To lead their business. In which regard,
Though I do hate him as I do hell pains,
Yet, for necessity of present life,
I must show out a flag and sign of love,
165   Which is indeed but sign. That you shall surely find him,
Lead to the Sagittary the raised search,
And there will I be with him. So, farewell.

                                              [Exit.]

Enter Brabantio with Servants and torches.

BRABANTIO.
It is too true an evil. Gone she is,
And what's to come of my despised time,
170   Is naught but bitterness. Now Roderigo,
Where didst thou see her? (O unhappy girl!)
With the Moor, say'st thou? (Who would be a father!)
How didst thou know 'twas she? (O, she deceives me
Past thought.) What said she to you? Get more tapers,
175   Raise all my kindred. Are they married, think you?

RODERIGO.
Truly I think they are.

BRABANTIO.
O heaven! How got she out? O treason of the blood!
Fathers, from hence trust not your daughters' minds
By what you see them act. Is there not charms
180   By which the property of youth and maidhood
May be abused? Have you not read, Roderigo,
Of some such thing?

RODERIGO.
Yes, sir, I have indeed.

BRABANTIO.
Call up my brother. O, would you had had her!
185   Some one way, some another. Do you know
Where we may apprehend her and the Moor?

RODERIGO.
I think I can discover him, if you please
To get good guard, and go along with me.

BRABANTIO.
Pray you lead on. At every house I'll call,
190   I may command at most. Get weapons, ho!
And raise some special officers of night.
On, good Roderigo. I will deserve your pains.

[Exeunt.]

SCENE II. VENICE. ANOTHER STREET.
Enter Othello, Iago and Attendants with torches.

IAGO.
Though in the trade of war I have slain men,
Yet do I hold it very stuff o' the conscience
To do no contriv'd murder; I lack iniquity
Sometimes to do me service: nine or ten times
5   I had thought to have yerk'd him here under the ribs.

OTHELLO.
'Tis better as it is.

IAGO.
Nay, but he prated,
And spoke such scurvy and provoking terms
Against your honour,
10   That with the little godliness I have,
I did full hard forbear him. But I pray you, sir,
Are you fast married? Be assur'd of this,
That the magnifico is much belov'd
And hath in his effect a voice potential
15   As double as the duke's; he will divorce you,
Or put upon you what restraint and grievance
The law (with all his might to enforce it on)
Will give him cable.

OTHELLO.
Let him do his spite;
20   My services, which I have done the signiory,
Shall out-tongue his complaints. 'Tis yet to know,—
Which, when I know that boasting is an honour,
I shall promulgate,—I fetch my life and being
From men of royal siege. And my demerits
25   May speak unbonneted to as proud a fortune
As this that I have reach'd. For know, Iago,
But that I love the gentle Desdemona,
I would not my unhoused free condition
Put into circumscription and confine
30   For the sea's worth. But look, what lights come yond?

IAGO.
Those are the raised father and his friends:
You were best go in.

OTHELLO.
 Not I; I must be found.
 My parts, my title, and my perfect soul
35 Shall manifest me rightly. Is it they?

IAGO.
 By Janus, I think no.

Enter Cassio and Officers with torches.

OTHELLO.
 The servants of the duke and my lieutenant.
 The goodness of the night upon you, friends!
 What is the news?

CASSIO.
40 The duke does greet you, general,
 And he requires your haste-post-haste appearance
 Even on the instant.

OTHELLO.
 What is the matter, think you?

CASSIO.
 Something from Cyprus, as I may divine.
45 It is a business of some heat. The galleys
 Have sent a dozen sequent messengers
 This very night at one another's heels;
 And many of the consuls, rais'd and met,
 Are at the duke's already. You have been hotly call'd for,
50 When, being not at your lodging to be found,
 The senate hath sent about three several quests
 To search you out.

OTHELLO.
 'Tis well I am found by you.
 I will but spend a word here in the house,
55 And go with you.

[Exit.]

CASSIO.
 Ancient, what makes he here?

IAGO.
 Faith, he tonight hath boarded a land carrack:
 If it prove lawful prize, he's made forever.

CASSIO.
I do not understand.

IAGO.
60   He's married.

CASSIO.
To who?

Enter Othello.

IAGO.
Marry to—Come, captain, will you go?

OTHELLO.
Have with you.

CASSIO.
Here comes another troop to seek for you.

Enter Brabantio, Roderigo and Officers with torches and weapons.

IAGO.
65   It is Brabantio. General, be advis'd,
He comes to bad intent.

OTHELLO.
Holla, stand there!

RODERIGO.
Signior, it is the Moor.

BRABANTIO.
Down with him, thief!

[They draw on both sides.]

IAGO.
70   You, Roderigo! Come, sir, I am for you.

OTHELLO.
Keep up your bright swords, for the dew will rust them.
Good signior, you shall more command with years
Than with your weapons.

BRABANTIO.
O thou foul thief, where hast thou stow'd my daughter?
75   Damn'd as thou art, thou hast enchanted her,
For I'll refer me to all things of sense,
(If she in chains of magic were not bound)

Whether a maid so tender, fair, and happy,
So opposite to marriage, that she shunn'd
80   The wealthy curled darlings of our nation,
Would ever have, to incur a general mock,
Run from her guardage to the sooty bosom
Of such a thing as thou—to fear, not to delight.
Judge me the world, if 'tis not gross in sense,
85   That thou hast practis'd on her with foul charms,
Abus'd her delicate youth with drugs or minerals
That weakens motion. I'll have't disputed on;
'Tis probable, and palpable to thinking.
I therefore apprehend and do attach thee
90   For an abuser of the world, a practiser
Of arts inhibited and out of warrant.—
Lay hold upon him, if he do resist,
Subdue him at his peril.

OTHELLO.
Hold your hands,
95   Both you of my inclining and the rest:
Were it my cue to fight, I should have known it
Without a prompter. Where will you that I go
To answer this your charge?

BRABANTIO.
To prison, till fit time
100   Of law and course of direct session
Call thee to answer.

OTHELLO.
What if I do obey?
How may the duke be therewith satisfied,
Whose messengers are here about my side,
105   Upon some present business of the state,
To bring me to him?

OFFICER.
'Tis true, most worthy signior,
The duke's in council, and your noble self,
I am sure is sent for.

BRABANTIO.
110   How? The duke in council?
In this time of the night? Bring him away;
Mine's not an idle cause. The duke himself,
Or any of my brothers of the state,
Cannot but feel this wrong as 'twere their own.

115 For if such actions may have passage free,
Bond-slaves and pagans shall our statesmen be.

[*Exeunt.*]

SCENE III. VENICE. A COUNCIL CHAMBER.
The Duke and Senators sitting at a table; Officers attending.

DUKE.
There is no composition in these news
That gives them credit.

FIRST SENATOR.
Indeed, they are disproportion'd;
My letters say a hundred and seven galleys.

DUKE.
5 And mine a hundred and forty.

SECOND SENATOR
And mine two hundred:
But though they jump not on a just account,
(As in these cases, where the aim reports,
'Tis oft with difference,) yet do they all confirm
10 A Turkish fleet, and bearing up to Cyprus.

DUKE.
Nay, it is possible enough to judgement:
I do not so secure me in the error,
But the main article I do approve
In fearful sense.

SAILOR.
15 [*Within.*] What, ho! what, ho! what, ho!

OFFICER.
A messenger from the galleys.

Enter Sailor.

DUKE.
Now,—what's the business?

SAILOR.
The Turkish preparation makes for Rhodes,
So was I bid report here to the state
20 By Signior Angelo.

DUKE.
How say you by this change?

FIRST SENATOR.
This cannot be
By no assay of reason. 'Tis a pageant
To keep us in false gaze. When we consider
25 The importancy of Cyprus to the Turk;
And let ourselves again but understand
That, as it more concerns the Turk than Rhodes,
So may he with more facile question bear it,
For that it stands not in such warlike brace,
30 But altogether lacks the abilities
That Rhodes is dress'd in. If we make thought of this,
We must not think the Turk is so unskilful
To leave that latest which concerns him first,
Neglecting an attempt of ease and gain,
35 To wake and wage a danger profitless.

DUKE.
Nay, in all confidence, he's not for Rhodes.

OFFICER.
Here is more news.

Enter a Messenger.

MESSENGER.
The Ottomites, reverend and gracious,
Steering with due course toward the isle of Rhodes,
40 Have there injointed them with an after fleet.

FIRST SENATOR.
Ay, so I thought. How many, as you guess?

MESSENGER.
Of thirty sail, and now they do re-stem
Their backward course, bearing with frank appearance
Their purposes toward Cyprus. Signior Montano,
45 Your trusty and most valiant servitor,
With his free duty recommends you thus,
And prays you to believe him.

DUKE.
'Tis certain, then, for Cyprus.
Marcus Luccicos, is not he in town?

FIRST SENATOR.
50 He's now in Florence.

DUKE.
Write from us to him; post-post-haste dispatch.

FIRST SENATOR.
Here comes Brabantio and the valiant Moor.

Enter Brabantio, Othello, Iago, Roderigo and Officers.

DUKE.
Valiant Othello, we must straight employ you
Against the general enemy Ottoman.
55 [*To Brabantio.*] I did not see you; welcome, gentle signior,
We lack'd your counsel and your help tonight.

BRABANTIO.
So did I yours. Good your grace, pardon me.
Neither my place, nor aught I heard of business
Hath rais'd me from my bed, nor doth the general care
60 Take hold on me; for my particular grief
Is of so flood-gate and o'erbearing nature
That it engluts and swallows other sorrows,
And it is still itself.

DUKE.
Why, what's the matter?

BRABANTIO.
65 My daughter! O, my daughter!

DUKE and SENATORS.
Dead?

BRABANTIO.
Ay, to me.
She is abused, stol'n from me, and corrupted
By spells and medicines bought of mountebanks;
70 For nature so preposterously to err,
Being not deficient, blind, or lame of sense,
Sans witchcraft could not.

DUKE.
Whoe'er he be, that in this foul proceeding,
Hath thus beguil'd your daughter of herself,
75 And you of her, the bloody book of law
You shall yourself read in the bitter letter,
After your own sense, yea, though our proper son
Stood in your action.

BRABANTIO.
Humbly I thank your grace.
80 Here is the man, this Moor, whom now it seems

Your special mandate for the state affairs
Hath hither brought.

ALL.
We are very sorry for 't.

DUKE.
[*To Othello.*] What, in your own part, can you say to this?

BRABANTIO.
85 Nothing, but this is so.

OTHELLO.
Most potent, grave, and reverend signiors,
My very noble and approv'd good masters:
That I have ta'en away this old man's daughter,
It is most true; true, I have married her.
90 The very head and front of my offending
Hath this extent, no more. Rude am I in my speech,
And little bless'd with the soft phrase of peace;
For since these arms of mine had seven years' pith,
Till now some nine moons wasted, they have us'd
95 Their dearest action in the tented field,
And little of this great world can I speak,
More than pertains to feats of broil and battle,
And therefore little shall I grace my cause
In speaking for myself. Yet, by your gracious patience,
100 I will a round unvarnish'd tale deliver
Of my whole course of love: what drugs, what charms,
What conjuration, and what mighty magic,
(For such proceeding I am charged withal)
I won his daughter.

BRABANTIO.
105 A maiden never bold:
Of spirit so still and quiet that her motion
Blush'd at herself; and she, in spite of nature,
Of years, of country, credit, everything,
To fall in love with what she fear'd to look on!
110 It is judgement maim'd and most imperfect
That will confess perfection so could err
Against all rules of nature, and must be driven
To find out practices of cunning hell,
Why this should be. I therefore vouch again,
115 That with some mixtures powerful o'er the blood,
Or with some dram conjur'd to this effect,
He wrought upon her.

DUKE.
 To vouch this is no proof;
 Without more wider and more overt test
120 Than these thin habits and poor likelihoods
 Of modern seeming do prefer against him.

FIRST SENATOR.
 But, Othello, speak:
 Did you by indirect and forced courses
 Subdue and poison this young maid's affections?
125 Or came it by request, and such fair question
 As soul to soul affordeth?

OTHELLO.
 I do beseech you,
 Send for the lady to the Sagittary,
 And let her speak of me before her father.
130 If you do find me foul in her report,
 The trust, the office I do hold of you,
 Not only take away, but let your sentence
 Even fall upon my life.

DUKE.
 Fetch Desdemona hither.

OTHELLO.
135 Ancient, conduct them, you best know the place.

                               [*Exeunt Iago and Attendants.*]

 And till she come, as truly as to heaven
 I do confess the vices of my blood,
 So justly to your grave ears I'll present
 How I did thrive in this fair lady's love,
140 And she in mine.

DUKE.
 Say it, Othello.

OTHELLO.
 Her father lov'd me, oft invited me,
 Still question'd me the story of my life,
 From year to year—the battles, sieges, fortunes,
 That I have pass'd.
145 I ran it through, even from my boyish days
 To the very moment that he bade me tell it,
 Wherein I spake of most disastrous chances,
 Of moving accidents by flood and field;
 Of hair-breadth scapes i' th' imminent deadly breach;

150 Of being taken by the insolent foe,
And sold to slavery, of my redemption thence,
And portance in my traveler's history,
Wherein of antres vast and deserts idle,
Rough quarries, rocks, and hills whose heads touch heaven,
155 It was my hint to speak,—such was the process;
And of the Cannibals that each other eat,
The Anthropophagi, and men whose heads
Do grow beneath their shoulders. This to hear
Would Desdemona seriously incline.
160 But still the house affairs would draw her thence,
Which ever as she could with haste dispatch,
She'd come again, and with a greedy ear
Devour up my discourse; which I observing,
Took once a pliant hour, and found good means
165 To draw from her a prayer of earnest heart
That I would all my pilgrimage dilate,
Whereof by parcels she had something heard,
But not intentively. I did consent,
And often did beguile her of her tears,
170 When I did speak of some distressful stroke
That my youth suffer'd. My story being done,
She gave me for my pains a world of sighs.
She swore, in faith, 'twas strange, 'twas passing strange;
'Twas pitiful, 'twas wondrous pitiful.
175 She wish'd she had not heard it, yet she wish'd
That heaven had made her such a man: she thank'd me,
And bade me, if I had a friend that lov'd her,
I should but teach him how to tell my story,
And that would woo her. Upon this hint I spake:
180 She lov'd me for the dangers I had pass'd,
And I lov'd her that she did pity them.
This only is the witchcraft I have us'd.
Here comes the lady. Let her witness it.

Enter Desdemona, Iago and Attendants.

DUKE.
I think this tale would win my daughter too.
185 Good Brabantio,
Take up this mangled matter at the best.
Men do their broken weapons rather use
Than their bare hands.

BRABANTIO.
I pray you hear her speak.

190   If she confess that she was half the wooer,
Destruction on my head, if my bad blame
Light on the man!—Come hither, gentle mistress:
Do you perceive in all this noble company
Where most you owe obedience?

DESDEMONA.
195   My noble father,
I do perceive here a divided duty:
To you I am bound for life and education.
My life and education both do learn me
How to respect you. You are the lord of duty,
200   I am hitherto your daughter: but here's my husband.
And so much duty as my mother show'd
To you, preferring you before her father,
So much I challenge that I may profess
Due to the Moor my lord.

BRABANTIO.
205   God be with you! I have done.
Please it your grace, on to the state affairs.
I had rather to adopt a child than get it.—
Come hither, Moor:
I here do give thee that with all my heart
210   Which, but thou hast already, with all my heart
I would keep from thee.—For your sake, jewel,
I am glad at soul I have no other child,
For thy escape would teach me tyranny,
To hang clogs on them.—I have done, my lord.

DUKE.
215   Let me speak like yourself, and lay a sentence,
Which as a grise or step may help these lovers
Into your favour.
When remedies are past, the griefs are ended
By seeing the worst, which late on hopes depended.
220   To mourn a mischief that is past and gone
Is the next way to draw new mischief on.
What cannot be preserved when fortune takes,
Patience her injury a mockery makes.
The robb'd that smiles steals something from the thief;
225   He robs himself that spends a bootless grief.

BRABANTIO.
So let the Turk of Cyprus us beguile,
We lose it not so long as we can smile;

He bears the sentence well, that nothing bears
But the free comfort which from thence he hears;
230   But he bears both the sentence and the sorrow
That, to pay grief, must of poor patience borrow.
These sentences to sugar or to gall,
Being strong on both sides, are equivocal:
But words are words; I never yet did hear
235   That the bruis'd heart was pierced through the ear.
I humbly beseech you, proceed to the affairs of state.

DUKE.
The Turk with a most mighty preparation makes for Cyprus. Othello, the
fortitude of the place is best known to you. And though we have there a sub-
stitute of most allowed sufficiency, yet opinion, a sovereign mistress of effects,
240   throws a more safer voice on you: you must therefore be content to slubber the
gloss of your new fortunes with this more stubborn and boisterous expedition.

OTHELLO.
The tyrant custom, most grave senators,
Hath made the flinty and steel couch of war
My thrice-driven bed of down: I do agnize
245   A natural and prompt alacrity
I find in hardness, and do undertake
This present wars against the Ottomites.
Most humbly, therefore, bending to your state,
I crave fit disposition for my wife,
250   Due reference of place and exhibition,
With such accommodation and besort
As levels with her breeding.

DUKE.
If you please,
Be't at her father's.

BRABANTIO.
255   I'll not have it so.

OTHELLO.
Nor I.

DESDEMONA.
Nor I. I would not there reside,
To put my father in impatient thoughts,
By being in his eye. Most gracious duke,
260   To my unfolding lend your prosperous ear,
And let me find a charter in your voice
T' assist my simpleness.

DUKE.
What would you, Desdemona?

DESDEMONA.
That I did love the Moor to live with him,
265   My downright violence and storm of fortunes
May trumpet to the world: my heart's subdued
Even to the very quality of my lord.
I saw Othello's visage in his mind,
And to his honours and his valiant parts
270   Did I my soul and fortunes consecrate.
So that, dear lords, if I be left behind,
A moth of peace, and he go to the war,
The rites for which I love him are bereft me,
And I a heavy interim shall support
275   By his dear absence. Let me go with him.

OTHELLO.
Let her have your voice.
Vouch with me, heaven, I therefore beg it not
To please the palate of my appetite,
Nor to comply with heat, the young affects
280   In me defunct, and proper satisfaction,
But to be free and bounteous to her mind.
And heaven defend your good souls that you think
I will your serious and great business scant
For she is with me. No, when light-wing'd toys
285   Of feather'd Cupid seel with wanton dullness
My speculative and offic'd instruments,
That my disports corrupt and taint my business,
Let housewives make a skillet of my helm,
And all indign and base adversities
290   Make head against my estimation.

DUKE.
Be it as you shall privately determine,
Either for her stay or going. The affair cries haste,
And speed must answer it.

FIRST SENATOR.
You must away tonight.

OTHELLO.
295   With all my heart.

DUKE.
At nine i' the morning here we'll meet again.

Othello, leave some officer behind,
And he shall our commission bring to you,
With such things else of quality and respect
300 As doth import you.

OTHELLO.
So please your grace, my ancient,
A man he is of honesty and trust,
To his conveyance I assign my wife,
With what else needful your good grace shall think
305 To be sent after me.

DUKE.
Let it be so.
Good night to everyone. [*To Brabantio.*] And, noble signior,
If virtue no delighted beauty lack,
Your son-in-law is far more fair than black.

FIRST SENATOR.
310 Adieu, brave Moor, use Desdemona well.

BRABANTIO.
Look to her, Moor, if thou hast eyes to see:
She has deceiv'd her father, and may thee.
[*Exeunt Duke, Senators, Officers, &c.*]

OTHELLO.
My life upon her faith! Honest Iago,
My Desdemona must I leave to thee.
315 I prithee, let thy wife attend on her,
And bring them after in the best advantage.—
Come, Desdemona, I have but an hour
Of love, of worldly matters, and direction,
To spend with thee. We must obey the time.
[*Exeunt Othello and Desdemona.*]

RODERIGO.
320 Iago—

IAGO.
What sayst thou, noble heart?

RODERIGO.
What will I do, thinkest thou?

IAGO.
Why, go to bed and sleep.

RODERIGO.
I will incontinently drown myself.

IAGO.
325   If thou dost, I shall never love thee after. Why, thou silly gentleman!

RODERIGO.
It is silliness to live, when to live is torment; and then have we a prescription to die when death is our physician.

IAGO.
O villainous! I have looked upon the world for four times seven years, and since I could distinguish betwixt a benefit and an injury, I never found man
330   that knew how to love himself. Ere I would say I would drown myself for the love of a guinea-hen, I would change my humanity with a baboon.

RODERIGO.
What should I do? I confess it is my shame to be so fond, but it is not in my virtue to amend it.

IAGO.
Virtue! a fig! 'Tis in ourselves that we are thus or thus. Our bodies are gar-
335   dens, to the which our wills are gardeners. So that if we will plant nettles or sow lettuce, set hyssop and weed up thyme, supply it with one gender of herbs or distract it with many, either to have it sterile with idleness or manured with industry, why, the power and corrigible authority of this lies in our wills. If the balance of our lives had not one scale of reason to
340   poise another of sensuality, the blood and baseness of our natures would conduct us to most preposterous conclusions. But we have reason to cool our raging motions, our carnal stings, our unbitted lusts; whereof I take this, that you call love, to be a sect, or scion.

RODERIGO.
It cannot be.

IAGO.
345   It is merely a lust of the blood and a permission of the will. Come, be a man. Drown thyself? Drown cats and blind puppies. I have professed me thy friend, and I confess me knit to thy deserving with cables of perdura-ble toughness; I could never better stead thee than now. Put money in thy purse; follow thou the wars; defeat thy favour with an usurped beard; I say,
350   put money in thy purse. It cannot be that Desdemona should long continue her love to the Moor,—put money in thy purse,—nor he his to her. It was a violent commencement, and thou shalt see an answerable sequestration— put but money in thy purse. These Moors are changeable in their wills. Fill thy purse with money. The food that to him now is as luscious as locusts
355   shall be to him shortly as acerb as the coloquintida. She must change for

youth. When she is sated with his body, she will find the error of her choice. She must have change, she must. Therefore put money in thy purse. If thou wilt needs damn thyself, do it a more delicate way than drowning. Make all the money thou canst. If sanctimony and a frail vow betwixt an erring
360 barbarian and a supersubtle Venetian be not too hard for my wits and all the tribe of hell, thou shalt enjoy her; therefore make money. A pox of drowning thyself! It is clean out of the way: seek thou rather to be hanged in compassing thy joy than to be drowned and go without her.

RODERIGO.
 Wilt thou be fast to my hopes if I depend on the issue?

IAGO.
365 Thou art sure of me. Go, make money. I have told thee often, and I retell thee again and again, I hate the Moor. My cause is hearted; thine hath no less reason. Let us be conjunctive in our revenge against him: if thou canst cuckold him, thou dost thyself a pleasure, me a sport. There are many events in the womb of time which will be delivered. Traverse, go,
370 provide thy money. We will have more of this tomorrow. Adieu.

RODERIGO.
 Where shall we meet i' the morning?

IAGO.
 At my lodging.

RODERIGO.
 I'll be with thee betimes.

IAGO.
 Go to, farewell. Do you hear, Roderigo?

RODERIGO.
375 What say you?

IAGO.
 No more of drowning, do you hear?

RODERIGO.
 I am changed. I'll sell all my land.

[Exit.]

IAGO.
 Thus do I ever make my fool my purse.
 For I mine own gain'd knowledge should profane
380 If I would time expend with such a snipe
 But for my sport and profit. I hate the Moor,
 And it is thought abroad that 'twixt my sheets
 He has done my office. I know not if 't be true,

But I, for mere suspicion in that kind,
385 Will do as if for surety. He holds me well,
The better shall my purpose work on him.
Cassio's a proper man. Let me see now,
To get his place, and to plume up my will
In double knavery. How, how? Let's see.
390 After some time, to abuse Othello's ear
That he is too familiar with his wife.
He hath a person and a smooth dispose,
To be suspected, fram'd to make women false.
The Moor is of a free and open nature
395 That thinks men honest that but seem to be so,
And will as tenderly be led by the nose
As asses are.
I have't. It is engender'd. Hell and night
Must bring this monstrous birth to the world's light.

[Exit.]

ACT II

SCENE I. A seaport in Cyprus. A Platform.
Enter Montano and two Gentlemen.

MONTANO.
What from the cape can you discern at sea?

FIRST GENTLEMAN.
Nothing at all, it is a high-wrought flood.
I cannot 'twixt the heaven and the main
Descry a sail.

MONTANO.
5 Methinks the wind hath spoke aloud at land.
A fuller blast ne'er shook our battlements.
If it hath ruffian'd so upon the sea,
What ribs of oak, when mountains melt on them,
Can hold the mortise? What shall we hear of this?

SECOND GENTLEMAN.
10 A segregation of the Turkish fleet.
For do but stand upon the foaming shore,
The chidden billow seems to pelt the clouds,
The wind-shak'd surge, with high and monstrous main,
Seems to cast water on the burning Bear,
15 And quench the guards of the ever-fixed pole;
I never did like molestation view
On the enchafed flood.

MONTANO.
 If that the Turkish fleet
 Be not enshelter'd, and embay'd, they are drown'd.
20 It is impossible to bear it out.

Enter a third Gentleman.

THIRD GENTLEMAN.
 News, lads! Our wars are done.
 The desperate tempest hath so bang'd the Turks
 That their designment halts. A noble ship of Venice
 Hath seen a grievous wreck and sufferance
25 On most part of their fleet.

MONTANO.
 How? Is this true?

THIRD GENTLEMAN.
 The ship is here put in,
 A Veronessa; Michael Cassio,
 Lieutenant to the warlike Moor Othello,
30 Is come on shore; the Moor himself at sea,
 And is in full commission here for Cyprus.

MONTANO.
 I am glad on't. 'Tis a worthy governor.

THIRD GENTLEMAN.
 But this same Cassio, though he speak of comfort
 Touching the Turkish loss, yet he looks sadly,
35 And prays the Moor be safe; for they were parted
 With foul and violent tempest.

MONTANO.
 Pray heavens he be;
 For I have serv'd him, and the man commands
 Like a full soldier. Let's to the sea-side, ho!
40 As well to see the vessel that's come in
 As to throw out our eyes for brave Othello,
 Even till we make the main and the aerial blue
 An indistinct regard.

THIRD GENTLEMAN.
 Come, let's do so;
45 For every minute is expectancy
 Of more arrivance.

Enter Cassio.

CASSIO.
Thanks, you the valiant of this warlike isle,
That so approve the Moor! O, let the heavens
Give him defence against the elements,
50   For I have lost him on a dangerous sea.

MONTANO.
Is he well shipp'd?

CASSIO.
His bark is stoutly timber'd, and his pilot
Of very expert and approv'd allowance;
Therefore my hopes, not surfeited to death,
55   Stand in bold cure.

                                    [*Within.*] A sail, a sail, a sail!

                Enter a Messenger.

CASSIO.
What noise?

MESSENGER.
The town is empty; on the brow o' the sea
Stand ranks of people, and they cry "A sail!"

CASSIO.
My hopes do shape him for the governor.

                                              [*A shot.*]

SECOND GENTLEMAN.
60   They do discharge their shot of courtesy.
Our friends at least.

CASSIO.
I pray you, sir, go forth,
And give us truth who 'tis that is arriv'd.

SECOND GENTLEMAN.
I shall.

                                              [*Exit.*]

MONTANO.
65   But, good lieutenant, is your general wiv'd?

CASSIO.
Most fortunately: he hath achiev'd a maid
That paragons description and wild fame,
One that excels the quirks of blazoning pens,

And in the essential vesture of creation
70   Does tire the ingener.

Enter second Gentleman.

How now? Who has put in?

SECOND GENTLEMAN.
 'Tis one Iago, ancient to the general.

CASSIO.
 He has had most favourable and happy speed:
 Tempests themselves, high seas, and howling winds,
75   The gutter'd rocks, and congregated sands,
 Traitors ensteep'd to clog the guiltless keel,
 As having sense of beauty, do omit
 Their mortal natures, letting go safely by
 The divine Desdemona.

MONTANO.
80   What is she?

CASSIO.
 She that I spake of, our great captain's captain,
 Left in the conduct of the bold Iago;
 Whose footing here anticipates our thoughts
 A se'nnight's speed. Great Jove, Othello guard,
85   And swell his sail with thine own powerful breath,
 That he may bless this bay with his tall ship,
 Make love's quick pants in Desdemona's arms,
 Give renew'd fire to our extincted spirits,
 And bring all Cyprus comfort!

Enter Desdemona, Iago, Roderigo, and Emilia.

90   O, behold,
 The riches of the ship is come on shore!
 Ye men of Cyprus, let her have your knees.
 Hail to thee, lady! and the grace of heaven,
 Before, behind thee, and on every hand,
95   Enwheel thee round!

DESDEMONA.
 I thank you, valiant Cassio.
 What tidings can you tell me of my lord?

CASSIO.
 He is not yet arrived, nor know I aught
 But that he's well, and will be shortly here.

DESDEMONA.
100   O, but I fear—How lost you company?

                                          [*Within.*] A sail, a sail!

CASSIO.
 The great contention of the sea and skies
 Parted our fellowship. But, hark! a sail.

                                          [*Guns within.*]

SECOND GENTLEMAN.
 They give their greeting to the citadel.
 This likewise is a friend.

CASSIO.
105   See for the news.

                                          [*Exit Gentleman.*]
 Good ancient, you are welcome. [*To Emilia.*] Welcome, mistress.
 Let it not gall your patience, good Iago,
 That I extend my manners; 'tis my breeding
 That gives me this bold show of courtesy.

                                          [*Kissing her.*]

IAGO.
110   Sir, would she give you so much of her lips
 As of her tongue she oft bestows on me,
 You would have enough.

DESDEMONA.
 Alas, she has no speech.

IAGO.
 In faith, too much.
115   I find it still when I have list to sleep.
 Marry, before your ladyship, I grant,
 She puts her tongue a little in her heart,
 And chides with thinking.

EMILIA.
 You have little cause to say so.

IAGO.
120   Come on, come on; you are pictures out of doors,
 Bells in your parlours, wild-cats in your kitchens,
 Saints in your injuries, devils being offended,
 Players in your housewifery, and housewives in your beds.

DESDEMONA.
 O, fie upon thee, slanderer!

IAGO.
125   Nay, it is true, or else I am a Turk.
       You rise to play, and go to bed to work.

EMILIA.
       You shall not write my praise.

IAGO.
       No, let me not.

DESDEMONA.
       What wouldst thou write of me, if thou shouldst praise me?

IAGO.
130   O gentle lady, do not put me to't,
       For I am nothing if not critical.

DESDEMONA.
       Come on, assay.—There's one gone to the harbour?

IAGO.
       Ay, madam.

DESDEMONA.
       I am not merry, but I do beguile
135   The thing I am, by seeming otherwise.—
       Come, how wouldst thou praise me?

IAGO.
       I am about it, but indeed, my invention
       Comes from my pate as birdlime does from frieze,
       It plucks out brains and all: but my Muse labours,
140   And thus she is deliver'd.
       If she be fair and wise, fairness and wit,
       The one's for use, the other useth it.

DESDEMONA.
       Well prais'd! How if she be black and witty?

IAGO.
       If she be black, and thereto have a wit,
145   She'll find a white that shall her blackness fit.

DESDEMONA.
       Worse and worse.

EMILIA.
       How if fair and foolish?

IAGO.
She never yet was foolish that was fair,
For even her folly help'd her to an heir.

DESDEMONA.
150   These are old fond paradoxes to make fools laugh i' the alehouse. What
miserable praise hast thou for her that's foul and foolish?

IAGO.
There's none so foul and foolish thereunto,
But does foul pranks which fair and wise ones do.

DESDEMONA.
O heavy ignorance! Thou praisest the worst best. But what praise couldst
155   thou bestow on a deserving woman indeed, one that in the authority of her
merit did justly put on the vouch of very malice itself?

IAGO.
She that was ever fair and never proud,
Had tongue at will and yet was never loud,
Never lack'd gold and yet went never gay,
160   Fled from her wish, and yet said, "Now I may";
She that, being anger'd, her revenge being nigh,
Bade her wrong stay and her displeasure fly;
She that in wisdom never was so frail
To change the cod's head for the salmon's tail;
165   She that could think and ne'er disclose her mind,
See suitors following and not look behind;
She was a wight, if ever such wight were—

DESDEMONA.
To do what?

IAGO.
To suckle fools and chronicle small beer.

DESDEMONA.
170   O most lame and impotent conclusion!—Do not learn of him, Emilia,
though he be thy husband.—How say you, Cassio? is he not a most profane
and liberal counsellor?

CASSIO.
He speaks home, madam. You may relish him more in the soldier than in
the scholar.

IAGO.
175   [*Aside.*] He takes her by the palm. Ay, well said, whisper. With as little a web
as this will I ensnare as great a fly as Cassio. Ay, smile upon her, do. I will

gyve thee in thine own courtship. You say true, 'tis so, indeed. If such tricks as these strip you out of your lieutenantry, it had been better you had not kissed your three fingers so oft, which now again you are most apt to play the sir in. Very good; well kissed, an excellent courtesy! 'Tis so, indeed. Yet again your fingers to your lips? Would they were clyster-pipes for your sake!

[*Trumpets within.*]

The Moor! I know his trumpet.

CASSIO.
'Tis truly so.

DESDEMONA.
Let's meet him, and receive him.

CASSIO.
Lo, where he comes!

Enter Othello and Attendants.

OTHELLO.
O my fair warrior!

DESDEMONA.
My dear Othello!

OTHELLO.
It gives me wonder great as my content
To see you here before me. O my soul's joy!
If after every tempest come such calms,
May the winds blow till they have waken'd death!
And let the labouring bark climb hills of seas
Olympus-high, and duck again as low
As hell's from heaven! If it were now to die,
'Twere now to be most happy, for I fear
My soul hath her content so absolute
That not another comfort like to this
Succeeds in unknown fate.

DESDEMONA.
The heavens forbid
But that our loves and comforts should increase
Even as our days do grow!

OTHELLO.
Amen to that, sweet powers!
I cannot speak enough of this content.

It stops me here; it is too much of joy:
205   And this, and this, the greatest discords be. [*They kiss.*]
       That e'er our hearts shall make!

IAGO.
[*Aside.*] O, you are well tun'd now,
But I'll set down the pegs that make this music,
As honest as I am.

OTHELLO.
210   Come, let us to the castle.—
       News, friends, our wars are done, the Turks are drown'd.
       How does my old acquaintance of this isle?
       Honey, you shall be well desir'd in Cyprus;
       I have found great love amongst them. O my sweet,
215   I prattle out of fashion, and I dote
       In mine own comforts.—I prithee, good Iago,
       Go to the bay and disembark my coffers.
       Bring thou the master to the citadel;
       He is a good one, and his worthiness
220   Does challenge much respect.—Come, Desdemona,
       Once more well met at Cyprus.
                          [*Exeunt Othello, Desdemona and Attendants.*]

IAGO.
Do thou meet me presently at the harbour. Come hither. If thou be'st
valiant—as, they say, base men being in love have then a nobility in their na-
tures more than is native to them—list me. The lieutenant tonight watches
225   on the court of guard: first, I must tell thee this: Desdemona is directly in
love with him.

RODERIGO.
With him? Why, 'tis not possible.

IAGO.
Lay thy finger thus, and let thy soul be instructed. Mark me with what vio-
lence she first loved the Moor, but for bragging, and telling her fantastical lies.
230   And will she love him still for prating? Let not thy discreet heart think it. Her
eye must be fed. And what delight shall she have to look on the devil? When
the blood is made dull with the act of sport, there should be, again to inflame
it and to give satiety a fresh appetite, loveliness in favour, sympathy in years,
manners, and beauties; all which the Moor is defective in: now, for want of
235   these required conveniences, her delicate tenderness will find itself abused,
begin to heave the gorge, disrelish and abhor the Moor, very nature will in-
struct her in it, and compel her to some second choice. Now sir, this granted
(as it is a most pregnant and unforced position) who stands so eminently in

240 the degree of this fortune as Cassio does? a knave very voluble; no further conscionable than in putting on the mere form of civil and humane seem-ing, for the better compassing of his salt and most hidden loose affection? Why, none, why, none! A slipper and subtle knave, a finder out of occasions; that has an eye can stamp and counterfeit advantages, though true advantage never present itself: a devilish knave! Besides, the knave is handsome, young,

245 and hath all those requisites in him that folly and green minds look after. A pestilent complete knave, and the woman hath found him already.

RODERIGO.
I cannot believe that in her, she is full of most blessed condition.

IAGO.
Blest fig's end! the wine she drinks is made of grapes: if she had been blessed, she would never have loved the Moor. Blessed pudding! Didst

250 thou not see her paddle with the palm of his hand? Didst not mark that?

RODERIGO.
Yes, that I did. But that was but courtesy.

IAGO.
Lechery, by this hand. An index and obscure prologue to the history of lust and foul thoughts. They met so near with their lips that their breaths embrac'd together. Villainous thoughts, Roderigo! When these mutualities

255 so marshal the way, hard at hand comes the master and main exercise, the incorporate conclusion. Pish! But, sir, be you ruled by me. I have brought you from Venice. Watch you tonight. For the command, I'll lay't upon you. Cassio knows you not. I'll not be far from you. Do you find some occasion to anger Cassio, either by speaking too loud, or tainting his dis-

260 cipline, or from what other course you please, which the time shall more favourably minister.

RODERIGO.
Well.

IAGO.
Sir, he is rash, and very sudden in choler, and haply with his truncheon may strike at you: provoke him that he may, for even out of that will I

265 cause these of Cyprus to mutiny, whose qualification shall come into no true taste again but by the displanting of Cassio. So shall you have a shorter journey to your desires by the means I shall then have to prefer them, and the impediment most profitably removed, without the which there were no expectation of our prosperity.

RODERIGO.
270 I will do this, if I can bring it to any opportunity.

IAGO.

I warrant thee. Meet me by and by at the citadel: I must fetch his necessaries
ashore. Farewell.

RODERIGO.

Adieu.

                         [*Exit.*]

IAGO.

  That Cassio loves her, I do well believe it;
275 That she loves him, 'tis apt, and of great credit:
  The Moor, howbeit that I endure him not,
  Is of a constant, loving, noble nature;
  And, I dare think, he'll prove to Desdemona
  A most dear husband. Now, I do love her too,
280 Not out of absolute lust (though peradventure
  I stand accountant for as great a sin)
  But partly led to diet my revenge,
  For that I do suspect the lusty Moor
  Hath leap'd into my seat. The thought whereof
285 Doth, like a poisonous mineral, gnaw my inwards,
  And nothing can or shall content my soul
  Till I am even'd with him, wife for wife,
  Or, failing so, yet that I put the Moor
  At least into a jealousy so strong
290 That judgement cannot cure. Which thing to do,
  If this poor trash of Venice, whom I trash
  For his quick hunting, stand the putting on,
  I'll have our Michael Cassio on the hip,
  Abuse him to the Moor in the rank garb
295 (For I fear Cassio with my night-cap too)
  Make the Moor thank me, love me, and reward me
  For making him egregiously an ass
  And practicing upon his peace and quiet
  Even to madness. 'Tis here, but yet confus'd.
300 Knavery's plain face is never seen till us'd.

                         [*Exit.*]

SCENE II. A street.
Enter Othello's Herald with a proclamation.

HERALD.

It is Othello's pleasure, our noble and valiant general, that upon certain
tidings now arrived, importing the mere perdition of the Turkish fleet, ev-

ery man put himself into triumph: some to dance, some to make bonfires, each man to what sport and revels his addition leads him. For besides these
5　beneficial news, it is the celebration of his nuptial. So much was his pleasure should be proclaimed. All offices are open, and there is full liberty of feasting from this present hour of five till the bell have told eleven. Heaven bless the isle of Cyprus and our noble general Othello!

[Exit.]

SCENE III. A HALL IN THE CASTLE.
Enter Othello, Desdemona, Cassio and Attendants.

OTHELLO.
　Good Michael, look you to the guard tonight.
　Let's teach ourselves that honourable stop,
　Not to outsport discretion.

CASSIO.
　Iago hath direction what to do.
5　But notwithstanding with my personal eye
　Will I look to't.

OTHELLO.
　Iago is most honest.
　Michael, good night. Tomorrow with your earliest
　Let me have speech with you. [To Desdemona.] Come, my dear love,
10　The purchase made, the fruits are to ensue;
　That profit's yet to come 'tween me and you.—
　Good night.

[Exeunt Othello, Desdemona and Attendants.]

Enter Iago.

CASSIO.
　Welcome, Iago. We must to the watch.

IAGO.
　Not this hour, lieutenant. 'Tis not yet ten o' th' clock. Our general cast us
15　thus early for the love of his Desdemona; who let us not therefore blame: he hath not yet made wanton the night with her; and she is sport for Jove.

CASSIO.
　She's a most exquisite lady.

IAGO.
　And, I'll warrant her, full of game.

CASSIO.
　Indeed, she is a most fresh and delicate creature.

IAGO.

20   What an eye she has! methinks it sounds a parley to provocation.

CASSIO.

An inviting eye, and yet methinks right modest.

IAGO.

And when she speaks, is it not an alarm to love?

CASSIO.

She is indeed perfection.

IAGO.

Well, happiness to their sheets! Come, lieutenant, I have a stoup of wine; and
25   here without are a brace of Cyprus gallants that would fain have a measure to
the health of black Othello.

CASSIO.

Not tonight, good Iago. I have very poor and unhappy brains for drinking. I
could well wish courtesy would invent some other custom of entertainment.

IAGO.

O, they are our friends; but one cup: I'll drink for you.

CASSIO.

30   I have drunk but one cup tonight, and that was craftily qualified too, and
behold, what innovation it makes here: I am unfortunate in the infirmity,
and dare not task my weakness with any more.

IAGO.

What, man! 'Tis a night of revels. The gallants desire it.

CASSIO.

Where are they?

IAGO.

35   Here at the door. I pray you, call them in.

CASSIO.

I'll do't; but it dislikes me.

                             [Exit.]

IAGO.

If I can fasten but one cup upon him,
With that which he hath drunk tonight already,
He'll be as full of quarrel and offence
40   As my young mistress' dog. Now my sick fool Roderigo,
Whom love hath turn'd almost the wrong side out,
To Desdemona hath tonight carous'd

Potations pottle-deep; and he's to watch:
Three lads of Cyprus, noble swelling spirits,
45   That hold their honours in a wary distance,
The very elements of this warlike isle,
Have I tonight fluster'd with flowing cups,
And they watch too. Now, 'mongst this flock of drunkards,
Am I to put our Cassio in some action
50   That may offend the isle. But here they come:
If consequence do but approve my dream,
My boat sails freely, both with wind and stream.

Enter Cassio, Montano and Gentlemen; followed by Servant with wine.

CASSIO.
'Fore God, they have given me a rouse already.

MONTANO.
Good faith, a little one; not past a pint, as I am a soldier.

IAGO.
55   Some wine, ho!
[*Sings.*]

    And let me the cannikin clink, clink,
    And let me the cannikin clink, clink:
      A soldier's a man,
      O, man's life's but a span,
60   *Why then let a soldier drink.*
Some wine, boys!

CASSIO.
'Fore God, an excellent song.

IAGO.
I learned it in England, where indeed they are most potent in potting: your
Dane, your German, and your swag-bellied Hollander,—drink, ho!—are
65   nothing to your English.

CASSIO.
Is your Englishman so expert in his drinking?

IAGO.
Why, he drinks you, with facility, your Dane dead drunk; he sweats not
to overthrow your Almain; he gives your Hollander a vomit ere the next
pottle can be filled.

CASSIO.
70   To the health of our general!

MONTANO.
I am for it, lieutenant; and I'll do you justice.

IAGO.
O sweet England!
[*Sings.*]
    King Stephen was a worthy peer,
        His breeches cost him but a crown;
75   *He held them sixpence all too dear,*
        With that he call'd the tailor lown.
    He was a wight of high renown,
        And thou art but of low degree:
    'Tis pride that pulls the country down,
80   *Then take thine auld cloak about thee.*
Some wine, ho!

CASSIO.
'Fore God, this is a more exquisite song than the other.

IAGO.
Will you hear 't again?

CASSIO.
No, for I hold him to be unworthy of his place that does those things. Well,
85 God's above all, and there be souls must be saved, and there be souls must
not be saved.

IAGO.
It's true, good lieutenant.

CASSIO.
For mine own part, no offence to the general, nor any man of quality, I
hope to be saved.

IAGO.
90 And so do I too, lieutenant.

CASSIO.
Ay, but, by your leave, not before me; the lieutenant is to be saved before
the ancient. Let's have no more of this; let's to our affairs. Forgive us our
sins! Gentlemen, let's look to our business. Do not think, gentlemen, I am
drunk. This is my ancient, this is my right hand, and this is my left. I am not
95 drunk now. I can stand well enough, and I speak well enough.

ALL.
Excellent well.

CASSIO.
Why, very well then. You must not think, then, that I am drunk.

[*Exit.*]

MONTANO.
To the platform, masters. Come, let's set the watch.

IAGO.
You see this fellow that is gone before,
100   He is a soldier fit to stand by Cæsar
And give direction: and do but see his vice,
'Tis to his virtue a just equinox,
The one as long as th' other. 'Tis pity of him.
I fear the trust Othello puts him in,
105   On some odd time of his infirmity,
Will shake this island.

MONTANO.
But is he often thus?

IAGO.
'Tis evermore the prologue to his sleep:
He'll watch the horologe a double set
110   If drink rock not his cradle.

MONTANO.
It were well
The general were put in mind of it.
Perhaps he sees it not, or his good nature
Prizes the virtue that appears in Cassio,
115   And looks not on his evils: is not this true?

Enter Roderigo.

IAGO.
[*Aside to him.*] How now, Roderigo?
I pray you, after the lieutenant; go.

[*Exit Roderigo.*]

MONTANO.
And 'tis great pity that the noble Moor
Should hazard such a place as his own second
120   With one of an ingraft infirmity:
It were an honest action to say so
To the Moor.

IAGO.
Not I, for this fair island.

I do love Cassio well and would do much
125   To cure him of this evil. But, hark! What noise?

[Cry within: "Help! help!"]

Enter Cassio, driving in Roderigo.

CASSIO.
Zounds, you rogue, you rascal!

MONTANO.
What's the matter, lieutenant?

CASSIO.
A knave teach me my duty! I'll beat the knave into a twiggen bottle.

RODERIGO.
Beat me?

CASSIO.
130   Dost thou prate, rogue?

[Striking Roderigo.]

MONTANO.
Nay, good lieutenant;
I pray you, sir, hold your hand.

CASSIO.
Let me go, sir,
Or I'll knock you o'er the mazard.

MONTANO.
135   Come, come, you're drunk.

CASSIO.
Drunk?

[They fight.]

IAGO.
[Aside to Roderigo.] Away, I say! Go out and cry a mutiny.

[Exit Roderigo.]

Nay, good lieutenant, God's will, gentlemen.
Help, ho!—Lieutenant,—sir,—Montano,—sir:—
140   Help, masters! Here's a goodly watch indeed!

[A bell rings.]

Who's that which rings the bell?—Diablo, ho!
The town will rise. God's will, lieutenant, hold,
You will be sham'd forever.

Enter Othello and Attendants.

OTHELLO.
 What is the matter here?

MONTANO.
145 Zounds, I bleed still, I am hurt to the death.

OTHELLO.
 Hold, for your lives!

IAGO.
 Hold, ho! lieutenant,— sir,— Montano,— gentlemen,—
 Have you forgot all place of sense and duty?
 Hold! The general speaks to you; hold, hold, for shame!

OTHELLO.
150 Why, how now, ho! From whence ariseth this?
 Are we turn'd Turks, and to ourselves do that
 Which heaven hath forbid the Ottomites?
 For Christian shame, put by this barbarous brawl:
 He that stirs next to carve for his own rage
155 Holds his soul light; he dies upon his motion.
 Silence that dreadful bell, it frights the isle
 From her propriety. What is the matter, masters?
 Honest Iago, that looks dead with grieving,
 Speak, who began this? On thy love, I charge thee.

IAGO.
160 I do not know. Friends all but now, even now,
 In quarter, and in terms like bride and groom
 Devesting them for bed; and then, but now,
 As if some planet had unwitted men,
 Swords out, and tilting one at other's breast,
165 In opposition bloody. I cannot speak
 Any beginning to this peevish odds;
 And would in action glorious I had lost
 Those legs that brought me to a part of it!

OTHELLO.
 How comes it, Michael, you are thus forgot?

CASSIO.
170 I pray you, pardon me; I cannot speak.

OTHELLO.
 Worthy Montano, you were wont be civil.
 The gravity and stillness of your youth
 The world hath noted, and your name is great

In mouths of wisest censure: what's the matter,
175 That you unlace your reputation thus,
And spend your rich opinion for the name
Of a night-brawler? Give me answer to it.

MONTANO.
Worthy Othello, I am hurt to danger.
Your officer, Iago, can inform you,
180 While I spare speech, which something now offends me,
Of all that I do know; nor know I aught
By me that's said or done amiss this night,
Unless self-charity be sometimes a vice,
And to defend ourselves it be a sin
185 When violence assails us.

OTHELLO.
Now, by heaven,
My blood begins my safer guides to rule,
And passion, having my best judgement collied,
Assays to lead the way. Zounds, if I stir,
190 Or do but lift this arm, the best of you
Shall sink in my rebuke. Give me to know
How this foul rout began, who set it on,
And he that is approv'd in this offence,
Though he had twinn'd with me, both at a birth,
195 Shall lose me. What! in a town of war,
Yet wild, the people's hearts brimful of fear,
To manage private and domestic quarrel,
In night, and on the court and guard of safety?
'Tis monstrous. Iago, who began't?

MONTANO.
200 If partially affin'd, or leagu'd in office,
Thou dost deliver more or less than truth,
Thou art no soldier.

IAGO.
Touch me not so near.
I had rather have this tongue cut from my mouth
205 Than it should do offence to Michael Cassio.
Yet I persuade myself, to speak the truth
Shall nothing wrong him. Thus it is, general:
Montano and myself being in speech,
There comes a fellow crying out for help,
210 And Cassio following him with determin'd sword,
To execute upon him. Sir, this gentleman

Steps in to Cassio and entreats his pause.
Myself the crying fellow did pursue,
Lest by his clamour (as it so fell out)
215   The town might fall in fright: he, swift of foot,
Outran my purpose: and I return'd the rather
For that I heard the clink and fall of swords,
And Cassio high in oath, which till tonight
I ne'er might say before. When I came back,
220   (For this was brief) I found them close together,
At blow and thrust, even as again they were
When you yourself did part them.
More of this matter cannot I report.
But men are men; the best sometimes forget;
225   Though Cassio did some little wrong to him,
As men in rage strike those that wish them best,
Yet surely Cassio, I believe, receiv'd
From him that fled some strange indignity,
Which patience could not pass.

OTHELLO.
230   I know, Iago,
Thy honesty and love doth mince this matter,
Making it light to Cassio. Cassio, I love thee,
But never more be officer of mine.

> Enter Desdemona, attended.

Look, if my gentle love be not rais'd up!
235   I'll make thee an example.

DESDEMONA.
What's the matter?

OTHELLO.
All's well now, sweeting; come away to bed.
Sir, for your hurts, myself will be your surgeon.
Lead him off.

> [*Montano is led off.*]

240   Iago, look with care about the town,
And silence those whom this vile brawl distracted.
Come, Desdemona: 'tis the soldiers' life
To have their balmy slumbers wak'd with strife.

> [*Exeunt all but Iago and Cassio.*]

IAGO.
What, are you hurt, lieutenant?

CASSIO.

245   Ay, past all surgery.

IAGO.

 Marry, Heaven forbid!

CASSIO.

 Reputation, reputation, reputation! O, I have lost my reputation! I have lost
the immortal part of myself, and what remains is bestial. My reputation,
Iago, my reputation!

IAGO.

250   As I am an honest man, I thought you had received some bodily wound;
there is more sense in that than in reputation. Reputation is an idle and most
false imposition, oft got without merit and lost without deserving. You have
lost no reputation at all, unless you repute yourself such a loser. What, man,
there are ways to recover the general again: you are but now cast in his mood,
255   a punishment more in policy than in malice, even so as one would beat his
offenceless dog to affright an imperious lion: sue to him again, and he's yours.

CASSIO.

 I will rather sue to be despised than to deceive so good a commander
with so slight, so drunken, and so indiscreet an officer. Drunk? and speak
parrot? and squabble? swagger? swear? and discourse fustian with one's
260   own shadow? O thou invisible spirit of wine, if thou hast no name to be
known by, let us call thee devil!

IAGO.

 What was he that you followed with your sword? What had he done to you?

CASSIO.

 I know not.

IAGO.

 Is't possible?

CASSIO.

265   I remember a mass of things, but nothing distinctly; a quarrel, but nothing
wherefore. O God, that men should put an enemy in their mouths to steal
away their brains! That we should with joy, pleasance, revel, and applause,
transform ourselves into beasts!

IAGO.

 Why, but you are now well enough: how came you thus recovered?

CASSIO.

270   It hath pleased the devil drunkenness to give place to the devil wrath. One
unperfectness shows me another, to make me frankly despise myself.

IAGO.

Come, you are too severe a moraler. As the time, the place, and the condi-
tion of this country stands, I could heartily wish this had not befallen; but
since it is as it is, mend it for your own good.

CASSIO.

275   I will ask him for my place again; he shall tell me I am a drunkard! Had I
as many mouths as Hydra, such an answer would stop them all. To be now
a sensible man, by and by a fool, and presently a beast! O strange! Every
inordinate cup is unbless'd, and the ingredient is a devil.

IAGO.

Come, come, good wine is a good familiar creature, if it be well used. Ex-
280   claim no more against it. And, good lieutenant, I think you think I love you.

CASSIO.
I have well approved it, sir.—I drunk!

IAGO.

You, or any man living, may be drunk at a time, man. I'll tell you what you
shall do. Our general's wife is now the general; I may say so in this respect,
for that he hath devoted and given up himself to the contemplation, mark,
285   and denotement of her parts and graces. Confess yourself freely to her.
Importune her help to put you in your place again. She is of so free, so kind,
so apt, so blessed a disposition, she holds it a vice in her goodness not to do
more than she is requested. This broken joint between you and her husband
entreat her to splinter, and, my fortunes against any lay worth naming, this
290   crack of your love shall grow stronger than it was before.

CASSIO.
You advise me well.

IAGO.
I protest, in the sincerity of love and honest kindness.

CASSIO.

I think it freely; and betimes in the morning I will beseech the virtuous
Desdemona to undertake for me; I am desperate of my fortunes if they
295   check me here.

IAGO.
You are in the right. Good night, lieutenant, I must to the watch.

CASSIO.
Good night, honest Iago.

[Exit.]

IAGO.
And what's he then, that says I play the villain?
When this advice is free I give and honest,
300   Probal to thinking, and indeed the course
To win the Moor again? For 'tis most easy
The inclining Desdemona to subdue
In any honest suit. She's fram'd as fruitful
As the free elements. And then for her
305   To win the Moor, were't to renounce his baptism,
All seals and symbols of redeemed sin,
His soul is so enfetter'd to her love
That she may make, unmake, do what she list,
Even as her appetite shall play the god
310   With his weak function. How am I then, a villain
To counsel Cassio to this parallel course,
Directly to his good? Divinity of hell!
When devils will the blackest sins put on,
They do suggest at first with heavenly shows,
315   As I do now: for whiles this honest fool
Plies Desdemona to repair his fortune,
And she for him pleads strongly to the Moor,
I'll pour this pestilence into his ear,
That she repeals him for her body's lust;
320   And by how much she strives to do him good,
She shall undo her credit with the Moor.
So will I turn her virtue into pitch,
And out of her own goodness make the net
That shall enmesh them all.

Enter Roderigo.

325   How now, Roderigo?

RODERIGO.
I do follow here in the chase, not like a hound that hunts, but one that fills
up the cry. My money is almost spent, I have been tonight exceedingly well
cudgelled; and I think the issue will be, I shall have so much experience for my
pains, and so, with no money at all and a little more wit, return again to Venice.

IAGO.
330   How poor are they that have not patience!
What wound did ever heal but by degrees?
Thou know'st we work by wit, and not by witchcraft,
And wit depends on dilatory time.
Does't not go well? Cassio hath beaten thee,
335   And thou, by that small hurt, hast cashier'd Cassio;

Though other things grow fair against the sun,
Yet fruits that blossom first will first be ripe.
Content thyself awhile. By the mass, 'tis morning;
Pleasure and action make the hours seem short.
340   Retire thee; go where thou art billeted.
Away, I say, thou shalt know more hereafter.
Nay, get thee gone.

[Exit Roderigo.]

Two things are to be done,
My wife must move for Cassio to her mistress.
345   I'll set her on;
Myself the while to draw the Moor apart,
And bring him jump when he may Cassio find
Soliciting his wife. Ay, that's the way.
Dull not device by coldness and delay.

[Exit.]

ACT III

SCENE I. CYPRUS. BEFORE THE CASTLE.
Enter Cassio and some Musicians.

CASSIO.
Masters, play here, I will content your pains,
Something that's brief; and bid "Good morrow, general."

[Music.]

Enter Clown.

CLOWN.
Why, masters, have your instruments been in Naples, that they speak i'
the nose thus?

FIRST MUSICIAN.
5   How, sir, how?

CLOWN.
Are these, I pray you, wind instruments?

FIRST MUSICIAN.
Ay, marry, are they, sir.

CLOWN.
O, thereby hangs a tail.

FIRST MUSICIAN.
Whereby hangs a tale, sir?

CLOWN.

10 Marry, sir, by many a wind instrument that I know. But, masters, here's money for you: and the general so likes your music, that he desires you, for love's sake, to make no more noise with it.

FIRST MUSICIAN.
Well, sir, we will not.

CLOWN.
If you have any music that may not be heard, to't again. But, as they say, to
15 hear music the general does not greatly care.

FIRST MUSICIAN.
We have none such, sir.

CLOWN.
Then put up your pipes in your bag, for I'll away. Go, vanish into air, away!
[*Exeunt Musicians.*]

CASSIO.
Dost thou hear, mine honest friend?

CLOWN.
No, I hear not your honest friend. I hear you.

CASSIO.
20 Prithee, keep up thy quillets. There's a poor piece of gold for thee: if the gentlewoman that attends the general's wife be stirring, tell her there's one Cassio entreats her a little favour of speech. Wilt thou do this?

CLOWN.
She is stirring, sir; if she will stir hither, I shall seem to notify unto her.

CASSIO.
Do, good my friend.
[*Exit Clown.*]
Enter Iago.

25 In happy time, Iago.

IAGO.
You have not been a-bed, then?

CASSIO.
Why, no. The day had broke
Before we parted. I have made bold, Iago,
To send in to your wife. My suit to her
30 Is, that she will to virtuous Desdemona
Procure me some access.

IAGO.
 I'll send her to you presently,
 And I'll devise a mean to draw the Moor
 Out of the way, that your converse and business
35 May be more free.

CASSIO.
 I humbly thank you for't.

[*Exit Iago.*]

 I never knew
 A Florentine more kind and honest.

Enter Emilia.

EMILIA.
 Good morrow, good lieutenant; I am sorry
 For your displeasure, but all will sure be well.
40 The general and his wife are talking of it,
 And she speaks for you stoutly: the Moor replies
 That he you hurt is of great fame in Cyprus
 And great affinity, and that in wholesome wisdom
 He might not but refuse you; but he protests he loves you
45 And needs no other suitor but his likings
 To take the safest occasion by the front
 To bring you in again.

CASSIO.
 Yet, I beseech you,
 If you think fit, or that it may be done,
50 Give me advantage of some brief discourse
 With Desdemona alone.

EMILIA.
 Pray you, come in.
 I will bestow you where you shall have time
 To speak your bosom freely.

CASSIO.
55 I am much bound to you.

[*Exeunt.*]

SCENE II. Cyprus. A Room in the Castle.
Enter Othello, Iago and Gentlemen.

OTHELLO.
 These letters give, Iago, to the pilot,
 And by him do my duties to the senate.

That done, I will be walking on the works,
Repair there to me.

IAGO.
5   Well, my good lord, I'll do't.

OTHELLO.
This fortification, gentlemen, shall we see't?

GENTLEMEN.
We'll wait upon your lordship.

[*Exeunt.*]

SCENE III. CYPRUS. THE GARDEN OF THE CASTLE.
Enter Desdemona, Cassio and Emilia.

DESDEMONA.
Be thou assured, good Cassio, I will do
All my abilities in thy behalf.

EMILIA.
Good madam, do. I warrant it grieves my husband
As if the cause were his.

DESDEMONA.
5   O, that's an honest fellow. Do not doubt, Cassio,
But I will have my lord and you again
As friendly as you were.

CASSIO.
Bounteous madam,
Whatever shall become of Michael Cassio,
10   He's never anything but your true servant.

DESDEMONA.
I know't. I thank you. You do love my lord.
You have known him long; and be you well assur'd
He shall in strangeness stand no farther off
Than in a politic distance.

CASSIO.
15   Ay, but, lady,
That policy may either last so long,
Or feed upon such nice and waterish diet,
Or breed itself so out of circumstance,
That, I being absent, and my place supplied,
20   My general will forget my love and service.

DESDEMONA.
 Do not doubt that. Before Emilia here
 I give thee warrant of thy place. Assure thee,
 If I do vow a friendship, I'll perform it
 To the last article. My lord shall never rest,
25   I'll watch him tame, and talk him out of patience;
 His bed shall seem a school, his board a shrift;
 I'll intermingle everything he does
 With Cassio's suit. Therefore be merry, Cassio,
 For thy solicitor shall rather die
30   Than give thy cause away.

Enter Othello and Iago.

EMILIA.
 Madam, here comes my lord.

CASSIO.
 Madam, I'll take my leave.

DESDEMONA.
 Why, stay, and hear me speak.

CASSIO.
 Madam, not now. I am very ill at ease,
35   Unfit for mine own purposes.

DESDEMONA.
 Well, do your discretion.

[Exit Cassio.]

IAGO.
 Ha, I like not that.

OTHELLO.
 What dost thou say?

IAGO.
 Nothing, my lord; or if—I know not what.

OTHELLO.
40   Was not that Cassio parted from my wife?

IAGO.
 Cassio, my lord? No, sure, I cannot think it,
 That he would steal away so guilty-like,
 Seeing you coming.

OTHELLO.
 I do believe 'twas he.

DESDEMONA.
45 How now, my lord?
I have been talking with a suitor here,
A man that languishes in your displeasure.

OTHELLO.
Who is't you mean?

DESDEMONA.
Why, your lieutenant, Cassio. Good my lord,
50 If I have any grace or power to move you,
His present reconciliation take;
For if he be not one that truly loves you,
That errs in ignorance and not in cunning,
I have no judgement in an honest face.
55 I prithee call him back.

OTHELLO.
Went he hence now?

DESDEMONA.
Ay, sooth; so humbled
That he hath left part of his grief with me
To suffer with him. Good love, call him back.

OTHELLO.
60 Not now, sweet Desdemon, some other time.

DESDEMONA.
But shall't be shortly?

OTHELLO.
The sooner, sweet, for you.

DESDEMONA.
Shall't be tonight at supper?

OTHELLO.
No, not tonight.

DESDEMONA.
65 Tomorrow dinner then?

OTHELLO.
I shall not dine at home;
I meet the captains at the citadel.

DESDEMONA.
Why then tomorrow night, or Tuesday morn,
On Tuesday noon, or night; on Wednesday morn.

70 I prithee name the time, but let it not
Exceed three days. In faith, he's penitent;
And yet his trespass, in our common reason,
(Save that, they say, the wars must make examples
Out of their best) is not almost a fault
75 To incur a private check. When shall he come?
Tell me, Othello: I wonder in my soul,
What you would ask me, that I should deny,
Or stand so mammering on. What? Michael Cassio,
That came a-wooing with you, and so many a time,
80 When I have spoke of you dispraisingly,
Hath ta'en your part, to have so much to do
To bring him in! Trust me, I could do much.

OTHELLO.
Prithee no more. Let him come when he will;
I will deny thee nothing.

DESDEMONA.
85 Why, this is not a boon;
'Tis as I should entreat you wear your gloves,
Or feed on nourishing dishes, or keep you warm,
Or sue to you to do a peculiar profit
To your own person: nay, when I have a suit
90 Wherein I mean to touch your love indeed,
It shall be full of poise and difficult weight,
And fearful to be granted.

OTHELLO.
I will deny thee nothing.
Whereon, I do beseech thee, grant me this,
95 To leave me but a little to myself.

DESDEMONA.
Shall I deny you? No, farewell, my lord.

OTHELLO.
Farewell, my Desdemona. I'll come to thee straight.

DESDEMONA.
Emilia, come. Be as your fancies teach you.
Whate'er you be, I am obedient.

[Exit with Emilia.]

OTHELLO.
100 Excellent wretch! Perdition catch my soul,
But I do love thee! And when I love thee not,
Chaos is come again.

IAGO.
My noble lord,—

OTHELLO.
What dost thou say, Iago?

IAGO.
105 Did Michael Cassio, when you woo'd my lady,
Know of your love?

OTHELLO.
He did, from first to last. Why dost thou ask?

IAGO.
But for a satisfaction of my thought.
No further harm.

OTHELLO.
110 Why of thy thought, Iago?

IAGO.
I did not think he had been acquainted with her.

OTHELLO.
O yes, and went between us very oft.

IAGO.
Indeed?

OTHELLO.
Indeed? Ay, indeed. Discern'st thou aught in that?
115 Is he not honest?

IAGO.
Honest, my lord?

OTHELLO.
Honest? ay, honest.

IAGO.
My lord, for aught I know.

OTHELLO.
What dost thou think?

IAGO.
120 Think, my lord?

OTHELLO.
Think, my lord? By heaven, he echoes me,
As if there were some monster in his thought

Too hideous to be shown. Thou dost mean something.
I heard thee say even now, thou lik'st not that,
125 When Cassio left my wife. What didst not like?
And when I told thee he was of my counsel
In my whole course of wooing, thou criedst, "Indeed?"
And didst contract and purse thy brow together,
As if thou then hadst shut up in thy brain
130 Some horrible conceit: if thou dost love me,
Show me thy thought.

IAGO.
My lord, you know I love you.

OTHELLO.
I think thou dost;
And for I know thou'rt full of love and honesty
135 And weigh'st thy words before thou giv'st them breath,
Therefore these stops of thine fright me the more:
For such things in a false disloyal knave
Are tricks of custom; but in a man that's just,
They're close dilations, working from the heart,
140 That passion cannot rule.

IAGO.
For Michael Cassio,
I dare be sworn I think that he is honest.

OTHELLO.
I think so too.

IAGO.
Men should be what they seem;
145 Or those that be not, would they might seem none!

OTHELLO.
Certain, men should be what they seem.

IAGO.
Why then, I think Cassio's an honest man.

OTHELLO.
Nay, yet there's more in this:
I prithee, speak to me as to thy thinkings,
150 As thou dost ruminate, and give thy worst of thoughts
The worst of words.

IAGO.
Good my lord, pardon me.
Though I am bound to every act of duty,

I am not bound to that all slaves are free to.
155　Utter my thoughts? Why, say they are vile and false:
As where's that palace whereinto foul things
Sometimes intrude not? Who has a breast so pure
But some uncleanly apprehensions
Keep leets and law-days, and in session sit
160　With meditations lawful?

OTHELLO.
Thou dost conspire against thy friend, Iago,
If thou but think'st him wrong'd and mak'st his ear
A stranger to thy thoughts.

IAGO.
I do beseech you,
165　Though I perchance am vicious in my guess,
As, I confess, it is my nature's plague
To spy into abuses, and of my jealousy
Shapes faults that are not,—that your wisdom
From one that so imperfectly conceits,
170　Would take no notice; nor build yourself a trouble
Out of his scattering and unsure observance.
It were not for your quiet nor your good,
Nor for my manhood, honesty, or wisdom,
To let you know my thoughts.

OTHELLO.
175　What dost thou mean?

IAGO.
Good name in man and woman, dear my lord,
Is the immediate jewel of their souls.
Who steals my purse steals trash. 'Tis something, nothing;
'Twas mine, 'tis his, and has been slave to thousands.
180　But he that filches from me my good name
Robs me of that which not enriches him
And makes me poor indeed.

OTHELLO.
By heaven, I'll know thy thoughts.

IAGO.
You cannot, if my heart were in your hand,
185　Nor shall not, whilst 'tis in my custody.

OTHELLO.
Ha?

IAGO.
  O, beware, my lord, of jealousy;
  It is the green-ey'd monster which doth mock
  The meat it feeds on. That cuckold lives in bliss
190 Who, certain of his fate, loves not his wronger;
  But O, what damned minutes tells he o'er
  Who dotes, yet doubts, suspects, yet strongly loves!

OTHELLO.
  O misery!

IAGO.
  Poor and content is rich, and rich enough;
195 But riches fineless is as poor as winter
  To him that ever fears he shall be poor.
  Good heaven, the souls of all my tribe defend
  From jealousy!

OTHELLO.
  Why, why is this?
200 Think'st thou I'd make a life of jealousy,
  To follow still the changes of the moon
  With fresh suspicions? No. To be once in doubt
  Is once to be resolv'd: exchange me for a goat
  When I shall turn the business of my soul
205 To such exsufflicate and blown surmises,
  Matching thy inference. 'Tis not to make me jealous,
  To say my wife is fair, feeds well, loves company,
  Is free of speech, sings, plays, and dances well;
  Where virtue is, these are more virtuous:
210 Nor from mine own weak merits will I draw
  The smallest fear or doubt of her revolt,
  For she had eyes, and chose me. No, Iago,
  I'll see before I doubt; when I doubt, prove;
  And on the proof, there is no more but this:
215 Away at once with love or jealousy!

IAGO.
  I am glad of it, for now I shall have reason
  To show the love and duty that I bear you
  With franker spirit: therefore, as I am bound,
  Receive it from me. I speak not yet of proof.
220 Look to your wife; observe her well with Cassio;
  Wear your eye thus, not jealous nor secure.
  I would not have your free and noble nature,
  Out of self-bounty, be abus'd. Look to't.

I know our country disposition well;
225 In Venice they do let heaven see the pranks
They dare not show their husbands. Their best conscience
Is not to leave undone, but keep unknown.

OTHELLO.
Dost thou say so?

IAGO.
She did deceive her father, marrying you;
230 And when she seem'd to shake and fear your looks,
She loved them most.

OTHELLO.
And so she did.

IAGO.
Why, go to then.
She that so young could give out such a seeming,
235 To seal her father's eyes up close as oak,
He thought 'twas witchcraft. But I am much to blame.
I humbly do beseech you of your pardon
For too much loving you.

OTHELLO.
I am bound to thee for ever.

IAGO.
240 I see this hath a little dash'd your spirits.

OTHELLO.
Not a jot, not a jot.

IAGO.
Trust me, I fear it has.
I hope you will consider what is spoke
Comes from my love. But I do see you're mov'd.
245 I am to pray you not to strain my speech
To grosser issues nor to larger reach
Than to suspicion.

OTHELLO.
I will not.

IAGO.
Should you do so, my lord,
250 My speech should fall into such vile success
Which my thoughts aim'd not. Cassio's my worthy friend.
My lord, I see you're mov'd.

OTHELLO.
No, not much mov'd.
I do not think but Desdemona's honest.

IAGO.
255   Long live she so! And long live you to think so!

OTHELLO.
And yet, how nature erring from itself—

IAGO.
Ay, there's the point. As, to be bold with you,
Not to affect many proposed matches,
Of her own clime, complexion, and degree,
260   Whereto we see in all things nature tends;
Foh! One may smell in such a will most rank,
Foul disproportion, thoughts unnatural.
But pardon me: I do not in position
Distinctly speak of her, though I may fear
265   Her will, recoiling to her better judgement,
May fall to match you with her country forms,
And happily repent.

OTHELLO.
Farewell, farewell:
If more thou dost perceive, let me know more;
270   Set on thy wife to observe. Leave me, Iago.

IAGO.
[*Going.*] My lord, I take my leave.

OTHELLO.
Why did I marry? This honest creature doubtless
Sees and knows more, much more, than he unfolds.

IAGO.
[*Returning.*] My lord, I would I might entreat your honour
275   To scan this thing no further. Leave it to time:
Though it be fit that Cassio have his place,
For sure he fills it up with great ability,
Yet if you please to hold him off awhile,
You shall by that perceive him and his means.
280   Note if your lady strain his entertainment
With any strong or vehement importunity,
Much will be seen in that. In the meantime,
Let me be thought too busy in my fears
(As worthy cause I have to fear I am)
285   And hold her free, I do beseech your honour.

OTHELLO.
Fear not my government.

IAGO.
I once more take my leave.

[*Exit.*]

OTHELLO.
This fellow's of exceeding honesty,
And knows all qualities, with a learned spirit,
290   Of human dealings. If I do prove her haggard,
Though that her jesses were my dear heartstrings,
I'd whistle her off, and let her down the wind
To prey at fortune. Haply, for I am black,
And have not those soft parts of conversation
295   That chamberers have, or for I am declin'd
Into the vale of years,—yet that's not much—
She's gone, I am abus'd, and my relief
Must be to loathe her. O curse of marriage,
That we can call these delicate creatures ours,
300   And not their appetites! I had rather be a toad,
And live upon the vapour of a dungeon,
Than keep a corner in the thing I love
For others' uses. Yet, 'tis the plague of great ones,
Prerogativ'd are they less than the base,
305   'Tis destiny unshunnable, like death:
Even then this forked plague is fated to us
When we do quicken. Desdemona comes.
If she be false, O, then heaven mocks itself!
I'll not believe't.

Enter Desdemona and Emilia.

DESDEMONA.
310   How now, my dear Othello?
Your dinner, and the generous islanders
By you invited, do attend your presence.

OTHELLO.
I am to blame.

DESDEMONA.
Why do you speak so faintly?
315   Are you not well?

OTHELLO.
I have a pain upon my forehead here.

DESDEMONA.
 Faith, that's with watching, 'twill away again;
 Let me but bind it hard, within this hour
 It will be well.

OTHELLO.
320 Your napkin is too little;

                    [*He puts the handkerchief from him, and she drops it.*]
 Let it alone. Come, I'll go in with you.

DESDEMONA.
 I am very sorry that you are not well.

                              [*Exeunt Othello and Desdemona.*]

EMILIA.
 I am glad I have found this napkin;
 This was her first remembrance from the Moor.
325 My wayward husband hath a hundred times
 Woo'd me to steal it. But she so loves the token,
 For he conjur'd her she should ever keep it,
 That she reserves it evermore about her
 To kiss and talk to. I'll have the work ta'en out,
330 And give't Iago. What he will do with it
 Heaven knows, not I,
 I nothing but to please his fantasy.

                    Enter Iago.

IAGO.
 How now? What do you here alone?

EMILIA.
 Do not you chide. I have a thing for you.

IAGO.
335 A thing for me? It is a common thing—

EMILIA.
 Ha?

IAGO.
 To have a foolish wife.

EMILIA.
 O, is that all? What will you give me now
 For that same handkerchief?

IAGO.
340 What handkerchief?

EMILIA.
 What handkerchief?
 Why, that the Moor first gave to Desdemona,
 That which so often you did bid me steal.

IAGO.
 Hast stol'n it from her?

EMILIA.
345　No, faith, she let it drop by negligence,
 And, to the advantage, I being here, took 't up.
 Look, here it is.

IAGO.
 A good wench, give it me.

EMILIA.
 What will you do with't, that you have been so earnest
350　To have me filch it?

IAGO.
 [*Snatching it.*] Why, what's that to you?

EMILIA.
 If it be not for some purpose of import,
 Give 't me again. Poor lady, she'll run mad
 When she shall lack it.

IAGO.
355　Be not acknown on't, I have use for it.
 Go, leave me.

[*Exit Emilia.*]

 I will in Cassio's lodging lose this napkin,
 And let him find it. Trifles light as air
 Are to the jealous confirmations strong
360　As proofs of holy writ. This may do something.
 The Moor already changes with my poison:
 Dangerous conceits are in their natures poisons,
 Which at the first are scarce found to distaste,
 But with a little act upon the blood
365　Burn like the mines of sulphur. I did say so.

Enter Othello.

 Look, where he comes. Not poppy, nor mandragora,
 Nor all the drowsy syrups of the world,
 Shall ever medicine thee to that sweet sleep
 Which thou ow'dst yesterday.

OTHELLO.

370   Ha! ha! false to me?

IAGO.

Why, how now, general? No more of that.

OTHELLO.

Avaunt! be gone! Thou hast set me on the rack.
I swear 'tis better to be much abus'd
Than but to know't a little.

IAGO.

375   How now, my lord?

OTHELLO.

What sense had I of her stol'n hours of lust?
I saw't not, thought it not, it harm'd not me.
I slept the next night well, was free and merry;
I found not Cassio's kisses on her lips.
380   He that is robb'd, not wanting what is stol'n,
Let him not know't, and he's not robb'd at all.

IAGO.

I am sorry to hear this.

OTHELLO.

I had been happy if the general camp,
Pioners and all, had tasted her sweet body,
385   So I had nothing known. O, now, for ever
Farewell the tranquil mind! Farewell content!
Farewell the plumed troops and the big wars
That make ambition virtue! O, farewell,
Farewell the neighing steed and the shrill trump,
390   The spirit-stirring drum, the ear-piercing fife,
The royal banner, and all quality,
Pride, pomp, and circumstance of glorious war!
And, O you mortal engines, whose rude throats
The immortal Jove's dread clamours counterfeit,
395   Farewell! Othello's occupation's gone!

IAGO.

Is't possible, my lord?

OTHELLO.

Villain, be sure thou prove my love a whore;
Be sure of it. Give me the ocular proof,
Or, by the worth of man's eternal soul,

400   Thou hadst been better have been born a dog
       Than answer my wak'd wrath.

       IAGO.
        Is't come to this?

       OTHELLO.
        Make me to see't, or at the least so prove it,
        That the probation bear no hinge nor loop
405   To hang a doubt on, or woe upon thy life!

       IAGO.
        My noble lord,—

       OTHELLO.
        If thou dost slander her and torture me,
        Never pray more. Abandon all remorse;
        On horror's head horrors accumulate;
410   Do deeds to make heaven weep, all earth amaz'd;
        For nothing canst thou to damnation add
        Greater than that.

       IAGO.
        O grace! O heaven defend me!
        Are you a man? Have you a soul or sense?
415   God be wi' you. Take mine office.—O wretched fool,
        That liv'st to make thine honesty a vice!
        O monstrous world! Take note, take note, O world,
        To be direct and honest is not safe.
        I thank you for this profit, and from hence
420   I'll love no friend, sith love breeds such offence.

       OTHELLO.
        Nay, stay. Thou shouldst be honest.

       IAGO.
        I should be wise; for honesty's a fool,
        And loses that it works for.

       OTHELLO.
        By the world,
425   I think my wife be honest, and think she is not.
        I think that thou art just, and think thou art not.
        I'll have some proof: her name, that was as fresh
        As Dian's visage, is now begrim'd and black
        As mine own face. If there be cords or knives,
430   Poison or fire, or suffocating streams,
        I'll not endure 't. Would I were satisfied!

IAGO.
I see, sir, you are eaten up with passion.
I do repent me that I put it to you.
You would be satisfied?

OTHELLO.
435 Would? Nay, I will.

IAGO.
And may; but how? How satisfied, my lord?
Would you, the supervisor, grossly gape on,
Behold her topp'd?

OTHELLO.
Death and damnation! O!

IAGO.
440 It were a tedious difficulty, I think,
To bring them to that prospect. Damn them then,
If ever mortal eyes do see them bolster
More than their own! What then? How then?
What shall I say? Where's satisfaction?
445 It is impossible you should see this,
Were they as prime as goats, as hot as monkeys,
As salt as wolves in pride, and fools as gross
As ignorance made drunk. But yet I say,
If imputation and strong circumstances,
450 Which lead directly to the door of truth,
Will give you satisfaction, you may have't.

OTHELLO.
Give me a living reason she's disloyal.

IAGO.
I do not like the office,
But sith I am enter'd in this cause so far,
455 Prick'd to 't by foolish honesty and love,
I will go on. I lay with Cassio lately,
And being troubled with a raging tooth,
I could not sleep.
There are a kind of men so loose of soul,
460 That in their sleeps will mutter their affairs.
One of this kind is Cassio:
In sleep I heard him say, "Sweet Desdemona,
Let us be wary, let us hide our loves;"
And then, sir, would he gripe and wring my hand,

465 Cry "O sweet creature!" and then kiss me hard,
 As if he pluck'd up kisses by the roots,
 That grew upon my lips, then laid his leg
 Over my thigh, and sigh'd and kiss'd, and then
 Cried "Cursed fate that gave thee to the Moor!"

OTHELLO.
470 O monstrous! monstrous!

IAGO.
 Nay, this was but his dream.

OTHELLO.
 But this denoted a foregone conclusion.
 'Tis a shrewd doubt, though it be but a dream.

IAGO.
 And this may help to thicken other proofs
475 That do demonstrate thinly.

OTHELLO.
 I'll tear her all to pieces.

IAGO.
 Nay, but be wise. Yet we see nothing done,
 She may be honest yet. Tell me but this,
 Have you not sometimes seen a handkerchief
480 Spotted with strawberries in your wife's hand?

OTHELLO.
 I gave her such a one, 'twas my first gift.

IAGO.
 I know not that: but such a handkerchief
 (I am sure it was your wife's) did I today
 See Cassio wipe his beard with.

OTHELLO.
485 If it be that,—

IAGO.
 If it be that, or any that was hers,
 It speaks against her with the other proofs.

OTHELLO.
 O, that the slave had forty thousand lives!
 One is too poor, too weak for my revenge!
490 Now do I see 'tis true. Look here, Iago;

All my fond love thus do I blow to heaven.
'Tis gone.
Arise, black vengeance, from thy hollow hell!
Yield up, O love, thy crown and hearted throne
495 To tyrannous hate! Swell, bosom, with thy fraught,
For 'tis of aspics' tongues!

IAGO.
Yet be content.

OTHELLO.
O, blood, Iago, blood!

IAGO.
Patience, I say. Your mind perhaps may change.

OTHELLO.
500 Never, Iago. Like to the Pontic Sea,
Whose icy current and compulsive course
Ne'er feels retiring ebb, but keeps due on
To the Propontic and the Hellespont;
Even so my bloody thoughts, with violent pace
505 Shall ne'er look back, ne'er ebb to humble love,
Till that a capable and wide revenge
Swallow them up. Now by yond marble heaven,
In the due reverence of a sacred vow [*Kneels.*]
I here engage my words.

IAGO.
510 Do not rise yet. [*Kneels.*]
Witness, you ever-burning lights above,
You elements that clip us round about,
Witness that here Iago doth give up
The execution of his wit, hands, heart,
515 To wrong'd Othello's service! Let him command,
And to obey shall be in me remorse,
What bloody business ever.

           [*They rise.*]

OTHELLO.
I greet thy love,
Not with vain thanks, but with acceptance bounteous,
520 And will upon the instant put thee to 't.
Within these three days let me hear thee say
That Cassio's not alive.

IAGO.
 My friend is dead. 'Tis done at your request.
 But let her live.

OTHELLO.
525 Damn her, lewd minx! O, damn her, damn her!
 Come, go with me apart, I will withdraw
 To furnish me with some swift means of death
 For the fair devil. Now art thou my lieutenant.

IAGO.
 I am your own for ever.

[Exeunt.]

SCENE IV. Cyprus. Before the Castle.
Enter Desdemona, Emilia and Clown.

DESDEMONA.
 Do you know, sirrah, where Lieutenant Cassio lies?

CLOWN.
 I dare not say he lies anywhere.

DESDEMONA.
 Why, man?

CLOWN.
 He's a soldier; and for one to say a soldier lies is stabbing.

DESDEMONA.
5 Go to. Where lodges he?

CLOWN.
 To tell you where he lodges is to tell you where I lie.

DESDEMONA.
 Can anything be made of this?

CLOWN.
 I know not where he lodges; and for me to devise a lodging, and say he lies
 here, or he lies there, were to lie in mine own throat.

DESDEMONA.
10 Can you inquire him out, and be edified by report?

CLOWN.
 I will catechize the world for him, that is, make questions and by them answer.

DESDEMONA.
Seek him, bid him come hither. Tell him I have moved my lord on his behalf,
and hope all will be well.

CLOWN.
To do this is within the compass of man's wit, and therefore I will attempt
15   the doing it.

[Exit.]

DESDEMONA.
Where should I lose that handkerchief, Emilia?

EMILIA.
I know not, madam.

DESDEMONA.
Believe me, I had rather have lost my purse
Full of crusadoes. And but my noble Moor
20   Is true of mind and made of no such baseness
As jealous creatures are, it were enough
To put him to ill thinking.

EMILIA.
Is he not jealous?

DESDEMONA.
Who, he? I think the sun where he was born
25   Drew all such humours from him.

EMILIA.
Look, where he comes.

Enter Othello.

DESDEMONA.
I will not leave him now till Cassio
Be call'd to him. How is't with you, my lord?

OTHELLO.
Well, my good lady. *[Aside.]* O, hardness to dissemble!
30   How do you, Desdemona?

DESDEMONA.
Well, my good lord.

OTHELLO.
Give me your hand. This hand is moist, my lady.

DESDEMONA.
It yet hath felt no age nor known no sorrow.

OTHELLO.
This argues fruitfulness and liberal heart.
35 Hot, hot, and moist. This hand of yours requires
A sequester from liberty, fasting and prayer,
Much castigation, exercise devout;
For here's a young and sweating devil here
That commonly rebels. 'Tis a good hand,
40 A frank one.

DESDEMONA.
You may indeed say so,
For 'twas that hand that gave away my heart.

OTHELLO.
A liberal hand. The hearts of old gave hands,
But our new heraldry is hands, not hearts.

DESDEMONA.
45 I cannot speak of this. Come now, your promise.

OTHELLO.
What promise, chuck?

DESDEMONA.
I have sent to bid Cassio come speak with you.

OTHELLO.
I have a salt and sorry rheum offends me.
Lend me thy handkerchief.

DESDEMONA.
50 Here, my lord.

OTHELLO.
That which I gave you.

DESDEMONA.
I have it not about me.

OTHELLO.
Not?

DESDEMONA.
No, faith, my lord.

OTHELLO.
55 That is a fault. That handkerchief
Did an Egyptian to my mother give.
She was a charmer, and could almost read
The thoughts of people. She told her, while she kept it,

'Twould make her amiable and subdue my father
60   Entirely to her love. But if she lost it,
     Or made a gift of it, my father's eye
     Should hold her loathed, and his spirits should hunt
     After new fancies: she, dying, gave it me,
     And bid me, when my fate would have me wive,
65   To give it her. I did so; and take heed on't,
     Make it a darling like your precious eye.
     To lose't or give't away were such perdition
     As nothing else could match.

DESDEMONA.
 Is't possible?

OTHELLO.
70   'Tis true. There's magic in the web of it.
     A sibyl, that had number'd in the world
     The sun to course two hundred compasses,
     In her prophetic fury sew'd the work;
     The worms were hallow'd that did breed the silk,
75   And it was dyed in mummy, which the skillful
     Conserv'd of maiden's hearts.

DESDEMONA.
 Indeed? Is't true?

OTHELLO.
 Most veritable, therefore look to 't well.

DESDEMONA.
 Then would to God that I had never seen 't!

OTHELLO.
80   Ha? wherefore?

DESDEMONA.
 Why do you speak so startingly and rash?

OTHELLO.
 Is't lost? is't gone? speak, is it out of the way?

DESDEMONA.
 Heaven bless us!

OTHELLO.
 Say you?

DESDEMONA.
85   It is not lost, but what and if it were?

OTHELLO.
How?

DESDEMONA.
I say it is not lost.

OTHELLO.
Fetch't, let me see 't.

DESDEMONA.
Why, so I can, sir, but I will not now.
90 This is a trick to put me from my suit.
Pray you, let Cassio be receiv'd again.

OTHELLO.
Fetch me the handkerchief! My mind misgives.

DESDEMONA.
Come, come.
You'll never meet a more sufficient man.

OTHELLO.
95 The handkerchief!

DESDEMONA.
I pray, talk me of Cassio.

OTHELLO.
The handkerchief!

DESDEMONA.
A man that all his time
Hath founded his good fortunes on your love,
100 Shar'd dangers with you,—

OTHELLO.
The handkerchief!

DESDEMONA.
In sooth, you are to blame.

OTHELLO.
Away!

[*Exit.*]

EMILIA.
Is not this man jealous?

DESDEMONA.
105   I ne'er saw this before.
       Sure there's some wonder in this handkerchief,
       I am most unhappy in the loss of it.

EMILIA.
       'Tis not a year or two shows us a man:
       They are all but stomachs and we all but food;
110   They eat us hungerly, and when they are full,
       They belch us.

                    Enter Cassio and Iago.

Look you, Cassio and my husband.

IAGO.
       There is no other way; 'tis she must do 't,
       And, lo, the happiness! Go and importune her.

DESDEMONA.
115   How now, good Cassio, what's the news with you?

CASSIO.
       Madam, my former suit: I do beseech you
       That by your virtuous means I may again
       Exist, and be a member of his love,
       Whom I, with all the office of my heart,
120   Entirely honour. I would not be delay'd.
       If my offence be of such mortal kind
       That nor my service past, nor present sorrows,
       Nor purpos'd merit in futurity,
       Can ransom me into his love again,
125   But to know so must be my benefit;
       So shall I clothe me in a forc'd content,
       And shut myself up in some other course
       To fortune's alms.

DESDEMONA.
       Alas, thrice-gentle Cassio,
130   My advocation is not now in tune;
       My lord is not my lord; nor should I know him
       Were he in favour as in humour alter'd.
       So help me every spirit sanctified,
       As I have spoken for you all my best,
135   And stood within the blank of his displeasure
       For my free speech! You must awhile be patient.
       What I can do I will; and more I will
       Than for myself I dare. Let that suffice you.

IAGO.
Is my lord angry?

EMILIA.
140   He went hence but now,
And certainly in strange unquietness.

IAGO.
Can he be angry? I have seen the cannon,
When it hath blown his ranks into the air
And, like the devil, from his very arm
145   Puff'd his own brother, and can he be angry?
Something of moment then. I will go meet him.
There's matter in't indeed if he be angry.

DESDEMONA.
I prithee do so.

[*Exit Iago.*]

Something sure of state,
150   Either from Venice, or some unhatch'd practice
Made demonstrable here in Cyprus to him,
Hath puddled his clear spirit, and in such cases
Men's natures wrangle with inferior things,
Though great ones are their object. 'Tis even so.
155   For let our finger ache, and it indues
Our other healthful members even to that sense
Of pain. Nay, we must think men are not gods,
Nor of them look for such observancy
As fits the bridal. Beshrew me much, Emilia,
160   I was (unhandsome warrior as I am)
Arraigning his unkindness with my soul;
But now I find I had suborn'd the witness,
And he's indicted falsely.

EMILIA.
Pray heaven it be state matters, as you think,
165   And no conception nor no jealous toy
Concerning you.

DESDEMONA.
Alas the day, I never gave him cause!

EMILIA.
But jealous souls will not be answer'd so;
They are not ever jealous for the cause,
170   But jealous for they are jealous: 'tis a monster
Begot upon itself, born on itself.

DESDEMONA.
Heaven keep that monster from Othello's mind!

EMILIA.
Lady, amen.

DESDEMONA.
I will go seek him. Cassio, walk hereabout:
175   If I do find him fit, I'll move your suit,
And seek to effect it to my uttermost.

CASSIO.
I humbly thank your ladyship.

[Exeunt Desdemona and Emilia.]

Enter Bianca.

BIANCA.
Save you, friend Cassio!

CASSIO.
What make you from home?
180   How is it with you, my most fair Bianca?
I' faith, sweet love, I was coming to your house.

BIANCA.
And I was going to your lodging, Cassio.
What, keep a week away? Seven days and nights?
Eight score eight hours, and lovers' absent hours,
185   More tedious than the dial eight score times?
O weary reckoning!

CASSIO.
Pardon me, Bianca.
I have this while with leaden thoughts been press'd,
But I shall in a more continuate time
190   Strike off this score of absence. Sweet Bianca,

[Giving her Desdemona's handkerchief.]

Take me this work out.

BIANCA.
O Cassio, whence came this?
This is some token from a newer friend.
To the felt absence now I feel a cause.
195   Is't come to this? Well, well.

CASSIO.
Go to, woman!
Throw your vile guesses in the devil's teeth,

From whence you have them. You are jealous now
That this is from some mistress, some remembrance.
200   No, in good troth, Bianca.

BIANCA.
Why, whose is it?

CASSIO.
I know not neither. I found it in my chamber.
I like the work well. Ere it be demanded,
As like enough it will, I'd have it copied.
205   Take it, and do 't, and leave me for this time.

BIANCA.
Leave you, wherefore?

CASSIO.
I do attend here on the general,
And think it no addition, nor my wish,
To have him see me woman'd.

BIANCA.
210   Why, I pray you?

CASSIO.
Not that I love you not.

BIANCA.
But that you do not love me.
I pray you bring me on the way a little,
And say if I shall see you soon at night.

CASSIO.
215   'Tis but a little way that I can bring you,
For I attend here. But I'll see you soon.

BIANCA.
'Tis very good; I must be circumstanc'd.

[Exeunt.]

ACT IV

SCENE I. CYPRUS. BEFORE THE CASTLE.
Enter Othello and Iago.

IAGO.
Will you think so?

OTHELLO.
Think so, Iago?

IAGO.
 What,
 To kiss in private?

OTHELLO.
5 An unauthoriz'd kiss.

IAGO.
 Or to be naked with her friend in bed
 An hour or more, not meaning any harm?

OTHELLO.
 Naked in bed, Iago, and not mean harm?
 It is hypocrisy against the devil:
10 They that mean virtuously and yet do so,
 The devil their virtue tempts, and they tempt heaven.

IAGO.
 So they do nothing, 'tis a venial slip.
 But if I give my wife a handkerchief—

OTHELLO.
 What then?

IAGO.
15 Why then, 'tis hers, my lord, and being hers,
 She may, I think, bestow't on any man.

OTHELLO.
 She is protectress of her honour too.
 May she give that?

IAGO.
 Her honour is an essence that's not seen;
20 They have it very oft that have it not:
 But for the handkerchief—

OTHELLO.
 By heaven, I would most gladly have forgot it.
 Thou said'st (O, it comes o'er my memory,
 As doth the raven o'er the infected house,
25 Boding to all) he had my handkerchief.

IAGO.
 Ay, what of that?

OTHELLO.
 That's not so good now.

IAGO.
What If I had said I had seen him do you wrong?
Or heard him say (as knaves be such abroad,
30   Who having, by their own importunate suit,
Or voluntary dotage of some mistress,
Convinced or supplied them, cannot choose
But they must blab.)

OTHELLO.
Hath he said anything?

IAGO.
35   He hath, my lord, but be you well assur'd,
No more than he'll unswear.

OTHELLO.
What hath he said?

IAGO.
Faith, that he did—I know not what he did.

OTHELLO.
What? What?

IAGO.
40   Lie.

OTHELLO.
With her?

IAGO.
With her, on her, what you will.

OTHELLO.
Lie with her! lie on her!—We say lie on her when they belie her.—Lie with
her! that's fulsome. Handkerchief— confessions— handkerchief! To con-
45   fess, and be hanged for his labour. First, to be hanged, and then to confess.
I tremble at it. Nature would not invest herself in such shadowing passion
without some instruction. It is not words that shake me thus. Pish! Noses,
ears, and lips. Is't possible?— Confess?— handkerchief?— O devil!—

[*Falls in a trance.*]

IAGO.
Work on,
50   My medicine, work! Thus credulous fools are caught,
And many worthy and chaste dames even thus,
All guiltless, meet reproach. What, ho! my lord!
My lord, I say! Othello!

Enter Cassio.

How now, Cassio!

CASSIO.
55 What's the matter?

IAGO.
 My lord is fallen into an epilepsy.
 This is his second fit. He had one yesterday.

CASSIO.
 Rub him about the temples.

IAGO.
 No, forbear;
60 The lethargy must have his quiet course.
 If not, he foams at mouth, and by and by
 Breaks out to savage madness. Look, he stirs:
 Do you withdraw yourself a little while,
 He will recover straight. When he is gone,
65 I would on great occasion speak with you.

[Exit Cassio.]

How is it, general? Have you not hurt your head?

OTHELLO.
 Dost thou mock me?

IAGO.
 I mock you? No, by heaven.
 Would you would bear your fortune like a man!

OTHELLO.
70 A horned man's a monster and a beast.

IAGO.
 There's many a beast, then, in a populous city,
 And many a civil monster.

OTHELLO.
 Did he confess it?

IAGO.
 Good sir, be a man.
75 Think every bearded fellow that's but yok'd
 May draw with you. There's millions now alive
 That nightly lie in those unproper beds
 Which they dare swear peculiar: your case is better.

O, 'tis the spite of hell, the fiend's arch-mock,
80 To lip a wanton in a secure couch,
And to suppose her chaste! No, let me know,
And knowing what I am, I know what she shall be.

OTHELLO.
O, thou art wise, 'tis certain.

IAGO.
Stand you awhile apart,
85 Confine yourself but in a patient list.
Whilst you were here o'erwhelmed with your grief,
(A passion most unsuiting such a man)
Cassio came hither. I shifted him away,
And laid good 'scuse upon your ecstasy,
90 Bade him anon return, and here speak with me,
The which he promis'd. Do but encave yourself,
And mark the fleers, the gibes, and notable scorns,
That dwell in every region of his face;
For I will make him tell the tale anew,
95 Where, how, how oft, how long ago, and when
He hath, and is again to cope your wife:
I say, but mark his gesture. Marry, patience,
Or I shall say you are all in all in spleen,
And nothing of a man.

OTHELLO.
100 Dost thou hear, Iago?
I will be found most cunning in my patience;
But,—dost thou hear?—most bloody.

IAGO.
That's not amiss.
But yet keep time in all. Will you withdraw?

                                        [*Othello withdraws.*]

105 Now will I question Cassio of Bianca,
A housewife that by selling her desires
Buys herself bread and clothes: it is a creature
That dotes on Cassio, (as 'tis the strumpet's plague
To beguile many and be beguil'd by one.)
110 He, when he hears of her, cannot refrain
From the excess of laughter. Here he comes.

                        Enter Cassio.

As he shall smile Othello shall go mad,
And his unbookish jealousy must construe

Poor Cassio's smiles, gestures, and light behaviour
115 Quite in the wrong. How do you now, lieutenant?

CASSIO.
The worser that you give me the addition
Whose want even kills me.

IAGO.
Ply Desdemona well, and you are sure on't.
[*Speaking lower.*] Now, if this suit lay in Bianca's power,
120 How quickly should you speed!

CASSIO.
Alas, poor caitiff!

OTHELLO.
[*Aside.*] Look how he laughs already!

IAGO.
I never knew a woman love man so.

CASSIO.
Alas, poor rogue! I think, i' faith, she loves me.

OTHELLO.
125 [*Aside.*] Now he denies it faintly and laughs it out.

IAGO.
Do you hear, Cassio?

OTHELLO.
Now he importunes him
To tell it o'er. Go to, well said, well said.

IAGO.
She gives it out that you shall marry her.
130 Do you intend it?

CASSIO.
Ha, ha, ha!

OTHELLO.
Do you triumph, Roman? Do you triumph?

CASSIO.
I marry her? What? A customer? I prithee, bear some charity to my wit,
do not think it so unwholesome. Ha, ha, ha!

OTHELLO.
135 So, so, so, so. They laugh that wins.

IAGO.
Faith, the cry goes that you shall marry her.

CASSIO.
Prithee say true.

IAGO.
I am a very villain else.

OTHELLO.
Have you scored me? Well.

CASSIO.
140   This is the monkey's own giving out. She is persuaded I will marry her, out of her own love and flattery, not out of my promise.

OTHELLO.
Iago beckons me. Now he begins the story.

CASSIO.
She was here even now. She haunts me in every place. I was the other day talking on the sea-bank with certain Venetians, and thither comes the bauble, 145   and falls thus about my neck.

OTHELLO.
Crying, "O dear Cassio!" as it were: his gesture imports it.

CASSIO.
So hangs, and lolls, and weeps upon me; so hales and pulls me. Ha, ha, ha!

OTHELLO.
Now he tells how she plucked him to my chamber. O, I see that nose of yours, but not that dog I shall throw it to.

CASSIO.
150   Well, I must leave her company.

IAGO.
Before me! look where she comes.

Enter Bianca.

CASSIO.
'Tis such another fitchew! Marry, a perfum'd one.
What do you mean by this haunting of me?

BIANCA.
Let the devil and his dam haunt you! What did you mean by that same 155   handkerchief you gave me even now? I was a fine fool to take it. I must take out the work? A likely piece of work, that you should find it in your

chamber and not know who left it there! This is some minx's token, and I must take out the work? There, give it your hobby-horse. Wheresoever you had it, I'll take out no work on't.

CASSIO.
160   How now, my sweet Bianca? How now, how now?

OTHELLO.
By heaven, that should be my handkerchief!

BIANCA.
If you'll come to supper tonight, you may. If you will not, come when you are next prepared for.

[Exit.]

IAGO.
After her, after her.

CASSIO.
165   Faith, I must; she'll rail in the street else.

IAGO.
Will you sup there?

CASSIO.
Faith, I intend so.

IAGO.
Well, I may chance to see you, for I would very fain speak with you.

CASSIO.
Prithee come, will you?

IAGO.
170   Go to; say no more.

[Exit Cassio.]

OTHELLO.
[*Coming forward.*] How shall I murder him, Iago?

IAGO.
Did you perceive how he laughed at his vice?

OTHELLO.
O Iago!

IAGO.
And did you see the handkerchief?

OTHELLO.

175   Was that mine?

IAGO.

Yours, by this hand: and to see how he prizes the foolish woman your wife! she gave it him, and he hath given it his whore.

OTHELLO.

I would have him nine years a-killing. A fine woman, a fair woman, a sweet woman!

IAGO.

180   Nay, you must forget that.

OTHELLO.

Ay, let her rot, and perish, and be damned tonight, for she shall not live. No, my heart is turned to stone; I strike it, and it hurts my hand. O, the world hath not a sweeter creature. She might lie by an emperor's side, and command him tasks.

IAGO.

185   Nay, that's not your way.

OTHELLO.

Hang her, I do but say what she is. So delicate with her needle, an admira-ble musician! O, she will sing the savageness out of a bear! Of so high and plenteous wit and invention!

IAGO.

She's the worse for all this.

OTHELLO.

190   O, a thousand, a thousand times: and then of so gentle a condition!

IAGO.

Ay, too gentle.

OTHELLO.

Nay, that's certain. But yet the pity of it, Iago! O Iago, the pity of it, Iago!

IAGO.

If you are so fond over her iniquity, give her patent to offend, for if it touch not you, it comes near nobody.

OTHELLO.

195   I will chop her into messes. Cuckold me!

IAGO.

O, 'tis foul in her.

OTHELLO.
With mine officer!

IAGO.
That's fouler.

OTHELLO.
Get me some poison, Iago; this night. I'll not expostulate with her, lest her
200   body and beauty unprovide my mind again. This night, Iago.

IAGO.
Do it not with poison, strangle her in her bed, even the bed she hath
contaminated.

OTHELLO.
Good, good. The justice of it pleases. Very good.

IAGO.
And for Cassio, let me be his undertaker. You shall hear more by midnight.

OTHELLO.
205   Excellent good. [*A trumpet within.*] What trumpet is that same?

          Enter Lodovico, Desdemona and Attendant.

IAGO.
Something from Venice, sure. 'Tis Lodovico
Come from the duke. See, your wife is with him.

LODOVICO.
Save you, worthy general!

OTHELLO.
With all my heart, sir.

LODOVICO.
210   The duke and senators of Venice greet you.

                        [*Gives him a packet.*]

OTHELLO.
I kiss the instrument of their pleasures.

                     [*Opens the packet and reads.*]

DESDEMONA.
And what's the news, good cousin Lodovico?

IAGO.
I am very glad to see you, signior.
Welcome to Cyprus.

LODOVICO.
215   I thank you. How does Lieutenant Cassio?

IAGO.
Lives, sir.

DESDEMONA.
Cousin, there's fall'n between him and my lord
An unkind breach, but you shall make all well.

OTHELLO.
Are you sure of that?

DESDEMONA.
220   My lord?

OTHELLO.
[*Reads.*] "This fail you not to do, as you will—"

LODOVICO.
He did not call; he's busy in the paper.
Is there division 'twixt my lord and Cassio?

DESDEMONA.
A most unhappy one. I would do much
225   To atone them, for the love I bear to Cassio.

OTHELLO.
Fire and brimstone!

DESDEMONA.
My lord?

OTHELLO.
Are you wise?

DESDEMONA.
What, is he angry?

LODOVICO.
230   May be the letter mov'd him;
For, as I think, they do command him home,
Deputing Cassio in his government.

DESDEMONA.
Trust me, I am glad on't.

OTHELLO.
Indeed!

DESDEMONA.
235   My lord?

OTHELLO.
 I am glad to see you mad.

DESDEMONA.
 Why, sweet Othello?

OTHELLO.
 Devil!

[Striking her.]

DESDEMONA.
 I have not deserv'd this.

LODOVICO.
240   My lord, this would not be believ'd in Venice,
 Though I should swear I saw't: 'tis very much.
 Make her amends. She weeps.

OTHELLO.
 O devil, devil!
 If that the earth could teem with woman's tears,
245   Each drop she falls would prove a crocodile.
 Out of my sight!

DESDEMONA.
 I will not stay to offend you.

[Going.]

LODOVICO.
 Truly, an obedient lady.
 I do beseech your lordship, call her back.

OTHELLO.
250   Mistress!

DESDEMONA.
 My lord?

OTHELLO.
 What would you with her, sir?

LODOVICO.
 Who, I, my lord?

OTHELLO.
 Ay, you did wish that I would make her turn.

255   Sir, she can turn, and turn, and yet go on,
      And turn again. And she can weep, sir, weep;
      And she's obedient, as you say, obedient,
      Very obedient. Proceed you in your tears.
      Concerning this, sir,—O well-painted passion!
260   I am commanded home.—Get you away;
      I'll send for you anon.—Sir, I obey the mandate,
      And will return to Venice.—Hence, avaunt!

                                        [*Exit Desdemona.*]

      Cassio shall have my place. And, sir, tonight,
      I do entreat that we may sup together.
265   You are welcome, sir, to Cyprus. Goats and monkeys!

                                                  [*Exit.*]

LODOVICO.
  Is this the noble Moor, whom our full senate
  Call all in all sufficient? Is this the nature
  Whom passion could not shake? whose solid virtue
  The shot of accident nor dart of chance
270   Could neither graze nor pierce?

IAGO.
  He is much chang'd.

LODOVICO.
  Are his wits safe? Is he not light of brain?

IAGO.
  He's that he is. I may not breathe my censure
  What he might be. If what he might he is not,
275   I would to heaven he were!

LODOVICO.
  What, strike his wife?

IAGO.
  Faith, that was not so well; yet would I knew
  That stroke would prove the worst!

LODOVICO.
  Is it his use?
280   Or did the letters work upon his blood,
  And new-create this fault?

IAGO.
  Alas, alas!
  It is not honesty in me to speak

What I have seen and known. You shall observe him,
285 And his own courses will denote him so
That I may save my speech: do but go after,
And mark how he continues.

LODOVICO.
I am sorry that I am deceiv'd in him.

[Exeunt.]

SCENE II. CYPRUS. A ROOM IN THE CASTLE.
Enter Othello and Emilia.

OTHELLO.
You have seen nothing, then?

EMILIA.
Nor ever heard, nor ever did suspect.

OTHELLO.
Yes, you have seen Cassio and she together.

EMILIA.
But then I saw no harm, and then I heard
5 Each syllable that breath made up between them.

OTHELLO.
What, did they never whisper?

EMILIA.
Never, my lord.

OTHELLO.
Nor send you out o' the way?

EMILIA.
Never.

OTHELLO.
10 To fetch her fan, her gloves, her mask, nor nothing?

EMILIA.
Never, my lord.

OTHELLO.
That's strange.

EMILIA.
I durst, my lord, to wager she is honest,
Lay down my soul at stake: if you think other,

15 Remove your thought, it doth abuse your bosom.
If any wretch have put this in your head,
Let heaven requite it with the serpent's curse,
For if she be not honest, chaste, and true,
There's no man happy. The purest of their wives
20 Is foul as slander.

OTHELLO.
Bid her come hither. Go.

[Exit Emilia.]

She says enough. Yet she's a simple bawd
That cannot say as much. This is a subtle whore,
A closet lock and key of villainous secrets.
25 And yet she'll kneel and pray. I have seen her do 't.

Enter Desdemona and Emilia.

DESDEMONA.
My lord, what is your will?

OTHELLO.
Pray, chuck, come hither.

DESDEMONA.
What is your pleasure?

OTHELLO.
Let me see your eyes.
30 Look in my face.

DESDEMONA.
What horrible fancy's this?

OTHELLO.
[To Emilia.] Some of your function, mistress,
Leave procreants alone, and shut the door.
Cough, or cry hem, if anybody come.
35 Your mystery, your mystery. Nay, dispatch.

[Exit Emilia.]

DESDEMONA.
Upon my knees, what doth your speech import?
I understand a fury in your words,
But not the words.

OTHELLO.
Why, what art thou?

DESDEMONA.
40   Your wife, my lord, your true and loyal wife.

OTHELLO.
  Come, swear it, damn thyself,
  Lest, being like one of heaven, the devils themselves
  Should fear to seize thee. Therefore be double-damn'd.
  Swear thou art honest.

DESDEMONA.
45   Heaven doth truly know it.

OTHELLO.
  Heaven truly knows that thou art false as hell.

DESDEMONA.
  To whom, my lord? With whom? How am I false?

OTHELLO.
  O Desdemona, away! away! away!

DESDEMONA.
  Alas the heavy day, why do you weep?
50   Am I the motive of these tears, my lord?
  If haply you my father do suspect
  An instrument of this your calling back,
  Lay not your blame on me. If you have lost him,
  Why, I have lost him too.

OTHELLO.
55   Had it pleas'd heaven
  To try me with affliction, had they rain'd
  All kinds of sores and shames on my bare head,
  Steep'd me in poverty to the very lips,
  Given to captivity me and my utmost hopes,
60   I should have found in some place of my soul
  A drop of patience. But, alas, to make me
  A fixed figure for the time of scorn
  To point his slow unmoving finger at.
  Yet could I bear that too, well, very well:
65   But there, where I have garner'd up my heart,
  Where either I must live or bear no life,
  The fountain from the which my current runs,
  Or else dries up, to be discarded thence,
  Or keep it as a cistern for foul toads
70   To knot and gender in!—turn thy complexion there,
  Patience, thou young and rose-lipp'd cherubin,

Ay, there, look grim as hell!

DESDEMONA.
I hope my noble lord esteems me honest.

OTHELLO.
O, ay, as summer flies are in the shambles,
75   That quicken even with blowing. O thou weed,
Who art so lovely fair, and smell'st so sweet,
That the sense aches at thee,
Would thou hadst ne'er been born!

DESDEMONA.
Alas, what ignorant sin have I committed?

OTHELLO.
80   Was this fair paper, this most goodly book,
Made to write "whore" upon? What committed?
Committed! O thou public commoner!
I should make very forges of my cheeks,
That would to cinders burn up modesty,
85   Did I but speak thy deeds. What committed!
Heaven stops the nose at it, and the moon winks;
The bawdy wind, that kisses all it meets,
Is hush'd within the hollow mine of earth,
And will not hear it. What committed!
90   Impudent strumpet!

DESDEMONA.
By heaven, you do me wrong.

OTHELLO.
Are not you a strumpet?

DESDEMONA.
No, as I am a Christian:
If to preserve this vessel for my lord
95   From any other foul unlawful touch
Be not to be a strumpet, I am none.

OTHELLO.
What, not a whore?

DESDEMONA.
No, as I shall be sav'd.

OTHELLO.
Is't possible?

DESDEMONA.
100   O, heaven forgive us!

OTHELLO.
I cry you mercy then.
I took you for that cunning whore of Venice
That married with Othello.—You, mistress,

Enter Emilia.

That have the office opposite to Saint Peter,
105   And keeps the gate of hell. You, you, ay, you!
We have done our course; there's money for your pains.
I pray you turn the key, and keep our counsel.

[*Exit.*]

EMILIA.
Alas, what does this gentleman conceive?
How do you, madam? How do you, my good lady?

DESDEMONA.
110   Faith, half asleep.

EMILIA.
Good madam, what's the matter with my lord?

DESDEMONA.
With who?

EMILIA.
Why, with my lord, madam.

DESDEMONA.
Who is thy lord?

EMILIA.
115   He that is yours, sweet lady.

DESDEMONA.
I have none. Do not talk to me, Emilia,
I cannot weep, nor answer have I none
But what should go by water. Prithee, tonight
Lay on my bed my wedding sheets, remember,
120   And call thy husband hither.

EMILIA.
Here's a change indeed!

[*Exit.*]

DESDEMONA.
'Tis meet I should be us'd so, very meet.
How have I been behav'd, that he might stick
The small'st opinion on my least misuse?

             Enter Iago and Emilia.

IAGO.
125   What is your pleasure, madam? How is't with you?

DESDEMONA.
I cannot tell. Those that do teach young babes
Do it with gentle means and easy tasks.
He might have chid me so, for, in good faith,
I am a child to chiding.

IAGO.
130   What's the matter, lady?

EMILIA.
Alas, Iago, my lord hath so bewhor'd her,
Thrown such despite and heavy terms upon her,
As true hearts cannot bear.

DESDEMONA.
Am I that name, Iago?

IAGO.
135   What name, fair lady?

DESDEMONA.
Such as she says my lord did say I was.

EMILIA.
He call'd her whore: a beggar in his drink
Could not have laid such terms upon his callet.

IAGO.
Why did he so?

DESDEMONA.
140   I do not know. I am sure I am none such.

IAGO.
Do not weep, do not weep: alas the day!

EMILIA.
Hath she forsook so many noble matches,
Her father, and her country, and her friends,
To be call'd whore? would it not make one weep?

DESDEMONA.
145   It is my wretched fortune.

IAGO.
 Beshrew him for't!
 How comes this trick upon him?

DESDEMONA.
 Nay, heaven doth know.

EMILIA.
 I will be hang'd, if some eternal villain,
150   Some busy and insinuating rogue,
 Some cogging, cozening slave, to get some office,
 Have not devis'd this slander. I'll be hang'd else.

IAGO.
 Fie, there is no such man. It is impossible.

DESDEMONA.
 If any such there be, heaven pardon him!

EMILIA.
155   A halter pardon him, and hell gnaw his bones!
 Why should he call her whore? who keeps her company?
 What place? what time? what form? what likelihood?
 The Moor's abused by some most villainous knave,
 Some base notorious knave, some scurvy fellow.
160   O heaven, that such companions thou'dst unfold,
 And put in every honest hand a whip
 To lash the rascals naked through the world
 Even from the east to the west!

IAGO.
 Speak within door.

EMILIA.
165   O, fie upon them! Some such squire he was
 That turn'd your wit the seamy side without,
 And made you to suspect me with the Moor.

IAGO.
 You are a fool. Go to.

DESDEMONA.
 Alas, Iago,
170   What shall I do to win my lord again?
 Good friend, go to him. For by this light of heaven,

I know not how I lost him. Here I kneel.
If e'er my will did trespass 'gainst his love,
Either in discourse of thought or actual deed,
175 Or that mine eyes, mine ears, or any sense,
Delighted them in any other form,
Or that I do not yet, and ever did,
And ever will, (though he do shake me off
To beggarly divorcement) love him dearly,
180 Comfort forswear me! Unkindness may do much;
And his unkindness may defeat my life,
But never taint my love. I cannot say "whore,"
It does abhor me now I speak the word;
To do the act that might the addition earn
185 Not the world's mass of vanity could make me.

IAGO.
I pray you, be content. 'Tis but his humour.
The business of the state does him offence,
And he does chide with you.

DESDEMONA.
If 'twere no other,—

IAGO.
190 'Tis but so, I warrant.

[Trumpets within.]

Hark, how these instruments summon to supper.
The messengers of Venice stay the meat.
Go in, and weep not. All things shall be well.

[Exeunt Desdemona and Emilia.]

Enter Roderigo.

How now, Roderigo?

RODERIGO.
195 I do not find that thou dealest justly with me.

IAGO.
What in the contrary?

RODERIGO.
Every day thou daffest me with some device, Iago, and rather, as it seems
to me now, keepest from me all conveniency than suppliest me with the
least advantage of hope. I will indeed no longer endure it. Nor am I yet
200 persuaded to put up in peace what already I have foolishly suffered.

IAGO.
Will you hear me, Roderigo?

RODERIGO.

Faith, I have heard too much, for your words and performances are no kin together.

IAGO.

You charge me most unjustly.

RODERIGO.

205 With naught but truth. I have wasted myself out of my means. The jewels you have had from me to deliver to Desdemona would half have corrupted a votarist: you have told me she hath received them, and returned me expectations and comforts of sudden respect and acquaintance, but I find none.

IAGO.

Well, go to, very well.

RODERIGO.

210 Very well, go to, I cannot go to, man, nor 'tis not very well. Nay, I say 'tis very scurvy, and begin to find myself fopped in it.

IAGO.

Very well.

RODERIGO.

I tell you 'tis not very well. I will make myself known to Desdemona. If she will return me my jewels, I will give over my suit and repent my unlawful 215 solicitation. If not, assure yourself I will seek satisfaction of you.

IAGO.

You have said now.

RODERIGO.

Ay, and said nothing but what I protest intendment of doing.

IAGO.

Why, now I see there's mettle in thee, and even from this instant do build on thee a better opinion than ever before. Give me thy hand, Roderigo. 220 Thou hast taken against me a most just exception, but yet I protest, I have dealt most directly in thy affair.

RODERIGO.

It hath not appeared.

IAGO.

I grant indeed it hath not appeared, and your suspicion is not without wit and judgement. But, Roderigo, if thou hast that in thee indeed, which I have 225 greater reason to believe now than ever,—I mean purpose, courage, and valour,—this night show it. If thou the next night following enjoy not Desdemona, take me from this world with treachery and devise engines for my life.

RODERIGO.
Well, what is it? Is it within reason and compass?

IAGO.
Sir, there is especial commission come from Venice to depute Cassio in
230 Othello's place.

RODERIGO.
Is that true? Why then Othello and Desdemona return again to Venice.

IAGO.
O, no; he goes into Mauritania, and takes away with him the fair Desdemona,
unless his abode be lingered here by some accident: wherein none can be so
determinate as the removing of Cassio.

RODERIGO.
235 How do you mean "removing" of him?

IAGO.
Why, by making him uncapable of Othello's place: knocking out his brains.

RODERIGO.
And that you would have me to do?

IAGO.
Ay, if you dare do yourself a profit and a right. He sups tonight with a
harlotry, and thither will I go to him. He knows not yet of his honourable
240 fortune. If you will watch his going thence, which I will fashion to fall out
between twelve and one, you may take him at your pleasure: I will be near to
second your attempt, and he shall fall between us. Come, stand not amazed
at it, but go along with me. I will show you such a necessity in his death that
you shall think yourself bound to put it on him. It is now high supper-time,
245 and the night grows to waste. About it.

RODERIGO.
I will hear further reason for this.

IAGO.
And you shall be satisfied.

[Exeunt.]

SCENE III. Cyprus. Another Room in the Castle.
Enter Othello, Lodovico, Desdemona, Emilia and Attendants.

LODOVICO.
I do beseech you, sir, trouble yourself no further.

OTHELLO.
O, pardon me; 'twill do me good to walk.

LODOVICO.
Madam, good night. I humbly thank your ladyship.

DESDEMONA.
Your honour is most welcome.

OTHELLO.
5   Will you walk, sir?—
O, Desdemona,—

DESDEMONA.
My lord?

OTHELLO.
Get you to bed on th' instant, I will be return'd forthwith. Dismiss your attendant there. Look 't be done.

DESDEMONA.
10   I will, my lord.

[Exeunt Othello, Lodovico and Attendants.]

EMILIA.
How goes it now? He looks gentler than he did.

DESDEMONA.
He says he will return incontinent,
He hath commanded me to go to bed,
And bade me to dismiss you.

EMILIA.
15   Dismiss me?

DESDEMONA.
It was his bidding. Therefore, good Emilia,
Give me my nightly wearing, and adieu.
We must not now displease him.

EMILIA.
I would you had never seen him!

DESDEMONA.
20   So would not I. My love doth so approve him,
That even his stubbornness, his checks, his frowns,—
Prithee, unpin me,—have grace and favour in them.

EMILIA.
I have laid those sheets you bade me on the bed.

DESDEMONA.
All's one. Good faith, how foolish are our minds!
25   If I do die before thee, prithee, shroud me
In one of those same sheets.

EMILIA.
Come, come, you talk.

DESDEMONA.
My mother had a maid call'd Barbary,
She was in love, and he she lov'd prov'd mad
30   And did forsake her. She had a song of "willow",
An old thing 'twas, but it express'd her fortune,
And she died singing it. That song tonight
Will not go from my mind. I have much to do
But to go hang my head all at one side
35   And sing it like poor Barbary. Prithee dispatch.

EMILIA.
Shall I go fetch your night-gown?

DESDEMONA.
No, unpin me here.
This Lodovico is a proper man.

EMILIA.
A very handsome man.

DESDEMONA.
40   He speaks well.

EMILIA.
I know a lady in Venice would have walked barefoot to Palestine for a
touch of his nether lip.

DESDEMONA.
[*Singing.*]
The poor soul sat sighing by a sycamore tree,
    Sing all a green willow.
45   *Her hand on her bosom, her head on her knee,*
    Sing willow, willow, willow.
The fresh streams ran by her, and murmur'd her moans,
    Sing willow, willow, willow;
Her salt tears fell from her, and soften'd the stones;——

50   Lay by these:——

[*Sings.*]
    Sing willow, willow, willow.

Prithee hie thee. He'll come anon.

[*Sings.*]
> *Sing all a green willow must be my garland.*
> *Let nobody blame him, his scorn I approve,—*

55 Nay, that's not next. Hark! who is't that knocks?

EMILIA.
It's the wind.

DESDEMONA.
[*Sings.*]
> *I call'd my love false love; but what said he then?*
>   *Sing willow, willow, willow:*
> *If I court mo women, you'll couch with mo men.*

60 So get thee gone; good night. Mine eyes do itch;
Doth that bode weeping?

EMILIA.
'Tis neither here nor there.

DESDEMONA.
I have heard it said so. O, these men, these men!
Dost thou in conscience think,—tell me, Emilia,—
65 That there be women do abuse their husbands
In such gross kind?

EMILIA.
There be some such, no question.

DESDEMONA.
Wouldst thou do such a deed for all the world?

EMILIA.
Why, would not you?

DESDEMONA.
70 No, by this heavenly light!

EMILIA.
Nor I neither by this heavenly light,
I might do't as well i' the dark.

DESDEMONA.
Wouldst thou do such a deed for all the world?

EMILIA.
The world's a huge thing. It is a great price for a small vice.

DESDEMONA.

75 In troth, I think thou wouldst not.

EMILIA.
In troth, I think I should, and undo't when I had done. Marry, I would not
do such a thing for a joint-ring, nor for measures of lawn, nor for gowns,
petticoats, nor caps, nor any petty exhibition; but, for the whole world—
why, who would not make her husband a cuckold to make him a monarch?
80 I should venture purgatory for 't.

DESDEMONA.
Beshrew me, if I would do such a wrong for the whole world.

EMILIA.
Why, the wrong is but a wrong i' the world; and having the world for your
labour, 'tis a wrong in your own world, and you might quickly make it right.

DESDEMONA.
I do not think there is any such woman.

EMILIA.
85 Yes, a dozen; and as many to the vantage as would store the world they
played for.
But I do think it is their husbands' faults
If wives do fall: say that they slack their duties,
And pour our treasures into foreign laps;
90 Or else break out in peevish jealousies,
Throwing restraint upon us. Or say they strike us,
Or scant our former having in despite.
Why, we have galls; and though we have some grace,
Yet have we some revenge. Let husbands know
95 Their wives have sense like them: they see, and smell
And have their palates both for sweet and sour,
As husbands have. What is it that they do
When they change us for others? Is it sport?
I think it is. And doth affection breed it?
100 I think it doth. Is't frailty that thus errs?
It is so too. And have not we affections,
Desires for sport, and frailty, as men have?
Then let them use us well: else let them know,
The ills we do, their ills instruct us so.

DESDEMONA.
105 Good night, good night. Heaven me such usage send,
Not to pick bad from bad, but by bad mend!

[Exeunt.]

ACT V

SCENE I. Cyprus. A Street.
Enter Iago and Roderigo.

IAGO.
Here, stand behind this bulk. Straight will he come.
Wear thy good rapier bare, and put it home.
Quick, quick, fear nothing; I'll be at thy elbow.
It makes us, or it mars us, think on that,
5   And fix most firm thy resolution.

RODERIGO.
Be near at hand, I may miscarry in 't.

IAGO.
Here, at thy hand. Be bold, and take thy stand.

            [Retires to a little distance.]

RODERIGO.
I have no great devotion to the deed;
And yet he hath given me satisfying reasons.
10   'Tis but a man gone. Forth, my sword; he dies.

              [Goes to his stand.]

IAGO.
I have rubb'd this young quat almost to the sense,
And he grows angry. Now, whether he kill Cassio,
Or Cassio him, or each do kill the other,
Every way makes my gain. Live Roderigo,
15   He calls me to a restitution large
Of gold and jewels that I bobb'd from him,
As gifts to Desdemona.
It must not be. If Cassio do remain,
He hath a daily beauty in his life
20   That makes me ugly. And besides, the Moor
May unfold me to him; there stand I in much peril.
No, he must die. But so, I hear him coming.

Enter Cassio.

RODERIGO.
I know his gait; 'tis he. Villain, thou diest!

      [Rushes out, and makes a pass at Cassio.]

CASSIO.
That thrust had been mine enemy indeed,
25   But that my coat is better than thou know'st.
I will make proof of thine.

[Draws, and wounds Roderigo.]

RODERIGO.
 O, I am slain!

 [Iago rushes from his post, cuts Cassio behind in the leg, and exit.]

CASSIO.
 I am maim'd forever. Help, ho! murder, murder!

[Falls.]

Enter Othello.

OTHELLO.
 The voice of Cassio. Iago keeps his word.

RODERIGO.
30 O, villain that I am!

OTHELLO.
 It is even so.

CASSIO.
 O, help, ho! light! a surgeon!

OTHELLO.
 'Tis he. O brave Iago, honest and just,
 That hast such noble sense of thy friend's wrong!
35 Thou teachest me,—minion, your dear lies dead,
 And your unbless'd fate hies. Strumpet, I come!
 Forth of my heart those charms, thine eyes, are blotted;
 Thy bed, lust-stain'd, shall with lust's blood be spotted.

[Exit.]

Enter Lodovico and Gratiano.

CASSIO.
 What, ho! No watch? No passage? murder, murder!

GRATIANO.
40 'Tis some mischance; the cry is very direful.

CASSIO.
 O, help!

LODOVICO.
 Hark!

RODERIGO.
 O wretched villain!

LODOVICO.
Two or three groan. It is a heavy night.
45 These may be counterfeits. Let's think't unsafe
To come in to the cry without more help.

RODERIGO.
Nobody come? Then shall I bleed to death.

Enter Iago with a light.

LODOVICO.
Hark!

GRATIANO.
Here's one comes in his shirt, with light and weapons.

IAGO.
50 Who's there? Whose noise is this that cries on murder?

LODOVICO.
We do not know.

IAGO.
Did not you hear a cry?

CASSIO.
Here, here! for heaven's sake, help me!

IAGO.
What's the matter?

GRATIANO.
55 This is Othello's ancient, as I take it.

LODOVICO.
The same indeed, a very valiant fellow.

IAGO.
What are you here that cry so grievously?

CASSIO.
Iago? O, I am spoil'd, undone by villains!
Give me some help.

IAGO.
60 O me, lieutenant! What villains have done this?

CASSIO.
I think that one of them is hereabout,
And cannot make away.

IAGO.
 O treacherous villains!
 [*To Lodovico and Gratiano.*] What are you there?
65 Come in and give some help.

RODERIGO.
 O, help me here!

CASSIO.
 That's one of them.

IAGO.
 O murderous slave! O villain!

[*Stabs Roderigo.*]

RODERIGO.
 O damn'd Iago! O inhuman dog!

IAGO.
70 Kill men i' the dark! Where be these bloody thieves?
 How silent is this town! Ho! murder! murder!
 What may you be? Are you of good or evil?

LODOVICO.
 As you shall prove us, praise us.

IAGO.
 Signior Lodovico?

LODOVICO.
75 He, sir.

IAGO.
 I cry you mercy. Here's Cassio hurt by villains.

GRATIANO.
 Cassio!

IAGO.
 How is't, brother?

CASSIO.
 My leg is cut in two.

IAGO.
80 Marry, heaven forbid!
 Light, gentlemen, I'll bind it with my shirt.

Enter Bianca.

BIANCA.
 What is the matter, ho? Who is't that cried?

IAGO.
 Who is't that cried?

BIANCA.
 O my dear Cassio, my sweet Cassio! O Cassio, Cassio, Cassio!

IAGO.
85   O notable strumpet! Cassio, may you suspect
 Who they should be that have thus mangled you?

CASSIO.
 No.

GRATIANO.
 I am sorry to find you thus; I have been to seek you.

IAGO.
 Lend me a garter. So.—O, for a chair,
90   To bear him easily hence!

BIANCA.
 Alas, he faints! O Cassio, Cassio, Cassio!

IAGO.
 Gentlemen all, I do suspect this trash
 To be a party in this injury.
 Patience awhile, good Cassio. Come, come;
95   Lend me a light. Know we this face or no?
 Alas, my friend and my dear countryman
 Roderigo? No. Yes, sure; O heaven! Roderigo.

GRATIANO.
 What, of Venice?

IAGO.
 Even he, sir. Did you know him?

GRATIANO.
100   Know him? Ay.

IAGO.
 Signior Gratiano? I cry you gentle pardon.
 These bloody accidents must excuse my manners,
 That so neglected you.

                                    WILLIAM SHAKESPEARE

GRATIANO.
I am glad to see you.

IAGO.
105   How do you, Cassio? O, a chair, a chair!

GRATIANO.
Roderigo!

IAGO.
He, he, 'tis he.
                                                        [*A chair brought in.*]
O, that's well said; the chair.
Some good man bear him carefully from hence,
110   I'll fetch the general's surgeon. [*To Bianca*] For you, mistress,
Save you your labour. He that lies slain here, Cassio,
Was my dear friend. What malice was between you?

CASSIO.
None in the world. Nor do I know the man.

IAGO.
[*To Bianca.*] What, look you pale?—O, bear him out o' the air.
                                      [*Cassio and Roderigo are borne off.*]
115   Stay you, good gentlemen.—Look you pale, mistress?
Do you perceive the gastness of her eye?
Nay, if you stare, we shall hear more anon.
Behold her well. I pray you, look upon her.
Do you see, gentlemen? Nay, guiltiness will speak
120   Though tongues were out of use.

                            Enter Emilia.

EMILIA.
'Las, what's the matter? What's the matter, husband?

IAGO.
Cassio hath here been set on in the dark
By Roderigo, and fellows that are 'scap'd.
He's almost slain, and Roderigo dead.

EMILIA.
125   Alas, good gentleman! alas, good Cassio!

IAGO.
This is the fruit of whoring. Prithee, Emilia,
Go know of Cassio where he supp'd tonight.
What, do you shake at that?

BIANCA.
  He supp'd at my house, but I therefore shake not.

IAGO.
130 O, did he so? I charge you go with me.

EMILIA.
  Fie, fie upon thee, strumpet!

BIANCA.
  I am no strumpet, but of life as honest
  As you that thus abuse me.

EMILIA.
  As I? Foh! fie upon thee!

IAGO.
135 Kind gentlemen, let's go see poor Cassio dress'd.
  Come, mistress, you must tell's another tale.
  Emilia, run you to the citadel,
  And tell my lord and lady what hath happ'd.
  Will you go on afore? [*Aside.*] This is the night
140 That either makes me or fordoes me quite.

[Exeunt.]

SCENE II. Cyprus. A Bedchamber in the castle.
Desdemona in bed asleep; a light burning.
Enter Othello.

OTHELLO.
  It is the cause, it is the cause, my soul,
  Let me not name it to you, you chaste stars!
  It is the cause. Yet I'll not shed her blood,
  Nor scar that whiter skin of hers than snow,
5 And smooth as monumental alabaster.
  Yet she must die, else she'll betray more men.
  Put out the light, and then put out the light:
  If I quench thee, thou flaming minister,
  I can again thy former light restore,
10 Should I repent me. But once put out thy light,
  Thou cunning'st pattern of excelling nature,
  I know not where is that Promethean heat
  That can thy light relume. When I have pluck'd thy rose,
  I cannot give it vital growth again,
15 It must needs wither. I'll smell it on the tree.

[Kissing her.]

  O, balmy breath, that dost almost persuade

Justice to break her sword! One more, one more.
Be thus when thou art dead, and I will kill thee,
And love thee after. One more, and this the last.
20   So sweet was ne'er so fatal. I must weep,
But they are cruel tears. This sorrow's heavenly,
It strikes where it doth love. She wakes.

DESDEMONA.
Who's there? Othello?

OTHELLO.
Ay, Desdemona.

DESDEMONA.
25   Will you come to bed, my lord?

OTHELLO.
Have you pray'd tonight, Desdemona?

DESDEMONA.
Ay, my lord.

OTHELLO.
If you bethink yourself of any crime
Unreconcil'd as yet to heaven and grace,
30   Solicit for it straight.

DESDEMONA.
Alack, my lord, what may you mean by that?

OTHELLO.
Well, do it, and be brief, I will walk by.
I would not kill thy unprepared spirit,
No, heaven forfend! I would not kill thy soul.

DESDEMONA.
35   Talk you of killing?

OTHELLO.
Ay, I do.

DESDEMONA.
Then heaven have mercy on me!

OTHELLO.
Amen, with all my heart!

DESDEMONA.
If you say so, I hope you will not kill me.

OTHELLO.
40   Hum!

DESDEMONA.
 And yet I fear you, for you are fatal then
 When your eyes roll so: why I should fear I know not,
 Since guiltiness I know not, but yet I feel I fear.

OTHELLO.
 Think on thy sins.

DESDEMONA.
45   They are loves I bear to you.

OTHELLO.
 Ay, and for that thou diest.

DESDEMONA.
 That death's unnatural that kills for loving.
 Alas, why gnaw you so your nether lip?
 Some bloody passion shakes your very frame.
50   These are portents; but yet I hope, I hope,
 They do not point on me.

OTHELLO.
 Peace, and be still!

DESDEMONA.
 I will so. What's the matter?

OTHELLO.
 That handkerchief which I so loved and gave thee,
55   Thou gav'st to Cassio.

DESDEMONA.
 No, by my life and soul!
 Send for the man and ask him.

OTHELLO.
 Sweet soul, take heed, take heed of perjury,
 Thou'rt on thy death-bed.

DESDEMONA.
60   Ay, but not yet to die.

OTHELLO.
 Yes, presently:
 Therefore confess thee freely of thy sin.

For to deny each article with oath
Cannot remove nor choke the strong conception
65   That I do groan withal. Thou art to die.

DESDEMONA.
Then, Lord have mercy on me!

OTHELLO.
I say, amen.

DESDEMONA.
And have you mercy too! I never did
Offend you in my life,   never lov'd Cassio
70   But with such general warranty of heaven
As I might love. I never gave him token.

OTHELLO.
By heaven, I saw my handkerchief in 's hand.
O perjur'd woman, thou dost stone my heart,
And mak'st me call what I intend to do
75   A murder, which I thought a sacrifice.
I saw the handkerchief.

DESDEMONA.
He found it then.
I never gave it him. Send for him hither.
Let him confess a truth.

OTHELLO.
80   He hath confess'd.

DESDEMONA.
What, my lord?

OTHELLO.
That he hath us'd thee.

DESDEMONA.
How? Unlawfully?

OTHELLO.
Ay.

DESDEMONA.
85   He will not say so.

OTHELLO.
No, his mouth is stopp'd.
Honest Iago hath ta'en order for 't.

DESDEMONA.
 O, my fear interprets! What, is he dead?

OTHELLO.
 Had all his hairs been lives, my great revenge
90   Had stomach for them all.

DESDEMONA.
 Alas, he is betray'd, and I undone!

OTHELLO.
 Out, strumpet! Weep'st thou for him to my face?

DESDEMONA.
 O, banish me, my lord, but kill me not!

OTHELLO.
 Down, strumpet!

DESDEMONA.
95   Kill me tomorrow, let me live tonight!

OTHELLO.
 Nay, if you strive,—

DESDEMONA.
 But half an hour!

OTHELLO.
 Being done, there is no pause.

DESDEMONA.
 But while I say one prayer!

OTHELLO.
100   It is too late.

[Smothers her.]

EMILIA.
 [Within.] My lord, my lord! what, ho! my lord, my lord!

OTHELLO.
 What noise is this? Not dead? Not yet quite dead?
 I that am cruel am yet merciful,
 I would not have thee linger in thy pain.
105   So, so.

EMILIA.
 [Within.] What, ho! my lord, my lord!

OTHELLO.
Who's there?

EMILIA.
[*Within.*] O, good my lord, I would speak a word with you!

OTHELLO.
Yes. 'Tis Emilia, by and by. She's dead.
110   'Tis like she comes to speak of Cassio's death;
The noise was high.—Ha! no more moving?
Still as the grave. Shall she come in? Were't good?
I think she stirs again; no. What's best to do?
If she come in, she'll sure speak to my wife.
115   My wife! my wife! what wife? I have no wife.
O, insupportable! O heavy hour!
Methinks it should be now a huge eclipse
Of sun and moon, and that the affrighted globe
Should yawn at alteration.

EMILIA.
120   [*Within.*] I do beseech you
That I may speak with you, O, good my lord!

OTHELLO.
I had forgot thee: O, come in, Emilia.
Soft, by and by; let me the curtains draw.
Where art thou?

[*Unlocks the door.*]

Enter Emilia.

125   What's the matter with thee now?

EMILIA.
O, my good lord, yonder's foul murders done!

OTHELLO.
What, now?

EMILIA.
But now, my lord.

OTHELLO.
It is the very error of the moon,
130   She comes more nearer earth than she was wont
And makes men mad.

EMILIA.
Cassio, my lord, hath kill'd a young Venetian
Call'd Roderigo.

OTHELLO.
Roderigo kill'd?
135 And Cassio kill'd?

EMILIA.
No, Cassio is not kill'd.

OTHELLO.
Not Cassio kill'd! Then murder's out of tune,
And sweet revenge grows harsh.

DESDEMONA.
O, falsely, falsely murder'd!

EMILIA.
140 Alas, what cry is that?

OTHELLO.
That? What?

EMILIA.
Out, and alas! That was my lady's voice.
Help! help, ho! help! O lady, speak again,
Sweet Desdemona! O sweet mistress, speak!

DESDEMONA.
145 A guiltless death I die.

EMILIA.
O, who hath done this deed?

DESDEMONA.
Nobody; I myself. Farewell.
Commend me to my kind lord. O, farewell!

[*She dies.*]

OTHELLO.
Why, how should she be murder'd?

EMILIA.
150 Alas, who knows?

OTHELLO.
You heard her say herself, it was not I.

EMILIA.
She said so. I must needs report the truth.

OTHELLO.
She's like a liar, gone to burning hell.
'Twas I that kill'd her.

EMILIA.
155   O, the more angel she,
And you the blacker devil!

OTHELLO.
She turn'd to folly, and she was a whore.

EMILIA.
Thou dost belie her, and thou art a devil.

OTHELLO.
She was false as water.

EMILIA.
160   Thou art rash as fire, to say
That she was false: O, she was heavenly true!

OTHELLO.
Cassio did top her; ask thy husband else.
O, I were damn'd beneath all depth in hell,
But that I did proceed upon just grounds
165   To this extremity. Thy husband knew it all.

EMILIA.
My husband?

OTHELLO.
Thy husband.

EMILIA.
That she was false to wedlock?

OTHELLO.
Ay, with Cassio. Nay, had she been true,
170   If heaven would make me such another world
Of one entire and perfect chrysolite,
I'd not have sold her for it.

EMILIA.
My husband?

OTHELLO.
Ay, 'twas he that told me first.
175   An honest man he is, and hates the slime
That sticks on filthy deeds.

EMILIA.
 My husband?

OTHELLO.
 What needs this iterance, woman? I say thy husband.

EMILIA.
 O mistress, villainy hath made mocks with love!
180 My husband say that she was false?

OTHELLO.
 He, woman;
 I say thy husband: dost understand the word?
 My friend, thy husband, honest, honest Iago.

EMILIA.
 If he say so, may his pernicious soul
185 Rot half a grain a day! he lies to the heart.
 She was too fond of her most filthy bargain.

OTHELLO.
 Ha!

EMILIA.
 Do thy worst:
 This deed of thine is no more worthy heaven
190 Than thou wast worthy her.

OTHELLO.
 Peace, you were best.

EMILIA.
 Thou hast not half that power to do me harm
 As I have to be hurt. O gull! O dolt!
 As ignorant as dirt! Thou hast done a deed
195 (I care not for thy sword) I'll make thee known,
 Though I lost twenty lives. Help! help, ho! help!
 The Moor hath kill'd my mistress! Murder, murder!

Enter Montano, Gratiano and Iago.

MONTANO.
 What is the matter? How now, general?

EMILIA.
 O, are you come, Iago? You have done well,
200 That men must lay their murders on your neck.

GRATIANO.
 What is the matter?

EMILIA.
Disprove this villain, if thou be'st a man.
He says thou told'st him that his wife was false.
I know thou didst not, thou'rt not such a villain.
205 Speak, for my heart is full.

IAGO.
I told him what I thought, and told no more
Than what he found himself was apt and true.

EMILIA.
But did you ever tell him she was false?

IAGO.
I did.

EMILIA.
210 You told a lie, an odious, damned lie;
Upon my soul, a lie; a wicked lie.
She false with Cassio? Did you say with Cassio?

IAGO.
With Cassio, mistress. Go to, charm your tongue.

EMILIA.
I will not charm my tongue; I am bound to speak.
215 My mistress here lies murder'd in her bed.

ALL.
O heavens forfend!

EMILIA.
And your reports have set the murder on.

OTHELLO.
Nay, stare not, masters, it is true indeed.

GRATIANO.
'Tis a strange truth.

MONTANO.
220 O monstrous act!

EMILIA.
Villany, villany, villany!
I think upon't, I think I smell't; O villany!
I thought so then. I'll kill myself for grief.
O villany, villany!

IAGO.
225   What, are you mad? I charge you, get you home.

EMILIA.
  Good gentlemen, let me have leave to speak.
  'Tis proper I obey him, but not now.
  Perchance, Iago, I will ne'er go home.

OTHELLO.
  O! O! O!

                                        [*Hanging over his wife.*]

EMILIA.
230   Nay, lay thee down and roar;
  For thou hast kill'd the sweetest innocent
  That e'er did lift up eye.

OTHELLO.
  [*Rising.*] O, she was foul!
  I scarce did know you, uncle, there lies your niece,
235   Whose breath indeed these hands have newly stopp'd.
  I know this act shows horrible and grim.

GRATIANO.
  Poor Desdemona! I am glad thy father's dead.
  Thy match was mortal to him, and pure grief
  Shore his old thread in twain: did he live now,
240   This sight would make him do a desperate turn,
  Yea, curse his better angel from his side,
  And fall to reprobance.

OTHELLO.
  'Tis pitiful. But yet Iago knows
  That she with Cassio hath the act of shame
245   A thousand times committed; Cassio confess'd it,
  And she did gratify his amorous works
  With that recognizance and pledge of love
  Which I first gave her; I saw it in his hand.
  It was a handkerchief, an antique token
250   My father gave my mother.

EMILIA.
  O heaven! O heavenly powers!

IAGO.
  Come, hold your peace.

EMILIA.
 'Twill out, 'twill out. I peace?
 No, I will speak as liberal as the north.
255 Let heaven and men and devils, let them all,
 All, all, cry shame against me, yet I'll speak.

IAGO.
 Be wise, and get you home.

EMILIA.
 I will not.

             [Iago goes to stab his wife.]

GRATIANO.
 Fie!
260 Your sword upon a woman?

EMILIA.
 O thou dull Moor, that handkerchief thou speak'st of
 I found by fortune and did give my husband;
 For often with a solemn earnestness,
 More than indeed belong'd to such a trifle,
265 He begg'd of me to steal it.

IAGO.
 Villanous whore!

EMILIA.
 She give it Cassio! no, alas, I found it,
 And I did give't my husband.

IAGO.
 Filth, thou liest!

EMILIA.
270 By heaven, I do not, I do not, gentlemen.
 O murderous coxcomb! What should such a fool
 Do with so good a wife?

OTHELLO
 Are there not stones in heaven
 But what serve for thunder? Precious villain!

          [Iago stabs Emilia and then runs out.]

GRATIANO.
275 The woman falls. Sure, he hath kill'd his wife.

EMILIA.
 Ay, ay. O, lay me by my mistress' side.

GRATIANO.
 He's gone, but his wife's kill'd.

MONTANO.
 'Tis a notorious villain. Take you this weapon,
 Which I have here recover'd from the Moor.
280 Come, guard the door without, let him not pass,
 But kill him rather. I'll after that same villain,
 For 'tis a damned slave.

[Exit Montano and Gratiano.]

OTHELLO.
 I am not valiant neither,
 But every puny whipster gets my sword.
285 But why should honour outlive honesty?
 Let it go all.

EMILIA.
 What did thy song bode, lady?
 Hark, canst thou hear me? I will play the swan,
 And die in music.
290 [*Sings.*] *Willow, willow, willow.*
 Moor, she was chaste. She lov'd thee, cruel Moor,
 So come my soul to bliss, as I speak true;
 So speaking as I think, I die, I die.

[She dies.]

OTHELLO.
 I have another weapon in this chamber,
295 It is a sword of Spain, the ice-brook's temper.
 O, here it is. Uncle, I must come forth.

GRATIANO.
 [*Within.*] If thou attempt it, it will cost thee dear;
 Thou hast no weapon, and perforce must suffer.

OTHELLO.
 Look in upon me then, and speak with me,
300 Or, naked as I am, I will assault thee.

Enter Gratiano.

GRATIANO.
 What is the matter?

OTHELLO.
Behold, I have a weapon.
A better never did itself sustain
Upon a soldier's thigh: I have seen the day
305 That with this little arm and this good sword
I have made my way through more impediments
Than twenty times your stop. But, O vain boast!
Who can control his fate? 'Tis not so now.
Be not afraid, though you do see me weapon'd.
310 Here is my journey's end, here is my butt,
And very sea-mark of my utmost sail.
Do you go back dismay'd? 'Tis a lost fear.
Man but a rush against Othello's breast,
And he retires. Where should Othello go?
315 Now, how dost thou look now? O ill-starr'd wench,
Pale as thy smock, when we shall meet at compt,
This look of thine will hurl my soul from heaven,
And fiends will snatch at it. Cold, cold, my girl!
Even like thy chastity.
320 O cursed, cursed slave! Whip me, ye devils,
From the possession of this heavenly sight!
Blow me about in winds, roast me in sulphur,
Wash me in steep-down gulfs of liquid fire!
O Desdemon! Dead, Desdemon! dead! Oh, oh!

*Enter Lodovico, Montano, Cassio carried in a chair, and Officers
with Iago prisoner.*

LODOVICO.
325 Where is this rash and most unfortunate man?

OTHELLO.
That's he that was Othello. Here I am.

LODOVICO.
Where is that viper? Bring the villain forth.

OTHELLO.
I look down towards his feet; but that's a fable.
If that thou be'st a devil, I cannot kill thee.

[Wounds Iago.]

LODOVICO.
330 Wrench his sword from him.

IAGO.
I bleed, sir, but not kill'd.

OTHELLO.
I am not sorry neither. I'd have thee live,
For in my sense 'tis happiness to die.

LODOVICO.
O thou Othello, that wert once so good,
335 Fall'n in the practice of a damned slave,
What shall be said to thee?

OTHELLO.
Why, anything;
An honourable murderer, if you will.
For naught did I in hate, but all in honour.

LODOVICO.
340 This wretch hath part confess'd his villany.
Did you and he consent in Cassio's death?

OTHELLO.
Ay.

CASSIO.
Dear general, I never gave you cause.

OTHELLO.
I do believe it, and I ask your pardon.
345 Will you, I pray, demand that demi-devil
Why he hath thus ensnar'd my soul and body?

IAGO.
Demand me nothing. What you know, you know.
From this time forth I never will speak word.

LODOVICO.
What, not to pray?

GRATIANO.
350 Torments will ope your lips.

OTHELLO.
Well, thou dost best.

LODOVICO.
Sir, you shall understand what hath befall'n,
Which, as I think, you know not. Here is a letter
Found in the pocket of the slain Roderigo,
355 And here another. The one of them imports
The death of Cassio, to be undertook
By Roderigo.

OTHELLO.
O villain!

CASSIO.
Most heathenish and most gross!

LODOVICO.
360   Now here's another discontented paper,
Found in his pocket too; and this, it seems,
Roderigo meant to have sent this damned villain,
But that, belike, Iago in the interim
Came in and satisfied him.

OTHELLO.
365   O the pernicious caitiff!
How came you, Cassio, by that handkerchief
That was my wife's?

CASSIO.
I found it in my chamber.
And he himself confess'd but even now,
370   That there he dropp'd it for a special purpose
Which wrought to his desire.

OTHELLO.
O fool! fool! fool!

CASSIO.
There is besides in Roderigo's letter,
How he upbraids Iago, that he made him
375   Brave me upon the watch, whereon it came
That I was cast. And even but now he spake,
After long seeming dead, Iago hurt him,
Iago set him on.

LODOVICO.
You must forsake this room, and go with us.
380   Your power and your command is taken off,
And Cassio rules in Cyprus. For this slave,
If there be any cunning cruelty
That can torment him much and hold him long,
It shall be his. You shall close prisoner rest,
385   Till that the nature of your fault be known
To the Venetian state. Come, bring away.

OTHELLO.
Soft you; a word or two before you go.
I have done the state some service, and they know't.

No more of that. I pray you, in your letters,
390   When you shall these unlucky deeds relate,
Speak of me as I am. Nothing extenuate,
Nor set down aught in malice. Then must you speak
Of one that loved not wisely, but too well;
Of one not easily jealous, but being wrought,
395   Perplex'd in the extreme; of one whose hand,
Like the base Judean, threw a pearl away
Richer than all his tribe; of one whose subdu'd eyes,
Albeit unused to the melting mood,
Drop tears as fast as the Arabian trees
400   Their medicinal gum. Set you down this.
And say besides, that in Aleppo once,
Where a malignant and a turban'd Turk
Beat a Venetian and traduc'd the state,
I took by the throat the circumcised dog,
405   And smote him, thus.

[Stabs himself.]

LODOVICO.
 O bloody period!

GRATIANO.
 All that's spoke is marr'd.

OTHELLO.
 I kiss'd thee ere I kill'd thee. No way but this,
 Killing myself, to die upon a kiss.

[Falling upon Desdemona.]

CASSIO.
410   This did I fear, but thought he had no weapon,
 For he was great of heart.

LODOVICO.
 [To Iago.] O Spartan dog,
 More fell than anguish, hunger, or the sea,
 Look on the tragic loading of this bed.
415   This is thy work. The object poisons sight,
 Let it be hid. Gratiano, keep the house,
 And seize upon the fortunes of the Moor,
 For they succeed on you. To you, lord governor,
 Remains the censure of this hellish villain.
420   The time, the place, the torture, O, enforce it!
 Myself will straight aboard, and to the state
 This heavy act with heavy heart relate.

[Exeunt.]

THE SONNET

Originating with court poets in Italy during the thirteenth century, the sonnet reached its height in the fourteenth century with the sonnets of Petrarch. After Sir Thomas Wyatt and Henry Howard, Earl of Surrey, introduced the form to the English court, it caught on quickly in England in the 1500s. One of the most popular poetic forms of all time, sonnets were composed by many authors in this collection, including Ben Jonson, William Shakespeare, John Donne, and John Milton. Other famous writers of the period not represented here also wrote sonnets, such as Edmund Spenser and Philip Sidney. The sonnet has remained popular since it became widespread. More recent poets like Elizabeth Barrett Browning and Gerard Manley Hopkins wrote sonnets in the Victorian era, as well as numerous contemporary poets.

A sonnet consists of fourteen lines, generally in iambic pentameter. There are two main types of sonnets: the Italian or Petrarchan sonnet and the English or Shakespearean sonnet. The Italian sonnet is ideal for languages like Italian that have a lot of rhyming words, because it uses a rhyme scheme with a lot of repetition: ABBAABBA/CDECDE (or CDCDCD). It consists of a stanza with eight lines, the octave, followed by a stanza with six lines, the sestet. The octave, with the rhyme scheme ABBAABBA, usually sets up a problem or question, while the sestet, CDECDE or CDCDCD, answers the question or resolves the problem. An example of this form is John Donne's "Holy Sonnet 7" (page 850):

> At the round earth's imagin'd corners, blow
> Your trumpets, angels, and arise, arise
> From death, you numberless infinities
> Of souls, and to your scatter'd bodies go;
> All whom the flood did, and fire shall o'erthrow,
> All whom war, dearth, age, agues, tyrannies,
> Despair, law, chance hath slain, and you whose eyes
> Shall behold God and never taste death's woe.
>> But let them sleep, Lord, and me mourn a space,
>> For if above all these my sins abound,
>> 'Tis late to ask abundance of thy grace
>> When we are there; here on this lowly ground
>> Teach me how to repent; for that's as good
>> As if thou hadst seal'd my pardon with thy blood.

Donne sets up the problem in the octave, which in this case is the impending Day of Judgment. The resolution in the sestet asks to postpone that judgment by "let[ting] them sleep," so that the speaker has time to repent and request God's forgiveness.

Because English offers fewer rhyming words than Italian, it can be difficult to write Petrarchan sonnets in the English language. The English or Shakespearean sonnet with its ABAB/CDCD/EFEF/GG rhyme scheme, solves that dilemma by requiring just one rhyme for each line. It consists of three stanzas with four lines each, called quatrains, and a final rhyming couplet. Whereas in the Petrarchan sonnet six lines are provided to resolve the question or problem, the Shakespearean sonnet sets up the problem in the three quatrains, leaving only the couplet for resolution. An example is Shakespeare's famous "Sonnet 18:"

> Shall I compare thee to a summer's day?
> Thou art more lovely and more temperate:
> Rough winds do shake the darling buds of May,
> And summer's lease hath all too short a date;
> Sometime too hot the eye of heaven shines,
> And often is his gold complexion dimm'd;
> And every fair from fair sometime declines,
> By chance or nature's changing course untrimm'd;
> But thy eternal summer shall not fade,
> Nor lose possession of that fair thou ow'st;
> Nor shall death brag thou wander'st in his shade,
> When in eternal lines to time thou grow'st:
>> So long as men can breathe or eyes can see,
>> So long lives this, and this gives life to thee.

Shakespeare uses twelve lines to set up the problem that the young man's beauty must eventually fade. The final couplet presents the solution: the youth will live on through "this," the poem itself.

Sonnets in English are usually written in iambic pentameter, which consists of five *iambs*: two-syllable units that contain an unstressed syllable followed by a stressed syllable. Hence, each line in iambic pentameter has ten syllables. Shakespeare wrote all of his poems, and many speeches in his plays, in iambic pentameter. For example, the first line of *Twelfth Night* (pages 364-452) reads "if music be the food of love, play on." Here's what that looks like with the stressed syllables in bold:

> If **mu**sic **be** the **food** of **love**, play **on**.

Another example is from John Milton's *Paradise Lost* (pages 892-1017).

> Mine **eyes** he **closed** but **op**en **left** the **cell**.

Many poets use variations of the Italian or English sonnet forms. Gerard Manley Hopkins wrote shorter sonnets with as few as ten lines, and longer sonnets with additional codas. Edmund Spenser created the Spenserian sonnet, which contributes an interlinked rhyme scheme to the English sonnet. Its rhyme scheme is ABAB/BCBC/CDCD/EE. An important use of sonnets during the Elizabethan era can be found in sonnet cycles, famously written by Spenser, Sidney, Shakespeare, and Lady Mary Wroth, among many others. Sonnet cycles are long collections of sonnets that contain a central theme, often a loose, overarching plot, and sometimes the same characters developed repeatedly. While each individual sonnet is an independent work with its own conflict and resolution, the cycles can also be treated as complete poetic entities.

Shakespeare's Sonnets

1

From fairest creatures we desire increase,
That thereby beauty's rose might never die,
But as the riper should by time decease,
His tender heir might bear his memory:
5 But thou, contracted to thine own bright eyes,
Feed'st thy light's flame with self-substantial fuel,
Making a famine where abundance lies,
Thyself thy foe, to thy sweet self too cruel:
Thou that art now the world's fresh ornament,
10 And only herald to the gaudy spring,
Within thine own bud buriest thy content,
And tender churl mak'st waste in niggarding[1]:
        Pity the world, or else this glutton be,
        To eat the world's due, by the grave and thee.

2

When forty winters shall besiege thy brow,
And dig deep trenches in thy beauty's field,
Thy youth's proud livery so gazed on now,
Will be a tatter'd weed of small worth held:
5 Then being asked, where all thy beauty lies,
Where all the treasure of thy lusty days;
To say, within thine own deep sunken eyes,
Were an all-eating shame, and thriftless praise.
How much more praise deserv'd thy beauty's use,
10 If thou couldst answer 'This fair child of mine
Shall sum my count, and make my old excuse,'
Proving his beauty by succession thine!
        This were to be new made when thou art old,
        And see thy blood warm when thou feel'st it cold.

3

Look in thy glass and tell the face thou viewest
Now is the time that face should form another;
Whose fresh repair if now thou not renewest,
Thou dost beguile the world, unbless some mother.
5 For where is she so fair whose unear'd womb

1: Being stingy or miserly; no relation to the similar racial slur.

Disdains the tillage of thy husbandry?
Or who is he so fond will be the tomb,
Of his self-love to stop posterity?
Thou art thy mother's glass and she in thee
10 Calls back the lovely April of her prime;
So thou through windows of thine age shalt see,
Despite of wrinkles this thy golden time.
       But if thou live, remember'd not to be,
       Die single and thine image dies with thee.

5

Those hours, that with gentle work did frame
The lovely gaze where every eye doth dwell,
Will play the tyrants to the very same
And that unfair which fairly doth excel;
5 For never-resting time leads summer on
To hideous winter, and confounds him there;
Sap checked with frost, and lusty leaves quite gone,
Beauty o'er-snowed and bareness every where:
Then were not summer's distillation left,
10 A liquid prisoner pent in walls of glass,
Beauty's effect with beauty were bereft,
Nor it, nor no remembrance what it was:
       But flowers distill'd, though they with winter meet,
       Leese but their show; their substance still lives sweet.

10

For shame! deny that thou bear'st love to any,
Who for thyself art so unprovident.
Grant, if thou wilt, thou art belov'd of many,
But that thou none lov'st is most evident:
5 For thou art so possess'd with murderous hate,
That 'gainst thyself thou stick'st not to conspire,
Seeking that beauteous roof to ruinate
Which to repair should be thy chief desire.
O! change thy thought, that I may change my mind:
10 Shall hate be fairer lodg'd than gentle love?
Be, as thy presence is, gracious and kind,
Or to thyself at least kind-hearted prove:
       Make thee another self for love of me,
       That beauty still may live in thine or thee.

12

When I do count the clock that tells the time,
And see the brave day sunk in hideous night;

When I behold the violet past prime,
And sable curls, all silvered o'er with white;
5 When lofty trees I see barren of leaves,
Which erst from heat did canopy the herd,
And summer's green all girded up in sheaves,
Borne on the bier with white and bristly beard,
Then of thy beauty do I question make,
10 That thou among the wastes of time must go,
Since sweets and beauties do themselves forsake
And die as fast as they see others grow;
    And nothing 'gainst Time's scythe can make defence
    Save breed, to brave him when he takes thee hence.

14

Not from the stars do I my judgement pluck;
And yet methinks I have astronomy,
But not to tell of good or evil luck,
Of plagues, of dearths, or seasons' quality;
5 Nor can I fortune to brief minutes tell,
Pointing to each his thunder, rain and wind,
Or say with princes if it shall go well
By oft predict that I in heaven find:
But from thine eyes my knowledge I derive,
10 And constant stars in them I read such art
As 'Truth and beauty shall together thrive,
If from thyself, to store thou wouldst convert';
    Or else of thee this I prognosticate:
    'Thy end is truth's and beauty's doom and date.'

15

When I consider everything that grows
Holds in perfection but a little moment,
That this huge stage presenteth nought but shows
Whereon the stars in secret influence comment;
5 When I perceive that men as plants increase,
Cheered and checked even by the self-same sky,
Vaunt in their youthful sap, at height decrease,
And wear their brave state out of memory;
Then the conceit of this inconstant stay
10 Sets you most rich in youth before my sight,
Where wasteful Time debateth with Decay
To change your day of youth to sullied night,
    And all in war with Time for love of you,
    As he takes from you, I engraft you new.

18

Shall I compare thee to a summer's day?
Thou art more lovely and more temperate:
Rough winds do shake the darling buds of May,
And summer's lease hath all too short a date:
5 Sometime too hot the eye of heaven shines,
And often is his gold complexion dimm'd,
And every fair from fair sometime declines,
By chance, or nature's changing course untrimm'd:
But thy eternal summer shall not fade,
10 Nor lose possession of that fair thou ow'st,
Nor shall death brag thou wander'st in his shade,
When in eternal lines to time thou grow'st,
      So long as men can breathe, or eyes can see,
      So long lives this, and this gives life to thee.

19

Devouring Time, blunt thou the lion's paws,
And make the earth devour her own sweet brood;
Pluck the keen teeth from the fierce tiger's jaws,
And burn the long-liv'd phoenix, in her blood;
5 Make glad and sorry seasons as thou fleets,
And do whate'er thou wilt, swift-footed Time,
To the wide world and all her fading sweets;
But I forbid thee one most heinous crime:
O! carve not with thy hours my love's fair brow,
10 Nor draw no lines there with thine antique pen;
Him in thy course untainted do allow
For beauty's pattern to succeeding men.
      Yet do thy worst, old Time; despite thy wrong,
      My love shall in my verse ever live young.

20

A woman's face with nature's own hand painted,
Hast thou, the master mistress of my passion;
A woman's gentle heart, but not acquainted
With shifting change, as is false women's fashion:
5 An eye more bright than theirs, less false in rolling,
Gilding the object whereupon it gazeth;
A man in hue all 'hues' in his controlling,
Which steals men's eyes and women's souls amazeth.
And for a woman wert thou first created;
10 Till Nature, as she wrought thee, fell a-doting,
And by addition me of thee defeated,
By adding one thing to my purpose nothing.

But since she prick'd thee out for women's pleasure,
Mine be thy love and thy love's use their treasure.

21

So is it not with me as with that Muse,
Stirr'd by a painted beauty to his verse,
Who heaven itself for ornament doth use
And every fair with his fair doth rehearse,
5 Making a couplement of proud compare.
With sun and moon, with earth and sea's rich gems,
With April's first-born flowers, and all things rare,
That heaven's air in this huge rondure hems.
O! let me, true in love, but truly write,
10 And then believe me, my love is as fair
As any mother's child, though not so bright
As those gold candles fix'd in heaven's air:
     Let them say more that like of hearsay well;
     I will not praise that purpose not to sell.

23

As an unperfect actor on the stage,
Who with his fear is put beside his part,
Or some fierce thing replete with too much rage,
Whose strength's abundance weakens his own heart;
5 So I, for fear of trust, forget to say
The perfect ceremony of love's rite,
And in mine own love's strength seem to decay,
O'ercharg'd with burthen of mine own love's might.
O! let my looks be then the eloquence
10 And dumb presagers of my speaking breast,
Who plead for love, and look for recompense,
More than that tongue that more hath more express'd.
     O! learn to read what silent love hath writ:
     To hear with eyes belongs to love's fine wit.

26

Lord of my love, to whom in vassalage
Thy merit hath my duty strongly knit,
To thee I send this written embassage,
To witness duty, not to show my wit:
5 Duty so great, which wit so poor as mine
May make seem bare, in wanting words to show it,
But that I hope some good conceit of thine
In thy soul's thought, all naked, will bestow it:
Till whatsoever star that guides my moving,

10   Points on me graciously with fair aspect,
      And puts apparel on my tatter'd loving,
      To show me worthy of thy sweet respect:
            Then may I dare to boast how I do love thee;
            Till then, not show my head where thou mayst prove me.

29

      When in disgrace with fortune and men's eyes
      I all alone beweep my outcast state,
      And trouble deaf heaven with my bootless cries,
      And look upon myself, and curse my fate,
5   Wishing me like to one more rich in hope,
      Featur'd like him, like him with friends possess'd,
      Desiring this man's art, and that man's scope,
      With what I most enjoy contented least;
      Yet in these thoughts my self almost despising,
10   Haply I think on thee, and then my state,
      Like to the lark at break of day arising
      From sullen earth, sings hymns at heaven's gate;
            For thy sweet love remember'd such wealth brings
            That then I scorn to change my state with kings.

30

      When to the sessions of sweet silent thought
      I summon up remembrance of things past,
      I sigh the lack of many a thing I sought,
      And with old woes new wail my dear time's waste:
5   Then can I drown an eye, unused to flow,
      For precious friends hid in death's dateless night,
      And weep afresh love's long since cancell'd woe,
      And moan the expense of many a vanish'd sight:
      Then can I grieve at grievances foregone,
10   And heavily from woe to woe tell o'er
      The sad account of fore-bemoaned moan,
      Which I new pay as if not paid before.
            But if the while I think on thee, dear friend,
            All losses are restor'd and sorrows end.

33

      Full many a glorious morning have I seen
      Flatter the mountain tops with sovereign eye,
      Kissing with golden face the meadows green,
      Gilding pale streams with heavenly alchemy;
5   Anon permit the basest clouds to ride
      With ugly rack on his celestial face,

And from the forlorn world his visage hide,
Stealing unseen to west with this disgrace:
Even so my sun one early morn did shine,
10 With all triumphant splendour on my brow;
But out! alack! he was but one hour mine,
The region cloud hath mask'd him from me now.
　　　Yet him for this my love no whit disdaineth;
　　　Suns of the world may stain when heaven's sun staineth.

35

No more be griev'd at that which thou hast done:
Roses have thorns, and silver fountains mud:
Clouds and eclipses stain both moon and sun,
And loathsome canker lives in sweetest bud.
5 All men make faults, and even I in this,
Authorizing thy trespass with compare,
Myself corrupting, salving thy amiss,
Excusing thy sins more than thy sins are;
For to thy sensual fault I bring in sense;
10 Thy adverse party is thy advocate,
And 'gainst myself a lawful plea commence:
Such civil war is in my love and hate,
　　　That I an accessary needs must be,
　　　To that sweet thief which sourly robs from me.

38

How can my Muse want subject to invent,
While thou dost breathe, that pour'st into my verse
Thine own sweet argument, too excellent
For every vulgar paper to rehearse?
5 O! give thyself the thanks, if aught in me
Worthy perusal stand against thy sight;
For who's so dumb that cannot write to thee,
When thou thyself dost give invention light?
Be thou the tenth Muse, ten times more in worth
10 Than those old nine which rhymers invocate;
And he that calls on thee, let him bring forth
Eternal numbers to outlive long date.
　　　If my slight Muse do please these curious days,
　　　The pain be mine, but thine shall be the praise.

44

If the dull substance of my flesh were thought,
Injurious distance should not stop my way;
For then despite of space I would be brought,

From limits far remote, where thou dost stay.
5 No matter then although my foot did stand
Upon the farthest earth remov'd from thee;
For nimble thought can jump both sea and land,
As soon as think the place where he would be.
But, ah! thought kills me that I am not thought,
10 To leap large lengths of miles when thou art gone,
But that so much of earth and water wrought,
I must attend time's leisure with my moan;
      Receiving nought by elements so slow
      But heavy tears, badges of either's woe.

55

Not marble, nor the gilded monuments
Of princes, shall outlive this powerful rhyme;
But you shall shine more bright in these contents
Than unswept stone, besmear'd with sluttish time.
5 When wasteful war shall statues overturn,
And broils root out the work of masonry,
Nor Mars his sword, nor war's quick fire shall burn
The living record of your memory.
'Gainst death, and all-oblivious enmity
10 Shall you pace forth; your praise shall still find room
Even in the eyes of all posterity
That wear this world out to the ending doom.
      So, till the judgement that yourself arise,
      You live in this, and dwell in lovers' eyes.

56

Sweet love, renew thy force; be it not said
Thy edge should blunter be than appetite,
Which but to-day by feeding is allay'd,
To-morrow sharpened in his former might:
5 So, love, be thou, although to-day thou fill
Thy hungry eyes, even till they wink with fulness,
To-morrow see again, and do not kill
The spirit of love, with a perpetual dulness.
Let this sad interim like the ocean be
10 Which parts the shore, where two contracted new
Come daily to the banks, that when they see
Return of love, more blest may be the view;
      Or call it winter, which being full of care,
      Makes summer's welcome, thrice more wished, more rare.

60

Like as the waves make towards the pebbled shore,
So do our minutes hasten to their end;
Each changing place with that which goes before,
In sequent toil all forwards do contend.
5 Nativity, once in the main of light,
Crawls to maturity, wherewith being crown'd,
Crooked eclipses 'gainst his glory fight,
And Time that gave doth now his gift confound.
Time doth transfix the flourish set on youth
10 And delves the parallels in beauty's brow,
Feeds on the rarities of nature's truth,
And nothing stands but for his scythe to mow:
      And yet to times in hope, my verse shall stand.
      Praising thy worth, despite his cruel hand.

62

Sin of self-love possesseth all mine eye
And all my soul, and all my every part;
And for this sin there is no remedy,
It is so grounded inward in my heart.
5 Methinks no face so gracious is as mine,
No shape so true, no truth of such account;
And for myself mine own worth do define,
As I all other in all worths surmount.
But when my glass shows me myself indeed
10 Beated and chopp'd with tanned antiquity,
Mine own self-love quite contrary I read;
Self so self-loving were iniquity.
      'Tis thee, myself, that for myself I praise,
      Painting my age with beauty of thy days.

63

Against my love shall be as I am now,
With Time's injurious hand crush'd and o'erworn;
When hours have drain'd his blood and fill'd his brow
With lines and wrinkles; when his youthful morn
5 Hath travell'd on to age's steepy night;
And all those beauties whereof now he's king
Are vanishing, or vanished out of sight,
Stealing away the treasure of his spring;
For such a time do I now fortify
10 Against confounding age's cruel knife,
That he shall never cut from memory
My sweet love's beauty, though my lover's life:

His beauty shall in these black lines be seen,
And they shall live, and he in them still green.

65

Since brass, nor stone, nor earth, nor boundless sea,
But sad mortality o'ersways their power,
How with this rage shall beauty hold a plea,
Whose action is no stronger than a flower?
5   O! how shall summer's honey breath hold out,
Against the wrackful siege of battering days,
When rocks impregnable are not so stout,
Nor gates of steel so strong but Time decays?
O fearful meditation! where, alack,
10 Shall Time's best jewel from Time's chest lie hid?
Or what strong hand can hold his swift foot back?
Or who his spoil of beauty can forbid?
      O! none, unless this miracle have might,
      That in black ink my love may still shine bright.

71

No longer mourn for me when I am dead
Than you shall hear the surly sullen bell
Give warning to the world that I am fled
From this vile world with vilest worms to dwell:
5   Nay, if you read this line, remember not
The hand that writ it, for I love you so,
That I in your sweet thoughts would be forgot,
If thinking on me then should make you woe.
O if, I say, you look upon this verse,
10 When I perhaps compounded am with clay,
Do not so much as my poor name rehearse;
But let your love even with my life decay;
      Lest the wise world should look into your moan,
      And mock you with me after I am gone.

73

That time of year thou mayst in me behold
When yellow leaves, or none, or few, do hang
Upon those boughs which shake against the cold,
Bare ruin'd choirs, where late the sweet birds sang.
5   In me thou see'st the twilight of such day
As after sunset fadeth in the west;
Which by and by black night doth take away,
Death's second self, that seals up all in rest.
In me thou see'st the glowing of such fire,

10   That on the ashes of his youth doth lie,
     As the death-bed, whereon it must expire,
     Consum'd with that which it was nourish'd by.
             This thou perceiv'st, which makes thy love more strong,
             To love that well, which thou must leave ere long.

74

     But be contented: when that fell arrest
     Without all bail shall carry me away,
     My life hath in this line some interest,
     Which for memorial still with thee shall stay.
5   When thou reviewest this, thou dost review
     The very part was consecrate to thee:
     The earth can have but earth, which is his due;
     My spirit is thine, the better part of me:
     So then thou hast but lost the dregs of life,
10   The prey of worms, my body being dead;
     The coward conquest of a wretch's knife,
     Too base of thee to be remembered.
             The worth of that is that which it contains,
             And that is this, and this with thee remains.

79

     Whilst I alone did call upon thy aid,
     My verse alone had all thy gentle grace;
     But now my gracious numbers are decay'd,
     And my sick Muse doth give an other place.
5   I grant, sweet love, thy lovely argument
     Deserves the travail of a worthier pen;
     Yet what of thee thy poet doth invent
     He robs thee of, and pays it thee again.
     He lends thee virtue, and he stole that word
10   From thy behaviour; beauty doth he give,
     And found it in thy cheek: he can afford
     No praise to thee, but what in thee doth live.
             Then thank him not for that which he doth say,
             Since what he owes thee, thou thyself dost pay.

80

     O how I faint when I of you do write,
     Knowing a better spirit doth use your name,
     And in the praise thereof spends all his might,
     To make me tongue-tied speaking of your fame!
5   But since your worth, wide as the ocean is,
     The humble as the proudest sail doth bear,

My saucy bark, inferior far to his,
On your broad main doth wilfully appear.
Your shallowest help will hold me up afloat,
10   Whilst he upon your soundless deep doth ride;
Or, being wrack'd, I am a worthless boat,
He of tall building, and of goodly pride:
      Then if he thrive and I be cast away,
      The worst was this: my love was my decay.

81

Or I shall live your epitaph to make,
Or you survive when I in earth am rotten;
From hence your memory death cannot take,
Although in me each part will be forgotten.
5   Your name from hence immortal life shall have,
Though I, once gone, to all the world must die:
The earth can yield me but a common grave,
When you entombed in men's eyes shall lie.
Your monument shall be my gentle verse,
10   Which eyes not yet created shall o'er-read;
And tongues to be, your being shall rehearse,
When all the breathers of this world are dead;
      You still shall live, such virtue hath my pen,
      Where breath most breathes, even in the mouths of men.

87

Farewell! thou art too dear for my possessing,
And like enough thou know'st thy estimate,
The charter of thy worth gives thee releasing;
My bonds in thee are all determinate.
5   For how do I hold thee but by thy granting?
And for that riches where is my deserving?
The cause of this fair gift in me is wanting,
And so my patent back again is swerving.
Thyself thou gav'st, thy own worth then not knowing,
10   Or me to whom thou gav'st it, else mistaking;
So thy great gift, upon misprision growing,
Comes home again, on better judgement making.
      Thus have I had thee, as a dream doth flatter,
      In sleep a king, but waking no such matter.

97

How like a winter hath my absence been
From thee, the pleasure of the fleeting year!
What freezings have I felt, what dark days seen!

What old December's bareness everywhere!
5 And yet this time removed was summer's time;
The teeming autumn, big with rich increase,
Bearing the wanton burden of the prime,
Like widow'd wombs after their lords' decease:
Yet this abundant issue seem'd to me
10 But hope of orphans, and unfather'd fruit;
For summer and his pleasures wait on thee,
And, thou away, the very birds are mute:
       Or, if they sing, 'tis with so dull a cheer,
       That leaves look pale, dreading the winter's near.

98

From you have I been absent in the spring,
When proud-pied April, dress'd in all his trim,
Hath put a spirit of youth in every thing,
That heavy Saturn laugh'd and leap'd with him.
5 Yet nor the lays of birds, nor the sweet smell
Of different flowers in odour and in hue,
Could make me any summer's story tell,
Or from their proud lap pluck them where they grew:
Nor did I wonder at the lily's white,
10 Nor praise the deep vermilion in the rose;
They were but sweet, but figures of delight,
Drawn after you, you pattern of all those.
       Yet seem'd it winter still, and you away,
       As with your shadow I with these did play.

100

Where art thou Muse that thou forget'st so long,
To speak of that which gives thee all thy might?
Spend'st thou thy fury on some worthless song,
Darkening thy power to lend base subjects light?
5 Return forgetful Muse, and straight redeem,
In gentle numbers time so idly spent;
Sing to the ear that doth thy lays esteem
And gives thy pen both skill and argument.
Rise, resty Muse, my love's sweet face survey,
10 If Time have any wrinkle graven there;
If any, be a satire to decay,
And make time's spoils despised every where.
       Give my love fame faster than Time wastes life,
       So thou prevent'st his scythe and crooked knife.

105

Let not my love be call'd idolatry,
Nor my beloved as an idol show,
Since all alike my songs and praises be
To one, of one, still such, and ever so.
5 Kind is my love to-day, to-morrow kind,
Still constant in a wondrous excellence;
Therefore my verse to constancy confin'd,
One thing expressing, leaves out difference.
'Fair, kind, and true,' is all my argument,
10 'Fair, kind, and true,' varying to other words;
And in this change is my invention spent,
Three themes in one, which wondrous scope affords.
      Fair, kind, and true, have often liv'd alone,
      Which three till now, never kept seat in one.

106

When in the chronicle of wasted time
I see descriptions of the fairest wights,
And beauty making beautiful old rime,
In praise of ladies dead and lovely knights,
5 Then, in the blazon of sweet beauty's best,
Of hand, of foot, of lip, of eye, of brow,
I see their antique pen would have express'd
Even such a beauty as you master now.
So all their praises are but prophecies
10 Of this our time, all you prefiguring;
And for they looked but with divining eyes,
They had not skill enough your worth to sing:
      For we, which now behold these present days,
      Have eyes to wonder, but lack tongues to praise.

107

Not mine own fears, nor the prophetic soul
Of the wide world dreaming on things to come,
Can yet the lease of my true love control,
Supposed as forfeit to a confin'd doom.
5 The mortal moon hath her eclipse endur'd,
And the sad augurs mock their own presage;
Incertainties now crown themselves assur'd,
And peace proclaims olives of endless age.
Now with the drops of this most balmy time,
10 My love looks fresh, and Death to me subscribes,
Since, spite of him, I'll live in this poor rime,
While he insults o'er dull and speechless tribes:

    And thou in this shalt find thy monument,
    When tyrants' crests and tombs of brass are spent.

116

    Let me not to the marriage of true minds
    Admit impediments. Love is not love
    Which alters when it alteration finds,
    Or bends with the remover to remove:
5   O, no! it is an ever-fixed mark,
    That looks on tempests and is never shaken;
    It is the star to every wandering bark,
    Whose worth's unknown, although his height be taken.
    Love's not Time's fool, though rosy lips and cheeks
10   Within his bending sickle's compass come;
    Love alters not with his brief hours and weeks,
    But bears it out even to the edge of doom.
        If this be error and upon me prov'd,
        I never writ, nor no man ever lov'd.

119

    What potions have I drunk of Siren tears,
    Distill'd from limbecks foul as hell within,
    Applying fears to hopes, and hopes to fears,
    Still losing when I saw myself to win!
5   What wretched errors hath my heart committed,
    Whilst it hath thought itself so blessed never!
    How have mine eyes out of their spheres been fitted,
    In the distraction of this madding fever!
    O benefit of ill! now I find true
10   That better is, by evil still made better;
    And ruin'd love, when it is built anew,
    Grows fairer than at first, more strong, far greater.
        So I return rebuk'd to my content,
        And gain by ill thrice more than I have spent.

126

    O thou, my lovely boy, who in thy power
    Dost hold Time's fickle glass, his fickle hour;
    Who hast by waning grown, and therein show'st
    Thy lovers withering, as thy sweet self grow'st.
5   If Nature, sovereign mistress over wrack,
    As thou goest onwards, still will pluck thee back,
    She keeps thee to this purpose, that her skill
    May time disgrace and wretched minutes kill.
    Yet fear her, O thou minion of her pleasure!

10 She may detain, but not still keep, her treasure:
      Her audit (though delayed) answered must be,
      And her quietus is to render thee.

127

In the old age black was not counted fair,
Or if it were, it bore not beauty's name;
But now is black beauty's successive heir,
And beauty slander'd with a bastard shame:
5 For since each hand hath put on Nature's power,
Fairing the foul with Art's false borrowed face,
Sweet beauty hath no name, no holy bower,
But is profan'd, if not lives in disgrace.
Therefore my mistress' eyes are raven black,
10 Her eyes so suited, and they mourners seem
At such who, not born fair, no beauty lack,
Sland'ring creation with a false esteem:
      Yet so they mourn becoming of their woe,
      That every tongue says beauty should look so.

128

How oft when thou, my music, music play'st,
Upon that blessed wood whose motion sounds
With thy sweet fingers when thou gently sway'st
The wiry concord that mine ear confounds,
5 Do I envy those jacks that nimble leap,
To kiss the tender inward of thy hand,
Whilst my poor lips which should that harvest reap,
At the wood's boldness by thee blushing stand!
To be so tickled, they would change their state
10 And situation with those dancing chips,
O'er whom thy fingers walk with gentle gait,
Making dead wood more bless'd than living lips.
      Since saucy jacks so happy are in this,
      Give them thy fingers, me thy lips to kiss.

129

The expense of spirit in a waste of shame
Is lust in action: and till action, lust
Is perjur'd, murderous, bloody, full of blame,
Savage, extreme, rude, cruel, not to trust;
5 Enjoy'd no sooner but despised straight;
Past reason hunted; and no sooner had,
Past reason hated, as a swallow'd bait,
On purpose laid to make the taker mad:

Mad in pursuit and in possession so;
10   Had, having, and in quest, to have extreme;
A bliss in proof, and proved, a very woe;
Before, a joy propos'd; behind a dream.
          All this the world well knows; yet none knows well
          To shun the heaven that leads men to this hell.

130

My mistress' eyes are nothing like the sun;
Coral is far more red, than her lips red:
If snow be white, why then her breasts are dun;
If hairs be wires, black wires grow on her head.
5   I have seen roses damask'd, red and white,
But no such roses see I in her cheeks;
And in some perfumes is there more delight
Than in the breath that from my mistress reeks.
I love to hear her speak, yet well I know
10   That music hath a far more pleasing sound:
I grant I never saw a goddess go;
My mistress, when she walks, treads on the ground:
          And yet by heaven, I think my love as rare,
          As any she belied with false compare.

135

Whoever hath her wish, thou hast thy 'Will,'
And 'Will' to boot, and 'Will' in over-plus;
More than enough am I that vex'd thee still,
To thy sweet will making addition thus.
5   Wilt thou, whose will is large and spacious,
Not once vouchsafe to hide my will in thine?
Shall will in others seem right gracious,
And in my will no fair acceptance shine?
The sea, all water, yet receives rain still,
10   And in abundance addeth to his store;
So thou, being rich in 'Will,' add to thy 'Will'
One will of mine, to make thy large will more.
          Let no unkind 'No' fair beseechers kill;
          Think all but one, and me in that one 'Will.'

138

When my love swears that she is made of truth,
I do believe her though I know she lies,
That she might think me some untutor'd youth,
Unlearned in the world's false subtleties.
5   Thus vainly thinking that she thinks me young,

Although she knows my days are past the best,
Simply I credit her false-speaking tongue:
On both sides thus is simple truth suppressed:
But wherefore says she not she is unjust?
10 And wherefore say not I that I am old?
O! love's best habit is in seeming trust,
And age in love, loves not to have years told:
       Therefore I lie with her, and she with me,
       And in our faults by lies we flatter'd be.

141

In faith I do not love thee with mine eyes,
For they in thee a thousand errors note;
But 'tis my heart that loves what they despise,
Who, in despite of view, is pleased to dote.
5 Nor are mine ears with thy tongue's tune delighted;
Nor tender feeling, to base touches prone,
Nor taste, nor smell, desire to be invited
To any sensual feast with thee alone:
But my five wits nor my five senses can
10 Dissuade one foolish heart from serving thee,
Who leaves unsway'd the likeness of a man,
Thy proud heart's slave and vassal wretch to be:
       Only my plague thus far I count my gain,
       That she that makes me sin awards me pain.

144

Two loves I have of comfort and despair,
Which like two spirits do suggest me still:
The better angel is a man right fair,
The worser spirit a woman colour'd ill.
5 To win me soon to hell, my female evil,
Tempteth my better angel from my side,
And would corrupt my saint to be a devil,
Wooing his purity with her foul pride.
And whether that my angel be turn'd fiend,
10 Suspect I may, yet not directly tell;
But being both from me, both to each friend,
I guess one angel in another's hell:
       Yet this shall I ne'er know, but live in doubt,
       Till my bad angel fire my good one out.

146

Poor soul, the centre of my sinful earth,
My sinful earth these rebel powers array,

Why dost thou pine within and suffer dearth,
Painting thy outward walls so costly gay?
5   Why so large cost, having so short a lease,
Dost thou upon thy fading mansion spend?
Shall worms, inheritors of this excess,
Eat up thy charge? Is this thy body's end?
Then soul, live thou upon thy servant's loss,
10   And let that pine to aggravate thy store;
Buy terms divine in selling hours of dross;
Within be fed, without be rich no more:
      So shall thou feed on Death, that feeds on men,
      And Death once dead, there's no more dying then.

147

My love is as a fever longing still,
For that which longer nurseth the disease;
Feeding on that which doth preserve the ill,
The uncertain sickly appetite to please.
5   My reason, the physician to my love,
Angry that his prescriptions are not kept,
Hath left me, and I desperate now approve
Desire is death, which physic did except.
Past cure I am, now Reason is past care,
10   And frantic-mad with evermore unrest;
My thoughts and my discourse as madmen's are,
At random from the truth vainly express'd;
      For I have sworn thee fair, and thought thee bright,
      Who art as black as hell, as dark as night.

154

The little Love-god lying once asleep,
Laid by his side his heart-inflaming brand,
Whilst many nymphs that vow'd chaste life to keep
Came tripping by; but in her maiden hand
5   The fairest votary took up that fire
Which many legions of true hearts had warm'd;
And so the general of hot desire
Was, sleeping, by a virgin hand disarm'd.
This brand she quenched in a cool well by,
10   Which from Love's fire took heat perpetual,
Growing a bath and healthful remedy,
For men diseased; but I, my mistress' thrall,
      Came there for cure and this by that I prove,
      Love's fire heats water, water cools not love.

BEN JONSON

Benjamin Jonson was born in June of 1572, a month after the death of his father, whose name is unknown. Before the elder Jonson's death, Queen Mary's government seized his property because of his Protestant faith. Two years later, Ben Jonson's mother Rebecca married Robert Brett, a bricklayer. Jonson attended the prestigious Westminster School, where his teacher, historian William Camden, befriended him. Jonson started school at Cambridge but, unwilling to be apprenticed to his stepfather, he volunteered to fight in the Netherlands for Dutch independence from Spain.

When Jonson returned to England, he began to work as an actor. He played the protagonist of Thomas Kyd's *The Spanish Tragedy*, which scholars identify as the first Elizabethan revenge tragedy. He may also have married his wife, whose identity is obscure, in 1594. They had three children, all of whom died before their father. By 1597, Jonson had begun worked as a playwright for producer Philip Henslowe. That same year, Parliament censored *The Isle of Dogs*, a play that Jonson co-wrote with satirist Thomas Nashe, after its first performance. The play has been lost, but scholars believe it satirized an important member of the British nobility, possibly even Queen Elizabeth herself. Jonson was imprisoned for three months, and Nashe's home was raided. This was the first of many run-ins with the law throughout Jonson's life. The following year he was again imprisoned, this time for killing his opponent in a duel. He converted to Catholicism while in jail.

1598 saw the first performance of *Every Man in His Humour*, which established Jonson's reputation as a dramatist. William Shakespeare acted in the play, and Jonson released a sequel, *Every Man out of His Humour*, the following year. Performances of these plays caused Jonson to become known for writing "comedies of humours," which focused on characters defined by certain traits that they possessed.[1] Jonson employed the genre to satirize society. In 1600, he released *Cynthia's Revels*, which satirized fellow poets and playwrights Thomas Dekker and John Marston. Jonson mocked both of them again in 1601's *Poetaster*. He went on, however, to collaborate with Dekker in 1603 and Marston in 1605, suggesting reconciliation.

Jonson's next play, *Sejanus His Fall*, was performed by the King's Men in 1604, but it was not well received. The Privy Council accused Jonson of treason because of *Sejanus*, but they took no action against him; it is uncertain what was considered

---

1: A popular medical theory at the time described the "four humours" which controlled emotions: blood, phlegm, black bile, and yellow bile.

treasonous about the play. During this time, Jonson also wrote masques for the court of King James VI and I, including *The Satyr* and *The Masque of Blackness*. Writing masques was more prestigious than being a common playwright, and Jonson wrote about two dozen masques for James throughout his reign. In 1605, Jonson released *Eastward Ho!*, a collaboration with John Marston and George Chapman. The drama's satire of Scottish people so offended King James so much that he had Chapman and Jonson imprisoned for four months. The Crown banned *Eastward Ho!* until 1614.

Jonson's next play, the 1606 comedy *Volpone* was well-received and remains Jonson's most-performed work to this day. Centering on a wealthy Venetian gentleman, it satirizes greed and gullibility. Throughout the next decade, Jonson wrote the comedies *Epicene* (1609), *The Alchemist* (1610), *Bartholomew Fair* (1614), and *The Devil is an Ass* (1616), as well as the tragedy *Catiline His Conspiracy* (1611). None of them were as famous— or as controversial— as his earlier plays. Jonson began receiving a yearly salary from King James for his masques in 1616, so he retired from writing plays for a decade to focus on masques. Oxford University also granted Jonson an honorary Master of Arts degree in 1619.

After King James I died in 1625, his son Charles was crowned king. Charles's ascension decreased the demand for Jonson's court masques, so he began to write plays for the general public again. Contemporary scholars find 1625's *The Staple of News* interesting because of its portrayal of early English journalism, but it was not well received at the time. 1629's *The New Inn* was a complete failure, earning resounding boos from audiences. The "Sons of Ben," a group of younger poets inspired by Jonson's work, even criticized *The New Inn* and mocked Jonson's poetic response to its failure, "An Ode to Himself." Jonson suffered multiple strokes in the 1620s. His last play performed in his lifetime was *The Magnetic Lady* in 1632, which received lukewarm reviews.

Jonson's health steadily declined throughout the 1630s. He died of unknown causes on August 18th, 1637, at the age of sixty-five. He received an elaborate funeral the following day, and was buried in Westminster Abbey. Jonson's grave is notable because he was buried upright, possibly due to economic circumstances or by his own request. A monument to Jonson was erected in Westminster Abbey's Poets' Corner in 1723. At the time of his death, Jonson left two plays unfinished: *Mortimer His Fall*, a history play, and *The Sad Shepherd*, a pastoral drama.

TIMELINE

1572	Jonson is born, immediately after his father's death.
1589	Jonson graduates from Westminster School and is apprenticed to his stepfather.
c. 1590	Jonson goes to the Netherlands as a soldier.
c. 1594	Jonson marries his wife, who may have been named Ann Lewis.
1597	Jonson is employed as a playwright; *The Isle of Dogs* is censored and Jonson is imprisoned for its contents.
1598	Jonson kills actor Gabriel Spenser in a duel and is imprisoned; he converts to Catholicism in jail; *Every Man in His Humour* is released with great success.
1599	*Every Man out of His Humour.*
1603	*Sejanus His Fall.*
1603	King James I is crowned and begins commissioning court masques.
1605	*Eastward Ho!* offends King James I because of its anti-Scottish sentiments; Jonson and Chapman are briefly imprisoned.
c. 1606	*Volpone.*
1609	*Epicene.*
1610	*The Alchemist.*
1611	*Catiline His Conspiracy.*
1614	*Bartholomew Fair.*
1616	*The Devil is an Ass.*
1619	Jonson is awarded an honorary degree from Oxford.
1625	King James I dies; King Charles I is crowned.
1625	*The Staple of News.*
1629	*The New Inn*, a catastrophic failure for Jonson.
1632	*The Magnetic Lady.*
1637	Jonson dies.

Volpone

By Ben Jonson

Dramatis Personae

VOLPONE, a Magnifico.
MOSCA, his Parasite.
VOLTORE, an Advocate.
CORBACCIO, an old Gentleman.
CORVINO, a Merchant.
BONARIO, son to Corbaccio.
SIR POLITICK WOULD-BE, a Knight.
PEREGRINE, a Gentleman Traveller.
NANO, a Dwarf.
CASTRONE, an Eunuch.
ANDROGYNO, an Hermaphrodite.
GREGE (or Mob).
COMMANDADORI, Officers of Justice.
MERCATORI, three Merchants.
AVOCATORI, four Magistrates.
NOTARIO, the Register.
LADY WOULD-BE, Sir Politick's Wife.
CELIA, Corvino's Wife.
SERVITORI, Servants, two Waiting-women, etc.

The Argument.

Volpone, childless, rich, feigns sick, despairs,
Offers his state to hopes of several heirs,
Lies languishing: his parasite receives
Presents of all, assures, deludes; then weaves
Other cross plots, which ope themselves, are told.
New tricks for safety are sought; they thrive: when bold,
Each tempts the other again, and all are sold.

Prologue.

Now, luck yet sends us, and a little wit
Will serve to make our play hit;
(According to the palates of the season)
Here is rhime, not empty of reason.
5   This we were bid to credit from our poet,
Whose true scope, if you would know it,

In all his poems still hath been this measure,
To mix profit with your pleasure;
And not as some, whose throats their envy failing,
10 Cry hoarsely, All he writes is railing:
And when his plays come forth, think they can flout them,
With saying, he was a year about them.
To this there needs no lie, but this his creature,
Which was two months since no feature;
15 And though he dares give them five lives to mend it,
'Tis known, five weeks fully penn'd it,
From his own hand, without a co-adjutor,
Novice, journey-man, or tutor.
Yet thus much I can give you as a token
20 Of his play's worth, no eggs are broken,
Nor quaking custards with fierce teeth affrighted,
Wherewith your rout are so delighted;
Nor hales he in a gull old ends reciting,
To stop gaps in his loose writing;
25 With such a deal of monstrous and forced action,
As might make Bethlem a faction:
Nor made he his play for jests stolen from each table,
But makes jests to fit his fable;
And so presents quick comedy refined,
30 As best critics have designed;
The laws of time, place, persons he observeth,
From no needful rule he swerveth.
All gall and copperas from his ink he draineth,
Only a little salt remaineth,
35 Wherewith he'll rub your cheeks, till red, with laughter,
They shall look fresh a week after.

ACT 1. SCENE 1.1.
A ROOM IN VOLPONE'S HOUSE.

ENTER VOLPONE AND MOSCA.

VOLP: Good morning to the day; and next, my gold:
Open the shrine, that I may see my Saint.
 [MOSCA WITHDRAWS THE CURTAIN, AND DISCOVERS PILES
 OF GOLD, PLATE, JEWELS, ETC.]
Hail the world's soul, and mine! more glad than is
The teeming earth to see the long'd-for sun
5 Peep through the horns of the celestial Ram,
Am I, to view thy splendour darkening his;
That lying here, amongst my other hoards,

Shew'st like a flame by night; or like the day
Struck out of chaos, when all darkness fled
10   Unto the centre. O thou son of Sol,
But brighter than thy father, let me kiss,
With adoration, thee, and every relick
Of sacred treasure, in this blessed room.
Well did wise poets, by thy glorious name,
15   Title that age which they would have the best;
Thou being the best of things: and far transcending
All style of joy, in children, parents, friends,
Or any other waking dream on earth:
Thy looks when they to Venus did ascribe,
20   They should have given her twenty thousand Cupids;
Such are thy beauties and our loves! Dear saint,
Riches, the dumb God, that giv'st all men tongues;
That canst do nought, and yet mak'st men do all things;
The price of souls; even hell, with thee to boot,
25   Is made worth heaven. Thou art virtue, fame,
Honour, and all things else. Who can get thee,
He shall be noble, valiant, honest, wise,—

MOS: And what he will, sir. Riches are in fortune
A greater good than wisdom is in nature.

30   VOLP: True, my beloved Mosca. Yet I glory
More in the cunning purchase of my wealth,
Than in the glad possession; since I gain
No common way; I use no trade, no venture;
I wound no earth with plough-shares; fat no beasts,
35   To feed the shambles; have no mills for iron,
Oil, corn, or men, to grind them into powder:
I blow no subtle glass; expose no ships
To threat'nings of the furrow-faced sea;
I turn no monies in the public bank,
40   Nor usure private.

MOS: No sir, nor devour
Soft prodigals. You shall have some will swallow
A melting heir as glibly as your Dutch
Will pills of butter, and ne'er purge for it;
45   Tear forth the fathers of poor families
Out of their beds, and coffin them alive
In some kind clasping prison, where their bones
May be forth-coming, when the flesh is rotten:
But your sweet nature doth abhor these courses;

50 You lothe the widdow's or the orphan's tears
    Should wash your pavements, or their piteous cries
    Ring in your roofs, and beat the air for vengeance.

VOLP: Right, Mosca; I do lothe it.

MOS: And besides, sir,
55 You are not like a thresher that doth stand
    With a huge flail, watching a heap of corn,
    And, hungry, dares not taste the smallest grain,
    But feeds on mallows, and such bitter herbs;
    Nor like the merchant, who hath fill'd his vaults
60 With Romagnia, and rich Candian wines,
    Yet drinks the lees of Lombard's vinegar:
    You will not lie in straw, whilst moths and worms
    Feed on your sumptuous hangings and soft beds;
    You know the use of riches, and dare give now
65 From that bright heap, to me, your poor observer,
    Or to your dwarf, or your hermaphrodite,
    Your eunuch, or what other household-trifle
    Your pleasure allows maintenance.

VOLP: Hold thee, Mosca,

                                          [GIVES HIM MONEY.]

70 Take of my hand; thou strik'st on truth in all,
    And they are envious term thee parasite.
    Call forth my dwarf, my eunuch, and my fool,
    And let them make me sport.

                                          [EXIT MOS.]

    What should I do,
75 But cocker up my genius, and live free
    To all delights my fortune calls me to?
    I have no wife, no parent, child, ally,
    To give my substance to; but whom I make
    Must be my heir: and this makes men observe me:
80 This draws new clients daily, to my house,
    Women and men of every sex and age,
    That bring me presents, send me plate, coin, jewels,
    With hope that when I die (which they expect
    Each greedy minute) it shall then return
85 Ten-fold upon them; whilst some, covetous
    Above the rest, seek to engross me whole,
    And counter-work the one unto the other,
    Contend in gifts, as they would seem in love:
    All which I suffer, playing with their hopes,

90 And am content to coin them into profit,
    To look upon their kindness, and take more,
    And look on that; still bearing them in hand,
    Letting the cherry knock against their lips,
    And draw it by their mouths, and back again.—
95 How now!

[RE-ENTER MOSCA WITH NANO, ANDROGYNO, AND
CASTRONE.]

    NAN: Now, room for fresh gamesters, who do will you to know,
    They do bring you neither play, nor university show;
    And therefore do entreat you, that whatsoever they rehearse,
    May not fare a whit the worse, for the false pace of the verse.
100 If you wonder at this, you will wonder more ere we pass,
    For know, here is inclosed the soul of Pythagoras,
    That juggler divine, as hereafter shall follow;
    Which soul, fast and loose, sir, came first from Apollo,
    And was breath'd into Aethalides; Mercurius his son,
105 Where it had the gift to remember all that ever was done.
    From thence it fled forth, and made quick transmigration
    To goldy-lock'd Euphorbus, who was killed in good fashion,
    At the siege of old Troy, by the cuckold of Sparta.
    Hermotimus was next (I find it in my charta)
110 To whom it did pass, where no sooner it was missing
    But with one Pyrrhus of Delos it learn'd to go a fishing;
    And thence did it enter the sophist of Greece.
    From Pythagore, she went into a beautiful piece,
    Hight Aspasia, the meretrix; and the next toss of her
115 Was again of a whore, she became a philosopher,
    Crates the cynick, as it self doth relate it:
    Since kings, knights, and beggars, knaves, lords and fools gat it,
    Besides, ox and ass, camel, mule, goat, and brock,
    In all which it hath spoke, as in the cobler's cock.
120 But I come not here to discourse of that matter,
    Or his one, two, or three, or his greath oath, BY QUATER!
    His musics, his trigon, his golden thigh,
    Or his telling how elements shift, but I
    Would ask, how of late thou best suffered translation,
125 And shifted thy coat in these days of reformation.

    AND: Like one of the reformed, a fool, as you see,
    Counting all old doctrine heresy.

    NAN: But not on thine own forbid meats hast thou ventured?

AND: On fish, when first a Carthusian I enter'd.

130   NAN: Why, then thy dogmatical silence hath left thee?

AND: Of that an obstreperous lawyer bereft me.

NAN: O wonderful change, when sir lawyer forsook thee!
For Pythagore's sake, what body then took thee?

AND: A good dull mule.

135   NAN: And how! by that means
Thou wert brought to allow of the eating of beans?

AND: Yes.

NAN: But from the mule into whom didst thou pass?

AND: Into a very strange beast, by some writers call'd an ass;
140   By others, a precise, pure, illuminate brother,
Of those devour flesh, and sometimes one another;
And will drop you forth a libel, or a sanctified lie,
Betwixt every spoonful of a nativity pie.

NAN: Now quit thee, for heaven, of that profane nation;
145   And gently report thy next transmigration.

AND: To the same that I am.

NAN: A creature of delight,
And, what is more than a fool, an hermaphrodite!
Now, prithee, sweet soul, in all thy variation,
150   Which body would'st thou choose, to keep up thy station?

AND: Troth, this I am in: even here would I tarry.

NAN: 'Cause here the delight of each sex thou canst vary?

AND: Alas, those pleasures be stale and forsaken;
No, 'tis your fool wherewith I am so taken,
155   The only one creature that I can call blessed:
For all other forms I have proved most distressed.

NAN: Spoke true, as thou wert in Pythagoras still.
This learned opinion we celebrate will,

Fellow eunuch, as behoves us, with all our wit and art,
160   To dignify that whereof ourselves are so great and special a part.

VOLP: Now, very, very pretty! Mosca, this
Was thy invention?

MOS: If it please my patron,
Not else.

165   VOLP: It doth, good Mosca.

MOS: Then it was, sir.

NANO AND CASTRONE [SING.]: Fools, they are the only nation
Worth men's envy, or admiration:
Free from care or sorrow-taking,
170   Selves and others merry making:
All they speak or do is sterling.
Your fool he is your great man's darling,
And your ladies' sport and pleasure;
Tongue and bauble are his treasure.
175   E'en his face begetteth laughter,
And he speaks truth free from slaughter;
He's the grace of every feast,
And sometimes the chiefest guest;
Hath his trencher and his stool,
180   When wit waits upon the fool:
O, who would not be
He, he, he?

[KNOCKING WITHOUT.]

VOLP: Who's that? Away!

[EXEUNT NANO AND CASTRONE.]

Look, Mosca. Fool, begone!

[EXIT ANDROGYNO.]

185   MOS: 'Tis Signior Voltore, the advocate;
I know him by his knock.

VOLP: Fetch me my gown,
My furs and night-caps; say, my couch is changing,
And let him entertain himself awhile
190   Without i' the gallery.

[EXIT MOSCA.]

Now, now, my clients
Begin their visitation! Vulture, kite,
Raven, and gorcrow, all my birds of prey,
That think me turning carcase, now they come;
195   I am not for them yet—
           [RE-ENTER MOSCA, WITH THE GOWN, ETC.]
How now! the news?

MOS: A piece of plate, sir.

VOLP: Of what bigness?

MOS: Huge,
200   Massy, and antique, with your name inscribed,
And arms engraven.

VOLP: Good! and not a fox
Stretch'd on the earth, with fine delusive sleights,
Mocking a gaping crow? ha, Mosca?

205   MOS: Sharp, sir.

VOLP: Give me my furs.
                      [PUTS ON HIS SICK DRESS.]
Why dost thou laugh so, man?

MOS: I cannot choose, sir, when I apprehend
What thoughts he has without now, as he walks:
210   That this might be the last gift he should give;
That this would fetch you; if you died to-day,
And gave him all, what he should be to-morrow;
What large return would come of all his ventures;
How he should worship'd be, and reverenced;
215   Ride with his furs, and foot-cloths; waited on
By herds of fools, and clients; have clear way
Made for his mule, as letter'd as himself;
Be call'd the great and learned advocate:
And then concludes, there's nought impossible.

220   VOLP: Yes, to be learned, Mosca.

MOS: O no: rich
Implies it. Hood an ass with reverend purple,
So you can hide his two ambitious ears,
And he shall pass for a cathedral doctor.

225   VOLP: My caps, my caps, good Mosca. Fetch him in.

       MOS: Stay, sir, your ointment for your eyes.

       VOLP: That's true;
       Dispatch, dispatch: I long to have possession
       Of my new present.

230   MOS: That, and thousands more,
       I hope, to see you lord of.

       VOLP: Thanks, kind Mosca.

       MOS: And that, when I am lost in blended dust,
       And hundred such as I am, in succession—

235   VOLP: Nay, that were too much, Mosca.

       MOS: You shall live,
       Still, to delude these harpies.

       VOLP: Loving Mosca!
       'Tis well: my pillow now, and let him enter.

                                                   [EXIT MOSCA.]

240   Now, my fain'd cough, my pthisic, and my gout,
       My apoplexy, palsy, and catarrhs,
       Help, with your forced functions, this my posture,
       Wherein, this three year, I have milk'd their hopes.
       He comes; I hear him—Uh! [COUGHING.] uh! uh! uh! O—

              [RE-ENTER MOSCA, INTRODUCING VOLTORE, WITH A
                            PIECE OF PLATE.]

245   MOS: You still are what you were, sir. Only you,
       Of all the rest, are he commands his love,
       And you do wisely to preserve it thus,
       With early visitation, and kind notes
       Of your good meaning to him, which, I know,
250   Cannot but come most grateful. Patron! sir!
       Here's signior Voltore is come—

       VOLP [FAINTLY.]: What say you?

       MOS: Sir, signior Voltore is come this morning
       To visit you.

255 VOLP: I thank him.

MOS: And hath brought
A piece of antique plate, bought of St Mark,
With which he here presents you.

VOLP: He is welcome.
260 Pray him to come more often.

MOS: Yes.

VOLT: What says he?

MOS: He thanks you, and desires you see him often.

VOLP: Mosca.

265 MOS: My patron!

VOLP: Bring him near, where is he?
I long to feel his hand.

MOS: The plate is here, sir.

VOLT: How fare you, sir?

270 VOLP: I thank you, signior Voltore;
Where is the plate? mine eyes are bad.

VOLT [PUTTING IT INTO HIS HANDS.]: I'm sorry,
To see you still thus weak.

MOS [ASIDE.]: That he's not weaker.

275 VOLP: You are too munificent.

VOLT: No sir; would to heaven,
I could as well give health to you, as that plate!

VOLP: You give, sir, what you can: I thank you. Your love
Hath taste in this, and shall not be unanswer'd:
280 I pray you see me often.

VOLT: Yes, I shall sir.

VOLP: Be not far from me.

MOS: Do you observe that, sir?

VOLP: Hearken unto me still; it will concern you.

285 MOS: You are a happy man, sir; know your good.

VOLP: I cannot now last long—

MOS: You are his heir, sir.

VOLT: Am I?

VOLP: I feel me going; Uh! uh! uh! uh!
290 I'm sailing to my port, Uh! uh! uh! uh!
And I am glad I am so near my haven.

MOS: Alas, kind gentleman! Well, we must all go—

VOLT: But, Mosca—

MOS: Age will conquer.

295 VOLT: 'Pray thee hear me:
Am I inscribed his heir for certain?

MOS: Are you!
I do beseech you, sir, you will vouchsafe
To write me in your family. All my hopes
300 Depend upon your worship: I am lost,
Except the rising sun do shine on me.

VOLT: It shall both shine, and warm thee, Mosca.

MOS: Sir,
I am a man, that hath not done your love
305 All the worst offices: here I wear your keys,
See all your coffers and your caskets lock'd,
Keep the poor inventory of your jewels,
Your plate and monies; am your steward, sir.
Husband your goods here.

310 VOLT: But am I sole heir?

MOS: Without a partner, sir; confirm'd this morning:
The wax is warm yet, and the ink scarce dry
Upon the parchment.

VOLT: Happy, happy, me!
315   By what good chance, sweet Mosca?

MOS: Your desert, sir;
I know no second cause.

VOLT: Thy modesty
Is not to know it; well, we shall requite it.

320   MOS: He ever liked your course sir; that first took him.
I oft have heard him say, how he admired
Men of your large profession, that could speak
To every cause, and things mere contraries,
Till they were hoarse again, yet all be law;
325   That, with most quick agility, could turn,
And [re-] return; [could] make knots, and undo them;
Give forked counsel; take provoking gold
On either hand, and put it up: these men,
He knew, would thrive with their humility.
330   And, for his part, he thought he should be blest
To have his heir of such a suffering spirit,
So wise, so grave, of so perplex'd a tongue,
And loud withal, that would not wag, nor scarce
Lie still, without a fee; when every word
335   Your worship but lets fall, is a chequin!—
[LOUD KNOCKING WITHOUT.]
Who's that? one knocks; I would not have you seen, sir.
And yet—pretend you came, and went in haste:
I'll fashion an excuse.—and, gentle sir,
When you do come to swim in golden lard,
340   Up to the arms in honey, that your chin
Is born up stiff, with fatness of the flood,
Think on your vassal; but remember me:
I have not been your worst of clients.

VOLT: Mosca!—

345   MOS: When will you have your inventory brought, sir?
Or see a copy of the will?—Anon!—
I will bring them to you, sir. Away, be gone,
Put business in your face.

[EXIT VOLTORE.]

VOLP [SPRINGING UP.]: Excellent Mosca!
350   Come hither, let me kiss thee.

MOS: Keep you still, sir.
Here is Corbaccio.

VOLP: Set the plate away:
The vulture's gone, and the old raven's come!

355   MOS: Betake you to your silence, and your sleep:
Stand there and multiply.
                        [PUTTING THE PLATE TO THE REST.]
Now, shall we see
A wretch who is indeed more impotent
Than this can feign to be; yet hopes to hop
360   Over his grave.—
                [ENTER CORBACCIO.]
Signior Corbaccio!
You're very welcome, sir.

CORB: How does your patron?

MOS: Troth, as he did, sir; no amends.

365   CORB: What! mends he?

MOS: No, sir: he's rather worse.

CORB: That's well. Where is he?

MOS: Upon his couch sir, newly fall'n asleep.

CORB: Does he sleep well?

370   MOS: No wink, sir, all this night.
Nor yesterday; but slumbers.

CORB: Good! he should take
Some counsel of physicians: I have brought him
An opiate here, from mine own doctor.

375   MOS: He will not hear of drugs.

CORB: Why? I myself
Stood by while it was made; saw all the ingredients:
And know, it cannot but most gently work:
My life for his, 'tis but to make him sleep.

380   VOLP [ASIDE.]: Ay, his last sleep, if he would take it.

MOS: Sir,
He has no faith in physic.

CORB: 'Say you? 'say you?

MOS: He has no faith in physic: he does think
385   Most of your doctors are the greater danger,
And worse disease, to escape. I often have
Heard him protest, that your physician
Should never be his heir.

CORB: Not I his heir?

390   MOS: Not your physician, sir.

CORB: O, no, no, no,
I do not mean it.

MOS: No, sir, nor their fees
He cannot brook: he says, they flay a man,
395   Before they kill him.

CORB: Right, I do conceive you.

MOS: And then they do it by experiment;
For which the law not only doth absolve them,
But gives them great reward: and he is loth
400   To hire his death, so.

CORB: It is true, they kill,
With as much license as a judge.

MOS: Nay, more;
For he but kills, sir, where the law condemns,
405   And these can kill him too.

CORB: Ay, or me;
Or any man. How does his apoplex?
Is that strong on him still?

MOS: Most violent.
410   His speech is broken, and his eyes are set,
His face drawn longer than 'twas wont—

CORB: How! how!
Stronger then he was wont?

MOS: No, sir: his face
415   Drawn longer than 'twas wont.

CORB: O, good!

MOS: His mouth
Is ever gaping, and his eyelids hang.

CORB: Good.

420   MOS: A freezing numbness stiffens all his joints,
And makes the colour of his flesh like lead.

CORB: 'Tis good.

MOS: His pulse beats slow, and dull.

CORB: Good symptoms, still.

425   MOS: And from his brain—

CORB: I conceive you; good.

MOS: Flows a cold sweat, with a continual rheum,
Forth the resolved corners of his eyes.

CORB: Is't possible? yet I am better, ha!
430   How does he, with the swimming of his head?

CORB: O, sir, 'tis past the scotomy; he now
Hath lost his feeling, and hath left to snort:
You hardly can perceive him, that he breathes.

CORB: Excellent, excellent! sure I shall outlast him:
435   This makes me young again, a score of years.

MOS: I was a coming for you, sir.

CORB: Has he made his will?
What has he given me?

MOS: No, sir.

440   CORB: Nothing! ha?

MOS: He has not made his will, sir.

CORB: Oh, oh, oh!
But what did Voltore, the Lawyer, here?

MOS: He smelt a carcase, sir, when he but heard
445 My master was about his testament;
As I did urge him to it for your good—

CORB: He came unto him, did he? I thought so.

MOS: Yes, and presented him this piece of plate.

CORB: To be his heir?

450 MOS: I do not know, sir.

CORB: True:
I know it too.

MOS [ASIDE.]: By your own scale, sir.

CORB: Well,
455 I shall prevent him, yet. See, Mosca, look,
Here, I have brought a bag of bright chequines,
Will quite weigh down his plate.

MOS [TAKING THE BAG.]: Yea, marry, sir.
This is true physic, this your sacred medicine,
460 No talk of opiates, to this great elixir!

CORB: 'Tis aurum palpabile, if not potabile.

MOS: It shall be minister'd to him, in his bowl.

CORB: Ay, do, do, do.

MOS: Most blessed cordial!
465 This will recover him.

CORB: Yes, do, do, do.

MOS: I think it were not best, sir.

CORB: What?

MOS: To recover him.

470   CORB: O, no, no, no; by no means.

MOS: Why, sir, this
Will work some strange effect, if he but feel it.

CORB: 'Tis true, therefore forbear; I'll take my venture:
Give me it again.

475   MOS: At no hand; pardon me:
You shall not do yourself that wrong, sir. I
Will so advise you, you shall have it all.

CORB: How?

MOS: All, sir; 'tis your right, your own; no man
480   Can claim a part: 'tis yours, without a rival,
Decreed by destiny.

CORB: How, how, good Mosca?

MOS: I'll tell you sir. This fit he shall recover.

CORB: I do conceive you.

485   MOS: And, on first advantage
Of his gain'd sense, will I re-importune him
Unto the making of his testament:
And shew him this.

                         [POINTING TO THE MONEY.]

CORB: Good, good.

490   MOS: 'Tis better yet,
If you will hear, sir.

CORB: Yes, with all my heart.

MOS: Now, would I counsel you, make home with speed;
There, frame a will; whereto you shall inscribe
495   My master your sole heir.

CORB: And disinherit
My son!

MOS: O, sir, the better: for that colour
Shall make it much more taking.

500   CORB: O, but colour?

MOS: This will sir, you shall send it unto me.
Now, when I come to inforce, as I will do,
Your cares, your watchings, and your many prayers,
Your more than many gifts, your this day's present,
505   And last, produce your will; where, without thought,
Or least regard, unto your proper issue,
A son so brave, and highly meriting,
The stream of your diverted love hath thrown you
Upon my master, and made him your heir:
510   He cannot be so stupid, or stone-dead,
But out of conscience, and mere gratitude—

CORB: He must pronounce me his?

MOS: 'Tis true.

CORB: This plot
515   Did I think on before.

MOS: I do believe it.

CORB: Do you not believe it?

MOS: Yes, sir.

CORB: Mine own project.

520   MOS: Which, when he hath done, sir.

CORB: Publish'd me his heir?

MOS: And you so certain to survive him—

CORB: Ay.

MOS: Being so lusty a man—

525   CORB: 'Tis true.

MOS: Yes, sir—

CORB: I thought on that too. See, how he should be
The very organ to express my thoughts!

MOS: You have not only done yourself a good—

530   CORB: But multiplied it on my son.

MOS: 'Tis right, sir.

CORB: Still, my invention.

MOS: 'Las, sir! heaven knows,
It hath been all my study, all my care,
535   (I e'en grow gray withal,) how to work things—

CORB: I do conceive, sweet Mosca.

MOS: You are he,
For whom I labour here.

CORB: Ay, do, do, do:
540   I'll straight about it.

[GOING.]

MOS: Rook go with you, raven!

CORB: I know thee honest.

MOS [ASIDE.]: You do lie, sir!

CORB: And—

545   MOS: Your knowledge is no better than your ears, sir.

CORB: I do not doubt, to be a father to thee.

MOS: Nor I to gull my brother of his blessing.

CORB: I may have my youth restored to me, why not?

MOS: Your worship is a precious ass!

550   CORB: What say'st thou?

MOS: I do desire your worship to make haste, sir.

CORB: 'Tis done, 'tis done, I go.

[EXIT.]

VOLP [LEAPING FROM HIS COUCH.]: O, I shall burst!
Let out my sides, let out my sides—

555   MOS: Contain
Your flux of laughter, sir: you know this hope
Is such a bait, it covers any hook.

VOLP: O, but thy working, and thy placing it!
I cannot hold; good rascal, let me kiss thee:
560   I never knew thee in so rare a humour.

MOS: Alas sir, I but do as I am taught;
Follow your grave instructions; give them words;
Pour oil into their ears, and send them hence.

VOLP: 'Tis true, 'tis true. What a rare punishment
565   Is avarice to itself!

MOS: Ay, with our help, sir.

VOLP: So many cares, so many maladies,
So many fears attending on old age,
Yea, death so often call'd on, as no wish
570   Can be more frequent with them, their limbs faint,
Their senses dull, their seeing, hearing, going,
All dead before them; yea, their very teeth,
Their instruments of eating, failing them:
Yet this is reckon'd life! nay, here was one;
575   Is now gone home, that wishes to live longer!
Feels not his gout, nor palsy; feigns himself
Younger by scores of years, flatters his age
With confident belying it, hopes he may,
With charms, like Aeson, have his youth restored:
580   And with these thoughts so battens, as if fate
Would be as easily cheated on, as he,
And all turns air!

                                 [KNOCKING WITHIN.]
Who's that there, now? a third?

MOS: Close, to your couch again; I hear his voice:
585   It is Corvino, our spruce merchant.

VOLP [LIES DOWN AS BEFORE.]: Dead.

MOS: Another bout, sir, with your eyes.
                                   [ANOINTING THEM.]
—Who's there?
                      [ENTER CORVINO.]
Signior Corvino! come most wish'd for! O,
590   How happy were you, if you knew it, now!

CORV: Why? what? wherein?

MOS: The tardy hour is come, sir.

CORV: He is not dead?

MOS: Not dead, sir, but as good;
595   He knows no man.

CORV: How shall I do then?

MOS: Why, sir?

CORV: I have brought him here a pearl.

MOS: Perhaps he has
600   So much remembrance left, as to know you, sir:
       He still calls on you; nothing but your name
       Is in his mouth: Is your pearl orient, sir?

CORV: Venice was never owner of the like.

VOLP [FAINTLY.]: Signior Corvino.

605   MOS: Hark.

VOLP: Signior Corvino!

MOS: He calls you; step and give it him.—He's here, sir,
       And he has brought you a rich pearl.

CORV: How do you, sir?
610   Tell him, it doubles the twelfth caract.

MOS: Sir,
       He cannot understand, his hearing's gone;
       And yet it comforts him to see you—

CORV: Say,
615   I have a diamond for him, too.

MOS: Best shew it, sir;
       Put it into his hand; 'tis only there
       He apprehends: he has his feeling, yet.
       See how he grasps it!

620   CORV: 'Las, good gentleman!
       How pitiful the sight is!

MOS: Tut! forget, sir.
The weeping of an heir should still be laughter
Under a visor.

625   CORV: Why, am I his heir?

  MOS: Sir, I am sworn, I may not shew the will,
Till he be dead; but, here has been Corbaccio,
Here has been Voltore, here were others too,
I cannot number 'em, they were so many;
630 All gaping here for legacies: but I,
Taking the vantage of his naming you,
"Signior Corvino, Signior Corvino," took
Paper, and pen, and ink, and there I asked him,
Whom he would have his heir? "Corvino." Who
635 Should be executor? "Corvino." And,
To any question he was silent too,
I still interpreted the nods he made,
Through weakness, for consent: and sent home th' others,
Nothing bequeath'd them, but to cry and curse.

640   CORV: O, my dear Mosca!

                                         [THEY EMBRACE.]

  Does he not perceive us?

  MOS: No more than a blind harper. He knows no man,
No face of friend, nor name of any servant,
Who 'twas that fed him last, or gave him drink:
645 Not those he hath begotten, or brought up,
Can he remember.

  CORV: Has he children?

  MOS: Bastards,
Some dozen, or more, that he begot on beggars,
650 Gipsies, and Jews, and black-moors, when he was drunk.
Knew you not that, sir? 'tis the common fable.
The dwarf, the fool, the eunuch, are all his;
He's the true father of his family,
In all, save me:—but he has giv'n them nothing.

655   CORV: That's well, that's well. Art sure he does not hear us?

  MOS: Sure, sir! why, look you, credit your own sense.
                                    [SHOUTS IN VOL.'S EAR.]

The pox approach, and add to your diseases,
If it would send you hence the sooner, sir,
For your incontinence, it hath deserv'd it
660　Thoroughly, and thoroughly, and the plague to boot!—
You may come near, sir.—Would you would once close
Those filthy eyes of yours, that flow with slime,
Like two frog-pits; and those same hanging cheeks,
Cover'd with hide, instead of skin—Nay help, sir—
665　That look like frozen dish-clouts, set on end!

CORV [ALOUD.]: Or like an old smoked wall, on which the rain
Ran down in streaks!

MOS: Excellent! sir, speak out:
You may be louder yet: A culverin
670　Discharged in his ear would hardly bore it.

CORV: His nose is like a common sewer, still running.

MOS: 'Tis good! And what his mouth?

CORV: A very draught.

MOS: O, stop it up—

675　CORV: By no means.

MOS: 'Pray you, let me.
Faith I could stifle him, rarely with a pillow,
As well as any woman that should keep him.

CORV: Do as you will: but I'll begone.

680　MOS: Be so:
It is your presence makes him last so long.

CORV: I pray you, use no violence.

MOS: No, sir! why?
Why should you be thus scrupulous, pray you, sir?

685　CORV: Nay, at your discretion.

MOS: Well, good sir, begone.

CORV: I will not trouble him now, to take my pearl.

MOS: Puh! nor your diamond. What a needless care
Is this afflicts you? Is not all here yours?
690 Am not I here, whom you have made your creature?
That owe my being to you?

CORV: Grateful Mosca!
Thou art my friend, my fellow, my companion,
My partner, and shalt share in all my fortunes.

695 MOS: Excepting one.

CORV: What's that?

MOS: Your gallant wife, sir,—

[EXIT CORV.]

Now is he gone: we had no other means
To shoot him hence, but this.

700 VOLP: My divine Mosca!
Thou hast to-day outgone thyself.

[KNOCKING WITHIN.]

—Who's there?
I will be troubled with no more. Prepare
Me music, dances, banquets, all delights;
705 The Turk is not more sensual in his pleasures,
Than will Volpone.

[EXIT MOS.]

Let me see; a pearl!
A diamond! plate! chequines! Good morning's purchase,
Why, this is better than rob churches, yet;
710 Or fat, by eating, once a month, a man.
[RE-ENTER MOSCA.]
Who is't?

MOS: The beauteous lady Would-be, sir.
Wife to the English knight, Sir Politick Would-be,
(This is the style, sir, is directed me,)
715 Hath sent to know how you have slept to-night,
And if you would be visited?

VOLP: Not now:
Some three hours hence—

MOS: I told the squire so much.

720   VOLP: When I am high with mirth and wine; then, then:
       'Fore heaven, I wonder at the desperate valour
       Of the bold English, that they dare let loose
       Their wives to all encounters!

       MOS: Sir, this knight
725   Had not his name for nothing, he is politick,
       And knows, howe'er his wife affect strange airs,
       She hath not yet the face to be dishonest:
       But had she signior Corvino's wife's face—

       VOLP: Has she so rare a face?

730   MOS: O, sir, the wonder,
       The blazing star of Italy! a wench
       Of the first year! a beauty ripe as harvest!
       Whose skin is whiter than a swan all over,
       Than silver, snow, or lilies! a soft lip,
735   Would tempt you to eternity of kissing!
       And flesh that melteth in the touch to blood!
       Bright as your gold, and lovely as your gold!

       VOLP: Why had not I known this before?

       MOS: Alas, sir,
740   Myself but yesterday discover'd it.

       VOLP: How might I see her?

       MOS: O, not possible;
       She's kept as warily as is your gold;
       Never does come abroad, never takes air,
745   But at a window. All her looks are sweet,
       As the first grapes or cherries, and are watch'd
       As near as they are.

       VOLP: I must see her.

       MOS: Sir,
750   There is a guard of spies ten thick upon her,
       All his whole household; each of which is set
       Upon his fellow, and have all their charge,
       When he goes out, when he comes in, examined.

       VOLP: I will go see her, though but at her window.

755   MOS: In some disguise, then.

VOLP: That is true; I must
Maintain mine own shape still the same: we'll think.

[EXEUNT.]

ACT 2.
SCENE 2.1.
ST. MARK'S PLACE; A RETIRED CORNER BEFORE
CORVINO'S HOUSE.

ENTER SIR POLITICK WOULD-BE, AND PEREGRINE.

SIR P: Sir, to a wise man, all the world's his soil:
It is not Italy, nor France, nor Europe,
That must bound me, if my fates call me forth.
Yet, I protest, it is no salt desire
5 Of seeing countries, shifting a religion,
Nor any disaffection to the state
Where I was bred, and unto which I owe
My dearest plots, hath brought me out; much less,
That idle, antique, stale, gray-headed project
10 Of knowing men's minds, and manners, with Ulysses!
But a peculiar humour of my wife's
Laid for this height of Venice, to observe,
To quote, to learn the language, and so forth—
I hope you travel, sir, with license?

15 PER: Yes.

SIR P: I dare the safelier converse—How long, sir,
Since you left England?

PER: Seven weeks.

SIR P: So lately!
20 You have not been with my lord ambassador?

PER: Not yet, sir.

SIR P: Pray you, what news, sir, vents our climate?
I heard last night a most strange thing reported
By some of my lord's followers, and I long
25 To hear how 'twill be seconded.

PER: What was't, sir?

SIR P: Marry, sir, of a raven that should build
In a ship royal of the king's.

PER [ASIDE.]: This fellow,
30 Does he gull me, trow? or is gull'd?
—Your name, sir.

SIR P: My name is Politick Would-be.

PER [ASIDE.]: O, that speaks him.
—A knight, sir?

35 SIR P: A poor knight, sir.

PER: Your lady
Lies here in Venice, for intelligence
Of tires, and fashions, and behaviour,
Among the courtezans? the fine lady Would-be?

40 SIR P: Yes, sir; the spider and the bee, ofttimes,
Suck from one flower.

PER: Good Sir Politick,
I cry you mercy; I have heard much of you:
'Tis true, sir, of your raven.

45 SIR P: On your knowledge?

PER: Yes, and your lion's whelping, in the Tower.

SIR P: Another whelp!

PER: Another, sir.

SIR P: Now heaven!
50 What prodigies be these? The fires at Berwick!
And the new star! these things concurring, strange,
And full of omen! Saw you those meteors?

PER: I did, sir.

SIR P: Fearful! Pray you, sir, confirm me,
55 Were there three porpoises seen above the bridge,
As they give out?

PER: Six, and a sturgeon, sir.

SIR P: I am astonish'd.

PER: Nay, sir, be not so;
60   I'll tell you a greater prodigy than these.

SIR P: What should these things portend?

PER: The very day
(Let me be sure) that I put forth from London,
There was a whale discover'd in the river,
65   As high as Woolwich, that had waited there,
Few know how many months, for the subversion
Of the Stode fleet.

SIR P: Is't possible? believe it,
'Twas either sent from Spain, or the archdukes:
70   Spinola's whale, upon my life, my credit!
Will they not leave these projects? Worthy sir,
Some other news.

PER: Faith, Stone the fool is dead;
And they do lack a tavern fool extremely.

75   SIR P: Is Mass Stone dead?

PER: He's dead sir; why, I hope
You thought him not immortal?
[ASIDE.]
—O, this knight,
80   Were he well known, would be a precious thing
To fit our English stage: he that should write
But such a fellow, should be thought to feign
Extremely, if not maliciously.

SIR P: Stone dead!

85   PER: Dead.—Lord! how deeply sir, you apprehend it?
He was no kinsman to you?

SIR P: That I know of.
Well! that same fellow was an unknown fool.

PER: And yet you knew him, it seems?

90   SIR P: I did so. Sir,
I knew him one of the most dangerous heads
Living within the state, and so I held him.

PER: Indeed, sir?

SIR P: While he lived, in action.
95   He has received weekly intelligence,
Upon my knowledge, out of the Low Countries,
For all parts of the world, in cabbages;
And those dispensed again to ambassadors,
In oranges, musk-melons, apricocks,
100   Lemons, pome-citrons, and such-like: sometimes
In Colchester oysters, and your Selsey cockles.

PER: You make me wonder.

SIR P: Sir, upon my knowledge.
Nay, I've observed him, at your public ordinary,
105   Take his advertisement from a traveller
A conceal'd statesman, in a trencher of meat;
And instantly, before the meal was done,
Convey an answer in a tooth-pick.

PER: Strange!
110   How could this be, sir?

SIR P: Why, the meat was cut
So like his character, and so laid, as he
Must easily read the cipher.

PER: I have heard,
115   He could not read, sir.

SIR P: So 'twas given out,
In policy, by those that did employ him:
But he could read, and had your languages,
And to't, as sound a noddle—

120   PER: I have heard, sir,
That your baboons were spies, and that they were
A kind of subtle nation near to China:

SIR P: Ay, ay, your Mamuluchi. Faith, they had
Their hand in a French plot or two; but they
125   Were so extremely given to women, as
They made discovery of all: yet I
Had my advices here, on Wednesday last.
From one of their own coat, they were return'd,
Made their relations, as the fashion is,
130   And now stand fair for fresh employment.

PER: 'Heart!
[ASIDE.]
This sir Pol will be ignorant of nothing.
—It seems, sir, you know all?

135 SIR P: Not all sir, but
I have some general notions. I do love
To note and to observe: though I live out,
Free from the active torrent, yet I'd mark
The currents and the passages of things,
140 For mine own private use; and know the ebbs,
And flows of state.

PER: Believe it, sir, I hold
Myself in no small tie unto my fortunes,
For casting me thus luckily upon you,
145 Whose knowledge, if your bounty equal it,
May do me great assistance, in instruction
For my behaviour, and my bearing, which
Is yet so rude and raw.

SIR P: Why, came you forth
150 Empty of rules, for travel?

PER: Faith, I had
Some common ones, from out that vulgar grammar,
Which he that cried Italian to me, taught me.

SIR P: Why this it is, that spoils all our brave bloods,
155 Trusting our hopeful gentry unto pedants,
Fellows of outside, and mere bark. You seem
To be a gentleman, of ingenuous race:—
I not profess it, but my fate hath been
To be, where I have been consulted with,
160 In this high kind, touching some great men's sons,
Persons of blood, and honour.—

[ENTER MOSCA AND NANO DISGUISED, FOLLOWED BY
PERSONS WITH MATERIALS FOR ERECTING A STAGE.]

PER: Who be these, sir?

MOS: Under that window, there 't must be. The same.

SIR P: Fellows, to mount a bank. Did your instructor
165 In the dear tongues, never discourse to you
Of the Italian mountebanks?

PER: Yes, sir.

SIR P: Why,
Here shall you see one.

170 PER: They are quacksalvers;
Fellows, that live by venting oils and drugs.

SIR P: Was that the character he gave you of them?

PER: As I remember.

SIR P: Pity his ignorance.
175 They are the only knowing men of Europe!
Great general scholars, excellent physicians,
Most admired statesmen, profest favourites,
And cabinet counsellors to the greatest princes;
The only languaged men of all the world!

180 PER: And, I have heard, they are most lewd impostors;
Made all of terms and shreds; no less beliers
Of great men's favours, than their own vile med'cines;
Which they will utter upon monstrous oaths:
Selling that drug for two-pence, ere they part,
185 Which they have valued at twelve crowns before.

SIR P: Sir, calumnies are answer'd best with silence.
Yourself shall judge.—Who is it mounts, my friends?

MOS: Scoto of Mantua, sir.

SIR P: Is't he? Nay, then
190 I'll proudly promise, sir, you shall behold
Another man than has been phant'sied to you.
I wonder yet, that he should mount his bank,
Here in this nook, that has been wont t'appear
In face of the Piazza!—Here, he comes.

[ENTER VOLPONE, DISGUISED AS A MOUNTEBANK DOCTOR,
          AND FOLLOWED BY A CROWD OF PEOPLE.]

195 VOLP [TO NANO.]: Mount, zany.

MOB: Follow, follow, follow, follow!

SIR P: See how the people follow him! he's a man
May write ten thousand crowns in bank here. Note,

[VOLPONE MOUNTS THE STAGE.]

Mark but his gesture:—I do use to observe
200 The state he keeps in getting up.

PER: 'Tis worth it, sir.

VOLP: Most noble gentlemen, and my worthy patrons! It may seem strange, that I, your Scoto Mantuano, who was ever wont to fix my bank in face of the public Piazza, near the shelter of the Portico to the Procuratia, should now,
205 after eight months' absence from this illustrious city of Venice, humbly retire myself into an obscure nook of the Piazza.

SIR P: Did not I now object the same?

PER: Peace, sir.

VOLP: Let me tell you: I am not, as your Lombard proverb saith, cold on
210 my feet; or content to part with my commodities at a cheaper rate, than I accustomed: look not for it. Nor that the calumnious reports of that impudent detractor, and shame to our profession, (Alessandro Buttone, I mean,) who gave out, in public, I was condemn'd a sforzato to the galleys, for poisoning the cardinal Bembo's—cook, hath at all attached, much less
215 dejected me. No, no, worthy gentlemen; to tell you true, I cannot endure to see the rabble of these ground ciarlitani, that spread their cloaks on the pavement, as if they meant to do feats of activity, and then come in lamely, with their mouldy tales out of Boccacio, like stale Tabarine, the fabulist: some of them discoursing their travels, and of their tedious captivity in the
220 Turks' galleys, when, indeed, were the truth known, they were the Christians' galleys, where very temperately they eat bread, and drunk water, as a wholesome penance, enjoined them by their confessors, for base pilferies.

SIR P: Note but his bearing, and contempt of these.

VOLP: These turdy-facy-nasty-paty-lousy-fartical rogues, with one poor
225 groat's-worth of unprepared antimony, finely wrapt up in several scartoccios, are able, very well, to kill their twenty a week, and play; yet, these meagre, starved spirits, who have half stopt the organs of their minds with earthy oppilations, want not their favourers among your shrivell'd sallad-eating artizans, who are overjoyed that they may have their half-pe'rth of physic;
230 though it purge them into another world, it makes no matter.

SIR P: Excellent! have you heard better language, sir?

VOLP: Well, let them go. And, gentlemen, honourable gentlemen, know, that for this time, our bank, being thus removed from the clamours of the

canaglia, shall be the scene of pleasure and delight; for I have nothing to
235 sell, little or nothing to sell.

SIR P: I told you, sir, his end.

PER: You did so, sir.

VOLP: I protest, I, and my six servants, are not able to make of this pre-
cious liquor, so fast as it is fetch'd away from my lodging by gentlemen
240 of your city; strangers of the Terra-firma; worshipful merchants; ay, and
senators too: who, ever since my arrival, have detained me to their uses, by
their splendidous liberalities. And worthily; for, what avails your rich man
to have his magazines stuft with moscadelli, or of the purest grape, when
his physicians prescribe him, on pain of death, to drink nothing but water
245 cocted with aniseeds? O health! health! the blessing of the rich, the riches
of the poor! who can buy thee at too dear a rate, since there is no enjoying
this world without thee? Be not then so sparing of your purses, honourable
gentlemen, as to abridge the natural course of life—

PER: You see his end.

250 SIR P: Ay, is't not good?

VOLP: For, when a humid flux, or catarrh, by the mutability of air, falls
from your head into an arm or shoulder, or any other part; take you a ducat,
or your chequin of gold, and apply to the place affected: see what good ef-
fect it can work. No, no, 'tis this blessed unguento, this rare extraction, that
255 hath only power to disperse all malignant humours, that proceed either of
hot, cold, moist, or windy causes—

PER: I would he had put in dry too.

SIR P: 'Pray you, observe.

VOLP: To fortify the most indigest and crude stomach, ay, were it of one,
260 that, through extreme weakness, vomited blood, applying only a warm nap-
kin to the place, after the unction and fricace;—for the vertigine in the head,
putting but a drop into your nostrils, likewise behind the ears; a most sov-
ereign and approved remedy. The mal caduco, cramps, convulsions, paral-
ysies, epilepsies, tremor-cordia, retired nerves, ill vapours of the spleen,
265 stopping of the liver, the stone, the strangury, hernia ventosa, iliaca passio;
stops a disenteria immediately; easeth the torsion of the small guts: and
cures melancholia hypocondriaca, being taken and applied according to my
printed receipt.

[POINTING TO HIS BILL AND HIS VIAL.]
270 For, this is the physician, this the medicine; this counsels, this cures; this
gives the direction, this works the effect; and, in sum, both together may

be termed an abstract of the theorick and practick in the Aesculapian art.
'Twill cost you eight crowns. And,—Zan Fritada, prithee sing a verse ex-
tempore in honour of it.

275 SIR P: How do you like him, sir?

PER: Most strangely, I!

SIR P: Is not his language rare?

PER: But alchemy,
I never heard the like: or Broughton's books.

280 NANO [SINGS.]: Had old Hippocrates, or Galen,
That to their books put med'cines all in,
But known this secret, they had never
(Of which they will be guilty ever)
Been murderers of so much paper,
285 Or wasted many a hurtless taper;
No Indian drug had e'er been famed,
Tabacco, sassafras not named;
Ne yet, of guacum one small stick, sir,
Nor Raymund Lully's great elixir.
290 Ne had been known the Danish Gonswart,
Or Paracelsus, with his long-sword.

PER: All this, yet, will not do, eight crowns is high.

VOLP: No more.—Gentlemen, if I had but time to discourse to you the
miraculous effects of this my oil, surnamed Oglio del Scoto; with the
295 countless catalogue of those I have cured of the aforesaid, and many more
diseases; the pattents and privileges of all the princes and commonwealths
of Christendom; or but the depositions of those that appeared on my part,
before the signiory of the Sanita and most learned College of Physicians;
where I was authorised, upon notice taken of the admirable virtues of my
300 medicaments, and mine own excellency in matter of rare and unknown
secrets, not only to disperse them publicly in this famous city, but in all
the territories, that happily joy under the government of the most pious
and magnificent states of Italy. But may some other gallant fellow say, O,
there be divers that make profession to have as good, and as experimented
305 receipts as yours: indeed, very many have assayed, like apes, in imitation of
that, which is really and essentially in me, to make of this oil; bestowed great
cost in furnaces, stills, alembecks, continual fires, and preparation of the
ingredients, (as indeed there goes to it six hundred several simples, besides
some quantity of human fat, for the conglutination, which we buy of the
310 anatomists,) but, when these practitioners come to the last decoction, blow,

blow, puff, puff, and all flies in fumo: ha, ha, ha! Poor wretches! I rather pity
their folly and indiscretion, than their loss of time and money; for these
may be recovered by industry: but to be a fool born, is a disease incurable.
For myself, I always from my youth have endeavoured to get the rarest se-
crets, and book them, either in exchange, or for money; I spared nor cost
nor labour, where any thing was worthy to be learned. And gentlemen,
honourable gentlemen, I will undertake, by virtue of chemical art, out of
the honourable hat that covers your head, to extract the four elements; that
is to say, the fire, air, water, and earth, and return you your felt without burn
or stain. For, whilst others have been at the Balloo, I have been at my book;
and am now past the craggy paths of study, and come to the flowery plains
of honour and reputation.

SIR P: I do assure you, sir, that is his aim.

VOLP: But, to our price—

PER: And that withal, sir Pol.

VOLP: You all know, honourable gentlemen, I never valued this ampulla, or
vial, at less than eight crowns, but for this time, I am content, to be deprived
of it for six; six crowns is the price; and less, in courtesy I know you cannot
offer me; take it, or leave it, howsoever, both it and I am at your service.
I ask you not as the value of the thing, for then I should demand of you
a thousand crowns, so the cardinals Montalto, Fernese, the great Duke of
Tuscany, my gossip, with divers other princes, have given me; but I despise
money. Only to shew my affection to you, honourable gentlemen, and your
illustrious State here, I have neglected the messages of these princes, mine
own offices, framed my journey hither, only to present you with the fruits of
my travels.—Tune your voices once more to the touch of your instruments,
and give the honourable assembly some delightful recreation.

PER: What monstrous and most painful circumstance
Is here, to get some three or four gazettes,
Some three-pence in the whole! for that 'twill come to.

NANO [SINGS.]: You that would last long, list to my song,
Make no more coil, but buy of this oil.
Would you be ever fair and young?
Stout of teeth, and strong of tongue?
Tart of palate? quick of ear?
Sharp of sight? of nostril clear?
Moist of hand? and light of foot?
Or, I will come nearer to't,
Would you live free from all diseases?

350   Do the act your mistress pleases;
Yet fright all aches from your bones?
Here's a med'cine, for the nones.

VOLP: Well, I am in a humour at this time to make a present of the small
quantity my coffer contains; to the rich, in courtesy, and to the poor for
355   God's sake. Wherefore now mark: I ask'd you six crowns, and six crowns,
at other times, you have paid me; you shall not give me six crowns, nor five,
nor four, nor three, nor two, nor one; nor half a ducat; no, nor a moccinigo.
Sixpence it will cost you, or six hundred pound— expect no lower price, for,
by the banner of my front, I will not bate a bagatine, that I will have, only,
360   a pledge of your loves, to carry something from amongst you, to shew I am
not contemn'd by you. Therefore, now, toss your handkerchiefs, cheerfully,
cheerfully; and be advertised, that the first heroic spirit that deignes to grace
me with a handkerchief, I will give it a little remembrance of something,
beside, shall please it better, than if I had presented it with a double pistolet.

365   PER: Will you be that heroic spark, sir Pol?
[CELIA AT A WINDOW ABOVE, THROWS DOWN HER
HANDKERCHIEF.]
O see! the window has prevented you.

VOLP: Lady, I kiss your bounty; and for this timely grace you have done
your poor Scoto of Mantua, I will return you, over and above my oil, a se-
cret of that high and inestimable nature, shall make you for ever enamour'd
370   on that minute, wherein your eye first descended on so mean, yet not alto-
gether to be despised, an object. Here is a powder conceal'd in this paper, of
which, if I should speak to the worth, nine thousand volumes were but as
one page, that page as a line, that line as a word; so short is this pilgrimage
of man (which some call life) to the expressing of it. Would I reflect on the
375   price? why, the whole world is but as an empire, that empire as a province,
that province as a bank, that bank as a private purse to the purchase of it.
I will only tell you; it is the powder that made Venus a goddess (given her
by Apollo,) that kept her perpetually young, clear'd her wrinkles, firm'd her
gums, fill'd her skin, colour'd her hair; from her deriv'd to Helen, and at the
380   sack of Troy unfortunately lost: till now, in this our age, it was as happily
recovered, by a studious antiquary, out of some ruins of Asia, who sent a
moiety of it to the court of France, (but much sophisticated,) wherewith
the ladies there, now, colour their hair. The rest, at this present, remains
with me; extracted to a quintessence: so that, whereever it but touches, in
385   youth it perpetually preserves, in age restores the complexion; seats your
teeth, did they dance like virginal jacks, firm as a wall; makes them white as
ivory, that were black, as—

[ENTER CORVINO.]

COR: Spight o' the devil, and my shame! come down here;
Come down;—No house but mine to make your scene?
390 Signior Flaminio, will you down, sir? down?
What, is my wife your Franciscina, sir?
No windows on the whole Piazza, here,
To make your properties, but mine? but mine?

                 [BEATS AWAY VOLPONE, NANO, ETC.]

Heart! ere to-morrow, I shall be new-christen'd,
395 And call'd the Pantalone di Besogniosi,
About the town.

PER: What should this mean, sir Pol?

SIR P: Some trick of state, believe it. I will home.

PER: It may be some design on you:

400 SIR P: I know not.
I'll stand upon my guard.

PER: It is your best, sir.

SIR P: This three weeks, all my advices, all my letters,
They have been intercepted.

405 PER: Indeed, sir!
Best have a care.

SIR P: Nay, so I will.

PER: This knight,
I may not lose him, for my mirth, till night.

                           [EXEUNT.]

SCENE 2.2.
A ROOM IN VOLPONE'S HOUSE.

ENTER VOLPONE AND MOSCA.

VOLP: O, I am wounded!

MOS: Where, sir?

VOLP: Not without;
Those blows were nothing: I could bear them ever.

5   But angry Cupid, bolting from her eyes,
      Hath shot himself into me like a flame;
      Where, now, he flings about his burning heat,
      As in a furnace an ambitious fire,
      Whose vent is stopt. The fight is all within me.
10   I cannot live, except thou help me, Mosca;
      My liver melts, and I, without the hope
      Of some soft air, from her refreshing breath,
      Am but a heap of cinders.

      MOS: 'Las, good sir,
15   Would you had never seen her!

      VOLP: Nay, would thou
      Had'st never told me of her!

      MOS: Sir 'tis true;
      I do confess I was unfortunate,
20   And you unhappy: but I'm bound in conscience,
      No less than duty, to effect my best
      To your release of torment, and I will, sir.

      VOLP: Dear Mosca, shall I hope?

      MOS: Sir, more than dear,
25   I will not bid you to dispair of aught
      Within a human compass.

      VOLP: O, there spoke
      My better angel. Mosca, take my keys,
      Gold, plate, and jewels, all's at thy devotion;
30   Employ them how thou wilt; nay, coin me too:
      So thou, in this, but crown my longings, Mosca.

      MOS: Use but your patience.

      VOLP: So I have.

      MOS: I doubt not
35   To bring success to your desires.

      VOLP: Nay, then,
      I not repent me of my late disguise.

      MOS: If you can horn him, sir, you need not.

VOLP: True:
40 Besides, I never meant him for my heir.—
Is not the colour of my beard and eyebrows,
To make me known?

MOS: No jot.

VOLP: I did it well.

45 MOS: So well, would I could follow you in mine,
With half the happiness!
[ASIDE.]—and yet I would
Escape your Epilogue.

VOLP: But were they gull'd
50 With a belief that I was Scoto?

MOS: Sir,
Scoto himself could hardly have distinguish'd!
I have not time to flatter you now; we'll part;
And as I prosper, so applaud my art.

            [EXEUNT.]

SCENE 2.3.

A ROOM IN CORVINO'S HOUSE.

ENTER CORVINO, WITH HIS SWORD IN HIS HAND, DRAGGING IN CELIA.

CORV: Death of mine honour, with the city's fool!
A juggling, tooth-drawing, prating mountebank!
And at a public window! where, whilst he,
With his strain'd action, and his dole of faces,
5 To his drug-lecture draws your itching ears,
A crew of old, unmarried, noted letchers,
Stood leering up like satyrs; and you smile
Most graciously, and fan your favours forth,
To give your hot spectators satisfaction!
10 What; was your mountebank their call? their whistle?
Or were you enamour'd on his copper rings,
His saffron jewel, with the toad-stone in't,
Or his embroider'd suit, with the cope-stitch,
Made of a herse-cloth? or his old tilt-feather?
15 Or his starch'd beard? Well; you shall have him, yes!

He shall come home, and minister unto you
The fricace for the mother. Or, let me see,
I think you'd rather mount; would you not mount?
Why, if you'll mount, you may; yes truly, you may:
20 And so you may be seen, down to the foot.
Get you a cittern, lady Vanity,
And be a dealer with the virtuous man;
Make one: I'll but protest myself a cuckold,
And save your dowry. I'm a Dutchman, I!
25 For, if you thought me an Italian,
You would be damn'd, ere you did this, you whore!
Thou'dst tremble, to imagine, that the murder
Of father, mother, brother, all thy race,
Should follow, as the subject of my justice.

30 CEL: Good sir, have pacience.

CORV: What couldst thou propose
Less to thyself, than in this heat of wrath
And stung with my dishonour, I should strike
This steel into thee, with as many stabs,
35 As thou wert gaz'd upon with goatish eyes?

CEL: Alas, sir, be appeas'd! I could not think
My being at the window should more now
Move your impatience, than at other times.

CORV: No! not to seek and entertain a parley
40 With a known knave, before a multitude!
You were an actor with your handkerchief;
Which he most sweetly kist in the receipt,
And might, no doubt, return it with a letter,
And point the place where you might meet: your sister's,
45 Your mother's, or your aunt's might serve the turn.

CEL: Why, dear sir, when do I make these excuses,
Or ever stir abroad, but to the church?
And that so seldom—

CORV: Well, it shall be less;
50 And thy restraint before was liberty,
To what I now decree: and therefore mark me.
First, I will have this bawdy light damm'd up;
And till't be done, some two or three yards off,
I'll chalk a line: o'er which if thou but chance

55   To set thy desperate foot; more hell, more horror
      More wild remorseless rage shall seize on thee,
      Than on a conjurer, that had heedless left
      His circle's safety ere his devil was laid.
      Then here's a lock which I will hang upon thee;
60   And, now I think on't, I will keep thee backwards;
      Thy lodging shall be backwards; thy walks backwards;
      Thy prospect, all be backwards; and no pleasure,
      That thou shalt know but backwards: nay, since you force
      My honest nature, know, it is your own,
65   Being too open, makes me use you thus:
      Since you will not contain your subtle nostrils
      In a sweet room, but they must snuff the air
      Of rank and sweaty passengers.

                                                    [KNOCKING WITHIN.]

      —One knocks.
70   Away, and be not seen, pain of thy life;
      Nor look toward the window: if thou dost—
      Nay, stay, hear this—let me not prosper, whore,
      But I will make thee an anatomy,
      Dissect thee mine own self, and read a lecture
75   Upon thee to the city, and in public.
      Away!

                                                    [EXIT CELIA.]

                         [ENTER SERVANT.]

      Who's there?

      SERV: 'Tis signior Mosca, sir.

      CORV: Let him come in.

                                                    [EXIT SERVANT.]

80   His master's dead: There's yet
      Some good to help the bad.—
                         [ENTER MOSCA.]

      My Mosca, welcome!
      I guess your news.

      MOS: I fear you cannot, sir.

85   CORV: Is't not his death?

      MOS: Rather the contrary.

      CORV: Not his recovery?

MOS: Yes, sir.

CORV: I am curs'd,
90 I am bewitch'd, my crosses meet to vex me.
How? how? how? how?

MOS: Why, sir, with Scoto's oil;
Corbaccio and Voltore brought of it,
Whilst I was busy in an inner room—

95 CORV: Death! that damn'd mountebank; but for the law
Now, I could kill the rascal: it cannot be,
His oil should have that virtue. Have not I
Known him a common rogue, come fidling in
To the osteria, with a tumbling whore,
100 And, when he has done all his forced tricks, been glad
Of a poor spoonful of dead wine, with flies in't?
It cannot be. All his ingredients
Are a sheep's gall, a roasted bitch's marrow,
Some few sod earwigs pounded caterpillars,
105 A little capon's grease, and fasting spittle:
I know them to a dram.

MOS: I know not, sir,
But some on't, there, they pour'd into his ears,
Some in his nostrils, and recover'd him;
110 Applying but the fricace.

CORV: Pox o' that fricace.

MOS: And since, to seem the more officious
And flatt'ring of his health, there, they have had,
At extreme fees, the college of physicians
115 Consulting on him, how they might restore him;
Where one would have a cataplasm of spices,
Another a flay'd ape clapp'd to his breast,
A third would have it a dog, a fourth an oil,
With wild cats' skins: at last, they all resolved
120 That, to preserve him, was no other means,
But some young woman must be straight sought out,
Lusty, and full of juice, to sleep by him;
And to this servicè, most unhappily,
And most unwillingly, am I now employ'd,
125 Which here I thought to pre-acquaint you with,
For your advice, since it concerns you most;

Because, I would not do that thing might cross
Your ends, on whom I have my whole dependance, sir:
Yet, if I do it not, they may delate
130 My slackness to my patron, work me out
Of his opinion; and there all your hopes,
Ventures, or whatsoever, are all frustrate!
I do but tell you, sir. Besides, they are all
Now striving, who shall first present him; therefore—
135 I could entreat you, briefly conclude somewhat;
Prevent them if you can.

CORV: Death to my hopes,
This is my villainous fortune! Best to hire
Some common courtezan.

140 MOS: Ay, I thought on that, sir;
But they are all so subtle, full of art—
And age again doting and flexible,
So as—I cannot tell—we may, perchance,
Light on a quean may cheat us all.

145 CORV: 'Tis true.

MOS: No, no: it must be one that has no tricks, sir,
Some simple thing, a creature made unto it;
Some wench you may command. Have you no kinswoman?
Odso—Think, think, think, think, think, think, think, sir.
150 One o' the doctors offer'd there his daughter.

CORV: How!

MOS: Yes, signior Lupo, the physician.

CORV: His daughter!

MOS: And a virgin, sir. Why? alas,
155 He knows the state of's body, what it is;
That nought can warm his blood sir, but a fever;
Nor any incantation raise his spirit:
A long forgetfulness hath seized that part.
Besides sir, who shall know it? some one or two—

160 CORV: I prithee give me leave.
                                        [WALKS ASIDE.]

If any man
But I had had this luck—The thing in't self,

I know, is nothing—Wherefore should not I
As well command my blood and my affections,
165 As this dull doctor? In the point of honour,
The cases are all one of wife and daughter.

MOS [ASIDE.]: I hear him coming.

CORV: She shall do't: 'tis done.
Slight! if this doctor, who is not engaged,
170 Unless 't be for his counsel, which is nothing,
Offer his daughter, what should I, that am
So deeply in? I will prevent him: Wretch!
Covetous wretch!—Mosca, I have determined.

MOS: How, sir?

175 CORV: We'll make all sure. The party you wot of
Shall be mine own wife, Mosca.

MOS: Sir, the thing,
But that I would not seem to counsel you,
I should have motion'd to you, at the first:
180 And make your count, you have cut all their throats.
Why! 'tis directly taking a possession!
And in his next fit, we may let him go.
'Tis but to pull the pillow from his head,
And he is throttled: it had been done before,
185 But for your scrupulous doubts.

CORV: Ay, a plague on't,
My conscience fools my wit! Well, I'll be brief,
And so be thou, lest they should be before us:
Go home, prepare him, tell him with what zeal
190 And willingness I do it; swear it was
On the first hearing, as thou mayst do, truly,
Mine own free motion.

MOS: Sir, I warrant you,
I'll so possess him with it, that the rest
195 Of his starv'd clients shall be banish'd all;
And only you received. But come not, sir,
Until I send, for I have something else
To ripen for your good, you must not know't.

CORV: But do not you forget to send now.

200　MOS: Fear not.

[EXIT.]

CORV: Where are you, wife? my Celia? wife?

[RE-ENTER CELIA.]

—What, blubbering?
Come, dry those tears. I think thou thought'st me in earnest;
Ha! by this light I talk'd so but to try thee:
205　Methinks the lightness of the occasion
Should have confirm'd thee. Come, I am not jealous.

CEL: No!
CORV: Faith I am not I, nor never was;
It is a poor unprofitable humour.
210　Do not I know, if women have a will,
They'll do 'gainst all the watches of the world,
And that the feircest spies are tamed with gold?
Tut, I am confident in thee, thou shalt see't;
And see I'll give thee cause too, to believe it.
215　Come kiss me. Go, and make thee ready, straight,
In all thy best attire, thy choicest jewels,
Put them all on, and, with them, thy best looks:
We are invited to a solemn feast,
At old Volpone's, where it shall appear
220　How far I am free from jealousy or fear.

[EXEUNT.]

ACT 3.
SCENE 3.1.
A STREET.

ENTER MOSCA.

MOS: I fear, I shall begin to grow in love
With my dear self, and my most prosperous parts,
They do so spring and burgeon; I can feel
A whimsy in my blood: I know not how,
5　Success hath made me wanton. I could skip
Out of my skin, now, like a subtle snake,
I am so limber. O! your parasite
Is a most precious thing, dropt from above,
Not bred 'mongst clods, and clodpoles, here on earth.

10 I muse, the mystery was not made a science,
It is so liberally profest! almost
All the wise world is little else, in nature,
But parasites, or sub-parasites.—And yet,
I mean not those that have your bare town-art,
15 To know who's fit to feed them; have no house,
No family, no care, and therefore mould
Tales for men's ears, to bait that sense; or get
Kitchen-invention, and some stale receipts
To please the belly, and the groin; nor those,
20 With their court dog-tricks, that can fawn and fleer,
Make their revenue out of legs and faces,
Echo my lord, and lick away a moth:
But your fine elegant rascal, that can rise,
And stoop, almost together, like an arrow;
25 Shoot through the air as nimbly as a star;
Turn short as doth a swallow; and be here,
And there, and here, and yonder, all at once;
Present to any humour, all occasion;
And change a visor, swifter than a thought!
30 This is the creature had the art born with him;
Toils not to learn it, but doth practise it
Out of most excellent nature: and such sparks
Are the true parasites, others but their zanis.

[ENTER BONARIO.]

MOS: Who's this? Bonario, old Corbaccio's son?
35 The person I was bound to seek.—Fair sir,
You are happily met.

BON: That cannot be by thee.

MOS: Why, sir?

BON: Nay, pray thee know thy way, and leave me:
40 I would be loth to interchange discourse
With such a mate as thou art

MOS: Courteous sir,
Scorn not my poverty.

BON: Not I, by heaven;
45 But thou shalt give me leave to hate thy baseness.

MOS: Baseness!

BON: Ay; answer me, is not thy sloth
Sufficient argument? thy flattery?
Thy means of feeding?

50   MOS: Heaven be good to me!
These imputations are too common, sir,
And easily stuck on virtue when she's poor.
You are unequal to me, and however,
Your sentence may be righteous, yet you are not
55   That, ere you know me, thus proceed in censure:
St. Mark bear witness 'gainst you, 'tis inhuman.

[WEEPS.]

BON [ASIDE.]: What! does he weep? the sign is soft and good;
I do repent me that I was so harsh.

MOS: 'Tis true, that, sway'd by strong necessity,
60   I am enforced to eat my careful bread
With too much obsequy; 'tis true, beside,
That I am fain to spin mine own poor raiment
Out of my mere observance, being not born
To a free fortune: but that I have done
65   Base offices, in rending friends asunder,
Dividing families, betraying counsels,
Whispering false lies, or mining men with praises,
Train'd their credulity with perjuries,
Corrupted chastity, or am in love
70   With mine own tender ease, but would not rather
Prove the most rugged, and laborious course,
That might redeem my present estimation,
Let me here perish, in all hope of goodness.

BON [ASIDE.]: This cannot be a personated passion.—
75   I was to blame, so to mistake thy nature;
Prithee, forgive me: and speak out thy business.

MOS: Sir, it concerns you; and though I may seem,
At first to make a main offence in manners,
And in my gratitude unto my master;
80   Yet, for the pure love, which I bear all right,
And hatred of the wrong, I must reveal it.
This very hour your father is in purpose
To disinherit you—

BON: How!

85 MOS: And thrust you forth,
As a mere stranger to his blood; 'tis true, sir:
The work no way engageth me, but, as
I claim an interest in the general state
Of goodness and true virtue, which I hear
90 To abound in you: and, for which mere respect,
Without a second aim, sir, I have done it.

BON: This tale hath lost thee much of the late trust
Thou hadst with me; it is impossible:
I know not how to lend it any thought,
95 My father should be so unnatural.

MOS: It is a confidence that well becomes
Your piety; and form'd, no doubt, it is
From your own simple innocence: which makes
Your wrong more monstrous, and abhorr'd. But, sir,
100 I now will tell you more. This very minute,
It is, or will be doing; and, if you
Shall be but pleas'd to go with me, I'll bring you,
I dare not say where you shall see, but where
Your ear shall be a witness of the deed;
105 Hear yourself written bastard; and profest
The common issue of the earth.

BON: I am amazed!

MOS: Sir, if I do it not, draw your just sword,
And score your vengeance on my front and face;
110 Mark me your villain: you have too much wrong,
And I do suffer for you, sir. My heart
Weeps blood in anguish—

BON: Lead; I follow thee.

[EXEUNT.]

SCENE 3.2.
A ROOM IN VOLPONE'S HOUSE.

ENTER VOLPONE.

VOLP: Mosca stays long, methinks. Bring forth your sports,
And help to make the wretched time more sweet.

[ENTER NANO, ANDROGYNO, AND CASTRONE.]

NAN: Dwarf, fool, and eunuch, well met here we be.
A question it were now, whether of us three,
5 Being all the known delicates of a rich man,
In pleasing him, claim the precedency can?

CAS: I claim for myself.

AND: And so doth the fool.

NAN: 'Tis foolish indeed: let me set you both to school.
10 First for your dwarf, he's little and witty,
And every thing, as it is little, is pretty;
Else why do men say to a creature of my shape,
So soon as they see him, It's a pretty little ape?
And why a pretty ape, but for pleasing imitation
15 Of greater men's actions, in a ridiculous fashion?
Beside, this feat body of mine doth not crave
Half the meat, drink, and cloth, one of your bulks will have.
Admit your fool's face be the mother of laughter,
Yet, for his brain, it must always come after:
20 And though that do feed him, 'tis a pitiful case,
His body is beholding to such a bad face.

                                          [KNOCKING WITHIN.]

VOLP: Who's there? my couch; away! look! Nano, see:
                                        [EXEUNT AND. AND CAS.]
Give me my caps, first—go, enquire.
                                        [EXIT NANO.]
—Now, Cupid
25 Send it be Mosca, and with fair return!

NAN [WITHIN.]: It is the beauteous madam—

VOLP: Would-be?—is it?

NAN: The same.

VOLP: Now torment on me! Squire her in;
30 For she will enter, or dwell here for ever:
Nay, quickly.
                                        [RETIRES TO HIS COUCH.]
—That my fit were past! I fear
A second hell too, that my lothing this
Will quite expel my appetite to the other:
35 Would she were taking now her tedious leave.
Lord, how it threats me what I am to suffer!

[RE-ENTER NANO, WITH LADY POLITICK WOULD-BE.]

LADY P: I thank you, good sir. 'Pray you signify
Unto your patron, I am here.—This band
Shews not my neck enough.—I trouble you, sir;
40   Let me request you, bid one of my women
Come hither to me.—In good faith, I, am drest
Most favorably, to-day! It is no matter:
'Tis well enough.—
           [ENTER 1 WAITING-WOMAN.]

Look, see, these petulant things,
45   How they have done this!

VOLP [ASIDE.]: I do feel the fever
Entering in at mine ears; O, for a charm,
To fright it hence.

LADY P: Come nearer: Is this curl
50   In his right place, or this? Why is this higher
Then all the rest? You have not wash'd your eyes, yet!
Or do they not stand even in your head?
Where is your fellow? call her.

                                [EXIT 1 WOMAN.]

NAN: Now, St. Mark
55   Deliver us! anon, she will beat her women,
Because her nose is red.

          [RE-ENTER 1 WITH 2 WOMAN.]

LADY P: I pray you, view
This tire, forsooth; are all things apt, or no?

1 WOM: One hair a little, here, sticks out, forsooth.

60   LADY P: Does't so, forsooth? and where was your dear sight,
When it did so, forsooth! What now! bird-eyed?
And you too? 'Pray you, both approach and mend it.
Now, by that light, I muse you are not ashamed!
I, that have preach'd these things so oft unto you,
65   Read you the principles, argued all the grounds,
Disputed every fitness, every grace,
Call'd you to counsel of so frequent dressings—

NAN [ASIDE.]: More carefully than of your fame or honour.

LADY P: Made you acquainted, what an ample dowry
75   The knowledge of these things would be unto you,
Able, alone, to get you noble husbands
At your return: and you thus to neglect it!
Besides you seeing what a curious nation
The Italians are, what will they say of me?
70   "The English lady cannot dress herself."
Here's a fine imputation to our country:
Well, go your ways, and stay, in the next room.
This fucus was too course too, it's no matter.—
Good-sir, you will give them entertainment?

                      [EXEUNT NANO AND WAITING-WOMEN.]

75   VOLP: The storm comes toward me.

LADY P [GOES TO THE COUCH.]: How does my Volpone?

VOLP: Troubled with noise, I cannot sleep; I dreamt
That a strange fury enter'd, now, my house,
And, with the dreadful tempest of her breath,
80   Did cleave my roof asunder.

LADY P: Believe me, and I
Had the most fearful dream, could I remember't—

VOLP [ASIDE.]: Out on my fate! I have given her the occasion
How to torment me: she will tell me hers.

85   LADY P: Me thought, the golden mediocrity,
Polite and delicate—

VOLP: O, if you do love me,
No more; I sweat, and suffer, at the mention
Of any dream: feel, how I tremble yet.

90   LADY P: Alas, good soul! the passion of the heart.
Seed-pearl were good now, boil'd with syrup of apples,
Tincture of gold, and coral, citron-pills,
Your elicampane root, myrobalanes—

VOLP [ASIDE.]: Ah me, I have ta'en a grass-hopper by the wing!

95   LADY P: Burnt silk, and amber: you have muscadel
Good in the house—

VOLP: You will not drink, and part?

LADY P: No, fear not that. I doubt, we shall not get
Some English saffron, half a dram would serve;
100 Your sixteen cloves, a little musk, dried mints,
Bugloss, and barley-meal—

VOLP [ASIDE.]: She's in again!
Before I fain'd diseases, now I have one.

LADY P: And these applied with a right scarlet cloth.

105 VOLP [ASIDE.]: Another flood of words! a very torrent!

LADY P: Shall I, sir, make you a poultice?

VOLP: No, no, no;
I am very well: you need prescribe no more.

LADY P: I have a little studied physic; but now,
110 I'm all for music, save, in the forenoons,
An hour or two for painting. I would have
A lady, indeed, to have all, letters, and arts,
Be able to discourse, to write, to paint,
But principal, as Plato holds, your music,
115 And, so does wise Pythagoras, I take it,
Is your true rapture: when there is concent
In face, in voice, and clothes: and is, indeed,
Our sex's chiefest ornament.

VOLP: The poet
120 As old in time as Plato, and as knowing,
Says that your highest female grace is silence.

LADY P: Which of your poets? Petrarch, or Tasso, or Dante?
Guarini? Ariosto? Aretine?
Cieco di Hadria? I have read them all.

125 VOLP [ASIDE.]: Is every thing a cause to my distruction?

LADY P: I think I have two or three of them about me.

VOLP [ASIDE.]: The sun, the sea will sooner both stand still,
Then her eternal tongue; nothing can 'scape it.

LADY P: Here's pastor Fido—

130 VOLP [ASIDE.]: Profess obstinate silence,
That's now my safest.

LADY P: All our English writers,
I mean such as are happy in the Italian,
Will deign to steal out of this author, mainly:
135 Almost as much, as from Montagnie;
He has so modern and facile a vein,
Fitting the time, and catching the court-ear!
Your Petrarch is more passionate, yet he,
In days of sonetting, trusted them with much:
140 Dante is hard, and few can understand him.
But, for a desperate wit, there's Aretine;
Only, his pictures are a little obscene—
You mark me not.

VOLP: Alas, my mind is perturb'd.

145 LADY P: Why, in such cases, we must cure ourselves,
Make use of our philosophy—

VOLP: Oh me!

LADY P: And as we find our passions do rebel,
Encounter them with reason, or divert them,
150 By giving scope unto some other humour
Of lesser danger: as, in politic bodies,
There's nothing more doth overwhelm the judgment,
And cloud the understanding, than too much
Settling and fixing, and, as 'twere, subsiding
155 Upon one object. For the incorporating
Of these same outward things, into that part,
Which we call mental, leaves some certain faeces
That stop the organs, and as Plato says,
Assassinate our Knowledge.

160 VOLP [ASIDE.]: Now, the spirit
Of patience help me!

LADY P: Come, in faith, I must
Visit you more a days; and make you well:
Laugh and be lusty.

165 VOLP [ASIDE.]: My good angel save me!

LADY P: There was but one sole man in all the world,
With whom I e'er could sympathise; and he
Would lie you, often, three, four hours together
To hear me speak; and be sometimes so rapt,
170 As he would answer me quite from the purpose,
Like you, and you are like him, just. I'll discourse,
An't be but only, sir, to bring you asleep,
How we did spend our time and loves together,
For some six years.

175 VOLP: Oh, oh, oh, oh, oh, oh!

LADY P: For we were coaetanei, and brought up—

VOLP: Some power, some fate, some fortune rescue me!

[ENTER MOSCA.]

MOS: God save you, madam!

LADY P: Good sir.

180 VOLP: Mosca? welcome,
Welcome to my redemption.

MOS: Why, sir?

VOLP: Oh,
Rid me of this my torture, quickly, there;
185 My madam, with the everlasting voice:
The bells, in time of pestilence, ne'er made
Like noise, or were in that perpetual motion!
The Cock-pit comes not near it. All my house,
But now, steam'd like a bath with her thick breath.
190 A lawyer could not have been heard; nor scarce
Another woman, such a hail of words
She has let fall. For hell's sake, rid her hence.

MOS: Has she presented?

VOLP: O, I do not care;
195 I'll take her absence, upon any price,
With any loss.

MOS: Madam—

LADY P: I have brought your patron
A toy, a cap here, of mine own work.

200   MOS: 'Tis well.
I had forgot to tell you, I saw your knight,
Where you would little think it.—

LADY P: Where?

MOS: Marry,
205   Where yet, if you make haste, you may apprehend,
Rowing upon the water in a gondole,
With the most cunning courtezan of Venice.

LADY P: Is't true?

MOS: Pursue them, and believe your eyes;
210   Leave me, to make your gift.

                                       [EXIT LADY P. HASTILY.]

—I knew 'twould take:
For, lightly, they, that use themselves most license,
Are still most jealous.

VOLP: Mosca, hearty thanks,
215   For thy quick fiction, and delivery of me.
Now to my hopes, what say'st thou?

            [RE-ENTER LADY P. WOULD-BE.]

LADY P: But do you hear, sir?—

VOLP: Again! I fear a paroxysm.

LADY P: Which way
220   Row'd they together?

MOS: Toward the Rialto.

LADY P: I pray you lend me your dwarf.

MOS: I pray you, take him.—

                                            [EXIT LADY P.]

Your hopes, sir, are like happy blossoms, fair,
225   And promise timely fruit, if you will stay
But the maturing; keep you at your couch,

Corbaccio will arrive straight, with the Will;
When he is gone, I'll tell you more.

[EXIT.]

VOLP: My blood,
230 My spirits are return'd; I am alive:
And like your wanton gamester, at primero,
Whose thought had whisper'd to him, not go less,
Methinks I lie, and draw—for an encounter.

[THE SCENE CLOSES UPON VOLPONE.]

SCENE 3.3
THE PASSAGE LEADING TO VOLPONE'S CHAMBER.

ENTER MOSCA AND BONARIO.

MOS: Sir, here conceal'd,

[SHEWS HIM A CLOSET.]

you may here all. But, pray you,
Have patience, sir;

[KNOCKING WITHIN.]

—the same's your father knocks:
5 I am compell'd to leave you.

[EXIT.]

BON: Do so.—Yet,
Cannot my thought imagine this a truth.

[GOES INTO THE CLOSET.]

SCENE 3.4.
ANOTHER PART OF THE SAME.

ENTER MOSCA AND CORVINO, CELIA FOLLOWING.

MOS: Death on me! you are come too soon, what meant you?
Did not I say, I would send?

CORV: Yes, but I fear'd
You might forget it, and then they prevent us.

5 MOS [ASIDE.]: Prevent! did e'er man haste so, for his horns?
A courtier would not ply it so, for a place.
—Well, now there's no helping it, stay here;
I'll presently return.

[EXIT.]

CORV: Where are you, Celia?
10 You know not wherefore I have brought you hither?

CEL: Not well, except you told me.

CORV: Now, I will:
Hark hither.

[EXEUNT.]

SCENE 3.5.
A CLOSET OPENING INTO A GALLERY.

ENTER MOSCA AND BONARIO.

MOS: Sir, your father hath sent word,
It will be half an hour ere he come;
And therefore, if you please to walk the while
Into that gallery—at the upper end,
5 There are some books to entertain the time:
And I'll take care no man shall come unto you, sir.

BON: Yes, I will stay there.
[ASIDE.]—I do doubt this fellow.

[EXIT.]

MOS [LOOKING AFTER HIM.]: There; he is far enough;
10 he can hear nothing:
And, for his father, I can keep him off.

[EXIT.]

SCENE 3.6.
VOLPONE'S CHAMBER.—VOLPONE ON HIS COUCH.
MOSCA SITTING BY HIM.

ENTER CORVINO, FORCING IN CELIA.

CORV: Nay, now, there is no starting back, and therefore,
Resolve upon it: I have so decreed.
It must be done. Nor would I move't, afore,
Because I would avoid all shifts and tricks,
5 That might deny me.

CEL: Sir, let me beseech you,
Affect not these strange trials; if you doubt
My chastity, why, lock me up for ever:
Make me the heir of darkness. Let me live,
10   Where I may please your fears, if not your trust.
CORV: Believe it, I have no such humour, I.
All that I speak I mean; yet I'm not mad;
Nor horn-mad, see you? Go to, shew yourself
Obedient, and a wife.

15   CEL: O heaven!

CORV: I say it,
Do so.

CEL: Was this the train?

CORV: I've told you reasons;
20   What the physicians have set down; how much
It may concern me; what my engagements are;
My means; and the necessity of those means,
For my recovery: wherefore, if you be
Loyal, and mine, be won, respect my venture.

25   CEL: Before your honour?

CORV: Honour! tut, a breath:
There's no such thing, in nature: a mere term
Invented to awe fools. What is my gold
The worse, for touching, clothes for being look'd on?
30   Why, this is no more. An old decrepit wretch,
That has no sense, no sinew; takes his meat
With others' fingers; only knows to gape,
When you do scald his gums; a voice; a shadow;
And, what can this man hurt you?

35   CEL [ASIDE.]: Lord! what spirit
Is this hath enter'd him?

CORV: And for your fame,
That's such a jig; as if I would go tell it,
Cry it on the Piazza! who shall know it,
40   But he that cannot speak it, and this fellow,
Whose lips are in my pocket? save yourself,
(If you'll proclaim't, you may,) I know no other,
Shall come to know it.

CEL: Are heaven and saints then nothing?
45   Will they be blind or stupid?

CORV: How!

CEL: Good sir,
Be jealous still, emulate them; and think
What hate they burn with toward every sin.

50   CORV: I grant you: if I thought it were a sin,
I would not urge you. Should I offer this
To some young Frenchman, or hot Tuscan blood
That had read Aretine, conn'd all his prints,
Knew every quirk within lust's labyrinth,
55   And were professed critic in lechery;
And I would look upon him, and applaud him,
This were a sin: but here, 'tis contrary,
A pious work, mere charity for physic,
And honest polity, to assure mine own.

60   CEL: O heaven! canst thou suffer such a change?

VOLP: Thou art mine honour, Mosca, and my pride,
My joy, my tickling, my delight! Go bring them.

MOS [ADVANCING.]: Please you draw near, sir.

CORV: Come on, what—
65   You will not be rebellious? by that light—

MOS: Sir,
Signior Corvino, here, is come to see you.

VOLP: Oh!

MOS: And hearing of the consultation had,
70   So lately, for your health, is come to offer,
Or rather, sir, to prostitute—

CORV: Thanks, sweet Mosca.

MOS: Freely, unask'd, or unintreated—

CORV: Well.

75   MOS: As the true fervent instance of his love,
His own most fair and proper wife; the beauty,
Only of price in Venice—

CORV: 'Tis well urged.

MOS: To be your comfortress, and to preserve you.

80 VOLP: Alas, I am past, already! Pray you, thank him
For his good care and promptness; but for that,
'Tis a vain labour e'en to fight 'gainst heaven;
Applying fire to stone—
[COUGHING.] uh, uh, uh, uh!
85 Making a dead leaf grow again. I take
His wishes gently, though; and you may tell him,
What I have done for him: marry, my state is hopeless.
Will him to pray for me; and to use his fortune
With reverence, when he comes to't.

90 MOS: Do you hear, sir?
Go to him with your wife.

CORV: Heart of my father!
Wilt thou persist thus? come, I pray thee, come.
Thou seest 'tis nothing, Celia. By this hand,
95 I shall grow violent. Come, do't, I say.

CEL: Sir, kill me, rather: I will take down poison,
Eat burning coals, do any thing.—

CORV: Be damn'd!
Heart, I'll drag thee hence, home, by the hair;
100 Cry thee a strumpet through the streets; rip up
Thy mouth unto thine ears; and slit thy nose,
Like a raw rotchet!—Do not tempt me; come,
Yield, I am loth—Death! I will buy some slave
Whom I will kill, and bind thee to him, alive;
105 And at my window hang you forth: devising
Some monstrous crime, which I, in capital letters,
Will eat into thy flesh with aquafortis,
And burning corsives, on this stubborn breast.
Now, by the blood thou hast incensed, I'll do it!

110 CEL: Sir, what you please, you may, I am your martyr.

CORV: Be not thus obstinate, I have not deserved it:
Think who it is intreats you. 'Prithee, sweet;—
Good faith, thou shalt have jewels, gowns, attires,
What thou wilt think, and ask. Do but go kiss him.
115 Or touch him, but, for my sake.—At my suit.—

This once.—No! not! I shall remember this.
Will you disgrace me thus? Do you thirst my undoing?

MOS: Nay, gentle lady, be advised.

CORV: No, no.
120 She has watch'd her time. Ods precious, this is scurvy,
'Tis very scurvy: and you are—

MOS: Nay, good, sir.

CORV: An arrant Locust, by heaven, a locust!
Whore, crocodile, that hast thy tears prepared,
125 Expecting how thou'lt bid them flow—

MOS: Nay, 'Pray you, sir!
She will consider.

CEL: Would my life would serve
To satisfy—

130 CORV: S'death! if she would but speak to him,
And save my reputation, it were somewhat;
But spightfully to affect my utter ruin!

MOS: Ay, now you have put your fortune in her hands.
Why i'faith, it is her modesty, I must quit her.
135 If you were absent, she would be more coming;
I know it: and dare undertake for her.
What woman can before her husband? 'pray you,
Let us depart, and leave her here.

CORV: Sweet Celia,
140 Thou may'st redeem all, yet; I'll say no more:
If not, esteem yourself as lost,—Nay, stay there.
                    [SHUTS THE DOOR, AND EXIT WITH MOSCA.]

CEL: O God, and his good angels! whither, whither,
Is shame fled human breasts? that with such ease,
Men dare put off your honours, and their own?
145 Is that, which ever was a cause of life,
Now placed beneath the basest circumstance,
And modesty an exile made, for money?

VOLP: Ay, in Corvino, and such earth-fed minds,
                              [LEAPING FROM HIS COUCH.]
That never tasted the true heaven of love.

150   Assure thee, Celia, he that would sell thee,
      Only for hope of gain, and that uncertain,
      He would have sold his part of Paradise
      For ready money, had he met a cope-man.
      Why art thou mazed to see me thus revived?
155   Rather applaud thy beauty's miracle;
      'Tis thy great work: that hath, not now alone,
      But sundry times raised me, in several shapes,
      And, but this morning, like a mountebank;
      To see thee at thy window: ay, before
160   I would have left my practice, for thy love,
      In varying figures, I would have contended
      With the blue Proteus, or the horned flood.
      Now art thou welcome.

      CEL: Sir!

165   VOLP: Nay, fly me not.
      Nor let thy false imagination
      That I was bed-rid, make thee think I am so:
      Thou shalt not find it. I am, now, as fresh,
      As hot, as high, and in as jovial plight,
170   As when, in that so celebrated scene,
      At recitation of our comedy,
      For entertainment of the great Valois,
      I acted young Antinous; and attracted
      The eyes and ears of all the ladies present,
175   To admire each graceful gesture, note, and footing.

                                      [SINGS.]

      Come, my Celia, let us prove,
      While we can, the sports of love,
      Time will not be ours for ever,
      He, at length, our good will sever;
180   Spend not then his gifts in vain;
      Suns, that set, may rise again:
      But if once we loose this light,
      'Tis with us perpetual night.
      Why should we defer our joys?
185   Fame and rumour are but toys.
      Cannot we delude the eyes
      Of a few poor household spies?
      Or his easier ears beguile,
      Thus remooved by our wile?——
190   'Tis no sin love's fruits to steal:
      But the sweet thefts to reveal;

To be taken, to be seen,
These have crimes accounted been.

CEL: Some serene blast me, or dire lightning strike
195   This my offending face!

VOLP: Why droops my Celia?
Thou hast, in place of a base husband, found
A worthy lover: use thy fortune well,
With secrecy and pleasure. See, behold,
200   What thou art queen of; not in expectation,
As I feed others: but possess'd, and crown'd.
See, here, a rope of pearl; and each, more orient
Than that the brave Egyptian queen caroused:
Dissolve and drink them. See, a carbuncle,
205   May put out both the eyes of our St Mark;
A diamond, would have bought Lollia Paulina,
When she came in like star-light, hid with jewels,
That were the spoils of provinces; take these,
And wear, and lose them: yet remains an ear-ring
210   To purchase them again, and this whole state.
A gem but worth a private patrimony,
Is nothing: we will eat such at a meal.
The heads of parrots, tongues of nightingales,
The brains of peacocks, and of estriches,
215   Shall be our food: and, could we get the phoenix,
Though nature lost her kind, she were our dish.

CEL: Good sir, these things might move a mind affected
With such delights; but I, whose innocence
Is all I can think wealthy, or worth th' enjoying,
220   And which, once lost, I have nought to lose beyond it,
Cannot be taken with these sensual baits:
If you have conscience—

VOLP: 'Tis the beggar's virtue,
If thou hast wisdom, hear me, Celia.
225   Thy baths shall be the juice of July-flowers,
Spirit of roses, and of violets,
The milk of unicorns, and panthers' breath
Gather'd in bags, and mixt with Cretan wines.
Our drink shall be prepared gold and amber;
230   Which we will take, until my roof whirl round
With the vertigo: and my dwarf shall dance,
My eunuch sing, my fool make up the antic.

Whilst we, in changed shapes, act Ovid's tales,
Thou, like Europa now, and I like Jove,
235 Then I like Mars, and thou like Erycine:
So, of the rest, till we have quite run through,
And wearied all the fables of the gods.
Then will I have thee in more modern forms,
Attired like some sprightly dame of France,
240 Brave Tuscan lady, or proud Spanish beauty;
Sometimes, unto the Persian sophy's wife;
Or the grand signior's mistress; and, for change,
To one of our most artful courtezans,
Or some quick Negro, or cold Russian;
245 And I will meet thee in as many shapes:
Where we may so transfuse our wandering souls,
Out at our lips, and score up sums of pleasures,

[SINGS.]

That the curious shall not know
How to tell them as they flow;
250 And the envious, when they find
What there number is, be pined.

CEL: If you have ears that will be pierc'd—or eyes
That can be open'd—a heart that may be touch'd—
Or any part that yet sounds man about you—
255 If you have touch of holy saints—or heaven—
Do me the grace to let me 'scape—if not,
Be bountiful and kill me. You do know,
I am a creature, hither ill betray'd,
By one, whose shame I would forget it were:
260 If you will deign me neither of these graces,
Yet feed your wrath, sir, rather than your lust,
(It is a vice comes nearer manliness,)
And punish that unhappy crime of nature,
Which you miscall my beauty; flay my face,
265 Or poison it with ointments, for seducing
Your blood to this rebellion. Rub these hands,
With what may cause an eating leprosy,
E'en to my bones and marrow: any thing,
That may disfavour me, save in my honour—
270 And I will kneel to you, pray for you, pay down
A thousand hourly vows, sir, for your health;
Report, and think you virtuous—

VOLP: Think me cold,
Frosen and impotent, and so report me?

275 That I had Nestor's hernia, thou wouldst think.
I do degenerate, and abuse my nation,
To play with opportunity thus long;
I should have done the act, and then have parley'd.
Yield, or I'll force thee.

[SEIZES HER.]

280 CEL: O! just God!

VOLP: In vain—

BON [RUSHING IN]: Forbear, foul ravisher, libidinous swine!
Free the forced lady, or thou diest, impostor.
But that I'm loth to snatch thy punishment
285 Out of the hand of justice, thou shouldst, yet,
Be made the timely sacrifice of vengeance,
Before this altar, and this dross, thy idol.—
Lady, let's quit the place, it is the den
Of villany; fear nought, you have a guard:
290 And he, ere long, shall meet his just reward.

[EXEUNT BON. AND CEL.]

VOLP: Fall on me, roof, and bury me in ruin!
Become my grave, that wert my shelter! O!
I am unmask'd, unspirited, undone,
Betray'd to beggary, to infamy—

[ENTER MOSCA, WOUNDED AND BLEEDING.]

295 MOS: Where shall I run, most wretched shame of men,
To beat out my unlucky brains?

VOLP: Here, here.
What! dost thou bleed?

MOS: O that his well-driv'n sword
300 Had been so courteous to have cleft me down
Unto the navel; ere I lived to see
My life, my hopes, my spirits, my patron, all
Thus desperately engaged, by my error!

VOLP: Woe on thy fortune!

305 MOS: And my follies, sir.

VOLP: Thou hast made me miserable.

MOS: And myself, sir.
Who would have thought he would have harken'd, so?

VOLP: What shall we do?

310   MOS: I know not; if my heart
Could expiate the mischance, I'd pluck it out.
Will you be pleased to hang me? or cut my throat?
And I'll requite you, sir. Let us die like Romans,
Since we have lived like Grecians.
                                                    [KNOCKING WITHIN.]

315   VOLP: Hark! who's there?
I hear some footing; officers, the saffi,
Come to apprehend us! I do feel the brand
Hissing already at my forehead; now,
Mine ears are boring.

320   MOS: To your couch, sir, you,
Make that place good, however.
                            [VOLPONE LIES DOWN, AS BEFORE.]
—Guilty men
Suspect what they deserve still.
                            [ENTER CORBACCIO.]
325   Signior Corbaccio!

CORB: Why, how now, Mosca?

MOS: O, undone, amazed, sir.
Your son, I know not by what accident,
Acquainted with your purpose to my patron,
330   Touching your Will, and making him your heir,
Enter'd our house with violence, his sword drawn
Sought for you, call'd you wretch, unnatural,
Vow'd he would kill you.

CORB: Me!

335   MOS: Yes, and my patron.

CORB: This act shall disinherit him indeed;
Here is the Will.

MOS: 'Tis well, sir.

CORB: Right and well:
340 Be you as careful now for me.

                    [ENTER VOLTORE, BEHIND.]

MOS: My life, sir,
Is not more tender'd; I am only yours.

CORB: How does he? will he die shortly, think'st thou?

MOS: I fear
345 He'll outlast May.

CORB: To-day?

MOS: No, last out May, sir.

CORB: Could'st thou not give him a dram?

MOS: O, by no means, sir.

350 CORB: Nay, I'll not bid you.

VOLT [COMING FORWARD.]: This is a knave, I see.

MOS [SEEING VOLTORE.]: How! signior Voltore!
[ASIDE.] did he hear me?

VOLT: Parasite!

355 MOS: Who's that?—O, sir, most timely welcome—

VOLT: Scarce,
To the discovery of your tricks, I fear.
You are his, *only*? and mine, also? are you not?

MOS: Who? I, sir?

360 VOLT: You, sir. What device is this
About a Will?

MOS: A plot for you, sir.

VOLT: Come,
Put not your foists upon me; I shall scent them.

365 MOS: Did you not hear it?

VOLT: Yes, I hear Corbaccio
Hath made your patron there his heir.

MOS: 'Tis true,
By my device, drawn to it by my plot,
370 With hope—

VOLT: Your patron should reciprocate?
And you have promised?

MOS: For your good, I did, sir.
Nay, more, I told his son, brought, hid him here,
375 Where he might hear his father pass the deed:
Being persuaded to it by this thought, sir,
That the unnaturalness, first, of the act,
And then his father's oft disclaiming in him,
(Which I did mean t'help on,) would sure enrage him
380 To do some violence upon his parent,
On which the law should take sufficient hold,
And you be stated in a double hope:
Truth be my comfort, and my conscience,
My only aim was to dig you a fortune
385 Out of these two old rotten sepulchres—

VOLT: I cry thee mercy, Mosca.

MOS: Worth your patience,
And your great merit, sir. And see the change!

VOLT: Why, what success?

390 MOS: Most happless! you must help, sir.
Whilst we expected the old raven, in comes
Corvino's wife, sent hither by her husband—

VOLT: What, with a present?

MOS: No, sir, on visitation;
395 (I'll tell you how anon;) and staying long,
The youth he grows impatient, rushes forth,
Seizeth the lady, wounds me, makes her swear
(Or he would murder her, that was his vow)
To affirm my patron to have done her rape:
400 Which how unlike it is, you see! and hence,
With that pretext he's gone, to accuse his father,
Defame my patron, defeat you—

VOLT: Where is her husband?
405 Let him be sent for straight.

MOS: Sir, I'll go fetch him.

VOLT: Bring him to the Scrutineo.

MOS: Sir, I will.

VOLT: This must be stopt.

410   MOS: O you do nobly, sir.
Alas, 'twas labor'd all, sir, for your good;
Nor was there want of counsel in the plot:
But fortune can, at any time, o'erthrow
The projects of a hundred learned clerks, sir.

415   CORB [LISTENING]: What's that?

VOLT: Will't please you, sir, to go along?

             [EXIT CORBACCIO, FOLLOWED BY VOLTORE.]

MOS: Patron, go in, and pray for our success.

VOLP [RISING FROM HIS COUCH.]: Need makes devotion:
heaven your labour bless!

                    [EXEUNT.]

ACT 4.
SCENE 4.1.
A STREET.

[ENTER SIR POLITICK WOULD-BE AND PEREGRINE.]

SIR P: I told you, sir, it was a plot: you see
What observation is! You mention'd me,
For some instructions: I will tell you, sir,
(Since we are met here in this height of Venice,)
5   Some few perticulars I have set down,
Only for this meridian, fit to be known
Of your crude traveller, and they are these.
I will not touch, sir, at your phrase, or clothes,
For they are old.

10   PER: Sir, I have better.

SIR P: Pardon,
I meant, as they are themes.

PER: O, sir, proceed:
I'll slander you no more of wit, good sir.

15   SIR P: First, for your garb, it must be grave and serious,
      Very reserv'd, and lock'd; not tell a secret
      On any terms, not to your father; scarce
      A fable, but with caution; make sure choice
      Both of your company, and discourse; beware
20   You never speak a truth—

      PER: How!

      SIR P: Not to strangers,
      For those be they you must converse with, most;
      Others I would not know, sir, but at distance,
25   So as I still might be a saver in them:
      You shall have tricks else past upon you hourly.
      And then, for your religion, profess none,
      But wonder at the diversity, of all:
      And, for your part, protest, were there no other
30   But simply the laws o' the land, you could content you,
      Nic. Machiavel, and Monsieur Bodin, both
      Were of this mind. Then must you learn the use
      And handling of your silver fork at meals;
      The metal of your glass; (these are main matters
35   With your Italian;) and to know the hour
      When you must eat your melons, and your figs.

      PER: Is that a point of state too?

      SIR P: Here it is,
      For your Venetian, if he see a man
40   Preposterous in the least, he has him straight;
      He has; he strips him. I'll acquaint you, sir,
      I now have lived here, 'tis some fourteen months
      Within the first week of my landing here,
      All took me for a citizen of Venice:
45   I knew the forms, so well—

      PER [ASIDE.]: And nothing else.

      SIR P: I had read Contarene, took me a house,
      Dealt with my Jews to furnish it with moveables—
      Well, if I could but find one man, one man
50   To mine own heart, whom I durst trust, I would—

      PER: What, what, sir?

SIR P: Make him rich; make him a fortune:
He should not think again. I would command it.

PER: As how?

55 SIR P: With certain projects that I have;
Which I may not discover.

PER [ASIDE.]: If I had
But one to wager with, I would lay odds now,
He tells me instantly.

60 SIR P: One is, and that
I care not greatly who knows, to serve the state
Of Venice with red herrings for three years,
And at a certain rate, from Rotterdam,
Where I have correspendence. There's a letter,
65 Sent me from one of the states, and to that purpose:
He cannot write his name, but that's his mark.

PER: He's a chandler?

SIR P: No, a cheesemonger.
There are some others too with whom I treat
70 About the same negociation;
And I will undertake it: for, 'tis thus.
I'll do't with ease, I have cast it all: Your hoy
Carries but three men in her, and a boy;
And she shall make me three returns a year:
75 So, if there come but one of three, I save,
If two, I can defalk:—but this is now,
If my main project fail.

PER: Then you have others?

SIR P: I should be loth to draw the subtle air
80 Of such a place, without my thousand aims.
I'll not dissemble, sir: where'er I come,
I love to be considerative; and 'tis true,
I have at my free hours thought upon
Some certain goods unto the state of Venice,
85 Which I do call "my Cautions;" and, sir, which
I mean, in hope of pension, to propound
To the Great Council, then unto the Forty,
So to the Ten. My means are made already—

PER: By whom?

90 SIR P: Sir, one that, though his place be obscure,
Yet he can sway, and they will hear him. He's
A commandador.

PER: What! a common serjeant?

SIR P: Sir, such as they are, put it in their mouths,
95 What they should say, sometimes; as well as greater:
I think I have my notes to shew you—
[SEARCHING HIS POCKETS.]

PER: Good sir.

SIR P: But you shall swear unto me, on your gentry,
Not to anticipate—

100 PER: I, sir!

SIR P: Nor reveal
A circumstance—My paper is not with me.

PER: O, but you can remember, sir.

SIR P: My first is
105 Concerning tinder-boxes. You must know,
No family is here, without its box.
Now, sir, it being so portable a thing,
Put case, that you or I were ill affected
Unto the state, sir; with it in our pockets,
110 Might not I go into the Arsenal,
Or you, come out again, and none the wiser?

PER: Except yourself, sir.

SIR P: Go to, then. I therefore
Advertise to the state, how fit it were,
115 That none but such as were known patriots,
Sound lovers of their country, should be suffer'd
To enjoy them in their houses; and even those
Seal'd at some office, and at such a bigness
As might not lurk in pockets.

120 PER: Admirable!

      SIR P: My next is, how to enquire, and be resolv'd,
      By present demonstration, whether a ship,
      Newly arrived from Soria, or from
      Any suspected part of all the Levant,
125   Be guilty of the plague: and where they use
      To lie out forty, fifty days, sometimes,
      About the Lazaretto, for their trial;
      I'll save that charge and loss unto the merchant,
      And in an hour clear the doubt.

130   PER: Indeed, sir!

      SIR P: Or—I will lose my labour.

      PER: 'My faith, that's much.

      SIR P: Nay, sir, conceive me. It will cost me in onions,
      Some thirty livres—

135   PER: Which is one pound sterling.

      SIR P: Beside my water-works: for this I do, sir.
      First, I bring in your ship 'twixt two brick walls;
      But those the state shall venture: On the one
      I strain me a fair tarpauling, and in that
140   I stick my onions, cut in halves: the other
      Is full of loop-holes, out at which I thrust
      The noses of my bellows; and those bellows
      I keep, with water-works, in perpetual motion,
      Which is the easiest matter of a hundred.
145   Now, sir, your onion, which doth naturally
      Attract the infection, and your bellows blowing
      The air upon him, will show, instantly,
      By his changed colour, if there be contagion;
      Or else remain as fair as at the first.
150   —Now it is known, 'tis nothing.

      PER: You are right, sir.

      SIR P: I would I had my note.

      PER: 'Faith, so would I:
      But you have done well for once, sir.

155   SIR P: Were I false,
      Or would be made so, I could shew you reasons

How I could sell this state now, to the Turk;
Spite of their galleys, or their—

[EXAMINING HIS PAPERS.]

PER: Pray you, sir Pol.

160   SIR P: I have them not about me.

PER: That I fear'd.
They are there, sir.

SIR P: No. This is my diary,
Wherein I note my actions of the day.

165   PER: Pray you let's see, sir. What is here?

[READS.]

"Notandum,
A rat had gnawn my spur-leathers; notwithstanding,
I put on new, and did go forth: but first
I threw three beans over the threshold. Item,
170   I went and bought two tooth-picks, whereof one
I burst immediatly, in a discourse
With a Dutch merchant, 'bout ragion del stato.
From him I went and paid a moccinigo,
For piecing my silk stockings; by the way
175   I cheapen'd sprats; and at St. Mark's I urined."
'Faith, these are politic notes!

SIR P: Sir, I do slip
No action of my life, but thus I quote it.

PER: Believe me, it is wise!

180   SIR P: Nay, sir, read forth.

[ENTER, AT A DISTANCE, LADY POLITICK-WOULD BE,
NANO, AND TWO WAITING-WOMEN.]

LADY P: Where should this loose knight be, trow?
sure he's housed.

NAN: Why, then he's fast.

LADY P: Ay, he plays both with me.
185   I pray you, stay. This heat will do more harm

To my complexion, than his heart is worth;
(I do not care to hinder, but to take him.)

                                  [RUBBING HER CHEEKS.]

How it comes off!

1 WOM: My master's yonder.

190   LADY P: Where?

1 WOM: With a young gentleman.

LADY P: That same's the party;
In man's apparel! 'Pray you, sir, jog my knight:
I'll be tender to his reputation,
195   However he demerit.

SIR P [SEEING HER]: My lady!

PER: Where?

SIR P: 'Tis she indeed, sir; you shall know her. She is,
Were she not mine, a lady of that merit,
200   For fashion and behaviour; and, for beauty
I durst compare—

PER: It seems you are not jealous,
That dare commend her.

SIR P: Nay, and for discourse—

205   PER: Being your wife, she cannot miss that.

SIR P [INTRODUCING PER.]: Madam,
Here is a gentleman, pray you, use him fairly;
He seems a youth, but he is—

LADY P: None.

210   SIR P: Yes, one
Has put his face as soon into the world—

LADY P: You mean, as early? but to-day?

SIR P: How's this?

LADY P: Why, in this habit, sir; you apprehend me:—
215   Well, master Would-be, this doth not become you;

I had thought the odour, sir, of your good name,
Had been more precious to you; that you would not
Have done this dire massacre on your honour;
One of your gravity and rank besides!
220   But knights, I see, care little for the oath
They make to ladies; chiefly, their own ladies.

SIR P: Now by my spurs, the symbol of my knighthood,—

PER [ASIDE.]: Lord, how his brain is humbled for an oath!

SIR P: I reach you not.

225   LADY P: Right, sir, your policy
May bear it through, thus.
[TO PER.] Sir, a word with you.
I would be loth to contest publicly
With any gentlewoman, or to seem
230   Froward, or violent, as the courtier says;
It comes too near rusticity in a lady,
Which I would shun by all means: and however
I may deserve from master Would-be, yet
T'have one fair gentlewoman thus be made
235   The unkind instrument to wrong another,
And one she knows not, ay, and to persever;
In my poor judgment, is not warranted
From being a solecism in our sex,
If not in manners.

240   PER: How is this!

SIR P: Sweet madam,
Come nearer to your aim.

LADY P: Marry, and will, sir.
Since you provoke me with your impudence,
245   And laughter of your light land-syren here,
Your Sporus, your hermaphrodite—

PER: What's here?
Poetic fury, and historic storms?

SIR P: The gentleman, believe it, is of worth,
250   And of our nation.

LADY P: Ay, your White-friars nation.
Come, I blush for you, master Would-be, I;
And am asham'd you should have no more forehead,
Than thus to be the patron, or St. George,
255 To a lewd harlot, a base fricatrice,
A female devil, in a male outside.

SIR P: Nay,
And you be such a one, I must bid adieu
To your delights. The case appears too liquid.

[EXIT.]

260 LADY P: Ay, you may carry't clear, with your state-face!—
But for your carnival concupiscence,
Who here is fled for liberty of conscience,
From furious persecution of the marshal,
Her will I dis'ple.

265 PER: This is fine, i'faith!
And do you use this often? Is this part
Of your wit's exercise, 'gainst you have occasion?
Madam—

LADY P: Go to, sir.

270 PER: Do you hear me, lady?
Why, if your knight have set you to beg shirts,
Or to invite me home, you might have done it
A nearer way, by far:

LADY P: This cannot work you
275 Out of my snare.

PER: Why, am I in it, then?
Indeed your husband told me you were fair,
And so you are; only your nose inclines,
That side that's next the sun, to the queen-apple.

280 LADY P: This cannot be endur'd by any patience.

[ENTER MOSCA.]

MOS: What is the matter, madam?

LADY P: If the Senate
Right not my quest in this; I'll protest them
To all the world, no aristocracy.

285   MOS: What is the injury, lady?

LADY P: Why, the callet
You told me of, here I have ta'en disguised.

MOS: Who? this! what means your ladyship? the creature
I mention'd to you is apprehended now,
290   Before the senate; you shall see her—

LADY P: Where?

MOS: I'll bring you to her. This young gentleman,
I saw him land this morning at the port.

LADY P: Is't possible! how has my judgment wander'd?
295   Sir, I must, blushing, say to you, I have err'd;
And plead your pardon.

PER: What, more changes yet!

LADY P: I hope you have not the malice to remember
A gentlewoman's passion. If you stay
300   In Venice here, please you to use me, sir—

MOS: Will you go, madam?

LADY P: 'Pray you, sir, use me. In faith,
The more you see me, the more I shall conceive
You have forgot our quarrel.

[EXEUNT LADY WOULD-BE, MOSCA, NANO, AND WAITING-
WOMEN.]

305   PER: This is rare!
Sir Politick Would-be? no; sir Politick Bawd.
To bring me thus acquainted with his wife!
Well, wise sir Pol, since you have practised thus
Upon my freshman-ship, I'll try your salt-head,
310   What proof it is against a counter-plot.

[EXIT.]

SCENE 4.2.
THE SCRUTINEO, OR SENATE-HOUSE.

ENTER VOLTORE, CORBACCIO, CORVINO, AND MOSCA.

VOLT: Well, now you know the carriage of the business,
Your constancy is all that is required
Unto the safety of it.

MOS: Is the lie
5 Safely convey'd amongst us? is that sure?
Knows every man his burden?

CORV: Yes.

MOS: Then shrink not.

CORV: But knows the advocate the truth?

10 MOS: O, sir,
By no means; I devised a formal tale,
That salv'd your reputation. But be valiant, sir.

CORV: I fear no one but him, that this his pleading
Should make him stand for a co-heir—

15 MOS: Co-halter!
Hang him; we will but use his tongue, his noise,
As we do croakers here.

CORV: Ay, what shall he do?

MOS: When we have done, you mean?

20 CORV: Yes.

MOS: Why, we'll think:
Sell him for mummia; he's half dust already.
[TO VOLTORE.] Do not you smile, to see this buffalo,
How he does sport it with his head?
25 [ASIDE.] —I should,
If all were well and past.
[TO CORBACCIO.] —Sir, only you
Are he that shall enjoy the crop of all,
And these not know for whom they toil.

30 CORB: Ay, peace.

MOS [TURNING TO CORVINO.]: But you shall eat it.
Much! [ASIDE.]
[TO VOLTORE.] —Worshipful sir,
Mercury sit upon your thundering tongue,
35   Or the French Hercules, and make your language
As conquering as his club, to beat along,
As with a tempest, flat, our adversaries;
But much more yours, sir.

VOLT: Here they come, have done.

40   MOS: I have another witness, if you need, sir,
I can produce.

VOLT: Who is it?

MOS: Sir, I have her.

[ENTER AVOCATORI AND TAKE THEIR SEATS, BONARIO,
CELIA, NOTARIO, COMMANDADORI, SAFFI, AND OTHER
OFFICERS OF JUSTICE.]

1 AVOC: The like of this the senate never heard of.

45   2 AVOC: 'Twill come most strange to them when we report it.

4 AVOC: The gentlewoman has been ever held
Of unreproved name.

3 AVOC: So has the youth.

4 AVOC: The more unnatural part that of his father.

50   2 AVOC: More of the husband.

1 AVOC: I not know to give
His act a name, it is so monstrous!

4 AVOC: But the impostor, he's a thing created
To exceed example!

55   1 AVOC: And all after-times!

2 AVOC: I never heard a true voluptuary
Described, but him.

3 AVOC: Appear yet those were cited?

NOT: All, but the old magnifico, Volpone.

60   1 AVOC: Why is not he here?

MOS: Please your fatherhoods,
Here is his advocate: himself's so weak,
So feeble—

4 AVOC: What are you?

65   BON: His parasite,
His knave, his pandar—I beseech the court,
He may be forced to come, that your grave eyes
May bear strong witness of his strange impostures.

VOLT: Upon my faith and credit with your virtues,
70   He is not able to endure the air.

2 AVOC: Bring him, however.

3 AVOC: We will see him.

4 AVOC: Fetch him.

VOLT: Your fatherhoods fit pleasures be obey'd;
                                      [EXEUNT OFFICERS.]
75   But sure, the sight will rather move your pities,
Than indignation. May it please the court,
In the mean time, he may be heard in me;
I know this place most void of prejudice,
And therefore crave it, since we have no reason
80   To fear our truth should hurt our cause.

3 AVOC: Speak free.

VOLT: Then know, most honour'd fathers, I must now
Discover to your strangely abused ears,
The most prodigious and most frontless piece
85   Of solid impudence, and treachery,
That ever vicious nature yet brought forth
To shame the state of Venice. This lewd woman,
That wants no artificial looks or tears
To help the vizor she has now put on,

90   Hath long been known a close adulteress,
     To that lascivious youth there; not suspected,
     I say, but known, and taken in the act
     With him; and by this man, the easy husband,
     Pardon'd: whose timeless bounty makes him now
100 Stand here, the most unhappy, innocent person,
     That ever man's own goodness made accused.
     For these not knowing how to owe a gift
     Of that dear grace, but with their shame; being placed
     So above all powers of their gratitude,
105 Began to hate the benefit; and, in place
     Of thanks, devise to extirpe the memory
     Of such an act: wherein I pray your fatherhoods
     To observe the malice, yea, the rage of creatures
     Discover'd in their evils; and what heart
110 Such take, even from their crimes:—but that anon
     Will more appear.—This gentleman, the father,
     Hearing of this foul fact, with many others,
     Which daily struck at his too tender ears,
     And grieved in nothing more than that he could not
115 Preserve himself a parent, (his son's ills
     Growing to that strange flood,) at last decreed
     To disinherit him.

     1 AVOC: These be strange turns!

     2 AVOC: The young man's fame was ever fair and honest.

120 VOLT: So much more full of danger is his vice,
     That can beguile so under shade of virtue.
     But, as I said, my honour'd sires, his father
     Having this settled purpose, by what means
     To him betray'd, we know not, and this day
125 Appointed for the deed; that parricide,
     I cannot style him better, by confederacy
     Preparing this his paramour to be there,
     Enter'd Volpone's house, (who was the man,
     Your fatherhoods must understand, design'd
130 For the inheritance,) there sought his father:—
     But with what purpose sought he him, my lords?
     I tremble to pronounce it, that a son
     Unto a father, and to such a father,
     Should have so foul, felonious intent!
135 It was to murder him: when being prevented
     By his more happy absence, what then did he?

Not check his wicked thoughts; no, now new deeds,
(Mischief doth ever end where it begins)
An act of horror, fathers! he dragg'd forth
140   The aged gentleman that had there lain bed-rid
Three years and more, out of his innocent couch,
Naked upon the floor, there left him; wounded
His servant in the face: and, with this strumpet
The stale to his forged practice, who was glad
145   To be so active,—(I shall here desire
Your fatherhoods to note but my collections,
As most remarkable,—) thought at once to stop
His father's ends; discredit his free choice
In the old gentleman, redeem themselves,
150   By laying infamy upon this man,
To whom, with blushing, they should owe their lives.

1 AVOC: What proofs have you of this?

BON: Most honoured fathers,
I humbly crave there be no credit given
155   To this man's mercenary tongue.

2 AVOC: Forbear.

BON: His soul moves in his fee.

3 AVOC: O, sir.

BON: This fellow,
160   For six sols more, would plead against his Maker.

1 AVOC: You do forget yourself.

VOLT: Nay, nay, grave fathers,
Let him have scope: can any man imagine
That he will spare his accuser, that would not
165   Have spared his parent?

1 AVOC: Well, produce your proofs.

CEL: I would I could forget I were a creature.

VOLT: Signior Corbaccio.
[CORBACCIO COMES FORWARD.]

1 AVOC: What is he?

170 VOLT: The father.

2 AVOC: Has he had an oath?

NOT: Yes.

CORB: What must I do now?

NOT: Your testimony's craved.

175 CORB: Speak to the knave?
I'll have my mouth first stopt with earth; my heart
Abhors his knowledge: I disclaim in him.

1 AVOC: But for what cause?

CORB: The mere portent of nature!
180 He is an utter stranger to my loins.

BON: Have they made you to this?

CORB: I will not hear thee,
Monster of men, swine, goat, wolf, parricide!
Speak not, thou viper.

185 BON: Sir, I will sit down,
And rather wish my innocence should suffer,
Then I resist the authority of a father.

VOLT: Signior Corvino!

[CORVINO COMES FORWARD.]

2 AVOC: This is strange.

190 1 AVOC: Who's this?

NOT: The husband.

4 AVOC: Is he sworn?

NOT: He is.

3 AVOC: Speak, then.

195   CORV: This woman, please your fatherhoods, is a whore,
       Of most hot exercise, more than a partrich,
       Upon record—

       1 AVOC: No more.

       CORV: Neighs like a jennet.

200   NOT: Preserve the honour of the court.

       CORV: I shall,
       And modesty of your most reverend ears.
       And yet I hope that I may say, these eyes
       Have seen her glued unto that piece of cedar,
205   That fine well-timber'd gallant; and that here
       The letters may be read, through the horn,
       That make the story perfect.

       MOS: Excellent! sir.

       CORV [ASIDE TO MOSCA.]: There's no shame in this now, is there?

210   MOS: None.

       CORV: Or if I said, I hoped that she were onward
       To her damnation, if there be a hell
       Greater than whore and woman; a good catholic
       May make the doubt.

215   3 AVOC: His grief hath made him frantic.

       1 AVOC: Remove him hence.

       2 AVOC: Look to the woman.
                                                    [CELIA SWOONS.]

       CORV: Rare!
       Prettily feign'd, again!

220   4 AVOC: Stand from about her.

       1 AVOC: Give her the air.

       3 AVOC [TO MOSCA.]: What can you say?

       MOS: My wound,
       May it please your wisdoms, speaks for me, received

225 In aid of my good patron, when he mist
His sought-for father, when that well-taught dame
Had her cue given her, to cry out, A rape!

BON: O most laid impudence! Fathers—

3 AVOC: Sir, be silent;
230 You had your hearing free, so must they theirs.

2 AVOC: I do begin to doubt the imposture here.

4 AVOC: This woman has too many moods.

VOLT: Grave fathers,
She is a creature of a most profest
235 And prostituted lewdness.

CORV: Most impetuous,
Unsatisfied, grave fathers!

VOLT: May her feignings
Not take your wisdoms: but this day she baited
240 A stranger, a grave knight, with her loose eyes,
And more lascivious kisses. This man saw them
Together on the water in a gondola.

MOS: Here is the lady herself, that saw them too;
Without; who then had in the open streets
245 Pursued them, but for saving her knight's honour.

1 AVOC: Produce that lady.

2 AVOC: Let her come.

[EXIT MOSCA.]

4 AVOC: These things,
They strike with wonder!

250 3 AVOC: I am turn'd a stone.

[RE-ENTER MOSCA WITH LADY WOULD-BE.]

MOS: Be resolute, madam.

LADY P: Ay, this same is she.

[POINTING TO CELIA.]

Out, thou chameleon harlot! now thine eyes
Vie tears with the hyaena. Dar'st thou look
255 Upon my wronged face?—I cry your pardons,
I fear I have forgettingly transgrest
Against the dignity of the court—

2 AVOC: No, madam.

LADY P: And been exorbitant—

260 2 AVOC: You have not, lady.

4 AVOC: These proofs are strong.

LADY P: Surely, I had no purpose
To scandalise your honours, or my sex's.

3 AVOC: We do believe it.

265 LADY P: Surely, you may believe it.

2 AVOC: Madam, we do.

LADY P: Indeed, you may; my breeding
Is not so coarse—

1 AVOC: We know it.

270 LADY P: To offend
With pertinacy—

3 AVOC: Lady—

LADY P: Such a presence!
No surely.

275 1 AVOC: We well think it.

LADY P: You may think it.

1 AVOC: Let her o'ercome. What witnesses have you
To make good your report?

BON: Our consciences.

280 CEL: And heaven, that never fails the innocent.

4 AVOC: These are no testimonies.

BON: Not in your courts,
Where multitude, and clamour overcomes.

1 AVOC: Nay, then you do wax insolent.

[RE-ENTER OFFICERS, BEARING VOLPONE ON A COUCH.]

285   VOLT: Here, here,
The testimony comes, that will convince,
And put to utter dumbness their bold tongues:
See here, grave fathers, here's the ravisher,
The rider on men's wives, the great impostor,
290   The grand voluptuary! Do you not think
These limbs should affect venery? or these eyes
Covet a concubine? pray you mark these hands;
Are they not fit to stroke a lady's breasts?—
Perhaps he doth dissemble!

295   BON: So he does.

VOLT: Would you have him tortured?

BON: I would have him proved.

VOLT: Best try him then with goads, or burning irons;
Put him to the strappado: I have heard
300   The rack hath cured the gout; 'faith, give it him,
And help him of a malady; be courteous.
I'll undertake, before these honour'd fathers,
He shall have yet as many left diseases,
As she has known adulterers, or thou strumpets.—
305   O, my most equal hearers, if these deeds,
Acts of this bold and most exorbitant strain,
May pass with sufferance; what one citizen
But owes the forfeit of his life, yea, fame,
To him that dares traduce him? which of you
310   Are safe, my honour'd fathers? I would ask,
With leave of your grave fatherhoods, if their plot
Have any face or colour like to truth?
Or if, unto the dullest nostril here,
It smell not rank, and most abhorred slander?
315   I crave your care of this good gentleman,
Whose life is much endanger'd by their fable;
And as for them, I will conclude with this,
That vicious persons, when they're hot and flesh'd

In impious acts, their constancy abounds:
320 Damn'd deeds are done with greatest confidence.

1 AVOC: Take them to custody, and sever them.

2 AVOC: 'Tis pity two such prodigies should live.

1 AVOC: Let the old gentleman be return'd with care;
       [EXEUNT OFFICERS WITH VOLPONE.]
I'm sorry our credulity hath wrong'd him.

325 4 AVOC: These are two creatures!

3 AVOC: I've an earthquake in me.

2 AVOC: Their shame, even in their cradles, fled their faces.

4 AVOC [TO VOLT.]: You have done a worthy service to the state, sir,
In their discovery.

330 1 AVOC: You shall hear, ere night,
What punishment the court decrees upon them.
   [EXEUNT AVOCAT., NOT., AND OFFICERS WITH BONARIO
             AND CELIA.]

VOLT: We thank your fatherhoods.—How like you it?

MOS: Rare.
I'd have your tongue, sir, tipt with gold for this;
335 I'd have you be the heir to the whole city;
The earth I'd have want men, ere you want living:
They're bound to erect your statue in St. Mark's.
Signior Corvino, I would have you go
And shew yourself, that you have conquer'd.

340 CORV: Yes.

MOS: It was much better that you should profess
Yourself a cuckold thus, than that the other
Should have been prov'd.

CORV: Nay, I consider'd that:
345 Now it is her fault.

MOS: Then it had been yours.

CORV: True; I do doubt this advocate still.

MOS: I'faith,
You need not, I dare ease you of that care.

350 CORV: I trust thee, Mosca.

[EXIT.]

MOS: As your own soul, sir.

CORB: Mosca!

MOS: Now for your business, sir.

CORB: How! have you business?

355 MOS: Yes, your's, sir.

CORB: O, none else?

MOS: None else, not I.

CORB: Be careful, then.

MOS: Rest you with both your eyes, sir.

360 CORB: Dispatch it.

MOS: Instantly.

CORB: And look that all,
Whatever, be put in, jewels, plate, moneys,
Household stuff, bedding, curtains.

365 MOS: Curtain-rings, sir.
Only the advocate's fee must be deducted.

CORB: I'll pay him now; you'll be too prodigal.

MOS: Sir, I must tender it.

CORB: Two chequines is well?

370 MOS: No, six, sir.

CORB: 'Tis too much.

MOS: He talk'd a great while;
You must consider that, sir.

CORB: Well, there's three—

375   MOS: I'll give it him.

CORB: Do so, and there's for thee.

[EXIT.]

MOS [ASIDE.]: Bountiful bones! What horrid strange offence
Did he commit 'gainst nature, in his youth,
Worthy this age?
380   [TO VOLT.]—You see, sir, how I work
Unto your ends; take you no notice.

VOLT: No,
I'll leave you.

[EXIT.]

MOS: All is yours, the devil and all:
385   Good advocate!—Madam, I'll bring you home.

LADY P: No, I'll go see your patron.

MOS: That you shall not:
I'll tell you why. My purpose is to urge
My patron to reform his Will; and for
390   The zeal you have shewn to-day, whereas before
You were but third or fourth, you shall be now
Put in the first; which would appear as begg'd,
If you were present. Therefore—

LADY P: You shall sway me.

[EXEUNT.]

ACT 5.
SCENE 5.1
A ROOM IN VOLPONE'S HOUSE.

ENTER VOLPONE.

VOLP: Well, I am here, and all this brunt is past.
I ne'er was in dislike with my disguise
Till this fled moment; here 'twas good, in private;
But in your public,—cave whilst I breathe.
5   'Fore God, my left leg began to have the cramp,

And I apprehended straight some power had struck me
With a dead palsy: Well! I must be merry,
And shake it off. A many of these fears
Would put me into some villanous disease,
10 Should they come thick upon me: I'll prevent 'em.
Give me a bowl of lusty wine, to fright
This humour from my heart.

[DRINKS.]

Hum, hum, hum!
'Tis almost gone already; I shall conquer.
15 Any device, now, of rare ingenious knavery,
That would possess me with a violent laughter,
Would make me up again.

[DRINKS AGAIN.]

So, so, so, so!
This heat is life; 'tis blood by this time:—Mosca!

[ENTER MOSCA.]

20 MOS: How now, sir? does the day look clear again?
Are we recover'd, and wrought out of error,
Into our way, to see our path before us?
Is our trade free once more?

VOLP: Exquisite Mosca!

25 MOS: Was it not carried learnedly?

VOLP: And stoutly:
Good wits are greatest in extremities.

MOS: It were a folly beyond thought, to trust
Any grand act unto a cowardly spirit:
30 You are not taken with it enough, methinks?

VOLP: O, more than if I had enjoy'd the wench:
The pleasure of all woman-kind's not like it.

MOS: Why now you speak, sir. We must here be fix'd;
Here we must rest; this is our master-piece;
35 We cannot think to go beyond this.

VOLP: True.
Thou hast play'd thy prize, my precious Mosca.

MOS: Nay, sir,
To gull the court—

40 VOLP: And quite divert the torrent
Upon the innocent.

MOS: Yes, and to make
So rare a music out of discords—

VOLP: Right.
45 That yet to me's the strangest, how thou hast borne it!
That these, being so divided 'mongst themselves,
Should not scent somewhat, or in me or thee,
Or doubt their own side.

MOS: True, they will not see't.
50 Too much light blinds them, I think. Each of them
Is so possest and stuft with his own hopes,
That any thing unto the contrary,
Never so true, or never so apparent,
Never so palpable, they will resist it—

55 VOLP: Like a temptation of the devil.

MOS: Right, sir.
Merchants may talk of trade, and your great signiors
Of land that yields well; but if Italy
Have any glebe more fruitful than these fellows,
60 I am deceiv'd. Did not your advocate rare?

VOLP: O—"My most honour'd fathers, my grave fathers,
Under correction of your fatherhoods,
What face of truth is here? If these strange deeds
May pass, most honour'd fathers"—I had much ado
65 To forbear laughing.

MOS: It seem'd to me, you sweat, sir.

VOLP: In troth, I did a little.

MOS: But confess, sir,
Were you not daunted?

70 VOLP: In good faith, I was
A little in a mist, but not dejected;
Never, but still my self.

MOS: I think it, sir.
Now, so truth help me, I must needs say this, sir,
And out of conscience for your advocate:
He has taken pains, in faith, sir, and deserv'd,
In my poor judgment, I speak it under favour,
Not to contrary you, sir, very richly—
Well—to be cozen'd.

VOLP: Troth, and I think so too,
By that I heard him, in the latter end.

MOS: O, but before, sir: had you heard him first
Draw it to certain heads, then aggravate,
Then use his vehement figures—I look'd still
When he would shift a shirt: and, doing this
Out of pure love, no hope of gain—

VOLP: 'Tis right.
I cannot answer him, Mosca, as I would,
Not yet; but for thy sake, at thy entreaty,
I will begin, even now—to vex them all,
This very instant.

MOS: Good sir.

VOLP: Call the dwarf
And eunuch forth.

MOS: Castrone, Nano!

[ENTER CASTRONE AND NANO.]

NANO: Here.

VOLP: Shall we have a jig now?

MOS: What you please, sir.

VOLP: Go,
Straight give out about the streets, you two,
That I am dead; do it with constancy,
Sadly, do you hear? impute it to the grief
Of this late slander.

[EXEUNT CAST. AND NANO.]

MOS: What do you mean, sir?

105   VOLP: O,
       I shall have instantly my Vulture, Crow,
       Raven, come flying hither, on the news,
       To peck for carrion, my she-wolfe, and all,
       Greedy, and full of expectation—

110   MOS: And then to have it ravish'd from their mouths!

       VOLP: 'Tis true. I will have thee put on a gown,
       And take upon thee, as thou wert mine heir:
       Shew them a will; Open that chest, and reach
       Forth one of those that has the blanks; I'll straight
115   Put in thy name.

       MOS [GIVES HIM A PAPER.]: It will be rare, sir.

       VOLP: Ay,
       When they ev'n gape, and find themselves deluded—

       MOS: Yes.

120   VOLP: And thou use them scurvily!
       Dispatch, get on thy gown.

       MOS [PUTTING ON A GOWN.]: But, what, sir, if they ask
       After the body?

       VOLP: Say, it was corrupted.

125   MOS: I'll say it stunk, sir; and was fain to have it
       Coffin'd up instantly, and sent away.

       VOLP: Any thing; what thou wilt. Hold, here's my will.
       Get thee a cap, a count-book, pen and ink,
       Papers afore thee; sit as thou wert taking
130   An inventory of parcels: I'll get up
       Behind the curtain, on a stool, and hearken;
       Sometime peep over, see how they do look,
       With what degrees their blood doth leave their faces,
       O, 'twill afford me a rare meal of laughter!

       MOS [PUTTING ON A CAP, AND SETTING OUT THE TABLE, ETC.]:
135   Your advocate will turn stark dull upon it.

VOLP: It will take off his oratory's edge.

MOS: But your clarissimo, old round-back, he
Will crump you like a hog-louse, with the touch.

VOLP: And what Corvino?

140 MOS: O, sir, look for him,
To-morrow morning, with a rope and dagger,
To visit all the streets; he must run mad.
My lady too, that came into the court,
To bear false witness for your worship—

145 VOLP: Yes,
And kist me 'fore the fathers; when my face
Flow'd all with oils.

MOS: And sweat, sir. Why, your gold
Is such another med'cine, it dries up
150 All those offensive savours: it transforms
The most deformed, and restores them lovely,
As 'twere the strange poetical girdle. Jove
Could not invent t' himself a shroud more subtle
To pass Acrisius' guards. It is the thing
155 Makes all the world her grace, her youth, her beauty.

VOLP: I think she loves me.

MOS: Who? the lady, sir?
She's jealous of you.

VOLP: Dost thou say so?

[KNOCKING WITHIN.]

160 MOS: Hark,
There's some already.

VOLP: Look.

MOS: It is the Vulture:
He has the quickest scent.

165 VOLP: I'll to my place,
Thou to thy posture.

[GOES BEHIND THE CURTAIN.]

MOS: I am set.

VOLP: But, Mosca,
Play the artificer now, torture them rarely.

[ENTER VOLTORE.]

170   VOLT: How now, my Mosca?

MOS [WRITING.]: "Turkey carpets, nine"—

VOLT: Taking an inventory! that is well.

MOS: "Two suits of bedding, tissue"—

VOLT: Where's the Will?
175   Let me read that the while.

[ENTER SERVANTS, WITH CORBACCIO IN A CHAIR.]

CORB: So, set me down:
And get you home.

[EXEUNT SERVANTS.]

VOLT: Is he come now, to trouble us!

MOS: "Of cloth of gold, two more"—

180   CORB: Is it done, Mosca?

MOS: "Of several velvets, eight"—

VOLT: I like his care.

CORB: Dost thou not hear?

[ENTER CORVINO.]

CORB: Ha! is the hour come, Mosca?

185   VOLP [PEEPING OVER THE CURTAIN.]: Ay, now, they muster.

CORV: What does the advocate here,
Or this Corbaccio?

CORB: What do these here?

[ENTER LADY POL. WOULD-BE.]

LADY P: Mosca!
190   Is his thread spun?

MOS: "Eight chests of linen"—

VOLP: O,
My fine dame Would-be, too!

CORV: Mosca, the Will,
195   That I may shew it these, and rid them hence.

MOS: "Six chests of diaper, four of damask."—There.

      [GIVES THEM THE WILL CARELESSLY, OVER HIS SHOULDER.]

CORB: Is that the will?

MOS: "Down-beds, and bolsters"—

VOLP: Rare!
200   Be busy still. Now they begin to flutter:
They never think of me. Look, see, see, see!
How their swift eyes run over the long deed,
Unto the name, and to the legacies,
What is bequeath'd them there—

205   MOS: "Ten suits of hangings"—

VOLP: Ay, in their garters, Mosca. Now their hopes are at the gasp.

VOLT: Mosca the heir?

CORB: What's that?

VOLP: My advocate is dumb; look to my merchant,
210   He has heard of some strange storm, a ship is lost,
He faints; my lady will swoon. Old glazen eyes,
He hath not reach'd his despair yet.

CORB [TAKES THE WILL.]: All these
Are out of hope: I am sure, the man.

CORV: But, Mosca—

215   MOS: "Two cabinets."

       CORV: Is this in earnest?

       MOS: "One of ebony"—

       CORV: Or do you but delude me?

       MOS: The other, mother of pearl—I am very busy.
220   Good faith, it is a fortune thrown upon me—
       "Item, one salt of agate"—not my seeking.

       LADY P: Do you hear, sir?

       MOS: "A perfum'd box"—'Pray you forbear,
       You see I'm troubled—"made of an onyx"—

225   LADY P: How!

       MOS: To-morrow or next day, I shall be at leisure
       To talk with you all.

       CORV: Is this my large hope's issue?

       LADY P: Sir, I must have a fairer answer.

230   MOS: Madam!
       Marry, and shall: 'pray you, fairly quit my house.
       Nay, raise no tempest with your looks; but hark you,
       Remember what your ladyship offer'd me,
       To put you in an heir; go to, think on it:
235   And what you said e'en your best madams did
       For maintenance, and why not you? Enough.
       Go home, and use the poor sir Pol, your knight, well,
       For fear I tell some riddles; go, be melancholy.
                                        [EXIT LADY WOULD-BE.]

       VOLP: O, my fine devil!

240   CORV: Mosca, 'pray you a word.

       MOS: Lord! will you not take your dispatch hence yet?
       Methinks, of all, you should have been the example.
       Why should you stay here? with what thought? what promise?
       Hear you; do not you know, I know you an ass,

245 And that you would most fain have been a wittol,
If fortune would have let you? that you are
A declared cuckold, on good terms? This pearl,
You'll say, was yours? right: this diamond?
I'll not deny't, but thank you. Much here else?
250 It may be so. Why, think that these good works
May help to hide your bad. I'll not betray you;
Although you be but extraordinary,
And have it only in title, it sufficeth:
Go home, be melancholy too, or mad.

[EXIT CORVINO.]

255 VOLP: Rare Mosca! how his villany becomes him!

VOLT: Certain he doth delude all these for me.

CORB: Mosca the heir!

VOLP: O, his four eyes have found it.

CORB: I am cozen'd, cheated, by a parasite slave;
260 Harlot, thou hast gull'd me.

MOS: Yes, sir. Stop your mouth,
Or I shall draw the only tooth is left.
Are not you he, that filthy covetous wretch,
With the three legs, that, here, in hope of prey,
265 Have, any time this three years, snuff'd about,
With your most grovelling nose; and would have hired
Me to the poisoning of my patron, sir?
Are not you he that have to-day in court
Profess'd the disinheriting of your son?
270 Perjured yourself? Go home, and die, and stink.
If you but croak a syllable, all comes out:
Away, and call your porters!

[EXIT CORBACCIO.]

Go, go, stink.

VOLP: Excellent varlet!

275 VOLT: Now, my faithful Mosca,
I find thy constancy.

MOS: Sir!

VOLT: Sincere.

MOS [WRITING.]: "A table
280 Of porphyry"—I marle, you'll be thus troublesome.

VOLP: Nay, leave off now, they are gone.

MOS: Why? who are you?
What! who did send for you? O, cry you mercy,
Reverend sir! Good faith, I am grieved for you,
285 That any chance of mine should thus defeat
Your (I must needs say) most deserving travails:
But I protest, sir, it was cast upon me,
And I could almost wish to be without it,
But that the will o' the dead must be observ'd,
290 Marry, my joy is that you need it not,
You have a gift, sir, (thank your education,)
Will never let you want, while there are men,
And malice, to breed causes. Would I had
But half the like, for all my fortune, sir!
295 If I have any suits, as I do hope,
Things being so easy and direct, I shall not,
I will make bold with your obstreperous aid,
Conceive me,—for your fee, sir. In mean time,
You that have so much law, I know have the conscience,
300 Not to be covetous of what is mine.
Good sir, I thank you for my plate; 'twill help
To set up a young man. Good faith, you look
As you were costive; best go home and purge, sir.
                                        [EXIT VOLTORE.]

VOLP [COMES FROM BEHIND THE CURTAIN.]:
Bid him eat lettuce well.
305 My witty mischief,
Let me embrace thee. O that I could now
Transform thee to a Venus!—Mosca, go,
Straight take my habit of clarissimo,
And walk the streets; be seen, torment them more:
310 We must pursue, as well as plot. Who would
Have lost this feast?

MOS: I doubt it will lose them.

VOLP: O, my recovery shall recover all.
That I could now but think on some disguise
315 To meet them in, and ask them questions:
How I would vex them still at every turn!

MOS: Sir, I can fit you.

VOLP: Canst thou?

MOS: Yes, I know
320   One o' the commandadori, sir, so like you;
      Him will I straight make drunk, and bring you his habit.

VOLP: A rare disguise, and answering thy brain!
      O, I will be a sharp disease unto them.

MOS: Sir, you must look for curses—

325   VOLP: Till they burst;
      The Fox fares ever best when he is curst.

                                          [EXEUNT.]

SCENE 5.2.
A HALL IN SIR POLITICK'S HOUSE.

ENTER PEREGRINE DISGUISED, AND THREE MERCHANTS.

PER: Am I enough disguised?

1 MER: I warrant you.

PER: All my ambition is to fright him only.

2 MER: If you could ship him away, 'twere excellent.

5   3 MER: To Zant, or to Aleppo?

PER: Yes, and have his
    Adventures put i' the Book of Voyages.
    And his gull'd story register'd for truth.
    Well, gentlemen, when I am in a while,
10 And that you think us warm in our discourse,
    Know your approaches.

1 MER: Trust it to our care.

                              [EXEUNT MERCHANTS.]

[ENTER WAITING-WOMAN.]

PER: Save you, fair lady! Is sir Pol within?

WOM: I do not know, sir.

15 PER: Pray you say unto him,
Here is a merchant, upon earnest business,
Desires to speak with him.

WOM: I will see, sir.

                                                 [EXIT.]

PER: Pray you.—
20 I see the family is all female here.

                [RE-ENTER WAITING-WOMAN.]

WOM: He says, sir, he has weighty affairs of state,
That now require him whole; some other time
You may possess him.

PER: Pray you say again,
25 If those require him whole, these will exact him,
Whereof I bring him tidings.

                                        [EXIT WOMAN.]

—What might be
His grave affair of state now! how to make
Bolognian sausages here in Venice, sparing
30 One o' the ingredients?

                [RE-ENTER WAITING-WOMAN.]

WOM: Sir, he says, he knows
By your word "tidings," that you are no statesman,
And therefore wills you stay.

PER: Sweet, pray you return him;
35 I have not read so many proclamations,
And studied them for words, as he has done—
But—here he deigns to come.

                                        [EXIT WOMAN.]

                  [ENTER SIR POLITICK.]

SIR P: Sir, I must crave
Your courteous pardon. There hath chanced to-day,
40 Unkind disaster 'twixt my lady and me;
And I was penning my apology,
To give her satisfaction, as you came now.

PER: Sir, I am grieved I bring you worse disaster:
The gentleman you met at the port to-day,
45 That told you, he was newly arrived—

SIR P: Ay, was
A fugitive punk?

PER: No, sir, a spy set on you;
And he has made relation to the senate,
50 That you profest to him to have a plot
To sell the State of Venice to the Turk.

SIR P: O me!

PER: For which, warrants are sign'd by this time,
To apprehend you, and to search your study
55 For papers—

SIR P: Alas, sir, I have none, but notes
Drawn out of play-books—

PER: All the better, sir.

SIR P: And some essays. What shall I do?

60 PER: Sir, best
Convey yourself into a sugar-chest;
Or, if you could lie round, a frail were rare:
And I could send you aboard.

SIR P: Sir, I but talk'd so,
65 For discourse sake merely.

[KNOCKING WITHIN.]

PER: Hark! they are there.

SIR P: I am a wretch, a wretch!

PER: What will you do, sir?
Have you ne'er a currant-butt to leap into?
70 They'll put you to the rack, you must be sudden.

SIR P: Sir, I have an ingine—

3 MER [WITHIN.]: Sir Politick Would-be?

2 MER [WITHIN.]: Where is he?

SIR P: That I have thought upon before time.

75   PER: What is it?

SIR P: I shall ne'er endure the torture.
Marry, it is, sir, of a tortoise-shell,
Fitted for these extremities: pray you, sir, help me.
Here I've a place, sir, to put back my legs,
80   Please you to lay it on, sir,
   [LIES DOWN WHILE PEREGRINE PLACES THE SHELL UPON HIM.]
—with this cap,
And my black gloves. I'll lie, sir, like a tortoise,
'Till they are gone.

PER: And call you this an ingine?

85   SIR P: Mine own device—Good sir, bid my wife's women
To burn my papers.
                               [EXIT PEREGRINE.]

        [THE THREE MERCHANTS RUSH IN.]

1 MER: Where is he hid?

3 MER: We must,
And will sure find him.

90   2 MER: Which is his study?

          [RE-ENTER PEREGRINE.]

1 MER: What are you, sir?

PER: I am a merchant, that came here
To look upon this tortoise.

3 MER: How!

95   1 MER: St. Mark!
What beast is this!

PER: It is a fish.

2 MER: Come out here!

PER: Nay, you may strike him, sir, and tread upon him;
100 He'll bear a cart.

1 MER: What, to run over him?

PER: Yes, sir.

3 MER: Let's jump upon him.

2 MER: Can he not go?

105 PER: He creeps, sir.

1 MER: Let's see him creep.

PER: No, good sir, you will hurt him.

2 MER: Heart, I will see him creep, or prick his guts.

3 MER: Come out here!

110 PER: Pray you, sir!
[ASIDE TO SIR POLITICK.] —Creep a little.

1 MER: Forth.

2 MER: Yet farther.

PER: Good sir!—Creep.

2 MER: We'll see his legs.
[THEY PULL OFF THE SHELL AND DISCOVER HIM.]

115 3 MER: Ods so, he has garters!

1 MER: Ay, and gloves!

2 MER: Is this your fearful tortoise?

PER [DISCOVERING HIMSELF.]: Now, sir Pol, we are even;
For your next project I shall be prepared:
120 I am sorry for the funeral of your notes, sir.

1 MER: 'Twere a rare motion to be seen in Fleet-street.

2 MER: Ay, in the Term.

1 MER: Or Smithfield, in the fair.

3 MER: Methinks 'tis but a melancholy sight.

125   PER: Farewell, most politic tortoise!

                                   [EXEUNT PER. AND MERCHANTS.]

                      [RE-ENTER WAITING-WOMAN.]

SIR P: Where's my lady?
Knows she of this?

WOM: I know not, sir.

SIR P: Enquire.—
130   O, I shall be the fable of all feasts,
The freight of the gazetti; ship-boy's tale;
And, which is worst, even talk for ordinaries.

WOM: My lady's come most melancholy home,
And says, sir, she will straight to sea, for physic.

135   SIR P: And I to shun this place and clime for ever;
Creeping with house on back: and think it well,
To shrink my poor head in my politic shell.

                                             [EXEUNT.]

SCENE 5.3.
A ROOM IN VOLPONE'S HOUSE.

ENTER MOSCA IN THE HABIT OF A CLARISSIMO; AND
VOLPONE IN THAT OF A COMMANDADORE.

VOLP: Am I then like him?

MOS: O, sir, you are he;
No man can sever you.

VOLP: Good.

5   MOS: But what am I?

VOLP: 'Fore heaven, a brave clarissimo, thou becom'st it!
Pity thou wert not born one.

MOS [ASIDE.]: If I hold
My made one, 'twill be well.

10 VOLP: I'll go and see
What news first at the court.

[EXIT.]

MOS: Do so. My Fox
Is out of his hole, and ere he shall re-enter,
I'll make him languish in his borrow'd case,
15 Except he come to composition with me.—
Androgyno, Castrone, Nano!

[ENTER ANDROGYNO, CASTRONE AND NANO.]

ALL: Here.

MOS: Go, recreate yourselves abroad; go sport.—

[EXEUNT.]

So, now I have the keys, and am possest.
20 Since he will needs be dead afore his time,
I'll bury him, or gain by him: I am his heir,
And so will keep me, till he share at least.
To cozen him of all, were but a cheat
Well placed; no man would construe it a sin:
25 Let his sport pay for it, this is call'd the Fox-trap.

[EXIT.]

SCENE 5.4
A STREET.

ENTER CORBACCIO AND CORVINO.

CORB: They say, the court is set.

CORV: We must maintain
Our first tale good, for both our reputations.

CORB: Why, mine's no tale: my son would there have kill'd me.

5 CORV: That's true, I had forgot:—
[ASIDE.]—mine is, I am sure.
But for your Will, sir.

CORB: Ay, I'll come upon him
For that hereafter; now his patron's dead.

[ENTER VOLPONE.]

10   VOLP: Signior Corvino! and Corbaccio! sir,
Much joy unto you.

CORV: Of what?

VOLP: The sudden good,
Dropt down upon you—

15   CORB: Where?

VOLP: And, none knows how,
From old Volpone, sir.

CORB: Out, arrant knave!

VOLP: Let not your too much wealth, sir, make you furious.

20   CORB: Away, thou varlet!

VOLP: Why, sir?

CORB: Dost thou mock me?

VOLP: You mock the world, sir; did you not change Wills?

CORB: Out, harlot!

25   VOLP: O! belike you are the man,
Signior Corvino? 'faith, you carry it well;
You grow not mad withal: I love your spirit:
You are not over-leaven'd with your fortune.
You should have some would swell now, like a wine-fat,
30   With such an autumn—Did he give you all, sir?

CORB: Avoid, you rascal!

VOLP: Troth, your wife has shewn
Herself a very woman; but you are well,
You need not care, you have a good estate,
35   To bear it out sir, better by this chance:
Except Corbaccio have a share.

CORV: Hence, varlet.

VOLP: You will not be acknown, sir; why, 'tis wise.
Thus do all gamesters, at all games, dissemble:
40   No man will seem to win.

[EXEUNT CORVINO AND CORBACCIO.]
—Here comes my vulture,
Heaving his beak up in the air, and snuffing.

[ENTER VOLTORE.]

VOLT: Outstript thus, by a parasite! a slave,
Would run on errands, and make legs for crumbs?
45   Well, what I'll do—

VOLP: The court stays for your worship.
I e'en rejoice, sir, at your worship's happiness,
And that it fell into so learned hands,
That understand the fingering—

50   VOLT: What do you mean?

VOLP: I mean to be a suitor to your worship,
For the small tenement, out of reparations,
That, to the end of your long row of houses,
By the Piscaria: it was, in Volpone's time,
55   Your predecessor, ere he grew diseased,
A handsome, pretty, custom'd bawdy-house,
As any was in Venice, none dispraised;
But fell with him; his body and that house
Decay'd, together.

60   VOLT: Come sir, leave your prating.

VOLP: Why, if your worship give me but your hand,
That I may have the refusal, I have done.
'Tis a mere toy to you, sir; candle-rents;
As your learn'd worship knows—

65   VOLT: What do I know?

VOLP: Marry, no end of your wealth, sir, God decrease it!

VOLT: Mistaking knave! what, mockst thou my misfortune?

[EXIT.]

VOLP: His blessing on your heart, sir; would 'twere more!—
Now to my first again, at the next corner.

[EXIT.]

SCENE 5.5.
ANOTHER PART OF THE STREET.

ENTER CORBACCIO AND CORVINO;—
MOSCA PASSES OVER THE STAGE, BEFORE THEM.

CORB: See, in our habit! see the impudent varlet!

CORV: That I could shoot mine eyes at him like gun-stones.

[ENTER VOLPONE.]

VOLP: But is this true, sir, of the parasite?

CORB: Again, to afflict us! monster!

5   VOLP: In good faith, sir,
I'm heartily grieved, a beard of your grave length
Should be so over-reach'd. I never brook'd
That parasite's hair; methought his nose should cozen:
There still was somewhat in his look, did promise
10 The bane of a clarissimo.

CORB: Knave—

VOLP: Methinks
Yet you, that are so traded in the world,
A witty merchant, the fine bird, Corvino,
15 That have such moral emblems on your name,
Should not have sung your shame; and dropt your cheese,
To let the Fox laugh at your emptiness.

CORV: Sirrah, you think the privilege of the place,
And your red saucy cap, that seems to me
20 Nail'd to your jolt-head with those two chequines,
Can warrant your abuses; come you hither:
You shall perceive, sir, I dare beat you; approach.

VOLP: No haste, sir, I do know your valour well,
Since you durst publish what you are, sir.

25 CORV: Tarry,
I'd speak with you.

VOLP: Sir, sir, another time—

CORV: Nay, now.

VOLP: O lord, sir! I were a wise man,
30   Would stand the fury of a distracted cuckold.

            [AS HE IS RUNNING OFF, RE-ENTER MOSCA.]

CORB: What, come again!

VOLP: Upon 'em, Mosca; save me.

CORB: The air's infected where he breathes.

CORV: Let's fly him.
                                    [EXEUNT CORV. AND CORB.]
35   VOLP: Excellent basilisk! turn upon the vulture.

                  [ENTER VOLTORE.]

VOLT: Well, flesh-fly, it is summer with you now;
Your winter will come on.

MOS: Good advocate,
Prithee not rail, nor threaten out of place thus;
40   Thou'lt make a solecism, as madam says.
Get you a biggin more, your brain breaks loose.
                                            [EXIT.]

VOLT: Well, sir.

VOLP: Would you have me beat the insolent slave,
Throw dirt upon his first good clothes?

45   VOLT: This same
Is doubtless some familiar.

VOLP: Sir, the court,
In troth, stays for you. I am mad, a mule
That never read Justinian, should get up,
50   And ride an advocate. Had you no quirk
To avoid gullage, sir, by such a creature?
I hope you do but jest; he has not done it:
'Tis but confederacy, to blind the rest.
You are the heir.

55   VOLT: A strange, officious,
Troublesome knave! thou dost torment me.

VOLP: I know—
It cannot be, sir, that you should be cozen'd;
'Tis not within the wit of man to do it;
60 You are so wise, so prudent; and 'tis fit
That wealth and wisdom still should go together.

                                                    [EXEUNT.]

SCENE 5.6.
THE SCRUTINEO OR SENATE-HOUSE.

ENTER AVOCATORI, NOTARIO, BONARIO, CELIA,
CORBACCIO, CORVINO, COMMANDADORI, SAFFI, ETC.

1 AVOC: Are all the parties here?

NOT: All but the advocate.

2 AVOC: And here he comes.

                    [ENTER VOLTORE AND VOLPONE.]

1 AVOC: Then bring them forth to sentence.

5   VOLT: O, my most honour'd fathers, let your mercy
Once win upon your justice, to forgive—
I am distracted—

VOLP [ASIDE.]: What will he do now?

VOLT: O,
10 I know not which to address myself to first;
Whether your fatherhoods, or these innocents—

CORV [ASIDE.]: Will he betray himself?

VOLT: Whom equally
I have abused, out of most covetous ends—

15 CORV: The man is mad!

CORB: What's that?

CORV: He is possest.

VOLT: For which, now struck in conscience, here, I prostate
Myself at your offended feet, for pardon.

20 1, 2 AVOC: Arise.

CEL: O heaven, how just thou art!

VOLP [ASIDE.]: I am caught
In mine own noose—

CORV [TO CORBACCIO.]: Be constant, sir: nought now
25 Can help, but impudence.

1 AVOC: Speak forward.

COM: Silence!

VOLT: It is not passion in me, reverend fathers,
But only conscience, conscience, my good sires,
30 That makes me now tell trueth. That parasite,
That knave, hath been the instrument of all.

1 AVOC: Where is that knave? fetch him.

VOLP: I go.

[EXIT.]

CORV: Grave fathers,
35 This man's distracted; he confest it now:
For, hoping to be old Volpone's heir,
Who now is dead—

3 AVOC: How?

2 AVOC: Is Volpone dead?

40 CORV: Dead since, grave fathers—

BON: O sure vengeance!

1 AVOC: Stay,
Then he was no deceiver?

VOLT: O no, none:
45 The parasite, grave fathers.

CORV: He does speak
Out of mere envy, 'cause the servant's made

The thing he gaped for: please your fatherhoods,
This is the truth, though I'll not justify
50   The other, but he may be some-deal faulty.

VOLT: Ay, to your hopes, as well as mine, Corvino:
But I'll use modesty. Pleaseth your wisdoms,
To view these certain notes, and but confer them;
As I hope favour, they shall speak clear truth.

55   CORV: The devil has enter'd him!

BON: Or bides in you.

4 AVOC: We have done ill, by a public officer,
To send for him, if he be heir.

2 AVOC: For whom?

60   4 AVOC: Him that they call the parasite.

3 AVOC: 'Tis true,
He is a man of great estate, now left.

4 AVOC: Go you, and learn his name, and say, the court
Entreats his presence here, but to the clearing
65   Of some few doubts.

[EXIT NOTARY.]

2 AVOC: This same's a labyrinth!

1 AVOC: Stand you unto your first report?

CORV: My state,
My life, my fame—

70   BON: Where is it?

CORV: Are at the stake—

1 AVOC: Is yours so too?

CORB: The advocate's a knave,
And has a forked tongue—

75   2 AVOC: Speak to the point.

CORB: So is the parasite too.

1 AVOC: This is confusion.

VOLT: I do beseech your fatherhoods, read but those—
[GIVING THEM THE PAPERS.]

CORV: And credit nothing the false spirit hath writ:
80 It cannot be, but he's possest grave fathers.
[THE SCENE CLOSES.]

SCENE 5.7.
A STREET.

ENTER VOLPONE.

VOLP: To make a snare for mine own neck! and run
My head into it, wilfully! with laughter!
When I had newly 'scaped, was free, and clear,
Out of mere wantonness! O, the dull devil
5 Was in this brain of mine, when I devised it,
And Mosca gave it second; he must now
Help to sear up this vein, or we bleed dead.—
[ENTER NANO, ANDROGYNO, AND CASTRONE.]
How now! who let you loose? whither go you now?
What, to buy gingerbread? or to drown kitlings?

10 NAN: Sir, master Mosca call'd us out of doors,
And bid us all go play, and took the keys.

AND: Yes.

VOLP: Did master Mosca take the keys? why so!
I'm farther in. These are my fine conceits!
15 I must be merry, with a mischief to me!
What a vile wretch was I, that could not bear
My fortune soberly? I must have my crotchets,
And my conundrums! Well, go you, and seek him:
His meaning may be truer than my fear.
20 Bid him, he straight come to me to the court;
Thither will I, and, if't be possible,
Unscrew my advocate, upon new hopes:
When I provoked him, then I lost myself.
[EXEUNT.]

SCENE 5.8.
THE SCRUTINEO, OR SENATE-HOUSE.

AVOCATORI, BONARIO, CELIA, CORBACCIO, CORVINO,
COMMANDADORI, SAFFI, ETC., AS BEFORE.

1 AVOC: These things can ne'er be reconciled. He, here,
[SHEWING THE PAPERS.]
Professeth, that the gentleman was wrong'd,
And that the gentlewoman was brought thither,
Forced by her husband, and there left.

5   VOLT: Most true.

CEL: How ready is heaven to those that pray!

1 AVOC: But that
Volpone would have ravish'd her, he holds
Utterly false; knowing his impotence.

10   CORV: Grave fathers, he's possest; again, I say,
Possest: nay, if there be possession, and
Obsession, he has both.

3 AVOC: Here comes our officer.

[ENTER VOLPONE.]

VOLP: The parasite will straight be here, grave fathers.

4 AVOC: You might invent some other name, sir varlet.

15   3 AVOC: Did not the notary meet him?

VOLP: Not that I know.

4 AVOC: His coming will clear all.

2 AVOC: Yet, it is misty.

VOLT: May't please your fatherhoods—

20   VOLP [WHISPERS VOLT.]: Sir, the parasite
Will'd me to tell you, that his master lives;
That you are still the man; your hopes the same;
And this was only a jest—

VOLT: How?

25 VOLP: Sir, to try
If you were firm, and how you stood affected.

VOLT: Art sure he lives?

VOLP: Do I live, sir?

VOLT: O me!
30 I was too violent.

VOLP: Sir, you may redeem it,
They said, you were possest; fall down, and seem so:
I'll help to make it good.

[VOLTORE FALLS.]

—God bless the man!—
35 Stop your wind hard, and swell: See, see, see, see!
He vomits crooked pins! his eyes are set,
Like a dead hare's hung in a poulter's shop!
His mouth's running away! Do you see, signior?
Now it is in his belly!

40 CORV: Ay, the devil!

VOLP: Now in his throat.

CORV: Ay, I perceive it plain.

VOLP: 'Twill out, 'twill out! stand clear.
See, where it flies,
45 In shape of a blue toad, with a bat's wings!
Do you not see it, sir?

CORB: What? I think I do.

CORV: 'Tis too manifest.

VOLP: Look! he comes to himself!

50 VOLT: Where am I?

VOLP: Take good heart, the worst is past, sir.
You are dispossest.

1 AVOC: What accident is this!

2 AVOC: Sudden, and full of wonder!

55 3 AVOC: If he were
Possest, as it appears, all this is nothing.

CORV: He has been often subject to these fits.

1 AVOC: Shew him that writing:—do you know it, sir?

VOLP [WHISPERS VOLT.]: Deny it, sir, forswear it; know it not.

60 VOLT: Yes, I do know it well, it is my hand;
But all that it contains is false.

BON: O practice!

2 AVOC: What maze is this!

1 AVOC: Is he not guilty then,
65 Whom you there name the parasite?

VOLT: Grave fathers,
No more than his good patron, old Volpone.

4 AVOC: Why, he is dead.

VOLT: O no, my honour'd fathers,
70 He lives—

1 AVOC: How! lives?

VOLT: Lives.

2 AVOC: This is subtler yet!

3 AVOC: You said he was dead.

75 VOLT: Never.

3 AVOC: You said so.

CORV: I heard so.

4 AVOC: Here comes the gentleman; make him way.

[ENTER MOSCA.]

3 AVOC: A stool.

80   4 AVOC [ASIDE.]: A proper man; and, were Volpone dead,
A fit match for my daughter.

3 AVOC: Give him way.

VOLP [ASIDE TO MOSCA.]: Mosca, I was almost lost, the advocate
Had betrayed all; but now it is recovered;
85   All's on the hinge again—Say, I am living.

MOS: What busy knave is this!—Most reverend fathers,
I sooner had attended your grave pleasures,
But that my order for the funeral
Of my dear patron, did require me—

90   VOLP [ASIDE.]: Mosca!

MOS: Whom I intend to bury like a gentleman.

VOLP [ASIDE.]: Ay, quick, and cozen me of all.

2 AVOC: Still stranger!
More intricate!

95   1 AVOC: And come about again!

4 AVOC [ASIDE.]: It is a match, my daughter is bestow'd.

MOS [ASIDE TO VOLP.]: Will you give me half?

VOLP: First, I'll be hang'd.

MOS: I know,
100   Your voice is good, cry not so loud.

1 AVOC: Demand
The advocate.—Sir, did not you affirm,
Volpone was alive?

VOLP: Yes, and he is;
105   This gentleman told me so.
[ASIDE TO MOS.] —Thou shalt have half.—

MOS: Whose drunkard is this same? speak, some that know him:
I never saw his face.
[ASIDE TO VOLP.] —I cannot now
110 Afford it you so cheap.

VOLP: No!

1 AVOC: What say you?

VOLT: The officer told me.

VOLP: I did, grave fathers,
115 And will maintain he lives, with mine own life.
And that this creature [POINTS TO MOSCA.] told me.
[ASIDE.] —I was born,
With all good stars my enemies.

MOS: Most grave fathers,
120 If such an insolence as this must pass
Upon me, I am silent: 'twas not this
For which you sent, I hope.

2 AVOC: Take him away.

VOLP: Mosca!

125 3 AVOC: Let him be whipt.

VOLP: Wilt thou betray me?
Cozen me?

3 AVOC: And taught to bear himself
Toward a person of his rank.

130 4 AVOC: Away.
                              [THE OFFICERS SEIZE VOLPONE.]

MOS: I humbly thank your fatherhoods.

VOLP [ASIDE.]: Soft, soft: Whipt!
And lose all that I have! If I confess,
It cannot be much more.

135 4 AVOC: Sir, are you married?

VOLP: They will be allied anon; I must be resolute:
The Fox shall here uncase.

[THROWS OFF HIS DISGUISE.]

MOS: Patron!

VOLP: Nay, now,
140 My ruins shall not come alone; your match
I'll hinder sure: my substance shall not glue you,
Nor screw you into a family.

MOS: Why, patron!

VOLP: I am Volpone, and this is my knave;

[POINTING TO MOSCA.]

145 This [TO VOLT.], his own knave; This [TO CORB.], avarice's fool;
This [TO CORV.], a chimera of wittol, fool, and knave:
And, reverend fathers, since we all can hope
Nought but a sentence, let's not now dispair it.
You hear me brief.

150 CORV: May it please your fatherhoods—

COM: Silence.

1 AVOC: The knot is now undone by miracle.

2 AVOC: Nothing can be more clear.

3 AVOC: Or can more prove these innocent.

155 1 AVOC: Give them their liberty.

BON: Heaven could not long let such gross crimes be hid.

2 AVOC: If this be held the high-way to get riches, may I be poor!

3 AVOC: This is not the gain, but torment.

1 AVOC: These possess wealth, as sick men possess fevers,
160 Which trulier may be said to possess them.

2 AVOC: Disrobe that parasite.

CORV, MOS: Most honour'd fathers!—

1 AVOC: Can you plead aught to stay the course of justice?
If you can, speak.

165   CORV, VOLT: We beg favour,

CEL: And mercy.

1 AVOC: You hurt your innocence, suing for the guilty.
Stand forth; and first the parasite: You appear
T'have been the chiefest minister, if not plotter,
170   In all these lewd impostures; and now, lastly,
Have with your impudence abused the court,
And habit of a gentleman of Venice,
Being a fellow of no birth or blood:
For which our sentence is, first, thou be whipt;
175   Then live perpetual prisoner in our gallies.

VOLT: I thank you for him.

MOS: Bane to thy wolvish nature!

1 AVOC: Deliver him to the saffi.
                           [MOSCA IS CARRIED OUT.]
—Thou, Volpone,
180   By blood and rank a gentleman, canst not fall
Under like censure; but our judgment on thee
Is, that thy substance all be straight confiscate
To the hospital of the Incurabili:
And, since the most was gotten by imposture,
185   By feigning lame, gout, palsy, and such diseases,
Thou art to lie in prison, cramp'd with irons,
Till thou be'st sick, and lame indeed.—Remove him.
                  [HE IS TAKEN FROM THE BAR.]

VOLP: This is call'd mortifying of a Fox.

1 AVOC: Thou, Voltore, to take away the scandal
190   Thou hast given all worthy men of thy profession,
Art banish'd from their fellowship, and our state.
Corbaccio!—bring him near—We here possess
Thy son of all thy state, and confine thee
To the monastery of San Spirito;
195   Where, since thou knewest not how to live well here,
Thou shalt be learn'd to die well.

CORB: Ah! what said he?

AND: You shall know anon, sir.

1 AVOC: Thou, Corvino, shalt
200 Be straight embark'd from thine own house, and row'd
Round about Venice, through the grand canale,
Wearing a cap, with fair long asses' ears,
Instead of horns; and so to mount, a paper
Pinn'd on thy breast, to the Berlina—

205 CORV: Yes,
And have mine eyes beat out with stinking fish,
Bruised fruit and rotten eggs—'Tis well. I am glad
I shall not see my shame yet.

1 AVOC: And to expiate
210 Thy wrongs done to thy wife, thou art to send her
Home to her father, with her dowry trebled:
And these are all your judgments.

ALL: Honour'd fathers.—

1 AVOC: Which may not be revoked. Now you begin,
215 When crimes are done, and past, and to be punish'd,
To think what your crimes are: away with them.
Let all that see these vices thus rewarded,
Take heart and love to study 'em! Mischiefs feed
Like beasts, till they be fat, and then they bleed.

[EXEUNT.]

[VOLPONE COMES FORWARD.]

220 VOLPONE: The seasoning of a play, is the applause.
Now, though the Fox be punish'd by the laws,
He yet doth hope, there is no suffering due,
For any fact which he hath done 'gainst you;
If there be, censure him; here he doubtful stands:
225 If not, fare jovially, and clap your hands.

[EXIT.]

JOHN WEBSTER

We do not know much about John Webster's life. He was most likely born around 1578, soon after his parents' marriage in London. His father, also John Webster, was a carriage maker, and his mother Elizabeth Coates was the daughter of a blacksmith. Webster was educated at Merchant Taylors' School; his father and uncle were both members of the Merchant Taylors' Company, a guild of tailors. Because Webster's plays suggest knowledge of the law, he was most likely the John Webster who was admitted to the Middle Temple, one of London's legal Inns of Court, in 1598.

By 1602, Webster had collaborated with other playwrights. He worked with Thomas Dekker on *Christmas Comes but Once a Year* and with a larger group including Dekker and Michael Drayton on *Caesar's Fall*; neither play was ever performed. Webster continued to work with Dekker on the history play *Sir Thomas Wyatt* (1602) and the comedies *Westward Ho* (1604) and *Northward Ho* (1605). He also adapted John Marston's *The Malcontent* in 1604. In 1605, when he was about twenty-seven, Webster married seventeen-year-old Sara Peniall, who was seven months pregnant at the time. She soon gave birth to their first son, John Webster III, and the couple most likely had more children.

Webster's best known works include the tragedies that he wrote in the 1610s. *The White Devil* was first performed and published in 1612. Based on the life of Vittoria Accoramboni, an assassinated Italian noblewoman, the play originally failed, but later gained scholarly appreciation for its complexity and sophisticated satire. *The Duchess of Malfi*, which the King's Men first performed in 1614, received further admiration from educated audiences. Modern companies frequently stage these two plays, and scholars praise their darkness, subtlety, and memorable protagonists.

While none achieved the success of *The Duchess of Malfi*, Webster continued to write plays. He composed *The Devil's Law Case* in the late 1610s, a tragicomedy that implies Webster had detailed knowledge of legal work and supports the theory that he attended law school. He then returned to collaborative comedies such as 1621's *Anything for a Quiet Life* with Thomas Middleton and 1624's *A Cure for a Cuckold* with William Rowley. He also collaborated with Rowley, Dekker, and John Ford on *Keep the Widow Waking* in 1624, a lost play about a social scandal. Webster's last play is *Appius and Virginia*, probably a collaboration with Thomas Heywood, dated to the late 1620s. Webster most likely died of unknown causes around 1632. However, the details of his death are obscure; it may have been as early as 1625 or as late as 1638.

Timeline

c. 1578	Webster is born.
1598	Webster is probably admitted to law school.
1602	Webster collaborates with other playwrights on plays which are never performed, including *Christmas Comes but Once a Year* and *Caesar's Fall*.
1602	*Sir Thomas Wyatt*.
1604	*Westward Ho*; an adaptation of *The Malcontent*.
1605	*Northward Ho*; Webster hastily marries Sara Peniall, who is seven months pregnant.
1612	*The White Devil*.
1614	*The Duchess of Malfi* is first performed (published 1623).
c. 1618	*The Devil's Law Case* (published 1623).
c. 1621	*Anything for a Quiet Life*.
c. 1624	*A Cure for a Cuckold*; *Keep the Widow Waking*.
Late 1620s	*Appius and Virginia*.
c. 1632	Webster dies.

The Duchess of Malfi

By John Webster

Dramatis Personae:

FERDINAND, Duke of Calabria.
CARDINAL, his brother.
ANTONIO (BOLOGNA), Steward of the Household to the Duchess.
DELIO [his friend].
DANIEL DE BOSOLA, Gentleman of the Horse to the Duchess.
CASTRUCCIO, an old Lord.
MARQUIS OF PESCARA.
(COUNT) MALATESTI.
RODERIGO,
SILVIO,
GRISOLAN, lords.
DOCTOR.
The Several Madmen.

DUCHESS (OF MALFI).
CARIOLA, her woman.
JULIA, Castruccio's wife, and the Cardinal's mistress.
Old Lady.

Ladies, Three Young Children, Two Pilgrims, Executioners,
  Court Officers, and Attendants.

ACT I
SCENE I
Enter ANTONIO and DELIO.

DELIO. You are welcome to your country, dear Antonio;
You have been long in France, and you return
A very formal Frenchman in your habit:
How do you like the French court?

5   ANTONIO. I admire it:
In seeking to reduce both state and people
To a fix'd order, their judicious king
Begins at home; quits first his royal palace
Of flattering sycophants, of dissolute

10   And infamous persons,—which he sweetly terms
     His master's master-piece, the work of heaven;
     Considering duly that a prince's court
     Is like a common fountain, whence should flow
     Pure silver drops in general, but if 't chance
15   Some curs'd example poison 't near the head,
     Death and diseases through the whole land spread.
     And what is 't makes this blessed government
     But a most provident council, who dare freely
     Inform him the corruption of the times?
20   Though some o' the court hold it presumption
     To instruct princes what they ought to do,
     It is a noble duty to inform them
     What they ought to foresee.—Here comes Bosola,
     The only court-gall; yet I observe his railing
25   Is not for simple love of piety:
     Indeed, he rails at those things which he wants;
     Would be as lecherous, covetous, or proud,
     Bloody, or envious, as any man,
     If he had means to be so.—Here's the cardinal.

Enter CARDINAL and BOSOLA.

30   BOSOLA. I do haunt you still.

     CARDINAL. So.

     BOSOLA. I have done you better service than to be slighted thus. Miserable
     age, where only the reward of doing well is the doing of it!

     CARDINAL. You enforce your merit too much.

35   BOSOLA. I fell into the galleys in your service: where, for two years together,
     I wore two towels instead of a shirt, with a knot on the shoulder, after the
     fashion of a Roman mantle. Slighted thus! I will thrive some way. Black-birds
     fatten best in hard weather; why not I in these dog-days?

     CARDINAL. Would you could become honest!

40   BOSOLA. With all your divinity do but direct me the way to it. I have
     known many travel far for it, and yet return as arrant knaves as they went
     forth, because they carried themselves always along with them.
                                                    Exit CARDINAL.
     Are you gone? Some fellows, they say, are possessed with the devil, but this
     great fellow were able to possess the greatest devil, and make him worse.

45 ANTONIO. He hath denied thee some suit?

BOSOLA. He and his brother are like plum-trees that grow crooked over standing-pools; they are rich and o'erladen with fruit, but none but crows, pies, and caterpillars feed on them. Could I be one of their flattering panders, I would hang on their ears like a horseleech, till I were full, and then
50 drop off. I pray, leave me. Who would rely upon these miserable dependencies, in expectation to be advanc'd to-morrow? What creature ever fed worse than hoping Tantalus? Nor ever died any man more fearfully than he that hoped for a pardon. There are rewards for hawks and dogs when they have done us service; but for a soldier that hazards his limbs in a battle,
55 nothing but a kind of geometry is his last supportation.

DELIO. Geometry?

BOSOLA. Ay, to hang in a fair pair of slings, take his latter swing in the world upon an honourable pair of crutches, from hospital to hospital. Fare ye well, sir: and yet do not you scorn us; for places in the court are but like
60 beds in the hospital, where this man's head lies at that man's foot, and so lower and lower.

He exits.

DELIO. I knew this fellow seven years in the galleys
For a notorious murder; and 'twas thought
The cardinal suborn'd it: he was releas'd
65 By the French general, Gaston de Foix,
When he recover'd Naples.

ANTONIO.'Tis great pity
He should be thus neglected: I have heard
He's very valiant. This foul melancholy
70 Will poison all his goodness; for, I'll tell you,
If too immoderate sleep be truly said
To be an inward rust unto the soul,
If then doth follow want of action
Breeds all black malcontents; and their close rearing,
75 Like moths in cloth, do hurt for want of wearing.

SCENE II

Enter SILVIO, CASTRUCCIO, JULIA, RODERIGO and GRISOLAN.

DELIO. The presence 'gins to fill: you promis'd me
To make me the partaker of the natures
Of some of your great courtiers.

ANTONIO. The lord cardinal's
5   And other strangers' that are now in court?
I shall.—Here comes the great Calabrian duke.

Enter FERDINAND and Attendants.

FERDINAND. Who took the ring oftenest?

SILVIO. Antonio Bologna, my lord.

FERDINAND. Our sister duchess' great-master of her household? Give him
10   the jewel.—When shall we leave this sportive action, and fall to action indeed?

CASTRUCCIO. Methinks, my lord, you should not desire to go to war in
person.

FERDINAND. Now for some gravity.—Why, my lord?

CASTRUCCIO. It is fitting a soldier arise to be a prince, but not necessary
15   a prince descend to be a captain.

FERDINAND. No?

CASTRUCCIO. No, my lord; he were far better do it by a deputy.

FERDINAND. Why should he not as well sleep or eat by a deputy? This
might take idle, offensive, and base office from him, whereas the other de-
20   prives him of honour.

CASTRUCCIO. Believe my experience, that realm is never long in quiet
where the ruler is a soldier.

FERDINAND. Thou toldest me thy wife could not endure fighting.

CASTRUCCIO. True, my lord.

25   FERDINAND. And of a jest she broke of a captain she met full of wounds:
I have forgot it.

CASTRUCCIO. She told him, my lord, he was a pitiful fellow, to lie, like the
children of Ismael, all in tents.

FERDINAND. Why, there's a wit were able to undo all the chirurgeons o'
30   the city; for although gallants should quarrel, and had drawn their weapons,
and were ready to go to it, yet her persuasions would make them put up.

CASTRUCCIO. That she would, my lord.—How do you like my Spanish gennet?

RODERIGO. He is all fire.

FERDINAND. I am of Pliny's opinion, I think he was begot by the wind;
he runs as if he were ballass'd with quicksilver.

SILVIO. True, my lord, he reels from the tilt often.

RODERIGO, GRISOLAN. Ha, ha, ha!

FERDINAND. Why do you laugh? Methinks you that are courtiers should
be my touch-wood, take fire when I give fire; that is, laugh when I laugh,
were the subject never so witty.

CASTRUCCIO. True, my lord: I myself have heard a very good jest, and
have scorn'd to seem to have so silly a wit as to understand it.

FERDINAND. But I can laugh at your fool, my lord.

CASTRUCCIO. He cannot speak, you know, but he makes faces; my lady
cannot abide him.

FERDINAND. No?

CASTRUCCIO. Nor endure to be in merry company; for she says too
much laughing, and too much company, fills her too full of the wrinkle.

FERDINAND. I would, then, have a mathematical instrument made for
her face, that she might not laugh out of compass. —I shall shortly visit
you at Milan, Lord Silvio.

SILVIO. Your grace shall arrive most welcome.

FERDINAND. You are a good horseman, Antonio; you have excellent rid-
ers in France: what do you think of good horsemanship?

ANTONIO. Nobly, my lord: as out of the Grecian horse issued many
famous princes, so out of brave horsemanship arise the first sparks of
growing resolution, that raise the mind to noble action.

FERDINAND. You have bespoke it worthily.

SILVIO. Your brother, the lord cardinal, and sister duchess.

Enter CARDINAL, with DUCHESS, and CARIOLA.

CARDINAL. Are the galleys come about?

GRISOLAN. They are, my lord.

FERDINAND. Here's the Lord Silvio is come to take his leave.

DELIO. Now, sir, your promise: what's that cardinal?
I mean his temper? They say he's a brave fellow,

65   Will play his five thousand crowns at tennis, dance,
     Court ladies, and one that hath fought single combats.

ANTONIO. Some such flashes superficially hang on him for form; but
observe his inward character: he is a melancholy churchman. The spring in
his face is nothing but the engend'ring of toads; where he is jealous of any
70   man, he lays worse plots for them than ever was impos'd on Hercules, for
he strews in his way flatterers, panders, intelligencers, atheists, and a thou-
sand such political monsters. He should have been Pope; but instead of
coming to it by the primitive decency of the church, he did bestow bribes
so largely and so impudently as if he would have carried it away without
75   heaven's knowledge. Some good he hath done———

DELIO. You have given too much of him. What's his brother?

ANTONIO. The duke there? A most perverse and turbulent nature.
     What appears in him mirth is merely outside;
     If he laught heartily, it is to laugh
80   All honesty out of fashion.

DELIO. Twins?

ANTONIO. In quality.
     He speaks with others' tongues, and hears men's suits
     With others' ears; will seem to sleep o' the bench
85   Only to entrap offenders in their answers;
     Dooms men to death by information;
     Rewards by hearsay.

DELIO. Then the law to him
     Is like a foul, black cobweb to a spider,—
90   He makes it his dwelling and a prison
     To entangle those shall feed him.

ANTONIO. Most true:
     He never pays debts unless they be shrewd turns,
     And those he will confess that he doth owe.
95   Last, for this brother there, the cardinal,
     They that do flatter him most say oracles
     Hang at his lips; and verily I believe them,
     For the devil speaks in them.
     But for their sister, the right noble duchess,
100 You never fix'd your eye on three fair medals
     Cast in one figure, of so different temper.
     For her discourse, it is so full of rapture,

You only will begin then to be sorry
When she doth end her speech, and wish, in wonder,
105 She held it less vain-glory to talk much,
Than your penance to hear her. Whilst she speaks,
She throws upon a man so sweet a look
That it were able to raise one to a galliard,
That lay in a dead palsy, and to dote
110 On that sweet countenance; but in that look
There speaketh so divine a continence
As cuts off all lascivious and vain hope.
Her days are practis'd in such noble virtue,
That sure her nights, nay, more, her very sleeps,
115 Are more in heaven than other ladies' shrifts.
Let all sweet ladies break their flatt'ring glasses,
And dress themselves in her.

DELIO. Fie, Antonio,
You play the wire-drawer with her commendations.

120 ANTONIO. I'll case the picture up: only thus much;
All her particular worth grows to this sum,—
She stains the time past, lights the time to come.

CARIOLA. You must attend my lady in the gallery,
Some half and hour hence.

125 ANTONIO. I shall.

Exeunt ANTONIO and DELIO.

FERDINAND. Sister, I have a suit to you.

DUCHESS. To me, sir?

FERDINAND. A gentleman here, Daniel de Bosola,
One that was in the galleys——

130 DUCHESS. Yes, I know him.

FERDINAND. A worthy fellow he is: pray, let me entreat for
The provisorship of your horse.

DUCHESS. Your knowledge of him
Commends him and prefers him.

135 FERDINAND. Call him hither.

Exit Attendant.

We are now upon parting. Good Lord Silvio,
Do us commend to all our noble friends
At the leaguer.

SILVIO. Sir, I shall.

140 DUCHESS. You are for Milan?

SILVIO. I am.

DUCHESS. Bring the caroches.—We 'll bring you down
To the haven.
Exeunt DUCHESS, SILVIO, CASTRUCCIO, RODERIGO, GRISOLAN,
CARIOLA, JULIA, and Attendants.

CARDINAL. Be sure you entertain that Bosola
145 For your intelligence. I would not be seen in 't;
And therefore many times I have slighted him
When he did court our furtherance, as this morning.

FERDINAND. Antonio, the great-master of her household,
Had been far fitter.

150 CARDINAL. You are deceiv'd in him.
His nature is too honest for such business.—
He comes: I'll leave you.
Exit.

Re-enter BOSOLA.

BOSOLA. I was lur'd to you.

FERDINAND. My brother, here, the cardinal, could never
155 Abide you.

BOSOLA. Never since he was in my debt.

FERDINAND. May be some oblique character in your face
Made him suspect you.

BOSOLA. Doth he study physiognomy?
160 There's no more credit to be given to the face
Than to a sick man's urine, which some call
The physician's whore, because she cozens him.
He did suspect me wrongfully.

FERDINAND. For that
165 You must give great men leave to take their times.
Distrust doth cause us seldom be deceiv'd.
You see the oft shaking of the cedar-tree
Fastens it more at root.

BOSOLA. Yet take heed;
170 For to suspect a friend unworthily
Instructs him the next way to suspect you,
And prompts him to deceive you.

FERDINAND. There's gold.

BOSOLA. So:
175 What follows?(Aside:) Never rain'd such showers as these
Without thunderbolts i' the tail of them.—Whose throat must I cut?

FERDINAND. Your inclination to shed blood rides post
Before my occasion to use you. I give you that
To live i' the court here, and observe the duchess;
180 To note all the particulars of her haviour,
What suitors do solicit her for marriage,
And whom she best affects. She's a young widow:
I would not have her marry again.

BOSOLA. No, sir?

185 FERDINAND. Do not you ask the reason; but be satisfied.
I say I would not.

BOSOLA. It seems you would create me
One of your familiars.

FERDINAND. Familiar! What's that?

190 BOSOLA. Why, a very quaint invisible devil in flesh,—
An intelligencer.

FERDINAND. Such a kind of thriving thing
I would wish thee; and ere long thou mayst arrive
At a higher place by 't.

195 BOSOLA. Take your devils,
Which hell calls angels!These curs'd gifts would make
You a corrupter, me an impudent traitor;
And should I take these, they'd take me to hell.

FERDINAND. Sir, I'll take nothing from you that I have given.
200 There is a place that I procur'd for you
This morning, the provisorship o' the horse;
Have you heard on 't?

BOSOLA. No.

FERDINAND. 'Tis yours: is 't not worth thanks?

205 BOSOLA. I would have you curse yourself now, that your bounty
(Which makes men truly noble) e'er should make me
A villain. O, that to avoid ingratitude
For the good deed you have done me, I must do
All the ill man can invent! Thus the devil
210 Candies all sins o'er; and what heaven terms vile,
That names he complimental.

FERDINAND. Be yourself;
Keep your old garb of melancholy; 'twill express
You envy those that stand above your reach,
215 Yet strive not to come near 'em. This will gain
Access to private lodgings, where yourself
May, like a politic dormouse——

BOSOLA. As I have seen some
Feed in a lord's dish, half asleep, not seeming
220 To listen to any talk; and yet these rogues
Have cut his throat in a dream. What's my place?
The provisorship o' the horse? Say, then, my corruption
Grew out of horse-dung: I am your creature.

FERDINAND. Away!

Exit.

225 BOSOLA. Let good men, for good deeds, covet good fame,
Since place and riches oft are bribes of shame.
Sometimes the devil doth preach.

Exit.

SCENE III

Enter FERDINAND, DUCHESS, CARDINAL, and CARIOLA.

CARDINAL. We are to part from you; and your own discretion
Must now be your director.

FERDINAND. You are a widow:
You know already what man is; and therefore
5   Let not youth, high promotion, eloquence——

CARDINAL. No,
Nor anything without the addition, honour,
Sway your high blood.

FERDINAND. Marry! they are most luxurious
10   Will wed twice.

CARDINAL. O, fie!

FERDINAND. Their livers are more spotted
Than Laban's sheep.

DUCHESS. Diamonds are of most value,
15   They say, that have pass'd through most jewellers' hands.

FERDINAND. Whores by that rule are precious.

DUCHESS. Will you hear me?
I'll never marry.

CARDINAL. So most widows say;
20   But commonly that motion lasts no longer
Than the turning of an hour-glass: the funeral sermon
And it end both together.

FERDINAND. Now hear me:
You live in a rank pasture, here, i' the court;
25   There is a kind of honey-dew that's deadly;
'T will poison your fame; look to 't. Be not cunning;
For they whose faces do belie their hearts
Are witches ere they arrive at twenty years,
Ay, and give the devil suck.

30   DUCHESS. This is terrible good counsel.

FERDINAND. Hypocrisy is woven of a fine small thread,
Subtler than Vulcan's engine: yet, believe 't,
Your darkest actions, nay, your privat'st thoughts,
Will come to light.

35   CARDINAL. You may flatter yourself,
And take your own choice; privately be married
Under the eaves of night——

FERDINAND. Think 't the best voyage
That e'er you made; like the irregular crab,
40 Which, though 't goes backward, thinks that it goes right
Because it goes its own way: but observe,
Such weddings may more properly be said
To be executed than celebrated.

CARDINAL. The marriage night
45 Is the entrance into some prison.

FERDINAND. And those joys,
Those lustful pleasures, are like heavy sleeps
Which do fore-run man's mischief.

50 CARDINAL. Fare you well.
Wisdom begins at the end: remember it.

Exit.

DUCHESS. I think this speech between you both was studied,
It came so roundly off.

FERDINAND. You are my sister;
55 This was my father's poniard, do you see?
I 'd be loth to see 't look rusty, 'cause 'twas his.
I would have you give o'er these chargeable revels:
A visor and a mask are whispering-rooms
That were never built for goodness,—fare ye well—
60 And women like variety of courtship.
What cannot a neat knave with a smooth tale
Make a woman believe? Farewell, lusty widow.

Exit.

DUCHESS. Shall this move me? If all my royal kindred
Lay in my way unto this marriage,
65 I 'd make them my low footsteps. And even now,
Even in this hate, as men in some great battles,
By apprehending danger, have achiev'd
Almost impossible actions (I have heard soldiers say so),
So I through frights and threatenings will assay
70 This dangerous venture. Let old wives report
I wink'd and chose a husband.—Cariola,
To thy known secrecy I have given up
More than my life,—my fame.

CARIOLA. Both shall be safe;
75 For I'll conceal this secret from the world

As warily as those that trade in poison
Keep poison from their children.

DUCHESS. Thy protestation
Is ingenious and hearty; I believe it.
80   Is Antonio come?

CARIOLA. He attends you.

DUCHESS. Good dear soul,
Leave me; but place thyself behind the arras,
Where thou mayst overhear us. Wish me good speed;
85   For I am going into a wilderness,
Where I shall find nor path nor friendly clue
To be my guide.

Cariola goes behind the arras.

Enter ANTONIO.

 I sent for you: sit down;
Take pen and ink, and write: are you ready?

90   ANTONIO. Yes.

DUCHESS. What did I say?

ANTONIO. That I should write somewhat.

DUCHESS. O, I remember.
After these triumphs and this large expense
95   It's fit, like thrifty husbands, we inquire
What's laid up for to-morrow.

ANTONIO. So please your beauteous excellence.

DUCHESS. Beauteous!
Indeed, I thank you. I look young for your sake;
100   You have ta'en my cares upon you.

ANTONIO. I'll fetch your grace
The particulars of your revenue and expense.

DUCHESS. O, you are
An upright treasurer: but you mistook;
105   For when I said I meant to make inquiry
What's laid up for to-morrow, I did mean
What's laid up yonder for me.

ANTONIO. Where?

DUCHESS. In heaven.
110 I am making my will (as 'tis fit princes should,
In perfect memory), and, I pray, sir, tell me,
Were not one better make it smiling, thus,
Than in deep groans and terrible ghastly looks,
As if the gifts we parted with procur'd
115 That violent distraction?

ANTONIO. O, much better.

DUCHESS. If I had a husband now, this care were quit:
But I intend to make you overseer.
What good deed shall we first remember? Say.

120 ANTONIO. Begin with that first good deed began i' the world
After man's creation, the sacrament of marriage;
I 'd have you first provide for a good husband;
Give him all.

DUCHESS. All!

125 ANTONIO. Yes, your excellent self.

DUCHESS. In a winding-sheet?

ANTONIO. In a couple.

DUCHESS. Saint Winifred, that were a strange will!

ANTONIO.'Twere stranger if there were no will in you
130 To marry again.

DUCHESS. What do you think of marriage?

ANTONIO. I take 't, as those that deny purgatory,
It locally contains or heaven or hell;
There's no third place in 't.

135 DUCHESS. How do you affect it?

ANTONIO. My banishment, feeding my melancholy,
Would often reason thus.

DUCHESS. Pray, let's hear it.

ANTONIO. Say a man never marry, nor have children,
140 What takes that from him? Only the bare name

Of being a father, or the weak delight
To see the little wanton ride a-cock-horse
Upon a painted stick, or hear him chatter
Like a taught starling.

145 　DUCHESS. Fie, fie, what's all this?
One of your eyes is blood-shot; use my ring to 't.
They say 'tis very sovereign.'Twas my wedding-ring,
And I did vow never to part with it
But to my second husband.

150 　ANTONIO. You have parted with it now.

DUCHESS. Yes, to help your eye-sight.

ANTONIO. You have made me stark blind.

DUCHESS. How?

ANTONIO. There is a saucy and ambitious devil
155 　Is dancing in this circle.

DUCHESS. Remove him.

ANTONIO. How?

DUCHESS. There needs small conjuration, when your finger
May do it: thus. Is it fit?

She puts the ring upon his finger; he kneels.

160 　ANTONIO. What said you?

DUCHESS. Sir,
This goodly roof of yours is too low built;
I cannot stand upright in 't nor discourse,
Without I raise it higher. Raise yourself;
165 　Or, if you please, my hand to help you: so.

Raises him.

ANTONIO. Ambition, madam, is a great man's madness,
That is not kept in chains and close-pent rooms,
But in fair lightsome lodgings, and is girt
With the wild noise of prattling visitants,
170 　Which makes it lunatic beyond all cure.
Conceive not I am so stupid but I aim
Whereto your favours tend: but he's a fool

That, being a-cold, would thrust his hands i' the fire
To warm them.

175   DUCHESS. So, now the ground's broke,
      You may discover what a wealthy mine
      I make your lord of.

      ANTONIO. O my unworthiness!

      DUCHESS. You were ill to sell yourself:
180   This dark'ning of your worth is not like that
      Which tradesmen use i' the city; their false lights
      Are to rid bad wares off: and I must tell you,
      If you will know where breathes a complete man
      (I speak it without flattery), turn your eyes,
185   And progress through yourself.

      ANTONIO. Were there nor heaven nor hell,
      I should be honest: I have long serv'd virtue,
      And ne'er ta'en wages of her.

      DUCHESS. Now she pays it.
190   The misery of us that are born great!
      We are forc'd to woo, because none dare woo us;
      And as a tyrant doubles with his words,
      And fearfully equivocates, so we
      Are forc'd to express our violent passions
195   In riddles and in dreams, and leave the path
      Of simple virtue, which was never made
      To seem the thing it is not. Go, go brag
      You have left me heartless; mine is in your bosom:
      I hope 'twill multiply love there. You do tremble:
200   Make not your heart so dead a piece of flesh,
      To fear more than to love me. Sir, be confident:
      What is 't distracts you? This is flesh and blood, sir;
      'Tis not the figure cut in alabaster
      Kneels at my husband's tomb. Awake, awake, man!
205   I do here put off all vain ceremony,
      And only do appear to you a young widow
      That claims you for her husband, and, like a widow,
      I use but half a blush in 't.

      ANTONIO. Truth speak for me;
210   I will remain the constant sanctuary
      Of your good name.

DUCHESS. I thank you, gentle love:
And 'cause you shall not come to me in debt,
Being now my steward, here upon your lips
215   I sign your Quietus est. This you should have begg'd now.
I have seen children oft eat sweetmeats thus,
As fearful to devour them too soon.

ANTONIO. But for your brothers?

DUCHESS. Do not think of them:
220   All discord without this circumference
Is only to be pitied, and not fear'd:
Yet, should they know it, time will easily
Scatter the tempest.

ANTONIO. These words should be mine,
225   And all the parts you have spoke, if some part of it
Would not have savour'd flattery.

DUCHESS. Kneel.

Cariola comes from behind the arras.

ANTONIO. Ha!

DUCHESS. Be not amaz'd; this woman's of my counsel:
230   I have heard lawyers say, a contract in a chamber
Per verba de presenti is absolute marriage.

She and ANTONIO kneel.

Bless, heaven, this sacred gordian [knot] which let violence
Never untwine!

ANTONIO. And may our sweet affections, like the spheres,
235   Be still in motion!

DUCHESS. Quickening, and make
The like soft music!

ANTONIO. That we may imitate the loving palms,
Best emblem of a peaceful marriage,
240   That never bore fruit, divided!

DUCHESS. What can the church force more?

ANTONIO. That fortune may not know an accident,
Either of joy or sorrow, to divide
Our fixed wishes!

245 DUCHESS. How can the church build faster?
We now are man and wife, and 'tis the church
That must but echo this.—Maid, stand apart:
I now am blind.

ANTONIO. What's your conceit in this?

250 DUCHESS. I would have you lead your fortune by the hand
Unto your marriage-bed:
(You speak in me this, for we now are one:)
We 'll only lie and talk together, and plot
To appease my humorous kindred; and if you please,
255 Like the old tale in ALEXANDER AND LODOWICK,
Lay a naked sword between us, keep us chaste.
O, let me shrowd my blushes in your bosom,
Since 'tis the treasury of all my secrets!
                              Exeunt DUCHESS and ANTONIO.

CARIOLA. Whether the spirit of greatness or of woman
260 Reign most in her, I know not; but it shows
A fearful madness. I owe her much of pity.
                                                      Exit.

Act II

Scene I
Enter BOSOLA and CASTRUCCIO.

BOSOLA. You say you would fain be taken for an eminent courtier?

CASTRUCCIO.'Tis the very main of my ambition.

BOSOLA. Let me see: you have a reasonable good face for 't already, and
your night-cap expresses your ears sufficient largely. I would have you learn
5   to twirl the strings of your band with a good grace, and in a set speech, at
th' end of every sentence, to hum three or four times, or blow your nose till
it smart again, to recover your memory. When you come to be a president
in criminal causes, if you smile upon a prisoner, hang him; but if you frown
upon him and threaten him, let him be sure to scape the gallows.

10   CASTRUCCIO. I would be a very merry president.

BOSOLA. Do not sup o' nights; 'twill beget you an admirable wit.

CASTRUCCIO. Rather it would make me have a good stomach to quarrel;
for they say, your roaring boys eat meat seldom, and that makes them so
valiant. But how shall I know whether the people take me for an eminent
15   fellow?

BOSOLA. I will teach a trick to know it: give out you lie a-dying, and if you hear the common people curse you, be sure you are taken for one of the prime night-caps.

Enter an Old Lady.

You come from painting now.

20   OLD LADY. From what?

BOSOLA. Why, from your scurvy face-physic. To behold thee not painted inclines somewhat near a miracle. These in thy face here were deep ruts and foul sloughs the last progress. There was a lady in France that, having had the small-pox, flayed the skin off her face to make it more level; and whereas before she
25   looked like a nutmeg-grater, after she resembled an abortive hedge-hog.

OLD LADY. Do you call this painting?

BOSOLA. No, no, but you call it careening of an old morphewed lady, to make her disembogue again: there's rough-cast phrase to your plastic.

OLD LADY. It seems you are well acquainted with my closet.

30   BOSOLA. One would suspect it for a shop of witchcraft, to find in it the fat of serpents, spawn of snakes, Jews' spittle, and their young children's ordure; and all these for the face. I would sooner eat a dead pigeon taken from the soles of the feet of one sick of the plague, than kiss one of you fasting. Here are two of you, whose sin of your youth is the very patrimo-
35   ny of the physician; makes him renew his foot-cloth with the spring, and change his high-pric'd courtezan with the fall of the leaf. I do wonder you do not loathe yourselves.
Observe my meditation now.
What thing is in this outward form of man
40   To be belov'd? We account it ominous,
If nature do produce a colt, or lamb,
A fawn, or goat, in any limb resembling
A man, and fly from 't as a prodigy:
Man stands amaz'd to see his deformity
45   In any other creature but himself.
But in our own flesh though we bear diseases
Which have their true names only ta'en from beasts,—
As the most ulcerous wolf and swinish measle,—
Though we are eaten up of lice and worms,
50   And though continually we bear about us
A rotten and dead body, we delight
To hide it in rich tissue: all our fear,
Nay, all our terror, is, lest our physician

Should put us in the ground to be made sweet.—
55 Your wife's gone to Rome: you two couple, and get you to the wells at Lucca
to recover your aches. I have other work on foot.

Exeunt CASTRUCCIO and Old Lady.

I observe our duchess
Is sick a-days, she pukes, her stomach seethes,
The fins of her eye-lids look most teeming blue,
60 She wanes i' the cheek, and waxes fat i' the flank,
And, contrary to our Italian fashion,
Wears a loose-bodied gown: there's somewhat in 't.
I have a trick may chance discover it,
A pretty one; I have bought some apricocks,
65 The first our spring yields.

Enter ANTONIO and DELIO, talking together apart.

DELIO. And so long since married?
You amaze me.

ANTONIO. Let me seal your lips for ever:
For, did I think that anything but th' air
70 Could carry these words from you, I should wish
You had no breath at all.—Now, sir, in your contemplation?
You are studying to become a great wise fellow.

BOSOLA. O, sir, the opinion of wisdom is a foul tetter that runs all over a man's
body: if simplicity direct us to have no evil, it directs us to a happy being; for
75 the subtlest folly proceeds from the subtlest wisdom: let me be simply honest.

ANTONIO. I do understand your inside.

BOSOLA. Do you so?

ANTONIO. Because you would not seem to appear to th' world
Puff'd up with your preferment, you continue
80 This out-of-fashion melancholy: leave it, leave it.

BOSOLA. Give me leave to be honest in any phrase, in any compliment
whatsoever. Shall I confess myself to you? I look no higher than I can
reach: they are the gods that must ride on winged horses. A lawyer's mule of
a slow pace will both suit my disposition and business; for, mark me, when
85 a man's mind rides faster than his horse can gallop, they quickly both tire.

ANTONIO. You would look up to heaven, but I think
The devil, that rules i' th' air, stands in your light.

BOSOLA. O, sir, you are lord of the ascendant, chief man with the duchess:
a duke was your cousin-german remov'd. Say you were lineally descended
90 from King Pepin, or he himself, what of this? Search the heads of the great-
est rivers in the world, you shall find them but bubbles of water. Some would
think the souls of princes were brought forth by some more weighty cause
than those of meaner persons: they are deceiv'd, there's the same hand to
them; the like passions sway them; the same reason that makes a vicar go
95 to law for a tithe-pig, and undo his neighbours, makes them spoil a whole
province, and batter down goodly cities with the cannon.

Enter DUCHESS and Ladies.

DUCHESS. Your arm, Antonio: do I not grow fat?
I am exceeding short-winded.—Bosola,
I would have you, sir, provide for me a litter;
100 Such a one as the Duchess of Florence rode in.

BOSOLA. The duchess us'd one when she was great with child.

DUCHESS. I think she did.—Come hither, mend my ruff:
Here, when? thou art such a tedious lady; and
Thy breath smells of lemon-pills: would thou hadst done!
105 Shall I swoon under thy fingers? I am
So troubled with the mother!

BOSOLA. (Aside.) I fear too much.

DUCHESS. I have heard you say that the French courtiers
Wear their hats on 'fore that king.

110 ANTONIO. I have seen it.

DUCHESS. In the presence?

ANTONIO. Yes.

DUCHESS. Why should not we bring up that fashion?
'Tis ceremony more than duty that consists
115 In the removing of a piece of felt.
Be you the example to the rest o' th' court;
Put on your hat first.

ANTONIO. You must pardon me:
I have seen, in colder countries than in France,
120 Nobles stand bare to th' prince; and the distinction
Methought show'd reverently.

BOSOLA. I have a present for your grace.

DUCHESS. For me, sir?

BOSOLA. Apricocks, madam.

125 DUCHESS. O, sir, where are they?
I have heard of none to-year.

BOSOLA.(Aside.) Good; her colour rises.

DUCHESS. Indeed, I thank you: they are wondrous fair ones.
What an unskilful fellow is our gardener!
130 We shall have none this month.

BOSOLA. Will not your grace pare them?

DUCHESS. No: they taste of musk, methinks; indeed they do.

BOSOLA. I know not: yet I wish your grace had par'd 'em.

DUCHESS. Why?

135 BOSOLA. I forgot to tell you, the knave gardener,
Only to raise his profit by them the sooner,
Did ripen them in horse-dung.

DUCHESS. O, you jest.—
You shall judge: pray, taste one.

140 ANTONIO. Indeed, madam,
I do not love the fruit.

DUCHESS. Sir, you are loth
To rob us of our dainties.'Tis a delicate fruit;
They say they are restorative.

145 BOSOLA.'Tis a pretty art,
This grafting.

DUCHESS.'Tis so; a bettering of nature.

BOSOLA. To make a pippin grow upon a crab,
A damson on a black-thorn.—(Aside.) How greedily she eats them!
150 A whirlwind strike off these bawd farthingales!
For, but for that and the loose-bodied gown,
I should have discover'd apparently
The young springal cutting a caper in her belly.

DUCHESS. I thank you, Bosola: they were right good ones,
155 If they do not make me sick.

ANTONIO. How now, madam!

DUCHESS. This green fruit and my stomach are not friends:
How they swell me!

BOSOLA.(Aside.) Nay, you are too much swell'd already.

160 DUCHESS. O, I am in an extreme cold sweat!

BOSOLA. I am very sorry.

Exit.

DUCHESS. Lights to my chamber!—O good Antonio,
I fear I am undone!

DELIO. Lights there, lights!

Exeunt DUCHESS and Ladies.

165 ANTONIO. O my most trusty Delio, we are lost!
I fear she's fall'n in labour; and there's left
No time for her remove.

DELIO. Have you prepar'd
Those ladies to attend her; and procur'd
170 That politic safe conveyance for the midwife
Your duchess plotted?

ANTONIO. I have.

DELIO. Make use, then, of this forc'd occasion.
Give out that Bosola hath poison'd her
175 With these apricocks; that will give some colour
For her keeping close.

ANTONIO. Fie, fie, the physicians
Will then flock to her.

DELIO. For that you may pretend
180 She'll use some prepar'd antidote of her own,
Lest the physicians should re-poison her.

ANTONIO. I am lost in amazement: I know not what to think on 't.

Exeunt.

Scene II

Enter BOSOLA and Old Lady.

BOSOLA. So, so, there's no question but her techiness and most vulturous eating of the apricocks are apparent signs of breeding, now?

OLD LADY. I am in haste, sir.

5 BOSOLA. There was a young waiting-woman had a monstrous desire to see the glass-house——

OLD LADY. Nay, pray, let me go. I will hear no more of the glass-house. You are still abusing women!

BOSOLA. Who, I? No; only, by the way now and then, mention your frailties. The orange-tree bears ripe and green fruit and blossoms all to-
10 gether; and some of you give entertainment for pure love, but more for more precious reward. The lusty spring smells well; but drooping autumn tastes well. If we have the same golden showers that rained in the time of Jupiter the thunderer, you have the same Danaes still, to hold up their laps to receive them. Didst thou never study the mathematics?

15 OLD LADY. What's that, sir?

BOSOLA. Why, to know the trick how to make a many lines meet in one centre. Go, go, give your foster-daughters good counsel: tell them, that the devil takes delight to hang at a woman's girdle, like a false rusty watch, that she cannot discern how the time passes.

Exit Old Lady.

Enter ANTONIO, RODERIGO, and GRISOLAN.

20 ANTONIO. Shut up the court-gates.

RODERIGO. Why, sir? What's the danger?

ANTONIO. Shut up the posterns presently, and call
All the officers o' th' court.

GRISOLAN. I shall instantly.

Exit.

25 ANTONIO. Who keeps the key o' th' park-gate?

RODERIGO. Forobosco.

ANTONIO. Let him bring 't presently.

Re-enter GRISOLAN with Servants.

FIRST SERVANT. O, gentleman o' th' court, the foulest treason!

BOSOLA.(Aside.) If that these apricocks should be poison'd now,
30   Without my knowledge?

FIRST SERV. There was taken even now a Switzer in the duchess'
bed-chamber—

SECOND SERVANT. A Switzer!

FIRST SERV. With a pistol——

35   SECOND SERV. There was a cunning traitor!

FIRST SERV And all the moulds of his buttons were leaden bullets.

SECOND SERV. O wicked cannibal!

FIRST SERV. 'Twas a French plot, upon my life.

SECOND SERV. To see what the devil can do!

40   ANTONIO. Are all the officers here?

SERVANTS. We are.

ANTONIO. Gentlemen,
We have lost much plate, you know; and but this evening
Jewels, to the value of four thousand ducats,
45   Are missing in the duchess' cabinet.
Are the gates shut?

SERVANT. Yes.

ANTONIO. 'Tis the duchess' pleasure
Each officer be lock'd into his chamber
50   Till the sun-rising; and to send the keys
Of all their chests and of their outward doors
Into her bed-chamber. She is very sick.

RODERIGO. At her pleasure.

ANTONIO. She entreats you take 't not ill: the innocent
55   Shall be the more approv'd by it.

BOSOLA. Gentlemen o' the wood-yard, where's your Switzer now?

FIRST SERV. By this hand, 'twas credibly reported by one o' the black guard.

Exeunt all except ANTONIO and DELIO.

DELIO. How fares it with the duchess?

ANTONIO. She's expos'd
60 Unto the worst of torture, pain, and fear.

DELIO. Speak to her all happy comfort.

ANTONIO. How I do play the fool with mine own danger!
You are this night, dear friend, to post to Rome:
My life lies in your service.

65 DELIO. Do not doubt me.

ANTONIO. O, 'tis far from me: and yet fear presents me
Somewhat that looks like danger.

DELIO. Believe it,
'Tis but the shadow of your fear, no more:
70 How superstitiously we mind our evils!
The throwing down salt, or crossing of a hare,
Bleeding at nose, the stumbling of a horse,
Or singing of a cricket, are of power
To daunt whole man in us. Sir, fare you well:
75 I wish you all the joys of a bless'd father;
And, for my faith, lay this unto your breast,—
Old friends, like old swords, still are trusted best.

Exit.

Enter CARIOLA.

CARIOLA. Sir, you are the happy father of a son:
Your wife commends him to you.

80 ANTONIO. Blessed comfort!—
For heaven' sake, tend her well: I'll presently
Go set a figure for's nativity.

Exeunt.

SCENE III

Enter BOSOLA, with a dark lantern.

BOSOLA. Sure I did hear a woman shriek: list, ha!
And the sound came, if I receiv'd it right,
From the duchess' lodgings. There's some stratagem
In the confining all our courtiers

5   To their several wards: I must have part of it;
    My intelligence will freeze else. List, again!
    It may be 'twas the melancholy bird,
    Best friend of silence and of solitariness,
    The owl, that screamed so.—Ha! Antonio!

Enter ANTONIO with a candle, his sword drawn.

10   ANTONIO. I heard some noise.—Who's there? What art thou? Speak.

     BOSOLA. Antonio, put not your face nor body
     To such a forc'd expression of fear;
     I am Bosola, your friend.

     ANTONIO. Bosola!—
15   (Aside.) This mole does undermine me.—Heard you not
     A noise even now?

     BOSOLA. From whence?

     ANTONIO. From the duchess' lodging.

     BOSOLA. Not I: did you?

20   ANTONIO. I did, or else I dream'd.

     BOSOLA. Let's walk towards it.

     ANTONIO. No: it may be 'twas
     But the rising of the wind.

     BOSOLA. Very likely.
25   Methinks 'tis very cold, and yet you sweat:
     You look wildly.

     ANTONIO. I have been setting a figure
     For the duchess' jewels.

     BOSOLA. Ah, and how falls your question?
30   Do you find it radical?

     ANTONIO. What's that to you?
     'Tis rather to be question'd what design,
     When all men were commanded to their lodgings,
     Makes you a night-walker.

35   BOSOLA. In sooth, I'll tell you:
     Now all the court's asleep, I thought the devil
     Had least to do here; I came to say my prayers;
     And if it do offend you I do so,
     You are a fine courtier.

40   ANTONIO. (Aside.) This fellow will undo me.—
     You gave the duchess apricocks to-day:
     Pray heaven they were not poison'd!

     BOSOLA. Poison'd! a Spanish fig
     For the imputation!

45   ANTONIO. Traitors are ever confident
     Till they are discover'd. There were jewels stol'n too:
     In my conceit, none are to be suspected
     More than yourself.

     BOSOLA. You are a false steward.

50   ANTONIO. Saucy slave, I'll pull thee up by the roots.

     BOSOLA. May be the ruin will crush you to pieces.

     ANTONIO. You are an impudent snake indeed, sir:
     Are you scarce warm, and do you show your sting?
     You libel well, sir?

55   BOSOLA. No, sir: copy it out,
     And I will set my hand to 't.

     ANTONIO. (Aside.) My nose bleeds.
     One that were superstitious would count
     This ominous, when it merely comes by chance.
60   Two letters, that are wrought here for my name,
     Are drown'd in blood!
     Mere accident.—For you, sir, I'll take order
     I' the morn you shall be safe.—(Aside.) 'Tis that must colour
     Her lying-in.—Sir, this door you pass not:
65   I do not hold it fit that you come near
     The duchess' lodgings, till you have quit yourself.—
     (Aside.) The great are like the base, nay, they are the same,
     When they seek shameful ways to avoid shame.

                                             Exit.

BOSOLA. Antonio hereabout did drop a paper:—
70 Some of your help, false friend.—O, here it is.
    What's here? a child's nativity calculated!

                                                                    Reads.

    'The duchess was deliver'd of a son, 'tween the hours twelve and one in the
    night, Anno Dom. 1504,'—that's this year—'decimo nono Decembris,'—
    that's this night— 'taken according to the meridian of Malfi,'—that's our
75 duchess: happy discovery!—'The lord of the first house being combust in
    the ascendant, signifies short life; and Mars being in a human sign, joined to
    the tail of the Dragon, in the eighth house, doth threaten a violent death.
    Caetera non scrutantur.'
    Why, now 'tis most apparent; this precise fellow
80 Is the duchess' bawd:—I have it to my wish!
    This is a parcel of intelligency
    Our courtiers were cas'd up for: it needs must follow
    That I must be committed on pretence
    Of poisoning her; which I'll endure, and laugh at.
85 If one could find the father now! but that
    Time will discover. Old Castruccio
    I' th' morning posts to Rome: by him I'll send
    A letter that shall make her brothers' galls
    O'erflow their livers. This was a thrifty way!
90 Though lust do mask in ne'er so strange disguise,
    She's oft found witty, but is never wise.

                                                                    Exit.

SCENE IV

Enter CARDINAL and JULIA.

CARDINAL. Sit: thou art my best of wishes. Prithee, tell me
    What trick didst thou invent to come to Rome
    Without thy husband?

JULIA. Why, my lord, I told him
5   I came to visit an old anchorite
    Here for devotion.

CARDINAL. Thou art a witty false one,—
    I mean, to him.

JULIA. You have prevail'd with me
10 Beyond my strongest thoughts; I would not now
    Find you inconstant.

CARDINAL. Do not put thyself
    To such a voluntary torture, which proceeds
    Out of your own guilt.

15   JULIA. How, my lord!

CARDINAL. You fear
My constancy, because you have approv'd
Those giddy and wild turnings in yourself.

JULIA. Did you e'er find them?

20   CARDINAL. Sooth, generally for women,
A man might strive to make glass malleable,
Ere he should make them fixed.

JULIA. So, my lord.

CARDINAL. We had need go borrow that fantastic glass
25   Invented by Galileo the Florentine
To view another spacious world i' th' moon,
And look to find a constant woman there.

JULIA. This is very well, my lord.

CARDINAL. Why do you weep?
30   Are tears your justification? The self-same tears
Will fall into your husband's bosom, lady,
With a loud protestation that you love him
Above the world. Come, I'll love you wisely,
That's jealously; since I am very certain
35   You cannot make me cuckold.

JULIA. I'll go home
To my husband.

CARDINAL. You may thank me, lady,
I have taken you off your melancholy perch,
40   Bore you upon my fist, and show'd you game,
And let you fly at it.—I pray thee, kiss me.—
When thou wast with thy husband, thou wast watch'd
Like a tame elephant:—still you are to thank me:—
Thou hadst only kisses from him and high feeding;
45   But what delight was that?'Twas just like one
That hath a little fing'ring on the lute,
Yet cannot tune it:—still you are to thank me.

JULIA. You told me of a piteous wound i' th' heart,
And a sick liver, when you woo'd me first,
50   And spake like one in physic.

CARDINAL. Who's that?————

Enter Servant.

Rest firm, for my affection to thee,
Lightning moves slow to 't.

SERVANT. Madam, a gentleman,
55 That's come post from Malfi, desires to see you.

CARDINAL. Let him enter: I'll withdraw.

Exit.

SERVANT. He says
Your husband, old Castruccio, is come to Rome,
Most pitifully tir'd with riding post.

Exit.

Enter DELIO.

60 JULIA. (Aside.) Signior Delio! 'tis one of my old suitors.

DELIO. I was bold to come and see you.

JULIA. Sir, you are welcome.

DELIO. Do you lie here?

JULIA. Sure, your own experience
65 Will satisfy you no: our Roman prelates
Do not keep lodging for ladies.

DELIO. Very well:
I have brought you no commendations from your husband,
For I know none by him.

70 JULIA. I hear he's come to Rome.

DELIO. I never knew man and beast, of a horse and a knight,
So weary of each other. If he had had a good back,
He would have undertook to have borne his horse,
His breech was so pitifully sore.

75 JULIA. Your laughter
Is my pity.

DELIO. Lady, I know not whether
You want money, but I have brought you some.

JULIA. From my husband?

80   DELIO. No, from mine own allowance.

JULIA. I must hear the condition, ere I be bound to take it.

DELIO. Look on 't, 'tis gold; hath it not a fine colour?

JULIA. I have a bird more beautiful.

DELIO. Try the sound on 't.

85   JULIA. A lute-string far exceeds it.
It hath no smell, like cassia or civet;
Nor is it physical, though some fond doctors
Persuade us seethe 't in cullises. I'll tell you,
This is a creature bred by——

Re-enter Servant.

90   SERVANT. Your husband's come,
Hath deliver'd a letter to the Duke of Calabria
That, to my thinking, hath put him out of his wits.

Exit.

JULIA. Sir, you hear:
Pray, let me know your business and your suit
95   As briefly as can be.

DELIO. With good speed: I would wish you,
At such time as you are non-resident
With your husband, my mistress.

JULIA. Sir, I'll go ask my husband if I shall,
100   And straight return your answer.

Exit.

DELIO. Very fine!
Is this her wit, or honesty, that speaks thus?
I heard one say the duke was highly mov'd
With a letter sent from Malfi. I do fear
105   Antonio is betray'd. How fearfully
Shows his ambition now! Unfortunate fortune!
They pass through whirl-pools, and deep woes do shun,
Who the event weigh ere the action's done.

Exit.

SCENE V

Enter CARDINAL and FERDINAND with a letter.

FERDINAND. I have this night digg'd up a mandrake.

CARDINAL. Say you?

FERDINAND. And I am grown mad with 't.

CARDINAL. What's the prodigy?

5　FERDINAND. Read there,—a sister damn'd: she's loose i' the hilts;
Grown a notorious strumpet.

CARDINAL. Speak lower.

FERDINAND. Lower!
Rogues do not whisper 't now, but seek to publish 't
10　(As servants do the bounty of their lords)
Aloud; and with a covetous searching eye,
To mark who note them. O, confusion seize her!
She hath had most cunning bawds to serve her turn,
And more secure conveyances for lust
15　Than towns of garrison for service.

CARDINAL. Is 't possible?
Can this be certain?

FERDINAND. Rhubarb, O, for rhubarb
To purge this choler!Here's the cursed day
20　To prompt my memory; and here 't shall stick
Till of her bleeding heart I make a sponge
To wipe it out.

CARDINAL. Why do you make yourself
So wild a tempest?

25　FERDINAND. Would I could be one,
That I might toss her palace 'bout her ears,
Root up her goodly forests, blast her meads,
And lay her general territory as waste
As she hath done her honours.

30　CARDINAL. Shall our blood,
The royal blood of Arragon and Castile,
Be thus attainted?

FERDINAND. Apply desperate physic:
We must not now use balsamum, but fire,

35 The smarting cupping-glass, for that's the mean
To purge infected blood, such blood as hers.
There is a kind of pity in mine eye,—
I'll give it to my handkercher; and now 'tis here,
I'll bequeath this to her bastard.

40 CARDINAL. What to do?

FERDINAND. Why, to make soft lint for his mother's wounds,
When I have hew'd her to pieces.

CARDINAL. Curs'd creature!
Unequal nature, to place women's hearts
45 So far upon the left side!

FERDINAND. Foolish men,
That e'er will trust their honour in a bark
Made of so slight weak bulrush as is woman,
Apt every minute to sink it!

50 CARDINAL. Thus ignorance, when it hath purchas'd honour,
It cannot wield it.

FERDINAND. Methinks I see her laughing,—
Excellent hyena!Talk to me somewhat quickly,
Or my imagination will carry me
55 To see her in the shameful act of sin.

CARDINAL. With whom?

FERDINAND. Happily with some strong-thigh'd bargeman,
Or one o' th' wood-yard that can quoit the sledge
Or toss the bar, or else some lovely squire
60 That carries coals up to her privy lodgings.

CARDINAL. You fly beyond your reason.

FERDINAND. Go to, mistress!
'Tis not your whore's milk that shall quench my wild-fire,
But your whore's blood.

65 CARDINAL. How idly shows this rage, which carries you,
As men convey'd by witches through the air,
On violent whirlwinds!This intemperate noise
Fitly resembles deaf men's shrill discourse,
Who talk aloud, thinking all other men
70 To have their imperfection.

FERDINAND. Have not you my palsy?

CARDINAL. Yes, but I can be angry
Without this rupture. There is not in nature
A thing that makes man so deform'd, so beastly,
75   As doth intemperate anger. Chide yourself.
You have divers men who never yet express'd
Their strong desire of rest but by unrest,
By vexing of themselves. Come, put yourself
In tune.

80   FERDINAND. So I will only study to seem
The thing I am not. I could kill her now,
In you, or in myself; for I do think
It is some sin in us heaven doth revenge
By her.

85   CARDINAL. Are you stark mad?

FERDINAND. I would have their bodies
Burnt in a coal-pit with the ventage stopp'd,
That their curs'd smoke might not ascend to heaven;
Or dip the sheets they lie in in pitch or sulphur,
90   Wrap them in 't, and then light them like a match;
Or else to-boil their bastard to a cullis,
And give 't his lecherous father to renew
The sin of his back.

CARDINAL. I'll leave you.

95   FERDINAND. Nay, I have done.
I am confident, had I been damn'd in hell,
And should have heard of this, it would have put me
Into a cold sweat. In, in; I'll go sleep.
Till I know who loves my sister, I'll not stir:
100   That known, I'll find scorpions to string my whips,
And fix her in a general eclipse.

Exeunt.

Act III
Scene I
Enter ANTONIO and DELIO.

ANTONIO. Our noble friend, my most beloved Delio!
O, you have been a stranger long at court:
Came you along with the Lord Ferdinand?

DELIO. I did, sir: and how fares your noble duchess?

5 ANTONIO. Right fortunately well: she's an excellent
Feeder of pedigrees; since you last saw her,
She hath had two children more, a son and daughter.

DELIO. Methinks 'twas yesterday. Let me but wink,
And not behold your face, which to mine eye
10 Is somewhat leaner, verily I should dream
It were within this half hour.

ANTONIO. You have not been in law, friend Delio,
Nor in prison, nor a suitor at the court,
Nor begg'd the reversion of some great man's place,
15 Nor troubled with an old wife, which doth make
Your time so insensibly hasten.

DELIO. Pray, sir, tell me,
Hath not this news arriv'd yet to the ear
Of the lord cardinal?

20 ANTONIO. I fear it hath:
The Lord Ferdinand, that's newly come to court,
Doth bear himself right dangerously.

DELIO. Pray, why?

ANTONIO. He is so quiet that he seems to sleep
25 The tempest out, as dormice do in winter.
Those houses that are haunted are most still
Till the devil be up.

DELIO. What say the common people?

ANTONIO. The common rabble do directly say
30 She is a strumpet.

DELIO. And your graver heads
Which would be politic, what censure they?

35 ANTONIO. They do observe I grow to infinite purchase,
The left hand way; and all suppose the duchess
Would amend it, if she could; for, say they,
Great princes, though they grudge their officers
Should have such large and unconfined means
40 To get wealth under them, will not complain,
Lest thereby they should make them odious

Unto the people. For other obligation
Of love or marriage between her and me
They never dream of.

45 DELIO. The Lord Ferdinand
Is going to bed.

Enter DUCHESS, FERDINAND, and Attendants.

FERDINAND. I'll instantly to bed,
For I am weary.—I am to bespeak
A husband for you.

50 DUCHESS. For me, sir! Pray, who is 't?

FERDINAND. The great Count Malatesti.

DUCHESS. Fie upon him!
A count! He's a mere stick of sugar-candy;
You may look quite through him. When I choose
55 A husband, I will marry for your honour.

FERDINAND. You shall do well in 't.—How is 't, worthy Antonio?

DUCHESS. But, sir, I am to have private conference with you
About a scandalous report is spread
Touching mine honour.

60 FERDINAND. Let me be ever deaf to 't:
One of Pasquil's paper-bullets, court-calumny,
A pestilent air, which princes' palaces
Are seldom purg'd of. Yet, say that it were true,
I pour it in your bosom, my fix'd love
65 Would strongly excuse, extenuate, nay, deny
Faults, were they apparent in you. Go, be safe
In your own innocency.

DUCHESS. (Aside.) O bless'd comfort! This deadly air is purg'd.
Exeunt DUCHESS, ANTONIO, DELIO, and Attendants.

FERDINAND. Her guilt treads on
70 Hot-burning coulters.
Enter BOSOLA.
 Now, Bosola,
How thrives our intelligence?

BOSOLA. Sir, uncertainly:
'Tis rumour'd she hath had three bastards, but
75 By whom we may go read i' the stars.

FERDINAND. Why, some
Hold opinion all things are written there.

BOSOLA. Yes, if we could find spectacles to read them.
I do suspect there hath been some sorcery
80 Us'd on the duchess.

FERDINAND. Sorcery! to what purpose?

BOSOLA. To make her dote on some desertless fellow
She shames to acknowledge.

FERDINAND. Can your faith give way
85 To think there's power in potions or in charms,
To make us love whether we will or no?

BOSOLA. Most certainly.

FERDINAND. Away! these are mere gulleries, horrid things,
Invented by some cheating mountebanks
90 To abuse us. Do you think that herbs or charms
Can force the will? Some trials have been made
In this foolish practice, but the ingredients
Were lenitive poisons, such as are of force
To make the patient mad; and straight the witch
95 Swears by equivocation they are in love.
The witch-craft lies in her rank blood. This night
I will force confession from her. You told me
You had got, within these two days, a false key
Into her bed-chamber.

100 BOSOLA. I have.

FERDINAND. As I would wish.

BOSOLA. What do you intend to do?

FERDINAND. Can you guess?

BOSOLA. No.

105 FERDINAND. Do not ask, then:
He that can compass me, and know my drifts,
May say he hath put a girdle 'bout the world,
And sounded all her quick-sands.

BOSOLA. I do not
110 Think so.

FERDINAND. What do you think, then, pray?

BOSOLA. That you
Are your own chronicle too much, and grossly
Flatter yourself.

115 FERDINAND. Give me thy hand; I thank thee:
I never gave pension but to flatterers,
Till I entertained thee. Farewell.
That friend a great man's ruin strongly checks,
Who rails into his belief all his defects.

Exeunt.

SCENE II
Enter DUCHESS, ANTONIO, and CARIOLA.

DUCHESS. Bring me the casket hither, and the glass.—
You get no lodging here to-night, my lord.

ANTONIO. Indeed, I must persuade one.

DUCHESS. Very good:
5 I hope in time 'twill grow into a custom,
That noblemen shall come with cap and knee
To purchase a night's lodging of their wives.

ANTONIO. I must lie here.

DUCHESS. Must! You are a lord of mis-rule.

10 ANTONIO. Indeed, my rule is only in the night.

DUCHESS. I'll stop your mouth.

Kisses him.

ANTONIO. Nay, that's but one; Venus had two soft doves
To draw her chariot; I must have another.—

She kisses him again.

When wilt thou marry, Cariola?

15 CARIOLA. Never, my lord.

ANTONIO. O, fie upon this single life! forgo it.
We read how Daphne, for her peevish flight,
Became a fruitless bay-tree; Syrinx turn'd

To the pale empty reed; Anaxarete
20   Was frozen into marble: whereas those
Which married, or prov'd kind unto their friends,
Were by a gracious influence transhap'd
Into the olive, pomegranate, mulberry,
Became flowers, precious stones, or eminent stars.

25   CARIOLA. This is a vain poetry: but I pray you, tell me,
If there were propos'd me, wisdom, riches, and beauty,
In three several young men, which should I choose?

ANTONIO.'Tis a hard question. This was Paris' case,
And he was blind in 't, and there was a great cause;
30   For how was 't possible he could judge right,
Having three amorous goddesses in view,
And they stark naked?'Twas a motion
Were able to benight the apprehension
Of the severest counsellor of Europe.
35   Now I look on both your faces so well form'd,
It puts me in mind of a question I would ask.

CARIOLA. What is 't?

ANTONIO. I do wonder why hard-favour'd ladies,
For the most part, keep worse-favour'd waiting-women
40   To attend them, and cannot endure fair ones.

DUCHESS. O, that's soon answer'd.
Did you ever in your life know an ill painter
Desire to have his dwelling next door to the shop
Of an excellent picture-maker?'Twould disgrace
45   His face-making, and undo him. I prithee,
When were we so merry?—My hair tangles.

ANTONIO. Pray thee, Cariola, let's steal forth the room,
And let her talk to herself: I have divers times
Serv'd her the like, when she hath chaf'd extremely.
50   I love to see her angry. Softly, Cariola.

Exeunt ANTONIO and CARIOLA.

DUCHESS. Doth not the colour of my hair 'gin to change?
When I wax gray, I shall have all the court
Powder their hair with arras, to be like me.
You have cause to love me; I ent'red you into my heart

Enter FERDINAND unseen.

55 Before you would vouchsafe to call for the keys.
We shall one day have my brothers take you napping.
Methinks his presence, being now in court,
Should make you keep your own bed; but you 'll say
Love mix'd with fear is sweetest. I'll assure you,
60 You shall get no more children till my brothers
Consent to be your gossips. Have you lost your tongue?
'Tis welcome:
For know, whether I am doom'd to live or die,
I can do both like a prince.

65 FERDINAND. Die, then, quickly!   *Giving her a poniard.*
Virtue, where art thou hid? What hideous thing
Is it that doth eclipse thee?

DUCHESS. Pray, sir, hear me.

FERDINAND. Or is it true thou art but a bare name,
70 And no essential thing?

DUCHESS. Sir——

FERDINAND. Do not speak.

DUCHESS. No, sir:
I will plant my soul in mine ears, to hear you.

75 FERDINAND. O most imperfect light of human reason,
That mak'st us so unhappy to foresee
What we can least prevent!Pursue thy wishes,
And glory in them: there's in shame no comfort
But to be past all bounds and sense of shame.

80 DUCHESS. I pray, sir, hear me: I am married.

FERDINAND. So!

DUCHESS. Happily, not to your liking: but for that,
Alas, your shears do come untimely now
To clip the bird's wings that's already flown!
85 Will you see my husband?

FERDINAND. Yes, if I could change
Eyes with a basilisk.

DUCHESS. Sure, you came hither
By his confederacy.

90 FERDINAND. The howling of a wolf
Is music to thee, screech-owl: prithee, peace.—
Whate'er thou art that hast enjoy'd my sister,
For I am sure thou hear'st me, for thine own sake
Let me not know thee. I came hither prepar'd

95 To work thy discovery; yet am now persuaded
It would beget such violent effects
As would damn us both. I would not for ten millions
I had beheld thee: therefore use all means
I never may have knowledge of thy name;

100 Enjoy thy lust still, and a wretched life,
On that condition.—And for thee, vile woman,
If thou do wish thy lecher may grow old
In thy embracements, I would have thee build
Such a room for him as our anchorites

105 To holier use inhabit. Let not the sun
Shine on him till he's dead; let dogs and monkeys
Only converse with him, and such dumb things
To whom nature denies use to sound his name;
Do not keep a paraquito, lest she learn it;

110 If thou do love him, cut out thine own tongue,
Lest it bewray him.

DUCHESS. Why might not I marry?
I have not gone about in this to create
Any new world or custom.

115 FERDINAND. Thou art undone;
And thou hast ta'en that massy sheet of lead
That hid thy husband's bones, and folded it
About my heart.

DUCHESS. Mine bleeds for 't.

120 FERDINAND. Thine! thy heart!
What should I name 't unless a hollow bullet
Fill'd with unquenchable wild-fire?

DUCHESS. You are in this
Too strict; and were you not my princely brother,

125 I would say, too wilful: my reputation
Is safe.

FERDINAND. Dost thou know what reputation is?
I'll tell thee,—to small purpose, since the instruction
Comes now too late.

130 Upon a time Reputation, Love, and Death,
Would travel o'er the world; and it was concluded
That they should part, and take three several ways.
Death told them, they should find him in great battles,
Or cities plagu'd with plagues: Love gives them counsel
135 To inquire for him 'mongst unambitious shepherds,
Where dowries were not talk'd of, and sometimes
'Mongst quiet kindred that had nothing left
By their dead parents: 'Stay,' quoth Reputation,
'Do not forsake me; for it is my nature,
140 If once I part from any man I meet,
I am never found again.' And so for you:
You have shook hands with Reputation,
And made him invisible. So, fare you well:
I will never see you more.

145 DUCHESS. Why should only I,
Of all the other princes of the world,
Be cas'd up, like a holy relic? I have youth
And a little beauty.

FERDINAND. So you have some virgins
150 That are witches. I will never see thee more.

Exit.

Re-enter ANTONIO with a pistol, and CARIOLA.

DUCHESS. You saw this apparition?

ANTONIO. Yes: we are
Betray'd. How came he hither? I should turn
This to thee, for that.

155 CARIOLA. Pray, sir, do; and when
That you have cleft my heart, you shall read there
Mine innocence.

DUCHESS. That gallery gave him entrance.

ANTONIO. I would this terrible thing would come again,
160 That, standing on my guard, I might relate
My warrantable love.——

(She shows the poniard.)

Ha! what means this?

DUCHESS. He left this with me.

ANTONIO. And it seems did wish
165 You would use it on yourself.

DUCHESS. His action seem'd
To intend so much.

ANTONIO. This hath a handle to 't,
As well as a point: turn it towards him, and
170 So fasten the keen edge in his rank gall.

Knocking within.

How now! who knocks? More earthquakes?

DUCHESS. I stand
As if a mine beneath my feet were ready
To be blown up.

175 CARIOLA. 'Tis Bosola.

DUCHESS. Away!
O misery! methinks unjust actions
Should wear these masks and curtains, and not we.
You must instantly part hence: I have fashion'd it already.

Exit ANTONIO.

Enter BOSOLA.

180 BOSOLA. The duke your brother is ta'en up in a whirlwind;
Hath took horse, and's rid post to Rome.

DUCHESS. So late?

BOSOLA. He told me, as he mounted into the saddle,
You were undone.

185 DUCHESS. Indeed, I am very near it.

BOSOLA. What's the matter?

DUCHESS. Antonio, the master of our household,
Hath dealt so falsely with me in's accounts.
My brother stood engag'd with me for money
190 Ta'en up of certain Neapolitan Jews,
And Antonio lets the bonds be forfeit.

BOSOLA. Strange!—(Aside.) This is cunning.

DUCHESS. And hereupon
My brother's bills at Naples are protested
195 Against.—Call up our officers.

BOSOLA. I shall.

                Exit.

     Re-enter ANTONIO.

DUCHESS. The place that you must fly to is Ancona:
Hire a house there; I'll send after you
My treasure and my jewels. Our weak safety
200 Runs upon enginous wheels: short syllables
Must stand for periods. I must now accuse you
Of such a feigned crime as Tasso calls
Magnanima menzogna, a noble lie,
'Cause it must shield our honours.—Hark! they are coming.

     Re-enter BOSOLA and Officers.

205 ANTONIO. Will your grace hear me?

DUCHESS. I have got well by you; you have yielded me
A million of loss: I am like to inherit
The people's curses for your stewardship.
You had the trick in audit-time to be sick,
210 Till I had sign'd your quietus; and that cur'd you
Without help of a doctor.—Gentlemen,
I would have this man be an example to you all;
So shall you hold my favour; I pray, let him;
For h'as done that, alas, you would not think of,
215 And, because I intend to be rid of him,
I mean not to publish.—Use your fortune elsewhere.

ANTONIO. I am strongly arm'd to brook my overthrow,
As commonly men bear with a hard year.
I will not blame the cause on 't; but do think
220 The necessity of my malevolent star
Procures this, not her humour. O, the inconstant
And rotten ground of service!You may see,
'Tis even like him, that in a winter night,
Takes a long slumber o'er a dying fire,
225 A-loth to part from 't; yet parts thence as cold
As when he first sat down.

DUCHESS. We do confiscate,
Towards the satisfying of your accounts,
All that you have.

230 ANTONIO. I am all yours; and 'tis very fit
All mine should be so.

DUCHESS. So, sir, you have your pass.

ANTONIO. You may see, gentlemen, what 'tis to serve
A prince with body and soul.

Exit.

235 BOSOLA. Here's an example for extortion: what moisture is drawn out of
the sea, when foul weather comes, pours down, and runs into the sea again.

DUCHESS. I would know what are your opinions
Of this Antonio.

SECOND OFFICER. He could not abide to see a pig's head gaping: I
240 thought your grace would find him a Jew.

THIRD OFFICER. I would you had been his officer, for your own sake.

FOURTH OFFICER. You would have had more money.

FIRST OFFICER. He stopped his ears with black wool, and to those came
to him for money said he was thick of hearing.

245 SECOND OFFICER. Some said he was an hermaphrodite, for he could
not abide a woman.

FOURTH OFFICER. How scurvy proud he would look when the treasury
was full! Well, let him go.

FIRST OFFICER. Yes, and the chippings of the buttery fly after him, to
250 scour his gold chain.

DUCHESS. Leave us.

Exeunt Officers.

What do you think of these?

BOSOLA. That these are rogues that in's prosperity,
But to have waited on his fortune, could have wish'd
255 His dirty stirrup riveted through their noses,
And follow'd after's mule, like a bear in a ring;
Would have prostituted their daughters to his lust;
Made their first-born intelligencers; thought none happy
But such as were born under his blest planet,
260 And wore his livery: and do these lice drop off now?
Well, never look to have the like again:
He hath left a sort of flattering rogues behind him;

Their doom must follow. Princes pay flatterers
In their own money: flatterers dissemble their vices,
265   And they dissemble their lies; that's justice.
Alas, poor gentleman!

DUCHESS. Poor! he hath amply fill'd his coffers.

BOSOLA. Sure, he was too honest. Pluto, the god of riches,
When he's sent by Jupiter to any man,
270   He goes limping, to signify that wealth
That comes on God's name comes slowly; but when he's sent
On the devil's errand, he rides post and comes in by scuttles.
Let me show you what a most unvalu'd jewel
You have in a wanton humour thrown away,
275   To bless the man shall find him. He was an excellent
Courtier and most faithful; a soldier that thought it
As beastly to know his own value too little
As devilish to acknowledge it too much.
Both his virtue and form deserv'd a far better fortune:
280   His discourse rather delighted to judge itself than show itself:
His breast was fill'd with all perfection,
And yet it seemed a private whisp'ring-room,
It made so little noise of 't.

DUCHESS. But he was basely descended.

285   BOSOLA. Will you make yourself a mercenary herald,
Rather to examine men's pedigrees than virtues?
You shall want him:
For know an honest statesman to a prince
Is like a cedar planted by a spring;
290   The spring bathes the tree's root, the grateful tree
Rewards it with his shadow: you have not done so.
I would sooner swim to the Bermoothes on
Two politicians' rotten bladders, tied
Together with an intelligencer's heart-string,
295   Than depend on so changeable a prince's favour.
Fare thee well, Antonio! Since the malice of the world
Would needs down with thee, it cannot be said yet
That any ill happen'd unto thee, considering thy fall
Was accompanied with virtue.

300   DUCHESS. O, you render me excellent music!

BOSOLA. Say you?

DUCHESS. This good one that you speak of is my husband.

BOSOLA. Do I not dream? Can this ambitious age
Have so much goodness in 't as to prefer
305   A man merely for worth, without these shadows
Of wealth and painted honours? Possible?

DUCHESS. I have had three children by him.

BOSOLA. Fortunate lady!
For you have made your private nuptial bed
310   The humble and fair seminary of peace,
No question but: many an unbenefic'd scholar
Shall pray for you for this deed, and rejoice
That some preferment in the world can yet
Arise from merit. The virgins of your land
315   That have no dowries shall hope your example
Will raise them to rich husbands. Should you want
Soldiers, 'twould make the very Turks and Moors
Turn Christians, and serve you for this act.
Last, the neglected poets of your time,
320   In honour of this trophy of a man,
Rais'd by that curious engine, your white hand,
Shall thank you, in your grave, for 't; and make that
More reverend than all the cabinets
Of living princes. For Antonio,
325   His fame shall likewise flow from many a pen,
When heralds shall want coats to sell to men.

DUCHESS. As I taste comfort in this friendly speech,
So would I find concealment.

BOSOLA. O, the secret of my prince,
330   Which I will wear on th' inside of my heart!

DUCHESS. You shall take charge of all my coin and jewels,
And follow him; for he retires himself
To Ancona.

BOSOLA. So.

335   DUCHESS. Whither, within few days,
I mean to follow thee.

BOSOLA. Let me think:
I would wish your grace to feign a pilgrimage
To our Lady of Loretto, scarce seven leagues

340   From fair Ancona; so may you depart
      Your country with more honour, and your flight
      Will seem a princely progress, retaining
      Your usual train about you.

      DUCHESS. Sir, your direction
345   Shall lead me by the hand.

      CARIOLA. In my opinion,
      She were better progress to the baths at Lucca,
      Or go visit the Spa
      In Germany; for, if you will believe me,
350   I do not like this jesting with religion,
      This feigned pilgrimage.

      DUCHESS. Thou art a superstitious fool:
      Prepare us instantly for our departure.
      Past sorrows, let us moderately lament them,
355   For those to come, seek wisely to prevent them.
                              Exeunt DUCHESS and CARIOLA.

      BOSOLA. A politician is the devil's quilted anvil;
      He fashions all sins on him, and the blows
      Are never heard: he may work in a lady's chamber,
      As here for proof. What rests but I reveal
360   All to my lord? O, this base quality
      Of intelligencer! Why, every quality i' the world
      Prefers but gain or commendation:
      Now, for this act I am certain to be rais'd,
      And men that paint weeds to the life are prais'd.
                                                      Exit.

                              SCENE III
      *Enter CARDINAL, FERDINAND, MALATESTI, PESCARA,
                        DELIO, and SILVIO.*

      CARDINAL. Must we turn soldier, then?

      MALATESTI. The emperor,
      Hearing your worth that way, ere you attain'd
      This reverend garment, joins you in commission
5   With the right fortunate soldier the Marquis of Pescara,
      And the famous Lannoy.

      CARDINAL. He that had the honour
      Of taking the French king prisoner?

MALATESTI. The same.
10   Here's a plot drawn for a new fortification
At Naples.

FERDINAND. This great Count Malatesti, I perceive,
Hath got employment?

DELIO. No employment, my lord;
15   A marginal note in the muster-book, that he is
A voluntary lord.

FERDINAND. He's no soldier.

DELIO. He has worn gun-powder in's hollow tooth for the tooth-ache.

SILVIO. He comes to the leaguer with a full intent
20   To eat fresh beef and garlic, means to stay
Till the scent be gone, and straight return to court.

DELIO. He hath read all the late service
As the City-Chronicle relates it;
And keeps two pewterers going, only to express
25   Battles in model.

SILVIO. Then he 'll fight by the book.

DELIO. By the almanac, I think,
To choose good days and shun the critical;
That's his mistress' scarf.

30   SILVIO. Yes, he protests
He would do much for that taffeta.

DELIO. I think he would run away from a battle,
To save it from taking prisoner.

SILVIO. He is horribly afraid
35   Gun-powder will spoil the perfume on 't.

DELIO. I saw a Dutchman break his pate once
For calling him pot-gun; he made his head
Have a bore in 't like a musket.

SILVIO. I would he had made a touch-hole to 't.
40   He is indeed a guarded sumpter-cloth,
Only for the remove of the court.

Enter BOSOLA.

PESCARA. Bosola arriv'd! What should be the business?
Some falling-out amongst the cardinals.
These factions amongst great men, they are like
45   Foxes, when their heads are divided,
They carry fire in their tails, and all the country
About them goes to wrack for 't.

SILVIO. What's that Bosola?

DELIO. I knew him in Padua,—a fantastical scholar, like such who study to
50   know how many knots was in Hercules' club, of what colour Achilles' beard
was, or whether Hector were not troubled with the tooth-ache. He hath
studied himself half blear-eyed to know the true symmetry of Caesar's nose
by a shoeing-horn; and this he did to gain the name of a speculative man.

PESCARA. Mark Prince Ferdinand:
55   A very salamander lives in's eye,
To mock the eager violence of fire.

SILVIO. That cardinal hath made more bad faces with his oppression than
ever Michael Angelo made good ones. He lifts up's nose, like a foul por-
poise before a storm.

60   PESCARA. The Lord Ferdinand laughs.

DELIO. Like a deadly cannon
That lightens ere it smokes.

PESCARA. These are your true pangs of death,
The pangs of life, that struggle with great statesmen.

65   DELIO. In such a deformed silence witches whisper their charms.

CARDINAL. Doth she make religion her riding-hood
To keep her from the sun and tempest?

FERDINAND. That, that damns her. Methinks her fault and beauty,
Blended together, show like leprosy,
70   The whiter, the fouler. I make it a question
Whether her beggarly brats were ever christ'ned.

CARDINAL. I will instantly solicit the state of Ancona
To have them banish'd.

FERDINAND. You are for Loretto:
75 I shall not be at your ceremony; fare you well.—
Write to the Duke of Malfi, my young nephew
She had by her first husband, and acquaint him
With's mother's honesty.

BOSOLA. I will.

80 FERDINAND. Antonio!
A slave that only smell'd of ink and counters,
And never in's life look'd like a gentleman,
But in the audit-time.—Go, go presently,
Draw me out an hundred and fifty of our horse,
85 And meet me at the foot-bridge.

Exeunt.

SCENE IV

Enter Two Pilgrims to the Shrine of our Lady of Loretto.

FIRST PILGRIM. I have not seen a goodlier shrine than this;
Yet I have visited many.

SECOND PILGRIM. The Cardinal of Arragon
Is this day to resign his cardinal's hat:
5 His sister duchess likewise is arriv'd
To pay her vow of pilgrimage. I expect
A noble ceremony.

FIRST PILGRIM. No question.—They come.

Here the ceremony of the Cardinal's instalment, in the habit of a soldier, perform'd in delivering up his cross, hat, robes, and ring, at the shrine, and investing him with sword, helmet, shield, and spurs; then ANTONIO, the DUCHESS and their children, having presented themselves at the shrine, are, by a form of banishment in dumb-show expressed towards them by the CARDINAL and the state of Ancona, banished: during all which ceremony, this ditty is sung, to very solemn music, by divers churchmen: and then exeunt all except the Two Pilgrims.

Arms and honours deck thy story,
10 To thy fame's eternal glory!
Adverse fortune ever fly thee;
No disastrous fate come nigh thee!
I alone will sing thy praises,
Whom to honour virtue raises,
15 And thy study, that divine is,
Bent to martial discipline is,

Lay aside all those robes lie by thee;
Crown thy arts with arms, they 'll beautify thee.
O worthy of worthiest name, adorn'd in this manner,
20   Lead bravely thy forces on under war's warlike banner!
O, mayst thou prove fortunate in all martial courses!
Guide thou still by skill in arts and forces!
Victory attend thee nigh, whilst fame sings loud thy powers;
Triumphant conquest crown thy head, and blessings pour down showers!

25   FIRST PILGRIM. Here's a strange turn of state! who would have thought
So great a lady would have match'd herself
Unto so mean a person? Yet the cardinal
Bears himself much too cruel.

SECOND PILGRIM. They are banish'd.

30   FIRST PILGRIM. But I would ask what power hath this state
Of Ancona to determine of a free prince?

SECOND PILGRIM. They are a free state, sir, and her brother show'd
How that the Pope, fore-hearing of her looseness,
Hath seiz'd into th' protection of the church
35   The dukedom which she held as dowager.

FIRST PILGRIM. But by what justice?

SECOND PILGRIM. Sure, I think by none,
Only her brother's instigation.

FIRST PILGRIM. What was it with such violence he took
40   Off from her finger?

SECOND PILGRIM. 'Twas her wedding-ring;
Which he vow'd shortly he would sacrifice
To his revenge.

FIRST PILGRIM. Alas, Antonio!
45   If that a man be thrust into a well,
No matter who sets hand to 't, his own weight
Will bring him sooner to th' bottom. Come, let's hence.
Fortune makes this conclusion general,
All things do help th' unhappy man to fall.

                                                        Exeunt.

SCENE V

Enter DUCHESS, ANTONIO, Children, CARIOLA, and Servants.

DUCHESS. Banish'd Ancona!

ANTONIO. Yes, you see what power
Lightens in great men's breath.

DUCHESS. Is all our train
5   Shrunk to this poor remainder?

ANTONIO. These poor men
Which have got little in your service, vow
To take your fortune: but your wiser buntings,
Now they are fledg'd, are gone.

10   DUCHESS. They have done wisely.
This puts me in mind of death: physicians thus,
With their hands full of money, use to give o'er
Their patients.

ANTONIO. Right the fashion of the world:
15   From decay'd fortunes every flatterer shrinks;
Men cease to build where the foundation sinks.

DUCHESS. I had a very strange dream to-night.

ANTONIO. What was 't?

DUCHESS. Methought I wore my coronet of state,
20   And on a sudden all the diamonds
Were chang'd to pearls.

ANTONIO. My interpretation
Is, you 'll weep shortly; for to me the pearls
Do signify your tears.

25   DUCHESS. The birds that live i' th' field
On the wild benefit of nature live
Happier than we; for they may choose their mates,
And carol their sweet pleasures to the spring.

Enter BOSOLA with a letter.

BOSOLA. You are happily o'erta'en.

30   DUCHESS. From my brother?

BOSOLA. Yes, from the Lord Ferdinand your brother
All love and safety.

DUCHESS. Thou dost blanch mischief,
Would'st make it white. See, see, like to calm weather
35 At sea before a tempest, false hearts speak fair
To those they intend most mischief.
(Reads.) 'Send Antonio to me; I want his head in a business.'
A politic equivocation!
He doth not want your counsel, but your head;
40 That is, he cannot sleep till you be dead.
And here's another pitfall that's strew'd o'er
With roses; mark it, 'tis a cunning one:
(Reads.) 'I stand engaged for your husband for several debts at Naples: let
not that trouble him; I had rather have his heart than his money':—
45 And I believe so too.

BOSOLA. What do you believe?

DUCHESS. That he so much distrusts my husband's love,
He will by no means believe his heart is with him
Until he see it: the devil is not cunning enough
50 To circumvent us In riddles.

BOSOLA. Will you reject that noble and free league
Of amity and love which I present you?

DUCHESS. Their league is like that of some politic kings,
Only to make themselves of strength and power
55 To be our after-ruin; tell them so.

BOSOLA. And what from you?

ANTONIO. Thus tell him; I will not come.

BOSOLA. And what of this?

ANTONIO. My brothers have dispers'd
60 Bloodhounds abroad; which till I hear are muzzl'd,
No truce, though hatch'd with ne'er such politic skill,
Is safe, that hangs upon our enemies' will.
I'll not come at them.

BOSOLA. This proclaims your breeding.
65 Every small thing draws a base mind to fear,

As the adamant draws iron. Fare you well, sir;
You shall shortly hear from's.

Exit.

DUCHESS. I suspect some ambush;
Therefore by all my love I do conjure you
70   To take your eldest son, and fly towards Milan.
Let us not venture all this poor remainder
In one unlucky bottom.

ANTONIO. You counsel safely.
Best of my life, farewell. Since we must part,
75   Heaven hath a hand in 't; but no otherwise
Than as some curious artist takes in sunder
A clock or watch, when it is out of frame,
To bring 't in better order.

DUCHESS. I know not which is best,
80   To see you dead, or part with you.—Farewell, boy:
Thou art happy that thou hast not understanding
To know thy misery; for all our wit
And reading brings us to a truer sense
Of sorrow.—In the eternal church, sir,
85   I do hope we shall not part thus.

ANTONIO. O, be of comfort!
Make patience a noble fortitude,
And think not how unkindly we are us'd:
Man, like to cassia, is prov'd best, being bruis'd.

90   DUCHESS. Must I, like to slave-born Russian,
Account it praise to suffer tyranny?
And yet, O heaven, thy heavy hand is in 't!
I have seen my little boy oft scourge his top,
And compar'd myself to 't: naught made me e'er
95   Go right but heaven's scourge-stick.

ANTONIO. Do not weep:
Heaven fashion'd us of nothing; and we strive
To bring ourselves to nothing.—Farewell, Cariola,
And thy sweet armful.—If I do never see thee more,
100   Be a good mother to your little ones,
And save them from the tiger: fare you well.

DUCHESS. Let me look upon you once more, for that speech
Came from a dying father. Your kiss is colder

Than that I have seen an holy anchorite
105   Give to a dead man's skull.

ANTONIO. My heart is turn'd to a heavy lump of lead,
With which I sound my danger: fare you well.

Exeunt ANTONIO and his son.

DUCHESS. My laurel is all withered.

CARIOLA. Look, madam, what a troop of armed men
110   Make toward us!

Re-enter BOSOLA visarded, with a Guard.

DUCHESS. O, they are very welcome:
When Fortune's wheel is over-charg'd with princes,
The weight makes it move swift: I would have my ruin
Be sudden.—I am your adventure, am I not?

115   BOSOLA. You are: you must see your husband no more.

DUCHESS. What devil art thou that counterfeit'st heaven's thunder?

BOSOLA. Is that terrible? I would have you tell me whether
Is that note worse that frights the silly birds
Out of the corn, or that which doth allure them
120   To the nets? You have heark'ned to the last too much.

DUCHESS. O misery! like to a rusty o'ercharg'd cannon,
Shall I never fly in pieces?—Come, to what prison?

BOSOLA. To none.

DUCHESS. Whither, then?

125   BOSOLA. To your palace.

DUCHESS. I have heard
That Charon's boat serves to convey all o'er
The dismal lake, but brings none back again.

BOSOLA. Your brothers mean you safety and pity.

130   DUCHESS. Pity!
With such a pity men preserve alive
Pheasants and quails, when they are not fat enough
To be eaten.

BOSOLA. These are your children?

135 DUCHESS. Yes.

BOSOLA. Can they prattle?

DUCHESS. No:
But I intend, since they were born accurs'd,
Curses shall be their first language.

140 BOSOLA. Fie, madam!
Forget this base, low fellow——

DUCHESS. Were I a man,
I 'd beat that counterfeit face into thy other.

BOSOLA. One of no birth.

145 DUCHESS. Say that he was born mean,
Man is most happy when's own actions
Be arguments and examples of his virtue.

BOSOLA. A barren, beggarly virtue.

DUCHESS. I prithee, who is greatest? Can you tell?
150 Sad tales befit my woe: I'll tell you one.
A salmon, as she swam unto the sea.
Met with a dog-fish, who encounters her
With this rough language; 'Why art thou so bold
To mix thyself with our high state of floods,
155 Being no eminent courtier, but one
That for the calmest and fresh time o' th' year
Dost live in shallow rivers, rank'st thyself
With silly smelts and shrimps? And darest thou
Pass by our dog-ship without reverence?'
160 'O,' quoth the salmon,'sister, be at peace:
Thank Jupiter we both have pass'd the net!
Our value never can be truly known,
Till in the fisher's basket we be shown:
I' th' market then my price may be the higher,
165 Even when I am nearest to the cook and fire.'
So to great men the moral may be stretched;
Men oft are valu'd high, when they're most wretched.—
But come, whither you please. I am arm'd 'gainst misery;
Bent to all sways of the oppressor's will:
170 There's no deep valley but near some great hill.

Exeunt.

ACT IV

SCENE I

Enter FERDINAND and BOSOLA.

FERDINAND. How doth our sister duchess bear herself
In her imprisonment?

BOSOLA. Nobly: I'll describe her.
She's sad as one long us'd to 't, and she seems
5   Rather to welcome the end of misery
Than shun it; a behaviour so noble
As gives a majesty to adversity:
You may discern the shape of loveliness
More perfect in her tears than in her smiles:
10 She will muse for hours together; and her silence,
Methinks, expresseth more than if she spake.

FERDINAND. Her melancholy seems to be fortified
With a strange disdain.

BOSOLA.'Tis so; and this restraint,
15 Like English mastives that grow fierce with tying,
Makes her too passionately apprehend
Those pleasures she is kept from.

FERDINAND. Curse upon her!
I will no longer study in the book
20 Of another's heart. Inform her what I told you.

Exit.

Enter DUCHESS and Attendants.

BOSOLA. All comfort to your grace!

DUCHESS. I will have none.
Pray thee, why dost thou wrap thy poison'd pills
In gold and sugar?

25 BOSOLA. Your elder brother, the Lord Ferdinand,
Is come to visit you, and sends you word,
'Cause once he rashly made a solemn vow
Never to see you more, he comes i' th' night;
And prays you gently neither torch nor taper
30 Shine in your chamber. He will kiss your hand,
And reconcile himself; but for his vow
He dares not see you.

DUCHESS. At his pleasure.—
Take hence the lights.—He's come.

Exeunt Attendants with lights.

Enter FERDINAND.

35 FERDINAND. Where are you?

DUCHESS. Here, sir.

FERDINAND. This darkness suits you well.

DUCHESS. I would ask you pardon.

FERDINAND. You have it;
40 For I account it the honorabl'st revenge,
Where I may kill, to pardon.—Where are your cubs?

DUCHESS. Whom?

FERDINAND. Call them your children;
For though our national law distinguish bastards
45 From true legitimate issue, compassionate nature
Makes them all equal.

DUCHESS. Do you visit me for this?
You violate a sacrament o' th' church
Shall make you howl in hell for 't.

50 FERDINAND. It had been well,
Could you have liv'd thus always; for, indeed,
You were too much i' th' light:—but no more;
I come to seal my peace with you. Here's a hand
 Gives her a dead man's hand.
55 To which you have vow'd much love; the ring upon 't
You gave.

DUCHESS. I affectionately kiss it.

FERDINAND. Pray, do, and bury the print of it in your heart.
I will leave this ring with you for a love-token;
60 And the hand as sure as the ring; and do not doubt
But you shall have the heart too. When you need a friend,
Send it to him that ow'd it; you shall see
Whether he can aid you.

DUCHESS. You are very cold:
65   I fear you are not well after your travel.—
Ha! lights!——O, horrible!

FERDINAND. Let her have lights enough.

Exit.

DUCHESS. What witchcraft doth he practise, that he hath left
A dead man's hand here?
*Here is discovered, behind a traverse, the artificial figures of ANTONIO and his
children, appearing as if they were dead.*

70   BOSOLA. Look you, here's the piece from which 'twas ta'en.
He doth present you this sad spectacle,
That, now you know directly they are dead,
Hereafter you may wisely cease to grieve
For that which cannot be recovered.

75   DUCHESS. There is not between heaven and earth one wish
I stay for after this. It wastes me more
Than were 't my picture, fashion'd out of wax,
Stuck with a magical needle, and then buried
In some foul dunghill; and yon's an excellent property
80   For a tyrant, which I would account mercy.

BOSOLA. What's that?

DUCHESS. If they would bind me to that lifeless trunk,
And let me freeze to death.

BOSOLA. Come, you must live.

85   DUCHESS. That's the greatest torture souls feel in hell,
In hell, that they must live, and cannot die.
Portia, I'll new kindle thy coals again,
And revive the rare and almost dead example
Of a loving wife.

90   BOSOLA. O, fie! despair? Remember
You are a Christian.

DUCHESS. The church enjoins fasting:
I'll starve myself to death.

BOSOLA. Leave this vain sorrow.
95   Things being at the worst begin to mend: the bee

When he hath shot his sting into your hand,
May then play with your eye-lid.

DUCHESS. Good comfortable fellow,
Persuade a wretch that's broke upon the wheel
100 To have all his bones new set; entreat him live
To be executed again. Who must despatch me?
I account this world a tedious theatre,
For I do play a part in 't 'gainst my will.

BOSOLA. Come, be of comfort; I will save your life.

105 DUCHESS. Indeed, I have not leisure to tend so small a business.

BOSOLA. Now, by my life, I pity you.

DUCHESS. Thou art a fool, then,
To waste thy pity on a thing so wretched
As cannot pity itself. I am full of daggers.
110 Puff, let me blow these vipers from me.
                              Enter Servant.
What are you?

SERVANT. One that wishes you long life.

DUCHESS. I would thou wert hang'd for the horrible curse
Thou hast given me: I shall shortly grow one
115 Of the miracles of pity. I'll go pray;—
                                                   Exit Servant.
No, I'll go curse.

BOSOLA. O, fie!

DUCHESS. I could curse the stars.

BOSOLA. O, fearful!

120 DUCHESS. And those three smiling seasons of the year
Into a Russian winter; nay, the world
To its first chaos.

BOSOLA. Look you, the stars shine still.

DUCHESS. O, but you must
125 Remember, my curse hath a great way to go.—
Plagues, that make lanes through largest families,
Consume them!—

BOSOLA. Fie, lady!

DUCHESS. Let them, like tyrants,
130 Never be remembered but for the ill they have done;
Let all the zealous prayers of mortified
Churchmen forget them!—

BOSOLA. O, uncharitable!

DUCHESS. Let heaven a little while cease crowning martyrs,
135 To punish them!—
Go, howl them this, and say, I long to bleed:
It is some mercy when men kill with speed.

Exit.

Re-enter FERDINAND.

FERDINAND. Excellent, as I would wish; she's plagu'd in art.
These presentations are but fram'd in wax
140 By the curious master in that quality,
Vincentio Lauriola, and she takes them
For true substantial bodies.

BOSOLA. Why do you do this?

FERDINAND. To bring her to despair.

145 BOSOLA. Faith, end here,
And go no farther in your cruelty:
Send her a penitential garment to put on
Next to her delicate skin, and furnish her
With beads and prayer-books.

150 FERDINAND. Damn her! that body of hers.
While that my blood run pure in 't, was more worth
Than that which thou wouldst comfort, call'd a soul.
I will send her masques of common courtezans,
Have her meat serv'd up by bawds and ruffians,
155 And, 'cause she 'll needs be mad, I am resolv'd
To move forth the common hospital
All the mad-folk, and place them near her lodging;
There let them practise together, sing and dance,
And act their gambols to the full o' th' moon:
160 If she can sleep the better for it, let her.
Your work is almost ended.

BOSOLA. Must I see her again?

FERDINAND. Yes.

BOSOLA. Never.

165 FERDINAND. You must.

BOSOLA. Never in mine own shape;
That's forfeited by my intelligence
And this last cruel lie: when you send me next,
The business shall be comfort.

170 FERDINAND. Very likely;
Thy pity is nothing of kin to thee, Antonio
Lurks about Milan: thou shalt shortly thither,
To feed a fire as great as my revenge,
Which nev'r will slack till it hath spent his fuel:
175 Intemperate agues make physicians cruel.

Exeunt.

SCENE II
Enter DUCHESS and CARIOLA.

DUCHESS. What hideous noise was that?

CARIOLA. 'Tis the wild consort
Of madmen, lady, which your tyrant brother
Hath plac'd about your lodging. This tyranny,
5   I think, was never practis'd till this hour.

DUCHESS. Indeed, I thank him. Nothing but noise and folly
Can keep me in my right wits; whereas reason
And silence make me stark mad. Sit down;
Discourse to me some dismal tragedy.

10 CARIOLA. O, 'twill increase your melancholy!

DUCHESS. Thou art deceiv'd:
To hear of greater grief would lessen mine.
This is a prison?

CARIOLA. Yes, but you shall live
15 To shake this durance off.

DUCHESS. Thou art a fool:
The robin-red-breast and the nightingale
Never live long in cages.

CARIOLA. Pray, dry your eyes.
20 What think you of, madam?

DUCHESS. Of nothing;
When I muse thus, I sleep.

CARIOLA. Like a madman, with your eyes open?

DUCHESS. Dost thou think we shall know one another
25 In th' other world?

CARIOLA. Yes, out of question.

DUCHESS. O, that it were possible we might
But hold some two days' conference with the dead!
From them I should learn somewhat, I am sure,
30 I never shall know here. I'll tell thee a miracle:
I am not mad yet, to my cause of sorrow:
Th' heaven o'er my head seems made of molten brass,
The earth of flaming sulphur, yet I am not mad.
I am acquainted with sad misery
35 As the tann'd galley-slave is with his oar;
Necessity makes me suffer constantly,
And custom makes it easy. Who do I look like now?

CARIOLA. Like to your picture in the gallery,
A deal of life in show, but none in practice;
40 Or rather like some reverend monument
Whose ruins are even pitied.

DUCHESS. Very proper;
And Fortune seems only to have her eye-sight
To behold my tragedy.—How now!
45 What noise is that?

Enter Servant.

SERVANT. I am come to tell you
Your brother hath intended you some sport.
A great physician, when the Pope was sick
Of a deep melancholy, presented him
50 With several sorts of madmen, which wild object
Being full of change and sport, forc'd him to laugh,
And so the imposthume broke: the self-same cure
The duke intends on you.

DUCHESS. Let them come in.

55 SERVANT. There's a mad lawyer; and a secular priest;
A doctor that hath forfeited his wits
By jealousy; an astrologian
That in his works said such a day o' the month
Should be the day of doom, and, failing of 't,
60 Ran mad; an English tailor craz'd i' the brain
With the study of new fashions; a gentleman-usher
Quite beside himself with care to keep in mind
The number of his lady's salutations
Or 'How do you,' she employ'd him in each morning;
65 A farmer, too, an excellent knave in grain,
Mad 'cause he was hind'red transportation:
And let one broker that's mad loose to these,
You'd think the devil were among them.

DUCHESS. Sit, Cariola.—Let them loose when you please,
70 For I am chain'd to endure all your tyranny.

Enter Madman.

Here by a Madman this song is sung to a dismal kind of music:

O, let us howl some heavy note,
Some deadly dogged howl,
Sounding as from the threatening throat
Of beasts and fatal fowl!
75 As ravens, screech-owls, bulls, and bears,
We 'll bell, and bawl our parts,
Till irksome noise have cloy'd your ears
And corrosiv'd your hearts.
At last, whenas our choir wants breath,
80 Our bodies being blest,
We 'll sing, like swans, to welcome death,
And die in love and rest.

FIRST MADMAN. Doom's-day not come yet! I'll draw it nearer by a perspective, or make a glass that shall set all the world on fire upon an instant.
85 I cannot sleep; my pillow is stuffed with a litter of porcupines.

SECOND MADMAN. Hell is a mere glass-house, where the devils are continually blowing up women's souls on hollow irons, and the fire never goes out.

FIRST MADMAN. I have skill in heraldry.

SECOND MADMAN. Hast?

90 FIRST MADMAN. You do give for your crest a woodcock's head with the brains picked out on 't; you are a very ancient gentleman.

THIRD MADMAN. Greek is turned Turk: we are only to be saved by the Helvetian translation.

FIRST MADMAN. Come on, sir, I will lay the law to you.

95 SECOND MADMAN. O, rather lay a corrosive: the law will eat to the bone.

THIRD MADMAN. He that drinks but to satisfy nature is damn'd.

FOURTH MADMAN. If I had my glass here, I would show a sight should make all the women here call me mad doctor.

FIRST MADMAN. What's he? a rope-maker?

100 SECOND MADMAN. No, no, no, a snuffling knave that, while he shows the tombs, will have his hand in a wench's placket.

THIRD MADMAN. Woe to the caroche that brought home my wife from the masque at three o'clock in the morning! It had a large feather-bed in it.

FOURTH MADMAN. I have pared the devil's nails forty times, roasted
105 them in raven's eggs, and cured agues with them.

THIRD MADMAN. Get me three hundred milch-bats, to make possets to procure sleep.

FOURTH MADMAN. All the college may throw their caps at me: I have made a soap-boiler costive; it was my masterpiece.

Here the dance, consisting of Eight Madmen, with music answerable thereunto; after which, BOSOLA, like an old man, enters.

110 DUCHESS. Is he mad too?

SERVANT. Pray, question him. I'll leave you.
Exeunt Servant and Madmen.

BOSOLA. I am come to make thy tomb.

DUCHESS. Ha! my tomb!
Thou speak'st as if I lay upon my death-bed,
115 Gasping for breath. Dost thou perceive me sick?

BOSOLA. Yes, and the more dangerously, since thy sickness is insensible.

DUCHESS. Thou art not mad, sure: dost know me?

BOSOLA. Yes.

DUCHESS. Who am I?

120 BOSOLA. Thou art a box of worm-seed, at best but a salvatory of green
     mummy. What's this flesh? a little crudded milk, fantastical puff-paste. Our
     bodies are weaker than those paper- prisons boys use to keep flies in; more
     contemptible, since ours is to preserve earth-worms. Didst thou ever see a
     lark in a cage? Such is the soul in the body: this world is like her little turf
125 of grass, and the heaven o'er our heads like her looking-glass, only gives us a
     miserable knowledge of the small compass of our prison.

     DUCHESS. Am not I thy duchess?

     BOSOLA. Thou art some great woman, sure, for riot begins to sit on thy
     forehead (clad in gray hairs) twenty years sooner than on a merry milk-maid's.
130 Thou sleepest worse than if a mouse should be forced to take up her lodging
     in a cat's ear: a little infant that breeds its teeth, should it lie with thee, would
     cry out, as if thou wert the more unquiet bedfellow.

     DUCHESS. I am Duchess of Malfi still.

     BOSOLA. That makes thy sleep so broken:
135 Glories, like glow-worms, afar off shine bright,
     But, look'd to near, have neither heat nor light.

     DUCHESS. Thou art very plain.

     BOSOLA. My trade is to flatter the dead, not the living;
     I am a tomb-maker.

140 DUCHESS. And thou comest to make my tomb?

     BOSOLA. Yes.

     DUCHESS. Let me be a little merry:—of what stuff wilt thou make it?

     BOSOLA. Nay, resolve me first, of what fashion?

     DUCHESS. Why, do we grow fantastical on our deathbed?
145 Do we affect fashion in the grave?

     BOSOLA. Most ambitiously. Princes' images on their tombs do not lie, as
     they were wont, seeming to pray up to heaven; but with their hands under
     their cheeks, as if they died of the tooth-ache. They are not carved with
     their eyes fix'd upon the stars, but as their minds were wholly bent upon the
150 world, the selfsame way they seem to turn their faces.

     DUCHESS. Let me know fully therefore the effect
     Of this thy dismal preparation,
     This talk fit for a charnel.

BOSOLA. Now I shall:—

    Enter Executioners, with a coffin, cords, and a bell.

155 Here is a present from your princely brothers;
And may it arrive welcome, for it brings
Last benefit, last sorrow.

DUCHESS. Let me see it:
I have so much obedience in my blood,
160 I wish it in their veins to do them good.

BOSOLA. This is your last presence-chamber.

CARIOLA. O my sweet lady!

DUCHESS. Peace; it affrights not me.

BOSOLA. I am the common bellman
165 That usually is sent to condemn'd persons
The night before they suffer.

DUCHESS. Even now thou said'st
Thou wast a tomb-maker.

BOSOLA.'Twas to bring you
170 By degrees to mortification. Listen.
Hark, now everything is still,
The screech-owl and the whistler shrill
Call upon our dame aloud,
And bid her quickly don her shroud!
175 Much you had of land and rent;
Your length in clay's now competent:
A long war disturb'd your mind;
Here your perfect peace is sign'd.
Of what is 't fools make such vain keeping?
180 Sin their conception, their birth weeping,
Their life a general mist of error,
Their death a hideous storm of terror.
Strew your hair with powders sweet,
Don clean linen, bathe your feet,
185 And (the foul fiend more to check)
A crucifix let bless your neck.
'Tis now full tide 'tween night and day;
End your groan, and come away.

CARIOLA. Hence, villains, tyrants, murderers! Alas!
190 What will you do with my lady?—Call for help!

DUCHESS. To whom? To our next neighbours? They are mad-folks.

BOSOLA. Remove that noise.

DUCHESS. Farewell, Cariola.
In my last will I have not much to give:
195 A many hungry guests have fed upon me;
Thine will be a poor reversion.

CARIOLA. I will die with her.

DUCHESS. I pray thee, look thou giv'st my little boy
Some syrup for his cold, and let the girl
200 Say her prayers ere she sleep.
Cariola is forced out by the Executioners.
Now what you please:
What death?

BOSOLA. Strangling; here are your executioners.

DUCHESS. I forgive them:
205 The apoplexy, catarrh, or cough o' th' lungs,
Would do as much as they do.

BOSOLA. Doth not death fright you?

DUCHESS. Who would be afraid on 't,
Knowing to meet such excellent company
210 In th' other world?

BOSOLA. Yet, methinks,
The manner of your death should much afflict you:
This cord should terrify you.

DUCHESS. Not a whit:
215 What would it pleasure me to have my throat cut
With diamonds? or to be smothered
With cassia? or to be shot to death with pearls?
I know death hath ten thousand several doors
For men to take their exits; and 'tis found
220 They go on such strange geometrical hinges,
You may open them both ways: any way, for heaven-sake,
So I were out of your whispering. Tell my brothers
That I perceive death, now I am well awake,
Best gift is they can give or I can take.
225 I would fain put off my last woman's-fault,
I 'd not be tedious to you.

FIRST EXECUTIONER. We are ready.

DUCHESS. Dispose my breath how please you; but my body
Bestow upon my women, will you?

230   FIRST EXECUTIONER. Yes.

DUCHESS. Pull, and pull strongly, for your able strength
Must pull down heaven upon me:—
Yet stay; heaven-gates are not so highly arch'd
As princes' palaces; they that enter there
235   Must go upon their knees. *Kneels.*—Come, violent death,
Serve for mandragora to make me sleep!—
Go tell my brothers, when I am laid out,
They then may feed in quiet.

> *They strangle her.*

BOSOLA. Where's the waiting-woman??
240   Fetch her: some other strangle the children.
> *Enter CARIOLA.*
Look you, there sleeps your mistress.

CARIOLA. O, you are damn'd
Perpetually for this!My turn is next;
Is 't not so ordered?

245   BOSOLA. Yes, and I am glad
You are so well prepar'd for 't.

CARIOLA. You are deceiv'd, sir,
I am not prepar'd for 't, I will not die;
I will first come to my answer, and know
250   How I have offended.

BOSOLA. Come, despatch her.—
You kept her counsel; now you shall keep ours.

CARIOLA. I will not die, I must not; I am contracted
To a young gentleman.

255   FIRST EXECUTIONER. Here's your wedding-ring.

CARIOLA. Let me but speak with the duke. I'll discover
Treason to his person.

BOSOLA. Delays:—throttle her.

FIRST EXECUTIONER. She bites and scratches.

250 CARIOLA. If you kill me now,
I am damn'd; I have not been at confession
This two years.

BOSOLA.(To Executioners.) When?

CARIOLA. I am quick with child.

265 BOSOLA. Why, then, your credit's saved.
Executioners strangle Cariola.
 Bear her into the next room;
Let these lie still.
Exeunt the Executioners with the body of CARIOLA.

Enter FERDINAND.

FERDINAND. Is she dead?

BOSOLA. She is what you'd have her. But here begin your pity:
Shows the Children strangled.
270 Alas, how have these offended?

FERDINAND. The death
Of young wolves is never to be pitied.

BOSOLA. Fix your eye here.

FERDINAND. Constantly.

275 BOSOLA. Do you not weep?
Other sins only speak; murder shrieks out.
The element of water moistens the earth,
But blood flies upwards and bedews the heavens.

FERDINAND. Cover her face; mine eyes dazzle: she died young.

280 BOSOLA. I think not so; her infelicity
Seem'd to have years too many.

FERDINAND. She and I were twins;
And should I die this instant, I had liv'd
Her time to a minute.

285 BOSOLA. It seems she was born first:
You have bloodily approv'd the ancient truth,
That kindred commonly do worse agree
Than remote strangers.

FERDINAND. Let me see her face

290 Again. Why didst thou not pity her? What
An excellent honest man mightst thou have been,
If thou hadst borne her to some sanctuary!
Or, bold in a good cause, oppos'd thyself,
With thy advanced sword above thy head,

295 Between her innocence and my revenge!
I bade thee, when I was distracted of my wits,
Go kill my dearest friend, and thou hast done 't.
For let me but examine well the cause:
What was the meanness of her match to me?

300 Only I must confess I had a hope,
Had she continu'd widow, to have gain'd
An infinite mass of treasure by her death:
And that was the main cause,—her marriage,
That drew a stream of gall quite through my heart.

305 For thee, as we observe in tragedies
That a good actor many times is curs'd
For playing a villain's part, I hate thee for 't,
And, for my sake, say, thou hast done much ill well.

BOSOLA. Let me quicken your memory, for I perceive
310 You are falling into ingratitude: I challenge
The reward due to my service.

FERDINAND. I'll tell thee
What I'll give thee.

BOSOLA. Do.

315 FERDINAND. I'll give thee a pardon
For this murder.

BOSOLA. Ha!

FERDINAND. Yes, and 'tis
The largest bounty I can study to do thee.
320 By what authority didst thou execute
This bloody sentence?

BOSOLA. By yours.

FERDINAND. Mine! was I her judge?
Did any ceremonial form of law
325 Doom her to not-being? Did a complete jury
Deliver her conviction up i' the court?
Where shalt thou find this judgment register'd,

Unless in hell? See, like a bloody fool,
Thou'st forfeited thy life, and thou shalt die for 't.

330 BOSOLA. The office of justice is perverted quite
When one thief hangs another. Who shall dare
To reveal this?

FERDINAND. O, I'll tell thee;
The wolf shall find her grave, and scrape it up,
335 Not to devour the corpse, but to discover
The horrid murder.

BOSOLA. You, not I, shall quake for 't.

FERDINAND. Leave me.

BOSOLA. I will first receive my pension.

340 FERDINAND. You are a villain.

BOSOLA. When your ingratitude
Is judge, I am so.

FERDINAND. O horror,
That not the fear of him which binds the devils
345 Can prescribe man obedience!—
Never look upon me more.

BOSOLA. Why, fare thee well.
Your brother and yourself are worthy men!
You have a pair of hearts are hollow graves,
350 Rotten, and rotting others; and your vengeance,
Like two chain'd-bullets, still goes arm in arm:
You may be brothers; for treason, like the plague,
Doth take much in a blood. I stand like one
That long hath ta'en a sweet and golden dream:
355 I am angry with myself, now that I wake.

FERDINAND. Get thee into some unknown part o' the world,
That I may never see thee.

BOSOLA. Let me know
Wherefore I should be thus neglected. Sir,
360 I serv'd your tyranny, and rather strove
To satisfy yourself than all the world:

And though I loath'd the evil, yet I lov'd
You that did counsel it; and rather sought
To appear a true servant than an honest man.

365   FERDINAND. I'll go hunt the badger by owl-light:
'Tis a deed of darkness.

Exit.

BOSOLA. He's much distracted. Off, my painted honour!
While with vain hopes our faculties we tire,
We seem to sweat in ice and freeze in fire.
370   What would I do, were this to do again?
I would not change my peace of conscience
For all the wealth of Europe.—She stirs; here's life:—
Return, fair soul, from darkness, and lead mine
Out of this sensible hell:—she's warm, she breathes:—
375   Upon thy pale lips I will melt my heart,
To store them with fresh colour.—Who's there?
Some cordial drink!—Alas!I dare not call:
So pity would destroy pity.—Her eye opes,
And heaven in it seems to ope, that late was shut,
380   To take me up to mercy.

DUCHESS. Antonio!

BOSOLA. Yes, madam, he is living;
The dead bodies you saw were but feign'd statues.
He's reconcil'd to your brothers; the Pope hath wrought
385   The atonement.

DUCHESS. Mercy!

Dies.

BOSOLA. O, she's gone again! there the cords of life broke.
O sacred innocence, that sweetly sleeps
On turtles' feathers, whilst a guilty conscience
390   Is a black register wherein is writ
All our good deeds and bad, a perspective
That shows us hell!That we cannot be suffer'd
To do good when we have a mind to it!
This is manly sorrow;
395   These tears, I am very certain, never grew
In my mother's milk. My estate is sunk
Below the degree of fear: where were
These penitent fountains while she was living?

O, they were frozen up! Here is a sight
400 As direful to my soul as is the sword
Unto a wretch hath slain his father.
Come, I'll bear thee hence,
And execute thy last will; that's deliver
Thy body to the reverend dispose
405 Of some good women: that the cruel tyrant
Shall not deny me. Then I'll post to Milan,
Where somewhat I will speedily enact
Worth my dejection.

Exit with the body.

ACT V
SCENE I
Enter ANTONIO and DELIO.

ANTONIO. What think you of my hope of reconcilement
To the Arragonian brethren?

DELIO. I misdoubt it;
For though they have sent their letters of safe-conduct
5 For your repair to Milan, they appear
But nets to entrap you. The Marquis of Pescara,
Under whom you hold certain land in cheat,
Much 'gainst his noble nature hath been mov'd
To seize those lands; and some of his dependants
10 Are at this instant making it their suit
To be invested in your revenues.
I cannot think they mean well to your life
That do deprive you of your means of life,
Your living.

15 ANTONIO. You are still an heretic
To any safety I can shape myself.

DELIO. Here comes the marquis: I will make myself
Petitioner for some part of your land,
To know whither it is flying.

20 ANTONIO. I pray, do.

Withdraws.

Enter PESCARA.
DELIO. Sir, I have a suit to you.

PESCARA. To me?

DELIO. An easy one:
There is the Citadel of Saint Bennet,
25 With some demesnes, of late in the possession
Of Antonio Bologna,—please you bestow them on me.

PESCARA. You are my friend; but this is such a suit,
Nor fit for me to give, nor you to take.

DELIO. No, sir?

30 PESCARA. I will give you ample reason for 't
Soon in private:—here's the cardinal's mistress.

Enter JULIA.

JULIA. My lord, I am grown your poor petitioner,
And should be an ill beggar, had I not
A great man's letter here, the cardinal's,
35 To court you in my favour.

Gives a letter.

PESCARA. He entreats for you
The Citadel of Saint Bennet, that belong'd
To the banish'd Bologna.

JULIA. Yes.

40 PESCARA. I could not have thought of a friend I could rather
Pleasure with it: 'tis yours.

JULIA. Sir, I thank you;
And he shall know how doubly I am engag'd
Both in your gift, and speediness of giving
45 Which makes your grant the greater.

Exit.

ANTONIO. How they fortify
Themselves with my ruin!

DELIO. Sir, I am
Little bound to you.

50 PESCARA. Why?

DELIO. Because you deni'd this suit to me, and gave 't
To such a creature.

PESCARA. Do you know what it was?
It was Antonio's land; not forfeited
55 By course of law, but ravish'd from his throat
By the cardinal's entreaty. It were not fit
I should bestow so main a piece of wrong
Upon my friend; 'tis a gratification
Only due to a strumpet, for it is injustice.
60 Shall I sprinkle the pure blood of innocents
To make those followers I call my friends
Look ruddier upon me? I am glad
This land, ta'en from the owner by such wrong,
Returns again unto so foul an use
65 As salary for his lust. Learn, good Delio,
To ask noble things of me, and you shall find
I'll be a noble giver.

DELIO. You instruct me well.

ANTONIO. Why, here's a man now would fright impudence from
70 sauciest beggars.

PESCARA. Prince Ferdinand's come to Milan,
Sick, as they give out, of an apoplexy;
But some say 'tis a frenzy: I am going
To visit him.

Exit.

75 ANTONIO. 'Tis a noble old fellow.

DELIO. What course do you mean to take, Antonio?

ANTONIO. This night I mean to venture all my fortune,
Which is no more than a poor ling'ring life,
To the cardinal's worst of malice. I have got
80 Private access to his chamber; and intend
To visit him about the mid of night,
As once his brother did our noble duchess.
It may be that the sudden apprehension
Of danger,—for I'll go in mine own shape,—
85 When he shall see it fraight with love and duty,
May draw the poison out of him, and work
A friendly reconcilement. If it fail,
Yet it shall rid me of this infamous calling;
For better fall once than be ever falling.

90 DELIO. I'll second you in all danger; and howe'er,
My life keeps rank with yours.

ANTONIO. You are still my lov'd and best friend.

Exeunt.

SCENE II

Enter PESCARA and DOCTOR.

PESCARA. Now, doctor, may I visit your patient?

DOCTOR. If 't please your lordship; but he's instantly
To take the air here in the gallery
By my direction.

5   PESCARA. Pray thee, what's his disease?

DOCTOR. A very pestilent disease, my lord,
They call lycanthropia.

PESCARA. What's that?
I need a dictionary to 't.

10   DOCTOR. I'll tell you.
In those that are possess'd with 't there o'erflows
Such melancholy humour they imagine
Themselves to be transformed into wolves;
Steal forth to church-yards in the dead of night,
15   And dig dead bodies up: as two nights since
One met the duke 'bout midnight in a lane
Behind Saint Mark's church, with the leg of a man
Upon his shoulder; and he howl'd fearfully;
Said he was a wolf, only the difference
20   Was, a wolf's skin was hairy on the outside,
His on the inside; bade them take their swords,
Rip up his flesh, and try. Straight I was sent for,
And, having minister'd to him, found his grace
Very well recover'd.

25   PESCARA. I am glad on 't.

DOCTOR. Yet not without some fear
Of a relapse. If he grow to his fit again,
I'll go a nearer way to work with him
Than ever Paracelsus dream'd of; if
30   They 'll give me leave, I'll buffet his madness out of him.
Stand aside; he comes.

Enter FERDINAND, CARDINAL, MALATESTI, and BOSOLA.

FERDINAND. Leave me.

MALATESTI. Why doth your lordship love this solitariness?

FERDINAND. Eagles commonly fly alone: they are crows, daws, and
35 starlings that flock together. Look, what's that follows me?

MALATESTI. Nothing, my lord.

FERDINAND. Yes.

MALATESTI. 'Tis your shadow.

FERDINAND. Stay it; let it not haunt me.

40 MALATESTI. Impossible, if you move, and the sun shine.

FERDINAND. I will throttle it.

> *Throws himself down on his shadow.*

MALATESTI. O, my lord, you are angry with nothing.

FERDINAND. You are a fool: how is 't possible I should catch my shadow,
unless I fall upon 't? When I go to hell, I mean to carry a bribe; for, look you,
45 good gifts evermore make way for the worst persons.

PESCARA. Rise, good my lord.

FERDINAND. I am studying the art of patience.

PESCARA. 'Tis a noble virtue.

FERDINAND. To drive six snails before me from this town to Moscow;
50 neither use goad nor whip to them, but let them take their own time; —the
patient'st man i' th' world match me for an experiment:— an I'll crawl after
like a sheep-biter.

CARDINAL. Force him up.

> *They raise him.*

FERDINAND. Use me well, you were best. What I have done, I have done:
55 I'll confess nothing.

DOCTOR. Now let me come to him.—Are you mad, my lord? are you out
of your princely wits?

FERDINAND. What's he?

PESCARA. Your doctor.

60 FERDINAND. Let me have his beard saw'd off, and his eye-brows fil'd
more civil.

DOCTOR. I must do mad tricks with him, for that's the only way on 't.—I
have brought your grace a salamander's skin to keep you from sun-burning.

FERDINAND. I have cruel sore eyes.

65 DOCTOR. The white of a cockatrix's egg is present remedy.

FERDINAND. Let it be a new-laid one, you were best.
Hide me from him: physicians are like kings,—
They brook no contradiction.

DOCTOR. Now he begins to fear me: now let me alone with him.

70 CARDINAL. How now! put off your gown!

DOCTOR. Let me have some forty urinals filled with rosewater: he and
I'll go pelt one another with them.—Now he begins to fear me.—Can you
fetch a frisk, sir?—Let him go, let him go, upon my peril: I find by his eye
he stands in awe of me; I'll make him as tame as a dormouse.

75 FERDINAND. Can you fetch your frisks, sir!—I will stamp him into a
cullis, flay off his skin to cover one of the anatomies this rogue hath set i'
th' cold yonder in Barber-Chirurgeon's-hall. —Hence, hence! you are all of
you like beasts for sacrifice.
                              Throws the DOCTOR down and beats him.
There's nothing left of you but tongue and belly, flattery and lechery.
                                                                    Exit.

80 PESCARA. Doctor, he did not fear you thoroughly.

DOCTOR. True; I was somewhat too forward.

BOSOLA. Mercy upon me, what a fatal judgment
Hath fall'n upon this Ferdinand!

PESCARA. Knows your grace
85 What accident hath brought unto the prince
This strange distraction?

CARDINAL. (Aside.) I must feign somewhat.—Thus they say it grew.
You have heard it rumour'd, for these many years
None of our family dies but there is seen
90 The shape of an old woman, which is given
By tradition to us to have been murder'd

By her nephews for her riches. Such a figure
One night, as the prince sat up late at's book,
Appear'd to him; when crying out for help,
95 The gentleman of's chamber found his grace
All on a cold sweat, alter'd much in face
And language: since which apparition,
He hath grown worse and worse, and I much fear
He cannot live.

100 BOSOLA. Sir, I would speak with you.

PESCARA. We 'll leave your grace,
Wishing to the sick prince, our noble lord,
All health of mind and body.

CARDINAL. You are most welcome.
Exeunt PESCARA, MALATESTI, and DOCTOR.
105 Are you come? so.—(Aside.) This fellow must not know
By any means I had intelligence
In our duchess' death; for, though I counsell'd it,
The full of all th' engagement seem'd to grow
]From Ferdinand.—Now, sir, how fares our sister?
110 I do not think but sorrow makes her look
Like to an oft-dy'd garment: she shall now
Take comfort from me. Why do you look so wildly?
O, the fortune of your master here the prince
Dejects you; but be you of happy comfort:
115 If you 'll do one thing for me I'll entreat,
Though he had a cold tomb-stone o'er his bones,
I 'd make you what you would be.

BOSOLA. Any thing;
Give it me in a breath, and let me fly to 't.
120 They that think long small expedition win,
For musing much o' th' end cannot begin.

Enter JULIA.

JULIA. Sir, will you come into supper?

CARDINAL. I am busy; leave me.

JULIA (Aside.) What an excellent shape hath that fellow!
Exit.

125 CARDINAL. 'Tis thus. Antonio lurks here in Milan:
Inquire him out, and kill him. While he lives,
Our sister cannot marry; and I have thought

Of an excellent match for her. Do this, and style me
Thy advancement.

130 BOSOLA. But by what means shall I find him out?

CARDINAL. There is a gentleman call'd Delio
Here in the camp, that hath been long approv'd
His loyal friend. Set eye upon that fellow;
Follow him to mass; may be Antonio,
135 Although he do account religion
But a school-name, for fashion of the world
May accompany him; or else go inquire out
Delio's confessor, and see if you can bribe
Him to reveal it. There are a thousand ways
140 A man might find to trace him; as to know
What fellows haunt the Jews for taking up
Great sums of money, for sure he's in want;
Or else to go to the picture-makers, and learn
Who bought her picture lately: some of these
145 Happily may take.

BOSOLA. Well, I'll not freeze i' th' business:
I would see that wretched thing, Antonio,
Above all sights i' th' world.

CARDINAL. Do, and be happy.

Exit.

150 BOSOLA. This fellow doth breed basilisks in's eyes,
He's nothing else but murder; yet he seems
Not to have notice of the duchess' death.
'Tis his cunning: I must follow his example;
There cannot be a surer way to trace
155 Than that of an old fox.

Re-enter JULIA, with a pistol.

JULIA. So, sir, you are well met.

BOSOLA. How Now!

JULIA. Nay, the doors are fast enough:
Now, sir, I will make you confess your treachery.

160 BOSOLA. Treachery!

JULIA. Yes, confess to me
Which of my women 'twas you hir'd to put
Love-powder into my drink?

BOSOLA. Love-powder!

165 JULIA. Yes, when I was at Malfi.
Why should I fall in love with such a face else?
I have already suffer'd for thee so much pain,
The only remedy to do me good
Is to kill my longing.

170 BOSOLA. Sure, your pistol holds
Nothing but perfumes or kissing-comfits.
Excellent lady!
You have a pretty way on 't to discover
Your longing. Come, come, I'll disarm you,
175 And arm you thus: yet this is wondrous strange.

JULIA. Compare thy form and my eyes together,
You 'll find my love no such great miracle.
Now you 'll say
I am wanton: this nice modesty in ladies
180 Is but a troublesome familiar
That haunts them.

BOSOLA. Know you me, I am a blunt soldier.

JULIA. The better:
Sure, there wants fire where there are no lively sparks
185 Of roughness.

BOSOLA. And I want compliment.

JULIA. Why, ignorance
In courtship cannot make you do amiss,
If you have a heart to do well.

190 BOSOLA. You are very fair.

JULIA. Nay, if you lay beauty to my charge,
I must plead unguilty.

BOSOLA. Your bright eyes
Carry a quiver of darts in them sharper
195 Than sun-beams.

JULIA. You will mar me with commendation,
Put yourself to the charge of courting me,
Whereas now I woo you.

BOSOLA. (Aside.) I have it, I will work upon this creature.—
200 Let us grow most amorously familiar:
     If the great cardinal now should see me thus,
     Would he not count me a villain?

     JULIA. No; he might count me a wanton,
     Not lay a scruple of offence on you;
205 For if I see and steal a diamond,
     The fault is not i' th' stone, but in me the thief
     That purloins it. I am sudden with you.
     We that are great women of pleasure use to cut off
     These uncertain wishes and unquiet longings,
210 And in an instant join the sweet delight
     And the pretty excuse together. Had you been i' th' street,
     Under my chamber-window, even there
     I should have courted you.

     BOSOLA. O, you are an excellent lady!

215 JULIA. Bid me do somewhat for you presently
     To express I love you.

     BOSOLA. I will; and if you love me,
     Fail not to effect it.
     The cardinal is grown wondrous melancholy;
220 Demand the cause, let him not put you off
     With feign'd excuse; discover the main ground on 't.

     JULIA. Why would you know this?

     BOSOLA. I have depended on him,
     And I hear that he is fall'n in some disgrace
225 With the emperor: if he be, like the mice
     That forsake falling houses, I would shift
     To other dependance.

     JULIA. You shall not need
     Follow the wars: I'll be your maintenance.

230 BOSOLA. And I your loyal servant: but I cannot
     Leave my calling.

     JULIA. Not leave an ungrateful
     General for the love of a sweet lady!
     You are like some cannot sleep in feather-beds,
235 But must have blocks for their pillows.

BOSOLA. Will you do this?

JULIA. Cunningly.

BOSOLA. To-morrow I'll expect th' intelligence.

JULIA. To-morrow! get you into my cabinet;
240 You shall have it with you. Do not delay me,
No more than I do you: I am like one
That is condemn'd; I have my pardon promis'd,
But I would see it seal'd. Go, get you in:
You shall see my wind my tongue about his heart
245 Like a skein of silk.

Exit BOSOLA.

Re-enter CARDINAL.

CARDINAL. Where are you?

Enter Servants.

SERVANTS. Here.

CARDINAL. Let none, upon your lives, have conference
With the Prince Ferdinand, unless I know it.—
250 (Aside.) In this distraction he may reveal
The murder.

Exeunt Servants.

Yond's my lingering consumption:
I am weary of her, and by any means
Would be quit of.

255 JULIA. How now, my lord! what ails you?

CARDINAL. Nothing.

JULIA. O, you are much alter'd:
Come, I must be your secretary, and remove
This lead from off your bosom: what's the matter?

260 CARDINAL. I may not tell you.

JULIA. Are you so far in love with sorrow
You cannot part with part of it? Or think you
I cannot love your grace when you are sad
As well as merry? Or do you suspect
265 I, that have been a secret to your heart

These many winters, cannot be the same
Unto your tongue?

CARDINAL. Satisfy thy longing,—
The only way to make thee keep my counsel
270   Is, not to tell thee.

JULIA. Tell your echo this,
Or flatterers, that like echoes still report
What they hear though most imperfect, and not me;
For if that you be true unto yourself,
275   I'll know.

CARDINAL. Will you rack me?

JULIA. No, judgment shall
Draw it from you: it is an equal fault,
To tell one's secrets unto all or none.

280   CARDINAL. The first argues folly.

JULIA. But the last tyranny.

CARDINAL. Very well: why, imagine I have committed
Some secret deed which I desire the world
May never hear of.

285   JULIA. Therefore may not I know it?
You have conceal'd for me as great a sin
As adultery. Sir, never was occasion
For perfect trial of my constancy
Till now: sir, I beseech you——

290   CARDINAL. You 'll repent it.

JULIA. Never.

CARDINAL. It hurries thee to ruin: I'll not tell thee.
Be well advis'd, and think what danger 'tis
To receive a prince's secrets. They that do,
295   Had need have their breasts hoop'd with adamant
To contain them. I pray thee, yet be satisfi'd;
Examine thine own frailty; 'tis more easy
To tie knots than unloose them. 'Tis a secret
That, like a ling'ring poison, may chance lie
300   Spread in thy veins, and kill thee seven year hence.

JULIA. Now you dally with me.

CARDINAL. No more; thou shalt know it.
By my appointment the great Duchess of Malfi
And two of her young children, four nights since,
305   Were strangl'd.

JULIA. O heaven! sir, what have you done!

CARDINAL. How now? How settles this? Think you your bosom
Will be a grave dark and obscure enough
For such a secret?

310   JULIA. You have undone yourself, sir.

CARDINAL. Why?

JULIA. It lies not in me to conceal it.

CARDINAL. No? Come, I will swear you to 't upon this book.

JULIA. Most religiously.

315   CARDINAL. Kiss it.

She kisses the book.

Now you shall never utter it; thy curiosity
Hath undone thee; thou 'rt poison'd with that book.
Because I knew thou couldst not keep my counsel,
I have bound thee to 't by death.

Re-enter BOSOLA.

320   BOSOLA. For pity-sake, hold!

CARDINAL. Ha, Bosola!

JULIA. I forgive you
This equal piece of justice you have done;
For I betray'd your counsel to that fellow.
325   He over-heard it; that was the cause I said
It lay not in me to conceal it.

BOSOLA. O foolish woman,
Couldst not thou have poison'd him?

JULIA. 'Tis weakness,
330   Too much to think what should have been done. I go, I know not whither.

Dies.

CARDINAL. Wherefore com'st thou hither?

BOSOLA. That I might find a great man like yourself,
Not out of his wits, as the Lord Ferdinand,
To remember my service.

335 CARDINAL. I'll have thee hew'd in pieces.

BOSOLA. Make not yourself such a promise of that life
Which is not yours to dispose of.

CARDINAL. Who plac'd thee here?

BOSOLA. Her lust, as she intended.

340 CARDINAL. Very well:
Now you know me for your fellow-murderer.

BOSOLA. And wherefore should you lay fair marble colours
Upon your rotten purposes to me?
Unless you imitate some that do plot great treasons,
345 And when they have done, go hide themselves i' th' grave
Of those were actors in 't?

CARDINAL. No more; there is
A fortune attends thee.

BOSOLA. Shall I go sue to Fortune any longer?
350 'Tis the fool's pilgrimage.

CARDINAL. I have honours in store for thee.

BOSOLA. There are a many ways that conduct to seeming
Honour, and some of them very dirty ones.

CARDINAL. Throw to the devil
355 Thy melancholy. The fire burns well;
What need we keep a stirring of 't, and make
A greater smother? Thou wilt kill Antonio?

BOSOLA. Yes.

CARDINAL. Take up that body.

360 BOSOLA. I think I shall
Shortly grow the common bier for church-yards.

CARDINAL. I will allow thee some dozen of attendants
To aid thee in the murder.

BOSOLA. O, by no means. Physicians that apply horse-leeches to any rank
365   swelling use to cut off their tails, that the blood may run through them the
faster: let me have no train when I go to shed blood, less it make me have a
greater when I ride to the gallows.

CARDINAL. Come to me after midnight, to help to remove
That body to her own lodging. I'll give out
370   She died o' th' plague; 'twill breed the less inquiry
After her death.

BOSOLA. Where's Castruccio her husband?

CARDINAL. He's rode to Naples, to take possession
Of Antonio's citadel.

375   BOSOLA. Believe me, you have done a very happy turn.

CARDINAL. Fail not to come. There is the master-key
Of our lodgings; and by that you may conceive
What trust I plant in you.

BOSOLA. You shall find me ready.
Exit CARDINAL.

380   O poor Antonio, though nothing be so needful
To thy estate as pity, yet I find
Nothing so dangerous!I must look to my footing:
In such slippery ice-pavements men had need
To be frost-nail'd well, they may break their necks else;
385   The precedent's here afore me. How this man
Bears up in blood! seems fearless!Why, 'tis well;
Security some men call the suburbs of hell,
Only a dead wall between. Well, good Antonio,
I'll seek thee out; and all my care shall be
390   To put thee into safety from the reach
Of these most cruel biters that have got
Some of thy blood already. It may be,
I'll join with thee in a most just revenge.
The weakest arm is strong enough that strikes
395   With the sword of justice. Still methinks the duchess
Haunts me: there, there!—'Tis nothing but my melancholy.
O Penitence, let me truly taste thy cup,
That throws men down only to raise them up!
Exit.

SCENE III

Enter ANTONIO and DELIO. Echo from the DUCHESS'S Grave.

DELIO. Yond's the cardinal's window. This fortification
Grew from the ruins of an ancient abbey;
And to yond side o' th' river lies a wall,
Piece of a cloister, which in my opinion
5 Gives the best echo that you ever heard,
So hollow and so dismal, and withal
So plain in the distinction of our words,
That many have suppos'd it is a spirit
That answers.

10 ANTONIO. I do love these ancient ruins.
We never tread upon them but we set
Our foot upon some reverend history;
And, questionless, here in this open court,
Which now lies naked to the injuries
15 Of stormy weather, some men lie interr'd
Lov'd the church so well, and gave so largely to 't,
They thought it should have canopied their bones
Till dooms-day. But all things have their end;
Churches and cities, which have diseases like to men,
20 Must have like death that we have.

ECHO. Like death that we have.

DELIO. Now the echo hath caught you.

ANTONIO. It groan'd methought, and gave
A very deadly accent.

25 ECHO. Deadly accent.

DELIO. I told you 'twas a pretty one. You may make it
A huntsman, or a falconer, a musician,
Or a thing of sorrow.

ECHO. A thing of sorrow.

30 ANTONIO. Ay, sure, that suits it best.

ECHO. That suits it best.

ANTONIO. 'Tis very like my wife's voice.

ECHO. Ay, wife's voice.

DELIO. Come, let us walk further from t.
35 I would not have you go to the cardinal's to-night:
Do not.

ECHO. Do not.

DELIO. Wisdom doth not more moderate wasting sorrow
Than time. Take time for 't; be mindful of thy safety.

40 ECHO. Be mindful of thy safety.

ANTONIO. Necessity compels me.
Make scrutiny through the passages
Of your own life, you 'll find it impossible
To fly your fate.

45 ECHO. O, fly your fate!

DELIO. Hark! the dead stones seem to have pity on you,
And give you good counsel.

ANTONIO. Echo, I will not talk with thee,
For thou art a dead thing.

50 ECHO. Thou art a dead thing.

ANTONIO. My duchess is asleep now,
And her little ones, I hope sweetly. O heaven,
Shall I never see her more?

ECHO. Never see her more.

55 ANTONIO. I mark'd not one repetition of the echo
But that; and on the sudden a clear light
Presented me a face folded in sorrow.

DELIO. Your fancy merely.

ANTONIO. Come, I'll be out of this ague,
60 For to live thus is not indeed to live;
It is a mockery and abuse of life.
I will not henceforth save myself by halves;
Lose all, or nothing.

DELIO. Your own virtue save you!
65 I'll fetch your eldest son, and second you.
It may be that the sight of his own blood

Spread in so sweet a figure may beget
The more compassion. However, fare you well.
Though in our miseries Fortune have a part,
70   Yet in our noble sufferings she hath none.
Contempt of pain, that we may call our own.

Exeunt.

Scene IV
Enter CARDINAL, PESCARA, MALATESTI, RODERIGO, and
GRISOLAN.

CARDINAL. You shall not watch to-night by the sick prince;
His grace is very well recover'd.

MALATESTI. Good my lord, suffer us.

CARDINAL. O, by no means;
5   The noise, and change of object in his eye,
Doth more distract him. I pray, all to bed;
And though you hear him in his violent fit,
Do not rise, I entreat you.

PESCARA. So, sir; we shall not.

10   CARDINAL. Nay, I must have you promise
Upon your honours, for I was enjoin'd to 't
By himself; and he seem'd to urge it sensibly.

PESCARA. Let our honours bind this trifle.

CARDINAL. Nor any of your followers.

15   MALATESTI. Neither.

CARDINAL. It may be, to make trial of your promise,
When he's asleep, myself will rise and feign
Some of his mad tricks, and cry out for help,
And feign myself in danger.

20   MALATESTI. If your throat were cutting,
I 'd not come at you, now I have protested against it.

CARDINAL. Why, I thank you.

GRISOLAN. 'Twas a foul storm to-night.

RODERIGO. The Lord Ferdinand's chamber shook like an osier.

25 MALATESTI. 'Twas nothing put pure kindness in the devil
To rock his own child.

Exeunt all except the CARDINAL.

CARDINAL. The reason why I would not suffer these
About my brother, is, because at midnight
I may with better privacy convey
30 Julia's body to her own lodging. O, my conscience!
I would pray now; but the devil takes away my heart
For having any confidence in prayer.
About this hour I appointed Bosola
To fetch the body. When he hath serv'd my turn, he dies.

Exit.

Enter BOSOLA.

35 BOSOLA. Ha! 'twas the cardinal's voice; I heard him name
Bosola and my death. Listen; I hear one's footing.

Enter FERDINAND.

FERDINAND. Strangling is a very quiet death.

BOSOLA. (Aside.) Nay, then, I see I must stand upon my guard.

FERDINAND. What say to that? Whisper softly: do you agree to 't?
40 So; it must be done i' th' dark; the cardinal would not for
a thousand pounds the doctor should see it.

Exit.

BOSOLA. My death is plotted; here's the consequence of murder.
We value not desert nor Christian breath,
When we know black deeds must be cur'd with death.

Enter ANTONIO and Servant.

45 SERVANT. Here stay, sir, and be confident, I pray; I'll fetch you a dark lantern.

Exit.

ANTONIO. Could I take him at his prayers,
There were hope of pardon.

BOSOLA. Fall right, my sword!—

Stabs him.

I'll not give thee so much leisure as to pray.

50 ANTONIO. O, I am gone! Thou hast ended a long suit in a minute.

BOSOLA. What art thou?

ANTONIO. A most wretched thing,
That only have thy benefit in death,
To appear myself.

Re-enter Servant with a lantern.

55   SERVANT. Where are you, sir?

ANTONIO. Very near my home.—Bosola!

SERVANT. O, misfortune!

BOSOLA. Smother thy pity, thou art dead else.—Antonio!
The man I would have sav'd 'bove mine own life!
60   We are merely the stars' tennis-balls, struck and banded
Which way please them.—O good Antonio,
I'll whisper one thing in thy dying ear
Shall make thy heart break quickly! Thy fair duchess
And two sweet children——

65   ANTONIO. Their very names kindle a little life in me.

BOSOLA. Are murder'd.

ANTONIO. Some men have wish'd to die
At the hearing of sad tidings; I am glad
That I shall do 't in sadness.would not now
70   Wish my wounds balm'd nor heal'd, for I have no use
To put my life to. In all our quest of greatness,
Like wanton boys whose pastime is their care,
We follow after bubbles blown in th' air.
Pleasure of life, what is 't? Only the good hours
75   Of an ague; merely a preparative to rest,
To endure vexation. I do not ask
The process of my death; only commend me to Delio.

BOSOLA. Break, heart!

ANTONIO. And let my son fly the courts to princes.

Dies.

80   BOSOLA. Thou seem'st to have lov'd Antonio.

SERVANT. I brought him hither,
To have reconcil'd him to the cardinal.

BOSOLA. I do not ask thee that.
Take him up, if thou tender thine own life,
85 And bear him where the lady Julia
Was wont to lodge.—O, my fate moves swift!
I have this cardinal in the forge already;
Now I'll bring him to th' hammer. O direful misprision!
I will not imitate things glorious.
90 No more than base; I'll be mine own example.—
On, on, and look thou represent, for silence,
The thing thou bear'st.

Exeunt.

SCENE V

Enter CARDINAL, with a book.

CARDINAL. I am puzzl'd in a question about hell;
He says, in hell there's one material fire,
And yet it shall not burn all men alike.
Lay him by. How tedious is a guilty conscience!
5 When I look into the fish-ponds in my garden,
Methinks I see a thing arm'd with a rake,
That seems to strike at me.

   Enter BOSOLA, and Servant bearing ANTONIO'S body.

Now, art thou come?
Thou look'st ghastly;
10 There sits in thy face some great determination
Mix'd with some fear.

BOSOLA. Thus it lightens into action:
I am come to kill thee.

CARDINAL. Ha!—Help! our guard!

15 BOSOLA. Thou art deceiv'd; they are out of thy howling.

CARDINAL. Hold; and I will faithfully divide revenues with thee.

BOSOLA. Thy prayers and proffers
Are both unseasonable.

CARDINAL. Raise the watch! We are betray'd!

20 BOSOLA. I have confin'd your flight: I'll suffer your retreat to Julia's
chamber, but no further.

CARDINAL. Help! we are betray'd!

Enter, above, PESCARA, MALATESTI, RODERIGO, and GRISOLAN.

MALATESTI. Listen.

CARDINAL. My dukedom for rescue!

25   RODERIGO. Fie upon his counterfeiting!

MALATESTI. Why, 'tis not the cardinal.

RODERIGO. Yes, yes, 'tis he: But, I'll see him hang'd ere I'll go down to him.

CARDINAL. Here's a plot upon me; I am assaulted! I am lost, unless some rescue!

30   GRISOLAN. He doth this pretty well; but it will not serve to laugh me out of mine honour.

CARDINAL. The sword's at my throat!

RODERIGO. You would not bawl so loud then.

MALATESTI. Come, come, let's go to bed: he told us this much aforehand.

35   PESCARA. He wish'd you should not come at him; but, believe 't, the accent of the voice sounds not in jest: I'll down to him, howsoever, and with engines force ope the doors.

Exit above.

RODERIGO. Let's follow him aloof, and note how the cardinal will laugh at him.

Exeunt, above, MALATESTI, RODERIGO, and GRISOLAN.

40   BOSOLA. There's for you first, 'cause you shall not unbarricade the door to let in rescue.

Kills the Servant.

CARDINAL. What cause hast thou to pursue my life?

BOSOLA. Look there.

CARDINAL. Antonio!

45   BOSOLA. Slain by my hand unwittingly. Pray, and be sudden. When thou kill'd'st thy sister, thou took'st from Justice her most equal balance, and left her naught but her sword.

CARDINAL. O, mercy!

BOSOLA. Now it seems thy greatness was only outward; for thou fall'st fast-
50   er of thyself than calamity can drive thee. I'll not waste longer time; there!

Stabs him.

CARDINAL. Thou hast hurt me.

BOSOLA. Again!

CARDINAL. Shall I die like a leveret, without any resistance?—Help, help, help! I am slain!

Enter FERDINAND.

55 FERDINAND. Th' alarum! Give me a fresh horse; rally the vaunt-guard, or the day is lost, yield, yield! I give you the honour of arms, shake my sword over you; will you yield?

CARDINAL. Help me; I am your brother!

FERDINAND. The devil! My brother fight upon the adverse party!
  He wounds the CARDINAL, and, in the scuffle, gives BOSOLA his death-wound.
60 There flies your ransom.

CARDINAL. O justice! I suffer now for what hath former bin: sorrow is held the eldest child of sin.

FERDINAND. Now you're brave fellows. Caesar's fortune was harder than Pompey's; Caesar died in the arms of prosperity, Pompey at the feet of
65 disgrace. You both died in the field. The pain's nothing; pain many times is taken away with the apprehension of greater, as the tooth-ache with the sight of a barber that comes to pull it out. There's philosophy for you.

BOSOLA. Now my revenge is perfect.—Sink, thou main cause
Kills FERDINAND.
Of my undoing!—The last part of my life hath done me best service.

70 FERDINAND. Give me some wet hay; I am broken-winded. I do account this world but a dog-kennel: I will vault credit and affect high pleasures beyond death.

BOSOLA. He seems to come to himself, now he's so near the bottom.

FERDINAND. My sister, O my sister! there's the cause on 't. Whether we
75 fall by ambition, blood, or lust, like diamonds, we are cut with our own dust.
Dies.

CARDINAL. Thou hast thy payment too.

BOSOLA. Yes, I hold my weary soul in my teeth; 'tis ready to part from me. I do glory that thou, which stood'st like a huge pyramid begun upon a large and ample base, shalt end in a little point, a kind of nothing.

Enter, below, PESCARA, MALATESTI, RODERIGO, and GRISOLAN.

80   PESCARA. How now, my lord!

MALATESTI. O sad disaster!

RODERIGO. How comes this?

BOSOLA. Revenge for the Duchess of Malfi murdered by the Arragonian
brethren; for Antonio slain by this hand; for lustful Julia poison'd by this
85   man; and lastly for myself, that was an actor in the main of all much 'gainst
mine own good nature, yet i' the end neglected.

PESCARA. How now, my lord!

CARDINAL. Look to my brother: he gave us these large wounds, as we
were struggling here i' th' rushes. And now, I pray, let me be laid by and never
90   thought of.

Dies.

PESCARA. How fatally, it seems, he did withstand his own rescue!

MALATESTI. Thou wretched thing of blood, how came Antonio by his death?

BOSOLA. In a mist; I know not how: such a mistake as I have often seen
in a play. O, I am gone! We are only like dead walls or vaulted graves, that,
95   ruin'd, yield no echo. Fare you well. It may be pain, but no harm, to me to
die in so good a quarrel. O, this gloomy world! In what a shadow, or deep
pit of darkness, doth womanish and fearful mankind live! Let worthy minds
ne'er stagger in distrust to suffer death or shame for what is just: mine is
another voyage.

Dies.

100   PESCARA. The noble Delio, as I came to th' palace, told me of Antonio's
being here, and show'd me a pretty gentleman, his son and heir.

Enter DELIO, and ANTONIO'S Son.

MALATESTI. O sir, you come too late!

DELIO. I heard so, and was arm'd for 't, ere I came. Let us make noble
use of this great ruin; and join all our force to establish this young hopeful
105   gentleman in's mother's right. These wretched eminent things leave no more
fame behind 'em, than should one fall in a frost, and leave his print in snow;
as soon as the sun shines, it ever melts, both form and matter. I have ever
thought Nature doth nothing so great for great men as when she's pleas'd to
make them lords of truth: integrity of life is fame's best friend, which nobly,
110   beyond death, shall crown the end.

Exeunt.

The Seventeenth Century

Abstract

The early seventeenth century was a tumultuous period in Britain. After Elizabeth I's almost 45-year reign, the Stuart kings were tasked with continuing the stability that she established. James I experienced limited success, dealing with financial troubles that started before his time, factionalism in his government, and increasing unpopularity. James did, however, enjoy plays and court masques, establishing himself as a significant patron of the arts. His son Charles I's reign was so disastrous that the monarchy was dissolved for eleven years and the idea of the divine right of kings was shattered—England became ruled by a commonwealth and then a protectorate before restoring its monarchy in 1660. The Wars of the Three Kingdoms, comprising many smaller conflicts within England, Ireland and Scotland, killed around 6% of Britain's population over fourteen years. Puritan control caused Parliament to shut down London's theaters. As could be expected, most of the literature from this later period deals with the issues Britain faced, whether this be discussions of war, religion, politics, or the nation's identity. Opposing camps of writers formed from those that supported the monarchy versus those that supported Parliament. Major authors like John Milton became increasingly drawn into political currents.

King James VI and I: the Jacobean Period

Born James Charles Stuart in 1556, James became King James VI of Scotland at the age of one upon the exile of his mother Mary, Queen of Scots. As King of Scotland, regents controlled James until he began to govern personally at about age sixteen. James was able to establish a relative peace amidst the Scottish lords, who were often crippled by infighting. He also had a good diplomatic relationhip with England. Queen Elizabeth executed James's mother Mary, Queen of Scots in 1587, but also sent James an annual subsidy starting in 1586. Rumors consistently circulated that James was gay; he was, indeed, close with several male favorites throughout his life. However, in 1589 he married Anne of Denmark, the fourteen-year-old daughter of King Frederick II of Denmark. Between 1594 and 1606 they would go have seven children, three of whom survived infancy.

James became King James I of England when Queen Elizabeth I died in 1603. The English people feared that the childless Elizabeth's death would cause a succession crisis, but none came since the Queen and her chief ministers had corresponded with James for years in preparation for him to assume the throne. His ascension was announced the same day Elizabeth died, 24 March 1603, to much celebration in London. Though his coronation went smoothly, two plots to kidnap the King failed in the first year of his reign.

James retained Elizabeth's important advisors, such as Robert Cecil, on the Privy Council but also added several Scottish nobles. He chose new English advisors as well, like Henry Howard, who later became Earl of Northampton. After James ascended the throne, he immediately began supporting the arts. He became the patron of William Shakespeare's acting, and throughout his reign he commissioner court masques, festive pageants with elaborate music, dance, costuming, and sets.

King James felt strongly that England and Scotland should be a single nation governed by one parliament, a view opposed by the parliaments of both countries. He styled himself "King of Great Britain" in official Scottish business and on coinage in both kingdoms, though Parliament prevented him from using the title officially in England. James was more politically successful abroad in his 1604 treaty with Spain, the Treaty of London, which established peace after nineteen years. Robert Cecil and Henry Howard were instrumental in the treaty's success.

The King also sponsored an updated *Book of Common Prayer* in 1604, establishing further reforms in the Church of England. The most serious attempt on James's life, the Gunpowder Plot, occurred in 1605. A group of Roman Catholic conspirators led by Robert Catesby planned to blow up the House of Lords during the opening of a new session of Parliament when the King would be in attendance. They then wanted to install the nine-year-old Princess Elizabeth, James's second child, on the throne. The plot was discovered through an anonymous tip; the conspirators, including Guy Fawkes, were hanged then drawn and quartered while still alive, a tortuous method of execution. In response to the plot, Parliament passed the Popish Recusants Act requiring subjects to explicitly swear allegiance to the King over the Pope. James, however, remained privately tolerant of Catholics as long as they swore the oath.

James also supported exploration and colonization. In 1607, England established the Jamestown Colony in Virginia. It was the first successful English colony in the modern-day United States after the failure of the Roanoke Colony. Colonization of North America continued throughout the seventeenth century.

Expenditures resulting from James's varied interests often resulted in a strained relationship with his Parliament. He incurred significant debt which Parliament was reluctant to finance. In 1610, James dismissed Parliament after they failed to reach a financial agreement, while the failure of 1614's so-called Addled Parliament to pass any bills at all led the King to rule without Parliamentary assistance until 1621.

In 1611, the *King James Bible* was published to public approbation. This poetic translation, which James sponsored, remains in widespread use today. In 1612, James's eldest son Henry Frederick died of typhoid fever at the age of eighteen, leaving second-son Charles as heir to the throne. Diplomatic successes abroad continued with Princess Elizabeth's marriage to Frederick V, a prince of the German kingdom of Bohemia.

James's own relationship with his most important favorite, George Villiers, later the Duke of Buckingham, began in 1614. Villiers was one of the most influential members of James's court, and his relationship with the King was controversial. In 1617, James justified his public friendship with Villiers to the Privy Council:

> I, James, am neither a god nor an angel, but a man like any other. Therefore I act like a man and confess to loving those dear to me more than other men. You may be sure that I love the Earl of Buckingham more than anyone else, and more than you who are here assembled. I wish to speak in my own behalf and not to have it thought to be a defect, for Jesus Christ did the same, and therefore I cannot be blamed. Christ had John, and I have George.

Having experienced a rocky start and a successful midseason, King James's reign became more troubled in its latter half. In 1615, the public speculated that some of James's advisors murdered essayist and courtier Thomas Overbury over a romantic affair with another courtier's wife. As a result, James's court developed a reputation for corruption, factionalism, and dysfunction.

Additionally, issues arose in foreign policy. James visited Scotland in 1617 for the only time during his English reign, attempting to reform the Scottish Kirk (church) to become more Anglican. The Kirk, however, strongly opposed this change. In 1618, James allowed the execution of the popular courtier Sir Walter Raleigh because he engaged in battle with Spanish forces in South America against the King's instructions. The English public widely opposed the execution, which was seen as an unfair appeasement of Spain. The rest of Europe was also in conflict—the Thirty Years' War started over Catholicism in 1618, with most of the German kingdoms, Scandinavia, and the Netherlands on one side versus Spain and the Holy Roman Empire on the other.

In 1621, James finally called Parliament back into session in an attempt to fund assistance for the Protestants, specifically his son-in-law Frederick V of Bohemia, in the Thirty Years' War. Parliament asked the King to declare war on Spain and marry his son Charles to a Protestant. James refused, dissolving Parliament again. This issue continued in 1623, when Charles travelled to Spain with George Villiers to arrange a wedding between Charles and Maria Anna, a daughter of King Philip III. Maria Anna refused to marry a Protestant. Charles and Villiers, who had become an increasingly powerful faction, pressured James throughout the rest of his reign to recall Parliament and declare war on Spain.

King James's health declined quickly beginning in 1624. Suffering from multiple diseases including malaria, arthritis, and gout, he died on March 27th, 1625, of dysentery at the age of 58. Despite the failures of his later reign, James was widely mourned and the recipient of a magnificent funeral. He was buried in Westminster Abbey alongside his wife, who had died in 1619, in the vault of Henry VII.

KING CHARLES I: THE CAROLINE PERIOD

Born in 1600 as the second son of King James I, Charles's chances of becoming regent were slim until his older brother, Henry Frederick, died of typhoid in 1612. Charles was a sickly child who stood five feet four inches tall as an adult. During his father's reign, Charles had hoped to marry Princess Maria Anna of Spain, but negotiations with Catholic Spain became unpopular with the English people. Having become close with his father's favorite George Villiers, he and Villiers pressured James to declare war on Spain at the end of James's reign.

After King James died in March 1625, Charles ascended the throne as King Charles I of England, Scotland, and Ireland. He was married in May to Henrietta Maria of France, a Catholic who did not attend his coronation because it was a Protestant ceremony. Charles immediately began having problems with Parliament—his first parliament became known as the Useless Parliament, as it met for only two months. Charles lied to this body, promising not to loosen religious restrictions on Catholics, while simultaneously promising to do so in his marriage treaty. Additionally, though Charles had been advocating for war with Spain prior to his father's death, Parliament only approved funds to attack Spanish colonies in the Americas.

George Villiers remained Charles's close advisor after James's death. Villiers became, however, increasingly unpopular with Parliament and the Privy Council. He led a failed naval expedition against Spain shortly after Charles's ascension to the throne after which the House of Commons began attempting to remove him from power. The following year, Parliament asked Charles to remove Villiers from court, causing Charles to dissolve the assembly again. In 1627, Villiers led another unsuccessful attack, this time to defend Protestants in France. He was assassinated in 1628, which devastated the King but prevented war with Spain.

In 1625 Charles passed the Act of Revocation in Scotland, which reclaimed for the Crown all land given to lords by the Crown and the Church since 1540. This made Charles very unpopular in Scotland. The next year saw the beginning of the six-year-long Western Rising, a series of rebellions in the west of England, ensuing from Charles's enclosure and sale of previously protected forest land. This involved seizing land that had been public for the crown, then selling it to private owners. The tactic resulted from Charles's efforts to raise money himself rather than cooperating with Parliament. In 1627, he levied a tax without Parliamentary concession, causing the assembly to pass the Petition of Right, which asserted that Charles could not levy taxes without permission, use martial law to imprison civilians without due process, or force citizens to quarter soldiers in their homes. In response, the King again dissolved Parliament.

1629 became the last year in which Charles summoned a parliament prior to the eleven years known both as "personal rule" and the "Eleven Years' Tyranny." Continuing to clash with the assembly on tax issues, Charles moved to dissolve Parliament but not before the Speaker of the House of Commons read resolutions against Catholicism, Charles's taxations, and Arminism, a school of anti-Calvinist Protestant thought that advocated free will. Lacking a parliament, the King could not raise money for war, so he was forced to make peace with France and Spain rather than attempt to gain the upper hand militarily.

The kingdom's financial troubles only worsened during "personal rule." Citizens of all three kingdoms continued to protest taxation; Charles's next attempt to strengthen the treasury angered them further. The King brought back a medieval tax called "ship money" which, in its original use, required England's coastal counties to pay for military ships. Charles extended the tax to every county, including those inland, and used the money for business unrelated to the military. This proved one of his least popular policies.

Religious matters also created strife during this period. In 1633, Charles appointed William Laud as Archbishop of Canterbury. Laud quickly introduced unpopular reforms in an attempt to increase the Anglican church's uniformity, angering both those who leaned Puritan and those who held onto Catholic traditions. In 1637, the King insisted that the Scottish Kirk begin using the *Book of Common Prayer*, to great opposition from the Kirk. The following year, the General Assembly of the Church of Scotland condemned the *Book*.

In 1639, the First Bishops' War took place between Scottish rebels and the King's forces. The two armies met to fight, but no battle ever occurred—Charles conceded by finally calling the Scottish Parliament into session. This conflict began the Wars of the Three Kingdoms, which officially continued until 1653, comprising many smaller wars in England, Scotland, and Ireland.

The King was officially bankrupted in 1640. The City of London refused to lend him money, so he seized silver from the Royal Mint, promising to pay it back. These financial troubles, in addition to his desire to declare war on Spain, led Charles to summon the English and Irish parliaments later the same year. The English assembly refused to fund a war unless the King ended ship money; the so-called Short Parliament was in session for less than a month before Charles dissolved it again.

In Scotland, Parliament announced itself independent from the King's approval, deciding to pass acts without his input. A Scottish army then invaded England with significant success and occupied the city of Newcastle in the Second Bishops' War. Charles, badly losing, recalled the English Parliament. He made peace with Scotland in October with the embarrassing Treaty of Ripon, promising significant payment to the Scottish army. In November, the Long Parliament commenced its session, during which it began prosecuting the King's advisors for treason.

Parliament passed the Triennial Act in 1641, requiring a parliament to be convened every three years at minimum. The King reluctantly signed the act because it was attached to a subsidy bill—he needed the money. Charles was also made to agree that Parliament could not be dissolved without its consent. The House of Commons then persisted in prosecuting his advisors, specifically the Earl of Strafford. Parliament was unable to prove the charges of treason against the Earl, but it passed a bill of attainder declaring his guilt anyway, executing him shortly afterwards.

The Long Parliament quickly took measures to remove the King's unpopular taxes, including ship money. Charles additionally conceded to the rule of Presbyterianism in the Scottish Kirk, earning him additional goodwill in Scotland, but that feeling soon dissipated due to a Royalist plot, known as The Incident, to kidnap powerful Presbyterian Scottish lords. Ireland then began armed conflict against England, known as the Irish Confederate Wars, to combat anti-Catholic discrimination and gain more self-government. These wars lasted until the overall end of the Wars of the Three Kingdoms in 1653.

1642 saw the outbreak of the first English Civil War, brought on by the irreconcilable differences between the King and Parliament. The war's immediate catalyst was Charles's attempt to enter the House of Commons to arrest five members he suspected of supporting the Scottish army in the Second Bishops' War. The chambers of Parliament are meant to be free from interference, including interference by the monarch; Parliament responded to this affront by taking control of London and the English navy and raising a volunteer militia. During this period, Parliament, now largely controlled by anti-theater Puritans, closed London's theaters to support the war effort, as they believed plays "representative of lascivious mirth and levity" were incompatible with the "times of humiliation." King Charles fled north, raising an army as he went. The forces met several times throughout the next three years, but no major victories were won on either side until 1645.

In 1644, Charles summoned his own Royalist parliament to his encampment at Oxford. At first, the majority of the original Parliamentarians joined him, but popular support quickly waned as peace talks with the opposition failed. Among those figures who supported Parliament was John Milton, who spent the war writing political pamphlets attacking the way that Charles governed the Church of England. Milton also published the *Aeropagitica*, a defense of free speech, in 1644.

The following year, the tides of the war turned in Parliament's favor with several Royalist defeats. The Parliamentary forces turned from local, individual forces to the New Model Army, a united English standing army. In 1646, the King was forced to flee Oxford, which was under siege, disguised as a servant. He was taken in by the Presbyterian Scottish army; however, it came to an agreement with Parliament in 1647 to hand Charles over in exchange for a sum of 400,000 pounds.

Once the King was in captivity, tensions arose between the New Model Army and Parliament. The Army favored local government and a powerful military while Parliament preferred central government and the dissolution of the army during peacetime. Meanwhile, Charles signed a secret treaty with the Scots, promising to make England Presbyterian if the Scottish army invaded and restored him to the throne.

The second English Civil War began in 1648 with the promised Scottish invasion. They were quickly defeated, marking the decisive end of the Royalist forces. Oliver Cromwell, an important commander in the New Model Army, gained power by winning an important battle. Parliament attempted to continue negotiating with the King, but the Army essentially staged a coup, removing all members of Parliament who did not want to prosecute Charles for treason. With these members removed, the Long Parliament became the Rump[1] Parliament.

In January 1649, the House of Commons indicted King Charles. Amid objections from the House of Lords, the Commons created a separate court to try the monarch. Of the commissioners summoned to this court, only about half accepted—those that held contempt for the King. Answering the accusation of treason against England, Charles insisted that no one could try a king and that the trial was illegitimate. The court found the King responsible for the ~300,000 deaths in the Wars of the Three Kingdoms, and on January 26th condemned him to death. He was executed on January 30th, 1649. Parliament refused to allow Charles' burial in Westminster Abbey, so he was buried alongside King Henry VIII and Jane Seymour in Windsor.

1: Remnant.

THE ENGLISH COMMONWEALTH AND PROTECTORATE

In May, after the King's January execution, Parliament declared England a commonwealth, eliminated the House of Lords, and replaced the Privy Council with the Council of State. The New Model Army also put down multiple internal rebellions from dissatisfied soldiers who wanted voting rights. In addition to closing the theaters, Parliament outlawed the celebration of Christmas and Easter on moral grounds because they originated from pagan traditions. The Parliamentary government soon began to clash with the Army's leaders. The Army Council insisted that Parliament tolerate various Protestant sects; in 1650, the Act of Uniformity was repealed, granting citizens greater freedom of worship within the Church of England by relaxing the Church's regulations on attendance, tithing, and more.

Parliament got little done between 1649 and 1653, suffering from internal factionalism, economic problems, and threats of invasion by Scotland and Ireland. Meanwhile, Oliver Cromwell led a brutal invasion of Ireland in order to squash an alliance of English Royalists and self-governing Irish Catholics. Because Cromwell hated the Irish on religious grounds, his tactics were incredibly bloody. His forces killed thousands of civilians, especially during the numerous sieges that took place. Though Cromwell left Ireland in 1650, the Cromwellian conquest portion of the Irish Confederate Wars continued until 1653, when Ireland was fully subjugated by English forces.

In 1650, the son of King Charles I, also Charles and subsequently Charles II, signed a treaty with the Parliament of Scotland sanctioning Presbyterianism across the three kingdoms after months of negotiating to be declared King of Scotland. He then travelled to Scotland. The Scottish Parliament declared Charles II King of Great Britain, France[2], and Ireland. In response, Cromwell left Ireland to lead an invasion into Scotland. While not as brutal as the invasion of Ireland, Cromwell's forces nonetheless killed hundreds of civilians. Charles responded by counter-invading England, but he had little success gaining followers. By the end of 1651, the New Model Army defeated the Royalist forces and Charles returned to the continent.

1652 saw major infighting in the English Parliament, with no agreement on church matters, holding elections, or unity between the kingdoms. This lack of progress led Cromwell to forcibly dissolve Parliament in April 1653. He then convened what came to be known as Barebone's Parliament, an assembly of primarily religious men nominated by the Army Council. The goal was to create a permanent constitution, but the group voted to dissolve itself after five months out of fear that the contingent of radical members that wanted to do away with common law would come to power.

In December of 1653, Oliver Cromwell was sworn in as Lord Protector, beginning the period known as the Protectorate. He governed alongside a new Council of State, with members that Cromwell chose himself, and a new parliament, which he dissolved in January 1655 when they opposed his

2: All English monarchs considered themselves rulers of France between 1340 and 1801.

reforms. After the Penruddock Uprising, a Royalist revolt, took place in March, Cromwell divided England into military-controlled districts. Conflict overseas also resumed: in 1655 England captured Jamaica from Spain, and in 1657 the Protectorate allied itself with France in a war against Spain.

A second Protectorate Parliament came together in 1656. Barring Catholics and Royalists from membership, it aligned closely with Cromwell. However, it ended military rule before proposing major constitutional changes. The most important reforms involved giving Parliament the sole right to levy taxes, reviving the House of Lords in all but name, making Lord Protector into a hereditary position, and making the Lord Protector an official king. Cromwell opposed regency while approving the rest of the changes, which went into effect in 1657.

No more major reforms occurred before Cromwell's death in 1658. He died suddenly, likely of malaria, and was buried in Westminster Abbey. Cromwell was succeeded as Lord Protector by his son, Richard, who was unpopular with the Army Council, his father's most loyal faction. Richard summoned a parliament in 1659. Because it was crippled by infighting, he quickly dissolved it. The Army leadership then removed Richard from power and reinstated the Rump Parliament.

After a complex series of power transfers, General George Monck, the leader of the English army in Scotland, returned to England and took power without opposition. He recalled the Presbyterian parliamentarians who had originally been removed by the Army Council, reforming the Long Parliament. It, however, voted to dissolve itself almost immediately. Monck then formed a new parliament and contacted Charles II. Charles issued the Declaration of Breda, promising a general pardon, religious tolerance, and payment for the army. He was officially declared King of England, Scotland, and Ireland in May 1660, restoring the monarchy.

Restoration was broadly welcomed by Parliament and England's citizens, who generally agreed that the Commonwealth had been unsuccessful. Fifty people were excluded from the general pardon—John Milton was almost among them—and nine people who signed the warrant for Charles I's execution were executed. Those executed, since their offense was considered high treason, were hanged, drawn, and quartered. Oliver Cromwell's body was also disinterred and decapitated in a posthumous execution ritual.

Charles II had twelve illegitimate children but no heirs. He was succeeded in 1685 by his brother James II, who ruled for three years as the last Catholic King of England, Scotland, and Ireland. James was deposed in the largely nonviolent Glorious Revolution by his daughter Mary and her husband William of Orange, permanently establishing Protestantism as the state religion of England.

Timeline

1557   James becomes King James VI of Scotland at the age of one.

1589   King James marries Anne of Denmark; he is twenty-three and she is
            fourteen.

1600   The future king Charles I is born.

1603   Queen Elizabeth I dies and is succeeded by King James I; this estab-
            lishes the royal house of Stuart in England.

1605   King James VI and I survives the Gunpowder Plot, a plan by Catholic
            dissident Guy Fawkes to blow up Parliament.

1609   William Shakespeare's sonnets are published in quarto.

c. 1606   Ben Jonson writes and releases *Volpone*.

1611   The *King James Bible* is finished and published.

1614   John Webster's *The Duchess of Malfi* is first performed.

1616   Shakespeare dies.

1621   John Donne becomes Dean of St. Paul's.

1625   James I dies and is succeeded by his son, King Charles I.

1628   Parliament passes the "Petition of Right;" George Villiers, Duke of
            Buckingham is assassinated.

c. 1631   John Milton writes "L'Allegro" and "Il Penseroso."

1633   Donne's *Songs and Sonnets* and *Holy Sonnets* are published posthumously.
            George Herbert publishes *The Temple*.

1639-53   The Wars of the Three Kingdoms take place.

1649   Charles I is tried and executed for treason.

1650   Richard Lovelace publishes his poetry collection *Lucasta*. Henry
            Vaughan publishes *Silex scintillans*.

1650s   Andrew Marvell writes "To His Coy Mistress."

1652   Richard Crashaw's "The Flaming Heart" and "On our crucified Lord
            naked and bloody" are published.

1653   Oliver Cromwell becomes governor of England as Lord Protector.

1658   Cromwell dies.

1660   The Restoration: King Charles II becomes King of England, Scotland,
            and Ireland.

1667   John Milton's *Paradise Lost* is published.

John Donne

Because of the coexisting Julian and Gregorian calendars, the year of John Donne's birth is unknown. Donne was born in London between January and June in either 1571 or 1572. He was born into a recusant Catholic family during a time when Catholics were widely discriminated against and were legally obligated to attend Church of England services. His father, a successful merchant also named John Donne, died in 1576. Donne and his siblings were raised by their mother, Elizabeth Heywood, daughter of playwright John Heywood. She soon married physician Dr. John Syminges.

Donne was educated privately until the age of eleven when he and his brother Henry began studying at Hart Hall, part of the University of Oxford. He attended the University of Cambridge three years later but did not receive a degree from either university because he would have been required to take the Oath of Supremacy. All nobles, degree recipients, public officials, and many others in England were compelled to take the Oath, which stated that Queen Elizabeth was "the only supreme governor of this realm, and of all other her Highness's dominions and countries, as well in all spiritual or ecclesiastical things." As a Catholic, Donne refused to swear the Oath, because it involved declaring Elizabeth head of the church instead of the Pope. Instead, he studied law at London's Thavies Inn beginning in 1591 and was accepted into a professional legal organization, Lincoln's Inn, in 1592, also in London.

In 1593, Queen Elizabeth issued "An Act for restraining Popish recusants." It claimed to help "discover and avoid… wicked and seditious persons, who, terming themselves Catholics, and being indeed spies and intelligencers… corrupt and seduce her majesty's subjects." The Act seized the assets of Catholics as property of the Crown and forbade them from traveling more than five miles from their home unless they were summoned by a court. The same year, Donne's younger brother died of disease in Newgate Prison after being arrested for harboring a Catholic priest. Many scholars believe that this made Donne start to question his Catholic faith, having also examined the differences between Catholic and Protestant doctrine during his legal studies. He probably wrote his first book of poems, titled *Satires*, around this time, and perhaps his *Songs and Sonnets*.

Donne inherited a fortune from his father and developed a reputation as a womanizer during his younger years, nicknamed Jack Donne. He frequented the London theaters and befriended poets and playwrights such as Christopher Brooke and Ben Jonson. He joined a naval expedition to Spain led by the Earl of Essex in 1596; he and Essex then joined Sir Walter Raleigh in a campaign for the Spanish-occupied Azores Islands in 1597, which became a disastrous naval loss for England. Afterwards, Donne returned to London, where he was appointed secretary to Sir Thomas Egerton, the Lord Keeper of the Great Seal (Lord Chancellor, an important member of Parliament). A practicing Catholic would not have been given this position, meaning that Donne was no longer at least publicly Catholic.

After four years in the secretarial position, Donne was elected to Parliament for the constituency of Brackley, north of London. However, he secretly married Egerton's niece Anne More in December of 1601. Because Anne was only seventeen at the time, her father, Sir George More, Lieutenant of the Tower, was furious. He had Donne dismissed from his employment and briefly imprisoned. The marriage ruined Donne's career prospects; when he wrote to Anne about losing his post, he signed the letter "John Donne, Anne Donne, Un-Done." After his release Donne and his family lived in poverty, relying on the charity of friends and noble patrons to live. Anne had twelve children in sixteen years, only seven of whom survived childhood.

The decade after Donne's marriage to Anne became a dark period in his life. He barely made enough to support his growing family by working intermittently as a lawyer. Donne's desperation is apparent when he began working for Bishop Thomas Morton, a writer and publisher of anti-Catholic pamphlets, as a co-writer. Donne wrote his *Divine Poems* during this time (1607) as well as passionately studying theology and the Catholic canon. *Biathanatos*, written in 1608 but published posthumously in 1644, reflects Donne's depressed mental state, highlighted by his use of biblical evidence to argue that suicide is not a sin. He even argued that Christ committed suicide by allowing himself to be crucified.

Donne's fortunes changed when he reconciled with his father-in-law George More and received his wife's dowry after eight years of marriage. In 1610, Donne met Sir Robert Drury, a member of Parliament who became his most important patron. Donne and Drury traveled together throughout continental Europe, and Drury gave Donne's family housing on his London estate. Donne wrote many of his works under Drury's patronage, including *A Funeral Elegy*, *An Anatomy of the World*, and *Of the Progress of the Soul*, as well as two anti-Catholic polemics (critical persuasive essays). *Pseudo-Martyr* (1610), which argued that English Catholics should pledge allegiance to King James I, caught the attention of the King. James told Donne that the only post he would receive would be in the church, despite Donne's desire for a secular position.

Donne capitulated to the King's wishes and took holy orders in 1615, receiving an honorary doctorate of divinity from Cambridge University. James then made him a Royal Chaplain. In the following years, he held various ministerial positions, including presiding over the chapel of Lincoln's Inn and the parishes of Keyston, Sevenoaks, and Blunham. Working in the Church finally allowed Donne financial security. However, his wife Anne died in 1617 after giving birth to a stillborn child. Heartbroken, Donne vowed never to marry again. He went to Germany as an ambassador's chaplain in 1618. He wrote *Hymn to Christ at the Author's Last Going into Germany* before the journey, and wrote his *Holy Sonnets* in the same year, both religious works that reflect on death. After his return to London, he was named Dean of St Paul's, an important position that he held for the rest of his life.

Donne gained a wide reputation as a talented preacher during the last decade of his life; 160 of his sermons have survived. His performances before King James I and King Charles I earned him additional ecclesiastical positions. He published his private meditations, *Devotions upon Emergent Occasions*, in 1624. Their emphasis on sickness and pain may result from the serious illness he endured and recovered from. Before his death in 1631, Donne preached a sermon to Charles I titled "Death's Duel," which critiques human mortality and resurrection. Many scholars consider this Donne's own funeral sermon. His last writing, just before his death, was *Hymn to God, My God, in my Sickness*. Donne died, probably of stomach cancer, on March 31, 1631, at the age of fifty-nine. He was buried in St. Paul's Cathedral.

TIMELINE[1]

1572	Donne is born in London.
1576	Donne's father dies and his mother marries Dr. John Syminges.
1591	Donne begins studying law.
1593	Elizabeth's *Act for Restraining Popish Recusants*; Donne's brother Henry dies in prison after harboring a priest.
c. 1595	*Satires*; *Songs and Sonnets*.
1597	Donne receives a secretarial position from Sir Thomas Egerton
1601	Donne secretly marries Anne More.
1607	*Divine Poems*.
1608	*Biathanatos*.
1609	Donne is reconciled with his father-in-law George More.
1610	Donne meets patron Sir Robert Drury; *Pseudo-Martyr*; *A Funeral Elegy*.
1611	*Ignatious His Conclave*; *An Anatomy of the World*.
1612	*Of the Progress of the Soul*.
1616	Donne is appointed parish priest of Keyston and Sevenoaks.
1617	Anne dies aged 33 due to childbirth.
1618	*Hymn to Christ at the Author's Last Going Into Germany*; *Holy Sonnets*.
1621	Donne is made dean of St Paul's.
1623-24	*Devotions upon Emergent Occasions*.
1625	King James I dies and is succeeded by King Charles I; Donne first preaches for Charles.
1631	*Hymn to God, my God, in my Sickness*; *Death's Duel* (sermon).
1631	Donne dies of an illness at the age of fifty-nine.

1: Since most of Donne's important works were published posthumously, this timeline lists the dates of composition, not publication.

Songs and Sonnets

By John Donne

The Good-Morrow

I wonder by my troth, what thou, and I
Did, till we lov'd? were we not wean'd till then?
But suck'd on countrey pleasures, childishly?
Or snorted we in the seaven sleepers den?
5 T'was so; But this, all pleasures fancies bee.
If ever any beauty I did see,
Which I desir'd, and got, t'was but a dreame of thee.

And now good morrow to our waking soules,
Which watch not one another out of feare;
10 For love, all love of other sights controules,
And makes one little roome, an every where.
Let sea-discoverers to new worlds have gone,
Let Maps to other, worlds on worlds have showne,
Let us possesse one world, each hath one, and is one.

15 My face in thine eye, thine in mine appeares,
And true plaine hearts doe in the faces rest,
Where can we finde two better hemispheares
Without sharpe North, without declining West?
What ever dyes, was not mixt equally;
20 If our two loves be one, or, thou and I
Love so alike, that none doe slacken, none can die.

Song

Goe, and catche a falling starre,
Get with child a mandrake roote,
Tell me, where all past yeares are,
Or who cleft the Divels foot,
5 Teach me to heare Mermaides singing,
Or to keep off envies stinging,
And finde
What winde
Serves to advance an honest minde.
10 If thou beest borne to strange sights,
Things invisible to see,
Ride ten thousand daies and nights,

Till age snow white haires on thee,
Thou, when thou retorn'st, wilt tell mee
15 All strange wonders that befell thee,
And sweare
No where
Lives a woman true, and faire.

If thou findst one, let mee know,
20 Such a Pilgrimage were sweet;
Yet doe not, I would not goe,
Though at next doore wee might meet,
Though shee were true, when you met her,
And last, till you write your letter,
25 Yet shee
Will bee
False, ere I come, to two, or three.

THE SUNNE RISING

Busy old foole, unruly Sunne,
Why dost thou thus,
Through windowes, and through curtaines call on us?
Must to thy motions lovers seasons run?
5 Sawcy pedantique wretch, goe chide
Late schoole boyes, and sowre prentices,
Goe tell Court-huntsmen, that the King will ride,
Call countrey ants to harvest offices;
Love, all alike, no season knowes, nor clyme,
10 Nor houres, dayes, moneths, which are the rags of time.

Thy beames, so reverend, and strong
Why shouldst thou thinke?
I could eclipse and cloud them with a winke,
But that I would not lose her sight so long:
15 If her eyes have not blinded thine,
Looke, and to morrow late, tell mee,
Whether both the'India's of spice and Myne
Be where thou leftst them, or lie here with mee.
Aske for those Kings whom thou saw'st yesterday,
20 And thou shalt heare, All here in one bed lay.

She'is all States, and all Princes, I,
Nothing else is.
Princes doe but play us; compar'd to this,
All honor's mimique; All wealth alchimie.
25 Thou sunne art halfe as happy'as wee,
In that the world's contracted thus;

Thine age askes ease, and since thy duties bee
To warme the world, that's done in warming us.
Shine here to us, and thou art every where;
30 This bed thy center is, these walls, thy spheare.

THE INDIFFERENT

I can love both faire and browne,
Her whom abundance melts, and her whom want betraies,
Her who loves lonenesse best, and her who maskes and plaies,
Her whom the country form'd, and whom the town,
5 Her who beleeves, and her who tries,
Her who still weepes with spungie eyes,
And her who is dry corke, and never cries;
I can love her, and her, and you and you,
I can love any, so she be not true.

10 Will no other vice content you?
Wil it not serve your turn to do, as did your mothers?
Or have you all old vices spent, and now would finde out others?
Or doth a feare, that men are true, torment you?
Oh we are not, be not you so,
15 Let mee, and doe you, twenty know.
Rob mee, but binde me not, and let me goe.
Must I, who came to travaile thorow you,
Grow your fixt subject, because you are true?

Venus heard me sigh this song,
20 And by Loves sweetest Part, Variety, she swore,
She heard not this till now; and that it should be so no more.
She went, examin'd, and return'd ere long,
And said, alas, Some two or three
Poore Heretiques in love there bee,
25 Which thinke to stablish dangerous constancie.
But I have told them, since you will be true,
You shall be true to them, who'are false to you.

THE CANONIZATION

For Godsake hold your tongue, and let me love,
Or chide my palsie, or my gout,
My five gray haires, or ruin'd fortune flout,
With wealth your state, your minde with Arts improve,
5 Take you a course, get you a place,
Observe his honour, or his grace,
Or the Kings reall, or his stamped face
Contemplate, what you will, approve,
So you will let me love.

10 Alas, alas, who's injur'd by my love?
  What merchants ships have my sighs drown'd?
  Who saies my teares have overflow'd his ground?
  When did my colds a forward spring remove?
  When did the heats which my veines fill
15 Adde one more to the plaguie Bill?
  Soldiers finde warres, and Lawyers finde out still
  Litigious men, which quarrels move,
  Though she and I do love.

  Call us what you will, wee are made such by love;
20 Call her one, mee another flye,
  We'are Tapers too, and at our owne cost die,
  And wee in us finde the'Eagle and the Dove.
  The Phœnix ridle hath more wit
  By us, we two being one, are it.
25 So to one neutrall thing both sexes fit,
  Wee dye and rise the same, and prove
  Mysterious by this love.

  Wee can dye by it, if not live by love,
  And if unfit for tombes and hearse
30 Our legend bee, it will be fit for verse;
  And if no peece of Chronicle wee prove,
  We'll build in sonnets pretty roomes;
  As well a well wrought urne becomes
  The greatest ashes, as halfe-acre tombes,
35 And by these hymnes, all shall approve
  Us *Canoniz'd* for Love:

  And thus invoke us; You whom reverend love
  Made one anothers hermitage;
  You, to whom love was peace, that now is rage;
40 Who did the whole worlds soule contract, and drove
  Into the glasses of your eyes
  (So made such mirrors, and such spies,
  That they did all to you epitomize,)
  Countries, Townes, Courts: Beg from above
45 A patterne of your love!

AIRE AND ANGELS

Twice or thrice had I loved thee,
Before I knew thy face or name;
So in a voice, so in a shapelesse flame,
Angells affect us oft, and worship'd bee;

5 Still when, to where thou wert, I came,
   Some lovely glorious nothing I did see.
   But since my soule, whose child love is,
   Takes limmes of flesh, and else could nothing doe,
   More subtile then the parent is,
10 Love must not be, but take a body too,
   And therefore what thou wert, and who,
           I bid Love aske, and now
   That it assume thy body, I allow,
   And fixe it selfe in thy lip, eye, and brow.

15 Whilst thus to ballast love, I thought,
   And so more steddily to have gone,
   With wares which would sinke admiration,
   I saw, I had loves pinnace overfraught,
   Ev'ry thy haire for love to worke upon
20 Is much too much, some fitter must be sought;
   For, nor in nothing, nor in things
   Extreme, and scatt'ring bright, can love inhere;
   Then as an Angell, face, and wings
   Of aire, not pure as it, yet pure doth weare,
25 So thy love may be my loves spheare;
           Just such disparitie
   As is twixt Aire and Angells puritie,
   'Twixt womens love, and mens will ever bee.

BREAKE OF DAY

   'Tis true, 'tis day; what though it be?
   O wilt thou therefore rise from me?
   Why should we rise, because 'tis light?
   Did we lie downe, because 'twas night?
5 Love which in spight of darknesse brought us hether,
   Should in despight of light keepe us together.
   Light hath no tongue, but is all eye;
   If it could speake as well as spie,
   This were the worst, that it could say,
10 That being well, I faine would stay,
   And that I lov'd my heart and honor so,
   That I would not from him, that had them, goe.
   Must businesse thee from hence remove?
   Oh, that's the worst disease of love,
15 The poore, the foule, the false, love can
   Admit, but not the busied man.
   He which hath businesse, and makes love, doth doe
   Such wrong, as when a maryed man doth wooe.

The Flea

Marke but this flea, and marke in this,
How little that which thou deny'st me is;
It suck'd me first, and now sucks thee,
And in this flea, our two bloods mingled bee;
5 Thou know'st that this cannot be said
A sinne, nor shame, nor losse of maidenhead,
      Yet this enjoyes before it wooe,
      And pamper'd swells with one blood made of two,
      And this, alas, is more then wee would doe.

10 Oh stay, three lives in one flea spare,
Where wee almost, yea more then maryed are.
This flea is you and I, and this
Our mariage bed, and mariage temple is;
Though parents grudge, and you, w'are met,
15 And cloysterd in these living walls of Jet.
      Though use make you apt to kill mee,
      Let not to that, selfe murder added bee,
      And sacrilege, three sinnes in killing three.

Cruell and sodaine, hast thou since
20 Purpled thy naile, in blood of innocence?
Wherein could this flea guilty bee,
Except in that drop which it suckt from thee?
Yet thou triumph'st, and saist that thou
Find'st not thy selfe, nor mee the weaker now;
25   'Tis true, then learne how false, feares bee;
      Just so much honor, when thou yeeld'st to mee,
      Will wast, as this flea's death tooke life from thee.

The Baite

Come live with mee, and bee my love,
And wee will some new pleasures prove
Of golden sands, and christall brookes,
With silken lines, and silver hookes.

5 There will the river whispering runne
Warm'd by thy eyes, more then the Sunne.
And there the'inamor'd fish will stay,
Begging themselves they may betray.

When thou wilt swimme in that live bath,
10 Each fish, which every channell hath,
Will amorously to thee swimme,
Gladder to catch thee, then thou him.

If thou, to be so seene, beest loath,
By Sunne, or Moone, thou darknest both,
15   And if my selfe have leave to see,
I need not their light, having thee.

Let others freeze with angling reeds,
And cut their legges, with shells and weeds,
Or treacherously poore fish beset,
20   With strangling snare, or windowie net:

Let coarse bold hands, from slimy nest
The bedded fish in banks out-wrest,
Or curious traitors, sleavesilke flies
Bewitch poore fishes wandring eyes.

25   For thee, thou needst no such deceit,
For thou thy selfe art thine owne bait;
That fish, that is not catch'd thereby,
Alas, is wiser farre then I.

THE APPARITION

When by thy scorne, O murdresse, I am dead,
    And that thou thinkst thee free
From all solicitation from mee,
Then shall my ghost come to thy bed,
5   And thee, fain'd vestall, in worse armes shall see;
Then thy sicke taper will begin to winke,
And he, whose thou art then, being tyr'd before,
Will, if thou stirre, or pinch to wake him, thinke
    Thou call'st for more,
10   And in false sleepe will from thee shrinke,
And then poore Aspen wretch, neglected thou
Bath'd in a cold quicksilver sweat wilt lye
    A veryer ghost then I;
What I will say, I will not tell thee now,
15   Lest that preserve thee'; and since my love is spent,
I'had rather thou shouldst painfully repent,
Then by my threatnings rest still innocent.

A VALEDICTION: FORBIDDING MOURNING

As virtuous men passe mildly away,
And whisper to their soules, to goe,
Whilst some of their sad friends doe say,
The breath goes now, and some say, no:

5 So let us melt, and make no noise,
No teare-floods, nor sigh-tempests move,
T'were prophanation of our joyes
To tell the layetie our love.

Moving of th'earth brings harmes and feares,
10 Men reckon what it did and meant,
But trepidation of the spheares,
Though greater farre, is innocent.

Dull sublunary lovers love
(Whose soule is sense) cannot admit
15 Absence, because it doth remove
Those things which elemented it.

But we by a love, so much refin'd,
That our selves know not what it is,
Inter-assured of the mind,
20 Care lesse, eyes, lips, and hands to misse.

Our two soules therefore, which are one,
Though I must goe, endure not yet
A breach, but an expansion,
Like gold to ayery thinnesse beate.

25 If they be two, they are two so
As stiffe twin compasses are two,
Thy soule the fixt foot, makes no show
To move, but doth, if the'other doe.

And though it in the center sit,
30 Yet when the other far doth rome,
It leanes, and hearkens after it,
And growes erect, as that comes home.

Such wilt thou be to mee, who must
Like th'other foot, obliquely runne;
35 Thy firmnes makes my circle just,
And makes me end, where I begunne.

THE EXTASIE

Where, like a pillow on a bed,
A Pregnant banke swel'd up, to rest
The violets reclining head,
Sat we two, one anothers best.
5 Our hands were firmely cimented
With a fast balme, which thence did spring,
Our eye-beames twisted, and did thred

Our eyes, upon one double string;
So to'entergraft our hands, as yet
10   Was all the meanes to make us one,
And pictures in our eyes to get
Was all our propagation.
As 'twixt two equall Armies, Fate
Suspends uncertaine victorie,
15   Our soules, (which to advance their state,
Were gone out,) hung 'twixt her, and mee.
And whil'st our soules negotiate there,
Wee like sepulchrall statues lay;
All day, the same our postures were,
20   And wee said nothing, all the day.
If any, so by love refin'd,
That he soules language understood,
And by good love were growen all minde,
Within convenient distance stood,
25   He (though he knew not which soule spake,
Because both meant, both spake the same)
Might thence a new concoction take,
And part farre purer then he came.
This Extasie doth unperplex
30   (We said) and tell us what we love,
Wee see by this, it was not sexe,
Wee see, we saw not what did move:
But as all severall soules containe
Mixture of things, they know not what,
35   Love, these mixt soules, doth mixe againe,
And makes both one, each this and that.
A single violet transplant,
The strength, the colour, and the size,
(All which before was poore, and scant,)
40   Redoubles still, and multiplies.
When love, with one another so
Interinanimates two soules,
That abler soule, which thence doth flow,
Defects of lonelinesse controules.
45   Wee then, who are this new soule, know,
Of what we are compos'd, and made,
For, th'Atomies of which we grow,
Are soules, whom no change can invade.
But O alas, so long, so farre
50   Our bodies why doe wee forbeare?
They are ours, though they are not wee, Wee are
The intelligences, they the spheare.

We owe them thankes, because they thus,
Did us, to us, at first convay,
55   Yeelded their forces, sense, to us,
Nor are drosse to us, but allay.
On man heavens influence workes not so,
But that it first imprints the ayre,
Soe soule into the soule may flow,
60   Though it to body first repaire.
As our blood labours to beget
Spirits, as like soules as it can,
Because such fingers need to knit
That subtile knot, which makes us man:
65   So must pure lovers soules descend
T'affections, and to faculties,
Which sense may reach and apprehend,
Else a great Prince in prison lies.
To'our bodies turne wee then, that so
70   Weake men on love reveal'd may looke;
Loves mysteries in soules doe grow,
But yet the body is his booke.
And if some lover, such as wee,
Have heard this dialogue of one,
75   Let him still marke us, he shall see
Small change, when we'are to bodies gone.

THE DAMPE

When I am dead, and Doctors know not why,
     And my friends curiositie
Will have me cut up to survay each part,
When they shall finde your Picture in my heart,
5   You thinke a sodaine dampe of love
      Will through all their senses move,
And worke on them as mee, and so preferre
Your murder, to the name of Massacre.

Poore victories! But if you dare be brave,
10   And pleasure in your conquest have,
First kill th'enormous Gyant, your *Disdaine*,
And let th'enchantresse *Honor*, next be slaine,
      And like a Goth and Vandall rize,
      Deface Records, and Histories
15   Of your owne arts and triumphs over men,
And without such advantage kill me then.

For I could muster up as well as you
      My Gyants, and my Witches too,

Which are vast *Constancy*, and *Secretnesse*,
20   But these I neyther looke for, nor professe;
              Kill mee as Woman, let mee die
              As a meere man; doe you but try
Your passive valor, and you shall finde than,
In that you'have odds enough of any man.

LETTER TO MR. T. W.[1]
All haile sweet Poët, more full of more strong fire,
Then hath or shall enkindle any spirit,
I lov'd what nature gave thee, but this merit
Of wit and Art I love not but admire;
5   Who have before or shall write after thee,
Their workes, though toughly laboured, will bee
Like infancie or age to mans firme stay,
Or earely and late twilights to mid-day.

Men say, and truly, that they better be
10   Which be envyed then pittied: therefore I,
Because I wish thee best, doe thee envie:
O wouldst thou, by like reason, pitty mee!
But care not for mee: I, that ever was
In Natures, and in Fortunes gifts, alas,
15   (Before thy grace got in the Muses Schoole
A monster and a begger,) am now a foole.

Oh how I grieve, that late borne modesty
Hath got such root in easie waxen hearts,
That men may not themselves, their owne good parts
20   Extoll, without suspect of surquedrie,
For, but thy selfe, no subject can be found
Worthy thy quill, nor any quill resound
Thy worth but thine: how good it were to see
A Poëm in thy praise, and writ by thee.

25   Now if this song be too'harsh for rime, yet, as
The Painters bad god made a good devill,
'Twill be good prose, although the verse be evill,
If thou forget the rime as thou dost passe.
Then write, that I may follow, and so bee
30   Thy debter, thy'eccho, thy foyle, thy zanee.
I shall be thought, if mine like thine I shape,
All the worlds Lyon, though I be thy Ape.

1: Thomas Woodward, a student at Cambridge.

HOLY SONNETS

By John Donne

I.

Thou hast made me, And shall thy worke decay?
Repaire me now, for now mine end doth haste,
I runne to death, and death meets me as fast,
And all my pleasures are like yesterday;
5 I dare not move my dimme eyes any way,
Despaire behind, and death before doth cast
Such terrour, and my feeble flesh doth waste
By sinne in it, which it t'wards hell doth weigh;
Onely thou art above, and when towards thee
10 By thy leave I can looke, I rise againe;
But our old subtle foe so tempteth me,
That not one houre my selfe I can sustaine;
Thy Grace may wing me to prevent his art,
And thou like Adamant draw mine iron heart.

VII.

At the round earths imagin'd corners, blow
Your trumpets, Angells, and arise, arise
From death, you numberlesse infinities
Of soules, and to your scattred bodies goe,
5 All whom the flood did, and fire shall o'erthrow,
All whom warre, dearth, age, agues, tyrannies,
Despaire, law, chance, hath slaine, and you whose eyes,
Shall behold God, and never tast deaths woe.
      But let them sleepe, Lord, and mee mourne a space,
10   For, if above all these, my sinnes abound,
      'Tis late to aske abundance of thy grace,
      When wee are there; here on this lowly ground,
      Teach mee how to repent; for that's as good
      As if thou'hadst seal'd my pardon, with thy blood.

X.

Death be not proud, though some have called thee
Mighty and dreadfull, for, thou art not soe,
For, those, whom thou think'st, thou dost overthrow,
Die not, poore death, nor yet canst thou kill mee.
5 From rest and sleepe, which but thy pictures bee,

Much pleasure, then from thee, much more must flow,
And soonest our best men with thee doe goe,
Rest of their bones, and soules deliverie.
    Thou art slave to Fate, Chance, kings, and desperate men,
10   And dost with poyson, warre, and sicknesse dwell,
    And poppie, or charmes can make us sleepe as well,
    And better then thy stroake; why swell'st thou then?
    One short sleepe past, wee wake eternally,
    And death shall be no more; death, thou shalt die.

XI.

Spit in my face you Jewes, and pierce my side,
Buffet, and scoffe, scourge, and crucifie mee,
For I have sinn'd, and sinn'd, and onely hee,
Who could do no iniquitie, hath dyed:
5 But by my death can not be satisfied
My sinnes, which passe the Jewes impiety:
They kill'd once an inglorious man, but I
Crucifie him daily, being now glorified.
    Oh let mee then, his strange love still admire:
10   Kings pardon, but he bore our punishment.
    And *Iacob* came cloth'd in vile harsh attire
    But to supplant, and with gainfull intent:
    God cloth'd himselfe in vile mans flesh, that so
    Hee might be weake enough to suffer woe.

XIV.

Batter my heart, three person'd God; for, you
As yet but knocke, breathe, shine, and seeke to mend;
That I may rise, and stand, o'erthrow mee,'and bend
Your force, to breake, blowe, burn and make me new.
5 I, like an usurpt towne, to'another due,
Labour to'admit you, but Oh, to no end,
Reason your viceroy in mee, mee should defend,
But is captiv'd, and proves weake or untrue.
    Yet dearely'I love you,'and would be loved faine,
10   But am betroth'd unto your enemie:
    Divorce mee,'untie, or breake that knot againe,
    Take mee to you, imprison mee, for I
    Except you'enthrall mee, never shall be free,
    Nor ever chaste, except you ravish mee.

XV.

Wilt thou love God, as he thee! then digest,
My Soule, this wholsome meditation,
How God the Spirit, by Angels waited on
In heaven, doth make his Temple in thy brest.
5 The Father having begot a Sonne most blest,
And still begetting, (for he ne'r begonne)
Hath deign'd to chuse thee by adoption,
Coheire to'his glory,'and Sabbaths endlesse rest.
        And as a robb'd man, which by search doth finde
10   His stolne stuffe sold, must lose or buy'it againe:
        The Sonne of glory came downe, and was slaine,
        Us whom he'had made, and Satan stolne, to unbinde.
        'Twas much, that man was made like God before,
        But, that God should be made like man, much more.

XVIII.

Show me deare Christ, thy spouse, so bright and clear.
What! is it She, which on the other shore
Goes richly painted? or which rob'd and tore
Laments and mournes in Germany and here?
5 Sleepes she a thousand, then peepes up one yeare?
Is she selfe truth and errs? now new, now outwore?
Doth she, and did she, and shall she evermore
On one, on seaven, or on no hill appeare?
        Dwells she with us, or like adventuring knights
10   First travaile we to seeke and then make Love?
        Betray kind husband thy spouse to our sights,
        And let myne amorous soule court thy mild Dove,
        Who is most trew, and pleasing to thee, then
        When she'is embrac'd and open to most men.

ODE: OF OUR SENSE OF SINNE.

1. Vengeance will sit above our faults; but till
        She there doth sit,
We see *her* not, nor *them*. Thus, blinde, yet still
We leade her way; and thus, whil'st we doe ill,
5   We suffer it.

2. Unhappy he, whom youth makes not beware
        Of doing ill.
Enough we labour under age, and care;
In number, th'errours of the last place, are
10   The greatest still.

3. Yet we, that should the ill we now begin
      As soone repent,
(Strange thing!) perceive not; our faults are not seen,
But past us; neither felt, but onely in
15   The punishment.

4. But we know our selves least; Mere outward shews
      Our mindes so store,
That our soules, no more than our eyes disclose
But forme and colour. Onely he who knowes
20   Himselfe, knowes more.

A Hymne to Christ, at the Authors last going into Germany.

In what torne ship soever I embarke,
That ship shall be my embleme of thy Arke;
What sea soever swallow mee, that flood
Shall be to mee an embleme of thy blood;
5 Though thou with clouds of anger do disguise
Thy race; yet through that maske I know those eyes,
Which, though they turne away sometimes,
      They never will despise.

I sacrifice this Iland unto thee,
10 And all whom I lov'd there, and who lov'd mee;
When I have put our seas twixt them and mee,
Put thou thy sea betwixt my sinnes and thee.
As the trees sap doth seeke the root below
In winter, in my winter now I goe,
15 Where none but thee, th'Eternall root
      Of true Love I may know.

Nor thou nor thy religion dost controule,
The amorousnesse of an harmonious Soule,
But thou would'st have that love thy selfe: As thou
20 Art jealous, Lord, so I am jealous now,
Thou lov'st not, till from loving more, thou free
My soule: Who ever gives, takes libertie:
O, if thou car'st not whom I love
      Alas, thou lov'st not mee.

25 Seale then this bill of my Divorce to All,
On whom those fainter beames of love did fall;
Marry those loves, which in youth scattered bee
On Fame, Wit, Hopes (false mistresses) to thee.
Churches are best for Prayer, that have least light:
30   To see God only, I goe out of sight:

And to scape stormy dayes, I chuse
An Everlasting night.

Hymne to God my God, in my sicknesse.

Since I am comming to that Holy roome,
Where, with thy Quire of Saints for evermore,
I shall be made thy Musique; As I come
I tune the Instrument here at the dore,
5   And what I must doe then, thinke here before.

Whilst my Physitians by their love are growne
Cosmographers, and I their Mapp, who lie
Flat on this bed, that by them may be showne
That this is my South-west discoverie
10 *Per fretum febris*, by these streights to die,

I joy, that in these straits, I see my West;
For, though theire currants yeeld returne to none,
What shall my West hurt me? As West and East
In all flatt Maps (and I am one) are one,
15 So death doth touch the Resurrection.

Is the Pacifique Sea my home? Or are
The Easterne riches? Is *Ierusalem?*
Anyan, and *Magellan*, and *Gibraltare*,
All streights, and none but streights, are wayes to them,
20 Whether where *Iaphet* dwelt, or *Cham*, or *Sem*.

We thinke that *Paradise* and *Calvarie*,
Christs Crosse, and *Adams* tree, stood in one place;
Looke Lord, and finde both *Adams* met in me;
As the first *Adams* sweat surrounds my face,
25 May the last *Adams* blood my soule embrace.

So, in his purple wrapp'd receive mee Lord,
By these his thornes give me his other Crowne;
And as to others soules I preach'd thy word,
Be this my Text, my Sermon to mine owne,
30 Therfore that he may raise the Lord throws down.

Excerpt from *Devotions upon Emergent Occasions*, "Meditation 17."

No man is an island, entire of itself; every man is a piece of the continent, a part of the main. If a clod be washed away by the sea, Europe is the less, as well as if a promontory were, as well as if a manor of thy friend's or of thine own were: any man's death diminishes me, because I am involved in mankind, and therefore never send to know for whom the bells tolls; it tolls for thee.

DEATH'S DUEL

Buildings stand by the benefit of their foundations that sustain and support them, and of their buttresses that comprehend and embrace them, and of their contignations that knit and unite them. The foundations suffer them not to sink, the buttresses suffer them not to swerve, and the contignation and knitting suffers them not to cleave. The body of our building is in the former part of this verse. It is this: *He that is our God is the God of salvation; ad salutes*, of salvations in the plural, so it is in the original; the God that gives us spiritual and temporal salvation too. But of this building, the foundation, the buttresses, the contignations, are in this part of the verse which constitutes our text, and in the three divers acceptations of the words amongst our expositors: *Unto God the Lord belong the issues from death*, for, first, the foundation of this building (that our God is the God of all salvation) is laid in this, that *unto* this *God the Lord belong the issues of death*; that is, it is in his power to give us an issue and deliverance, even then when we are brought to the jaws and teeth of death, and to the lips of that whirlpool, the grave. And so in this acceptation, this *exitus mortis*, this issue of death is *liberatio á morte*, a deliverance from death, and this is the most obvious and most ordinary acceptation of these words, and that upon which our translation lays hold, the *issues from death*. And then, secondly, the buttresses that comprehend and settle this building, that he that is our God is the God of all salvation, are thus raised; *unto God the Lord belong the issues of death*, that is, the disposition and manner of our death; what kind of issue and transmigration we shall have out of this world, whether prepared or sudden, whether violent or natural, whether in our perfect senses or shaken and disordered by sickness, there is no condemnation to be argued out of that, no judgment to be made upon that, for, howsoever they die, *precious in his sight is the death of his saints*, and with him are the issues of death; the ways of our departing out of this life are in his hands. And so in this sense of the words, this *exitus mortis*, the issues of death, is *liberatio in morte*, a deliverance in death; not that God will deliver us from dying, but that he will have a care of us in the hour of death, of what kind soever our passage be. And in this sense and acceptation of the words, the natural frame and contexture doth well and pregnantly administer unto us. And then, lastly, the contignation and knitting of this building, that he that is our God is the God of all salvations, consists in this, *Unto* this *God the Lord belong the issues of death*; that is, that this God the Lord having united and knit both natures in one, and being God, having also come into this world in our flesh, he could have no other means to save us, he could have no other issue out of this world, nor return to his former glory, but by death. And so in this sense, this *exitus mortis*, this issue of death, is *liberatio per mortem*, a deliverance by death, by the death of this God, our Lord Christ Jesus. And this is Saint Augustine's acceptation of the words, and those many and great persons that have adhered to him. In all these three lines, then, we shall look upon these words, first, as the God of power, the Almighty Father rescues his servants from the jaws of death; and then as the God of mercy, the glorious Son rescued us by taking upon himself this issue of death; and then, between these two, as the God of comfort, the Holy Ghost rescues us from all discomfort by his blessed impressions beforehand, that what manner of death soever be ordained for us, yet this *exitus mortis* shall be *introitus in vitam*, our issue in death shall be an entrance into everlasting life. And these three considerations: our deliverance *à morte, in morte, per mortem*, from death, in death, and by death, will abundantly do all the offices of the foundations, of the buttresses, of the contignation, of this our building; that he that is our God is the God of all salvation, because *unto* this *God the Lord belong the issues of death.*

First, then, we consider this *exitus mortis* to be *liberatio à morte*, that with *God the Lord are the issues of death*; and therefore in all our death, and deadly calamities of this life, we may justly hope of a good issue from him. In all our periods and transitions in this life, are so many passages from death to death; our very birth and entrance into this life is *exitus à morte*, an issue from death, for in our mother's womb we are dead, so as that we do not know we live, not so much as we do in our sleep, neither is there any grave so close or so putrid a prison, as the womb would be unto us if we stayed in it beyond our time, or died there before our time. In the grave the worms do not kill us; we breed, and feed, and then kill those worms which we ourselves produced. In the womb the dead child kills the mother that conceived it, and is a murderer, nay, a parricide, even after it is dead. And if we be not dead so in the womb, so as that being dead we kill her that gave us our first life, our life of vegetation, yet we are dead so as David's idols are dead. In the womb we have *eyes and see not, ears and hear not.* There in the womb we are fitted for works of darkness, all the while deprived of light; and there in the womb we are taught cruelty, by being fed with blood, and may be damned, though we be never born. Of our very making in the womb, David says, *I am wonderfully and fearfully made,* and *such knowledge is too excellent for me,* for even that *is the Lord's doing, and it is wonderful in our eyes*; ipse fecit nos, *it is he that made us, and not we ourselves,* nor our parents neither. *Thy hands have made and fashioned me round about,* saith Job, *and* (as the original word is) *thou hast taken pains about me, and yet* (says he) *thou dost destroy me.* Though I be the masterpiece of the greatest master (man is so), yet if thou do no more for me, if thou leave me where thou madest me, destruction will follow. The womb, which should be the house of life, becomes death itself if God leave us there. That which God threatens so often, the shutting of a womb, is not so heavy nor so discomfortable a curse in the first as in the latter shutting, nor in the shutting of barrenness as in the shutting of weakness, when *children are come to the birth, and no strength to bring forth.*

It is the exaltation of misery to fall from a near hope of happiness. And in that vehement imprecation, the prophet expresses the highest of God's anger, *Give them, O Lord, what wilt thou give them? give them a miscarrying womb.* Therefore as soon as we are men (that is, inanimated, quickened in the womb), though we cannot ourselves, our parents have to say in our behalf, *Wretched man that he is, who shall deliver him from this body of death?* if there be no deliverer. It must be he that said to Jeremiah, *Before I formed thee I knew thee, and before thou camest out of the womb I sanctified thee.* We are not sure that there was no kind of ship nor boat to fish in, nor to pass by, till God prescribed Noah that absolute form of the ark. That word which the Holy Ghost, by Moses, useth for the ark, is common to all kind of boats, *thebah*;

and is the same word that Moses useth for the boat that he was exposed in, that his mother laid him in an ark of bulrushes. But we are sure that Eve had no midwife when she was delivered of Cain, therefore she might well say, *Possedi virum à Domino, I have gotten a man from the Lord*, wholly, entirely from the Lord; it is the Lord that enabled me to conceive, the Lord that infused a quickening soul into that conception, the Lord that brought into the world that which himself had quickened; without all this might Eve say, my body had been but the house of death, and *Domini Domini sunt exitus mortis, To God the Lord belong the issues of death*. But then this *exitus à morte* is but *introitus in mortem*; this issue, this deliverance, from that death, the death of the womb, is an entrance, a delivering over to another death, the manifold deaths of this world; we have a winding-sheet in our mother's womb which grows with us from our conception, and we come into the world wound up in that winding-sheet, for we come to seek a grave. And as prisoners discharged of actions may lie for fees, so when the womb hath discharged us, yet we are bound to it by cords of hestæ, by such a string as that we cannot go thence, nor stay there; we celebrate our own funerals with cries even at our birth; as though our threescore and ten years' life were spent in our mother's labour, and our circle made up in the first point thereof; we beg our baptism with another sacrament, with tears; and we come into a world that lasts many ages, but we last not. *In domo Patris*, says our Saviour, speaking of heaven, *multæ mansiones*, divers and durable; so that if a man cannot possess a martyr's house (he hath shed no blood for Christ), yet he may have a confessor's, he hath been ready to glorify God in the shedding of his blood. And if a woman cannot possess a virgin's house (she hath embraced the holy state of marriage), yet she may have a matron's house, she hath brought forth and brought up children in the fear of God. *In domo Patris, in my Father's house*, in heaven, there *are many mansions*; but here, upon earth, the *Son of man hath not where to lay his head*, saith he himself. *Nonne terram dedit filiis hominum?* How then hath God given this earth to the sons of men? He hath given them earth for their materials to be made of earth, and he hath given them earth for their grave and sepulchre, to return and resolve to earth, but not for their possession. *Here we have no continuing city*, nay, no cottage that continues, nay, no persons, no bodies, that continue. Whatsoever moved Saint Jerome to call the journeys of the Israelites in the wilderness, mansions; the word (the word is *nasang*) signifies but a journey, but a peregrination. Even the Israel of God hath no mansions, but journeys, pilgrimages in this life. By what measure did Jacob measure his life to Pharaoh? *The days of the years of my pilgrimage*. And though the apostle would not say *morimur*, that whilst we are in the body we are dead, yet he says, *perigrinamur*, whilst we are in the body we are but in a pilgrimage, and we are *absent from the Lord*: he might have said dead, for this whole world is but an universal churchyard, but our common grave, and the life and motion that the greatest persons have in it is but as the shaking of buried bodies in their grave, by an earthquake. That which we call life is but *hebdomada mortium*, a week of death, seven days, seven periods of our life spent in dying, a dying seven times over; and there is an end. Our birth dies in infancy, and our infancy dies in youth, and youth and the rest die in age, and age also dies and determines all. Nor do all these, youth out of infancy, or age out of youth, arise so, as the phœnix out of the ashes of another phœnix formerly dead, but as a wasp or a serpent out of a carrion, or as a snake out of dung. Our youth is worse than our infancy, and our age worse than our youth. Our youth is hungry and thirsty after those sins which our infancy knew not; and our age is sorry and angry, that it cannot pursue those sins which our youth did; and besides, all the way, so many deaths, that is, so many deadly calamities accompany every condition and every period of this life, as that death itself would be an ease to them that suffer them. Upon this sense doth Job wish that God had not given him an issue from the first death, from the womb, *Wherefore thou hast brought me forth out of the womb? Oh that I had given up the ghost, and no eye seen me! I should have been as though I had not been.* And not only the impatient Israelites in their murmuring (*would to God we had died by the hand of the Lord in the land of Egypt*), but Elijah himself, when he fled from Jezebel, and went for his life, as that text says, under the juniper tree, requested that he might die, and said, *It is enough now, O Lord, take away my life.* So Jonah justifies his impatience, nay, his anger, towards God himself: *Now, O Lord, take, I beseech thee, my life from me, for it is better to die than to live.* And when God asked him, *Dost thou well to be angry for this?* he replies, *I do well to be angry, even unto death.* How much worse a death than death is this life, which so good men would so often change for death! But if my case be as Saint Paul's case, *quotidiè morior,* that I die daily, that something heavier than death fall upon me every day; if my case be David's case, *tota die mortificamur; all the day long we are killed,* that not only every day, but every hour of the day, something heavier than death fall upon me; though that be true of me, *Conceptus in peccatis, I was shapen in iniquity, and in sin did my mother conceive me* (there I died one death); though that be true of me, *Natus filius iræ,* I was born not only the child of sin, but the child of wrath, of the wrath of God for sin, which is a heavier death: yet *Domini Domini sunt exitus mortis, with God the Lord are the issues of death;* and after a Job, and a Joseph, and a Jeremiah, and a Daniel, I cannot doubt of a deliverance. And if no other deliverance conduce more to his glory and my good, yet he hath the keys of death, and he can let me out at that door, that is, deliver me from the manifold deaths of this world, the *omni die,* and the *tota die,* the every day's death and every hour's death, by that one death, the final dissolution of body and soul, the end of all. But then is that the end of all? Is that dissolution of body and soul the last death that the body shall suffer (for of spiritual death we speak not now). It is not, though this be *exitus à morte*: it is *introitus in mortem*; though it be an issue from manifold deaths of this world, yet it is an entrance into the death of corruption and putrefaction, and vermiculation, and incineration, and dispersion in and from the grave, in which every dead man dies over again. It was a prerogative peculiar to Christ, not to die this death, not to see corruption. What gave him this privilege? Not Joseph's great proportion of gums and spices, that might have preserved his body from corruption and incineration longer than he needed it, longer than three days, but it would not have done it for ever. What preserved him then? Did his exemption and freedom from original sin preserve him from this corruption and incineration? It is true that original sin hath induced this corruption and incineration upon us; if we had not sinned in Adam, *mortality had not put on immor-*

tality (as the apostle speaks), nor *corruption had not put on incorruption*, but we had had our transmigration from this to the other world without any mortality, any corruption at all. But yet since Christ took sin upon him, so far as made him mortal, he had it so far too as might have made him see this corruption and incineration, though he had no original sin in himself; what preserved him then? Did the hypostatical union of both natures, God and man, preserve him from this corruption and incineration? It is true that this was a most powerful embalming, to be embalmed with the Divine Nature itself, to be embalmed with eternity, was able to preserve him from corruption and incineration for ever. And he was embalmed so, embalmed with the Divine Nature itself, even in his body as well as in his soul; for the Godhead, the Divine Nature, did not depart, but remained still united to his dead body in the grave; but yet for all this powerful embalming, his hypostatical union of both natures, we see Christ did die; and for all his union which made him God and man, he became no man (for the union of the body and soul makes the man, and he whose soul and body are separated by death as long as that state lasts, is properly no man). And therefore as in him the dissolution of body and soul was no dissolution of the hypostatical union, so there is nothing that constrains us to say, that though the flesh of Christ had seen corruption and incineration in the grave, this had not been any dissolution of the hypostatical union, for the Divine nature, the Godhead, might have remained with all the elements and principles of Christ's body, as well as it did with the two constitutive parts of his person, his body and his soul. This incorruption then was not in Joseph's gums and spices, nor was it in Christ's innocency, and exemption from original sin, nor was it (that is, it is not necessary to say it was) in the hypostatical union. But this incorruptibleness of his flesh is most conveniently placed in that; *Non dabis, thou wilt not suffer thy Holy One to see corruption*; we look no further for causes or reasons in the mysteries of religion, but to the will and pleasure of God; Christ himself limited his inquisition in that *ita est, even so, Father, for so it seemeth good in thy sight.* Christ's body did not see corruption, therefore, because God had decreed it should not. The humble soul (and only the humble soul is the religious soul) rests himself upon God's purposes and the decrees of God which he hath declared and manifested, not such as are conceived and imagined in ourselves, though upon some probability, some verisimilitude; so in our present case Peter proceeds in his sermon at Jerusalem, and so Paul in his at Antioch. They preached Christ to have been risen without seeing corruption, not only because God had decreed it, but because he had manifested that decree in his prophet, therefore doth Saint Paul cite by special number the second Psalm for that decree, and therefore both Saint Peter and Saint Paul cite for it that place in the sixteenth Psalm; for when God declares his decree and purpose in the express words of his prophet, or when he declares it in the real execution of the decree, then he makes it ours, then he manifests it to us. And therefore, as the mysteries of our religion are not the objects of our reason, but by faith we rest on God's decree and purpose—(it is so, O God, because it is thy will it should be so)—so God's decrees are ever to be considered in the manifestation thereof. All manifestation is either in the word of God, or in the execution of the decree; and when these two concur and meet it is the strongest demonstration that can be: when therefore I find those marks of adoption and spiritual filiation which are delivered in the word of God to be upon me; when I find that real execution of his good purpose upon me, as that actually I do live under the obedience and under the conditions which are evidences of adoption and spiritual filiation; then, so long as I see these marks and live so, I may safely comfort myself in a holy certitude and a modest infallibility of my adoption. Christ determines himself in that, the purpose of God was manifest to him; Saint Peter and Saint Paul determine themselves in those two ways of knowing the purpose of God, the word of God before the execution of the decree in the fulness of time. It was prophesied before, said they, and it is performed now, Christ is risen without seeing corruption. Now, this which is so singularly peculiar to him, that his flesh should not see corruption, at his second coming, his coming to judgment, shall extend to all that are then alive; their hestæ shall not see corruption, because, as the apostle says, and says as a secret, as a mystery, *Behold I shew you a mystery, we shall not all sleep* (that is, not continue in the state of the dead in the grave), *but we shall all be changed in an instant,* we shall have a dissolution, and in the same instant a redintegration, a recompacting of body and soul, and that shall be truly a death and truly a resurrection, but no sleeping in corruption; but for us that die now and sleep in the state of the dead, we must all pass this posthume death, this death after death, nay, this death after burial, this dissolution after dissolution, this death of corruption and putrefaction, of vermiculation and incineration, of dissolution and dispersion in and from the grave, when these bodies that have been the children of royal parents, and the parents of royal children, must say with Job, *Corruption, thou art my father, and to the worm, Thou art my mother and my sister.* Miserable riddle, when the same worm must be my mother, and my sister and myself! Miserable incest, when I must be married to my mother and my sister, and be both father and mother to my own mother and sister, beget and bear that worm which is all that miserable penury; when my mouth shall be filled with dust, and the *worm shall feed, and feed sweetly* upon me; when the ambitious man shall have no satisfaction, if the poorest alive tread upon him, nor the poorest receive any contentment in being made equal to princes, for they shall be equal but in dust. *One dieth at his full strength, being wholly at ease and in quiet; and another dies in the bitterness of his soul, and never eats with pleasure;* but *they lie down alike in the dust, and the worm covers them.* In Job and in Isaiah, it covers them and is spread under them, *the worm is spread under thee, and the worm covers thee.* There are the mats and the carpets that lie under, and there are the state and the canopy that hang over the greatest of the sons of men. Even those bodies that were *the temples of the Holy Ghost* come to this dilapidation, to ruin, to rubbish, to dust; even the Israel of the Lord, and Jacob himself, hath no other specification, no other denomination, but that *vermis Jacob,* thou worm of Jacob. Truly the consideration of this posthume death, this death after burial, that after God (with whom are the issues of death) hath delivered me from the death of the womb, by bringing me into the world, and from the manifold deaths of the world, by laying me in the grave, I must die again in an incineration of this flesh, and in a dispersion of that dust. That that monarch, who spread over many nations alive, must in his dust lie in a corner of that sheet of lead, and there but so long as that lead will last; and that private and retired man, that thought himself his own for ever, and never came forth, must in his dust of the grave be published, and (such are the revolutions of the grave) be mingled with the dust of every highway and of every dunghill, and swallowed in every puddle and pond. This is the most inglorious and contemptible vilification, the most deadly and peremptory nullification of man, that we can consider. God seems to have carried the declaration of his power to a great height, when he sets the prophet Ezekiel in the valley of dry bones, and says, *Son of man, can these bones live?* as though it had been impossible, and yet they did; the Lord laid *sinews upon them, and flesh, and breathed into them, and they did live.* But in that case there were bones to be seen, something visible, of which it might be said, Can this thing live? But in this death of incineration and dispersion of dust, we see nothing that we call that man's. If we say, Can this dust live? Perchance it cannot; it may be the mere dust of the earth, which never did live, never shall. It may be the dust of that man's worm, which did live, but shall no more. It may be the dust of another man, that concerns not him of whom it was asked. This death of incineration and dispersion is, to natural reason, the most irrecoverable death of all; and yet *Domini Domini sunt exitus mortis, unto God the Lord belong the issues of death*; and by recompacting this dust into the same body, and remaining the same body with the same soul, he shall in a blessed and glorious resurrection give me such an issue from this death as shall never pass into any other death, but establish me into a life that shall last as long as the Lord of Life himself.

And so have you that that belongs to the first acceptation of these words (*unto God the Lord belong the issues of death*); That though from the womb to the grave, and in the grave itself, we pass from death to death, yet, as Daniel speaks, *the Lord our God is able to deliver us, and he will deliver us.*

And so we pass unto our second accommodation of these words (*unto God the Lord belong the issues of death*); that it belongs to God, and not to man, to pass a judgment upon us at our death, or to conclude a dereliction on God's part upon the manner thereof.

Those indications which the physicians receive, and those presagitions which they give for death or recovery in the patient, they receive and they give out of the grounds and the rules of their art; but we have no such rule or art to give a presagition of spiritual death and damnation upon any such indication as we see in any dying man; we see often enough to be sorry, but not to despair; we may be deceived both ways: we use to comfort ourself in the death of a friend, if it be testified that he went away like a lamb, that is, without any reluctation; but God knows that may be accompanied with a dangerous damp and stupefaction, and insensibility of his present state. Our blessed Saviour suffered colluctations with death, and a *sadness even in his soul to death*, and an agony even to a bloody sweat in his body, and expostulations with God, and exclamations upon the cross. He was a devout man who said upon his death-bed, or death-turf (for he was a hermit), *Septuaginta annos Domino servivisti, et mori times?* Hast thou served a good master threescore and ten years, and now art thou loth to go into his presence? Yet Hilarion was loth. Barlaam was a devout man (a hermit too) that said that day he died,

Cogita te hodie cæpisse servire Domino, et hodie finiturum, Consider this to be the first day's service that ever thou didst thy Master, to glorify him in a Christianly and a constant death, and if thy first day be thy last day too, how soon dost thou come to receive thy wages! Yet Barlaam could have been content to have stayed longer forth. Make no ill conclusions upon any man's lothness to die, for the mercies of God work momentarily in minutes, and many times insensibly to bystanders, or any other than the party departing. And then upon violent deaths inflicted as upon malefactors, Christ himself hath forbidden us by his own death to make any ill conclusion; for his own death had those impressions in it; he was reputed, he was executed as a malefactor, and no doubt many of them who concurred to his death did believe him to be so. Of sudden death there are scarce examples be found in the Scriptures upon good men, for death in battle cannot be called sudden death; but God governs not by examples but by rules, and therefore make no ill conclusion upon sudden death nor upon distempers neither, though perchance accompanied with some words of diffidence and distrust in the mercies of God. The tree lies as it falls, it is true, but it is not the last stroke that fells the tree, nor the last word nor gasp that qualifies the soul. Still pray we for a peaceable life against violent death, and for time of repentance against sudden death, and for sober and modest assurance against distempered and diffident death, but never make ill conclusions upon persons overtaken with such deaths; *Domini Domini sunt exitus mortis, to God the Lord belong the issues of death.* And he received Samson, who went out of this world in such a manner (consider it actively, consider it passively in his own death, and in those whom he slew with himself) as was subject to interpretation hard enough. Yet the Holy Ghost hath moved Saint Paul to celebrate Samson in his great catalogue, and so doth all the church. Our critical day is not the very day of our death, but the whole course of our life. I thank him that prays for me when the bell tolls, but I thank him much more that catechises me, or preaches to me, or instructs me how to live. *Fac hoc et vive,* there is my security, the mouth of the Lord hath said it, *do this and thou shalt live.* But though I do it, yet I shall die too, die a bodily, a natural death. But God never mentions, never seems to consider that death, the bodily, the natural death. God doth not say, Live well, and thou shalt die well, that is, an easy, a quiet death; but, Live well here, and thou shalt live well for ever. As the first part of a sentence pieces well with the last, and never respects, never hearkens after the parenthesis that comes between, so doth a good life here flow into an eternal life, without any consideration what manner of death we die. But whether the gate of my prison be opened with an oiled key (by a gentle and preparing sickness), or the gate be hewn down by a violent death, or the gate be burnt down by a raging and frantic fever, a gate into heaven I shall have, for from the Lord is the cause of my life, and *with God the Lord are the issues of death.* And further we carry not this second acceptation of the words, as this *issue of death* is *liberatio in morte,* God's care that the soul be safe, what agonies soever the body suffers in the hour of death.

But pass to our third part and last part: As this issue of death is *liberatio per mortem,* a deliverance by the death of another. *Sufferentiam Job audiisti, et vidisti finem Domini,* says Saint James, *You have heard of the patience of Job,* says he: all this while you have done that, for in every man, calamitous, miserable man, a Job speaks. Now, *see the end of the Lord*, sayeth that apostle, which is not that end that the Lord proposed to himself (salvation to us), nor the end which he proposes to us (conformity to him), but *see the end of the Lord*, says he, the end that the Lord himself came to, death, and a painful and a shameful death. But why did he die? and why die so? *Quia Domini Domini sunt exitus mortis* (as Saint Augustine, interpreting this text, answers that question), because to this *God our Lord belonged the issues of death. Quid apertius diceretur?* says he there, what can be more obvious, more manifest than this sense of these words? In the former part of this verse it is said, He that is *our God is the God of salvation; Deus salvos faciendi*, so he reads it, the God that must save us. Who can that be, says he, but Jesus? For therefore that name was given him because he was to save us. And to this Jesus, says he, this Saviour, *belong the issues of death; Nec oportuit eum de hac vita alios exitus habere quam mortis*: being come into this life in our mortal nature, he could not go out of this life any other way but by death. *Ideo dictum*, says he, therefore it is said, *to God the Lord belonged the issues of death; ut ostenderetur moriendo nos salvos facturum*, to show that his way to save us was to die. And from this text doth Saint Isidore prove that Christ was truly man (which as many sects of heretics denied, as that he was truly God), because to him, though he were *Dominus Dominus* (as the text doubles it), God the Lord, yet to *him, to God the Lord belonged the issues of death; oportuit eum pati*; more cannot be said than Christ himself says of himself; *These things Christ ought to suffer*, he had no other way but death: so then this part of our sermon must needs be a passion sermon, since all his life was a continual passion, all our Lent may well be a continual Good Friday. Christ's painful life took off none of the pains of his death, he felt not the less then for having felt so much before. Nor will any thing that shall be said before lessen, but rather enlarge the devotion, to that which shall be said of his passion at the time of due solemnization thereof. Christ bled not a drop the less at the last for having bled at his circumcision before, nor will you a tear the less then if you shed some now. And therefore be now content to consider with me how *to this God the Lord belonged the issues of death*. That God, this Lord, the Lord of life, could die, is a strange contemplation; that the Red Sea could be dry, that the sun could stand still, that an oven could be seven times heat and not burn, that lions could be hungry and not bite, is strange, miraculously strange, but super-miraculous that God *could* die; but that God *would* die is an exaltation of that. But even of that also it is a super-exaltation, that God should die, must die, and *non exitus* (said Saint Augustine), God the Lord had no issue but by death, and *oportuit pati* (says Christ himself), all this Christ ought to suffer, was bound to suffer; *Deus ultimo Deus*, says David, God is the God of revenges, he would not pass over the son of man unrevenged, unpunished. But then *Deus ultionum libere egit* (says that place), the God of revenges works freely, he punishes, he spares whom he will. And would he not spare himself? he would not: *Dilectio fortis ut mors, love is strong as death*; stronger, it drew in death, that naturally is not welcome. *Si possibile* says Christ, *if it be possible, let this cup pass*, when his love, expressed in a former decree with his Father, had made it impossible. *Many waters quench not love.* Christ tried many: he was baptised out of his love, and his love determined not there; he mingled blood with water in his agony, and that determined not his love; he wept pure blood, all his blood at all his eyes, at all his pores, in his flagellation and thorns (*to the Lord our God belonged the issues of blood*), and these expressed, but these did not quench his love. He would not spare, nay, he could not spare himself. There was nothing more free, more voluntary, more spontaneous than the death of Christ. It is true, *libere egit*, he died voluntarily; but yet when we consider the contract that had passed between his Father and him, there was an *oportuit*, a kind of necessity upon him: all this *Christ ought to suffer.* And when shall we date this obligation, this *oportuit*, this necessity? When shall we say that began? Certainly this decree by which Christ was to suffer all this was an eternal decree, and was there any thing before that that was eternal? Infinite love, eternal love; be pleased to follow this home, and to consider it seriously, that what liberty soever we can conceive in Christ to die or not to die; this necessity of dying, this decree is as eternal as that liberty; and yet how small a matter made he of this necessity and this dying? His Father calls it but a bruise, and but a bruising of his heel (the serpent shall bruise his heel), and yet that was, that the serpent should practise and compass his death. Himself calls it but a baptism, as though he were to be the better for it. I *have a baptism to be baptised with*, and he was in pain till it was accomplished, and yet this baptism was his death. The Holy Ghost calls it joy (*for the joy which was set before him he endured the cross*), which was not a joy of his reward after his passion, but a joy that filled him even in the midst of his torments, and arose from him; when Christ calls his *calicem* a cup, and no worse (*Can ye drink of my cup*), he speaks not odiously, not with detestation of it. Indeed it was a cup, *salus mundo*, a health to all the world. And *quid retribuam*, says David, *What shall I render to the Lord?* Answer you with David, *Accipiam calicem, I will take the cup of salvation*; take it, that cup is salvation, his passion, if not into your present imitation, yet into your present contemplation. And behold how that Lord that was God, yet could die, would die, must die for our salvation. That Moses and Elias talked with Christ in the transfiguration, both Saint Matthew and Saint Mark tells us, but what they talked of, only Saint Luke; *Dicebant excessum ejus*, says he, *They talked of his disease, of his death, which was to be accomplished at Jerusalem*. The word is of his *exodus*, the very word of our text, *exitus*, his *issue by death*. Moses, who in his exodus had prefigured this issue of our Lord, and in passing Israel out of Egypt through the Red Sea, had foretold in that actual prophecy, Christ passing of mankind through the sea of his blood; and Elias, whose exodus and issue of this world was a figure of Christ's ascension; had no doubt a great satisfaction in talking with our blessed Lord, *de excessu ejus*, of the full consummation of all this in his death, which was to be accomplished at Jerusalem. Our meditation of his death should be more visceral, and affect us more, because it is of a thing already done. The ancient Romans had a certain tenderness and detestation of the name of death; they could not name death, no, not in their wills; there they could not say, *Si mori contigerit*, but *si quid humanitas contingat*, not if or when I die, but when the course of nature is accomplished upon me. To us that speak daily of the death of Christ (he was crucified, dead, and buried), can the memory or the mention of our own death be irksome or bitter? There are in these latter times amongst us that name death freely enough, and the death of God, but in blasphemous oaths and execrations. Miserable men, who shall therefore be said never to have named Jesus, because they have named him too often; and therefore hear Jesus say, *Nescivi vos, I never knew you*, because they made themselves too familiar with him. Moses and Elias talked with Christ of his death only in a holy and joyful sense, of the benefit which they and all the world were to receive by that. Discourses of religion should not be out of curiosity, but to edification. And then they talked with Christ of his death at that time when he was in the greatest height of glory, that ever he admitted in this world, that is, his transfiguration. And we are afraid to speak to the great men of this world of their death, but nourish in them a vain imagination of immortality and immutability. But *bonum est nobis esse hic* (as Saint Peter said there), *It is good to dwell here*, in this consideration of his death, and therefore transfer we our tabernacle (our devotions) through some of those steps which God the Lord made to his *issue of death* that day. Take in the whole day from the hour that Christ received the passover upon Thursday unto the hour in which he died the next day. Make this present day that day in thy devotion, and consider what he did, and remember what you have done. Before he instituted and celebrated the sacrament (which was after the eating of the passover), he proceeded to that act of humility, to wash his disciples' feet, even Peter's, who for a while resisted him. In thy preparation to the holy and blessed sacrament, hast thou with a sincere humility sought a reconciliation with all the world, even with those that have been averse from it, and refused that reconciliation from thee? If so, and not else, thou hast spent that first part of his last day in a conformity with him. After the sacrament he spent the time till night in prayer, in preaching, in psalms: hast thou considered that a worthy receiving of the sacrament consists in a continuation of holiness after, as well as in a preparation before? If so, thou hast therein also conformed thyself to him; so Christ spent his time till night. At night he went into the garden to pray, and he prayed prolixious, he spent much time in prayer, how much? Because it is literally expressed, that he prayed there three several times, and that returning to his disciples after his first prayer, and finding them asleep, said, *Could ye not watch with me one hour*, it is collected that he spent three hours in prayer. I dare scarce ask thee whither thou wentest, or how thou disposedst of thyself, when it grew dark and after last night. If that time were spent in a holy recommendation of thyself to God, and a submission of thy will to his, it was spent in a conformity to him. In that time, and in those prayers, was his agony and bloody sweat. I will hope that thou didst pray; but not every ordinary and customary prayer, but prayer actually accompanied with shedding of tears and dispositively in a readiness to shed blood for his glory in necessary cases, puts thee into a conformity with him. About midnight he was taken and bound with a kiss, art thou not too conformable to him in that? Is not that too literally, too exactly thy case, at midnight to have been taken and bound with a kiss? From thence he was carried back to Jerusalem, first to Annas, then to Caiaphas, and (as late as it was) then he was examined and buffeted, and delivered over to the custody of those officers from whom he received all those irrisions, and violences, the covering of his face, the spitting upon his face, the blasphemies of words, and the smartness of blows, which that gospel mentions: in which compass fell that gallicinium, that crowing of the cock which called up Peter to his repentance. How thou passedst all that time thou knowest. If thou didst any thing that needest Peter's tears, and hast not shed them, let me be thy cock, do it now. Now, thy Master (in the unworthiest of his servants) looks back upon thee, do it now. Betimes, in the morning, so soon as it was day, the Jews held a council in the high priest's hall, and agreed upon their evidence against him, and then carried him to Pilate, who was to be his judge; didst thou accuse thyself when thou wakedst this morning, and wast thou content even with false accusations, that is, rather to suspect actions to have been sin, which were not, than to smother and justify such as were truly sins? Then thou spentest that hour in conformity to him; Pilate found no evidence against him, and therefore to ease himself, and to pass a compliment upon Herod, tetrarch of Galilee, who was at that time at Jerusalem (because Christ, being a Galilean, was of Herod's jurisdiction), Pilate sent him to Herod, and rather as a madman than a malefactor; Herod remanded him (with scorn) to Pilate, to proceed against him; and this was about eight of the clock. Hast thou been content to come to this inquisition, this examination, this agitation, this cribration, this pursuit of thy conscience; to sift it, to follow it from the sins of thy youth to thy present sins, from the sins of thy bed to the sins of thy board, and from the substance to the circumstance of thy sins? That is time spent like thy Saviour's. Pilate would have saved Christ, by using the privilege of the day in his behalf, because that day one prisoner was to be delivered, but they choose Barabbas; he would have saved him from death, by satisfying their fury with inflicting other torments upon him, scourging and crowning with thorns, and loading him with many scornful and ignominious contumelies; but they regarded him not, they pressed a crucifying. Hast thou gone about to redeem thy sin, by fasting, by alms, by disciplines and mortifications, in way of satisfaction to the justice of God? That will not serve, that is not the right way; we press an utter crucifying of that sin that governs thee: and that conforms thee to Christ. Towards noon Pilate gave judgment, and they made such haste to execution as that by noon he was upon the cross. There now hangs that sacred body upon the cross, rebaptized in his own tears, and sweat, and embalmed in his own blood alive. There are those bowels of compassion which are so conspicuous, so manifested, as that you may see them through his wounds. There those glorious eyes grew faint in their sight, so as the sun, ashamed to survive them, departed with his light too. And then that Son of God, who was never from us, and yet had now come a new way unto us in assuming our nature, delivers that soul (which was never out of his Father's hands) by a *new way*, a voluntary emission of it into his Father's hands; for though *to this God our Lord belonged these issues of death*, so that considered in his own contract, he must necessarily die, yet at no breach or battery which they had made upon his sacred body issued his soul; but *emisit*, he gave up the ghost; and as God breathed a soul into the first Adam, so this second Adam breathed his soul into God, into the hands of God.

There we leave you in that blessed dependency, to hang upon him that hangs upon the cross, there bathe in his tears, there suck at his wounds, and lie down in peace in his grave, till he vouchsafe you a resurrection, and an ascension into that kingdom which He hath prepared for you with the inestimable price of his incorruptible blood. Amen.

Metaphysical poetry spans a time frame broader than the Wars of the Three Kingdoms. The term "metaphysical" originated from a disparaging comment about John Donne by seventeenth-century literary critic John Dryden: "[Donne] affects the metaphysics, not only in his satires, but in his amorous verses, where nature only should reign; and perplexes the minds of the fair sex with nice speculations of philosophy." The label of *metaphysical* to describe these poets did not become popular until the twentieth century, when they began to achieve wider scholarly recognition. Metaphysical poetry refers to traditional works that center upon the sacred and rely heavily upon conceits which compare two dissimilar subjects and exaggerate conventional emotions. Metaphysical conceits specifically interface the physical with the abstract to create an extended metaphor, linking the unlike subjects or things together logically. Scholars have applied the term "metaphysical" to numerous poets, such as Herbert, Vaughan, Crashaw, Marvell, and even Shakespeare—but Donne epitomizes the label. Within the context of the English Civil Wars, Metaphysical poets were likely to support Parliament rather than King Charles I, whose religious doctrines were highly unpopular. This helps to contrast them with Cavalier poets.

GEORGE HERBERT

George Herbert was one of the first metaphysical poets to follow in John Donne's footsteps. In fact, Herbert died the same year that Donne's *Songs and Sonnets* and *Holy Sonnets* were first published, 1633, indicating that any inspiration Herbert took from Donne came from his sermons or poems shared privately. Born into a distinguished family and highly educated, Herbert wrote in Latin and Greek as well as in English. Because he was devoutly religious, opting ultimately to pursue the vocation of parish priest, all his surviving poems focus on religious subjects. Before his death at the age of thirty-nine, Herbert sent his poems to a friend, instructing him to publish the works only if they could "turn to the advantage of any dejected poor soul."

Born in Wales but reared in England, George Herbert had nine siblings. After his father died when Herbert was three, John Donne, a close family friend, served as his godfather. At first, Herbert intended to pursue the political career expected of a highly born gentleman. Upon graduating from Cambridge, he became a fellow at his alma mater, then a public orator. In 1624, Herbert was elected to Parliament, but he left politics behind with the death of his patron King James I in 1625. Herbert then joined the clergy in 1629, electing to serve, unlike his powerful preaching godfather, as a humble country parson. He simultaneously wrote and painstakingly revised religious poetry. Fellow poet Henry Vaughan remembered him as an incredibly caring and charitable clergyman, "a most glorious saint."

Herbert, who was sickly throughout his life, died in 1633. His collection *The Temple: Sacred Poems and Private Ejaculations* was published posthumously the same year.

HENRY VAUGHAN

Henry Vaughan started his literary career with secular writing but switched to religious compositions after a painful illness in the late 1640s. Had his life gone differently, he might have been a Cavalier poet in support of King Charles I—he was secretary to a Royalist judge and briefly served in the Royalist army. Instead, Vaughan was influenced by his illness and the works of George Herbert to become devoutly religious. Many of the pieces included in Vaughan's *Silex Scintillans* were inspired by Herbert's poetry.

Vaughan was born in 1621 to a wealthy Welsh family. He had a twin brother, Thomas, who became a philosopher and alchemist. Vaughan was reared in Wales; he left to attend Oxford sometime around 1640, then returned home upon the outbreak of the English Civil War. Sometime during the war, Vaughan began to study and make a living from the practice of medicine. He and his wife Catherine had four children, living a quiet life in the countryside until Vaughan's death in 1695. His writing went largely unappreciated during his life, though *Silex Scintillans* was published in 1650 and received a second volume in 1655. Twentieth and twenty-first century scholars have particularly appreciated Vaughan's work for its strong imagery and devotion.

RICHARD CRASHAW

Richard Crashaw's father, William Crashaw was a well-known Anglican preacher who strongly opposed Catholicism. Richard was born around 1612 in London. His mother died when he was an infant, and his father died when he was thirteen. Crashaw's first poems were Protestant-leaning epigrams that he composed in Latin while studying at Cambridge. After graduating, he became curate of the university's chapel in 1638. Crashaw was motivated by his church's Catholic history and the fact that many of Cambridge's fellows drew from Catholicism in their practice of the Anglican faith to decorate the chapel more traditionally, provoking ire from Puritans. This forced him to relocate to the Netherlands, where he converted to Catholicism. Crashaw went on to live in Paris, then traveled to Rome as a pilgrim in 1646, where he was introduced to the Pope. He wrote most of his celebrated poems after his conversion to Catholicism; his best-known works, including "The Flaming Heart," are about Spanish Catholic nun Saint Teresa of Avila. Soon upon Crashaw's acquisition of a seminary post in Rome in 1647, his health declined, and he died in 1649.

<h1 style="text-align:center">Cavalier poets: Royalist sentiments</h1>

The tradition of Cavalier poetry is much more specific than that of metaphysical poetry. During the Wars of the Three Kingdoms (1639-1653) and especially the English Civil Wars when King Charles I was deposed, a group of poets emerged who steadfastly supported the monarch. Most of them were courtiers; the term *cavalier* was coined as a pejorative term comparing these poets to boisterous, hedonistic knights. Cavalier poems are characterized by themes of war, pleasure, and aesthetic beauty in contrast to more traditional poetry on subjects like religion or deeply complex love. Cavelier texts also glorify the Crown, producing nostalgia for fading Royalist ideals and rituals. Since the genre emerged during a specific period of upheaval, it was inherently short-lived, fading after the defeat of the Royalist cause.

Robert Herrick

Robert Herrick exemplifies Cavalier poetry, especially his earlier poems. The most common subjects of these poems are female sexuality and *carpe diem*, "seize the day," or the warning that life is short, a theme that Herrick helped to repopularize. He wrote thousands of short poems that critics have called "tiny, charmingly exquisite jewels," publishing his major collection *Hesperides* in 1648 just after the conclusion of the English Civil Wars. For Herrick the good life which he termed "cleanly wantonness" involved love devoid of high passion, the power of poetry as ballast against the ravages of time, and the pleasures of food, drink, and song.

Herrick was born in London in 1591 to a wealthy family. He was apprenticed to his uncle, a court jeweler, before being accepted to Cambridge where he became a member of the Sons of Ben, a group of poets who emulated Ben Jonson's work. After Cambridge, Herrick joined the Church of England and acquired a vicarage. However, he was removed from this position in 1647 because of his Royalist sympathies. He finished and published *Hesperides* partly to make a living during this time. Upon the restoration in 1660, Herrick garnered favor with King Charles II through poetry that ultimately reinforced the conservative values of social stability, tradition, and order that had been threatened by the Puritan revolution. Charles restored Herrick's vicarage. Despite the playfully sexual content of his poems, Herrick remained a bachelor until his death in 1674 at the age of eighty-three.

Richard Lovelace

A poet who fought for King Charles I's cause during the Wars of the Three Kingdoms, Richard Lovelace is another quintessential example of the Cavalier style. After the defeat of the Royalist cause, Lovelace turned to literature, publishing his collection of poetry *Lucasta* in 1649. These early poems of his deal primarily with his experiences in war, glorifying the nobility of fighting for one's country.

From a well-known military family, Lovelace was born in 1617. His father, Sir William Lovelace, died at war with Spain when Richard was nine. At eighteen, Lovelace graduated from the University of Oxford, where he wrote his first poems. He joined the Bishops' Wars in 1639, which inspired his first war poems. In 1642, Lovelace was imprisoned for various Royalist actions taken against the House of Commons; though he was quickly released, the Commons prevented him from fighting in the first English Civil War. This experience inspired Lovelace's poetry about imprisonment, including "To Althea, From Prison." He was incarcerated again between 1648 and 1649, during which time King Charles I was executed. Lovelace continued to write poems but never achieved notability again. He died in 1657.

Andrew Marvell

Andrew Marvell is an exceptional case. Scholars consider him a metaphysical poet because he sat in Parliament and remained good friends with the staunch anti-Royalist John Milton. However, his most famous poem, "To His Coy Mistress," exemplifies the *carpe diem* attitude displayed by Cavalier poets. This poem exhibits the playful eroticism and appreciation of beauty that are cornerstones of the Cavalier style. Most of Marvell's other poetry falls squarely in the metaphysical genre while his prose works criticize the monarchy.

Marvell was born in 1621 to an Anglican clergyman. After his education at Trinity College, Cambridge, he spent most of the English Civil War on the continent. Having mastered Latin and Greek at Cambridge, Marvell learned French, Italian, and Spanish during his travels. He worked with John Milton on Latin translations for Oliver Cromwell's government before being elected to Parliament in 1659, serving until his death. During the 1660 restoration of the monarchy, Marvell became instrumental in saving Milton from execution for his anti-Royalist writing. Marvell also wrote anonymous satires about the corruption within Parliament while he was a member. He died suddenly in 1678 while reportedly in perfect health; some contemporaries rumored that he was poisoned for political reasons.

THE TEMPLE: SACRED POEMS AND PRIVATE EJACULATIONS
(EXCERPTS)

BY GEORGE HERBERT

The dedication of this work having been made by the Authour to the *Divine Majestie* onely, how should we now presume to interest any mortall man in the patronage of it? Much lesse think we it meet to seek the recommendation of the Muses, for that which himself was confident to have been inspired by a diviner breath then flows from *Helicon*. The world therefore shall receive it in that naked simplicitie, with which he left it, without any addition either of support or ornament, more then is included in it self. We leave it free and unforestalled to every mans judgement, and to the benefit that he shall finde by perusall. Onely for the clearing of some passages, we have thought it not unfit to make the common Reader privie to some few particularities of the condition and disposition of the Person;

Being nobly born, and as eminently endued with gifts of the minde, and having by industrie and happy education perfected them to that great height of excellencie, whereof his fellowship of Trinitie Colledge in Cambridge, and his Orator-ship in the Universitie, together with that knowledge which the Kings Court had taken of him, could make relation farre above ordinarie. Quitting both his deserts and all the opportunities that he had for worldly preferment, he betook himself to the Sanctuarie and Temple of God, choosing rather to serve at Gods Altar, then to seek the honour of State-employments. As for those inward enforcements to this course (for outward there was none) which many of these ensuing verses bear witnesse of, they detract not from the freedome, but adde to the honour of this resolution in him. As God had enabled him, so he accounted him meet not onely to be called, but to be compelled to this service: Wherein his faith full discharge was such, as may make him justly a companion to the primitive Saints, and a pattern or more for the age he lived in.

To testifie his independencie upon all others, and to quicken his diligence in this kinde, he used in his ordinarie speech, when he made mention of the blessed name of our Lord and Saviour Jesus Christ, to adde, *My Master*.

Next God, he loved that which God himself hath magnified above all things, that is, his Word: so as he hath been heard to make solemne protestation, that he would not part with one leaf thereof for the whole world, if it were offered him in exchange.

His obedience and conformitie to the Church and the discipline thereof was singularly remarkable Though he abounded in private devotions, yet went he every morning and evening with his familie to the Church; and by his example, exhortations, and encouragements drew the greater part of his parishioners to accompanie him dayly in the publick celebration of Divine Service.

As for worldly matters, his love and esteem to them was so little, as no man can more ambitiously seek, then he did earnestly endeavour the resignation of an Ecclesiasticall dignitie, which he was possessour of. But God permitted not the accomplishment of this desire, having ordained him his instrument for reed-ifying of the Church belonging thereunto, that had layen ruinated almost twenty yeares. The reparation whereof, having been uneffectually attempted by publick colllections, was in the end by his own and some few others private free-will-of-ferings succesfully effected. With the remembrance whereof, as of an especiall good work, when a friend went about to comfort him on his death-bed, he made answer, *It is a good work, if it be sprinkled with the bloud of Christ:* otherwise then in this respect he could finde nothing to glorie or comfort himself with, neither in this, nor in any other thing.

And these are but a few of many that might be said, which we have chosen to premise as a glance to some parts of the ensuing book, and for an example to the Reader. We conclude all with his own Motto, with which he used to conclude all things that might seem to tend any way to his own honour;
Lesse then the least of Gods mercies.

The Dedication.

LOrd, my first fruits present themselves to thee;
Yet not mine neither: for from thee they came,
And must return. Accept of them and me,
And make us strive, who shall sing best thy name.
Turn their eyes hither, who shall make a gain:
Theirs, who shall hurt themselves or me, refrain.

Upon Julia's Breasts

By Robert Herrick

Display thy breasts, my Julia—there let me
Behold that circummortal purity,
Between whose glories there my lips I'll lay,
Ravish'd in that fair *via lactea.*[1]

To the Virgins, to Make Much of Time

By Robert Herrick

Gather ye rosebuds while ye may,
  Old time is still a-flying:
And this same flower that smiles to-day
  To-morrow will be dying.

5 The glorious lamp of heaven, the sun,
    The higher he's a-getting,
The sooner will his race be run,
    And nearer he's to setting.

1: Milky way.

That age is best which is the first,
10   When youth and blood are warmer;
But being spent, the worse, and worst
    Times still succeed the former.

Then be not coy, but use your time,
    And while ye may go marry:
15 For having lost but once your prime
    You may for ever tarry.

To Lucasta, Going to the Warres

By Richard Lovelace

Tell me not, (sweet,) I am unkinde,
That from the nunnerie
Of thy chaste breast and quiet minde
To warre and armes I flie.

5 True: a new Mistresse now I chase,
The first foe in the field;
And with a stronger faith imbrace
A sword, a horse, a shield.

Yet this inconstancy is such,
10 As you too shall adore;
I could not love thee, dear, so much,
Lov'd I not Honour more.

Silex Scintillans

(Excerpts)

By Henry Vaughan

Death. A Dialogue.

Soule:
'TIs a sad Land, that in one day
Hath dull'd thee thus, when death shall freeze
Thy bloud to Ice, and thou must stay
Tenant for Yeares, and Centuries,
5 How wilt thou brook't? —

Body:
I cannot tell,—
But if all sence wings not with thee,
And something still be left the dead,
I'le wish my Curtaines off to free
10 Me from so darke, and sad a bed;

A neast of nights, a gloomie sphere,
Where shadowes thicken, and the Cloud
Sits on the Suns brow all the yeare,
And nothing moves without a shrowd;

Soule:
15 'Tis so: But as thou sawest that night
Wee travell'd in, our first attempts
Were dull, and blind, but Custome straight
Our feares, and falls brought to contempt,

Then, when the gastly twelve was past
20 We breath'd still for a blushing East,
And bad the lazie Sunne make hast,
And on sure hopes, though long, did feast;

But when we saw the Clouds to crack
And in those Cranies light appear'd,
25 We thought the day then was not slack,
And pleas'd our selves with what wee feard;

Just so it is in death. But thou
Shalt in thy mothers bosome sleepe
Whilst I each minute grone to know
30 How neere Redemption creepes.

Then shall wee meet to mixe again, and met,
'Tis last good-night, our Sunne shall never set.

DAY OF JUDGEMENT.

When through the North a fire shall rush
And rowle into the East,
And like a firie torrent brush
And sweepe up South, and West,

5 When all shall streame, and lighten round
And with surprizing flames
Both stars, and Elements confound
And quite blot out their names,

When thou shalt spend thy sacred store
10 Of thunders in that heate
And low as ere they lay before
Thy six-dayes-buildings beate,

When like a scrowle the heavens shal passe
And vanish cleane away,
15 And nought must stand of that vast space
Which held up night, and day,

When one lowd blast shall rend the deepe,
And from the wombe of earth
Summon up all that are asleepe
20 Unto a second birth,

When thou shalt make the Clouds thy seate,
And in the open aire
The Quick, and dead, both small and great
Must to thy barre repaire;

25 O then it wilbe all too late
To say, what shall I doe?
Repentance there is out of date
And so is mercy too;

Prepare, prepare me then, O God!
30 And let me now begin
To feele my loving fathers Rod
Killing the man of sinne!

Give me, O give me Crosses here,
Still more afflictions lend,
35 That pill, though bitter, is most deare
That brings health in the end;

Lord, God! I beg nor friends, nor wealth
But pray against them both;
Three things I'de have, my soules chief health!
40 And one of these seme loath,

A living FAITH, a HEART of flesh,
The WORLD an Enemie,
This last will keepe the first two fresh,
And bring me, where I'de be.

THE FLAMING HEART

BY RICHARD CRASHAW

UPON THE BOOK AND PICTURE OF THE SERAPHICAL SAINT TERESA, AS SHE IS USUALLY
EXPRESSED WITH A SERAPHIM BISIDE HER.

Wel-meaning readers! you that come as freinds
And catch the pretious name this peice pretends;
Make not too much hast to admire
That fair-cheek't fallacy of fire.
5 That is a seraphim, they say
And this the great Teresia.

Readers, be rul'd by me; and make
Here a well-plact and wise mistake:
You must transpose the picture quite,
10   And spell it wrong to read it right;
Read him for her, and her for him,
And call the saint the seraphim.
Painter, what didst thou understand
To put her dart into his hand?
15   See, even the yeares and size of him
Showes this the mother seraphim.
This is the mistresse flame; and duteous he
Her happy fire-works here, comes down to see.
O most poor-spirited of men!
20   Had thy cold pencil kist her pen,
Thou couldst not so unkindly err
To show vs this faint shade for her.
Why, man, this speakes pure mortall frame;
And mockes with female frost Love's manly flame.
25   One would suspect thou meant'st to paint
Some weak, inferiour, woman-saint.
But had thy pale-fac't purple took
Fire from the burning cheeks of that bright booke,
Thou wouldst on her have heap't up all
30   That could be found seraphicall;
What e're this youth of fire, weares fair,
Rosy fingers, radiant hair,
Glowing cheek, and glistering wings,
All those fair and fragrant things
35   But before all, that fiery dart
Had fill'd the hand of this great heart.

Doe then, as equall right requires,
Since his the blushes be, and her's the fires,
Resume and rectify thy rude design,
40   Undresse thy seraphim into mine;
Redeem this iniury of thy art,
Give him the vail, give her the dart.
Give him the vail; that he may cover
The red cheeks of a rivall'd lover.
45   Asham'd that our world now can show
Nests of new seraphims here below.

Give her the dart, for it is she
(Fair youth) shootes both thy shaft, and thee;
Say, all ye wise and well-peirc't hearts
50   That live and dy amidst her darts,

What is't your tastfull spirits doe prove
In that rare life of her, and Love?
Say, and bear witnes. Sends she not
A seraphim at every shott?
55   What magazins of immortall armes there shine!
Heavn's great artillery in each love-spun line.
Give then the dart to her who gives the flame;
Give him the veil, who gives the shame.

But if it be the frequent fate
60   Of worst faults to be fortunate;
If all's præscription; and proud wrong
Hearkens not to an humble song;
For all the gallantry of him,
Give me the suffring seraphim.
65   His be the bravery of all those bright things,
The glowing cheekes, the glistering wings;
The rosy hand, the radiant dart;
Leave her alone the flaming heart.

Leave her that; and thou shalt leave her
70   Not one loose shaft but Love's whole quiver.
For in Love's feild was never found
A nobler weapon then a wound.
Love's passives are his activ'st part,
The wounded is the wounding heart.
75   O heart! the æquall poise of Love's both parts
Bigge alike with wound and darts.
Live in these conquering leaves; live all the same,
And walk through all tongues one triumphant flame.
Live here, great heart; and love and dy and kill;
80   And bleed and wound; and yeild and conquer still.
Let this immortall life wherere it comes
Walk in a crowd of loves and martyrdomes.
Let mystick deaths wait on't; and wise soules be
The love-slain wittnesses of this life of thee.
85   O sweet incendiary! shew here thy art,
Upon this carcasse of a hard, cold hart;
Let all thy scatter'd shafts of light, that play
Among the leaves of thy larg books of day.
Combin'd against this brest at once break in
90   And take away from me my self and sin;
This gratious robbery shall thy bounty be,
And my best fortunes such fair spoiles of me.
O thou undanted daughter of desires!
By all thy dowr of lights and fires;

95   By all the eagle in thee, all the dove;
     By all thy lives and deaths of love;
     By thy larg draughts of intellectuall day,
     And by thy thirsts of love more large then they;
     By all thy brim-fill'd bowles of feirce desire,
100   By thy last morning's draught of liquid fire;
     By the full kingdome of that finall kisse
     That seiz'd thy parting soul, and seal'd thee His;
     By all the Heav'n thou hast in Him
     (Fair sister of the seraphim!)
105   By all of Him we have in thee;
     Leave nothing of my self in me.
     Let me so read thy life, that I
     Unto all life of mine may dy.

ON OUR CRUCIFIED LORD NAKED AND BLOODY

By Richard Crashaw

Th' have left Thee naked, Lord: O that they had!
This garment too I would they had deny'd.
Thee with Thyselfe they have too richly clad,
Opening the purple wardrobe of Thy side.
5   O never could bee found garments too good
        For Thee to weare, but these of Thine own blood.

TO HIS COY MISTRESS

By Andrew Marvell

Had we but world enough and time,
This coyness, lady, were no crime.
We would sit down and think which way
To walk, and pass our long love's day.
5   Thou by the Indian Ganges' side
     Should'st rubies find: I by the tide
     Of Humber would complain. I would
     Love you ten years before the Flood,
     And you should, if you please, refuse
10   Till the conversion of the Jews.
     My vegetable love should grow
     Vaster than empires and more slow.
     An hundred years should go to praise
     Thine eyes, and on thy forehead gaze;
15   Two hundred to adore each breast,
     But thirty thousand to the rest;
     An age at least to every part,

And the last age should show your heart.
For, lady, you deserve this state,
20 Nor would I love at lower rate.

But at my back I always hear
Time's wingèd chariot hurrying near,
And yonder all before us lie
Deserts of vast eternity.
25 Thy beauty shall no more be found,
Nor in thy marble vault shall sound
My echoing song; then worms shall try
That long-preserved virginity,
And your quaint honour turn to dust,
30 And into ashes all my lust.
The grave's a fine and private place,
But none, I think, do there embrace.

Now, therefore, while the youthful hue
Sits on thy skin like morning dew,
35 And while thy willing soul transpires
At every pore with instant fires,
Now, let us sport us while we may;
And now, like amorous birds of prey,
Rather at once our time devour,
40 Than languish in his slow-chapt power!
Let us roll all our strength, and all
Our sweetness up into one ball;
And tear our pleasures with rough strife,
Through the iron gates of life!
45 Thus, though we cannot make our sun
Stand still, yet we will make him run.

John Milton

John Milton was born in London on December 9th, 1608. His father, also John Milton, made a prosperous living as a scrivener (a copier and transcriber) and was a talented music composer. His mother, Sara Jeffrey Milton, was the daughter of a successful tailor. Milton was baptized in the Church of England when he was three days old. He had two surviving siblings: an older sister, Anne, and a younger brother, Christopher.

Milton began his education with private tutors around the age of nine, enrolling in St. Paul's School in 1620. He likely heard John Donne give sermons at St. Paul's Cathedral after Donne became its Dean in 1621. He studied Latin and Greek, which inspired the elevated language he used in his later works. Milton would also write some of his later works in Latin, aiming them at a continental and scholarly audience. He wrote his first known compositions, two psalms, at the age of fifteen, demonstrating his strong interest in religion from a young age.

Milton enrolled at sixteen in Christ's College, Cambridge University, probably with intentions to join the ministry. He did not enjoy his time at Cambridge—his classmates called him "The Lady of Christ's College" because of his feminine appearance and disinterest in sports. He also likely considered the curriculum boring and stilted. Nonetheless, Milton was successful academically, earning a bachelor's degree in 1629 and a master's degree in 1632. Milton wrote several poems by the time he graduated, including "On the Morning of Christ's Nativity," "L'Allegro," "Il Penseroso," and an epitaph "On Shakespeare."

Although his education prepared him to become a minister, Milton returned home after earning his MA. We're not certain why he did not enter the ministry, but scholars speculate that he was already too religiously radical to take oaths to the Church of England, or that he did not wish to be part of the church's hierarchy. This decision could be early evidence of Milton's subsequent Puritan beliefs. He may have returned home to care for his aging parents or simply because he wanted to become a poet. With generous financial support from his father, Milton spent six years learning independently, reading classical authors in Latin and Greek and extensively studying history. He also wrote during this time, composing two masques commissioned to be performed at court, *Arcades* and *Comus*, and his pastoral elegy *Lycidas*.

Milton's mother died in 1637, and in 1638 he departed for a fifteen-month tour in Italy. By then, Milton was fluent in English, French, Spanish, Italian, Dutch, Latin, Greek, and Hebrew. Later, he learned to read Old English as well. He met other intellectuals and formed close friendships with several Italian poets, who admired his ability to write in their language. He also met the astronomer

Galileo, who was under house arrest by the Roman Catholic church. Milton refers to Galileo and his telescope in *Paradise Lost*. In 1639, Milton returned to London due to the deaths of his sister Anne and close friend Charles Diodati, as well as the likelihood of an English civil war.

Back in London, Milton tutored Anne's two sons and several other students. His main writings became political prose tracts attacking the leadership of the Church of England. Milton supported Parliament, opposing King Charles I and the Archbishop of Canterbury (for a complete overview of the Wars of the Three Kingdoms, see pages 827-834). He published the pamphlets *Of Reformation touching Church Discipline in England*, *Of Prelatical Episcopacy*, and *The Reason of Church-Government Urged against Prelaty* in 1641 and 1642, among others. All of these pamphlets argue for a Presbyterian-style government of the Church of England by a council of elders, rather than by bishops.

In 1642, thirty-four-year-old Milton married seventeen-year-old Mary Powell. The beginning of their marriage was difficult, with Mary returning to her family for three years after the wedding. Speculated causes of the separation include the outbreak of the first English Civil War, Mary's dislike for the comparative lack of luxury in her husband's household, and a clash between Milton's anti-Royalist views and the Royalist inclinations of Mary's family. Milton wrote four tracts advocating for the right of divorce during their years of separation, the first being 1643's *The Doctrine and Discipline of Divorce*. These tracts were not well received by the English print authorities—this close brush with censorship inspired Milton to write his defense of free speech in the publishing industry. *Areopagitica; A speech of Mr. John Milton for the Liberty of Unlicenc'd Printing, to the Parlament of England*, referred to simply as the *Areopagitica*, became one of his most celebrated essays. Also in 1644, Milton published a tract titled *Of Education* which advocated for national education reforms. Mary returned to her husband in 1645, after which they had three daughters (Anne, Mary, and Deborah). Mary Powell Milton died in 1652.

The first English Civil war ended in 1646, with King Charles I executed for treason by a Parliamentary court in January 1649. Two weeks later, Milton published *The Tenure of Kings and Magistrates*, probably written during Charles's trial, which argues that citizens have a right to depose tyrants. The ruling Council of State appointed Milton Secretary for Foreign Tongues the next month. His position called for him to write correspondence for England in foreign languages. Milton's next several essays responded to various Royalist texts published during this time. His *Eikonoklastes* refuted the *Eikon Basilike*, a Royalist book that portrayed Charles as a martyr. The Council of State then ordered Milton to write a book defending the English people, which he published in 1652, titled *Defensio pro Populo Anglicano*. He published more of these defenses in 1654 and 1655 (*Defensio secunda* and *Defensio pro se*, respectively), in response to Royalist treatises that became increasingly personal attacks on Milton.

By 1652, Milton was completely blind. His eyesight had been in decline for years, likely the result of eyestrain from so much reading. He dictated his writing to copiers after this point. In 1656, he married Katherine Woodcock, who died along with their infant daughter less than two years later. Though Milton served as the Secretary for Foreign Tongues until the Restoration of the monarchy in 1660, his deputies carried out most of his duties after he went blind. Milton wrote several treatises after Oliver Cromwell, Lord Protector (the leader of the English Republic) died in 1658, including *A Treatise of Civil Power* and *The Ready and Easy Way to Establishing a Free Commonwealth*. Because of his anti-Royalist writings, Milton was forced into hiding when the monarchy was restored in 1660. He emerged from seclusion when Charles passed the Indemnity and Oblivion Act, which issued "the general Pardon.; Treasons and other Offences mentioned since 1st Jan. 1637." Milton's friends in Parliament, including fellow poet Andrew Marvell, prevented him from being excluded from the general pardon. Nevertheless, he was imprisoned for several months, and his books were burned.

Milton married his third wife in 1663. Elizabeth Mynshull was twenty-four to Milton's fifty-five. While the couple had no children, their marriage was reportedly happy. In 1667, he published his most famous work, *Paradise Lost*, which comprised over ten thousand lines of blank verse, or unrhymed iambic pentameter. Originally published in ten volumes, Milton revised the second 1674 edition to include twelve books. Books 1–4, 9, 10, and 12 are included in this anthology. Milton began to compose his major work in 1658, dictating the epic in its entirety to his various scribes and publishing it with minor revisions. Milton defines *Paradise Lost* as a text that would "justify the ways of God to men." It was not initially heralded, but by the end of the 1600s seven editions were issued, including an annotated critical edition. *Paradise Lost*'s sequel, *Paradise Regained*, presents Jesus Christ as the main character. It was published in 1671, along with the closet drama *Samson Agonistes*, which describes the activities of Samson in the biblical Book of Judges.

Milton also wrote important prose works during the last decade of his life. In 1670, he published *The History of Britain*, which had taken him decades to complete. In 1672, he published *Artis Logicae*, a textbook on logic written in Latin. He never finished *De Doctrina Christiana*, his comprehensive treatise on Christian theology. It was discovered in 1823, translated, and published in 1825. His last major work was *Of True Religion*, an anti-Catholic treatise that argues for religious tolerance for Protestant sects. Milton died on November 8, 1674, at the age of sixty-five. His cause of death is usually recorded as complications caused by gout, but other health issues may have been involved. He was survived by his third wife and his three daughters.

After Milton's death, critical examination of his writings increased. Politics often influenced appreciation for his work because of his anti-Royalist and Puritan leanings, but over time, he became almost universally admired by readers. Some biographers have named him second only to Shakespeare in his adroitness with the English language and his importance as a British writer.

Timeline

1608	Milton is born in London.
1625	Milton enters Christ's College, Cambridge.
1629	"Christ's Nativity."
1630	"On Shakespeare."
1631	"L'Allegro"; "Il Penserosa."
1632	Milton leaves Cambridge with a master's degree.
1632-34	*Arcades*; *Comus* (court masques).
1637	*Lycidas*.
1638-39	Milton travels in continental Europe, then returns to England because of impending civil war and deaths in his personal life.
1641	*Of Reformation touching Church Discipline in England*.
1642	*The Reason of Church-Government Urged against Prelaty*.
1642	Milton marries his first wife, Mary Powell, who is half his age.
1643	*The Doctrine and Discipline of Divorce*.
1644	*Areopagitica*; *Of Education*.
1649	*The Tenure of Kings and Magistrates*; *Eikonoklastes*.
1649	Milton becomes Secretary for Foreign Tongues.
1652	*Defensio pro Populo Anglicano*.
1654	*Defensio secunda*.
1655	*Defensio pro se*.
1656	Milton marries Katherine Woodcock.
1659	*A Treatise of Civil Power*.
1660	*The Ready and Easy Way to Establishing a Free Commonwealth*.
1660	The ascension of King Charles II to the throne of England brings the Restoration of the monarchy; Milton goes into hiding until the passage of the Indemnity and Oblivion Act.
1663	Milton marries his third wife, Elizabeth Mynshull.
1667	*Paradise Lost*.
1670	*History of Britain*.
1671	*Paradise Regained*; *Samson Agonistes*.
1672	*Artis Logicae*.
1673	*Of True Religion*.
1674	Milton dies.

L'Allegro

Hence, loathed Melancholy,
Of Cerberus and blackest Midnight born
In Stygian cave forlorn
'Mongst horrid shapes, and shrieks, and sights unholy!
5 Find out some uncouth cell,
Where brooding Darkness spreads his jealous wings,
And the night-raven sings;
There, under ebon shades and low-browed rocks,
As ragged as thy locks,
10 In dark Cimmerian desert ever dwell.
But come, thou Goddess fair and free,
In heaven yclept Euphrosyne,
And by men heart-easing Mirth;
Whom lovely Venus, at a birth,
15 With two sister Graces more,
To ivy-crowned Bacchus bore:
Or whether (as some sager sing)
The frolic wind that breathes the spring,
Zephyr, with Aurora playing,
20 As he met her once a-Maying,
There, on beds of violets blue,
And fresh-blown roses washed in dew,
Filled her with thee, a daughter fair,
So buxom, blithe, and debonair.
25 Haste thee, Nymph, and bring with thee
Jest, and youthful Jollity,
Quips and cranks and wanton wiles,
Nods and becks and wreathed smiles
Such as hang on Hebe's cheek,
30 And love to live in dimple sleek;
Sport that wrinkled Care derides,
And Laughter holding both his sides.
Come, and trip it, as you go,
On the light fantastic toe;
35 And in thy right hand lead with thee
The mountain-nymph, sweet Liberty;
And, if I give thee honour due,
Mirth, admit me of thy crew,
To live with her, and live with thee,
40 In unreproved pleasures free:

To hear the lark begin his flight,
And, singing, startle the dull night,
From his watch-tower in the skies,
Till the dappled dawn doth rise;
45 Then to come, in spite of sorrow,
And at my window bid good-morrow,
Through the sweet-briar or the vine,
Or the twisted eglantine;
While the cock, with lively din,
50 Scatters the rear of darkness thin,
And to the stack, or the barn-door,
Stoutly struts his dames before:
Oft listening how the hounds and horn
Cheerly rouse the slumbering morn,
55 From the side of some hoar hill,
Through the high wood echoing shrill:
Sometime walking, not unseen,
By hedgerow elms, on hillocks green,
Right against the eastern gate
60 Where the great Sun begins his state,
Robed in flames and amber light,
The clouds in thousand liveries dight;
While the ploughman, near at hand,
Whistles o'er the furrowed land,
65 And the milkmaid singeth blithe,
And the mower whets his scythe,
And every shepherd tells his tale
Under the hawthorn in the dale.
Straight mine eye hath caught new pleasures,
70 Whilst the landskip round it measures:
Russet lawns, and fallows grey,
Where the nibbling flocks do stray;
Mountains on whose barren breast
The labouring clouds do often rest;
75 Meadows trim, with daisies pied;
Shallow brooks, and rivers wide;
Towers and battlements it sees
Bosomed high in tufted trees,
Where perhaps some beauty lies,
80 The cynosure of neighbouring eyes.
Hard by a cottage chimney smokes
From betwixt two aged oaks,
Where Corydon and Thyrsis met
Are at their savoury dinner set
85 Of herbs and other country messes,

Which the neat-handed Phyllis dresses;
And then in haste her bower she leaves,
With Thestylis to bind the sheaves;
Or, if the earlier season lead,
90   To the tanned haycock in the mead.
Sometimes, with secure delight,
The upland hamlets will invite,
When the merry bells ring round,
And the jocund rebecks sound
95   To many a youth and many a maid
Dancing in the chequered shade,
And young and old come forth to play
On a sunshine holiday,
Till the livelong daylight fail:
100   Then to the spicy nut-brown ale,
With stories told of many a feat,
How Faery Mab the junkets eat.
She was pinched and pulled, she said;
And he, by Friar's lantern led,
105   Tells how the drudging goblin sweat
To earn his cream-bowl duly set,
When in one night, ere glimpse of morn,
His shadowy flail hath threshed the corn
That ten day-labourers could not end;
110   Then lies him down, the lubber fiend,
And, stretched out all the chimney's length,
Basks at the fire his hairy strength,
And crop-full out of doors he flings,
Ere the first cock his matin rings.
115   Thus done the tales, to bed they creep,
By whispering winds soon lulled asleep.
Towered cities please us then,
And the busy hum of men,
Where throngs of knights and barons bold,
120   In weeds of peace, high triumphs hold
With store of ladies, whose bright eyes
Rain influence, and judge the prize
Of wit or arms, while both contend
To win her grace whom all commend.
125   There let Hymen oft appear
In saffron robe, with taper clear,
And pomp, and feast, and revelry,
With mask and antique pageantry;
Such sights as youthful poets dream
130   On summer eves by haunted stream.

Then to the well-trod stage anon,
If Jonson's learned sock be on,
Or sweetest Shakespeare, Fancy's child,
Warble his native wood-notes wild.
135 And ever, against eating cares,
Lap me in soft Lydian airs,
Married to immortal verse,
Such as the meeting soul may pierce,
In notes with many a winding bout
140 Of linked sweetness long drawn out
With wanton heed and giddy cunning,
The melting voice through mazes running,
Untwisting all the chains that tie
The hidden soul of harmony;
145 That Orpheus' self may heave his head
From golden slumber on a bed
Of heaped Elysian flowers, and hear
Such strains as would have won the ear
Of Pluto to have quite set free
150 His half-regained Eurydice.
These delights if thou canst give,
Mirth, with thee I mean to live.

Il Pinseroso

Hence, vain deluding Joys,
The brood of Folly without father bred!
How little you bested
Or fill the fixed mind with all your toys!
5 Dwell in some idle brain,
And fancies fond with gaudy shapes possess,
As thick and numberless
As the gay motes that people the sun-beams,
Or likest hovering dreams,
10 The fickle pensioners of Morpheus' train.
But, hail! thou Goddess sage and holy!
Hail, divinest Melancholy!
Whose saintly visage is too bright
To hit the sense of human sight,
15 And therefore to our weaker view
O'erlaid with black, staid Wisdom's hue;
Black, but such as in esteem

Prince Memnon's sister might beseem,
Or that starred Ethiop queen that strove
20   To set her beauty's praise above
The Sea-Nymphs, and their powers offended.
Yet thou art higher far descended:
Thee bright-haired Vesta long of yore
To solitary Saturn bore;
25   His daughter she; in Saturn's reign
Such mixture was not held a stain.
Oft in glimmering bowers and glades
He met her, and in secret shades
Of woody Ida's inmost grove,
30   Whilst yet there was no fear of Jove.
Come, pensive Nun, devout and pure,
Sober, steadfast, and demure,
All in a robe of darkest grain,
Flowing with majestic train,
35   And sable stole of cypress lawn
Over thy decent shoulders drawn.
Come; but keep thy wonted state,
With even step, and musing gait,
And looks commercing with the skies,
40   Thy rapt soul sitting in thine eyes:
There, held in holy passion still,
Forget thyself to marble, till
With a sad leaden downward cast
Thou fix them on the earth as fast.
45   And join with thee calm Peace and Quiet,
Spare Fast, that oft with gods doth diet,
And hears the Muses in a ring
Aye round about Jove's altar sing;
And add to these retired Leisure,
50   That in trim gardens takes his pleasure;
But, first and chiefest, with thee bring
Him that yon soars on golden wing,
Guiding the fiery-wheeled throne,
The Cherub Contemplation;
55   And the mute Silence hist along,
'Less Philomel will deign a song,
In her sweetest saddest plight,
Smoothing the rugged brow of Night,
While Cynthia checks her dragon yoke
60   Gently o'er the accustomed oak.
Sweet bird, that shunn'st the noise of folly,
Most musical, most melancholy!

Thee, chauntress, oft the woods among
I woo, to hear thy even-song;
65 And, missing thee, I walk unseen
On the dry smooth-shaven green,
To behold the wandering moon,
Riding near her highest noon,
Like one that had been led astray
70 Through the heaven's wide pathless way,
And oft, as if her head she bowed,
Stooping through a fleecy cloud.
Oft, on a plat of rising ground,
I hear the far-off curfew sound,
75 Over some wide-watered shore,
Swinging slow with sullen roar;
Or, if the air will not permit,
Some still removed place will fit,
Where glowing embers through the room
80 Teach light to counterfeit a gloom,
Far from all resort of mirth,
Save the cricket on the hearth,
Or the bellman's drowsy charm
To bless the doors from nightly harm.
85 Or let my lamp, at midnight hour,
Be seen in some high lonely tower,
Where I may oft outwatch the Bear,
With thrice great Hermes, or unsphere
The spirit of Plato, to unfold
90 What worlds or what vast regions hold
The immortal mind that hath forsook
Her mansion in this fleshly nook;
And of those demons that are found
In fire, air, flood, or underground,
95 Whose power hath a true consent
With planet or with element.
Sometime let gorgeous Tragedy
In sceptred pall come sweeping by,
Presenting Thebes, or Pelops' line,
100 Or the tale of Troy divine,
Or what (though rare) of later age
Ennobled hath the buskined stage.
But, O sad Virgin! that thy power
Might raise Musaeus from his bower;
105 Or bid the soul of Orpheus sing
Such notes as, warbled to the string,
Drew iron tears down Pluto's cheek,

And made Hell grant what love did seek;
Or call up him that left half-told
110 The story of Cambuscan bold,
Of Camball, and of Algarsife,
And who had Canace to wife,
That owned the virtuous ring and glass,
And of the wondrous horse of brass
115 On which the Tartar king did ride;
And if aught else great bards beside
In sage and solemn tunes have sung,
Of turneys, and of trophies hung,
Of forests, and enchantments drear,
120 Where more is meant than meets the ear.
Thus, Night, oft see me in thy pale career,
Till civil-suited Morn appear,
Not tricked and frounced, as she was wont
With the Attic boy to hunt,
125 But kerchieft in a comely cloud
While rocking winds are piping loud,
Or ushered with a shower still,
When the gust hath blown his fill,
Ending on the rustling leaves,
130 With minute-drops from off the eaves.
And, when the sun begins to fling
His flaring beams, me, Goddess, bring
To arched walks of twilight groves,
And shadows brown, that Sylvan loves,
135 Of pine, or monumental oak,
Where the rude axe with heaved stroke
Was never heard the nymphs to daunt,
Or fright them from their hallowed haunt.
There, in close covert, by some brook,
140 Where no profaner eye may look,
Hide me from day's garish eye,
While the bee with honeyed thigh,
That at her flowery work doth sing,
And the waters murmuring,
145 With such consort as they keep,
Entice the dewy-feathered Sleep.
And let some strange mysterious dream
Wave at his wings, in airy stream
Of lively portraiture displayed,
150 Softly on my eyelids laid;
And, as I wake, sweet music breathe
Above, about, or underneath,

Sent by some Spirit to mortals good,
Or the unseen Genius of the wood.
155 But let my due feet never fail
To walk the studious cloister's pale,
And love the high embowed roof,
With antique pillars massy proof,
And storied windows richly dight,
160 Casting a dim religious light.
There let the pealing organ blow,
To the full-voiced quire below,
In service high and anthems clear,
As may with sweetness, through mine ear,
165 Dissolve me into ecstasies,
And bring all Heaven before mine eyes.
And may at last my weary age
Find out the peaceful hermitage,
The hairy gown and mossy cell,
170 Where I may sit and rightly spell
Of every star that heaven doth shew,
And every herb that sips the dew,
Till old experience do attain
To something like prophetic strain.
175 These pleasures, Melancholy, give;
And I with thee will choose to live.

Paradise Lost

Book I

Of Man's first disobedience, and the fruit
Of that forbidden tree whose mortal taste
Brought death into the World, and all our woe,
With loss of Eden, till one greater Man
5   Restore us, and regain the blissful seat,
Sing, Heavenly Muse, that, on the secret top
Of Oreb, or of Sinai, didst inspire
That shepherd who first taught the chosen seed
In the beginning how the heavens and earth
10   Rose out of Chaos: or, if Sion hill
Delight thee more, and Siloa's brook that flowed
Fast by the oracle of God, I thence
Invoke thy aid to my adventurous song,
That with no middle flight intends to soar
15   Above th' Aonian mount, while it pursues
Things unattempted yet in prose or rhyme.
And chiefly thou, O Spirit, that dost prefer
Before all temples th' upright heart and pure,
Instruct me, for thou know'st; thou from the first
20   Wast present, and, with mighty wings outspread,
Dove-like sat'st brooding on the vast Abyss,
And mad'st it pregnant: what in me is dark
Illumine, what is low raise and support;
That, to the height of this great argument,
25   I may assert Eternal Providence,
And justify the ways of God to men.

Say first—for Heaven hides nothing from thy view,
Nor the deep tract of Hell—say first what cause
Moved our grand parents, in that happy state,
30   Favoured of Heaven so highly, to fall off
From their Creator, and transgress his will
For one restraint, lords of the World besides.
Who first seduced them to that foul revolt?

Th' infernal Serpent; he it was whose guile,
35   Stirred up with envy and revenge, deceived
The mother of mankind, what time his pride
Had cast him out from Heaven, with all his host

Of rebel Angels, by whose aid, aspiring
To set himself in glory above his peers,
40 He trusted to have equalled the Most High,
If he opposed, and with ambitious aim
Against the throne and monarchy of God,
Raised impious war in Heaven and battle proud,
With vain attempt. Him the Almighty Power
45 Hurled headlong flaming from th' ethereal sky,
With hideous ruin and combustion, down
To bottomless perdition, there to dwell
In adamantine chains and penal fire,
Who durst defy th' Omnipotent to arms.

50 Nine times the space that measures day and night
To mortal men, he, with his horrid crew,
Lay vanquished, rolling in the fiery gulf,
Confounded, though immortal. But his doom
Reserved him to more wrath; for now the thought
55 Both of lost happiness and lasting pain
Torments him: round he throws his baleful eyes,
That witnessed huge affliction and dismay,
Mixed with obdurate pride and steadfast hate.
At once, as far as Angels ken, he views
60 The dismal situation waste and wild.
A dungeon horrible, on all sides round,
As one great furnace flamed; yet from those flames
No light; but rather darkness visible
Served only to discover sights of woe,
65 Regions of sorrow, doleful shades, where peace
And rest can never dwell, hope never comes
That comes to all, but torture without end
Still urges, and a fiery deluge, fed
With ever-burning sulphur unconsumed.
70 Such place Eternal Justice has prepared
For those rebellious; here their prison ordained
In utter darkness, and their portion set,
As far removed from God and light of Heaven
As from the centre thrice to th' utmost pole.
75 Oh how unlike the place from whence they fell!
There the companions of his fall, o'erwhelmed
With floods and whirlwinds of tempestuous fire,
He soon discerns; and, weltering by his side,
One next himself in power, and next in crime,
80 Long after known in Palestine, and named
Beelzebub. To whom th' Arch-Enemy,

And thence in Heaven called Satan, with bold words
Breaking the horrid silence, thus began:—

"If thou beest he—but O how fallen! how changed
85 From him who, in the happy realms of light
Clothed with transcendent brightness, didst outshine
Myriads, though bright!—if he whom mutual league,
United thoughts and counsels, equal hope
And hazard in the glorious enterprise
90 Joined with me once, now misery hath joined
In equal ruin; into what pit thou seest
From what height fallen: so much the stronger proved
He with his thunder; and till then who knew
The force of those dire arms? Yet not for those,
95 Nor what the potent Victor in his rage
Can else inflict, do I repent, or change,
Though changed in outward lustre, that fixed mind,
And high disdain from sense of injured merit,
That with the Mightiest raised me to contend,
100 And to the fierce contentions brought along
Innumerable force of Spirits armed,
That durst dislike his reign, and, me preferring,
His utmost power with adverse power opposed
In dubious battle on the plains of Heaven,
105 And shook his throne. What though the field be lost?
All is not lost—the unconquerable will,
And study of revenge, immortal hate,
And courage never to submit or yield:
And what is else not to be overcome?
110 That glory never shall his wrath or might
Extort from me. To bow and sue for grace
With suppliant knee, and deify his power
Who, from the terror of this arm, so late
Doubted his empire—that were low indeed;
115 That were an ignominy and shame beneath
This downfall; since, by fate, the strength of Gods,
And this empyreal substance, cannot fail;
Since, through experience of this great event,
In arms not worse, in foresight much advanced,
120 We may with more successful hope resolve
To wage by force or guile eternal war,
Irreconcilable to our grand Foe,
Who now triumphs, and in th' excess of joy
Sole reigning holds the tyranny of Heaven."

125 So spake th' apostate Angel, though in pain,
Vaunting aloud, but racked with deep despair;
And him thus answered soon his bold compeer:—

"O Prince, O Chief of many throned Powers
That led th' embattled Seraphim to war
130 Under thy conduct, and, in dreadful deeds
Fearless, endangered Heaven's perpetual King,
And put to proof his high supremacy,
Whether upheld by strength, or chance, or fate,
Too well I see and rue the dire event
135 That, with sad overthrow and foul defeat,
Hath lost us Heaven, and all this mighty host
In horrible destruction laid thus low,
As far as Gods and heavenly Essences
Can perish: for the mind and spirit remains
140 Invincible, and vigour soon returns,
Though all our glory extinct, and happy state
Here swallowed up in endless misery.
But what if he our Conqueror (whom I now
Of force believe almighty, since no less
145 Than such could have o'erpowered such force as ours)
Have left us this our spirit and strength entire,
Strongly to suffer and support our pains,
That we may so suffice his vengeful ire,
Or do him mightier service as his thralls
150 By right of war, whate'er his business be,
Here in the heart of Hell to work in fire,
Or do his errands in the gloomy Deep?
What can it then avail though yet we feel
Strength undiminished, or eternal being
155 To undergo eternal punishment?"

Whereto with speedy words th' Arch-Fiend replied:—
"Fallen Cherub, to be weak is miserable,
Doing or suffering: but of this be sure—
To do aught good never will be our task,
160 But ever to do ill our sole delight,
As being the contrary to his high will
Whom we resist. If then his providence
Out of our evil seek to bring forth good,
Our labour must be to pervert that end,
165 And out of good still to find means of evil;
Which ofttimes may succeed so as perhaps
Shall grieve him, if I fail not, and disturb

His inmost counsels from their destined aim.
But see! the angry Victor hath recalled
170　His ministers of vengeance and pursuit
Back to the gates of Heaven: the sulphurous hail,
Shot after us in storm, o'erblown hath laid
The fiery surge that from the precipice
Of Heaven received us falling; and the thunder,
175　Winged with red lightning and impetuous rage,
Perhaps hath spent his shafts, and ceases now
To bellow through the vast and boundless Deep.
Let us not slip th' occasion, whether scorn
Or satiate fury yield it from our Foe.
180　Seest thou yon dreary plain, forlorn and wild,
The seat of desolation, void of light,
Save what the glimmering of these livid flames
Casts pale and dreadful? Thither let us tend
From off the tossing of these fiery waves;
185　There rest, if any rest can harbour there;
And, re-assembling our afflicted powers,
Consult how we may henceforth most offend
Our enemy, our own loss how repair,
How overcome this dire calamity,
190　What reinforcement we may gain from hope,
If not, what resolution from despair."

Thus Satan, talking to his nearest mate,
With head uplift above the wave, and eyes
That sparkling blazed; his other parts besides
195　Prone on the flood, extended long and large,
Lay floating many a rood, in bulk as huge
As whom the fables name of monstrous size,
Titanian or Earth-born, that warred on Jove,
Briareos or Typhon, whom the den
200　By ancient Tarsus held, or that sea-beast
Leviathan, which God of all his works
Created hugest that swim th' ocean-stream.
Him, haply slumbering on the Norway foam,
The pilot of some small night-foundered skiff,
205　Deeming some island, oft, as seamen tell,
With fixed anchor in his scaly rind,
Moors by his side under the lee, while night
Invests the sea, and wished morn delays.
So stretched out huge in length the Arch-fiend lay,
210　Chained on the burning lake; nor ever thence
Had risen, or heaved his head, but that the will

And high permission of all-ruling Heaven
Left him at large to his own dark designs,
That with reiterated crimes he might
215 Heap on himself damnation, while he sought
Evil to others, and enraged might see
How all his malice served but to bring forth
Infinite goodness, grace, and mercy, shewn
On Man by him seduced, but on himself
220 Treble confusion, wrath, and vengeance poured.

Forthwith upright he rears from off the pool
His mighty stature; on each hand the flames
Driven backward slope their pointing spires, and rolled
In billows, leave i' th' midst a horrid vale.
225 Then with expanded wings he steers his flight
Aloft, incumbent on the dusky air,
That felt unusual weight; till on dry land
He lights—if it were land that ever burned
With solid, as the lake with liquid fire,
230 And such appeared in hue as when the force
Of subterranean wind transports a hill
Torn from Pelorus, or the shattered side
Of thundering Etna, whose combustible
And fuelled entrails, thence conceiving fire,
235 Sublimed with mineral fury, aid the winds,
And leave a singed bottom all involved
With stench and smoke. Such resting found the sole
Of unblest feet. Him followed his next mate;
Both glorying to have scaped the Stygian flood
240 As gods, and by their own recovered strength,
Not by the sufferance of supernal Power.

"Is this the region, this the soil, the clime,"
Said then the lost Archangel, "this the seat
That we must change for Heaven?—this mournful gloom
245 For that celestial light? Be it so, since he
Who now is sovereign can dispose and bid
What shall be right: farthest from him is best
Whom reason hath equalled, force hath made supreme
Above his equals. Farewell, happy fields,
250 Where joy for ever dwells! Hail, horrors! hail,
Infernal world! and thou, profoundest Hell,
Receive thy new possessor—one who brings
A mind not to be changed by place or time.
The mind is its own place, and in itself

255 Can make a Heaven of Hell, a Hell of Heaven.
What matter where, if I be still the same,
And what I should be, all but less than he
Whom thunder hath made greater? Here at least
We shall be free; th' Almighty hath not built
260 Here for his envy, will not drive us hence:
Here we may reign secure; and, in my choice,
To reign is worth ambition, though in Hell:
Better to reign in Hell than serve in Heaven.
But wherefore let we then our faithful friends,
265 Th' associates and co-partners of our loss,
Lie thus astonished on th' oblivious pool,
And call them not to share with us their part
In this unhappy mansion, or once more
With rallied arms to try what may be yet
270 Regained in Heaven, or what more lost in Hell?"

So Satan spake; and him Beelzebub
Thus answered:—"Leader of those armies bright
Which, but th' Omnipotent, none could have foiled!
If once they hear that voice, their liveliest pledge
275 Of hope in fears and dangers—heard so oft
In worst extremes, and on the perilous edge
Of battle, when it raged, in all assaults
Their surest signal—they will soon resume
New courage and revive, though now they lie
280 Grovelling and prostrate on yon lake of fire,
As we erewhile, astounded and amazed;
No wonder, fallen such a pernicious height!"

He scarce had ceased when the superior Fiend
Was moving toward the shore; his ponderous shield,
285 Ethereal temper, massy, large, and round,
Behind him cast. The broad circumference
Hung on his shoulders like the moon, whose orb
Through optic glass the Tuscan artist views
At evening, from the top of Fesole,
290 Or in Valdarno, to descry new lands,
Rivers, or mountains, in her spotty globe.
His spear—to equal which the tallest pine
Hewn on Norwegian hills, to be the mast
Of some great ammiral, were but a wand—
295 He walked with, to support uneasy steps
Over the burning marl, not like those steps
On Heaven's azure; and the torrid clime

Smote on him sore besides, vaulted with fire.
Nathless he so endured, till on the beach
300 Of that inflamed sea he stood, and called
His legions—Angel Forms, who lay entranced
Thick as autumnal leaves that strow the brooks
In Vallombrosa, where th' Etrurian shades
High over-arched embower; or scattered sedge
305 Afloat, when with fierce winds Orion armed
Hath vexed the Red-Sea coast, whose waves o'erthrew
Busiris and his Memphian chivalry,
While with perfidious hatred they pursued
The sojourners of Goshen, who beheld
310 From the safe shore their floating carcases
And broken chariot-wheels. So thick bestrown,
Abject and lost, lay these, covering the flood,
Under amazement of their hideous change.
He called so loud that all the hollow deep
315 Of Hell resounded:—"Princes, Potentates,
Warriors, the Flower of Heaven—once yours; now lost,
If such astonishment as this can seize
Eternal Spirits! Or have ye chosen this place
After the toil of battle to repose
320 Your wearied virtue, for the ease you find
To slumber here, as in the vales of Heaven?
Or in this abject posture have ye sworn
To adore the Conqueror, who now beholds
Cherub and Seraph rolling in the flood
325 With scattered arms and ensigns, till anon
His swift pursuers from Heaven-gates discern
Th' advantage, and, descending, tread us down
Thus drooping, or with linked thunderbolts
Transfix us to the bottom of this gulf?
330 Awake, arise, or be for ever fallen!"

They heard, and were abashed, and up they sprung
Upon the wing, as when men wont to watch
On duty, sleeping found by whom they dread,
Rouse and bestir themselves ere well awake.
335 Nor did they not perceive the evil plight
In which they were, or the fierce pains not feel;
Yet to their General's voice they soon obeyed
Innumerable. As when the potent rod
Of Amram's son, in Egypt's evil day,
340 Waved round the coast, up-called a pitchy cloud
Of locusts, warping on the eastern wind,

That o'er the realm of impious Pharaoh hung
Like Night, and darkened all the land of Nile;
So numberless were those bad Angels seen
345   Hovering on wing under the cope of Hell,
'Twixt upper, nether, and surrounding fires;
Till, as a signal given, th' uplifted spear
Of their great Sultan waving to direct
Their course, in even balance down they light
350   On the firm brimstone, and fill all the plain:
A multitude like which the populous North
Poured never from her frozen loins to pass
Rhene or the Danaw, when her barbarous sons
Came like a deluge on the South, and spread
355   Beneath Gibraltar to the Libyan sands.
Forthwith, form every squadron and each band,
The heads and leaders thither haste where stood
Their great Commander—godlike Shapes, and Forms
Excelling human; princely Dignities;
360   And Powers that erst in Heaven sat on thrones,
Though on their names in Heavenly records now
Be no memorial, blotted out and rased
By their rebellion from the Books of Life.
Nor had they yet among the sons of Eve
365   Got them new names, till, wandering o'er the earth,
Through God's high sufferance for the trial of man,
By falsities and lies the greatest part
Of mankind they corrupted to forsake
God their Creator, and th' invisible
370   Glory of him that made them to transform
Oft to the image of a brute, adorned
With gay religions full of pomp and gold,
And devils to adore for deities:
Then were they known to men by various names,
375   And various idols through the heathen world.

Say, Muse, their names then known, who first, who last,
Roused from the slumber on that fiery couch,
At their great Emperorr's call, as next in worth
Came singly where he stood on the bare strand,
380   While the promiscuous crowd stood yet aloof?

The chief were those who, from the pit of Hell
Roaming to seek their prey on Earth, durst fix
Their seats, long after, next the seat of God,
Their altars by his altar, gods adored

385 Among the nations round, and durst abide
Jehovah thundering out of Sion, throned
Between the Cherubim; yea, often placed
Within his sanctuary itself their shrines,
Abominations; and with cursed things
390 His holy rites and solemn feasts profaned,
And with their darkness durst affront his light.
First, Moloch, horrid king, besmeared with blood
Of human sacrifice, and parents' tears;
Though, for the noise of drums and timbrels loud,
395 Their children's cries unheard that passed through fire
To his grim idol. Him the Ammonite
Worshiped in Rabba and her watery plain,
In Argob and in Basan, to the stream
Of utmost Arnon. Nor content with such
400 Audacious neighbourhood, the wisest heart
Of Solomon he led by fraud to build
His temple right against the temple of God
On that opprobrious hill, and made his grove
The pleasant valley of Hinnom, Tophet thence
405 And black Gehenna called, the type of Hell.
Next Chemos, th' obscene dread of Moab's sons,
From Aroar to Nebo and the wild
Of southmost Abarim; in Hesebon
And Horonaim, Seon's real, beyond
410 The flowery dale of Sibma clad with vines,
And Eleale to th' Asphaltic Pool:
Peor his other name, when he enticed
Israel in Sittim, on their march from Nile,
To do him wanton rites, which cost them woe.
415 Yet thence his lustful orgies he enlarged
Even to that hill of scandal, by the grove
Of Moloch homicide, lust hard by hate,
Till good Josiah drove them thence to Hell.
With these came they who, from the bordering flood
420 Of old Euphrates to the brook that parts
Egypt from Syrian ground, had general names
Of Baalim and Ashtaroth—those male,
These feminine. For Spirits, when they please,
Can either sex assume, or both; so soft
425 And uncompounded is their essence pure,
Not tried or manacled with joint or limb,
Nor founded on the brittle strength of bones,
Like cumbrous flesh; but, in what shape they choose,
Dilated or condensed, bright or obscure,

430 Can execute their airy purposes,
And works of love or enmity fulfil.
For those the race of Israel oft forsook
Their Living Strength, and unfrequented left
His righteous altar, bowing lowly down
435 To bestial gods; for which their heads as low
Bowed down in battle, sunk before the spear
Of despicable foes. With these in troop
Came Astoreth, whom the Phoenicians called
Astarte, queen of heaven, with crescent horns;
440 To whose bright image nightly by the moon
Sidonian virgins paid their vows and songs;
In Sion also not unsung, where stood
Her temple on th' offensive mountain, built
By that uxorious king whose heart, though large,
445 Beguiled by fair idolatresses, fell
To idols foul. Thammuz came next behind,
Whose annual wound in Lebanon allured
The Syrian damsels to lament his fate
In amorous ditties all a summer's day,
450 While smooth Adonis from his native rock
Ran purple to the sea, supposed with blood
Of Thammuz yearly wounded: the love-tale
Infected Sion's daughters with like heat,
Whose wanton passions in the sacred porch
455 Ezekiel saw, when, by the vision led,
His eye surveyed the dark idolatries
Of alienated Judah. Next came one
Who mourned in earnest, when the captive ark
Maimed his brute image, head and hands lopt off,
460 In his own temple, on the grunsel-edge,
Where he fell flat and shamed his worshippers:
Dagon his name, sea-monster, upward man
And downward fish; yet had his temple high
Reared in Azotus, dreaded through the coast
465 Of Palestine, in Gath and Ascalon,
And Accaron and Gaza's frontier bounds.
Him followed Rimmon, whose delightful seat
Was fair Damascus, on the fertile banks
Of Abbana and Pharphar, lucid streams.
470 He also against the house of God was bold:
A leper once he lost, and gained a king—
Ahaz, his sottish conqueror, whom he drew
God's altar to disparage and displace
For one of Syrian mode, whereon to burn

475   His odious offerings, and adore the gods
      Whom he had vanquished. After these appeared
      A crew who, under names of old renown—
      Osiris, Isis, Orus, and their train—
      With monstrous shapes and sorceries abused
480   Fanatic Egypt and her priests to seek
      Their wandering gods disguised in brutish forms
      Rather than human. Nor did Israel scape
      Th' infection, when their borrowed gold composed
      The calf in Oreb; and the rebel king
485   Doubled that sin in Bethel and in Dan,
      Likening his Maker to the grazed ox—
      Jehovah, who, in one night, when he passed
      From Egypt marching, equalled with one stroke
      Both her first-born and all her bleating gods.
490   Belial came last; than whom a Spirit more lewd
      Fell not from Heaven, or more gross to love
      Vice for itself. To him no temple stood
      Or altar smoked; yet who more oft than he
      In temples and at altars, when the priest
495   Turns atheist, as did Eli's sons, who filled
      With lust and violence the house of God?
      In courts and palaces he also reigns,
      And in luxurious cities, where the noise
      Of riot ascends above their loftiest towers,
500   And injury and outrage; and, when night
      Darkens the streets, then wander forth the sons
      Of Belial, flown with insolence and wine.
      Witness the streets of Sodom, and that night
      In Gibeah, when the hospitable door
505   Exposed a matron, to avoid worse rape.

      These were the prime in order and in might:
      The rest were long to tell; though far renowned
      Th' Ionian gods—of Javan's issue held
      Gods, yet confessed later than Heaven and Earth,
510   Their boasted parents;—Titan, Heaven's first-born,
      With his enormous brood, and birthright seized
      By younger Saturn: he from mightier Jove,
      His own and Rhea's son, like measure found;
      So Jove usurping reigned. These, first in Crete
515   And Ida known, thence on the snowy top
      Of cold Olympus ruled the middle air,
      Their highest heaven; or on the Delphian cliff,
      Or in Dodona, and through all the bounds

Of Doric land; or who with Saturn old
520 Fled over Adria to th' Hesperian fields,
And o'er the Celtic roamed the utmost Isles.

All these and more came flocking; but with looks
Downcast and damp; yet such wherein appeared
Obscure some glimpse of joy to have found their Chief
525 Not in despair, to have found themselves not lost
In loss itself; which on his countenance cast
Like doubtful hue. But he, his wonted pride
Soon recollecting, with high words, that bore
Semblance of worth, not substance, gently raised
530 Their fainting courage, and dispelled their fears.
Then straight commands that, at the warlike sound
Of trumpets loud and clarions, be upreared
His mighty standard. That proud honour claimed
Azazel as his right, a Cherub tall:
535 Who forthwith from the glittering staff unfurled
Th' imperial ensign; which, full high advanced,
Shone like a meteor streaming to the wind,
With gems and golden lustre rich emblazed,
Seraphic arms and trophies; all the while
540 Sonorous metal blowing martial sounds:
At which the universal host up-sent
A shout that tore Hell's concave, and beyond
Frighted the reign of Chaos and old Night.
All in a moment through the gloom were seen
545 Ten thousand banners rise into the air,
With orient colours waving: with them rose
A forest huge of spears; and thronging helms
Appeared, and serried shields in thick array
Of depth immeasurable. Anon they move
550 In perfect phalanx to the Dorian mood
Of flutes and soft recorders—such as raised
To height of noblest temper heroes old
Arming to battle, and instead of rage
Deliberate valour breathed, firm, and unmoved
555 With dread of death to flight or foul retreat;
Nor wanting power to mitigate and swage
With solemn touches troubled thoughts, and chase
Anguish and doubt and fear and sorrow and pain
From mortal or immortal minds. Thus they,
560 Breathing united force with fixed thought,
Moved on in silence to soft pipes that charmed
Their painful steps o'er the burnt soil. And now

Advanced in view they stand—a horrid front
Of dreadful length and dazzling arms, in guise
565 Of warriors old, with ordered spear and shield,
Awaiting what command their mighty Chief
Had to impose. He through the armed files
Darts his experienced eye, and soon traverse
The whole battalion views—their order due,
570 Their visages and stature as of gods;
Their number last he sums. And now his heart
Distends with pride, and, hardening in his strength,
Glories: for never, since created Man,
Met such embodied force as, named with these,
575 Could merit more than that small infantry
Warred on by cranes—though all the giant brood
Of Phlegra with th' heroic race were joined
That fought at Thebes and Ilium, on each side
Mixed with auxiliar gods; and what resounds
580 In fable or romance of Uther's son,
Begirt with British and Armoric knights;
And all who since, baptized or infidel,
Jousted in Aspramont, or Montalban,
Damasco, or Marocco, or Trebisond,
585 Or whom Biserta sent from Afric shore
When Charlemain with all his peerage fell
By Fontarabbia. Thus far these beyond
Compare of mortal prowess, yet observed
Their dread Commander. He, above the rest
590 In shape and gesture proudly eminent,
Stood like a tower. His form had yet not lost
All her original brightness, nor appeared
Less than Archangel ruined, and th' excess
Of glory obscured: as when the sun new-risen
595 Looks through the horizontal misty air
Shorn of his beams, or, from behind the moon,
In dim eclipse, disastrous twilight sheds
On half the nations, and with fear of change
Perplexes monarchs. Darkened so, yet shone
600 Above them all th' Archangel: but his face
Deep scars of thunder had intrenched, and care
Sat on his faded cheek, but under brows
Of dauntless courage, and considerate pride
Waiting revenge. Cruel his eye, but cast
605 Signs of remorse and passion, to behold
The fellows of his crime, the followers rather
(Far other once beheld in bliss), condemned

For ever now to have their lot in pain—
Millions of Spirits for his fault amerced
610 Of Heaven, and from eternal splendours flung
For his revolt—yet faithful how they stood,
Their glory withered; as, when heaven's fire
Hath scathed the forest oaks or mountain pines,
With singed top their stately growth, though bare,
615 Stands on the blasted heath. He now prepared
To speak; whereat their doubled ranks they bend
From wing to wing, and half enclose him round
With all his peers: attention held them mute.
Thrice he assayed, and thrice, in spite of scorn,
620 Tears, such as Angels weep, burst forth: at last
Words interwove with sighs found out their way:—

"O myriads of immortal Spirits! O Powers
Matchless, but with th' Almighty!—and that strife
Was not inglorious, though th' event was dire,
625 As this place testifies, and this dire change,
Hateful to utter. But what power of mind,
Forseeing or presaging, from the depth
Of knowledge past or present, could have feared
How such united force of gods, how such
630 As stood like these, could ever know repulse?
For who can yet believe, though after loss,
That all these puissant legions, whose exile
Hath emptied Heaven, shall fail to re-ascend,
Self-raised, and repossess their native seat?
635 For me, be witness all the host of Heaven,
If counsels different, or danger shunned
By me, have lost our hopes. But he who reigns
Monarch in Heaven till then as one secure
Sat on his throne, upheld by old repute,
640 Consent or custom, and his regal state
Put forth at full, but still his strength concealed—
Which tempted our attempt, and wrought our fall.
Henceforth his might we know, and know our own,
So as not either to provoke, or dread
645 New war provoked: our better part remains
To work in close design, by fraud or guile,
What force effected not; that he no less
At length from us may find, who overcomes
By force hath overcome but half his foe.
650 Space may produce new Worlds; whereof so rife
There went a fame in Heaven that he ere long

Intended to create, and therein plant
A generation whom his choice regard
Should favour equal to the Sons of Heaven.
655 Thither, if but to pry, shall be perhaps
Our first eruption—thither, or elsewhere;
For this infernal pit shall never hold
Celestial Spirits in bondage, nor th' Abyss
Long under darkness cover. But these thoughts
660 Full counsel must mature. Peace is despaired;
For who can think submission? War, then, war
Open or understood, must be resolved."

He spake; and, to confirm his words, outflew
Millions of flaming swords, drawn from the thighs
665 Of mighty Cherubim; the sudden blaze
Far round illumined Hell. Highly they raged
Against the Highest, and fierce with grasped arms
Clashed on their sounding shields the din of war,
Hurling defiance toward the vault of Heaven.
670 There stood a hill not far, whose grisly top
Belched fire and rolling smoke; the rest entire
Shone with a glossy scurf—undoubted sign
That in his womb was hid metallic ore,
The work of sulphur. Thither, winged with speed,
675 A numerous brigade hastened: as when bands
Of pioneers, with spade and pickaxe armed,
Forerun the royal camp, to trench a field,
Or cast a rampart. Mammon led them on—
Mammon, the least erected Spirit that fell
680 From Heaven; for even in Heaven his looks and thoughts
Were always downward bent, admiring more
The riches of heaven's pavement, trodden gold,
Than aught divine or holy else enjoyed
In vision beatific. By him first
685 Men also, and by his suggestion taught,
Ransacked the centre, and with impious hands
Rifled the bowels of their mother Earth
For treasures better hid. Soon had his crew
Opened into the hill a spacious wound,
690 And digged out ribs of gold. Let none admire
That riches grow in Hell; that soil may best
Deserve the precious bane. And here let those
Who boast in mortal things, and wondering tell
Of Babel, and the works of Memphian kings,
695 Learn how their greatest monuments of fame

And strength, and art, are easily outdone
By Spirits reprobate, and in an hour
What in an age they, with incessant toil
And hands innumerable, scarce perform.
700   Nigh on the plain, in many cells prepared,
That underneath had veins of liquid fire
Sluiced from the lake, a second multitude
With wondrous art founded the massy ore,
Severing each kind, and scummed the bullion-dross.
705   A third as soon had formed within the ground
A various mould, and from the boiling cells
By strange conveyance filled each hollow nook;
As in an organ, from one blast of wind,
To many a row of pipes the sound-board breathes.
710   Anon out of the earth a fabric huge
Rose like an exhalation, with the sound
Of dulcet symphonies and voices sweet—
Built like a temple, where pilasters round
Were set, and Doric pillars overlaid
715   With golden architrave; nor did there want
Cornice or frieze, with bossy sculptures graven;
The roof was fretted gold. Not Babylon
Nor great Alcairo such magnificence
Equalled in all their glories, to enshrine
720   Belus or Serapis their gods, or seat
Their kings, when Egypt with Assyria strove
In wealth and luxury. Th' ascending pile
Stood fixed her stately height, and straight the doors,
Opening their brazen folds, discover, wide
725   Within, her ample spaces o'er the smooth
And level pavement: from the arched roof,
Pendent by subtle magic, many a row
Of starry lamps and blazing cressets, fed
With naptha and asphaltus, yielded light
730   As from a sky. The hasty multitude
Admiring entered; and the work some praise,
And some the architect. His hand was known
In Heaven by many a towered structure high,
Where sceptred Angels held their residence,
735   And sat as Princes, whom the supreme King
Exalted to such power, and gave to rule,
Each in his Hierarchy, the Orders bright.
Nor was his name unheard or unadored
In ancient Greece; and in Ausonian land
740   Men called him Mulciber; and how he fell

From Heaven they fabled, thrown by angry Jove
Sheer o'er the crystal battlements: from morn
To noon he fell, from noon to dewy eve,
A summer's day, and with the setting sun
745 Dropt from the zenith, like a falling star,
On Lemnos, th' Aegaean isle. Thus they relate,
Erring; for he with this rebellious rout
Fell long before; nor aught availed him now
To have built in Heaven high towers; nor did he scape
750 By all his engines, but was headlong sent,
With his industrious crew, to build in Hell.
Meanwhile the winged Heralds, by command
Of sovereign power, with awful ceremony
And trumpet's sound, throughout the host proclaim
755 A solemn council forthwith to be held
At Pandemonium, the high capital
Of Satan and his peers. Their summons called
From every band and squared regiment
By place or choice the worthiest: they anon
760 With hundreds and with thousands trooping came
Attended. All access was thronged; the gates
And porches wide, but chief the spacious hall
(Though like a covered field, where champions bold
Wont ride in armed, and at the Soldan's chair
765 Defied the best of Paynim chivalry
To mortal combat, or career with lance),
Thick swarmed, both on the ground and in the air,
Brushed with the hiss of rustling wings. As bees
In spring-time, when the Sun with Taurus rides.
770 Pour forth their populous youth about the hive
In clusters; they among fresh dews and flowers
Fly to and fro, or on the smoothed plank,
The suburb of their straw-built citadel,
New rubbed with balm, expatiate, and confer
775 Their state-affairs: so thick the airy crowd
Swarmed and were straitened; till, the signal given,
Behold a wonder! They but now who seemed
In bigness to surpass Earth's giant sons,
Now less than smallest dwarfs, in narrow room
780 Throng numberless—like that pygmean race
Beyond the Indian mount; or faery elves,
Whose midnight revels, by a forest-side
Or fountain, some belated peasant sees,
Or dreams he sees, while overhead the Moon
785 Sits arbitress, and nearer to the Earth

Wheels her pale course: they, on their mirth and dance
Intent, with jocund music charm his ear;
At once with joy and fear his heart rebounds.
Thus incorporeal Spirits to smallest forms
790   Reduced their shapes immense, and were at large,
Though without number still, amidst the hall
Of that infernal court. But far within,
And in their own dimensions like themselves,
The great Seraphic Lords and Cherubim
795   In close recess and secret conclave sat,
A thousand demi-gods on golden seats,
Frequent and full. After short silence then,
And summons read, the great consult began.

Book II

High on a throne of royal state, which far
Outshone the wealth of Ormus and of Ind,
Or where the gorgeous East with richest hand
Showers on her kings barbaric pearl and gold,
5   Satan exalted sat, by merit raised
To that bad eminence; and, from despair
Thus high uplifted beyond hope, aspires
Beyond thus high, insatiate to pursue
Vain war with Heaven; and, by success untaught,
10   His proud imaginations thus displayed:—

"Powers and Dominions, Deities of Heaven!—
For, since no deep within her gulf can hold
Immortal vigour, though oppressed and fallen,
I give not Heaven for lost: from this descent
15   Celestial Virtues rising will appear
More glorious and more dread than from no fall,
And trust themselves to fear no second fate!—
Me though just right, and the fixed laws of Heaven,
Did first create your leader—next, free choice
20   With what besides in council or in fight
Hath been achieved of merit—yet this loss,
Thus far at least recovered, hath much more
Established in a safe, unenvied throne,
Yielded with full consent. The happier state
25   In Heaven, which follows dignity, might draw
Envy from each inferior; but who here
Will envy whom the highest place exposes
Foremost to stand against the Thunderer's aim
Your bulwark, and condemns to greatest share

30 Of endless pain? Where there is, then, no good
    For which to strive, no strife can grow up there
    From faction: for none sure will claim in Hell
    Precedence; none whose portion is so small
    Of present pain that with ambitious mind
35 Will covet more! With this advantage, then,
    To union, and firm faith, and firm accord,
    More than can be in Heaven, we now return
    To claim our just inheritance of old,
    Surer to prosper than prosperity
40 Could have assured us; and by what best way,
    Whether of open war or covert guile,
    We now debate. Who can advise may speak."

    He ceased; and next him Moloch, sceptred king,
    Stood up—the strongest and the fiercest Spirit
45 That fought in Heaven, now fiercer by despair.
    His trust was with th' Eternal to be deemed
    Equal in strength, and rather than be less
    Cared not to be at all; with that care lost
    Went all his fear: of God, or Hell, or worse,
50 He recked not, and these words thereafter spake:—

    "My sentence is for open war. Of wiles,
    More unexpert, I boast not: them let those
    Contrive who need, or when they need; not now.
    For, while they sit contriving, shall the rest—
55 Millions that stand in arms, and longing wait
    The signal to ascend—sit lingering here,
    Heaven's fugitives, and for their dwelling-place
    Accept this dark opprobrious den of shame,
    The prison of his tyranny who reigns
60 By our delay? No! let us rather choose,
    Armed with Hell-flames and fury, all at once
    O'er Heaven's high towers to force resistless way,
    Turning our tortures into horrid arms
    Against the Torturer; when, to meet the noise
65 Of his almighty engine, he shall hear
    Infernal thunder, and, for lightning, see
    Black fire and horror shot with equal rage
    Among his Angels, and his throne itself
    Mixed with Tartarean sulphur and strange fire,
70 His own invented torments. But perhaps
    The way seems difficult, and steep to scale
    With upright wing against a higher foe!

Let such bethink them, if the sleepy drench
Of that forgetful lake benumb not still,
75   That in our proper motion we ascend
Up to our native seat; descent and fall
To us is adverse. Who but felt of late,
When the fierce foe hung on our broken rear
Insulting, and pursued us through the Deep,
80   With what compulsion and laborious flight
We sunk thus low? Th' ascent is easy, then;
Th' event is feared! Should we again provoke
Our stronger, some worse way his wrath may find
To our destruction, if there be in Hell
85   Fear to be worse destroyed! What can be worse
Than to dwell here, driven out from bliss, condemned
In this abhorred deep to utter woe!
Where pain of unextinguishable fire
Must exercise us without hope of end
90   The vassals of his anger, when the scourge
Inexorably, and the torturing hour,
Calls us to penance? More destroyed than thus,
We should be quite abolished, and expire.
What fear we then? what doubt we to incense
95   His utmost ire? which, to the height enraged,
Will either quite consume us, and reduce
To nothing this essential—happier far
Than miserable to have eternal being!—
Or, if our substance be indeed divine,
100 And cannot cease to be, we are at worst
On this side nothing; and by proof we feel
Our power sufficient to disturb his Heaven,
And with perpetual inroads to alarm,
Though inaccessible, his fatal throne:
105 Which, if not victory, is yet revenge."

He ended frowning, and his look denounced
Desperate revenge, and battle dangerous
To less than gods. On th' other side up rose
Belial, in act more graceful and humane.
110 A fairer person lost not Heaven; he seemed
For dignity composed, and high exploit.
But all was false and hollow; though his tongue
Dropped manna, and could make the worse appear
The better reason, to perplex and dash
115 Maturest counsels: for his thoughts were low—
To vice industrious, but to nobler deeds

Timorous and slothful. Yet he pleased the ear,
And with persuasive accent thus began:—

"I should be much for open war, O Peers,
120   As not behind in hate, if what was urged
Main reason to persuade immediate war
Did not dissuade me most, and seem to cast
Ominous conjecture on the whole success;
When he who most excels in fact of arms,
125   In what he counsels and in what excels
Mistrustful, grounds his courage on despair
And utter dissolution, as the scope
Of all his aim, after some dire revenge.
First, what revenge? The towers of Heaven are filled
130   With armed watch, that render all access
Impregnable: oft on the bordering Deep
Encamp their legions, or with obscure wing
Scout far and wide into the realm of Night,
Scorning surprise. Or, could we break our way
135   By force, and at our heels all Hell should rise
With blackest insurrection to confound
Heaven's purest light, yet our great Enemy,
All incorruptible, would on his throne
Sit unpolluted, and th' ethereal mould,
140   Incapable of stain, would soon expel
Her mischief, and purge off the baser fire,
Victorious. Thus repulsed, our final hope
Is flat despair: we must exasperate
Th' Almighty Victor to spend all his rage;
145   And that must end us; that must be our cure—
To be no more. Sad cure! for who would lose,
Though full of pain, this intellectual being,
Those thoughts that wander through eternity,
To perish rather, swallowed up and lost
150   In the wide womb of uncreated Night,
Devoid of sense and motion? And who knows,
Let this be good, whether our angry Foe
Can give it, or will ever? How he can
Is doubtful; that he never will is sure.
155   Will he, so wise, let loose at once his ire,
Belike through impotence or unaware,
To give his enemies their wish, and end
Them in his anger whom his anger saves
To punish endless? "Wherefore cease we, then?"
160   Say they who counsel war; "we are decreed,

Reserved, and destined to eternal woe;
Whatever doing, what can we suffer more,
What can we suffer worse?" Is this, then, worst—
Thus sitting, thus consulting, thus in arms?
165 What when we fled amain, pursued and struck
With Heaven's afflicting thunder, and besought
The Deep to shelter us? This Hell then seemed
A refuge from those wounds. Or when we lay
Chained on the burning lake? That sure was worse.
170 What if the breath that kindled those grim fires,
Awaked, should blow them into sevenfold rage,
And plunge us in the flames; or from above
Should intermitted vengeance arm again
His red right hand to plague us? What if all
175 Her stores were opened, and this firmament
Of Hell should spout her cataracts of fire,
Impendent horrors, threatening hideous fall
One day upon our heads; while we perhaps,
Designing or exhorting glorious war,
180 Caught in a fiery tempest, shall be hurled,
Each on his rock transfixed, the sport and prey
Or racking whirlwinds, or for ever sunk
Under yon boiling ocean, wrapt in chains,
There to converse with everlasting groans,
185 Unrespited, unpitied, unreprieved,
Ages of hopeless end? This would be worse.
War, therefore, open or concealed, alike
My voice dissuades; for what can force or guile
With him, or who deceive his mind, whose eye
190 Views all things at one view? He from Heaven's height
All these our motions vain sees and derides,
Not more almighty to resist our might
Than wise to frustrate all our plots and wiles.
Shall we, then, live thus vile—the race of Heaven
195 Thus trampled, thus expelled, to suffer here
Chains and these torments? Better these than worse,
By my advice; since fate inevitable
Subdues us, and omnipotent decree,
The Victor's will. To suffer, as to do,
200 Our strength is equal; nor the law unjust
That so ordains. This was at first resolved,
If we were wise, against so great a foe
Contending, and so doubtful what might fall.
I laugh when those who at the spear are bold
205 And venturous, if that fail them, shrink, and fear

What yet they know must follow—to endure
Exile, or ignominy, or bonds, or pain,
The sentence of their Conqueror. This is now
Our doom; which if we can sustain and bear,
210 Our Supreme Foe in time may much remit
His anger, and perhaps, thus far removed,
Not mind us not offending, satisfied
With what is punished; whence these raging fires
Will slacken, if his breath stir not their flames.
215 Our purer essence then will overcome
Their noxious vapour; or, inured, not feel;
Or, changed at length, and to the place conformed
In temper and in nature, will receive
Familiar the fierce heat; and, void of pain,
220 This horror will grow mild, this darkness light;
Besides what hope the never-ending flight
Of future days may bring, what chance, what change
Worth waiting—since our present lot appears
For happy though but ill, for ill not worst,
225 If we procure not to ourselves more woe."

Thus Belial, with words clothed in reason's garb,
Counselled ignoble ease and peaceful sloth,
Not peace; and after him thus Mammon spake:—

"Either to disenthrone the King of Heaven
230 We war, if war be best, or to regain
Our own right lost. Him to unthrone we then
May hope, when everlasting Fate shall yield
To fickle Chance, and Chaos judge the strife.
The former, vain to hope, argues as vain
235 The latter; for what place can be for us
Within Heaven's bound, unless Heaven's Lord supreme
We overpower? Suppose he should relent
And publish grace to all, on promise made
Of new subjection; with what eyes could we
240 Stand in his presence humble, and receive
Strict laws imposed, to celebrate his throne
With warbled hymns, and to his Godhead sing
Forced hallelujahs, while he lordly sits
Our envied sovereign, and his altar breathes
245 Ambrosial odours and ambrosial flowers,
Our servile offerings? This must be our task
In Heaven, this our delight. How wearisome
Eternity so spent in worship paid

To whom we hate! Let us not then pursue,
250   By force impossible, by leave obtained
Unacceptable, though in Heaven, our state
Of splendid vassalage; but rather seek
Our own good from ourselves, and from our own
Live to ourselves, though in this vast recess,
255   Free and to none accountable, preferring
Hard liberty before the easy yoke
Of servile pomp. Our greatness will appear
Then most conspicuous when great things of small,
Useful of hurtful, prosperous of adverse,
260   We can create, and in what place soe'er
Thrive under evil, and work ease out of pain
Through labour and endurance. This deep world
Of darkness do we dread? How oft amidst
Thick clouds and dark doth Heaven's all-ruling Sire
265   Choose to reside, his glory unobscured,
And with the majesty of darkness round
Covers his throne, from whence deep thunders roar.
Mustering their rage, and Heaven resembles Hell!
As he our darkness, cannot we his light
270   Imitate when we please? This desert soil
Wants not her hidden lustre, gems and gold;
Nor want we skill or art from whence to raise
Magnificence; and what can Heaven show more?
Our torments also may, in length of time,
275   Become our elements, these piercing fires
As soft as now severe, our temper changed
Into their temper; which must needs remove
The sensible of pain. All things invite
To peaceful counsels, and the settled state
280   Of order, how in safety best we may
Compose our present evils, with regard
Of what we are and where, dismissing quite
All thoughts of war. Ye have what I advise."

He scarce had finished, when such murmur filled
285   Th' assembly as when hollow rocks retain
The sound of blustering winds, which all night long
Had roused the sea, now with hoarse cadence lull
Seafaring men o'erwatched, whose bark by chance
Or pinnace, anchors in a craggy bay
290   After the tempest. Such applause was heard
As Mammon ended, and his sentence pleased,
Advising peace: for such another field

They dreaded worse than Hell; so much the fear
Of thunder and the sword of Michael
295 Wrought still within them; and no less desire
To found this nether empire, which might rise,
By policy and long process of time,
In emulation opposite to Heaven.
Which when Beelzebub perceived—than whom,
300 Satan except, none higher sat—with grave
Aspect he rose, and in his rising seemed
A pillar of state. Deep on his front engraven
Deliberation sat, and public care;
And princely counsel in his face yet shone,
305 Majestic, though in ruin. Sage he stood
With Atlantean shoulders, fit to bear
The weight of mightiest monarchies; his look
Drew audience and attention still as night
Or summer's noontide air, while thus he spake:—

310 "Thrones and Imperial Powers, Offspring of Heaven,
Ethereal Virtues! or these titles now
Must we renounce, and, changing style, be called
Princes of Hell? for so the popular vote
Inclines—here to continue, and build up here
315 A growing empire; doubtless! while we dream,
And know not that the King of Heaven hath doomed
This place our dungeon, not our safe retreat
Beyond his potent arm, to live exempt
From Heaven's high jurisdiction, in new league
320 Banded against his throne, but to remain
In strictest bondage, though thus far removed,
Under th' inevitable curb, reserved
His captive multitude. For he, to be sure,
In height or depth, still first and last will reign
325 Sole king, and of his kingdom lose no part
By our revolt, but over Hell extend
His empire, and with iron sceptre rule
Us here, as with his golden those in Heaven.
What sit we then projecting peace and war?
330 War hath determined us and foiled with loss
Irreparable; terms of peace yet none
Vouchsafed or sought; for what peace will be given
To us enslaved, but custody severe,
And stripes and arbitrary punishment
335 Inflicted? and what peace can we return,
But, to our power, hostility and hate,

Untamed reluctance, and revenge, though slow,
Yet ever plotting how the Conqueror least
May reap his conquest, and may least rejoice
340 In doing what we most in suffering feel?
Nor will occasion want, nor shall we need
With dangerous expedition to invade
Heaven, whose high walls fear no assault or siege,
Or ambush from the Deep. What if we find
345 Some easier enterprise? There is a place
(If ancient and prophetic fame in Heaven
Err not)—another World, the happy seat
Of some new race, called Man, about this time
To be created like to us, though less
350 In power and excellence, but favoured more
Of him who rules above; so was his will
Pronounced among the Gods, and by an oath
That shook Heaven's whole circumference confirmed.
Thither let us bend all our thoughts, to learn
355 What creatures there inhabit, of what mould
Or substance, how endued, and what their power
And where their weakness: how attempted best,
By force or subtlety. Though Heaven be shut,
And Heaven's high Arbitrator sit secure
360 In his own strength, this place may lie exposed,
The utmost border of his kingdom, left
To their defence who hold it: here, perhaps,
Some advantageous act may be achieved
By sudden onset—either with Hell-fire
365 To waste his whole creation, or possess
All as our own, and drive, as we were driven,
The puny habitants; or, if not drive,
Seduce them to our party, that their God
May prove their foe, and with repenting hand
370 Abolish his own works. This would surpass
Common revenge, and interrupt his joy
In our confusion, and our joy upraise
In his disturbance; when his darling sons,
Hurled headlong to partake with us, shall curse
375 Their frail original, and faded bliss—
Faded so soon! Advise if this be worth
Attempting, or to sit in darkness here
Hatching vain empires." Thus Beelzebub
Pleaded his devilish counsel—first devised
380 By Satan, and in part proposed: for whence,
But from the author of all ill, could spring

So deep a malice, to confound the race
Of mankind in one root, and Earth with Hell
To mingle and involve, done all to spite
385   The great Creator? But their spite still serves
His glory to augment. The bold design
Pleased highly those infernal States, and joy
Sparkled in all their eyes: with full assent
They vote: whereat his speech he thus renews:—
390   "Well have ye judged, well ended long debate,
Synod of Gods, and, like to what ye are,
Great things resolved, which from the lowest deep
Will once more lift us up, in spite of fate,
Nearer our ancient seat—perhaps in view
395   Of those bright confines, whence, with neighbouring arms,
And opportune excursion, we may chance
Re-enter Heaven; or else in some mild zone
Dwell, not unvisited of Heaven's fair light,
Secure, and at the brightening orient beam
400   Purge off this gloom: the soft delicious air,
To heal the scar of these corrosive fires,
Shall breathe her balm. But, first, whom shall we send
In search of this new World? whom shall we find
Sufficient? who shall tempt with wandering feet
405   The dark, unbottomed, infinite Abyss,
And through the palpable obscure find out
His uncouth way, or spread his airy flight,
Upborne with indefatigable wings
Over the vast abrupt, ere he arrive
410   The happy Isle? What strength, what art, can then
Suffice, or what evasion bear him safe,
Through the strict senteries and stations thick
Of Angels watching round? Here he had need
All circumspection: and we now no less
415   Choice in our suffrage; for on whom we send
The weight of all, and our last hope, relies."

This said, he sat; and expectation held
His look suspense, awaiting who appeared
To second, or oppose, or undertake
420   The perilous attempt. But all sat mute,
Pondering the danger with deep thoughts; and each
In other's countenance read his own dismay,
Astonished. None among the choice and prime
Of those Heaven-warring champions could be found
425   So hardy as to proffer or accept,

Alone, the dreadful voyage; till, at last,
Satan, whom now transcendent glory raised
Above his fellows, with monarchal pride
Conscious of highest worth, unmoved thus spake:—

430 "O Progeny of Heaven! Empyreal Thrones!
With reason hath deep silence and demur
Seized us, though undismayed. Long is the way
And hard, that out of Hell leads up to light.
Our prison strong, this huge convex of fire,
435 Outrageous to devour, immures us round
Ninefold; and gates of burning adamant,
Barred over us, prohibit all egress.
These passed, if any pass, the void profound
Of unessential Night receives him next,
440 Wide-gaping, and with utter loss of being
Threatens him, plunged in that abortive gulf.
If thence he scape, into whatever world,
Or unknown region, what remains him less
Than unknown dangers, and as hard escape?
445 But I should ill become this throne, O Peers,
And this imperial sovereignty, adorned
With splendour, armed with power, if aught proposed
And judged of public moment in the shape
Of difficulty or danger, could deter
450 Me from attempting. Wherefore do I assume
These royalties, and not refuse to reign,
Refusing to accept as great a share
Of hazard as of honour, due alike
To him who reigns, and so much to him due
455 Of hazard more as he above the rest
High honoured sits? Go, therefore, mighty Powers,
Terror of Heaven, though fallen; intend at home,
While here shall be our home, what best may ease
The present misery, and render Hell
460 More tolerable; if there be cure or charm
To respite, or deceive, or slack the pain
Of this ill mansion: intermit no watch
Against a wakeful foe, while I abroad
Through all the coasts of dark destruction seek
465 Deliverance for us all. This enterprise
None shall partake with me." Thus saying, rose
The Monarch, and prevented all reply;
Prudent lest, from his resolution raised,
Others among the chief might offer now,

470 Certain to be refused, what erst they feared,
And, so refused, might in opinion stand
His rivals, winning cheap the high repute
Which he through hazard huge must earn. But they
Dreaded not more th' adventure than his voice
475 Forbidding; and at once with him they rose.
Their rising all at once was as the sound
Of thunder heard remote. Towards him they bend
With awful reverence prone, and as a God
Extol him equal to the Highest in Heaven.
480 Nor failed they to express how much they praised
That for the general safety he despised
His own: for neither do the Spirits damned
Lose all their virtue; lest bad men should boast
Their specious deeds on earth, which glory excites,
485 Or close ambition varnished o'er with zeal.

Thus they their doubtful consultations dark
Ended, rejoicing in their matchless Chief:
As, when from mountain-tops the dusky clouds
Ascending, while the north wind sleeps, o'erspread
490 Heaven's cheerful face, the louring element
Scowls o'er the darkened landscape snow or shower,
If chance the radiant sun, with farewell sweet,
Extend his evening beam, the fields revive,
The birds their notes renew, and bleating herds
495 Attest their joy, that hill and valley rings.
O shame to men! Devil with devil damned
Firm concord holds; men only disagree
Of creatures rational, though under hope
Of heavenly grace, and, God proclaiming peace,
500 Yet live in hatred, enmity, and strife
Among themselves, and levy cruel wars
Wasting the earth, each other to destroy:
As if (which might induce us to accord)
Man had not hellish foes enow besides,
505 That day and night for his destruction wait!

The Stygian council thus dissolved; and forth
In order came the grand infernal Peers:
Midst came their mighty Paramount, and seemed
Alone th' antagonist of Heaven, nor less
510 Than Hell's dread Emperor, with pomp supreme,
And god-like imitated state: him round
A globe of fiery Seraphim enclosed
With bright emblazonry, and horrent arms.

Then of their session ended they bid cry
515 With trumpet's regal sound the great result:
Toward the four winds four speedy Cherubim
Put to their mouths the sounding alchemy,
By herald's voice explained; the hollow Abyss
Heard far and wide, and all the host of Hell
520 With deafening shout returned them loud acclaim.
Thence more at ease their minds, and somewhat raised
By false presumptuous hope, the ranged Powers
Disband; and, wandering, each his several way
Pursues, as inclination or sad choice
525 Leads him perplexed, where he may likeliest find
Truce to his restless thoughts, and entertain
The irksome hours, till his great Chief return.
Part on the plain, or in the air sublime,
Upon the wing or in swift race contend,
530 As at th' Olympian games or Pythian fields;
Part curb their fiery steeds, or shun the goal
With rapid wheels, or fronted brigades form:
As when, to warn proud cities, war appears
Waged in the troubled sky, and armies rush
535 To battle in the clouds; before each van
Prick forth the airy knights, and couch their spears,
Till thickest legions close; with feats of arms
From either end of heaven the welkin burns.
Others, with vast Typhoean rage, more fell,
540 Rend up both rocks and hills, and ride the air
In whirlwind; Hell scarce holds the wild uproar:—
As when Alcides, from Oechalia crowned
With conquest, felt th' envenomed robe, and tore
Through pain up by the roots Thessalian pines,
545 And Lichas from the top of Oeta threw
Into th' Euboic sea. Others, more mild,
Retreated in a silent valley, sing
With notes angelical to many a harp
Their own heroic deeds, and hapless fall
550 By doom of battle, and complain that Fate
Free Virtue should enthrall to Force or Chance.
Their song was partial; but the harmony
(What could it less when Spirits immortal sing?)
Suspended Hell, and took with ravishment
555 The thronging audience. In discourse more sweet
(For Eloquence the Soul, Song charms the Sense)
Others apart sat on a hill retired,
In thoughts more elevate, and reasoned high

     Of Providence, Foreknowledge, Will, and Fate—
560 Fixed fate, free will, foreknowledge absolute,
     And found no end, in wandering mazes lost.
     Of good and evil much they argued then,
     Of happiness and final misery,
     Passion and apathy, and glory and shame:
565 Vain wisdom all, and false philosophy!—
     Yet, with a pleasing sorcery, could charm
     Pain for a while or anguish, and excite
     Fallacious hope, or arm th' obdured breast
     With stubborn patience as with triple steel.
570 Another part, in squadrons and gross bands,
     On bold adventure to discover wide
     That dismal world, if any clime perhaps
     Might yield them easier habitation, bend
     Four ways their flying march, along the banks
575 Of four infernal rivers, that disgorge
     Into the burning lake their baleful streams—
     Abhorred Styx, the flood of deadly hate;
     Sad Acheron of sorrow, black and deep;
     Cocytus, named of lamentation loud
580 Heard on the rueful stream; fierce Phlegeton,
     Whose waves of torrent fire inflame with rage.
     Far off from these, a slow and silent stream,
     Lethe, the river of oblivion, rolls
     Her watery labyrinth, whereof who drinks
585 Forthwith his former state and being forgets—
     Forgets both joy and grief, pleasure and pain.
     Beyond this flood a frozen continent
     Lies dark and wild, beat with perpetual storms
     Of whirlwind and dire hail, which on firm land
590 Thaws not, but gathers heap, and ruin seems
     Of ancient pile; all else deep snow and ice,
     A gulf profound as that Serbonian bog
     Betwixt Damiata and Mount Casius old,
     Where armies whole have sunk: the parching air
595 Burns frore, and cold performs th' effect of fire.
     Thither, by harpy-footed Furies haled,
     At certain revolutions all the damned
     Are brought; and feel by turns the bitter change
     Of fierce extremes, extremes by change more fierce,
600 From beds of raging fire to starve in ice
     Their soft ethereal warmth, and there to pine
     Immovable, infixed, and frozen round
     Periods of time,—thence hurried back to fire.

          They ferry over this Lethean sound
605   Both to and fro, their sorrow to augment,
          And wish and struggle, as they pass, to reach
          The tempting stream, with one small drop to lose
          In sweet forgetfulness all pain and woe,
          All in one moment, and so near the brink;
610   But Fate withstands, and, to oppose th' attempt,
          Medusa with Gorgonian terror guards
          The ford, and of itself the water flies
          All taste of living wight, as once it fled
          The lip of Tantalus. Thus roving on
615   In confused march forlorn, th' adventurous bands,
          With shuddering horror pale, and eyes aghast,
          Viewed first their lamentable lot, and found
          No rest. Through many a dark and dreary vale
          They passed, and many a region dolorous,
620   O'er many a frozen, many a fiery alp,
          Rocks, caves, lakes, fens, bogs, dens, and shades of death—
          A universe of death, which God by curse
          Created evil, for evil only good;
          Where all life dies, death lives, and Nature breeds,
625   Perverse, all monstrous, all prodigious things,
          Obominable, inutterable, and worse
          Than fables yet have feigned or fear conceived,
          Gorgons, and Hydras, and Chimeras dire.

          Meanwhile the Adversary of God and Man,
630   Satan, with thoughts inflamed of highest design,
          Puts on swift wings, and toward the gates of Hell
          Explores his solitary flight: sometimes
          He scours the right hand coast, sometimes the left;
          Now shaves with level wing the deep, then soars
635   Up to the fiery concave towering high.
          As when far off at sea a fleet descried
          Hangs in the clouds, by equinoctial winds
          Close sailing from Bengala, or the isles
          Of Ternate and Tidore, whence merchants bring
640   Their spicy drugs; they on the trading flood,
          Through the wide Ethiopian to the Cape,
          Ply stemming nightly toward the pole: so seemed
          Far off the flying Fiend. At last appear
          Hell-bounds, high reaching to the horrid roof,
645   And thrice threefold the gates; three folds were brass,
          Three iron, three of adamantine rock,
          Impenetrable, impaled with circling fire,

Yet unconsumed. Before the gates there sat
On either side a formidable Shape.
650   The one seemed woman to the waist, and fair,
But ended foul in many a scaly fold,
Voluminous and vast—a serpent armed
With mortal sting. About her middle round
A cry of Hell-hounds never-ceasing barked
655   With wide Cerberean mouths full loud, and rung
A hideous peal; yet, when they list, would creep,
If aught disturbed their noise, into her womb,
And kennel there; yet there still barked and howled
Within unseen. Far less abhorred than these
660   Vexed Scylla, bathing in the sea that parts
Calabria from the hoarse Trinacrian shore;
Nor uglier follow the night-hag, when, called
In secret, riding through the air she comes,
Lured with the smell of infant blood, to dance
665   With Lapland witches, while the labouring moon
Eclipses at their charms. The other Shape—
If shape it might be called that shape had none
Distinguishable in member, joint, or limb;
Or substance might be called that shadow seemed,
670   For each seemed either—black it stood as Night,
Fierce as ten Furies, terrible as Hell,
And shook a dreadful dart: what seemed his head
The likeness of a kingly crown had on.
Satan was now at hand, and from his seat
675   The monster moving onward came as fast
With horrid strides; Hell trembled as he strode.
Th' undaunted Fiend what this might be admired—
Admired, not feared (God and his Son except,
Created thing naught valued he nor shunned),
680   And with disdainful look thus first began:—

"Whence and what art thou, execrable Shape,
That dar'st, though grim and terrible, advance
Thy miscreated front athwart my way
To yonder gates? Through them I mean to pass,
685   That be assured, without leave asked of thee.
Retire; or taste thy folly, and learn by proof,
Hell-born, not to contend with Spirits of Heaven."

To whom the Goblin, full of wrath, replied:—
"Art thou that traitor Angel? art thou he,
690   Who first broke peace in Heaven and faith, till then
Unbroken, and in proud rebellious arms

Drew after him the third part of Heaven's sons,
Conjured against the Highest—for which both thou
And they, outcast from God, are here condemned
695 To waste eternal days in woe and pain?
And reckon'st thou thyself with Spirits of Heaven
Hell-doomed, and breath'st defiance here and scorn,
Where I reign king, and, to enrage thee more,
Thy king and lord? Back to thy punishment,
700 False fugitive; and to thy speed add wings,
Lest with a whip of scorpions I pursue
Thy lingering, or with one stroke of this dart
Strange horror seize thee, and pangs unfelt before."

So spake the grisly Terror, and in shape,
705 So speaking and so threatening, grew tenfold,
More dreadful and deform. On th' other side,
Incensed with indignation, Satan stood
Unterrified, and like a comet burned,
That fires the length of Ophiuchus huge
710 In th' arctic sky, and from his horrid hair
Shakes pestilence and war. Each at the head
Levelled his deadly aim; their fatal hands
No second stroke intend; and such a frown
Each cast at th' other as when two black clouds,
715 With heaven's artillery fraught, came rattling on
Over the Caspian,—then stand front to front
Hovering a space, till winds the signal blow
To join their dark encounter in mid-air.
So frowned the mighty combatants that Hell
720 Grew darker at their frown; so matched they stood;
For never but once more was wither like
To meet so great a foe. And now great deeds
Had been achieved, whereof all Hell had rung,
Had not the snaky Sorceress, that sat
725 Fast by Hell-gate and kept the fatal key,
Risen, and with hideous outcry rushed between.

"O father, what intends thy hand," she cried,
"Against thy only son? What fury, O son,
Possesses thee to bend that mortal dart
730 Against thy father's head? And know'st for whom?
For him who sits above, and laughs the while
At thee, ordained his drudge to execute
Whate'er his wrath, which he calls justice, bids—
His wrath, which one day will destroy ye both!"

735 She spake, and at her words the hellish Pest
Forbore: then these to her Satan returned:—

"So strange thy outcry, and thy words so strange
Thou interposest, that my sudden hand,
Prevented, spares to tell thee yet by deeds
740 What it intends, till first I know of thee
What thing thou art, thus double-formed, and why,
In this infernal vale first met, thou call'st
Me father, and that phantasm call'st my son.
I know thee not, nor ever saw till now
745 Sight more detestable than him and thee."

T' whom thus the Portress of Hell-gate replied:—
"Hast thou forgot me, then; and do I seem
Now in thine eye so foul?—once deemed so fair
In Heaven, when at th' assembly, and in sight
750 Of all the Seraphim with thee combined
In bold conspiracy against Heaven's King,
All on a sudden miserable pain
Surprised thee, dim thine eyes and dizzy swum
In darkness, while thy head flames thick and fast
755 Threw forth, till on the left side opening wide,
Likest to thee in shape and countenance bright,
Then shining heavenly fair, a goddess armed,
Out of thy head I sprung. Amazement seized
All th' host of Heaven; back they recoiled afraid
760 At first, and called me Sin, and for a sign
Portentous held me; but, familiar grown,
I pleased, and with attractive graces won
The most averse—thee chiefly, who, full oft
Thyself in me thy perfect image viewing,
765 Becam'st enamoured; and such joy thou took'st
With me in secret that my womb conceived
A growing burden. Meanwhile war arose,
And fields were fought in Heaven: wherein remained
(For what could else?) to our Almighty Foe
770 Clear victory; to our part loss and rout
Through all the Empyrean. Down they fell,
Driven headlong from the pitch of Heaven, down
Into this Deep; and in the general fall
I also: at which time this powerful key
775 Into my hands was given, with charge to keep
These gates for ever shut, which none can pass
Without my opening. Pensive here I sat

Alone; but long I sat not, till my womb,
Pregnant by thee, and now excessive grown,
780 Prodigious motion felt and rueful throes.
At last this odious offspring whom thou seest,
Thine own begotten, breaking violent way,
Tore through my entrails, that, with fear and pain
Distorted, all my nether shape thus grew
785 Transformed: but he my inbred enemy
Forth issued, brandishing his fatal dart,
Made to destroy. I fled, and cried out Death!
Hell trembled at the hideous name, and sighed
From all her caves, and back resounded Death!
790 I fled; but he pursued (though more, it seems,
Inflamed with lust than rage), and, swifter far,
Me overtook, his mother, all dismayed,
And, in embraces forcible and foul
Engendering with me, of that rape begot
795 These yelling monsters, that with ceaseless cry
Surround me, as thou saw'st—hourly conceived
And hourly born, with sorrow infinite
To me; for, when they list, into the womb
That bred them they return, and howl, and gnaw
800 My bowels, their repast; then, bursting forth
Afresh, with conscious terrors vex me round,
That rest or intermission none I find.
Before mine eyes in opposition sits
Grim Death, my son and foe, who set them on,
805 And me, his parent, would full soon devour
For want of other prey, but that he knows
His end with mine involved, and knows that I
Should prove a bitter morsel, and his bane,
Whenever that shall be: so Fate pronounced.
810 But thou, O father, I forewarn thee, shun
His deadly arrow; neither vainly hope
To be invulnerable in those bright arms,
Through tempered heavenly; for that mortal dint,
Save he who reigns above, none can resist."

815 She finished; and the subtle Fiend his lore
Soon learned, now milder, and thus answered smooth:—

"Dear daughter—since thou claim'st me for thy sire,
And my fair son here show'st me, the dear pledge
Of dalliance had with thee in Heaven, and joys
820 Then sweet, now sad to mention, through dire change

Befallen us unforeseen, unthought-of—know,
I come no enemy, but to set free
From out this dark and dismal house of pain
Both him and thee, and all the heavenly host
825   Of Spirits that, in our just pretences armed,
Fell with us from on high. From them I go
This uncouth errand sole, and one for all
Myself expose, with lonely steps to tread
Th' unfounded Deep, and through the void immense
830   To search, with wandering quest, a place foretold
Should be—and, by concurring signs, ere now
Created vast and round—a place of bliss
In the purlieus of Heaven; and therein placed
A race of upstart creatures, to supply
835   Perhaps our vacant room, though more removed,
Lest Heaven, surcharged with potent multitude,
Might hap to move new broils. Be this, or aught
Than this more secret, now designed, I haste
To know; and, this once known, shall soon return,
840   And bring ye to the place where thou and Death
Shall dwell at ease, and up and down unseen
Wing silently the buxom air, embalmed
With odours. There ye shall be fed and filled
Immeasurably; all things shall be your prey."

845   He ceased; for both seemed highly pleased, and Death
Grinned horrible a ghastly smile, to hear
His famine should be filled, and blessed his maw
Destined to that good hour. No less rejoiced
His mother bad, and thus bespake her sire:—

850   "The key of this infernal Pit, by due
And by command of Heaven's all-powerful King,
I keep, by him forbidden to unlock
These adamantine gates; against all force
Death ready stands to interpose his dart,
855   Fearless to be o'ermatched by living might.
But what owe I to his commands above,
Who hates me, and hath hither thrust me down
Into this gloom of Tartarus profound,
To sit in hateful office here confined,
860   Inhabitant of Heaven and heavenly born—
Here in perpetual agony and pain,
With terrors and with clamours compassed round
Of mine own brood, that on my bowels feed?

Thou art my father, thou my author, thou
865 My being gav'st me; whom should I obey
But thee? whom follow? Thou wilt bring me soon
To that new world of light and bliss, among
The gods who live at ease, where I shall reign
At thy right hand voluptuous, as beseems
870 Thy daughter and thy darling, without end."
Thus saying, from her side the fatal key,
Sad instrument of all our woe, she took;
And, towards the gate rolling her bestial train,
Forthwith the huge portcullis high up-drew,
875 Which, but herself, not all the Stygian Powers
Could once have moved; then in the key-hole turns
Th' intricate wards, and every bolt and bar
Of massy iron or solid rock with ease
Unfastens. On a sudden open fly,
880 With impetuous recoil and jarring sound,
Th' infernal doors, and on their hinges grate
Harsh thunder, that the lowest bottom shook
Of Erebus. She opened; but to shut
Excelled her power: the gates wide open stood,
885 That with extended wings a bannered host,
Under spread ensigns marching, might pass through
With horse and chariots ranked in loose array;
So wide they stood, and like a furnace-mouth
Cast forth redounding smoke and ruddy flame.
890 Before their eyes in sudden view appear
The secrets of the hoary Deep—a dark
Illimitable ocean, without bound,
Without dimension; where length, breadth, and height,
And time, and place, are lost; where eldest Night
895 And Chaos, ancestors of Nature, hold
Eternal anarchy, amidst the noise
Of endless wars, and by confusion stand.
For Hot, Cold, Moist, and Dry, four champions fierce,
Strive here for mastery, and to battle bring
900 Their embryon atoms: they around the flag
Of each his faction, in their several clans,
Light-armed or heavy, sharp, smooth, swift, or slow,
Swarm populous, unnumbered as the sands
Of Barca or Cyrene's torrid soil,
905 Levied to side with warring winds, and poise
Their lighter wings. To whom these most adhere
He rules a moment: Chaos umpire sits,
And by decision more embroils the fray

By which he reigns: next him, high arbiter,
910 Chance governs all. Into this wild Abyss,
The womb of Nature, and perhaps her grave,
Of neither sea, nor shore, nor air, nor fire,
But all these in their pregnant causes mixed
Confusedly, and which thus must ever fight,
915 Unless th' Almighty Maker them ordain
His dark materials to create more worlds—
Into this wild Abyss the wary Fiend
Stood on the brink of Hell and looked a while,
Pondering his voyage; for no narrow frith
920 He had to cross. Nor was his ear less pealed
With noises loud and ruinous (to compare
Great things with small) than when Bellona storms
With all her battering engines, bent to rase
Some capital city; or less than if this frame
925 Of Heaven were falling, and these elements
In mutiny had from her axle torn
The steadfast Earth. At last his sail-broad vans
He spread for flight, and, in the surging smoke
Uplifted, spurns the ground; thence many a league,
930 As in a cloudy chair, ascending rides
Audacious; but, that seat soon failing, meets
A vast vacuity. All unawares,
Fluttering his pennons vain, plumb-down he drops
Ten thousand fathom deep, and to this hour
935 Down had been falling, had not, by ill chance,
The strong rebuff of some tumultuous cloud,
Instinct with fire and nitre, hurried him
As many miles aloft. That fury stayed—
Quenched in a boggy Syrtis, neither sea,
940 Nor good dry land—nigh foundered, on he fares,
Treading the crude consistence, half on foot,
Half flying; behoves him now both oar and sail.
As when a gryphon through the wilderness
With winged course, o'er hill or moory dale,
945 Pursues the Arimaspian, who by stealth
Had from his wakeful custody purloined
The guarded gold; so eagerly the Fiend
O'er bog or steep, through strait, rough, dense, or rare,
With head, hands, wings, or feet, pursues his way,
950 And swims, or sinks, or wades, or creeps, or flies.
At length a universal hubbub wild
Of stunning sounds, and voices all confused,
Borne through the hollow dark, assaults his ear

With loudest vehemence. Thither he plies
955 Undaunted, to meet there whatever Power
Or Spirit of the nethermost Abyss
Might in that noise reside, of whom to ask
Which way the nearest coast of darkness lies
Bordering on light; when straight behold the throne
960 Of Chaos, and his dark pavilion spread
Wide on the wasteful Deep! With him enthroned
Sat sable-vested Night, eldest of things,
The consort of his reign; and by them stood
Orcus and Ades, and the dreaded name
965 Of Demogorgon; Rumour next, and Chance,
And Tumult, and Confusion, all embroiled,
And Discord with a thousand various mouths.

T' whom Satan, turning boldly, thus:—"Ye Powers
And Spirits of this nethermost Abyss,
970 Chaos and ancient Night, I come no spy
With purpose to explore or to disturb
The secrets of your realm; but, by constraint
Wandering this darksome desert, as my way
Lies through your spacious empire up to light,
975 Alone and without guide, half lost, I seek,
What readiest path leads where your gloomy bounds
Confine with Heaven; or, if some other place,
From your dominion won, th' Ethereal King
Possesses lately, thither to arrive
980 I travel this profound. Direct my course:
Directed, no mean recompense it brings
To your behoof, if I that region lost,
All usurpation thence expelled, reduce
To her original darkness and your sway
985 (Which is my present journey), and once more
Erect the standard there of ancient Night.
Yours be th' advantage all, mine the revenge!"

Thus Satan; and him thus the Anarch old,
With faltering speech and visage incomposed,
990 Answered: "I know thee, stranger, who thou art—
That mighty leading Angel, who of late
Made head against Heaven's King, though overthrown.
I saw and heard; for such a numerous host
Fled not in silence through the frighted Deep,
995 With ruin upon ruin, rout on rout,
Confusion worse confounded; and Heaven-gates

Poured out by millions her victorious bands,
Pursuing. I upon my frontiers here
Keep residence; if all I can will serve
1000 That little which is left so to defend,
Encroached on still through our intestine broils
Weakening the sceptre of old Night: first, Hell,
Your dungeon, stretching far and wide beneath;
Now lately Heaven and Earth, another world
1005 Hung o'er my realm, linked in a golden chain
To that side Heaven from whence your legions fell!
If that way be your walk, you have not far;
So much the nearer danger. Go, and speed;
Havoc, and spoil, and ruin, are my gain."

1010 He ceased; and Satan stayed not to reply,
But, glad that now his sea should find a shore,
With fresh alacrity and force renewed
Springs upward, like a pyramid of fire,
Into the wild expanse, and through the shock
1015 Of fighting elements, on all sides round
Environed, wins his way; harder beset
And more endangered than when Argo passed
Through Bosporus betwixt the justling rocks,
Or when Ulysses on the larboard shunned
1020 Charybdis, and by th' other whirlpool steered.
So he with difficulty and labour hard
Moved on, with difficulty and labour he;
But, he once passed, soon after, when Man fell,
Strange alteration! Sin and Death amain,
1025 Following his track (such was the will of Heaven)
Paved after him a broad and beaten way
Over the dark Abyss, whose boiling gulf
Tamely endured a bridge of wondrous length,
From Hell continued, reaching th' utmost orb
1030 Of this frail World; by which the Spirits perverse
With easy intercourse pass to and fro
To tempt or punish mortals, except whom
God and good Angels guard by special grace.

But now at last the sacred influence
1035 Of light appears, and from the walls of Heaven
Shoots far into the bosom of dim Night
A glimmering dawn. Here Nature first begins
Her farthest verge, and Chaos to retire,
As from her outmost works, a broken foe,

1040 With tumult less and with less hostile din;
That Satan with less toil, and now with ease,
Wafts on the calmer wave by dubious light,
And, like a weather-beaten vessel, holds
Gladly the port, though shrouds and tackle torn;
1045 Or in the emptier waste, resembling air,
Weighs his spread wings, at leisure to behold
Far off th' empyreal Heaven, extended wide
In circuit, undetermined square or round,
With opal towers and battlements adorned
1050 Of living sapphire, once his native seat;
And, fast by, hanging in a golden chain,
This pendent World, in bigness as a star
Of smallest magnitude close by the moon.
Thither, full fraught with mischievous revenge,
1055 Accursed, and in a cursed hour, he hies.

Book III

Hail, holy Light, offspring of Heaven firstborn,
Or of the Eternal coeternal beam
May I express thee unblam'd? since God is light,
And never but in unapproached light
5 Dwelt from eternity, dwelt then in thee
Bright effluence of bright essence increate.
Or hear'st thou rather pure ethereal stream,
Whose fountain who shall tell? before the sun,
Before the Heavens thou wert, and at the voice
10 Of God, as with a mantle, didst invest
The rising world of waters dark and deep,
Won from the void and formless infinite.
Thee I re-visit now with bolder wing,
Escap'd the Stygian pool, though long detain'd
15 In that obscure sojourn, while in my flight
Through utter and through middle darkness borne,
With other notes than to the Orphean lyre
I sung of Chaos and eternal Night;
Taught by the heavenly Muse to venture down
20 The dark descent, and up to re-ascend,
Though hard and rare: Thee I revisit safe,
And feel thy sovran vital lamp; but thou
Revisit'st not these eyes, that roll in vain
To find thy piercing ray, and find no dawn;
25 So thick a drop serene hath quench'd their orbs,
Or dim suffusion veil'd. Yet not the more
Cease I to wander, where the Muses haunt,

Clear spring, or shady grove, or sunny hill,
Smit with the love of sacred song; but chief
30 Thee, Sion, and the flowery brooks beneath,
That wash thy hallow'd feet, and warbling flow,
Nightly I visit: nor sometimes forget
Those other two equaled with me in fate
So were I equall'd with them in renown,
35 Thy sovran command, that Man should find grace;
Blind Thamyris, and blind Maeonides,
And Tiresias, and Phineus, prophets old:
Then feed on thoughts, that voluntary move
Harmonious numbers; as the wakeful bird
40 Sings darkling, and in shadiest covert hid
Tunes her nocturnal note. Thus with the year
Seasons return; but not to me returns
Day, or the sweet approach of even or morn,
Or sight of vernal bloom, or summer's rose,
45 Or flocks, or herds, or human face divine;
But cloud instead, and ever-during dark
Surrounds me, from the cheerful ways of men
Cut off, and for the book of knowledge fair
Presented with a universal blank
50 Of nature's works to me expung'd and ras'd,
And wisdom at one entrance quite shut out.
So much the rather thou, celestial Light,
Shine inward, and the mind through all her powers
Irradiate; there plant eyes, all mist from thence
55 Purge and disperse, that I may see and tell
Of things invisible to mortal sight.
Now had the Almighty Father from above,
From the pure empyrean where he sits
High thron'd above all highth, bent down his eye
60 His own works and their works at once to view:
About him all the Sanctities of Heaven
Stood thick as stars, and from his sight receiv'd
Beatitude past utterance; on his right
The radiant image of his glory sat,
65 His only son; on earth he first beheld
Our two first parents, yet the only two
Of mankind in the happy garden plac'd
Reaping immortal fruits of joy and love,
Uninterrupted joy, unrivall'd love,
70 In blissful solitude; he then survey'd
Hell and the gulf between, and Satan there
Coasting the wall of Heaven on this side Night

In the dun air sublime, and ready now
To stoop with wearied wings, and willing feet,
75 On the bare outside of this world, that seem'd
Firm land imbosom'd, without firmament,
Uncertain which, in ocean or in air.
Him God beholding from his prospect high,
Wherein past, present, future, he beholds,
80 Thus to his only Son foreseeing spake.
Only begotten Son, seest thou what rage
Transports our Adversary? whom no bounds
Prescrib'd no bars of Hell, nor all the chains
Heap'd on him there, nor yet the main abyss
85 Wide interrupt, can hold; so bent he seems
On desperate revenge, that shall redound
Upon his own rebellious head. And now,
Through all restraint broke loose, he wings his way
Not far off Heaven, in the precincts of light,
90 Directly towards the new created world,
And man there plac'd, with purpose to assay
If him by force he can destroy, or, worse,
By some false guile pervert; and shall pervert;
For man will hearken to his glozing lies,
95 And easily transgress the sole command,
Sole pledge of his obedience: So will fall
He and his faithless progeny: Whose fault?
Whose but his own? ingrate, he had of me
All he could have; I made him just and right,
100 Sufficient to have stood, though free to fall.
Such I created all the ethereal Powers
And Spirits, both them who stood, and them who fail'd;
Freely they stood who stood, and fell who fell.
Not free, what proof could they have given sincere
105 Of true allegiance, constant faith or love,
Where only what they needs must do appear'd,
Not what they would? what praise could they receive?
What pleasure I from such obedience paid,
When will and reason (reason also is choice)
110 Useless and vain, of freedom both despoil'd,
Made passive both, had serv'd necessity,
Not me. They therefore, as to right belong'd,
So were created, nor can justly accuse
Their Maker, or their making, or their fate,
115 As if predestination over-rul'd
Their will dispos'd by absolute decree
Or high foreknowledge they themselves decreed

Their own revolt, not I; if I foreknew,
Foreknowledge had no influence on their fault,
120 Which had no less proved certain unforeknown.
So without least impulse or shadow of fate,
Or aught by me immutably foreseen,
They trespass, authors to themselves in all
Both what they judge, and what they choose; for so
125 I form'd them free: and free they must remain,
Till they enthrall themselves; I else must change
Their nature, and revoke the high decree
Unchangeable, eternal, which ordain'd
Their freedom: they themselves ordain'd their fall.
130 The first sort by their own suggestion fell,
Self-tempted, self-deprav'd: Man falls, deceiv'd
By the other first: Man therefore shall find grace,
The other none: In mercy and justice both,
Through Heaven and Earth, so shall my glory excel;
135 But Mercy, first and last, shall brightest shine.
Thus while God spake, ambrosial fragrance fill'd
All Heaven, and in the blessed Spirits elect
Sense of new joy ineffable diffus'd.
Beyond compare the Son of God was seen
140 Most glorious; in him all his Father shone
Substantially express'd; and in his face
Divine compassion visibly appear'd,
Love without end, and without measure grace,
Which uttering, thus he to his Father spake.
145 O Father, gracious was that word which clos'd
Thy sovran command, that Man should find grace;
For which both Heaven and earth shall high extol
Thy praises, with the innumerable sound
Of hymns and sacred songs, wherewith thy throne
150 Encompass'd shall resound thee ever blest.
For should Man finally be lost, should Man,
Thy creature late so lov'd, thy youngest son,
Fall circumvented thus by fraud, though join'd
With his own folly? that be from thee far,
155 That far be from thee, Father, who art judge
Of all things made, and judgest only right.
Or shall the Adversary thus obtain
His end, and frustrate thine? shall he fulfill
His malice, and thy goodness bring to nought,
160 Or proud return, though to his heavier doom,
Yet with revenge accomplish'd, and to Hell
Draw after him the whole race of mankind,

By him corrupted? or wilt thou thyself
Abolish thy creation, and unmake
165 For him, what for thy glory thou hast made?
So should thy goodness and thy greatness both
Be question'd and blasphem'd without defence.
To whom the great Creator thus replied.
O son, in whom my soul hath chief delight,
170 Son of my bosom, Son who art alone.
My word, my wisdom, and effectual might,
All hast thou spoken as my thoughts are, all
As my eternal purpose hath decreed;
Man shall not quite be lost, but sav'd who will;
175 Yet not of will in him, but grace in me
Freely vouchsaf'd; once more I will renew
His lapsed powers, though forfeit; and enthrall'd
By sin to foul exorbitant desires;
Upheld by me, yet once more he shall stand
180 On even ground against his mortal foe;
By me upheld, that he may know how frail
His fallen condition is, and to me owe
All his deliverance, and to none but me.
Some I have chosen of peculiar grace,
185 Elect above the rest; so is my will:
The rest shall hear me call, and oft be warn'd
Their sinful state, and to appease betimes
The incensed Deity, while offer'd grace
Invites; for I will clear their senses dark,
190 What may suffice, and soften stony hearts
To pray, repent, and bring obedience due.
To prayer, repentance, and obedience due,
Though but endeavour'd with sincere intent,
Mine ear shall not be slow, mine eye not shut.
195 And I will place within them as a guide,
My umpire Conscience; whom if they will hear,
Light after light, well us'd, they shall attain,
And to the end, persisting, safe arrive.
This my long sufferance, and my day of grace,
200 They who neglect and scorn, shall never taste;
But hard be harden'd, blind be blinded more,
That they may stumble on, and deeper fall;
And none but such from mercy I exclude.
But yet all is not done; Man disobeying,
205 Disloyal, breaks his fealty, and sins
Against the high supremacy of Heaven,
Affecting God-head, and, so losing all,

To expiate his treason hath nought left,
But to destruction sacred and devote,
210 He, with his whole posterity, must die,
Die he or justice must; unless for him
Some other able, and as willing, pay
The rigid satisfaction, death for death.
Say, heavenly Powers, where shall we find such love?
215 Which of you will be mortal, to redeem
Man's mortal crime, and just the unjust to save?
Dwells in all Heaven charity so dear?
He ask'd, but all the heavenly quire stood mute,
And silence was in Heaven: on Man's behalf
220 Patron or intercessour none appear'd,
Much less that durst upon his own head draw
The deadly forfeiture, and ransom set.
And now without redemption all mankind
Must have been lost, adjudg'd to Death and Hell
225 By doom severe, had not the Son of God,
In whom the fulness dwells of love divine,
His dearest mediation thus renew'd.
Father, thy word is past, Man shall find grace;
And shall grace not find means, that finds her way,
230 The speediest of thy winged messengers,
To visit all thy creatures, and to all
Comes unprevented, unimplor'd, unsought?
Happy for Man, so coming; he her aid
Can never seek, once dead in sins, and lost;
235 Atonement for himself, or offering meet,
Indebted and undone, hath none to bring;
Behold me then: me for him, life for life
I offer: on me let thine anger fall;
Account me Man; I for his sake will leave
240 Thy bosom, and this glory next to thee
Freely put off, and for him lastly die
Well pleased; on me let Death wreak all his rage.
Under his gloomy power I shall not long
Lie vanquished. Thou hast given me to possess
245 Life in myself for ever; by thee I live;
Though now to Death I yield, and am his due,
All that of me can die, yet, that debt paid,
Thou wilt not leave me in the loathsome grave
His prey, nor suffer my unspotted soul
250 For ever with corruption there to dwell;
But I shall rise victorious, and subdue
My vanquisher, spoiled of his vaunted spoil.

Death his death's wound shall then receive, and stoop
Inglorious, of his mortal sting disarmed;
255   I through the ample air in triumph high
Shall lead Hell captive maugre Hell, and show
The powers of darkness bound. Thou, at the sight
Pleased, out of Heaven shalt look down and smile,
While, by thee raised, I ruin all my foes;
260   Death last, and with his carcase glut the grave;
Then, with the multitude of my redeemed,
Shall enter Heaven, long absent, and return,
Father, to see thy face, wherein no cloud
Of anger shall remain, but peace assured
265   And reconcilement: wrath shall be no more
Thenceforth, but in thy presence joy entire.

His words here ended; but his meek aspect
Silent yet spake, and breathed immortal love
To mortal men, above which only shone
270   Filial obedience: as a sacrifice
Glad to be offered, he attends the will
Of his great Father. Admiration seized
All Heaven, what this might mean, and whither tend,
Wondering; but soon th' Almighty thus replied:

275   O thou in Heaven and Earth the only peace
Found out for mankind under wrath, O thou
My sole complacence! Well thou know'st how dear
To me are all my works; nor Man the least,
Though last created, that for him I spare
280   Thee from my bosom and right hand, to save,
By losing thee a while, the whole race lost.
Thou, therefore, whom thou only canst redeem,
Their nature also to thy nature join;
And be thyself Man among men on Earth,
285   Made flesh, when time shall be, of virgin seed,
By wondrous birth; be thou in Adam's room
The head of all mankind, though Adam's son.
As in him perish all men, so in thee,
As from a second root, shall be restored
290   As many as are restored, without thee none.
His crime makes guilty all his sons; thy merit,
Imputed, shall absolve them who renounce
Their own both righteous and unrighteous deeds,
And live in thee transplanted, and from thee
295   Receive new life. So Man, as is most just,

Shall satisfy for Man, be judged and die,
And dying rise, and rising with him raise
His brethren, ransomed with his own dear life.
So heavenly love shall outdo hellish hate,
300   Giving to death, and dying to redeem,
So dearly to redeem what hellish hate
So easily destroyed, and still destroys
In those who, when they may, accept not grace.
Nor shalt thou, by descending to assume
305   Man's nature, lessen or degrade thine own.
Because thou hast, though throned in highest bliss
Equal to God, and equally enjoying
God-like fruition, quitted all, to save
A world from utter loss, and hast been found
310   By merit more than birthright Son of God,
Found worthiest to be so by being good,
Far more than great or high; because in thee
Love hath abounded more than glory abounds;
Therefore thy humiliation shall exalt
315   With thee thy manhood also to this throne:
Here shalt thou sit incarnate, here shalt reign
Both God and Man, Son both of God and Man,
Anointed universal King; all power
I give thee; reign for ever, and assume
320   Thy merits; under thee, as head supreme,
Thrones, Princedoms, Powers, Dominions, I reduce:
All knees to thee shall bow, of them that bide
In Heaven, or Earth, or under Earth in Hell.
When thou, attended gloriously from Heaven,
325   Shalt in the sky appear, and from thee send
The summoning Arch-Angels to proclaim
Thy dread tribunal; forthwith from all winds,
The living, and forthwith the cited dead
Of all past ages, to the general doom
330   Shall hasten; such a peal shall rouse their sleep.
Then, all thy saints assembled, thou shalt judge
Bad Men and Angels; they, arraigned, shall sink
Beneath thy sentence; Hell, her numbers full,
Thenceforth shall be for ever shut. Mean while
335   The world shall burn, and from her ashes spring
New Heaven and Earth, wherein the just shall dwell,
And, after all their tribulations long,
See golden days, fruitful of golden deeds,
With joy and peace triumphing, and fair truth.
340   Then thou thy regal scepter shalt lay by,

For regal scepter then no more shall need,
God shall be all in all. But, all ye Gods,
Adore him, who to compass all this dies;
Adore the Son, and honour him as me.
345 No sooner had the Almighty ceased, but all
The multitude of Angels, with a shout
Loud as from numbers without number, sweet
As from blest voices, uttering joy, Heaven rung
With jubilee, and loud Hosannas filled
350 The eternal regions: Lowly reverent
Towards either throne they bow, and to the ground
With solemn adoration down they cast
Their crowns inwove with amarant and gold;
Immortal amarant, a flower which once
355 In Paradise, fast by the tree of life,
Began to bloom; but soon for man's offence
To Heaven removed, where first it grew, there grows,
And flowers aloft shading the fount of life,
And where the river of bliss through midst of Heaven
360 Rolls o'er Elysian flowers her amber stream;
With these that never fade the Spirits elect
Bind their resplendent locks inwreathed with beams;
Now in loose garlands thick thrown off, the bright
Pavement, that like a sea of jasper shone,
365 Impurpled with celestial roses smiled.
Then, crowned again, their golden harps they took,
Harps ever tuned, that glittering by their side
Like quivers hung, and with preamble sweet
Of charming symphony they introduce
370 Their sacred song, and waken raptures high;
No voice exempt, no voice but well could join
Melodious part, such concord is in Heaven.
Thee, Father, first they sung Omnipotent,
Immutable, Immortal, Infinite,
375 Eternal King; the Author of all being,
Fountain of light, thyself invisible
Amidst the glorious brightness where thou sit'st
Throned inaccessible, but when thou shadest
The full blaze of thy beams, and, through a cloud
380 Drawn round about thee like a radiant shrine,
Dark with excessive bright thy skirts appear,
Yet dazzle Heaven, that brightest Seraphim
Approach not, but with both wings veil their eyes.
Thee next they sang of all creation first,
385 Begotten Son, Divine Similitude,

In whose conspicuous countenance, without cloud
Made visible, the Almighty Father shines,
Whom else no creature can behold; on thee
Impressed the effulgence of his glory abides,
390 Transfused on thee his ample Spirit rests.
He Heaven of Heavens and all the Powers therein
By thee created; and by thee threw down
The aspiring Dominations: Thou that day
Thy Father's dreadful thunder didst not spare,
395 Nor stop thy flaming chariot-wheels, that shook
Heaven's everlasting frame, while o'er the necks
Thou drovest of warring Angels disarrayed.
Back from pursuit thy Powers with loud acclaim
Thee only extolled, Son of thy Father's might,
400 To execute fierce vengeance on his foes,
Not so on Man: Him through their malice fallen,
Father of mercy and grace, thou didst not doom
So strictly, but much more to pity incline:
No sooner did thy dear and only Son
405 Perceive thee purposed not to doom frail Man
So strictly, but much more to pity inclined,
He to appease thy wrath, and end the strife
Of mercy and justice in thy face discerned,
Regardless of the bliss wherein he sat
410 Second to thee, offered himself to die
For Man's offence. O unexampled love,
Love no where to be found less than Divine!
Hail, Son of God, Saviour of Men! Thy name
Shall be the copious matter of my song
415 Henceforth, and never shall my heart thy praise
Forget, nor from thy Father's praise disjoin.
Thus they in Heaven, above the starry sphere,
Their happy hours in joy and hymning spent.
Mean while upon the firm opacous globe
420 Of this round world, whose first convex divides
The luminous inferiour orbs, enclosed
From Chaos, and the inroad of Darkness old,
Satan alighted walks: A globe far off
It seemed, now seems a boundless continent
425 Dark, waste, and wild, under the frown of Night
Starless exposed, and ever-threatening storms
Of Chaos blustering round, inclement sky;
Save on that side which from the wall of Heaven,
Though distant far, some small reflection gains
430 Of glimmering air less vexed with tempest loud:

Here walked the Fiend at large in spacious field.
As when a vultur on Imaus bred,
Whose snowy ridge the roving Tartar bounds,
Dislodging from a region scarce of prey
435   To gorge the flesh of lambs or yeanling kids,
On hills where flocks are fed, flies toward the springs
Of Ganges or Hydaspes, Indian streams;
But in his way lights on the barren plains
Of Sericana, where Chineses drive
440   With sails and wind their cany waggons light:
So, on this windy sea of land, the Fiend
Walked up and down alone, bent on his prey;
Alone, for other creature in this place,
Living or lifeless, to be found was none;
445   None yet, but store hereafter from the earth
Up hither like aereal vapours flew
Of all things transitory and vain, when sin
With vanity had filled the works of men:
Both all things vain, and all who in vain things
450   Built their fond hopes of glory or lasting fame,
Or happiness in this or the other life;
All who have their reward on earth, the fruits
Of painful superstition and blind zeal,
Nought seeking but the praise of men, here find
455   Fit retribution, empty as their deeds;
All the unaccomplished works of Nature's hand,
Abortive, monstrous, or unkindly mixed,
Dissolved on earth, fleet hither, and in vain,
Till final dissolution, wander here;
460   Not in the neighbouring moon as some have dreamed;
Those argent fields more likely habitants,
Translated Saints, or middle Spirits hold
Betwixt the angelical and human kind.
Hither of ill-joined sons and daughters born
465   First from the ancient world those giants came
With many a vain exploit, though then renowned:
The builders next of Babel on the plain
Of Sennaar, and still with vain design,
New Babels, had they wherewithal, would build:
470   Others came single; he, who, to be deemed
A God, leaped fondly into Aetna flames,
Empedocles; and he, who, to enjoy
Plato's Elysium, leaped into the sea,
Cleombrotus; and many more too long,
475   Embryos, and idiots, eremites, and friars

White, black, and gray, with all their trumpery.
Here pilgrims roam, that strayed so far to seek
In Golgotha him dead, who lives in Heaven;
And they, who to be sure of Paradise,
480   Dying, put on the weeds of Dominick,
Or in Franciscan think to pass disguised;
They pass the planets seven, and pass the fixed,
And that crystalline sphere whose balance weighs
The trepidation talked, and that first moved;
485   And now Saint Peter at Heaven's wicket seems
To wait them with his keys, and now at foot
Of Heaven's ascent they lift their feet, when lo
A violent cross wind from either coast
Blows them transverse, ten thousand leagues awry
490   Into the devious air: Then might ye see
Cowls, hoods, and habits, with their wearers, tost
And fluttered into rags; then reliques, beads,
Indulgences, dispenses, pardons, bulls,
The sport of winds: All these, upwhirled aloft,
495   Fly o'er the backside of the world far off
Into a Limbo large and broad, since called
The Paradise of Fools, to few unknown
Long after; now unpeopled, and untrod.
All this dark globe the Fiend found as he passed,
500   And long he wandered, till at last a gleam
Of dawning light turned thither-ward in haste
His travelled steps: far distant he descries
Ascending by degrees magnificent
Up to the wall of Heaven a structure high;
505   At top whereof, but far more rich, appeared
The work as of a kingly palace-gate,
With frontispiece of diamond and gold
Embellished; thick with sparkling orient gems
The portal shone, inimitable on earth
510   By model, or by shading pencil, drawn.
These stairs were such as whereon Jacob saw
Angels ascending and descending, bands
Of guardians bright, when he from Esau fled
To Padan-Aram, in the field of Luz
515   Dreaming by night under the open sky
And waking cried, This is the gate of Heaven.
Each stair mysteriously was meant, nor stood
There always, but drawn up to Heaven sometimes
Viewless; and underneath a bright sea flowed
520   Of jasper, or of liquid pearl, whereon

Who after came from earth, failing arrived
Wafted by Angels, or flew o'er the lake
Rapt in a chariot drawn by fiery steeds.
The stairs were then let down, whether to dare
525   The Fiend by easy ascent, or aggravate
His sad exclusion from the doors of bliss:
Direct against which opened from beneath,
Just o'er the blissful seat of Paradise,
A passage down to the Earth, a passage wide,
530   Wider by far than that of after-times
Over mount Sion, and, though that were large,
Over the Promised Land to God so dear;
By which, to visit oft those happy tribes,
On high behests his angels to and fro
535   Passed frequent, and his eye with choice regard
From Paneas, the fount of Jordan's flood,
To Beersaba, where the Holy Land
Borders on Egypt and the Arabian shore;
So wide the opening seemed, where bounds were set
540   To darkness, such as bound the ocean wave.
Satan from hence, now on the lower stair,
That scaled by steps of gold to Heaven-gate,
Looks down with wonder at the sudden view
Of all this world at once. As when a scout,
545   Through dark and desert ways with peril gone
All night; at last by break of cheerful dawn
Obtains the brow of some high-climbing hill,
Which to his eye discovers unaware
The goodly prospect of some foreign land
550   First seen, or some renowned metropolis
With glistering spires and pinnacles adorned,
Which now the rising sun gilds with his beams:
Such wonder seised, though after Heaven seen,
The Spirit malign, but much more envy seised,
555   At sight of all this world beheld so fair.
Round he surveys (and well might, where he stood
So high above the circling canopy
Of night's extended shade,) from eastern point
Of Libra to the fleecy star that bears
560   Andromeda far off Atlantick seas
Beyond the horizon; then from pole to pole
He views in breadth, and without longer pause
Down right into the world's first region throws
His flight precipitant, and winds with ease
565   Through the pure marble air his oblique way

Amongst innumerable stars, that shone
Stars distant, but nigh hand seemed other worlds;
Or other worlds they seemed, or happy isles,
Like those Hesperian gardens famed of old,
570 Fortunate fields, and groves, and flowery vales,
Thrice happy isles; but who dwelt happy there
He staid not to inquire: Above them all
The golden sun, in splendour likest Heaven,
Allured his eye; thither his course he bends
575 Through the calm firmament, (but up or down,
By center, or eccentrick, hard to tell,
Or longitude,) where the great luminary
Aloof the vulgar constellations thick,
That from his lordly eye keep distance due,
580 Dispenses light from far; they, as they move
Their starry dance in numbers that compute
Days, months, and years, towards his all-cheering lamp
Turn swift their various motions, or are turned
By his magnetick beam, that gently warms
585 The universe, and to each inward part
With gentle penetration, though unseen,
Shoots invisible virtue even to the deep;
So wonderously was set his station bright.
There lands the Fiend, a spot like which perhaps
590 Astronomer in the sun's lucent orb
Through his glazed optick tube yet never saw.
The place he found beyond expression bright,
Compared with aught on earth, metal or stone;
Not all parts like, but all alike informed
595 With radiant light, as glowing iron with fire;
If metal, part seemed gold, part silver clear;
If stone, carbuncle most or chrysolite,
Ruby or topaz, to the twelve that shone
In Aaron's breast-plate, and a stone besides
600 Imagined rather oft than elsewhere seen,
That stone, or like to that which here below
Philosophers in vain so long have sought,
In vain, though by their powerful art they bind
Volatile Hermes, and call up unbound
605 In various shapes old Proteus from the sea,
Drained through a limbeck to his native form.
What wonder then if fields and regions here
Breathe forth Elixir pure, and rivers run
Potable gold, when with one virtuous touch
610 The arch-chemick sun, so far from us remote,

Produces, with terrestrial humour mixed,
Here in the dark so many precious things
Of colour glorious, and effect so rare?
Here matter new to gaze the Devil met
615   Undazzled; far and wide his eye commands;
For sight no obstacle found here, nor shade,
But all sun-shine, as when his beams at noon
Culminate from the equator, as they now
Shot upward still direct, whence no way round
620   Shadow from body opaque can fall; and the air,
No where so clear, sharpened his visual ray
To objects distant far, whereby he soon
Saw within ken a glorious Angel stand,
The same whom John saw also in the sun:
625   His back was turned, but not his brightness hid;
Of beaming sunny rays a golden tiar
Circled his head, nor less his locks behind
Illustrious on his shoulders fledge with wings
Lay waving round; on some great charge employed
630   He seemed, or fixed in cogitation deep.
Glad was the Spirit impure, as now in hope
To find who might direct his wandering flight
To Paradise, the happy seat of Man,
His journey's end and our beginning woe.
635   But first he casts to change his proper shape,
Which else might work him danger or delay:
And now a stripling Cherub he appears,
Not of the prime, yet such as in his face
Youth smiled celestial, and to every limb
640   Suitable grace diffused, so well he feigned:
Under a coronet his flowing hair
In curls on either cheek played; wings he wore
Of many a coloured plume, sprinkled with gold;
His habit fit for speed succinct, and held
645   Before his decent steps a silver wand.
He drew not nigh unheard; the Angel bright,
Ere he drew nigh, his radiant visage turned,
Admonished by his ear, and straight was known
The Arch-Angel Uriel, one of the seven
650   Who in God's presence, nearest to his throne,
Stand ready at command, and are his eyes
That run through all the Heavens, or down to the Earth
Bear his swift errands over moist and dry,
O'er sea and land: him Satan thus accosts.
655   Uriel, for thou of those seven Spirits that stand

In sight of God's high throne, gloriously bright,
The first art wont his great authentick will
Interpreter through highest Heaven to bring,
Where all his sons thy embassy attend;
660   And here art likeliest by supreme decree
Like honour to obtain, and as his eye
To visit oft this new creation round;
Unspeakable desire to see, and know
All these his wonderous works, but chiefly Man,
665   His chief delight and favour, him for whom
All these his works so wonderous he ordained,
Hath brought me from the quires of Cherubim
Alone thus wandering. Brightest Seraph, tell
In which of all these shining orbs hath Man
670   His fixed seat, or fixed seat hath none,
But all these shining orbs his choice to dwell;
That I may find him, and with secret gaze
Or open admiration him behold,
On whom the great Creator hath bestowed
675   Worlds, and on whom hath all these graces poured;
That both in him and all things, as is meet,
The universal Maker we may praise;
Who justly hath driven out his rebel foes
To deepest Hell, and, to repair that loss,
680   Created this new happy race of Men
To serve him better: Wise are all his ways.
So spake the false dissembler unperceived;
For neither Man nor Angel can discern
Hypocrisy, the only evil that walks
685   Invisible, except to God alone,
By his permissive will, through Heaven and Earth:
And oft, though wisdom wake, suspicion sleeps
At wisdom's gate, and to simplicity
Resigns her charge, while goodness thinks no ill
690   Where no ill seems: Which now for once beguiled
Uriel, though regent of the sun, and held
The sharpest-sighted Spirit of all in Heaven;
Who to the fraudulent impostor foul,
In his uprightness, answer thus returned.
695   Fair Angel, thy desire, which tends to know
The works of God, thereby to glorify
The great Work-master, leads to no excess
That reaches blame, but rather merits praise
The more it seems excess, that led thee hither
700   From thy empyreal mansion thus alone,

To witness with thine eyes what some perhaps,
Contented with report, hear only in Heaven:
For wonderful indeed are all his works,
Pleasant to know, and worthiest to be all
705 Had in remembrance always with delight;
But what created mind can comprehend
Their number, or the wisdom infinite
That brought them forth, but hid their causes deep?
I saw when at his word the formless mass,
710 This world's material mould, came to a heap:
Confusion heard his voice, and wild uproar
Stood ruled, stood vast infinitude confined;
Till at his second bidding Darkness fled,
Light shone, and order from disorder sprung:
715 Swift to their several quarters hasted then
The cumbrous elements, earth, flood, air, fire;
And this ethereal quintessence of Heaven
Flew upward, spirited with various forms,
That rolled orbicular, and turned to stars
720 Numberless, as thou seest, and how they move;
Each had his place appointed, each his course;
The rest in circuit walls this universe.
Look downward on that globe, whose hither side
With light from hence, though but reflected, shines;
725 That place is Earth, the seat of Man; that light
His day, which else, as the other hemisphere,
Night would invade; but there the neighbouring moon
(So call that opposite fair star) her aid
Timely interposes, and her monthly round
730 Still ending, still renewing, through mid Heaven,
With borrowed light her countenance triform
Hence fills and empties to enlighten the Earth,
And in her pale dominion checks the night.
That spot, to which I point, is Paradise,
735 Adam's abode; those lofty shades, his bower.
Thy way thou canst not miss, me mine requires.
Thus said, he turned; and Satan, bowing low,
As to superiour Spirits is wont in Heaven,
Where honour due and reverence none neglects,
740 Took leave, and toward the coast of earth beneath,
Down from the ecliptick, sped with hoped success,
Throws his steep flight in many an aery wheel;
Nor staid, till on Niphates' top he lights.

Book IV

Lines 1-848 have been omitted.

Hail, wedded Love, mysterious law, true source
Of human offspring, sole propriety
In Paradise of all things common else!
By thee adulterous Lust was driven from men
5   Among the bestial herds to range; by thee
Founded in reason, loyal, just, and pure,
Relations dear, and all the charities
Of father, son, and brother, first were known.
Far be it, that I should write thee sin or blame,
10 Or think thee unbefitting holiest place,
Perpetual fountain of domestick sweets,
Whose bed is undefiled and chaste pronounced,
Present, or past, as saints and patriarchs used.
Here Love his golden shafts employs, here lights
15 His constant lamp, and waves his purple wings,
Reigns here and revels; not in the bought smile
Of harlots, loveless, joyless, unendeared,
Casual fruition; nor in court-amours,
Mixed dance, or wanton mask, or midnight ball,
20 Or serenate, which the starved lover sings
To his proud fair, best quitted with disdain.
These, lulled by nightingales, embracing slept,
And on their naked limbs the flowery roof
Showered roses, which the morn repaired. Sleep on,
25 Blest pair; and O! yet happiest, if ye seek
No happier state, and know to know no more.

Book IX

No more of talk where God or Angel guest
With Man, as with his friend, familiar us'd,
To sit indulgent, and with him partake
Rural repast; permitting him the while
5 Venial discourse unblam'd. I now must change
Those notes to tragick; foul distrust, and breach
Disloyal on the part of Man, revolt,
And disobedience: on the part of Heaven
Now alienated, distance and distaste,
10 Anger and just rebuke, and judgement given,
That brought into this world a world of woe,
Sin and her shadow Death, and Misery
Death's harbinger: Sad task! yet argument
Not less but more heroick than the wrath

15 Of stern Achilles on his foe pursued
    Thrice fugitive about Troy wall; or rage
    Of Turnus for Lavinia disespous'd;
    Or Neptune's ire, or Juno's, that so long
    Perplexed the Greek, and Cytherea's son:
20 If answerable style I can obtain
    Of my celestial patroness, who deigns
    Her nightly visitation unimplor'd,
    And dictates to me slumbering; or inspires
    Easy my unpremeditated verse:
25 Since first this subject for heroick song
    Pleas'd me long choosing, and beginning late;
    Not sedulous by nature to indite
    Wars, hitherto the only argument
    Heroick deem'd chief mastery to dissect
30 With long and tedious havock fabled knights
    In battles feign'd; the better fortitude
    Of patience and heroick martyrdom
    Unsung; or to describe races and games,
    Or tilting furniture, imblazon'd shields,
35 Impresses quaint, caparisons and steeds,
    Bases and tinsel trappings, gorgeous knights
    At joust and tournament; then marshall'd feast
    Serv'd up in hall with sewers and seneshals;
    The skill of artifice or office mean,
40 Not that which justly gives heroick name
    To person, or to poem. Me, of these
    Nor skill'd nor studious, higher argument
    Remains; sufficient of itself to raise
    That name, unless an age too late, or cold
45 Climate, or years, damp my intended wing
    Depress'd; and much they may, if all be mine,
    Not hers, who brings it nightly to my ear.
    The sun was sunk, and after him the star
    Of Hesperus, whose office is to bring
50 Twilight upon the earth, short arbiter
    'Twixt day and night, and now from end to end
    Night's hemisphere had veil'd the horizon round:
    When satan, who late fled before the threats
    Of Gabriel out of Eden, now improv'd
55 In meditated fraud and malice, bent
    On Man's destruction, maugre what might hap
    Of heavier on himself, fearless returned
    By night he fled, and at midnight returned
    From compassing the earth; cautious of day,

60 Since Uriel, regent of the sun, descried
His entrance, and foreworned the Cherubim
That kept their watch; thence full of anguish driven,
The space of seven continued nights he rode
With darkness; thrice the equinoctial line
65 He circled; four times crossed the car of night
From pole to pole, traversing each colure;
On the eighth returned; and, on the coast averse
From entrance or Cherubick watch, by stealth
Found unsuspected way. There was a place,
70 Now not, though sin, not time, first wrought the change,
Where Tigris, at the foot of Paradise,
Into a gulf shot under ground, till part
Rose up a fountain by the tree of life:
In with the river sunk, and with it rose
75 Satan, involved in rising mist; then sought
Where to lie hid; sea he had searched, and land,
From Eden over Pontus and the pool
Maeotis, up beyond the river Ob;
Downward as far antarctick; and in length,
80 West from Orontes to the ocean barred
At Darien; thence to the land where flows
Ganges and Indus: Thus the orb he roamed
With narrow search; and with inspection deep
Considered every creature, which of all
85 Most opportune might serve his wiles; and found
The Serpent subtlest beast of all the field.
Him after long debate, irresolute
Of thoughts revolved, his final sentence chose
Fit vessel, fittest imp of fraud, in whom
90 To enter, and his dark suggestions hide
From sharpest sight: for, in the wily snake
Whatever sleights, none would suspicious mark,
As from his wit and native subtlety
Proceeding; which, in other beasts observed,
95 Doubt might beget of diabolick power
Active within, beyond the sense of brute.
Thus he resolved, but first from inward grief
His bursting passion into plaints thus poured.
More justly, seat worthier of Gods, as built
100 With second thoughts, reforming what was old!
O Earth, how like to Heaven, if not preferred
For what God, after better, worse would build?
Terrestrial Heaven, danced round by other Heavens
That shine, yet bear their bright officious lamps,

105   Light above light, for thee alone, as seems,
      In thee concentring all their precious beams
      Of sacred influence! As God in Heaven
      Is center, yet extends to all; so thou,
      Centring, receivest from all those orbs: in thee,
110   Not in themselves, all their known virtue appears
      Productive in herb, plant, and nobler birth
      Of creatures animate with gradual life
      Of growth, sense, reason, all summed up in Man.
      With what delight could I have walked thee round,
115   If I could joy in aught, sweet interchange
      Of hill, and valley, rivers, woods, and plains,
      Now land, now sea and shores with forest crowned,
      Rocks, dens, and caves! But I in none of these
      Find place or refuge; and the more I see
120   Pleasures about me, so much more I feel
      Torment within me, as from the hateful siege
      Of contraries: all good to me becomes
      Bane, and in Heaven much worse would be my state.
      But neither here seek I, no nor in Heaven
125   To dwell, unless by mastering Heaven's Supreme;
      Nor hope to be myself less miserable
      By what I seek, but others to make such
      As I, though thereby worse to me redound:
      For only in destroying I find ease
130   To my relentless thoughts; and, him destroyed,
      Or won to what may work his utter loss,
      For whom all this was made, all this will soon
      Follow, as to him linked in weal or woe;
      In woe then; that destruction wide may range:
135   To me shall be the glory sole among
      The infernal Powers, in one day to have marred
      What he, Almighty styled, six nights and days
      Continued making; and who knows how long
      Before had been contriving? though perhaps
140   Not longer than since I, in one night, freed
      From servitude inglorious well nigh half
      The angelick name, and thinner left the throng
      Of his adorers: He, to be avenged,
      And to repair his numbers thus impaired,
145   Whether such virtue spent of old now failed
      More Angels to create, if they at least
      Are his created, or, to spite us more,
      Determined to advance into our room
      A creature formed of earth, and him endow,

150 Exalted from so base original,
    With heavenly spoils, our spoils: What he decreed,
    He effected; Man he made, and for him built
    Magnificent this world, and earth his seat,
    Him lord pronounced; and, O indignity!
155 Subjected to his service angel-wings,
    And flaming ministers to watch and tend
    Their earthly charge: Of these the vigilance
    I dread; and, to elude, thus wrapt in mist
    Of midnight vapour glide obscure, and pry
160 In every bush and brake, where hap may find
    The serpent sleeping; in whose mazy folds
    To hide me, and the dark intent I bring.
    O foul descent! that I, who erst contended
    With Gods to sit the highest, am now constrained
165 Into a beast; and, mixed with bestial slime,
    This essence to incarnate and imbrute,
    That to the highth of Deity aspired!
    But what will not ambition and revenge
    Descend to? Who aspires, must down as low
170 As high he soared; obnoxious, first or last,
    To basest things. Revenge, at first though sweet,
    Bitter ere long, back on itself recoils:
    Let it; I reck not, so it light well aimed,
    Since higher I fall short, on him who next
175 Provokes my envy, this new favourite
    Of Heaven, this man of clay, son of despite,
    Whom, us the more to spite, his Maker raised
    From dust: Spite then with spite is best repaid.
    So saying, through each thicket dank or dry,
180 Like a black mist low-creeping, he held on
    His midnight-search, where soonest he might find
    The serpent; him fast-sleeping soon he found
    In labyrinth of many a round self-rolled,
    His head the midst, well stored with subtile wiles:
185 Not yet in horrid shade or dismal den,
    Nor nocent yet; but, on the grassy herb,
    Fearless unfeared he slept: in at his mouth
    The Devil entered; and his brutal sense,
    In heart or head, possessing, soon inspired
190 With act intelligential; but his sleep
    Disturbed not, waiting close the approach of morn.
    Now, when as sacred light began to dawn
    In Eden on the humid flowers, that breathed
    Their morning incense, when all things, that breathe,

195 From the Earth's great altar send up silent praise
To the Creator, and his nostrils fill
With grateful smell, forth came the human pair,
And joined their vocal worship to the quire
Of creatures wanting voice; that done, partake
200 The season prime for sweetest scents and airs:
Then commune, how that day they best may ply
Their growing work: for much their work out-grew
The hands' dispatch of two gardening so wide,
And Eve first to her husband thus began.
205 Adam, well may we labour still to dress
This garden, still to tend plant, herb, and flower,
Our pleasant task enjoined; but, till more hands
Aid us, the work under our labour grows,
Luxurious by restraint; what we by day
210 Lop overgrown, or prune, or prop, or bind,
One night or two with wanton growth derides
Tending to wild. Thou therefore now advise,
Or hear what to my mind first thoughts present:
Let us divide our labours; thou, where choice
215 Leads thee, or where most needs, whether to wind
The woodbine round this arbour, or direct
The clasping ivy where to climb; while I,
In yonder spring of roses intermixed
With myrtle, find what to redress till noon:
220 For, while so near each other thus all day
Our task we choose, what wonder if so near
Looks intervene and smiles, or object new
Casual discourse draw on; which intermits
Our day's work, brought to little, though begun
225 Early, and the hour of supper comes unearned?
To whom mild answer Adam thus returned.
Sole Eve, associate sole, to me beyond
Compare above all living creatures dear!
Well hast thou motioned, well thy thoughts employed,
230 How we might best fulfil the work which here
God hath assigned us; nor of me shalt pass
Unpraised: for nothing lovelier can be found
In woman, than to study houshold good,
And good works in her husband to promote.
235 Yet not so strictly hath our Lord imposed
Labour, as to debar us when we need
Refreshment, whether food, or talk between,
Food of the mind, or this sweet intercourse
Of looks and smiles; for smiles from reason flow,

240   To brute denied, and are of love the food;
      Love, not the lowest end of human life.
      For not to irksome toil, but to delight,
      He made us, and delight to reason joined.
      These paths and bowers doubt not but our joint hands
245   Will keep from wilderness with ease, as wide
      As we need walk, till younger hands ere long
      Assist us; But, if much converse perhaps
      Thee satiate, to short absence I could yield:
      For solitude sometimes is best society,
250   And short retirement urges sweet return.
      But other doubt possesses me, lest harm
      Befall thee severed from me; for thou knowest
      What hath been warned us, what malicious foe
      Envying our happiness, and of his own
255   Despairing, seeks to work us woe and shame
      By sly assault; and somewhere nigh at hand
      Watches, no doubt, with greedy hope to find
      His wish and best advantage, us asunder;
      Hopeless to circumvent us joined, where each
260   To other speedy aid might lend at need:
      Whether his first design be to withdraw
      Our fealty from God, or to disturb
      Conjugal love, than which perhaps no bliss
      Enjoyed by us excites his envy more;
265   Or this, or worse, leave not the faithful side
      That gave thee being, still shades thee, and protects.
      The wife, where danger or dishonour lurks,
      Safest and seemliest by her husband stays,
      Who guards her, or with her the worst endures.
270   To whom the virgin majesty of Eve,
      As one who loves, and some unkindness meets,
      With sweet austere composure thus replied.
      Offspring of Heaven and Earth, and all Earth's Lord!
      That such an enemy we have, who seeks
275   Our ruin, both by thee informed I learn,
      And from the parting Angel over-heard,
      As in a shady nook I stood behind,
      Just then returned at shut of evening flowers.
      But, that thou shouldst my firmness therefore doubt
280   To God or thee, because we have a foe
      May tempt it, I expected not to hear.
      His violence thou fearest not, being such
      As we, not capable of death or pain,
      Can either not receive, or can repel.

285   His fraud is then thy fear; which plain infers
       Thy equal fear, that my firm faith and love
       Can by his fraud be shaken or seduced;
       Thoughts, which how found they harbour in thy breast,
       Adam, mis-thought of her to thee so dear?
290   To whom with healing words Adam replied.
       Daughter of God and Man, immortal Eve!
       For such thou art; from sin and blame entire:
       Not diffident of thee do I dissuade
       Thy absence from my sight, but to avoid
295   The attempt itself, intended by our foe.
       For he who tempts, though in vain, at least asperses
       The tempted with dishonour foul; supposed
       Not incorruptible of faith, not proof
       Against temptation: Thou thyself with scorn
300   And anger wouldst resent the offered wrong,
       Though ineffectual found: misdeem not then,
       If such affront I labour to avert
       From thee alone, which on us both at once
       The enemy, though bold, will hardly dare;
305   Or daring, first on me the assault shall light.
       Nor thou his malice and false guile contemn;
       Subtle he needs must be, who could seduce
       Angels; nor think superfluous other's aid.
       I, from the influence of thy looks, receive
310   Access in every virtue; in thy sight
       More wise, more watchful, stronger, if need were
       Of outward strength; while shame, thou looking on,
       Shame to be overcome or over-reached,
       Would utmost vigour raise, and raised unite.
315   Why shouldst not thou like sense within thee feel
       When I am present, and thy trial choose
       With me, best witness of thy virtue tried?
       So spake domestick Adam in his care
       And matrimonial love; but Eve, who thought
320   Less attributed to her faith sincere,
       Thus her reply with accent sweet renewed.
       If this be our condition, thus to dwell
       In narrow circuit straitened by a foe,
       Subtle or violent, we not endued
325   Single with like defence, wherever met;
       How are we happy, still in fear of harm?
       But harm precedes not sin: only our foe,
       Tempting, affronts us with his foul esteem
       Of our integrity: his foul esteem

330 Sticks no dishonour on our front, but turns
Foul on himself; then wherefore shunned or feared
By us? who rather double honour gain
From his surmise proved false; find peace within,
Favour from Heaven, our witness, from the event.
335 And what is faith, love, virtue, unassayed
Alone, without exteriour help sustained?
Let us not then suspect our happy state
Left so imperfect by the Maker wise,
As not secure to single or combined.
340 Frail is our happiness, if this be so,
And Eden were no Eden, thus exposed.
To whom thus Adam fervently replied.
O Woman, best are all things as the will
Of God ordained them: His creating hand
345 Nothing imperfect or deficient left
Of all that he created, much less Man,
Or aught that might his happy state secure,
Secure from outward force; within himself
The danger lies, yet lies within his power:
350 Against his will he can receive no harm.
But God left free the will; for what obeys
Reason, is free; and Reason he made right,
But bid her well be ware, and still erect;
Lest, by some fair-appearing good surprised,
355 She dictate false; and mis-inform the will
To do what God expressly hath forbid.
Not then mistrust, but tender love, enjoins,
That I should mind thee oft; and mind thou me.
Firm we subsist, yet possible to swerve;
360 Since Reason not impossibly may meet
Some specious object by the foe suborned,
And fall into deception unaware,
Not keeping strictest watch, as she was warned.
Seek not temptation then, which to avoid
365 Were better, and most likely if from me
Thou sever not: Trial will come unsought.
Wouldst thou approve thy constancy, approve
First thy obedience; the other who can know,
Not seeing thee attempted, who attest?
370 But, if thou think, trial unsought may find
Us both securer than thus warned thou seemest,
Go; for thy stay, not free, absents thee more;
Go in thy native innocence, rely
On what thou hast of virtue; summon all!

375 For God towards thee hath done his part, do thine.
So spake the patriarch of mankind; but Eve
Persisted; yet submiss, though last, replied.
With thy permission then, and thus forewarned
Chiefly by what thy own last reasoning words
380 Touched only; that our trial, when least sought,
May find us both perhaps far less prepared,
The willinger I go, nor much expect
A foe so proud will first the weaker seek;
So bent, the more shall shame him his repulse.
385 Thus saying, from her husband's hand her hand
Soft she withdrew; and, like a Wood-Nymph light,
Oread or Dryad, or of Delia's train,
Betook her to the groves; but Delia's self
In gait surpassed, and Goddess-like deport,
390 Though not as she with bow and quiver armed,
But with such gardening tools as Art yet rude,
Guiltless of fire, had formed, or Angels brought.
To Pales, or Pomona, thus adorned,
Likest she seemed, Pomona when she fled
395 Vertumnus, or to Ceres in her prime,
Yet virgin of Proserpina from Jove.
Her long with ardent look his eye pursued
Delighted, but desiring more her stay.
Oft he to her his charge of quick return
400 Repeated; she to him as oft engaged
To be returned by noon amid the bower,
And all things in best order to invite
Noontide repast, or afternoon's repose.
O much deceived, much failing, hapless Eve,
405 Of thy presumed return! event perverse!
Thou never from that hour in Paradise
Foundst either sweet repast, or sound repose;
Such ambush, hid among sweet flowers and shades,
Waited with hellish rancour imminent
410 To intercept thy way, or send thee back
Despoiled of innocence, of faith, of bliss!
For now, and since first break of dawn, the Fiend,
Mere serpent in appearance, forth was come;
And on his quest, where likeliest he might find
415 The only two of mankind, but in them
The whole included race, his purposed prey.
In bower and field he sought, where any tuft
Of grove or garden-plot more pleasant lay,
Their tendance, or plantation for delight;

420   By fountain or by shady rivulet
He sought them both, but wished his hap might find
Eve separate; he wished, but not with hope
Of what so seldom chanced; when to his wish,
Beyond his hope, Eve separate he spies,
425   Veiled in a cloud of fragrance, where she stood,
Half spied, so thick the roses blushing round
About her glowed, oft stooping to support
Each flower of slender stalk, whose head, though gay
Carnation, purple, azure, or specked with gold,
430   Hung drooping unsustained; them she upstays
Gently with myrtle band, mindless the while
Herself, though fairest unsupported flower,
From her best prop so far, and storm so nigh.
Nearer he drew, and many a walk traversed
435   Of stateliest covert, cedar, pine, or palm;
Then voluble and bold, now hid, now seen,
Among thick-woven arborets, and flowers
Imbordered on each bank, the hand of Eve:
Spot more delicious than those gardens feigned
440   Or of revived Adonis, or renowned
Alcinous, host of old Laertes' son;
Or that, not mystick, where the sapient king
Held dalliance with his fair Egyptian spouse.
Much he the place admired, the person more.
445   As one who long in populous city pent,
Where houses thick and sewers annoy the air,
Forth issuing on a summer's morn, to breathe
Among the pleasant villages and farms
Adjoined, from each thing met conceives delight;
450   The smell of grain, or tedded grass, or kine,
Or dairy, each rural sight, each rural sound;
If chance, with nymph-like step, fair virgin pass,
What pleasing seemed, for her now pleases more;
She most, and in her look sums all delight:
455   Such pleasure took the Serpent to behold
This flowery plat, the sweet recess of Eve
Thus early, thus alone: Her heavenly form
Angelick, but more soft, and feminine,
Her graceful innocence, her every air
460   Of gesture, or least action, overawed
His malice, and with rapine sweet bereaved
His fierceness of the fierce intent it brought:
That space the Evil-one abstracted stood
From his own evil, and for the time remained

465 Stupidly good; of enmity disarmed,
Of guile, of hate, of envy, of revenge:
But the hot Hell that always in him burns,
Though in mid Heaven, soon ended his delight,
And tortures him now more, the more he sees
470 Of pleasure, not for him ordained: then soon
Fierce hate he recollects, and all his thoughts
Of mischief, gratulating, thus excites.
Thoughts, whither have ye led me! with what sweet
Compulsion thus transported, to forget
475 What hither brought us! hate, not love; nor hope
Of Paradise for Hell, hope here to taste
Of pleasure; but all pleasure to destroy,
Save what is in destroying; other joy
To me is lost. Then, let me not let pass
480 Occasion which now smiles; behold alone
The woman, opportune to all attempts,
Her husband, for I view far round, not nigh,
Whose higher intellectual more I shun,
And strength, of courage haughty, and of limb
485 Heroick built, though of terrestrial mould;
Foe not informidable! exempt from wound,
I not; so much hath Hell debased, and pain
Enfeebled me, to what I was in Heaven.
She fair, divinely fair, fit love for Gods!
490 Not terrible, though terrour be in love
And beauty, not approached by stronger hate,
Hate stronger, under show of love well feigned;
The way which to her ruin now I tend.
So spake the enemy of mankind, enclosed
495 In serpent, inmate bad! and toward Eve
Addressed his way: not with indented wave,
Prone on the ground, as since; but on his rear,
Circular base of rising folds, that towered
Fold above fold, a surging maze! his head
500 Crested aloft, and carbuncle his eyes;
With burnished neck of verdant gold, erect
Amidst his circling spires, that on the grass
Floated redundant: pleasing was his shape
And lovely; never since of serpent-kind
505 Lovelier, not those that in Illyria changed,
Hermione and Cadmus, or the god
In Epidaurus; nor to which transformed
Ammonian Jove, or Capitoline, was seen;
He with Olympias; this with her who bore

510 Scipio, the highth of Rome. With tract oblique
    At first, as one who sought access, but feared
    To interrupt, side-long he works his way.
    As when a ship, by skilful steersmen wrought
    Nigh river's mouth or foreland, where the wind
515 Veers oft, as oft so steers, and shifts her sail:
    So varied he, and of his tortuous train
    Curled many a wanton wreath in sight of Eve,
    To lure her eye; she, busied, heard the sound
    Of rusling leaves, but minded not, as used
520 To such disport before her through the field,
    From every beast; more duteous at her call,
    Than at Circean call the herd disguised.
    He, bolder now, uncalled before her stood,
    But as in gaze admiring: oft he bowed
525 His turret crest, and sleek enamelled neck,
    Fawning; and licked the ground whereon she trod.
    His gentle dumb expression turned at length
    The eye of Eve to mark his play; he, glad
    Of her attention gained, with serpent-tongue
530 Organick, or impulse of vocal air,
    His fraudulent temptation thus began.
    Wonder not, sovran Mistress, if perhaps
    Thou canst, who art sole wonder! much less arm
    Thy looks, the Heaven of mildness, with disdain,
535 Displeased that I approach thee thus, and gaze
    Insatiate; I thus single; nor have feared
    Thy awful brow, more awful thus retired.
    Fairest resemblance of thy Maker fair,
    Thee all things living gaze on, all things thine
540 By gift, and thy celestial beauty adore
    With ravishment beheld! there best beheld,
    Where universally admired; but here
    In this enclosure wild, these beasts among,
    Beholders rude, and shallow to discern
545 Half what in thee is fair, one man except,
    Who sees thee? and what is one? who should be seen
    A Goddess among Gods, adored and served
    By Angels numberless, thy daily train.
    So glozed the Tempter, and his proem tuned:
550 Into the heart of Eve his words made way,
    Though at the voice much marvelling; at length,
    Not unamazed, she thus in answer spake.
    What may this mean? language of man pronounced
    By tongue of brute, and human sense expressed?

560　The first, at least, of these I thought denied
　　　To beasts; whom God, on their creation-day,
　　　Created mute to all articulate sound:
　　　The latter I demur; for in their looks
　　　Much reason, and in their actions, oft appears.
565　Thee, Serpent, subtlest beast of all the field
　　　I knew, but not with human voice endued;
　　　Redouble then this miracle, and say,
　　　How camest thou speakable of mute, and how
　　　To me so friendly grown above the rest
570　Of brutal kind, that daily are in sight?
　　　Say, for such wonder claims attention due.
　　　To whom the guileful Tempter thus replied.
　　　Empress of this fair world, resplendent Eve!
　　　Easy to me it is to tell thee all
575　What thou commandest; and right thou shouldst be obeyed:
　　　I was at first as other beasts that graze
　　　The trodden herb, of abject thoughts and low,
　　　As was my food; nor aught but food discerned
　　　Or sex, and apprehended nothing high:
580　Till, on a day roving the field, I chanced
　　　A goodly tree far distant to behold
　　　Loaden with fruit of fairest colours mixed,
　　　Ruddy and gold: I nearer drew to gaze;
　　　When from the boughs a savoury odour blown,
585　Grateful to appetite, more pleased my sense
　　　Than smell of sweetest fennel, or the teats
　　　Of ewe or goat dropping with milk at even,
　　　Unsucked of lamb or kid, that tend their play.
　　　To satisfy the sharp desire I had
590　Of tasting those fair apples, I resolved
　　　Not to defer; hunger and thirst at once,
　　　Powerful persuaders, quickened at the scent
　　　Of that alluring fruit, urged me so keen.
　　　About the mossy trunk I wound me soon;
595　For, high from ground, the branches would require
　　　Thy utmost reach or Adam's: Round the tree
　　　All other beasts that saw, with like desire
　　　Longing and envying stood, but could not reach.
　　　Amid the tree now got, where plenty hung
600　Tempting so nigh, to pluck and eat my fill
　　　I spared not; for, such pleasure till that hour,
　　　At feed or fountain, never had I found.
　　　Sated at length, ere long I might perceive
　　　Strange alteration in me, to degree

605   Of reason in my inward powers; and speech
      Wanted not long; though to this shape retained.
      Thenceforth to speculations high or deep
      I turned my thoughts, and with capacious mind
      Considered all things visible in Heaven,
610   Or Earth, or Middle; all things fair and good:
      But all that fair and good in thy divine
      Semblance, and in thy beauty's heavenly ray,
      United I beheld; no fair to thine
      Equivalent or second! which compelled
615   Me thus, though importune perhaps, to come
      And gaze, and worship thee of right declared
      Sovran of creatures, universal Dame!
      So talked the spirited sly Snake; and Eve,
      Yet more amazed, unwary thus replied.
620   Serpent, thy overpraising leaves in doubt
      The virtue of that fruit, in thee first proved:
      But say, where grows the tree? from hence how far?
      For many are the trees of God that grow
      In Paradise, and various, yet unknown
625   To us; in such abundance lies our choice,
      As leaves a greater store of fruit untouched,
      Still hanging incorruptible, till men
      Grow up to their provision, and more hands
      Help to disburden Nature of her birth.
630   To whom the wily Adder, blithe and glad.
      Empress, the way is ready, and not long;
      Beyond a row of myrtles, on a flat,
      Fast by a fountain, one small thicket past
      Of blowing myrrh and balm: if thou accept
635   My conduct, I can bring thee thither soon
      Lead then, said Eve. He, leading, swiftly rolled
      In tangles, and made intricate seem straight,
      To mischief swift. Hope elevates, and joy
      Brightens his crest; as when a wandering fire,
640   Compact of unctuous vapour, which the night
      Condenses, and the cold environs round,
      Kindled through agitation to a flame,
      Which oft, they say, some evil Spirit attends,
      Hovering and blazing with delusive light,
645   Misleads the amazed night-wanderer from his way
      To bogs and mires, and oft through pond or pool;
      There swallowed up and lost, from succour far.
      So glistered the dire Snake, and into fraud
      Led Eve, our credulous mother, to the tree

650 Of prohibition, root of all our woe;
Which when she saw, thus to her guide she spake.
Serpent, we might have spared our coming hither,
Fruitless to me, though fruit be here to excess,
The credit of whose virtue rest with thee;
655 Wonderous indeed, if cause of such effects.
But of this tree we may not taste nor touch;
God so commanded, and left that command
Sole daughter of his voice; the rest, we live
Law to ourselves; our reason is our law.
660 To whom the Tempter guilefully replied.
Indeed! hath God then said that of the fruit
Of all these garden-trees ye shall not eat,
Yet Lords declared of all in earth or air?
To whom thus Eve, yet sinless. Of the fruit
665 Of each tree in the garden we may eat;
But of the fruit of this fair tree amidst
The garden, God hath said, Ye shall not eat
Thereof, nor shall ye touch it, lest ye die.
She scarce had said, though brief, when now more bold
670 The Tempter, but with show of zeal and love
To Man, and indignation at his wrong,
New part puts on; and, as to passion moved,
Fluctuates disturbed, yet comely and in act
Raised, as of some great matter to begin.
675 As when of old some orator renowned,
In Athens or free Rome, where eloquence
Flourished, since mute! to some great cause addressed,
Stood in himself collected; while each part,
Motion, each act, won audience ere the tongue;
680 Sometimes in highth began, as no delay
Of preface brooking, through his zeal of right:
So standing, moving, or to highth up grown,
The Tempter, all impassioned, thus began.
O sacred, wise, and wisdom-giving Plant,
685 Mother of science! now I feel thy power
Within me clear; not only to discern
Things in their causes, but to trace the ways
Of highest agents, deemed however wise.
Queen of this universe! do not believe
690 Those rigid threats of death: ye shall not die:
How should you? by the fruit? it gives you life
To knowledge; by the threatener? look on me,
Me, who have touched and tasted; yet both live,
And life more perfect have attained than Fate

695 Meant me, by venturing higher than my lot.
Shall that be shut to Man, which to the Beast
Is open? or will God incense his ire
For such a petty trespass? and not praise
Rather your dauntless virtue, whom the pain
700 Of death denounced, whatever thing death be,
Deterred not from achieving what might lead
To happier life, knowledge of good and evil;
Of good, how just? of evil, if what is evil
Be real, why not known, since easier shunned?
705 God therefore cannot hurt ye, and be just;
Not just, not God; not feared then, nor obeyed:
Your fear itself of death removes the fear.
Why then was this forbid? Why, but to awe;
Why, but to keep ye low and ignorant,
710 His worshippers? He knows that in the day
Ye eat thereof, your eyes that seem so clear,
Yet are but dim, shall perfectly be then
Opened and cleared, and ye shall be as Gods,
Knowing both good and evil, as they know.
715 That ye shall be as Gods, since I as Man,
Internal Man, is but proportion meet;
I, of brute, human; ye, of human, Gods.
So ye shall die perhaps, by putting off
Human, to put on Gods; death to be wished,
720 Though threatened, which no worse than this can bring.
And what are Gods, that Man may not become
As they, participating God-like food?
The Gods are first, and that advantage use
On our belief, that all from them proceeds:
725 I question it; for this fair earth I see,
Warmed by the sun, producing every kind;
Them, nothing: if they all things, who enclosed
Knowledge of good and evil in this tree,
That whoso eats thereof, forthwith attains
730 Wisdom without their leave? and wherein lies
The offence, that Man should thus attain to know?
What can your knowledge hurt him, or this tree
Impart against his will, if all be his?
Or is it envy? and can envy dwell
735 In heavenly breasts? These, these, and many more
Causes import your need of this fair fruit.
Goddess humane, reach then, and freely taste!
He ended; and his words, replete with guile,
Into her heart too easy entrance won:

740   Fixed on the fruit she gazed, which to behold
       Might tempt alone; and in her ears the sound
       Yet rung of his persuasive words, impregned
       With reason, to her seeming, and with truth:
       Mean while the hour of noon drew on, and waked
745   An eager appetite, raised by the smell
       So savoury of that fruit, which with desire,
       Inclinable now grown to touch or taste,
       Solicited her longing eye; yet first
       Pausing a while, thus to herself she mused.
750   Great are thy virtues, doubtless, best of fruits,
       Though kept from man, and worthy to be admired;
       Whose taste, too long forborn, at first assay
       Gave elocution to the mute, and taught
       The tongue not made for speech to speak thy praise:
755   Thy praise he also, who forbids thy use,
       Conceals not from us, naming thee the tree
       Of knowledge, knowledge both of good and evil;
       Forbids us then to taste! but his forbidding
       Commends thee more, while it infers the good
760   By thee communicated, and our want:
       For good unknown sure is not had; or, had
       And yet unknown, is as not had at all.
       In plain then, what forbids he but to know,
       Forbids us good, forbids us to be wise?
765   Such prohibitions bind not. But, if death
       Bind us with after-bands, what profits then
       Our inward freedom? In the day we eat
       Of this fair fruit, our doom is, we shall die!
       How dies the Serpent? he hath eaten and lives,
770   And knows, and speaks, and reasons, and discerns,
       Irrational till then. For us alone
       Was death invented? or to us denied
       This intellectual food, for beasts reserved?
       For beasts it seems: yet that one beast which first
775   Hath tasted envies not, but brings with joy
       The good befallen him, author unsuspect,
       Friendly to man, far from deceit or guile.
       What fear I then? rather, what know to fear
       Under this ignorance of good and evil,
780   Of God or death, of law or penalty?
       Here grows the cure of all, this fruit divine,
       Fair to the eye, inviting to the taste,
       Of virtue to make wise: What hinders then
       To reach, and feed at once both body and mind?

785 So saying, her rash hand in evil hour
Forth reaching to the fruit, she plucked, she eat!
Earth felt the wound; and Nature from her seat,
Sighing through all her works, gave signs of woe,
That all was lost. Back to the thicket slunk
790 The guilty Serpent; and well might; for Eve,
Intent now wholly on her taste, nought else
Regarded; such delight till then, as seemed,
In fruit she never tasted, whether true
Or fancied so, through expectation high
795 Of knowledge; not was Godhead from her thought.
Greedily she ingorged without restraint,
And knew not eating death: Satiate at length,
And hightened as with wine, jocund and boon,
Thus to herself she pleasingly began.
800 O sovran, virtuous, precious of all trees
In Paradise! of operation blest
To sapience, hitherto obscured, infamed.
And thy fair fruit let hang, as to no end
Created; but henceforth my early care,
805 Not without song, each morning, and due praise,
Shall tend thee, and the fertile burden ease
Of thy full branches offered free to all;
Till, dieted by thee, I grow mature
In knowledge, as the Gods, who all things know;
810 Though others envy what they cannot give:
For, had the gift been theirs, it had not here
Thus grown. Experience, next, to thee I owe,
Best guide; not following thee, I had remained
In ignorance; thou openest wisdom's way,
815 And givest access, though secret she retire.
And I perhaps am secret: Heaven is high,
High, and remote to see from thence distinct
Each thing on Earth; and other care perhaps
May have diverted from continual watch
820 Our great Forbidder, safe with all his spies
About him. But to Adam in what sort
Shall I appear? shall I to him make known
As yet my change, and give him to partake
Full happiness with me, or rather not,
825 But keeps the odds of knowledge in my power
Without copartner? so to add what wants
In female sex, the more to draw his love,
And render me more equal; and perhaps,
A thing not undesirable, sometime

830 Superiour; for, inferiour, who is free
This may be well: But what if God have seen,
And death ensue? then I shall be no more!
And Adam, wedded to another Eve,
Shall live with her enjoying, I extinct;
835 A death to think! Confirmed then I resolve,
Adam shall share with me in bliss or woe:
So dear I love him, that with him all deaths
I could endure, without him live no life.
So saying, from the tree her step she turned;
840 But first low reverence done, as to the Power
That dwelt within, whose presence had infused
Into the plant sciential sap, derived
From nectar, drink of Gods. Adam the while,
Waiting desirous her return, had wove
845 Of choicest flowers a garland, to adorn
Her tresses, and her rural labours crown;
As reapers oft are wont their harvest-queen.
Great joy he promised to his thoughts, and new
Solace in her return, so long delayed:
850 Yet oft his heart, divine of something ill,
Misgave him; he the faltering measure felt;
And forth to meet her went, the way she took
That morn when first they parted: by the tree
Of knowledge he must pass; there he her met,
855 Scarce from the tree returning; in her hand
A bough of fairest fruit, that downy smiled,
New gathered, and ambrosial smell diffused.
To him she hasted; in her face excuse
Came prologue, and apology too prompt;
860 Which, with bland words at will, she thus addressed.
Hast thou not wondered, Adam, at my stay?
Thee I have missed, and thought it long, deprived
Thy presence; agony of love till now
Not felt, nor shall be twice; for never more
865 Mean I to try, what rash untried I sought,
The pain of absence from thy sight. But strange
Hath been the cause, and wonderful to hear:
This tree is not, as we are told, a tree
Of danger tasted, nor to evil unknown
870 Opening the way, but of divine effect
To open eyes, and make them Gods who taste;
And hath been tasted such: The serpent wise,
Or not restrained as we, or not obeying,
Hath eaten of the fruit; and is become,

875 Not dead, as we are threatened, but thenceforth
Endued with human voice and human sense,
Reasoning to admiration; and with me
Persuasively hath so prevailed, that I
Have also tasted, and have also found
880 The effects to correspond; opener mine eyes,
Dim erst, dilated spirits, ampler heart,
And growing up to Godhead; which for thee
Chiefly I sought, without thee can despise.
For bliss, as thou hast part, to me is bliss;
885 Tedious, unshared with thee, and odious soon.
Thou therefore also taste, that equal lot
May join us, equal joy, as equal love;
Lest, thou not tasting, different degree
Disjoin us, and I then too late renounce
890 Deity for thee, when Fate will not permit.
Thus Eve with countenance blithe her story told;
But in her cheek distemper flushing glowed.
On the other side Adam, soon as he heard
The fatal trespass done by Eve, amazed,
895 Astonied stood and blank, while horrour chill
Ran through his veins, and all his joints relaxed;
From his slack hand the garland wreathed for Eve
Down dropt, and all the faded roses shed:
Speechless he stood and pale, till thus at length
900 First to himself he inward silence broke.
O fairest of Creation, last and best
Of all God's works, Creature in whom excelled
Whatever can to sight or thought be formed,
Holy, divine, good, amiable, or sweet!
905 How art thou lost! how on a sudden lost,
Defaced, deflowered, and now to death devote!
Rather, how hast thou yielded to transgress
The strict forbiddance, how to violate
The sacred fruit forbidden! Some cursed fraud
910 Of enemy hath beguiled thee, yet unknown,
And me with thee hath ruined; for with thee
Certain my resolution is to die:
How can I live without thee! how forego
Thy sweet converse, and love so dearly joined,
915 To live again in these wild woods forlorn!
Should God create another Eve, and I
Another rib afford, yet loss of thee
Would never from my heart: no, no! I feel
The link of Nature draw me: flesh of flesh,

920   Bone of my bone thou art, and from thy state
       Mine never shall be parted, bliss or woe.
       So having said, as one from sad dismay
       Recomforted, and after thoughts disturbed
       Submitting to what seemed remediless,
925   Thus in calm mood his words to Eve he turned.
       Bold deed thou hast presumed, adventurous Eve,
       And peril great provoked, who thus hast dared,
       Had it been only coveting to eye
       That sacred fruit, sacred to abstinence,
930   Much more to taste it under ban to touch.
       But past who can recall, or done undo?
       Not God Omnipotent, nor Fate; yet so
       Perhaps thou shalt not die, perhaps the fact
       Is not so heinous now, foretasted fruit,
935   Profaned first by the serpent, by him first
       Made common, and unhallowed, ere our taste;
       Nor yet on him found deadly; yet he lives;
       Lives, as thou saidst, and gains to live, as Man,
       Higher degree of life; inducement strong
940   To us, as likely tasting to attain
       Proportional ascent; which cannot be
       But to be Gods, or Angels, demi-Gods.
       Nor can I think that God, Creator wise,
       Though threatening, will in earnest so destroy
945   Us his prime creatures, dignified so high,
       Set over all his works; which in our fall,
       For us created, needs with us must fail,
       Dependant made; so God shall uncreate,
       Be frustrate, do, undo, and labour lose;
950   Not well conceived of God, who, though his power
       Creation could repeat, yet would be loth
       Us to abolish, lest the Adversary
       Triumph, and say; "Fickle their state whom God
       Most favours; who can please him long? Me first
955   He ruined, now Mankind; whom will he next?"
       Matter of scorn, not to be given the Foe.
       However I with thee have fixed my lot,
       Certain to undergo like doom: If death
       Consort with thee, death is to me as life;
960   So forcible within my heart I feel
       The bond of Nature draw me to my own;
       My own in thee, for what thou art is mine;
       Our state cannot be severed; we are one,
       One flesh; to lose thee were to lose myself.

965 So Adam; and thus Eve to him replied.
O glorious trial of exceeding love,
Illustrious evidence, example high!
Engaging me to emulate; but, short
Of thy perfection, how shall I attain,
970 Adam, from whose dear side I boast me sprung,
And gladly of our union hear thee speak,
One heart, one soul in both; whereof good proof
This day affords, declaring thee resolved,
Rather than death, or aught than death more dread,
975 Shall separate us, linked in love so dear,
To undergo with me one guilt, one crime,
If any be, of tasting this fair fruit;
Whose virtue for of good still good proceeds,
Direct, or by occasion, hath presented
980 This happy trial of thy love, which else
So eminently never had been known?
Were it I thought death menaced would ensue
This my attempt, I would sustain alone
The worst, and not persuade thee, rather die
985 Deserted, than oblige thee with a fact
Pernicious to thy peace; chiefly assured
Remarkably so late of thy so true,
So faithful, love unequalled: but I feel
Far otherwise the event; not death, but life
990 Augmented, opened eyes, new hopes, new joys,
Taste so divine, that what of sweet before
Hath touched my sense, flat seems to this, and harsh.
On my experience, Adam, freely taste,
And fear of death deliver to the winds.
995 So saying, she embraced him, and for joy
Tenderly wept; much won, that he his love
Had so ennobled, as of choice to incur
Divine displeasure for her sake, or death.
In recompence (for such compliance bad
1000 Such recompence best merits) from the bough
She gave him of that fair enticing fruit
With liberal hand: he scrupled not to eat,
Against his better knowledge; not deceived,
But fondly overcome with female charm.
1005 Earth trembled from her entrails, as again
In pangs; and Nature gave a second groan;
Sky loured; and, muttering thunder, some sad drops
Wept at completing of the mortal sin
Original: while Adam took no thought,

1010 Eating his fill; nor Eve to iterate
  Her former trespass feared, the more to sooth
  Him with her loved society; that now,
  As with new wine intoxicated both,
  They swim in mirth, and fancy that they feel
1015 Divinity within them breeding wings,
  Wherewith to scorn the earth: But that false fruit
  Far other operation first displayed,
  Carnal desire inflaming; he on Eve
  Began to cast lascivious eyes; she him
1020 As wantonly repaid; in lust they burn:
  Till Adam thus 'gan Eve to dalliance move.
  Eve, now I see thou art exact of taste,
  And elegant, of sapience no small part;
  Since to each meaning savour we apply,
1025 And palate call judicious; I the praise
  Yield thee, so well this day thou hast purveyed.
  Much pleasure we have lost, while we abstained
  From this delightful fruit, nor known till now
  True relish, tasting; if such pleasure be
1030 In things to us forbidden, it might be wished,
  For this one tree had been forbidden ten.
  But come, so well refreshed, now let us play,
  As meet is, after such delicious fare;
  For never did thy beauty, since the day
1035 I saw thee first and wedded thee, adorned
  With all perfections, so inflame my sense
  With ardour to enjoy thee, fairer now
  Than ever; bounty of this virtuous tree!
  So said he, and forbore not glance or toy
1040 Of amorous intent; well understood
  Of Eve, whose eye darted contagious fire.
  Her hand he seised; and to a shady bank,
  Thick over-head with verdant roof imbowered,
  He led her nothing loth; flowers were the couch,
1045 Pansies, and violets, and asphodel,
  And hyacinth; Earth's freshest softest lap.
  There they their fill of love and love's disport
  Took largely, of their mutual guilt the seal,
  The solace of their sin; till dewy sleep
1050 Oppressed them, wearied with their amorous play,
  Soon as the force of that fallacious fruit,
  That with exhilarating vapour bland
  About their spirits had played, and inmost powers
  Made err, was now exhaled; and grosser sleep,

1055 Bred of unkindly fumes, with conscious dreams
Incumbered, now had left them; up they rose
As from unrest; and, each the other viewing,
Soon found their eyes how opened, and their minds
How darkened; innocence, that as a veil
1060 Had shadowed them from knowing ill, was gone;
Just confidence, and native righteousness,
And honour, from about them, naked left
To guilty Shame; he covered, but his robe
Uncovered more. So rose the Danite strong,
1065 Herculean Samson, from the harlot-lap
Of Philistean Dalilah, and waked
Shorn of his strength. They destitute and bare
Of all their virtue: Silent, and in face
Confounded, long they sat, as strucken mute:
1070 Till Adam, though not less than Eve abashed,
At length gave utterance to these words constrained.
O Eve, in evil hour thou didst give ear
To that false worm, of whomsoever taught
To counterfeit Man's voice; true in our fall,
1075 False in our promised rising; since our eyes
Opened we find indeed, and find we know
Both good and evil; good lost, and evil got;
Bad fruit of knowledge, if this be to know;
Which leaves us naked thus, of honour void,
1080 Of innocence, of faith, of purity,
Our wonted ornaments now soiled and stained,
And in our faces evident the signs
Of foul concupiscence; whence evil store;
Even shame, the last of evils; of the first
1085 Be sure then.—How shall I behold the face
Henceforth of God or Angel, erst with joy
And rapture so oft beheld? Those heavenly shapes
Will dazzle now this earthly with their blaze
Insufferably bright. O! might I here
1090 In solitude live savage; in some glade
Obscured, where highest woods, impenetrable
To star or sun-light, spread their umbrage broad
And brown as evening: Cover me, ye Pines!
Ye Cedars, with innumerable boughs
1095 Hide me, where I may never see them more!—
But let us now, as in bad plight, devise
What best may for the present serve to hide
The parts of each from other, that seem most
To shame obnoxious, and unseemliest seen;

1100   Some tree, whose broad smooth leaves together sewed,
        And girded on our loins, may cover round
        Those middle parts; that this new comer, Shame,
        There sit not, and reproach us as unclean.
        So counselled he, and both together went
1105   Into the thickest wood; there soon they chose
        The fig-tree; not that kind for fruit renowned,
        But such as at this day, to Indians known,
        In Malabar or Decan spreads her arms
        Branching so broad and long, that in the ground
1110   The bended twigs take root, and daughters grow
        About the mother tree, a pillared shade
        High over-arched, and echoing walks between:
        There oft the Indian herdsman, shunning heat,
        Shelters in cool, and tends his pasturing herds
1115   At loop-holes cut through thickest shade: Those leaves
        They gathered, broad as Amazonian targe;
        And, with what skill they had, together sewed,
        To gird their waist; vain covering, if to hide
        Their guilt and dreaded shame! O, how unlike
1120   To that first naked glory! Such of late
        Columbus found the American, so girt
        With feathered cincture; naked else, and wild
        Among the trees on isles and woody shores.
        Thus fenced, and, as they thought, their shame in part
1125   Covered, but not at rest or ease of mind,
        They sat them down to weep; nor only tears
        Rained at their eyes, but high winds worse within
        Began to rise, high passions, anger, hate,
        Mistrust, suspicion, discord; and shook sore
1130   Their inward state of mind, calm region once
        And full of peace, now tost and turbulent:
        For Understanding ruled not, and the Will
        Heard not her lore; both in subjection now
        To sensual Appetite, who from beneath
1135   Usurping over sovran Reason claimed
        Superiour sway: From thus distempered breast,
        Adam, estranged in look and altered style,
        Speech intermitted thus to Eve renewed.
        Would thou hadst hearkened to my words, and staid
1140   With me, as I besought thee, when that strange
        Desire of wandering, this unhappy morn,
        I know not whence possessed thee; we had then
        Remained still happy; not, as now, despoiled
        Of all our good; shamed, naked, miserable!

1145 Let none henceforth seek needless cause to approve
The faith they owe; when earnestly they seek
Such proof, conclude, they then begin to fail.
To whom, soon moved with touch of blame, thus Eve.
What words have passed thy lips, Adam severe!
1150 Imputest thou that to my default, or will
Of wandering, as thou callest it, which who knows
But might as ill have happened thou being by,
Or to thyself perhaps? Hadst thou been there,
Or here the attempt, thou couldst not have discerned
1155 Fraud in the Serpent, speaking as he spake;
No ground of enmity between us known,
Why he should mean me ill, or seek to harm.
Was I to have never parted from thy side?
As good have grown there still a lifeless rib.
1160 Being as I am, why didst not thou, the head,
Command me absolutely not to go,
Going into such danger, as thou saidst?
Too facile then, thou didst not much gainsay;
Nay, didst permit, approve, and fair dismiss.
1165 Hadst thou been firm and fixed in thy dissent,
Neither had I transgressed, nor thou with me.
To whom, then first incensed, Adam replied.
Is this the love, is this the recompence
Of mine to thee, ingrateful Eve! expressed
1170 Immutable, when thou wert lost, not I;
Who might have lived, and joyed immortal bliss,
Yet willingly chose rather death with thee?
And am I now upbraided as the cause
Of thy transgressing? Not enough severe,
1175 It seems, in thy restraint: What could I more
I warned thee, I admonished thee, foretold
The danger, and the lurking enemy
That lay in wait; beyond this, had been force;
And force upon free will hath here no place.
1180 But confidence then bore thee on; secure
Either to meet no danger, or to find
Matter of glorious trial; and perhaps
I also erred, in overmuch admiring
What seemed in thee so perfect, that I thought
1185 No evil durst attempt thee; but I rue
The errour now, which is become my crime,
And thou the accuser. Thus it shall befall
Him, who, to worth in women overtrusting,
Lets her will rule: restraint she will not brook;

1190   And, left to herself, if evil thence ensue,
       She first his weak indulgence will accuse.
       Thus they in mutual accusation spent
       The fruitless hours, but neither self-condemning;
       And of their vain contest appeared no end.

Book X

       Mean while the heinous and despiteful act
       Of Satan, done in Paradise; and how
       He, in the serpent, had perverted Eve,
       Her husband she, to taste the fatal fruit,
5   Was known in Heaven; for what can 'scape the eye
       Of God all-seeing, or deceive his heart
       Omniscient? who, in all things wise and just,
       Hindered not Satan to attempt the mind
       Of Man, with strength entire and free will armed,
10   Complete to have discovered and repulsed
       Whatever wiles of foe or seeming friend.
       For still they knew, and ought to have still remembered,
       The high injunction, not to taste that fruit,
       Whoever tempted; which they not obeying,
15   (Incurred what could they less?) the penalty;
       And, manifold in sin, deserved to fall.
       Up into Heaven from Paradise in haste
       The angelick guards ascended, mute, and sad,
       For Man; for of his state by this they knew,
20   Much wondering how the subtle Fiend had stolen
       Entrance unseen. Soon as the unwelcome news
       From Earth arrived at Heaven-gate, displeased
       All were who heard; dim sadness did not spare
       That time celestial visages, yet, mixed
25   With pity, violated not their bliss.
       About the new-arrived, in multitudes
       The ethereal people ran, to hear and know
       How all befel: They towards the throne supreme,
       Accountable, made haste, to make appear,
30   With righteous plea, their utmost vigilance
       And easily approved; when the Most High
       Eternal Father, from his secret cloud,
       Amidst in thunder uttered thus his voice.
       Assembled Angels, and ye Powers returned
35   From unsuccessful charge; be not dismayed,
       Nor troubled at these tidings from the earth,
       Which your sincerest care could not prevent;
       Foretold so lately what would come to pass,

When first this tempter crossed the gulf from Hell.
40 I told ye then he should prevail, and speed
On his bad errand; Man should be seduced,
And flattered out of all, believing lies
Against his Maker; no decree of mine
Concurring to necessitate his fall,
45 Or touch with lightest moment of impulse
His free will, to her own inclining left
In even scale. But fallen he is; and now
What rests, but that the mortal sentence pass
On his transgression,—death denounced that day?
50 Which he presumes already vain and void,
Because not yet inflicted, as he feared,
By some immediate stroke; but soon shall find
Forbearance no acquittance, ere day end.
Justice shall not return as bounty scorned.
55 But whom send I to judge them? whom but thee,
Vicegerent Son? To thee I have transferred
All judgement, whether in Heaven, or Earth, or Hell.
Easy it may be seen that I intend
Mercy colleague with justice, sending thee
60 Man's friend, his Mediator, his designed
Both ransom and Redeemer voluntary,
And destined Man himself to judge Man fallen.
So spake the Father; and, unfolding bright
Toward the right hand his glory, on the Son
65 Blazed forth unclouded Deity: He full
Resplendent all his Father manifest
Expressed, and thus divinely answered mild.
Father Eternal, thine is to decree;
Mine, both in Heaven and Earth, to do thy will
70 Supreme; that thou in me, thy Son beloved,
Mayest ever rest well pleased. I go to judge
On earth these thy transgressours; but thou knowest,
Whoever judged, the worst on me must light,
When time shall be; for so I undertook
75 Before thee; and, not repenting, this obtain
Of right, that I may mitigate their doom
On me derived; yet I shall temper so
Justice with mercy, as may illustrate most
Them fully satisfied, and thee appease.
80 Attendance none shall need, nor train, where none
Are to behold the judgement, but the judged,
Those two; the third best absent is condemned,
Convict by flight, and rebel to all law:

Conviction to the serpent none belongs.
85　Thus saying, from his radiant seat he rose
Of high collateral glory: Him Thrones, and Powers,
Princedoms, and Dominations ministrant,
Accompanied to Heaven-gate; from whence
Eden, and all the coast, in prospect lay.
90　Down he descended straight; the speed of Gods
Time counts not, though with swiftest minutes winged.
Now was the sun in western cadence low
From noon, and gentle airs, due at their hour,
To fan the earth now waked, and usher in
95　The evening cool; when he, from wrath more cool,
Came the mild Judge, and Intercessour both,
To sentence Man: The voice of God they heard
Now walking in the garden, by soft winds
Brought to their ears, while day declined; they heard,
100　And from his presence hid themselves among
The thickest trees, both man and wife; till God,
Approaching, thus to Adam called aloud.
Where art thou, Adam, wont with joy to meet
My coming seen far off? I miss thee here,
105　Not pleased, thus entertained with solitude,
Where obvious duty ere while appeared unsought:
Or come I less conspicuous, or what change
Absents thee, or what chance detains?—Come forth!
He came; and with him Eve, more loth, though first
110　To offend; discountenanced both, and discomposed;
Love was not in their looks, either to God,
Or to each other; but apparent guilt,
And shame, and perturbation, and despair,
Anger, and obstinacy, and hate, and guile.
115　Whence Adam, faltering long, thus answered brief.
I heard thee in the garden, and of thy voice
Afraid, being naked, hid myself. To whom
The gracious Judge without revile replied.
My voice thou oft hast heard, and hast not feared,
120　But still rejoiced; how is it now become
So dreadful to thee? That thou art naked, who
Hath told thee? Hast thou eaten of the tree,
Whereof I gave thee charge thou shouldst not eat?
To whom thus Adam sore beset replied.
125　O Heaven! in evil strait this day I stand
Before my Judge; either to undergo
Myself the total crime, or to accuse
My other self, the partner of my life;

Whose failing, while her faith to me remains,
130   I should conceal, and not expose to blame
By my complaint: but strict necessity
Subdues me, and calamitous constraint;
Lest on my head both sin and punishment,
However insupportable, be all
135   Devolved; though should I hold my peace, yet thou
Wouldst easily detect what I conceal.—
This Woman, whom thou madest to be my help,
And gavest me as thy perfect gift, so good,
So fit, so acceptable, so divine,
140   That from her hand I could suspect no ill,
And what she did, whatever in itself,
Her doing seemed to justify the deed;
She gave me of the tree, and I did eat.
To whom the Sovran Presence thus replied.
145   Was she thy God, that her thou didst obey
Before his voice? or was she made thy guide,
Superiour, or but equal, that to her
Thou didst resign thy manhood, and the place
Wherein God set thee above her made of thee,
150   And for thee, whose perfection far excelled
Hers in all real dignity? Adorned
She was indeed, and lovely, to attract
Thy love, not thy subjection; and her gifts
Were such, as under government well seemed;
155   Unseemly to bear rule; which was thy part
And person, hadst thou known thyself aright.
So having said, he thus to Eve in few.
Say, Woman, what is this which thou hast done?
To whom sad Eve, with shame nigh overwhelmed,
160   Confessing soon, yet not before her Judge
Bold or loquacious, thus abashed replied.
The Serpent me beguiled, and I did eat.
Which when the Lord God heard, without delay
To judgement he proceeded on the accused
165   Serpent, though brute; unable to transfer
The guilt on him, who made him instrument
Of mischief, and polluted from the end
Of his creation; justly then accursed,
As vitiated in nature: More to know
170   Concerned not Man, (since he no further knew)
Nor altered his offence; yet God at last
To Satan first in sin his doom applied,
Though in mysterious terms, judged as then best:

And on the Serpent thus his curse let fall.
175   Because thou hast done this, thou art accursed
Above all cattle, each beast of the field;
Upon thy belly groveling thou shalt go,
And dust shalt eat all the days of thy life.
Between thee and the woman I will put
180   Enmity, and between thine and her seed;
Her seed shall bruise thy head, thou bruise his heel.
So spake this oracle, then verified
When Jesus, Son of Mary, second Eve,
Saw Satan fall, like lightning, down from Heaven,
185   Prince of the air; then, rising from his grave
Spoiled Principalities and Powers, triumphed
In open show; and, with ascension bright,
Captivity led captive through the air,
The realm itself of Satan, long usurped;
190   Whom he shall tread at last under our feet;
Even he, who now foretold his fatal bruise;
And to the Woman thus his sentence turned.
Thy sorrow I will greatly multiply
By thy conception; children thou shalt bring
195   In sorrow forth; and to thy husband's will
Thine shall submit; he over thee shall rule.
On Adam last thus judgement he pronounced.
Because thou hast hearkened to the voice of thy wife,
And eaten of the tree, concerning which
200   I charged thee, saying, Thou shalt not eat thereof:
Cursed is the ground for thy sake; thou in sorrow
Shalt eat thereof, all the days of thy life;
Thorns also and thistles it shall bring thee forth
Unbid; and thou shalt eat the herb of the field;
205   In the sweat of thy face shalt thou eat bread,
Till thou return unto the ground; for thou
Out of the ground wast taken, know thy birth,
For dust thou art, and shalt to dust return.
So judged he Man, both Judge and Saviour sent;
210   And the instant stroke of death, denounced that day,
Removed far off; then, pitying how they stood
Before him naked to the air, that now
Must suffer change, disdained not to begin
Thenceforth the form of servant to assume;
215   As when he washed his servants feet; so now,
As father of his family, he clad
Their nakedness with skins of beasts, or slain,
Or as the snake with youthful coat repaid;

And thought not much to clothe his enemies;
220   Nor he their outward only with the skins
      Of beasts, but inward nakedness, much more.
      Opprobrious, with his robe of righteousness,
      Arraying, covered from his Father's sight.
      To him with swift ascent he up returned,
225   Into his blissful bosom reassumed
      In glory, as of old; to him appeased
      All, though all-knowing, what had passed with Man
      Recounted, mixing intercession sweet.
      Mean while, ere thus was sinned and judged on Earth,
230   Within the gates of Hell sat Sin and Death,
      In counterview within the gates, that now
      Stood open wide, belching outrageous flame
      Far into Chaos, since the Fiend passed through,
      Sin opening; who thus now to Death began.
235   O Son, why sit we here each other viewing
      Idly, while Satan, our great author, thrives
      In other worlds, and happier seat provides
      For us, his offspring dear? It cannot be
      But that success attends him; if mishap,
240   Ere this he had returned, with fury driven
      By his avengers; since no place like this
      Can fit his punishment, or their revenge.
      Methinks I feel new strength within me rise,
      Wings growing, and dominion given me large
245   Beyond this deep; whatever draws me on,
      Or sympathy, or some connatural force,
      Powerful at greatest distance to unite,
      With secret amity, things of like kind,
      By secretest conveyance. Thou, my shade
250   Inseparable, must with me along;
      For Death from Sin no power can separate.
      But, lest the difficulty of passing back
      Stay his return perhaps over this gulf
      Impassable, impervious; let us try
255   Adventurous work, yet to thy power and mine
      Not unagreeable, to found a path
      Over this main from Hell to that new world,
      Where Satan now prevails; a monument
      Of merit high to all the infernal host,
260   Easing their passage hence, for intercourse,
      Or transmigration, as their lot shall lead.
      Nor can I miss the way, so strongly drawn
      By this new-felt attraction and instinct.

Whom thus the meager Shadow answered soon.
265 Go, whither Fate, and inclination strong,
Leads thee; I shall not lag behind, nor err
The way, thou leading; such a scent I draw
Of carnage, prey innumerable, and taste
The savour of death from all things there that live:
270 Nor shall I to the work thou enterprisest
Be wanting, but afford thee equal aid.
So saying, with delight he snuffed the smell
Of mortal change on earth. As when a flock
Of ravenous fowl, though many a league remote,
275 Against the day of battle, to a field,
Where armies lie encamped, come flying, lured
With scent of living carcasses designed
For death, the following day, in bloody fight:
So scented the grim Feature, and upturned
280 His nostril wide into the murky air;
Sagacious of his quarry from so far.
Then both from out Hell-gates, into the waste
Wide anarchy of Chaos, damp and dark,
Flew diverse; and with power (their power was great)
285 Hovering upon the waters, what they met
Solid or slimy, as in raging sea
Tost up and down, together crouded drove,
From each side shoaling towards the mouth of Hell;
As when two polar winds, blowing adverse
290 Upon the Cronian sea, together drive
Mountains of ice, that stop the imagined way
Beyond Petsora eastward, to the rich
Cathaian coast. The aggregated soil
Death with his mace petrifick, cold and dry,
295 As with a trident, smote; and fixed as firm
As Delos, floating once; the rest his look
Bound with Gorgonian rigour not to move;
And with Asphaltick slime, broad as the gate,
Deep to the roots of Hell the gathered beach
300 They fastened, and the mole immense wrought on
Over the foaming deep high-arched, a bridge
Of length prodigious, joining to the wall
Immoveable of this now fenceless world,
Forfeit to Death; from hence a passage broad,
305 Smooth, easy, inoffensive, down to Hell.
So, if great things to small may be compared,
Xerxes, the liberty of Greece to yoke,
From Susa, his Memnonian palace high,

    Came to the sea: and, over Hellespont
310 Bridging his way, Europe with Asia joined,
    And scourged with many a stroke the indignant waves.
    Now had they brought the work by wonderous art
    Pontifical, a ridge of pendant rock,
    Over the vexed abyss, following the track
315 Of Satan to the self-same place where he
    First lighted from his wing, and landed safe
    From out of Chaos, to the outside bare
    Of this round world: With pins of adamant
    And chains they made all fast, too fast they made
320 And durable! And now in little space
    The confines met of empyrean Heaven,
    And of this World; and, on the left hand, Hell
    With long reach interposed; three several ways
    In sight, to each of these three places led.
325 And now their way to Earth they had descried,
    To Paradise first tending; when, behold!
    Satan, in likeness of an Angel bright,
    Betwixt the Centaur and the Scorpion steering
    His zenith, while the sun in Aries rose:
330 Disguised he came; but those his children dear
    Their parent soon discerned, though in disguise.
    He, after Eve seduced, unminded slunk
    Into the wood fast by; and, changing shape,
    To observe the sequel, saw his guileful act
335 By Eve, though all unweeting, seconded
    Upon her husband; saw their shame that sought
    Vain covertures; but when he saw descend
    The Son of God to judge them, terrified
    He fled; not hoping to escape, but shun
340 The present; fearing, guilty, what his wrath
    Might suddenly inflict; that past, returned
    By night, and listening where the hapless pair
    Sat in their sad discourse, and various plaint,
    Thence gathered his own doom; which understood
345 Not instant, but of future time, with joy
    And tidings fraught, to Hell he now returned;
    And at the brink of Chaos, near the foot
    Of this new wonderous pontifice, unhoped
    Met, who to meet him came, his offspring dear.
350 Great joy was at their meeting, and at sight
    Of that stupendous bridge his joy encreased.
    Long he admiring stood, till Sin, his fair
    Enchanting daughter, thus the silence broke.

O Parent, these are thy magnifick deeds,
355 Thy trophies! which thou viewest as not thine own;
Thou art their author, and prime architect:
For I no sooner in my heart divined,
My heart, which by a secret harmony
Still moves with thine, joined in connexion sweet,
360 That thou on earth hadst prospered, which thy looks
Now also evidence, but straight I felt,
Though distant from thee worlds between, yet felt,
That I must after thee, with this thy son;
Such fatal consequence unites us three!
365 Hell could no longer hold us in our bounds,
Nor this unvoyageable gulf obscure
Detain from following thy illustrious track.
Thou hast achieved our liberty, confined
Within Hell-gates till now; thou us impowered
370 To fortify thus far, and overlay,
With this portentous bridge, the dark abyss.
Thine now is all this world; thy virtue hath won
What thy hands builded not; thy wisdom gained
With odds what war hath lost, and fully avenged
375 Our foil in Heaven; here thou shalt monarch reign,
There didst not; there let him still victor sway,
As battle hath adjudged; from this new world
Retiring, by his own doom alienated;
And henceforth monarchy with thee divide
380 Of all things, parted by the empyreal bounds,
His quadrature, from thy orbicular world;
Or try thee now more dangerous to his throne.
Whom thus the Prince of darkness answered glad.
Fair Daughter, and thou Son and Grandchild both;
385 High proof ye now have given to be the race
Of Satan (for I glory in the name,
Antagonist of Heaven's Almighty King,)
Amply have merited of me, of all
The infernal empire, that so near Heaven's door
390 Triumphal with triumphal act have met,
Mine, with this glorious work; and made one realm,
Hell and this world, one realm, one continent
Of easy thorough-fare. Therefore, while I
Descend through darkness, on your road with ease,
395 To my associate Powers, them to acquaint
With these successes, and with them rejoice;
You two this way, among these numerous orbs,
All yours, right down to Paradise descend;

There dwell, and reign in bliss; thence on the earth
400 Dominion exercise and in the air,
Chiefly on Man, sole lord of all declared;
Him first make sure your thrall, and lastly kill.
My substitutes I send ye, and create
Plenipotent on earth, of matchless might
405 Issuing from me: on your joint vigour now
My hold of this new kingdom all depends,
Through Sin to Death exposed by my exploit.
If your joint power prevail, the affairs of Hell
No detriment need fear; go, and be strong!
410 So saying he dismissed them; they with speed
Their course through thickest constellations held,
Spreading their bane; the blasted stars looked wan,
And planets, planet-struck, real eclipse
Then suffered. The other way Satan went down
415 The causey to Hell-gate: On either side
Disparted Chaos overbuilt exclaimed,
And with rebounding surge the bars assailed,
That scorned his indignation: Through the gate,
Wide open and unguarded, Satan passed,
420 And all about found desolate; for those,
Appointed to sit there, had left their charge,
Flown to the upper world; the rest were all
Far to the inland retired, about the walls
Of Pandemonium; city and proud seat
425 Of Lucifer, so by allusion called
Of that bright star to Satan paragoned;
There kept their watch the legions, while the Grand
In council sat, solicitous what chance
Might intercept their emperour sent; so he
430 Departing gave command, and they observed.
As when the Tartar from his Russian foe,
By Astracan, over the snowy plains,
Retires; or Bactrin Sophi, from the horns
Of Turkish crescent, leaves all waste beyond
435 The realm of Aladule, in his retreat
To Tauris or Casbeen: So these, the late
Heaven-banished host, left desart utmost Hell
Many a dark league, reduced in careful watch
Round their metropolis; and now expecting
440 Each hour their great adventurer, from the search
Of foreign worlds: He through the midst unmarked,
In show plebeian Angel militant
Of lowest order, passed; and from the door

Of that Plutonian hall, invisible
445 Ascended his high throne; which, under state
Of richest texture spread, at the upper end
Was placed in regal lustre. Down a while
He sat, and round about him saw unseen:
At last, as from a cloud, his fulgent head
450 And shape star-bright appeared, or brighter; clad
With what permissive glory since his fall
Was left him, or false glitter: All amazed
At that so sudden blaze the Stygian throng
Bent their aspect, and whom they wished beheld,
455 Their mighty Chief returned: loud was the acclaim:
Forth rushed in haste the great consulting peers,
Raised from their dark Divan, and with like joy
Congratulant approached him; who with hand
Silence, and with these words attention, won.
460 Thrones, Dominations, Princedoms, Virtues, Powers;
For in possession such, not only of right,
I call ye, and declare ye now; returned
Successful beyond hope, to lead ye forth
Triumphant out of this infernal pit
465 Abominable, accursed, the house of woe,
And dungeon of our tyrant: Now possess,
As Lords, a spacious world, to our native Heaven
Little inferiour, by my adventure hard
With peril great achieved. Long were to tell
470 What I have done; what suffered; with what pain
Voyaged th' unreal, vast, unbounded deep
Of horrible confusion; over which
By Sin and Death a broad way now is paved,
To expedite your glorious march; but I
475 Toiled out my uncouth passage, forced to ride
The untractable abyss, plunged in the womb
Of unoriginal Night and Chaos wild;
That, jealous of their secrets, fiercely opposed
My journey strange, with clamorous uproar
480 Protesting Fate supreme; thence how I found
The new created world, which fame in Heaven
Long had foretold, a fabrick wonderful
Of absolute perfection! therein Man
Placed in a Paradise, by our exile
485 Made happy: Him by fraud I have seduced
From his Creator; and, the more to encrease
Your wonder, with an apple; he, thereat
Offended, worth your laughter! hath given up

Both his beloved Man, and all his world,
490 To Sin and Death a prey, and so to us,
Without our hazard, labour, or alarm;
To range in, and to dwell, and over Man
To rule, as over all he should have ruled.
True is, me also he hath judged, or rather
495 Me not, but the brute serpent in whose shape
Man I deceived: that which to me belongs,
Is enmity which he will put between
Me and mankind; I am to bruise his heel;
His seed, when is not set, shall bruise my head:
500 A world who would not purchase with a bruise,
Or much more grievous pain?—Ye have the account
Of my performance: What remains, ye Gods,
But up, and enter now into full bliss?
So having said, a while he stood, expecting
505 Their universal shout, and high applause,
To fill his ear; when, contrary, he hears
On all sides, from innumerable tongues,
A dismal universal hiss, the sound
Of publick scorn; he wondered, but not long
510 Had leisure, wondering at himself now more,
His visage drawn he felt to sharp and spare;
His arms clung to his ribs; his legs entwining
Each other, till supplanted down he fell
A monstrous serpent on his belly prone,
515 Reluctant, but in vain; a greater power
Now ruled him, punished in the shape he sinned,
According to his doom: he would have spoke,
But hiss for hiss returned with forked tongue
To forked tongue; for now were all transformed
520 Alike, to serpents all, as accessories
To his bold riot: Dreadful was the din
Of hissing through the hall, thick swarming now
With complicated monsters head and tail,
Scorpion, and Asp, and Amphisbaena dire,
525 Cerastes horned, Hydrus, and Elops drear,
And Dipsas; (not so thick swarmed once the soil
Bedropt with blood of Gorgon, or the isle
Ophiusa,) but still greatest he the midst,
Now Dragon grown, larger than whom the sun
530 Ingendered in the Pythian vale or slime,
Huge Python, and his power no less he seemed
Above the rest still to retain; they all
Him followed, issuing forth to the open field,

Where all yet left of that revolted rout,
535　Heaven-fallen, in station stood or just array;
Sublime with expectation when to see
In triumph issuing forth their glorious Chief;
They saw, but other sight instead! a croud
Of ugly serpents; horrour on them fell,
540　And horrid sympathy; for, what they saw,
They felt themselves, now changing; down their arms,
Down fell both spear and shield; down they as fast;
And the dire hiss renewed, and the dire form
Catched, by contagion; like in punishment,
545　As in their crime. Thus was the applause they meant,
Turned to exploding hiss, triumph to shame
Cast on themselves from their own mouths. There stood
A grove hard by, sprung up with this their change,
His will who reigns above, to aggravate
550　Their penance, laden with fair fruit, like that
Which grew in Paradise, the bait of Eve
Used by the Tempter: on that prospect strange
Their earnest eyes they fixed, imagining
For one forbidden tree a multitude
555　Now risen, to work them further woe or shame;
Yet, parched with scalding thirst and hunger fierce,
Though to delude them sent, could not abstain;
But on they rolled in heaps, and, up the trees
Climbing, sat thicker than the snaky locks
560　That curled Megaera: greedily they plucked
The fruitage fair to sight, like that which grew
Near that bituminous lake where Sodom flamed;
This more delusive, not the touch, but taste
Deceived; they, fondly thinking to allay
565　Their appetite with gust, instead of fruit
Chewed bitter ashes, which the offended taste
With spattering noise rejected: oft they assayed,
Hunger and thirst constraining; drugged as oft,
With hatefullest disrelish writhed their jaws,
570　With soot and cinders filled; so oft they fell
Into the same illusion, not as Man
Whom they triumphed once lapsed. Thus were they plagued
And worn with famine, long and ceaseless hiss,
Till their lost shape, permitted, they resumed;
575　Yearly enjoined, some say, to undergo,
This annual humbling certain numbered days,
To dash their pride, and joy, for Man seduced.
However, some tradition they dispersed

Among the Heathen, of their purchase got,
580 And fabled how the Serpent, whom they called
Ophion, with Eurynome, the wide—
Encroaching Eve perhaps, had first the rule
Of high Olympus; thence by Saturn driven
And Ops, ere yet Dictaean Jove was born.
585 Mean while in Paradise the hellish pair
Too soon arrived; Sin, there in power before,
Once actual; now in body, and to dwell
Habitual habitant; behind her Death,
Close following pace for pace, not mounted yet
590 On his pale horse: to whom Sin thus began.
Second of Satan sprung, all-conquering Death!
What thinkest thou of our empire now, though earned
With travel difficult, not better far
Than still at Hell's dark threshold to have sat watch,
595 Unnamed, undreaded, and thyself half starved?
Whom thus the Sin-born monster answered soon.
To me, who with eternal famine pine,
Alike is Hell, or Paradise, or Heaven;
There best, where most with ravine I may meet;
600 Which here, though plenteous, all too little seems
To stuff this maw, this vast unhide-bound corps.
To whom the incestuous mother thus replied.
Thou therefore on these herbs, and fruits, and flowers,
Feed first; on each beast next, and fish, and fowl;
605 No homely morsels! and, whatever thing
The sithe of Time mows down, devour unspared;
Till I, in Man residing, through the race,
His thoughts, his looks, words, actions, all infect;
And season him thy last and sweetest prey.
610 This said, they both betook them several ways,
Both to destroy, or unimmortal make
All kinds, and for destruction to mature
Sooner or later; which the Almighty seeing,
From his transcendent seat the Saints among,
615 To those bright Orders uttered thus his voice.
See, with what heat these dogs of Hell advance
To waste and havock yonder world, which I
So fair and good created; and had still
Kept in that state, had not the folly of Man
620 Let in these wasteful furies, who impute
Folly to me; so doth the Prince of Hell
And his adherents, that with so much ease
I suffer them to enter and possess

A place so heavenly; and, conniving, seem
625 To gratify my scornful enemies,
That laugh, as if, transported with some fit
Of passion, I to them had quitted all,
At random yielded up to their misrule;
And know not that I called, and drew them thither,
630 My Hell-hounds, to lick up the draff and filth
Which Man's polluting sin with taint hath shed
On what was pure; til, crammed and gorged, nigh burst
With sucked and glutted offal, at one sling
Of thy victorious arm, well-pleasing Son,
635 Both Sin, and Death, and yawning Grave, at last,
Through Chaos hurled, obstruct the mouth of Hell
For ever, and seal up his ravenous jaws.
Then Heaven and Earth renewed shall be made pure
To sanctity, that shall receive no stain:
640 Till then, the curse pronounced on both precedes.
He ended, and the heavenly audience loud
Sung Halleluiah, as the sound of seas,
Through multitude that sung: Just are thy ways,
Righteous are thy decrees on all thy works;
645 Who can extenuate thee? Next, to the Son,
Destined Restorer of mankind, by whom
New Heaven and Earth shall to the ages rise,
Or down from Heaven descend.—Such was their song;
While the Creator, calling forth by name
650 His mighty Angels, gave them several charge,
As sorted best with present things. The sun
Had first his precept so to move, so shine,
As might affect the earth with cold and heat
Scarce tolerable; and from the north to call
655 Decrepit winter; from the south to bring
Solstitial summer's heat. To the blanc moon
Her office they prescribed; to the other five
Their planetary motions, and aspects,
In sextile, square, and trine, and opposite,
660 Of noxious efficacy, and when to join
In synod unbenign; and taught the fixed
Their influence malignant when to shower,
Which of them rising with the sun, or falling,
Should prove tempestuous: To the winds they set
665 Their corners, when with bluster to confound
Sea, air, and shore; the thunder when to roll
With terrour through the dark aereal hall.
Some say, he bid his Angels turn ascanse

The poles of earth, twice ten degrees and more,
670 From the sun's axle; they with labour pushed
Oblique the centrick globe: Some say, the sun
Was bid turn reins from the equinoctial road
Like distant breadth to Taurus with the seven
Atlantick Sisters, and the Spartan Twins,
675 Up to the Tropick Crab: thence down amain
By Leo, and the Virgin, and the Scales,
As deep as Capricorn; to bring in change
Of seasons to each clime; else had the spring
Perpetual smiled on earth with vernant flowers,
680 Equal in days and nights, except to those
Beyond the polar circles; to them day
Had unbenighted shone, while the low sun,
To recompense his distance, in their sight
Had rounded still the horizon, and not known
685 Or east or west; which had forbid the snow
From cold Estotiland, and south as far
Beneath Magellan. At that tasted fruit
The sun, as from Thyestean banquet, turned
His course intended; else, how had the world
690 Inhabited, though sinless, more than now,
Avoided pinching cold and scorching heat?
These changes in the Heavens, though slow, produced
Like change on sea and land; sideral blast,
Vapour, and mist, and exhalation hot,
695 Corrupt and pestilent: Now from the north
Of Norumbega, and the Samoed shore,
Bursting their brazen dungeon, armed with ice,
And snow, and hail, and stormy gust and flaw,
Boreas, and Caecias, and Argestes loud,
700 And Thrascias, rend the woods, and seas upturn;
With adverse blast upturns them from the south
Notus, and Afer black with thunderous clouds
From Serraliona; thwart of these, as fierce,
Forth rush the Levant and the Ponent winds,
705 Eurus and Zephyr, with their lateral noise,
Sirocco and Libecchio. Thus began
Outrage from lifeless things; but Discord first,
Daughter of Sin, among the irrational
Death introduced, through fierce antipathy:
710 Beast now with beast 'gan war, and fowl with fowl,
And fish with fish; to graze the herb all leaving,
Devoured each other; nor stood much in awe
Of Man, but fled him; or, with countenance grim,

Glared on him passing. These were from without
715　The growing miseries, which Adam saw
Already in part, though hid in gloomiest shade,
To sorrow abandoned, but worse felt within;
And, in a troubled sea of passion tost,
Thus to disburden sought with sad complaint.
720　O miserable of happy! Is this the end
Of this new glorious world, and me so late
The glory of that glory, who now become
Accursed, of blessed? hide me from the face
Of God, whom to behold was then my highth
725　Of happiness!—Yet well, if here would end
The misery; I deserved it, and would bear
My own deservings; but this will not serve:
All that I eat or drink, or shall beget,
Is propagated curse. O voice, once heard
730　Delightfully, Encrease and multiply;
Now death to hear! for what can I encrease,
Or multiply, but curses on my head?
Who of all ages to succeed, but, feeling
The evil on him brought by me, will curse
735　My head? Ill fare our ancestor impure,
For this we may thank Adam! but his thanks
Shall be the execration: so, besides
Mine own that bide upon me, all from me
Shall with a fierce reflux on me rebound;
740　On me, as on their natural center, light
Heavy, though in their place. O fleeting joys
Of Paradise, dear bought with lasting woes!
Did I request thee, Maker, from my clay
To mould me Man? did I solicit thee
745　From darkness to promote me, or here place
In this delicious garden? As my will
Concurred not to my being, it were but right
And equal to reduce me to my dust;
Desirous to resign and render back
750　All I received; unable to perform
Thy terms too hard, by which I was to hold
The good I sought not. To the loss of that,
Sufficient penalty, why hast thou added
The sense of endless woes? Inexplicable
755　Thy justice seems; yet to say truth, too late
I thus contest; then should have been refused
Those terms whatever, when they were proposed:
Thou didst accept them; wilt thou enjoy the good,

Then cavil the conditions? And, though God
760 Made thee without thy leave, what if thy son
Prove disobedient, and reproved, retort,
"Wherefore didst thou beget me? I sought it not!"
Wouldst thou admit for his contempt of thee
That proud excuse? yet him not thy election,
765 But natural necessity begot.
God made thee of choice his own, and of his own
To serve him; thy reward was of his grace;
Thy punishment then, justly is at his will.
Be it so, for I submit; his doom is fair,
770 That dust I am, and shall to dust return.
O welcome hour whenever! Why delays
His hand to execute what his decree
Fixed on this day? Why do I overlive,
Why am I mocked with death, and lengthened out
775 To deathless pain? How gladly would I meet
Mortality my sentence, and be earth
Insensible! How glad would lay me down
As in my mother's lap! There I should rest,
And sleep secure; his dreadful voice no more
780 Would thunder in my ears; no fear of worse
To me, and to my offspring, would torment me
With cruel expectation. Yet one doubt
Pursues me still, lest all I cannot die;
Lest that pure breath of life, the spirit of Man
785 Which God inspired, cannot together perish
With this corporeal clod; then, in the grave,
Or in some other dismal place, who knows
But I shall die a living death? O thought
Horrid, if true! Yet why? It was but breath
790 Of life that sinned; what dies but what had life
And sin? The body properly had neither,
All of me then shall die: let this appease
The doubt, since human reach no further knows.
For though the Lord of all be infinite,
795 Is his wrath also? Be it, Man is not so,
But mortal doomed. How can he exercise
Wrath without end on Man, whom death must end?
Can he make deathless death? That were to make
Strange contradiction, which to God himself
800 Impossible is held; as argument
Of weakness, not of power. Will he draw out,
For anger's sake, finite to infinite,
In punished Man, to satisfy his rigour,

      Satisfied never? That were to extend
805   His sentence beyond dust and Nature's law;
      By which all causes else, according still
      To the reception of their matter, act;
      Not to the extent of their own sphere. But say
      That death be not one stroke, as I supposed,
810   Bereaving sense, but endless misery
      From this day onward; which I feel begun
      Both in me, and without me; and so last
      To perpetuity;—Ay me! that fear
      Comes thundering back with dreadful revolution
815   On my defenceless head; both Death and I
      Am found eternal, and incorporate both;
      Nor I on my part single; in me all
      Posterity stands cursed: Fair patrimony
      That I must leave ye, Sons! O, were I able
820   To waste it all myself, and leave ye none!
      So disinherited, how would you bless
      Me, now your curse! Ah, why should all mankind,
      For one man's fault, thus guiltless be condemned,
      It guiltless? But from me what can proceed,
825   But all corrupt; both mind and will depraved
      Not to do only, but to will the same
      With me? How can they then acquitted stand
      In sight of God? Him, after all disputes,
      Forced I absolve: all my evasions vain,
830   And reasonings, though through mazes, lead me still
      But to my own conviction: first and last
      On me, me only, as the source and spring
      Of all corruption, all the blame lights due;
      So might the wrath! Fond wish! couldst thou support
835   That burden, heavier than the earth to bear;
      Than all the world much heavier, though divided
      With that bad Woman? Thus, what thou desirest,
      And what thou fearest, alike destroys all hope
      Of refuge, and concludes thee miserable
840   Beyond all past example and future;
      To Satan only like both crime and doom.
      O Conscience! into what abyss of fears
      And horrours hast thou driven me; out of which
      I find no way, from deep to deeper plunged!
845   Thus Adam to himself lamented loud,
      Through the still night; not now, as ere Man fell,
      Wholesome, and cool, and mild, but with black air
      Accompanied; with damps, and dreadful gloom;

Which to his evil conscience represented
850 All things with double terrour: On the ground
Outstretched he lay, on the cold ground; and oft
Cursed his creation; Death as oft accused
Of tardy execution, since denounced
The day of his offence. Why comes not Death,
855 Said he, with one thrice-acceptable stroke
To end me? Shall Truth fail to keep her word,
Justice Divine not hasten to be just?
But Death comes not at call; Justice Divine
Mends not her slowest pace for prayers or cries,
860 O woods, O fountains, hillocks, dales, and bowers!
With other echo late I taught your shades
To answer, and resound far other song.—
Whom thus afflicted when sad Eve beheld,
Desolate where she sat, approaching nigh,
865 Soft words to his fierce passion she assayed:
But her with stern regard he thus repelled.
Out of my sight, thou Serpent! That name best
Befits thee with him leagued, thyself as false
And hateful; nothing wants, but that thy shape,
870 Like his, and colour serpentine, may show
Thy inward fraud; to warn all creatures from thee
Henceforth; lest that too heavenly form, pretended
To hellish falshood, snare them! But for thee
I had persisted happy; had not thy pride
875 And wandering vanity, when least was safe,
Rejected my forewarning, and disdained
Not to be trusted; longing to be seen,
Though by the Devil himself; him overweening
To over-reach; but, with the serpent meeting,
880 Fooled and beguiled; by him thou, I by thee
To trust thee from my side; imagined wise,
Constant, mature, proof against all assaults;
And understood not all was but a show,
Rather than solid virtue; all but a rib
885 Crooked by nature, bent, as now appears,
More to the part sinister, from me drawn;
Well if thrown out, as supernumerary
To my just number found. O! why did God,
Creator wise, that peopled highest Heaven
890 With Spirits masculine, create at last
This novelty on earth, this fair defect
Of nature, and not fill the world at once
With Men, as Angels, without feminine;

Or find some other way to generate
895 Mankind? This mischief had not been befallen,
And more that shall befall; innumerable
Disturbances on earth through female snares,
And strait conjunction with this sex: for either
He never shall find out fit mate, but such
900 As some misfortune brings him, or mistake;
Or whom he wishes most shall seldom gain
Through her perverseness, but shall see her gained
By a far worse; or, if she love, withheld
By parents; or his happiest choice too late
905 Shall meet, already linked and wedlock-bound
To a fell adversary, his hate or shame:
Which infinite calamity shall cause
To human life, and houshold peace confound.
He added not, and from her turned; but Eve,
910 Not so repulsed, with tears that ceased not flowing
And tresses all disordered, at his feet
Fell humble; and, embracing them, besought
His peace, and thus proceeded in her plaint.
Forsake me not thus, Adam! witness Heaven
915 What love sincere, and reverence in my heart
I bear thee, and unweeting have offended,
Unhappily deceived! Thy suppliant
I beg, and clasp thy knees; bereave me not,
Whereon I live, thy gentle looks, thy aid,
920 Thy counsel, in this uttermost distress,
My only strength and stay: Forlorn of thee,
Whither shall I betake me, where subsist?
While yet we live, scarce one short hour perhaps,
Between us two let there be peace; both joining,
925 As joined in injuries, one enmity
Against a foe by doom express assigned us,
That cruel Serpent: On me exercise not
Thy hatred for this misery befallen;
On me already lost, me than thyself
930 More miserable! Both have sinned; but thou
Against God only; I against God and thee;
And to the place of judgement will return,
There with my cries importune Heaven; that all
The sentence, from thy head removed, may light
935 On me, sole cause to thee of all this woe;
Me, me only, just object of his ire!
She ended weeping; and her lowly plight,
Immoveable, till peace obtained from fault

        Acknowledged and deplored, in Adam wrought
940 Commiseration: Soon his heart relented
        Towards her, his life so late, and sole delight,
        Now at his feet submissive in distress;
        Creature so fair his reconcilement seeking,
        His counsel, whom she had displeased, his aid:
945 As one disarmed, his anger all he lost,
        And thus with peaceful words upraised her soon.
        Unwary, and too desirous, as before,
        So now of what thou knowest not, who desirest
        The punishment all on thyself; alas!
950 Bear thine own first, ill able to sustain
        His full wrath, whose thou feelest as yet least part,
        And my displeasure bearest so ill. If prayers
        Could alter high decrees, I to that place
        Would speed before thee, and be louder heard,
955 That on my head all might be visited;
        Thy frailty and infirmer sex forgiven,
        To me committed, and by me exposed.
        But rise;—let us no more contend, nor blame
        Each other, blamed enough elsewhere; but strive
960 In offices of love, how we may lighten
        Each other's burden, in our share of woe;
        Since this day's death denounced, if aught I see,
        Will prove no sudden, but a slow-paced evil;
        A long day's dying, to augment our pain;
965 And to our seed (O hapless seed!) derived.
        To whom thus Eve, recovering heart, replied.
        Adam, by sad experiment I know
        How little weight my words with thee can find,
        Found so erroneous; thence by just event
970 Found so unfortunate: Nevertheless,
        Restored by thee, vile as I am, to place
        Of new acceptance, hopeful to regain
        Thy love, the sole contentment of my heart
        Living or dying, from thee I will not hide
975 What thoughts in my unquiet breast are risen,
        Tending to some relief of our extremes,
        Or end; though sharp and sad, yet tolerable,
        As in our evils, and of easier choice.
        If care of our descent perplex us most,
980 Which must be born to certain woe, devoured
        By Death at last; and miserable it is
        To be to others cause of misery,
        Our own begotten, and of our loins to bring

Into this cursed world a woeful race,
985 That after wretched life must be at last
Food for so foul a monster; in thy power
It lies, yet ere conception to prevent
The race unblest, to being yet unbegot.
Childless thou art, childless remain: so Death
990 Shall be deceived his glut, and with us two
Be forced to satisfy his ravenous maw.
But if thou judge it hard and difficult,
Conversing, looking, loving, to abstain
From love's due rights, nuptial embraces sweet;
995 And with desire to languish without hope,
Before the present object languishing
With like desire; which would be misery
And torment less than none of what we dread;
Then, both ourselves and seed at once to free
1000 From what we fear for both, let us make short,—
Let us seek Death;—or, he not found, supply
With our own hands his office on ourselves:
Why stand we longer shivering under fears,
That show no end but death, and have the power,
1005 Of many ways to die the shortest choosing,
Destruction with destruction to destroy?—
She ended here, or vehement despair
Broke off the rest: so much of death her thoughts
Had entertained, as dyed her cheeks with pale.
1010 But Adam, with such counsel nothing swayed,
To better hopes his more attentive mind
Labouring had raised; and thus to Eve replied.
Eve, thy contempt of life and pleasure seems
To argue in thee something more sublime
1015 And excellent, than what thy mind contemns;
But self-destruction therefore sought, refutes
That excellence thought in thee; and implies,
Not thy contempt, but anguish and regret
For loss of life and pleasure overloved.
1020 Or if thou covet death, as utmost end
Of misery, so thinking to evade
The penalty pronounced; doubt not but God
Hath wiselier armed his vengeful ire, than so
To be forestalled; much more I fear lest death,
1025 So snatched, will not exempt us from the pain
We are by doom to pay; rather, such acts
Of contumacy will provoke the Highest
To make death in us live: Then let us seek

Some safer resolution, which methinks
1030 I have in view, calling to mind with heed
Part of our sentence, that thy seed shall bruise
The Serpent's head; piteous amends! unless
Be meant, whom I conjecture, our grand foe,
Satan; who, in the serpent, hath contrived
1035 Against us this deceit: To crush his head
Would be revenge indeed! which will be lost
By death brought on ourselves, or childless days
Resolved, as thou proposest; so our foe
Shal 'scape his punishment ordained, and we
1040 Instead shall double ours upon our heads.
No more be mentioned then of violence
Against ourselves; and wilful barrenness,
That cuts us off from hope; and savours only
Rancour and pride, impatience and despite,
1045 Reluctance against God and his just yoke
Laid on our necks. Remember with what mild
And gracious temper he both heard, and judged,
Without wrath or reviling; we expected
Immediate dissolution, which we thought
1050 Was meant by death that day; when lo! to thee
Pains only in child-bearing were foretold,
And bringing forth; soon recompensed with joy,
Fruit of thy womb: On me the curse aslope
Glanced on the ground; with labour I must earn
1055 My bread; what harm? Idleness had been worse;
My labour will sustain me; and, lest cold
Or heat should injure us, his timely care
Hath, unbesought, provided; and his hands
Clothed us unworthy, pitying while he judged;
1060 How much more, if we pray him, will his ear
Be open, and his heart to pity incline,
And teach us further by what means to shun
The inclement seasons, rain, ice, hail, and snow!
Which now the sky, with various face, begins
1065 To show us in this mountain; while the winds
Blow moist and keen, shattering the graceful locks
Of these fair spreading trees; which bids us seek
Some better shroud, some better warmth to cherish
Our limbs benummed, ere this diurnal star
1070 Leave cold the night, how we his gathered beams
Reflected may with matter sere foment;
Or, by collision of two bodies, grind
The air attrite to fire; as late the clouds

Justling, or pushed with winds, rude in their shock,
1075 Tine the slant lightning; whose thwart flame, driven down
Kindles the gummy bark of fir or pine;
And sends a comfortable heat from far,
Which might supply the sun: Such fire to use,
And what may else be remedy or cure
1080 To evils which our own misdeeds have wrought,
He will instruct us praying, and of grace
Beseeching him; so as we need not fear
To pass commodiously this life, sustained
By him with many comforts, till we end
1085 In dust, our final rest and native home.
What better can we do, than, to the place
Repairing where he judged us, prostrate fall
Before him reverent; and there confess
Humbly our faults, and pardon beg; with tears
1090 Watering the ground, and with our sighs the air
Frequenting, sent from hearts contrite, in sign
Of sorrow unfeigned, and humiliation meek.
Undoubtedly he will relent, and turn
From his displeasure; in whose look serene,
1095 When angry most he seemed and most severe,
What else but favour, grace, and mercy, shone?
So spake our father penitent; nor Eve
Felt less remorse: they, forthwith to the place
Repairing where he judged them, prostrate fell
1100 Before him reverent; and both confessed
Humbly their faults, and pardon begged; with tears
Watering the ground, and with their sighs the air
Frequenting, sent from hearts contrite, in sign
Of sorrow unfeigned, and humiliation meek.

Book XII

As one who in his journey bates at noon,
Though bent on speed; so here the Arch-Angel paused
Betwixt the world destroyed and world restored,
If Adam aught perhaps might interpose;
5 Then, with transition sweet, new speech resumes.
Thus thou hast seen one world begin, and end;
And Man, as from a second stock, proceed.
Much thou hast yet to see; but I perceive
Thy mortal sight to fail; objects divine
10 Must needs impair and weary human sense:
Henceforth what is to come I will relate;
Thou therefore give due audience, and attend.

This second source of Men, while yet but few,
And while the dread of judgement past remains
15 Fresh in their minds, fearing the Deity,
With some regard to what is just and right
Shall lead their lives, and multiply apace;
Labouring the soil, and reaping plenteous crop,
Corn, wine, and oil; and, from the herd or flock,
20 Oft sacrificing bullock, lamb, or kid,
With large wine-offerings poured, and sacred feast,
Shall spend their days in joy unblamed; and dwell
Long time in peace, by families and tribes,
Under paternal rule: till one shall rise
25 Of proud ambitious heart; who, not content
With fair equality, fraternal state,
Will arrogate dominion undeserved
Over his brethren, and quite dispossess
Concord and law of nature from the earth;
30 Hunting (and men not beasts shall be his game)
With war, and hostile snare, such as refuse
Subjection to his empire tyrannous:
A mighty hunter thence he shall be styled
Before the Lord; as in despite of Heaven,
35 Or from Heaven, claiming second sovranty;
And from rebellion shall derive his name,
Though of rebellion others he accuse.
He with a crew, whom like ambition joins
With him or under him to tyrannize,
40 Marching from Eden towards the west, shall find
The plain, wherein a black bituminous gurge
Boils out from under ground, the mouth of Hell:
Of brick, and of that stuff, they cast to build
A city and tower, whose top may reach to Heaven;
45 And get themselves a name; lest, far dispersed
In foreign lands, their memory be lost;
Regardless whether good or evil fame.
But God, who oft descends to visit men
Unseen, and through their habitations walks
50 To mark their doings, them beholding soon,
Comes down to see their city, ere the tower
Obstruct Heaven-towers, and in derision sets
Upon their tongues a various spirit, to rase
Quite out their native language; and, instead,
55 To sow a jangling noise of words unknown:
Forthwith a hideous gabble rises loud,
Among the builders; each to other calls

Not understood; till hoarse, and all in rage,
As mocked they storm: great laughter was in Heaven,
60 And looking down, to see the hubbub strange,
And hear the din: Thus was the building left
Ridiculous, and the work Confusion named.
Whereto thus Adam, fatherly displeased.
O execrable son! so to aspire
65 Above his brethren; to himself assuming
Authority usurped, from God not given:
He gave us only over beast, fish, fowl,
Dominion absolute; that right we hold
By his donation; but man over men
70 He made not lord; such title to himself
Reserving, human left from human free.
But this usurper his encroachment proud
Stays not on Man; to God his tower intends
Siege and defiance: Wretched man! what food
75 Will he convey up thither, to sustain
Himself and his rash army; where thin air
Above the clouds will pine his entrails gross,
And famish him of breath, if not of bread?
To whom thus Michael. Justly thou abhorrest
80 That son, who on the quiet state of men
Such trouble brought, affecting to subdue
Rational liberty; yet know withal,
Since thy original lapse, true liberty
Is lost, which always with right reason dwells
85 Twinned, and from her hath no dividual being:
Reason in man obscured, or not obeyed,
Immediately inordinate desires,
And upstart passions, catch the government
From reason; and to servitude reduce
90 Man, till then free. Therefore, since he permits
Within himself unworthy powers to reign
Over free reason, God, in judgement just,
Subjects him from without to violent lords;
Who oft as undeservedly enthrall
95 His outward freedom: Tyranny must be;
Though to the tyrant thereby no excuse.
Yet sometimes nations will decline so low
From virtue, which is reason, that no wrong,
But justice, and some fatal curse annexed,
100 Deprives them of their outward liberty;
Their inward lost: Witness the irreverent son
Of him who built the ark; who, for the shame

Done to his father, heard this heavy curse,
Servant of servants, on his vicious race.
105 Thus will this latter, as the former world,
Still tend from bad to worse; till God at last,
Wearied with their iniquities, withdraw
His presence from among them, and avert
His holy eyes; resolving from thenceforth
110 To leave them to their own polluted ways;
And one peculiar nation to select
From all the rest, of whom to be invoked,
A nation from one faithful man to spring:
Him on this side Euphrates yet residing,
115 Bred up in idol-worship: O, that men
(Canst thou believe?) should be so stupid grown,
While yet the patriarch lived, who 'scaped the flood,
As to forsake the living God, and fall
To worship their own work in wood and stone
120 For Gods! Yet him God the Most High vouchsafes
To call by vision, from his father's house,
His kindred, and false Gods, into a land
Which he will show him; and from him will raise
A mighty nation; and upon him shower
125 His benediction so, that in his seed
All nations shall be blest: he straight obeys;
Not knowing to what land, yet firm believes:
I see him, but thou canst not, with what faith
He leaves his Gods, his friends, and native soil,
130 Ur of Chaldaea, passing now the ford
To Haran; after him a cumbrous train
Of herds and flocks, and numerous servitude;
Not wandering poor, but trusting all his wealth
With God, who called him, in a land unknown.
135 Canaan he now attains; I see his tents
Pitched about Sechem, and the neighbouring plain
Of Moreh; there by promise he receives
Gift to his progeny of all that land,
From Hameth northward to the Desart south;
140 (Things by their names I call, though yet unnamed;)
From Hermon east to the great western Sea;
Mount Hermon, yonder sea; each place behold
In prospect, as I point them; on the shore
Mount Carmel; here, the double-founted stream,
145 Jordan, true limit eastward; but his sons
Shall dwell to Senir, that long ridge of hills.
This ponder, that all nations of the earth

Shall in his seed be blessed: By that seed
Is meant thy great Deliverer, who shall bruise
150 The Serpent's head; whereof to thee anon
Plainlier shall be revealed. This patriarch blest,
Whom faithful Abraham due time shall call,
A son, and of his son a grand-child, leaves;
Like him in faith, in wisdom, and renown:
155 The grandchild, with twelve sons increased, departs
From Canaan to a land hereafter called
Egypt, divided by the river Nile
See where it flows, disgorging at seven mouths
Into the sea. To sojourn in that land
160 He comes, invited by a younger son
In time of dearth, a son whose worthy deeds
Raise him to be the second in that realm
Of Pharaoh. There he dies, and leaves his race
Growing into a nation, and now grown
165 Suspected to a sequent king, who seeks
To stop their overgrowth, as inmate guests
Too numerous; whence of guests he makes them slaves
Inhospitably, and kills their infant males:
Till by two brethren (these two brethren call
170 Moses and Aaron) sent from God to claim
His people from enthralment, they return,
With glory and spoil, back to their promised land.
But first, the lawless tyrant, who denies
To know their God, or message to regard,
175 Must be compelled by signs and judgements dire;
To blood unshed the rivers must be turned;
Frogs, lice, and flies, must all his palace fill
With loathed intrusion, and fill all the land;
His cattle must of rot and murren die;
180 Botches and blains must all his flesh emboss,
And all his people; thunder mixed with hail,
Hail mixed with fire, must rend the Egyptians sky,
And wheel on the earth, devouring where it rolls;
What it devours not, herb, or fruit, or grain,
185 A darksome cloud of locusts swarming down
Must eat, and on the ground leave nothing green;
Darkness must overshadow all his bounds,
Palpable darkness, and blot out three days;
Last, with one midnight stroke, all the first-born
190 Of Egypt must lie dead. Thus with ten wounds
The river-dragon tamed at length submits
To let his sojourners depart, and oft

Humbles his stubborn heart; but still, as ice
More hardened after thaw; till, in his rage
195   Pursuing whom he late dismissed, the sea
Swallows him with his host; but them lets pass,
As on dry land, between two crystal walls;
Awed by the rod of Moses so to stand
Divided, till his rescued gain their shore:
200   Such wondrous power God to his saint will lend,
Though present in his Angel; who shall go
Before them in a cloud, and pillar of fire;
By day a cloud, by night a pillar of fire;
To guide them in their journey, and remove
205   Behind them, while the obdurate king pursues:
All night he will pursue; but his approach
Darkness defends between till morning watch;
Then through the fiery pillar, and the cloud,
God looking forth will trouble all his host,
210   And craze their chariot-wheels: when by command
Moses once more his potent rod extends
Over the sea; the sea his rod obeys;
On their embattled ranks the waves return,
And overwhelm their war: The race elect
215   Safe toward Canaan from the shore advance
Through the wild Desart, not the readiest way;
Lest, entering on the Canaanite alarmed,
War terrify them inexpert, and fear
Return them back to Egypt, choosing rather
220   Inglorious life with servitude; for life
To noble and ignoble is more sweet
Untrained in arms, where rashness leads not on.
This also shall they gain by their delay
In the wide wilderness; there they shall found
225   Their government, and their great senate choose
Through the twelve tribes, to rule by laws ordained:
God from the mount of Sinai, whose gray top
Shall tremble, he descending, will himself
In thunder, lightning, and loud trumpets' sound,
230   Ordain them laws; part, such as appertain
To civil justice; part, religious rites
Of sacrifice; informing them, by types
And shadows, of that destined Seed to bruise
The Serpent, by what means he shall achieve
235   Mankind's deliverance. But the voice of God
To mortal ear is dreadful: They beseech
That Moses might report to them his will,

And terrour cease; he grants what they besought,
Instructed that to God is no access
240 Without Mediator, whose high office now
Moses in figure bears; to introduce
One greater, of whose day he shall foretel,
And all the Prophets in their age the times
Of great Messiah shall sing. Thus, laws and rites
245 Established, such delight hath God in Men
Obedient to his will, that he vouchsafes
Among them to set up his tabernacle;
The Holy One with mortal Men to dwell:
By his prescript a sanctuary is framed
250 Of cedar, overlaid with gold; therein
An ark, and in the ark his testimony,
The records of his covenant; over these
A mercy-seat of gold, between the wings
Of two bright Cherubim; before him burn
255 Seven lamps as in a zodiack representing
The heavenly fires; over the tent a cloud
Shall rest by day, a fiery gleam by night;
Save when they journey, and at length they come,
Conducted by his Angel, to the land
260 Promised to Abraham and his seed:—The rest
Were long to tell; how many battles fought
How many kings destroyed; and kingdoms won;
Or how the sun shall in mid Heaven stand still
A day entire, and night's due course adjourn,
265 Man's voice commanding, "Sun, in Gibeon stand,
And thou moon in the vale of Aialon,
Till Israel overcome!" so call the third
From Abraham, son of Isaac; and from him
His whole descent, who thus shall Canaan win.
270 Here Adam interposed. O sent from Heaven,
Enlightener of my darkness, gracious things
Thou hast revealed; those chiefly, which concern
Just Abraham and his seed: now first I find
Mine eyes true-opening, and my heart much eased;
275 Erewhile perplexed with thoughts, what would become
Of me and all mankind: But now I see
His day, in whom all nations shall be blest;
Favour unmerited by me, who sought
Forbidden knowledge by forbidden means.
280 This yet I apprehend not, why to those
Among whom God will deign to dwell on earth
So many and so various laws are given;

So many laws argue so many sins
Among them; how can God with such reside?
285   To whom thus Michael. Doubt not but that sin
Will reign among them, as of thee begot;
And therefore was law given them, to evince
Their natural pravity, by stirring up
Sin against law to fight: that when they see
290   Law can discover sin, but not remove,
Save by those shadowy expiations weak,
The blood of bulls and goats, they may conclude
Some blood more precious must be paid for Man;
Just for unjust; that, in such righteousness
295   To them by faith imputed, they may find
Justification towards God, and peace
Of conscience; which the law by ceremonies
Cannot appease; nor Man the mortal part
Perform; and, not performing, cannot live.
300   So law appears imperfect; and but given
With purpose to resign them, in full time,
Up to a better covenant; disciplined
From shadowy types to truth; from flesh to spirit;
From imposition of strict laws to free
305   Acceptance of large grace; from servile fear
To filial; works of law to works of faith.
And therefore shall not Moses, though of God
Highly beloved, being but the minister
Of law, his people into Canaan lead;
310   But Joshua, whom the Gentiles Jesus call,
His name and office bearing, who shall quell
The adversary-Serpent, and bring back
Through the world's wilderness long-wandered Man
Safe to eternal Paradise of rest.
315   Mean while they, in their earthly Canaan placed,
Long time shall dwell and prosper, but when sins
National interrupt their publick peace,
Provoking God to raise them enemies;
From whom as oft he saves them penitent
320   By Judges first, then under Kings; of whom
The second, both for piety renowned
And puissant deeds, a promise shall receive
Irrevocable, that his regal throne
For ever shall endure; the like shall sing
325   All Prophecy, that of the royal stock
Of David (so I name this king) shall rise
A Son, the Woman's seed to thee foretold,

Foretold to Abraham, as in whom shall trust
All nations; and to kings foretold, of kings
330　The last; for of his reign shall be no end.
But first, a long succession must ensue;
And his next son, for wealth and wisdom famed,
The clouded ark of God, till then in tents
Wandering, shall in a glorious temple enshrine.
335　Such follow him, as shall be registered
Part good, part bad; of bad the longer scroll;
Whose foul idolatries, and other faults
Heaped to the popular sum, will so incense
God, as to leave them, and expose their land,
340　Their city, his temple, and his holy ark,
With all his sacred things, a scorn and prey
To that proud city, whose high walls thou sawest
Left in confusion; Babylon thence called.
There in captivity he lets them dwell
345　The space of seventy years; then brings them back,
Remembering mercy, and his covenant sworn
To David, stablished as the days of Heaven.
Returned from Babylon by leave of kings
Their lords, whom God disposed, the house of God
350　They first re-edify; and for a while
In mean estate live moderate; till, grown
In wealth and multitude, factious they grow;
But first among the priests dissention springs,
Men who attend the altar, and should most
355　Endeavour peace: their strife pollution brings
Upon the temple itself: at last they seise
The scepter, and regard not David's sons;
Then lose it to a stranger, that the true
Anointed King Messiah might be born
360　Barred of his right; yet at his birth a star,
Unseen before in Heaven, proclaims him come;
And guides the eastern sages, who inquire
His place, to offer incense, myrrh, and gold:
His place of birth a solemn Angel tells
365　To simple shepherds, keeping watch by night;
They gladly thither haste, and by a quire
Of squadroned Angels hear his carol sung.
A virgin is his mother, but his sire
The power of the Most High: He shall ascend
370　The throne hereditary, and bound his reign
With Earth's wide bounds, his glory with the Heavens.
He ceased, discerning Adam with such joy

Surcharged, as had like grief been dewed in tears,
Without the vent of words; which these he breathed.
375   O prophet of glad tidings, finisher
Of utmost hope! now clear I understand
What oft my steadiest thoughts have searched in vain;
Why our great Expectation should be called
The seed of Woman: Virgin Mother, hail,
380   High in the love of Heaven; yet from my loins
Thou shalt proceed, and from thy womb the Son
Of God Most High: so God with Man unites!
Needs must the Serpent now his capital bruise
Expect with mortal pain: Say where and when
385   Their fight, what stroke shall bruise the victor's heel.
To whom thus Michael. Dream not of their fight,
As of a duel, or the local wounds
Of head or heel: Not therefore joins the Son
Manhood to Godhead, with more strength to foil
390   Thy enemy; nor so is overcome
Satan, whose fall from Heaven, a deadlier bruise,
Disabled, not to give thee thy death's wound:
Which he, who comes thy Saviour, shall recure,
Not by destroying Satan, but his works
395   In thee, and in thy seed: Nor can this be,
But by fulfilling that which thou didst want,
Obedience to the law of God, imposed
On penalty of death, and suffering death;
The penalty to thy transgression due,
400   And due to theirs which out of thine will grow:
So only can high Justice rest appaid.
The law of God exact he shall fulfil
Both by obedience and by love, though love
Alone fulfil the law; thy punishment
405   He shall endure, by coming in the flesh
To a reproachful life, and cursed death;
Proclaiming life to all who shall believe
In his redemption; and that his obedience,
Imputed, becomes theirs by faith; his merits
410   To save them, not their own, though legal, works.
For this he shall live hated, be blasphemed,
Seised on by force, judged, and to death condemned
A shameful and accursed, nailed to the cross
By his own nation; slain for bringing life:
415   But to the cross he nails thy enemies,
The law that is against thee, and the sins
Of all mankind, with him there crucified,

Never to hurt them more who rightly trust
In this his satisfaction; so he dies,
420 But soon revives; Death over him no power
Shall long usurp; ere the third dawning light
Return, the stars of morn shall see him rise
Out of his grave, fresh as the dawning light,
Thy ransom paid, which Man from death redeems,
425 His death for Man, as many as offered life
Neglect not, and the benefit embrace
By faith not void of works: This God-like act
Annuls thy doom, the death thou shouldest have died,
In sin for ever lost from life; this act
430 Shall bruise the head of Satan, crush his strength,
Defeating Sin and Death, his two main arms;
And fix far deeper in his head their stings
Than temporal death shall bruise the victor's heel,
Or theirs whom he redeems; a death, like sleep,
435 A gentle wafting to immortal life.
Nor after resurrection shall he stay
Longer on earth, than certain times to appear
To his disciples, men who in his life
Still followed him; to them shall leave in charge
440 To teach all nations what of him they learned
And his salvation; them who shall believe
Baptizing in the profluent stream, the sign
Of washing them from guilt of sin to life
Pure, and in mind prepared, if so befall,
445 For death, like that which the Redeemer died.
All nations they shall teach; for, from that day,
Not only to the sons of Abraham's loins
Salvation shall be preached, but to the sons
Of Abraham's faith wherever through the world;
450 So in his seed all nations shall be blest.
Then to the Heaven of Heavens he shall ascend
With victory, triumphing through the air
Over his foes and thine; there shall surprise
The Serpent, prince of air, and drag in chains
455 Through all his realm, and there confounded leave;
Then enter into glory, and resume
His seat at God's right hand, exalted high
Above all names in Heaven; and thence shall come,
When this world's dissolution shall be ripe,
460 With glory and power to judge both quick and dead;
To judge the unfaithful dead, but to reward
His faithful, and receive them into bliss,

Whether in Heaven or Earth; for then the Earth
Shall all be Paradise, far happier place
465 Than this of Eden, and far happier days.
So spake the Arch-Angel Michael; then paused,
As at the world's great period; and our sire,
Replete with joy and wonder, thus replied.
O Goodness infinite, Goodness immense!
470 That all this good of evil shall produce,
And evil turn to good; more wonderful
Than that which by creation first brought forth
Light out of darkness! Full of doubt I stand,
Whether I should repent me now of sin
475 By me done, and occasioned; or rejoice
Much more, that much more good thereof shall spring;
To God more glory, more good-will to Men
From God, and over wrath grace shall abound.
But say, if our Deliverer up to Heaven
480 Must re-ascend, what will betide the few
His faithful, left among the unfaithful herd,
The enemies of truth? Who then shall guide
His people, who defend? Will they not deal
Worse with his followers than with him they dealt?
485 Be sure they will, said the Angel; but from Heaven
He to his own a Comforter will send,
The promise of the Father, who shall dwell
His Spirit within them; and the law of faith,
Working through love, upon their hearts shall write,
490 To guide them in all truth; and also arm
With spiritual armour, able to resist
Satan's assaults, and quench his fiery darts;
What man can do against them, not afraid,
Though to the death; against such cruelties
495 With inward consolations recompensed,
And oft supported so as shall amaze
Their proudest persecutors: For the Spirit,
Poured first on his Apostles, whom he sends
To evangelize the nations, then on all
500 Baptized, shall them with wonderous gifts endue
To speak all tongues, and do all miracles,
As did their Lord before them. Thus they win
Great numbers of each nation to receive
With joy the tidings brought from Heaven: At length
505 Their ministry performed, and race well run,
Their doctrine and their story written left,
They die; but in their room, as they forewarn,

Wolves shall succeed for teachers, grievous wolves,
Who all the sacred mysteries of Heaven
510　To their own vile advantages shall turn
Of lucre and ambition; and the truth
With superstitions and traditions taint,
Left only in those written records pure,
Though not but by the Spirit understood.
515　Then shall they seek to avail themselves of names,
Places, and titles, and with these to join
Secular power; though feigning still to act
By spiritual, to themselves appropriating
The Spirit of God, promised alike and given
520　To all believers; and, from that pretence,
Spiritual laws by carnal power shall force
On every conscience; laws which none shall find
Left them inrolled, or what the Spirit within
Shall on the heart engrave. What will they then
525　But force the Spirit of Grace itself, and bind
His consort Liberty? what, but unbuild
His living temples, built by faith to stand,
Their own faith, not another's? for, on earth,
Who against faith and conscience can be heard
530　Infallible? yet many will presume:
Whence heavy persecution shall arise
On all, who in the worship persevere
Of spirit and truth; the rest, far greater part,
Will deem in outward rites and specious forms
535　Religion satisfied; Truth shall retire
Bestuck with slanderous darts, and works of faith
Rarely be found: So shall the world go on,
To good malignant, to bad men benign;
Under her own weight groaning; till the day
540　Appear of respiration to the just,
And vengeance to the wicked, at return
Of him so lately promised to thy aid,
The Woman's Seed; obscurely then foretold,
Now ampler known thy Saviour and thy Lord;
545　Last, in the clouds, from Heaven to be revealed
In glory of the Father, to dissolve
Satan with his perverted world; then raise
From the conflagrant mass, purged and refined,
New Heavens, new Earth, ages of endless date,
550　Founded in righteousness, and peace, and love;
To bring forth fruits, joy and eternal bliss.
He ended; and thus Adam last replied.

How soon hath thy prediction, Seer blest,
Measured this transient world, the race of time,
555 Till time stand fixed! Beyond is all abyss,
Eternity, whose end no eye can reach.
Greatly-instructed I shall hence depart;
Greatly in peace of thought; and have my fill
Of knowledge, what this vessel can contain;
560 Beyond which was my folly to aspire.
Henceforth I learn, that to obey is best,
And love with fear the only God; to walk
As in his presence; ever to observe
His providence; and on him sole depend,
565 Merciful over all his works, with good
Still overcoming evil, and by small
Accomplishing great things, by things deemed weak
Subverting worldly strong, and worldly wise
By simply meek: that suffering for truth's sake
570 Is fortitude to highest victory,
And, to the faithful, death the gate of life;
Taught this by his example, whom I now
Acknowledge my Redeemer ever blest.
To whom thus also the Angel last replied.
575 This having learned, thou hast attained the sum
Of wisdom; hope no higher, though all the stars
Thou knewest by name, and all the ethereal powers,
All secrets of the deep, all Nature's works,
Or works of God in Heaven, air, earth, or sea,
580 And all the riches of this world enjoyedst,
And all the rule, one empire; only add
Deeds to thy knowledge answerable; add faith,
Add virtue, patience, temperance; add love,
By name to come called charity, the soul
585 Of all the rest: then wilt thou not be loth
To leave this Paradise, but shalt possess
A Paradise within thee, happier far.—
Let us descend now therefore from this top
Of speculation; for the hour precise
590 Exacts our parting hence; and see the guards,
By me encamped on yonder hill, expect
Their motion; at whose front a flaming sword,
In signal of remove, waves fiercely round:
We may no longer stay: go, waken Eve;
595 Her also I with gentle dreams have calmed
Portending good, and all her spirits composed
To meek submission: thou, at season fit,

Let her with thee partake what thou hast heard;
Chiefly what may concern her faith to know,
600 The great deliverance by her seed to come
(For by the Woman's seed) on all mankind:
That ye may live, which will be many days,
Both in one faith unanimous, though sad,
With cause, for evils past; yet much more cheered
605 With meditation on the happy end.
He ended, and they both descend the hill;
Descended, Adam to the bower, where Eve
Lay sleeping, ran before; but found her waked;
And thus with words not sad she him received.
610 Whence thou returnest, and whither wentest, I know;
For God is also in sleep; and dreams advise,
Which he hath sent propitious, some great good
Presaging, since with sorrow and heart's distress
Wearied I fell asleep: But now lead on;
615 In me is no delay; with thee to go,
Is to stay here; without thee here to stay,
Is to go hence unwilling; thou to me
Art all things under Heaven, all places thou,
Who for my wilful crime art banished hence.
620 This further consolation yet secure
I carry hence; though all by me is lost,
Such favour I unworthy am vouchsafed,
By me the Promised Seed shall all restore.
So spake our mother Eve; and Adam heard
625 Well pleased, but answered not: For now, too nigh
The Arch-Angel stood; and, from the other hill
To their fixed station, all in bright array
The Cherubim descended; on the ground
Gliding meteorous, as evening-mist
630 Risen from a river o'er the marish glides,
And gathers ground fast at the labourer's heel
Homeward returning. High in front advanced,
The brandished sword of God before them blazed,
Fierce as a comet; which with torrid heat,
635 And vapour as the Libyan air adust,
Began to parch that temperate clime; whereat
In either hand the hastening Angel caught
Our lingering parents, and to the eastern gate
Led them direct, and down the cliff as fast
640 To the subjected plain; then disappeared.
They, looking back, all the eastern side beheld
Of Paradise, so late their happy seat,

Waved over by that flaming brand; the gate
With dreadful faces thronged, and fiery arms:
645 Some natural tears they dropt, but wiped them soon;
The world was all before them, where to choose
Their place of rest, and Providence their guide:
They, hand in hand, with wandering steps and slow,
Through Eden took their solitary way.

The King James Bible

The First Book of Moses: Called Genesis

1:1 In the beginning God created the heaven and the earth.

1:2 And the earth was without form, and void; and darkness was upon the face of the deep. And the Spirit of God moved upon the face of the waters.

1:3 And God said, Let there be light: and there was light.

1:4 And God saw the light, that it was good: and God divided the light from the darkness.

1:5 And God called the light Day, and the darkness he called Night. And the evening and the morning were the first day.

1:6 And God said, Let there be a firmament in the midst of the waters, and let it divide the waters from the waters.

1:7 And God made the firmament, and divided the waters which were under the firmament from the waters which were above the firmament: and it was so.

1:8 And God called the firmament Heaven. And the evening and the morning were the second day.

1:9 And God said, Let the waters under the heaven be gathered together unto one place, and let the dry land appear: and it was so.

1:10 And God called the dry land Earth; and the gathering together of the waters called he Seas: and God saw that it was good.

1:11 And God said, Let the earth bring forth grass, the herb yielding seed, and the fruit tree yielding fruit after his kind, whose seed is in itself, upon the earth: and it was so.

1:12 And the earth brought forth grass, and herb yielding seed after his kind, and the tree yielding fruit, whose seed was in itself, after his kind: and God saw that it was good.

1:13 And the evening and the morning were the third day.

1:14 And God said, Let there be lights in the firmament of the heaven to divide the day from the night; and let them be for signs, and for seasons, and for days, and years:

1:15 And let them be for lights in the firmament of the heaven to give light upon the earth: and it was so.

1:16 And God made two great lights; the greater light to rule the day, and the lesser light to rule the night: he made the stars also.

1:17 And God set them in the firmament of the heaven to give light upon the earth,

1:18 And to rule over the day and over the night, and to divide the light from the darkness: and God saw that it was good.

1:19 And the evening and the morning were the fourth day.

1:20 And God said, Let the waters bring forth abundantly the moving creature that

hath life, and fowl that may fly above the earth in the open firmament of heaven.
1:21 And God created great whales, and every living creature that moveth, which the waters brought forth abundantly, after their kind, and every winged fowl after his kind: and God saw that it was good.
1:22 And God blessed them, saying, Be fruitful, and multiply, and fill the waters in the seas, and let fowl multiply in the earth.
1:23 And the evening and the morning were the fifth day.
1:24 And God said, Let the earth bring forth the living creature after his kind, cattle, and creeping thing, and beast of the earth after his kind: and it was so.
1:25 And God made the beast of the earth after his kind, and cattle after their kind, and every thing that creepeth upon the earth after his kind: and God saw that it was good.
1:26 And God said, Let us make man in our image, after our likeness: and let them have dominion over the fish of the sea, and over the fowl of the air, and over the cattle, and over all the earth, and over every creeping thing that creepeth upon the earth.
1:27 So God created man in his own image, in the image of God created he him; male and female created he them.
1:28 And God blessed them, and God said unto them, Be fruitful, and multiply, and replenish the earth, and subdue it: and have dominion over the fish of the sea, and over the fowl of the air, and over every living thing that moveth upon the earth.
1:29 And God said, Behold, I have given you every herb bearing seed, which is upon the face of all the earth, and every tree, in the which is the fruit of a tree yielding seed; to you it shall be for meat.
1:30 And to every beast of the earth, and to every fowl of the air, and to every thing that creepeth upon the earth, wherein there is life, I have given every green herb for meat: and it was so.
1:31 And God saw every thing that he had made, and, behold, it was very good. And the evening and the morning were the sixth day.

2:1 Thus the heavens and the earth were finished, and all the host of them.
2:2 And on the seventh day God ended his work which he had made; and he rested on the seventh day from all his work which he had made.
2:3 And God blessed the seventh day, and sanctified it: because that in it he had rested from all his work which God created and made.
2:4 These are the generations of the heavens and of the earth when they were created, in the day that the LORD God made the earth and the heavens,
2:5 And every plant of the field before it was in the earth, and every herb of the field before it grew: for the LORD God had not caused it to rain upon the earth, and there was not a man to till the ground.
2:6 But there went up a mist from the earth, and watered the whole face of the ground.
2:7 And the LORD God formed man of the dust of the ground, and breathed into his nostrils the breath of life; and man became a living soul.
2:8 And the LORD God planted a garden eastward in Eden; and there he put the

man whom he had formed.

2:9 And out of the ground made the LORD God to grow every tree that is pleasant to the sight, and good for food; the tree of life also in the midst of the garden, and the tree of knowledge of good and evil.

2:10 And a river went out of Eden to water the garden; and from thence it was parted, and became into four heads.

2:11 The name of the first is Pison: that is it which compasseth the whole land of Havilah, where there is gold;

2:12 And the gold of that land is good: there is bdellium and the onyx stone.

2:13 And the name of the second river is Gihon: the same is it that compasseth the whole land of Ethiopia.

2:14 And the name of the third river is Hiddekel: that is it which goeth toward the east of Assyria. And the fourth river is Euphrates.

2:15 And the LORD God took the man, and put him into the garden of Eden to dress it and to keep it.

2:16 And the LORD God commanded the man, saying, Of every tree of the garden thou mayest freely eat:

2:17 But of the tree of the knowledge of good and evil, thou shalt not eat of it: for in the day that thou eatest thereof thou shalt surely die.

2:18 And the LORD God said, It is not good that the man should be alone; I will make him an help meet for him.

2:19 And out of the ground the LORD God formed every beast of the field, and every fowl of the air; and brought them unto Adam to see what he would call them: and whatsoever Adam called every living creature, that was the name thereof.

2:20 And Adam gave names to all cattle, and to the fowl of the air, and to every beast of the field; but for Adam there was not found an help meet for him.

2:21 And the LORD God caused a deep sleep to fall upon Adam, and he slept: and he took one of his ribs, and closed up the flesh instead thereof;

2:22 And the rib, which the LORD God had taken from man, made he a woman, and brought her unto the man.

2:23 And Adam said, This is now bone of my bones, and flesh of my flesh: she shall be called Woman, because she was taken out of Man.

2:24 Therefore shall a man leave his father and his mother, and shall cleave unto his wife: and they shall be one flesh.

2:25 And they were both naked, the man and his wife, and were not ashamed.

3:1 Now the serpent was more subtil than any beast of the field which the LORD God had made. And he said unto the woman, Yea, hath God said, Ye shall not eat of every tree of the garden?

3:2 And the woman said unto the serpent, We may eat of the fruit of the trees of the garden:

3:3 But of the fruit of the tree which is in the midst of the garden, God hath said, Ye shall not eat of it, neither shall ye touch it, lest ye die.

3:4 And the serpent said unto the woman, Ye shall not surely die:

3:5 For God doth know that in the day ye eat thereof, then your eyes shall be opened, and ye shall be as gods, knowing good and evil.

3:6 And when the woman saw that the tree was good for food, and that it was pleasant to the eyes, and a tree to be desired to make one wise, she took of the fruit thereof, and did eat, and gave also unto her husband with her; and he did eat.

3:7 And the eyes of them both were opened, and they knew that they were naked; and they sewed fig leaves together, and made themselves aprons.

3:8 And they heard the voice of the LORD God walking in the garden in the cool of the day: and Adam and his wife hid themselves from the presence of the LORD God amongst the trees of the garden.

3:9 And the LORD God called unto Adam, and said unto him, Where art thou?

3:10 And he said, I heard thy voice in the garden, and I was afraid, because I was naked; and I hid myself.

3:11 And he said, Who told thee that thou wast naked? Hast thou eaten of the tree, whereof I commanded thee that thou shouldest not eat?

3:12 And the man said, The woman whom thou gavest to be with me, she gave me of the tree, and I did eat.

3:13 And the LORD God said unto the woman, What is this that thou hast done? And the woman said, The serpent beguiled me, and I did eat.

3:14 And the LORD God said unto the serpent, Because thou hast done this, thou art cursed above all cattle, and above every beast of the field; upon thy belly shalt thou go, and dust shalt thou eat all the days of thy life:

3:15 And I will put enmity between thee and the woman, and between thy seed and her seed; it shall bruise thy head, and thou shalt bruise his heel.

3:16 Unto the woman he said, I will greatly multiply thy sorrow and thy conception; in sorrow thou shalt bring forth children; and thy desire shall be to thy husband, and he shall rule over thee.

3:17 And unto Adam he said, Because thou hast hearkened unto the voice of thy wife, and hast eaten of the tree, of which I commanded thee, saying, Thou shalt not eat of it: cursed is the ground for thy sake; in sorrow shalt thou eat of it all the days of thy life;

3:18 Thorns also and thistles shall it bring forth to thee; and thou shalt eat the herb of the field;

3:19 In the sweat of thy face shalt thou eat bread, till thou return unto the ground; for out of it wast thou taken: for dust thou art, and unto dust shalt thou return.

3:20 And Adam called his wife's name Eve; because she was the mother of all living.

3:21 Unto Adam also and to his wife did the LORD God make coats of skins, and clothed them.

3:22 And the LORD God said, Behold, the man is become as one of us, to know good and evil: and now, lest he put forth his hand, and take also of the tree of life, and eat, and live for ever:

3:23 Therefore the LORD God sent him forth from the garden of Eden, to till the ground from whence he was taken.

3:24 So he drove out the man; and he placed at the east of the garden of Eden Cherubims, and a flaming sword which turned every way, to keep the way of the tree of life.

4:1 And Adam knew Eve his wife; and she conceived, and bare Cain, and said, I have gotten a man from the LORD.

4:2 And she again bare his brother Abel. And Abel was a keeper of sheep, but Cain was a tiller of the ground.

4:3 And in process of time it came to pass, that Cain brought of the fruit of the ground an offering unto the LORD.

4:4 And Abel, he also brought of the firstlings of his flock and of the fat thereof. And the LORD had respect unto Abel and to his offering:

4:5 But unto Cain and to his offering he had not respect. And Cain was very wroth, and his countenance fell.

4:6 And the LORD said unto Cain, Why art thou wroth? and why is thy countenance fallen?

4:7 If thou doest well, shalt thou not be accepted? and if thou doest not well, sin lieth at the door. And unto thee shall be his desire, and thou shalt rule over him.

4:8 And Cain talked with Abel his brother: and it came to pass, when they were in the field, that Cain rose up against Abel his brother, and slew him.

4:9 And the LORD said unto Cain, Where is Abel thy brother? And he said, I know not: Am I my brother's keeper?

4:10 And he said, What hast thou done? the voice of thy brother's blood crieth unto me from the ground.

4:11 And now art thou cursed from the earth, which hath opened her mouth to receive thy brother's blood from thy hand;

4:12 When thou tillest the ground, it shall not henceforth yield unto thee her strength; a fugitive and a vagabond shalt thou be in the earth.

4:13 And Cain said unto the LORD, My punishment is greater than I can bear.

4:14 Behold, thou hast driven me out this day from the face of the earth; and from thy face shall I be hid; and I shall be a fugitive and a vagabond in the earth; and it shall come to pass, that every one that findeth me shall slay me.

4:15 And the LORD said unto him, Therefore whosoever slayeth Cain, vengeance shall be taken on him sevenfold. And the LORD set a mark upon Cain, lest any finding him should kill him.

4:16 And Cain went out from the presence of the LORD, and dwelt in the land of Nod, on the east of Eden.

FURTHER READING

LITERATURE

The Complete Old English Poems. Translated by Craig Williamson with an introduction by Tom Shippey, University of Pennsylvania Press, 2017.

Heaney, Seamus, translator. *Beowulf: A New Verse Translation*. Farrar, Straus, and Giroux, New York, 2000.

Kempe, Margery. *The Book of Margery Kempe*. Edited by Lynn Staley, Medieval Institute Publications, 1996.

Old English Poetry: An Anthology. Translated and edited by R. M. Liuzza, Broadview Press, 2000.

Shakespeare, William. *Richard III*. Edited by Barbara A. Mowat and Paul Werstine, Folger Shakespeare Library edition, Simon & Schuster, 2015.

HISTORY

Guy, John. *Queen of Scots: The True Life of Mary Stuart*. Mariner Books, 2005.

Jones, Dan. *The Plantagenets: The Kings Who Made England*. HarperCollins, 2012.

Mate, Mavis E. *Women in Medieval English Society*. Cambridge University Press, 2001.

Royle, Trevor. *Civil War: The Wars of the Three Kingdoms, 1638-1660*. Abacus, 2005.

Watson, Nicholas and Jaqueline Jenkins. *The Writings of Julian of Norwich: A Vision Showed to a Devout Woman and A Revelation of Love*. Penn State Press, 2006.

9 781943 115570